BIRMINGHAM CITY

THE COMPLETE RECORD

BIRMINGHAM CITY

THE COMPLETE RECORD

TONY MATTHEWS

DEDICATION

This book is dedicated to Gil Merrick,
who passed away in February 2010.

First published in Great Britain in 2010 by The Derby Books Publishing Company Limited,
3 The Parker Centre, Derby, DE21 4SZ.

© Tony Matthews, 2010

ISBN 978-1-85983-853-2
Printed and Bound in Rzeszowskie Zakłady Graficzne S.A., Poland.

CONTENTS

FOREWORD

by **GIL MERRICK**

Former Blues' goalkeeper and manager, and the club's record appearance-maker

Birmingham City Football Club has a very rich, proud and distinguished history.

Founded in 1875, the Blues have long been at the very heart of the community, despite having arch-rivals Aston Villa and Black Country neighbours West Bromwich Albion based just a few miles away.

St Andrew's has been the club's home for over 100 years and is now regarded as one of the best-equipped stadiums in the country, albeit with a moderate capacity.

Over the course of time, Blues have been served by a host of great players, far too many to list on this page, but they are all mentioned in this excellent book, and I know that when I played in the 1940s and 1950s that several were really top-class footballers, including the entire team that won the Second Division title in 1955, finished sixth in the top flight (the highest position any Blues side has claimed), reached the FA Cup Final of 1956, lost in the semi-final of 1957 and played in a major European competition.

In front of me at that time were the likes of full-backs Jeff Hall and Ken Green, skipper Len Boyd, tough defenders Trevor Smith and Roy Warhurst, flying winger Gordon Astall, the Welsh workhorse Noel Kinsey, two brilliant marksmen – Eddie Brown and Peter Murphy – and goalscoring outside-left Alex Govan.

Plenty more followed, including teenage sensation and football's first £1 million player Trevor Francis, his strike partner Bob Latchford, the long-serving duo of Malcolm Beard and Malcolm Page and the likeable Frank Worthington, while before them the fans turned out in their thousands to cheer on that brilliant goal-machine Joe Bradford, Scottish-born schemer Johnny Crosbie, the durable Don Dearson, left-winger George Edwards, captain sensible Fred Harris, England's number-one goalkeeper Harry Hibbs, the versatile Dennis Jennings, who seemed to go on forever, centre-forward Charlie Wilson Jones, defender and penalty expert Frank Mitchell, goalscoring outside-right Jackie Stewart, the ever-reliable Lew Stoker and Frank Womack, who holds the club's League appearance record.

And it must be said that Blues have also had some excellent managers, too. Some won honours, some did not; some turned ordinary players into international stars, some sold players when they should not have done…but that is part and parcel of being the boss, and I know all about that and the pressure it brings.

Reading about all the star players and digesting reports on important games played by Blues over the years will bring the memories flooding back.

Being a Brummie myself, and having had the pleasure and, indeed, the honour to have been associated with Birmingham City Football Club as a player and manager for 26 years, I have always appreciated how important football is to supporters…to many people it is the single most important thing in life outside their family. Hundreds, perhaps thousands simply live and breathe Blues – the club, the players, everything connected with the name Birmingham City is in their blood. And why not…

This book: *Birmingham City: The Complete Record* tells you everything you need to know about this great Midland club. You can check out the career details of every single player who has played in a senior competitive game for the Blues; how many appearances he made, how many goals he scored. You can check out your first-ever match at St Andrew's, look back at all the highs and lows of past teams and relive all the glory days. Yes, there have been quite a few, believe me. It is all here.

And on that note, I must once again congratulate author Tony Matthews, along with his researchers, assistants and indeed the publishers, for compiling such a magnificent book.

Read it, enjoy it – this is another splendid acquisition to add to the Birmingham City collection.

Gil Merrick
(b. 26 January 1922 – d. 3 February 2010)

NB: Gil penned this foreword three months before his death in February 2010.

INTRODUCTION

This book, *The Complete History of Birmingham City: 1875 to 2010*, contains virtually everything there is to know about the famous Midlands club.

The club's roots can be traced back to a group of cricket-loving churchgoers who, in 1875, formed Small Heath Alliance FC to further their interest in an alternative sport.

With the three Edden brothers and the brothers James prominent, the club grew fast and in 1885 turned professional, joining the Football Alliance four years later and gaining a place in the Football League (Division Two) in 1892. The team continued to make steady progress and, with several quality players in their ranks, did reasonably well.

After the club had changed its name to Birmingham, Blues moved from Muntz Street to their current home, St Andrew's, in December 1906 and after demotion and promotion, once as Second Division champions (1921), the club made its first appearance at Wembley – losing 2–1 to local rivals West Bromwich Albion in the FA Cup Final.

Joe Bradford was now banging in the goals season after season and he went on to score 249 in the Football League alone for Blues, a record which still stands today.

After holding their own in the First Division, attracting the biggest-ever crowd to St Andrew's – 67,341 for an FA Cup tie with Everton in February 1939 – and adding City to their name during World War Two, Blues had an excellent 1945–46 season, the most successful in the club's 70-year existence at that time as they won the Football League (South) and reached the semi-final of the FA Cup. The Second Division title followed in 1947–48 and after relegation (again) promotion was achieved once more to the top flight in 1954–55, Blues going up as champions under manager Arthur Turner. Blues' best ever season followed in 1955–56 when they finished sixth in Division One – their highest League placing to date – and were beaten in the FA Cup Final by Manchester City.

In 1960, Blues became the first League club from Great Britain to reach a major European Cup Final, but unfortunately lost over two legs to Spanish giants CF Barcelona in the Inter Cities Fairs Cup. They repeated that feat a year later, losing in the 1961 Final to AS Roma from Italy.

A major trophy finally arrived at St Andrew's in 1963 when Blues – under the shrewd guidance of former goalkeeper Gil Merrick – defeated second city rivals Aston Villa 3–1 on aggregate in the two-legged League Cup Final, skipper Trevor Smith celebrating by collecting the trophy at Villa Park.

However, after some enterprising campaigns, more Cup disappointments, several relegation campaigns (some won, some lost), a spell in the Third Division (1989–92) and a handful of promotions, 'Brummie' fans finally had something extra to cheer about in 1991 when manager Barry Fry's team won the Leyland DAF Trophy by beating Tranmere Rovers 3–2 at Wembley. Four years later, with Lou Macari in charge, Blues triumphed for a second time at the Empire Stadium, recording a 1–0 victory over Carlisle United in the Final of the Auto Windscreens Shield.

After seven years in the second tier of English football (1995–2002), a League Cup Final defeat at the hands of Liverpool and a handful of Play-off defeats, Blues at long last reached the Premier League at the fourth time of asking through the Play-off route, with a penalty shoot-out victory over Norwich City at Cardiff's Millennium Stadium in 2002.

The team remained in the top flight for four seasons, slipping into the Championship in 2006, but to the delight of the fans they bounced back straight away, only to repeat that relegation/promotion cycle once again in 2007 and 2008.

Now, with an established team and a fine manager in Alex McLeish, Blues will be looking ahead to another sound and exciting season in the Premier League when hopefully, perhaps not in 2010–11, but in the very near future, they can claim a top-six finish in the world's greatest Football League.

So, as they say and sing: 'Keep Right On To The End Of The Road'…and further!

Honours achieved by Blues:
Football League Championship runners-up: 2006–07, 2008–09
Division Two champions: 1892–93, 1920–21, 1947–48, 1954–55, 1994–95
Division Two runners-up: 1893–94, 1900–01, 1902–03, 1971–72, 1984–85
Division Three runners-up: 1991–92
FA Cup runners-up: 1930–31, 1955–56
League Cup winners: 1962–63
League Cup runners-up: 2000–01
Leyland DAF Cup winners 1990–91
Auto Windscreens Shield winners: 1994–95
Inter Cities Fairs Cup runners-up: 1958–60, 1960–61

Tony Matthews, August 2010

ACKNOWLEDGEMENTS

First and foremost I must say a special big thank you to Steve Caron and Alex Morton at DB Publishing, Derby, for their valuable assistance and co-operation in respect of this book.

A hearty thank you, also, to Chris Kershaw at Birmingham City Football Club. To the *Birmingham Mail* for the loan of certain photographs. To my long-time friends and ardent Blues supporters Dave Drage (now resident in Northampton) and Gordon Andrews (who lives in Shipston-on-Stour, Warwickshire), to Rob Hawkins (Redditch), to Ivan Barnsley (secretary of the ex-Blues Players' Association), to John Harrison (Buxton), to Richard Harvey (Saltash, Cornwall), to ex-players Neil Dougall and Gil Merrick (sadly now departed), and last but by no means least to my darling wife Margaret for all her help, support and encouragement, as always – it's getting something of a habit, compiling all these books, even in Spain!

Note: The majority of pictures used in this book have come from scrapbooks, photograph albums and old programmes owned by ex-players, avid Blues supporters and serious collectors of football memorabilia. I have been unable to establish clear copyright on some of these pictures and therefore both myself and/or the publishers would be pleased to hear from anyone whose copyright has unintentionally been infringed.

THE HISTORY OF BIRMINGHAM CITY 1875-2010

THE EARLY YEARS: 1875–81

Like so many football clubs that started up during the late 19th century, Birmingham City's origins lie firmly in the church. Formed by a group of young, enthusiastic sportsmen, mostly cricketers who regularly attended the Holy Church in Bordesley Green in September 1875, the club was originally called Small Heath Alliance.

Interest was keen, and in no time at all there were enough players ready and willing to play football. A 12-a-side match was quickly organised against a team of Aston Villa supporters who played under the name of Holte Wanderers. This fixture took place on a strip of waste land in Arthur Street, Bordesley Green, in November 1875 and ended in a 1–1 draw, David Keys scoring for the 'Heathens', whose team was: Will Edden (goalkeeper), Arthur Wright, Fred James, Tommy James, George Edden, Billy Edmunds (captain and first honorary secretary of the club, 1875–84) and Tom Edden (defenders/half-backs) and Keys, Charles Barmore, Charlie Barr, Jack Sparrow and Richard Morris (forwards).

At least a dozen games were completed during that first season, with twice as many being played in 1876–77. And with an annual subscription charge of 3d for each player, competition for places in the team was fierce, so much so that when Blues moved to their first enclosed ground, Muntz Street, in the summer of 1877, the club was well blessed with good quality players and had money in the bank.

The neat, compact Muntz Street ground was rented from the Gessey family for an annual fee of £5, and Blues would continue playing there for 29 years, eventually leaving in December 1906, by which time the yearly rent had risen to £375. Home attendances slowly increased, and with much stronger opposition the team itself slowly but surely became one of the better clubs in the Midlands region.

On 27 September 1879 Blues met their second city neighbours, Aston Villa, for the very first time, thus laying the foundation stones for what is today, certainly to the respective supporters, a great tradition of football rivalry. For the record, Blues won that inaugural 'local derby' at Muntz Street by a goal and a 'disputed goal' to nil in front of 3,000 spectators. After the game, both sets of players complained about the state of the pitch, and as a result a party of experts were brought in to sort it out.

Blues did very well in their first campaign at Muntz Street, remaining undefeated in 22 games and scoring plenty of goals, with Barr, Sparrow and Tom Edden leading the way.

Arthur James was now skipper, and he would continue to lead the side right through to 1885. Very popular with players and supporters alike, he was affectionately known as the

'People's Pet.' He represented the Birmingham Association several times in annual challenge matches against Sheffield, London and Glasgow, as well as playing against other significant selected sides.

Blues (or the Heathens as they were still called) suffered very few major upsets during the first six years of their existence.

Entering all the local Cup competitions, they eventually participated in the FA (English) Cup for the first time in 1881. Yet surprisingly, there seemed very little interest as barely 1,000 spectators attended their first-ever tie, which resulted in a 4–1 home win over Derby Town, Slater having the honour of scoring the club's first goal in this prestigious tournament. Unfortunately, Blues were knocked out in the next round, hammered 6–0 by a strong Wednesbury Old Athletic side.

FIRST TROPHY, HARRY MORRIS, MUNTZ STREET

In 1882–83, Blues won their first local trophy – the Walsall Cup – beating the favourites Walsall Swifts 4–1 in the Final. They also took part (again) in the FA Cup, receiving a bye through to the first round proper where they lost, in a replay, to Stafford Road FC, a team of Wolverhampton railway workers. Bringing in new faces all the time, the squad now comprised 20 'useful' footballers, among them Walter Hards, Walter Jones, Tom Morgan and Eddie Stanley.

Blues played an FA Cup tie on a neutral ground for the first time in 1883–84, losing to Birmingham Excelsior in a first-round replay at the Aston Lower Grounds. They also signed goalkeeper Tom Hedges, later to become a Director of West Bromwich Albion, while the James brothers were still turning out regularly.

A name of the future, 18-year-old Harry Morris, made his senior debut for Blues in an FA Cup defeat by Birmingham Excelsior in 1884–85. An apprentice plumber when he joined the club, Morris banked the money he received from playing football carefully and when he retired he bought a handcart, a few tools and set up his own business as a master plumber…and as you will read later, it was he who showed great foresight when he spotted 'a wilderness of stagnant water and muddy slopes' off Garrison Lane, Bordesley Green, which was subsequently developed into Birmingham City's home ground of today, St Andrew's. Morris remained as a player with the club until May 1893, acting as captain for a number of years. He returned to the fold in 1903 as a Director and served on the Board until his death in 1931. He was a massive influence and was held in high esteem by everyone who knew him.

Alf 'Inky' Jones was appointed secretary of the club in July 1885. And it was he who officially signed the paperwork to enable Blues to become a professional organisation in August of that year, while at the same time he struck up an agreement with all the first team players whereby half of the gate money from each home game would be divided between them. That season saw Eddie Stanley score Blues' first FA Cup hat-trick (a four-timer in fact) against Burton Wanderers. Blues reached the semi-finals for the first time, but after unveiling a new strip – chocolate-and-blue-halved shirts – this team was well and truly hammered 4–0 by West Bromwich Albion. The team for that game was: goalkeeper Hedges; full-backs Jerry Hare and Bob Evetts; half-backs Fred James, heavyweight Charlie Simms and Wally Felton and forwards Morris, Tom Davenport, Stanley, Ted Hill and Bill Figures.

In 1886–87 Blues went out of the FA Cup in the first round proper for the fourth time in six seasons, ousted by Mitchell's St George. Chris Charsley had now taken over in goal and would later play for England. In a Birmingham Senior Cup tie in November 1886, Coseley were thrashed 13–0, Blues' biggest-ever win at first-team level. For the first time in their history, Blues played in front of a five-figure crowd (12,000) when losing 4–0 in a second-round FA Cup tie away to the holders Aston Villa in 1887–88. The team was swapped around quite a lot, and at least half-a-dozen new players arrived on the scene, among them two Dixons, George and Walter, and centre-forward Austin Smith who scored over 30 goals in all matches this season before being released after upsetting the committee.

In July 1888, three years after adopting professionalism, Blues were registered as a Limited Liability Company – the first football club in the country to adopt such a title. At this juncture, the official share capital of the club was believed to be around £650. Influential secretary Alf Jones was the man behind the move. The club also changed its name from Small Heath Alliance to Small Heath, and under this new title they started off exceedingly well.

Two splendid footballing brothers, Ted and Will Devey, both scored four goals in Blues' 9–0 FA Cup win over Burton Wanderers – a club record – but progress in this competition was halted in the first round proper by Blues' bogey team at the time, West Bromwich Albion, who won a close contest at Muntz Street. Having failed to gain membership to the newly formed Football League the year before, Blues settled for a place in the Football Alliance in 1889–90 and began well with a 3–2 win over Birmingham St George, their first goal in the competition being scored by George Short.

Regulars in the team at this juncture were Charsley in goal, full-backs Walter Gittins and Fred Speller, Harry Morris who had now switched to right-half, the two Devey brothers, rugged Welsh centre-half Caesar Jenkyns, forwards Fred Heath and Stanley, plus left-winger Short. Jack Hallam was to sign in February. Although blessed with a seemingly big squad, Blues fielded only nine players (due to injury and ill-health) in their Alliance game at Sheffield Wednesday in December. It proved to be an unhappy debut for goalkeeper Francis Banks, and the Owls rattled nine goals past him. On a positive note, Will Devey became the first Blues player to score a double hat-trick – striking six times in the 12–0 win over Nottingham Forest in March. The powerful Devey finished up as leading scorer with 27 goals.

One interesting yet annoying thing that happened in 1890–91 was that Blues were disqualified from the FA Cup…for fielding an unregistered player, Charlie Short, in the first qualifying round against Hednesford Town. It was a blow, because before being thrown out, Blues had reached the first round proper by defeating Wednesbury Old Athletic and were quietly confident of making further progress. In the Alliance, Blues stuttered along and finished 10th (third from bottom). The problem was that they failed to keep a clean sheet, conceding 66 goals in 22 games, securing only 16 points.

Two major signings that season were full-back Tom Bayley and winger Tommy Hands. Tough defender Caesar Jenkyns became Blues' first full international in 1891–92 – capped by Wales against Ireland at Bangor in February. He was one heck of a player, totally committed and, due to his rather robust approach, was often in trouble with the referee. In fact, he was the first Blues player to be sent off in a competitive game, banished against Liverpool in October 1893.

In January 1892, Arsenal lost their first competitive game, thumped 5–1 by Blues in an FA Cup tie at Muntz Street. Blues came third in the Alliance this season, four points behind the champions Nottingham Forest and two short of the runners-up, Newton Heath. They actually fulfilled their last fixture against Crewe Alexandra with only 10 men and still won 2–0. During the summer of 1892, election was gained to the newly-formed Second Division of the Football League. Goalkeeper George Hollis and right-half Billy Ollis (both from Warwick County) boosted Blues' squad this season.

INTO THE LEAGUE, CHAMPIONS, WALTER ABBOTT

In July 1892, Alf Jones was upgraded to secretary-manager, a position he would retain until 1908. He saw Blues win their first-ever game in the Football League Division Two in great style, beating Burslem Port Vale 5–1 at home, with inside-left Fred Wheldon from Oldbury among the scorers. He was a wonderful player who went on to net 82 goals for Blues in 129 appearances before going on to play for Aston Villa, West Bromwich Albion and also England.

Blues followed up that initial victory over the Vale by winning their first away game against Walsall Town Swifts by 3–1 at the Chuckery, and a comprehensive 12–0 home League win over Walsall Town Swifts in December 1892 remains the club's joint-biggest senior win to date. The versatile Billy Walton and centre-forward Frank Mobley (from Coventry) who would go on and score 65 goals in 103 appearances in four seasons, both bagged hat-tricks against the Saddlers, and as time progressed became valuable members of the team.

Blues won the Second Division Championship that season, but in those days there was no automatic promotion, and as a result contesting teams had to play a Test Match (forerunner of the current Play-off) to decide who went up, stayed up or came down! Blues were paired with Newton Heath (later Manchester United), who had finished bottom of the First Division. At the time all such 'Tests' were played on neutral grounds, and on this occasion Blues met Newton Heath at the Victoria Ground (Stoke). After a 1–1 draw, the replay took place at Bramall Lane (Sheffield), but unfortunately Blues were blown away to the tune of 5–2, meaning another season in Division Two.

For their second season in Division Two (1893–94) Blues had a very strong squad and this time gained a place in the top-flight. After finishing runners-up to Liverpool, they defeated Darwen, somewhat nervously, in another Test Match at Stoke. During the course of the campaign, Blues won 7–0 at Northwich Victoria, a winning margin that would not be equalled for 104 years. They also recorded their 13th successive League win, nine having been carried over from the previous season. Blues, with a terrific forward-line, became the first team to score 100 League goals in a season, reaching the milestone against Arsenal in March. With Wheldon (22 goals) and Mobley (24), it meant that for the first time since 1888 two players from the same club had bagged 20 or more goals in the same League season, while Charlie Izon, secured from Halesowen in September, scored a hat-trick on his

Blues debut against Walsall Town Swifts. Two other new signings who would go on to do well were the versatile Ted Jolly and left-back Tom Reynolds.

On the whole, 1894–95 was not a good season, Blues ending their 30–match programme in 12th position – just three points clear of relegation. A poor away record of 11 defeats (including 7–1 at Sunderland and 9–1 at Blackburn) let them down badly. Fred Wheldon scored Blues' first-ever penalty in the 2–2 draw with Aston Villa in October, but late in the game Dennis Hodgetts equalised from the spot for Villa. Blues lost to rivals West Bromwich Albion three times in that term, twice in the League and once in the FA Cup, beaten 2–1 at home in the first round. Ex-Sunderland full-back John 'Dowk' Oliver played in the first of his 62 games for Blues while another full-back, Billy Pratt, acquired from works football, would go on playing for the club until May 1902, making 139 appearances.

As a result of slipping down to 15th in 1895–96, Blues once again had to compete in the Test Match system, playing both Liverpool and Manchester City twice.

Despite thumping Manchester City 8–0 at home when both Jack Jones and Fred Wheldon scored hat-tricks, unfortunately this time round Blues were relegated back to the Second Division after losing two and drawing one of their other three games. Aston Villa scored 11 goals in the two 'Second City' derbies, winning 7–3 at Perry Barr and 4–1 at Muntz Street. Blues debutants that season included Walter Abbott, a local-born inside-left who would become a champion goalscorer in 1898–99, Tom Farnall, a wing-half from Gloucester, Jack Jones (ex-Halesowen), Frank Lester from Walsall Trinity, Welshman Bill Robertson (from Abercorn) and the club's first £100 player, Danny Bruce from Sheffield United.

In 1896–97 Blues came fourth in Division Two. They dropped 11 points at home, and probably as a result missed out on the chance of regaining their top-flight status. An eight-match unbeaten run at the end of the season was not quite good enough as the top two teams, Notts County and Grimsby Town, were well away by then. Blues met and beat Newcastle for the first time in a League game during that term, but they went out of the FA Cup to Notts County, their fifth successive first-round elimination.

New players at the club included winger Billy Bennett from Crewe Alexandra, Scottish-born right-back Tom Dunlop, Charlie Hare (ex-Arsenal), Dennis Hodgetts (an England international from Aston Villa), Jack Inglis, a winger from Airdrieonians, defender Alex Leake, who would go on and play for England, forward Tom Oakes and Sparkbrook-born goalkeeper Ernie Pointer.

Blues set a club record that still stands in September 1897 when they beat Loughborough Town 2–0. It was their ninth successive away win, but generally they had a disappointing season, finishing sixth in Division Two, 12 points behind the champions Burnley. And once again they went out of the FA Cup in the opening round. Into the Blues camp came full-back Arthur Archer, a £50 buy from Burton Wanderers, goalkeeper Harry Clutterbuck and forward Wilson Lewis (both from Hereford Thistle), centre-forward Jimmy Higgins from Stourbridge and Sid Wharton, a splendid outside-left from Smethwick Wesleyan Rovers, who would go on and score 25 goals in 167 outings for the club before retiring in 1903.

Blues slipped down to eighth in 1898–99, despite Walter Abbott's goals. The burly inside-left became the first Blues player to score five times in a League game – doing so against Darwen (home) in late November – and he ended the season with a total of 42 goals, 34 in the League, which remains a club record to this day. Another fine marksman, Bob McRoberts, was signed from Gainsborough Trinity for £150 in August 1898. The Scotsman would go on to score 86 goals in 188 appearances for Blues up to 1905. He later returned to the club as manager.

In the FA Cup, for the first time since 1892, Blues reached the second round proper only to lose in a home replay to Stoke. In March 1899, Blues signed centre-half Walter Wigmore from Gainsborough Trinity. Arthur Gardner and Stourbridge-born George Layton were two more useful signings.

Despite an excellent start, with eight wins in their opening 10 games, which sent them to the top of the table, Blues could only manage third spot in Division Two in 1899–1900, and they failed to reach the first round proper of the FA Cup, knocked out in the fifth qualifying round by neighbours Walsall in a replay. They performed moderately from November onwards, and as a unit only occasionally hit top form. Six different players figured on the scoresheet when Oswestry Town were defeated 10–2 in the FA Cup, while leading marksman McRoberts (24 goals) claimed four hat-tricks. Wigmore also had an excellent first full season, scoring eight times in 29 appearances. Goalkeeper Nat Robinson made his senior debut this season, along with forwards Jack 'Soldier' Aston from Arsenal and Walter Main from Airdrieonians.

PROMOTION, RELEGATION, ST ANDREW'S

Runners-up and promoted at the end of 1900–01, Blues lost only five games, one at home, and scored 57 goals, conceding just 24, eight in front of their own supporters. McRoberts top-scored with 17 goals, Aston netted 10 and Johnny McMillan 13. The latter was signed in January from Leicester Fosse and scored 28 goals in 52 games for Blues before transferring to Bradford City in May 1903. Six years later, he returned to the club as a trainer. Blues' first FA Cup experience against Aston Villa ended in disappointment with a third-round defeat after a replay.

In 1901–02 Blues finished 17th (next to bottom) in Division One and were relegated after just one season with the 'big boys'. Surprisingly, despite a poor campaign, for the first time in the club's history the average home League attendance climbed into five figures to over 13,000, with 23,000 the highest, for the visit of Aston Villa in October. Blues, who were ousted by Southern League Portsmouth in the first round of the FA Cup, were blessed with the services of several new players, among them the former Aston Villa and England winger Charlie Athersmith, Billy Beer, who would later become the club's manager, right-back Archie Goldie, outside-left Charlie Field, formerly of Brentford and Sheffield United, future 100-goal, all-action centre-forward Billy 'Bullet' Jones and inside-right Arthur Leonard, a £120 buy from Glentoran. They also signed goalkeeper Jack Dorrington from Kidderminster Harriers, who would appear in over 100 games for the club before retiring in 1913, left-half Jim Dougherty from New Brighton Tower and Harry Wassall from Brierley Hill Alliance, while future England international Jimmy Windridge became a full-time professional.

'Up and down' Blues gained promotion once again in 1902–03, this time as runners-up to Manchester City (54 points to 51). They also equalled their best-ever League win, whipping hapless Doncaster Rovers 12–0 at home in mid-April. Two players, Arthur Leonard and Fed Wilcox, both scored four-timers in this rather one-sided contest.

Promotion was clinched on the very last day of the season with a 2–1 victory over Manchester United at Muntz Street. Only Arsenal could have denied Blues their moment of glory. The Gunners had to win well against Leicester Fosse (they drew 0–0) while Blues had to lose to United. Hot-shots Leonard and McRoberts shared 30 goals between them this term while another fine goalscorer, Fred Wilcox, was recruited from Bristol Rovers. In the summer of 1903, former player Harry Morris joined the Board of Directors, and with William Adams already bedded in as president things, it was hoped, would start to improve; however, 1903–04 was not a good season, Blues finishing in the middle of Division One. They never really got going and failed to win any of their first eight League games, while managing only two victories in their opening 15. In fact, they only started to play from March onwards, recording six victories in their last nine matches. That was far too late!

Sheffield United ended Blues' 20–game unbeaten League run (carried over from the previous season) with a 3–1 win in September, and Billy Jones and Fred Wilcox finished up as joint top-scorers with eight goals each. Full-backs Jack Glover and Frank Stokes, who joined the club this season, would go on to make a combined total of 337 appearances for Blues. And the player who would later score the first-ever goal at St Andrew's, Benny Green, was recruited from Barnsley, while Charlie Tickle arrived from Bournbrook.

After a lengthy meeting at Muntz Street on 23 March 1905, it was decided unanimously that the club's name should be changed from Small Heath to Birmingham, to take effect from 1 August 1905. Blues went on to finish seventh that season – mainly due to a poor ending when they won only two of their last 10 matches. And if it had not been for Billy Jones's haul of 16 goals, they might well have ended up in a relegation dog-fight. His efforts won points off Arsenal (twice), Blackburn, Newcastle and Sunderland (twice), and he was inspirational in a 5–0 home drubbing of Bury. For the second time in four years, Portsmouth dumped Blues out of the FA Cup in the first round. In April 1905, Arthur Mounteney, a well-groomed cricketer-footballer, was signed from Leicester Fosse. He would go on and score 30 goals in almost 100 appearances for Blues in four years. Also recruited was Arthur Cornan, a tough-tackling left-half from Barnsley.

A year or so earlier, in the winter of 1904, Director Harry Morris had spotted some wasteland in Bordesley Green on which he knew a decent-sized football stadium could be built. He put his thoughts forward, convinced his fellow directors that the Garrison Lane site was the right one for the club, and with the backing of his chairman, Walter Hart, a downpayment was made to secure the land on a 21-year lease on what was described as 'advantageous terms', allowing the necessary development work to commence in late February 1906. The person put in charge of this enormous project was Thomas Turley. Along with a enthusiastic committee which comprised Messrs Hart and Morris, Richard Todd, Thomas Wittell and Walter Bull, encouragement was at hand all down the line. Plans were drawn up by a local, reliable plumber and avid supporter of the team, Harry Pumfrey, who had studied at the Birmingham School of Art. 'His plans', said one spokesman, 'would have done credit to the most expensive professional architect in the land.

Blues could only finish in seventh position in 1905–06. They huffed and puffed, but never really threatened the top four teams. Their best spell came during the first third of the campaign when they bagged 20 points out of a possible 28. They whipped Nottingham Forest 5–0 and Middlesbrough 7–0 (Benny Green scored five) in successive home matches either side of Christmas, but in the end they were well off the pace, finishing 10 points behind the champions Liverpool. The biggest-ever crowd at Muntz Street – 34,000 – saw Blues beat Tottenham Hotspur 2–0 in a third-round FA Cup replay. Newcastle United ended their run the following month. In April 1906, Blues paid Coventry City £100 for left-back Jack Kearn.

Season 1906–07 saw Blues move to their new ground, which was completed after 10 months of non-stop hard work. St Andrew's was officially declared 'open' by Sir John Holder, a leading figure in the city, on Boxing Day 1906, and on a snow-covered pitch a crowd of 32,000 saw Middlesbrough hold Blues to a goalless draw. Three days later Benny Green had the pleasure of scoring the first goal on Blues' new ground, a diving header through the snow in a 3–0 victory over Preston. Despite having a new, and better, pitch to play on, Blues could only finish ninth this season. They said farewell to Muntz Street with a 3–1 victory over Bury in December, Arthur Mounteney scoring the last goal, before embarking on a new life at St Andrew's. The first 'Second City' derby at St Andrew's ended in a 3–1 win for Blues in front of a record 49,950 crowd. Blues' average home League attendance this season (at two grounds) was, at that time, a record high of just over 15,000. In June 1907, Edmund 'Ninty' Eyre was signed from Rotherham Town.

DEMOTION AGAIN, NEW MANAGERS, WORLD WAR ONE

Down and out…Blues were relegated yet again in 1907–08 after finishing bottom of the table with 30 points out of a possible 76. They won only nine games (out of 38) and were three points adrift of Bolton and 22 worse off than the champions Manchester United. Blues suffered their first League defeat at St Andrew's, losing 1–0 to Bury in September, and they also lost their first FA Cup tie there as well, going down 2–1 to West Bromwich Albion in January. Surprisingly, Blues' average home League attendance rose slightly and 45,000 saw the game against Aston Villa in September.

Blues spent £1,000 in the transfer market for the first time in December 1907 when they signed Yorkshire county cricketer Alonso Drake from Sheffield United. Unfortunately, the utility player never settled at St Andrew's and left after just eight months. Full-back Walter Corbett, signed in 1907, won a soccer gold medal for Great Britain at the 1908 Olympics. With Alex Watson now installed as their new manager, Blues had a terrible second-half to the 1908–09 season, winning only four of their last 19 matches. As a result, they had to settle for 11th place in Division Two.

Jack Dorrington, who had been at the club since 1901, had now taken over in goal from Nat Robinson, Bob Fairman had been replaced by Tom Daykin at left-half, and George Anderson, Jim Bumphrey, Fred Chapple, Ted King and Billy Smith had all come into the forward-line. In the reserves was a confident-looking full-back named Frank Womack. He would remain at the club until 1928, captaining the team for 17 years and amassing a then record 515 appearances, while playing in 100 wartime games as well. He was a truly great player and dedicated club man. Bogey team Portsmouth put paid to Blues' FA Cup hopes in round one – again.

Winger Jack Wilcox was signed in November 1908 from Aston Villa, with George Travers moving in the opposite direction. Albert Gardner, who was profoundly deaf, also arrived at the club from BSA Sports, as did Jack Needham, signed from Mansfield Town in June 1909 and winger Bob Firth, later to play for Nottingham Forest and Port Vale.

Blues finished rock bottom in 1909–10 but were not relegated, as there was no Third Division…yet! Blues were poor, winning only eight of their 38 matches and mustering a mere 42 goals, Walter Freeman top-scoring with 10. Just prior to the start of that season, in July 1909, centre-half Frank Buckley was signed from Manchester City, and on the opening day of the League programme Frank Womack made his senior debut. Wing-half Jim Moles, who was to stay at the club for two years, was signed from Leyton, forward Walter Freeman and right-winger Charlie Millington arrived from Fulham (for £600), George Gallimore was secured from Sheffield United and Frank Foxall from their neighbours Wednesday.

In July 1910, former player Bob McRoberts took over as team manager, but under his leadership Blues plodded along and finished in 16th position after a very disappointing season. They suffered 18 defeats, 13 away from home and, in fact, were only eight points clear of bottom club Lincoln City. And for the fifth season running they went out of the FA Cup in the first round. Full-backs Bill 'Kosher' Ball and Bob Bonthron, George Robertson (from Clyde), England goalkeeper Horace Bailey who had stood between the posts for Leicester Fosse when they were thrashed 12–0 by Nottingham Forest in 1908, another 'keeper Herbert Crossthwaite (Exeter City), centre-forward Jack Hall (Leicester Fosse) and Walter Abbott (for a second spell) were among the players who joined Blues that season.

After a disastrous start to the 1911–12 season when they lost six of their opening seven League games, five on the trot, Blues scrambled up to 12th spot in the table. Even so, they were only six points better off than next-to-bottom club Leeds United, while another 13 away defeats did not help matters one iota. There was no joy either in the FA Cup as Blues slipped out of the competition in the first round for the 16th time in 20 seasons. This term Blues recruited winger Dick Gibson, three centre-halves, Bill Gildea, Alex McClure and Alf Tinkler, winger Jim Conlin (Manchester City) and Billy 'Bullet' Jones, who returned to St Andrew's after an excellent spell with Brighton, while inside-right Frank Hodges became a full-time professional.

In 1912–13 a much more determined Blues side missed out on automatic promotion from the Second Division by just four points. They lost four of their last seven games, allowing Preston North End and Burnley to claim the top two positions. With Billy Jones and George Robertson scoring well up front, the team looked quite capable of returning to the top flight, but in the end, pressure told and they had to settle for third spot. In the FA Cup it was back to normal…ousted in the first round, this time by Manchester City.

New faces at St Andrew's that term included Scotsmen Jack Ballantyne from Vale of Leven and Charlie Duncan from Dunfermline Athletic, Billy 'Mollie' Morgan from Cradley St Luke's, right-half Joe Roulson via Sheffield works football and Arthur 'Nipper' Smith from Queen's Park Rangers.

Somewhat disappointingly, Blues claimed 14th place in Division Two in 1913–14 after winning only two away games and conceding a total of 60 goals in 38 matches. With an average home League crowd of more than 17,000, this was the highest so far in Blues'

Blues' first and second team players, along with the manager, training staff, club members and directors face the camera before a public practice match at St Andrew's at the start of the 1912–13 season.

history. And they actually reached the third round of the FA Cup for the first time since 1906, only to lose 2–1 to Southern League side Queen's Park Rangers at St Andrew's. In January 1914, Blues signed future England international Percy Barton from Sultan FC, goalkeepers Billy Robb and former St Andrew's trialist Stan Hauser and ex-West Bromwich Albion amateur Ernie Edwards. In May 1914 Blues went on their first overseas tour to Denmark, winning both games.

The last season before World War One (1914–15) saw Blues claim sixth place in Division Two, 10 points behind the champions Derby County and seven adrift of second-placed Preston North End. They suffered two bad spells which knocked them back considerably – three wins in their first 10 games and only two from their last 12. Only 500 spectators attended the 3–3 draw at Glossop in September – the lowest crowd any Blues team has played in front of at League level. In contrast, there were 8,000 present at St Andrew's to see the return fixture, which Blues won 11–1, Jimmy Windridge (five) and future Albion player Andy Smith (four) leading the goal charge.

Two players, 19-year-old goalkeeper Billy Robb and right-winger Richard Gibson, were both ever-presents. Blues went out of the FA Cup in the third round for the second season running, but they did win some silverware, beating Aston Villa 1–0 in the Staffordshire Cup Final. At the end of this season, and to see Blues through the difficulties of the war, Frank Richards was appointed team manager in place of Bob McRoberts.

League and FA Cup football was postponed for the duration of World War One. Blues played in the Midland Section, Principal Section and subsidiary competitions in seasons 1915–16, 1917–18 and 1918–19, but did not play serious football at all in 1916–17. In fact, the club was asked to help the cause by offering the use of St Andrew's as a rifle range to

During World War One, Blues signed several guest players, including five from West Bromwich Albion, two of whom are pictured in this 1916–17 team group: goalkeeper Hubert Pearson (centre, back row) and outside-right Claude Jephcott (extreme left, front row).

train Britain's soldiers. Blues played competitive games during the war, and several internationals turned out for the club as guests, among them Harry Hampton, Harold Edgley, Charlie Wallace and Tom Weston of Aston Villa, Hubert Pearson, Sid Bowser, Claude Jephcott, Jesse Pennington and Sammy Richardson from West Bromwich Albion, Arthur Brooks, Sammy Brooks and Teddy Peers of Wolves and the legendary Charlie Buchan of Sunderland. (See Wartime Football).

SECOND DIVISION CHAMPIONS, JOE BRADFORD

For the resumption of League football in 1919–20, Blues had a pretty strong first-team squad, the main body comprising goalkeeper Dan Tremelling, full-backs Billy Ball, Tom White and Frank Womack, half-backs Percy Barton, Alex McClure and Joe Roulson and forwards Lol Burkinshaw, Ben Millward, 'Mollie' Morgan, Jack Whitehouse and Billy Walker. Jack Daws (from Mansfield Town), Jack Short (from Notts County), centre-forward Harry Hampton (Aston Villa) and record signing from Blackpool, Joe Lane, all arrived after Christmas, as did a certain Joe Bradford, who was destined to become Blues' greatest-ever goalscorer. He was signed as a professional in February 1920 after trials with Aston Villa and Derby County. Thanks Villa!

The biggest of Blues' 24 League wins this season was 8–0 versus Nottingham Forest at home when Hampton scored four times. But despite all their efforts, they could only finish in third spot, 14 points behind the champions and eight behind runners-up Huddersfield Town. And they went out of the FA Cup in the third round, beaten by a strong Liverpool team which came fourth in Division One. The average League attendance at St Andrew's this season shot up to over 23,000, the best in the club's history so far. In May 1920, George Liddell signed as a professional for the club. He would go on to make 345 appearances, play in the 1931 FA Cup Final and after retiring would manage Blues for six years: 1933–39.

Blues won the Second Division Championship in 1920–21, making certain by winning at Port Vale on the very last day of the season. A draw or defeat would have handed the title to Cardiff City. Blessed with a steady defence of Tremelling (who conceded only 38 goals), full-backs Womack and Jack Jones (signed from Sunderland in May 1920) and a middle-line of Roulson, McClure and Barton, Blues also had some excellent forwards in winger Lol Burkinshaw, Hampton, Lane, Johnny Crosbie (a record £3,700 buy from Ayr United in May 1920) and Whitehouse. All told, the team netted 79 goals. A 10-match winning run from mid-October to mid-December set them on their way and when the pressure began to tell, the team, despite two defeats in March, won eight and drew three of their last 13 fixtures to take the honours.

Joe Bradford scored on his debut against West Ham on Christmas Day – the first of a record 267 goals he would net for the club in 15 years. And for the first time, Blues' average home League attendance topped the 31,000 mark, the best turnout being a new record of

Birmingham in 1921–22. Back row, left to right: W. Kendrick (assistant trainer), P. Neill, F. Sharp, G. Getgood, H. Reddington, D. Tremelling, W. Hunter, G. Liddell, W.H. Jenkins, H. Brown, S. Scholey (masseur), J. Eccles (trainer). Third row: F.H. Richards (secretary-manager), L. Burkinshaw, M.J. Harris (director), J. Roulson, Mr H. Cant (chairman), M.W. Hart (director), M.T. Turley (director), T. White, Mr H.S. Thomas (director), Mr S. Richards (assistant secretary). Second row: R. Booth, J. Whitehouse, H. Hampton, A. McClure, F. Womack, P. Barton, J. Elkes, J. Lane, J. Jones, G. Davies, W.H. Harvey. Front row: E. Cameron, D. Dixon, J. Crosbie, E. Linley, J. Bradford. J. Daws.

60,017 for the return fixture against West Ham shortly after Christmas; however, less than a fortnight later Blues went out of the FA Cup to Luton Town in the first round. Among the other new recruits this term was Ted Linley, a knock-kneed winger who cost £800, plus Tom Pike, from Worksop.

Unfortunately, owing to a complete mix-up in the club's offices, secretary-manager Frank Richards failed to submit Blues' entry form for the FA Cup, and therefore in 1921–22 they failed to take part in the competition for the first time since entering in 1881. In the League, the team finished 18th out of 22, avoiding relegation by five points – after managing three wins and a draw in their last five matches. Always struggling at the wrong end of the table, their two heaviest defeats came at Arsenal (5–2) and Newcastle United (4–0), while Blues themselves failed to score in 13 of 42 League matches.

Defender George Getgood (from Reading), winger Billy Harvey (from Sheffield Wednesday who later became manager), Joe Barratt (who had played for the club as a guest in 1917), Fred Foxall (from Aston Villa) and Eli Ashurst, brother of England full-back Bill, were among the players who made their debuts for Blues this term. And Johnny Crosbie became the first Blues player to win a Scottish cap (versus England).

Rising one place to 17th in 1922–23, Blues were only seven points clear of the drop-zone when the curtain came down. They had struggled for long periods, losing nine games on the trot (eight League, one FA Cup) between Christmas and mid-February, and only Joe Bradford's 18 League goals kept them out of trouble. In fact, it took some willpower right at the death (eight points gained from six games) to stay up. Huddersfield, the holders, knocked Blues out of the FA Cup in the first round. Right-half Dickie Dale, who had been signed in March 1922, made his mark this term, as did winger Charlie Bosbury from Southampton and Albert Rawson from Sheffield United, while Wallace Clark (from Leeds United) would feature later. As the season ended, Frank Richards handed over his managerial duties to former player Billy Beer.

Blues did not have a good season in 1923–24, finishing a disappointing 14th in the table. They were in deep trouble up until February, but somehow got themselves sorted out, won eight games out of 11 and climbed to safety.

On the final day of the League programme, Blues' 'keeper Dan Tremelling saved a 90th-minute penalty from Cardiff City's Len Davies. The Welsh club needed to win to clinch the League title but had to be content with a draw, leaving Huddersfield Town as champions by 0.024 of a goal. For the second season running it was the Yorkshire club who knocked Blues out of the FA Cup in the first round. Jimmy Cringan made the first of his 285 appearances for Blues that season, while Moses Lane, ex-Walsall, scored four goals in 13 outings as partner to Joe Bradford. Another debutant was Ernie Islip, who had won the FA Cup with Huddersfield in 1922.

Blues crept up to eighth in 1924–25, having topped the table following a 1–0 away win over the reigning champions Huddersfield Town in October. Only a six-match unbeaten run at the end of the campaign saw them gain some respectability. Joe Bradford, who missed 17 games mainly through injury, hit his first hat-trick for the club in a 5–2 win over Liverpool in November. He was ably supported up front by Ernie Islip and George Briggs. In fact, all three players ended up with 11 goals apiece. The third-biggest crowd of the season at Anfield, over 44,000, saw Liverpool knock Blues out of the FA Cup in the third round. Two wingers who joined Blues on the same day in December 1923, Aubrey Scriven and George Briggs, finally had decent runs in the first team along with Edmund 'Martin' Harvey, formerly of Huddersfield Town.

Season 1925–26 saw the current offside law introduced, but Blues could not make it pay and slumped to 14th in the table. The team never functioned properly despite eight players making 32 or more League appearances. With goals flying in all over the country (several teams scored over 80) Blues managed only 66, and one feels that if it had not been for Bradford's tally of 26, there might well been a relegation battle on the cards. Blues made one of the longest possible journeys north in the FA Cup, only to lose 2–1 to South Shields in the fourth round. Former Bromsgrove Rovers star Jack Russell did well as Scriven's deputy on the left-wing this season, while Billy Hunter did likewise as Jimmy Cringan's replacement at centre-half.

Ex-player Billy Beer was replaced as Blues manager in March 1927 by another former player, Bill Harvey, who had been Beer's assistant since August 1926; however, Harvey remained in office for just under two months before Frank Richards returned for a second spell which would end in July 1928. Without any consistency, Blues hiccupped along to finish eight points clear of the relegation zone in a poor 17th position in 1926–27. They lost half of their 42 matches, and they slipped out of the FA Cup in the fourth round, beaten by Southampton. Johnny Crosbie (18) and Joe Bradford (23) scored roughly two-thirds of Blues' goals between them. But there was something to cheer about (within the club) as the average League attendance was over 22,000.

Bill Thirlaway, signed in May 1926 from South Shields, shared the left-wing spot with Scriven; Benny Bond, who had signed professional forms at the end of the previous season, was given 19 League outings on the right-wing; the former West Bromwich Albion and England right-back Joe Smith deputised for the injured Frank Womack while Alex Leslie was also given his League baptism at left-half.

WOMACK RETIRES, FA CUP FINAL AGONY

Blues settled for 11th position in the First Division in 1927–28, thanks mainly to a decent late run which saw them pocket 18 points out of a possible 28, but even then they were only three points clear of the relegation zone! In fact, at one point they were in deep trouble, along with no fewer than 10 other clubs. The champions Everton eventually amassed 53 points, while bottom club Middlesbrough gained 37. And there were only 10 points separating third-placed Leicester from Tottenham Hotspur, who finished 21st.

For the first time in his career Joe Bradford topped the 30-goal mark, four of his strikes coming in the exciting 4–4 draw at Blackburn in September. In-form Bradford also scored a treble to save Blues' blushes against non-League side Peterborough & Fletton United in the FA Cup, and he netted another hat-trick against Burnley in the home League game. An Old Trafford crowd of 52,568 saw Manchester United knock Blues out of the FA Cup in the fifth round, the first time the club had ever reached this stage of the competition proper. Long-serving captain Frank Womack made his farewell appearance for Blues this term, in the 2–0 home defeat by Newcastle in April.

Among those who made their first appearances for the club were Ernie Curtis, Welsh international Stan Davies (formerly of West Bromwich Albion), Billy Ellis (from Sunderland), Jack Firth, George 'Lofty' Morrell and Jack Randle (ex-Coventry City). Curtis, Firth, Morrell and Randle went on to amass a combined total of 660 first-class appearances for Blues. One-time Arsenal manager Leslie Knighton took over as boss at St Andrew's from Bill Harvey in July 1928, yet his presence and experience failed to inspire Blues, who had another moderate season. They finished 15th in Division One with 40 points, 12 fewer than champions Sheffield Wednesday and 11 more than bottom club Cardiff City. Bradford finished up as top-scorer again with 24 goals in League and Cup, while George Hicks, a promising left-winger from Manchester City, netted 12. Another new signing, Ned Barkas, brought in to partner Jack Randle at full-back, scored with a penalty against his former club Huddersfield in his second game. Other new faces at St Andrew's included India-born Paddy Mills (ex-Notts County), forwards George Haywood and Tom Robinson (both from Gresley Rovers), winger Bill Horsman (signed from Selby Town, who would remain at the club for seven years), ex-miner Harold Booton (from Shirebrook) and Billy Blyth from Arsenal.

Blues had a slightly better season in 1929–30, edging up to 11th place, but 12 defeats on the road proved difficult to digest. In fact, they gained 41 points in total, only five more than relegated Burnley. Manager Knighton – whose old club Arsenal knocked Blues out of the Cup – introduced some fresh faces, but generally the team lacked spark and enterprise, despite playing some terrific football at times. A 12-goal thriller at Blackburn ended in a 7–5 defeat; Newcastle United got whipped 5–1 at St Andrew's and four goals were fired past West Ham, Huddersfield, Everton and Manchester City in that order.

Birmingham's first team squad with manager A.L. Knighton (left) and trainer A. Taylor (right), photographed at the start of the 1930–31 season.

1931 FA Cup Final programme cover.

Leading scorer (again) was Joe Bradford, who netted four hat-tricks during the month of September – one for the Football League and three for Blues, one of them in that ding-dong battle at Ewood Park when Syd Puddefoot struck four times for Rovers. Harry Hibbs effectively took over from Dan Tremelling as Blues' first-choice goalkeeper, while

Birmingham 1930–31: back row, left to right: A.L. Knighton (manager), J. Crosbie, G. Morrall, H. Hibbs, A. Leslie, G. Curtis, A Taylor (trainer). Middle row: J. Cringan, G. Briggs, J. Bradford, E. Barkas, J. Firth, R. Gregg. On ground: G. Liddell, W. Horsman.

giant defender Tom Fillingham and amateur 'keeper Ken Tewksbury made their debuts for the club.

Bradford scored his 13th and last hat-trick (a four-timer) for Blues in a 4–1 win over Blackburn (one of his favourite clubs!) in 1930–31, while his seven more goals helped Blues reach their first-ever FA Cup Final. At Wembley, against Second Division West Bromwich Albion, Bradford equalised on a soggy pitch, but a second 'W.G.' Richardson goal ensured the trophy went to the Hawthorns. However, it might well have been a different story had Bob Gregg's 'goal' not been disallowed for offside by the referee and not by the linesman. Blues played very well to reach the Final, ousting Liverpool (at Anfield), Port Vale, Watford, Chelsea in a replay before a near 75,000 crowd at Stamford Bridge, and Sunderland in the semis.

By concentrating too much on the Cup, Blues struggled in the League, finishing in 19th position, just five points clear of relegation. They managed a mere 55 goals (only bottom club Manchester United scored fewer), and of their 19 defeats the worst was a 9–1 battering by Sheffield Wednesday at Hillsborough, this being Blues' joint-heaviest in League football to this day. New 'pro' Lew Stoker and wing-half Charlie Calladine (ex-Scunthorpe) were among the other players who made their League debuts for Blues this season.

After their exploits of the previous season, Blues upped their game in the League to claim ninth place in 1931–32, but sadly went out in the fourth round of the FA Cup at Grimsby. They won their last four matches to move up three places and might well have finished higher but for a disastrous March during which they lost five games on the bounce.

Twelve different players scored goals for Blues that season, Bradford yet again finishing up as leading marksman with 28, his best return since 1927–28. And Blues also gained sweet revenge for that FA Cup Final defeat by doubling-up over newly promoted West Bromwich Albion. Tom Grosvenor, who had been with Blues since 1928, finally got his chance in the first team and within two years was an England international. Tamworth-born right-winger Frank White was one of the few new faces at St Andrew's.

MANAGER LIDDELL, RECORD CROWDS AT ST ANDREW'S

Down four places to 13th in 1932–33, Blues had a poor October and November, and in truth they never recovered. They did much better in the Cup, reaching the quarter-finals before losing 4–0 at West Ham, their heaviest defeat in the competition for 20 years. Three players suffered bad injuries that season – Jimmy Cringan, Tom Fillingham and Bill Horsman – and all missed several matches. And Blues' average home League attendance dropped to under 17,000, the lowest since 1914–15.

In May 1933 manager Leslie Knighton left to take over the hot-seat at Chelsea. Into his place stepped former full-back and captain George Liddell, who had always said (as a player) that he would return one day to manage. It was Chairman Harry Morris who gave him the job, and there is no doubt he inherited a fine bunch of players, although one or two were perhaps past their best.

Harry Hibbs was still firmly established in goal; Harry Booton (an ever-present) and Ned Barkas were the regular full-backs; Lew Stoker, George Morrall and Tom Fillingham or Charlie Calladine were the half-backs, with George Briggs, Tom Grosvenor (also an ever-present), Joe Bradford, Bob Gregg and Ernie Curtis the front five. With so much talent available, or so everyone thought, Blues were expected to do well in 1933–34 but, in fact, they were poor, and only avoided relegation by the skin of their teeth, escaping the drop by just two points. They won two and drew one of their last four matches to stay up above Newcastle United and Sheffield United. Prior to that results had been varied, some good wins, some scrambled wins and plenty of bad defeats, 18 in all, including heavy thrashings at Derby, Liverpool and Sunderland.

An emphatic 7–3 victory at Leicester in the penultimate game came completely out of the blue, but it was vitally important in the circumstances. Billy Guest, who had signed for Blues in 1928 and turned professional in 1932, scored a smart hat-trick against the Foxes, his first treble for the club. Frank McGurk (signed from Clyde), Dave Mangnall (bought from Huddersfield), West Bromwich-born Fred Roberts and Frank White all contributed well this season, while Frank Clack proved a reliable stand-in for Harry Hibbs. A new record crowd at St Andrew's – 66,544 – witnessed the FA Cup semi-final between Leicester City and Portsmouth.

Thanks to three other teams playing poorly in 1934–35 – Tottenham Hotspur, Leicester City and Middlesbrough – Blues escaped relegation by three points as they finished in 19th position. Always in trouble, they lost five games on the bounce in December, won only twice in 15 starts up to mid-March and recorded just one victory in seven outings at the end of the campaign. They were involved in some very tight matches, losing 5–4 at Liverpool, 4–3 at Grimsby and 3–2 at home to both Leicester and Everton. They also lost 3–2 to Burnley in the sixth round of the FA Cup – the furthest they had gone in the competition since 1931. But generally far too many goals were conceded (81 in the League and five in the Cup).

Bradford scored his 267th and last goal for the club in 3–1 win at Grimsby in March before appearing in his last game against Everton on 4 May. Fred Harris, signed in March 1933, scored on his Blues debut against Aston Villa. He would remain at St Andrew's until May 1950. Charlie Wilson Jones also came to the fore this season. Signed for £1,500 from Wrexham, he would effectively take over from Bradford and started well by scoring 17 goals in 18 senior appearances. Joe Devine (from QPR) and Billy Steel (a £5,000 buy from Liverpool) also did well in their first season with the club, while future Welsh international Don Dearson made his senior debut in the 4–0 home defeat by Huddersfield.

There was a huge improvement in Blues' form in 1935–36 as they lifted themselves up to 12th in the table, although they were only six points ahead of relegated Aston Villa. And it was back to the bad old days when they slipped out of the FA Cup in round three. A new record League crowd at St Andrew's – 60,250 – attended the local derby with Villa, and there were almost 50,000 fans present for the return fixture later in the campaign when Blues featured two 18-year-olds in Cyril Trigg and Billy Hughes – the youngest full-back pairing ever to appear in the Football League. Other Blues debutants in 1935–36 included goalkeeper Frank Clack, Joe Loughran (a wing-half from Durham), Yorkshireman Jack Sykes and the versatile Dennis Jennings, who would carry on playing for the club until he was almost 40 years of age, eventually retiring in May 1950 with almost 380 first-team appearances under his belt.

From late October 1936 to early February 1937, Blues won only two of 16 League games and fell 10 places in the table, eventually finishing in 11th position – and they suffered another early exit from the FA Cup, beaten by Stoke in round three. Manager George Liddell used 29 players, handing debuts to former Oldham Athletic star Norman Brunskill, one-time colliery worker Herbert Butler, ex-Blackburn Rovers forward Jack Beattie and Welsh international Dai Richards.

Two wins in the last two games saved Blues from relegation in 1937–38. They finished in 18th position, only two points better off than relegated Manchester City in 21st spot. They actually drew 18 of their 42 matches – a club record. And for the third season running they were eliminated from the FA Cup in round three. Not one player reached double figures in the scoring

Team page from the away League game against West Bromwich Albion, which at the time was described as a 'relegation battle'.

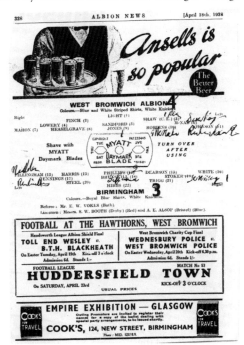

charts, but one pleasing note was that the average League attendance at St Andrew's was the best since 1922 (24,543 against 27,443).

At this juncture, it must be said that Blues had a very good squad, comprising Hibbs in goal, full-backs Trigg and Hughes, half-backs Brunskill, Fillingham and Richards, forwards White, Beattie, Wilson, Jones, Harris, Dearson and Seymour Morris with Jennings, Stoker, Owen Madden (a £2,000 buy from Norwich) and Welsh international Charlie Phillips (secured from Aston Villa) also available.

At the end of the last full pre-World War Two season (1938–39), Blues were relegated with a dismal record – 22 defeats, 84 goals conceded and a mere 32 points, their lowest tally since 1911. On the brink of the drop with four matches remaining, they gave themselves a fighting chance with victories over Brentford and Blackpool; however, a home draw with Chelsea proved the final nail in the coffin, while the point gained kept the Londoners up.

Never again will 67,341 spectators cram themselves into St Andrew's like they did for the Blues-Everton FA Cup tie in February 1939. This attendance record has now stood for 71 years. Manager George Liddell used 32 players that season, including a new goalkeeper, Jack Wheeler, two new centre-halves in Bill Meacock from Lincoln and Arthur Turner, a £6,000 buy from Stoke who would later become manager, Irish-born winger Jackie Brown, ex-Coventry, inside-right Harold Bodle from Rotherham, Tom Farrage, who sadly would lose his life during World War Two, and Charlie Craven, an inside-forward from Grimsby. He also signed Dave Massart from Bells Athletic and recruited a fine goalkeeper by the name of Gil Merrick who was to stay at St Andrew's as a player and then manager until April 1964, making a record 551 appearances.

WORLD WAR TWO, SECOND DIVISION CHAMPIONS

Only three 'League' games were played at the start of the 1939–40 season before World War Two was declared, at which point George Liddell resigned as Blues manager. The normal League programme was cancelled, and after a short break Blues began playing in the Midland Regional League and Cup competitions. Their best win that season was an 8–1 home thumping of Walsall, while their heaviest defeat came at the Hawthorns, where West Bromwich Albion won 6–1.

Several guest players turned out for the club and this would be the theme throughout the hostilities. Legendary goalkeeper Harry Hibbs retired in May 1940 after appearing in 389 competitive games for Blues. He had spent 16 years at St Andrew's and was the only player during wartime football to have a benefit match (Blues versus Aston Villa).

Initially under the guidance of temporary manager Bill Camkin, who was in office from October 1939 until November 1944, and then Ted Goodier, who took over until May 1945, Blues played 'competitively' in all but one season of wartime football, missing out in 1941–42 when they contested only friendly matches. The team did reasonably well in the Midland Regional League, Football League (South), Football League (North), League Cup, League North Cup and Midland League Cup competitions, recording some excellent victories, but also suffering several heavy defeats. (See Wartime Football).

During the hostilities, St Andrew's was badly damaged by enemy bombs. Both the Railway End and the Main Stand suffered badly, while the roof over the Spion Kop crashed

An official team sheet issued for the wartime game between Walsall and Blues at Fellows Park on 15 April 1944. The final score was 2–2 and Cyril Trigg scored both goals for Blues.

to the ground. The German Luftwaffe, in fact, scored no fewer than 20 direct hits on the ground, and it meant that some of Blues' home games had to be staged at Villa Park and also on the grounds of Leamington and Solihull.

When Blues moved back to St Andrew's in 1943, the club added City to its name, but the players had to change in a nearby factory as the dressing rooms were unusable and had no water supply. At that point a massive clean-up operation was launched, and an apple tree was found to be growing through debris on the Kop. After weeks of hard work, the ground was virtually back to normal (internally at least) for the start of the 1945–46 season.

During the war years Blues used several guest players, including seven from Aston Villa, namely Jimmy Allen, Frank Broome, George Cummings, George Edwards, Bob Iverson, Alex Massie and Frank Moss; two goalkeepers in Sam Bartram (Charlton) and Ted Ditchburn (Spurs), the Arsenal full-back Eddie Hapgood, classy Irishman Peter Doherty (Manchester City) and Ipswich Town winger Jock Mulraney, who would join the club permanently in October 1945. On 14 April 1945, the Blues–Wolves League (South) game lasted for over two and a half hours – it started at 3pm and finished around 5.45pm (153 minutes of playing time).

Harry Storer was appointed Blues' manager in June 1945 and he certainly got the team back on track. In what was referred to as the 'transitional League season' when teams from the north of the country were placed in one Division and teams from the south in another, under his

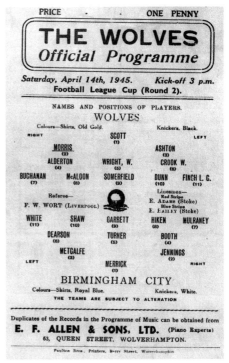

Team sheet for the Wolves v Blues Football League Cup (South) game at Molineux on 14 April 1945. This game lasted for 153 minutes before Wolves won 1–0 with a Bill Morris goal.

Gil Merrick is beaten by Tommy Lawton's looping header in Blues' 3–2 Football League South win at Stamford Bridge in November 1945. Len Goulden (Chelsea), centre, and Fred Harris (Blues) are the other players looking on.

shrewd guidance, Blues won the Football League (S) Championship, edging out rivals Aston Villa on goal-average after a titanic battle. On the last day of the campaign, having just played 10 League games in the month of April, Blues won 3–0 at Luton while Villa beat Millwall 2–0; a goal either way in both games would have handed the title to the team from Villa Park. A crowd of 63,820 – the biggest ever for a 'Second City' derby – saw Blues' goalkeeper Merrick save Harry Parkes's fifth-minute penalty in the 2–2 League draw at Villa in January. This was to prove crucial when the last ball was kicked on 4 May.

'Goal' for Harold Bodle in Blues' 5–0 victory over Watford in a fourth-round FA Cup tie at bomb-damaged St Andrew's in January 1946.

Blues face the camera in August 1946: back row, left to right: F. Harris, D. Jennings, G. Merrick, F. Mitchell, W. Hughes. Front row: A. Mulraney, N. Dougall, A. turner, C. Trigg. N. Bodle, G. Edwards. At front: J. Goodwin.

Ted Duckhouse netted from 50 yards in Blues' 8–0 home win over Spurs, and five players reached double figures in the goal stakes – the first time this had happened since 1893–94. Flying Scotsman Jock Mulraney scored twice in less than a minute in the first half of Blues' 5–0 FA Cup win over Watford. Thirty seconds later he hit the post, thus just missing out on what could have been the fastest hat-trick ever! Blues reached the semi-finals of the competition, but after Duckhouse had been carried off with a broken leg they lost 4–0 to Derby County after extra-time in a replay at Maine Road. A combined total of 145,420 spectators attended the two semi-final matches, with 80,407 witnessing the replay. This is a record for a midweek game away from Wembley involving two League clubs.

Several new players had now boosted the senior squad. Some had arrived during the war, others in 1945–46, among them rugged defender Jack Badham, winger Johnny Berry who would later become a 'Busby Babe', wing-half Don Dorman from Shirley Juniors, Neil

Blues' centre-forward Charlie Wilson Jones (no. 9) scoring with a powerful header in a 2–1 League win at Tottenham on 31 August 1946.

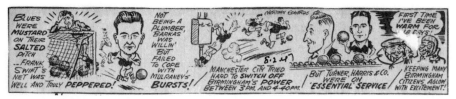

Newspaper cartoon celebrating Blues' 5–0 FA Cup win over Manchester City in February 1947.

Dougall from Burnley, Frank Mitchell and George Edwards from Coventry, Jack Goodwin from Worcester City, former Millwall amateur full-back Ken Green, 5ft 5in winger Bobby Laing from Falkirk and centre-half Sid Owen. Blues finished third in Division Two in 1946–47, the first League season after World War Two. They missed promotion by three points, despite a splendid run-in which saw them lose only once in their last 10 games. The average home attendance rose to a new high of 33,665 and several players who had been with the club before and during the hostilities were back in the team, still managed by Storer.

In 1947–48, despite drawing their last three League games 0–0, Blues won the Second Division Championship by three points from Newcastle United (59–56). Surprisingly, they scored just 55 goals in 42 matches, but thanks to a rock-solid defence and some brilliant displays by Gil Merrick, they conceded only 24, six coming in two home matches, against

A cartoon of Blues, Second Division Champions in 1947–48 with official team photograph and the trophy: Back row, left to right: D. Fairhurst (physiotherapist), K. Green. E. Duckhouse, G. Merrick, F. Mitchell, D. Jennings. Front row: J. Stewart, N. Dougall, F. Harris, H. Storer (manager), C. Trigg, H. Bodle, G. Edwards.

Barnsley and Bradford. The average League attendance at St Andrew's rose to a healthy 38,341, and not once did the crowd figure for a single game drop below 29,000.

Prior to the start of the season, defender Martin McDonnell, a huge favourite of manager Harry Storer, joined the club from Southport. Forwards Archie Garrett, Frank McKee, Fred Slater and Jackie Stewart were also signed from Northampton, Dundee United, Burton Albion and Raith Rovers respectively. A lack of goals (only 36 scored in 42 games) meant that Blues finished a disappointing 17th in the First Division in 1948–49. And the club's unbeaten away run of 15 matches also came to an end in September.

Storer who had left his post as manager in November 1948, was replaced by Bob Brocklebank in January 1949, just as Blues slipped out of the FA Cup in a third round second replay to Leicester – the club's 'longest' tie since their four-match epic with Manchester United in 1903–04. Having started the campaign with this team – Merrick; Green, Jennings; Harris, Duckhouse, Badham; Stewart Dougall, Trigg, Bodle and Edwards – as the weeks rolled by, the new boss rang the changes, bringing in Berry, wing-half Len Boyd (signed from Plymouth for £17,500 and who later skippered Blues at Wembley), Jim Dailey (from Sheffield Wednesday), Don Dorman, Irishman Ray Ferris (from Crewe), Garrett, Johnny Jordan (from Juventus), Laing, McKee, Mitchell and Harry Roberts (from Chesterfield) plus a few others in an attempt to get the right balance. Stewart finished up as top-scorer with 11 goals, including a four-timer in the home win over Manchester City. Blues' average home League attendance that season increased to a record 38,452, which still stands today.

Brocklebank had a disastrous first full season in charge at St Andrew's. There is no getting away from it, Blues played poorly in 1949–50, and their away form was unbelievably bad, losing 14 of their 21 matches. As a result they slipped back into the Second Division by finishing rock bottom with 28 points, their lowest tally since 1910. With the team goalless in 20 League matches, Jim Dailey was leading marksman with just nine goals, and for the second season running Blues went out of the FA Cup in the third round. Bobby Brennan, an Irish international, signed from Luton Town for £20,000, centre-forward Jimmy Higgins from Dundalk, Billy Smith from Northampton and Arthur Atkins from Paget Rangers, were new recruits, while Roy Warhurst was given his debut on the left wing. He later became a prominent wing-half and stayed at the club until 1957.

INTO THE 1950S, PROMOTION, FA CUP DISAPPOINTMENT

Beaten FA Cup semi-finalists and fourth in Division Two, 1950–51 was not a bad season for Blues. In fact, their points tally was only three fewer than runners-up Manchester City, and poor spells in November and just after Christmas proved crucial in the end. Two huge crowds of over 70,000 attended each of the two semi-final encounters with Blackpool, but the average League attendance at St Andrew's dropped alarmingly, with 10 crowds under 25,000.

Merrick, Atkins and Welsh international Aubrey Powell (signed from Everton in August) were ever-presents, while a converted Cyril Trigg top-scored with 19 goals, 17 in the League. Full-back Jeff Hall, later to play for England, made his debut against Bury in January. 'Roy' Martin and ex-Wolves player Ken Rowley were also given their League baptisms this season.

Blues failed to win promotion on goal-average in 1951–52. Cardiff City went up as runners'-up behind champions Sheffield Wednesday after Blues lost two of their last three

Blues' line-up before the home League game with Chesterfield in February in 1951. Back row, left to right: J. Badham, D. Dorman, A. Atkins, G. Merrick, R. Martin, R. Ferris. Front row: J. Stewart, J. Higgins, C. Trigg, W. Smith, J. Berry. Blues won 2–1.

games, one of them crucially against the Welsh club at Ninian Park. In with a great chance to rejoin the big boys in the top flight, Blues looked well on course after winning seven out of eight games in March and April, but in the end they ran out of steam and had nothing to show for their bold efforts at the end of the day. Once again the average League attendance at St Andrew's was rather disappointing, around 24,500. Centre-forward Ted Purdon (signed from the Maritz Brothers club in South Africa), half-backs Johnny Watts and Johnny Newman,

winger Billy Wardle (from Blackpool) and Tommy Briggs (from Coventry) were among the other debutants for Blues this season, while Len Boyd became Blues' first England B international, capped against Holland.

Season 1952–53 was not a good one for Blues. Always off the pace, they finished in sixth place, 10 points behind runners-up Huddersfield Town. Yet it could have been much

Blues wing-half Ray Ferris assists Blackpool's Stan Mortensen during the 1951 FA Cup semi-final at Maine Road in March 1951. Arthur Atkins, the Blues centre-half, looks on.

A mixed Blues team including Dennis Jennings, Jim Dailey, goalkeeper Bill Robertson and Jeff Hall, poses for the camera along with their opponents before a local charity match in 1951.

worse – they actually picked up seven points out of eight from their last four games to move up six places! Murphy proved his worth by top-scoring with 26 goals. Tottenham Hotspur put paid to Blues' hopes of reaching the FA Cup Final with a sixth-round second replay win at Molineux. And the average League attendance at St Andrew's this season was a shade under 20,000 – the lowest since 1933. Goalkeeper Johnny Schofield, Merrick's successor, made his debut that season, the first of 237 appearances for the club. In June 1953, Blues paid £6,500 for

Blues of 1951–52. Back row, left to right: R. Shaw (trainer), C. Trigg, J. Badham, G. Merrick, L. Boyd, A. Atkins, R. Martin, K. Rowley. Front row: J. Stewart, D. Dorman, R. Warhurst, W. Smith, R. Ferris, E. Purdon.

Blues line up before their League game against Blackburn Rovers at Ewood Park in November 1952. Back row, left to right: C. Trigg, K. Green, G. Merrick, A. Atkins, R. Warhurst, R. Martin. Front row: J. Stewart, T. Briggs, L. Boyd, P. Murphy, G. Cox. Murphy scored twice in a 2–1 win.

left-winger Alex Govan from Plymouth Argyle and £4,000 for inside-right Noel Kinsey from Norwich City. Both players would give the club excellent service for a number of years.

Blues had a moderate 1953–54 season, finishing seventh in Division Two, nine points behind the two promoted clubs, Everton and Leicester City, but they did have the pleasure of knocking the subsequent League champions Wolves out of the FA Cup in the third round.

With Gil Merrick behind him, Blues' skipper Len Boyd rises to meet a high cross during the home FA Cup tie with Tottenham Hotspur in February 1953 which ended in a 1–1 draw.

After drawing 1–1 with Tottenham Hotspur at St Andrew's in the sixth round of the FA Cup in February 1953, Blues held the Londoners at 2–2 in the replay at White Hart Lane. Here Blues goalkeeper Gil Merrick punches clear off the head of the Spurs centre-forward Len Duquemin. Spurs went on to win the second replay 1–0.

Another signing from Plymouth Argyle, outside-right Gordon Astall, was outstanding, as were Govan, Kinsey and Smith, while Blues gave a debut to full-back George Allen.

As Second Division champions, just, and FA Cup quarter-finalists, 1954–55 turned out to be an excellent season for Blues. By defeating Doncaster Rovers 5–1 on the last day of the League programme, they sneaked ahead of Luton Town and Rotherham on goal average after

Blues' trainer putting Alex Govan, Len Boyd and Jackie Stewart through their strides in 1953.

The Blues of 1954–55. Back row, left to right: D. Fairhurst (physiotherapist), J. Lane, J. Badham, J. Schofield, G. Merrick, J. Newman, K. Green, G. Allen, R. Shaw (trainer). Seated: G. Astall, M. Kinsey, L. Boyd, A. Turner (manager), P. Murphy, A. Govan. On ground: E. Brown, J. Hall, R. Warhurst.

Scenes of joy in the Belle Vue dressing room as Blues players raise their cups of tea in celebration after winning the Second Division Championship with a 5–1 victory over Doncaster Rovers on the last day of the 1954–55 season.

all three clubs had finished with 54 points. In fact, this was the tightest race ever for honours in League football. Former player Arthur Turner returned to the club as manager in November, and from thereon in he was able to field a relatively settled team as the fans were treated to some superb attacking football.

Liverpool suffered their heaviest League defeat ever when Blues thrashed them 9–1 in December;

The team page from the matchday programme issued for the historic game against Liverpool in December 1954.

OFFICIAL PROGRAMME   PRICE ONE PENNY

BIRMINGHAM CITY FOOTBALL CLUB LTD.

FOOTBALL LEAGUE

WEDNESDAY, MARCH 2nd, 1955

Kick-off 3.0 p.m.

BIRMINGHAM CITY

MERRICK

(2) HALL   (3) GREEN

(4) BOYD   (5) SMITH   (6) WARHURST

(7) ASTALL   (8) KINSEY   (10) MURPHY   (11) GOVAN

(9) LANE

Referee:
Mr. J. G. WILLIAMS
(Notts)

Linesmen:
Messrs. J. W. MALCOLM (red)
D. W. SMITH (Yellow)

BROOK (9)

WILLIAMS (11)   VICKERS (10)   NIGHTINGALE (8)   WEBB (7)

KERFOOT (6)   CHARLES (5)   RIPLEY (4)

HAIR (3)   DUNN (2)

WOOD

LEEDS UNITED

KEY TO SCORE BOARD

A { BOLTON WANDERERS / SUNDERLAND   B { NEWCASTLE UNITED / NOTTINGHAM FOREST

SATURDAY NEXT, MARCH 5th, 3.0 p.m.   FOOTBALL COMBINATION

LUTON TOWN RESERVES

Printed by The Studio Press (B'ham) Ltd., Elkington Street, Birmingham, 6

The rare single-sheet programme issued for the rearranged League game between Blues and Leeds United on 2 March 1955. Only 10,774 fans saw Blues win 2–0.

Port Vale were hammered 7–2 in late November and four goals were scored in 19 second-half minutes as Middlesbrough were defeated 5–2 in April. Blues hit 92 League goals in total, their biggest haul since 1893–94, and five players got into double-figures, 'Spud' Murphy again topping the charts with 20 goals, followed by Eddie Brown (signed from Coventry in October) with 17 and Govan 16.

Back in the top flight, Blues did exceedingly well in 1955–56. They achieved their highest-ever position

Blues prepare for life back in the First Division (August 1955). Back row, left to right: J. Hall, E. Brown, J. Watts, J. Schofield, T. Smith, J. Badham. Front row: N. Kinsey, J. Lane, L. Boyd, P. Murphy, A. Govan.

Blues goalkeeper Gil Merrick saves at the feet of Manchester City's Joe Hayes during the 1956 FA Cup Final.

by finishing sixth with 45 points – just four behind runners-up Blackpool. They also reached their second FA Cup Final, losing 3–1 to Manchester City, whose German-born goalkeeper Bert Trautmann broke his neck when diving at the feet of Peter Murphy. Kinsey scored for Blues, who were second best on the day.

Earlier in the competition, a record crowd saw the 7–1 third round win at Torquay and in fact Blues played all their Cup ties away this season, with the semi-final being a repeat of their 1931 victory over Sunderland. There were plenty more exciting games during the campaign, including a 4–3 League win over Manchester City at St Andrew's when skipper

Blues' 1956 FA Cup Final squad. Back row, left to right: R. Shaw (trainer), J. Hall, J. Newman, T. Smith, G. Merrick, L. Boyd, K. Green, J. Badham, D. Fairhurst (physiotherapist). Front row: G. Astall, N. Kinsey, E. Brown, A. Turner (manager), R. Warhurst, P. Murphy, A. Govan. On ground: W. Finney, J. Watts.

Len Boyd thumped in a dramatic late goal, a 6–2 thrashing of Everton, a 5–2 victory over Bolton and 5–0 wins at Portsmouth and at home to Huddersfield.

Blues played their first-ever game in a major European competition, drawing 0–0 with Inter Milan in a group 'B' match in the Inter Cities Fairs Cup in mid-May. Eddie Brown then grabbed Blues' first goal in this competition in the return leg, to become the first Blues player to score in three different major competitions in the same season (League, FA Cup and Fairs Cup). Two signings that term were Bill Finney from Stoke City and Bryan Orritt from Bangor.

TWO EUROPEAN FINALS, RELEGATION BATTLES

Blues slipped down to 13th in the table in 1956–57 and they played their last-ever League

game on a Christmas Day, beating Sheffield Wednesday at home 4–0. A record crowd at Brunton Park of 27,445 saw Blues' third-round FA Cup clash with Carlisle United. Leading 3–1 with two minutes to go, the Cumbrians hit back to earn a replay. But with Wembley again in their sights, Blues eventually fell to the Busby Babes of Manchester United in the semi-final.

The captains of the 1957 FA Cup semi-finalists: Roy Warhurst (Blues), Ray Barlow (West Bromwich Albion) and Johnny Dixon (Aston Villa).

In October 1956, floodlights were switched on at St Andrew's for the first time as Blues drew 3–3 with the German club Borussia Dortmund in front of 45,000 spectators. Dick Neal (from Wolves), full-back Brian Farmer who had been with the club since 1950 and defender Graham Sissons all made their Blues debuts this season. Retaining 13th position in the First Division in 1957–58, Blues nevertheless completed the double over Aston Villa for the first time since 1905–06. In the Fairs Cup semi-final (carried over from the previous season) battling Blues lost in a replay to the Spanish giants Barcelona. In the first leg, it was 3–3 at half-time before Peter Murphy scored a 63rd-minute winner for Blues, only for Barcelona to bring the aggregate scores level at 4–4 in the Nou Camp and then win the replay in Basle, Switzerland by 2–1.

In February 1958, the former Arsenal and England player Pat Beasley was appointed joint manager of Blues. An annoyed Arthur Turner threatened to resign but was persuaded to stay on – for the time being! Dick Neal took over at left-half from Roy Warhurst this season while wingers Mike Hellawell (ex-Queen's Park Rangers) and Harry Hooper (signed from Wolves for £20,000) were among those who made their debuts. In September 1958, a disgruntled manager Arthur Turner left St Andrew's, leaving Pat Beasley in sole charge of the team, and under his guidance Blues claimed ninth place in the First Division, having started the campaign poorly – no wins in their opening six games, which included a 6–0 home drubbing by West Bromwich Albion. They did, however, make excellent progress in the Inter Cities Fairs Cup, once again qualifying for the semi-finals which would be played in October and November 1959. In a thrilling second round battle with Dinamo Zagreb, Blues came through 4–3 on aggregate to set up a semi-final clash with the Belgian club, Union St Gilloise.

Blues in Europe, 1959. Back row, left to right: R. Stubbs, R. Neal, G. Merrick, P. Murphy, J. Schofield, J. Watts, G. Allen. Second row: K. Fish (trainer), B. Farmer, G. Astall, T. Smith, B. Larkin, J. Gordon, W. Hume, P. Beasley (manager). On ground: B. Taylor, G. Sissons.

Johnny Gordon, a £10,000 buy from Portsmouth, scored 13 minutes into his Blues debut against Leicester in September, and the former Portsmouth star went on to finish second top-scorer behind Bunny Larkin (19 goals to 11). Winger Brian Taylor also contributed five League goals following his £10,000 move from Walsall. Sadly, right-back Jeff Hall played his last game for Blues against Portsmouth on 21 March 1959. He was diagnosed with polio soon afterwards and died on 4 April…a sad loss to both club and country. A promising young striker from Quinton, Robin Stubbs, burst on the scene this season, scoring nine goals in just 12 League games.

Blues were almost relegated in 1959–60. They scrambled clear of the trap-door after winning two of their last three games to finish in 19th position, just two points clear of demoted Leeds United. But in the FA Cup it was 'as you were' when Watford won a third-round tie 2–1 in front of a near full-house at Vicarage Road.

Three goals were scored in three minutes of a League game at Preston in September, two by Blues who eventually lost 3–2. And two England players, Ronnie Allen and Derek Kevan, both hit hat-tricks in West Bromwich Albion's 7–1 win at St Andrew's in April. This made it a total of 18 goals for the Baggies in three successive League visits to Blues' territory. After 22 years as a player, Gil Merrick made his 551st and final appearance for Blues in the 2–0 home League win over Leeds United.

Left-winger Brian Taylor broke his leg 12 minutes into the Inter Cities Fairs Cup semi-final home leg with Union St Gilloise in November. New signing Jim Barrett from Nottingham Forest was also injured, but Blues still won 4–2 (8–4 on aggregate) to become the first British club to reach a major European Final, which they subsequently lost 4–1 over two legs to Barcelona. Blues played well in their home leg (0–0), but with 75,000 fans present they were outplayed in the Nou Camp and were well beaten by the Spanish Cup winners. Don Weston, signed from Leeds United to replace the injured Robin Stubbs, netted three times in 16 games. Billy Rudd from Stalybridge Celtic was another debutant this season.

MERRICK AS MANAGER, LEAGUE CUP GLORY

Pat Beasley had been replaced as manager at St Andrew's by Gil Merrick in May 1960, but for the former goalkeeper, his first season in charge was nerve-wracking to say the least as Blues amazingly lost their last five matches yet somehow escaped demotion by the skin of their teeth, finishing in 19th position, two points clear of disaster. They looked safe after beating Cardiff City at home on 3 April, but then something went completely wrong as they lost, in turn, to Tottenham Hotspur, Manchester United, Blackpool, Burnley and Leicester City in the space of 26 days to slide down the table to the brink of disaster. If it had not been for Newcastle United (two wins in their last eight outings) and Preston North End (none in their last seven) then Blues would have sunk without trace.

When they beat Preston 3–2 in January, it was their first win at Deepdale for over 25 years. And they also took three points off Newcastle, but their awful away form, 15 defeats, let them down badly. In the game at White Hart Lane, Spurs were 3–0 up after 14 minutes and went on to double their score, making it a nightmare debut for Blues' 'keeper Colin Withers. Another goalkeeper, Johnny Schofield, was carried off with a fractured skull in the home game with Manchester United in November. He later had a metal plate inserted in his head.

Blues slipped out of the FA Cup in the fifth round at Leicester and were eliminated in round three of the inaugural League Cup competition, having earlier won their opening game at Bradford thanks to a Mike Hellawell goal, Blues' first in the competition. Surprisingly, in the context of their League form, Blues once more reached the Final of the Inter Cities Fairs Cup (to be played over two legs in September and October 1961). That had some thrilling victories over the Hungarian club Ujpesti Dozsa and Boldklub Copenhagen before twice beating Inter Milan 2–1 to set up a final showdown with another Italian club, AS Roma. And there have not been too many managers who, in their first season in charge, have led their team into a major Final, like Merrick did.

Despite having Johnny Gordon sent off, Blues scored twice in the last three minutes to beat Ujpesti Dozsa 2–1 in the second leg of their first round tie. All eight goals in the 4–4 away draw in Copenhagen were scored in the space of 47 minutes. Blues led 3–1 after an hour. In the return fixture, Blues netted three times in five minutes just before half-time before going on to win 9–4 on aggregate. Three stars of the future, Malcolm Beard, Winston Foster and Terry Hennessey, plus top-scorer Jimmy Harris, a £20,000 buy from Everton in December, midfield schemer Jimmy Bloomfield, bought for £7,000 from Arsenal, and Scottish winger Bertie Auld, who cost £15,000 from Celtic, all made their debuts this season, the latter in the second leg of the Fairs Cup semi-final against Inter Milan.

Blues rose to 17th place in the First Division table in 1961–62, but it could, and should, have been better. They lost three and drew one of their last four games and slipped down from near halfway. They also did poorly in both domestic Cup competitions and lost in the Fairs Cup Final over two legs to AS Roma. Diego Camps netted a hat-trick for Espanyol in their 5–2 second-round first-leg win of this tournament, while in the return leg four players were sent off. The average League attendance at St Andrew's this term was the lowest since 1955 (23,537).

Six players – Malcolm Beard, Trevor Smith, Mike Hellawell, Jimmy Harris, Bertie Auld and Johnny Schofield – all made over 40 senior appearances this term, Beard and Hellawell being ever-present. Two new signings, Stan Lynn, a £2,000 buy from Aston Villa, and Ken Leek, who cost £23,000 from Newcastle United, both played well, Leek top-scoring with 20 goals.

At long last, after 82 years of playing in competitive football, Blues finally won a major domestic trophy, lifting the Football League Cup by beating rivals Aston Villa 3–1 on aggregate in the two-legged Final of 1962–63. This victory certainly made up for another indifferent season of First Division football which saw Blues escape relegation by defeating FA Cup finalists Leicester City 3–2 at St Andrew's on the very last day. Prior to that they had staggered along, only occasionally producing a worthwhile performance, and as the games began to run out a wobbly defence started to leak goals alarmingly, Blackpool and Blackburn both smashing in six and Liverpool five as Blues battled for their lives at the base of the table. Full-back Colin Green, a £12,000 buy from Everton in December, made his debut this season.

In 1963–64, for the fourth season running, Blues came mighty close to losing their top-flight status. This time they stayed up after winning their last two games against Liverpool and Sheffield United to finish in 20th position once again, a point above Bolton Wanderers.

In fact they had to beat the Blades on the final day – a draw would have sent them down on goal-average! It was also a poor Cup campaign as well, Blues going out in both domestic competitions at the first hurdle. Alex Harley (a big-money signing from Manchester City) did reasonably well at centre-forward, and the ex-Wolves and Villa player Bobby Thomson battled tirelessly up front. Ray Martin made his debut at right-back and a young Johnny Vincent showed what he had to offer with a couple of impressive displays in midfield.

RELEGATION, STAN CULLIS, TWO SEMI-FINALS

Gil Merrick was sacked as Blues manager in April 1964 and was replaced by Joe Mallett, but neither he nor the players could do a thing right, and this time there was no saving sad Blues, who were relegated in bottom spot in 1964–65, three points below Midland neighbours Wolves. Blues lost 16 of their 21 away games and gave away 96 goals, the most ever in a single season. They conceded four or more goals in a game on 10 occasions and at times were lucky not to have been beaten more heavily.

Blues were 2–0 up after 27 minutes of their FA Cup tie at West Ham, only to lose 4–2 and they also lost in the opening round of the League Cup to Chelsea. Wingers Alec Jackson, bought from West Bromwich Albion, and Dennis Thwaites tried their hardest, as did another newcomer and joint top-scorer Geoff Vowden from Nottingham Forest. Malcolm Page, Ronnie Fenton (another ex-Albion player) and Cammie Fraser made decent starts to their Blues' careers, while Winston Foster was now first choice centre-half (in place of Trevor Smith).

Playing in the Second Division for the first time in a decade, Blues found themselves in the lower reaches of the table by December 1965, at which point the club decided to swap managers, enticing the former Wolves boss Stan Cullis out of retirement to take over from Joe Mallett. Cullis did reasonably well by introducing a more attacking approach, but in the end the team finished a disappointing 10th. Unfortunately, Blues were beaten by lowly Mansfield Town in the League Cup and by Leicester City in the FA Cup. Blues' average home League attendance this season was the lowest at St Andrew's since 1914–15.

Former Dunfermline Athletic stopper Jim Herriot was now in goal, ex-Notts County and Aston Villa star Ron Wylie was in midfield and, just before Mallett left, Welshman Trevor Hockey moved to St Andrew's from Newcastle United to add some much-needed bite and commitment to the team. And Tommy Rae became Blues' first loan signing, although he never made a senior appearance.

Besides a poor ending to the 1966–67 season – four defeats on the trot – Blues again finished 10th in the League table. They also reached the sixth round of the FA Cup and the semi-finals of the League Cup. Manager Cullis certainly got the players focused in the latter competition, but they simply could not come to grips with Third Division leaders Queen's Park Rangers inspired by a developing Rodney Marsh in the semis and lost 7–2 on aggregate. Blues also crashed out of the FA Cup to another London club, Tottenham Hotspur, losing 6–0 in a replay at White Hart Lane. Both QPR and Spurs went on to win the respective competitions.

The Chelsea duo of Barry Bridges (bought for a record £55,000) and Albert Murray and Fulham's Scottish international Graham Leggatt were among the new faces brought into St Andrew's this season, while forward Phil Summerill, a young player from Erdington who

Blues skipper Ron Wylie with his manager Stan Cullis.

would do well in later years, made his Blues debut in March. That season Blues' teenagers lost 2–0 on aggregate to Sunderland in the two-legged FA Youth Cup Final.

Blues took fourth place in the Division in 1967–68, six points short of the runners'-up spot, and they reached another Cup semi-final. A poor spell either side of the New Year, when they won only once in six League starts, knocked the stuffing out of the team, and to be fair after that Blues were always playing catch up. Knocked out in the third round of the League Cup, Blues did much better in the FA Cup, beating two top First Division sides, Arsenal and Chelsea, before losing, perhaps unluckily, to neighbours West Bromwich Albion in the semi-final at Villa Park when it was a case of Fred Pickering against the Baggies' goalkeeper John Osborne. Former England centre-forward Pickering cost £50,000 from Blackburn Rovers, and he scored 15 goals this term, while top marksman Barry Bridges netted a 16-minute hat-trick in Blues' 4–1 win over Rotherham United in October.

After a woeful start when they registered only two wins in their opening nine League games, Blues struggled thereafter to make ground on the leaders and eventually settled for seventh place in 1968–69, 12 points adrift of runners-up Crystal Palace. In the FA Cup they did enough to beat the European Cup-holders Manchester United in round five but after a 2–2 home draw they lost the replay 6–2 in front of almost 62,000 fans at Old Trafford. Denis Law hit a hat-trick for the Reds. In the League Cup, Chelsea won a second-round tie courtesy of an own-goal by Blues' defender Winston Foster. Jimmy Greenhoff, a £70,000 capture from Leeds United, arrived at the club just after gaining a Fairs Cup-winners' medal. Defender Dave Robinson, Garry Pendrey and the Latchford brothers, goalkeeper Dave and striker Bob, also made their Blues' debuts this season, while former England full-back Bobby Thomson was a £40,000 signing from Wolves.

Blues played well below par throughout the 1969–70 season – and at times they were really dreadful. They finished in 18th position, just four points clear of relegation, went out of both Cups in the opening round and in March manager Cullis packed up. Twenty League games were lost and 78 goals conceded as Blues' defence, at times, simply collapsed. They were hammered 6–2 at Millwall, 6–0 at Norwich City and 6–0 at Sheffield United and also lost heavily at Preston and Swindon…and it was not as if goalkeeper Jim Herriot played badly. Far from it, it was the players in front of him who failed to do the business.

Tony Hateley, the former Notts County, Aston Villa, Liverpool and Coventry City striker, was signed for £72,000 in August, while George Johnston (from Arsenal) was another debutant this season.

TREVOR FRANCIS, PROMOTION, MORE SEMI-FINAL GLOOM

Brian Clough, Don Revie and Ronnie Allen had all been on Blues' wanted list before they appointed Freddie Goodwin as the club's new manager in May 1970. He did a decent enough job in his first season, Blues edging up to ninth in the table, well off the pace in terms of promotion, but with a much stronger and tighter defence. In February, Trevor Francis became the first 16-year-old to score four goals in a League game, achieving the feat against Bolton.

Blues, 2–0 down in their League Cup replay against Wrexham, hit back to win 3–2 but failed to reach the fifth round, while exiting the FA Cup in the third. Besides Francis, other debutants this season included goalkeeper Mike Kelly (from Queen's Park Rangers), midfielders Alan Campbell (from Cardiff City) and George Smith (from Middlesbrough), strapping centre-half Roger Hynd (from Crystal Palace, once of Rangers) and winger Gordon Taylor (from Bolton Wanderers).

By beating Hull City 2–0 in April 1972, Blues completed their 36th consecutive home League game without defeat, and it also set them up for promotion, which they achieved on the very last day of the season with a 1–0 win at Orient. They also reached the semi-finals of the FA Cup, only to lose to double-chasing Leeds United at Hillsborough. It turned out to be an excellent campaign for manager Goodwin, who got his players working for each other from the word go. Blues produced some splendid performances, winning 19 and drawing 18 of their 42 matches and thoroughly deserving their success, and the fans celebrated too, with the average attendance at St Andrew's topping 32,000, the best since 1957.

Tommy Carroll (from Ipswich Town) was the first loan signing to play for Blues, making his debut (with Bob Hatton) at Burnley in October. Youngster Steve Phillips, goalkeeper Paul Cooper, the versatile Kenny Burns, who became a firm favourite with the St Andrew's fans, defender Stan Harland, former captain of 1969 League Cup winners Swindon Town, winger Mike O'Grady (on loan from Wolves) and striker Bob Hatton, who would prove a great aide to Francis and Bob Latchford, were some of manager Goodwin's new introductions this season.

The *Blues News* programme from 1972.

Back in the top flight for the first time in seven years, Blues did reasonably well in 1972–73, finishing a creditable 10th, but failed to do much in the Cup competitions. They claimed some good scalps in the League – Everton, Leeds United, the champions Liverpool and Manchester United among them – and were unlucky not to have beaten runners-up Arsenal and Liverpool at Anfield. In fact, Blues led 3–1 on Merseyside before eventually losing 4–3. Full-back Tony Want (from Tottenham), experienced midfielder Bobby Hope (from West Bromwich Albion), centre-half John Roberts (the club's first six-figure fee at £140,000 from Arsenal) and youngsters Jimmy Calderwood and Paul Hendrie all made their Blues debuts that season.

In football, things can change so quickly. After doing well the previous season, Blues struggled throughout 1973–74 and, due to a poor away record, they finished a disappointing 19th in the League with 37 points, only five clear of relegation. They also failed again in all of the Cup competitions. Only occasionally did they produce a worthwhile display, their best wins coming against Arsenal, Leicester City and Queen's Park Rangers. Full-back Dennis Clarke, the first substitute to appear in an FA Cup Final (for WBA in 1968), Welsh international goalkeeper Gary Sprake (from Leeds United), able-bodied defender Joe Gallagher and the former Everton duo of Howard Kendall and Archie Styles all made their Blues debuts that term. The latter arrived at St Andrew's as part of the record £350,000 deal which saw Bob Latchford move to Goodison Park.

For the second time in three seasons and for the seventh time since World War Two, Blues reached the semi-finals of the FA Cup in 1974–75. This time they were desperately unlucky to lose to a last-minute goal in the dying seconds of extra-time in their replay with Fulham. But in the League it was a struggle, and 17th place was the best Freddie Goodwin's side could manage. They could well have been relegated, but in the end poor results on the part of Chelsea, Luton and a few others, meant that disaster was averted by just four points. Ricky Sbragia, Steve Bryant, Gary Emmanuel and Ian Smith were among Blues' debutants that season, while future Blues star Colin Todd (Derby County) was voted Footballer of the Year.

SIR ALF RAMSEY, JIM SMITH, FIRST £1 MILLION FOOTBALLER

Season 1975–76 was another nail-biting one for Blues, who escaped relegation once again, thanks to other clubs dropping points at crucial times. Freddie Goodwin was replaced in the manager's chair by Willie Bell in September and the former Leeds United defender certainly had a tough time, results going against him all the time, although it must be said that the team on the whole played well below par on a number of occasions.

Seven points from their last four games effectively kept Blues up in 19th position. But it was close. Going into their final match, it was either Blues or Wolves for the drop, along with Burnley and Sheffield United who were already doomed. Blues were at Bramall Lane, while Wolves entertained Championship-chasing Liverpool. Blues scraped their vital point while Wolves lost 3–1...that was how close it was in the end. Striker Peter Withe and wide-midfielder Terry Hibbitt (brother of Wolves' star Kenny) were two players introduced to Blues' first team this season. For the first time, the charge to stand on the terraces at St Andrew's rose to £1.

Manager Willie Bell steered Blues up to 13th place in the table in 1976–77 – yet they were still only four points clear of relegation, and there was no joy in any of the Cup competitions. The two best performances of the campaign came in the League with 6–2 and 5–1 wins over Leicester City (away) and Derby County (home) respectively. In fact, at Filbert Street, Blues led 4–0 at half-time and then 6–0. Wingers John Connolly and Gary Jones (both from Everton), seasoned goalkeeper and star of Sunderland's 1973 FA Cup Final victory over Leeds United, Jim Montgomery, and star of the future Kevan Broadhurst were among the handful of Blues debutants that season, while Keith Bertschin became Blues' first-ever England Under-21 player, capped against Scotland.

Blues had three managers during the 1977–78 season – Bell until September 1977, then former England boss Sir Alf Ramsey until March 1978 and finally Jim Smith. In the end the team finished 11th in the table, well clear of danger and nowhere near the top six! In the Cup competitions it was the usual story. Midfielder Tony Towers, a League Cup-winner with Manchester City in 1976, striker Keith Bertschin from Ipswich Town and teenager Kevin Dillon were all given their Blues debuts this season.

It was all downhill for Blues from December 1978 onwards – and they fell faster once Trevor Francis had been sold to Nottingham Forest in February to officially become Britain's first £1 million footballer (sold for £1.18 million to be precise). In fact, Blues mustered only two wins during the first half of the campaign, lost eight in a row from early December to mid-February (to equal the club record) and in the end amassed just

The Birmingham City programme from August 1978.

22 points (out of a possible 126), their lowest total ever from a full 42-match programme, and their lowest tally overall since 1895–96. A lack of goals, only 37 scored, was the main problem, but generally performances in both League and Cup were pretty poor, although that horrid record run of 18 successive away defeats finally came to an end in May with a 3–1 victory at Queen's Park Rangers. New faces at St Andrew's that season included defender Pat Howard (from Arsenal), wingers Stewart Barrowclough (from Newcastle) and Steve Lynex (from Shamrock Rovers), midfielders Alan Ainscow (ex-Blackpool) and former Aston Villa star Bruce Rioch (on loan from Derby), forwards Alan Buckley (from Walsall) and Don Givens (from QPR). Also introduced to League football were two young full-backs, Mark Dennis and Belgium-born Pat Van den Hauwe.

PROMOTION, RELEGATION AND PROMOTION (AGAIN)

What a difference a year and a few new players make! After the dismal showing the previous year, Jim Smith and Blues got it all right in 1979–80, gaining promotion in third place behind Leicester City and Sunderland. They clinched a place in the top flight with a last-

The Birmingham City programme from August 1980.

match home draw with Notts County in front of 33,863 fans. With everything going well in the League, Blues failed to make progress in the Cup competitions, but who cared? Top-flight football had arrived yet again.

Experienced defender Colin Todd signed from Everton for £300,000 and made the 500th League appearance of his career when he played against Swansea in October, and another wily campaigner, Scottish international midfielder Archie Gemmill, secured from Nottingham Forest for £150,000, also made his 500th League appearance at club level, celebrating with a penalty against his former club Preston. One of the game's characters, Frank Worthington, was another excellent signing by manager Jim Smith. He cost £150,000 from Bolton Wanderers. Another useful forward was Tony Evans who arrived from Cardiff City; goalkeeper Jeff Wealands was transferred from Hull City, who in 1986 would return to St Andrew's and helped Altrincham knock Blues out of the FA Cup. Terry Lees was recruited from Dutch football and fiery left-winger Willie Johnston, once of West Bromwich Albion and Rangers, came on loan from Vancouver Whitecaps. A few months earlier, he had been 'sent home' from the 1978 World Cup for drug abuse.

Unfortunately, 1980–81 was not a great season by a long chalk as Blues plodded along to finish 13th in the Division while going out in the fourth round of the FA Cup and the fifth round of the League Cup. Due to so many poor performances (the worst coming at Ipswich, lost 5–1), the average attendance at St Andrew's dropped below the 20,000 mark for the first time since 1967. Young goalkeeper Tony Coton saved a 52nd-minute penalty on his Blues' debut against Sunderland in December, while others who made their first appearances for Blues this term included Solihull-born Ian Handysides, who was to die tragically at the age of 28 in 1990, defender Phil Hawker who, in later years would do well at Walsall, and full-back David Langan, a £350,000 buy from Derby County.

Manager Jim Smith remained in office until February 1982 before being replaced, somewhat surprisingly, by Ron Saunders who, the previous season, had guided Aston Villa to their first League Championship success in 71 years. Ironically, Saunders's first game in charge ended in a 1–0 defeat by his old club, Aston Villa, ex-Blues player Peter Withe scoring the goal.

Blues were struggling by the time Smith left. Sitting on the edge of the drop-zone and out of both Cups, they had limped along and did not do much better under Saunders, eventually finishing a disappointing 16th, only two points away from relegation. In fact, they stayed up thanks to a draw (at Leeds) and a win (at Coventry) in their last two matches.

New faces in the St Andrew's camp this season included Dutchmen Tony van Mierlo and Bud Brocken from SV Willem, Roger Jones (on loan from Derby), defenders Geoff Scott (from Leicester) and Byron Stevenson (from Leeds) and forwards Neil Whatmore (a £350,000 signing from Bolton) and Mick Harford. The latter cost £100,000 from Newcastle and scored nine goals in his first 12 outings for the club, one coming on his debut against Brighton. Blues' average home League attendance in 1981–82 was 17,116, their lowest since 1966.

Yet again Blues struggled badly on the pitch, winning only 12 of their 42 League matches in 1982–83, but thanks to a late flourish (five victories and a draw in their last six games) they managed to climb up to 17th position, just three points away from relegation. They actually went into their final game at Southampton needing to win. Brighton and Swansea were already down, and effectively it was between Blues (47 points), Luton Town (46) and Manchester City (47), who met at Maine Road, as to who would join them in Division Two. The outcome was that both Blues and Luton escaped with 1–0 wins while Manchester City went down. Kevin Summerfield, recalled from his loan spell at Walsall just 24 hours earlier, scored the winning goal against the Saddlers in the third-round FA Cup tie.

Thirty players were called up for first-team duty this season, including 11 new signings – goalkeeper Jim Blyth and Jim Hagan (from Coventry City), three former Aston Villa players, Frank Carrodus from Wrexham, Robert Hopkins and Noel Blake, midfielder Mick Halsall on loan from Liverpool, Colin Brazier from NASL club the Jackson Teamen, loan strikers Kevin Bremner (from Colchester) and Mick Ferguson (from Everton, who was later signed permanently), winger Howard Gayle (from Liverpool) and Wayne Mumford (from Manchester City), while two youngsters, Carlos Francis and Martin Kuhl, also made their senior debuts.

Season 1983–84 turned out to be a horrible one all round for Blues. They were relegated in 20th position after scoring only 39 League goals, missed out on a place in the FA Cup semi-finals by losing at home to Watford in round six and succumbed to Liverpool in the fourth round of the League Cup. And to make things even worse, the average League attendance at St Andrew's (14,106) was the lowest since 1915, meaning that gate receipts were alarmingly low. Billy Wright, signed from Everton to bolster up the defence, did a reasonable job, as did forward Tony Rees from Aston Villa, ex-West Bromwich Albion apprentice midfielder Mark McCarrick and full-back 'Harry' Roberts from Coventry City.

In 1984–85, against all the pre-season forecasts, and indeed, against all the odds, Blues stunned everyone – even their own fans – by returning to the top flight at the first attempt, amassing a record 82 points to finish runners-up behind Oxford United (84), clinching promotion with a 2–0 win over Cardiff with two matches remaining. A record number of games were won (25 – 13 away from home) while a much tighter defence conceded only 33 goals, the fewest since 1971–72. An eight-match unbeaten run at the end of the season paved the way for promotion, new

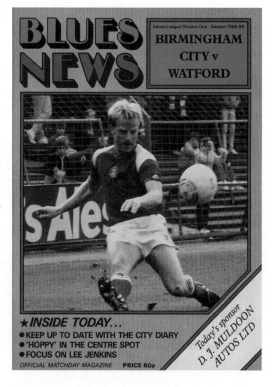

A Birmingham City programme from the 1985–86 season.

signings David Geddis (from Barnsley) and Andy Kennedy (from Rangers), along with earlier recruit Wayne Clarke from Wolves, scoring crucial goals. In the FA Cup, Blues were involved in a four-match battle with Norwich City before going out in the third round. Other new signings who were totally committed included midfielders Des Bremner (ex-Aston Villa) and one-time Manchester United star Gerry Daly, centre-half Ken Armstrong (from Southampton) and full-back Ray Ranson from Manchester City, while star of the future (for Arsenal and England) goalkeeper David Seaman, a £100,000 buy from Peterborough United, took over from Tony Coton.

DOWN AGAIN, WORST SEASON EVER, LOW CROWDS

In May 1986, one local newspaper headline stated: 'Blues are up and down like a yo-yo' after another frustrating season which saw them relegated back to the Second Division. All round it was a disastrous campaign – only eight League games were won, a record 29 lost, 30 goals scored, 73 conceded and just 29 points obtained, and to add insult to injury non-League side Altrincham (with ex-Blues goalkeeper Jeff Wealands in their line-up) came to St Andrew's and knocked Blues out of the FA Cup in the third round.

On 16 January, two days after that humiliating Cup defeat and on the back of a record 17-match winless League run, Ron Saunders resigned as manager, replaced in the hot-seat by John Bond, who had previously been in charge of Swansea City. He did his best, but Blues were bad, and this was clearly emphasised by poor attendances. Indeed, only 5,833 bothered to turn up for the game against Southampton in April, the lowest for a League match at St Andrew's since March 1955. Afterwards it was hinted that Blues just might seek a ground-sharing plan with Walsall or Wolves! Mark Jones, who had arrived at the club the previous season in a player-exchange deal with Brighton for Mick Ferguson, forward Steve Whitton (from West Ham) and up-and-coming youngsters Julian Dicks and John Frain all made their Blues debuts. The latter would remain at St Andrew's until 1997, making 337 appearances for the club.

Blues had another poor season in 1986–87. They struggled desperately at times before clinging on to 19th position in the League, avoiding successive relegations by just two points, and falling out of both Cup competitions early on. In fact, it was a good job that there were three other Division Two teams worse than Blues this term! The attendance for the home League game with Sheffield United in December (a mere 5,007) was the lowest at St Andrew's for 61 years. Blues' average home crowd of 7,426 was the worst-ever at the ground. On the injury front, defender Paul Hart (signed from Sheffield Wednesday) collided with Tommy Williams (ex-Leicester City) in the home League game against Plymouth Argyle and never played for Blues again. And Brian 'Harry' Roberts broke his leg in the 60th minute of the League game against West Bromwich Albion, but played on despite the pain.

Following David Seaman's move to Queen's Park Rangers, Blues replaced him with Roger Hansbury from Cambridge United before introducing Paul Tomlinson from Sheffield United. Vince Overson (from Burnley) took over at centre-half; Dennis Mortimer, Aston Villa's League and European Cup-winning captain, was brought into midfield, while young full-back Kevin Ashley, Luton Town striker Marc North and winger Steve Wigley (from Sheffield United in an exchange deal with Martin Kuhl) were given chances late on.

For Blues, 1987–88 was another poor season. The team finished 19th in the table, avoiding the drop by just two points. The fans continued to stay away in their thousands – the season's average at St Andrew's being just over 8,500 – although the last 30,000 crowd at the ground (34,494) witnessed the 1–0 FA Cup defeat by Nottingham Forest. The former West Bromwich Albion trio of goalkeeper Tony Godden and midfielders Gary Childs and John Trewick, a returning Peter Withe from Portland Timbers, Colin Robinson from Shrewsbury Town, Ian Atkins from Ipswich and Kevin Langley from Manchester City were among the players who signed for Blues this season.

Even the most dedicated and avid Blues supporters agree that 1988–89 was the worst season in the club's history. With another new manager in charge, their eighth in 20 years, Blues crashed through the floorboards of the Second Division and into the Third for the first time ever. They finished 23rd, no less than 12 points from safety, won only eight and lost a record 27 of their 46 matches, scored 31 goals (only 10 away), mustered 35 points out of a possible 138 and attracted an all-time average home League attendance to St Andrew's of 6,289, with only 4,026 fans bothering to show their faces for the clash with Swindon Town in mid-April – the lowest League crowd at St Andrew's for 76 years.

Ex-player Garry Pendrey was the man chosen to get Blues back into the top flight, but his players never responded and of the 29 he chose, it would be fair to say that only half-a-dozen pulled their weight. After crashing 5–0 to Aston Villa in their away League Cup tie in October (eventually losing 7–0 on aggregate), Blues trailed their neighbours 5–0 at half-time in a Simod Cup tie a month later before losing 6–0 – this being their heaviest defeat in any major competition against their arch-rivals. Youngsters Ian Clarkson, Dean Peer and Simon Sturridge, goalkeeper Martin Thomas (from Newcastle United) and striker Carl Richards (from Bournemouth) all did well in their first season of League action with the club.

With the former Spurs and Derby player Dave Mackay installed as manager, in August 1989 Blues won their first-ever game in Division Three, beating Crewe Alexandra 3–0, Mark Yates scoring the first goal at this level. But after a decent enough start (six wins in their opening 10 matches) they fell off the pace and eventually finished in seventh position, a massive 27 points behind the champions Bristol Rovers and 21 adrift of third-placed Notts County. Blues also failed to make much progress in the Cup competitions. Defenders Phil Sprosen (signed from Port Vale) and Trevor

A Birmingham City programme from the 1988–89 season.

Matthewson (from Lincoln), striker Dennis Bailey (acquired from Crystal Palace) and midfielders Nigel Gleghorn (ex-Ipswich and Manchester City) and Dougie Bell (recruited from Shrewsbury Town) made their Blues debuts this season.

THIRD DIVISION FOOTBALL, WEMBLEY TRIUMPH

In 1990–91, for the first time in modern day history, Blues failed to reach the third round of the FA Cup following their defeat by Brentford, but they did give their supporters something to cheer about by winning the Leyland DAF Cup at Wembley. In late January, after making their best start to a League campaign for 91 years (unbeaten in 12 games, eight of them consecutive draws, a record), Blues found themselves down in 15th place.

At this point, Mackay resigned, handing over his duties to fellow Scot Lou Macari. The former Manchester United player certainly turned things round, and when a ball was kicked for the last time in May Blues lay in 12th position and, of course, they had a trophy under their belts after beating Tranmere Rovers 3–2 in the Leyland DAF Final, their first visit to the Empire Stadium for 44 years. Full-back Greg Downs (from Coventry City), striker Trevor Aylott (ex- Bournemouth), big John Gayle (from Wimbledon) and wide-man Ian Rodgerson (from Cardiff City) were among the new faces at St Andrew's.

Somewhat surprisingly, Macari left St Andrew's in June 1991 and was replaced two months later by Terry Cooper, who quickly got things sorted out on the pitch, and only two League defeats were suffered in the first four months of the season. Blues were flying and, despite an early FA Cup exit, they powered on in the League, eventually claiming the runners'-up spot behind Brentford. Their home form was the key factor (15 wins and six draws), while on the road they ran up eight victories including important ones at

Peterborough and West Bromwich Albion. The win at the Hawthorns saw Blues replace the Baggies at the top of the table.

Martin Thomas, Alan Miller (on loan from Arsenal) and Kevin Dearden (from Hull City) shared the goalkeeping position; centre-half Martin Hicks was recruited from Reading to replace Overson (sold to Stoke City); Louie Donowa and David Rennie (from Bristol City) and the manager's son Mark Cooper (from Exeter City) came into midfield while South African John Paskin (ex-West Bromwich Albion and Wolves) and Coventry old boy Kevin Drinkell were utilised up front.

Blues were back to their bad ways in 1992–93, clinging on to their First Division

A Birmingham City programme from the 1990–91 season in the third division.

(old Second) status by two points thanks to a win over Charlton Athletic on the very last day. After a good start (four straight wins), Blues huffed and puffed after that and in the end just about deserved to survive – although some say they were lucky! In the Anglo-Italian Cup, only 139 spectators paid to watch the tie in Lucchese in mid-December – the lowest crowd ever to attend a competitive match involving Blues, home or away. Four goalkeepers, Bob Catlin (from Notts County), young David Foy, Andy Gosney (from Portsmouth) and 35-year-old former Manchester United stopper Les Sealey, two full-backs, Paul Holmes (from Torquay), Scott Hiley (from Exeter) and young Graham Potter, defenders Darren Rogers (from West Bromwich Albion) and Paul Mardon (from Bristol City), midfielder George Parris (from West Ham) and forwards Paul Peschisolido (from Toronto Blizzard), the lanky Mark Sale (from Rocester) and Darren Rowbotham (also from Torquay) were all called up by manager Cooper.

BARRY FRY, WEMBLEY GLORY (AGAIN), LOADS OF PLAYERS!

Cooper was Blues' manager for the first half of the 1993–94 season, Barry Fry (brought in from Southend United) for the second half, and it was the latter who, unfortunately, took Blues down once again. With the introduction of the Premier League the previous season, Blues finished third from bottom in Division One and were relegated with Oxford United and Peterborough. A poor away record (14 defeats) and only nine home wins did not help matters whatsoever – but the football was better overall, and the average League attendance at St Andrew's rose to 14,378 – the highest since 1983; however, there was a crowd of just 2,710 for Blues' Anglo-Italian Cup tie against Wolves – the lowest for a competitive game at St Andrew's since 1910.

Signed from Benfica, Jose Dominguez, at 5ft 3ins tall, became the smallest player ever to appear for Blues when he made his League debut at Grimsby in March. Other debutants this season included goalkeepers Ian Bennett (from Peterborough) and Kevin Miller (from Exeter), full-back Paul Fenwick (from Canadian club Winnipeg Fury), centre-halves Liam Daish (Cambridge United), Richard Dryden (Notts County) and former Arsenal and West Bromwich Albion star Chris Whyte (from Leeds), midfielders Gary Cooper (from Peterborough), Paul Harding (Notts County) and Kenny Lowe (Stoke), wingers Ted McMinn (Derby) and David Smith (Coventry) and forwards Neil Doherty (Barrow), Steve McGavin (Colchester), Steve Claridge (a £150,000 capture from Cambridge United), Paul Moulden (Oldham), Andy Saville (£155,000 from Hartlepool), Carl Shutt (Leeds) and Danny Wallace (£250,000 from Manchester United). And Blues, as a club, were fined a record £55,000 by the Football League for illegally approaching manager Fry before he had resigned his position at Roots Hall.

In 1994–95, Blues had an unbeaten run of 23 games, 20 in the League – a club record – as they won the Division Two Championship in style with a total of 89 points – their best ever. Manager Barry Fry used a record 41 players in completing 63 matches (League and Cup), and in-form goalkeeper Ian Bennett kept a club record 19 clean sheets. That gave Blues a 'minor' double – having won the Auto-Windscreen Shield at Wembley a fortnight earlier against Carlisle United. Paul Tait's 'golden goal' decided the contest in the 103rd minute, and in fact the same player had scored Blues' first-ever 'golden goal' in the semi-final victory over Swansea City.

Blues achieved their biggest League win, home or away, since 1959 when beating Blackpool 7–1 at St Andrew's on New Year's Eve, having been 1–0 down after eight minutes. Jonathan Hunt, a £50,000 buy from Southend United, hit a hat-trick in a 5–3 AWS win at Peterborough – the first treble by a Blues player since David Geddis's nine years earlier. In January 1995, the tallest and heaviest footballer ever to play for Blues (at that time), striker Kevin Francis, was signed from Stockport County for £800,000. Standing 6ft 7in and weighing 16st 10lb, this giant of a man went on to score some excellent goals for the club. Three other signings this term from manager Fry's former club Southend were right-back Gary Poole, centre-half Mick Bodley and winger Ricky Otto, while striker Gary Bull was secured on loan from Nottingham Forest, defender Dave Barnett arrived from Barnet and forward Paul Williams from Crystal Palace.

In 1995–96 manager Barry Fry called on a staggering 47 players as Blues re-established themselves in the second tier of English football, although not without a fight. They had to put in a lot of hard graft before finally settling in 15th place, just six points (two wins) from relegation. Although their League form was moderate, in the League Cup Blues played exceptionally well, reaching the semi-finals before losing 5–1 on aggregate to Premier League side Leeds United.

Veteran goalkeeper Fred Barber, Paul Barnes (from York City) Jonathan Bass, Jason Bowen (from Swansea), Gary Breen (from Peterborough), Steve Castle (ex-Plymouth Argyle), Ken Charlery (Peterborough), John Cornforth (also from Swansea), Andy Edwards (Southend), Steve Finnan (Welling United), Richard Forsyth (Kidderminster Harriers), Martin Grainger (Brentford), Dutch 'keeper Bart Griemink (WK Emmen), Danny Hill (on loan from Spurs), Michael Johnson (Notts County), Jae Martin (Southend), David Preece (on loan from Derby), young defender Simon Rea, Ian Richardson (from Dagenham & Redbridge), Sigurd Rushfeldt, Vinny Samways, John Sheridan and Mark Ward were among the players who made their senior debuts for Blues this season, while striker Paul Peschisolido returned for a second spell at St Andrew's, signed for £400,000 from Stoke City. Blues' average home League attendance this term was 18,086 – the best since 1981.

In May 1996, 17 years after leaving St Andrew's, Trevor Francis returned to the club, this time as manager and, to give him credit, he did not have a bad first season in charge. Blues finished a respectable 10th in the Division, only five points from a Play-off spot. Drawing 15 of their 46 League matches did make things difficult at times, but a tight defence (only 48 goals conceded) was a big plus in Francis's strategy, and it certainly boded well for the future.

£100,000 Swedish international winger Anders Limpar was one of four players signed from Everton. The other three were full-back Gary Ablett for £390,000, midfielder Barry Horne for £250,000 and defender Matt Jackson (on loan). Also on view were two strikers, Marco Gabbiadini (on loan from Derby) and Mike Newell (a £775,000 buy from Blackburn), midfielders Chris Holland (Newcastle), Bryan Hughes (who cost £750,000 from Wrexham) and Martyn O'Connor (a £500,000 signing from Peterborough) as well as two more Derby players, goalkeeper Steve Sutton and defender Darren Wassall.

Blues needed to beat Charlton Athletic at St Andrew's on the last day of the 1997–98 season to clinch a Play-off spot. Unfortunately, they could only draw and therefore finished in seventh position, one place below Sheffield United on goals scored. To get as close as they did, Blues had goalkeeper Ian Bennett to thank. He broke his own club record by keeping 23 clean sheets, 21 in the League, two in the League Cup. It was a bitter disappointment for manager Francis and his players, because Blues had produced some excellent displays during the course of the season, the highlight being a resounding and record-equalling 7–0 away win at Stoke in January. They completed the double over the Potters and did likewise over Manchester City, scoring a last-gasp winner in each game. In fact, they were 1–0 down going into stoppage time in the home clash in December, but Nicky Forster (a £700,000 signing from Brentford) netted an equaliser before Martyn O'Connor bagged the winner in the 97th minute.

Among the new faces at St Andrew's this season were midfielder Chris Marsden (a £500,000 recruit from Stockport), striker Dele Adebola from Crewe Alexandra (for £1 million), fellow goal-getter Paul Furlong (£1.5 million from Chelsea), left-back Simon Charlton (who cost £250,000 from Huddersfield Town), former England striker Tony Cottee (on loan from Leicester), German 'Tony' Hey (from Fortuna Cologne), winger Jon McCarthy (a £1.85 million signing from York City), the versatile Zimbabwean Peter Ndlovu (who was bought for £1.6 million from Coventry City) and defender Darren Purse (transferred for £800,000 from Oxford United).

PLAY-OFF DISAPPOINTMENT, FRANCIS AS MANAGER

It was a case of so near yet so far for Blues in 1998–99. After playing some excellent football, they finished their League programme with four wins out of six to claim fourth position, thus qualifying for the Play-offs, but after a 1–1 aggregate draw with Watford, the Hornets won the resulting penalty shoot-out 7–6 to leave Trevor Francis, his players and the supporters totally devastated. Blues actually went to the top of the First Division table in September after beating Stockport 2–0 at home...this being their highest position all season. Players who arrived at St Andrew's this term included £1.2 million defender David Holdsworth from Sheffield United, midfielder Graham Hyde, on a free transfer from Sheffield Wednesday, and full-backs Simon Marsh from Oxford United for £250,000 and Gary Rowett, who cost £1 million from Derby County, while the former Aston Villa goalkeeper Kevin Poole was brought in from Leicester City. England Youth international striker Andrew Johnson also made his debut.

It was Play-off disappointment yet again for Blues in 1999–2000. After a fifth-place finish in Division One, they capitulated 4–0 in their semi-final first-leg at St Andrew's against Barnsley and, in truth, there was no way back for Trevor Francis's men, although they did salvage some pride with a 2–1 win at Oakwell. Among Blues' debutants this season were several loanees, including ex-Portsmouth and Newcastle United full-back John Beresford, West Ham's future England international and Manchester United midfielder Michael Carrick, Scottish international Allan Johnston (from Sunderland), two goalkeepers, Richard Knight (from Derby) and the Norwegian Thomas Myhre (from Everton), Isaiah Rankin (from Bradford City) and the Liberian international striker Chris Wreh (from Arsenal). Other debutants included former trainee James Dyson, the Zambian Jimmy Haarhoff, Australian wide-man Stan Lazaridis, Brazilian striker Marcelo and the former Chelsea midfielder Eddie Newton.

In 2000–01, for the third season running, Blues missed out on the chance of reaching the Premier League by losing in the semi-final Play-off, this time in a penalty shoot-out at Preston North End, who had actually missed from the spot in normal time. Manager Trevor Francis was distraught after the game at Deepdale. With time fast running out, Blues were leading 2–1 on aggregate and virtually booked in at Millennium Stadium, Cardiff.. But then it all went wrong as 'Izzy' Rankine struck a dramatic last-minute equaliser to take the game into extra-time and then to penalties. A raging Francis disputed the referee's choice of ends for the shoot-out and twice led his players off the pitch in an angry protest before finally agreeing to continue. To make things worse, Jon McCarthy broke his leg for a third time as a Blues player.

Geoff Horsfield became the club's first £2 million-plus footballer (signed from Fulham), while other Blues debutants this term included defenders Peter Atherton, former Albion and Liverpool left-back David Burrows, two ex-Villa players, Gary Charles and Carl Tiler, Nicky Eaden from Barnsley, midfielders Jamie Pollock (on loan from Crystal Palace) and Danny Sonner (from Sheffield Wednesday) and forwards Mark Burchill, on loan from Celtic, Jacques Williams (secured from the French club, Bordeaux) and Curtis Woodhouse (a £1 million buy from Sheffield United).

INTO THE PREMIER LEAGUE WITH STEVE BRUCE

Premier League here we come! At long last, Blues reached the 'promised land' by succeeding in the Football League Play-offs at the end of the 2001–02 season. Around 35,000 fans celebrated in style at Cardiff's Millennium Stadium after Norwich City were defeated 4–2 in a penalty shoot-out following an initial 1–1 draw in the Final.

Blues' goalkeeper Nico Vaesen (signed from Huddersfield for £800,000) saved one Norwich penalty before Brummie-born youngster Darren Carter cracked in the match-winning, money-spinning 12-yard kick to trigger off joyous celebrations. Blues boss Steve Bruce said: 'The courage of the players is incredible. They've fought to the death and I'm proud of them. They've done remarkably well and all credit to them – they're fantastic.'

Having sacked manager Francis in December and eventually replaced him with former Manchester United defender Bruce, Blues lost only two of their last 15 League games, as they slowly but competently moved up the table to finish fifth, clinching a Play-off spot with a final-day home victory over Sheffield United. Two months after being sacked, Francis returned to St Andrew's as boss of Crystal Palace. Directly after the match, former Eagles boss Bruce, who had resigned his position at Selhurst Park two weeks earlier, was handed the job at St Andrew's.

Peschisolido netted twice for Sheffield United against his former club in November. Debutants this season included overseas-born players Arek Bak (from Poland), Bjorn Otto Bragstad (Norway), Carlos Ferrari (Brazil), Stern John (Trinidad), Tresor Luntala (France) and Olivier Tebily (Ivory Coast), plus 33-year-old Curtis Fleming (on loan from Middlesbrough), Northern Ireland international midfielder Damien Johnson and experienced on-loan goalkeeper Alan Kelly and right-back Jeff Kenna (all from Blackburn) and former Aston Villa trainee forward Tommy Mooney (from Watford).

To finish 13th in the Premier League in 2002–03 was described by manager Bruce as being 'Excellent, better then we anticipated'. Blues had several experienced players in their line-up, including French international and World Cup-winner Christophe Dugarry (on

Penalty shoot-out star Darren Carter (left), goalkeeper Nico Vaesen and goalscorer Geoff Horsfield celebrate after Blues had beaten Norwich City in the 2003 First Division Play-off final at the Millennium Stadium, Cardiff to gain a place in the Premiership for the very first time.

loan from Bordeaux), Senegalese star Alious Cissé, Republic of Ireland star Kenny Cunningham (from Wimbledon), the American Jovan Kirovski and Republic of Ireland striker Clinton Morrison (both from Crystal Palace), Welsh internationals Andy Marriott and Robbie Savage (from Barnsley and Leicester City respectively, the latter costing £2.5 million).

They were certainly never out of their depth when mixing it with most of the top-line clubs. In fact, they took four points off Liverpool and only struggled against one of the big boys, losing 2–0 away and 4–0 at home to runners-up Arsenal who, in fact, were Blues' first-ever Premier League opponents at Highbury, when £1.5 million signing from the French club Montpellier, Cissé, was sent-off on his debut. This, incidentally, was the Gunners' record-breaking 14th successive top-flight win. An early exit from both domestic competitions was elementary as Blues played some decent football at times, especially when twice beating arch-rivals Aston Villa. There is no doubt the fans appreciated it, as the average Premier League attendance at St Andrew's was 28,813 – up by almost 7,000 on the previous season and the biggest since 1975. Players who made their debuts for Blues this season were Jamie Clapham (a £1 million signing from Ipswich Town), midfielder Stephen Clemence (bought for £250,000 from Spurs), Ferdinand Coly (also from Senegal), former Jamaican international full-back Darryl Powell (from Derby County, who moved to Sheffield Wednesday halfway through the campaign), young full-back Mat Sadler, Polish international Piotr Swierczerski (who made just one substitute appearance against Chelsea at St Andrew's in February), Matthew Upson (a £1 million signing from Arsenal and a future England centre-back) and 34-year-old defender Steve Vickers (from Middlesbrough).

Blues climbed three places in the Premier League table to finish 10th in 2003–04 – their highest position in the top flight since 1973. Yet it could have been even better. Earlier in the campaign they occupied fourth spot and, in fact, had an excellent chance of qualifying for the UEFA Cup, but managed only one win and five draws in their last nine matches and slipped disappointingly down the ladder from fifth to halfway. The 17 'PL' goals scored by on-loan Finnish international striker Mikael Forssell from Chelsea were vitally important, while the contributions made by goalkeeper Maik Taylor (a bargain buy from Fulham), defender Kenny Cunningham, midfielders David Dunn (who cost £5.5 million from Blackburn Rovers), Damien Johnson and Stephen Clemence, and the strong-running of Aussie international Stan Lazaridis, were all outstanding.

Perhaps the best team performances came against Everton, Fulham, Leeds United and Manchester City at home and Newcastle away, although they were involved in a real ding-dong thriller at Middlesbrough which ended in a 5–3 defeat. The average League attendance at St Andrew's increased to over 29,000, with a record turnout for the redesigned stadium of 29,588 witnessing the November defeat by champions-elect Arsenal. Other debutants in the Blues ranks this term were young Andrew Barrowman (one outing as a substitute), the Argentine international Luciano Figueroa (secured for £2.5 million from Rosario Central) and Martin Taylor, bought from Blackburn Rovers for £1.25 million.

RELEGATION AND ANOTHER NEW MANAGER

Blues had their moments in season 2004–05, ending with a 2–1 win over runners-up Arsenal. Ninth place was the highest they achieved, in late December after four straight wins, two coming against near-neighbours Aston Villa and West Bromwich Albion, before finally finishing 12th. Early Cup exits may well have disrupted the momentum when they happened, but overall Steve Bruce's side, blessed with a fair sprinkling of good quality players, did alright.

Several new faces arrived at St Andrew's this term, including former England forward Darren Anderton (on a free transfer from Tottenham Hotspur), striker Robbie Blake (who cost £1.25 million from Burnley), the boss's son Alex Bruce (from Blackburn Rovers), Senegalese international Salif Diao (on loan from Liverpool), Julian Gray (another free transfer from Crystal Palace), Danish international winger Jesper Gronkjaer (a £2.2 million buy from Chelsea), ex-Leicester City and England striker Emile Heskey (a £3.5 million recruit from Liverpool, with extra payments to follow regarding appearances), midfielder Muzzy Izzet (also a 'free' from Leicester City), Dutch right-back Mario Melchiot (a giveaway from Chelsea), on-loan Tunisian midfielder Mehdi Nafti (from Racing Santander), bulky Uruguayan striker Walter Pandiani (on loan from Deportivo La Coruna), pacy winger Jermaine Pennant (a £3 million signing from Arsenal) and the former Aston Villa, Manchester United and Trinidad & Tobago international Dwight Yorke (also from Blackburn).

Having been promoted together at the end of the 2001–02 season, Blues and West Bromwich Albion returned to the Championship after finishing 18th and 19th respectively in the Premier League in 2005–06. For Blues it was a poor campaign. They lost 20 of their 38 'PL' matches and scored only 28 goals, their lowest total ever as a Football League club. In fact, they failed to find the net in 20 outings, having one five-match goalless run in October and November, but somehow they managed to net five times in the game against Portsmouth in January! The highest position the team attained was 13th (at the end of August) and from late October onwards they were never out of the bottom four.

Blues played much better in the two Cup competitions, reaching the quarter-finals of both before being humiliated 7–0 at home by Liverpool in the FA Cup and beaten 3–1 by Manchester United in the League Cup, also at St Andrew's. Blues' debutants this season included teenager Matt Birley, the former Manchester United and England midfielder Nicky Butt (on loan from Newcastle United), striker 'DJ' Campbell (a £500,000 buy from Brentford), Czech Republic international midfielder Jiri Jarosik (on a season-long loan spell from Chelsea), the club's 'Young Player of the Year' Neil Kilkenny, Czech Republic Under-21 international Martin Latka (on loan from Slavia Prague), former Arsenal trainee Sam Oji, Republic of Ireland Under-21 international Marcus Painter, ex-England, Norwich City, Chelsea and Blackburn Rovers striker Chris Sutton (signed on a free transfer from Celtic) and young Peter Till, who made one substitute outing against Scunthorpe in the League Cup.

Putting the disappointment of relegation behind them, Blues regained Premier League status at the first attempt, finishing runners-up to Sunderland in 2006–07. In fact, one extra victory (three points) would have clinched the League One Championship. Blues won five of their opening seven matches and after that, with the exception of a slight hiccup here and there, they always looked strong promotion contenders, confirming their place in the Premier League on 29 April following third-placed Derby County's defeat by Crystal Palace. A total of 26 games were won and only 12 lost, three at home. And with Mikael Forssell struggling with injuries throughout the campaign, it was left to on-loan Danish striker Nicklas Bendtner from Arsenal and £3 million signing from Coventry City Gary McSheffrey, plus 'DJ' Campbell, to get the goals.

Other debutants and new signings this season were 35-year-old striker Andy Cole (on loan from Portsmouth), Neil Danns (a £500,000 buy from Colchester), 6ft 4in Tunisian centre-back Radhi Ben Abdelmajid Jaidi (bought from Bolton Wanderers for £2 million), £3 million striker Cameron Jerome (from Cardiff City), Republic of Ireland right-back Stephen Kelly (secured for £750,000 from Tottenham Hotspur), Swedish forward Sebastian Larsson (sold by Arsenal for £500,000 with DR Congo star Fabrice Muamba also joining from Arsenal on loan), defender Bruno N'Gotty (Jaidi's defensive partner from Bolton) and forward Rowan Vine, who arrived from Luton Town for £2.5 million. On the credit side, Blues accepted a club record fee of £6.7 million from Liverpool for winger Jermaine Pennant.

Up, down, up and down again in 2007–08 – this is Blues' record over a four-year period. Yet they could and should have avoided relegation this time round. When the final ball was kicked, only eight points separated Blues in 19th position from Newcastle in 12th. In late November, after a 2–1 defeat by Aston Villa and with the team lying 16th, manager Steve Bruce left St Andrew's to take over at Wigan Athletic. Eric Black acted as caretaker boss for a short time before Alex McLeish, the Scotland boss, who like Bruce had also been a fine defender, took charge. He made a flying start, 10-man Blues winning 3–2 at Tottenham, courtesy of Sebastian Larsson's 35-yard rocket in the 90th minute. McLeish quickly introduced some ideas and slowly bought in fresh faces, but the damage had already been done and Blues went down. They won only eight Premier League games and lost 19, while a goal-a-game was never going to be enough. In fact, their worst run surprisingly came after McLeish had moved in – only five victories being recorded in 24 matches; it had been three in 14 under Bruce. The heaviest defeat of the campaign was hard to take – a 5–1 hammering at Villa Park – while a 2–1 reverse at relegated Reading was also painful. Blues ended on a high, nevertheless, whipping Blackburn Rovers 4–1 in the Premier League, but this fixture was marred by a pitch invasion as several disillusioned fans called for the board to resign.

Owner David Sullivan, in reaction to all this, pointed the finger at former manager Steve Bruce for the club's relegation, saying: 'He bought poorly during the previous summer' and named Franck Queudrue (a £2 million capture from Fulham) and Ghanaian international goalkeeper Richard Kingson in particular as poor signings. Indeed, he called Kingson a 'waste of space'. This lead to Queudrue hitting back at Sullivan for his comments, saying that he had 'not played enough to be judged so harshly.'

Also into the St Andrew's camp this season came Stuart Parnaby (on a free from Middlesbrough), Garry O'Connor (who cost £2.7 million from Lokomotiv Moscow), Olivier Kapo (a £3 million buy from Juventus), Daniel de Ridder (from Celta Vigo), Liam Ridgewell (sold for £2 million by rivals Aston Villa), David Murphy (a £1.5 million signing from Hibernian), James McFadden (enrolled for £5.75 million from Everton), Mauro Zarate (from the Qatar side Al-Sadd) and loan signings Johan Djourou (Arsenal) and Wilson Palacios (Deportivo Olimpia).

Out of St Andrew's, either before, during or immediately after the season, went no fewer than 15 players, namely Fabrice Muamba (sold to Bolton Wanderers for £5 million), Mikael Forssell (on a free to the German club Hannover '96), Olivier Kapo and Daniel de Ridder (to Wigan Athletic), Sone Aluko (to Aberdeen), 'DJ' Campbell, Stephen Clemence and Bruno N'Gotty (all to Leicester City), Julian Gray (to Coventry City), Mat Sadler (to Watford), Neil Danns (to Crystal Palace), Neil Kilkenny (to Leeds United) and Rowan Vine (to Queen's Park Rangers), while Ulises De la Cruz and Olivier Tebily were both released, the latter eventually joining Toronto.

BACK INTO THE PREMIER LEAGUE, TAKEOVER OF THE CLUB

After a good pre-season tour to Austria when all three games were won, Blues started their 2008–09 Championship campaign well, former Aston Villa and West Bromwich Albion striker Kevin Phillips scoring in each of his first three games to set up wins over Sheffield United, Southampton and Barnsley. But after that it was another hard battle, which some diehard supporters had expected, as Blues crept back into the Premier League. They gained automatic promotion (as runners-up) on the very last day of the League season with a 2–1 win at Reading who, if they had won, would have gone up with Wolves, leaving Alex McLeish's men contemplating the Play-offs yet again.

During the season Blues won four League games and salvaged a point from four others, with extremely late goals – proving a point that the team kept battling all down the line until the very last ball was kicked.

A total of 34 players were used by McLeish this season, and besides top-scorer Phillips, other debutants included striker Marcus Bent (bought from Charlton Athletic for £1.1 million), midfielder Lee Carsley (acquired from Everton), full-back Stephen Carr (released by Newcastle United) and loan signings Lee Bowyer and Nigel Quashie (both from West Ham), Nicky Hunt (from Bolton), Scott Sinclair (from Chelsea), Djimi Traore (from Portsmouth) and the Ghanaian international and former Arsenal star Quincy Owusu-Abeyei (from Spartak Moscow). The average League attendance at St Andrew's of just over 19,000 was the lowest for 11 years, and this despite gaining promotion!

After a rather indifferent build-up to the 2009–10 season, which included a goalless tour to Austria, Blues started their sixth season in the Premier League with a 1–0 defeat against the reigning champions Manchester United in front of 75,000 fans at Old Trafford, in which manager Alex McLeish gave debuts to no fewer than six players – Ecuadorean international striker Christian 'Chucho' Benitez from the Mexico League club Santos Laguna, Scottish international and former Blackburn Rovers midfielder Barry Ferguson (signed from Rangers), England Under-21 goalkeeper Joe Hart (on loan from Manchester City), central defender Roger Johnson (a £5 million buy from Cardiff City), Irish-born midfielder James O'Shea and the former Arsenal centre-back Gregory Vignal (on loan from French club Lens). Also in waiting were two other newcomers, Giovanny Espinoza, another Ecuadorean international, secured on a two-year deal from Barcelona Sporting, and a former St Andrew's trainee, Krystian Pearce, on loan from Peterborough United. And then into the camp came Finnish international Teemu Tainio (on loan from Sunderland).

An early home defeat to arch-rivals Aston Villa did little to boost confidence in the camp. In fact, Blues won only three of their first 12 Premier League matches, and they also made an early exit from the League Cup (beaten by Sunderland). In September 2009, wealthy businessman Carson Yeung took over Birmingham City Football Club. The Hong Kong entrepreneur secured a significant investment from China to confirm the takeover. Two years earlier, in 2007, Yeung's attempted takeover bit the dust amid farcical circumstances. The board allowed him to buy 29.9 per cent of their shares for £15 million in July of that year, on the understanding that the rest of the money would follow for absolute control by December. It never came, and manager Steve Bruce quit to join Wigan Athletic in November, fearing for his future. Blues were plunged into turmoil. Yeung tried and failed to get a seat on the board, and all went quiet – that is until September 2009 when the takeover was officially confirmed. Sources in Hong Kong said that Mr Yueng's company, Grandtop International, is worth around HK $500 million (£39 million). Yeung himself is the club's largest single shareholder, through Grandtop, which has since changed its name to Birmingham International Holdings.

Soon after the takeover, David Sullivan, Karren Brady and Ralph Gold said goodbye via this statement:

'Since coming to the club over 16 years ago there have been many changes on and off the field. The day we came to St Andrew's in 1993 the facilities were tired and in desperate need of refurbishment, the gates were averaging under 7,000 a game and the business was in dire need of stability.

'During our time at the club we have made tremendous developments to both St Andrew's and Wast Hills Training Ground…75 per cent of St Andrew's has now been rebuilt; plans for a new 55,000-seater stadium are with Birmingham City Council and we have spent over £5 million on a development that rivals any other Premier League training ground with state-of-the-art facilities.

'Through many initiatives and offers here at the club we have nurtured a national and international fan base.

'We have a supporter-base of over 250,000 nationally and internationally; last season (2008–09) we were the 10th-best supported club in the Championship and still gained promotion, and we averaged 26,000 at St Andrew's the last time we were in the Premier League.

'We brought the football club back to the top flight of English football for the first time in 16 years. For the last nine seasons we have been in the Premier League or promoted to it at the first time of asking. Before this we made three Play-off semi-finals; played in the final of the Worthington Cup at the Millennium Stadium and this last close season (summer of 2009) we were the 10th biggest net spenders in the Premier League which was more than Arsenal.

'The club is now financially solvent and holds a highly valued status in English football to date. We are one of the only football clubs in the Premier League to run a successful and efficient business. But, we realised 18 months ago when we were relegated from the Premier League, that large sections of supporters wanted a change of ownership. With great effort we have sourced a multi-millionaire, backed by other mega-rich Chinese investors who we hope can achieve for the club what we have failed to achieve.

'It is with a feeling of great sadness that we say goodbye to the club.

'We will always be Blues supporters, we will watch the results every week with interest and we hope that when you all look back you will realise we did a pretty good job during our time at St Andrew's. All that's left to say is Keep Right On!'

Moving on, resilient manager McLeish and his players slowly but surely got things together out on the pitch, and over a period of three months, from 24 October to 23 January, Blues went 15 matches without defeat (12 in the Premier League). This excellent run ended with a 3–0 defeat at champions-elect Chelsea. Thankfully, Blues got themselves back on track, and although their performances were not as good as they had been, points were banked from wins over Wolves, Wigan and Portsmouth and also from draws with Spurs and Everton.

Ousted from the FA Cup by lowly Portsmouth in the sixth round, Blues, obviously disappointed, battled on gamely in the Premier League, but their form waned, and they managed only one win in their last 10 League games and also lost the return fixture with rivals Aston Villa, a dubious late penalty deciding a tight contest. Midfielder Craig Gardner, who had been signed earlier in the year from Villa, lined up against his former club, along with Phillips and Ridgewell.

With a total of 50 points, Blues claimed their highest League position for 51 years, equalling their 1958–59 placing of ninth, and it was down to an excellent home record. Indeed, Blues held the top six clubs – Chelsea, Manchester United, Arsenal, Tottenham Hotspur, Manchester City and Liverpool – to a draw at St Andrew's, and that was no mean feat. McLeish used 29 players in League and Cup action, with Ferguson (43), Johnson (43), Bowyer (42), Hart (41), McFadden (41), Ridgewell (37), Benitez (36), Jerome (36) and Dann (35) making most appearances. Jerome was leading scorer with 11 goals. The average Premier League attendance at St Andrew's (19 games played) was 25,246, a rise of 6,156 on the 2008–09 Championship campaign.

So, as they say, 'Keep Right On To The End Of The Road', and Blues will certainly do that as they embark on another season in what many say is the toughest and best football league in the world – the Premier League. But with some more new faces around St Andrew's, including giant 6ft 8in Serbian striker Nikola Zigic, who cost £6 million from Valencia and played for his country in the World Cup in South Africa, who knows what might be achieved by Alex McLeish and his adopted Blues.

Blues manager Alex McLeish and his Aston Villa counterpart Martin O'Neill shake hands after another derby defeat!

JACK WISEMAN – MR BIRMINGHAM CITY

On Friday 14 August 2009, Jack Wiseman, former Chairman of the club, died at the age of 92. He had enjoyed a 53-year association with Blues, having joined the Board of Directors in 1956 and latterly serving as vice-chairman.

During his lifetime in football, Jack also served on the FA Council for 35 years, joining in 1974, represented the Football League for 13 years from 1974 and also Division Four for eight years up to 1994, when he was made a life vice-president.

A member of the International Committee for 30 years (1975–2005), the Match & Grounds Committee for 27 years (1974–2001) and the Disciplinary Committee for 12 years (1974–86), he also served on the Commercial Committee…you can say he was a dedicated follower of football.

The FA's vice-chairman Sir Dave Richards said: 'Jack Wiseman's tireless work for The FA marked him out as a true stalwart of the game. His effort and commitment to all aspects of the running and the development of English football was recognised by colleagues throughout the game. Jack always made time for the staff and players, which earned him the trust and respect that was typical of his time at the FA.

'It was an honour and a privilege not only to have worked with Jack, but to be able to count him as a friend – his contribution to football was significant. He will be sadly missed.'

He was presented with a lifetime achievement award by Blues in 2008 when the then chairman David Gold revealed: 'He was a real stalwart who had played a major role in the club's history. He was "Mr Football"…one of the greatest sadnesses for me is that Jack never received a Knighthood for his work in football. He was so popular and so respected by everyone. He'll be missed.'

Michael Wiseman has been a director of Birmingham City since 1997, and his appointment as vice-president continues the link between the Wiseman family and the club which has existed since 1928. Michael graduated from Sheffield University with a degree in economics and subsequently qualified as a chartered accountant in 1982. He is currently the managing director of property company, Haunch Lane Developments Ltd, a Governor of University College Birmingham and director of Metal Packaging Ltd.

BLUES GROUNDS

EARLY GROUNDS

Blues played their first home games on a bare but flat strip of wasteland off Arthur Street, in the Bordesley Green district of the city, near to where St Andrew's stands today. In the summer of 1876 the club made a temporary move to a fenced-off field in Ladypool Road, Sparkbrook, which could house around 3,000 spectators and, because the field itself was enclosed, the public were charged an entry fee.

Interest in the team grew quickly, and within 12 months Blues moved 'home' again, this time to a rented field in Small Heath, situated in a built-up area, near to the main A45 Birmingham-Coventry road. An annual rent of £5 was fixed by the owner 'Father Sam' Gessey, an avid supporter and able defender who played in four games for the club between 1877 and 1884. This compact ground, known as Muntz Street, had four sides of open terracing, a small wooden stand, painted off-white, with a solid roof, ornate fittings, pointed gables and flagpoles, as well as two decent changing-rooms for home and away players.

With a capacity of 10,000, the 'new' ground was officially opened on 11 September 1877 when Blues defeated a local team, Saltley College, 5–0 in a friendly in front of just 50 onlookers who paid 6s 8d in gate receipts. Over the years, a lot of maintenance work was carried out at the ground, both internally and externally. The pitch, which was initially full of pot holes, was flattened and twice returfed.

In 1897 a decent old stand was purchased from Aston Villa for £90. This was 'transferred' by 10 lorries from Perry Barr to Muntz Street and was erected behind one of the goals, while the height of the terracing was raised, thus increasing the overall capacity to around 30,000. Surprisingly, this became insufficient to cope with the demand, as the attendance for the home League match with Aston Villa in September 1905 attracted a full house, although it was reported that 4,000 more spectators climbed walls or broke through turnstiles to gain entry, thus pushing the 'unofficial attendance' up to around the 34,000 mark. After several requests, the first in the summer of 1903, landlord Mr Gessey refused to sell the freehold of the ground, nor would he permit major extensions to be made. As a result, Blues' financial secretary advised the board of directors that staying at Muntz Street was costing the club at least £2,000 a year and stated that there was no alternative but to search for a large enough site, on which a new ground could be built.

MUNTZ STREET FACT FILE

* Muntz Street, known locally as the 'celery trenches' was used by Blues for 29 years – from September 1877 until December 1906.

* In their first season at the ground Blues were unbeaten in 22 home matches.
* The record attendance at Muntz Street was 34,000 for the Blues versus Tottenham Hotspur FA Cup third-round replay on 28 February 1906.
* The last competitive game staged at Muntz Street was a League Division Two fixture between Blues and Bury on 22 December 1906. A crowd of 10,000 saw Blues win 3–1, with Arthur Mounteney scoring the last goal.
* When Blues left the ground, the annual rent was £300.
* Four Junior internationals were staged at Muntz Street, all featuring a Birmingham representative side (made up of players from Blues, Aston Villa and West Bromwich Albion) against a Scotland XI. The 'home' team was victorious by 5–2 in 1898, 2–1 in 1904 and 2–0 in 1906, while the Scots won 2–1 in 1900.
* Two Inter-Association games were also staged at Muntz Street – a team representing Birmingham (the city) beating London 3–0 in 1887 and 6–1 in 1890.

St Andrew's

In 1905, knowing that the club urgently required a new, more substantial and, indeed, more centralised ground, a young, keen and enthusiastic director and former player, Harry Morris, identified a site in Bordesley Green, only three-quarters of a mile (1km) away from Muntz Street, and nearer to the city centre. Covering an area of some 7.5 acres and bordered by Cattell Road, Coventry Road, Tilton Road, Garrison Lane and a main railway line, it had been used previously by a local brickworks company.

Morris described his find as 'a wilderness of stagnant water and muddy slopes'. It was certainly just the sort of area the club required, and after some serious talking the official documents were signed, Blues securing the land on a 21-year lease. There followed a search for a surveyor/engineer to take control of designing the new ground, and in the end it was a local carpenter and former art student, Harry Pumfrey, who, despite a lack of qualifications, came up with the plans 'which would have done credit to the most expensive professional architect', said a delighted Harry Morris.

Another director, Thomas Turley, a well-known builder, was appointed clerk of works, and it is estimated that the club saved over £2,000 in professional fees by keeping the building work 'in-house'. It is believed that a band of gypsies laid a curse on the club when they were evicted from the site shortly before work began. But these days this assumption is taken with a pinch of salt by ardent supporters and, in truth, nothing has really occurred which can be readily put down to a gypsy's curse!

Work effectively commenced on the building of the new ground (St Andrew's) in February 1906. Initially, Artesian springs, which kept the land flooded, had to be completely drained and blocked off with loads of rubble before tons of good-quality soil could be laid on top. To create height for the terracing on the Coventry Road side, the club offered the site as a tip to local people who, over a short period of time, quickly paid a total of £800 for the pleasure of dumping an estimated 100,000 loads of rubbish on Blues' newly acquired piece of land. This embankment – known from the outset as the Spion Kop – had 110 steps at its highest point. It could accommodate 48,000 spectators comfortably, each paying 6d. The grandstand (or main stand) erected on the Garrison Lane side of the ground was 123yds long and comprised 6,000 seats which were split into six sections of 1,000. They cost from 1s to 2s each per match.

Gangways to the seats were all lit by electricity, and in front of the seating area there was ample room for another 5,000 spectators to stand under cover. Underneath there were three refreshment rooms, two changing rooms, a training area with plunge bath, a good-sized billiard room (courtesy of local brewery magnate Sir John Holder) and the official boardroom and offices, which hitherto had been situated in premises a few miles away. Behind the left-hand goal (known as the railway end) there was enough standing room for a further 4,000 spectators, and access to three parts of the ground was gained via a number of turnstiles.

When the ground was completed and ready for use, having cost just £10,000, it was revealed that capacity was 75,000 (with 6,000 seats and room for 22,000 spectators under cover). The playing surface, which measured 115 by 75yds (105m × 69m), was said to be one of the largest in the country (at that time) and was bordered by a strip of grass 4yds wide, with a cinder running track around the outside.

Blues' new ground – St Andrew's – was officially opened by Sir John Holder on Boxing Day 1906, when Birmingham played hosts to Middlesbrough in a First Division match. There had been a heavy snowfall overnight, and hundreds of volunteers, including members of the club's board, worked all morning to clear the pitch in time for the kick-off, which was put back an hour to allow the fans to get into position. Unfortunately it was not a great game, as the 32,000 crowd witnessed a 0–0 draw. *The Birmingham Daily Post* reported that 'The fact that so many spectators attended under such adverse conditions augurs well for the step that the directors have taken' and that the directors were 'to be congratulated in having provided their supporters with a ground second to none in the country'.

Following further development work and some major readjustments, the capacity of St Andrew's had been reduced to 68,000 by 1930. And nine years later, a record crowd of 67,341 packed into the ground for Birmingham's fifth-round FA Cup tie against Everton in February 1939.

During the early months of World War Two, part of St Andrew's was badly damaged by German bombs. Immediately the Chief Constable of Birmingham closed the entire ground in fear of further raids being carried out. But local MPs were annoyed with this attitude and raised the matter in Parliament. Unfortunately, the Home Office secretary refused to over-rule the Chief Constable's decision; however, the ground, surprisingly, was the only one in the whole country that was closed during the first part of the war. The ban, thankfully for Blues, was lifted in March 1940 when Walsall lost 2–1 in a Regional League game in front of 12,000 spectators.

In mid-January 1942, Blues received another blow when the main stand at St Andrew's was completely gutted by a raging fire…started by accident and not by German warfare! The National Fire Service was utilising the ground as its base when a small fire flared out of control in a brazier. An officer grabbed hold of a bucket and threw what he thought was water over the flames, but to his amazement the bucket was full of petrol and not water. The blaze caused several thousand pounds worth of damage, and at the same time all the club's records and files went up in smoke.

At that point, St Andrew's looked in a very sorry state – the steel framework that had formed part of the stand was twisted in all directions. There were huge cracks in almost every section of terracing, and there was one gigantic crater in the middle of the pitch. Blues had nowhere to play, so they asked if they could borrow Leamington's ground, while also enquiring about the available of nearby Villa Park. Both venues were subsequently used, and when the war ended Blues set about raising funds to rebuild the damaged areas of St Andrew's, but it was going to take an enormous amount of money.

In the meantime, in July 1943, City was added to Birmingham's name, and the official programme for the 1943–44 season carried the new title on the front cover – Birmingham City Football Club. Work started on building a new stand in 1951, and five years later (in October 1956) floodlights were installed, Blues playing out a 3–3 draw with German side Borussia Dortmund to officially 'switch on' the lights in front of 45,000 spectators.

The Spion Kop, situated opposite the main (new) stand, which ran from corner flag to corner flag, was now capable of housing around 40,000 fans, making it one of the biggest standing areas on a football ground anywhere in the country. This was finally repaired in full by 1952, after which a modern roof was erected over the entire 120-plus yards of terracing. A replica 'main' stand was then erected at the 'Railway End' of the ground and over the next 10 years, St Andrew's saw redevelopment work carried out in several other places.

A scoreboard and clock were installed at the City End of the ground in memory of the club's former player Jeff Hall who sadly died from polio in April 1959. And later, to commemorate the 50th anniversary of the full-back's death, the club commissioned a memorial clock to replace the original one, which did not survive the 1990s renovations. Placed centrally above the main stand, it was unveiled in September 2008 by Hall's former teammates Alex Govan and the late Gil Merrick; however, adverse reaction to the clock's size and position provoked the club into ordering a larger replacement.

In 1963, the capacity of St Andrew's was reduced to 43,204, with 9,280 seats situated in the Main Stand and behind the goal at the Railway End.

In the 1970s, the Asda chain proposed to share the cost of a new stand as part of a supermarket development on land behind the Spion Kop which had become vacant due to slum clearance regulations; however, in the face of strong opposition from commercial rivals, this proposal fell through. Some years later, in the summer of 1988, the capacity of St Andrew's was reduced again, this time to 38,200, but the seating had been increased to over 10,000, and there was a family section available as well.

Following the tragedies at Valley Parade (Bradford) and Hillsborough (Sheffield), the subsequent Taylor Report of 1992 resulted in another cut in the ground capacity. And this time it was a huge one, down to just 26,000 for safety reasons. This was increased to 28,235 within a year, but at this juncture it was unanimously agreed that the entire stadium required a massive revamp. That was given the green light after the club had been taken over in March 1993 by millionaire businessman David Sullivan, the Gold brothers and Karren Brady, who moved in *en bloc* to rescue the club from bankruptcy. The new regime quickly agreed plans to turn St Andrew's into an all-seater stadium with a capacity of 30,000.

Chairman David Gold recalled his first visit to St Andrew's after the takeover: 'It was a shock. I had a picture in my mind of what I was expecting, but it was in such a state of disrepair that it

Work underway on transforming the pitch at St Andrew's into a quality surface ready for the Premier League. Contractors and groundstaff joined forces to rip up the old turf and remove tonnes of earth so that a state-of-the-art undersoil heating system, incorporating 18 miles of pipes could be fitted. The £500,000 work was complete in time for the start of the 2009–10 season.

was hard to comprehend. Only two-thirds of the bulbs on the floodlights were working and the Football League had threatened action if we didn't do something to improve the lights. It was raining. It was a dour game. It was dark. It was dull. There were people standing in the rain looking extremely uncomfortable and unhappy. This First Division club was penniless and near to extinction. There were corrugated-iron fences round the ground and it looked as though it hadn't seen a lick of paint since Birmingham reached the FA Cup Final in 1956.'

The first phase of this massive redevelopment project commenced soon after a somewhat emotional home game against Bristol City in mid-April 1994 when around 19,000 ardent Blues fans (in a crowd of 20,316) waved goodbye to the beloved Tilton Road End stand and the famous Spion Kop. Several supporters grabbed anything they could as souvenirs, including slabs of terracing, doors and door-frames, concrete pillars, parts of crash barriers, even rusty old screws, bolts, hinges or a simple letter from off the old scoreboard…and a few even lifted up a chunk of turf as well!

The 1970s forward-line trio of Trevor Francis, Bob Hatton and Bob Latchford came along to set the building work in motion, and it was soon revealed that the cost of the revamping would be around £4.5 million, the majority of which would go on an elaborate 7,000 all-seater stand at the Tilton Road End which, it was stated, would be ready for use at the Chester City home game in late August 1994. It was, and with a huge flag draped over the seats saying 'Thank You David Sullivan' 12,188 fans saw Louie Donowa score the deciding goal to give Blues a 1–0 win.

The 'new' Kop, with its 9,500 seats, was 'officially' opened soon afterwards for the League Cup tie against Blackburn Rovers (4 October), and the all-seater ground itself was finally completed and given clearance by health and safety officials in November 1994. Soon after receiving the 'go ahead' to stage matches, a crowd of almost 20,000 attended the 'official' opening of the 'new' St Andrew's as Blues and Aston Villa played out a 1–1 'friendly match' draw after Baroness Trumpington, spokeswoman for the Department of National Heritage at the House of

Commons, had unveiled a commemorative plaque and also presented a cheque for £2.5 million (a grant from the Football Trust) to Blues chairman Jack Wiseman.

A continuous L-shaped single-tier stand links the 'Kop' and Tilton Road end, and there is seating room for almost 17,000 spectators spread over the remaining half of the ground, with a smart walkway separating the back and front sections. Seating in the Kop Stand includes the director's box and a row of executive suites, while under the stand itself there are a number of excellent function rooms and hospitality areas. The stadium now has floodlight pylons only on the north side; the south side is lit by a single row of lights which are affixed along the front of the Kop roof. The Tilton Road Stand contains 9,000 seats and is the only stand on the ground without a single hospitality box.

Planning permission for an all-seater 'Railway Stand' was granted in March 1995, but work was delayed by a dispute over land owned by Railtrack, and the opening of the 'new' stand was put back almost four years before being opened in 1999, thus guaranteeing extra seating for another 8,000 spectators. Situated on the west side of the ground, the Railway Stand is free-standing. It was officially opened in 1999 and comprises two tiers – the upper is the smaller of the two and is known as the Olympic Gallery. This overhangs the lower tier, at the back of which is a row of excellent Executive Boxes. Visiting supporters have been allocated the lower section of this stand and are segregated from home fans by rolls of plastic netting which are draped over the seats. The family area is situated in the paddocks of the Main Stand and also in the lower section of the Railway Stand, though for the start of the 2009–10 season it was switched to the Kop. The function rooms and corporate boxes are available for hire for business or social events, and St Andrew's itself is licensed to carry out civil weddings (a few couples have already tied the knot on Blues territory). There are wheelchair areas in all parts of the ground with commentary headsets for visually-impaired spectators.

St Andrew's football ground in Small Heath, photographed on Tuesday 26 January 2010. It has been the home ground of Birmingham City Football Club for more than a century.

75

The playing area of St Andrew's measures 110yds by 74yds (101m x 68m), and the pitch itself was actually relaid three times in 2007. The first attempt – made because the surface had deteriorated to a dangerous condition – was deemed unsuccessful due to a freak rainfall, resulting in the postponement of the next match, the first time such an event had happened in senior English football. The essential groundwork was then repeated, and again it was not right, so a third attempt was made in the close season, and this time all was well. The postponement of an FA Cup tie in January 2009 clearly highlighted the lack of under-soil heating, which the club duly installed at the end of that season – after promotion had been gained to the Premier League. This project comprised 18 miles of piping and cost in the region of £500,000.

Nowadays, St Andrew's is regarded, internally and externally, as one of the best-equipped stadiums in the Premier League, with a capacity of 30,079; however, in time that figure will rise if certain plans and ideas come to fruition. It has been mentioned that, hopefully by 2015, the overall capacity could rise to 40,000, even a shade higher, possibly topping Villa Park's capacity of 42,573, to make it the biggest and most spacious football ground in the Midlands.

For the 2010–11 season, the old main stand at St Andrew's will be known as the Garrison Lane Stand.

ST ANDREW'S FACT FILE

* In 2004, a proposal was put forward to build a 'sports village' which would comprise a brand new 55,000-capacity ground for the club, to be known as the City of Birmingham Stadium. Provisions for other sports and leisure facilities as well as a casino would be made. The project itself would have been financed by the Birmingham City Council, Birmingham City Football Club (via the proceeds of the sale of St Andrew's) and the US Casino Group, Las Vegas Sands. The feasibility of the plan depended on the Government issuing a licence for a super casino as permitted under the Gambling Act 2005, and Birmingham being chosen as the venue. Unfortunately this did not materialise. Not to be outdone, the club subsequently gained planning permission to redevelop the Main Stand, but the club and the council have continued to seek alternative sources of funding for the City of Birmingham Stadium project.
* St Andrew's, at 123m above sea level, is the sixth highest League ground (above sea level) in the UK.
* The semi-final of 1907 between Arsenal and Sheffield Wednesday was the first FA Cup tie ever staged at St Andrew's.
* The 1934 FA Cup semi-final between Leicester City and Portsmouth attracted a then record crowd to St Andrew's of 66,544. This stood for five years.
* Blues' last home League game of their 1984–85 promotion season against Leeds United was marred by rioting, culminating in the death of a boy when a wall collapsed on him. This tragic event happened on the same day as the Bradford City fire disaster.
* Since the stadium has become all-seater, the top attendance has been 29,588, for the Premier League game with Arsenal in November 2003. The 2010 capacity is set at 30,079.
* St Andrew's was the venue for the first-ever penalty shoot-out at the end of a major game. It

happened after the FA Cup third/fourth place Play-off between Blues and Stoke City in August 1972 had finished level at 0–0 after 90 minutes. The spot-kicks favoured Blues, who took third place by winning the shoot-out 4–3.

* The fourth qualifying round tie between Alvechurch and Oxford City in 1971–72 became the longest FA Cup encounter ever, lasting a total of 11 hours before Alvechurch won the fifth replay 1–0. The fifth of the six meetings took place at St Andrew's.

OTHER GAMES AT ST ANDREW'S

Wartime International

October 1941	England 2 Wales 1	Att. 25,145

Inter-League

February 1919	Football League 3 Scottish League 1	Att. 21,990

B Internationals

February 1957	England 4 Scotland 1	Att. 40,000
November 1980	England 1 Australia 0	Att. 3,292

Under-23 Internationals

November 1962	England 5 Greece 0	Att. 20,530
November 1968	England 2 Holland 2	Att. 24,258

Under-21 International

February 2001	England 0 Spain 4	Att. 13,761

Youth Internationals

April 1983	England 1 Belgium 1	Att. 3,000
May 1983	England 4 Scotland 1	Att. 3,500

England Schoolboy/Junior Internationals

May 1952	England 2 Scotland 2	Att. 4,000
April 1966	England 2 Northern Ireland 0	Att. 2,486

FA Vase Finals

May 2004	Winchester City 2 Sudbury 0	Att. 5,080
May 2006	Nantwich Town 3 Hillingdon Borough 1	Att. 3,286

FA Cup semi-finals

March 1907	Arsenal 1 Sheffield Wednesday 3	Att. 35,940
March 1909	Bristol City 2 Derby County 1 (replay)	Att. 27,600
March 1911	Chelsea 0 Newcastle United 3	Att. 40,264
April 1913	Sunderland 3 Burnley 2 (replay)	Att. 45,000
March 1924	Manchester City 0 Newcastle United 2	Att. 50,039
March 1934	Leicester City 1 Portsmouth 4	Att. 66,544
March 1957	Aston Villa 1 West Brom Albion 0 (replay)	Att. 58,067
March 1959	Luton Town 1 Norwich City 0 (replay)	Att. 49,488
March 1961	Leicester City 2 Sheffield United 0 (replay)	Att. 37,190

Amateur FA Senior Challenge Cup Final

May 1948	Boldmere St Michael's 2 Cambridge Town 1	Att. 2,000

FA Amateur Cup semi-finals

March 1967	Hendon 2 Skelmersdale 2	Att. 5,600
March 1969	Sutton Town 4 Whitley Bay 2	Att. 4,000

First Division Play-off

May 1987	Charlton Athletic 2 Leeds United 1	Att. 15,841

FA Cup second/third replays

November 1926	Kettering Town 1 Worcester City 0	Att. 1,560
February 1956	Burnley 2 Chelsea 2	Att. 21,921
November 1957	Aldershot 2 Worcester City 0	Att. 3,000
January 1970	Cardiff City 1 York City 3	Att. 7,347
October 1970	Nuneaton Borough 1 Tamworth 3	Att. 2,000
November 1971	Alvechurch 0 Oxford City 0	Att. 2,500

Football League Cup second replay

October 1976	Bolton Wanderers 2 Fulham 1	Att. 9,315

Other Fixtures

April 1910	Birmingham County FA 1 Scottish FA 1	Att. 3,000
May 1923	Birmingham County FA 1 Scottish FA 0	Att. 2,500
April 1933	Birmingham County FA 1 Scottish FA 2	Att. 2,500
May 1950	ATC semi-final: England 2 Wales 2	Att. 1,500
March 1958	RAF 2 Royal Navy 0	Att. 1,000
February 1964	FA XI 3 Universities Athletic Union 1	Att. 1,200

Other Sporting Events

* Small Heath Harriers Athletic Club, whose headquarters had been at the club's old Muntz Street ground, trained at St Andrew's until the 1920s.
* The 1960 South African touring Rugby Union team beat a Midland Counties XV by 16 points to 5 on a muddy St Andrew's pitch in front of a 17,000 crowd.
* In 1949, Dick Turpin beat Albert Finch on points to retain his British and Empire Middleweight Boxing title; and Turpin's brothers Jack and future world middleweight champion Randolph fought on the same bill.
* In 1965, Henry Cooper defeated Johnny Prescott at St Andrew's to retain his British and Empire Heavyweight title. Due to heavy rain 48 hours before, the fight actually took place two days after originally scheduled, which prompted debate as to the feasibility of outdoor boxing promotions in light of the unpredictable British weather.
* St Andrew's was also the location for the 'stadium rally scene' in Peter Watkins's 1967 film *Privilege*.
* The ground has also staged music/pop concerts, including gigs by UB40 (supported by The Pogues) in 1989, the 2002 'Party in the Park' (when Westlife and the Sugababes were the star attractions) and Duran Duran in 2005.
* HRH the Prince of Wales visited St Andrew's on his official tour of Birmingham in the summer of 1980.
* The legendary world heavyweight boxing champion Mohammad Ali also visited St Andrew's in May 1984 (when Blues played Liverpool in a League game).

MATCHES TO REMEMBER

SMALL HEATH 0 WEST BROMWICH ALBION 4
6 March 1886   Attendance: 4,100

This FA Cup semi-final at the Aston Lower Grounds was a one-sided contest. On a bitterly cold afternoon, Blues were outplayed and could have lost by an ever bigger margin. Albion took an early lead through Arthur Loach and after Tommy Green and George Woodhall had both shaved the woodwork, the latter made it 2–0 before half-time. After a 'goal' by Albion's Jem Bayliss had been disallowed, Loach made it 3–0 on the hour before completing his hat-trick from George Bell's corner with 15 minutes remaining. At this point, a group of Birmingham hooligans raced onto the pitch and surrounded some of the Albion players, who came in for some rough treatment. As police and stewards intervened, the unruly mob dashed towards the exits, hurling clumps of ice, bricks, tin cans, buckets and chairs at anyone who got in their way. One carriage driver lost an ear when he was struck by an open-ended metal can. This was a day Blues wanted to forget quickly.

SMALL HEATH 5 BURSLEM PORT VALE 1
3 September 1892   Attendance: 2,500

Blues commenced life in the Football League with this resounding victory at Muntz Street. On a wet, miserable afternoon and with a strong wind behind them, Blues, with a 'rush', took the lead on five minutes through Fred Wheldon. After prolonged pressure, George Short made it 2–0 on 37 minutes and six minutes later Wheldon struck again to give Blues a healthy half-time lead. Five minutes into the second period Jack Hallam's 20-yard rocket made it 4–0 and after Bert Bliss had grabbed a consolation for Vale, Harry Edwards rounded things off with a fifth for Blues late on.

BLACKBURN ROVERS 9 SMALL HEATH 1
5 January 1895   Attendance: 3,000

Right-back Tilson Pritchard made his debut at right-back and winger Bill Lewis was appearing in only his second League game for the club in this heavy defeat at Ewood Park. The 22-year-old Pritchard was given the run-around by Rovers' left-winger Harry Chippendale, who scored a hat-trick as well as having a hand in three more of his side's goals. Blues, who had defeated Liverpool 3–0 seven days earlier, were outclassed as Ted Kilean also netted a treble while Geordie Anderson, Pat Gordon and Jock Sorley were the other scorers. Billy Walter grabbed a consolation goal for Blues.

MANCHESTER CITY 3 SMALL HEATH 0
1 January 1897   Attendance: 16,000

This was Blues' first-ever League game on a New Year's Day and ended in a disappointing 3–0 defeat to a moderate Manchester City side. Although the Lancashire club had most of the play, Blues created far more chances but wasted them with sloppy finishing. Charlie Bannister, Jack Gunn and Jim Sharples scored the decisive goals and Gunn even missed a late penalty.

SMALL HEATH 4 WEST BROMWICH ALBION 7
13 September 1897 Attendance: 3,000

This all-action second-round Birmingham Charity Cup tie went to extra-time before Albion finally triumphed and went through to meet Aston Villa in the semi-final. After a quiet opening, Walter Abbott fired Blues ahead in the 25th minute, only for Ben Garfield to equalise 45 seconds later from Arthur Watson's side pass. Pressing forward, Blues then scored twice more before half-time, first through Billy Walton and then Tom Oakes to take a 3–1 lead. And after Joe Reader had saved well from Walton, Charlie Hare made it 4–1 in the 52nd minute. Albion, however, regrouped and quickly reduced the deficit when Albert Flewitt scored from distance. Tom Perry then had a goal disallowed as Blues back-pedalled, and after Garfield had made it 4–3 with a rising cross-shot in the 70th minute, it was game on. Albion were buzzing and deservedly grabbed an equaliser with five minutes remaining, Garfield completing a fine hat-trick with a shot on the run. Just before the end of the first period of extra-time Garfield scored his fourth goal of the afternoon and soon afterwards chased a seemingly lost cause, gained control of the bouncing ball and blasted a shot at goal, the ball taking a slight deflection before flying past Harry Clutterbuck for goal number six. With defenders struggling to sort things out at the back, Alex McKenzie pounced to ram the final nail into Blues' coffin to complete a remarkable come-back for the Baggies.

SMALL HEATH 3 WEST BROMWICH ALBION 4
12 September 1898 Attendance: 3,000

This was another second-round Birmingham Charity Cup tie which Blues seemed to have won but lost! Tom Oakes's drive put Blues in front in the fifth minute and Albion were hardly in the game during a one-sided first-half which ended with two more goals for the home side, Walter Abbott and Jack Good beating opposition 'keeper Joe Reader with well-struck ground shots. But it was a different story after the break. It was all Albion. Five-goal hero from the previous season, Ben Garfield, continued to hit the target, making it 3–1 on the hour. Ralph Brett, finding space, netted from 12 yards to bring the scores even closer and soon afterwards Jack Banks squeezed in the Baggies' equaliser after some good work down the right by England international Billy Bassett. With Blues firmly on the rack, it came as no surprise when Garfield grabbed the winning goal a minute from time, netting from Bassett's low cross.

SMALL HEATH 12 DONCASTER ROVERS 0
11 April 1903 Attendance: 8,000

Rovers were completely overwhelmed in the second half as Blues virtually dominated throughout. Arthur Leonard (18 minutes) and Fred Wilcox (29 and 40) scored before the interval. And with the visitors in total disarray, both Leonard and Wilcox went on to claim four-timers, the former scoring his third with a terrific drive from 40 yards. Bob McRoberts (2), Charlie Athersmith, Charlie Field (with another superb effort) and Jack Dougherty (the last) completed the massacre.

SUNDERLAND 1 BIRMINGHAM 4
26 November 1904   Attendance: 12,000

Blues outplayed Sunderland on a bone hard pitch. Unbeaten at home since March, the Wearsiders, who never got to grips with the surface, fell behind in the ninth minute when Fred Wilcox scored from 10 yards. However, against the run of play, Alf Common equalised on 24 minutes before Billy 'Bullit' Jones barged ball and 'keeper over the line seven minutes later to edge Blues back in front. Tempers boiled over after the break and several players, including three from Blues, were spoken to by Derby referee Dick Chesterman. Then, in the 80th minute, Jones cut inside and lashed in Blues' third goal before Benny Green popped in number four after 'keeper Tommy Rowlandson had dropped Charlie Field's high cross from the left.

BIRMINGHAM 4 BURNLEY 0
6 April 1912   Attendance: 35,000

Top-of-the-table Burnley were brought down to earth with a bump after a splendid display by Blues. Following several near misses, Blues took the lead on 20 minutes when Jack Hall converted Albert Gardner's pass from 10 yards. Debutant Arthur Reed made it 2–0 six minutes later, after Hall and Walter Hastings had done the spadework, and just past the hour mark Hastings, cutting inside, converted Dickie Gibson's cross to make it three. With 15 minutes remaining and the visitors down and out, Reed darted forward to net his second and Blues' fourth to round off a fine victory.

HUDDERSFIELD TOWN 7 BIRMINGHAM 0
25 October 1913   Attendance: 10,000

In April 1911, Blues had been battered 7–1 by Huddersfield. On this occasion, the Terriers scored seven goals again, but this time without reply as the visitors were outplayed in every department. In the first half, dominated entirely by Huddersfield, Tom Elliott set up Bert Smith for the first goal on five minutes followed by Fred Fayers's 30-yard thunderbolt which made it 2–0 on the half-hour. After the break it was all Huddersfield and the goals came thick and fast. Joe Jee's shot deflected off Billy Ball for goal number three in the 49th minute while Jimmy Macaulay, who scored a hat-trick in 1911, made it 4–0 with a 15-yard drive in the 54th minute. Then it was Elliott who took centre stage, netting a quick-fire hat-trick between the 60th and 69th minutes. His first goal was down to a mistake by 'keeper Herbert Crossthwaite, but his other two were classic individual efforts. Dismal Blues had only two shots on target all afternoon.

BIRMINGHAM 8 NOTTINGHAM FOREST 0
10 March 1920   Attendance: 15,000

Two headlines in local papers read 'Forest felled by Birmingham's new blood' and 'Scoring was like clockwork' after Blues had cantered home in style. Harry Hampton, signed from Aston Villa, scored in the 20th and 26th minutes and another new boy, Joe Lane, a record buy from Blackpool, made it 3–0 in the 48th minute. Hampton completed his hat-trick with a close range header on 63 minutes before Lol Burkinshaw slammed in a 30-yard pile-driver to make it 5–0 in the 68th minute, following up with number six five minutes later after some superb work by George Davies. After Hampton had knocked in his fourth goal of the afternoon in the 75th minute, Lane rounded things off with an eighth with seconds remaining.

REAL MADRID 0 BIRMINGHAM 3
1 July 1923   Attendance: 15,000

Blues caused a minor upset with this friendly win at the Santiago Bernabeu Stadium…and in the end they triumphed with only 10 men. Defender Alex McClure was sent off late in the second-half for telling his goalkeeper, Dan Tremelling, where to stand when facing a penalty-kick which had been awarded for handball by full-back Jack Jones, who, in fact, brought his hands up in front of his face to protect his teeth. McClure told Tremelling to stand nearer to his right-hand upright rather than in the middle of the goal. The referee kept on saying 'ready, are you ready?' Tremelling didn't react, McClure kept talking and at this point the ref told him to 'buzz off' and sent him to the dressing room. After the game the official agreed he should never have awarded a penalty (which was subsequently missed by Victor Del Campo) and he was asked to apologise in the local newspaper. Joe Bradford (two) and Billy Harvey scored Blues' goals. Two years later Blues repeated their 3–0 victory over the Madrid club in a return fixture at St Andrew's in front of 10,000 spectators.

BIRMINGHAM 1 BURNLEY 7
10 April 1926   Attendance: 16,616

Left-winger Louis Page was switched to centre-forward for this game and what an impact he made – scoring six goals as Blues were swept aside by a rampaging Burnley side, battling to stay in the First Division. After a quiet opening 20 minutes, Page got his teeth into the home defence. He scored his first goal halfway through the half, added a second seven minutes later and completed his 'first' hat-trick just before the break. After striking a post, Jack Bruton's shot was fisted into his own net by Blues' 'keeper Dan Tremelling for Burnley's fourth goal on 58 minutes and then it was back to Page, who bagged his 'second' hat-trick in the space of just three minutes right on the hour. Firstly he tucked away Jack Hill's pass from six yards, then he netted from close range after John Steel's free-kick had been saved by Tremelling and finally he headed in James Tonner's precise centre. Never-say-die Joe Bradford hit an 86th-minute consolation goal for poor Blues.

BIRMINGHAM 6 BOLTON WANDERERS 1
4 April 1927   Attendance: 6,321

This was technically a must-win game for lowly Blues – and they cantered to an impressive victory with a vintage display of attacking football which destroyed Bolton, who at the time were lying fourth in Division One. Blues took the lead in the sixth minute when Joe Bradford converted a cross from Benny Bond. George Gibson then bundled goalkeeper Dan Tremelling over the line to claim an equaliser before Blues regained the lead in the 23rd minute through George Briggs. In the second half it was one-way traffic. Jimmy Cringan made it 3–1 and inspirational Scot Johnny Crosbie bagged a couple either side of a second from the lively Bradford.

BIRMINGHAM 4 PETERBOROUGH & FLETTON UNITED 3
14 January 1928   Attendance: 38,128

Non-Leaguers, backed by 4,000 travelling supporters, battled long and hard in this third-round FA Cup tie before losing a seven-goal thriller at St Andrew's. Stan Davies shot Blues in front on seven minutes, but the home fans were stunned when the visitors equalised through Les Bruton in the 19th minute, after 'keeper Dan Tremelling had mishandled a shot from Jack Willis. Under severe pressure, Blues slipped behind five minutes later when Bruton capitalised on another error by Tremelling and amazingly, just before the interval, Charlie McGuigan got on the end of Willis's low cross to make it 3–1. Blues looked down and out, but in the second half they hit top form. Johnny Crosbie began to run the show in centre-field and his shrewd pass allowed Joe Bradford to reduce the arrears on the hour. The Scot then set up Bradford for the equaliser 15 minutes later, and with time fast running out, he sent a 30-yard pass right to Bradford's feet for the centre-forward to complete his hat-trick and send Blues through to the next round.

BIRMINGHAM 5 LEEDS UNITED 1
22 December 1928   Attendance: 16,057

Blues went into Christmas on a high with their first victory in three months, virtually controlling the game from the first to the last whistle. Joe Bradford scored early on after both Johnny Crosbie and George Hicks had tested Leeds 'keeper Jimmy Potts. In the 19th minute Bradford netted again following good work by Crosbie and George Briggs. At this juncture Blues had Leeds reeling, raining in shots from all angles. Then, in the 51st minute, the visitors won a penalty when Jimmy Cringan fouled Charlie Keetley in the area. Russell Wainscoat took the kick only to see Dan Tremelling pull off a brilliant diving save. Four minutes later, however, Turnbull reduced the deficit with a shot on the turn, only for George Liddell to restore Blues' two-goal lead in the 63rd minute, following a corner by Hicks. The Blues left-winger got on the score sheet himself with 20 minutes remaining, squeezing the ball over the line after Briggs had seen his effort saved. And Bradford completed his hat-trick five minutes later with a shot from 15 yards.

SHEFFIELD WEDNESDAY 9 BIRMINGHAM 1
13 December 1930   Attendance: 21,226

Prior to this League game at Hillsborough, Wednesday had scored 30 goals in seven games. As it turned out they were no match for Blues, who succumbed under heavy pressure. Harry Burgess fired the Owls in front in the 16th minute and in the last quarter-of-an-hour's action of the first half they increased their advantage to 5–0 with excellent goals from Jack Ball (30 minutes), Ellis Rimmer (31), Mark Hooper (38) and Ball again (41). Jimmy Seed made it 6–0 early in the second half before George Briggs netted what was to prove only a consolation effort for Blues in the 61st minute. Rampant Wednesday then upped the pace once more and three further goals were scored between the 63rd and 73rd minutes through Hooper (2) and Seed as Blues were pegged back inside their own half for long periods. Seed even hit the bar late on as the home side went in search of a 10th goal. This victory put the Owls on top of the First Division table, while at the same time it was Blues' joint heaviest defeat in the club's history, following the one at Blackburn in 1895.

BIRMINGHAM 2 SUNDERLAND 0
14 March 1931   Attendance: 43,570

Blues reached their first-ever FA Cup Final with this hard-earned but deserved victory over Sunderland at Elland Road. With 15,000 supporters behind them, Blues soaked up a lot of first-half pressure before Ernie Curtis scored the opening goal in the 32nd minute, his low shot fizzing past 'keeper Middleton from 15 yards. Sunderland hit back and Bob Gurney scraped the woodwork, O'Connor headed inches over and Harry Hibbs saved brilliantly from Eden and Devine. With three minutes left and only two players up front – Joe Bradford and Curtis – Blues secured a place at Wembley when the latter converted a rebound after the former had picked him out with a wonderful cross-field pass.

BIRMINGHAM 1 WEST BROMWICH ALBION 2
25 April 1931   Attendance: 90,368

After 50 years of trying Blues appeared in their first FA Cup Final – and it was the first all-Midland clash for 36 years. On a sodden pitch, the Second Division side from the Hawthorns made the early running and on six minutes Bob Gregg thought he had scored but his downward header was ruled out for offside – a dubious decision. In the 25th minute Albion edged in front when 'W.G.' Richardson latched on to the loose ball to find the net from close range after Harry Hibbs had saved his first effort. It was nip and tuck through to half-time and for the first 10 minutes of the second period, and then, out of the blue, Joe Bradford, with his left shoulder facing the Baggies' goal, suddenly turned and belted the ball past Harold Pearson for the equaliser. Yet straight from the restart, and with the Blues fans still cheering, Albion went straight downfield and regained the lead, 'W.G.' toe-ending the ball past Hibbs from two yards after George Liddell's failed clearance. As hard as they tried, Blues couldn't grab a second equaliser and, in fact, Albion might well have scored two more goals, Hibbs denying them with brilliant saves.

BIRMINGHAM 4 PORTSMOUTH 0
24 December 1932   Attendance: 15,716

Blues' centre-forward Joe Bradford netted the 233rd goal of his career in this easy victory over Pompey and, by doing so, passed Steve Bloomer's total of 232 for Derby County to become the most prolific marksman for a single club in Football League history. In the fourth minute, the sparse crowd cheered the first goal, scored by Tom Grosvenor after the Pompey defence had failed to clear Lew Stoker's free-kick. Forty-seconds later it was 2–0 when Bradford fired the ball past John Gilfillan from 20 yards after a pass by George Briggs had been missed by Jerry Mackie. Blues increased their lead in the 27th minute when Grosvenor drove home from 25 yards and, although the home side continued to attack, they had to wait until the 80th minute before netting a fourth goal. This time Bob Gregg, who had earlier been off the field with an injury, was in the right place at the right time to find the net after Gilfillan had saved from Bradford.

LEICESTER CITY 3 BIRMINGHAM 7
28 April 1934   Attendance: 16,981

This was a League game Blues had to win. Deep in relegation trouble, they went to Filbert Street full of confidence and came away with two valuable points after producing a wonderful display of attacking football. On a slippery wet pitch, Blues took the lead in the fourth minute when Sid Moffatt netted from Billy Guest's astute left-wing cross. Leicester hit back and equalised in the 25th minute through Arthur Chandler, only for Blues to regain control six minutes later when Guest robbed Septimus Smith to score with ease. Fifty seconds later Guest made it 3–1 with a powerful left-footer, only for Leicester to hit back strongly and equalise with smartly-taken goals by Chandler and Arthur Maw. At this point, with 25 minutes remaining, Blues went into overdrive and Dave Mangnall immediately edged them back in front. Dai Jones then conceded a silly own-goal to put Blues 5–3 ahead and in the 75th minute Fred Roberts cracked in number six before Guest crowned a great afternoon's work by grabbing his hat-trick and Blues' seventh goal with five minutes remaining. Blues stayed up; Newcastle United and Sheffield United went down.

BIRMINGHAM 5 COVENTRY CITY 1
12 January 1935   Attendance: 40,349

There looked to be a shock in store when Coventry took an early lead through Billy Jones's penalty after George Liddell had handled. But in the end, this third-round FA Cup tie ended in a resounding victory for Blues. Responding quickly, Blues, on a strength-sapping pitch, peppered the visitors' goal before finally equalising in the 22nd minute through Fred Harris. Then, in a devastating spell between the 60th and 66th minutes, Blues scored three times through Dave Mangnall, Billy Guest and Harris again, before the latter claimed his hat-trick goal with eight minutes remaining. Blues drew Southampton away in the next round.

WEST BROMWICH ALBION 4 BIRMINGHAM 3
18 April 1938   Attendance: 34,406

This was a crucial relegation battle with both Albion and Blues deep in trouble at the foot of the First Division. After an even but tense opening, Dennis Jennings unleashed a speculative 50-yard 'drive' which flew past debutant goalkeeper Harry Baldwin to give Blues a ninth-minute lead. Ten minutes later 'W.G.' Richardson headed Albion level, only for Charlie Phillips to net twice in three minutes just before half-time to put Blues firmly in control. However, after the break it was all Albion. Full-back Cecil Shaw made it 3–2 with a 47th-minute penalty; Richardson equalised seven minutes later and the grounded Harry Jones stuck out his leg to divert Jack Mahon's low cross past Harry Hibbs for the winning goal with four minutes remaining. Victory, though, was not enough. Albion still went down and Blues stayed up by two points (38–36).

BIRMINGHAM 2 EVERTON 2
11 February 1939   Attendance: 67,341

A record St Andrew's attendance saw this entertaining fifth-round FA Cup tie. At the time Everton were top of the First Division while Blues were struggling at the opposite end of the table. But as so often happens in football, the underdogs played well above par and in the end were unlucky not to have won. Up until the 44th minute it had been a fairly even contest, but then amazingly two goals were scored in sixty seconds. Owen Madden's shot for Blues took a slight deflection off Norman Greenhalgh and flew past 'keeper Ted Sagar, and straight from the kick-off Irish international Alex Stevenson equalised for Everton with a crisp low drive from 12 yards. Walter Boyes, the former West Brom winger, then fired the Merseysiders in front on 61 minutes before Madden headed home the equaliser with 10 minutes remaining. Everton won the replay 2–1.

BIRMINGHAM CITY 8 TOTTENHAM HOTSPUR 0
6 October 1945   Attendance: 21,608

Spurs were completely outplayed by a virile and well-balanced Blues side in this Football League South fixture. Arthur Turner blotted out the threat of Spurs' centre-forward Gibbons, and as a result the visitors hardly managed a worthwhile effort on target. Ted Duckhouse scored the opening goal with a swinging effort from fully 50 yards, and before half-time Dave Massart (crisp right-footed shot) and Neil Dougall (from a free-kick) increased the lead. Harold Bodle added a fourth; Massart hit number five; George Edwards tucked away number six and winger Jock Mulraney netted twice late on to send the Londoners packing with their tails between their legs.

BIRMINGHAM CITY 6 LEICESTER CITY 2
25 December 1945   Attendance: 30,228

Blues went into the League South game in good form, especially winger Jock Mulraney. Indeed, it was the Scotsman who destroyed the Leicester defence, setting up three goals and scoring another himself. This was the first of the afternoon when he diverted Wilson Jones's effort between the posts in the fourth minute. Wilson Jones made it 2–0 soon afterwards and the same player scored a third in the 20th minute as the Leicester defence back-pedalled. Dewis reduced the arrears on the half-hour mark, but rampant Blues continued to drive forward and Neil Dougall made it 4–1, only for Dewis to strike again just before half-time. Harold Bodle and George Edwards added two more goals to Blues' tally in a relatively calm second half in which Mulraney also hit the woodwork. Blues maintained their form and went on to win the Championship on goal-average from rivals Aston Villa.

BIRMINGHAM CITY 0 PLYMOUTH ARGYLE 1
16 March 1946   Attendance: 22,135

This was a shock result. For this League South fixture Blues put out their strongest side while Argyle fielded four regulars, one guest and six reserves, two of whom were juniors. Blues, beaten once in their previous 14 games and the Division leaders, were confident of victory over bottom club Argyle, who had won only one of their 33 League and Cup games all season. Argyle's 'keeper Bill Shortt was brilliant in the first half, pulling off a string of fine saves. Harold Bodle and Neil Dougall, later to join the Devon club, missed easy chances after the break and, as the visitors grew in confidence, Blues began to struggle. Then, completely by surprise, with four minutes remaining, Argyle broke away and snatched the winning goal, Paddy Brown heading Horace Cumner's cross past a stunned Gil Merrick. Blues picked themselves up and went on to win the Championship, while Plymouth finished rock bottom, 47 points behind Blues (14–61).

BIRMINGHAM CITY 5 MANCHESTER CITY 0
8 February 1947   Attendance: 56,056

A big St Andrew's crowd saw Blues ease into the sixth round of the FA Cup with a splendid victory over Manchester City. On a freezing afternoon, on a bone-hard, sand-covered pitch, Blues took the lead on nine minutes, Harold Bodle driving the ball low into the net off

England 'keeper Frank Swift's left hand after a smart build-up involving Jock Mulraney and Fred Harris. After the visitors had twice hit the woodwork, Cyril Trigg capitalised on a mistake by Les McDowell to put Blues 2–0 in front in the 62nd minute. And in the 79th minute Trigg added a third from Mulraney's pass. With time running out and Blues well on top, Bert Sproston handled in the box, allowing Frank Mitchell to net a fourth, and right on time Mulraney crowned a fine display of wing play by scoring number five.

BIRMINGHAM CITY 4 WEST BROMWICH ALBION 0
29 March 1948   Attendance: 47,047

Blues retained the leadership of the Second Division with this emphatic victory over their Midland rivals at St Andrew's. On a slippery pitch, Blues took the lead in the second minute when Jackie Stewart followed up George Edwards's corner to score from two yards. A quarter of an hour later it was 2–0 when Stewart's corner was headed home by Harold Bodle. Albion hit back and Dave Walsh struck a post before Cyril Trigg made it 3–0 halfway through the second half. Near the end Stewart charged in to make it 4–0 and so inflict upon the Baggies their heaviest League defeat (in terms of goal-difference) for 18 months.

BIRMINGHAM CITY 4 MANCHESTER CITY 1
15 September 1948   Attendance: 35,593

Not too many wingers score four goals in a competitive game – but Jackie Stewart of Birmingham did precisely that in this First Division clash with Manchester City at St Andrew's. The Scotsman netted his first goal in the 25th minute after some intelligent play between Neil Dougall and Fred Harris. Then, during a second-half blitz, he destroyed City's defence with some powerhouse shooting. His second goal came in the 56th minute, his third, and best, 12 minutes later and his fourth 15 minutes from time. Frank Swift, the opposition goalkeeper, never knew what hit him, saying afterwards: 'I never saw two of Jackie's shots.' George Smith scored a late consolation goal for the visitors.

ASTON VILLA 0 BIRMINGHAM CITY 3
4 December 1948   Attendance: 62,424

This was the first League meeting between the two Second City teams since 1939. And it was Blues who dictated most of the play, new signing Jackie Stewart scoring twice and Harold Bodle once. Stewart, fed in by a clever back-heeler from Neil Dougall, put his side ahead in the 15th minute and his second came on 66 minutes after a deliberately flighted free-kick by Fred Harris. Blues' third goal was netted by Harold Bodle in the 71st minute after some fine work by Johnny Berry down the right.

DONCASTER ROVERS 0 BIRMINGHAM CITY 5
19 January 1952   Attendance: 20,282

This was only the second time since 1934 that Blues had scored five goals in an away game. The star of the show was debutant inside-left Peter Murphy, who notched a hat-trick. The former Tottenham Hotspur and Coventry City player netted his first on 11 minutes after a neat flicked pass by Wardle. His second came six minutes before half-time when he took

Roy Warhurst's pass in his stride before stroking the ball past 'keeper Hardwick. After Jackie Stewart had scored a magnificent third goal in the 67th minute, Murphy completed his hat-trick five minutes later when he glided the ball past Hardwick from eight yards. And the Scotsman wasn't finished yet. With eight minutes remaining he got free down the right and crossed for Tommy Briggs to knock in goal number five.

BIRMINGHAM CITY 4 HULL CITY 3
15 November 1952 Attendance: 17,529

This seven-goal thriller was decided late on by Blues' reserve left-winger Geoff Cox. In fact, Hull found themselves 3–0 down early in the second half after Blues had produced some excellent football. Jackie Stewart scored the first goal in the 10th minute, touching home Cyril Trigg's short pass. Peter Murphy added a second just before the break with a lob over 'keeper Billy Bly and Trigg's 50th-minute penalty (after Murphy had been tripped) made it three. But the Tigers roared back in style and netted three times themselves in 10 minutes to bring the scores level. Denis Durham and young 17-year-old debutant Cliff Bursell (2) were on target as the home defenders relaxed! And the visitors should have taken the lead through Viggo Jensen before Blues squeezed out victory with Cox's 84th-minute strike through a crowd of players.

CHELSEA 0 BIRMINGHAM CITY 4
14 February 1953 Attendance: 45,872

This was certainly a 'St Valentine's Day Massacre' as Blues smashed four past Chelsea in a one-sided second half of this fifth-round FA Cup tie. Having knocked out West Bromwich Albion in the previous round in a third replay, the Londoners looked strong during the first 45 minutes, but once Blues had taken the lead, they never threatened again. Ted Purdon headed Blues in front from Jackie Stewart's high cross in the 57th minute, and 13 minutes later, following a free-kick, the South African centre-forward made it 2–0 with another free header. Twelve minutes from time Peter Murphy took Stewart's pass in his stride to net number three and on 80 minutes Keith Bannister's shot was deflected home by Cyril Trigg for goal number four.

BIRMINGHAM CITY 6 SWANSEA TOWN 0
22 August 1953 Attendance: 26,817

Despite torrential rain, a decent crowd turned up at St Andrew's to see Blues hammer the 10 men of Swansea by six clear goals. Ted Purdon scored the opener in the fifth minute with a side-foot shot from six yards. The visitors tried to get back into the game, but fell further behind in the 18th minute when Peter Murphy nipped in for an easy tap-in following Jackie Stewart's cross from the right. Nine minutes before the interval, Noel Kinsey added a third, bravely heading home, low down, from Stewart's right-wing corner. Without Billy Lucas (injured ankle) for the second half, Swansea fell further behind in the 57th minute when Murphy netted after a superb display of individual dribbling. The same player then completed his hat-trick 10 minutes later by drilling the ball home after Alex Govan had jumped over Stewart's low cross. The final nail went into the Welsh club's coffin in the 73rd minute when Purdon got on the end of Roy Warhurst's cross to fire past 'keeper Gwynfryn Groves. Right at the end a sneaky Govan shot was cleared off the line by full-back Tom Keane.

BIRMINGHAM CITY 5 BRENTFORD 1
24 October 1953   Attendance: 23,582

All five of Blues' goals were scored in the space of 26 first-half minutes as the London Bees were well and truly stung at St Andrew's. Having already netted a six, a five and two threes in early season games, Blues were gifted their opening goal when Brentford full-back Walter Bragg steered the ball past his own 'keeper Reg Newton following an inviting right-wing cross from debut-boy Gordon Astall. In the 14th minute it was 2–0 when Peter Murphy belted in a 25-yard special and on 27 minutes Noel Kinsey wriggled through a flimsy defence to make it 3–0. Two attacks later and Ted Purdon got on the scoresheet with a header from Alex Govan's perfect cross and the latter grabbed a fifth four minutes later, nodding home Jeff Hall's deep cross. Brentford, who included future Blues star Jimmy Bloomfield in their line-up, did better after the break and in the 58th minute set up Billy Dare for a consolation goal.

WOLVERHAMPTON WANDERERS 1 BIRMINGHAM CITY 2
9 January 1954   Attendance: 36,784

Wolves went on to win the First Division Championship this season, so this third-round FA Cup victory by Blues was something special…and it was no fluke! Fielding their full team (except for the injured goalkeeper Bert Williams), Wolves were strong favourites to progress into the next round, but Blues matched them kick for kick and in the end were deserving winners. Dennis Wilshaw put the home side in front in the 14th minute only for former Wolves player Ken Rowley to equalise soon afterwards. Driving forward Wolves then twice hit the woodwork before Peter Murphy fired home a dramatic winner halfway through the second half. Blues defended brilliantly to hold on to their lead.

LEICESTER CITY 3 BIRMINGHAM CITY 4
16 January 1954   Attendance: 34,704

This Second Division match had everything…and in the end it was Blues who came out on top. After defending stoutly, Blues suddenly went into overdrive and scored twice in the 14th and 15th minutes through Ken Rowley and Alex Govan. Leicester struck back through Derek Hines halfway through the first half and, after Arthur Rowley had seen his 'rocket' saved at full length by Gil Merrick, Hines equalised five minutes into the second period, after Merrick had failed to collect an inswinging corner. Undeterred, Blues battled on and regained the lead in the 65th minute through Govan, while four minutes later Peter Murphy netted with a crisp drive high past 'keeper Anderson. Although Rowley netted a third for Leicester with four minutes remaining, Blues held on for an impressive victory.

BIRMINGHAM CITY 7 PORT VALE 2
27 November 1954   Attendance: 16,352

Blues started this Second Division game like a house on fire, scoring twice through Peter Murphy inside the first 18 minutes. Vale, though, were always dangerous on the break and England 'keeper Gil Merrick was called into action several times. A minute after the interval Alex Govan made it 3–0 before Albert Mullard reduced the deficit with a 51st-minute penalty after a foul by Merrick on Basil Hayward. In the 55th minute Vale's skipper Tom Cheadle left the field injured, and as a result Blues made hay, dashing into a 5–1 lead with goals from Noel Kinsey and Murphy, who thus completed his hat-trick. Vale replied with a 74th-minute strike from Hayward before Eddie Brown and Kinsey completed a resounding victory.

BIRMINGHAM CITY 9 LIVERPOOL 1
11 December 1954   Attendance: 17,067

Never before or since have Liverpool conceded nine goals in a League game. In this Second Division fixture at St Andrew's they were 'murdered' by Blues who seemed to score at will. Blues took the lead on 48 seconds, Jackie Lane scoring via Ray Lambert's left boot. Eddie Brown made it 2–0 in the 11th minute and five minutes later goalkeeper Doug Rudham dropped Gordon Astall's corner allowing Brown to tap in number three. After Trevor Smith had slipped, Billy Liddell raced away to reduce the arrears after 19 minutes before Blues grabbed a fourth goal through Astall before half-time. The barrage continued after the break. Lane's presence enabled Astall to chest the ball over the line for goal number five in the 49th minute. Peter Murphy's high-speed rocket made it 6–1 five minutes later and after both Astall and Jeff Hall had hit the Liverpool crossbar, left-winger Alex Govan blasted in goal number seven in the 77th minute. Still Blues drove forward and, with six minutes remaining, Brown set up Murphy for number eight before the latter completed his hat-trick with a toe-ender a minute later. It was a pity that such a small crowd saw this memorable victory.

DONCASTER ROVERS 1 BIRMINGHAM CITY 5
4 May 1955   Attendance: 21,305

Blues clinched the Second Division Championship with this superb win at Belle Vue. A fairly even first half saw each side score once. Gordon Astall fired Blues ahead from a rebound in the 38th minute before Jimmy Walker equalised six minutes later with a powerful header from Alick Jeffrey's cross. The second half was all Blues. Rovers were not in it at all and three goals in the space of 18 minutes sewed things up for Arthur Turner's side. Ten minutes after the restart Peter Murphy scored via a post; 10 minutes later Eddie Brown weaved his way through a sloppy defence to make it 3–1 and in the 73rd minute Astall netted his second of the game with a stunning volley from 15 yards. Right on time Alex Govan got in on the act with a fifth goal to trigger the celebrations.

BIRMINGHAM CITY 4 MANCHESTER CITY 3
22 October 1955   Attendance: 28,398

Len Boyd decided this splendid game in Blues' favour with just two minutes remaining. In a ding-dong contest, played at an amazing pace, there were chances at both ends of the field and the final result could well have been 6–6, even 7–7. It was so close. Blues led 1–0 on 24 minutes when Peter Murphy hooked in Jackie Lane's long throw to the far post. Joe Hayes equalised for the visitors 11 minutes later, heading the ball over Gil Merrick from 10 yards. But Blues hit back and scored twice more in six minutes either side of half-time – first through Lane (41) after a superb Eddie Brown run, and then through Alex Govan (47) with a side-footer after another fine run by Brown. The Manchester side, though, never gave up and debutant Roy Faulkner converted Bobby Cunliffe's cross from the right in the 63rd minute before Jack Dyson equalised from the penalty spot six minutes later after Jack Badham had brought down Cunliffe. Boyd, however, made the headlines with his late free-kick winner from 20 yards.

BIRMINGHAM CITY 3 CHELSEA 0
5 November 1955   Attendance: 30,499

The reigning League champions were well beaten by Blues at St Andrew's. Alex Govan set up Gordon Astall to volley in the first goal in the 10th minute. After several close shaves, at both ends of the field, Astall bagged a second three minutes before half-time, firing the ball home after Eddie Brown had hit the bar from Govan's corner. Victory was sealed in the first attack of the second-half, skipper Len Boyd slamming a 20-yarder past the former Blues 'keeper Bill Robertson.

TORQUAY UNITED 1 BIRMINGHAM CITY 7
7 January 1956   Attendance: 18,730

Despite the foggy conditions, a record crowd packed Torquay's Plainmoor ground to see this third-round FA Cup tie. In the end it was a cake-walk for Blues, who cruised to an impressive victory. On a bumpy pitch, Blues dominated the first half and scored four times. Gordon Astall grabbed the first in the 22nd minute, Eddie Brown the next two and Noel Kinsey the fourth with a neat header. Brown completed his hat-trick in the 47th minute and Peter Murphy made it 6–0 just 90 seconds later before Ronnie Shaw hit a consolation goal for the Gulls, only for Murphy, with a complete miss-cue, to find the net for Blues' seventh with 17 minutes remaining. This was a great way to start a Cup run.

BIRMINGHAM CITY 4 CHARLTON ATHLETIC 0
4 February 1956   Attendance: 24,447

Eddie Brown was the star of the show as Blues completely outplayed the Addicks at St Andrew's. The centre-forward netted a sublime hat-trick on a slippery pitch, scoring in the sixth, 47th and 70th minutes. His first goal was a smart volley past goalkeeper Sam Bartram's right hand following Gordon Astall's corner; his second was a tap-in also from a corner, this time taken by Peter Murphy, and his third was the pick of the bunch, a cracking drive from 20 yards. Blues' other goal was bagged by Murphy after Bartram had fumbled Astall's free-kick. This was Charlton's seventh away defeat on the bounce.

WEST BROMWICH ALBION 0 BIRMINGHAM CITY 1
18 February 1956   Attendance: 57,213

This fifth-round FA Cup tie at the Hawthorns was only given the go-ahead 75 minutes before kick-off. The pitch was covered in snow, bone hard and very uneven in places, but Blues adapted to the conditions far better than the Baggies and deserved their victory. Under-strength Albion had three chances in the first half, Ray Barlow, Maurice Setters and George Lee all going close, while Eddie Brown (twice), Noel Kinsey and Alex Govan did likewise for Blues. After the break, Gil Merrick touched Frank Griffin's shot onto a post and Barlow fired over, while at the other end Brown, Gordon Astall (twice) and Peter Murphy all had decent efforts saved by Albion's 'keeper Jimmy Sanders. The deciding goal came nine minutes from time, Murphy driving his shot wide of the diving Sanders at the 'Brummie End' to send the 10,000 Blues supporters wild with delight at the other end of the ground.

BIRMINGHAM CITY 3 SUNDERLAND 0
17 March 1956   Attendance: 65,107

As they had done exactly 25 years earlier, Blues reached the FA Cup Final by knocking Sunderland out at the semi-final stage. This time at Hillsborough they went one better than they did in 1931, by recording an excellent 3–0 victory. Noel Kinsey struck the first blow, putting Blues in front in the 11th minute, converting Alex Govan's splendid cross from the left with sweet aplomb. After two near misses, Blues increased their lead in the 65th minute when Gordon Astall touched the ball home from close range following a six-man move down the right. As Sunderland pressed forward, so Blues counter-attacked and it was no surprise when Eddie Brown swept in number three with seven minutes remaining to set off a rousing chorus of *Keep Right On To the End of the Road*. Drawn away in every round, Blues now had to travel again, this time to Wembley for the final showdown with Manchester City.

BIRMINGHAM CITY 1 MANCHESTER CITY 3
5 May 1956   Attendance: 98,982

Unfortunately Blues did not play at all well in their second FA Cup Final. Lacking thrust and drive, they were outplayed at times by a stronger, more active side and in the end they got off lightly with a score-line of 3–1. In front of HM the Queen, Joe Hayes put the Maine Road club into a second-minute lead, taking Don Revie's deft back-heeler in his stride before shooting low past Gil Merrick. Blues hit back and in the 13th minute drew level through Noel Kinsey, whose shot went past Bert Trautmann via a post. That, in truth, was the only good thing about Blues on an afternoon they wanted to forget. The fighting spirit was missing and although certain players did their best, overall the team was well below par. Manchester City always looked confident with the ball, especially Revie, Ken Barnes and Bobby Johnstone, and they went in front again in the 64th minute when Jack Dyson, the Lancashire cricketer, banged home Johnstone's astute pass from 12 yards. Soon afterwards Johnstone raced clear and made it 3–1. That was it for Blues. Soon afterwards Trautmann was injured when he dived at the feet of Peter Murphy, but carried on after treatment, although later it was revealed he had broken a bone in his neck. The gate receipts for this Final amounted to £49,886.

PORTSMOUTH 3 BIRMINGHAM CITY 4
29 August 1956   Attendance: 25,686

Alex Govan was the star of this narrow victory at Fratton Park. The Scottish-born left-winger scored a hat-trick as Blues came back three times to claim both points. Pompey took the lead through the head of future Blues star Johnny Gordon in the third minute. Govan equalised five minutes later from Eddie Brown's pass before an unlucky own-goal by 'keeper Gil Merrick put the home side back in front. Gordon Astall, from a Johnny Watts through ball, made it 2–2 just on the half-hour only for Jimmy Harris, another future Blues player, to edge Portsmouth into a 3–2 lead just after the interval, beating the offside trap to slip the ball home unchallenged. Blues, though, kept going, and Govan squared things up in the 54th minute (after an exquisite pass by Noel Kinsey) before driving in the winner from Peter Murphy's cross with a quarter of an hour remaining.

BIRMINGHAM CITY 6 NEWCASTLE UNITED 1
5 September 1956   Attendance: 32,506

Blues scored a total of 22 goals in their opening six League games of the 1956–57 season, half a dozen coming against Newcastle at St Andrew's. Alex Govan, once again, was in superb form and he netted yet another hat-trick, to take his tally to the season to 10. Firing on all cylinders, Blues scored twice in the first 20 minutes through Peter Murphy via Noel Kinsey's delicate lob (12) and Govan, following a surging run and shot by Eddie Brown. Murphy added a third before half-time (from Govan's low cross) and, after Vic Keeble had reduced the arrears in the 56th minute, Blues hit three more in eight minutes (71st–79th) through Kinsey with a top-corner chip and two from Govan, a breakaway followed by an easy tap-in after Brown had done the donkey work.

BIRMINGHAM CITY 3 MANCHESTER UNITED 1
15 December 1956   Attendance: 36,146

Pouring rain and a gale-force wind couldn't stop Blues from pulling off a terrific win over the League leaders, who had suffered only two defeats all season (in 20 games). The Busby Babes fell behind as early as the fourth minute when Bryan Orritt tucked his shot wide of Ray Wood after good work by Alex Govan and a neat header by Eddie Brown. Pushing United back, Blues attacked in force and in the 24th minute were gifted a second goal when Mark Jones misjudged Gil Merrick's long kick downfield, allowing Brown to race on and fire home unchallenged. Six minutes later it was 3–0 – and game over – when Brown fired in his second goal after Peter Murphy and sent him clear. United came more and more into the game during the second half and Billy Whelan found the net in the 62nd minute, putting away a cross from former Blues winger Johnny Berry. Roy Warhurst later cleared a Duncan Edwards effort off the line, Merrick saved well from Whelan and Tommy Taylor's shot flew inches wide. This was a great win for Blues – their first over United for six years.

SOUTHEND UNITED 1 BIRMINGHAM CITY 6
26 January 1957   Attendance: 28,964

Blues left-winger Alex Govan destroyed plucky Southend in this fourth-round FA Cup tie at Roots Hall. Peter Murphy set the ball rolling in the fourth minute and six minutes later the unfortunate Jim Lawler screwed the ball past his own 'keeper to put Blues 2–0 in front. That soon changed to 3–0 when the unstoppable Govan netted in the 15th and 24th minutes. However, backed by the majority of the crowd, the Shrimpers found a way through five minutes after the break when Roy Hollis scored following a corner, but further strikes from Cox and the impressive Govan, who thus completed his hat-trick, saw Blues safely through to the next round.

BIRMINGHAM CITY 6 LEEDS UNITED 2
20 April 1957   Attendance: 30,642

Blues' left-winger Alex Govan scored his fifth hat-trick of the season as Leeds United crashed to their heaviest League defeat for nine years. The Scot tore holes in the Yorkshire club's defence and in the end the jovial Scot could well have scored at least another three times. Leeds scored first through John Charles in the fifth minute, but Blues responded quickly and Gordon Astall equalised from Govan's low cross 90 seconds later. In the 16th minute Eddie Brown lobbed Blues into the lead before Govan netted the first of his three goals from the penalty spot halfway through the half after Kerfoot had handled Astall's centre. His second followed a minute later when Peter Murphy's pass left him clear on goal to fire past 'keeper Wood. Immediately after that Govan hit a post before Charles reduced the deficit to 4–2 with a header on 32 minutes and the same player should have netted again soon afterwards but shot wide from close range. Brown then hit an upright as Blues counter-attacked, but 10 minutes after the interval he did score, albeit somewhat freakishly when the ball bounced over the line off his stomach after Wood had fly-kicked it straight at him. Govan completed his hat-trick in the 67th minute with an unstoppable low drive and then, late on, shot wide when it looked easier to score.

BIRMINGHAM CITY 4   CF BARCELONA 3
23 October 1957   Attendance: 30,791

This Inter-Cities Fairs Cup semi-final first leg at St Andrew's had everything – excitement, seven goals, scores of mistakes, some brilliant skill and some great goalkeeping. Blues struck first, Eddie Brown driving the ball home after Barca's goalkeeper Ramallets had spilled Bunny Larkin's low drive. But the Spanish giants hit back immediately, Tejada equalising with a centre-cum-shot from the left, the ball falling beyond Gil Merrick and into the far corner of the net. The visitors, who at this point were running Blues ragged, then swept in front on 18 minutes when Evaristo scored with a toe-ender after a terrific run and cross by Martinez. Blues, though, regrouped and, against the run of play, equalised on 32 minutes through Bryan Orritt, who netted on the turn after the Barca defence had failed to clear their lines. However, the Blues fans were still cheering when Martinez fed Vilaverde, who volleyed home spectacularly from 30 yards. Blues responded again and within two minutes Peter Murphy had made it 3–3 when Brown turned Gordon Astall's pass across goal for the inside-left to head home from five yards. After that there were at least four chances created by both sides. In the end it was Blues who stole the winner, Murphy cracking the ball home in the 62nd minute after Johnny Watts had broken up a Barca attack. Ramallets saved well from Brown and Astall late on, while Vilaverde fired over from eight yards. Three weeks later Blues lost the second leg 1–0 before 60,000 fans in the Nou Camp stadium and therefore ,with the aggregate score level at 4–4, a third game was staged in neutral Switzerland. Blues battled to the end, but despite an excellent Peter Murphy goal went down 2–1 in front of 20,000 fans.

BIRMINGHAM CITY 3   WEST BROMWICH ALBION 5
26 December 1957   Attendance: 48,396

With only one win in their previous six games, Albion struck form with an excellent victory at St Andrew's. Despite plenty of attacking football, the first goal in this thrilling contest didn't arrive until 26th minute. Albion won three quick corners and scored from the third. Frank Griffin's right-wing flag-kick was headed back into the danger-zone by Derek Kevan for Bobby Robson to fire home off Brian Farmer. Blues stuck in there and a minute before half-time Eddie Brown slid in the equaliser from Noel Kinsey's astute pass. However, four minutes after the break Albion were back in front when Robson, collecting Ray Barlow's through ball, strode through the Blues defence before driving a low shot past Gil Merrick. Following near misses at both ends, Albion went 3–1 up in the 66th minute when Kevan rose majestically to meet Griffin's free-kick, sending the ball into the net via the crossbar. Back came City and five minutes later, from Harry Hooper's corner, Kinsey missed with a header only for Dick Neal to pop behind him and net from close range. Albion continued to drive forward and in the 78th minute Joe Kennedy, having carried the ball 40 yards unchallenged, passed to Griffin, whose cross was converted by Kevan. Blues were not finished yet though, and in the 83rd minute Hooper scored from the spot after Maurice Setters was adjudged to have handled Trevor Smith's long downfield ball aimed for Peter Murphy. But it was Albion who finished the stronger, Ronnie Allen sealing victory with a brilliant overhead kick after Kevan had nodded Griffin's corner back across goal. This was great entertainment for the big holiday crowd.

BIRMINGHAM CITY 4 ARSENAL 1
1 March 1958   Attendance: 26,834

After losing 5–1 at Wolves and 8–0 at Preston in their two previous games, Blues turned things round against the Gunners to record an excellent victory at St Andrew's. Star of the show was new £20,000 signing Harry Hooper, who found the net inside the first minute with a cracking shot after a 40-yard run and then had a hand in Peter Murphy's goal in the 42nd minute and Eddie Brown's second in the 85th. The latter's first strike came just after half-time, a side-foot tap-in from three yards following a cross by Gordon Astall. Future Blues star Jimmy Bloomfield scored a consolation goal for the Gunners.

SUNDERLAND 1 BIRMINGHAM CITY 6
5 April 1958   Attendance: 34,184

Sunderland were deep in relegation trouble when they entertained Blues at Roker Park, but no-one really expected this emphatic score-line, especially as the visitors had already been thrashed 5–1 (twice), 7–1 and 8–0 on their travels earlier in the season. The action was all at the wrong end of the pitch as far as the Wearsiders were concerned. Bryan Orritt set the ball rolling, giving Blues a two-minute lead with a header. Harry Hooper made it 2–0 in the ninth minute following a rebound, and soon afterwards Peter Murphy clipped in a third before Orritt struck again before the quarter of an hour mark to put rampant Blues completely in charge at 4–0. It got better early in the second-half when Alex Govan grabbed a fifth goal and, after Don Revie had netted a consolation effort for Sunderland, Eddie Brown completed the rout with a sixth for Blues three minutes from time. At the death, Brown all but made it seven, his shot flying back off the woodwork.

BIRMINGHAM CITY 0 WEST BROMWICH ALBION 6
3 September 1958   Attendance: 35,983

With heavy rain pouring down on an already sodden pitch, Blues had no answer to Albion's purposeful attack. Derek Hogg darted down the left-wing, sped past Jeff Hall and crossed for Ronnie Allen to volley Albion into a fifth-minute lead. Gil Merrick kept his side in the game with four fine saves before Blues conceded three times in the space of four minutes. Just past the half-hour mark, Davey Burnside cracked home a fierce left-footer from the edge of the box; Derek Kevan made it 3–0 two minutes later with a powerful drive from 20 yards and Jimmy Campbell poked the ball over the line following a mêlée inside the Blues' six-yard area in the 37th minute. It was more of the same after the interval. Impish winger

Campbell streaked away unchallenged to make it 5–0 in the 47th minute and, after Kevan, Allen and Hogg had all gone close, Burnside ran in his second and Albion's sixth halfway through the half. With the rain teeming down, Allen hit a post, Hogg headed inches wide and Merrick saved twice from Kevan as Albion powered forward. This was Blues' heaviest home defeat since 1925 and it was Albion's biggest away win in terms of goal-difference, since 1935 when they beat Aston Villa 7–0.

BIRMINGHAM CITY 4 LEEDS UNITED 1
17 September 1958 Attendance: 24,068

Eddie Brown was Blues' hero in this fine victory over Leeds at St Andrew's. The centre-forward scored all his side's goals, had another ruled out for offside, struck the outside of a post and also missed two of the simplest chances imaginable. Behind to a 19th-minute goal scored by Jim Forrest, Blues equalised five minutes later when Brown turned in Brian Taylor's cross. In the 32nd minute Dick Neal picked out Brown, who turned and fired low past 'keeper Wood for his second and, after Forrest had bent the Blues' crossbar, Brown completed his hat-trick four minutes after half-time with a rising shot that flew into the net near the angle. His fourth effort arrived in the 69th minute when he cut inside full-back Grenville Hair and beat Wood at his near post. Gil Merrick had only one shot to save in the second half, so much were Blues on top.

TOTTENHAM HOTSPUR 0 BIRMINGHAM CITY 4
22 November 1958 Attendance: 28,708

Despite being without two key players, Gil Merrick and Jeff Hall, Blues played out of their skins to inflict upon Spurs their heaviest home League defeat, in terms of goal-difference, for two and a half years. Ahead in the 15th minute thanks to Bunny Larkin's low right-footed drive, Blues increased their lead just past the half-hour mark when Harry Hooper drove home at the second attempt after good work by Larkin and Brian Taylor. With Spurs seemingly always under pressure, goal number three arrived in the 57th minute when Larkin latched on to Trevor Smith's long ball to shoot low past John Hollowbread. Five minutes later it was all over when Taylor, drifting in unnoticed, cracked in Hooper's pull-back for goal number four. Blues created and missed four more chances later in the game as they toyed with the opposition.

BIRMINGHAM CITY 6 MANCHESTER CITY 1
26 December 1958 Attendance: 34,290

This was Blues' biggest win of the season, giving their Manchester rivals a real pounding. Bunny Larkin hit the City crossbar in the first minute and Bert Trautmann saved superbly from Johnny Gordon before Alex Jackson put Blues ahead after a weak back pass by Cliff Sear. Five minutes before half-time Larkin slid home Dick Neal's cross-shot to make it 2–0. Following a spell of three corners in quick succession, Blues increased their lead in the 62nd minute when Jackson stabbed the ball home after some smart build-up play by Brian Taylor and Gordon Astall, and in the 73rd minute Gordon's shot bounced awkwardly in front of Trautmann and into the net for goal number four. A powerful drive by Larkin flew in off Dave Ewing on 76 minutes to make it 5–0, only for George Hannah to grab a consolation goal for City before Taylor completed the scoring seconds later as the fog descended on St Andrew's.

NOTTINGHAM FOREST 1 BIRMINGHAM CITY 7
7 March 1959   Attendance: 18,977

Having been thumped 5–0 by Forest in a fifth-round FA Cup second replay two weeks earlier, Blues gained sweet revenge with this brilliant League win at the City Ground. After Roy Dwight had put the home side ahead on 17 minutes, teenage centre-forward Robin Stubbs scored twice in 10 minutes and Gordon Astall stroked in a third to give Blues a comfortable half-time lead. Four minutes after the break Harry Hooper netted at the second attempt to make it 4–1, and on the hour mark Johnny Gordon smashed in number five from Astall's drag-back. Two minutes later a rare goal, belted in from 15 yards by Johnny Watts, made it six before Astall rounded things off with number seven in the 84th minute, spearing an unstoppable shot past Willie Fraser. By now at least three-quarters of the crowd had left the ground!

BIRMINGHAM CITY 1 WEST BROMWICH ALBION 7
18 April 1960   Attendance: 28,685

After taking a fourth-minute lead through Johnny Gordon, Blues were swept aside as the Baggies produced a superb display of attacking football. In the 10th minute Derek Hogg crossed from the left and Derek Kevan headed down for Ronnie Allen to fire in the equaliser. Albion dictated play after that, but it was not until the 40th minute that they made their pressure tell, Allen netting from close range after Johnny Schofield had saved his first shot. Two minutes later future Blues winger Alec Jackson took Joe Kennedy's pass in his stride to make it 3–1. Albion came again in the 57th minute when Kevan drove through the Blues defence to slam the ball past Schofield. Six minutes later the England striker made it 5–1 with a superb header from Hogg's free-kick and in Albion's next raid the 'Tank' completed his hat-trick after George Allen had failed to clear his lines. At 6–1 down and looking shell-shocked, Blues managed one worthwhile attack in the 80th minute, but were thwarted by Baggies goalkeeper Jock Wallace, who fly-kicked the ball hard and low into the midst of the home supporters to the right of his goal, injuring a young boy. With seconds remaining the unfortunate Allen conceded a late penalty, allowing his namesake Ronnie to net his hat-trick goal from the spot to give Albion a resounding 7–1 victory and so make it 18 goals for the Baggies in their last three visits to St Andrew's, following 5–3 and 6–0 victories. At the final whistle Wallace had to be escorted from the pitch by two policemen. Near the tunnel he was involved in a scuffle with Blues' Dick Neal and as a result both players were booked.

BIRMINGHAM CITY 5 KB COPENHAGEN 0
7 December 1960   Attendance: 22,486

This easy win over KB Copenhagen booked Blues their place in the Inter-Cities Fairs Cup semi-final. Having drawn the first leg 4–4 in Denmark, they overpowered their opponents at St Andrew's to register a comfortable 9–4 aggregate victory. Robin Stubbs started the ball rolling with a fourth-minute goal, hammering the ball home in style following Johnny Watts's astute pass. Although dominating play, Blues had to wait until the 48th minute before scoring again and again and again – three in just five minutes immediately after half-time and all came from mistakes. The men on target were Jimmy Harris, Mike Hellawell and Jimmy Bloomfield, the last two capitalising on goalkeeping howlers. Stubbs struck the last goal in the 67th minute, firing across the 'keeper from 18 yards.

INTER MILAN 1 BIRMINGHAM CITY 2
19 April 1961 Attendance: 29,530

Even today, there aren't many teams who win in the San Siro stadium. But back in 1961 Blues achieved a wonderful victory there in the first leg of their Inter-Cities Fairs Cup semi-final clash with the Italian giants Inter Milan. In front of a partisan home crowd, Blues played exceptionally well throughout and, after Jimmy Bloomfield had gone close early on, the former Arsenal player set up the first goal for Jimmy Harris in the 12th minute. Inter hit back and Colin Withers pulled off two fine saves in the Blues goal before Robin Stubbs missed a chance at the other end. Then Bloomfield was tripped inside the penalty area, but the referee dismissed claims for a spot-kick. Five minutes before half-time Blues, perhaps against the run of play, went 2–0 up when Stubbs went up for a high cross with Inter defender David Balleri. The Italian got his head to the ball first and deflected past 'keeper Vittorio Da Pozzo. Inter were shell-shocked but they battled on and 12 minutes from time the former Charlton Athletic forward Eddie Firmani reduced the deficit with a close-range shot after a brilliant pass by Mario Carso. Blues were now just 90 minutes away from reaching their second Fairs Cup Final in successive years.

BIRMINGHAM CITY 2 AS ROMA 2
27 September 1961 Attendance: 21,005

Blues were disappointed at not gaining some sort of advantage from the first leg of their Inter-Cities Fairs Cup Final clash with Roma. In front of a moderate crowd, they missed three clear-cut chances in the first-half before allowing the Italians to take a 2–0 lead with some sloppy defending. First Orlando evaded a clumsy challenge by Graham Sissons to cross for Argentinian striker Pedro Manfredini to net with ease past Johnny Schofield in the 32nd minute, and on the hour Roberto Menichelli collected a rebound off Malcolm Beard to score with ease from eight yards. To their credit Blues fought back strongly. After two near misses, and three outstanding saves by Roma's agile goalkeeper Fabio Cudicini, Mike Hellawell netted with a low drive on 80 minutes, and three minutes from time Bryan Orritt equalised with a close-range effort after Jimmy Harris's shot had come back off the crossbar. Blues therefore had a tough task ahead when they visited Rome for the return leg on 11 October. They played well enough in front of a hostile 50,000 crowd but the home side netted twice, in the 56th minute through Lojocona and in the 90th minute through Manolo Pestrin, to take the trophy 4–2 on aggregate.

BIRMINGHAM CITY 3 TOTTENHAM HOTSPUR 3
6 January 1962 Attendance: 46,096

Blues fought back from being 3–0 down in this third-round FA Cup tie against the holders Tottenham Hotspur...and they almost won it in the end. After an early chance had gone begging, Blues were pushed back by a swift-moving Spurs forward-line. Jimmy Greaves put the Londoners in front in the seventh minute, tucking away the rebound after Johnny Schofield had saved his first effort. Left-winger Cliff Jones made it 2–0 just before the half-hour and three minutes later Greaves headed in a third after a smart move involving Les Allen and Dave Mackay. Blues hit back immediately, however, Jimmy Harris reducing the deficit from Stan Lynn's free-kick. Then, four minutes after the interval, Harris popped up again to make it 2–3. Spurs were on the rack – Blues were on the march. The home supporters ran on the pitch, and off again, before Ken Leek amazingly cracked in the equaliser in the 54th minute. Blues had the ball in the net again later on but it was ruled out for offside, a decision that upset Malcolm Beard, who said: 'Our fourth goal was the best of the lot. I saw nothing wrong with it at all – but Ken Howley the referee did.' Unfortunately Spurs won the replay 4–2 and they went on to retain the trophy by defeating Burnley in the Final.

BIRMINGHAM CITY 5 BARROW 1
29 October 1962   Attendance: 11,765

After a moderate display in the first half of this third-round League Cup replay, when all they managed was a Ken Leek goal in the sixth minute, Blues took control after the break and eased comfortably through to the next round. Robin Stubbs collected Leek's pass to make it 2–0 in the 58th minute and Brian Arrowsmith gave away an own-goal three minutes later before Jimmy Harris netted twice – a header in the 67th minute and a close-range shot seconds from the end. Barrow's 80th-minute consolation was scored by Johnny Kemp.

IPSWICH TOWN 1 BIRMINGHAM CITY 5
17 November 1962   Attendance: 16,775

League champions in their first-ever season in top-flight football in 1961–62, Ipswich were well below the following term and only just managed to avoid relegation. Blues also stayed up by the skin of their teeth and, although this game at Portman Road was staged early in the campaign, it proved to be a significant victory for the visitors. Jimmy Harris scored first for Blues in the 16th minute, after Robin Stubbs and Bertie Auld had created the opening. Sixty seconds later it was 2–0 when Auld was on hand to fire home after Ken Leek had missed his kick in front of an open goal. Ted Phillips reduced the deficit on 35 minutes with a low drive from Ray Crawford's pass, but Blues came again in the second half with two smartly-taken goals from Leek in the 55th minute (from Terry Hennessey's pass) and right at the death (from Auld's corner). Jimmy Harris scored Blues' fourth goal in between times.

BIRMINGHAM CITY 3 BURY 2
27 March 1963   Attendance: 11,293

Blues were made to fight every inch of the way before winning this first leg of their 1963 League Cup semi-final against Bury. Blues were well below par in the first half and fell behind in the 29th minute when Griffin scored with a high shot past Johnny Schofield. Following a half-time pep talk, everything changed after the break and the Shakers were really shaken as Blues scored three times in 18 minutes to seemingly take control of the tie. Mickey Bullock equalised on the hour; Bertie Auld made it 2–1 four minutes later when he nodded in Mike Hellawell's cross and then Ken Leek scored a third on 79 minutes from another perfect Hellawell delivery. But Bury stunned the St Andrew's faithful with a late goal by Billy Calder and it was now all to play for at Gigg Lane. As it turned out, Ken Leek's goal in the second leg earned Blues a 1–1 draw and an overall victory of 4–3 to set up a Final with rivals Aston Villa.

BIRMINGHAM CITY 3 ASTON VILLA 1
23 May 1963   Attendance: 31,902

This victory in the first leg of the 1963 League Cup Final paved the way for Blues to go on and lift their major Cup trophy in the club's history. Villa 'keeper Nigel Sims saved well from Jimmy Harris and Ken Leek early on before the latter gave Blues the lead in the 14th minute, firing home Bertie Auld's precise cross from eight yards. Jimmy Bloomfield was then injured but carried on with his thigh heavily strapped before Bobby Thomson grabbed a surprise equaliser four minutes from half-time. Gordon Lee found space down the right and whipped over a low cross for Thomson to drive past Johnny Schofield. With both teams down to 10 men, defenders John Sleeuwenhoek (Villa) and Trevor Smith having gone off for treatment, Blues edged back in front in the 52nd minute. It was Leek again who found the net from another hard, low cross from the impressive Auld. As the game hotted up and tempers rose, Blues scored a third goal in the 66th minute, Bloomfield sneaking in on the blind side to steer Harris's cunning cross past a bewildered Sims. Late on Sims saved well from Leek and Auld, but that two-goal advantage was just what Blues had hoped for. And so it proved. The return leg was played at Villa Park four days later and ended goalless. Delighted Blues skipper Trevor Smith duly lifted the silver trophy on opposition soil to the delight of the travelling fans in the near 38,000 crowd.

BIRMINGHAM CITY 3 LIVERPOOL 1
22 April 1964   Attendance: 22,630

Blues had to win this home game to give themselves a fighting chance of avoiding relegation and they won in some style, despite having Bertie Auld sent-off in the second-half. Handball by Gerry Byrne enabled Stan Lynn to 'blast' Blues in front from the penalty spot on seven minutes. Twice Bobby Thomson came close to extending the lead before Ken Leek made it 2–0 in the 16th minute. With the crowd roaring them on Blues drove forward and in the 38th minute Mike Hellawell smashed in a wonderful cross-shot to increase the advantage. Three-nil up at half-time, Blues were cruising and they continued to press hard after the break. Liverpool responded and twice hit the woodwork before Roger Hunt squeezed in a consolation goal 10 minutes from time, although they were facing nine men, Ray Martin having left the field injured while Auld was in the bath. Three days later Blues defeated Sheffield United 3–0 at St Andrew's to retain their First Division status.

BIRMINGHAM CITY 5 BLACKBURN ROVERS 5
24 April 1965   Attendance: 8,887

There haven't been all that many 5–5 draws in League football over the years. Indeed, Blues have only ever figured in two – and both came within a year of each other, against Blackburn Rovers in 1965 and Derby County in 1966. Prior to this encounter with the Rovers, Blues, in all fairness, had been relegated to the Second Division, so realistically there was nothing at stake and therefore both sets of players enjoyed their afternoon out – none more than Malcolm Beard! In front of their loyal supporters, the goals flowed thick and fast. Rovers took a 2–0 lead inside the first 20 minutes through Andy McEvoy's header and Mike Ferguson's power-drive. Blues drew level before half-time with a second-attempt strike from Geoff Vowden and a ferociously-struck penalty from Stan Lynn. An unfortunate own-goal by Terry Hennessey, who deflected Mike England's speculative long-range effort wide of debutant 'keeper Billy Beel, edged the visitors back in front in the 51st minute and England star Bryan Douglas's downward header made it 4–2 from Rovers' next attack. Then, seconds later, after Vowden's shot had been charged down, up stepped Malcolm Beard to reduce the deficit, only for Douglas to race 50 yards upfield to make it 5–3. Blues pressed on and the unlikely figure of Beard completed his hat-trick with goals in the 71st and 78th minutes to earn his side a point. What a game.

BIRMINGHAM CITY 3 LEEDS UNITED 3
26 April 1965   Attendance: 16,638

Leeds United needed to win this final game of the season to pip Manchester United for the First Division title. Blues, already doomed to relegation, put up a terrific fight and were unlucky not to win despite having 10 men for most of the game. Dennis Thwaites scored first for Blues in the fourth minute before Alex Jackson left the field with a shoulder injury (remember substitutes were not used until August 1965). Amazingly, though, Blues threw caution to the wind and drove forward, increasing their lead to 3–0 with two smartly-taken goals in the space of 10 minutes just before half-time through Malcolm Beard and Geoff Vowden. Leeds, stunned into silence, came out of the blocks for the second half and, after three near misses, Johnny Giles reduced the deficit with a 65th-minute penalty. Eleven minutes later Paul Reaney netted from close range and with four minutes remaining Jack Charlton grabbed the equaliser. Elsewhere Manchester United lost 2–1 at Villa Park, but were declared champions on goal-average from Leeds, both clubs ending the season with 61 points.

BIRMINGHAM CITY 4 BURY 0
18 December 1965   Attendance: 10,998

In this game Ronnie Fenton became the first substitute to score for Blues in a League game. He came on when goalkeeper Jim Herriot went off injured in the 84th minute and six minutes later headed home Blues' fourth goal from Cammie Fraser's cross to sew up this rather easy victory over the Shakers on a very soggy St Andrew's pitch. Dennis Thwaites netted twice – in the 25th minute from Bobby Thomson's cross and on the hour after some smart work by his opposite winger Alec Jackson. In between times Trevor Hockey made Blues' second goal for Thomson, who netted with a vicious volley past 'keeper Chris Harker in the 27th minute.

BIRMINGHAM CITY 5 DERBY COUNTY 5
9 April 1966   Attendance: 13,078

This 10-goal thriller had everything but it was a pity, once again, that such a small crowd saw the action. After a quiet start, Trevor Hockey put Blues in front in the 13th minute. Derby hit back and netted twice in 45 seconds with a brace from Hockey's fellow Welshman Alan Durban, only for Malcolm Beard to equalise with a 25th-minute penalty, awarded after Bobby Saxton had brought down Alec Jackson. Eight minutes later Blues edged back in front, courtesy of an own-goal by Saxton, who diverted Cammie Fraser's low cross past 'keeper Reg Matthews. Following a series of close shaves, at both ends of the field, Rovers drew level early in the second half through Ian Buxton before goals from Beard – a rocket in off the bar on 50 minutes – and Geoff Vowden's header (67) put Blues back in control. County, though, battled on gamely and earned themselves a point when Bobby Thomson conceded an own-goal in the 84th minute and Durban completed his hat-trick seconds later.

PORTSMOUTH 4 BIRMINGHAM CITY 5
24 August 1966   Attendance: 16,934

Blues started the 1966–67 season like a house on fire, scoring 12 goals in their opening four League games, five of them coming in this thrilling encounter at Fratton Park. Blues established a 2–0 first-half lead through Geoff Vowden (19 minutes) and Barry Bridges (40). After plenty of end-to-end excitement, Pompey hit back on the hour through Brian Lewis, but a 73rd-minute penalty by Malcolm Beard (after Alex Wilson had handled) made it 3–1, only for Ray Hiron to bring Pompey back into the game a minute later. Further strikes from Vowden (81 minutes) and Bert Murray (86) put Blues firmly in control, but the home side produced a storming finish and scored twice in 40 seconds through Bert McCann and future Aston Villa manager Tony Barton to make it look a much closer contest than it really was.

BIRMINGHAM CITY 3 WOLVERHAMPTON WANDERERS 2
17 December 1966   Attendance: 27,542

Two-nil down with 19 minutes remaining, Blues turned things round in style by scoring three times to win this local derby and so clinch their first League double over Wolves for 46 years. Dave Wagstaffe gave the visitors a first-minute lead after Terry Wharton had headed Mike Bailey's cross against a post. After good Blues pressure, Wolves broke clear and went 2–0 up 10 minutes before half-time when Bailey powered the ball home from 30 yards. It was a different Blues in the second half and after Trevor Hockey and Bobby Thomson, against his former club, had both gone close, Barry Bridges converted Geoff Vowden's measured pass to make it 2–1. Eight minutes later Mickey Bullock crashed in the equaliser off the underside of Fred Davies's crossbar and with two minutes remaining Vowden raced through the middle to smash in the winner.

BIRMINGHAM CITY 6 HULL CITY 2
4 September 1967   Attendance: 25,931

Five goals were scored in the space of 16 minutes either side of half-time in this Second Division match at St Andrew's. Blues got off to a flying start, Barry Bridges netting in the ninth minute with a header after Ron Wylie's shot had rebounded to him off the crossbar. Both sides had chances after that but the crowd had to wait until the 42nd minute before Bridges's former Chelsea teammate Bert Murray made it 2–0 after Fred Pickering's shot had come back to him off a defender. Then, in Blues' next attack, Bridges grabbed his second goal and Blues' third when he latched onto Trevor Hockey's overhead kick to drive his shot past 'keeper Maurice Swan. The Tigers came roaring out for the second half and pegged Blues back by scoring twice in two minutes through Chris Chilton (50) and Dave Wagstaff (51), both from defensive mistakes. But Blues had plenty left in the tank and in the 58th minute Pickering made it 4–2 with a smart header from Hockey's cross; Geoff Vowden netted number five in the 71st minute with another header, this time from Murray's cross; and with 10 minutes remaining, Johnny Vincent, who had a superb game, made it six after some neat work involving Bridges and Pickering.

BIRMINGHAM CITY 6 MIDDLESBROUGH 1
26 September 1967   Attendance: 28,885

This was an emphatic win by Blues. Middlesbrough, who had conceded nine goals in their previous eight League games, proved no match for Freddie Goodwin's team, who produced some brilliant attacking football. Fred Pickering opened the scoring for Blues in the seventh minute when he just managed to convert Bert Murray's right-wing cross. After three previous efforts had passed him by, Geoff Vowden finally got on the score sheet in the 24th minute with Blues' second goal after good work by Trevor Hockey. Just before the interval Malcolm Beard netted a third from the penalty spot after Hockey had been fouled by Worthington. Seven minutes into the second half, after John O'Rourke had struck a post, Barry Bridges made it 4–0 with a crisp 30-yard strike following Ron Wylie's free-kick, and although Johnny Crossan reduced the arrears soon afterwards, Johnny Vincent (75 minutes) and Pickering (76) rounded off a brilliant afternoon for Blues.

ASTON VILLA 2 BIRMINGHAM CITY 4
7 October 1967   Attendance: 50,067

A crowd of over 50,000 saw Blues bounce back from being 1–0 and then 2–1 down to win this highly entertaining local derby at Villa Park in style. Brian Greenhalgh put the hosts in front in the second minute, heading in Willie Anderson's cross, before Barry Bridges equalised in the 21st minute when he nodded in Geoff Vowden's flick-on from Johnny Vincent's long throw. Back came Villa, and on the half-hour Brian Godfrey slotted the ball past Jim Herriot after some fine work by winger Dave Rudge. Blues battled on and won a penalty in the 37th minute when Lew Chatterley handled, allowing Malcolm Beard to fire his spot-kick past ex-Blues 'keeper Colin Withers. In the second half Blues were the masters and scored twice more, through Vowden on 59 minutes, from Vincent's pass, and Bridges 90 seconds later after a wonderful cross from ex-Villa man Ron Wylie.

BIRMINGHAM CITY 6 HUDDERSFIELD TOWN 1
23 December 1967   Attendance: 26,163

This was a great early Christmas present for Blues, who annihilated a poor Huddersfield Town side on a slippery St Andrew's pitch. It took Stan Cullis's side 38 minutes to score their first goal, Fred Pickering tapping in after Geoff Vowden's shot had been saved. This was surprisingly cancelled out by future Blues star Frank Worthington's header just before the interval, but the second half was one-way traffic as Blues ran rings around their Yorkshire opponents. Johnny Vincent made it 2–1 on 55 minutes from Ron Wylie's flick. Winger Graham Leggatt scored from Vincent's pass on 59 minutes (3–1). A Vowden rocket on 65 minutes made it 4–1; number five came courtesy of Pickering's second in the 67th minute and Barry Bridges rounded things off with number six seven minutes from time.

BIRMINGHAM CITY 0 WEST BROMWICH ALBION 2
27 March 1968   Attendance: 60,831

Blues played very well in this FA Cup semi-final and if it had not been for Baggies goalkeeper John Osborne, who pulled off a string of fine saves, mostly from Fred Pickering, then who knows what the final score might have been. Skippered by future Albion manager

Ron Wylie, Blues slipped behind in the 13th minute when Jim Herriot dived to save Tony Brown's free-kick, only for the ball to fall kindly for Jeff Astle to net from close range. Geoff Vowden should have equalised before the Pickering-Osborne show came into force. Three times 'Ossie' saved from the burly striker, while Albion's John Talbut cleared another effort off the line. Unfortunately Barry Bridges was out of sorts and it was left to Pickering to pit his wits against Albion's tough defence, Osborne again denying the former Everton star with splendid saves from a shot a powerful header, Then, in the 67th minute, Blues' hopes were shattered when Tony Brown drilled in Albion's second goal after Kenny Stephens had intercepted Bert Murray's pass to Malcolm Beard. The winger fed future Blues midfielder Bobby Hope, who then set up Brown to fire his 20-yard shot past Herriot. Albion defended in numbers after that and, in fact, Astle and Clive Clark could well have scored at the other end as Blues pressed forward to no avail.

BIRMINGHAM CITY 5 HUDDERSFIELD TOWN 1
7 September 1968   Attendance: 25,001

In this Second Division game, Blues forward Geoff Vowden became the first substitute to score a hat-trick in a League game. Leading 2–0 at the interval with goals from Jimmy Greenhoff's brilliant shot in the 26th minute and Fred Pickering's volley on 40 minutes, future St Andrew's favourite Frank Worthington got his side back into the game with a fine 63rd-minute strike before Vowden got to work on the Terriers' defence. Having replaced skipper Ron Wylie for the second half, he headed his first and second goals in the 71st and 74th minutes before shooting in his third a minute from time after Johnny Vincent had set him up. A decent-sized crowd saw history made.

BIRMINGHAM CITY 4 ASTON VILLA 0
21 September 1968   Attendance: 40,527

This was an impressive victory by Blues. Villa were outclassed and in the end the foe from Aston were let off lightly. After defender Dave Robinson had made two important first-half interventions, Blues took control after the break and tore Villa apart. Phil Summerill opened the door with the first goal after 63 minutes, following Jimmy Greenhoff's knock-down. Three minutes later Greenhoff himself made it 2–0 with a neat header from a Geoff Vowden centre. Despite dictating the play, Blues had to wait until the last seven minutes before completing the scoring, Johnny Vincent netting the third (from Vowden's inch-perfect cross) and Vowden the fourth after Greenhoff had set him free.

BIRMINGHAM CITY 5 FULHAM 4
5 October 1968   Attendance: 28,448

This nine-goal thriller included a four-timer for Blues forward Jimmy Greenhoff, who also missed a penalty. It was Johnny Vincent, however, who opened the scoring for Blues in the second minute, netting with ease from Geoff Vowden's angled pass. Then Greenhoff netted twice in quick succession. He raced onto Ron Wylie's splendid through ball to crack in his first in the 19th minute before making it 3–0 with a powerful header from Vincent's cross six minutes later. Then, amazingly, Fulham stormed back to score three times themselves in the space of eight minutes straight after half-time through Frank Large (2) and a Dave Robinson own-goal. In the 64th minute Greenhoff was upended by Reg Matthewson but missed hopelessly from the spot before making amends 50 seconds later by completing his hat-trick to edge Blues back in front at 4–3. Back came Fulham and Malcolm Macdonald swooped to equalise again for the Cottagers before Greenhoff nudged home the winner in the 71st minute after goalkeeper McClelland had made a hash of collecting Vincent's cross. And just as Hereford referee Jim Finney blew the final whistle, a shot from Greenhoff skimmed an upright.

BIRMINGHAM CITY 5 HULL CITY 2
30 November 1968   Attendance: 21,352

Phil Summerill was the star of this Blues' victory. He scored a seven-minute hat-trick to secure both points after the Tigers had fought back from 2–0 down to draw level with less than 20 minutes remaining. Jimmy Greenhoff (21 minutes) and Fred Pickering (32) put Blues in charge, but back came Hull and after Roy Greenwood had made it 2–1 with a skimming 20-yard drive before half-time, Dennis Butler made it 2–2 from Greenwood's cross before Summerill took over. The Erdington-born striker put Blues back in front in the 72nd minute when his looping centre eluded Ian McKechnie and dropped behind the 'keeper. His second goal, which made it 4–2, came five minutes later with a neat effort from the edge of the area before he completed his hat-trick in the 79th minute after Pickering's shot had rebounded off the crossbar.

BIRMINGHAM CITY 5 BOLTON WANDERERS 0
25 March 1969   Attendance: 20,454

Phil Summerill scored his second hat-trick of the season as Blues demolished Bolton. After having six shots and a goal disallowed in the first 25 minutes, Blues finally took the lead just before the half-hour mark when Johnny Vincent robbed a dithering Geoff Bromilow before firing past Eddie Hopkinson. Eight minutes after the break Summerill netted the first of his three goals, sliding the ball home after Hopkinson had saved from Jimmy Greenhoff. Seven minutes later Malcolm Beard unleashed a thunderbolt from fully 35 yards to make it 3–0 and two minutes later Summerill grabbed his second and Blues' fourth when he headed in Beard's measured cross. Bolton had given up by this time and, to rub salt into the wounds, Summerill duly completed his hat-trick in the last minute when he coolly headed in Vincent's cross.

BIRMINGHAM CITY 4 BOLTON WANDERERS 0
20 February 1971   Attendance: 25,600

This was the game in which 16-year-old Trevor Francis scored four goals as Blues overwhelmed Bolton with a wonderful display of attacking football. The Devon teenager opened his account in the 16th minute with a smart finish from Gordon Taylor's knock-back. Three minutes later he struck again after Taylor and Phil Summerill had done the spade-work. With the visitors permanently on the back foot and Blues driving forward at will, Francis gleefully clipped home his hat-trick goal in the 78th minute, driving the ball home following Summerill's smart pass. Then, with time running out, Alan Campbell broke down the right and, from his teasing cross, Francis bravely darted in to head the ball wide of the former Wolves 'keeper Alan Boswell. Right at the death Taylor almost made it 5–0 with a shot that hit the Bolton crossbar.

BIRMINGHAM CITY 6 PORTSMOUTH 3
8 January 1972   Attendance: 22,410

In wet, horrible conditions, Blues did very well to beat luckless Portsmouth in this Second Division encounter at St Andrew's. Pompey scored twice in the first eight minutes through Bert McCann and George Ley before Blues got going. Then poacher Bob Hatton made it 2–1 halfway through the half, Alan Campbell equalised with a 31st-minute penalty (awarded after Trevor Francis had been brought down) and Hatton again netted a third just before the break. The visitors drew level at 3–3 with a Ray Hiron goal 12 minutes after the interval and twice came mighty close to regaining the lead, but Blues finished the stronger, scoring three times in the last seven minutes through Bob Latchford (2) and Francis to move up to fifth place in the table.

BIRMINGHAM CITY 0 LEEDS UNITED 3
15 April 1972   Attendance: 54,723

At the time of this FA Cup semi-final, Blues were on course to emulate West Bromwich Albion's 1931 feat of winning the Cup and gaining promotion from the Second Division in the same season. But in front of a near full-house at Hillsborough they were beaten convincingly by Don Revie's Leeds United side, who scored twice in seven minutes during the first half and sewed things up with a third halfway through the second. In a hard fought game, Bob Latchford and Trevor Francis both went close for Blues before Mick Jones opened the scoring in the 18th minute. After considerable pressure, Leeds increased their lead in the 25th minute through Peter Lorimer and, although Blues battled on bravely, they never looked like getting back into the game and conceded a third goal to Jones in the 65th minute. Leeds went on to beat Arsenal 1–0 in the Final.

LEYTON ORIENT 0 BIRMINGHAM CITY 1
2 May 1972   Attendance: 33,383

Less than three weeks after losing their FA Cup semi-final tie with Leeds, Blues clinched promotion to the First Division with this single goal win at Brisbane Road on the last night of the season. In front of 18,000 travelling fans, Freddie Goodwin's side had plenty of nervous moments during the course of the 100 minutes (referee Martin Lowe added 10 minutes on at the end because of two pitch invasions by both home and away supporters). The former St Andrew's player Mickey Bullock twice went agonisingly close for Orient before Bob Latchford scored the all-important goal in the 58th minute. A left-wing corner by Gordon Taylor was headed home by the centre-forward despite having his shirt tugged by 'keeper Goddard. Even the announcement that there could be a bomb inside the ground failed to prevent the end-of-match celebrations. This was quite a night in East London… and it certainly made up for losing that semi-final in Sheffield.

LIVERPOOL 4 BIRMINGHAM CITY 3
2 December 1972   Attendance: 45,407

There are not too many teams who have scored three goals at Anfield (other than Liverpool) and lost. But this is precisely what happened to Blues in 1972 and, in all fairness, they were robbed of at least a point. Two-nil up inside 20 minutes through Gordon Taylor, whose shot went in off Trevor Storton's back, and Bobby Hope, who was on hand to place the ball over the line from Bob Latchford's deft header, Liverpool hit back in the 32nd minute when left-back Alec Lindsay was sent clear by an Emlyn Hughes free-kick. However, 10 minutes later Bob Latchford converted Bob Hatton's pass to give Blues a 3–1 cushion, only for Peter Cormack to make it 3–2 on the stroke of half-time. Nine minutes into the second half, the Hughes-Lindsay free-kick operation worked again as the latter equalised. Kevin Keegan and Ian Callaghan both went close for the Reds and Hatton had a goal ruled out for a push inside the box before John Toshack rose to head home the 78th-minute winner from Keegan's measured cross.

BIRMINGHAM CITY 5 CARDIFF CITY 2
5 January 1974   Attendance: 22,435

After recovering manfully from two-goal deficit, Cardiff City were eventually swept aside by in-form Blues in this third-round FA Cup tie at St Andrew's. Trevor Francis opened the scoring in the third minute and his strike partner Bob Latchford increased Blues' lead on 35 minutes. Then the visitors found their feet and drew level with two goals from John Impey and Andy McCulloch in the space of 90 seconds just on the hour before further efforts from Latchford (75) and Bob Hatton (75 and 88) sent Blues comfortably into the next round.

BIRMINGHAM CITY 3 LIVERPOOL 1
21 December 1974   Attendance: 26,608

This was an excellent victory for Blues over the FA Cup-holders Liverpool. After Gordon Taylor had gone close early on, Alan Campbell's 17th-minute penalty (awarded after a foul on Bob Hatton) was saved by Ray Clemence. Continuing to play football, Blues pressed on and deservedly took the lead on the half-hour through Taylor, who controlled and then converted Campbell's pass with a low angled drive. Liverpool hit back immediately and after some clever inter-play between Peter Cormack and Terry McDermott, John Toshack rose to power home the latter's cross. Then, right on half-time, Exeter referee Ron Crabb awarded Blues a second spot-kick for another foul on Hatton. This time Howard Kendall stepped forward to drive the ball past Clemence. After the break both teams had chances to add to their score and it was Blues who secured the points with a last-minute goal from Hatton, who headed home Taylor's cross from the left.

FULHAM 1 BIRMINGHAM CITY 0
9 April 1975   Attendance: 35,205

Blues suffered last-minute heartbreak at the end of extra-time in this FA Cup semi-final replay at Maine Road. After playing out a 1–1 draw at Hillsborough, when 54,166 fans saw John Mitchell's spectacular goal for Fulham cancelled out by Blues' defender Joe Gallagher, the teams met again four days later and once again it proved to be a tight encounter. There was plenty of dour defending at both ends of the pitch, Bobby Moore being outstanding for the Cottagers and Garry Pendrey and Gallagher likewise for Blues. With extra-time fast running out, Fulham somehow found themselves with four players inside Blues' six-yard box. After a shot by Viv Busby and a bit of a scramble, the ball rebounded off Blues' 'keeper Dave Latchford, struck Mitchell and rolled tantalisingly over the line to send the Londoners to Wembley and Blues back to St Andrew's with a lot of pain and sorrow. Fulham lost to Moore's former club West Ham United in the Final.

BIRMINGHAM CITY 5 DERBY COUNTY 1
2 October 1976   Attendance: 29,190

This was the day the Rams really got 'burned up' – by Blues centre-forward Kenny Burns, who snapped up four goals in this splendid victory at St Andrew's. On a wet, slippery pitch, Burns notched a hat-trick in the first half-hour to knock the stuffing out of Derby. His first goal was a deft header from Gray Jones's high cross; his second was a scrambled effort in the 22nd minute after some smart work by Trevor Francis and Terry Hibbitt, and his third was a stab-in on 30 minutes from Francis's pass. County netted just on half-time through Leighton James, but they were no match for Blues as Burns bagged his fourth of the afternoon in the 70th minute, before John Connolly curled in a fifth three minutes from time.

LEICESTER CITY 2 BIRMINGHAM CITY 6
4 December 1976   Attendance: 20,388

This was 'The Kenny Burns Show On Ice' as the Blues' makeshift centre-forward scored an excellent hat-trick on a slippery Filbert Street pitch to clinch a splendid victory. In fact, Blues were 6–0 up before Leicester began to play and in the end the final score could well have been 10–2 (even 10–0), so well did Blues play in difficult conditions. Gary Emmanuel opened the scoring in the 12th minute with a clear shot at goal. Trevor Francis drifted in to make it 2–0 soon afterwards before Burns netted twice in a four-minute spell before half-time, both with the help of Terry Hibbitt. After Denis Rofe had conceded an own-goal on 53 minutes, Burns duly completed his hat-trick 11 minutes later. Leicester were stunned and so were their fans, but they plodded on and were rewarded with two late strikes, courtesy of a Steve Kember shot and a Frank Worthington penalty.

BIRMINGHAM CITY 3 ARSENAL 3
18 January 1977   Attendance: 23,247

Very rarely do you see two players score a hat-trick and neither ends up a winner. This was the case in this First Division match at St Andrew's when Trevor Francis netted three times for Blues and Malcolm MacDonald likewise for Arsenal. Blues led 2–0 after 37 minutes and 3–1 following Francis's third goal from the penalty spot, given away by David O'Leary in the 51st minute. But two late strikes from 'Super Mac' earned the Gunners a point.

BIRMINGHAM CITY 5 MANCHESTER UNITED 1
11 November 1978   Attendance: 23,550

Rarely does Manchester United concede five goals in a game, but they did just that at St Andrew's on a cold winter's afternoon in 1978 as Blues turned on a super show to record their first League win of the season. In fact, it was their first victory of any kind for 17 matches, since beating Leicester City on 15 April 1978. Joe Jordan put United ahead in the 13th minute but Blues picked themselves up and went for the kill. Kevin Dillon equalised with a low right-footer on 23 minutes and nine minutes later Alan Buckley was on hand to steer home ex-United forward Don Givens's header from Alberto Tarantini's cross. Two minutes later the former Walsall striker bagged his second and Blues' third, converting Givens's measured pass. Six minutes after the interval, Blues went 4–1 up when Givens netted from eight yards and, with virtually the last kick of the game, Jimmy Calderwood raced in to give Blues five.

BIRMINGHAM CITY 5 CHELSEA 1
11 March 1980   Attendance: 27,297

Blues went to the top of the Second Division with this resounding victory over promotion rivals Chelsea at St Andrew's. Kevan Broadhurst's speculative long-range shot deflected off Kevin Hales and flew past 'keeper Petar Borota for the opening goal on two minutes. Then the unfortunate Borota conceded an own-goal in the 20th minute, dropping the ball over the line when challenged by Keith Bertschin. Chelsea hit back through Tommy Langley in the 35th minute, but seven minutes after half-time Blues regained their two-goal lead when Alan Ainscow scored following a pass from Colin Todd. Driving on, Blues cruised into a 4–1 lead in the 72nd minute when Ainscow scored his second after neat work by Frank Worthington, and the final nail was hammered into the visitors' coffin by Kevin Dillon's curling 20-yard drive a minute from time.

BIRMINGHAM CITY 3 NOTTS COUNTY 3
3 May 1980   Attendance: 33,863

Blues needed a point from their last game of the season against Notts County to stay in the First Division – and they got it, just! In a tension-packed encounter, the visitors gave as good as they got and came back from 2–0 down to equalise before half-time. They then pegged Blues back again with 17 minutes to go. Keith Bertschin opened the scoring from Kevin Dillon's pass in the 18th minute and four minutes later Alan Curbishley made it 2–0 with a 25-yard free-kick. Then it was all County. Some poor defending in the 36th minute allowed Gordon Mair to drift in unmarked to convert David Hunt's cross from the left and four minutes later Trevor Christie smashed in the equaliser after Kevan Broadhurst had slipped. But back came Blues and shortly before half-time Dillon was well placed to steer Bertschin's low return past 'keeper Raddy Avramovic. As the tension mounted, Don Masson's shot was brilliantly saved by Blues 'keeper Jeff Wealands before Kevin Kilcline brought the scores level again on 67 minutes with a close-range effort following a set piece on the right. Christie and Hunt went close to winning the game for the visitors, but Blues held out and a pitch invasion at the end meant that First Division football would be staged at St Andrew's for at least another season.

BIRMINGHAM CITY 4 SOUTHAMPTON 0
10 October 1981   Attendance: 16,938

Two goals apiece for Frank Worthington and Neil Whatmore in the second half destroyed a poor Southampton side. Blues dictated most of the 45 minutes but couldn't find a way past 'keeper Peter Wells. After the break it was much the same, but this time the goals flowed freely. 'Worthy' netted his first in the 50th minute, when he was on hand to slam the ball home after Wells had beaten out his penalty-kick after he was fouled in the area by Dave Watson. Eight minutes later the Elvis Presley fan made it 2–0 with a stunning volley he created himself from Kevin Dillon's pass. Then, in the 73rd minute, Whatmore got in on the act by converting Bud Brocken's cross and the former Bolton player grabbed a fourth goal five minutes from time when he was on hand to head home after Worthington's shot rebounded off a post. Saints' midfielder Alan Ball was booked while Mick Channon and Kevin Keegan were well below par.

BIRMINGHAM CITY 3 WEST BROMWICH ALBION 3
31 October 1981   Attendance: 21,601

Albion were the better side early on, but against the run of play, and it was Blues who took the lead on 35 minutes when goalkeeper Tony Godden failed to hold Bud Brocken's low shot, allowing Archie Gemmill to score with ease. Three minutes later it was 1–1, Cyrille Regis firing hard and low past Jeff Wealands from 25 yards. The same player netted Albion's second goal in their next attack, cracking home Gary Owen's through ball. There was action at both ends of the field after that, but it wasn't until the 73rd minute that a fourth goal was scored, again by Regis, who completed his hat-trick with a deft finish from the tightest of angles after Wealands had dropped John Wile's knock-on header. Owen then missed a sitter before Blues got back in the game in the 76th minute, Tony Evans, looking two yards offside, converting Gemmill's smart pass. This set up a terrific climax which resulted in a Blues' equaliser, Frank Worthington netting an 80th minute penalty, awarded by referee Don Shaw for a push on Ian Handysides by Godden. The future Blues number one was dropped for the next game, ending his record-breaking run of 226 consecutive appearances for the Baggies.

BIRMINGHAM CITY 2 IPSWICH TOWN 3
2 January 1982   Attendance: 17,236

Ipswich Town, with slightly more attacking flair, won this entertaining third-round FA Cup by the odd goal in five. Alan Brazil (35 minutes) gave the visitors the lead before Frank Worthington equalised with a penalty 90 seconds before half-time. Midfielder Alan Curbishley then edged Blues in front in the 50th minute before John Wark and Brazil again netted in the 72nd and 79th minutes to send the 1978 winners through.

NOTTS COUNTY 1 BIRMINGHAM CITY 4
1 May 1982   Attendance: 10,704

After a run of 31 away games without a win, Blues finally got rid of their travel sickness by whipping Notts County at Meadow Lane. Settled by a first-minute goal by Les Phillips, Blues conceded an equaliser to McCulloch in the 12th minute and, although they controlled the game, the first half ended with the scores level. After the interval, it all became too easy for Ron Saunders's side as the Magpies succumbed under severe pressure. Blues regained the lead in the 47th minute when Tony Evans smashed home Phillips's looped cross from the left. Halfway through the half Mick Harford made it 3–1 after some smart inter-play between Kevin Dillon and Phillips, and with nine minutes remaining Evans netted his second and Blues' fourth goal with a side-foot tap-in after a splendid four-man move.

SHEFFIELD UNITED 3 BIRMINGHAM CITY 4
1 January 1985   Attendance: 16,571

This was Blues' first victory over the Blades in Yorkshire for 12 years. Two-nil down just past the hour mark following goals by Hefferman and Edwards, Blues stormed back to take a commanding lead with four goals in the space of 16 minutes from Robert Hopkins, David Geddis, Wayne Clarke's deft header and Gary West, who diverted Hopkins' cross past his own 'keeper John Burridge. United made it 4–3 with a Colin Morris penalty, after he had been fouled by 'Harry' Roberts and only a fine save late on by David Seaman earned Blues all three points.

BIRMINGHAM CITY 4 CRYSTAL PALACE 1
18 October 1986   Attendance: 5,987

Without a win in the previous eight games, Blues finally came to life with this excellent victory over the Eagles, but fewer than 6,000 spectators were present – the second lowest League crowd at St Andrew's since March 1955. From Wayne Clarke's pass, midfielder Des Bremner scored first for Blues in the 20th minute. Vince Overson, up for a corner, glided in number two seven minutes later, only for Taylor to pull one back for Palace six minutes after half-time. A stunning 30-yarder by Steve Whitton put Blues back in control in the 65th minute and Clarke nipped in to make it 4–1 with barely a minute remaining. For the record, Palace gained sweet revenge by hammering Blues 6–0 in the return game at Selhurst Park in mid-March.

BIRMINGHAM CITY 3 TRANMERE ROVERS 2
26 May 1991   Attendance: 58,756

This was Blues' first trip to Wembley since 1956 and around 35,000 of their fans were there to see them win the Leyland DAF Trophy at the expense of Tranmere Rovers. After a strong start, Blues took the lead in the 21st minute through Simon Sturridge, who latched onto John Gayle's header before beating Eric Nixon with a low drive. Play was fairly even after that, although Martyn Thomas in the Blues goal was hardly troubled. Then, two minutes before the interval, Gayle made it 2–0 with a powerful shot from just outside the box. Blues looked comfortable during the early stages of the second half but then, unexpectedly, Rovers scored twice in six minutes just past the hour mark, first through Steve Cooper and then via big Jim Steel. Blues were wobbling, errors were creeping in to their play and Rovers were on top. But with time fast running out, a free-kick was launched forward by Ian Clarkson. Vince Overson beat Dave Higgins in the air and the ball hung just right for Gayle to swoop and smash it past Nixon. It was a great goal – one of the best seen at Wembley for years – and it won the trophy for Blues.

BIRMINGHAM CITY 1 SHREWSBURY TOWN 0
25 April 1992   Attendance: 19,868

Nigel Gleghorn's 34th-minute goal decided this one-sided encounter at St Andrew's when victory clinched promotion back to the second tier of English football for Blues. Virtually running the show from start to finish, Blues found Ken Hughes in the Shrews' goal in terrific form. He saved brilliantly from Simon Sturridge (twice) and Paul Mardon, Darren Rowbottom and Ian Rodgerson, while Mark Cooper fired over and Sturridge hit the side-netting. Former St Andrew's star Robert Hopkins twice came close for the visitors who also had Kevin Summerfield in their line-up.

BIRMINGHAM CITY 4 SWINDON TOWN 6
12 April 1993   Attendance: 17,903

This was a real ding-dong contest. Blues needed a point at least to keep alive their hopes of avoiding relegation while Swindon were in a play-off position. After a rather relaxed opening 20 minutes, Blues suddenly went into overdrive and took a two-goal lead through Dean Peer and full-back John Frain, but a header from centre-half Shaun Taylor just before half-time brought the visitors back into the game. Then two goals in four minutes by Paul Moulden (47) and Andy Saville (51) put Blues well in control, but nobody in the stadium could have envisaged what would happen in the last half-hour. Throwing caution to the wind, Glenn Hoddle moved forward and Swindon suddenly clicked into gear. They pegged Blues back in their own half and the goals simply rained in. On 60 minutes Craig Maskell made it 4–2 from Micky Hazard's superb pass. Five minutes later Dave Mitchell headed a third for the visitors and on 76 minutes the same player netted the equaliser after some great build-up play involving the former Spurs duo of Hoddle and Hazard. Two minutes on, and with Blues reeling under pressure, Maskell grabbed his second and Swindon's fifth from Paul Bodin's corner and 50 seconds from time Mitchell, after outpacing Trevor Matthewson, completed his hat-trick to earn his side a memorable victory. Blues stayed up while Swindon went on to win the Play-off Final and gain a place in the Premier League.

WEST BROMWICH ALBION 2 BIRMINGHAM CITY 4
27 April 1994   Attendance: 20,316

This was a crucial relegation match and it was never-say-die Blues who came out on top. Played off the park for half an hour and 1–0 down due to Kevin Donovan's 24th-minute goal, Blues equalised in the 38th minute through Steve Claridge. Five minutes after half-time Louie Donowa netted with a sensational 40-yard chip and in the 56th minute, after former Blues defender Paul Mardon had slipped, home 'keeper Stuart Naylor presented Andy Saville with a simple tap-in to make it 3–1. Daryl Burgess headed Albion back into the game in the 64th minute and the Baggies should have levelled, but Bob Taylor, Andy Hunt and Donovan all fluffed easy chances. In the last minute Claridge raced through to fire home Blues' fourth goal to sew up the points. Sadly Blues still went down while Albion stayed up.

BIRMINGHAM CITY 5 CREWE ALEXANDRA 0
1 November 1994   Attendance: 14,212

Jonathan Hunt scored a hat-trick in this easy Second Division victory over the Alex at St Andrew's. The midfielder opened his account in the 24th minute from Louie Donowa's cross and the same player made it 2–0 seven minutes later by smashing in Gary Bull's knockdown. Five minutes before the break Donowa nipped in with a third after a superb solo run and Steve Claridge finished off José Dominguez's pass for number four six minutes from time before Hunt completed his hat-trick with the last kick of the game.

CHESTER CITY 0 BIRMINGHAM CITY 4
10 December 1994   Attendance: 3,946

In front of one of the lowest League crowds ever to watch Blues in action, Chester were completely outplayed by Barry Fry's team. After a lot of pressure, Liam Daish opened the scoring in the 24th minute when he headed home Chris Whyte's flick-on. On the stroke of half-time Steve Claridge added a second when he nodded in Steve McGavin's cross and it was McGavin himself who netted the third on 66 minutes after a poor clearance by Jenkins. As the players celebrated the goal, one of them, Daish, was booked by Lichfield referee Brandwood for picking up and playing a child's trumpet in front of the Blues fans. Substitute Kenny Lowe hit number four with a quarter of an hour remaining.

BIRMINGHAM CITY 7 BLACKPOOL 1
31 December 1994   Attendance: 18,025

This was Blues' biggest win since 1959 and the three points gained took them to the top of the Second Division table for the first time in the season. Against the run of play, the visitors had the cheek to take an eighth-minute lead through Bradshaw, but the same player conceded an own-goal four minutes later to bring Blues level. After that it was end to end action despite the final result that seems to show everything in a different light. Louie Donowa made it 2–1 in the 25th minute with a rising shot and 12 minutes later Steve Claridge ripped home a 30-yarder. Kenny Lowe grabbed a goal eight minutes into the second half, heading in Ricky Otto's cross, and 11 minutes later Lowe set up Donowa for number five. Blackpool kept going, but so did Blues, and Claridge claimed his second in the 73rd minute after a smart back-heeler by McGavin before George Parris tapped in from close range with four minutes remaining. This was a fine performance by Blues.

BIRMINGHAM CITY 1 CARLISLE UNITED 0
23 April 1995   Attendance: 73,663

There were well over 40,000 Blues supporters present for this Auto Windscreens Shield Final at Wembley. Unfortunately, it turned out to be a rather dour contest that Blues just about deserved to win – although they had to wait until the 103rd minute before substitute Paul Tait scored the vital 'golden' goal – the first in Wembley history. Former Aston Villa defender Derek Mountfield had held the Carlisle defence together and, in a game of few chances, it was the Cumbrians who came closest to scoring before Tait's decisive winner from Ricky Otto's floated left-wing cross.

HUDDERSFIELD TOWN 1 BIRMINGHAM CITY 2
6 May 1995   Attendance: 18,775

Blues needed just a single point from their last League game of 1994–95 to clinch the Second Division title – they got three and deservedly so after a thoroughly professional performance in front of a record crowd at the Alfred McAlpine stadium. After a shaky start Blues took control, although the first half was scoreless. Blues pressed continually after the interval and the breakthrough came in the 73rd minute when Steve Claridge turned to smash an unstoppable shot past Terriers' 'keeper Francis. With five minutes remaining substitute Paul Tait netted a second to ease the nerves and, although Bullock grabbed a consolation goal for the home side late on, 4,000 Brummie fans celebrated in style when referee Jeff Winter sounded the final whistle.

BARNSLEY 0 BIRMINGHAM CITY 5
2 September 1995   Attendance: 11,121

This was a splendid win for Blues at Oakwell. After a goalless first half, Blues turned up the gas after the break and tore Barnsley apart. Jonathan Hunt started the rout with a 54th-minute penalty, awarded for a trip on Steve Claridge by 'keeper David Watson, who was sent off. Six minutes later Claridge took Chris Whyte's long pass in his stride before smacking home a corker from 18 yards and, seven minutes after that, Chris Charlery was left unmarked to fire in number three. With the Tykes' defence at sixes and sevens, Richard

Forsyth found space to net a fourth goal in the 76th minute and six minutes from time Neil Doherty made it five from a deft Claridge pass. With time ticking by Bishop handled Forsyth's shot on the line; he was also dismissed but Claridge missed the resulting penalty. It was pretty good afternoon's work overall.

BIRMINGHAM CITY 2 MANCHESTER CITY 1
13 December 1997   Attendance: 21,014

This League game lasted for 97 minutes. The visitors had taken the lead with just two minutes of normal time remaining but then, quite unexpectedly, Blues stormed forward and struck two hammer blows in the last two minutes of added time to steal all three points. Seven players were booked in this robust encounter, which did not really liven up until the last quarter of an hour. Then, after a couple of close shaves, Georgian striker Murtaz Shelia drifted in unchallenged to nod the visitors in front. Gritty Blues rolled up their sleeves and in the 96th minute Nicky Forster equalised from a yard out. And then, amazingly, in the final attack of the game, Forster's shot was diverted 30 yards away from goal. Martyn O'Connor picked up the loose ball, moved forward, dummied a couple of defenders and 'keeper Martyn Margetson and then chipped it into the far corner for a dramatic winning goal. St Andrew's erupted. No one could believe what they had seen…what an ending.

STOKE CITY 0 BIRMINGHAM CITY 7
10 January 1998   Attendance: 14,940

Around 2,500 Blues supporters saw their team demolish the Potters to equal the club's best-ever away win in the Football League. On top from the start, Bryan Hughes headed the first goal on four minutes and followed up with a second five minutes later. After a 20-minute 'rest' Nicky Forster surged downfield to make it 3–0 at the break. Three more goals followed during the first 25 minutes of the second half, Paul Furlong (2) and Jon McCarthy finding Carl Muggleton's net with consummate ease. Then, with hordes of irate Stoke supporters surrounding the pitch, Furlong completed his hat-trick with two minutes remaining. At the final whistle scores of home fans charged onto the pitch, demanding the resignation of Chairman Peter Coates. Mounted police in riot gear thankfully maintained reasonable calm.

OXFORD UNITED 1 BIRMINGHAM CITY 7
12 December 1998   Attendance: 7,189

This was Blues' second seven-goal romp of 1998 and five different players figured on the scoresheet. Gary Rowett got things going with a 16th-minute goal. Paul Furlong made it 2–0 fifty seconds later and, after Rowett had added a third in the 31st minute, Furlong claimed his second and Blues' fourth just before half-time after a bulldozing run by Dele Adebola. Full-back Martin Grainger moved forward to make it 5–0 10 minutes after the break and, with just under 20 minutes remaining, Peter Ndlovu scored a fine individual goal for number six and substitute Bryan Hughes volleyed home Nicky Forster's cross for the seventh. Dean Windass somehow headed a late consolation goal for United.

LEICESTER CITY 4 BIRMINGHAM CITY 2

2 January 1999   Attendance: 19,846

Defenders Frank Sinclair and Rob Ullathorne put the Foxes 2–0 up inside the first 27 minutes of this highly entertaining third-round FA Cup tie at Filbert Street. Steve Robinson reduced the deficit before half-time but further goals, against the run of play, by Tony Cottee (51 minutes) and winger Steve Guppy (70) gave Leicester a huge advantage. Blues battled on gamely and, after three easy chances had gone begging, a late strike from Dele Adebola made the final scoreline much more respectable.

BIRMINGHAM CITY 4 WEST BROMWICH ALBION 0

13 March 1999   Attendance: 29,060

This was Blues' biggest home win over the Baggies for 51 years. From the outset the visitors were put under pressure and, if the truth be known, Blues virtually dominated the game throughout. Dele Adebola, with a sweetly-struck left-footer, opened the scoring on 15 minutes. After several near misses, Blues' second goal arrived in the 50th minute when Peter Ndlovu sidestepped two Albion defenders before firing high past 'keeper Phil Whitehead. Twelve minutes later it was 3–0 – and game over – when Adebola grabbed his second, slipping the ball into the corner of the net after skipping past Aussie full-back Andy McDermott. And to wrap things up, Martin Grainger rifled the ball home from six yards with two minutes remaining after Whitehead, under pressure from Paul Furlong, could only parry the ball into his path.

TOTTENHAM HOTSPUR 1 BIRMINGHAM CITY 3

31 October 2000   Attendance: 27,096

Blues played some splendid football in the first 45 minutes to set up this excellent victory over Spurs in the third round of the League Cup at White Hart Lane. Dele Adebola gave them the lead in the 15th minute, from Stan Lazaridis's low cross, and just before the half-hour mark the Nigerian bagged a second, sending a wonderful 35-yard left-footed curler past 'keeper Neil Sullivan. Then, in the last minute of the first half, Mark Burchill made it 3–0 with a side-footer from Martin Grainger's centre. Darren Anderton converted a 60th-minute penalty for Spurs, after Lazaridis tripped future Blues midfielder Stephen Clemence.

BIRMINGHAM CITY 4 IPSWICH TOWN 1

31 January 2001   Attendance: 28,624

Blues reached their first major Cup Final for 45 years by defeating Ipswich Town over two legs in the League Cup semi-final. After the aggregate scores had finished level at 2–2, Blues scored twice in extra-time of the second leg to win 4–1 on the night and 4–2 on aggregate to book a place at the Millennium Stadium against Liverpool. In a thrilling match watched by a full house at St Andrew's, Blues, 1–0 down from the first leg, drew level overall in the 42nd minute through Martin Grainger. Then, 10 minutes into the second half, Geoff Horsfield scored a second to put Blues in front, only for Scowcroft to equalise almost immediately. It was nail-biting stuff which continued into extra-time. With two minutes of the first period remaining Danny Sonner fed Horsfield and the striker smacked Blues back in front. With Ipswich pushing forward, Andy Johnson netted a fourth goal to seal the tie and send the Blues fans wild with delight.

BIRMINGHAM CITY 1 LIVERPOOL 1
25 February 2001   Attendance: 73,500
(Blues lost 5–4 on pens)

For the first time since 1963, Blues reached the League Cup Final and, instead of playing at Wembley, they took on the favourites Liverpool at Cardiff's Millennium Stadium. After dominating the early proceedings, the Reds took the lead in the 29th minute when Robbie Fowler volleyed home Emile Heskey's knock-on following a long punt downfield by 'keeper Sander Westerveld. But Blues stuck in there, growing in confidence all the time. Andrew Johnson almost equalised and then shot wide before referee David Elleray awarded Blues a 90th-minute penalty when Didier Hamann tripped Martyn O'Connor. Defender Darren Purse stepped forward to fire the ball home and take the game into extra-time. It was tense stuff and with the scores still level after 30 minutes, it came down to the dreaded penalty shoot-out. Sadly, it all ended in disappointment for the 35,000 Blues fans when Johnson's spot-kick was saved by Westerveld, thus handing Liverpool a 5–4 victory on penalties. The Anfield club went from strength to strength after this victory and duly completed a memorable treble.

BIRMINGHAM CITY 1 NORWICH CITY 1
12 May 2002   Attendance: 71,597
(Blues won 4–2 on penalties)

Blues gained promotion to the Premier League for the first time in their history after beating Norwich City in a nail-biting penalty shoot-out at the Millennium Stadium in Cardiff. After a goalless 90 minutes, Iwan Roberts put the Canaries in front in the first minute of extra-time and, after some wonderful aggressive play, Geoff Horsfield grabbed an equaliser for Blues in the 102nd minute to take the game to a dreaded shoot-out. Roberts scored first for Norwich (1–0)…Stern John levelled for Blues…Vaesen then saved from Mulryne while Devlin netted to put Blues 2–1 in front. Sutch became the second Norwich player to miss, but Lazaridis stepped up and scored (3–1 to Blues). Easton made it 3–2, only for local boy Darren Carter to clinch victory with Blues' fourth decisive kick to send 35,000 blue and white clad supporters wild with delight. A smiling Steve Bruce said after the game: 'I think we've only lost one game in 17 now – the courage of the players is incredible. They've fought to the death and I'm proud of them. They've done remarkably well and all credit to them – they're fantastic.'

ARSENAL 2 BIRMINGHAM CITY 0
18 August 2002   Attendance: 38,018

Around 2,700 travelling supporters saw Birmingham City's first-ever Premier League game end in a 2–0 defeat at the hands of the reigning champions at Highbury. The Gunners were far too strong on the day and, despite some hard graft and solid commitment by the Blues players, the Londoners deserved their victory. Both goals came in the first half through the French duo of Thierry Henry, who struck with a ninth-minute free-kick after a foul by Damien Johnson, and Sylvan Wiltord, who netted with a wonderful 24th-minute strike. Stern John and the hard-working Johnson came closest for Blues, but some fine saves by Vaesen in the second half kept the score to a minimum. Aliou Cissé (Blues) was sent off.

MIDDLESBROUGH 5 BIRMINGHAM CITY 3
20 March 2004   Attendance: 29,369

Middlesbrough shaded this thrilling game thanks to their goalkeeper Mark Schwarzer, who produced at least half a dozen splendid saves, mostly from Mikael Forssell. It could have been 5–5 at half-time as both teams attacked at will. Mendieta put the home side in front in the fifth minute before Maccarone made it 2–0 halfway through the first half. Martin Taylor reduced the deficit two minutes later, only for Middlesbrough to score again through Gareth Southgate's toe-poke from eight yards on the half-hour. With both defences stretched to the limit, Forssell hit the woodwork with a header before Schwarzer saved from Bryan Hughes and Stan Lazaridis. A minute before half-time, a move involving Forssell and Clinton Morrison ended with the latter tapping home from close range. The action continued…and 45 seconds later Maccarone bent a marvellous effort into the top corner (4–2). Birmingham came back again. Morrison and Forssell were both thwarted by Schwarzer, Stern John flashed a half-chance high and wide before Forssell grabbed his second of the game in the 59th minute to put Blues right back in the hunt. Mendieta then volleyed across goal as 'Boro tried to ease the pressure. Schwarzer made another great save from Lazaridis before substitute Nemeth ended the contest in the 90th minute with a fifth 'Boro goal, rounding Maik Taylor after a slip by Matthew Upson.

BIRMINGHAM CITY 4 WEST BROMWICH ALBION 0
18 December 2004   Attendance: 28,880

This easy victory saw Blues equal their best-ever League win over Albion – and they may well have scored more goals had 'keeper Russell Hoult not been in such good form. Bernt Haas impeded David Dunn to allow Robbie Savage to set the ball rolling with a fourth-minute penalty. Clinton Morrison converted Darren Carter's pass to make it 2–0 in the 24th minute and on the half-hour Emile Heskey netted a third from another Carter pass. Albion tried their best but rarely threatened Maik Taylor's goal and with nine minutes remaining Darren Anderton whipped in a free-kick to seal victory.

BIRMINGHAM CITY 5 PORTSMOUTH 0
21 January 2006   Attendance: 29,138

Blues moved above Portsmouth in the Premier League after this superb victory. Steve Bruce's side went ahead in the fifth minute when Mario Melchiot crossed for Jiri Jarosik to head home. After continuous pressure, Jermaine Pennant drilled Emile Heskey's pass past 'keeper Ashdown to double Blues' advantage on 37 minutes and after half-time further goals from Matthew Upson (a powerful header on 56 minutes), substitute Mikael Forssell (a penalty on 89) and David Dunn sealed Pompey's fate.

BIRMINGHAM CITY 2 SHEFFIELD WEDNESDAY 0
28 April 2007   Attendance: 29,317

Blues clinched an instant return to the Premier League with this 2–0 victory over Wednesday. Manager Steve Bruce said: 'This has been my greatest achievement in the game and I'm absolutely delighted for everyone. It's been my toughest-ever season. A few people have doubted me at times but I've come through it. We seem to lurch from one crisis to another at this club, yet the facts are that we have been outside the top six for only two weeks this season.' After a tension-packed 75 minutes when chances were at a premium, and playing with 10 men from the 68th minute following Fabrice Muamba's sending-off, Cameron Jerome broke the deadlock by hooking in Blues' first goal after Owls' keeper Chris Adamson had failed to deal with a corner. With six minutes remaining Sebastian Larsson secured victory with a fine individual effort. By losing their final game at Preston, Blues had to settle for runners'-up spot behind Sunderland.

BIRMINGHAM CITY 4 TOTTENHAM HOTSPUR 1
1 March 2008   Attendance: 26,055

Mikael Forssell was the star of this impressive win over Spurs. The Finn, who had struggled with injury for four years, netted his first Premier League hat-trick and Blues collected three precious points in their fight to avoid relegation. This was Blues' first League victory since Boxing Day and their first double over Spurs for 32 years, and a delighted Alex McLeish said: 'We needed that and all credit to Mika. He's a great finisher, one of the best I've seen.' With Forssell and James McFadden causing problems for a makeshift Spurs defence, Blues, with a strong wind in their favour, went ahead after seven minutes. Gary McSheffrey's cross picked out Liam Ridgewell, whose header looked to be going wide, but McFadden reacted quickly and turned the ball back across goal for Forssell to head in from close range. Then a mix-up between Fabrice Muamba and Radhi Jaidi allowed Dimitov Berbatov to fire a 20-yard shot against Maik Taylor's post. Blues started the second half on the offensive, Spurs 'keeper Paul Robinson saving well from McFadden and Forssell. On 55 minutes Sebastian Larsson fired home a superb free-kick to double Blues' lead and the cheering had hardly died down before Forssell grabbed his second to make it 3–0. Denied his hat-trick by Chimbonda, Forssell duly completed his treble in the 81st minute with a cool finish from McFadden's pass. Jenas scored a consolation goal in injury-time for woeful Spurs.

READING 1 BIRMINGHAM CITY 2
3 May 2009   Attendance: 23,879

Blues clinched automatic promotion to the Premier League with this hard-earned victory at the Madejski Stadium on the last day of the season. After an uneventful opening quarter of an hour, Reading's American 'keeper Marcus Hahnemann allowed a weak Keith Fahey effort to squirm under him and give the visitors the lead in the 23rd minute. The Royals barely threatened for the remainder of the first half, Liam Rosenior's dangerous cross being the only worry to a tight away defence. Blues doubled their lead on the hour when poor Reading marking allowed Kevin Phillips a clear run on goal and the self-proclaimed 'Super Kev' made no mistake by rolling the ball into the net. The travelling fans thought their side had already done enough to clinch promotion, but substitute Marek Matejovsky halved the deficit almost immediately when he curled into the corner after being found by Dave

Kitson. Reading threw caution to the wind as they went in search of the two goals that would have seen them automatically promoted, but the final clear-cut chance of the game went to Blues' Garry O'Connor, whose effort struck the inside of the post with Hahnemann well beaten.

LIVERPOOL 2 BIRMINGHAM CITY 2

9 November 2009   Attendance: 42,560

Blues thoroughly deserved a share of the points at Anfield. In fact, they should have won – Liverpool's skipper Steve Gerrard equalising with a controversial penalty on 70 minutes after David Ngog had clearly dived when challenged by Lee Carsley. Even the most avid 'Kop-ite' agreed that it was a 'shameful, play-acting fall' by the Frenchman. Ngog had given the Reds an early lead, but Blues fought back strongly and drew level via the head of Christian Benitez in the 25th minute. Pressing forward, the visitors then stunned the home fans by going 2–1 in front shortly after half-time. Cameron Jerome collected Scott Dann's headed clearance and went on to beat Pepe Reina with a low, crisp drive. Then referee Peter Walton was conned into awarding a spot-kick and Blues had to settle for a point.

BIRMINGHAM CITY 2 WOLVERHAMPTON WANDERERS 1

7 February 2010   Attendance: 24,165

Veteran striker Kevin Phillips came off the bench to rescue Blues, scoring twice in the last 11 minutes to secure a 2–1 derby victory over Wolves. Having suffered one defeat in 15 games, Blues fell behind in the 42nd minute when Wolves sharp-shooter Kevin Doyle slotted home from close range. Blues felt aggrieved, but once Phillips had entered the action, taking over from Christian Benitez just past the hour mark, things started to change dramatically. Phillips equalised in the 79th minute after good work by Keith Fahey and £3 million debutant Craig Gardner. The goal inspired Blues and, five minutes later, skipper Stephen Carr advanced down the right and his cross was hooked home in familiar style by the inspirational Phillips.

BLUES' STARS

WALTER ABBOTT, born in Birmingham on 7 December 1877, was a powerful inside-left and later a resilient left-half. Joining Blues from Rosewood Villa in April 1896, he remained at the club until July 1899 when he moved to Everton. He scored a record 42 goals (34 in the League) in his last season with Blues, netting 65 in 83 games in all. He played in successive FA Cup Finals for Everton in 1906 and 1907, gaining a winners' medal in the first before switching to Burnley. Rejoining Blues for the 1910–11 season, he was injured in his first game and never played again. Abbott, who was capped for England versus Wales in March 1902, also represented the Football League on four occasions. Later employed in the car industry, he died in Birmingham on 1 February 1941. His son, Walter junior, played for Grimsby Town in 1920–21.

ARTHUR ARCHER, born in Ashby-de-la-Zouch on 19 November 1877, played full-back for Burton St Edmund's, Tutbury Hampton, Swadlincote and Burton Wanderers before joining Blues in August 1897. He spent four and a half years with the club, netting three goals in 170 appearances and helping Blues win promotion in 1901. A year later he moved to New Brompton (now Gillingham) and later assisted Wingfield House FC, Tottenham Hotspur, Norwich, Brighton and Millwall, retiring in 1909. Later a coach in Germany, Italy and Belgium and also at Watford, he died in Hertfordshire in 1940.

GORDON ASTALL was a brilliant outside-right, fast, direct and clever with a powerful shot. Born in Horwich on 22 September

1927, and a former Royal Marine, he played for Southampton and had a trial with Bolton Wanderers before helping Plymouth Argyle win the Third Division (South) title in 1952, the same year he represented England 'B'. He was transferred to Birmingham City for £14,000 in October 1953 and two years later helped Blues gain promotion from Division Two. An FA Cup finalist in 1956, gaining two full caps for his country against Finland and Germany soon afterwards, Astall also played for the Football League XI. He scored 67 goals in 263 games for Blues before joining Torquay United in July 1961, retiring two years later. He later coached the non-League Devon club Upton Vale for a short time and still lives in Torbay.

CHARLIE ATHERSMITH was one of the most famous names in Aston Villa's late 19th-century history. One of the fastest wingers of his day, wonderfully consistent, he was especially adept at racing 40 yards down the field without anyone getting near him and he always seemed to rise to the big occasion. One feels that if it had not been for West Brom's outside-right Billy Bassett, Athersmith would have gained far more than the 12 caps he won for England. Born in Bloxwich on 10 May 1872 and a pupil at Walsall Road Council School, he assisted the Unity Gas works team before joining Villa in 1891. Over the next decade he scored 86 goals in 311 appearances, won five League Championship-winning medals, two FA Cup-winners' medals and was instrumental when Villa completed the double in 1897. Athersmith also played in two international trials, twice for an England XI and on nine occasions for the Football League. He joined Blues in June 1901 and remained at the club for two seasons, helping them win promotion while netting 13 goals in 106 appearances. Selected for the unsanctioned Tagg & Campbell FA tour to Germany in 1903, he regretted going because, along with several other players, some of them internationals, he was subsequently suspended. His career at top level ended there and then, although he did assist Bloxwich Strollers while serving his ban. He became Grimsby's trainer in 1907 but fell ill two years later and moved to Shifnal, where he died on 18 September 1910.

BERTIE AULD upset the Celtic chairman and directors and was sold to Blues in April 1961 for £15,000. He made his debut immediately in the second leg of the 1961 Fairs Cup semi-final against Inter Milan, the first of 145 appearances he made for the club (31 goals scored). Born in Glasgow on 23 March 1938, Auld joined Celtic in March

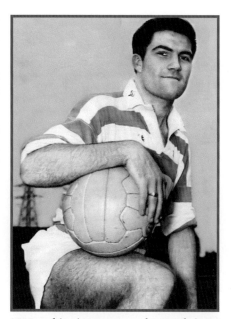

1955 and in six years scored 24 goals in 86 appearances, gained three caps for Scotland and played twice for the Scottish League. Auld's fiery temper also saw him sent off five times in his career, once as a Blues player against Español in the Fairs Cup. In 1962–63 he was outstanding as Blues avoided relegation and beat Aston Villa in the League Cup Final. However, in January 1965, Celtic boss Jock Stein enticed Auld back to Parkhead for £12,000. Rehoused at his old stomping ground, he became a star of the team, helping the Bhoys win five Scottish League titles in succession (1966–70), three Scottish Cups, four League Cups and the European Cup in 1967, as well as playing in the World Club Championship. In May 1971 he joined Hibernian, later becoming coach at Easter Road before taking charge of Partick Thistle, Hibs, Hamilton Academical and Dumbarton.

JACK BADHAM served Blues for 24 years, as a player and later as a coach. Born in Birmingham on 31 January 1919, he joined the club from Shirley Juniors in 1934 but

lost six years of his career to the war. He twice helped Blues win promotion from the Second Division (1948 and 1955), but missed the 1956 FA Cup Final when manager Turner chose Johnny Newman to replace the injured Roy Warhurst. A lion-hearted defender who occupied eight different positions during his time at St Andrew's, Badham was best at right-back. He skippered Blues' second XI for two seasons before leaving for Stourbridge in 1957, having scored four goals in 190 appearances. Returning to Blues as coach to the juniors in 1959, he was later player-coach of Moorlands Athletic and manager of Moor Green. He died in Birmingham on 1 January 1992.

BILLY 'KOSHER' BALL made 165 appearances at full-back for Blues in 10 years up to October 1921. A Second Division Championship-winner in his last season at St Andrew's, he gained one Victory cap for England in October 1919 v Wales. Born in Woodside, Derby on 9 April 1886, he played for Dudley Welfare,

Stourbridge and Wellington Town before joining Blues and after leaving assisted Cannock Town and Wellington Town for a second time, retiring in June 1924. He died in Shropshire on 30 September 1942.

NED BARKAS was born in Wardley, Northumberland on 21 November 1901. Initially a centre forward with Bedlington United, he joined Huddersfield as a professional in 1921, and was immediately converted into a full-back. A strong tackler, he helped the Terriers win the League title in 1923 and 1924, played in the 1928 FA Cup Final defeat by Blackburn Rovers and toured Canada with the FA in 1926. In December 1928, he signed for Blues for £4,000 and over the next eight and a half years, scored nine goals in 288 games, skippering the team in the 1931 Cup Final. Teaming up with his former manager Leslie Knighton at Chelsea in 1937, he remained at Stamford Bridge until May 1939. He was later player-manager of Solihull Town and assisted Willmott Breedon & Nuffield Mechanics during World War Two. Barkas died in Little Bromwich on 24 April 1962.
NB: Four Barkas brothers played professional football and collectively appeared in 1,125 League games between 1920 and 1949. Ned himself made 404 appearances.

PERCY BARTON was a thickset wing-half or left-back. With Blues from January 1914 to August 1929, his career was disrupted by World War One, but from August 1919 until his departure he produced some exquisite performances, helping Blues gain promotion in 1921, winning seven England caps and appearing in 358 games, scoring 14 goals, one a stunning header from 30 yards in a 4–1 victory over Wolves in November 1920. On leaving St Andrew's, Barton joined Stourbridge, retiring in May 1933. Born in Plaistow, London on 19

August 1895, he died in Edmonton on 20 October 1961.

MALCOLM BEARD served Blues for 16 years, 14 as a player. Born in Cannock on 3 May 1942, he represented Cannock & District and Staffordshire Schools before joining Blues in June 1957, turning professional in May 1959. He scored 32 goals (including a hat-trick v Blackburn in April 1965) in 405 appearances for the club, gaining League Cup honours in 1963 and playing in the 1967 and 1968 League Cup and FA Cup semi-finals. Sent off in his last game for Blues at Millwall, Beard left St Andrew's in July 1971 for Aston Villa, whom he helped win the Third Division. Later with Atherstone Town, he also coached in Saudi Arabia before returning to St Andrew's as a scout in 1979, taking a similar position at Villa Park in 1982. Coach at Middlesbrough and Portsmouth and scout for Leicester, he returned to Villa Park for a third time in 1994 as Chief Scout, becoming second team manager in 1997.

JIMMY BLOOMFIELD was a skilful inside-forward, born in Kensington, London on 15 February 1934, who played for Walthamstow Avenue and Brentford before joining Arsenal, with whom he won two England Under-23 caps, represented the Football League and played for a London XI in the first Inter-Cities Fairs Cup Final in 1958. Signed by Blues for £20,000 in November 1960, he spent four seasons at St Andrew's, losing in another

Fairs Cup Final in 1961 but starring in the 1963 League Cup triumph when he scored in the two-legged Final against Aston Villa. In June 1964 – after netting 31 goals in 147 appearances – he returned to Brentford and later had spells with West Ham, Plymouth and Leyton Orient, the latter as player-manager, successfully guiding the O's to the Third Division Championship. Taking over as manager of Leicester City in 1971, he kept the Foxes in the First Division for six years and led them to the FA Cup semi-finals. Returning to Brisbane Road as manager in 1977, he took Orient to the FA Cup semi-finals the following year. Appointed coach at Luton Town soon afterwards, he was with the Hatters when he died from cancer on 3 April 1983 in Chingford, Essex.

HAROLD BODLE was born in Woodlands near Doncaster on 4 October 1920. An inside-forward for Doncaster schoolboys, he worked at and played for Silverwood Colliery, assisted Ridgehill Athletic and had trials for Doncaster Rovers and Bradford before joining Rotherham United in 1938. Transferred to Birmingham for £2,000 within six months, he played once before World War Two and made several appearances during the hostilities, helping Blues win the Football League (South) title, reach the FA Cup semi-finals in 1946 and gain promotion in 1948. After netting 36 goals in 110 outings for the club, Bodle moved to Bury in March 1949 for £9,500. Later player-manager, coach and trainer at Betteshanger Colliery Welfare in the Kent League, he returned to League action with Stockport County and Accrington Stanley, retiring in May 1957. He was then manager at Peel Park and also at Burton Albion, and he died in Bournemouth on 1 January 2005.

LEE BOWYER was born in Canning Town, London on 3 January 1977 and played in the same Sunday League team as Darren Purse. He began his career with Charlton Athletic, turning professional in April 1994. He scored 14 goals in 58 appearances for the Addicks before joining Leeds United for £2.6 million in July 1996 – a record fee for a British teenager. He became a key player at Elland Road, helping Leeds reach the semi-finals of the UEFA Cup in 2000 and twice being voted the club's player of the year. After netting 55 goals in 265 appearances, he left Leeds in January 2003 for West Ham in a £100,000 deal. He never settled at Upton Park and was subsequently transferred to Newcastle United on a free in July 2003. Two years later he was involved in an on-pitch brawl with teammate Kieron Dyer during the home game with Aston Villa. Red-carded, he was given a three-match ban; Dyer received the same punishment. Bowyer was also fined six weeks wages by the club for throwing the first punch. A year later, he was fined £600 and ordered to pay £1,000 in costs after using threatening behaviour towards Dyer. Bowyer made almost 100 appearances for the Geordies before returning to West Ham in June 2006. He joined Blues on loan in January 2009 and signed a two-year contract in July of the same year. Second top-scorer for Blues in 2009–10, he had seven goals to his name in 59 appearances when the 2010–11 season began. On the international front, Bowyer played for England at Youth team level and has one full cap to his name (v Portugal in 2002) and 13 at Under-21 level. Unfortunately his life outside football has had its problems. He failed a test for cannabis use in 1994 and was banned. Shortly after joining Leeds, he was convicted of affray following an alleged racist incident at McDonald's in London. In January 2000, he and his Leeds colleague Jonathan Woodgate were arrested and charged with causing grievous bodily harm with intent and affray, after an Asian student was seriously injured. After a second trial, which ended in December 2001, Bowyer was cleared of both charges. Woodgate was not. Then, in June 2005, after a brawl, he was charged by Northumbria Police with public order offences, under section four of the Public Order Act.

LEN BOYD skippered Birmingham City to the Second Division Championship in 1955 and then led them in the FA Cup Final against Manchester City the following season. Born in Plaistow, London on 11 November 1923, he attended the same West Ham School as another Blues player, Ken Green, before starting his career with Ilford. He served in Malta with the Royal Navy during the war before joining Plymouth Argyle, for whom he scored five goals in 80 senior appearances in four years. Transferred to St Andrew's for £17,500 in January 1949, he was the first player to leave the Devon club for a five-figure fee, and Blues certainly benefited from his experience. He joined Fred Harris and Ted Duckhouse in the half-back line and

quickly established himself as a regular member of the team. Taking over as captain, Boyd proved to be an inspirational leader and was outstanding when Blues regained their top-flight status in 1955, going up as champions. A year later he played in the FA Cup Final and also tasted European football for the first time. Capped by England B against Holland B in 1951–52, his only representative honour, Boyd was a fine player, a hard-working footballer who was successfully converted into a wing-half after starting out as a useful inside-forward while serving in the Royal Navy. He gave Blues great service, scoring 13 goals in 282 appearances, figuring prominently with two England internationals on the right flank – Jeff Hall and Gordon Astall. In the summer of 1956 Boyd announced his retirement due to a knee injury that had plagued him for six months. He was out of football for two and a half years before making a mini comeback with Hinckley Athletic (January 1959). He later worked as a coach and chief scout for Redditch United before becoming the first traffic warden in Melton Mowbray, where he lived for the rest of his life. He died in Melton Mowbray on 14 February 2008.

JOE BRADFORD holds several scoring records for Birmingham. A dynamic, all-action centre forward, who had trials with both Aston Villa and Derby County as a teenager, he served Blues from February 1920 (signed for just £125 from Green Victoria FC in Leicestershire) until May 1935, when he was transferred to Bristol City. Born in Peggs Green, Leicester on 22 January 1901, Bradford once netted 15 goals in a local Leicester Junior League game and was immediately offered a trial by Aston Villa and then Derby before Blues stepped in and secured his services a month after his 19th birthday. With Joe Lane, Johnny Crosbie and Harry Hampton firmly

by West Bromwich Albion. Capped 12 times by England, Bradford also represented the Football League on five occasions, and when he left St Andrew's for Bristol City in May 1935, after a stay of 15 years, his record was quite outstanding – 267 League and Cup goals in a total of 445 senior appearances. Joe eventually quit playing after one season at Ashton Gate, returning to the Midlands to run a café. He later became a licensee, first in Birmingham, then in Droitwich and finally in Stourbridge. After pulling pints for a living, Bradford went on to help the former Aston Villa star Eric Houghton run a sports shop in Sutton Coldfield. Appointed president of the local football team (Sutton Coldfield Town) Bradford did some scouting for Arsenal during season 1946–47 and also worked briefly in the pools office at St Andrew's. Blues' greatest-ever goalscorer was 79 when he died in Birmingham on 6 September 1980.

BARRY BRIDGES was a wartime baby, born in Horsfield near Norwich on 29 April 1941. He represented Norfolk Boys and England Schoolboys before joining Chelsea as a junior, turning professional in May 1958, the same year he gained an FA Youth Cup-winners' medal, followed by England Youth honours. The recipient of a League Cup-winners' tankard in 1965, he also played in four full internationals for his country and starred in a Football League XI. After 10 years at Stamford Bridge, during which time he scored 93 goals in 203 appearances, he moved to St Andrew's, signed for £55,000 in May 1966. In the next two seasons Bridges scored some stunning goals – perhaps his best being a wonderful over-kick that knocked Arsenal out of the FA Cup in 1968. Fast and direct, Bridges netted 46 times in 104 appearances for Blues and played in both the 1967 League Cup and 1968 FA Cup semi-finals. He moved to Queen's Park

installed in the three central forward positions at St Andrew's, Bradford bided his time in the reserves and was given only four outings when Blues won the Second Division Championship in 1920–21. However, the following term he made a huge impact, scoring 10 goals in 17 League appearances. He never looked back, got better and better, and over the next 11 seasons (1922–33 inclusive) he simply terrorised opposing goalkeepers (and defenders) by scoring totals of 19, 24, 11, 27, 23, 32, 24, 23, 22, 28 and 14 goals respectively. He bagged a club record 29 in the League alone in 1929–30 and he had the pleasure of scoring Blues' first-ever goal at Wembley, in their 1931 FA Cup Final defeat

Rangers in August 1968, switched to Millwall in 1970 and later assisted Brighton & Hove Albion and Highlands Park (South Africa), was player-manager of St Patrick's Athletic (Ireland) and also bossed Sligo Rovers, Dereham Town, Kings Lynn and Horsfield FC. After leaving football he went into the hotel business in Brighton before taking over a milk round in Hove.

GEORGE BRIGGS played in the 1931 FA Cup Final – one of 324 appearances he made for Blues (107 goals scored). A well-built right-winger, fast and clever, he was born in Wombwell, Yorkshire, on 23 May 1903 and starred for Denaby United before moving to St Andrew's in December 1923 for £400. He spent 10 years with Blues, leaving in 1933 for Plymouth Argyle and later assisting St Austell before retiring in 1937. He later worked and lived in Moseley, Birmingham, where he died in around 1980.

EDDIE BROWN wanted to join the church but was persuaded not to by a football-mad clergyman. He certainly made the right

decision, becoming a very useful centre forward, whose playing career spanned 16 years. Born in Preston on 28 February 1926, Brown started out with Preston North End in 1948 and, after spending a few years with both Southampton and Coventry City, he joined Birmingham City in October 1954. An instant success at St Andrew's, he averaged a goal every two games for Blues, and his haul of 14 in 1954–55 helped his side win the Second Division Championship. The following season he was again in tip-top form, netting another 28 goals, seven of them in the FA Cup as Blues reached the Final, only to lose to Manchester City. Quite often after scoring a goal, spectacular or not, Brown would peel away and perform a celebratory jig round one of the corner flags…he was a great character on and off the pitch. He netted a hat-trick when Blues thrashed Liverpool 9–1 at St Andrew's in 1954. Brown packed a fierce right-foot shot and was also good in the air, but his main asset was his anticipation – and on several occasions he would dart into the penalty area to knock home a loose ball or

glide in a low cross. After scoring 90 goals in 185 appearances for Blues, he left St Andrew's in January 1959 for Leyton Orient. Later with Scarborough and Stourbridge, Bedworth Town (as player-manager) and Wigan Athletic, he retired in December 1964. Brown subsequently became a sports master at a Preston Catholic school, and one of his great achievements was to 'discover' future Liverpool defender Mark Lawrenson.

STEVE BRUCE was born in Corbridge, Northumberland on 31 December 1960 and at one point was on the verge of quitting the game after being rejected by a number of top clubs. However, he was offered an apprenticeship at Gillingham in 1986 and never looked back, becoming a truly wonderful, consistent centre-back. He made 230 appearances for the Gills before joining Norwich City in August 1984 for £125,000. In December 1987, after gaining League Cup and Second Division Championship-winning medals and playing in another 180 matches, he switched to Manchester United

for £800,000. At Old Trafford, Bruce achieved great success, winning the Premier League three times, the FA Cup twice, the League Cup, the European Cup-winners' Cup, the European Super Cup and the FA Charity Shield on two occasions, as well as collecting several runners'-up prizes. He also became the first English player of the 20th century to captain a team to the coveted League and FA Cup double, doing so in 1994; however, despite his success on the field, he was never selected to play for the England at senior level, although he did gain Youth and 'B' team honours and represented the Football League. In June 1986, after making 425 appearances for United, Bruce left the Reds to join Blues. He did well at St Andrew's, scoring twice in 82 outings before leaving in July 1988 to take over as player-manager at Sheffield United. After short spells in charge of Huddersfield Town, Wigan Athletic and Crystal Palace, he returned to St Andrew's as manager in December 2001. He twice led Blues into the Premier League during his tenure of nearly six years, but resigned in November 2007 to begin a second spell in charge of Wigan. He did an excellent job at the JJB Stadium, on limited resources, before 'transferring' to Sunderland, replacing another ex-Blues player, Ricky Sbragia, as manager in June 2009. He was accompanied by his dedicated backroom staff of Eric Black (assistant-manager), coaches Mark Bowen, Nigel Spink and Keith Bertschin, while naming Sbragia as the club's chief scout. Several commentators and newspaper reporters, and quite a few players, have described Bruce as one of the best English players of the 1980s and 1990s never to play for his country at full international level. (See also managers).

KENNY BURNS could play anywhere and often did! Physically strong, he feared no one, was powerful in the air, tackled with purpose

and aggression and could shoot with both feet. Once a dominant centre-half, then a striker, he also played in midfield, as inside-forward, as emergency full-back and occasionally as a winger…and after leaving St Andrew's he reverted to a defensive role with Nottingham Forest. Born in Glasgow on 23 September 1953, Burns was on schoolboy forms with Rangers before joining Blues as apprentice in June 1970, turning professional the following year (July 1971). Remaining at St Andrew's until July 1977, he amassed a fine record with Blues, scoring a goal every four games. After a slow start to his League career, he helped Blues gain promotion to the top flight in 1972 and after a few years defending he was pushed forward following Bob Latchford's move to Everton in February 1974. And what a fine job he did as leader of the attack! Having had to deal with robust strikers in his early days, Burns had no trouble whatsoever in matching the physical strength of the array of defenders who opposed him in his new role and he quickly settled down alongside Trevor Francis and Bob Hatton in the Blues' attack, scoring a hat-trick in a 3–3 draw at Leicester in early April. He gained the first of his 20

full caps for Scotland soon after that, lining up as Denis Law's strike-partner in a 2–1 defeat by West Germany. His other 19 international appearances followed between October 1974 and May 1981. He played in the 1978 World Cup Finals in Argentina and also represented his country in two Under-23 matches. Second top-scorer for Blues behind Francis in his last season at St Andrew's, Kenny's haul included another hat-trick against Leicester in a 6-2 win at Filbert Street in December 1976 and a four-timer in a 5–1 win over Derby two months earlier. Burns, who failed to win any major prizes with Blues, other than promotion, scored 53 goals in 204 appearances before moving to Nottingham Forest for £150,000 in July 1977. At the City Ground he reverted to a defensive position and helped Brian Clough's team twice win the European Cup and the First Division Championship and League Cup double and in 1978 was voted PFA Footballer of the Year. In October 1981 – after almost 200 appearances for Forest – Burns moved to Leeds United for £400,000. Never the same player at Elland Road, in March 1984, after two loan spells with Derby County, he signed for the Rams on a permanent basis. Then, after assisting Notts County, Burns played his 424th and final League game for Barnsley against Crystal Palace in April 1986. He then went to Sweden and was assistant manager at Telford United from July 1993 to May 1994. Later a publican in Ilkeston and Stoke-on-Trent, in 2008 he was engaged by Nottingham Forest in the club's Corporate Department.

IAN CLARKSON made 172 appearances for Birmingham City, whom he served for nine years from 1987–96. Born in Solihull on 4 December 1970, he played mainly as a full-back and helped Blues win the Leyland DAF Trophy in 1991. On leaving St Andrew's, he joined Stoke City and later served with Northampton Town and Kidderminster Harriers where he became captain, helping the Aggborough club gain promotion to the Football League as Conference champions in his first season. When Jan Molby resigned as manager of Kidderminster in March 2002, Clarkson acted as assistant to caretaker boss Ian Britton but was released three months later for financial reasons. At that point Ian joined Nuneaton Borough and later had spells with Stafford Rangers, Leamington and Forest Green Rovers, before finally retiring. A qualified coach and coach educator, Clarkson has since worked for Birmingham City's Football in the Community programme and during the later years was employed as a football reporter and journalist by the *Birmingham Post* and *Sunday Mercury* newspapers and worked on the PFA website. In 2006 he became manager of a scheme designed to involve young people in sport and physical activity, as part of a wider programme of regeneration of the deprived areas of North Solihull.

JOHNNY CROSBIE was an expert at creating openings for his colleagues and contributed greatly to the impressive goal-tally of Birmingham's star striker Joe Bradford. A genuine craftsman who could use both feet, he was always involved in the action and, even if the game was rather dull, he seemed to sparkle. He simply loved his football and he gave Blues tremendous service for over 12 years. Born in the Gorbals district of Glasgow on 3 June 1896, he played for Glenbuck Cherrypickers, Muirbank Athletic and Saltcoats before joining Ayr United in August 1913. Active throughout World War One, he represented Scotland in a Victory international against England in 1919. He duly earned his first full cap versus Wales and soon afterwards signed Blues for a then record fee of £3,700 in May 1920. 'Too

much, far too much' claimed one director, but Crosbie turned out to be real bargain, rated as one of Blues' finest investments. In his first season at St Andrew's, Crosbie was an ever-present, producing some quality performances while scoring 14 goals as Blues won the Second Division Championship on goal-average from Cardiff. The following season he was joint top-scorer with Bradford and he also collected his second cap, starring in a 1–0 victory over England at Villa Park. Known as 'Peerless', he was the architect in centre-field when Blues reached the 1931 FA Cup Final in which they lost 2–1 to West Bromwich Albion. Crosbie's pen-picture in the programme for that Cup Final read: 'The master mind of the Birmingham attack…for Crosbie is a real star…Without Crosbie the Birmingham team would be sadly handicapped – it is fortunate for this unlucky club that Crosbie has escaped serious injury.' In the summer of 1932, having scored 72 goals in 432 appearances, Johnny left St Andrew's for Chesterfield but stayed at Saltergate barely four months before returning to the Midlands to become player-manager of Stourbridge. In February 1933 he took a coaching position in Gothenburg, Sweden and in 1934–35 ran a works team in Kidderminster. Crosbie, who was a button-maker by trade, died on 15 February 1992.

ERNIE CURTIS played on the left wing for Blues in the 1931 FA Cup Final against West Bromwich Albion. A confident footballer, he served with Cardiff Corinthians and Cardiff City, with whom he won the FA Cup in 1927, before joining Blues in 1928. He remained at St Andrew's for five and a half years, during which time he scored 53 goals in 180 appearances. Capped three times by Wales, he returned to Ninian Park in November 1933 and, after assisting Coventry City and Hartlepool United, he retired as a player to become Cardiff's assistant coach. Born in the Welsh capital on 10 June 1907, Curtis was 85 when he died in Cardiff on 15 November 1992.

DON DEARSON was born in Ynysybwl, South Wales on 13 May 1914. A rugged performer who preferred a wing-half role, he played for Llantwit Major Juniors and Barry Town before joining Blues in 1934. He remained at St Andrew's until 1947 and in the intervening years appeared in 136 League and Cup games plus 166 wartime fixtures, scoring a total of 44 goals. He also won 15 wartime and three full caps for Wales and helped Blues win the Football League (South) title in 1946. A guest with Northampton Town, Nottingham Forest, Wrexham and West Bromwich Albion during the hostilities, he also served in the Birmingham City Police Force. Don moved to Coventry City from St Andrew's and later played for Walsall (1949–51), Nuneaton Borough and Bilston United. He was 76 when he died in Sheldon, Birmingham on 24 December 1990.

WILL DEVEY was a terrific centre-forward, as keen as mustard, skilful, strong and blessed with a powerful right-foot shot. Born in Perry Barr on 12 April 1865, he played for Clarendon Montrose, Wellington Road FC, Aston Unity and Mitchell St George's before joining Blues in August 1885. A prolific scorer, he bagged 33 in 40 Football Alliance matches before moving to Wolves in August 1891. A year later he switched to Aston Villa, played next for Walsall Town Swifts in 1894–95, had spells with Burton Wanderers, Notts County, Walsall, Burton Wanderers (again) and Walsall Darlaston before returning to Blues in March 1899, retiring two years later having netted a total of 49 goals in 51 first-class matches for the club. Devey was 83 when he died in Handsworth, Birmingham on 24 October 1948.

NEIL DOUGALL was a valuable member of Birmingham City's League (South) and 1948 Second Division Championship-winning sides. A Scotsman from Falkirk,

born on 7 November 1921, he played for Burnley before joining Blues in 1945. A Scottish international, gaining one full and one Victory cap, Dougall was a classy inside-right who scored 18 goals in 108 appearances for Blues before moving to Plymouth Argyle in 1949. He spent 20 years at Home Park, as a player, assistant trainer, head trainer and caretaker manager. He helped the Pilgrims win the Third Division (South) and Third Division titles in 1952 and 1959 respectively. After retiring from football he ran a fitness club in Plymouth from which he retired in 1986. Dougall, who for many years suffered from Alzheimer's disease, died in Plymouth in December 2009, aged 88.

GEORGE EDWARDS was a wonderful outside-left who scored nine goals in 97 first-class appearances and 13 in 38 wartime fixtures during his four and a half years at St Andrew's from July 1944 to December 1948. He helped Blues win the League (South) title in 1946 and the Second Division Championship two years later.

Capped by Wales at both amateur and senior levels, he was born in Kilgetty, South Wales on 2 December 1920 and played for Swansea Town and Coventry City before joining Blues. On leaving St Andrew's he signed for Cardiff City for £12,000 and went on to win a Welsh Cup-winners' medal in 1951 before retiring in 1955. Edwards later became a director at Ninian Park, a position he held until 1977. He gained an MA degree at Birmingham University, his thesis being 'A History of the Pembroke Coalfields.' Edwards died on 22 October 2008, aged 87.

TREVOR FRANCIS became Britain's first £1 million footballer when Birmingham City sold him to Nottingham Forest for £975,000 plus VAT and levy charges in February 1979. And immediately the Forest manager Brian Clough said: 'He'll be worth double that amount – you see!' With electrifying pace, intricate ball skills, a powerful right-foot shot and amazing self-confidence, Francis was certainly a top-quality footballer. Born in Plymouth on 19 April 1954, he joined Blues straight from his school in July 1969 and turned professional in April 1971 – having already made his mark in League football. Indeed, he scored 15 goals in his first 16 League games, between September 1970 and March 1971, including a four-timer in a Second Division encounter with Bolton Wanderers two months before his 17th birthday. He starred in the club's promotion-winning campaign of 1971–72, netting 12 goals in 39 games, and continued to produce the goods in the First Division, although his goal-return was not half as good as it had been in previous seasons. In 1977–78 Francis recorded his best seasonal goal haul for Blues with 29, but by now it was inevitable he would soon be leaving St Andrew's. He eventually departed for the City Ground after scoring 133 goals in 330 first-class

matches for Blues. The fans were obviously bitterly disappointed to lose such a superstar player who had brought a breath of fresh air to the club. No sooner had he arrived at the City Ground, than Francis netted the winning goal for Forest in the 1979 European Cup Final win over FF Malmo, and a year later he gained a Super Cup-winners' medal and a League Cup runners'-up prize but missed out on a second European Cup prize through injury. After that Francis had a spell in the NASL with Detroit, assisted Manchester City, spent five seasons in Italy with Sampdoria

and Atalanta, gaining a Cup-winners' medal with the former in 1985, and added a Scottish League Cup-winners' medal to his collection in 1988 with Glasgow Rangers. After assisting Queen's Park Rangers, he then joined Sheffield Wednesday, whom he helped gain promotion from the Second Division while collecting a League Cup-winners' medal as a non-playing sub. A year later, as player-manager at Hillsborough, Francis received runners'-up medals in both the League Cup and FA Cup before returning to St Andrew's as manager in May 1996. During his five-year tenure, he guided

Blues to the First Division Play-offs three seasons running, losing each time, and he was also bitterly disappointed when Liverpool won the 2001 League Cup Final on penalties at the Millennium Stadium. Francis later had a spell in charge of Crystal Palace (2001–02) before becoming a TV soccer pundit. The recipient of five Under-23 and 52 full caps for England (the latter gained between February 1977 and April 1986), Francis scored 225 goals in 752 senior appearances during a wonderful playing career.

JOE GALLAGHER was a competent centre-half who scored 23 goals in 335 games for Birmingham City between 1970 and 1981, also gaining an England B cap v Australia (1980). Born in Liverpool on 11 January 1955, he was a big favourite with the St Andrew's crowd, and after leaving Blues for Wolves in a £350,000 deal Gallagher made just 34 appearances and netted one goal during an uneasy time at Molineux. Later with West Ham United, Burnley, Halifax Town (loan) and Padiham

(loan), he was in charge of non-League side Coleshill Town for five seasons, returned to Birmingham as Community Liaison Officer (1990) and spent his final years in the game as player-manager of Atherstone United and Kings Heath (1995–96). Later employed by Land Rover and a part-time reporter for the Press Association, Gallagher was also involved in corporate hospitality at Blues' home matches.

JACK GLOVER was a solid full-back, a shade on the small side, who after being released by Albion, joined Blackburn Rovers as a professional in 1897. Born in West Bromwich on 28 October 1876, Glover played for Great Bridge Unity, Halesowen and Rudge Whitworth FC before having a spell with the Baggies, for whom he played in a handful of second XI games. From Ewood Park he switched to New Brompton (now Gillingham) and in 1900 was signed for £100 by Liverpool. He spent three and a half years with the Merseysiders, up to January 1904 when he returned to the Midlands with Birmingham. He scored twice in 124 appearances for Blues,

eventually winding down his career with Brierley Hill Alliance before retiring in 1910. He gained a League Championship-winners' medal with Liverpool in 1901, represented the Football League and had a trial with England. Glover died in Dudley on 20 April 1955.

ALEX GOVAN was a terrific winger, industrious, fast and tricky, who regularly pushed the ball past his opponent and beat him for pace before getting in a dangerous cross. Not all that tall, he was nevertheless strong and willing and was never completely mastered by an opposing full-back. Govan, who was born in Glasgow on 16 June 1929 and played for the local Bridgton Boys Club as a youngster, joined Plymouth Argyle in 1944. He teamed up with two future Blues players, Len Boyd and Gordon Astall, at Home Park and helped the Pilgrims win the Third Division (South) title before moving to St Andrew's for £6,500 in June 1953. He averaged a goal every three games for Blues, netting 60 times in 186 appearances, gaining a Second Division Championship-winners' medal in 1955 and an FA Cup runners'-up medal a year later. Govan missed only five League games (all through injury) in 1954–55 and was brilliant in resounding home victories over Port Vale (7–2), Liverpool (9–1) and Ipswich (4–0). Two years later, in 1956–57, he set a new club record for a winger by netting 30 goals in all competitions. His tally included five hat-tricks – four in the League against Portsmouth, Newcastle United, Preston North End and Leeds United, and one in the FA Cup at Southend United. He actually claimed three trebles in four games in the space of 10 days. After playing in 17 of the first 20 games of 1957–58, Govan started to slow down and, after Astall had switched to the left to accommodate Harry Hooper, he dropped to the reserves. Sold to Portsmouth in

March 1958, after scoring 60 goals in 187 appearances for Blues, Govan returned to Plymouth at the end of that season and upped his Argyle record to 38 goals in 150 games before retiring in May 1960. He now resides at Hartley Vale near Plymouth and still follows Blues on TV.

KEN GREEN was one of the most durable defenders in League football between 1948 and 1958. A canny full-back, he formed excellent partnerships with Dennis Jennings, Jack Badham and Jeff Hall and shared in most of Blues' successes during the immediate post-war period and played in the 1956 FA Cup Final against Manchester City. Green, who was known affectionately as 'Slasher', was born in West Ham, London on 27 April 1924. Registered as an amateur with Millwall, he was serving in the Army when he wrote to the Blues secretary asking for a trial. He subsequently received a favourable reply in the post, kept his appointment, played well in a trial match and was immediately offered a contract in, of all places, the dressing room at Villa Park, signing as a professional in

November 1943. After serving in the forces, Green confidently bedded himself in at St Andrew's. He worked hard at his game and, after some fine displays in the reserves, made his League debut against Brentford in September 1947. He took to competitive League football like a duck to water and he happily collected a Second Division Championship-winners' medal at the end of the season. Green was a regular at right-back for five years before switching to the opposite flank to accommodate the fast-improving Jeff Hall. Thereafter, he was an inspirational defender, producing some terrific displays and captaining the side on several occasions. A stern tackler, he was never erratic in his challenges and always tried to jockey his opponent into a false sense of security by shepherding him close to the touchline. And it must be said that very few wingers got the better of Green. Adding a Second Division-winners' medal to his collection in 1955, Green had earlier gained two England B caps against Yugoslavia and Switzerland in 1953–54 as well as representing the Football League on two occasions in the early 1950s. After

appearing in 449 games for Blues (three goals scored) he finally called it a day by retiring in the summer of 1959. Green remained in Birmingham and later took over a post office in Handsworth, Birmingham. He died in Sutton Coldfield on 12 June 2001.

BOB GREGG believes he had a 'goal' wrongly disallowed for offside in the 1931 FA Cup Final defeat by West Bromwich Albion. That apart, he scored 15 times in 75 appearances for Birmingham between January 1931 and September 1933 when he was sold to Chelsea for £1,500. Born in Ferryhill, County Durham, on 19 February 1904, he played initially for Spennymoor United, then Charlton Colliery, Durham City, Ferryhill Athletic, Darlington and Sheffield Wednesday, with whom he gained a First Division Championship-winners' medal, before joining Blues for £2,200. He spent five years at Stamford Bridge and after a spell with Boston United played briefly for Sligo Rovers before retiring in May 1944. Gregg died in Durham in 1991.

JEFF HALL, despite being on the small side, was a wonderfully consistent right-back, highly efficient and strong with a first-rate temperament. His positional sense was superb, his tackling precise and very few wingers got the better of him. An England international who played in 17 consecutive internationals for his country over a period of two years (October 1955–October 1957), Hall was also a very perky sort of player, strong and enthusiastic and a fighter to the last. Born in Scunthorpe on 7 September 1929, he played for several local junior teams including St Anne's, Wilsden and Top Bank FC before signing amateur forms with Bradford Park Avenue in August 1949. After completing his national service he joined Blues as a professional in May 1950 and eventually took over the number-two shirt

JACK HALLAM was born in Oswestry on 20 February 1869. An outside-right, he was capped at full international level for Wales and scored 63 goals in 155 games for Birmingham (Small Heath) in the Football Alliance, Football League and FA Cup, and he also represented Swindon Town. Hallam started his career playing for clubs in his native town and it was as an Oswestry Town player that he won international honours, lining up against England in February 1889. The following year he moved to Small Heath of the Football Alliance. The strength of Hallam's game lay in his speed and in his first season in League football he helped Blues win the Second Division Championship before gaining promotion a year later. He switched to Swindon in August 1896 and after retiring worked for the Great Western Railway in Swindon, where he died on 7 March 1949.

halfway through the 1952–53 season when Ken Green moved across to the left. Hall retained his position competently thereafter, injuries and international duties apart, until he was tragically struck down with polio shortly after making his 265th and final appearance for Blues at Portsmouth in March 1959. He was only 29 years of age when he died a fortnight later (4 April). A member of Blues' Second Division Championship-winning side of 1954–55 and FA Cup Final team a year later, he also won a B cap and represented Young England (v England) in 1958, played for the Football League on four occasions and appeared twice for the FA when touring the West Indies in the summer of 1955. Hall's only goal for Blues came in the League game at Stoke in September 1953 when he was pushed forward by manager Arthur Turner into the outside-right position after Jackie Stewart had pulled out with an injury. Sadly, it was to no avail, as the Potters won 3–2.

FRED HARRIS was born in Solihull on 2 July 1912. He joined Birmingham as an inside-forward in 1933 and was the club's leading scorer in season 1938–39 with 14 League goals and 17 in all competitions. During World War Two he converted to

play as a wing-half and played out the rest of his career in that position. His strong tackling and constructive use of the ball impressed manager Harry Storer sufficiently to make him club captain. Harris helped Blues win the Football League (South) title in 1946 and the Second Division title two years later. The following season he gained representative honours for the Football League XI against the Scottish League. He retired from football in 1950, having made 312 appearances for Blues (68 goals scored) plus another 92 during World War Two. Continuing his practice as a chiropodist and physiotherapist in Acocks Green, he died in Birmingham on 11 October 1998.

BOB HATTON was born in Hull in April 1947. A splendid, much-travelled striker, he appeared in over 600 League matches for a variety of clubs and scored at a rate better than one goal in every three matches. Wolves recognised his potential early and gave him a trial before signing him as a professional in November 1964. He moved to Bolton Wanderers in 1967, switched to Northampton Town 12 months later, went north to Carlisle United in 1969 and eventually joined Blues in October 1971,

signed for £80,000, a year after helping the Cumbrian club reach the semi-finals of the League Cup. Hatton went on to shine brightly for Blues, sharing in and contributing to their success for nearly five full years, during which he was often linked with a possible international call-up before moving to Blackpool in 1976 for £60,000. At St Andrew's he struck up a superb understanding with Trevor Francis and Bob Latchford and went on to score 73 goals in 218 appearances, helping Blues reach the FA Cup semi-final in 1975. After his exploits at Bloomfield Road, Hatton moved to Luton Town in the summer of 1978, where he spent two years. There followed a further two seasons with Sheffield United before he rounded off his eventful career with a spell at Cardiff City, announcing his retirement as a player in 1983. Since then he has worked closely with the PFA in the Midlands.

TERRY HENNESSEY was born in Llay, Wrexham on 1 September 1942 and represented Wrexham & District Boys, was capped by Wales as a schoolboy inside-forward before joining Birmingham City as a junior in June 1958, turning professional in September 1959. Transformed into an attacking wing-half, he was rated by many as one of the best in that position in the game during the 1960s, producing some superb performances, especially for Blues, whom he skippered on several occasions. Instrumental when Blues reached the Final of the Inter-Cities Fairs Cup in 1961 and likewise when Aston Villa were defeated in the Final of the League Cup two years later, he was strong, athletic and a fine passer of the ball. Controversially in some people's minds, as time passed by, he was switched to a defensive position where, for most of the time, he performed as a sweeper – yet still produced great performances. He appeared in 202 games for Blues (three

of Tulsa Roughnecks before returning to England in 1978 as coach to Shepshed Charterhouse, holding office for two years. Following a second spell with the Roughnecks, initially as a coach in 1980, then as chief coach/manager (he won the NASL in 1983), his next appointment took him to Vancouver Whitecaps as assistant-manager/coach to former Wolves, Forest and Derby winger Alan Hinton. After that Hennessey coached in Toronto before spending the 1987–88 season as boss of the Australian club Heidelberg in Victoria. He still resides in Australia today.

JIM HERRIOT was born in Chapelhall near Airdrie on 20 December 1939 and played for Douglasdale Juniors before gaining a Scottish Cup runners'-up medal with Dunfermline Athletic in April 1965. The following month he joined Blues and became a big favourite at St Andrew's.

Known as the 'Clown Prince', he often daubed boot polish, American-football style, under his eyes to divert the glare of the floodlights during evening matches and often smeared dirt on his face to divert the glare of the sun…even if the sun wasn't shining!

goals scored) before transferring to Nottingham Forest for £45,000 in November 1965. Looking older than he really was due to his receding hairline, Hennessey became the driving force in the Forest midfield and captained the side which reached the FA Cup semi-final in 1967. After adding 183 appearances to his career tally and undergoing an operation for appendicitis, he surprisingly joined East Midlands rivals Derby County for £110,000. In 1972, under Brian Clough's managership, Hennessey gained both League Championship and Texaco Cup-winners' medals with the Rams, and before leaving the Baseball Ground he took his tally of full international caps with Wales up to 39 – having gained his first as a Blues player against Northern Ireland in April 1962. Earlier he had represented his country in six Under-23 internationals, all as a Blues player. In April 1974, after two cartilage operations, Hennessey became manager of Tamworth. Three years later he took charge of Kimberley Town and then had a spell in the NASL as assistant-coach

Infuriating at times, brilliant one minute, scary the next, Herriot could produce a stunning save and then let in a silly goal or drop the ball from a high, looping centre which invariably resulted in a scramble inside his area. Some fans and even his teammates, nicknamed him 'Dracula', simply because he hated crosses, but that apart, Herriot was a fine 'keeper who went on to appear in 212 matches for Blues after replacing Johnny Schofield for the 1965–66 season. Herriot played in both the 1967 League Cup and 1968 FA Cup semi-finals for Blues and was an ever-present in 1966–67 and in fact, missed only two League games out of a possible 148 between November 1965 and April 1969. Following loan spells with Aston Villa, Mansfield Town and Durban City, he left St Andrew's in August 1971 for Hibernian, with whom he gained Scottish League Cup and Dryburgh Cup-winners' medals. In February 1975, Herriot switched to Partick Thistle and, after a loan spell with Morton, returned to Dunfermline in 1976, ending his career back at Morton a year later. Capped eight times by Scotland, Herriot also played for his country's 'B' and Under-23 teams and twice represented the Scottish League as a Dunfermline player. Today he enjoys everlasting fame following the adoption of his surname by the famous veterinarian author and Blues supporter Alf Wright, whose pseudonym was, of course, James Herriot. Goalkeeper Herriot worked as a bricklayer in Larkhall until he was 65.

HARRY HIBBS was born in Wilnecote, Tamworth on 27 May 1906 and while training as a plumber, played for his local club sides Wilnecote Holy Trinity and Tamworth Castle, who had two horrendous seasons in the Birmingham & District Football League, conceding no fewer than 164 goals. Despite this, Hibbs managed to produce some outstanding performances,

his displays being noted by eagle-eyed scouts from St Andrew's. At the age of 17, Hibbs was offered a trial by Blues. He did well and was rewarded with a professional contract in May 1924. A regular feature of manager Billy Beer's side during a barren period in the club's history, things changed dramatically when new boss Leslie Knighton arrived in 1928, and a vast improvement took place in the fortunes of both Hibbs and the team. Selected for the FA tour to South Africa, Harry appeared in three Test Matches, his form earning him a full England cap against Wales at Stamford Bridge in 1929. Prior to Hibbs's international debut, the England selectors had tried 21 different goalkeepers in the nine years since Sam Hardy's retirement in 1920. Harry was almost a 'carbon copy' of Hardy. Unspectacular but extremely reliable, he preferred to do everything as simply as possible, a style that was to see him go on and win 25 caps for his country, keeping 10 clean sheets in the process. Blues reached the FA Cup Final in 1931 only to lose 2–1 to West Bromwich Albion, whose goalkeeper was none other than Hibbs's cousin, Harold Pearson. After making 389 first-class appearances for Blues, Harry's career at St Andrew's ended in May 1940, soon after he had played in his own testimonial match against Aston Villa. In August 1944, Harry was appointed manager-coach of Walsall where he remained for seven years. The highlight of this period was the club's appearance in the 1946 Third Division (South) Final against Bournemouth in front of 20,000 fans at Stamford Bridge. After that Hibbs, by now well into his thirties, kept goal for Havillands FC between February 1953 and the following summer before spending some time out of the game, only to return to manage Ware Town and then Welwyn Garden City, where he settled. He died there on 23 April 1984.

BILLY HUGHES was born in Llanelli on 6 March 1918. A splendid left-back, he made 169 appearances in the First Division for Birmingham City and Chelsea and, as an international, won 10 full and 14 wartime/Victory caps for Wales and also played for Great Britain against the Rest of Europe in 1947. He joined Blues from Llanelli in 1934 and made his first-team debut at the age of 17; by the time he was 19 he was a regular first choice. He developed into a ball-winning defender who used the ball constructively. During World War Two when he served in the RAF, he made 49 regional appearances for Blues and played as a guest for Blackpool, Swansea Town, Fulham and Chester. In all Hughes had 110 outings for Blues before joining Luton Town in July 1947. Eight months later he was sold to Chelsea for £12,000 and went on to assist Hereford United and Flint Town United, with whom he won his only major club honour, the

Welsh Cup, in 1954. A decade earlier, in 1944, he toured France and Belgium with an FA Combined Services XI and also played for a Royal Air Force XI in a 7–1 defeat against Scotland at Hillsborough. His teammates that day included Stanley Matthews, Stan Mortensen, Raich Carter and Frank Soo. After retiring in May 1955, Hughes scouted for Chester. He died in Birmingham on 16 June 1981.

CAESAR JENKYNS was born in Builth Wells on 24 August 1866. A strong, versatile player, he was registered with several clubs and gained eight caps for Wales. Caesar joined Small Heath (Birmingham) initially in August 1884, but left to play for the local Unity Gas team, only to return to Blues in July 1888. He played in both the Football Alliance and Football League Second Division, skippering Blues to promotion to the top flight in 1894. He went on to score 21 goals in 153 appearances for the club (in the Football League, FA Cup, Football Alliance and Test Matches) before being

released in April 1895 following an ugly incident at Derby the previous month whereby, after being sent off, he attempted to assault two spectators. Jenkyns next played for Woolwich Arsenal and after becoming the first Gunner to win a full cap, he left the Londoners for Newton Heath (now Manchester United) in May 1896. He later served with Walsall, Coventry City (as player-coach) and Saltley Wednesday as a guest before retiring in May 1905 to take over the George Inn pub at Moxley near Wednesbury. Before World War One, Jenkyns joined the Birmingham City Police Force, serving as a constable for over 20 years. He was almost 75 when he died in Birmingham on 23 July 1941.

DENNIS JENNINGS was born at Habberley Valley, Kidderminster on 20 July 1910 and played over 300 games in the top two Divisions of the Football League during his 21-year career. The oldest player ever to appear for Birmingham City in a competitive first-team match – he was 39 years, nine months and 17 days old when he lined up against Wolves in a First

Division game in May 1950 – Jennings was an amateur with West Bromwich Albion and also assisted Kidderminster Harriers before turning professional with Huddersfield Town in October 1930. He moved to Grimsby Town in 1932 and helped the Mariners to win the Second Division title two years later. In January 1936 Blues paid £1,200 for his services and over the next 15 years he gave the St Andrew's faithful plenty to cheer about. He scored 14 goals in 214 senior appearances and netted another three in 164 wartime matches when he occupied every outfield position apart from centre-half, contributing greatly to Blues winning the Championship of the Football League (South) in 1945–46. He also played as a guest for Nottingham Forest during the hostilities. After the war was over, Jennings spent five seasons playing as an attack-minded full-back, mostly on the left side. He helped Blues clinch the Second Division title and with it promotion in 1947–48 before making his final first team appearance at Molineux in 1950. At that

point Jennings returned to his former club, Kidderminster, as player-coach, before finishing his career with Lockheed Leamington. After retiring from football he moved south to Wadebridge in Cornwall where he and his brother ran a caravan park at Little Dinham. Dennis died in Cornwall on 16 March 1996, aged 85.

DAMIEN JOHNSON was born on 18 November 1978 in Lisburn, Northern Ireland. A hard-working midfielder, his first club was Portadown, from where he switched to Blackburn Rovers, turning professional in February 1996. Loaned to Nottingham Forest in January 1998, he made 83 appearances for the Ewood Park club before transferring to Birmingham City in March 2002. Soon after taking over the Blues' captaincy in 2006–07 he angered several fans when he first threw his skipper's armband and then his shirt on the floor after being substituted late on. Thankfully, that incident soon passed by and in October 2006 he had his jaw broken in two places following a challenge by West

Bromwich Albion's left-back Paul Robinson. Despite his injury, however, Johnson played on until the final whistle. The second most-capped player (with 42) behind goalkeeper Maik Taylor ever to play for Blues, he made the first of his 56 full international appearances for his country as a Blackburn player against the Republic of Ireland in May 1999 and reached the 50 mark 10 years later. Hugely popular with the 'Green and White Army' of Irish fans, not least for his 100 per cent effort and commitment, Johnson has also 11 Under-21 caps in his locker, having won four as a Youth team player. He scored four goals in 214 senior appearances for Blues before his transfer to relegation-threatened Plymouth Argyle in February 2010. He helped Blackburn reach the League Cup Final in 2002 and Blues clinch promotion to the Premier League in 2009.

MICHAEL JOHNSON was born in Nottingham in July 1973. A defender, he played for Clifton All Whites and represented Nottinghamshire Schoolboys before joining Notts County in 1989 and turning professional two years later. In September 1995 he was transferred to Birmingham City for £225,000 and went on to appear in 314 competitive games for Blues, scoring 18 goals. He played in the 2001 Football League Cup Final defeat by Liverpool and also in the Premier League before joining Derby County in August 2003. Nicknamed 'Magic' (after the famous American basketball player Earvin 'Magic' Johnson) he was a decidedly quick, clever centre-back with a terrific leap, which made him a force to be reckoned with at set pieces. He had a wholehearted approach to the game, was dedicated and gave nothing less than 100 per cent out on the pitch, After eight years service with Blues, Johnson was sold to Derby County in August 2003 and four years later he moved to Sheffield

Wednesday before returning to his former club, Notts County, in February 2008, initially on loan, prior to signing a one-year contract. On retiring in May 2009 he was appointed caretaker manager at Meadow Lane and later became youth-team coach. Johnson won 12 caps for Jamaica.

BILLY JONES – known as the 'Tipton Slasher' and 'Bullet' – was born in Tipton on 12 April 1880. A robust centre-forward, he had two spells with Birmingham, the first from August 1901 to June 1909 and the second from April 1912 to November 1913. He scored 102 goals in 253 appearances for Blues in all competitions, and was their leading scorer for four successive seasons from 1903–07 and again on his return to the club in 1912–13. In between times he twice served with Brighton & Hove Albion, first as a player, 1909–12 and 1913–15, and after the war he spent 19 years as assistant trainer with the Hove club, 1920–39. He helped Blues gain promotion to the First Division in 1903 and Brighton win the old Southern League in 1910. Upon the outbreak of World War One, Jones was one of the first players to sign up with the Footballers' Battalion of the Middlesex Regiment. He was 77 when he died in a Sussex nursing home in 1957.

CHARLIE WILSON JONES was born in Pentre Broughton near Wrexham on 29 April 1914. Frail-looking, he was nonetheless a prolific goalscorer and after trials with Blackburn Rovers and Bolton Wanderers, he played centre-forward for Wrexham before joining Birmingham for £1,500 in September 1934. Over the next 13 years, Jones scored 69 goals in 150 League and Cup games for Blues as well as netting 45 goals in 75 wartime fixtures, gaining a Football League (South) winners' medal in 1946. He was, in fact, leading scorer for Blues on three occasions during the 1930s.

A guest player with Blackpool, Huddersfield Town, West Bromwich Albion and Wrexham during the hostilities, Charlie left St Andrew's for Nottingham Forest in September 1947 and later assisted Redditch United and Kidderminster Harriers before retiring in June 1950 to enter the licensed trade. He died in Birmingham on 9 January 1986.

JACK JONES was born in Rotherham on 8 February 1891. A former miner, he was a rock-solid full-back, who played initially for Sunderland before transferring to St Andrew's for £2,000 in May 1930. Nicknamed 'Cracker', he served Blues for six seasons, during which time he scored one goal in 237 senior appearances, forming a formidable full-back partnership with skipper Frank Womack and helping the club win the Second Division Championship in 1920–21. He left Blues for Nelson in May 1927, and after that assisted Crewe Alexandra and Scarborough before retiring in 1931. He died in a Rotherham hospital on 20 July 1948.

HOWARD KENDALL was born in Ryton-on-Tyne on 22 May 1946 and joined Preston North End in 1961. Three years later he played in the FA Cup Final against West Ham at the age of 17 years and 345 days, making him the youngest Cup finalist of the 20th century. A defender when he joined Everton for £80,000 in March 1967, he was switched into midfield to link up with Alan Ball and Colin Harvey. This famous trio (nicknamed 'the Holy Trinity') played a major part when the Merseysiders won the League Championship in 1970. Kendall captained Everton for three seasons before his transfer to Birmingham City in February 1974 in a £350,000 deal that took Bob Latchford to Goodison Park and also saw Archie Styles arrive at St Andrew's. He scored 18 goals in 134 appearances for Blues and was no doubt one of the best all-round players the club had seen for many years. Leaving St Andrew's for Stoke City in August 1977 for £40,000, he became player-coach of the Potters, helping them gain promotion in 1979. Surprisingly Kendall never played for England, although he did win caps at Schoolboy, Youth and Under-23 levels, captaining the youth team

to victory in the 1964 Little World Cup. In June 1979 Kendall was appointed player-manager of Blackburn Rovers, whom he guided back into the Second Division in 1980 and then narrowly missed promotion to the First on goal difference. In May 1981 he returned to Everton as player-manager, retiring as a player after four games. He was on the verge of being sacked in January 1984, but results improved and Everton went on to reach the League Cup Final and won the FA Cup that season. Then, in 1984–85, Kendall's team won the League title, finishing 13 points clear of Liverpool, and they also lifted the European Cup-Winners' Cup, but missed out on the treble by losing to Manchester United in the FA Cup Final. The following year the Merseysiders narrowly failed to win the double – finishing second in both competitions – but in 1986–87 it was back to winning ways for Kendall when the League Championship trophy came back to Goodison Park. On leaving Everton in June 1987, Kendall took charge of the Spanish club Atletico Bilbao. He did not do too well in La Liga, and after turning down an offer to manage Newcastle, he was sacked by Bilbao in November 1989, returning to England as boss of Manchester City the following month. There followed another spell as boss at Everton from November 1990 to December 1993 and after that Kendall managed the Greek club Xanthi, Notts County, Sheffield United and Everton again (1997–99). He then returned to Greece to coach Ethnikos Piraeus, but was sacked after only four months. That was his last job in football and he remains the last English manager to win a major European competition.

NOEL KINSEY was born on Christmas Eve, 1925, in Treorchy in the Rhondda Valley. A clever, goalscoring inside-right, he played initially as an amateur for Cardiff City before joining Norwich City as a

League, while playing for Birmingham City, Sheffield United, Watford, Portsmouth, Derby County, Notts County and Bristol City. He later assisted Happy Valley in Hong Kong, and represented the Hong Kong League in matches against Mexico and Bulgaria, before returning to play in non-League football with Farnborough Town and Weymouth. He netted six times in 132 senior games for Blues, whom he served from June 1981 until March 1987 when he moved to Bramall Lane in an exchange deal involving Steve Wigley. He was a member of the club's promotion-winning team in 1985. A qualified coach, he was on the coaching staff of Aldershot Town in 2008–09, having acted as caretaker manager until the appointment of Gary Waddock in May 2007.

BOB LATCHFORD was born in Kings Heath, Birmingham on 18 January 1951. An old fashioned centre-forward, he had a terrific career which realised well over 250 goals in more than 550 club appearances. In fact, 211 of his goals were scored in 495 First Division games with four clubs – Birmingham City, Everton, Swansea City and Coventry City. He also gained 12 full caps for England. Especially good in the air and on the ground, he was six feet (1.83m) tall, quite fast over short distances and without doubt a great 'goal poacher' who scored well over 20 times with some great diving headers. An FA Youth Cup runner-up with Blues in 1967, he helped the team win promotion from the Second Division in 1972 and formed a wonderful strike-force with Trevor Francis and Bob Hatton. Bob was transferred to Everton in February 1974 in what was, at the time, a British record deal of £350,000, which also saw Howard Kendall and Archie Styles move from Goodison to St Andrew's. He finished up as the Merseyside club's top-scorer in six successive seasons, notching 30 goals in 1977–78 and receiving

professional in 1947, switching to Birmingham City in June 1953. Kinsey helped Blues win the Second Division Championship in 1955 and a year later scored against Manchester City in the FA Cup Final – one of 56 he netted for the club in 173 appearances. He left St Andrew's for Port Vale in February 1958 and later assisted King's Lynn and Lowestoft Town (as player-coach) before retiring in August 1966. During a fine career, Kinsey struck a total of 111 goals in 444 League games and won seven caps for Wales in the 1950s. After leaving football he worked for a firm of solicitors in the offices of the Norwich Union Insurance Company. Inducted into the inaugural Norwich City FC Hall of Fame in 2009, he is alive and well and is now one of Blues' oldest former players, residing in the village of Thorpe near Norwich.

MARTIN KUHL was born in Frimley, Surrey on 10 January 1965 and at the age of 14 was on the books of Chelsea. A wholehearted midfielder, he made over 500 club appearances, 474 in the Football

a cheque for £100,000 from a local newspaper for his achievement. During the mid-seventies, Latchford was widely considered one of the top English forwards of his generation and duly earned his first full cap in a World Cup qualifier against Italy in 1977. The closest he came to gaining a winners' medal in a major Cup competition came at Everton when he was a finalist in the League Cup in 1977. Latchford scored 84 goals in 194 appearances for Blues and followed up with 138 in 289 outings for Everton. A great inspiration to a whole generation of fans (at St Andrew's and Goodison Park) he moved to Swansea in 1981 and celebrated his arrival at the Vetch Field by scoring a hat-trick on his debut for the Welsh club. He later played for the Dutch club NAC Breda (13 goals in 15 outings), Coventry City, Lincoln City, Newport County and Merthyr Tydfil before retiring in 1987. After that Latchford was a director of non-League club Alvechurch and also worked in the commercial department at St Andrew's before becoming a coach with Blues in 1999–2000. He now resides in Germany. In April 2006 a book was published telling the story of Bob's 1977–78

season. Co-written with journalist Martin O'Boyle, the proceeds go to Everton's former players' charity.

DAVE LATCHFORD, the older brother of Bob, was born in Kings Heath, Birmingham on 9 April 1949. He joined Birmingham City from school in 1964 and signed professional forms at the age of 17. Called up for the England Youth squad with Peter Shilton, but not capped, he kept goal for Blues in the 1967 FA Youth Cup Final before making his League debut two years later at Bury. However, with Jim Herriot, Paul Cooper and Mike Kelly also at the club, it took another four years for Latchford to establish himself as undisputed first choice. Even then manager Freddie Goodwin brought in Welsh international Gary Sprake, but Latchford soon regained his place and went on to appear in 239 senior matches before handing over his duties to Jim Montgomery. Latchford left St Andrew's in July 1977 for Motherwell, managed at the time by his former teammate Roger Hynd. He followed up with spells at Bury, Barnsley, Redditch, Cheltenham Town and East Worle before retiring in 1992 to became a funeral director, later enjoying life as a superintendent of cemeteries in Solihull, while coaching for a time at Solihull Borough.

STAN LAZARIDIS was born in Perth, Australia on 16 August 1972. Basically a left-winger, who could perform adequately at left-back, his reputation as a young teenager began with Olympic Kingsway in his homeland where, despite his age, he tormented many a defender with his extraordinary change of pace. From there he switched to West Adelaide Hellas in 1992 and it was here where his dashing runs and lightning pace attracted the attention of scouts from England. At the end of the 1995 season he finally got his big move to Europe when West Ham boss Harry Redknapp paid £300,000 to bring him to Upton Park. Lazaridis made only 87 appearances for the Hammers in four seasons before dropping down a division to sign for Birmingham City in the summer of 1999. He settled much better at St Andrew's and played an important role in guiding the team into the Premier League in 2002, a year after playing in the League Cup Final. Despite several new signings, Lazaridis remained a regular in the Blues line-up, scoring the winner in the local derby against Aston Villa in March 2003, following up with a superb goal against Everton in February 2004. Lazaridis spent seven excellent years with Blues, during which time he set a new record for being the club's most capped player, gaining 33 for Australia, since bettered by two Irishmen, Damien Johnson (42) and Maik Taylor (52). Without doubt the fans' hero, he was released in June 2006 after scoring eight goals in 222 appearances for the club. Returning home, he signed for Aussie A-League club Perth Glory and was named in the Aussie 2006 World Cup squad, but never made it to Germany. Unfortunately his time with the Glory was tainted when, in January 2007, he registered a positive drug test for anti-androgen Finasteride, a prescription alopecia medication, which is banned due to its potential as a masking agent for other performance-enhancing substances. While noting his previous good character and making clear there was no evidence he had taken performance-enhancing drugs, Lazaridis was nevertheless found guilty by the Australian Sports Anti-Doping Authority and was handed a 12-month suspension from football. Two months after his return, in March 2008, Glory's manager Dave Mitchell cut him from the club's roster, at which point Lazaridis announced his retirement from competitive football.

ALEX LEAKE was born in Small Heath, Birmingham on 11 July 1871. After leaving Green Lane school he trained as a blacksmith with Hoskins & Sewell, manufacturers of metal bedsteads, in the Bordesley district of the city, and played for the works football team. He later helped Old Hill Wanderers win the 1893–94 Birmingham & District League Championship. His success with the Wanderers went unnoticed, and in July 1894 he was signed by newly-promoted Small Heath. He made his debut at left-half, but was switched to centre-half midway through a relegation season and thereafter, right through to 1899, he rarely missed a game, captaining the side on several occasions. Reverting to left-half later, he also filled in at inside-left when required. Leake helped Blues regain top-flight status in 1901, but then surprisingly, after scoring 23 goals in 221 appearances, he left the club in June 1902 after relegation had been suffered again. During his last season at St Andrew's he played in an England international trial match and also for an England XI in an unofficial international against Germany. Leake joined rivals Aston Villa in July 1902 and he remained there for five years, during which time he helped Villa take second spot in the First Division in 1904 and gained an FA Cup-winners' medal the following year. While at Villa

Park, he won five full caps for England, making his debut at the age of 32, and also found himself unwittingly at the centre of one of the great scandals of English football. On the last day of the 1904–05 season, Manchester City needed to beat Aston Villa to win the League title. It was a spiteful game, and Leake himself had been involved in several confrontations, both physical and verbal, with opponents. Afterwards he claimed that City's Billy Meredith had offered him a bribe of £10 for his team to throw the match. Meredith was found guilty by the Football Association, fined, and suspended from all levels of football for 18 months. Because his club refused to help him financially, Meredith made public the illegal payments Manchester City were making to their players. An FA investigation resulted in life bans for directors, long suspensions for players, and the club being forced to sell its playing staff. An Aston Villa match programme of 1906 describes Leake 'As a

good-tempered, honest worker; safe rather than showy; hard to beat in a tackle and good at spoiling an opponent's pass. Alert, keeps his head, and never tires in the hardest matches. His unfailing good humour has made him a general favourite.' He was certainly that. Moving to Burnley in December 1907, he stayed at Turf Moor for a further two and a half years, playing a significant part in building a team for the future and being named as an England reserve. Returning to the Midlands in 1910, he spent a season with Wednesbury Old Athletic in the Birmingham & District League before acting as trainer at Crystal Palace, Merthyr Town and Walsall. Leake, who also coached at school level, died in Birmingham on 29 March 1938.

KEN LEEK was an exceptionally fine goalscorer whose professional career ran from 1952 until 1970. Born next door to Don Dearson's family in Ynysybwl near Pontypridd on 26 July 1935, he joined Northampton Town as a 17-year-old, then moved to Leicester City in 1958 and to Newcastle United in June 1961. Birmingham City recruited him for £23,000 five months later and, after leaving St Andrew's in December 1964, he returned to Northampton before going on to play for Bradford City, Rhyl Town and Ton Pentre. Leek played for Wales in the 1958 World Cup Finals in Sweden and in all won 13 caps for his country, while also playing for the Under-23 team. While with Leicester he was mysteriously dropped for the 1961 FA Cup Final, despite having scored in all the previous rounds. His finest hour with Blues came in the 1963 League Cup Final when his two goals in the first leg helped set up an aggregate 3–1 victory over Aston Villa. Leek averaged a goal every two games for Blues – 61 in 120 games – and in all at club level he netted 147 goals in 397 appearances. He died in Daventry on 19 November 2007.

ALEC LESLIE was born in Greenock on 7 April 1902. A defensive left-half with a bone-crunching tackle, he was an influential player who appeared in 143 games for Birmingham, including 132 top-flight matches and the 1931 FA Cup Final, between April 1927 and May 1932 when he retired with a knee injury. Prior to his move to St Andrew's, Leslie had played for Greenock Wayfarers, Port Glasgow Junior, St Mirren, Houghton-le-Spring FC, Morton, St Mirren (again) and Torquay United. After football he ran the Freemason's Inn on Hawkes Street, Birmingham and later worked for the Inland Revenue before returning to Scotland. He died in Greenock in 1974.

GEORGE LIDDELL was born in Murton, County Durham on 14 July 1895 and was an amateur with newly-elected South Shields when League football resumed after World War One. He turned professional when he joined Birmingham in May 1920 and over the next 12 years he scored six goals in 345 appearances in all competitions for Blues, playing in the 1931 FA Cup Final. A powerfully built defender who read the game well, he was positive on the ball and

had superb positional sense. When Blues' manager Leslie Knighton left for Chelsea in 1933, Liddell succeeded him in the hot seat at St Andrew's. He stayed in the job until September 1939. During his six-year tenure he selected 70 different players for first-team duty. A trained teacher, Liddell taught at several schools in the Birmingham area, including Handsworth New Road Secondary Modern School where he was head teacher in the early 1950s. He died in Hampshire in 1975. (See also managers).

STAN LYNN was a rock-solid, no-nonsense hard-tackling, strong-kicking full-back who made 324 appearances for Aston Villa before adding 148 more to his tally with Blues. He also scored 38 goals for City's arch-rivals and netted 30 times during his time at St Andrew's. Born in Bolton on 18 June 1928, he started out with Accrington Stanley and moved south to Villa Park in March 1950 for a fee of £10,000. He gained FA Cup, Second Division Championship and League Cup winners' prizes in 1957, 1960 and 1961 respectively before moving to St Andrew's

in October 1961 and going on to help Blues win the League Cup in 1963, beating his former club Villa in the Final. Nicknamed 'Stan the Wham' for his blockbusting shooting, he once struck a hat-trick for Villa against Sunderland in January 1958, becoming the first full-back ever to score a hat-trick in a top-flight match. In 1964–65 he was Birmingham's joint leading scorer. In August 1966 Lynn moved down the ladder to sign for Stourbridge, retiring two years later, although he still made appearances for Aston Villa All Stars in charity matches until 1985. He worked in the tool room stores at Lucas in Birmingham for many years until his retirement in 1983. Twice married, Lynn was 74 years of age when he died of Alzheimer's disease in a Solihull nursing home on 28 April 2002.

ALEX McCLURE was born in Workington on 3 April 1892. A resolute centre-half, he played for Grangetown Juniors before joining Birmingham in January 1912. He went on to score four goals in 198 appearances in all competitions for Blues, helping them win the Second Division Championship in 1920–21. A very powerful defender with good positional ability, he skippered Blues' second XI before establishing himself as club captain and linchpin of the first team's defence. McClure, who represented the Football League against the Irish Football League in 1921, moved to Aston Villa in December 1923 and later played for Stoke, Coventry City and Walsall before becoming trainer of the Luton Town colts team. He then took over as trainer of Birmingham's Junior team, and in May 1932 was appointed assistant manager at St Andrew's under Leslie Knighton and later under George Liddell. After leaving football McClure worked for Rudge motorcycles and later ran a very successful haulage business in Small

Heath, Birmingham. During World War One he served in the Royal Navy and was involved in the Zeebrugge Raid. He died in Birmingham on 15 August 1973.

JAMES McFADDEN was born in Springburn, Glasgow on 14 April 1983. A utility forward, able to occupy virtually every front-line position, he made his senior debut for his first club, Motherwell, at the age of 17. Voted Scotland's 'Young Player of the Year' in 2003, he quickly moved to Everton for £1.25 million and did well at Goodison Park early on but then faded and was disappointed when a loan spell with his boyhood heroes Celtic fell through. After netting 19 goals in 139 outings for the Merseysiders McFadden joined Birmingham City for £5 million in January 2008 and this figure could rise to £6 million depending on appearances. He was in fine form in 2008–09, helping Blues finish second in the Championship and so regain their place in the Premier League. McFadden won the first of his 46 caps at the age of 19, on a Far East tour against South

Africa, and in September 2007 he became a cult hero when he scored spectacularly against France in a European Championship qualifier in the Parc des Princes, which is regarded as one of Scotland's most famous goals. He netted another beauty for his country in a World Cup qualifier against Macedonia at Hampden Park in September 2009 and now has 15 to his credit. A torn thigh muscle kept him out of action for several weeks during the 2009–10 season and he was sorely missed! By May 2010 he had hit 13 goals in 83 appearances for Blues.

BOB McROBERTS was born in Coatbridge, Scotland on 12 July 1874. A centre-forward with Airdrieonians and Albion Rovers north of the border, he moved south to play for Gainsborough Trinity in 1896 before joining Small Heath (Birmingham) in August 1898. After seven years with Blues, he signed for the League's newcomers Chelsea in August 1905. He also played as a defender at Stamford Bridge

before retiring in May 1909. McRoberts returned to Blues as manager the following year and held that position until August 1915. He scored 82 goals in 187 appearances for Blues, and was leading marksman three seasons running from 1899 to 1902, gaining a Second Division Championship-winners' medal in 1901. He was also Chelsea's first ever £100 signing. He died in Birkenhead on 27 February 1959. (See also managers).

GIL MERRICK was born in Sparkhill, Birmingham on 26 January 1922 – and was said to be one of the best, if not THE best, goalkeeper in Great Britain during the early 1950s – despite having the misfortune to be between the posts when the Hungarians put 13 goals past England in two internationals in 1953 and 1954. Merrick copied the style of Harry Hibbs, his illustrious predecessor in the Blues goal. Calm, unspectacular with a technique all of his own, that of unique positional sense, he also used the whole framework of his body to stop shots as well as having a huge pair of hands and strong kick. A powerfully built man with a dapper moustache, he made 715 first-team appearances for Blues including wartime competitions, and is still the club's record appearance-maker at senior level (551 games). Merrick also starred in a record 56 FA Cup matches. Over a period of eight years from August 1946 until April 1954, Merrick was very rarely absent from competitive match action, only international calls and the odd injury disrupting his progress. He helped Blues win the Football League (South) title in 1945–46, conceded only 24 goals in 41 League matches when the Second Division Championship was won in 1948–49, gained another Second Division-winners' medal in 1955 and a year later played in the FA Cup Final against Manchester City. Between November 1951 and June 1954 he

gained 23 caps for England. He also represented the Football League on 11 occasions between 1947 and 1954 and in 1945–46 he played for the Army Physical Training team. After assisting several local junior clubs Merrick joined Blues as amateur in 1938, but was loaned out to Solihull Town to gain experience. Returning to sign as a professional in readiness for the ill-fated 1939–40 campaign, he went on to play in 164 regional games during the hostilities. Eventually replaced by Johnny Schofield in April 1959, Gil had two more outings the following season before retiring in 1960 to take over as manager at St Andrew's…and what a terrific first season he had in charge, leading Blues to the Inter-Cities Fairs Cup Final. Two years later he celebrated again as Blues won the Football League Cup. In office for four years, Merrick later managed Bromsgrove Rovers and Atherstone Town. He resided in Sparkbrook for the remaining of his life, passing away on 3 February 2010, shortly after penning the foreword to this book. (See also managers).

FRANK MITCHELL was technically an Australian, born in Goulburn, New South Wales on 3 June 1922. A fine wing-half, he made over 350 appearances in the Football League, including 86 in the First Division and he also played county cricket for Warwickshire. Mitchell moved to England as a teenager, his main sport at the time being cricket. As a 15-year-old he joined the Edgbaston ground staff before starting his football career as an amateur with Coventry City. When on leave from the Royal Navy, he made guest appearances during World War Two for several clubs, including Arsenal, Portsmouth and Birmingham, and in fact, Blues were sufficiently impressed that they signed him as a full-time professional in September 1943. Blessed with a calm temperament and excellent football brain, Mitchell became Blues' regular penalty-taker and in 1946 played for an England XI against a Scotland XI in an unofficial friendly to raise funds for the families of the victims killed in the Bolton disaster. Mitchell, who also starred for the FA XI, made 106 appearances for Birmingham, gaining Football League (South) and Second Division

Championship-winning medals in 1946 and 1948 respectively. He eventually moved to Chelsea in January 1949 before ending his playing days with Watford in 1958. Mitchell played 17 first-class matches for Warwickshire between 1946 and 1948, taking 22 wickets at an average of 38.9 with his right-arm medium-pace or off-break bowling. He also scored 229 runs at an average of 8.29 and took seven catches. He later played for and then became groundsman and secretary of the Knowle and Dorridge Cricket Club and he also worked on the ground at Kynochs. Mitchell, who attended his last match at St Andrew's at the age of 60, died in Lapworth, Warwickshire on 2 April 1984.

FRANK MOBLEY was born in Handsworth, Birmingham on 21 November 1868. A big, strong, powerfully-built centre forward, he played for Hockley Belmont, Cape Hill and Singers FC (Coventry) before scoring 65 goals in 103 appearances in all competitions for Blues, whom he served for four years, from April 1892 until May 1896. Leading scorer in three successive seasons, 1893–96, he was also overall top scorer in the Second Division when Blues won the title in 1892 and then gained promotion the following season. On leaving Blues Mobley joined Bury. He later played for Warmley FC (Bristol) and Coventry City (briefly) before retiring in 1902 when he returned to live and work in Birmingham, where he died on 12 April 1940.

GEORGE MORRALL was a tough, reliable centre-half, born in Smethwick on 4 October 1905, who scored seven goals in 266 appearances for Birmingham, 243 in the First Division. Nicknamed 'Lofty' he joined the club in March 1927 (after an unsuccessful trial with West Bromwich Albion) and was an FA Cup finalist in 1931 (against the Baggies) before leaving St

Andrew's in June 1936 for Swindon Town, for whom he made over 100 appearances before retiring in 1940. Morrall died in Birmingham on 15 November 1955.

HARRY MORRIS was born in Birmingham on 11 April 1866. A pupil at Small Heath Council School, he was an apprentice plumber when he joined Small Heath Alliance (Blues) in 1883. Initially a centre-forward, he subsequently switched to half-back from where he captained the team. The majority of Morris's playing career preceded the formation of the Football Alliance and even the Football League, and when he retired in May 1893 he had scored four goals in 68 competitive games for Blues. As a player Morris had been able to save £85 from his wages and with this money he purchased the lease of a shop near the club's old Arthur Street ground and duly set up his own plumbing business. Within 10 years he had become a Blues director and it was down to Morris's business acumen that St Andrew's was built. Indeed, it was he who spotted the area of sloping wasteland near to a railway which was converted into Blues' new ground in 1906. Morris remained on the club's board of directors until 1929, when his son Harry

junior took over. Another son, Len, also served as a director. In fact, Morris junior was appointed chairman in 1933, and after 38 years unbroken service to the club was handed the presidency in 1967, the year of his death. Harry Morris senior died on 26 June 1931, just two months after watching Blues lose in the FA Cup Final – 45 years after he himself had played in a losing semi-final against the same team, West Bromwich Albion.

SEYMOUR MORRIS was born in Ynyshir, Glamorgan on 15 February 1908. He became a miner on leaving school and at the age of 15 joined the army, serving in the Welch Regiment. While stationed near Cardiff he played on the left-wing for Aberaman Athletic in the Welsh League where he was spotted by a scout from Huddersfield Town. In March 1933, aged 25, Morris joined the Terriers as a professional. Unfortunately he was unable to gain a regular first-team place at Leeds Road and in March 1935 moved to Birmingham for £1,500. At St Andrew's he played second fiddle to Billy Guest before making the outside-left berth his own in 1936. Top scorer for Blues in 1936–37 with 16 goals, Morris gained a total of five full caps for Wales that same season, helping his country win the Home International Championship. He worked as an aircraft service engineer at Elmdon aerodrome during World War Two, having the odd game with Blues. In fact, he made his 83rd and final appearance for the club in April 1945. He scored 31 goals. Thereafter, along with his wife, Morris ran a children's home in South Wales for many years before his death on 3 October 1991 at the age of 83.

ARTHUR MOUNTENEY was born in Belgrave, Leicester on 11 February 1883. Known as 'Pecker' he was a well-built, hard-shooting inside forward who played for

Leicester Imperial and Leicester Fosse before joining Birmingham in April 1905. He went on to score 30 goals in 97 appearances for Blues in four years, up to his transfer to Preston North End in April 1909. He later played for Grimsby Town, Portsmouth and Hinckley Athletic and retired in 1915. One thing which cannot be taken away from Mounteney is the fact that he had the pleasure of scoring Blues' last goal at their Muntz Street ground before the club moved to St Andrew's in December 1906. Besides being an excellent footballer, Mounteney was also a very capable cricketer. He was a middle-order right-hand batsman and occasional bowler for Leicestershire for 13 years from 1911. In that time he scored 5,306 runs, including six centuries, for an average of 20.8. He was 50 when he died in Leicester on 1 June 1933.

PETER MURPHY was born in West Hartlepool, County Durham on 7 March 1922. A utility forward, he represented Coventry Schools, had trials with Middlesbrough, was an amateur with both Coventry City and Birmingham City and played as a guest for Millwall during World War Two before signing professional forms at Highfield Road in May 1946. After four years with the Sky Blues, for whom he scored 37 goals, he was transferred to Tottenham Hotspur in June 1950 for £18,500. He helped the London club win the Second Division title in 1951, but became unsettled in the capital and in January 1952 he moved to St Andrew's in a £20,000 deal. He netted a hat-trick on his Blues debut in a 5–0 League win at Doncaster and continued to find the net on a regular basis thereafter. Top-scorer with 20 goals when Blues won the Second Division Championship in 1955, the following season he struck 17 times, five in the FA Cup, as Blues reached the Final only

to lose to Manchester City. It was Murphy, in fact, who collided with City's goalkeeper Bert Trautmann, causing the German to fracture his neck. Murphy announced his retirement in the summer of 1959 to become a coach at St Andrew's, but with Blues battling against relegation the following season he came back to help them avoid the drop, netting two goals in a 3–0 home win over Arsenal and two more in a 4–2 victory at Sheffield Wednesday to finish up with a total of 127 goals in 268 appearances. In 1961, Murphy guided non-League Rugby Town to promotion to the Southern League Premier Division and later returned to Highfield Road to manage Coventry City's A team before going into the licensed trade, working as a representative for Davenports Brewery. He was only 53 years of age when he died in Coventry on 7 April 1975.

DICK NEAL was born in Dinnington near Sheffield on 1 October 1933. A powerful, hard-working wing-back, he made over 350 League appearances while serving with

Lincoln City, Birmingham City and Middlesbrough. He also played for Blues in the Final of the Inter-Cities Fairs Cup in 1960. Nurtured through the junior ranks by Wolves, Neal played for the club's nursery side, Wath Wanderers, before turning professional in 1951. After failing to break into the first team at Molineux, Neal was sold to Lincoln City in July 1954. He played over 100 games for the Imps and gained both England Youth and Under-23 caps before switching to St Andrew's in April 1957 in a cash/player exchange deal involving Albert Linnecor. Neal went on to give Blues excellent service, amassing 197 appearances and scoring 18 goals, captaining the side in 1960–61. After losing his place to Terry Hennessey, he moved to Middlesbrough, where injury restricted his appearances during the two seasons at Ayresome Park. He returned to Lincoln as captain for another year before taking over as player-manager of Rugby Town, following up with similar roles at Hednesford Town, Brierley Hill Alliance and Blakenhall Town. When he quit

football in 1969 Neal went into the licensed trade, taking his first pub in Birmingham and his second in Penkridge. In 2006, to celebrate their 100th season in the Football League, Lincoln City fans voted Neal into 42nd place in the club's '100 Legends'. Neal's father, also named Dick, was a winger with Blackpool, Derby County, Southampton, Bristol City and Accrington Stanley before World War Two.

JOHNNY NEWMAN was born in Hereford on 13 December 1933. A wing-half or central defender, he began his professional career with Birmingham City in March 1951. Four years later he helped Blues win the Second Division title and in 1956 was on the losing side in an FA Cup Final. After making 65 appearances during his time at St Andrew's, the ever-reliable Newman moved on to Leicester City for £12,000 in November 1957 and onto Plymouth Argyle for £3,000 in January 1960. He made over 300 appearances for the Pilgrims in seven years and in 1966 he helped the Football League (which contained seven members of England's World Cup-winning team) beat the Irish League 12–0 at Home Park. Newman ended his playing days with another Devon club, Exeter City, initially as a player and then as player-manager from 1969 until his retirement in 1972. Newman's next move took him to Grimsby Town, whom he guided to promotion from the Fourth Division. After that he spent 11 uneasy months in charge at Derby County, before returning to his home-town to manage Hereford United (1983–87). After that Newman served as assistant-manager at both York City and Notts County, was Youth Development Officer at Mansfield, assistant-boss at Burton Albion and coach at Worcester City before pulling out of football for good in 1998, aged 65.

MALCOLM PAGE was born in Knuckles, Radnorshire on 5 February 1947 and represented Radnorshire & District Boys, Radnorshire County XI and Wales (four games) as a schoolboy. A versatile footballer – he wore every numbered outfield shirt for Blues – Page could defend with the best and hold his own in midfield with some of the finest players in the game. He scored 10 goals in 391 appearances for Blues, whom he served for 17 years, from July 1964 until February 1981, gaining a Second Division Championship-winners' medal in 1972 and playing in three FA Cup semi-finals. On leaving St Andrew's he joined Oxford United, eventually retiring in March 1982. He won his first full cap for Wales against Finland in 1971 and his final tally of 28 was a club record which stood for 25 years until beaten by Stan Lazaridis in 2005. Page, who also won six Under-23 caps, captained both his League clubs and his country. Page was born just inside Wales when his mother was visiting an aunt. She was unable to return to her home in England for the birth due to severe weather conditions.

GARRY PENDREY was born in Lozells, Birmingham on 9 February 1949 and signed for Blues on leaving school in July 1965, turning professional in October 1966.

A strong, competitive defender, he remained at St Andrew's until August 1979, and during his 14-year stay at St Andrew's he made 360 first-class appearances and scored five goals. He was an FA Youth Cup finalist in 1967 and in 1972 helped Blues gain promotion from the Second Division. In 1969 he became Blues' youngest-ever captain when he skippered the team at the age of 29 years and six months. Often referred to as 'Gazza' and 'Penders', Pendrey was a huge favourite with the St Andrew's crowd and when he left to join neighbours West Bromwich Albion in May 1979, just after his testimonial, some were rather surprised. He spent two years at the Hawthorns and after that played, in turn, for Torquay United, Bristol Rovers and Walsall, initially acting as player-coach with the Saddlers. On his retirement as a player in 1983, Pendrey became senior coach at the Bescot stadium, working alongside former Blues forward Alan Buckley. Two years after seeing the team reach the League

Cup semi-final, Pendrey was replaced when the club was sold to a new owner, Terry Ramsden. He spent a few months on the coaching staff at Wolverhampton Wanderers before returning to Birmingham City as manager in June 1987. However, with a dwindling squad and no money to spend on new players, he knew from the start he was fighting a losing battle. In April 1989, with relegation to the Third Division for the first time in the club's history confirmed, the new owners sacked him and appointed Dave Mackay as manager. After turning down an offer to become a coach at St Andrew's, Pendrey rejoined Wolves, where he remained until November 1996. He then surprised everyone by accepting the position of assistant-manager to Gordon Strachan at Coventry City. And when Strachan left the Sky Blues in 2001, Pendrey also departed…only for the pair to be re-united as manager and assistant at Southampton in October 2002. There was more to come when, in June 2005, Pendrey joined Celtic as Strachan's assistant manager and, when the Scotsman took over as boss of Middlesbrough in 2009, Pendrey followed him to the Riverside stadium.

KEVIN PHILLIPS started scoring goals when he was six years of age – and he has certainly grabbed some priceless ones in his two seasons with Blues, top-scoring with 14 in 2008–09, including a six-yard tap-in at Reading which clinched promotion to the Premier League in the final League game. In 2009–10 he netted the 200th of his club career while at the same taking his record with Blues to 18 goals in 62 appearances. Born in Hitchin on 25 July 1973, Phillips began his net-bulging exploits with Watford, signing professional forms at Vicarage Road in December 1994 after a spell with Baldock Town. In July 1997, he was transferred to Sunderland for £325,000; moved 400 miles south to join

Southampton for £3.25 million in August 2003; joined Aston Villa for £750,000 in July 2005; became a West Bromwich Albion player for £700,000 in August 2006 and two years later was recruited on a free transfer by Blues' boss Alex McLeish. A First Division winner in 1999 with Sunderland, he helped the Baggies win the Championship in 2008 and earlier in his career played in one 'B' and eight full internationals for England.

FRED PICKERING was originally a full-back before developing into a burly striker with an excellent first touch and powerful right-foot shot. Born in Blackburn on 19 January 1941, he started out with his hometown club in 1956 as a junior, turning professional at the age of 17. He spent four years at Ewood Park, during which time he averaged a goal every two games. In 1963, Pickering signed for Everton and over the same period of time he struck 70 goals in 115 appearances. Signed by Birmingham City for £50,000 in August 1967, Pickering

spent two seasons at St Andrew's. He maintained his form and hit 32 goals in 88 outings for Blues, helping them reach the 1968 FA Cup semi-final. Moving on, he played for Blackpool, Blackburn (again) and finally Brighton, retiring in 1972, having notched 168 goals in 354 League games. Pickering won three caps for England, scoring five times including a debut hat-trick in a 10–0 win over the USA in 1964. He also played for his country in three Under-23 internationals and represented the Football League. After leaving football Pickering worked as a fork-lift truck driver. He now lives in Blackburn.

TED PURDON was a blond centre-forward, strong and mobile, who scored 30 goals in 70 appearances for Birmingham City between August 1950 and January 1954. Born in Johannesburg, South Africa on 1 March 1930, he came to England on tour with the Maritz Brothers club at the age of 20 and was watched by scouts from several clubs, and it was Blues who got in first ahead of Arsenal and Manchester City.

The club's top scorer in 1953–54, Purdon was then sold to Sunderland for £15,000 and netted five goals in his first two games for the Wearsiders, one against Arsenal coming after just nine seconds of play – the fastest ever scored for that club. In 1954 he collided with the West Bromwich Albion goalkeeper Norman Heath during a League game at Roker Park. Heath never played again – and Purdon never really got over the tragedy. Along with several of his former Sunderland teammates, Purdon was punished by the Football Association for receiving illegal payments from the club. By the time this matter was investigated, he had left for Workington and later assisted Barrow, Bath City (Southern League champions 1960), Bristol Rovers, Toronto City (Canada), Polish White Eagles FC (also in Toronto) and New York Ukrainians (US Open Cup-winners in 1965) before retiring in 1966 to take up coaching in Canada. Besides being a fine footballer, Purdon was also a useful cricketer, being named as 12th man by Warwickshire in the County Championship. Founder member and honorary president of Sunderland's North

American supporters' club, in company with fellow supporters Purdon had just watched on television Sunderland defeat Burnley in the game which virtually clinched the club's 2007 promotion to the Premier League when he suffered a stroke. He sadly died in a Toronto hospital two days later.

ARTHUR 'NAT' ROBINSON holds the record for most ever-present seasons for Blues: four between 1898 and 1906. Born in Coventry on 28 February 1878, he was a real character but nonetheless a very fine goalkeeper who used to wind his arms around in circles in an attempt to put off his opponent. It is also said that he wore two jerseys irrespective of how hot or cold the weather was! He played for Allesley FC, Coventry Stars and Singers before joining Birmingham in August 1898. Over the next 10 years he made 306 appearances for Blues, twice helping them win promotion, in 1901 and 1903. He also represented the Football League on two occasions and featured in two international trials with England. In July 1908 Robinson moved to Chelsea before winding down his career with Coventry City. He retired in May 1910 to become licensee of the Red Lion Inn, Barras Green in Coventry. Robinson had a pet dog called 'Ninety', named after the number of minutes in a game of football. The former Blues goalkeeper died in Coventry on 15 May 1929.

JOHNNY SCHOFIELD was understudy to the great Gil Merrick for a number of years before finally establishing himself as Blues' first-choice goalkeeper in 1960. Born in Atherstone, Warwickshire on 8 February 1931, Schofield signed as a professional at St Andrew's on his 19th birthday, having previously played for Nuneaton Borough's reserve team. Once in control, he remained first choice between the posts until the mid-

1960s, amassing a total of 237 appearances, playing in two Inter-Cities Fairs Cup Finals and helping Blues beat Aston Villa to win the League Cup in 1963. As a second XI player in November 1957, Schofield survived a pit explosion at Baddesley Colliery in Warwickshire, and three years later he fractured his skull while playing against Manchester United in a League game. He recovered well from both mishaps. With advancing age, and the signing of Jim Herriot, Schofield lost his place in the first team and was transferred to Wrexham in July 1966. Two years later he became player-manager of Atherstone Town and, after retiring, ran a successful wines and spirits business in his home town, where he died on 1 November 2006.

TREVOR SMITH was born in Brierley Hill on 13 April 1936. He attended Quarry Bank Secondary Modern School and played in defence for the Brierley Hill & Sedgley Boys' side that finished runners-up in the English Schools Trophy Final of 1951. He also played with and against Duncan Edwards in trial games for Dudley Schools. Trevor

represented the Football League, played in Schoolboy and Youth internationals and appeared twice for an Army XI during his national service. In October 1964, following injury problems – and having scored three goals in 430 appearances for Blues – Smith was transferred to Walsall for £18,000. Blues, however, were called cheats for selling an injured player, because the unfortunate Smith only started 13 matches for the Saddlers before retiring in February 1966. Later a permit player in the Lichfield Sunday League, he was also in charge of Mile Oak Rovers (1970–71) before becoming a branch manager for Thresher's Wine Stores, first in Birmingham's Bull Ring and then in Dagenham, Essex, where he died on 9 August 2003.

worked hard at his game and developed into a muscular centre-half with Birmingham City, whom he served supremely well for 13 years, initially as an amateur before turning professional at the age of 17 in 1953. He had the misfortune to concede an own-goal on his debut at Derby, but he put that to one side to become an exceptionally fine player, a colossus at the heart of the Blues' defence. He helped the team win the Second Division title in 1955 and the following season starred in a great FA Cup run which saw Blues reach the Final (lost to Manchester City). Leading by example, Smith skippered the team several times, including in the 1960 Fairs Cup Final v Barcelona and in the 1963 League Cup Final victory over Aston Villa. When Wolves legend Billy Wright announced his retirement in 1959, it was widely thought that Smith would take over at centre-half in the England team. He played in two internationals in October 1959 but in the end manager Walter Winterbottom decided to go with Peter Swan instead. Besides his two full caps, Trevor won 15 at Under-23 level, two with the 'B' team, twice

JACKIE STEWART was born in Lochgelly, Fife on 4 September 1921. A former miner, he started his professional career with Raith Rovers in August 1939 and moved to Birmingham City in January 1948. Blessed with terrific pace, he had a direct style and in his first full season at St Andrew's (1948–49) he finished up as top scorer with

11 goals. Injury unfortunately started to affect his performances from 1952 onwards and this resulted in a return to Raith in February 1955. He made 218 appearances in all competitions for Blues, scoring 55 goals. Stewart went on to become Raith's trainer. Stewart died in Cowdenbeath in 1990.

LEW STOKER was born in Wheatley Hill, County Durham, on 31 March 1910. A talented right half and 'feeder of the attack', he played for Brandon Juniors, Esh Winning Juniors, Bearpark and West Stanley before having a successful trial at St Andrew's in 1930. Signed as a professional later that year, he spent most of his professional career with Birmingham, for whom he played 246 games in all competitions, including 230 in the First Division. In 1938 he moved on to Nottingham Forest and retired, through injury, during World War Two. Stoker won three full caps for England between 1932 and 1934 and also represented the Football League. After his football days were over Stoker worked for Wimbush's bakery in

Birmingham and died in the city on 26 May 1979. His younger brother, Bob, played for Bolton and Huddersfield Town in the 1930s.

FRANK STOKES, easily recognisable on the pitch by the ungainly way he carried his arms, scored one goal (a smartly taken 15-yarder against Notts County in October 1906) in 213 appearances for Birmingham between October 1903 and August 1910 before injury forced him to retire. Born in Burslem, Stoke-on-Trent on 7 June 1881 and a defender with Burslem Port Vale and Reading before joining Blues, Stokes was a magnificent full-back, all muscle yet extremely mobile, who formed a wonderful partnership with Jack Glover. He appeared in four England trial matches but was not selected for international duty. He died in Birmingham in 1945.

GORDON TAYLOR, OBE, the PFAs current Chief Executive, was born in Ashton-under-Lyne on 28 December 1944. A direct touchline-hugging winger, he made over 250 appearances for Bolton Wanderers before joining Birmingham City in December 1970 for £18,000. Two years later he helped Blues gain promotion to the First Division and went on to net 10 times in 203 outings for the

club up to March 1976 when he signed for Blackburn Rovers. After spending the 1977 season in the NASL with Vancouver Whitecaps, Taylor returned to Ewood Park before switching to Bury in 1978. He retired from the game later that same year. In 1981 he was appointed Chief Executive of the Professional Footballers' Association, is a fully qualified FA Coach, has a degree in economics from London University and is a member of FIFA's football committee, acting as president from 1992–2005. He was awarded the OBE in the 2008 New Year Honours List. All of Gordon's English League clubs began with the letter 'B'.

MAIK TAYLOR is Blues' most capped player of all-time. A goalkeeper, born in Hildesheim, Germany on 4 September 1971, he began his career with ASC Neinburg before moving to Princess Marina College. He then played for Petersfield Town and Farnborough Town before joining Barnet in June 1995, switching to Southampton in January 1997 and then on to Fulham for £800,000. Ten months later, Cottagers' boss at the time, Kevin Keegan, rated him as the 'best taker of a cross in Britain'. Taylor helped the London club win the Second Division title in 1999 (when he also won his first cap for Northern Ireland against the country of his birth), take the First Division title in 2001 and a place in the Premier League to boot. After appearing in 232 games for Fulham, 6ft 4in Taylor was snapped up by Birmingham City in August 2003, initially on loan, before signing permanently for £1.5 million in January 2004. Since then he has produced a string of impressive performances, being chosen as the 'goalkeeper' for the Premier League team for 2003–04. A fine shot-stopper with good aerial ability, he was replaced as Blues' number one in February 2007 by Colin Doyle, but regained his place early in the

2007–08 Premier League season. With 83 Northern Ireland caps to his name, he has also played for his country's Under-21 and 'B' teams, and by May 2010 had amassed 238 appearances for Blues, whom he helped regain Premier League status in 2009.

MARTIN THOMAS was born on 28 November 1959 in the village of Senghenydd, Glamorgan. He joined Bristol Rovers as a youth player and after loan spells with Cardiff City, Tottenham Hotspur and Southend United, he moved to Newcastle United for £50,000 in 1983. While at St James' Park he won his first and only international cap for Wales in a European Championship qualifier against Finland. After another loan spell, this time with Middlesbrough, Martin was sold to Birmingham City for £75,000 in October 1988. Blues suffered relegation in 1989, but returned in 1992 when he played superbly well. However, in August 1994, having appeared in 176 games for Blues and after loan spells with Aston Villa and Crystal Palace, he joined Cheltenham Town, retiring in May 1995. Having earlier earned a preliminary coaching certificate with Newcastle he supplemented this with further coaching badges during his time at St Andrew's. He eventually gained a UEFA 'A' Coaching License, taking a position within the FA as a Regional Development Officer, based at Lilleshall, having previously coached at Norwich City, Swindon Town and Newcastle United. Working part-time, Thomas, with the assistance of other professional goalkeepers, including Steve Ogrizovic, Paul Barron and Andy Poole, helped train young up-and-coming players from the ages of 12 to 16 from various clubs across the Midlands, at a time when there were no qualified goalkeeping coaches around. In 1996, Thomas helped coach England's Under-16 'keepers before joining the FA full-time in 1997. Since then he has remained part of the England Youth coaching set-up, teaming up with former international Ray Clemence. Also part of the England Under-21 coaching staff which took the team to the semi-finals of Euro 2007, his current title is Assistant National Goalkeeping Coach.

COLIN TODD was involved in a British record transfer in February 1971 when he moved to Derby County from Sunderland for £180,000. A brilliant defender, he won two League titles with the Rams, forming a formidable partnership with Roy McFarland at both club and country level. Voted PFA Players' Player of the Year in 1975, Todd went on to appear in 371 games for Derby before moving to Everton in September 1978 for the unusual sum of £333,333.33. A year later he left Goodison Park for St Andrew's, signed by Jim Smith for £300,000, and over the next three seasons played in 108 games for Blues, helping them gain promotion in 1980. Sold to Nottingham Forest for £70,000 in August 1982, Todd went on to assist Oxford United,

Vancouver Whitecaps and Luton Town before retiring in 1984 with over 800 club appearances under his belt. He won 27 caps for England, starred in 14 Under-23 internationals and represented the Football League on three occasions. Entering football management with Whitley Bay in 1985, he then coached Middlesbrough for a year before taking over as boss at Ayresome Park in March 1990, succeeding Bruce Rioch. Leaving 'Boro in June 1991, he was out of the game until May 1992 when he was appointed as manager Rioch's assistant at Bolton, and when Rioch left to boss Arsenal, having achieved promotion in 1995, Todd stepped up to manager, recruiting his old buddy Roy McFarland as his running partner. Unfortunately Bolton struggled in the Premier League and as a result McFarland was dismissed early in 1996, leaving Todd in sole charge. Unable to prevent relegation, he nevertheless turned things round and gained promotion, only to slip back down in 1998. Despite this yo-yo situation, Todd remained loyal and led Bolton into the Play-off Final the following year, in which they lost to

Watford. He resigned seven games into the 1999–2000 season and, after a mini break, returned as manager of Swindon Town. He then resigned in November 2000 in order to return to Derby as assistant manager to his former Birmingham boss Jim Smith, and when Smith left in October 2001, Todd was promoted to manager, only to lose his job after just three months. Joining Bradford City in 2003 as assistant to manager Bryan Robson, he was upgraded when the former Manchester United skipper left in May 2004, making it the fourth time he had been promoted from assistant to manager. Battling on gamely, he became the longest-serving Bradford manager for 20 years before being sacked in February 2007, prior to the club's demotion to League Two. Remaining in football, Todd then took charge of the Danish side Randers FC in the summer of 2007, remaining in control until January 2009 when he decided to quit Scandinavian football. Four months later he 'joined' his 15th major League club when he was appointed manager of Darlington, staying until September 2009. Todd was born in Chester-le-Street, County Durham, on 12 December 1948. His son, Andy, has played as a defender for Middlesbrough, Swindon, Bolton, Charlton, Grimsby, Blackburn, Derby and Perth Glory in Australia.

DAN TREMELLING was born in Mansfield Woodhouse, Nottinghamshire, on 12 November 1897 and played initially as a full-back for his local team, Langwith Colliery Junction Wagon Works, before becoming a goalkeeper…taking over the job during an injury crisis! He did well, so much so that in August 1918 Lincoln City recruited him as a professional. He subsequently moved to Birmingham in May 1919 and went straight into the first team where he remained for 11 seasons, until Harry Hibbs took over in 1929–30.

Tremelling, who helped Blues win the Second Division title in 1921 and played for England against Wales in 1927, made 395 appearances in 13 years at St Andrew's before moving to Bury in May 1932. He returned to Birmingham as assistant trainer in June 1936, a position he held for five years. After retiring from football he went into the licensed trade. He died in Birmingham on 15 August 1970.

CYRIL TRIGG netted 72 goals in 291 appearances in senior competitions for Blues; he also scored 88 times in 95 wartime games. Twice leading scorer, firstly in 1946–47, despite playing a third of his matches at right-back, and secondly in 1950–51, he was by then exclusively a centre-forward. Born on 8 April 1917 in Measham, Leicestershire, he spent the whole of his League career – all 19 years – at St Andrew's, having joined the club as a junior from Bedworth Town in August 1935. World War Two began when he was 22 years old, so his time in football was severely disrupted by the conflict, as he served in the Royal Air Force in India and

FA Cup in 1946, it was not the same as competing in the Football League. In February 1948, having made 53 senior appearances for Blues, Turner moved to Southport as player-manager. Eight months later he took charge of Crewe Alexandra, where he stayed for three years before returning to Stoke in December 1951, as assistant to Bob McGrory, later working under Frank Taylor. In November 1954, Turner made it full circle back to St Andrew's when he replaced Bob Brocklebank as manager. Inheriting a fine set of players including Jeff Hall, Len Boyd, Roy Warhurst, Peter Murphy and Alex Govan, he quickly got the team playing as a unit. The Second Division Championship was won that season. In 1956, Turner guided the Blues to their highest-ever League finish – sixth place in the First Division – only four points behind runners-up Blackpool. He also took them into the FA Cup Final which Manchester City won 3–1 and soon afterwards became the first manager to take an English club side into a major European competition when Blues represented the City of Birmingham in the inaugural Inter-Cities Fairs Cup (May 1956). They went on to reach the semi-final stage before going out to the eventual winners Barcelona in a replay after a 4–4 aggregate draw. The following year Turner led Blues to the FA Cup semi-finals, only to lose to Manchester United's 'Busby Babes'. His record in the transfer market at St Andrew's was pretty sound. He signed England Under-23 international Dick Neal to replace Len Boyd, recruited two decent wingers in Harry Hooper and future England player Mike Hellawell, and gave professional contracts to Malcolm Beard and Colin Withers. In January 1958, the former Arsenal and Huddersfield player Pat Beasley joined Birmingham City. He believed he was moving in as Turner's assistant, but chairman Harry Morris announced to the

Burma and also played as a guest for Blackpool and Nottingham Forest. Trigg helped Blues win the Football League (South) title in 1946 and the Second Division Championship two years later, and he also played in the 1951 FA Cup semi-final. He moved to Stourbridge as player-coach in May 1954 and retired in May 1957. He died in Birmingham a day after his 76th birthday in 1993.

ARTHUR TURNER was born in Chesterton, Staffordshire, on 1 April 1909 and was an amateur with West Bromwich Albion before joining Stoke City in 1930. A strong defensive half-back, good in the air and on the ground, he won a Second Division Championship medal with the Potters in 1933 and appeared in over 300 games for the club before transferring to Birmingham for £6,000 in January 1939. Unfortunately, Blues were relegated at the end of that season and with war imminent, Turner's career suffered as a result. He was 30 when fighting broke out and although he played in 186 games during the hostilities, captaining the side to the League (South) Championship and to the semi-finals of the

press that he was to be appointed joint-manager. Turner, who found out about this arrangement not from the club but from the press, was not happy and threatened to resign, but was persuaded to stay 'for the time being', eventually quitting in September 1958. After that disappointing end to a fine spell with Blues, Turner took over as manager of Headington United (now Oxford United) in 1959. And not long after that, First Division Leeds United approached him to become their new boss. He turned the Yorkshire club down after Oxford's directors matched Leeds' salary offer. In those days there was no automatic promotion into the Football League (clubs had to be elected) and with some fine players at the club including the Atkinson brothers, Graham and Ron, Cyril Beavon and Maurice Kyle, Oxford were elected to the Fourth Division in 1962 in place of Accrington Stanley, who went bankrupt. Two years later Turner's team knocked Blackburn Rovers out of the FA Cup, becoming the first Fourth Division side to reach the quarter-finals of the competition. In 1964–65, Turner took the U's to promotion and three years later the Third Division Championship came to the Manor Ground. After a few seasons of mixed fortunes he went upstairs, taking over as Oxford's general manager in April 1969, leaving future Blues boss Ron Saunders to run the team. However, in February 1972 Turner was surprisingly dismissed when the club admitted they were unable to afford to keep him in post. Remaining in the game well into the 1980s, he was engaged as a scout by both Rotherham United and Sheffield Wednesday. He died in Sheffield on 12 January 1994, aged 84. (See also managers).

PAT VAN DEN HAUWE was a hard-tackling full-back with a vigorous and combative attitude. Nicknamed 'Toughie',

between July 1977 and September 1984, he made 143 appearances for Blues (scoring one goal). Born to an English father, René (who kept goal for Belgium) and a Welsh mother, in Dendermonde, Belgium on 16 December 1960, he came to England with his family at an early age and, after gaining UK citizenship, he qualified to play for any of the four home countries, eventually choosing Wales, for whom he gained 13 full caps in the 1980s. On leaving St Andrew's, Van den Hauwe joined Everton for £100,000, and in August 1989 moved to Tottenham Hotspur for £575,000, later assisting Millwall and Notts County before retiring in 1999. He won the First Division title twice, the European Cup-winners' Cup once and played in two losing FA Cup Finals while at Goodison Park and, as a Spurs player, won the FA Cup in 1991.

JOHNNY VINCENT was born in West Bromwich on 8 February 1947. An attacking midfielder or inside-forward, he scored 59 goals in almost 300 League appearances while playing for Birmingham City, Middlesbrough and Cardiff City. He then assisted Atherstone Town before ending his

career in America with the Connecticut Bicentennials, retiring in September 1978. He joined Blues straight from school, turned professional in February 1964 and made his first-team debut the very next month – the first of 194 outings for the club (44 goals scored). Vincent's style of play was elegant; he was consistent, a fine passer of the ball, was a strong and thrustful runner and possessed a stinging right-foot shot. He remained first choice under manager Stan Cullis, but when Freddie Goodwin took over he was traded in for the more physical approach of Middlesbrough's George Smith, both players being valued at £40,000, the deal going through in March 1971. Vincent spent one season at Ayresome Park, followed by three years with Cardiff City, before returning to the Midlands with Atherstone Town. In all he was in football for 13 years and on retiring ran a pub in Northfield, Birmingham and later in Oldbury and Warley. He died of cancer in a nursing home in Kidderminster, Worcestershire, on 23 December 2006, aged 59.

GEOFF VOWDEN was the first substitute in League football to come on and score a hat-trick – doing so for Blues against Huddersfield Town in a Second Division match at St Andrew's in September 1968. Born in Barnsley on 27 April 1941 and raised in Jersey, Vowden was 17 when he came over to England to join Nottingham Forest. He signed professional forms in January 1960 and went on to net 40 goals in 90 games for the Reds before being sold to Birmingham City for £25,000 in October 1964. He spent seven seasons with Blues and scored at a rate of a goal every three games, finishing as top marksman three seasons running: 1964–67. In March 1971, Vowden joined arch-rivals Aston Villa for £12,500 and in his first full season at Villa Park contributed 11 goals towards winning the Third Division title. In June 1974,

Vowden signed for New York Cosmos in the NASL and on his return to England later in the year he joined Kettering Town as player/assistant manager under Ron Atkinson, whom he succeeded as manager at the end of the year. He later coached domestically and also in Saudi Arabia before taking over as reserve-team manager at Sheffield United in 1980–81.

BILLY WALTON was born in Hockley Brook, Birmingham on 6 August 1871 and followed Small Heath from a young age, attending the 1886 FA Cup semi-final against West Bromwich Albion, who won 4–0. On leaving school he trained to be a silversmith in the jewellery quarter and remained employed in that trade while playing initially as a part-time inside-forward and later as a wing-half for Blues, whom he served for 15 years, from August 1888 until May 1903. Skilful, easy-moving and a powerful shooter, he helped win the Second Division Championship in 1892–93, gain promotion the following season and the same in 1901. Walton scored 70 goals in 232 senior appearances for Blues before leaving to join Dudley. The way he nurtured the younger players at the club earned him the nickname 'Mother.' Indeed, his support for Birmingham was life-long. He was a guest of the club for the official opening of St Andrew's on Boxing Day 1906 and, in fact, he helped clear snow from pitch and terraces so that the match against Middlesbrough could go ahead. He attended both of the FA Cup Finals involving Blues (in 1931 and 1956) and was a keen visitor to St Andrew's right up until his death in Dudley Road Hospital, Winson Green, on 10 February 1963 at the age of 91.

ROY WARHURST, a canny Yorkshireman, was born in Handsworth, Sheffield, on 18 September 1926. He started his career as a winger before developing into a stocky wing-half with a bone-crunching tackle. Totally committed, he gave nothing less than 100 per cent each and every time he took the field and, above all, was a down-to-earth character, a big hit with the fans and players who simply loved and enjoyed football. Warhurst was an amateur with Huddersfield Town before making 17 appearances for Sheffield United, whom he

joined in May 1944. He switched his allegiance to St Andrew's in March 1950, Blues paying just £8,000 for his signature, and he became the 10th player to be used by the club in the left-half position that season. Playing in the reserves for most of 1950–51, he became a first-team regular in September 1951 and never looked back. He was superb when Blues won the Second Division Championship in 1954–55 and the following season, after helping the team reach the FA Cup Final, he sadly missed the big day through injury. After scoring 10 goals in 239 appearances for Blues, it came as a surprise to several people when iron-man Warhurst was transferred to Manchester City in June 1957 for £10,000. He spent almost two years at Maine Road before moving to Crewe Alexandra, later serving with Oldham Athletic and Banbury Spencer before retiring in May 1964. Warhurst worked as a scrap metal dealer in Lichfield for many years afterwards.

JEFF WEALANDS was born in Darlington on 25 August 1951 and played for Star Juniors and Darlington Cleveland Bridge before turning professional with Wolverhampton Wanderers in 1968. Unable to break into the first team at Molineux, and following a loan spell with Northampton Town, he moved to his home town club, Darlington, in 1979, transferring to Hull City in 1972 and onto Birmingham City for £30,000 in July 1979. Blues won promotion to the top flight in his first season at St Andrew's, Wealands keeping 16 clean sheets and being voted 'Player of the Year.' He went on to appear in 119 games for the club before a difference of views with new manager Ron Saunders saw him dropped. Subsequently loaned out to Manchester United as cover for Gary Bailey, a recurring back injury restricted his chances at Old Trafford and, after further loan spells with Oldham Athletic and

Preston North End, he entered non-League football with Altrincham. Success came quickly as the minnows who knocked his former club Blues out of the FA Cup in 1986 also won the FA Trophy at Wembley. The following season he played in the Final of the Cheshire Senior Cup before joining Barrow, returning to Altrincham in 1988. He appeared in 273 games for the non-League club, his last at the age of 41. After retiring, Wealands served briefly on the board of directors of Altrincham and is now helping to coach goalkeepers at Bury. He now runs a property development company in Altrincham.

FRED WHELDON was born in Langley Green, Oldbury, on 1 November 1869. The youngest of 10 children, he was an extremely talented inside-left who played for Langley Green Victoria before joining Small Heath (Birmingham) in February 1890. A star in the Football Alliance, in which he scored virtually a goal a game, Wheldon was then a key member of the team that won the Second Division title in

1893, top-scoring with 25 goals. He continued to hit the target and finished with a Blues' record of 113 goals in 175 appearances before transferring to Aston Villa for £350 in June 1896. Instrumental in helping Villa complete the League and FA Cup double in 1897, he won the first of four full caps for England against Ireland in February of that year before collecting his second League Championship-winners' medal in 1899. After striking 74 goals in 140 games for Villa, he left to join West Bromwich Albion in August 1900, switching to Queen's Park Rangers a year later before winding down his career with Portsmouth and Worcester City, retiring in January 1907. Besides being a superb footballer, Wheldon was also a very capable cricketer. Between 1899 and 1906 he amassed 4,938 runs in 138 matches for Worcestershire for an average of 22.54. He also hit three centuries and took 95 catches. After ending his sporting career, Wheldon ran a public house in Worcester where he died on 13 January 1924.

WALTER WIGMORE was born in the Gloucestershire village of Pucklechurch on 25 February 1873, but as a child moved with his family to Kiveton Park, South Yorkshire. He played his early football with Worksop Town before joining Gainsborough Trinity in 1896, where he struck up an excellent strike partnership with future Blues player Bob McRoberts, and in March 1899 Birmingham paid £180 to reunite him with McRoberts. Tried at centre-half when Alex Leake was injured, Wigmore impressed so much that for nine years he remained first choice in that position, making the last of his 355 appearances for the club shortly before his 39th birthday. He also scored 25 goals – not bad for a defender – twice helped Blues gain promotion to the First Division, in 1901 and 1903, and played for the Players' Union

XI and the Football League. Often penalised for dangerous play due to his unusual reluctance to head the ball, preferring to use his feet, however high the ball came to him, Wigmore left St Andrew's in August 1912 for Brierley Hill Alliance, retiring in May 1913. He returned to Worksop soon afterwards and was only 58 when he died there on 8 September 1931.

JIMMY WINDRIDGE was born deep in Blues' terrority in Small Heath on 21 October 1882. He joined Blues in 1899 (from Small Heath Alma) and made the first of his 61 senior appearances in 1903, the year the club was promoted to the First Division. In April 1905 Windridge became one of the first players to join the newly-formed Chelsea club, signed for £190 along with teammates Jimmy Robertson and Bob McRoberts. His impact was immediate, scoring a hat-trick on his home debut against Blackpool, the first competitive football match ever played at Stamford Bridge. Later overshadowed by more high-profile forwards such as George Hilsdon and Vivian Woodward, he moved to Middlesbrough in 1911 and returned to Birmingham for a second spell in 1914, going on to equal the club's record of scoring five goals in a League match v Glossop in 1915. An England international, capped eight times, he scored in six consecutive matches for his country, including all four matches during the country's first overseas tour. Besides his football ability, Windridge also played cricket for Warwickshire, scoring 161 runs for an average of 14.64. The cousin of fellow England international and former Blues defender Alex Leake, Windridge died in Small Heath on 23 September 1939.

FRANK WOMACK, who began his professional career in July 1908 when he joined Birmingham from Rawmarsh Albion,

having previously played for Lapham Street FC, made the first of 515 appearances for Blues in September 1908 against Gainsborough Trinity. Out of that figure, 491 came in the Football League – a club record that still stands. He also played in 92 World War One fixtures, bringing his overall tally of first-team outings to 607, and only goalkeeper Gil Merrick has made more. Womack, suitably proportioned for a full-back, was a stern tackler and strong kicker, well-liked by all and a tremendous club man. He spent virtually all of his playing career at St Andrew's, never signing a contract, and was club captain for 16 years from 1912 to 1928. During his time at the club, Blues twice finished third in the Second Division (1913 and 1920) before winning the Championship in 1921. On par for ability with Jesse Pennington of West Bromwich Albion, Womack was an England international trialist (playing in three games); he also represented the Football League and at 39 years and 207 days he is the second oldest player ever to appear at senior level for Blues (behind Dennis Jennings). On leaving St Andrew's in May 1928, he joined

Worcester City as player-manager and in his first season at St George's Lane, Womack guided City to the Birmingham League title and into the first round of the FA Cup. Surprisingly, he returned to League football at the end of that season, joining Torquay United, for whom he played a further 20 games before retiring in July 1930. At that juncture he took over from Albert Hoskins as manager at Plainmoor, staying there until May 1932 when he was appointed boss of Grimsby Town, just after the Mariners had been relegated from the First Division. While in charge at Blundell Park, he guided his team to promotion to the First Division as champions and also to an all-time highest League placing of fifth in 1935 and an FA Cup semi-final the following year. In October 1936, Womack was on the move again, this time to Leicester City as manager. He turned things round at Filbert Street as City won the Second Division title and promotion. However, he resigned following the Foxes' relegation in May 1939. Just before World War Two was declared, the local Leicester newspapers published articles that claimed that Womack had several thousand pounds available to spend on players. He strongly disputed this and referred all enquirers to his board of directors. As a direct result, he resigned and moved to Fleetwood, Lancashire, in April 1940. Returning to management in July 1942 when he took over at Notts County, he left Meadow Lane early in 1945 to become Oldham Athletic's new manager (February), but resigned in April 1947 after the Latics had struggled in the first post-war season. Womack then chose to return to Grimsby as guest manager in January 1951, staying for five months while number one boss Charlie Spencer was recovering from an illness. He left in May 1951, after Grimsby's relegation. Womack was born in Wortley near Stannington, Sheffield, on 16 September 1888 and died at Caistor-on-Sea, Norfolk, on 8 October 1968. In November 1913, Womack was involved in a bribery scandal. He was approached by a man who offered him 55 guineas to fix the result of a League game between Birmingham and Grimsby Town. The necessary authorities were informed, a trap was set, the culprit duly arrested and at the next local Assize Court he was sentenced to six months in prison. Grimsby won the game 2–1.

FRANK WORTHINGTON was born in Halifax on 23 November 1948 and as a 15-year-old, just before signing for Huddersfield Town as an apprentice, he was ready to sign for Liverpool, but his medical test revealed he had high blood pressure, so Bill Shankly called the deal off. But Liverpool's loss was certainly someone else's gain, as Worthington went on to have a brilliant career as a professional footballer. He spent eight years with Huddersfield before transferring to Leicester City in 1972 to begin his trek around the country as a soccer nomad. In 1977 he switched to Bolton Wanderers and after a spell in the NASL with Philadelphia Fury he joined Birmingham City in November 1979 for £150,000. After scoring 33 goals in 88 appearances for Blues, whom he helped gain promotion to the First Division, he had a second spell in the NASL, this time with Tampa Bay Rowdies before transferring to Leeds United, later assisting Southampton, Brighton & Hove Albion, Tranmere Rovers, Preston North End, Stockport County, Cape Town Spurs (South Africa), Chorley, Stalybridge Celtic, Galway United, Weymouth, Radcliffe Borough, Guiseley, Hinckley Town (as player-manager-coach), Cemaes Bay, Halifax Town (player-coach) and finally Swindon Town (coach, December 1993–May 1994). Worthington, an avid Elvis Presley fan, played eight times for England at senior level and twice for the Under-23s, and he also represented the Football League. His career

(in this country and abroad) brought him 286 goals in 905 appearances (236 coming in 757 Football League games). He had his best years with Leicester (72 goals in 210 outings) and actually scored in each of 22 consecutive League seasons (1966 to 1988 inclusive). One can only speculate what he might have achieved if he had joined Liverpool instead of Huddersfield all those years ago!

RON WYLIE was an exceptionally fine inside-forward who later became a quality wing-half. He made his name at Notts County where he played (partly under the leadership of the former Aston Villa player Eric Houghton) for 10 years, making 238 appearances and netting 39 goals before transferring to Villa Park for £9,250 in November 1958. Always regarded as the main schemer in the side, he scored 26 goals in 244 games and helped Villa win the Second Division Championship and promotion to the First Division in 1959–60 and lift the League Cup a year later, as well as being voted 'Midland Footballer of the Year' in 1965. Highly regarded by the fans, Wylie played twice for Scotland as a schoolboy but never gained a full cap, due perhaps to the abundance of quality midfielders available at the time. Transferred to Birmingham City at the start of the 1965–66 season, he stayed at St Andrew's for five years, adding another 149 appearances (and two goals) to his tally, playing in two losing semi-finals (the 1967 League Cup and the 1968 FA Cup). Retiring in May 1970, Wylie remained with Blues as the club's Public Relations Officer for a month before becoming coach at Villa Park (1970–72) and then taking a similar role with Coventry City, where he also acted as assistant-manager. Thereafter he held an advisory post in Cyprus and Bulova (Hong Kong) before returning to England as manager of West Bromwich Albion in July 1982. He failed to do the business at the Hawthorns and left in February 1984, replaced by Johnny Giles. He returned to Villa Park to take charge of the reserve team, later working as a scout (1987–90) before rejoining Villa once again, this time as Community Liaison Officer, a post he held until he quit football in May 2003. Wylie, who was born in Kelvin, Glasgow, on 6 August 1933, played for Clydesdale Juniors before joining Notts County.

...AND THE OTHER PLAYERS' RECORDS

Key to text:

Positions: G (goalkeeper), RB (right-back), LB (left-back), FB (full-back), D (defender), CH (centre-half), WH (wing-half), HB (half-back), M (midfield), OR (outside-right), OL (outside-left), (W) winger, IF (inside-forward), F (forward) CF (centre-forward), S (striker), U (utility).

Record with Blues (all senior competitive games): i.e. 124 apps/2 goals. Apps include those made as a substitute.
Club with the letter (l) after its name: player signed on loan
Club with (NL) after name: non-League
From: the club from which the player was signed and the year (not season)
To: the club to which the player moved when leaving Blues (or his next club)

Player	Position	Record	From	To
GARY ABLETT	D	124/2	Everton 1996	Blackpool 2000
			won the FA Cup with both Everton and Liverpool	
RICHARD ADAMS	IF	2	Calthorpe 1887	Calthorpe 1888
DELE ADEBOLA	S	152/41	Crewe Alexandra 1998	Crystal Palace 2002
			had scored over 150 goals in more than 600 club appearances at 2010	
GEORGE ADEY	U	79/2	Stourbridge 1898	Kettering Town 1902
JIM ADLINGTON	W	6/4	Ironbridge 1895	Berwick Rangers (NL) 1896
KEMY AUGUSTIEN	M	20	AZ Alkmaar (Holland L) 2008	AZ Alkmaar 2008
ALAN AINSCOW	M	125/22	Blackpool 1971	Everton 1981
FRED ALLEN	OR	3	Spring Hill Methodists 1890	Lea Bank 1892
GARY ALLEN	F	1	Hillingdon Boys 1971	Wimbledon 1975
GEORGE ALLEN	FB	165	Coventry City 1952	Torquay United 1962
SONE ALUKO	S	1	School 2004	Aberdeen 2009
			played for England at Under-18/19 levels before winning a full cap for Nigeria (v. Eire) in 2009	
GEOFF ANDERSON	OR	1	Ramsgate 1962	Mansfield Town 1964
GEORGE ANDERSON	OL	80/10	Sunderland Royal Rovers 1905	Brentford 1909
DARREN ANDERTON	F	24/3	Tottenham Hotspur 2004	Wolverhampton W. 2005
KEN ARMSTRONG	D	69/1	Southampton 1984	Walsall 1986
			broke his ankle in his first training session with Walsall and never played again	
KEVIN ASHLEY	FB	62/1	School 1984	Wolves 1990
ELIAS ASHURST	FB	70/1	Stanley United 1922	Retired
			brother Bill played for England.	
JACK ASTON	IF	61/22	Woolwich Arsenal 1900	Doncaster Rovers 1902
PETER ATHERTON	F	13	Bradford City (l) 2001	Bradford City 2001
ARTHUR ATKINS	D	105	Paget Rangers 1948	Shrewsbury Town 1954
IAN ATKINS	M	117/9	Ipswich Town 1988	Colchester United 1990
			made over 550 League appearances during his career	
WALTER AVEYARD	CF	7/3	Sheffield Wednesday 1947	Port Vale 1948
TREVOR AYLOTT	F	31/1	Bournemouth 1990	Oxford United 1991
			netted over 100 goals in 500+ club appearances (1975–93)	
DENNIS BAILEY	S	93/25	Crystal Palace 1989	Queen's Park Rangers 1991

Player	Position	Record	From	To
EDWARD BAILEY	LB	1	Falling Heath Rangers 1882	Aston Unity 1884
HORACE BAILEY	G	53	Derby County 1910	Retired 1913
			conceded 12 goals playing for Leicester Fosse v Nottingham Forest in 1908	
ARKADIUSZ BAK	M	5	Polonia Warsaw (l) 2001	Polonia Warsaw 2001
JACK BALLANTYNE	OR	21/2	Vale of Leven 1913	Vale of Leven 1915
FRANCIS BANKS	G	3	All Saints 1889	Warwick County 1890
FRED BANKS	OL	1	Myrtle Villa 1909	Stourbridge 1910
KEITH BANNISTER	HB	27	Sheffield United 1950	King's Lynn 1954
ERIC BARBER	F	6/2	Shelbourne 1966	Chicago Spurs (USA) 1967
			won both League and Cup medals in Ireland	
FRED BARBER	G	1	Luton Town 1996	Retired 1996
FRED BARLOW	FB	3	Wednesbury Old Athletic	1885 Aston Villa 1887
RAY BARLOW	LH	7	West Brom Albion 1960	Stourbridge 1961
			made almost 500 appearances in 16 years with West Bromwich Albion	
PAUL BARNES	F	15/7	York City 1996	Burnley 1996
STEVE BARNES	W	5	Welling United 1995	Harlesden 1996
DAVE BARNETT	D	59	Barnet 1993	Dunfermline Athletic 1996
JIM BARRETT	IF	13/5	Nottingham Forest 1959	West Ham United 1960
JOE BARRETT	OR	31/1	Leicester City 1917	Southampton 1918
(2 spells)			Southampton 1922	Pontypridd 1923
STEW BARROWCLOUGH	OR	30/2	Newcastle United 1978	Bristol Rovers 1979
ARCHIE BARTON	FB	1	Coles Farm Unity 1889	Kings Heath Comrades 1890
JONATHAN BASS	FB	80	School 1992	Hartlepool United 2001
HARRY BATES	OR	3	Coventry City 1912	Walsall 1913
SAM BAYLEY	F	1/1	Leamington 1899	Leamington 1899
TOM BAYLEY	FB	69	Walsall Town Swifts 1890	Walsall Town Swifts 1893
JACK BEATTIE	IF	36/9	Blackburn Rovers 1937	Huddersfield Town 1938
JASON BECKFORD	F	8/1	Manchester City 1992	Stoke City 1994
BILLY BEEL	G	1	Shrewsbury Town 1965	Shifnal Town 1965
			conceded five goals on his League debut for Blues v Blackburn in 1965	
BILLY BEER	WH/F	250/35	Sheffield United 1902	Retired 1910
(See also managers)				
DOUGIE BELL	M	22	Shrewsbury Town 1989	Partick Thistle 1991
			gained three League and two Scottish Cup-winners' medals with Aberdeen	
SAM BELLAMY	RB	1	St Andrew's OSL 1937	Tamworth 1947
NICKLAS BENDTNER	S	48/13	Arsenal (l) 2006	Arsenal 2007
			played for Denmark in the 2010 World Cup	
CHRISTIAN BENITEZ	F)	36/4	Santo Laguna (Mexico, l) 2009	Santo Laguna 2010
BILLY BENNETT	OR	76/13	Crewe Alexandra 1896	Stafford Rangers 1901
IAN BENNETT	G	354	Peterborough United 1993	Leeds United 2005
			kept 27 clean sheets, 10 in succession, in 62 first-team games for Blues in 1994–95.	
MARCUS BENT	S	35/3	Wigan Athletic 2008	Still with club
JOHNNY BERRY	OR	114/6	Aldershot YMCA 1944	Manchester United 1951
			was badly injured in the Munich air crash in 1958	
KEITH BERTSCHIN	S	141/41	Ipswich Town 1977	Norwich City 1981
			scored with his first kick in League football for Ipswich v Arsenal in 1976	
BILLY BIDMEAD	LB	3	Brierley Hill Alliance 1903	Leighton FC 1906
JOE BIRCH	RB	1	Hednesford Town 1928	Bournemouth 1929
ADRIAN BIRD	CH	32/1	Boco Juniors 1985	Moor Green 1990
JACK BIRD	RH	1	Rowley United 1902	Walsall 1906
MATT BIRLEY	W	3	School 2003	Lincoln City 2006

Player	Position	Record	From	To
SIMON BLACK	F	4	School 1991	Doncaster Rovers 1996
RICHIE BLACKMORE	G	1	Bristol City 1971	Dundalk 1974
			helped Dundalk win three League titles and three Irish Cup Finals	
ANTHONY BLAKE	LB	2	Rubery Owen FC 1948	Gillingham 1952
NOEL BLAKE	CH	96/5	Aston Villa 1982	Portsmouth 1984
ROBBIE BLAKE	F	13/2	Burnley 2005	Leeds United 2005
ALBERT BLOXHAM	D	3	Torquay United 1926	Rhyl Athletic 1928
EDGAR BLUFF	IF	9/1	Sheffield United 1907	St Helens Town 1908
BILL BLYTH	U	21/4	Arsenal 1929	Retired 1931
			captained Arsenal in their 1927 FA Cup Final defeat by Cardiff City	
JIM BLYTH	G	16	Coventry City 1982	Nuneaton Borough 1985
JOHN BODENHAM	G	2	Aston Manor 1881	Birmingham Excelsior 1883
MICK BODLEY	D	3	Southend United (l) 1995	Southend United 1995
BENNY BOND	IF	85/13	Coseley 1926	Retired 1932
BOB BONTHRON	RB	12/1	Northampton Town 1910	Leith Athletic 1911
BOB BOOTH	WH	8/1	Blackpool 1920	Southend United 1922
HAROLD BOOTON	RB	163/2	Shirebrook 1929	Luton Town 1936
CHARLIE BOSBURY	OR	15	Southampton 1922	Preston North End 1925
HAMEUR BOUAZZA	W	16/1	Charlton Athletic (l) 2009	Charlton Athletic 2009
FRED BOWDEN	OL	1	Cradley Heath 1925	Kidderminster Harriers 1927
JASON BOWEN	F	65/11	Swansea City 1995	Reading 1997
KEITH BOWKER	U	23/5	School 1966	Exeter City 1973
ARTHUR BOX	G	29	Stoke 1909	Leek Victoria 1910
BILL BRADBURY	IF	3/2	Coventry City 1954	Hull City 1955
LEE BRADBURY	S	9	Crystal Palace (l) 1999	Crystal Palace 1999
BJORN BRAGSTAD	D	3	Derby County (l) 2001	Derby County 2001
COLIN BRAZIER	U	19/1	Jacksonville Teamen (1982)	AP Leamington 1983
GARY BREEN	D	45/2	Peterborough United 1996	Coventry City 1997
DES BREMNER	M	193/3	Aston Villa 1984	Fulham 1989
KEVIN BREMNER	F	4/1	Colchester United (l) 1982	Colchester United 1982
			played for five League clubs in 1982–83 (a record)	
BOBBY BRENNAN	OL	40/7	Luton Town 1949	Fulham 1953
MALCOLM BRIGGS	F	1	School 1977	Durham City 1980
			played only three minutes of first-team football for Blues (v. Manchester City in 1979)	
TOMMY BRIGGS	CF	52/23	Coventry City 1951	Blackburn Rovers 1952
			scored 286 goals in 390 League games during his career	
KEVAN BROADHURST	U	173/10	Bradford City (T) 1975	Walsall (L, retired) 1986
'BUD' BROCKEN	OR	19	SV Willem II (Holland) 1982	FC Groningen (Holland) 1982
			made over 500 League appearances in Dutch football	
IAN BROWN	W	1	Luton Town 1984	Felixstowe 1986
JACKIE BROWN	OR	38/7	Coventry City 1938	Barry Town (1948)
KEN BROWN	D	12	West Ham United 1996	Millwall 1997
WALTER BROWN	IF	2	Bloxwich 1891	Wednesbury Old Athletic 1892
ALEX BRUCE	D	12	Blackburn Rovers 2005	Ipswich Town 2006
DANNY BRUCE	F	10/2	Notts County 1895	Perth (Scotland) 1896
HARRY BRUCE	FB	8	Bishop Auckland 1925	Gillingham 1928
TED BRUETON	G	1	Stafford Rangers 1894	Willenhall Swifts 1894
NORMAN BRUNSKILL	WH	65/2	Oldham Athletic 1936	Barnsley 1938
STEVE BRYANT	LB	42/1	School 1970	Northampton Town 1976
ALAN BUCKLEY	F	29/8	Walsall 1979	Walsall 1979
			went on to manage Walsall, Grimsby Town (three spells), West Bromwich Albion and Lincoln City	

Player	Position	Record	From	To
FRANK BUCKLEY	D	56/4	Manchester City 1909	Derby County 1911
			was a Major with the Middlesex Regiment during World War One and	
				went on to manage six League clubs
GARY BULL	F	22/8	Nottingham Forest (l) 1994	Nottingham Forest 1995
(2 spells)			Brighton & Hove Albion 1995	York City 1996
MICKEY BULLOCK	CF	31/11	School 1962	Oxford United 1967
PETER BULLOCK	IF	28/3	Stoke City 1962	Southend United 1965
			the Bullock brothers (Michael & Peter) were together at Blues from 1962–65	
JIM BUMPHREY	WH	143/6	Ashington Alliance 1908	Durham City 1915
WALTER BUNCH	LB	3	Walsall 1901	Retired 1902
MARK BURCHILL	S	17/5	Celtic (l) 2000	Celtic 2000
LOL BURKINSHAW	OR	75/12	Stalybridge Celtic 1919	Halifax Town 1922
DAVID BURROWS	LB	30	Coventry City 2000	Sheffield Wednesday 2002
TED BURTON	CF	1	Highfield Villa 1891	Springfield Villa 1892
JACK BURTON	IL	4/3	West Ham United 1909	Cardiff City 1910
MICK BURTON	W	4	School 1986	Sheffield Wednesday 1991
HERBERT BUTLER	CH	11	Bestwood Colliery 1933	Crewe Alexandra 1939
NICKY BUTT	M	29/3	Newcastle United (l) 2005	Newcastle United 2006
JIMMY BYE	D	2	Shirley Juniors 1937	Retired 1944
JIMMY CALDERWOOD	U	159/5	Glasgow Amateurs 19781	SV Willem II (Holland) 1980
				spent 13 years in Dutch football (1980–93)
CHARLIE CALLADINE	WH	127/4	Scunthorpe United 1930	Blackburn Rovers 1936
EDDIE CAMERON	IF	6/1	Clydebank 1921	Walsall 1922
ALAN CAMPBELL	M	209/14	Charlton Athletic 1970	Cardiff City 1976
'D.J.' CAMPBELL	S	50/12	Brentford 2005	Leicester City 2007
STUART CAMPBELL	M	2	Leicester City (l) 2000	Leicester City 2000
TOMMY CAPEL	IF	8/1	Chesterfield 1949	Nottingham Forest 1949
DEREK CARR	U	4	Lockheed Leamington 1947	Rugby Town 1950
STEPHEN CARR	RB	53	Newcastle United 2009	Still with club
BILL CARRIER	RB	7	Non-League 1909	Worcester City 1912
MICHAEL CARRICK	M	2	West Ham United (l) 2000	West Ham United 2000
			was a member of England's 2010 World Cup squad	
FRANK CARRODUS	M)	9	Wrexham 1982	Bury 1983
TOMMY CARROLL	RB	47	Ipswich Town 1971	Retired 1973
LEE CARSLEY	M	53/3	Everton 2008	Coventry City 2010
DARREN CARTER	M	53/5	School 1999	West Brom Albion 2005
TIM CARTER	G	3	Sunderland (l) 1991	Sunderland 1991
FRED CASTLE	CF	3	Smethwick Highfield 1925	Shrewsbury Town 1927
STEVE CASTLE	M	38/2	Plymouth Argyle 1995	Peterborough United 1997
			career realised almost 600 club appearances and 123 goals	
BOB CATLIN	G	8	Notts County (l) 1993	Notts County 1993
ALF CHAPLIN	HB	4	Coventry City 1903	Woolwich Arsenal 1905
			once scored 24 goals in one match for St Paul's FC	
FRED CHAPPLE	IF	53/16	Aston Villa 1908	Crewe Alexandra 1910
KEN CHARLERY	S	24/6	Peterborough United 1995	Peterborough United 1996
GARY CHARLES	FB	3	West Ham United (l) 2000	West Ham United 2000
SIMON CHARLTON	FB	78	Southampton 1997	Bolton Wanderers 2000
CHRIS CHARSLEY	G	88	Stafford Rangers 1886	West Brom Albion 1894
(Had three separate spells with club in five years)				
			was Chief Constable of Coventry (1899–1918)	
WALTER CHARSLEY	WH	3	Harborne 1890	Edgbaston Royal 1891

Player	Position	Record	From	To
JOHN CHEESEWRIGHT	G	2	Kingsbury Town 1991	Dagenham & Redbridge 1992
GARY CHILDS	M	62/2	Walsall 1987	Grimsby Town 1989
ALIOU CISSE	M	38	Montpellier Herault (France) 2002	Portsmouth 2004
FRANK CLACK	G	66	Witney Town 1932	Brentford 1939
JAMIE CLAPHAM	LB	97/1	Ipswich Town 2003	Wolverhampton W. 2006
STEVE CLARIDGE	F	120/42	Cambridge United 1994	Leicester City 1996
			played his 1,000th competitive football match for Bournemouth v Port Vale	
			in December 2000. Appeared for 20 different clubs between 1982 and 2007	
WALLACE CLARKE	OL	32	Leeds United 1923	Coventry City 1924
ALBERT CLARKE	IF	31/9	Torquay United 1936	Blackburn Rovers 1938
DENNIS CLARKE	FB	21	Huddersfield Town 1973	Retired 1975
			was the first-ever substitute to play in an FA Cup Final	
			(for West Bromwich Albion in 1968).	
EDWARD CLARKE	LB	1	School 1889	Ward End Unity 1890
EDWARD. O. CLARKE	G	1	Harborne 1884	Knowle 1885
WAYNE CLARKE	S	105/43	Wolverhampton W. 1984	Everton 1987
			was one of five brothers who all played League football	
HARRY CLAYTON	IF	2	Calthorpe 1883	Birmingham CFC 1884
STEPHEN CLEMENCE	M	135/9	Tottenham Hotspur 2003	Leicester City 2007
HARRY CLUTTERBUCK	G	2	Hereford Thistle 1897	Queen's Park Rangers 1899
JIMMY COCHRANE	IR	3/1	School 1951	Walsall 1958
ANDY COLE	S	5/1	Portsmouth (l) 2007	Portsmouth 2007
			scored almost 300 goals (290 in League/Premier League) in almost 700 competitive	
			games in his 20-year-plus career; gained a First Division, five Premier League, two FA Cup,	
			League Cup and UEFA Cup-winners' medals with Manchester United (1995–2001)	
SAM COLE	CF	1	Smethwick Centaur 1898	Harborne 1900
FERDINAND COLY	RB	2	RC Lens (France, L) 1999	RC Lens 2000
			won 23 caps for Senegal	
JIMMY CONLIN	OL	23/2	Manchester City 1911	Airdrieonians 1912
JOHN CONNOLLY	OL	63/9	Everton 1976	Newcastle United 1978
RICHARD COOKE	W	5	Tottenham Hotspur (l) 1986	Tottenham Hotspur 1986
TERRY COOKE	F	4	Manchester United (l) 1996	Manchester United 1996
GARY COOPER	M	83/4	Peterborough United 1993	Welling United 1996
MARK COOPER	M	44/9	Southend United 1991	Liverpool (trial) 1992
			is the son of the former Blues' manager Terry Cooper	
PAUL COOPER	G	26	Sutton Coldfield Town 1971	Ipswich Town 1974
			made over 550 club appearances during his career, saving 16 penalties	
WALLY CORBETT	FB	48	Aston Villa 1907	Wellington Town 1911
			won a soccer gold medal for Great Britain at the 1908 Olympics	
FRANCIS CORNAN	LH	61/1	Barnsley 1905	Aston Villa 1908
JOHN CORNFORTH	M	8	Swansea City 1996	Wycombe Wanderers 1996
CARLOS COSTLY	S	8	GKS Belchatow (Honduras, L) 2009	GKS Belchatow 2009
TONY COTON	G	114	Mile Oak Rovers 1977	Watford 1984
			saved a first-half penalty on his League debut for Blues v Sunderland in 1980	
TONY COTTEE	S	5/1	Leicester City (l) 1997	Leicester City 1997
			scored 306 goals in 735 club appearances during his 21-year career	
GEOFF COX	W	38/5	Nuneaton Boys 1950	Torquay United 1957
JOHN COXFORD	CH	16	Sunderland 1927	Bournemouth 1930
CHARLIE CRAVEN	IF	21/2	Manchester United 1938	Tamworth 1939
RAY CRAWSHAW	CH	4	Accrington Stanley 1934	Bromsgrove Rovers 1935
JIMMY CRINGAN	WH	285/12	Bury (trial) 1922	Boston United 1934

Player	Position	Record	From	To
BERT CROSSTHWAITE	G	49	Exeter City 1910	Stoke 1914
KENNY CUNNINGHAM	FB	144	Wimbledon 2002	Sunderland 2006
ALAN CURBISHLEY	M	155/15	West Ham United 1979	Aston Villa 1983
			was manager of Charlton Athletic for 11 years to 2006	
LEN CURRYER	CF	2	Harborne 1885	Birmingham Excelsior 1887
JUAN MIGUEL DA SOUZA	F	19	Dagenham & Redbridge 1994	Wycombe Wanderers 1995
JIMMY DAILEY	CF	42/14	Sheffield Wednesday 1949	Exeter City 1952
LIAM DAISH	CH	98/6	Cambridge United 1994	Coventry City 1996
DICKY DALE	D)	150	Stanley United 1922	West Brom Albion 1928
GERRY DALY	M	76/2	Coventry City 1984	Shrewsbury Town 1985
SCOTT DANN	D	35/1	Coventry City 2009	Still with club
NEIL DANNS	M	39/3	Colchester United 2006	Crystal Palace 2008
TREVOR DARK	W	5/1	Merton Boys 1977	Hendon 1981
MICKY DARRELL	IF	18/2	School 1962	Peterborough United 1971
TOM DAVENPORT	IF	13/8	Hockley Belmont 1885	St Luke's 1886
(2 spells with club)			St Luke's 1888	Birmingham St George's 1889
GEORGE DAVIES	OL	29/7	Ironbridge 1918	Southend United 1922
STAN DAVIES	F	17/5	West Brom Albion 1928	Rotherham United 1929
			played in six different positions for his country (Wales); awarded the	
			Military medal and the Croix de Guerre in World War One	
JIM DAWS	RH	47/1	Mansfield Town 1920	Bristol Rovers 1924
TOM DAYKIN	WH	94/1	Sunderland 1908	South Shields 1912
DANIEL DE RIDDER	M	12	Celta Vigo 2007	Wigan Athletic 2008
ULISES DE LA CRUZ	RB	1	Reading 2008	LDU Quito (Ecuador) 2008
			won 94 caps for Ecuador	
HARRY DEACON	IF	3	Hallam FC 1920	Swansea Town 1922
JOHN DEAKIN	M	7	Shepshed Charterhouse 1989	Carlisle United 1991
KEVIN DEARDEN	G	12	Hull City (l) 1992	Hull City 1992
JIMMY DEELEY	OL	1	Worcester Rovers 1895	Hereford Thistle 1896
MARK DENNIS	LB	145/1	Chelsea Boys 1977	Southampton 1983
TED DEVEY	LH	153/6	Birmingham Excelsior 1888	Burton Wanderers 1896
RAY DEVEY	CH	1	Shirley Old Boys 1937	Mansfield Town 1947
JOE DEVINE	U	56/2	Queen's Park Rangers 1935	Chesterfield 1937
JIM DEVLIN	IF	2/1	King's Park 1924	Preston North End 1926
PAUL DEVLIN	F	137/35	Notts County 1996	Sheffield United 1998
(2 spells with club)			Sheffield United 2001	Watford 2002
SALIF DIAO	M	2	Liverpool (l) 2005	Liverpool 2005
JULIAN DICKS	LB	102/2	School 1984	West Ham United 1988
			became a professional golfer	
KEVIN DILLON	M	212/19	Durham Boys 1976	Portsmouth 1983
DAVE DIXON	RB	4	Preston Colliery 1920	Southend United 1925
GEORGE DIXON	LB	1	Oldbury FC 1887	Aston Unity 1888
WALTER DIXON	OR	2/2	Birmingham Excelsior 1887	Church FC 1888
JOHN DJOUROU-GBADJERE	D	13	Arsenal (l) 2007	Arsenal 2007
NEIL DOHERTY	F	30/2	Leeds United (trial) 1994	Kidderminster Harriers 1996
EAMONN DOLAN	F	16/1	West Ham United 1990	Exeter City 1991
JOSÉ DOMINGUEZ	W	45/4	AD Fafe (Portugal) 1994	Sporting Lisbon (Portugal) 1995
			at 5ft 3in, is one of the smallest players ever to appear for Blues	
LOUIE DONOWA	W	168/19	Bristol City 1991	Peterborough United 1996
DON DORMAN	F	64/6	Shirley Juniors 1945	Coventry City 1951
			was in football for over 40 years	

Player	Position	Record	From	To
JACK DORRINGTON	G	111	Kidderminster Harriers 1901	Retired 1913
JIM DOUGHERTY	LH	136/3	New Brighton Tower 1901	Coventry City 1908
KEITH DOWNING	M	2	Wolverhampton W. 1993	Stoke City 1994
GREG DOWNS	LB	23/1	Coventry City 1990	Hereford United 1991
COLIN DOYLE	G	30	School 2002	Still with club
ALONZO DRAKE	IF	13/2	Sheffield United 1907	Queen's Park Rangers 1908
			played in 157 county cricket matches for Yorkshire, scoring 4,816 runs	
			and taking 480 wickets, with a best return of 10-35 v Somerset	
HARRY DRAPER	IL	3	Rotherham Town 1910	Denaby United 1911
KEVIN DRINKELL	S	5/2	Coventry City (l) 1991	Coventry City 1991
RICHARD DRYDEN	D	54	Notts County 1993	Bristol City 1994
TED DUCKHOUSE	D	127/4	West Brom Albion 1938	Northampton Town 1950
CHRISTOPHE DUGARRY	F	29/6	Bordeaux (France) 2003	Qatar Sports Club 2004
			was a World Cup and European Championship-winner with France in 1998 and 2000	
CHARLIE DUNCAN	CF	24/9	Dunfermline Athletic 1913	Clyde 1915
			scored 52 goals for Blues when they won the Central League title in 1914–15	
TOM DUNLOP	D	62/2	Annbank 1896	Dundee Harp 1898
DAVID DUNN	M	69/8	Blackburn Rovers 2003	Blackburn Rovers 2007
NICKY EADEN	RB	90/5	Barnsley 2000	Wigan Athletic 2002
RICHARD EDGHILL	RB	3	Manchester City (l) 2000	Manchester City 2000
ANDY EDWARDS	D	58/3	Southend United 1995	Peterborough United 1996
ERNIE EDWARDS	HB	17	Redditch United 1913	Tipton Excelsior 1919
HARRY EDWARDS	IF	5/1	Singers FC 1892	Ryton Rovers 1893
BILLY EDWARDS	OL	5/1	Singers FC 1896	Rugby Town 1897
JACK ELKES	IR	35/15	Shifnal Town 1918	Southampton 1922
RICHARD ELLIMAN	LB	4	Sandwell FC 1882	Smethwick Highfield 1886
TONY ELLIOTT	G	1	FA Academy 1986	Hereford United 1988
BILL ELLIS	OL	36/8	Sunderland 1927	Lincoln City 1929
GARY EMMANUEL	M	78/6	School 1970	Bristol Rovers 1978
GIOVANNIY ESPINOZA	D	2	Barcelona S.C. (Ecuador) 2009	Union Espanola (Chile) 2009
			is current Ecuador's second-most capped player	
MANUEL ESTEVES	M	1	Vitoria Setubal (Portugal, L) 1995	Vitoria Setubal 1995
HUGH EVANS	IF	14	Redditch United 1947	Bournemouth 1950
LEN EVANS	G	2	Cardiff City 1933	FC Svenborg (Sweden) 1935
ROBERT EVANS	G	3	Coventry City 1913	Nuneaton Town 1914
TOM EVANS	RH	6	Cradley St Luke's 1917	Brighton & Hove Albion 1921
TONY EVANS	F	76/33	Cardiff City 1979	Crystal Palace 1983
ALBERT EVERS	HB	2	Royal Oak Rangers 1891	Yardley Victoria 1891
BOB EVETTS	FB	8/1	St Stephen's Church 1894	Warwick County 1887
EDMUND EYRE	OL	82/16	Rotherham Town 1907	Aston Villa 1908
CRAIG FAGAN	F	3	School 2000	Colchester United 2004
			helped Hull City reach the Premier League in 2008	
KEITH FAHEY	OL	59/4	St Patrick's Athletic 2009	Still with club
BOB FAIRMAN	D	39/1	Southampton 1907	West Ham United 1909
JACK FALL	G	2	Kettering Town 1895	Altrincham 1896
WALTER FARLEY	WH	1	Birmingham Excelsior 1885	Stourbridge 1887
BRIAN FARMER	RB	145	Stourbridge 1950	Bournemouth 1962
MICK FARMER	WH	1/1	School 1961	Lincoln City 1965
TOM FARNALL	WH	53/2	Eastville Rovers 1895	Eastville Rovers 1897
(2 spells with club)			Eastville Rovers 1899	Watford 1900
TOM FARRAGE	OL	7/2	Walker Celtic 1937	Killed in World War Two
			a pilot with the Air Army Corps	

Player	Position	Record	From	To
GREG FARRELL	OR	5	Small Heath Unity 1959	Cardiff City 1964
KEN FAULKNER	F	2	Smethwick Highfield 1943	Oldbury United 1947
WALTER FELTON	HB	7/1	The Grove FC 1884	Walsall Swifts 1886
RONNIE FENTON	IF	40/8	West Brom Albion 1965	Brentford 1968
PAUL FENWICK	D	24	Winnipeg Fury 1992	Dunfermline Athletic 1995
BARRY FERGUSON, MBE	M	43/2	Blackburn Rovers 2009	Still with club
			gained three Premier, three League Cup and three Scottish Cup-winners'	
				medals with Rangers
MIKE FERGUSON	S	25/9	Everton 1982	Brighton & Hove Albion 1984
CARLOS FERRARI	S	4	FC Mirassol (Brazil, L) 2001	FC Mirassol 2002
RAY FERRIS	WH	106/4	Crewe Alexandra 1949	Worcester City 1953
CHARLIE FIELD	OL	89/15	Sheffield United 1902	Retired 1906
BILL FIGURES	IL	9/2	St Andrew's Rovers 1885	Great Bridge Unity 1887
LUCIANO FIGUEROA	S	2	Rosario Central (Argentina) 2003	Cruz Azui (Mexico) 2003
			scored five goals for Rosario Central against Boca Juniors in 2004	
TOM FILLINGHAM	CH	192/9	Bromley United 1928	Ipswich Town 1938
STEVE FINNAN	RB	22/1	Welling United 1995	Notts County 1996
BILL FINNEY	IF	17/1	Stoke City 1955	Queen's Park Rangers 1957
BOB FIRTH	OR	26/2	Golder's Green FC 1909	Wellington Town 1911
JACK FIRTH	WH	98/8	Doncaster Rovers 1926	Swansea Town 1933
PAUL FITZPATRICK	M	7	Leicester City 1993	Northampton Town 1994
CURTIS FLEMING	FB	6	Middlesbrough (l) 2001	Middlesbrough 2001
TOM FLETCHER	IL	2	Willenhall 1900	Cradley St Luke's 1901
HOWARD FORINTON	S	10/1	Yeovil Town 1997	Peterborough United 1999
MIKAEL FORSSELL	S	119/37	Chelsea (l) 2003	Chelsea 2003
(2 spells with club)			Chelsea (l) 2004/2005	Hannover '96 (Germany) 2009
NICKY FORSTER	S	76/12	Brentford 1997	Reading 1999
			ended the 2009–10 season with over almost 200 goals and	
				710 club appearances safely under his belt
RICHARD FORSYTH	M	41/2	Kidderminster Harriers 1995	Stoke City 1996
ARTHUR FOSTER	IL	2/1	Birmingham Corinthians 1913	Acocks Green FC 1914
			is the brother of Bob Foster, the famous Warwickshire and England cricketer	
BEN FOSTER	G	**	Manchester United 2010	Still with club
WINSTON FOSTER	CH	170/2	Birmingham County FA 1955	Plymouth Argyle 1969
TED FOUNTAIN	IF	3	Small Heath Langley 1894	Birmingham St George's 1895
MATTHEW FOX	D	15	Hurley Colts 1987	Northampton Town 1993
STEPHEN FOX	OR	29/1	Tamworth 1975	Wrexham 1978
FRANK FOXALL	IF	22/3	Sheffield Wednesday 1910	Shrewsbury Town 1911
FRED FOXALL	OL	28/4	Aston Villa 1922	Watford 1923
DAVID FOY	M	4	School 1989	Scunthorpe United 1993
JOHN FRAIN	U	337/26	School 1984	Northampton Town 1997
			made 243 appearances for Northampton Town after leaving Blues	
CARLOS FRANCIS	W	5	School 1979	Enfield 1984
KEVIN FRANCIS	S	83/21	Stockport County 1995	Oxford United 1998
			at 6ft 7in, is the second-tallest player to join Blues, 2010 signing Zigic is taller	
SEAN FRANCIS	F	6	School 1988	Telford United 1992
ADAM FRASER	LB	24	Glasgow Northern 1895	Heart of Midlothian 1896
CAMMIE FRASER	FB	42	Aston Villa 1965	Falkirk 1966
NEIL FREEMAN	G	33	Southend United 1978	Peterborough United 1981
				became a police officer in Northampton
WALTER FREEMAN	IF	37/11	Fulham 1909	Walsall 1911

Player	Position	Record	From	To
PAUL FURLONG	S	153/56	Chelsea 1996	Queen's Park Rangers 2002
			was still scoring League goals for Barnet in 2010 at the age of 41	
MARCO GABBIADINI	S	2	Derby County (l) 1996	Derby County 1996
			scored 276 goals in 791 career appearances	
WALTER GADSBY	IR	4/3	Redditch Excelsior 1896	Watford 1898
GEORGE GALLIMORE	OL	18/1	Sheffield United 1910	Leek Town 1911
ALF GARD	OR	3	Trowbridge Town 1900	Maidenhead FC 1901
ALBERT GARDNER	WH	120/4	BSA Sports 1908	Kings Heath (l) 1914
				was profoundly deaf
EDWARD GARDNER	F	16/11	Smethwick Hall 1898	Oldbury Town 1899
CRAIG GARDNER	M	15/1	Aston Villa 2010	Still with club
ARCHIE GARRETT	S	18/6	Northampton Town 1947	Northampton Town 1948
BILLY GARTON	D	5	Manchester United (l) 1986	Manchester United 1986
HOWARD GAYLE	OR	59/11	Liverpool 1983	Sunderland 1984
JOHN GAYLE	S	55/14	Wimbledon 1990	Coventry City 1993
DAVID GEDDIS	S	56/21	Barnsley 1984	Shrewsbury Town 1987
ARCHIE GEMMILL	M	115/14	Nottingham Forest 1979	Jacksonville Teamen (USA) 1982
			won three First Division Championship medals, plus League Cup and European Cup-winners' prizes and made over 750 appearances (589 in League competition) during his 20-year career	
BILLY GEORGE	G	1	Aston Villa 1911	Retired 1912
			made 399 League appearances for Aston Villa and one for Blues, the latter when officially engaged as the club's trainer	
SAM GESSEY	D	4	Wolverhampton St Luke's 1877	Willenhall 1884
			owned the land on which Blues' former ground, Muntz Street, stood	
GEORGE GETGOOD	WH	10	Reading 1921	Southampton 1922
			changed his name from Goodman	
RICHARD GIBSON	OR	120/19	Sultan FC 1911	Manchester United 1921
BILL GILDEA	CH	20/1	Bradford City 1911	Celtic 1912
JERRY GILL	D	74	Yeovil Town 1997	Northampton Town 2002
WALTER GITTINS	FB	26	Lozells Sports Club 1889	Stafford Rangers 1890
DON GIVENS	F	62/10	Queen's Park Rangers 1978	Sheffield United 1981
			missed a penalty with his last kick in League football – for Sheffield United v Walsall – and as a result the Blades were relegated to the Fourth Division	
NIGEL GLEGHORN	M	176/42	Manchester City 1989	Stoke City 1992
TONY GODDEN	G	37	Chelsea 1986	Peterborough United 1989
			holds the record for most consecutive appearances for West Bromwich Albion (228)	
JOE GODFREY	CF	3/1	Nottingham Forest 1918	Coventry City 1919
			brother, Bruce, played in goal for Blues during World War One	
ARCHIE GOLDIE	RB	79	New Brighton Tower 1901	Crewe Alexandra 1904
PERCY GOOCH	CF	4/1	Norwich City 1907	Notts County 1908
MICHAEL GOOD	IF	16/1	Airdrieonians 1896	Watford 1898
TERRY GOODE	W	2	School 1977	Kettering Town 1982
JACK GOODWIN	OR	33/8	Worcester City 1946	Brentford 1949
			coached in the USA during the 1960s	
COLIN GORDON	F	30/3	Fulham 1989	Leicester City 1991
JOHNNY GORDON	F	115/40	Portsmouth 1958	Portsmouth 1961
			scored 105 goals in 443 League games for Portsmouth	
PAUL GORMAN	M	7	Arsenal 1984	Carlisle United 1985
ANDY GOSNEY	G	24	Portsmouth 1992	Exeter City 1993
HARRY GRAHAM	IF	12/4	Bradford City 1911	Raith Rovers 1912

Player	Position	Record	From	To
MARTIN GRAINGER	LB	266/28	Brentford 1996	Retired 2004
JULIAN GRAY	W	73/24	Crystal Palace 2004	Coventry City 2007
ARTHUR GREEN	RB	1	Mansfield Town 1911	Lincoln City 1912
COLIN GREEN	FB	217/1	Everton 1962	Tamworth 1971
			made his League debut for Everton against Stan Matthews and Blackpool.	
WALTER GREEN	F	2	Church football 1882	Nechells 1883
JIMMY GREENHOFF	F	36/15	Leeds United 1968	Stoke City 1969
			scored the winning goal for Manchester United in the 1977 FA Cup Final,	
			deflecting home Lou Macari's shot, this being one of 171 goals in 680 career games	
TOMMY GREER	CF	2	Coatbridge Rob Roy 1910	Reading 1912
BART GRIEMINK	G	26	WK Emmen (Holland) 1995	Peterborough United 1996
JESPER GRONKJAER	W	18/1	Chelsea 2004	Atletico Madrid (Spain) 2005
			won his 81st cap for Denmark in the 2010 World Cup Finals	
TOM GROSVENOR	U	115/18	Stourbridge 1928	Sheffield Wednesday 1936
BILLY GUEST	OL	84/17	Bromley Juniors 1928	Blackburn Rovers 1937
JIMMY HAARHOFF	S	1	School 1997	Chester City 2000
HARRY HADDON	CF	8/2	Army football 1896	Walsall Wood 1897
JIM HAGAN	D	167	Coventry City 1982	Celta Vigo (Spain) 1987
			was voted Ulster's 'Young Footballer of the Year' in 1976	
WILF HAINES	OR	3	Stafford Rangers 1908	Leek United 1909
FRED HALL	CF	5/2	Whitewell Old Boys 1947	Bedford Town 1949
JACK HALL	F	102/48	Leicester Fosse 1910	Hucknall Town 1915
JACK HALLWORTH	LH	1	Twyford Youth Club 1906	Leek Alexandra 1907
MICK HALSALL	M	46/3	Liverpool 1983	Carlisle United 1984
WALTER HALSALL	HB	24	Blackburn Rovers 1938	Chesterfield 1939
HARRY HAMPTON	CF	59/31	Aston Villa 1920	Wellington Town 1924
			scored 242 goals in 376 games for Aston Villa, gaining one League Championship	
			and three FA Cup-winners' medals plus four England caps	
TOMMY HANDLEY	CH	13	Kings Norton Metal Works 1907	Bradford Park Ave. 1909
TOMMY HANDS	OL	150/42	Small Heath Unity 1890	King's Heath 1896
IAN HANDYSIDES	M	133/12	Durham Boys 1978	Walsall 1984
(2 spells with club)			Walsall 1986	Retired 1988
ROGER HANSBURY	G	68	Cambridge United 1986	Cardiff City 1989
PAUL HARDING	M	26/1	Notts County (l) 1993/1994	Cardiff City 1997
WALTER HARDS	OL	5/2	Summerhill Works 1881	Stourbridge 1884
CHARLIE HARE	IF	45/14	Woolwich Arsenal 1895	Watford 1898
			served with the Warwickshire Yeomanry during the Boer War	
JEREMIAH HARE	RB	8	Pershore Saints 1884	King's Heath 1888
MICK HARFORD	S	109/33	Newcastle United 1982	Luton Town 1984
			retired in 1997 with a club record of 232 goals in 708 appearances	
STAN HARLAND	WH	52	Swindon Town 1971	Yeovil Town 1973
			captained Swindon Town to a famous 3–1 League Cup Final	
			victory over Arsenal in 1969	
ALEX HARLEY	CF	29/9	Manchester City 1963	Dundee 1964
			was a croupier at a Birmingham Casino at the time of his death in 1969	
DENNIS HARPER	IR	1	Darlaston 1955	Romford 1959
ROLY HARPER	OR	29/2	Walsall Wood 1904	Burton United 1907
ANDREW HARRIS	U	2	School 1988	Exeter City 1991
JIMMY HARRIS	F	115/53	Everton 1960	Oldham Athletic 1964
WALLY HARRIS	OR	94/15	Burton All Saints 1922	Walsall 1929
ARTHUR HARRISON	OR	4/3	Linton FC 1902	Brownhills Athletic 1903

Player	Position	Record	From	To
MICK HARRISON	D	3	School 1968	Southend United 1972
WILBERT HARRISON	CF	1/2	Birmingham St George's 1891	Summerfield Saints 1892
JOE HART	G	41	Manchester City (I) 2009	Manchester City 2010
			was a member of England's 2010 World Cup squad	
PAUL HART	D	1	Sheffield Wednesday 1986	Notts County 1987
			broke his leg on his debut for Blues v Plymouth Argyle in December 1986	
			(his only game for the club)	
WALTER HARTWELL	D	51/1	Erdington FC 1901	Bradford Park Avenue 1908
BILLY HARVEY	OR	79/2	Sheffield Wednesday 1921	Southend United 1925
CHARLIE HARVEY	OR	2	St Phillip's YMCA 1904	Leek 1907
EDMUND HARVEY	OR	14	Huddersfield Town 1924	Bradford City 1927
IAN HASTIE	OR	1	Edmonton Royal 1911	High Wycombe 1912
WALTER HASTINGS	OL	44/7	Brighton & Hove A. 1912	Watford 1914
TONY HATELEY	CF	30/6	Coventry City 1969	Notts County 1970
			scored 211 goals in 434 League games during his 17-year career	
STAN HAUSER	G	34	Handsworth Oakhill 1913	Stourbridge 1922
WILLIE HAVENGA	OR	1	Bremner Old Boys (S Africa) 1948	Luton Town 1950
PHIL HAWKER	LB	37/1	School 1978	Walsall 1983
FRED HAWLEY	CH	3	Coventry City 1920	Swindon Town 1920
HARRY HAYNES	CH	10	Wolverhampton W. 1895	Southampton St Mary's 1896
GEORGE HAYWOOD	CF	46/18	Gresley Rovers 1928	Chesterfield 1934
FRED HEATH	U	30/3	Cookham FC 1889	Stourbridge 1891
TOM HEDGES	G	8	Walsall Swifts 1883	Darlaston 1887
			became a director of West Bromwich Albion	
MIKE HELLAWELL	OR	213/33	Queen's Park Rangers 1957	Sunderland 1965
CROSBIE HENDERSON	LB	6	Grimsby Town 1910	Brighton & Hove Albion 1911
JOHN HENDERSON	IF	4	Leicester Fosse 1901	Maxwelltown Volunteers 1902
IAN HENDON	D	4	Leyton Orient (I) 1995	Leyton Orient 1995
PAUL HENDRIE	IF	32/1	Kirkintillock Rob Roy 1972	Portland Timbers 1976
EMILE HESKEY	S	78/16	Liverpool 2004	Wigan Athletic 2006
ANTOINE HEY	M	11/1	Fortuna Cologne (Germany) 1997	FC Wuppertoi (Germany) 1999
TERRY HIBBITT	M	122/11	Newcastle United 1975	Newcastle United 1978
			brother Kenny played for Wolves	
GEORGE HICKS	OL	80/18	Manchester City 1923	Manchester United 1932
MARTIN HICKS	D	73/2	Reading 1991	Newbury Town 1993
JACK HIGGINS	IL	1	Aston Villa 1907	Brierley Hill Alliance 1908
			played country cricket for Worcestershire between 1912–30,	
			scoring 4,149 runs in 121 matches	
JIMMY HIGGINS	CF	6/3	Stourbridge 1897	Netherton 1898
JIMMY HIGGINS	CF	54/14	Dundalk 1949	Hereford United 1953
JACK HIGGINSON	F	14/4	Dudley Town 1900	Stourbridge 1902
SCOTT HILEY	RB	58	Exeter City 1993	Manchester City 1996
DANNY HILL	M	7	Tottenham Hotspur (I) 1995	Tottenham Hotspur 1996
DENNIS HILL	OL	4	Leicester City 1951	Burton Albion 1957
TED HILL	OL	10/5	Walsall Phoenix 1885	Darlaston 1899
JACK HIRONS	OL	5	Walsall 1903	Walsall 1906
TREVOR HOCKEY	M	232/13	Newcastle United 1965	Sheffield United 1971
			became the youngest footballer, in 1968, to play on all 92 League grounds and	
			made over 600 appearances during his career; he used to own and play a	
			pink piano and died from a heart attack after playing in a five-a-side match in 1987	
FRANK HODGES	IR	32/5	Birmingham Gas FC 1911	Manchester United 1919

Player	Position	Record	From	To
DENNIS HODGETTS	IL	23/9	Aston Villa 1896	Retired 1898
			scored 91 goals in 215 appearances for Aston Villa, gaining two League	
			and two FA Cup-winners' medals	
TOM HOGAN	F	2	Cobh Ramblers 1991	Shamrock Rovers 1992
DAVID HOLDSWORTH	D	101/8	Sheffield United 1999	Bolton Wanderers 2002
			twin brother Dean was also a professional footballer	
CHRIS HOLLAND	M	87	Newcastle United 1996	Huddersfield Town 2002
GEORGE HOLLIS	G	41	Warwick County 1891	Bournbrook 1894
EZRA HOLMES	CF	2	Gainsborough Trinity 1907	Stamford 1908
PAUL HOLMES	RB	13	Torquay United 1992	Everton 1993
WILLIE HOLMES	OR	1	Notts County 1934	Heanor Town 1935
HARRY HOOPER	OR	119/42	Wolverhampton W. 1957	Sunderland 1960
LYNDON HOOPER	M	6	Toronto Blizzard (Canada) 1993	Cincinatti Silverbacks (USA) 1995
			went on to win 67 caps for Canada	
BOBBY HOPE	M	46/5	West Brom Albion 1972	Philadelphia Atoms (USA) 1975
			made 403 appearances for West Bromwich Albion, gaining both	
			League Cup and FA Cup-winners' medals	
ROBERT HOPKINS	W	205/33	Aston Villa 1983	Manchester City 1986
(2 spells with club)			West Brom Albion 1989	Shrewsbury Town 1991
BARRY HORNE	M	40	Everton 1996	Huddersfield Town 1997
			made 764 appearances during his career (over 500 before joining Blues)	
GEOFF HORSFIELD	S	126/28	Fulham 2000	Wigan Athletic 2003
			was diagnosed with testicular cancer in 2008, but after an	
			operation he resumed his career with Lincoln City	
BILLY HORSMAN	W	83/3	Selby Town 1928	Chester 1935
'BUD' HOUGHTON	CF	4/1	Bradford Park Avenue 1957	Southend United 1958
HARRY HOWARD	WH	51/1	Sheffield United 1902	Wisbech Town 1906
PAT HOWARD	CH	43	Arsenal 1978	Bury 1979
DAVID HOWELL	D	2	Southend United 1993	Retired 1994
			made his debut for Blues at the age of 38 in December 1994	
DAVE HOWITT	RB	3	School 1968	Bury 1973
WILF HOYLAND	OR	6	Glossop 1923	Brighton & Hove Albion 1924
ARTHUR HUBBARD	LB	5	Wright & Eagle Range FC 1932	Luton Town 1935
BRYAN HUGHES	M	293/42	Wrexham 1997	Charlton Athletic 2004
JACK HUGHES	CH	1	Birmingham Unity 1890	Lea Hall Cons. 1891
JOHN HUGHES	OL	7	Tamworth Castle 1947	Tamworth 1949
BILLY HUME	U	10/2	Dunfermline Athletic 1958	St Mirren 1960
JONATHAN HUNT	M	92/25	Southend United 1994	Derby County 1997
NICKY HUNT	RB	11	Bolton Wanderers (l) 2008	Bolton Wanderers 2009
BILLY HUNTER	CH	42	Brownhills Juniors 1921	Grimsby Town 1927
JON HUTCHINSON	D	7	School 1998	Darlington 2003
RICHARD HUXFORD	FB	5	Millwall (l) 1994	Millwall 1994
GRAHAM HYDE	M	59/2	Sheffield Wednesday 1999	Bristol Rovers 2002
ROGER HYND	CH	205/5	Crystal Palace 1970	Walsall 1975
			although a central defender, played centre-forward for	
			Rangers in the 1967 European Cup-winners' Cup Final	
JIMMY INGLIS	OR	62/28	Airdrieonians 1896	Luton Town 1899
DENNIS ISHERWOOD	RB	5/1	School 1962	Bromsgrove Rovers 1968
HARRY ISHERWOOD	LB	1	Sunderland 1927	Bournemouth 1928
ERNIE ISLIP	IF	89/24	Huddersfield Town 1923	Bradford City 1927
			won an FA Cup-winners' medal with Huddersfield in the	
			last Final before Wembley (1922)	

Player	Position	Record	From	To
PAUL IVEY	F	7	School 1977	Chesterfield 1982
CHARLIE IZON	F	26/8	Halesowen 1893	Walsall 1897
			scored a hat-trick on his League debut for Blues v Walsall Town Swifts in 1893	
MUZZY IZZET	M	28/1	Leicester City 2004	Retired 2006
ALEC JACKSON	F	85/12	West Brom Albion 1964	Walsall 1967
ALEX JACKSON	CF	10/7	Shettlestone Juniors 1958	Plymouth Argyle 1960
MATT JACKSON	D	10	Everton (l) 1996	Everton 1996
WALTER JACKSON	OR	4/1	Harborne 1893	Berwick Rangers (NL) 1894
RADHI JAIDI	D	93/6	Bolton Wanderers 2006	Southampton 2009
ARTHUR JAMES	OR	5/3	Birmingham Carriage Works FC 1874	Retired 1887
			Arthur, Fred and Tom James, all brothers, were registered together	
				as Blues players from 1875 to 1885
FRED JAMES	D	12	Birmingham Carriage Works FC 1874	Retired 1886
JIMMY JAMES	IF	7/2	Paget Rangers 1950	Torquay United 1955
TOM JAMES	WH	7/1	Birmingham Carriage Works FC 1875	Retired 1885
JIŘÍ JAROŠÍK	M	32/8	Chelsea (l) 2005	Chelsea 2006
LEE JENKINS	M	1	Rovaniemi Pal. (Finland) 1985	Finnairin Pal. (Finland) 1986
			broke his ankle in his only game for Blues v WBA in 1985	
LEIGH JENKINSON	F	3	Coventry City (l) 1993	Coventry City 1993
STEVE JENKINS	FB	4	Huddersfield Town (l) 2000	Huddersfield Town 2001
LINDLEY JENKINS	M	3	South Staffs Boys 1970	Walsall 1974
CAMERON JEROME	S	159/37	Cardiff City 2006	Still with club
JAKE JERVIS	S	1	School 2007	Still with club
STERN JOHN	S	85/21	Nottingham Forest 2002	Coventry City 2004
ANDREW JOHNSON	U	103/13	School 1996	Crystal Palace 2002
			missed the crucial last penalty in the shoot-out with Liverpool	
				at the end of the 2001 League Cup Final
ARTHUR JOHNSON	OL	9	Barnsley 1927	Bristol City 1928
DAMIEN JOHNSON	M	214/4	Blackburn Rovers 2002	Plymouth Argyle 2010
ROGER JOHNSON	D	43	Cardiff City 2009	Still with club
ALLAN JOHNSTON	W	10	Sunderland (l) 1999	Sunderland 1999
GEORGE JOHNSTON	IF	10/1	Arsenal 1969	Fulham 1970
WILLIE JOHNSTON	OL	18	Vancouver Whitecaps (Canada, L) 1979	Vancouver Whitecaps 1980
			won League Cup, Scottish Cup and European Cup-winners' medals with Rangers;	
			he was also suspended by the Scottish FA in 1971 for a record 67 days and was sent	
			home from the 1978 World Cup Finals in Argentina for drug abuse	
TED JOLLY	F	21/2	Lozells FC 1893	Berwick Rangers (NL) 1896
			scored a hat-trick of own-goals in a Birmingham League match in March 1895	
AARON JONES	F	5	Barnsley 1905	Notts County 1907
ABRAHAM JONES	CF	3/2	West Bromwich Sandwell 1919	Reading 1921
BILL JONES	FB	1	Calthorpe FC 1881	West Bromwich Standard 1883
CHARLIE JONES	OL	1	Verity's Works FC 1908	Bristol Rovers 1909
DAVID JONES	IF	9	Crewe Alexandra 1957	Millwall 1959
FRED JONES	IL	1	Leeds United 1934	Cheltenham Town 1935
FRED W. JONES	LB	9	Newton Heath 1892	Lincoln City 1893
GARY JONES	OR	38/1	Everton 1976	Fort Lauderdale Strikers (USA) 1978
JOHN JONES	IF	39/18	Halesowen 1894	Eastville Rovers 1897
MARK JONES	FB	40	Brighton & Hove Albion 1984	Shrewsbury Town 1987
PAUL JONES	W	2	Knowle Juniors 1990	Moor Green 1993
ROGER JONES	G	4	Derby County (l) 1982	Derby County 1982
			spent over 20 years keeping goal and made over 750 appearances	

Player	Position	Record	From	To
TOMMY JONES	IF	31/12	Everton 1910	Southport Central 1912
TOMMY T. JONES	OL	3	Shrewsbury Town 1904	Shifnal Town 1905
WALLY JONES	CF	4	The Grove FC 1881	Blackheath 1884
			scored four goals in four minutes during Blues' 16–0 friendly	
			win over Darlaston All Saints in 1881–82	
JOHNNY JORDAN	F	25/3	Juventus (Italy) 1949	Sheffield Wednesday 1950
OLIVIER KAPO	M	26/5	Juventus (Italy) 2007	Wigan Athletic 2008
JACK KEARNS	LB	64/1	Coventry City 1906	Aston Villa 1909
REG KEATING	IF	5/1	Stockport County 1931	Norwich City 1932
ALAN KELLY	G	6	Blackburn Rovers (l) 2001	Blackburn Rovers 2001
JACK KELLY	F	12/1	Leeds United 1939	Bury 1939
MIKE KELLY	G	74	Queen's Park Rangers 1970	Minnesota Kicks (USA) 1976
			became part of the England coaching set-up in the 2000s	
STEPHEN KELLY	RB	88	Tottenham Hotspur 2006	Fulham 2009
MARK KENDALL	G	1	Northampton Town 1984	Tamworth 1986
KEN KENDRICK	CF	10/1	Halesowen Town 1936	Retired 1944
WILLIAM KENDRICK	CH	1	Calthorpe 1891	Hockley St Luke's 1892
JEFF KENNA	RB	84	Blackburn Rovers (l) 2001/2002	Derby County 2004
ANDY KENNEDY	S	87/20	Glasgow Rangers 1985	Blackburn Rovers 1988
FRED KERNS	IR	1	Aston Villa 1908	Bristol Rovers 1909
JACK KIDD	IR	44/8	St Johnstone 1910	Brierley Hill Alliance 1912
NEIL KILKENNEY	D	39	Arsenal 2002	Leeds United 2008
HARRY 'TED' KING	CF	30/7	Worcester City 1907	Crewe Alexandra 1910
			scored 67 goals in 99 games for Northampton Town before World War One	
SID KING	G	2	Cradley Heath 1936	Hereford United 1946
RICHARD KINGSON	G	3	Ankaraspor (Turkey) 2007	Wigan Athletic 2008
			played for Ghana in the 2010 World Cup, when he upped his	
			total of international caps to 86	
EZEKIAL KINGSTON	OR	1	Wednesbury Old Athletic 1881	Bloxwich Strollers 1883
CONYERS KIRBY	OR	1	Fulham 1906	Blackpool 1907
			became a referee in Spain and was in charge of Blues' friendly with	
			Real Madrid in 1923 when he sent off Alex McClure	
JOVAN KIROVSKI	M	23/2	Crystal Palace 2002	Los Angeles Galaxy (USA) 2004
JACK KIRTON	OL	18/2	Lincoln City 1897	Sunderland 1898
HYMIE KLONER	RH	1	Marist Bros. (S. Africa) 1950	Transvaal (S. Africa) 1950
RICHARD KNIGHT	G	1	Derby County (l) 1999	Derby County 1999
BOBBY LAING	OL	19/2	Falkirk 1946	Watford 1950
HARRY LANE	F	2	Bloxwich Strollers 1930	Southend United 1933
JACKIE LANE	F	50/14	Boldmere St Michael's 1949	Notts County 1956
JOE LANE	CF	67/26	Blackpool 1920	Millwall 1922
			was a record signing by Blues in 1920, costing £3,600 from Blackpool	
MOSES LANE	CF	15/4	Willenhall 1922	Derby County 1924
			was awarded the Military Medal after serving in France	
			and Italy during World War One.	
DAVID LANGAN	RB	102/3	Derby County 1980	Oxford United 1984
			retired in 1992 with over 500 club appearances to his credit	
KEVIN LANGLEY	M)	88/2	Manchester City 1988	Wigan Athletic 1990
HUBERT LAPPIN	OL	12/2	Chester 1909	Chirk 1910
'BUNNY' LARKIN	U	92/29	Rockwood Albion 1952	Norwich City 1960
			was nicknamed 'Rip Van Winkle'	
SEBASTIAN LARSSON	F	164/21	Arsenal (l) 2006/2007	Still with club

Player	Position	Record	From	To
MARTIN LATKA	D	6	Slavia Prague (Czech Republic, L) 2006	Slavia Prague 2006
GEORGE LAYTON	U	17/3	Wesleyan Rovers 1898	Dudley Town 1901
GEORGE LEA	RH	28/1	Oakengates Town 1932	Millwall 1937
CHARLIE LEATHERBARROW	IR	5/3	Walsall Swifts 1894	Millwall 1895
JACK LEE	F	7/3	Walsall Unity 1893	Old Hill Wanderers 1895
TERRY LEES	D	19	Roda JC (Holland) 1979	Newport County 1981
ANDREW LEGG	U	49/5	Notts County 1996	Reading 1998

made well over 750 appearances during his playing career,
twice winning the Welsh Cup with Swansea City

Player	Position	Record	From	To
GRAHAM LEGGATT	OR	20/3	Fulham 1967	Rotherham United 1968
ARTHUR LEONARD	IR	75/26	Glentoran 1901	Stoke 1904

was christened Arthur Bamford

Player	Position	Record	From	To
JACK LEONARD	OR	9/1	Bristol City 1899	Cheltenham Town 1900
FRANK LESTER	FB	78	Walsall Unity 1895	Walsall 1901
BILL LEWIS	OR	3/2	Windsor St. Gas Depot 1894	Hereford Town 1896
WILSON LEWIS	OR	21/7	Hereford Thistle 1897	Bromyard 1898
ANDERS LIMPAR	F	5	Everton 1997	AIK Stockholm (Sweden) 1997
ALBERT LINDON	G	7	Birmingham Fruiters FC 1910	Aston Villa 1911

tipped the scales at 16st when playing for Charlton Athletic in 1927–28

Player	Position	Record	From	To
WILTON LINES	F	7/1	Calthorpe 1898	Hockley Belmont 1899
JOHN LINFORD	CF	2	Ipswich Town (I) 1984	Ipswich Town 1984

scored over 80 goals in Dutch football

Player	Position	Record	From	To
TED LINLEY	OL	118/11	Worksop Town 1920	Nottingham Forest 1926
ALBERT LINNECOR	U	18	Brookhill Juniors 1950	Lincoln City 1957

scored five goals for Boston United v Swindon Town in 1965

Player	Position	Record	From	To
DAVID LINNEY	M	1	School 1977	Oxford United 1982
IVOR LINTON	U	4	Peterborough United 1983	Bilston Town 1984
ARTHUR LITTLEFORD	RB	3	South Yardley 1893	Berwick Rangers (NL) 1895
LEWIS LODGE	RB	1	Corinthians 1896	Newbury Town 1897

was a Cambridge University Blue (three times)

Player	Position	Record	From	To
JOCK LOGAN	OL	1	Partick Thistle 1896	Musselburgh 1897
JOE LOUGHRAN	WH	34/2	Consett FC 1933	Dudley Town 1937
JIM LOVESEY	LB	1	Hockley Hill Transport FC 1886	Birmingham Belmont 1887
BERNARD LOWE	IL	16/3	Halesowen 1908	Darlaston 1911
KENNY LOWE	M	29/3	Stoke City 1993	Darlington 1997
TRESOR LUNTALA	M	16	Stade Rennais (France) 1999	Wolves (trial) 2002
STEVE LYNEX	OR	66/13	Shamrock Rovers 1979	Leicester City 1981
(2 spells with club)			Leicester City (I) 1986	Leicester City 1986
BILL McCAFFERTY	IF	4	Reading 1906	Bathgate 1907
MARK McCARRICK	RB	20	Witton Albion 1983	Lincoln City 1984
JON McCARTHY	OR	142/8	Port Vale 1997	Port Vale 2002

broke his leg three times in two years as a Blues player

Player	Position	Record	From	To
BILL McCOURTY	LH	1	North Seaton 1909	Ryton FC 1910
JIM McDONAGH	G	1	Notts County (I) 1984	Notts County 1984
MARTIN McDONNELL	CH	32	Southport 1947	Coventry City 1949

was signed by manager Harry Storer three times for three different clubs

Player	Position	Record	From	To
DUNCAN McDOWELL	CF	2	London Schools 1980	Leatherhead 1983
STEVE McGAVIN	F	33/7	Colchester United 1992	Wycombe Wanderers 1995
FRANK McGURK	OR	19/2	Clyde 1933	Bristol City 1935
ALEX McINTOSH	IF	23/4	Wolverhampton W. 1947	Coventry City 1948
JACK McKAY	F	21/2	Hebburn FC 1910	Blyth Spartans 1912

Player	Position	Record	From	To
FRANK McKEE	LH	24	Dundee United 1948	Gillingham 1952
JOHNNY McMILLAN	S	52/25	Leicester Fosse 1901	Bradford City 1903
			scored five goals in a League game for both Blues and Derby County	
TED McMINN	M	26	Derby County 1993	Burnley 1994
GARY McSHEFFREY	S	96/20	Coventry City 2006	Coventry City 2010
DAVE MADDEN	M	5/1	Crystal Palace (l) 1990	Crystal Palace 1990
OWEN MADDEN	F	15/5	Norwich City 1938	Cork City 1939
			after leaving Cork City, helped rivals Cork United win five Irish	
			League titles and two Cup Finals between 1941 and 1947.	
WALTER MAIN	IF	41/14	Airdrieonians 1899	St Bernard's FC 1901
DAVE MANGNALL	CF	39/15	Huddersfield Town 1934	West Ham United 1935
MARCELO (DOS SANTOS)	S	91/26	Sheffield United 1999	Walsall 2002
			was the first Brazilian to play for Blues, signed for £500,000 in 1999	
PAUL MARDON	D	63	Bristol City 1991	West Brom Albion 1993
CHRIS MARSDEN	M	59/6	Stockport County 1995	Southampton 1998
SIMON MARSH	FB	8	Oxford United 1998	Contract cancelled 2001
JAE MARTIN	M	9	Southend United 1995	Lincoln City 1996
RAY MARTIN	FB	374/1	Aston Villa 1961	Portland Timbers (USA) 1976
			made over 370 appearances for Blues after he was released by Aston Villa	
			after breaking manager Joe Mercer's toe in training	
'ROY' MARTIN	FB	74	Kilwinning Rangers 1950	Derby County 1956
DAVE MASSART	F	3	Bell's Athletic 1938	Walsall 1947
TREVOR MATTHEWSON	D	203/13	Lincoln City 1989	Preston North End 1993
BILL MEACOCK	CH	14	Lincoln City 1938	Bristol City 1939
BILL MEATES	G	17	Eastbourne 1895	Warmley 1897
MEHDI NAFTI	M	84/1	Racing Santander (Spain) 2005	FC Aris (Greece) 2009
MARIO MELCHIOT	RB	67/2	Chelsea 2004	Rennes (France) 2006
JOHN METCALFE	OL	2	Yardley Boys 1951	York City 1957
MICHEL (MIGUEL MARCOS MADERA)	M	9	Sporting Gijon (Spain) 2010	Still with club
ARTHUR MILLARD	F	4/3	Smethwick Centaur 1891	Lea Hall 1892
BERT MILLARD	U	33/15	Cardiff City 1919	Coventry City 1920
ALAN MILLER	G	16	Arsenal (l) 1992	Arsenal 1992
			went out on loan to seven different clubs during his career	
KEVIN MILLER	G	30	Exeter City 1993	Watford 1994
CHARLIE MILLINGTON	OR	87/13	Fulham 1909	Wellington Town 1912
BERT 'PADDY' MILLS	IF	13/3	Notts County 1929	Hull City 1929
JIM MITTELL	G	6	Wigan Borough 1931	Luton Town 1933
SID MOFFATT	OR	17/3	Congleton Town 1933	Millwall 1936
JIM MOLES	WH	33	Leyton 1909	Edmonton 1911
JIM MONTGOMERY	G	73	Sunderland 1977	Nottingham Forest 1979
			made more than 700 appearances during his career and will always be	
			remembered for his brilliant double save for Sunderland in their	
			1973 FA Cup Final win over Leeds United	
TOMMY MOONEY	M	39/15	Watford 2001	Swindon Town 2003
ERNIE MOORE	LB	1	Sparkhill Alliance 1893	Hockley Hill 1895
GEORGE MOORE	IF	3/1	Nuneaton Borough 1908	Leamington Town 1909
RICHARD MORAN	CF	9/1	FC Fujita (Japan) 1990	Waterlooville 1991
ARTHUR MORELAND	CF	3	Swindon Town 1938	Port Vale 1939
JACK MORFITT	CF	1	Mansfield Town 1928	Blackpool 1931
BILL MORGAN	OL	68/13	Cradley St Luke's 1912	Coventry City 1920

Player	Position	Record	From	To
JACK MORGAN	CH	1	Edinburgh Emmett 1924	Doncaster Rovers 1926
TOM MORGAN	CH	2	Walsall Town Swifts 1882	Darlaston 1883
TREVOR MORGAN	U	2	South China FC 1993	Solihull Borough 1993
			made 623 appearances during his career (481 in the Football League)	
TONY MORLEY	OL	4/3	West Brom Albion (l) 1984	West Brom Albion 1984
ARTHUR MORRIS	IL	4/2	Shrewsbury Town 1906	Shrewsbury Town 1908
DAVID MORRIS	IL	3	Darlaston 1910	Tipton Town 1912
RONNIE MORRIS	OL	15	FA School of Excellence 1986	Nuovo Pistoiese (Italy) 1989
SEYMOUR MORRIS	OL	83/31	Huddersfield Town 1935	Retired 1944
			was one of five Welsh internationals on Blues' books in 1938–39	
CLINTON MORRISON	S	97/16	Crystal Palace 2002	Crystal Palace 2005
DENNIS MORTIMER	M	37/6	Brighton & Hove Albion 1986	Kettering Town 1987
			made 406 appearances for Aston Villa, with whom he gained League,	
			League Cup, European Cup and Super Cup-winners' medals	
ROY MORTON	M	6/1	Manchester United 1973	Leamington Town 1977
PAUL MOULDEN	S	23/6	Oldham Athletic 1993	Huddersfield Town 1995
			scored a record 289 goals for Bolton Lads' Club Under-15s in 1981–82	
FABRICE MUAMBA	M	79/2	Arsenal (l) 2006 /2007	Bolton Wanderers 2008
IAN MUIR	IF	3	Queen's Park Rangers 1983	Brighton & Hove Albion 1984
(2 spells with club)			Tranmere Rovers 1995	Sing Tao (Hong Kong) 1996
			is Tranmere Rovers' record scorer with 142 League goals	
JOE MULLETT	D	3	Malt Mill United 1955	Norwich City 1959
AMBROSE MULRANEY	W	41/16	Ipswich Town 1945	Shrewsbury Town 1947
WAYNE MUMFORD	RB	8	Manchester City 1982	Worcester City 1984
WILLIAM MUMFORD	RB	3	Bournville 1920	Brighton & Hove Albion 1921
DAVID MURPHY	M	46/1	Hibernian 2008	Still with club
ALBERT MURRAY	U	160/23	Chelsea 1966	Brighton & Hove Albion 1971
			(nicknamed 'Ruby') made 595 League appearances during his 19-year career	
JIM MURRAY	IR	1/1	Aston Villa 1901	Watford 1902
JORDAN MUTCH	M	1	School 2007	Still with club
			became Blues' second-youngest player at the age of 16 years and 268 days	
			when he made his debut against Southampton in a League Cup tie in 2008	
THOMAS MYHRE	G	9	Everton (l) 2000	Everton 2000
PETER NDLOVU	F	134/28	Coventry City 1997	Sheffield United 2001
KEITH NEALE	IF	5/1	Metropolitan FC 1953	Lincoln City 1957
ANDY NEEDHAM	F	3/1	School 1971	Blackburn Rovers 1976
JACK NEEDHAM	IF	20/5	Mansfield Town 1909	Wolverhampton W. 1910
PETER NEIL	OR	5	East Fife 1921	Heart of Midlothian 1922
PETER NEILSON	OL	3/1	Airdrieonians 1913	Wallyford 1914
MIKE NEWELL	S	20/3	Blackburn Rovers 1996	Aberdeen 1997
			scored 166 goals in 655 senior appearances during his nomadic	
			career which saw him serve with 13 different clubs	
EDDIE NEWTON	M	9	Chelsea 1999	Oxford United 2000
			won the FA Cup, League Cup and European Cup-winners' Cup with Chelsea	
BRUNO N'GOTTY	D	27/2	Bolton Wanderers 2006	Leicester City 2007
MARC NORTH	F	5/1	Luton Town (l) 1987	Luton Town 1987
			was playing for Lincoln City on the day when	
			Bradford City's stand burned down in 1985	
ALF OAKES	IL	1	Worcester City 1927	Rhyl Athletic 1928
TOMMY OAKES	F	38/8	Hereford Thistle 1896	Gloucester City 1900
GARRY O'CONNOR	S	56/11	Lokomotiv Moscow (Russia) 2007	Still with club

Player	Position	Record	From	To
MARTYN O'CONNOR	M	223/19	Peterborough United 1996	Walsall 2002
MIKE O'GRADY	W	3	Wolverhampton W. (l) 1972	Wolverhampton W. 1972
EDDIE O'HARA	OL	6	Dundalk 1949	Hereford United 1951
SAM OJI	D	1	Arsenal 2004	Leyton Orient 2007
FOLORUNSO OKENLA	W	13/1	Exeter City 1991	Montreal Impact (Canada) 1993
JACK OLIVER	LB	62	Middlesbrough Ironopolis 1894	Durham 1896
BILLY OLLIS	RH	134/2	Warwick County 1891	Hereford Thistle 1896
JIM OLNEY	CH	3	Redditch United 1936	Swindon Town 1938
ALAN O'NEILL	F	4	Cobh Ramblers 1992	Cobh Ramblers 1993
GARY O'REILLY	D	1	Crystal Palace (l) 1991	Crystal Palace 1991
			scored for Crystal Palace in the 1990 FA Cup Final v Manchester United	
BRYAN ORRITT	U	119/27	Bangor City 1956	Middlesbrough 1962
				played as a junior for
			Llanfairpwllgwyngyllgogerychwyrndrobwllllantysiliogogogoch (shortened to Llanfair PG FC)	
IAN OSBORNE	RB	11	Mid-Leicester Boys 1968	Port Vale 1976
JAMES O'SHEA	S	3	Galway United 2009	Still with club
SID OTTEWELL	IF	5/2	Chesterfield 1947	Nottingham Forest 1948
RICKY OTTO	F	62/8	Southend United 1994	Halesowen Town 1997
			a huge Bob Marley fan, entered League football in 1990 shortly	
			after serving a prison sentence for armed robbery	
BORJA OUBINA	M	2	Celta Vigo (Spain, L) 2007	Celta Vigo 2007
VINCE OVERSON	D	212/5	Burnley 1986	Stoke City 1991
BILL OWEN	G	6	Nuneaton Borough 1926	Fulham 1929
SID OWEN	CH	5	Birmingham YMCA 1945	Luton Town 1947
			captained Luton Town in the 1959 FA Cup Final and was voted	
			'Footballer of the Year' that same season	
QUINCY OWUSU-ABEYIE	F	21/3	Spartak Moscow (l) 2008	Spartak Moscow 2009
MARCOS PAINTER	LB	11	School 2003	Swansea City 2006
WILSON PALACIOUS	M	8	Olimpia FC (Honduras, L) 2007	Olimpia 2007
WALTER PANDIANI	S	14/4	Deportivo La Coruna (Spain, L) 2005	Deportivo La Coruna 2005
STUART PARNABY	FB	50	Middlesbrough 2007	Still with club
HARRY PARR	RH	1	Wellington Town 1937	Dawley Rovers 1939
GEORGE PARRIS	M	52/2	West Ham United 1993	Norrkopping FC (Sweden) 1996
			made almost 500 appearances at various levels during his career	
CHARLIE PARTRIDGE	G	33	Wednesbury Old Athletic 1890	Willenhall Town 1896
JOHN PASKIN	S	11/3	Wolverhampton W. (l) 1991	Wolverhampton W. 1992
JACK PEART	CF	3	Notts County 1919	Derby County 1920
DEAN PEER	M	150/12	Stourbridge Falcons 1985	Northampton Town 1995
JERMAINE PENNANT	W	60/3	Arsenal 2005	Liverpool 2006
FRED PENTLAND	IL	1	Avondale Juniors 1900	Blackburn Rovers 1903
BILL PEPLOW	OR	17/1	Redditch Town 1907	Bristol Rovers 1908
PAUL PESCHISOLIDO	S	57/18	Toronto Blizzard (Canada) 1992	Stoke City 1994
(2 spells with club)			Stoke City 1996	West Brom Albion 1998
			is married to former Birmingham City managing director Karren Brady	
'CHARLIE' PHILLIPS	IF	25/10	Aston Villa 1938	Chelmsford City 1939
LES PHILLIPS	M	54/4	School 1979	Oxford United 1984
STEVE PHILLIPS	F	26/1	School 1970	Northampton Town 1980
			scored 255 goals in 710 appearances for his seven League clubs (1970–88)	
ARTHUR PHOENIX	IF	3	Glossop North End 1922	Aston Villa 1924
THEOPHILUS PIKE	OL	17/4	Bournemouth 1928	Southend United 1930
DOUG PIMBLEY	OL	2	Leicester City 1946	Notts County 1948
NICKY PLATNAUER	U	36/2	Coventry City 1984	Cardiff City 1986

Player	Position	Record	From	To
ERNIE POINTER	G	29	Redditch Town 1896	Berwick Rangers (NL) 1898
(2 spells with club)			Berwick Rangers (NL) 1900	Kidderminster Harriers 1901
TOM POINTON	OL	4/1	Redditch Town 1913	Redditch Town 1914

was played by Blues before his transfer from Redditch Town had been completed,
and the club were subsequently fined £5

JAMIE POLLOCK	M	5	Crystal Palace (l) 2001	Crystal Palace 2001
GARY POOLE	RB	103/4	Southend United 1994	Charlton Athletic 1996
KEVIN POOLE	G	67	Leicester City 1997	Bolton Wanderers 2001

was still engaged as Burton Albion's goalkeeper in 2010, at the age of 47

GRAHAM POTTER	D	32/2	School 1991	Stoke City 1993
AUBREY POWELL	IF	15/1	Everton 1950	Wellington Town 1951

was told by doctors that his career was over after breaking his leg in 1937,
but he continued playing until 1952

DARRYL POWELL	D	14	Derby County 2002	Sheffield Wednesday 2003
HERBERT POWELL	IF	5/1	Coventry City 1910	Rotherham Town 1911
BILL PRATT	OL	26/1	St John's FC 1888	Small Heath Unity 1892
BILLY PRATT	LB	140	Hoskins & Sewell FC 1894	Retired 1902
DAVID PREECE	M	7	Derby County (l) 1995	Derby County 1996

made 655 career appearances, 395 for Luton Town,
with whom he won the League Cup in 1988

DAN PRESTON	D	1	School 2008	Still with club
JOSIAH PRESTON	RB	7	Burton United 1908	Halesowen Town 1910
JACK PRICE	RH	1/1	Aston Villa 1885	Birmingham St Luke's FC 1888
JOHN PRICE	IR	1	Shenstone FC 1897	Watford 1900
RYAN PRICE	G	1	Stafford Rangers 1994	Macclesfield Town 1995

was 6ft 5in tall and weighed 14st

TILSON PRITCHARD	RB	1	Burntwood Swifts 1894	Lichfield Town 1895
MARK PRUDHOE	G	5	Sunderland 1984	Walsall 1986

made over 400 appearances with 14 different clubs during his 21-year career

BERNARD PUMFREY	LB	13/1	Birmingham St Mark's 1892	Gainsborough Trinity 1894
DARREN PURSE	D	200/11	Oxford United 1998	West Brom Albion 2004
BILL PURVES	RB	43	Glentoran 1893	Glentoran 1897
NIGEL QUASHIE	M	11	West Ham United (l) 2008	West Ham United 2008
FRANCK QUEUDRUE	LB	54/3	Fulham 2007	Released 2010
JAMES QUINN	F	4	School 1991	Blackpool 1993
WALTER QUINTON	LB	9	Rotherham United 1939	Brentford 1949
JACK RANDLE	FB	116/1	Coventry City 1927	Southend United 1933

scored a hat-trick of own-goals during his Coventry City days

RAY RANSON	RB	158	Manchester City 1984	Newcastle United 1988

bought Coventry City football club in December 2007

MICK RATHBONE	RB	25	Aston Villa Boys 1974	Blackburn Rovers 1979
ALBERT RAWSON	CF	19/9	Sheffield United 1923	Barnsley 1924
SIMON REA	D	3	School 1992	Peterborough United 1999
ARTHUR REED	IF	29/13	Doncaster Rovers 1912	Retired 1917
TONY REES	F	111/16	Aston Villa 1983	Grimsby Town 1989
MATTHEW REGAN	CF	7/2	Claines FC 1959	Shrewsbury Town 1964
DAVID REGIS	S	7/2	Stoke City 1994	Southend United 1994

is the brother of Cyrille, cousin of sprinter John and uncle to striker Jason Roberts

DAVID RENNIE	U	37/4	Bristol City 1992	Coventry City 1993

became Leicester City's physiotherapist

BILL REYNOLDS	LB	13	St Luke's FC 1893	Berwick Rangers (NL) 1894

Player	Position	Record	From	To
'CARL' RICHARDS	CF	19/2	Bournemouth 1988	Peterborough United 1989
DAI RICHARDS	LH	66/2	Brentford 1937	Walsall 1939
ERNIE RICHARDSON	OR	3	Leven FC 1936	Swansea Town 1938
IAN RICHARDSON	D	16	Dagenham & Redbridge 1995	Notts County 1996
LIAM RIDGEWELL	D	113/6	Aston Villa 2007	Still with club
HARRY RILEY	OR	1	Hunt FC 1928	Ashton National 1929
BRUCE RIOCH	M	3	Derby County (l) 1978	Derby County 1978
			was the first English-born player to captain Scotland, doing so at the	
			1978 World Cup; he scored 160 goals in 530 League games	
JIMMY ROACH	G	17	Hereford Thistle 1895	Hereford Town 1896
BILLY ROBB	G	45	Kirkintilloch Rob Roy 1914	Armadale 1915
			career spanned 27 years, and he holds the record for the longest gap between	
			League appearances, 17 years: 1915 with Blues, 1932 with Aldershot	
'HARRY' ROBERTS	FB	213	Coventry City 1984	Wolverhampton W. 1990
			wrote a book during his time at Wolves (Harry's Game)	
FRED ROBERTS	IL	32/10	Thomas Pigot's Works FC 1933	Luton Town 1934
HARRY ROBERTS	OL	38/3	Chesterfield 1948	Shrewsbury Town 1951
JOHN ROBERTS	D	79/1	Arsenal 1972	Wrexham 1976
JOSIAH ROBERTS	RB	1	Mitchell St George's 1892	Walsall Wood 1893
BILL ROBERTSON	U	103/15	Abercorn 1896	Eastville Rovers 1899
(2 spells with club)			Eastville Rovers 1902	Bristol Rovers 1903
BILL H. ROBERTSON	G	3	Chelsea 1948	Stoke City 1952
			initially a centre-forward, took up goalkeeping at the age of 20	
GEORGE ROBERTSON	U	87/17	Clyde 1910	Bloxwich Strollers 1914
JIM ROBERTSON	IR	7/2	Crewe Alexandra 1903	Chelsea 1905
JIM. E. ROBERTSON	CF	8/2	Dundee 1933	Kilmarnock 1934
COLIN ROBINSON	F	42/6	Shrewsbury Town 1988	Hereford United 1989
DAVE ROBINSON	D	127/4	School 1964	Walsall 1973
			saved the club £80,000, according to manager Stan Cullis	
PHIL ROBINSON	M	12	Notts County (l) 1991	Notts County 1991
			was 'given away' by Aston Villa (to Wolves)	
STEVE ROBINSON	M	95/2	School 1991	Swindon Town 2001
TOM ROBINSON	IL	10/1	Gresley Rovers 1928	Blackpool 1933
IAN RODGERSON	U	116/16	Cardiff City (l) 1990/1991	Sunderland 1993
ARCHIE ROE	IF	3	South Shields 1919	Gillingham 1920
DARREN ROGERS	D	26	West Brom Albion 1992	Walsall 1994
KEVIN ROGERS	M	9/1	Aston Villa 1983	Wrexham 1984
BILLY RONSON	M	2	Barnsley (l) 1985	Barnsley 1985
			became one of the most successful players around the US indoor circuit	
WALLY ROTHERHAM	IL	2	Wolverhampton St Luke's 1880	Leabrook 1883
JOE ROULSON	RH	125/4	Cammel Laird FC 19012	Swansea Town 1923
DARREN ROWBOTHAM	F	41/6	Torquay United 1992	Crewe Alexandra 1993
GARY ROWETT	D	103/11	Derby County 1998	Leicester City 2000
			was signed by former Blues star Alan Curbishley for Charlton Athletic in 2002	
KEN ROWLEY	IF	42/20	Wolverhampton W. 1951	Coventry City 1954
BILLY RUDD	F	26/4	Stalybridge Celtic 1959	York City 1961
			made well over 600 appearances during his career	
SIGURD RUSHFELDT	S	9/1	FC Tromso (Norway, L) 1995	FC Tromso 1995
BRIAN RUSHTON	RB	15	Dudley Boys 1959	Notts County 1967
CECIL RUSSELL	F	27/2	Bromsgrove Rovers 1924	Bristol Rovers 1927
GUY RUSSELL	CF	14	Knowle North Star 1984	Kemin Pallosuera (Finland) 1989

Player	Position	Record	From	To
MARTIN RUSSELL	M	6	Manchester United (l) 1986	Manchester United 1986
			from Portadown, was voted Northern Ireland's 'Player of the Year' in 1992	
MARK RUTHERFORD	W	5	School 1988	Shelbourne 1991
ALFRED SABIN	RH	2	Accles & Pollock Works FC 1930	Oldbury United 1930
MAT SADLER	D	61	School 2000	Watford 2008
DAN SAHLIN	S	1	Hammarby IF (Sweden, L) 1995	Hammarby IF 1995
			played just 20 minutes for Blues v Leicester City in 1995	
MARK SALE	S	27/3	Rocester 1992	Torquay United 1993
ASHLEY SAMMONS	M	1	School 2008	Still with club
ARTHUR SAMSON	G	2	Measham Town 1922	Burton Town 1923
VINNY SAMWAYS	M	12	Everton (l) 1996	Everton 1996
			won the FA Cup with Spurs in 1991	
PAUL SANSOME	G	2	Southend United (l) 1996	Southend United 1996
			racked up 525 League appearances during his career	
ROBBIE SAVAGE	M	88/12	Leicester City 2002	Blackburn Rovers 2005
ANDY SAVILLE	S	65/18	Hartlepool United 1993	Preston North End 1995
			struck 133 goals in 520 senior appearances in 17 years	
RICKY SBRAGIA	D	17/1	Glasgow Amateurs 1972	Walsall 1978
			was manager of Sunderland before handing over to Steve Bruce	
RAFAEL SCHMITZ	D	16	FC Lille (France, L) 2007	FC Lille 2008
GEOFF SCOTT	D	19	Leicester City 1982	Charlton Athletic 1982
RICHARD SCOTT	U	19	School 1991	Shrewsbury Town 1995
AUBREY SCRIVEN	OL	52/9	Denaby United 1923	Bradford City 1927
TOM SCRIVENS	IF	16/9	Smethwick Rovers 1897	Wellingborough 1898
DAVID SEAMAN, MBE	G	84	Peterborough United 1984	Queen's Park Rangers 1986
			made 1,049 club and international appearances, starring in two World Cups	
			and collecting medals galore with Arsenal between 1979 and 2004	
ALF SELLMAN	CH	1	Bridgetown Amateurs 1904	Leyton 1905
FRANK SHARP	IL	5	Barton Boys Sports Club 1922	Chesterfield 1923
BRIAN SHARPLES	CH	72/2	School 1959	Exeter City 1968
FRED SHAW	IF	5	Darlaston 1932	Notts County 1934
JACK SHAW	LH	11	Grimsby Town 1939	Watford 1945
RAY SHAW	WH	13	Darlaston 1937	Retired 1947
PETER SHEARER	F	38/13	Coventry City 1983	Rochdale 1986
(2 spells with club)			Bournemouth 1994	Peterborough United 1995
JOHN SHERIDAN	M	4	Sheffield Wednesday (l) 1996	Sheffield Wednesday 1996
			a League Cup-winner with Sheffield Wednesday,	
			made over 700 appearances at club level.	
CHARLIE SHORT	F	19/17	Birmingham Excelsior 1889	Unity Gas Depot FC 1890
(2 spells with club)			Unity Gas Depot FC 1890	Bloxwich Strollers 1892
			was not registered to play in an FA Cup tie against Wednesbury Old Athletic	
			in 1890, and as a result Blues were disqualified from the competition that season	
GEORGE SHORT	U	29/5	Unity Gas Depot FC 1887	Oldbury Town 1895
			was the elder brother of Charlie	
JACK SHORT	IF	17/10	Notts County 1919	Watford 1920
JAMES SHORT	IR	1	Stafford Road 1891	Bilston 1893
ROBIN SHROOT	W	1	Harrow 2009	Still with club
JACK SHUFFLEBOTTOM	CH	1	Old Mill FC 1905	Oldham Athletic 1907
CARL SHUTT	S	29/4	Leeds United 1993	Manchester City 1994
CHARLIE SIMMS	CH	23	Mitchell St George's 1884	Retired 1892
			served Blues, as a player, trainer and groundsman, for almost 30 years: 1884–1914	

Player	Position	Record	From	To
SCOTT SINCLAIR	F	14	Chelsea (l) 2009	Chelsea 2009
DENNIS SINGER	IF	31/15	Newport County 1960	Bournemouth 1962
GRAHAM SISSONS	D	106	Country Girl FC 1954	Peterborough United 1962
BILL SLATER	CF	5/4	Calthorpe 1879	Brades Heath 1884
FRED SLATER	CF	5/1	Burton Albion 1947	York City 1951
			broke his leg when making his League debut for Blues	
			against Huddersfield Town in 1948	
JOHN SLEEUWENHOEK	CH	32	Aston Villa 1967	Oldham Athletic 1971
			the son of a Dutch parachute instructor, played against	
			Blues in the 1963 League Cup Final	
BRYAN SMALL	LB	3	Aston Villa (l) 1994	Aston Villa 1994
SAM SMALL	CF	6	Bromsgrove Rovers 1934	West Ham United 1937
MARK SMALLEY	D	7	Nottingham Forest (l) 1986	Nottingham Forest 1986
ANDREW SMITH	IF	59/34	Crosswell's brewery 1912	West Brom Albion 1919
			won a League Championship with West Bromwich Albion in 1920,	
			a year after leaving Blues	
ARTHUR SMITH	OL	52/4	Queen's Park Rangers 1912	Brierley Hill Alliance 1914
AUSTIN SMITH	CF	2/2	Walsall Town 1887	Bournville 1888
BERNARD SMITH	LB	12	Derby County 1932	Coventry City 1935
BILLY A. SMITH	IR	17/5	Coventry City 1908	Coventry City 1909
BILLY H. SMITH	IF	62/23	Northampton Town 1950	Blackburn Rovers 1952
DAVID SMITH	M	44/3	Coventry City 1993	West Brom Albion 1994
			penalty for West Bromwich Albion knocked Blues out of the Anglo-Italian Cup in 1996	
GEORGE SMITH	LH	1	Edgbaston 1890	Handsworth Royal 1891
GEORGE SMITH	M	45	Middlesbrough 1971	Cardiff City 1973
GILBERT SMITH	RB	14	Causeway Green Villa 1893	Berwick Rangers (NL) 1894
JOHN SMITH	IL	6/1	Wolverhampton W. 1906	Bristol Rovers 1907
JOE SMITH	RB	50	West Brom Albion 1926	Worcester City 1929
JOE E. SMITH	LH	8	Hickleton Main Colliery 1912	Richmond FC 1915
SAM SMITH	CF	33/13	Walsall L.M.S. 1930	Chelsea 1934
STEVE SMITH	G	3	Cardiff City 1973	Bradford City 1978
WALTER SMITH	IF	26/6	Bury 1914	Altrincham 1916
GEORGE SMITHIES	CF	1	Preston North End 1931	Derby Dale FC 1932
DANNY SONNER	M	56/3	Sheffield Wednesday 2000	Walsall 2002
GEORGE SOUTHALL	OL	14	Stourbridge 1905	Halesowen 1907
JIM SOUTHAM	FB	3	Newport County 1946	Northampton Town 1949
FRED SPELLER	FB	95	Great Marlow 1888	Retired 1894
			career was cut short by a broken leg	
GARY SPRAKE	G	24	Leeds United 1973	Retired 1975
			was Wales's youngest-ever goalkeeper in 1963 (aged 18)	
CHARLIE SPRIGG	OL	16	Bilston United 1912	Redditch Town 1913
PHIL SPROSON	CH	16/1	Port Vale 1989	Stafford Rangers 1990
NEIL SPROSTON	CF	1	School 1986	Alvechurch 1990
BARRIE SQUIRES	OL	1	Bristol City 1953	Bradford City 1954
RON STAINTON	LB	1	Bournville 1927	King's Heath 1928
EDDIE STANLEY	F	35/17	Calthorpe 1881	Retired 1891
WILSON STANLEY	OR	1	Hockley Belmont 1886	Oldbury Broadwell 1887
ARTHUR STANTON	RB	6	Bloxwich Strollers 1913	Oldbury United 1919
PHIL STARBUCK	F	3	Nottingham Forest (l) 1988	Nottingham Forest 1988
BILLY STEEL	LB	91	Liverpool 1935	Derby County 1939
			was Scotland's trainer at the 1954 World Cup	

Player	Position	Record	From	To
BYRON STEVENSON	D	91/3	Leeds United 1982	Bristol Rovers 1985
				was sent-off playing for Wales in 1879
STUART STORER	OR	10	VS Rugby 1984	Everton 1987
ROBIN STUBBS	CF	70/20	Oldbury Boys 1956	Torquay United 1963
				wife Anthea Redfern left him to marry Bruce Forsyth
SIMON STURRIDGE	F	186/38	School 1985	Stoke City 1993
				scored Blues' first goal at Wembley for 60 years in 1991
CHRIS SUTTON	S	11/1	Celtic 2006	Aston Villa 2007
				scored 151 goals in 410 career League appearances
STEVE SUTTON	G	6	Derby County 1996	Grantham Town 1998
ARCHIE STYLES	LB	82/4	Everton 1974	Peterborough United 1978
KEVIN SUMMERFIELD	F	8/2	West Brom Albion 1982	Walsall 1983
				scored 89 goals in 460 League games
PHIL SUMMERILL	F	131/52	Aston Boys 1963	Huddersfield Town 1973
LARRY SUMMERS	D	2	The Grove 1880	Hockley Hill 1882
PIOTR SWIERCZEWSKI	M	1	Olympique Marseille (France) 2003	Lech Poznan (Poland) 2004
				was due to sign for Blues after a fee of £1 million had been agreed with Marseille
				after his loan spell, but the deal fell through; he went on to win 70 caps for Poland
ALBERT SYKES	LH	1	Maltby Town 1924	Brighton & Hove Albion 1926
ERNIE SYKES	RB	10	Sutton Town 1936	Cardiff City 1939
JACK SYKES	LB	34	Wombwell FC 1932	Millwall 1937
PAUL TAIT	U	212/18	Hurley Colts 1987	Oxford United 1999
TEEMO TAINHO	M	6	Sunderland (l) 2009	Sunderland 2010
ALBERTO TARANTINI	FB	24/1	Boca Juniors (Argentina) 1978	Talleres de Cordoba (Argentina) 1979
				the Argentinian World Cup-winner, cost Blues £295,000 in 1979
JOE TATTON	CH	1	St Mark's 1880	Nechells 1882
BILL TAYLOR	U	10	Langley Green Victoria 1891	Quinton FC 1893
BRIAN TAYLOR	OL	67/9	Walsall 1958	Rotherham United 1961
JOE TAYLOR	LB	3	Hockley Belmont 1881	Brookvale 1884
MARTIN TAYLOR	D	117/3	Blackburn Rovers 2004	Watford 2010
Dr IAN TAYLOR-SMITH	F	2	Queen's Park 1975	Heart of Midlothian 1977
JIMMY TEBBS	OL	4/1	Loughborough Town 1900	Leicester United 1902
OLIVIER TEBILY	U	95	Glasgow Celtic 2002	FC Toronto (Canada) 2008
KEN TEWKSBURY	G	5	Birmingham University 1929	Aston Villa 1931
				married the daughter of Blues' director Mr W.H. Bull
VIC TEYCHENNE	HB/CF	2	Wednesbury Old Athletic 1880	Smethwick Centaur 1882
BILL THIRLAWAY	OL	23/1	South Shields 1926	Cardiff City 1927
HORACE THOMPSON	OL)	1	Handsworth Victoria 1922	Lye Town 1923
LEN THOMPSON	OL	2	Hallam FC 1918	Swansea Town 1922
TOMMY THOMPSON	OL	1	Nettlefolds FC 1902	Oldbury Town 1903
BOBBY THOMSON	LB	69	Wolverhampton W. 1969	Luton Town 1971
				made 477 League appearances for his five clubs
BOBBY G. THOMSON	U	129/25	Aston Villa 1963	Stockport County 1967
				played against his former club (Aston Villa) in the 1963 League Cup Final
JACK THOROGOOD	OL	24/2	Frickley Colliery 1930	Millwall 1934
WILF THRELFALL	OL	5	Sunderland 1927	Bournemouth 1928
DENNIS THWAITES	OL	95/21	School 1960	Retired 1972 (Rover FC).
				is the uncle of ex-West Bromwich Albion defender Steve Lilwall
CHARLIE TICKLE	IL	91/15	Bournbrook 1904	Coventry City 1908
CARL TILER	D	1	Charlton Athletic (l) 2001	Charlton Athletic 2001
PETER TILL	W	1	School 2003	Grimsby Town 2006

Player	Position	Record	From	To
ALF TINKLER	CH	103/3	Ilkeston Town 1911	Burton United 1915
PAUL TOMLINSON	G	11	Sheffield United (l) 1987	Sheffield United 1987
TONY TOWERS	M	103/4	Sunderland 1977	Montreal Manic (Canada) 1981
DJIMI TRAORE	D	3	Portsmouth (l) 2009	Portsmouth 2009
			cost Liverpool £550,000, Charlton Athletic £2 million and Portsmouth £1 million	
'GEORGE' TRAVERS	CF	2	Wolverhampton W. 1907	Aston Villa 1908
			was an FA Cup-winner with Barnsley in 1912	
JOHN TREWICK	M	42	Newcastle United 1987	Hartlepool United 1989
			joined Newcastle United in 1980 for a fee of £234,567.89, and after West Bromwich Albion's trip to China in 1978 the midfielder, when questioned about the Great Wall, said: 'Once you've seen one wall, you've seen them all.'	
ARTHUR S. TURNER	IR	1	Aston Villa 1890	Stourbridge 1891
TERRY TWELL	G	2	Bourne Town 1964	Stamford Town 1968
MATTHEW UPSON	D	128/5	Arsenal 2003	West Ham United 2007
NICO VAESEN	G	63	Huddersfield Town 2001	FC Lierse (Belgium) 2006
ARCHIE VALE	G	2	Erdington R.C. 1882	Aston Villa 1883
ENRIC VALLES	M	**	NAC Breda (Holland) 2010	Still with club
			a Spaniard, was with Barcelona before NAC Breda	
TOINE VAN MIERLO	OL	47/4	SV Willem II (Holland) 1981	SV Willem 1982
STEVE VICKERS	D	23/1	Middlesbrough 2001	Retired 2003
			made nearly 400 appearances for Tranmere and over 300 for Middlesbrough.	
GREGORY VIGNAL	WB	9	Lens (France) 2009	Released 2010
ROWAN VINE	S	19/1	Luton Town 2007	Queen's Park Rangers 2007
GEORGE WADDELL	RH	2	Oldham Athletic 1922	Hamilton Academical 1923
BILLY WALKER	CF	30/10	Lanemark FC 1914	Coventry City 1920
ALEX WALLACE	OL	2/1	Baltimore (USA) 1897	Hereford Thistle 1898
'DANNY' WALLACE	F	19/2	Manchester United 1993	Wycombe Wanderers 1995
			was a European Cup-winner with Manchester United in 1991	
SID WALLINGTON	LH	2	Wolseley Sports 1928	Bristol Rovers 1933
TONY WANT	FB	127/2	Tottenham Hotspur (172)	Minnesota Kicks (USA) 1978
MARK WARD	M	82/8	Everton 1994	Huddersfield Town 1996
			was gaoled for eight years in 2005 for supplying cocaine	
WALTER WARD	G	5	Calthorpe 1890	Oldbury Broadwell 1891
BILLY WARDLE	OL	68/7	Blackpool 1951	Barnsley 1953
PETER WARMINGTON	IF	9/3	Redditch Juniors 1949	Bromsgrove Rovers 1957
DARREN WASSALL	D	30	Manchester City 1997	Burton Albion 2000
HARRY WASSALL	LB	60/1	Brierley Hill Alliance 1902	Bristol Rovers 1904
ERNIE WATKINS	IF	8/1	Finchley 1922	Southend United 1924
JACK WATSON	RB	2	Bloxwich Strollers 1919	Measham Town 1920
PERCY WATSON	LB	2	Rotherham Town 1893	Denaby United 1894
TOM WATSON	G	2	Yardley Victoria 1893	Birmingham Police Force 1895
			a full-back, kept goal for Blues' second XI in 1894–95	
ERNIE WATTS	IR	2	Hockley Hill 1889	Smethwick Highfield 1890
JOHNNY WATTS	WH	248/3	Saltley Old Boys 1948	Nuneaton Borough 1963
IKE WEBB	G	6	Wellington Town 1898	West Brom Albion 1901
MATT WEBB	W	1	School 1993	NL football 1997
SID WEBB	IF	3	Wednesbury Old Athletic 1911	Worcester City 1912
DON WESTON	CF	25/3	Wrexham 1960	Rotherham United 1960
SID WHARTON	OL	167/25	Smethwick Wesleyans 1897	Retired 1903
NEIL WHATMORE	F	27/7	Bolton Wanderers 1981	Oxford United 1983
JACK WHEELER	G	13	Cheltenham Town 1938	Huddersfield Town 1948
			was goalkeeper in Huddersfield Town's six-man defence which played in every game in 1952–53	

Player	Position	Record	From	To
FRANK WHITE	OR	156/50	Tamworth 1931	Preston North End 1938
HARRY WHITE	LH	2	Wednesbury Old Athletic 1921	Ellesmere Port 1922
TOM WHITE	RB	15	Notts County 1918	Worksop Town 1921
ALAN WHITEHEAD	D	6	School 1967	Kettering Town 1974
JIM WHIEHEAD	IL	2	Kings Norton Boys Club 1881	Lea Hall 1882
JACK WHITEHOUSE	F	115/35	Redditch Town 1916	Derby County 1923
STEVE WHITTON	F	119/36	West Ham United 1986	Sheffield Wednesday 1989
			scored 117 goals in 531 competitive appearances during his career	
CHRIS WHYTE	D	89/1	Leeds United 1993	Charlton Athletic 1996
STEVE WIGLEY	W	98/5	Sheffield United 1987	Portsmouth 1989
FRED WILCOX	IL	84/3	Bristol Rovers 1903	Middlesbrough 1906
			played alongside Steve Bloomer at Middlesbrough	
HARRY WILCOX	IF	17/3	Selly Oak St Mary's 1898	Watford 1900
JACK WILCOX	W	48/2	Aston Villa 1908	Southampton 1911
LES WILCOX	OL	4/2	West Bromwich Highfield 1889	Oldbury Town 1890
FRED WILKES	CF	5/4	Handsworth Boys Club 1891	Brownhills FC 1892
WALTER WILLETTS	OL	1	Langley Victoria 1884	Oldbury 1885
DEAN WILLIAMS	G	5	School 1988	Tamworth 1992
HARRY WILLIAMS	LB	1	Aston Manor 1896	Nechells 1897
JACQUES WILLIAMS	M	4	Bordeaux (France) 1999	Crewe Alexandra (trial) 2002
JIMMY WILLIAMS	IF	12/3	Accrington Stanley 1908	Accrington Stanley 1909
			was among a handful of footballers killed during World War One	
PAUL WILLIAMS	F	12/1	Crystal Palace (l) 1995	Crystal Palace 1995
TOMMY WILLIAMS	U	4	Peterborough United 2002	Peterborough United 2003
TOMMY E. WILLIAMS	D	74/2	Leicester City 1986	Grimsby Town 1988
ROGER WILLIS	U	20/5	Watford 1993	Southend United 1994
ALF WILSON	RB	2	Sheffield Wednesday 1919	Rotherham County 1921
JARED WILSON	FB	1	School 2005	Released 2010
PETER WITHE	S	48/11	Portland Timbers (USA) 1975	Nottingham Forest 1976
(2 spells with club)			Sheffield United (l) 1987	Sheffield United 1987
			scored 232 goals in 640 games during his lengthy career	
COLIN WITHERS	G	116	West Brom Albion 1957	Aston Villa 1964
			conceded six goals on his Blues' debut at Tottenham in 1960	
TREVOR WOLLASTON	RH	1	Yardley Victoria 1891	Stechford Royal Unity 1891
TREVOR WOLSTENHOLME	U	2/1	Chloride FC 1959	Torquay United 1963
EDMUND WOOD	CH	1	Northampton Town 1925	Rhyl Athletic 1928
CURTIS WOODHOUSE	M	55/2	Sheffield United 2001	Peterborough United 2003
BILLY WRAGG	D	1	Leicester Fosse 1901	Watford 1901
			scored Nottingham Forest's first goal in their 1898 FA Cup Final win	
ADAM WRATTEN	M	1/2	School 1991	Released 1995
			scored twice as a substitute against Wolves in an Anglo-Italian Cup tie in 1993, his only game for Blues	
CHRIS WREH	S	7/1	Arsenal (l) 1999	Arsenal 1999
BILLY WRIGHT	D	137/14	Everton 1983	Carlisle United 1986
PAT WRIGHT	FB	3	Springfield Boys Club 1959	Shrewsbury Town 1962
MARK YATES	U	65/7	Forest falcons 1986	Burnley 1991
DWIGHT YORKE	F	16/2	Blackburn Rovers 2004	Sydney FC (Australia) 2005
			scored 197 goals in 612 club games and gained 72 caps for Trindad & Tobago during his career	
MAURO ZARATE	W	14/4	Al-Sadd (Qatar, L) 2008	Al-Sadd 2008
NIKOLA ZIGIC	F	**	Valencia 2010	Still with club

Wartime Guests

The following are some of the many guest players used by Blues during World War One and World War Two:

1915–19

JOHN BELL A utility forward from Nottingham Forest (8 goals in 21 games).

SID BOWSER An England international inside-forward from West Bromwich Albion who made 42 appearances for Blues.

SAMMY BROOKS Outside-left from Wolves who netted twice in nine outings for Blues.

CHARLIE BUCHAN Classy inside-right of Sunderland and England who scored over 250 League goals during his career.

HAROLD EDGLEY Of Aston Villa, made seven appearances for Blues.

BERT FREEMAN The Burnley and England centre-forward.

GEORGE HUNTER A half-back from Manchester United who scored twice in 21 games for Blues.

CLAUDE JEPHCOTT Outside-right of West Bromwich Albion, who notched two goals in his 12 outings for Blues.

HARRY MONTGOMERY A right-winger from Glossop who hit seven goals in 19 starts for Blues.

TEDDY PEERS Wolves' Welsh international goalkeeper who played in 12 games for Blues.

JESSE PENNINGTON The England and West Bromwich Albion full-back.

SAMMY RICHARDSON Pennington's Baggies' teammate.

DANNY SHEA An England international forward from Blackburn Rovers.

SAMMY STEVENS Netherton-born centre-forward from Hull City who struck 12 goals in 15 games for Blues.

CHARLIE WALLACE Outside-left of Aston Villa and England who missed a penalty in the 1913 FA Cup Final.

TOM WESTON Wallace's Villa Park colleague who played in the 1920 FA Cup Final.

1939–46

JACK ACQUROFF Centre-forward from Norwich City, hit 10 goals in 44 appearances in two seasons for Blues (1942–44).

JIMMY ALLEN Aston Villa's England international.

SAM BARTRAM Charlton's goalkeeper.

JACKIE BRAY Manchester City and England left-half.

DICK BRIGHT A local lad, struck 10 goals in 27 games for Blues.

FRANK BROOME England international forward from Aston Villa, who made seven appearances for Blues.

GEORGE CUMMINGS Also from Aston Villa and a Scottish international defender.

TED DITCHBURN Spurs' goalkeeper.

PETER DOHERTY Of Manchester City and Ireland.

GEORGE EASTHAM Of Blackpool, father of George junior.

GEORGE EDWARDS Outside-left of Aston Villa.

BOB FINAN Centre-forward of Blackpool.

EDDIE HAPGOOD Arsenal and England full-back.

GEORGE HARDWICK Middlesbrough and England captain.

BOB IVERSON Of Aston Villa and formerly of Wolves.

CLARRIE JORDAN Centre-forward from Doncaster Rovers.

JIMMY McCORMICK Of Spurs, who made 28 appearances on the right-wing for Blues.

IAN McPHERSON A winger from Rangers who had also played for Arsenal.

ALEX MASSIE Aston Villa and Scotland wing-half who later became manager at Villa Park.

'LOL' MORGAN Half-back for Walsall.

FRANK MOSS Centre-half at Aston Villa.

AMBROSE MULRANEY Who signed for Blues permanently in 1945.

HUGH O'DONNELL Blackpool outside-left.

SID OTTEWELL Who joined Blues on contract in 1947.

TOM PEARSON Scottish international from Newcastle United.

CHARLIE REVELL From Charlton Athletic.

GEORGE ROBINSON From Charlton Athletic and ex-Sunderland.

JACK SHELTON A full-back from Walsall.

BILLY THAYNE Shelton's teammate at Fellows Park.

DOUG TRENTHAM From Everton, brother of Bert, ex-West Bromwich Albion.

BERT TURNER Of Charlton Athletic, who scored two goals in the 1946 FA Cup Final, one for each side.

PETER VAUSE An outside-left from Rochdale who also played for Blackburn Rovers and Blackpool.

Blues' Managers: 1892–2010

Name	Appointed	Left
ALF JONES	July 1892	June 1908
ALEX WATSON	July 1908	June 1910
BOB McROBERTS	July 1910	May 1915
FRANK RICHARDS	May 1915	May 1923
BILLY BEER	May 1923	March 1927
BILLY HARVEY	March 1927	May 1928
LESLIE KNIGHTON	July 1928	May 1933
GEORGE LIDDELL	July 1933	September 1939
WILLIAM CAMKIN	October 1939	November 1944
TED GOODIER	November 1944	May 1945
HARRY STORER	June 1945	November 1948
BOB BROCKLEBANK	January 1949	October 1954
ARTHUR TURNER	November 1954	February 1958
TURNER/PAT BEASLEY*	January 1958	September 1958
PAT BEASLEY	September 1958	May 1960
GIL MERRICK	May 1960	April 1964
JOE MALLETT	July 1964	December 1965
STAN CULLIS	December 1965	March 1970
FREDDIE GOODWIN	May 1970	September 1975
WILLIE BELL	September 1975	September 1977
SIR ALF RAMSEY	September 1977	March 1978
JIM SMITH	March 1978	February 1982
RON SAUNDERS	February 1982	January 1986
JOHN BOND	January 1986	May 1987
GARRY PENDREY	June 1987	April 1989
DAVE MACKAY	April 1989	January 1991
BILL COLDWELL+	January 1991	
LOU MACARI	February 1991	June 1991
BILL COLDWELL+	June 1991	August 1991
TERRY COOPER	August 1991	December 1993
BARRY FRY	December 1993	May 1996
TREVOR FRANCIS	May 1996	December 2001
STEVE BRUCE	December 2001	November 2007
ERIC BLACK +	November 2007	
ALEX McLEISH	November 2007	To date

* Beasley and Turner were joint managers for seven months.
+ Caretaker manager.

THE MEN IN CHARGE

The playing side of the football club was run by a selected five-man committee for almost 17 years, from 1875 to 1892. The team captain was a key member of the committee, along with the secretary and treasurer, vice-captain and one other – and it was the captain who had perhaps the biggest say regarding team selection.

ALF JONES was appointed Blues' first secretary-manager in the summer of 1892. Nicknamed 'Inky' – simply because he was always seen with a pen in his hand – Jones was in office for 16 years, having previously held the position as club secretary from 1885 when he replaced player Billy Edmunds. During his time as secretary Blues reached the semi-finals of the FA (English) Cup in 1886 and gained a place in the Football League in 1892. Then, when he became secretary-manager they won the Second Division title in 1893 and achieved promotion on three occasions, in 1894, 1901 and 1903. He was also at the helm when the move was made from Muntz Street to St Andrew's. Born in Small Heath in 1850, he was a much-respected gentleman and under his shrewd guidance Blues became a force to be reckoned with in English football. Jones remained close to the club after being replaced as secretary-manager by Alex Watson. In fact, he hardly missed a home game and was fast approaching his 80th birthday when he died in Birmingham in 1930.

ALEX WATSON was Blues' secretary-manager for two seasons, 1908–10. Born in Birmingham in 1855, the son of a wealthy businessman, Watson was responsible for signing Frank Womack, but under his supervision the team struggled in the Second Division, finishing 11th and 20th,

and crashed out of the FA Cup in the first round in both campaigns. He continued to support the club after his departure and it is understood that in later years he applied to become a member of the board of directors, but failed by a handful of votes. Watson died in around 1940 in Birmingham.

BOB McROBERTS was Blues' first official team manager, appointed by chairman Walter Hart in July 1910. He remained in charge for five years and although the team came close to gaining promotion in 1913, the overall performances on the field of play left a lot to be desired. McRoberts tried his best and got on well with the players, but one feels that he was not suited to be a manager of men. He recruited the former Aston Villa and England goalkeeper Billy George as his assistant and first-team trainer. (See Blues' Stars)

FRANK RICHARDS replaced Bob McRoberts and was effectively in charge of the team during World War One and for the first four years after the hostilities. In 1920 he recruited Joe Bradford, who would become Blues' greatest-ever goalscorer, and signed several other outstanding players during his eight-year tenure. However, Frank was more of an administrator than a team manager and, in fact, he did not always have the final say in the formation, or indeed, the selection of the team. It was Richards who, amazingly, failed to submit Blues' entry for the 1921–22 FA Cup competition, a season after the team had won promotion to the First Division. Born in Handsworth, Birmingham, in 1880, Richards worked in Hockley's jewellery quarter for two years before joining the office staff at St Andrew's in 1906, moving up to secretary in 1911 and then into the manager's hot-seat in 1915. In 1924–25, Richards served

Blues as club secretary before leaving St Andrew's to become secretary-manager of Preston North End, only to return for a second time as Blues' secretary (to assist Billy Harvey) in August 1927. He retained his post for just one season before ending his footballing career as secretary-manager of Bournemouth from July 1928–June 1930. Richards died in Edgbaston, Birmingham in 1963.

BILLY BEER was the second former player to manage the club. He was in charge at St Andrew's for almost four years, 1923–27, acting as secretary-manager for the last two. Born near Chesterfield in January 1879, he appeared in 250 first-class games for Blues and then worked in Australia and also had a spell as a licensee before returning to the club following Richards' departure. Beer signed several quality players for Blues including Benny Bond, Jimmy Cringan, George Briggs, Harry Hibbs and Alec Leslie and Joe Smith, an England international from West Bromwich Albion. However, although he was totally committed, he struggled to get the best out of his players and in fact he often complained about the attitude of certain first-team squad members. He resigned despite a vote of confidence from the club's directors. Blues finished 14th, 8th and 14th in Division One in his first three seasons in charge and were based in the lower regions when he departed. He was 62 when he died in Birmingham in 1941. (See Blues' Stars)

BILLY HARVEY, another ex-player, was manager at St Andrew's for a little over a year, guiding the team to 11th in the First Division table before leaving to take charge of Chesterfield, where he remained for six years, steering the Spireites to the Third Division North Championship in 1936. An England amateur international right-winger who also toured South Africa with the FA in 1920, Harvey also enjoyed cricket and played for Warwickshire and Border Province in South Africa after emigrating during World War Two. Born in Hampshire in 1886, he died in South Africa in 1970.

LESLIE KNIGHTON played intermediate football for Gresley Rovers, Burton Albion and Fazeley Swifts, retiring through injury in 1904, at which point he became manager of non-League side Castleford Town. Five years later Knighton was appointed secretary-assistant manager of Huddersfield Town and in 1912 took a similar position with Manchester City before being engaged as Arsenal's manager in May 1919. He remained in the Highbury hot seat for six years, leaving in 1925 to take over at Bournemouth, from where he switched to St Andrew's in July 1928. Five years later he left to become boss of Chelsea – accepting an offer he couldn't refuse – and later managed Shrewsbury Town. Quitting top-class football in December 1948, Knighton took over as secretary of a Bournemouth golf club before having a spell in charge of non-League Portishead FC. He signed and developed some superb players at Huddersfield and Manchester City, but struggled with Arsenal after his chairman told him 'You're getting no money to spend in the transfer market.' He assembled a very efficient side at St Andrew's and took Birmingham to the 1931 FA Cup Final. Born in Church Gresley, Derbyshire, in March 1884, Knighton died in Bournemouth in May 1959 after a short illness.

GEORGE LIDDELL, who had been a player for Blues for 12 years, from May 1920, making almost 350 senior appearances, took over from Knighton in July 1933 and remained in office for a little over six years. Liddell had always wanted to manage the club and his wish was granted by chairman Harry Morris, who said at the time: 'George will do a good job, just like he did as a player.' Unfortunately he struggled to find success on the field despite having some very talented players at his disposal. He also made a few good signings and introduced several promising youngsters via the St Andrew's youth channels. However, after a few near misses, Blues were relegated from the First Division at the end of the 1938–39 season and, just as World War Two kicked in, Liddell quit, having used no fewer than 70 players during his six years at the helm. Later headmaster of Handsworth Secondary Modern School (Birmingham), he eventually retired to Hampshire. (See Blues' Stars)

WILLIAM CAMKIN was the man who looked after Blues' fortunes for most of World War Two. He was in office for five years, from October 1939 until November 1944, being officially engaged as honorary managing director. Born in Birmingham in 1890, Camkin was assisted by the former Aston Villa player George Blackburn, who organised the training, while Camkin himself did the office work, pulling the club through a difficult period when St Andrew's was severely damaged by German bombs. Eventually ill-health caused him to quit the club, but he continued to attend home matches as a supporter until his death in 1960. His son, John Camkin, was a well-known sports journalist who later became a director of Coventry City.

* The Camkin Cup was a local competition for Midland-based non-League clubs during the 1960s.

TED GOODIER was a fair-haired wing-half with Huddersfield Town, Lancaster Town, Oldham Athletic, Queen's Park Rangers, Watford, Crewe Alexandra and Rochdale, acting as player-manager with the latter club for six years from 1938. He took over from Camkin as Blues' manager in November 1944 and remained at the forefront until May 1945, when Harry Storer moved into the proverbial hotseat at St Andrew's. He then returned to Rochdale and guided the Spotland club to victory in the Lancashire Cup Final over Blackpool in 1949. Later in charge of Wigan Athletic and his former club, Oldham Athletic. Born in 1902, Goodier died in his home town of Farnworth, Bolton, in November 1967 aged 65.

HARRY STORER was a forthright character, a strict disciplinarian, an economist, direct in his approach, harsh and blunt but blessed with a lot of common sense. He was, without doubt, a sharp-tongued football man with a heart of gold. Born into a sporting family in West Derby, Liverpool, on 2 February 1898, Storer played as an inside-forward in non-League circles for Heanor Wesleyans, Marehay FC, Codnor Park, Riddings St James, Eastwood Bible Class, Ripley Town and Eastwood Town before joining Notts County as an amateur in 1918. He was then a trialist with Millwall before turning professional with Grimsby Town in February 1919. Two years later he moved to Derby County for £2,500 and spent eight years at the Baseball Ground, until February 1929 when he was sold to Burnley for £4,250. Also capped twice by England, he retired in May 1931 to become Coventry City's manager, a position he held until June 1945 when he was engaged, surprisingly some thought, by Birmingham City. He stayed at St Andrew's until November 1948, when he returned to Highfield Road, remaining as manager for five years until December 1953 when he took over the reins of his former club Derby County. In charge of the Rams for seven years, Storer later became a senior scout for Everton in the 1960s.

Besides being a very good footballer, Storer was also a fine cricketer, starring for Derbyshire from 1920–36, during which time he scored 13,513 runs, including 18 centuries, at an average of 27.63. He also took over 200 wickets and helped his county win the county Championship in his last year.

Storer, with his shrewdness, tactical brain, astuteness and know-how, guided Blues to the Football League (South) title and FA Cup semi-final in 1946 and two years later led them to the Second Division Championship. He transformed a side without stars and designed his plans round a strong, efficient defence, which conceded only 24 goals in 42 League games in 1947–48. He signed some fine players and one of them, Martin O'Donnell, he actually recruited three times – for Coventry, Blues and Derby. Storer died in Derby on 1 September 1967, just after one of his close admirers, Brian Clough, had taken over as manager of Derby County.

BOB BROCKLEBANK was Blues' manager for just over five and a half years from January 1949–October 1954, steering the team into the FA Cup semi-finals in 1951. Brocklebank transferred and/or released over 40 players during his tenure at St Andrew's, although he did sign some exceptionally good ones as well, among them Gordon Astall, Len Boyd, Tommy Briggs, Alex Govan, Noel Kinsey, Peter Murphy, Ted Purdon and Roy Warhurst, and he also introduced Jeff Hall and Trevor Smith to League football. Born in Finchley on 23 May 1908, Brocklebank was an inside-forward with Aston Villa and Burnley before taking over as manager of Chesterfield in 1945. After leaving St

Andrew's he served as a coach and scout for West Bromwich Albion and managed both Hull City and Bradford City before retiring to Brixham in 1964. He died in the Devon seaside fishing town on 12 September 1981.

ARTHUR TURNER took over from Bob Brocklebank as Blues manager in November 1954 and remained in the hot seat until February 1958. A former player, he led Blues to the Second Division Championship in 1955, to the FA Cup Final 12 months later, into the FA Cup semi-finals in 1957 and was in charge when the team entered the Inter-Cities Fairs Cup, thus becoming the first manager to take an English club into a major European competition. He introduced some fine players to St Andrew's, including Terry Hennessey, Brian Farmer, Bryan Orritt and Johnny Watts.

Unfortunately, an unsavoury episode led to his departure (resignation). He was told via a reliable source that Pat Beasley was to be appointed as his assistant in January 1958. Beasley would concentrate on the reserves and deal with the general everyday chores in respect of the playing side of the club. It transpired that Beasley in fact was engaged as joint manager and, to make matters worse, Turner was not told of this by anyone in authority at the club. He received the information via the local press. He threatened to walk out but several players persuaded him to stay on, which he did until September 1958 when he resigned.

In January 1959 he took over as manager of Oxford United and signed many top players for the U's including the Atkinson brothers, Ron and Graham, Maurice Kyle and Cyril Beavon. Oxford won the Southern League title in 1961 and 1962 and as a result gained entry into the Football League, replacing Accrington

Stanley. In 1964 Turner took unfashionable Oxford into the quarter-finals of the FA Cup – the first Fourth Division team to achieve this feat – and four years later they won the Third Division title with a team that cost only £14,350. Turner remained in charge of the team for another year and was general manager after that before leaving the club in 1972. He later did some scouting for Rotherham United and Sheffield United. (See Blues' Stars).

PAT BEASLEY was joint manager with Turner (above) for eight months in 1958 and he then served as sole manager for some 20 months before ex-goalkeeper Gil Merrick took over the reins. Born in Stourbridge on 17 July 1913, he played intermediate football for Cookley and Stourbridge before spending five years with Arsenal (1931–36), during which time he gained two League Championship winning medals. On leaving Highbury he signed for Fulham before taking over as player-manager of Bristol City in July 1950, retiring as a player in 1952. He moved from Ashton Gate to St Andrew's in January 1958 and, during his time as manager, signed Johnny Gordon and Harry Hooper and handed Robin Stubbs his League debut. Unfortunately he didn't achieve a great deal with Blues, although he was in charge of the team which reached the Inter-Cities Fairs Cup Final in 1960. On leaving the club Beasley did some scouting for his former employers, Fulham, and was manager of Dover from 1961–64. He died in Taunton on 27 February 1986.

GIL MERRICK joined Blues as a player in 1938 and spent the next 22 years keeping goal for the club. On his retirement he was appointed team manager (May 1960) and retained his position for four seasons, during which time he took the team into a

European Cup Final (beaten by AS Roma in the Inter-Cities Fairs Cup in 1961) and also to glory (over arch-rivals Aston Villa) in the 1963 League Cup Final. He recruited three excellent wingers in Bertie Auld, Mike Hellawell and Brian Taylor, signed two splendid full-backs in Stan Lynn and Colin Green, secured two fine inside-forwards in Jimmy Bloomfield and Ken Leek and striker Jimmy Harris, and he also introduced Colin Withers, Malcolm Beard, Terry Hennessey, Winston Foster and Johnny Vincent into League football. Sadly, during his term in office Blues were always struggling in the First Division and eventually, after the team had finished 19th, 17th, 20th and 20th again, he was sacked at the end of the 1963–64 season. (See Blues' Stars).

JOE MALLETT replaced Gil Merrick as Blues' manager in July 1964 and held the position for barely 18 months until December 1965. Born in Gateshead on 8 January 1916, he played initially for

Charlton Athletic (from 1935) and thereafter assisted QPR, Fulham and West Ham United (as a wartime guest), Southampton and Leyton Orient before taking over as coach at Nottingham Forest (August 1954). Ten years later he moved to St Andrew's, working under Merrick in the same capacity and then, after taking over as boss, he signed Jim Herriot, Trevor Hockey, Roy Wylie, Geoff Vowden and the West Bromwich Albion duo of Alec Jackson and Ron Fenton, among others, while also handing future Welsh international Malcolm Page his Football League debut. Mallett was in charge when Blues went down into the Second Division. At the time there was a lot of discontent in the camp and he was seemingly always under pressure. Replaced by Stan Cullis halfway through the 1965–66 campaign, he went abroad to coach the Greek club Panionios, turning a poor side into a pretty good one. Although he suffered several problems when the junta was overthrown in Greece – he was even placed under arrest for a while – he later returned to that country as coach of Apollon FC. He also had two spells in the USA, first with New York Cosmos and then San Jose Earthquakes, while also acting as a scout for Southampton. Mallett died in Hastings in February 2004.

STAN CULLIS managed Blues for four and a quarter years – from December 1965 until March 1970. In that time the team reached the 1967 League Cup and 1968 FA Cup semi-finals and, if the truth be known, they were desperately unlucky to lose to West Bromwich Albion in the latter game at Villa Park. Vastly experienced in the game of football, Cullis's signings included full-back Bobby Thomson (from his former club Wolves), the Chelsea duo of Barry Bridges and Bert Murray, Scottish international winger Graham Leggatt,

England striker Fred Pickering, centre-forward Tony Hateley, the skilful Jimmy Greenhoff and reliable centre-half John Sleeuwenhoek. He also blooded four local-born youngsters, namely Garry Pendrey, Phil Summerill and the Latchford brothers, goalscorer Bob and goalkeeper Dave. A real hard man, with a stern approach to the game, Cullis was perhaps past his best when he was in charge of Blues, but he was certainly a manager to be reckoned with and the players loved him – or some of them did! Before taking over at St Andrew's, Cullis had won three League Championships and two FA Cup Finals as manager of Wolves, a position he held from 1947 to 1964. He had earlier served the Molineux club as a player, making 171 appearances, mainly as a centre-half. He was also capped 12 times at senior level and on 20 occasions during wartime football, captaining England at the age of 22. Born in Ellesmere Port, Cheshire on 25 October 1915, Cullis died in Malvern on 27 February 2001, aged 85.

FREDDIE GOODWIN was Blues' manager for a little over four seasons, from May 1970 until September 1975, and during that time he guided the team to promotion from Division Two and to two FA Cup semi-finals, which both ended in defeats, against Leeds United in 1972 and Fulham three years later. One of the most successful managers in the club's history, the former Manchester United player signed and gave debuts to some brilliant footballers including Trevor Francis, the versatile Kenny Burns, defenders Joe Gallagher and Stan Harland, striker Bob Hatton (who formed a lethal partnership with Bob Latchford), midfielders Alan Campbell, Bobby Hope and Howard Kendall and winger Gordon Taylor. He blended the team together superbly and in his second season in charge, 1971–72, most of the on-field performances were outstanding. The fans certainly appreciated his efforts.

Born in Heywood, Lancashire on 28 June 1933, Goodwin signed as a trainee for Manchester United via Cheshire Schoolboys as a 20-year-old and became one of the Busby Babes. A wing-half, he made his senior debut in November 1954 against Arsenal and helped the Reds win successive League titles in 1956 and 1957.

Thankfully he was not on the plane that crashed at Munich airport in February 1958, but he was in the team that made a comeback after that disaster and played in that season's FA Cup Final defeat by Bolton (the team he supported as a lad). He scored eight goals in 107 appearances for United before joining Leeds in March 1960 for £10,000. However, in January 1964 he suffered a triple fracture of his right leg after a collision with his teammate John Charles in an FA Cup tie against Cardiff City. He never really recovered and left Elland Road at the end of the year, having netted twice in 120 appearances for Leeds.

Goodwin went on to become a player-manager of Scunthorpe United, although he did not play many games due to his injury. He left the 'Iron' in June 1966 to take over as manager of the New York Generals, later bossing Brighton & Hove Albion before moving to St Andrew's. While at Birmingham, he introduced yoga, psychological testing and other new training techniques and there is no doubt his methods certainly worked! After leaving Blues he returned to the States to coach Minnesota Kicks (1976–79 and again in 1980–81) while also helping form the Indoor Soccer League. Goodwin also played in 11 county cricket matches for Lancashire, taking 27 wickets.

WILLIE BELL took over from Goodwin in September 1975 and remained in office for two years. Unfortunately he achieved nothing with Blues who just escaped relegation in 19th place and followed up by claiming 13th position in 1976–77. The team also made early exits from both domestic Cup competitions. He signed goalkeeper Jim Montgomery, former striker Peter Withe and winger John Connolly, but generally speaking he failed to get the best out of his squad. A Scotsman, born in Johnstone,

Renfrewshire, on 3 September 1937, Bell was a full-back with Neilston Juniors, Queen's Park, Leeds United (1960–67), Leicester City and Brighton & Hove Albion. He amassed over 350 League appearances, 204 for Leeds, and played alongside Freddie Goodwin at Elland Road. He also won two amateur and two full caps for his country. He was then player-coach under Goodwin at Brighton and also at St Andrew's, before taking over the hotseat in September 1975. He retained his position for two years before being sacked. Two months after leaving he took charge of Lincoln City and later coached Liberty University Flames in Lynchburg, Virginia, USA. Bell is a devout Christian and an ordained minister.

SIR ALF RAMSEY, as everyone knows, guided England to World Cup glory in 1966. He had been a Birmingham City director since January 1976 before being persuaded to take over from Bell as team manager in September 1977, a position he held until early March 1978 when he severed his links with the club. It is believed that at a board meeting three weeks earlier, on 20 February, Ramsey recommended that both Trevor Francis and Joe Gallagher should be transfer listed. The board agreed, but three days later changed their minds about Francis. Ramsey was furious, and admitted, at a later date, that this was when he decided to opt out because of the board's policy. He didn't really want the job in the first place, but agreed, in the end, to do his best until a successor was found. The players enjoyed his presence and worked well under his control. Indeed, they produced some decent performances and comfortably held their own in mid-table.

Born in Dagenham, Essex on 22 January 1920, Ramsey played for Five Elms FC, Portsmouth (as an amateur) and Southampton before joining Tottenham Hotspur in 1949. A very able and efficient right-back, he spent six years at White Hart Lane, gaining both Second and First Division Championship-winning medals with Spurs and collecting 32 England caps while also playing in one B international and five times for the Football League.

Retiring in May 1955, Ramsey was appointed manager of Ipswich Town three months later and remained at Portman Road until January 1963 when he took over from Walter Winterbottom as England manager, having led Ipswich to the Third, Second and then First Division titles in successive seasons. And then, in his third year in charge of his country, he celebrated with thousands of others when the Jules Rimet trophy was lifted by Bobby Moore at Wembley. Ramsey remained as England chief until May 1974 and was out of the game for almost two years before returning as a Blues director. Knighted in January 1967 (for services to football) he was a shrewd football tactician, both as a player and manager. He died in Ipswich on 28 April 1999.

JIM SMITH was Blues' manager for virtually four years, from March 1978 to February 1982, bringing with him his assistant Norman Bodell. It was hoped he would motivate the team, which had lost confidence, but unfortunately Blues were relegated from the First Division in his first full season in charge. However, he was able to rebuild the team and allowed many of the players who had won promotion in 1972 to leave and, most notably, he made one of his star players, Trevor Francis, the first £1 million footballer, which the club's board of directors had not allowed Ramsey to do!

Smith signed several experienced players while nurturing along some very promising youngsters. Among the players he brought to the club were Archie Gemmill, Don Givens, Willie Johnston, Colin Todd and Frank Worthington. All did exceptionally well, unlike the Argentinian World Cup-winner Alberto Tarantini and Walsall striker Alan Buckley, both of whom failed to do the business at St Andrew's. Known as 'Bald Eagle', Smith successfully guided Blues back into the top flight at the first time of asking and then

quietly but efficiently established them as a very capable and hardworking mid-table side in 1981–82 before being surprisingly sacked in favour of Ron Saunders (from rivals Aston Villa).

A Yorkshireman, born in Sheffield on 7 October 1949, Smith played for Sheffield United, Aldershot, Halifax Town and Lincoln City before spending four years as player-manager of Boston United (1988–72). The non-League club finished in the top four of the NPL in each of his first three seasons, and reached the third round proper of the FA Cup, while in his fourth season Boston extended their unbeaten League run to 51 games, a British record at professional level. In October 1972 Smith was appointed player-manager of Colchester United and led the Essex club to promotion from Division Four before 'transferring' his duties to Blackburn Rovers, newly promoted to the Second Division in 1975. He guided Rovers through one season of survival, one of establishment and was well into a promotion push in his third campaign when he left Ewood Park to take over as Blues manager.

Moving on four years, to March 1982, Smith became manager of Oxford United, leading them to the Third Division Championship in 1984. The following year the U's were again promoted as they reached the top flight of English football for the first time in their history, going up as Second Division champions. Despite this spectacular success, Oxford chairman Robert Maxwell failed to improve Smith's contract. This led to his resignation and he quickly took charge of Queen's Park Rangers (June 1985). After that he managed Newcastle United, was coach at Middlesbrough, bossed Portsmouth (taking Pompey to the FA Cup semi-final in 1992) and Derby County and was assistant manager-coach at Coventry City before returning to Fratton Park as assistant manager in 2002–03.

Smith, one of the game's great characters, who visited every Football League ground in the country in his capacity as a manager, was then enrolled as Harry Redknapp's assistant at Southampton before returning for a second spell as manager of Oxford United, who also gave him a seat on the board. Unfortunately his expertise failed to stave off relegation to the Conference and after a poor start to the 2007–08 season he quit as manager to concentrate on his director's role full-time. However, following the sacking of Darren Patterson a year later, never-say-die Smith was persuaded to take over as caretaker manager, holding office until the arrival of Chris Wilder. He is still a director of Oxford United who, last season, regained Football League status after an absence of five years.

* Smith was in charge for over 1,600 matches as a football club manager.

RON SAUNDERS was in the hot seat at St Andrews for four years, from February 1982 to January 1986. Already an experienced manager, having been in charge of Yeovil Town, Oxford United, Norwich City, Manchester City and Aston Villa, he led the Canaries to the Second Division title in 1972 and League Cup Final a year later, won the League Cup with Manchester City in 1974 and followed up by guiding Villa to promotion in 1975, then the First Division Championship in 1981, and twice winning the League Cup, in 1975 and 1977. When he left, Villa were well on their way to the European Cup Final.

Unyielding, blunt, hard-talking and a strict disciplinarian, Saunders turned things round late on in his first season at St Andrew's, steering relegation-threatened Blues to a respectable 16th in 1982–83 as the team gained 16 points from their remaining six games. However, despite bringing in several experienced players, including Colin Brazier, Mick Ferguson and Mickey Halsall, plus Robert Hopkins from his former club Villa, overall performances on the pitch did not improve a great deal in 1982–83, Blues taking 17th position. And in 1983–84 things got even worse when relegation was suffered. To his credit, though, Saunders stuck to his guns, and once again he recruited several senior players, among them goalkeeper David Seaman, full-back Ray Ranson, defender Ken Armstrong, midfielder Des Bremner and forward David Geddis (both from Villa) and striker Wayne Clarke, and blended together a team good enough (in his mind) to win promotion at the first attempt, Blues claiming the runners'-up spot behind Saunders's old club, Oxford United.

However, after a very poor first half of 1985–86 when only four League games were won, including a run of 16 without a win, plus an embarrassing FA Cup home defeat at the hands of non-League side Altrincham, he walked out on the club in January to take charge of local rivals and fellow strugglers West Bromwich Albion. He was unable to prevent the Baggies from slipping into the Second Division and was dismissed in September 1987, after failing to get them back into the top flight. He has not really been associated with football since then. As a player, between 1951 and 1967, Saunders starred as a robust centre-forward for Everton, Tonbridge Angels, Gillingham, Portsmouth, Watford and Charlton Athletic. He scored almost 200 goals in 400 League games, including 145 in 236 outings for Pompey.

Born in Birkenhead on 6 November 1932, Saunders now lives in Solihull and has property in Spain and still enjoys a round of golf.

JOHN BOND took over as manager at St Andrew's on 22 January 1986 but could not prevent Blues from suffering relegation for the second time in three years, seven consecutive defeats at the end of the campaigning sealing their fate. The following season, Blues struggled yet again, eventually finishing just one place away from demotion to the Third Division. This record was simply not good enough for the club's board of directors, and it came as no real surprise when Bond was sacked on 27 May 1987, lashing out at chairman Ken Wheldon on his departure by saying: 'You wouldn't treat a dog the way I have been treated here.'

After six months out of football, Bond returned as assistant manager to Asa Hartford at Shrewsbury Town in January 1990. A year later he took over as manager and remained in office until July 1993

when he and his chairman both resigned. Bond subsequently worked as a football commentator for BBC Radio 5 Live before returning to coaching, assisting his son Kevin who was manager of Stafford Rangers, acting mainly as a scout and advisor. In November 1998, he became manager of Witton Albion and after that came out of retirement to assist manager John Benson at Wigan Athletic. In November 2009, Bond appeared on the Sky Sports programme *Time Of Our Lives* in which, along with ex-players Ken Brown and Ronnie Boyce and presenter Jeff Stelling, he looked back on his career at West Ham.

Born in Colchester on 17 December 1932, Bond was mainly a full-back with Colchester Casuals, West Ham United (1949–66) and Torquay United, making 511 League appearances, 318 for the Hammers. Retiring in 1969, he became coach at Gillingham, managed Bournemouth for three and a half years and then, like his predecessor, Ron Saunders, took charge of both Norwich City (1973–80) and Manchester City (until 1983), followed by Burnley and Swansea City, spending just 12 months at the Vetch Field before moving to St Andrew's.

GARRY PENDREY, who had made 360 appearances for Blues, mainly in defence, between 1965 and 1979, and was very popular with the supporters, was the man chosen to replace Bond as manager, taking over almost immediately in June 1987 and staying until April 1989. He jumped at the chance of taking charge of his beloved club, saying: 'This is the only job I ever wanted.'

Since leaving St Andrew's as a player, he had played for West Bromwich Albion (under Ron Atkinson), Torquay United, Bristol Rovers, Walsall (as player-coach under ex-Blues forward Alan Buckley and then manager) and briefly acted as a coach

with Wolves. It is fair to say that he was rather inexperienced and although he tried his best, he had no money to spend to boost a dwindling squad. He was, in truth, fighting a losing battle and although he got the team performing with gusto and a certain amount of skill, there was something missing and, after two bad seasons, the second of which ended in relegation to the Third Division for the first time in the club's history, 'Penders' was sacked. He refused the offer of a coaching role (under his replacement Dave Mackay) and rejoined Wolves instead. Then, when his good friend Gordon Strachan took over as manager of Coventry City in November 1996, Pendrey was appointed as his assistant. Since then he has followed the former Manchester United, Leeds and Scottish international around the UK, working with him at Southampton, Celtic and Middlesbrough. (See Blues' Stars)

DAVE MACKAY spent just under two years as Birmingham City's manager. During his reign, the former Hearts, Spurs,

Derby County and Scotland wing-half signed Trevor Aylott, Dennis Bailey, Dougie Bell, Greg Downs, John Gayle, Nigel Gleghorn, Ian Rodgerson and Trevor Matthewson, among others, but could not get the team working as a unit and, after several heated arguments with the club's owners, it came as no surprise when he left St Andrew's early in January 1991.

Born in Edinburgh on 14 November 1934, Mackay made over 600 League appearances north and south of the border and won 22 caps for his country. He helped his local club Hearts win the League, Scottish Cup and League Cup twice in the 1950s. Then, after moving to London, he starred in Spurs' double-winning team of 1961 and collected two more FA Cup-winners' medals in 1962 and 1967 before playing his part in Derby's Second Division Championship-winning team of 1969, the same year he was voted joint Footballer of the Year (with Tony Book). Two years later Mackay was appointed player-manager of Swindon Town and after that went on to boss Nottingham Forest, his former club Derby (leading the Rams to First Division glory in 1975), Walsall, Al-Arabi Sporting Club (Kuwait), Alab Shabab (Dubai) and Doncaster Rovers, before taking over at St Andrew's. After his stint with Blues he had decent spells as coach with FC Zamalek (Egypt) and also in Qatar, eventually leaving football for good in 1997.

* George Best described Mackay as 'the hardest man I have ever played against – and certainly the bravest'.

BILL COLDWELL had two spells as caretaker manager at St Andrew's, firstly for a week or so in January 1991, prior to Lou Macari's appointment, and then for around 10 weeks later in the year ahead of Terry Cooper's arrival. Born in Petersfield,

Hampshire on 4 June 1932, he played football for Weymouth and cricket for the MCC. A scout and part-time coach for Blues in the late 1960s and early 1970s, he acted as caretaker manager on two occasions. The first time was for three unbeaten games between the departure of Dave Mackay and the arrival of Lou Macari in early 1971. Then, after Macari walked out in June 1971, Coldwell again took over as caretaker, this time persuading most of the significant number of out-of-contract players to sign new deals and not to follow Macari out of the club. He supervised pre-season training until the appointment of Cooper. Coldwell later managed his former club Weymouth for six months in 1993. He died in Bristol at the age of 63.

LOU MACARI was manager of Blues for just five months, from February to June 1991. He insisted upon a strict fitness regime, which included extra sessions in the players' free time and the banning of alcohol anywhere at the club. He certainly got everyone buzzing at St Andrew's, taking Blues to Wembley for the first time since 1956 when they played and beat Tranmere Rovers in the Final of the Leyland DAF Trophy. It came as a shock to the players and indeed to the supporters when he chose to leave the club to take over as manager of Stoke City, saying that the club 'lacked ambition'. He immediately guided the Potters to victory in the Auto-Glass Trophy Final at Wembley and followed up by winning promotion in 1993. Earlier Macari had managed Swindon Town from July 1984 (winning two promotions) and West Ham United, and later on he returned to Stoke for a second spell, took charge of his former club Celtic and also managed and scouted for Huddersfield Town. In 1990, he and the Swindon Town chairman Brian Hillier

were charged by the FA for unauthorised betting on a match involving Swindon.

Born in Largs, Ayrshire on 7 June 1949, Macari was an inside-forward with Kilmarnock Amateurs, Kilwinning Rangers, Celtic (1966–73) and Manchester United before taking over as player-manager of Swindon in 1984. Honoured by Scotland as a schoolboy, he went on to win two Under-23 and 24 full caps and, at club level, scored 125 goals in 525 first-class matches over a period of 20 years (88 in 391 for Manchester United alone). He gained two League, two Cup and two League Cup-winners' medals with Celtic and Second Division and FA Cup-winners' medals with Manchester United. Now a resident of Stoke-on-Trent, Macari works as a pundit for MUTV and occasionally for Sky Sports. He also writes in the local newspaper *The Sentinel* and owns the Lou Macari Chip Shop on Chester Road, near Old Trafford.
* Macari's sons, Michael and Paul, played for Stoke when he was manager of the club. His youngest son, Jonathan, committed suicide by hanging in 1999 after being released from his contract by Nottingham Forest.

TERRY COOPER was manager at St Andrew's for two and a half seasons, from August 1991 to December 1993. He confidently led Blues to promotion from the old Division Three in his first season at the helm and then kept them up on a nerve-wracking final day of the 1992–93 campaign. Indeed, the club has a lot to thank Cooper for, as he helped to steady the ship during that second season after the then-owners' business went into receivership and the club's very future looked in doubt. He departed after a disappointing start to 1993–94 when only five League games were won and rivals Aston Villa had eliminated Blues from the League Cup.

The former Leeds United, Middlesbrough, Bristol City, Bristol Rovers, Doncaster Rovers and England left-back bought in several players during his reign as Blues' manager, among them goalkeepers Kevin Dearden, Andy Gosney, Kevin Miller and Les Sealey, full-backs Scott Hiley, Paul Holmes and Graham Potter, defenders Richard Dryden, Martin Hicks, Paul Mardon, Darren Rogers and Chris Whyte, midfielders Mark Cooper (his son), Ted McMinn, David Rennie and George Parris, wingers Louie Donowa and David Smith, and strikers Kevin Drinkell, John Paskin, Paul Peschisolido, Darren Rowbotham, Mark Sale, Andy Saville, Carl Shutt and David Speedie.

Born in Castleford, Yorkshire on 12 July 1944, Cooper was an attacking left-back who represented England on 20 occasions and appeared in the 1970 World Cup Finals. He made over 350 appearances for Leeds United between 1961 and 1975, gaining League, League Cup and two Fairs Cup-winners' medals before moving to Middlesbrough, where a broken leg severely disrupted his career. He regained full fitness and later assisted Bristol City, Bristol Rovers (player-coach), Doncaster Rovers and Bristol City (again, as player-manager), retiring as a player in 1984 before becoming a director at Ashton Gate. In May 1988, he moved into full-time management with Exeter City and won the Fourth Division Championship with the Grecians in 1990 before his 'transfer' to Blues, where he also joined the board, only to leave the club and eventually return to Exeter in January 1994, staying until the summer of 1995 when ill-health forced him to quit the game.

BARRY FRY was manager at St Andrew's for two and a half years – from December 1993 until May 1996. Under his shrewd but stern and strict guidance, Blues won the double in 1995 (claiming the Division Two title and lifting the Auto-Windscreen Shield) and while in charge Fry signed a huge number of players, some on loan, in an effort to get the club 'back on track'. These included Dave Barnett, goalkeeper Ian Bennett, Mick Bodley, Gary Bull, Steve Claridge, Gary Cooper, Liam Daish, winger Jose Dominguez, Neil Doherty, giant striker Kevin Francis, Jonathan Hunt, Keith Lowe, Steve McGavin, Ricky Otto, Gary Poole, Dave Regis, Mark Ward and Paul Williams. In fact, Fry used a club record 47 players in competitive matches in season 1995–96. For the statistically minded, he utilised no fewer than 21 different players during the friendly with Walsall in July 1994.

Born in Bedford on 7 April 1945, he was a forward with Manchester United and Bolton Wanderers before moving to Luton Town in 1965. Later with Gravesend & Northfleet, Leyton Orient, Romford and Bedford Town, he retired in 1974 to take over as manager of Dunstable Town, receiving solid financial backing from chairman Keith Cheeseman. Indeed, in his autobiography Fry claims that he was often given blank, signed cheques, and two of his big-name signings were Jeff Astle and George Best. Dunstable gained promotion, but Fry was later dismissed by Cheeseman's successor, Billy Kitt, after poor performances in the Southern League. After managerial spells at Hillingdon Borough and Bedford (again) in 1979 Fry became Barnet's manager for the first of two spells covering almost 13 seasons…despite being sacked eight times and reinstated on each occasion by controversial chairman Stan Flashman. He was in charge when the club was in a precarious financial state and under threat of expulsion from the Football League. But he survived, as did Barnet.

His first spell at Underhill ended in December 1985 when he left to take over Maidstone United. He returned in August

1986 and stayed for a further seven seasons. The team finished runners-up three times in the Vauxhall Conference before winning the title in 1991. Then, two years later, with his team within striking distance of the new Division Two, Fry left just two months before the end of the season to manage Southend United who, at the time, were bottom of Division One. He kept the 'Shrimpers' up, but later in the year packed his bags and moved to St Andrew's. Leaving Blues for Peterborough United in 1996, Fry spent nine years in the manager's chair at London Road before handing over his duties to Mark Wright. Later acting as caretaker boss (2007), he is now the Director of Football at the club and has been associated with the game for 48 years.

TREVOR FRANCIS returned to St Andrew's as team manager in May 1996, almost 17 years after leaving Blues for a then record fee of £1.18 million (all add-ons included) in February 1979. He would remain in charge until December 2001. There is no doubt he did an excellent job and during his term in office his signings, several of them experienced professionals, included Gary Ablett, Paul Barnes, Jason Bowen, Gary Breen, future manager Steve Bruce, former West Brom left-back David Burrows, Steve Castle, Simon Charlton, ex-England striker Tony Cottee, Paul Devlin, Nicky Eaden, future Liverpool star Steve Finnan, Nicky Forster, Richard Forsyth, Paul Furlong, who was still playing and scoring goals in 2010 at the age of 41, Martin Grainger, goalkeeper Bart Griemink, Chris Holland, Bryan Hughes, David Holdsworth, Brian Horne, Geoff Horsfield, Graham Hyde, Michael Johnson, Australian international Stan Lazaridis, long-throw expert Andy Legg, the Swede Anders Limpar, Tresor Luntala, winger Jon

McCarthy, the Brazilian Marcelo, Chris Marsden, Peter Ndlovu, Mike Newell, Martin O'Connor, the returning Paul Peschisolido, centre-back Darren Purse, Izzy Rankin, Gary Rowett, Vinny Samways, Danny Sonner, Chris Sutton, two more goalkeepers in Steve Sutton and Nico Vaesen, Darren Wassall, Curtis Woodhouse and Chris Wreh. He even 'recruited' Michael Carrick, Jamie Pollock and Thomas Myhre and handed a debut to future England striker Andrew Johnson.

Francis, placing the emphasis on attack, steered Blues into the First Division Play-offs three seasons running, starting in 1998–99, but disappointingly the team lost in the semi-final of each one. He also guided Blues to the League Cup Final of 2001 and, like so many others that day, was bitterly disappointed when Liverpool won the penalty shoot-out at the Millennium Stadium. Football can be a cruel game, we all know that, and barely seven months later Francis was sacked and replaced by Steve Bruce.

Born on 19 April 1954 in Boxhill, Plymouth, Francis joined Blues as a schoolboy. He made rapid progress. Handed his League debut in September 1970 as a 16-year-old, he ended his first season with 15 goals from just 22 games. An out-and-out striker, he possessed terrific pace, could shoot, head and pass and had confidence in his own ability. He helped Blues gain promotion in 1972, reach two FA Cup semi-finals and scored 133 goals in 329 senior appearances for the club before his £1 million plus transfer to Nottingham Forest in February 1979, having spent the previous summer playing for Detroit Express in the fledgling NASL.

Reigning League champions Forest then reached the European Cup Final in May 1979 and Francis had the pleasure of heading the only goal of a tight game with FF Malmo. The following season he missed

Forest's second European Cup Final against Hamburg SV due to an injury to his Achilles tendon and was sold to Manchester City in 1981, again for £1 million. After that he played for Sampdoria, whom he helped win the Coppa Italia in 1985 before joining Atalanta. Returning to the UK in 1987, he signed for Glasgow Rangers and, after gaining a Scottish Cup-winners' medal in 1988 he left Ibrox Park for Queen's Park Rangers, where he eventually became player-manager. He then transferred himself to Sheffield Wednesday in February 1990, once again becoming player-manager at Hillsborough. With the Owls he won the League Cup and promotion before returning to his spiritual home at St Andrew's in 1996. Francis also won 52 England caps (12 goals) and in more than 750 club appearances he struck over 220 goals. (See Blues' Stars)

STEVE BRUCE twice led Blues to promotion to the Premier League during his tenure of nearly six years at St Andrew's, the first time after just six months in charge, thus ending a 16-year exodus from the top flight of English football for the club. Having reached and lost three successive Play-off semi-finals under Trevor Francis, Blues made it fourth time lucky by defeating Norwich City in a penalty shoot-out in the 2002 Play-off Final at Cardiff's Millennium Stadium. Amid great celebrations, a delighted and slightly overcome Bruce said: 'The courage of the players is incredible. They've fought to the death and I'm proud of them. They've done remarkably well and all credit to them – they're fantastic.' It was certainly a great achievement and the very next season his experience and expertise helped enormously as Blues finished a very creditable 13th in the top flight – their best placing since 1980–81. Tenth and 12th in the next two campaigns was competent

enough, but Bruce himself, the board of directors and especially the fans wanted a little bit extra. Unfortunately the team failed to deliver in 2005–06 and, after some very poor performances, when only eight wins were recorded in 38 Premier League matches, Blues were relegated back to the Championship with 34 points – their lowest tally for 20 years. Bruce was not a happy chappie and called for more effort and commitment from his players. He got it all right, as the team bounced back at the first attempt under his strict and bold leadership, taking the runners'-up spot with a total of 86 points, their highest since 1994–95. How times change! Unfortunately Blues simply couldn't keep hold of the former Manchester United defender and with the team struggling at the wrong end of the Premier League table, he upped and left St Andrew's to join Wigan in November 2007.

Among the players Bruce drafted into St Andrew's during his time as manager were Darren Anderton, Robbie Blake, his son Alex Bruce, former Manchester United

colleague Nicky Butt, Aliou Cissé, Jamie Clapham, Stephen Clemence, Kenny Cunningham, Neil Danns, Swiss international Johan Djourou-Gbadjere, French World Cup star Christophe Dugarry, David Dunn, striker Mikael Forssell, Julian Gray, Jesper Gronkjaer, Emile Heskey (a player he has always admired), Muzzy Izzet, Radhi Jaidi, Cameron Jerome, Stern John, Damien Johnson, Olivier Kapo, Jeff Kenna, Jovan Kirovski, Stephen Kelly, Sebastien Larsson, Gary McSheffrey, Mario Melchiot, Clinton Morrison, Fabrice Muamba, Tunisian international Medhi Nafti, Bruno N'Gotty, the Uruguayan Walter Pandianai, Stuart Parnaby, winger Jermaine Pennant, Daryl Powell, French defender Franck Queudrue, Liam Ridgewell (from rivals Aston Villa), Welsh midfielder Robbie Savage (who was a youngster at Old Trafford when Bruce was there), Rafael Schmitz, Maik Taylor, Martin Taylor, Olivier Tebily, future England centre-back Matthew Upson, Rowan Vine and – another ex-Villa man – Dwight Yorke. He also gave a debut to Blues' 2002 Wembley penalty shoot-out hero Darren Carter.

Born in Corbridge, Northumberland on 31 December 1960, Bruce was a promising schoolboy footballer but was rejected by a number of professional clubs. In fact, he was on the verge of quitting the game altogether when he was offered a trial at Gillingham. Bruce did well, was signed as an apprentice and went on to play over 200 games for the club before joining Norwich City in 1984. Three years later he moved to Manchester United, with whom he achieved great success, winning medals galore and skippering the Reds for several seasons, being the first English player of the 20th century to captain a team to the coveted League (Premier League) and FA Cup double. Despite his success on the field, Bruce never played for

England. Commentators and contemporaries have described him as one of the best defenders of the 1980s and 1990s never to play for his country at full international level.

He left Old Trafford in June 1996, being one of five ex-Premier League stars signed by his predecessor Trevor Francis for Blues. Appointed captain, unfortunately his playing career at St Andrew's was dogged by a series of disagreements with Francis. In fact, director David Sullivan felt the need to publicly deny rumours that Bruce was lined up to replace Francis as manager after the club's stock market flotation and during the 1997–98 season the central-defender was dropped for the first time in his career, for a match against former club Gillingham. Bruce described himself as being 'hurt and unhappy' at being omitted and by November 1997 he was being left out of the team on a regular basis. His omission against Nottingham Forest provoked a public war of words, which fuelled rumours that Francis was to be dismissed and that Bruce would take over as caretaker boss until the end of the season. That never happened, as Bruce accepted a one-year extension to his playing contract, at reduced wages, which included a clause allowing him to leave for a managerial post. Linked with several vacancies, including those at Wigan Athletic and his former club Norwich City, for which he was twice interviewed, he eventually accepted the position of player-manager of Sheffield United, the deal being delayed for a short time while Blues attempted to negotiate a transfer fee for his playing contract. He took up his new position at Bramall Lane in July 1998 and played 11 games before retiring as a player. He left the Blades in June 1999 and, after spending relatively short periods of time in charge of Huddersfield Town,

Wigan Athletic and Crystal Palace, he returned to St Andrew's as Blues' manager in December 2001. After six years in the hot seat he returned to Wigan (for a second spell as manager) and in June 2009 became boss of Sunderland. Bruce is an all-round decent guy. (See Blues' Stars)

ERIC BLACK was born on 1 October 1963 in Bellshill, Lanarkshire. He played as a forward for Aberdeen (scoring 70 goals in 180 League games) and FC Metz (France) and gained two full caps for Scotland in 1987. He managed Motherwell (2001–02) and Coventry City (2004) before being engaged as assistant manager to Steve Bruce at St Andrew's. Then, when Bruce departed, Black took over as caretaker boss for just 72 hours in November 2007, before teaming up again with the former Manchester United and Blues defender at Wigan, following him to Sunderland in 2009.

ALEX McLEISH was quickly named as the man to replace Steve Bruce. Scottish international James McFadden was an early signing, followed by many more, but the team, on the whole, failed to produce the goods, producing far too many lacklustre displays. As a result they were relegated back to the Championship for the second time in two seasons. An honest-to-goodness football man, McLeish got down to business in the summer of 2008 and drew up a plan, one which he knew, deep down, would bring the best out of his players and hopefully secure a return to the Premier League. He signed accomplished strikers Marcus Bent (from Charlton) and Kevin Phillips (from West Brom) and added some muscle to his midfield by recruiting Lee Carsley (from Everton). His team was almost complete, and what a great start the players made to the new season, winning nine, drawing three and

losing only one of their opening 13 games. They shot to the top of the table and remained there or thereabouts right through to the end of the campaign, gaining promotion as runners-up to Wolverhampton Wanderers.

Not at all confident that his squad was good enough to tackle the rigours of Premier League football, he went out and boosted it by signing Ecuadorian striker Christian Benitez, full-back Stephen Carr, two big centre-backs, Scott Dann and Roger Johnson, fellow countryman Barry Ferguson, the Spaniard Michel, England goalkeeper Joe Hart (on loan from Manchester City) and West Ham's experienced midfielder Lee Bowyer, who had been on loan at St Andrew's since January. By the end of the 2009–10 season he had signed virtually a whole new team! But it was worth it, as Blues claimed ninth place in the table, their highest League finish since 1959, and they matched the top six teams in the Premier League kick for kick at St Andrew's, remaining unbeaten against them all. Believing that Blues will still be strong enough to retain their top-flight status, McLeish added some more quality to his squad ahead of the 2010–11 season, signing giant Serbian striker Nikola Zigic from Valencia for £6 million ahead of the World Cup and also adding to his recruitment list England international goalkeeper Ben Foster from Manchester City and midfielder Enric Valles from NAC Breda (Holland), while at the same time Gary McSheffrey and Lee Carsley both moved to Coventry City and Franck Queudrue, Gregory Vignal and Jared Wilson were all released.

McLeish's able assistant Roy Aitken and the club's reserve-team coach Malky Thomson also left to team up with David O'Leary at Al Ahli (UAE). Peter Grant arrived as the new coach.

Born in January 1959 in Barrhead, Renfrewshire and nicknamed 'Big Eck', McLeish was a central defender with Aberdeen during their 1980s glory years, making around 600 appearances for the club while also gaining 77 caps for Scotland. He began his managerial career at Motherwell and served next with Hibernian before guiding Rangers to two League Championships and five winning Cup Finals in just five years. From January to November 2007 he managed the Scotland national team in 10 matches, narrowly failing to qualify for the 2008 UEFA European championships. After resigning his position, he took over at St Andrew's. In recognition of his distinguished service to Scottish sport, McLeish was awarded an honorary doctorate by the University of Aberdeen in 2008. He was also voted SPL Manager of the Month nine times between October 2000 and January 2006.

MANAGERIAL NOTEPAD

- Nine former Blues players have become the club's manager – McRoberts, Beer, Harvey, Liddell, Merrick, Turner, Pendrey, Francis and Bruce.
- Ex-Blues star Howard Kendall (with Everton in 1985) and future boss Ron Saunders (with Aston Villa in 1975 and 1981) both won Manager of the Year awards.
- As manager of Sheffield Wednesday, Trevor Francis lost in both the League Cup and FA Cup Finals of 1993.
- As a football club manager, Harry Storer signed Martin O'Donnell three times for three different clubs – for Blues in 1947, for Coventry City in 1949 and for Derby County in 1955.
- Seeking a replacement for Cullis in 1970, Blues approached Brian Clough, Don Revie and Ronnie Allen without success!

Down the years, well over 50 former Blues players, including the nine already mentioned, have found their way in to club management, among them:
Gary Ablett, Ian Atkins, Bertie Auld, Noel Blake, Jimmy Bloomfield, Harold Bodle, Barry Bridges, Tommy Briggs, Kevan Broadhurst, Alan Buckley, (Major) Frank Buckley, Micky Bullock, Jimmy Calderwood, Steve Claridge, Ian Clarkson, John Cornforth, Tony Cottee, Alan Curbishley, Stan Davies, Kevin Dillon, Neil Dougall, Don Dorman (joint caretaker), Neil Dougall (caretaker), Keith Downing, Greg Downs, Ronnie Fenton, Archie Gemmill, Jimmy Greenhoff, Jim Hagan, Mick Halsall, Mick Harford, Paul Hart, Ian Hendon, Terry Hennessey, Harry Hibbs, Trevor Hockey, Roger Hynd, Mike Kelly, Howard Kendall, Jeff Kenna, Martin Kuhl

(caretaker), Albert Lindon, Roy McDonough, Johnny McMillan, Dave Mangnall, Mike Newell, Johnny Newman, Syd Owen, Jack Peart, Paul Peschisolido, Mick Rathbone, Bruce Rioch, Ray Shaw, Ricky Sbragia, John Sheridan, Billy Smith (caretaker), Billy Steel, Chris Sutton, Colin Todd, John Trewick, Jack Wheeler, Steve Whitton, Steve Wigley, Peter Withe, Frank Womack, Frank Worthington, Ron Wylie and Mark Yates.

Several more ex-players have managed at non-League level, including:
Jack Badham, Ned Barkas, Keith Bowker, Eddie Brown, Kenny Burns, Alan Campbell, Simon Charlton, Wayne Clarke, John Connolly, Mark Cooper, Jimmy Cringan, Johnny Crosbie, Gerry Daly, Eamonn Dolan, Joe Gallagher, Billy Garton, John Gayle, Nigel Gleghorn, Tony Godden, Stan Harland, Terry Hibbitt, Trevor Hockey, David Holdsworth, Bobby Hope, Kevin Langley, Andrew Legg, Graham Leggatt, Alec McClure, Jim McDonagh, Steve McGavin, Owen Madden, Dennis Mortimer, Jock Mulraney, Peter Murphy, Dick Neal, Bryan Orritt, Sid Ottewell, George Parris, Steve Phillips, John Roberts, Craig Russell, Johnny Schofield, Geoff Scott, Carl Shutt, George Smith, Joe Smith, Bobby A. Thomson, Geoff Vowden, Billy Walker, Syd Wallington, Mark Ward, Jack Whitehouse, Billy Wright and Pat Wright.
* Don Givens acted as caretaker manager of the Republic of Ireland national team.

Coaches and assistant managers of Blues
Here is a list, in A-Z order, of the respective coaches, at various levels, and assistant-managers who have been associated with Blues over the years. Some posts also included the positions of club physiotherapist/masseur and even trainer.
Roy Aitken*, Ian Atkins, Jack Badham+,
Frank Barlow, Chic Bates, Willie Bell, Keith Bertschin+, Eric Black, George Blackburn, Norman Bodell, Mark Bowen*, Ian Bowyer, Keith Bradley, Steve Brannigan, Kevan Broadhurst+, Tony Brown*, Brian Caswell, George Dalton, Fred Davies, Reg Devey, Jack Eccles, Len Evans, Dave Fairhurst*, Bobby Ferguson*, Ken Fish, George Foster, Lil Fuccillo, Billy George*, Bill Gibson, Emilio Aldecoa Gomez*, Peter Grant, Harry Hampton*+, Paul Heath, Peter Henderson, David Howells, Derek Jefferson, Richard Johnson, Tom Johns, Mike Kelly+, Bill Kendrick, Bob Latchford*+, Keith Leonard, Abvel Lowe, Neil McDiarmid, Malky Mackay*, Johnny McMillan+, Joe Mallett, Mick Mills*, Trevor Morgan, Peter Murphy+, Olly Norman, Ken Oliver, George Penfield, John Pryce, Kevin Reeves, Ray Shaw+, Syd Scholey, Bill Shorthouse, Charlie Simms+, Nigel Spink*, Edwin Stein, Archie Taylor, Tony Taylor, Malky Thomson, Dan Tremelling+*, Kevin Walters, Mark Ward+, Andy Watson, Sid Wharton+, Jim Williams, Alex Wilson and Chris Woods*.

* Gained full international honours as players.
+ Was a player with Blues.

Coach's Clipboard
● Brian Eastick was appointed Director of Coaching at St Andrew's in 1999.
● Former Blues full-back Brian Farmer organised soccer camps, academies and tours at home and abroad, for clubs, youth centres, community groups and schools from his home in Great Barr, Birmingham in the 1990s (registered under Peershardy Soccer School & Academies 1995).

1889-90

Football Alliance

Manager: Committee

Match No.	Date		Venue	Opponents		Result	Scorers	Attendance
1	Sep	7	H	Birm. St. George	W	3-2	Short, Stanley, W.Devey	2,0
2		14	H	Bootle	D	2-2	W.Devey, Stanley	2,0
3		21	A	Walsall Town Swifts	D	1-1	W.Devey	1,5
4	Oct	12	A	Sunderland Albion	L	1-6	Davenport	1,0
5		19	H	Sheffield Wednesday	D	2-2	W.Devey 2	3,0
6	Nov	2	A	Nottingham Forest	D	0-0		1,0
7		9	H	Walsall Town Swifts	L	0-2		3,0
8		23	H	Grimsby Town	W	3-1	W.Devey 2, Heath	3,0
9	Dec	21	A	Sheffield Wednesday	L	1-9	Brayshaw (og)	1,5
10		25	A	Birm. St. George	L	1-4	Heath	5,0
11		26	A	Grimsby Town	L	0-4		3,0
12		28	H	Long Eaton Rangers	W	3-1	Stanley 2, Pratt	2,0
13	Jan	4	A	Crewe Alexandra	L	0-2		3,0
14		25	A	Long Eaton Rangers	W	2-0	W.Devey, Lines	5
15	Feb	15	H	Darwen	W	6-2	W.Devey, Jenkyns, Hallam, Wheldon 2, Wilcox	5
16		22	A	Crewe Alexandra	L	2-6	W.Devey, Stanley	2,0
17	Mar	8	H	Nottingham Forest	W	12-0	W.Devey 6, G Short 3, Hallam, E.Devey 2	1,0
18		15	H	Newton Heath	D	1-1	Wilcox	2,0
19		29	H	Sunderland Albion	L	1-3	W.Devey	2,0
20	Apr	4	A	Bootle	L	0-6		1,0
21		5	A	Darwen	L	2-4	Hallam, Morris	3,0
22		7	A	Newton Heath	L	1-9	W.Devey	4,0

Only 10 men in match 9.
One own-goal

Appearanc
Goa

FA Cup

	Date		Venue	Opponents		Result	Scorers	Attendance
Q2	Oct	26	A	Oldbury Town	W	3-1	W.Devey 2, Davenport	1,0
Q3	Nov	16	A	Wednesbury Old Ath.	W	5-1	Walton 2, W.Devey 2, Heath	2,0
Q4	Dec	7	H	Walsall Town Swifts	W	4-0	W.Devey 3, Stanley	2,0
R1	Jan	18	H	Clapton	W	3-1	W.Devey, Stanley 2	2,0
R2	Feb	1	A	Wolverhampton Wan.	L	1-2	W.Devey	3,0

Appearanc
Goa

Appearance / line-up grid

Bally C	Barton A	Speller F	Morris H	Jenkyns CAL	Devey EJ	Short GF	Stanley AE	Devey W	Heath F	Davenport E	Gittins W	Lines W	Simms C	Pratt W	Walton WH	Banks F	Watts E	Morgan A	Clarke E	Hallam J	Wheldon GF	Wilcox L	Short C
2	3	4	5	6	7	8	9	10	11														
2		4	5	6	7	10	9		11	3	8												
2		4		6	7	8	9		11	3	10	5											
2		4	5	6	7	10	9		11	3	8												
2		4	5	6	7		9	11	8	3			10										
2		4	5	6	7	10	9		11	3			8										
2		4	5	6	7	11	9	10		3			8										
2		4	5	6	7	11	9	10		3			8										
2		4	5	6		7			10	3	8		9		1								
2		4	5	6	7			9		3			11	10									
2		4	5	6	7	10		9		3			11		8								
2		4	5	6		9			10	3	7		11	8									
2		4			7		9	11		3		5	10	8		6							
2		4	5	6		10		9		3	7		11	8									
		4	5			9	6			2			8			3	7	10	11				
		5	6			10	9			2	7	4	11	8			3						
2		5	6	8		9	4			3			11			7		10					
2		4	5	6		9	10			3			8			7	11						
2		5	6	7		9	4			3	8		10			11							
2		5	6			9	4			3	8					7	10	11					
2	7		6			9	4			3	5		10	1		8		11					
2	7	5				8	9	4		3			6	11		10	1						
1	20	18	19	19	13	13	18	17	5	21	7	7	10	13	3	2	1	1	7	2	4	1	
		1	1	2	4	5	18	2	1		1		1					3	2	2			

Second grid

Bally C	Barton A	Speller F	Morris H	Jenkyns CAL	Devey EJ	Short GF	Stanley AE	Devey W	Heath F	Davenport E	Gittins W	Lines W	Simms C	Pratt W	Walton WH	Banks F	Watts E	Morgan A	Clarke E	Hallam J	Wheldon GF	Wilcox L	Short C
		3	4	5	6	7		9	10	8	2			11									
		3	4	5	6	7	11	9	10		2			8									
		3	4	5	6	7	11	9	10		2			8									
		3	4	5			7	9	10		2		6	11	8								
		3	4	5			7	9	6	10	2			11	8								
		5	5	5	3	4	5	5	2	5			1	3	4								
						3	9	1	1					2									

League Table

	P	W	D	L	F	A	Pts
Sheffield Wednesday	22	15	2	5	70	39	32
Bootle	22	13	2	7	66	39	28
Sunderland Albion*	21	12	2	7	64	39	28
Grimsby Town	22	12	2	8	58	47	26
Crewe Alexandra	22	11	2	9	68	59	24
Darwen	22	10	2	10	70	75	22
Birmingham St George	21	9	3	9	62	49	21
Newton Heath	22	9	2	11	40	44	20
Walsall Town Swifts	22	8	3	11	44	59	19
Small Heath	22	6	5	11	44	67	17
Nottingham Forest	22	6	5	11	31	62	17
Long Eaton Rangers	22	4	2	16	35	73	10

* Sunderland Albion awarded 2 pts when Birmingham St George refused to play a replayed fixture.

Football Alliance

Manager: Committee

Did you know that?

Five players were ever-presents for Blues this season.

Blues gained revenge over Sheffield Wednesday with a resounding 7–1 home win in January...but the attendance was only 500.

Blues conceded 21 goals in five Alliance matches over a period of six weeks between 22 November and 3 January.

They also conceded a total of 19 goals in four successive away matches.

The average home League attendance this season rose to 2,500, with a crowd of 5,000 being recorded on three separate occasions.

Match No.	Date		Venue	Opponents	Result		Scorers	Attendance
1	Sep	6	A	Walsall Town Swifts	L	2-5	W.Devey, Reynolds (og)	5,0
2		13	H	Sunderland Albion	L	0-3		5,0
3		27	A	Grimsby Town	L	1-3	Jenkyns	2,0
4	Oct	11	A	Sheffield Wednesday	D	3-3	Walton, W.Devey, Hallam	7,0
5		18	H	Walsall Town Swifts	L	0-1		5,0
6	Nov	1	H	Stoke	W	5-1	Short 3, Wheldon, W.Devey	2,5
7		8	A	Bootle	D	1-1	W.Devey	1,0
8		22	H	Darwen	L	3-4	Hallam 3	2,0
9		29	A	Birm. St. George	L	4-5	E.Devey, W.Devey, Short, Hallam	2,0
10	Dec	13	A	Newton Heath	L	1-3	Hallam	1,0
11		27	A	Stoke	L	2-4	Short 2	3,0
12	Jan	3	A	Darwen	L	3-5	W.Devey, Hallam, Wheldon	3,0
13		10	H	Sheffield Wednesday	W	7-1	Wheldon, Short 2, Jenkyns 2, W.Devey 2	5
14	Feb	7	H	Crewe Alexandra	W	4-3	W.Devey 3, Wheldon	2,0
15		21	H	Grimsby Town	L	1-2	Short	2,0
16		26	A	Nottingham Forest	W	5-4	Hallam, Jenkyns, W.Devey, Short, one og	2,5
17		28	H	Nottingham Forest	W	4-2	Short 3, Wheldon	5,0
18	Mar	7	H	Newton Heath	W	2-1	Wheldon 2	2,0
19		16	H	Birm. St. George	L	1-4	Hands	1,0
20		21	H	Bootle	W	7-1	Short 3, Hands 2, W.Devey, Wheldon	1,0
21		31	A	Sunderland Albion	L	0-4		3,0
22	Apr	11	A	Crewe Alexandra	L	2-6	W.Devey 2	1,0

Appearanc
Two own-goals   Go

FA Cup

Q1	Oct	4	H	Hednesford Town	W	8-0	Wheldon 3, Hallam, W.Devey 2, Jenkyns, Webster (og)	1,5
Q2	Dec	6	A	Wednesbury Old Ath.	W	2-0	Short, Hallam	2,0

Small Heath disqualified for fielding an unregistered player.   Appearanc
One own-goal   Go

…gie C	Bayley JT	Spilan F	Morris H	Hughes J	Devey EJ	Haslam J	Walton WH	Devey W	Wheldon GF	Pratt W	Charsley C	Jenkyns CAL	Heath F	Short C	Ward W	Turner AS	Hands T	Charsley W	Sierra C	Evans A	Wollaston J
2	3	4	5	6	7	8	9	10	11												
3	2	6		4	7	8	9	10	11	1	5										
2	3			6	7	8	9	10	11		5	4									
2	3	4		6	7	8	9	10	11	1	5										
2	3	4		6	7		9	10	11	1	5		8								
2	3	4		6	7		9	10	11	1	5		8								
2	3	4		6	7		9	10	11		5		8	1							
2	3	4		6	7		9	10	11	1	5				8						
2	3	4		6	7		9	10	11		5		8	1							
2	3			6	7		9			5	4	8				11					
2	3	4			7		9	10		5		8	1			11	6				
2	3			6	7		9	10		1	5		8			11	4				
2	3	4		6	7	8		10		1	5		9			11					
2	3	4		6	7	8		10		1	5		9			11					
2	3	4		6	7		9	10		1			8			11	5				
2	3			6	7	8		10		1	5	4	9			11					
2	3			6	7	8		10		1	5	4	9			11					
2	3			6	7	8		10		1	5		9			11					
2	3	4		6	7	8		10		1		5	9			11					
2	3			6	7	8		10			9	1				11	4		5		
2	3				7	8		10		5	4	9	1			11			6		
2	3			6	7	8		10	11	1		5	9						4		
22	22	13	1	20	22	4	22	22	10	14	17	8	17	5	1	12	3	1	2	1	
				1	8		1	15	8			4				16				3	

…gie C	Bayley JT	Spilan F	Morris H	Hughes J	Devey EJ	Haslam J	Walton WH	Devey W	Wheldon GF	Pratt W	Charsley C	Jenkyns CAL	Heath F	Short C	Ward W	Turner AS	Hands T	Charsley W	Sierra C	Evans A	Wollaston J
2	3	4		6	7	8	9	10	11	1	5										
2	3	4		6	7		9	10	11	1	5		8								
2	2	2		2	1	2	2	2	2	2	2		1								
				2			2	3					1			1					

League Table

	P	W	D	L	F	A	Pts
Stoke	22	13	7	2	57	39	33
Sunderland Albion	22	12	6	4	69	28	30
Grimsby Town	22	11	5	6	43	27	27
Birmingham St George	22	12	2	8	64	62	26
Nottingham Forest	22	9	7	6	66	39	25
Darwen	22	10	3	9	64	59	23
Walsall Town Swifts	22	9	3	10	34	61	21
Crewe Alexandra	22	8	4	10	59	67	20
Newton Heath	22	7	3	12	37	55	17
Small Heath	22	7	2	13	58	66	16
Bootle	22	3	7	12	40	61	13
Sheffield Wednesday	22	4	5	13	39	66	13

Football Alliance

Manager: Committee

Blues played with only 10 men in the last game of the season at Crewe, inside-right Billy Walton being the absentee.

Blues' average home League attendance this season was 2,045; the biggest single crowd being 3,500 versus Nottingham Forest in April.

Fred Wheldon scored in 12 of the 22 Alliance matches, bagging a hat-trick against Lincoln City (h).

Full-back Fred Speller took his total number of Alliance appearances to 64 out of a possible 66.

Match No.	Date		Venue	Opponents	Result		Scorers	Attendan
1	Sep	5	H	Burton Swifts	W	3-1	Hallam 2, Wilkes	2,0
2		12	H	Birm. St. George	D	2-2	Brown, Hands	3,0
3		19	A	Burton Swifts	L	3-6	E.Devey, Wheldon 2	2,0
4		26	H	Lincoln City	W	4-0	Wheldon 3, Brown	2,0
5	Oct	8	A	Nottingham Forest	L	0-2		2,0
6		10	H	Sheffield Wednesday	D	2-2	Millard	1,0
7		17	A	Walsall Town Swifts	W	4-1	Hands 2, Morris, Wheldon	2,0
8	Nov	21	A	Bootle	W	1-0	Jenkyns	3,0
9		28	A	Birm. St. George	L	0-1		5
10	Dec	12	H	Crewe Alexandra	W	3-1	Hallam 2, Jenkyns	6
11		19	H	Grimsby Town	W	2-1	Lundie (og), Hallam	1,0
12		26	A	Newton Heath	D	3-3	Walton, Wheldon 2	7,0
13	Jan	2	A	Ardwick	D	2-2	Harrison 2	4,0
14		9	A	Sheffield Wednesday	L	3-6	Hallam, Walton, McConnachie (og)	6,0
15	Feb	13	A	Lincoln City	D	1-1	Wheldon	2,0
16		20	H	Ardwick	W	4-0	Wheldon 2, Hallam, Walton	2,0
17		27	H	Newton Heath	W	3-2	Walton, Hallam, Wheldon	3,0
18	Mar	26	H	Bootle	W	4-1	Walton 2, Wheldon 2	2,0
19	Apr	2	H	Grimsby Town	W	3-0	Hallam, Wheldon 2	2,0
20		9	A	Walsall Town Swifts	W	4-3	Hallam, Wheldon 2, Hands	4,0
21		16	H	Nottingham Forest	L	1-2	Wheldon	3,5
22		20	A	Crewe Alexandra	W	2-0	Wheldon 2	1,0

Played with 10 men in game 22   Appearanc

Two own-goals   Go

FA Cup

	Date		Venue	Opponents	Result		Scorers	Attendan
Q1	Oct	3	A	Leicester Fosse	W	6-2	Hands, Millard 2, Hallam, Wheldon 2	1,0
Q2		24	A	Burton Wanderers	D	1-1	Wheldon	4,0
rep		31	A	Burton Wanderers	W	2-1	Taylor, Wheldon	2,0
Q3	Nov	14	H	Burton Swifts	W	4-2	Hands, Walton 2, Wheldon	3,0
Q4	Dec	5	H	Brierley Hill Alliance	W	6-2	Wheldon, Wilkes 3, Walton, Hands	1,4
R1	Jan	16	H	Royal Arsenal	W	5-1	Hallam 2, Wheldon 2, Walton	4,0
R2		30	A	Sheffield Wednesday	L	0-2		12,0

Drawn at home in R2 but sold the ground rights.   Appearanc

One unknown   Go

	Bayley JT	Spilier F	Ollis W	Jenkyns CAL	Devey EJ	Taylor W	Hallam J	Wilkes F	Wheldon GF	Brown WE	Walton WH	Hands T	Charsley C	Millard A	Morris H	Burton EG	Allen F	Pratt W	Harrison W	Simms C	Short J	Kendrick W	Comer L
	2	3	4	5	6	7	8	9	10	11													
	2	3	4	5	6		7		10	8	9	11											
	2	3	6	5	8	4	9		10		7	11											
	2	3	4	5	6	11	7	9	10	8					1								
		3	4	5	6	2	7		10		11	1		8	9								
		3	4	5	6	2	7		10		11	1	8			9							
	2	3	4	5	6		7		10		8	11			9								
	2	3	4	5	6		9		10		8	11					7						
	2	3	4	5	6		9		10		8	11					7	11					
	2	3	4	5	6		8	9	10			11					7						
	2	3	4	5	6		7	9	10			11											
	2	3	4	5	6		7		10		8	11			9								
	2	3	4	5	6		7		10		8	11	1				9						
	2	3	4	5	6		7		10		8	11			9								
	2	3	4	5	6		7		10			11		9				1	8				
	2	3	4		6	5	7		10		8	11			9								
	2	3	4		6		7		10		8	11			9					5	9		
	2	3	4	5	6		7		10		8	11			9								
	2	3	4	5	6		7		10		8	11			9								
	2	3	4	5	6		7		10			11										9	
20	22	22	20	22	6	22	4	22	3	15	19	4	3	9	1	3	1	1	1	1	1	2
		2	1		10	1	21	2	6	4			1	1			2						

	Bayley JT	Spilier F	Ollis W	Jenkyns CAL	Devey EJ	Taylor W	Hallam J	Wilkes F	Wheldon GF	Brown WE	Walton WH	Hands T	Charsley C	Millard A	Morris H	Burton EG	Allen F	Pratt W	Harrison W	Simms C	Short J	Kendrick W	Comer L
		3	4	5	6	2	9		10			11	1	8	7								
		3	4	5	6	2	7		10		8	11	1			9							
	2	3	4	5	6	11	7		10		8		1			9							
	2	3	4	5	6		7		10		8	11	1			9							
		3	4	5	6	2	7	9	10		8	11	1										
	2	3	4	5	6		7		10		8	11	1			9							
	2	3	4	5	6		7		10		8	11	1			9							
4	7	7	7	7	4	7	1	7		6	6	7	1		6								
			1	3	3	8			4	3			2										

League Table

	P	W	D	L	F	A	Pts
Nottingham Forest	22	14	5	3	59	22	33
Newton Heath	22	12	7	3	69	33	31
Small Heath	22	12	5	5	53	36	29
Sheffield Wednesday	22	12	4	6	65	35	28
Burton Swifts	22	12	2	8	54	52	26
Grimsby Town	22	6	6	10	40	39	18
Crewe Alexandra	22	7	4	11	44	49	18
Ardwick	22	6	6	10	39	51	18
Bootle	22	8	2	12	42	64	18
Lincoln City	22	6	5	11	37	65	17
Walsall Town Swifts	22	6	3	13	33	59	15
Birmingham St George	22	5	3	14	31	64	13

1892-93

Division Two

Secretary-manager: Alfred Jones

Match No.	Date	Venue	Opponents	Result		Scorers	Attendance
1	Sep 3	H	Burslem Port Vale	W	5-1	Wheldon 2, Short, Hallam, Edwards	2,5
2	10	A	Walsall Town Swifts	W	3-1	Wheldon, Jenkyns, Pinches (og)	2,0
3	17	A	Sheffield United	L	0-2		4,0
4	24	H	Lincoln City	W	4-1	Wheldon 2, Jenkyns, Mobley	2,5
5	Oct 1	A	Grimsby Town	L	2-3	Wheldon 2	3,0
6	3	A	Burton Swifts	W	3-2	Wheldon, Lawrence (og), Mobley	2,0
7	8	H	Crewe Alexandra	W	6-0	Walton, Wheldon, Hallam, Devey, Mobley, Hands	2,5
8	22	A	Ardwick	D	2-2	Wheldon 2	3,0
9	29	H	Darwen	W	3-2	Mobley, Hallam, Hands	2,0
10	Nov 5	A	Bootle	W	4-1	Walton, Mobley, Wheldon, Hands	1,5
11	12	H	Burton Swifts	W	3-2	Mobley, Walton, Jenkyns	4,0
12	Dec 3	H	Sheffield United	D	1-1	Wheldon	3,0
13	10	A	Darwen	L	3-4	Hallam 2, Hands	3,0
14	17	H	Walsall Town Swifts	W	12-0	Wheldon 2, Walton 3, Hallam 2, Mobley 3, Hands 2	2,0
15	24	A	Northwich Victoria	W	6-0	Mobley 2, Wheldon 2, Walton, Hands	2,0
16	31	A	Crewe Alexandra	W	3-1	Mobley, Hands, Hallam	1,5
17	Jan 7	A	Lincoln City	W	4-3	Wheldon 3, Hands	1,0
18	14	H	Northwich Victoria	W	6-2	Ollis, Wheldon 3, Walton, Hallam	2,0
19	Feb 18	H	Bootle	W	6-2	Hallam 3, Mobley 2, Wheldon	2,0
20	25	H	Grimsby Town	W	8-3	Hands 2, Hallam 2, Wheldon, Walton 3	2,5
21	Mar 25	A	Burslem Port Vale	W	3-0	Walton 2, Hallam	3,0
22	Apr 1	H	Ardwick	W	3-2	Hallam 2, Walton	1,0
						Appearances	
						Two own-goals	Goals

Test Matches

	Apr 22	N	Newton Heath	D	1-1	Wheldon	4,0
	27	N	Newton Heath	L	2-5	Walton, Mobley	6,0

Apr 22 match played at Victoria Ground, Stoke. Replay at Bramall Lane.

Appearances
Goals

FA Cup

R1	Jan 21	A	Burnley	L	0-2		7,5
						Appearances	

Bayley CG	Bayley JT	Spiller F	Ollis W	Jenkyns GAL	Devey EJ	Hallam J	Edwards HR	Short GF	Wheldon GF	Hands T	Walton WAT	Mobley F	Hollis G	Roberts JE	Pumfrey B	Jones FW	Simms C	Morris H
2	3	4	5	6	7	8	9	10	11									
2	3	4	5	6	7	8	9	10	11									
	3	4	5	6	7	8	2	10	11		9							
	3	4	5	6	7	8	2	10	11		9	1						
2	3	4	5	6		7		10	11	8	9	1						
2	3	4	5	6	7			10	11	8	9							
	3	4	5	6	7		2	10	11	8	9							
2	3	4	5	6	7			10	11	8	9	1						
2	3	4	5	6	7			10	11	8	9							
2		4	5	6	7			10	11	8	9				3			
2		4	5	6	7			10	11	8	9				3			
2		4	5	6	7			10	11	8	9				3			
2		4	5	6	7			10	11	8	9				3			
2		4	5	6	7			10	11	8	9				3			
2		4	5	6	7			10	11	8	9	1			3			
2		4	5	6	7			10	11	8	9				3			
		4		6	7		2	10	11	8	9	1			3	5		
2		4	5	6	7			10	11	8	9	1			3			
2		4	5		7	3		10	11	8	9				6			
2		4	5		7	6		10	11	8	9	1			3			
2		4	5		7	6		10	11	8	9				3			
2		4	5		7	6		10	11	8	9				3			
18	**9**	**22**	**21**	**18**	**21**	**5**	**10**	**22**	**22**	**19**	**19**	**8**	**1**	**3**	**8**	**1**	**1**	
	1		3	1		17	1	1	25	11	14	14						

Bayley CG	Bayley JT	Spiller F	Ollis W	Jenkyns GAL	Devey EJ	Hallam J	Edwards HR	Short GF	Wheldon GF	Hands T	Walton WAT	Mobley F	Hollis G	Roberts JE	Pumfrey B	Jones FW	Simms C	Morris H
2		4	5		7	6		10	11	8	9				3			
2		4	5		7	6		10		8	9				3	11		
2	2	2	2		2	2	1	2	2	2	2				2	1		
						1			1		2							
2		4	5		7	6		10	11	8	9				3			
1		1	1		1	1		1	1	1	1				1			

League Table

	P	W	D	L	F	A	Pts
Small Heath	22	17	2	3	90	35	36
Sheffield United	22	16	3	3	62	19	35
Darwen	22	14	2	6	60	36	30
Grimsby Town	22	11	1	10	42	41	23
Ardwick	22	9	3	10	45	40	21
Burton Swifts	22	9	2	11	47	47	20
Northwich Victoria	22	9	2	11	42	58	20
Bootle	22	8	3	11	49	63	19
Lincoln City	22	7	3	12	45	51	17
Crewe Alexandra	22	6	3	13	42	69	15
Burslem Port Vale	22	6	3	13	30	57	15
Walsall Town Swifts	22	5	3	14	37	75	13

Division Two

Secretary-manager: Alfred Jones

1893-94

Did you know that?

Caesar Jenkyns became the first Blues player to be sent-off in a League game when he was dismissed in the 4–3 home defeat by Liverpool in October.

Blues became the first club to score 100 League goals in a season. Jack Hallam scored the 100th at Arsenal in March while Frank Mobley and Fred Wheldon both netted over 20 times apiece – the first time two players from the same club had achieved this feat in the same season.

Blues' 7–0 away win at Northwich Victoria in January was to remain a club record for 104 years.

Blues registered their 13th successive League victory when beating Walsall Town Swifts in September.

Blues had four players ever-present this season.

Match No.	Date		Venue	Opponents	Result		Scorers	Attendance
1	Sep	2	A	Walsall Town Swifts	W	3-1	Lee 2, Wheldon	5,00
2		4	H	Rotherham Town	W	4-3	Wheldon, Hands, Mobley, Hallam	3,00
3		9	H	Burton Swifts	W	6-1	Wheldon 2, Jolley 2, Hands, Lee	3,00
4		16	H	Walsall Town Swifts	W	4-0	Jenkyns, Izon 3	2,00
5		23	A	Liverpool	L	1-3	Jenkyns	8,0
6		25	A	Burslem Port Vale	L	0-5		3,00
7		30	A	Ardwick	W	1-0	Wheldon	3,00
8	Oct	7	H	Grimsby Town	W	5-2	Walton 3, Izon, Hallam	3,00
9		14	H	Liverpool	L	3-4	Wheldon, Jenkyns, Hands	5,00
10		21	A	Woolwich Arsenal	W	4-1	Wheldon 2, Hallam, Hands	3,0
11		28	A	Newcastle United	W	2-0	Mobley, Wheldon	3,00
12	Nov	11	A	Lincoln City	W	5-2	Wheldon, Mobley 3, Walton	1,0
13		25	A	Middlesbro Ironopolis	L	0-3		20
14	Dec	2	H	Northwich Victoria	W	8-0	Wheldon 4, Mobley 3, Walton	1,50
15		6	A	Crewe Alexandra	W	6-1	Hallam, Mobley 2, Hands, Walton, Jenkyns	5
16		9	A	Burton Swifts	W	2-0	Mobley, Hands	1,50
17		16	H	Newcastle United	L	1-4	Hallam	2,0
18		23	H	Middlesbro Ironopolis	W	2-1	Pumfrey, Walton	1,50
19		30	H	Lincoln City	W	6-0	Devey, Wheldon 2, Mobley, Hands, Walton	2,0
20	Jan	6	A	Northwich Victoria	W	7-0	Walton, Mobley 3, Hands 2, Wheldon	2,0
21		13	A	Crewe Alexandra	W	5-3	Jackson, Walton 2, Mobley, Hands	1,00
22	Feb	3	A	Notts County	L	1-3	Mobley	5,0
23	Mar	3	A	Grimsby Town	L	1-2	Mobley	3,00
24		17	H	Ardwick	W	10-2	Mobley 3, Wheldon 2, Hallam 2, Hands, Jenkyns, Walton	2,0
25		23	A	Rotherham Town	W	3-2	Walton, Hallam, Wheldon	1,0
26		24	H	Burslem Port Vale	W	6-0	Hands, Walton 2, Mobley 2, Wheldon	4,0
27		31	A	Woolwich Arsenal	W	4-1	Jenkyns, Wheldon, Mobley, Hallam	3,5
28	Apr	7	H	Notts County	W	3-0	Hands 2, Walton	8,50
							Appearanc	
							Goa	

Test Match

	Apr	28	N	Darwen	W	3-1	Hallam, Walton, Wheldon	3,0

Played at the Victoria Ground, Stoke

							Appearanc	
							Goa	

FA Cup

R1	Jan	27	H	Bolton Wanderers	L	3-4	Hallam, Mobley, Wheldon	7,0
							Appearanc	
							Goa	

Jolley E	Pumfrey B	Ollis W	Jenkyns CAL	Devey EJ	Hallam J	Lee J	Mobley F	Wheldon GF	Hands T	Smith G	Short GF	Izon CJ	Spiller F	Walton WH	Reynolds WT	Jackson W	Littleford AG	Purves W	Partridge C	Charsley CC	Watson PC
2	3	4	5	6	7	8	9	10	11												
2	3	4	5	6	7	8	9	10	11												
7	3	4	5	6		8	9	10	11	2											
	3	4	5	6	7	8		10	11		2	9									
	3	4	5	6	7	8		10	11	2		9									
	3	4	5	6	7	8		10	11	2		9									
		4	5	6	7	8		10	11	2		9	3								
		4	5	6	7			10	11	2		9	3	8							
		4	5	6	7		9	10	11	2				8	3						
		4	5	6	7			10	11	2		9		8	3						
		4	5	6	7		9	10	11	2				8	3						
5		4		6	7		9	10	11	2				8	3						
5		4		6	7		9	10	11	2				8	3						
		4	5	6	7		9	10	11	2				8	3						
		4	5	6	7		9	10	11	2				8	3						
		4	5	6			9	10	11	2				8	3	7					
		4	5	6	7		9	10	11	2				8	3						
	8	4	5	6				10	11			9		7	3		2				
		4	5	6			9	10	11					8	3	7		2			
	3	4	5	6			9	10	11					8		7	2				
		4	5	6			9	10	11					8	3	7	2				
6		4	5	2	7		9	10	11		3			8					1		
6		4	5	2	7		9	10	11		3	8									
		4	5	6	7		9	10	11		2			8						1	3
		4	5	6	7		9	10	11		2			8							3
		4	5	6	7		9	10	11		3			8				2		1	
		4	5	6	7		9	10	11		3			8				2		1	
		4	5	6	7		9	10	11		3			8				2		1	
7	8	28	26	28	22	7	21	28	28	14	8	8	2	20	12	4	3	4	1	4	2
2	1		6	1	9	3	24	22	14			4		16		1					

Jolley E	Pumfrey B	Ollis W	Jenkyns CAL	Devey EJ	Hallam J	Lee J	Mobley F	Wheldon GF	Hands T	Smith G	Short GF	Izon CJ	Spiller F	Walton WH	Reynolds WT	Jackson W	Littleford AG	Purves W	Partridge C	Charsley CC	Watson PC
		4	5	6	7		9	10	11		3			8				2		1	
		1	1	1	1		1	1	1		1			1				1		1	
					1			1						1							

Jolley E	Pumfrey B	Ollis W	Jenkyns CAL	Devey EJ	Hallam J	Lee J	Mobley F	Wheldon GF	Hands T	Smith G	Short GF	Izon CJ	Spiller F	Walton WH	Reynolds WT	Jackson W	Littleford AG	Purves W	Partridge C	Charsley CC	Watson PC
		4	5	6	7		9	10	11					8	3		2				
		1	1	1	1		1	1	1					1	1		1				
					1		1	1													

League Table

	P	W	D	L	F	A	Pts
Liverpool	28	22	6	0	77	18	50
Small Heath	28	21	0	7	103	44	42
Notts County	28	18	3	7	70	31	39
Newcastle United	28	15	6	7	66	39	36
Grimsby Town	28	15	2	11	71	58	32
Burton Swifts	28	14	3	11	79	61	31
Burslem Port Vale	28	13	4	11	66	64	30
Lincoln City	28	11	6	11	59	58	28
Woolwich Arsenal	28	12	4	12	52	55	28
Walsall Town Swifts	28	10	3	15	51	61	23
Middlesbro' Ironopolis	28	8	4	16	37	72	20
Crewe Alexandra	28	6	7	15	42	73	19
Ardwick	28	8	2	18	47	71	18
Rotherham Town	28	6	3	19	44	91	15
Northwich Victoria	28	3	3	22	30	98	9

Division One

Secretary-manager: Alfred Jones

Did you know that?

Young right-back Tilson Pritchard was given the run-around by England left-winger and hat-trick hero Harry Chippendale when making his League debut in the 9–1 defeat at Blackburn in January.

Fred Wheldon scored Blues' first-ever penalty…in the 2–2 League draw with Aston Villa in October. Later in the game Blues conceded their first penalty in a League game, allowing Dennis Hodgetts to equalise.

Trailing 3–0 at half-time, Blues stormed back to record their first League win over Wolves by 4–3 in October.

Caesar Jenkyns scored and was then sent off in Blues' first-ever meeting with Derby on 16 March.

Blues played seven games in 55 days between 2 February and 28 March (six in the League).

Match No.	Date		Venue	Opponents	Result		Scorers	Attendance
1	Sep	1	A	Aston Villa	L	1-2	Hands	20,00
2		3	A	Everton	L	0-5		8,00
3		8	H	Bolton Wanderers	W	2-0	Wheldon 2	5,00
4		15	A	Wolverhampton Wan.	L	1-2	Wheldon	4,00
5		22	A	Preston North End	W	1-0	Hands	6,00
6		29	H	Preston North End	D	4-4	Hands, Wheldon, Mobley 2	4,00
7	Oct	6	H	Wolverhampton Wan.	W	4-3	Walton 2, Mobley, Wheldon	4,00
8		13	A	Burnley	L	1-3	Mobley	5,00
9		20	H	Aston Villa	D	2-2	Wheldon (pen), Hallam	15,00
10		27	A	Stoke	D	2-2	Mobley, Hands	1,00
11	Nov	3	H	Everton	D	4-4	Wheldon, Izon, Hallam, Jenkyns	10,00
12		10	A	West Bromwich Albion	L	1-4	Hands	4,52
13		17	H	Stoke	W	4-2	Walton, Hallam, Mobley, Wheldon	3,00
14		24	A	Bolton Wanderers	W	2-1	Hallam, Wheldon	4,00
15	Dec	1	H	Sheffield United	W	4-2	Leatherbarrow 3, Wheldon (pen)	6,00
16		8	A	Sunderland	L	1-7	Hallam	6,00
17		15	A	Liverpool	L	1-3	Mobley	3,00
18		22	H	Nottingham Forest	L	1-2	Mobley	3,00
19		26	A	Sheffield Wednesday	L	0-2		14,00
20		29	H	Liverpool	W	3-0	Mobley, Lewis, Walton	5,00
21	Jan	5	A	Blackburn Rovers	L	1-9	Walton	3,00
22		26	A	Nottingham Forest	L	0-2		4,00
23	Feb	9	H	Sunderland	D	1-1	Hands	15,00
24		23	H	West Bromwich Albion	L	1-2	Mobley	9,00
25	Mar	2	H	Blackburn Rovers	D	1-1	Mobley	3,00
26		16	H	Derby County	L	3-5	Walton, Hallam, Jenkyns	6,00
27		23	H	Burnley	W	1-0	Wheldon	5,00
28		25	H	Sheffield Wednesday	D	0-0		3,00
29		30	A	Derby County	L	1-4	Mobley	2,00
30	Apr	13	A	Sheffield United	W	2-0	Mobley, Hill (og)	4,00

Appearance
One own-goal
Goa

FA Cup

R1	Feb	2	H	West Bromwich Albion	L	1-2	Walton	10,20

Appearance
Goa

Appearances & Goals grid

Dudge C	Purves WM	Oliver JS	Ollis W	Jenayns CAL	Devey EJ	Hallam J	Walton WHT	Mobley F	Wheldon GF	Hands T	Bnetton EM	Izon CLJ	Leatherbarrow C	Jolley E	Moore EW	Lewis WJ	Pritchard T	Fosman EJ	Jones JT	Watson T
2	3	4	5	6	7	8	9	10	11											
2	3	4	5	6	7	8	9	10	11											
2	3	4	5	6	7	8	9	10	11											
2	3	4	5	6	7	8	9	10	11											
2	3	4	5	6	7	8	9	10	11											
2	3	4	5	6	7	8	9	10	11	1										
2	3	4	5	6	7	8	9	10	11											
2	3	4	5	6	7	8	9	10	11											
2	3	4	5	6	7	8	9	10	11											
2	3	4	5	6	7	8	9	10	11											
2	3	4	5	6	7	8			10	11		9								
2	3	4	5	6	7	8	9	10	11											
2	3	4	5	6	7	8	9	10	11											
2	3	4	5	6	7		9	10	11			8								
2	3	4	5	6	7		9	10	11			8								
2	3	4	5	6	7		9	10	11			8								
2	3	4	5	6	7		9	10	11			8								
2	3	4	5		7	8	9	10	11				6							
2	3	4	5		7	8	9	10	11				6							
2		4	5			8	9	10	11		3		6						7	
3		4		5		8	9		11		10		6					2	7	
2	3	4	5	6	7	8	9	10	11											
2	3	4	5	6	7	8	9		11						10					
2	3	4	5	6		8	9	10	11							7				
2	3	4	5	6	7	8	9	10	11								1			
2	3	4	5	6	7	8		10	11				9				1			
2	3	4	5	6	7	8	9	10							11					
2	3	4	5	6	7	8	9	10	11											
2	3	4	5	6	7	8	9	10	11											
2	3	4	5	6	7	8	9	10	11											
2	3	4												5						
30	**28**	**30**	**28**	**26**	**27**	**26**	**28**	**29**	**29**	**1**	**2**	**5**	**5**	**1**	**2**	**1**	**2**	**1**	**2**	
		2			6	6	13	11	6					1	3			1		

Cup grid

Dudge C	Purves WM	Oliver JS	Ollis W	Jenayns CAL	Devey EJ	Hallam J	Walton WHT	Mobley F	Wheldon GF	Hands T	Bnetton EM	Izon CLJ	Leatherbarrow C	Jolley E	Moore EW	Lewis WJ	Pritchard T	Fosman EJ	Jones JT	Watson T
2	3	4	5	6	7	8	9	10	11											
1	1	1	1	1	1	1	1	1	1											
		1																		

League Table

	P	W	D	L	F	A	Pts
Sunderland	30	21	5	4	80	37	47
Everton	30	18	6	6	82	50	42
Aston Villa	30	17	5	8	82	43	39
Preston North End	30	15	5	10	62	46	35
Blackburn Rovers	30	11	10	9	59	49	32
Sheffield United	30	14	4	12	57	55	32
Nottingham Forest	30	13	5	12	50	56	31
Sheffield Wednesday	30	12	4	14	50	55	28
Burnley	30	11	4	15	44	56	26
Bolton Wanderers	30	9	7	14	61	62	25
Wolverhampton W	30	9	7	14	43	63	25
Small Heath	30	9	7	14	50	74	25
West Bromwich Albion	30	10	4	16	51	66	24
Stoke	30	9	6	15	50	67	24
Derby County	30	7	9	14	45	68	23
Liverpool	30	7	8	15	51	70	22

Division One

Secretary-manager: Alfred Jones

Did you know that?

Blues used 32 players this season in all competitions.

Blues, in fact, conceded 22 goals in three games against Midland clubs, losing 7–3 to Aston Villa (for whom Johnny Campbell scored four times), 8–0 at Derby (when the defence concentrated on keeping Steve Bloomer quiet until very late on when he scored the Rams' last goal) and 7–2 at home to Wolves.

That latter scoreline at Muntz Street in January is still Wolves' biggest-ever victory on Blues soil.

Joey Schofield scored a hat-trick in Stoke's 6–1 win over Blues in October.

Match No.	Date		Venue	Opponents	Result		Scorers	Attendance
1	Sep	2	A	Sheffield United	L	0-2		7,00
2		7	A	Aston Villa	L	3-7	Walton, Mobley, Hands	14,00
3		14	H	Stoke	L	1-2	Hallam	8,00
4		21	A	Nottingham Forest	L	0-3		4,00
5		28	H	Bolton Wanderers	L	1-2	Mobley	4,00
6	Oct	5	A	Preston North End	L	2-3	Mobley 2	3,00
7		12	A	Bury	W	5-4	Wheldon 2, Mobley, Jones 2	6,00
8		19	A	Stoke	L	1-6	Jones	8,00
9		26	H	Aston Villa	L	1-4	Jones	10,00
10	Nov	9	H	Nottingham Forest	W	1-0	Mobley	5,00
11		23	H	Preston North End	W	5-2	Wheldon 2, Jones 2, Mobley	5,00
12		30	A	Derby County	L	0-8		7,00
13	Dec	7	H	Everton	L	0-3		3,00
14		14	A	Sunderland	L	1-2	Wheldon	4,00
15		21	H	West Bromwich Albion	D	2-2	Bruce, Adlington	6,00
16		26	H	Burnley	W	1-0	Adlington	5,50
17	Jan	4	H	Derby County	L	1-3	Adlington	10,00
18		18	H	Wolverhampton Wan.	W	3-2	Adlington, Bruce, Ollis	5,00
19		25	A	Wolverhampton Wan.	L	2-7	Wheldon, Mobley	4,00
20	Feb	3	A	Everton	L	0-3		8,00
21		8	H	Sheffield Wednesday	D	1-1	Leake	4,00
22		22	H	Bolton Wanderers	L	1-4	Mobley	8,00
23		29	H	Blackburn Rovers	W	2-1	Robertson, Wheldon	8,00
24	Mar	7	H	Bury	W	1-0	Haddon	5,00
25		21	A	Blackburn Rovers	L	1-2	Haddon	5,00
26	Apr	3	A	Burnley	D	1-1	Robertson	5,00
27		4	A	Sheffield Wednesday	L	0-3		4,00
28		6	A	West Bromwich Albion	D	0-0		3,75
29		7	H	Sheffield United	W	2-1	Mobley 2	6,00
30		11	H	Sunderland	L	0-1		8,00
							Appearances	
							Goals	

Test Matches

	Date		Venue	Opponents	Result		Scorers	Attendance
1	Apr	18	A	Liverpool	L	0-4		20,00
2		20	H	Liverpool	D	0-0		5,00
3		25	A	Manchester City	L	0-3		9,50
4		27	H	Manchester City	W	8-0	Jones 3, Wheldon 3, Abbott, Hallam	2,00
							Appearances	
							Goals	

FA Cup

	Date		Venue	Opponents	Result		Scorers	Attendance
R1	Feb	1	H	Bury	L	1-4	Lewis	15,00
							Appearances	
							Goals	

Player columns (left to right):

Wridge C · Parves WM · Oliver JS · Ollis W · Jolley E · Devey EJ · Hallam J · Walton WHT · Mobley F · Wheldon GF · Hands T · Roach J · Fall JW · Harnes AH · Jones JT · Icon CJ · Lester F · Leake A · Massies WP · Adlington JH · Fraser A · Bruce D · Farnall T · Haddon H · Robertson W · Lodge LV · Pratt W · Fountain EJ · Dunlop T · Devey J · Abbott WA · Lewis WJJ

Match-by-match appearance grid (values shown as they appear across the row):

	Visible numbers in row
	2 3 4 5 6 7 8 9 10 11
	2 3 4 5 6 7 8 9 10 11 1
	2 3 4 5 7 8 9 10 11 1 6
	2 3 4 5 6 7 10 11 1 8 9
	2 3 4 5 7 9 10 11 1 8 6
	3 4 5 7 9 10 11 1 8 2 6
	3 4 5 7 9 10 11 1 2 8 6
	2 3 4 5 7 9 10 8 11 6 1
	2 3 4 6 7 9 10 11 5 8 1
	3 4 6 7 9 10 11 1 5 8 2
	3 4 6 5 9 10 11 1 8 2 7
	3 4 5 8 10 11 1 7 2 6 9
	3 4 7 5 8 10 11 1 2 6 9
	3 4 7 5 8 10 11 1 2 6 9
	3 4 8 10 11 1 5 2 7 6 9
	3 4 9 10 11 1 5 8 2 7 6
	3 4 8 10 11 1 5 2 7 6 9
	3 4 8 11 1 5 9 2 7 6 10
	3 4 8 9 11 1 5 2 7 6 10
	3 7 10 11 9 2 5 1 6 8 4
	3 7 10 11 9 2 5 1 6 8 4
	3 7 10 11 8 2 5 1 6 4 9
	7 10 11 3 5 1 6 4 9 8 2
	3 7 10 11 2 5 1 6 4 9 8
	3 7 10 11 2 5 1 6 4 9 8
	3 7 10 9 5 1 6 4 8 2 11
	3 7 8 1 9 5 6 4 10 2 11
	3 7 10 11 9 5 1 6 4 8 2

Appearances total row:
7 29 19 11 3 12 9 28 30 25 15 2 9 14 6 20 14 12 6 19 9 11 5 8 1 1 2 1 0 0

Goals row:
1 · · 1 1 11 7 1 · · 6 · 1 · 4 · 2 · · 2 2

1896-97

Division Two

Secretary-manager: Alfred Jones

Match No.	Date	Venue	Opponents		Result	Scorers	Attendance
1	Sep 5	H	Newcastle United	W	3-1	Leake, Inglis, Jones	4,0
2	12	A	Newcastle United	L	3-4	Jones 2, Inglis	10,8
3	14	H	Darwen	W	5-1	Inglis, Walton, Robertson 2, Nixon (og)	8
4	19	H	Lincoln City	L	1-2	Edwards	6,0
5	26	A	Burton Swifts	D	1-1	Inglis	2,0
6	Oct 3	A	Burton Swifts	L	1-2	Inglis	4,0
7	10	A	Newton Heath	D	1-1	Jones	6,0
8	17	H	Gainsborough Trinity	D	2-2	Inglis, Leake	5,0
9	24	A	Walsall	W	6-1	Izon, Inglis 2, Walton 2, Jones	4,0
10	31	H	Grimsby Town	L	0-1		7,5
11	Nov 14	H	Woolwich Arsenal	W	5-2	Hodgetts, Farnall, Walton, Hare, Robertson	2,0
12	21	A	Darwen	L	0-2		3,0
13	28	H	Newton Heath	W	1-0	Jones	5,0
14	Dec 5	H	Grimsby Town	L	1-2	Inglis	4,0
15	19	A	Loughborough	L	0-2		1,0
16	25	H	Walsall	D	3-3	Inglis, Hare, Izon	7,5
17	Jan 1	A	Manchester City	L	0-3		16,0
18	2	A	Gainsborough Trinity	W	3-1	Hodgetts 2, Izon	1,5
19	23	A	Blackpool	W	3-1	Inglis 2, Hare	2,0
20	Feb 13	A	Burton Wanderers	W	6-2	Gadsby 2, Inglis, Hare, Walton, Hodgetts	2,0
21	27	H	Burton Wanderers	W	3-2	Hodgetts, Hare, Oakes	6,0
22	Mar 6	H	Blackpool	L	1-3	Hodgetts	6,0
23	13	A	Lincoln City	W	3-1	Inglis, Oakes, Jones	2,0
24	20	H	Loughborough	W	3-0	Jones 2, Leake	4,0
25	27	A	Leicester Fosse	W	1-0	Hodgetts	5,5
26	29	A	Woolwich Arsenal	W	3-2	Hodgetts 2, Hare	2,5
27	Apr 3	A	Notts County	W	2-1	Abbott 2	5,0
28	10	H	Notts County	W	3-1	Abbott 2, Inglis	7,0
29	16	H	Leicester Fosse	D	2-2	Hare, Inglis	2,0
30	19	H	Manchester City	W	3-1	Leake 2, Hare	6
							Appearanc
						One own-goal	Goa

FA Cup

R1	Jan 30	N	Notts County	L	1-2	Walton	10,0
							Appearanc
							Goa

238

	..llis VJP	Dunlop T	Lester F	Farnall T	Leake A	Walton WHT	Inglis JA	Robertson W	Jones JT	Abbott W	Edwards WH	Pointer E	Pratt W	Bennett WA	Izon CJ	Hodgetts D	Haddon H	Logan JT	Hare CB	Good MLH	Oakes TF	Gladdy W	Williams H
	2	3	4	5	6	7	8	9	10	11													
	2	3	4	5	6	7	8	9	10	11	1												
	2		4	5	6	7	8	9	10	11	1	3											
	2		4	5	6	7	8	9	10	11	1	3											
	2	3	4	5	6	11	8	9	10		1		7										
		2	4	5	6	7	8	9		11	1	3	8										
		2	4	5	6	7	8	9		11	1	3		10									
	4	2		5	6	7	8	9			1	3		11	10								
		2	4	5	6	7		8				3		11	10	9							
		2	4	5	6	7	9					3		11	10					8			
		2	4	5	6	7		9		11		3			10					8			
		2	4	5	6	7	9					3		11	10					8			
		2	4	5	6	7		9		11		3			10					8			
		2		5	6	7					1	3		11	10	9				8	4		
		2		5	6	7		8			1	3		11	10					9	4		
		2	4	5	6	7	8				1	3		11	10					9			
		2	4	5	8		10				1	3		9	11					7	6		
	4	2		5	6	7	8				1	3			10			9		11			
	4	2		5	6	7					1	3			10			9		11	8		
	4	2		5	6	7					1	3			10			9		11	8		
	4	2		5	6	7					1	3			10			9		11	8		
	4			5		7	6	8			1	3			10			9		11		2	
	4	2		5		7	6	8			1	3			10			9		11			
	4	2		5		7	6	8			1	3			10			9		11			
	4	2		5		7	6	8			1	3			10			9		11			
	4	2		5		7	6	8	10		1	3						9		11			
	4	2		5		7	6	8	10		1	3			11			9					
	4	2		5		7	6	8	10		1	3			11			9					
	4	2		5		7	6	8	10		1	3			11			9					
	18	27	15	30	21	29	23	20	12	5	28	27	2	9	22	3	1	20	3	9	3	1	
		1	5	5	16	3	9	4	1		3	9		8					2	2			

	..llis VJP	Dunlop T	Lester F	Farnall T	Leake A	Walton WHT	Inglis JA	Robertson W	Jones JT	Abbott W	Edwards WH	Pointer E	Pratt W	Bennett WA	Izon CJ	Hodgetts D	Haddon H	Logan JT	Hare CB	Good MLH	Oakes TF	Gladdy W	Williams H
	4	2		5	6	7	8			1	3			10			9		11				
	1	1		1	1	1	1			1	1			1			1		1				
				1																			

League Table

	P	W	D	L	F	A	Pts
Notts County	30	19	4	7	92	43	42
Newton Heath	30	17	5	8	56	34	39
Grimsby Town	30	17	4	9	66	45	38
Small Heath	30	16	5	9	69	47	37
Newcastle United	30	17	1	12	56	52	35
Manchester City	30	12	8	10	58	50	32
Gainsborough Trinity	30	12	7	11	50	47	31
Blackpool	30	13	5	12	59	56	31
Leicester Fosse	30	13	4	13	59	57	30
Woolwich Arsenal	30	13	4	13	68	70	30
Darwen	30	14	0	16	67	61	28
Walsall	30	11	4	15	54	69	26
Loughborough	30	12	1	17	50	64	25
Burton Swifts	30	9	6	15	46	61	24
Burton Wanderers	30	9	2	19	31	67	20
Lincoln City	30	5	2	23	27	85	12

Division Two

Secretary-manager: Alfred Jones

Did you know that?

Blues set a new, and still existing, club record when they beat Loughborough Town 2–0 in September. It was their ninth successive away win, commencing in January.

David Hannah scored a hat-trick (including one penalty) when Arsenal beat Blues 4–2 in March.

By beating Blues 4–1 at Turf Moor, League leaders Burnley stretched their unbeaten run to 14 matches.

Blackpool's win over Blues at Bloomfield Road was only their second of the season at the time.

Match No.	Date		Venue	Opponents	Result		Scorers	Attendance
1	Sep	4	A	Burton Swifts	W	3-1	Inglis 2, Abbott	1,5
2		11	H	Leicester Fosse	W	2-1	Abbott, Gadsby	3,0
3		18	A	Loughborough	W	2-0	Walton 2	2,0
4		25	H	Burton Swifts	W	2-1	Hare 2	7,5
5	Oct	2	A	Darwen	D	1-1	Walton	3,0
6		9	H	Gainsborough Trinity	W	4-3	Abbott 2, Robertson, Hare	4,5
7		16	A	Blackpool	L	1-4	Hare	1,5
8		23	H	Newton Heath	W	2-1	Lewis 2	3,0
9	Nov	6	H	Loughborough	W	1-0	Abbott	5,0
10		13	A	Grimsby Town	L	1-3	Wallace	2,0
11		27	A	Newcastle United	L	0-4		11,0
12	Dec	4	H	Walsall	W	6-0	Hare, Oakes 2, Abbott 2 (1 pen), Kirton	3,0
13		18	A	Walsall	W	2-1	Lewis 2	3,0
14		25	H	Darwen	W	5-1	Lewis, Abbott 3, Kirton	10,0
15		27	A	Manchester City	L	0-1		11,0
16	Jan	8	H	Burnley	D	2-2	Abbott, Leake	10,0
17		15	A	Lincoln City	W	2-1	Abbott, Lewis	2,5
18		29	H	Blackpool	L	2-3	Lewis, Robertson	5,0
19	Feb	5	A	Burnley	L	1-4	Oakes	4,0
20		12	H	Luton Town	W	4-2	Oakes, Abbott 2 (1 pen), McEwan (og)	4,0
21		19	A	Gainsborough Trinity	D	0-0		2,0
22	Mar	5	A	Woolwich Arsenal	L	2-4	Hare, Oakes	8,0
23		12	A	Grimsby Town	L	0-2		6,5
24		26	A	Leicester Fosse	L	0-2		2,0
25	Apr	2	A	Luton Town	W	2-1	Dunlop, Inglis	3,0
26		9	A	Newton Heath	L	1-3	Higgins	3,0
27		11	A	Manchester City	D	3-3	Abbott, Leake, Good	2,0
28		12	H	Newcastle United	W	1-0	Higgins	5,0
29		16	H	Lincoln City	W	4-0	Oakes, Abbott 2, Higgins	4,0
30		23	H	Woolwich Arsenal	W	2-1	Abbott 2	4,5

Appearances

One own-goal

Goals

FA Cup

| Q3 | Oct 30 | | A | Burslem Port Vale | L | 1-2 | Walton | 2,0 |

Appearances

Goals

240

	Buck HJ	Archer A	Lester F	Dunlop T	Leake A	Robertson W	Inglis JA	Lewis WA	Hare CB	Abbott W	Kernon JW	Oakes TT	Gaddy W	Walton WHT	Good M	Wallace A	Pratt W	Wharton SE	Webb I	Higgins J
	2	3	4	5	6	7	8	9	10	11										
	2	3	4	5	6			9	10	11	7	8								
	2	3	4	5	6	7		9	10	11				8						
	2	3	4	5	6	7		9	10	11				8						
	2	3	4	5	6	7		9	10	11				8						
	2	3	4	5	6	7	8	9	10	11										
	2	3	4	5	6			10	11	8		7			9					
		3	4	5	11		8	2	10		7		6	9						
	2	3	4	5	6			8	9	10		7					11			
	2	3	4	5				8	9	10		7		6			11			
	2		4	5		7	8	9	10			6					3	11		
	2		4	5	6		9	7	10	11	8						3			
	2		4	5	6		9	7	10	11	8						3			
	2		4	5	6		9	7	10	11	8						3			
	2		4	5	6		9	7	10	11	8						3			
	2		4	5	6		9	7	10	11	8						3			
	2		4	5	6		9	7	10	11	8						3			
	2		4	5	6		9	7	10	11	8						3			
	2		4	5	6	7	9		10	11	8						3			
	2		4	5	6		9	7	10		8						3	11		
	2		4	5	6		9	7	10		8						3	11		
	2		4		6		9	7	10	11	8			5			3			
	2		4	5	6		9	7	10	11	8						3			
	2		4		6	7	8	9	10	11				5			3			
	2		4	5	6	7		10		11				8			3		1	9
	2		4	5	6	7		10		11				8			3		1	9
	2		4	5	6			10	7					8			3	11		9
	2		4	5	6			10	7					8			3	11	1	9
	2		4	5	6			10	7					8			3	11	1	9
	2		4	5	6			10	7					8			3	11		9
	29	10	30	28	28	10	20	23	30	18	22	1	8	8	2	20	7	4	6	
		1	2	2	3	7	6	19	2	6	1	3		1	1				3	

	Buck HJ	Archer A	Lester F	Dunlop T	Leake A	Robertson W	Inglis JA	Lewis WA	Hare CB	Abbott W	Kernon JW	Oakes TT	Gaddy W	Walton WHT	Good M	Wallace A	Pratt W	Wharton SE	Webb I	Higgins J
	2	3		5	11		8	9	10		7		6	4						
	1	1		1	1		1	1	1		1		1	1						
									1											

League Table

	P	W	D	L	F	A	Pts
Burnley	30	20	8	2	80	24	48
Newcastle United	30	21	3	6	64	32	45
Manchester City	30	15	9	6	66	36	39
Newton Heath	30	16	6	8	64	35	38
Woolwich Arsenal	30	16	5	9	69	49	37
Small Heath	30	16	4	10	58	50	36
Leicester Fosse	30	13	7	10	46	35	33
Luton Town	30	13	4	13	68	50	30
Gainsborough Trinity	30	12	6	12	50	54	30
Walsall	30	12	5	13	58	58	29
Blackpool	30	10	5	15	49	61	25
Grimsby Town	30	10	4	16	52	62	24
Burton Swifts	30	8	5	17	38	69	21
Lincoln City	30	6	5	19	43	82	17
Darwen	30	6	2	22	31	76	14
Loughborough	30	6	2	22	24	87	14

Division Two

Secretary-manager: Alfred Jones

Match No.	Date		Venue	Opponents	Result		Scorers	Attendan
1	Sep	3	A	Burton Swifts	W	6-2	Abbott 2, McRoberts 2, Dunlop, Leake	3,0
2		5	H	Lincoln City	W	4-1	Bennett, Leake, Abbott 2	3,0
3		10	H	Burslem Port Vale	L	1-2	Abbott	10,0
4		17	H	Barnsley	W	3-1	McRoberts, Abbott, Wharton	5,0
5		24	A	Loughborough	D	1-1	McRoberts	2,0
6	Oct	8	A	Grimsby Town	L	0-2		3,0
7		15	H	Newton Heath	W	4-1	Abbott, Walton, Robertson, Inglis	5,0
8		22	A	New Brighton Tower	L	0-4		4,0
9	Nov	5	A	Woolwich Arsenal	L	0-2		7,0
10		12	H	Luton Town	W	9-0	Gardner 2, McRoberts, Wharton, Inglis, Robertson 3, Abbott	4,0
11		26	H	Darwen	W	8-0	Gardner 2, Abbott 5 (1 pen), Robertson	2,0
12	Dec	3	A	Gainsborough Trinity	D	1-1	Gardner	1,0
13		17	A	Glossop	W	2-1	Abbott, Inglis	2,0
14		24	H	Walsall	W	2-1	Gardner, McRoberts	7,0
15		26	H	Blackpool	W	5-0	Inglis, Walton, Abbott 2, McRoberts	4,0
16		27	H	Manchester City	W	4-1	Abbott 2, Inglis, McRoberts	10,0
17		31	H	Burton Swifts	W	4-1	Robertson, Gardner 2, Abbott	4,0
18	Jan	7	A	Burslem Port Vale	L	0-1		5,0
19		14	A	Barnsley	L	2-7	Gardner, Walton	2,0
20		21	H	Loughborough	W	6-0	Abbott 3, Wharton 2, Wilcox	3,0
21	Feb	4	H	Grimsby Town	W	2-1	Abbott, Robertson	6,0
22		18	H	New Brighton Tower	W	3-2	Abbott 2, Wilcox	10,0
23		25	A	Newton Heath	L	0-2		12,0
24	Mar	4	H	Woolwich Arsenal	W	4-1	Abbott 3, Wharton	3,0
25		8	A	Blackpool	D	1-1	Devey	1,0
26		11	A	Luton Town	W	3-2	Abbott 3 (1 pen)	2,0
27		18	H	Leicester Fosse	L	0-3		10,0
28		25	A	Darwen	D	1-1	McRoberts	2
29		31	A	Lincoln City	D	2-2	Wigmore, Bennett	5,0
30	Apr	1	H	Gainsborough Trinity	W	6-1	Abbott 3, Wigmore 2, Bennett	6,0
31		8	A	Manchester City	L	0-2		18,0
32		15	H	Glossop	D	1-1	McRoberts	6,0
33		22	A	Walsall	L	0-2		5,0
34		29	A	Leicester Fosse	D	0-0		5,0

Appearanc
Goa

FA Cup

Q3	Oct	29	H	Chirk	W	8-0	Walton 3, Inglis 2, Abbott 2, Leake	3,0
Q4	Nov	19	H	Druids	W	10-0	Abbott 2, McRoberts 3, Gardner, Inglis 2, Leake, Hughes (og)	4,0
Q5		10	H	Burslem Port Vale	W	7-0	Gardner, McRoberts, Abbott 3, Wharton, Inglis	7,0
R1	Jan	28	H	Manchester City	W	3-2	Abbott, McRoberts 2	15,3
R2		11	A	Stoke	D	2-2	Robertson, Wharton	12,0
rep		15	H	Stoke	L	1-2	Inglis	14,3

Appearanc
Goa

One own-goal

Player appearance grid (shirt numbers by match):

	Buck HJ	Archer A	Pratt W	Dunlop T	Leake A	Robertson W	Bennett WA	Good MHS	McRoberts R	Abbott W	Wharton SE	Webb I	Wilcox HM	Oakes TF	Inglis JA	Walton WHT	Gardner AE	Lester F	Layton G	Davey W	Wigmore W	Axby DW	Price JL
1	2	3	4	5	6	7	8	9	10	11													
2	2	3	4	5	6	7	8	9	10	11													
3	2	3	4	5	6	7	8	9	10	11													
4	2	3	4	5	6	7		9	10	11	1	8											
5	2	3	4	5	6	7		9	10	11		8											
6	2	3	4	5	6		10	9	8	11				7									
7	2	3	4	5	6			9	10	11				7	8								
8	2	3	4	5	6			9	10	11				7	8								
9	2	3	4	5	6			9	10	11				7	8								
10	2	3		5	6			9	10	11				7	4	8							
11	2	3		5	6			9	10	11				7	4	8							
12	2	3		5	6			9	10	11				7	4	8							
13	2	3		5	6			9	10	11				7	4	8							
14	2	3		5	6			9	10	11				7	4	8							
15	2	3		5	6			9	10	11				7	4	8							
16	2	3		5	6			9	10	11				7	4	8							
17	2	3		5	6			9	10	11				7	4	8							
18	2	3		5	6			9	10	11				7	4	8							
19	2	3		5	6			9	10	11				7	4	8							
20	2	3		5	6			9	10	11			8		7	4							
21	2	3		5	6			9	10	11				7	4	8							
22		3		5				9	10	11			8		7	4	2	6					
23	2	3		5	6				10	11			9		7	4	8						
24	2	3		5	6	7			10	11					4	8							
25	2	3		5	6	7			10	11					4	8			9				
26	2	3		5	6	7			10	11			9		4	8							
27	2	3		5	6	7			10	11			9		4	8							
28	2	3		5	6	7		8	10	11					4				9				
29	2	3		5	6	7		8	10	11					4				9				
30	2	3		5	6	7		8	10	11					4				9				
31	2			5	6	7		8	10	11					4		3		9				
32	2	3		5	6			8	10	11					4			7	9				
33	2	3		5	6				10	11			8		4				9	7			
34	2	3		5					10	11					4			6	9	7	8		
App	33	33	9	34	32	13	4	27	34	34	1	8	2	17	28	16	2	2	2	7	2	1	
Gls		1		2	7	3		10	34	6		2		5	2	9				1	3		

Cup appearances:

	Buck HJ	Archer A	Pratt W	Dunlop T	Leake A	Robertson W	Bennett WA	Good MHS	McRoberts R	Abbott W	Wharton SE	Webb I	Wilcox HM	Oakes TF	Inglis JA	Walton WHT	Gardner AE	Lester F	Layton G	Davey W	Wigmore W	Axby DW	Price JL
1	2	3		5	6			9	10	11				7	8								
2	2	3		5	6			9	10	11				7	4	8							
3	2	3		5	6			9	10	11				7	4	8							
4	2	3		5	6			9	10	11				7	4	8							
5	2	3		5	6			9	10	11			8		7	4							
6	2	3		5	6				10	11			9	8	7	4							
App	6	6	1	6	6			5	6	6			2	1	6	6	3						
Gls				2	1			6	8	2					6	3	2						

League Table

	P	W	D	L	F	A	Pts
Manchester City	34	23	6	5	92	35	52
Glossop	34	20	6	8	76	38	46
Leicester Fosse	34	18	9	7	64	42	45
Newton Heath	34	19	5	10	67	43	43
New Brighton Tower	34	18	7	9	71	52	43
Walsall	34	15	12	7	79	36	42
Woolwich Arsenal	34	18	5	11	72	41	41
Small Heath	34	17	7	10	85	50	41
Burslem Port Vale	34	17	5	12	56	34	39
Grimsby Town	34	15	5	14	71	60	35
Barnsley	34	12	7	15	52	56	31
Lincoln City	34	12	7	15	51	56	31
Burton Swifts	34	10	8	16	51	70	28
Gainsborough Trinity	34	10	5	19	56	72	25
Luton Town	34	10	3	21	51	95	23
Blackpool	34	8	4	22	49	90	20
Loughborough	34	6	6	22	38	92	18
Darwen	34	2	5	27	22	141	9

Division Two

Secretary-manager: Alfred Jones

Top of the table Sheffield Wednesday stretched their unbeaten run to nine League games when beating Blues 4–0 in October.

There were four hat-tricks in Bob McRoberts's total of 24 goals for Blues this season.

Blues utilised a different player at centre-forward in five successive League matches in February/March. Smethwick-born Sam Cole was one of them. When McRoberts cried off injured barely an hour before kick-off, and with reserve Billy Walton away playing for the reserves, Cole was called out of the crowd for his debut in the 2–0 home win over Burton Swifts in March. This was his only appearance for the club. Cole was related to Herbert and John Cole who both played for West Bromwich Albion in the early 1900s.

Match No.	Date	Venue	Opponents	Result		Scorers	Attendance
1	Sep 2	H	Walsall	W	3-2	Wigmore 2, Wharton	7,0
2	9	A	Middlesbrough	W	3-1	McRoberts 3	10,0
3	16	H	Chesterfield	W	5-3	McRoberts, Bennett 2, Main, Wilcox	7,0
4	23	A	Gainsborough Trinity	W	4-1	McRoberts, Wharton, Bennett 2	1,0
5	30	H	Bolton Wanderers	D	0-0		10,0
6	Oct 2	H	Lincoln City	W	5-0	Wigmore 2, McRoberts 3	4,0
7	7	A	Loughborough	W	2-1	Main, Farnell	2,0
8	14	H	Newton Heath	W	1-0	Main	10,0
9	21	A	Sheffield Wednesday	L	0-4		9,0
10	Nov 4	A	Burton Swifts	W	3-0	Archer (pen), Wharton, McRoberts	2,0
11	11	A	New Brighton Tower	D	2-2	Scrivens, Leake	2,0
12	25	A	Woolwich Arsenal	L	0-3		3,0
13	Dec 2	H	Barnsley	W	5-0	Main, McRoberts, Wigmore 2, Leonard	5,0
14	16	H	Luton Town	W	3-0	Bennett 2, Scrivens	2,0
15	23	A	Burslem Port Vale	L	0-3		2,0
16	30	A	Walsall	L	0-1		3,0
17	Jan 6	H	Middlesbrough	W	5-1	McRoberts 2, Scrivens, Bennett, Bayley	1,4
18	13	A	Chesterfield	D	0-0		2,0
19	20	H	Gainsborough Trinity	W	8-1	Wharton, McRoberts 3, Layton 2, Bennett, Main	4,0
20	27	H	Burslem Port Vale	W	2-1	Aston, Leake	4,0
21	Feb 3	A	Bolton Wanderers	D	1-1	McRoberts	6,2
22	10	H	Loughborough	W	6-0	Aston 3, Leake 2, Adey	2,0
23	12	H	Grimsby Town	L	0-1		2,0
24	17	A	Newton Heath	L	2-3	Aston, Wharton	14,0
25	24	H	Sheffield Wednesday	W	4-1	Layton, Wharton, Leake, Bennett	9,0
26	Mar 10	H	Burton Swifts	W	2-0	Leake, Aston	5,0
27	17	H	New Brighton Tower	W	2-0	Scrivens 2	5,3
28	24	A	Grimsby Town	L	0-2		5,0
29	31	H	Woolwich Arsenal	W	3-1	Leake, McRoberts, Aston	3,0
30	Apr 7	A	Barnsley	D	1-1	Leake	2,0
31	13	A	Lincoln City	D	0-0		5,0
32	14	H	Leicester Fosse	W	4-1	McRoberts, Wharton, Main, Wragg (og)	6,0
33	17	A	Leicester Fosse	L	0-2		6,0
34	21	A	Luton Town	W	2-1	Main, McRoberts	1,0

Appearanc

One own-goal Go

FA Cup

Q3	Oct 28	H	Oswestry United	W	10-2	Scrivens 2, Wharton 2, Main 2, Wigmore, McRoberts 2, Adey	1,0
Q4	Nov 22	H	Wrexham	W	6-1	McRoberts 3, Scrivens 2, Wigmore	1,5
Q5	Dec 9	H	Walsall	D	0-0		4,0
rep	14	A	Walsall	L	0-2		1,0

Appearanc
Go

Archer A	Pratt W	Walton WHT	Leake A	Farnall T	Bennett WA	Wigmore W	McRoberts R	Main WS	Wharton SE	Abey GW	Wilcox HM	Oakes TF	Scrivens T	Leonard J	Lester F	Layton G	Bayley S	Adam J	Cole S
2	3	4	5	6	7	8	9	10	11										
2	3	5	6	7	8	9	10	11	4										
2	3		6	7	5	9	10	11	4	8									
2	3		6	7	5	9	10	11	4	8									
2	3		6	7	5	9	10	11	4	8									
2	3		6		5	9	10	11	7	8	4								
2	3		6		5	9	10	11	7		4	8							
2	3	5	6		4	9	10	11		7		8							
2	3	5	6		8	9	10	11	4	7									
2	3	6	4		5	9	10	11	7			8							
2		5	6		3	9	10	11	4			8	7						
2	3	5	6			9	10	11	4			8	7						
2	3	5	6		8	9	10	11	4				7						
2		5	6	8			10	11	4			9	7	3					
2		5	6	8		10		11	4			9	7	3					
2	3	5	6	8		10		11	4			9	7						
2	3	5		7		9		11	4			8			6	10			
2	3	5		8		9		11	4			10	7		6				
2	3	5		7		9	10	11	4						6		8		
2	3	6		7	5	9	10	11	4								8		
2	3	10	6	7	5	9		11	4								8		
2	3	10	4		5	9		11	7						6		8		
2	3	10	4		5	9		11	7						6		8		
2	3	10		7	5	9		11	4						6		8		
2	3	7	8		9	5	10		11	4					6				
2	3	10		7	5			11	4						6		8	9	
2	3	10		7	5			11	4			9			6		8		
2	3	9	10		7	5		11	4						6		8		
2	3	5		7		9		11	4			10			6		8		
2	3	6		7	5			11	4			10					8		
2	3	6		7	5	9	10	11	4								8		
2	3	6		7	5	9	10	11	4								8		
2	3	6		7	5	9	10	11	4								8		
2	3	6		7	5	9	10	11	4								8		
34	31	3	29	19	24	26	30	20	34	32	6	2	13	7	2	11	1	15	1
1		8	1	9	6	19	7	7	1	1		5	1		3	1	7		

Archer A	Pratt W	Walton WHT	Leake A	Farnall T	Bennett WA	Wigmore W	McRoberts R	Main WS	Wharton SE	Abey GW	Wilcox HM	Oakes TF	Scrivens T	Leonard J	Lester F	Layton G	Bayley S	Adam J	Cole S
2	3	6	4		5	9	10	11	7						8				
2	3	6	4	7	5	9	10	11							8				
2	3	6	4		8	9	10	11	5				7						
2	3	5	6			10	8	11	4			9	7						
4	4	4	4	1	3	4	4	4	3				3	2					
			2	5	2	2	1						4						

League Table

	P	W	D	L	F	A	Pts
Sheffield Wednesday	34	25	4	5	84	22	54
Bolton Wanderers	34	22	8	4	79	25	52
Small Heath	34	20	6	8	78	38	46
Newton Heath	34	20	4	10	63	27	44
Leicester Fosse	34	17	9	8	53	36	43
Grimsby Town	34	17	6	11	67	46	40
Chesterfield	34	16	6	12	65	60	38
Woolwich Arsenal	34	16	4	14	61	43	36
Lincoln City	34	14	8	12	47	43	36
New Brighton Tower	34	13	9	12	66	58	35
Burslem Port Vale	34	14	6	14	39	50	34
Walsall	34	12	8	14	50	55	32
Gainsborough Trinity	34	9	7	18	47	75	25
Middlesbrough	34	8	8	18	39	69	24
Burton Swifts	34	9	6	19	43	84	24
Barnsley	34	8	7	19	46	79	23
Luton Town	34	5	8	21	40	75	18
Loughborough	34	1	6	27	18	100	8

Division Two

Secretary-manager: Alfred Jones

Match No.	Date		Venue	Opponents	Result		Scorers	Attendance
1	Sep	1	A	Burslem Port Vale	D	2-2	Aston, Main	3,0
2		8	H	Leicester Fosse	D	0-0		8,0
3		15	A	New Brighton Tower	D	0-0		4,0
4		22	H	Gainsborough Trinity	W	6-0	Leake 2, McRoberts 2, Walton, Thornley (og)	2,0
5		29	A	Walsall	D	2-2	McRoberts, Wigmore	3,0
6	Oct	6	H	Burton Swifts	W	2-0	Walton, Higginson	2,0
7		13	A	Barnsley	W	2-1	Higginson., Aston	4,0
8		20	H	Woolwich Arsenal	W	2-1	Aston, Higginson	8,0
9		27	A	Blackpool	D	0-0		3,0
10	Nov	10	H	Chesterfield	D	0-0		6,0
11		17	A	Grimsby Town	D	1-1	Higginson	5,0
12		24	H	Lincoln City	W	2-0	McRoberts, Leake	5,0
13	Dec	1	A	Newton Heath	W	1-0	McRoberts	6,0
14		8	H	Glossop	W	1-0	Aston (pen)	8,0
15		15	A	Middlesbrough	W	1-0	Archer	13,0
16		22	H	Burnley	L	0-1		10,0
17		26	H	Stockport County	W	2-0	Aston, McRoberts	7,0
18		29	H	Burslem Port Vale	W	2-1	McRoberts 2	6,0
19	Jan	5	A	Leicester Fosse	D	1-1	Aston	8,0
20		12	H	New Brighton Tower	W	4-0	McRoberts 2, Main 2	2,0
21		19	A	Gainsborough Trinity	W	2-1	Aston, McRoberts	1,0
22	Feb	16	H	Barnsley	W	3-1	McRoberts, Aston, Tebbs	8,0
23	Mar	2	H	Blackpool	W	10-1	McRoberts 5, McMillan 5	3,0
24		9	A	Stockport County	D	0-0		5,0
25		16	A	Chesterfield	D	1-1	McMillan	4,0
26		30	A	Lincoln City	L	1-3	McMillan	2,5
27	Apr	1	H	Grimsby Town	W	2-1	Aston, McMillan	3,5
28		6	H	Newton Heath	W	1-0	McMillan	5,0
29		8	H	Walsall	W	2-1	Aston, Main	4,0
30		13	A	Glossop	L	0-2		2,0
31		15	A	Burton Swifts	W	2-0	McMillan 2	2,0
32		20	H	Middlesbrough	W	2-1	McMillan 2	8,0
33		22	A	Woolwich Arsenal	L	0-1		3,5
34		27	A	Burnley	L	0-1		1,0

One own-goal

Appearanc
Goa

FA Cup

	Date		Venue	Opponents	Result		Scorers	Attendance
R1	Feb	9	A	Stoke	D	1-1	Main	12,0
rep		13	H	Stoke	W	2-1	Bennett, Wharton	10,0
R2		23	H	Burnley	W	1-0	McMillan	11,0
R3	Mar	23	H	Aston Villa	D	0-0		18,0
rep		27	A	Aston Villa	L	0-1		15,0

R1 replay a.e.t.

R3 replay a.e.t.

Appearanc
Goa

Appearance / line-up grid

	Wilkinson AC	Archer A	Pratt W	Aden GW	Wigmore W	Leake A	Tabbs JT	Aston J	McRoberts R	Main WS	Wharton SE	Bennett WA	Layton G	Webb I	Walton WHT	Lester F	Higginson J	Fletcher TW	Wing WA	Gant A	McMillan JS	Henderson JK
	2	3	4	5	6		8	9	10	11												
	2	3	4	5			8	9	10	11	7	6										
	2	3	4	5	6		8	9	10	11	7		1									
	2	3	4	5	10			9		11	7	6		8								
	2			5	10		8	9		11	7	6		4	3							
	2		4	5	6			9		11	7			8	3	10						
	2	3		5	6		8	9		11	7			4		10						
	2	3		5	6		8	9		11	7			4		10						
	2	3		5	6		8	9		11	7			4		10						
	2			5	6		8		9	11	7			4	3	10						
	2	3		5	6		8	9		11	7			4		10						
	2	3		5	6		8	9		11	7			4		10						
	2			5	6		8	9		11	7			4	3	10						
	2			5	6		8	9		11	7			4	3	10						
	2		4	5	6		8	9		11	7				3	10						
	2		4	5			8	9		11	7	6			3	10						
	2	3	4	5			8	9	10	11	7			6								
	2	3	4	5	6		8	9		11	7									10		
	3		4	5	2		8	9		11	7			6						10		
	3		2	5	6		8	9	10	11	7			4				2				
	3		2	5	6		8	9	10	11	7			4								
	3		2	5	6	11	8	9						4					7	10		
	3		2	5	6		8	9		11	7			4						10		
	3		2	5	6		9		7	11	8			4						10		
	3		2	5	6		8			11	7			4						9	10	
	2	3	4	5	6		8		10	11									7	9		
	2	3	7	5	6		8		10	11				4						9		
	2	3	4	5	6		8		10	11									7	9		
	2	3	4	5	6		8		10	11	7									9		
	3		2	5	6		8	9		11	7			4						10		
	3		2	5	6			9		11	7			4						10	8	
	3		2	5	6			9		11	7			4						10	8	
	3		2	5	6	11			7	10				4						9	8	
	34	16	24	34	31	3	29	26	13	33	28	4	1	24	7	11	2	1	3	13	4	
	1		1	3	1		10	17	4		2			4		13						

	Wilkinson AC	Archer A	Pratt W	Aden GW	Wigmore W	Leake A	Tabbs JT	Aston J	McRoberts R	Main WS	Wharton SE	Bennett WA	Layton G	Webb I	Walton WHT	Lester F	Higginson J	Fletcher TW	Wing WA	Gant A	McMillan JS	Henderson JK
	3		2	5	6		8	9	10	11	7			4								
	3		2	5	6		8	9	10	11	7			4								
	3		2	5	6		8	9		11	7			4		10						
	2	3	4	5	6		8		10	11	7					9						
	2	3		5	6		8		10	11	7			4		9						
	5	2	4	5	5		5	3	4	5	5			4		3						
							1	1	1							1						

League Table

	P	W	D	L	F	A	Pts
Grimsby Town	34	20	9	5	60	33	49
Small Heath	34	19	10	5	57	24	48
Burnley	34	20	4	10	53	29	44
New Brighton Tower	34	17	8	9	57	38	42
Glossop	34	15	8	11	51	33	38
Middlesbrough	34	15	7	12	50	40	37
Woolwich Arsenal	34	15	6	13	39	35	36
Lincoln City	34	13	7	14	43	39	33
Burslem Port Vale	34	11	11	12	45	47	33
Newton Heath	34	14	4	16	42	38	32
Leicester Fosse	34	11	10	13	39	37	32
Blackpool	34	12	7	15	33	58	31
Gainsborough Trinity	34	10	10	14	45	60	30
Chesterfield	34	9	10	15	46	58	28
Barnsley	34	11	5	18	47	60	27
Walsall	34	7	13	14	40	56	27
Stockport County	34	11	3	20	38	68	25
Burton Swifts	34	8	4	22	34	66	20

Division One

Secretary-manager: Alfred Jones

Match No.	Date		Venue	Opponents	Result		Scorers	Attendance
1	Sep	2	H	Liverpool	D	0-0		12,00
2		7	H	Bolton Wanderers	W	2-0	Aston, McRoberts	15,00
3		14	A	Manchester City	W	4-1	Aston 2, McRoberls, McMillan	23,00
4		21	H	Wolverhampton Wan.	L	1-2	Aston	16,00
5		28	A	Liverpool	L	1-3	McMillan	20,00
6	Oct	5	H	Newcastle United	W	3-1	Aston, McMillan, McRoberts	12,00
7		12	H	Aston Villa	L	0-2		23,00
8		19	H	Sheffield United	W	5-1	McMillan 2, Athersmith, Jones, McRoberts	20,00
9		26	A	Nottingham Forest	D	1-1	Jones	10,00
10	Nov	2	H	Bury	W	1-0	Wigmore	15,00
11		9	A	Blackburn Rovers	L	1-3	Archer (pen)	6,00
12		23	A	Everton	L	0-1		15,00
13		30	A	Sunderland	L	2-3	McMillan, Murray	18,00
14	Dec	7	A	Grimsby Town	L	0-1		8,00
15		21	H	Sheffield Wednesday	D	1-1	Leonard	12,00
16		26	A	Aston Villa	L	0-1		40,00
17		28	A	Notts County	L	1-6	Leonard	8,00
18	Jan	4	A	Bolton Wanderers	L	0-4		6,58
19		11	H	Manchester City	W	1-0	McRoberts (pen)	20,00
20		18	A	Wolverhampton Wan.	L	1-2	McRoberts	5,00
21	Feb	1	A	Newcastle United	L	0-2		13,00
22		15	H	Sheffield United	W	4-1	McRoberts, Field, Leonard, Wharton	9,00
23		17	H	Stoke	D	1-1	Athersmith	8,00
24		22	H	Grimsby Town	W	6-0	Field 2, Leonard, McRoberts, Wigmore, McConnell (og)	16,00
25	Mar	1	A	Bury	L	0-2		6,00
26		8	H	Blackburn Rovers	W	2-0	Wharton 2	15,00
27		15	A	Stoke	L	0-1		4,00
28		22	H	Everton	L	0-1		15,00
29		29	A	Sunderland	D	1-1	Athersmith	8,00
30		31	H	Derby County	D	0-0		7,00
31	Apr	5	H	Nottingham Forest	D	1-1	Athersmith	15,00
32		12	H	Derby County	W	5-1	Leonard 2, McMillan, McRoberts, Wharton	10,00
33		19	A	Sheffield Wednesday	W	2-1	McRoberts, Wharton	10,00
34		26	H	Notts County	D	0-0		20,00

Appearance
Goa

FA Cup

IR	Dec 14	A	Portsmouth	L	1-2	McRoberts	15,00

Appearance
Goa

Appearances & goals grid (shirt numbers worn per match)

	Goldie A	Archer A	Watson WHT	Wigmore W	Leake A	Bennett WA	Aston J	McRoberts R	McMillan JS	Wharton SE	Higginson J	Ainsworth WC	Apey GW	Jones WH	Tebb JT	Murray JA	Leonard AR	Bunch W	Pratt W	Dougherty J	Wassell H	Beer WU	Field CWF	Hartwell AW	Pemland F
2	3	4		5	6		7	8	9	10	11														
2	3	4		5	6		8	9	10	11	7														
2	3	4		5	6		8	9	10	11		7													
2	3	4		5	6		8	9	10	11		7													
2	3	4		5	6		8	9	10	11		7													
2	3	6			5	6	8	9	10	11		7	4												
2	3	4		5	6		8	9	10	11		7													
2	3			5	6			9	10		11	7	4	8											
2	3			5	6			9	10		11	7	4	8											
2	3	4		5	6		8	9	10	11		7													
2	3	4		5	6			9	10			7		8	11										
2	3			5	6	8		9	10	11		7	4												
2	3	4		5	6			9	10	11		7		8											
2	3			5	6	8		9	10	11		7	4												
2	3			5	6			9	10	11		7	4		8										
2				5	6			9	10	11		7	4		8	3									
2				5	6			9	10	11		7	4		8	2	3								
2		5			3			9	10	11		7	4		8			6							
2	3			5	6			9	10	11		7	4		8										
2					5	8	9	10			7	4		11					6	3					
2	3			5	6	8	9			7	4	10		11											
2	3			5	6		9		11		7				8							4	10		
2	3			5	6		9		11		7				8							4	10		
2	3			5	6		9		11		7				8							4	10		
2	3			5	6		9		11		7				8							4	10		
2	3			5	6		9		11		7				8							4	10		
2	3			5	6		9		11		7				8							4	10		
2	3				5		9		11		7	6			8							4	10		
2					6			9	11		7				8				3	4	10	5			
2					6			9	11		7				8				3	4	10	5			
2					6		9	10	11		7				8				3	4		5			
2		4			6		9	10	11		7				8				3			5			
2		5		6			9	10	11		7				8				3	4					
2		5		6			9		11		7				8				3	4	10				
33	**24**	**11**	**28**	**33**	**3**	**11**	**32**	**24**	**29**	**3**	**32**	**13**	**4**	**1**	**1**	**20**	**2**	**1**	**2**	**7**	**12**	**10**	**4**		
1		2			5	10	7	5		4		2		1	6				3						

Cup appearances & goals

	Goldie A	Archer A	Watson WHT	Wigmore W	Leake A	Bennett WA	Aston J	McRoberts R	McMillan JS	Wharton SE	Higginson J	Ainsworth WC	Apey GW	Jones WH	Tebb JT	Murray JA	Leonard AR	Bunch W	Pratt W	Dougherty J	Wassell H	Beer WU	Field CWF	Hartwell AW	Pemland F
2			5	6		8	9		11		7	4						3						10		
1		1	1	1		1	1		1	1	1	1						1						1	
									1																

League Table

	P	W	D	L	F	A	Pts
Sunderland	34	19	6	9	50	35	44
Everton	34	17	7	10	53	35	41
Newcastle United	34	14	9	11	48	34	37
Blackburn Rovers	34	15	6	13	52	48	36
Nottingham Forest	34	13	9	12	43	43	35
Derby County	34	13	9	12	39	41	35
Bury	34	13	8	13	44	38	34
Aston Villa	34	13	8	13	42	40	34
Sheffield Wednesday	34	13	8	13	48	52	34
Sheffield United	34	13	7	14	53	48	33
Liverpool	34	10	12	12	42	38	32
Bolton Wanderers	34	12	8	14	51	56	32
Notts County	34	14	4	16	51	57	32
Wolverhampton W	34	13	6	15	46	57	32
Grimsby Town	34	13	6	15	44	60	32
Stoke	34	11	9	14	45	55	31
Small Heath	34	11	8	15	47	45	30
Manchester City	34	11	6	17	42	58	28

1902-03

Division Two

Secretary-manager: Alfred Jones

Match No.	Date		Venue	Opponents	Result		Scorers	Attendance
1	Sep	6	A	Leicester Fosse	W	3-1	Field 2, McRoberts	6,0
2		13	H	Manchester City	W	4-0	Jones. McMillan, Leonard 2	12,0
3		20	A	Burnley	L	1-2	McMillan	3,0
4		27	H	Preston North End	W	3-1	Leonard, McMillan, Wigmore	10,0
5	Oct	4	A	Burslem Port Vale	D	2-2	McMillan, Athersmith	4,0
6		11	H	Barnsley	W	2-1	Athersmith, Leonard	7,0
7		18	A	Gainsborough Trinity	L	0-1		3,0
8		25	H	Burton United	W	2-0	Field, Athersmith	5,0
9	Nov	1	A	Bristol City	D	1-1	McRoberts	12,0
10		8	H	Glossop	W	3-1	McRoberts 2, Beer	5,0
11		15	A	Manchester United	W	1-0	Beer	24,0
12		22	H	Stockport County	W	2-0	Beer, McRoberts	5,0
13		29	A	Blackpool	W	1-0	Leonard	3,0
14	Dec	6	A	Woolwich Arsenal	W	2-0	Leonard, Wigmore	10,0
15		13	A	Doncaster Rovers	L	0-1		3,0
16		20	H	Lincoln City	W	3-1	Harrison 2, Leonard	7,0
17		26	H	Chesterfield	W	2-1	Athersmith, Beer	13,0
18		27	A	Chesterfield	D	1-1	McRoberts	6,0
19	Jan	3	H	Leicester Fosse	W	4-3	Leonard 2, Field, McRoberts	6,0
20		17	H	Burnley	W	3-0	Leonard, Field, Athersmith	7,0
21		24	A	Preston North End	L	1-2	Beer	7,0
22		31	H	Burslem Port Vale	W	5-1	McRoberts, Jones, Beer (pen), Windridge 2	6,0
23	Feb	14	H	Gainsborough Trinity	W	1-0	McRoberts	7,0
24		21	A	Burton United	W	1-0	McRoberts	3,0
25		23	A	Manchester City	L	0-4		20,0
26		28	H	Bristol City	W	2-0	Windridge 2	12,0
27	Mar	7	A	Glossop	W	1-0	Windridge	2,0
28		21	A	Stockport County	W	2-1	McRoberts, Harrison	4,0
29		28	H	Blackpool	W	5-1	Wilcox 2, McRoberts, Beer (pen), Wolstenholme (og)	7,0
30	Apr	4	A	Woolwich Arsenal	L	1-6	McRoberts	15,0
31		10	A	Lincoln City	W	1-0	Leonard	6,0
32		11	H	Doncaster Rovers	W	12-0	Leonard 4, Wilcox 4, Athersmith, Field, McRoberts, Dougherty	8,0
33		13	A	Barnsley	L	0-3		5,0
34		20	H	Manchester United	W	2-1	Leonard, Wilcox	4,0

Appearanc

One own-goal Goa

FA Cup

R1	Feb	7	A	Derby County	L	1-2	Windridge	15,0

Appearanc

Goa

Gibbins AC	Goldie A	Wassall H	Beer WJ	Wigmore W	Dougherty J	Aldersmith WC	Leonard AR	McRoberts R	Field CWF	Jones WH	McMillan JS	Hanwell AW	Wharton SE	Dorrington J	Tickle CH	Harrison A	Howard H	Thompson T	Woodridge JE	Hirons JW	Wilcox FJ
2	3	4	5	6	7	8	9	10	11												
2	3	4	5	6	7	8	9		11	10											
2	3	4	5	6	7	8	9		11	10											
2	3	4	9	6	7	8			10	5	11										
2	3	9	6	7	8				4	10	11	1									
2		4	5	3	7	8	9	10	6		11										
2	3	4		7	8	9		6		5	11		10								
2	3	4	5	6	7	8	9	10	11												
2	3	4	5	6	7	8	9	11		10											
2	3	4	5	6	7	8	9		10				11								
2	3	4	5	6	7	8	9			10		11									
2	3	4	5	6	7	8	9			10		11									
2	3	4	5	6	7	8	9			10		11									
2	3	4	5	6	7	8	9			10		11									
2	3	4	5	6	7	8	9			10		11									
2	3	4	5	6		8	9		10			11			7						
2	3	4	5	6	7	8	9	10				11									
2	3	4		5	7	8	9	10		11				6							
2	3	4	5	6	7	8	9	10				11									
2	3	4	5		7	8	9	10		11				6							
2	3	4	5	6	7		9	10	8								11				
2	3	4	5	6	7		9	11	8								10				
2	3		5	6	7	8	9	11	4								10				
2	3	4	5	6	7	8	9								10		11				
2	3	4	5	6	7	8	9		11								10				
2	3	4		6	7	8	9			5	11					7	10				
2	3	4	5	6		8	9	11								7	10				
2	3	4		6		8	9	11		5						7	10				
2	3	4		6	7	8	9			5								11	10		
2	3	4		6	7	8	9			5								11	10		
2	3	4	5	6	7	8	9	11				1					10				
2	3	4		5	7	8	9	11			1			6			10				
2	3	4		6	7	8	9	11	5		1						10				
2	3	4	5		8		11		9		1		7	6			10				
34	33	33	26	31	30	32	31	17	14	12	6	14	5	2	4	4	1	7	3	6	
	7	2	1	6	16	14	6	2	4					3				5	7		

Gibbins AC	Goldie A	Wassall H	Beer WJ	Wigmore W	Dougherty J	Aldersmith WC	Leonard AR	McRoberts R	Field CWF	Jones WH	McMillan JS	Hanwell AW	Wharton SE	Dorrington J	Tickle CH	Harrison A	Howard H	Thompson T	Woodridge JE	Hirons JW	Wilcox FJ
2	3		5	6	7	8	9	11	4								10				
1	1		1	1	1	1	1	1	1								1				
																	1				

League Table

	P	W	D	L	F	A	Pts
Manchester City	34	25	4	5	95	29	54
Small Heath	34	24	3	7	74	36	51
Woolwich Arsenal	34	20	8	6	66	30	48
Bristol City	34	17	8	9	59	38	42
Manchester United	34	15	8	11	53	38	38
Chesterfield	34	14	9	11	67	40	37
Preston North End	34	13	10	11	56	40	36
Barnsley	34	13	8	13	55	51	34
Burslem Port Vale	34	13	8	13	57	62	34
Lincoln City	34	12	6	16	46	53	30
Glossop	34	11	7	16	43	57	29
Gainsborough Trinity	34	11	7	16	41	59	29
Burton United	34	11	7	16	39	59	29
Blackpool	34	9	10	15	44	59	28
Leicester Fosse	34	10	8	16	41	65	28
Doncaster Rovers	34	9	7	18	35	72	25
Stockport County	34	7	6	21	38	74	20
Burnley	34	6	8	20	30	77	20

1903-04

Division One

Secretary-manager: Alfred Jones

Match No.	Date		Venue	Opponents	Result		Scorers	Attendance
1	Sep	1	A	Derby County	L	1-4	Leonard	5,0
2		5	H	Sheffield United	L	1-3	Wilcox	12,00
3		7	H	Nottingham Forest	D	3-3	Leonard, Wilcox, Athersmith	9,00
4		12	A	Newcastle United	L	1-3	Wilcox	6,00
5		19	H	Aston Villa	D	2-2	Wilcox, Robertson	25,00
6		26	A	Middlesbrough	L	1-3	Howard	20,00
7	Oct	3	H	Liverpool	L	1-2	Wigmore	10,00
8		10	A	Bury	L	0-1		4,00
9		17	A	Blackburn Rovers	W	2-1	Windridge 2	10,00
10		24	A	Nottingham Forest	W	1-0	Wilcox	7,00
11		31	H	Sheffield Wednesday	D	0-0		12,00
12	Nov	7	A	Sunderland	L	1-3	Wigmore	14,00
13		14	H	West Bromwich Albion	L	0-1		12,56
14		21	A	Wolverhampton Wan.	L	0-1		7,00
15		28	A	Everton	L	1-5	Leonard	5,00
16	Dec	5	H	Stoke	W	1-0	Robertson	5,00
17		19	A	Manchester City	L	0-3		15,00
18		26	A	Notts County	L	0-2		12,00
19	Jan	2	A	Sheffield United	D	1-1	Jones	12,00
20		9	H	Newcastle United	W	3-0	Beer 2, Jones	8,00
21		16	A	Aston Villa	D	1-1	Green	20,00
22		23	H	Middlesbrough	D	2-2	Athersmith, Field	11,00
23		30	A	Liverpool	W	2-0	Jones, Wilcox	20,00
24	Feb	13	A	Blackburn Rovers	D	1-1	Jones	2,00
25		27	A	Sheffield Wednesday	L	2-3	Jones 2	7,00
26	Mar	5	H	Sunderland	W	2-1	Beer 2	12,00
27		12	A	West Bromwich Albion	W	1-0	Green	22,76
28		19	H	Wolverhampton Wan.	W	3-0	Green, Beer, Wilcox	12,00
29		26	A	Everton	D	1-1	Beer	12,00
30	Apr	2	A	Stoke	L	0-1		6,00
31		4	H	Bury	W	1-0	Wilcox	15,00
32		9	H	Derby County	W	1-0	Jones	8,00
33		16	A	Manchester City	L	0-4		15,00
34		23	H	Notts County	W	2-0	Green, Jones	8,00

Appearance
Goa

FA Cup

	Date		Venue	Opponents	Result		Scorers	Attendance
IR	Dec	12	A	Manchester United	D	1-1	Wassell	10,00
rep		16	H	Manchester United	D	1-1	Leonard	4,00
rep2		21	N	Manchester United	D	1-1	Field	5,00
rep3	Jan	11	N	Manchester United	L	1-3	Athersmith	9,37

Replay and replay 2 a.e.t..
Replay 2 at Bramall Lane, Sheffield.
Replay 3 at Hyde Road, Manchester.

Appearance
Goa

252

	...ington J	Galán A	Wassell H	Dougherty J	Wigmore W	Howard H	Adamsmith WC	Leonard AR	McBeaha R	Wilcox FJ	Field CWF	Hartwell AW	Jones WH	Robinson AC	Robertson J	Birmead WH	Beer WU	Windridge JF	Stokes F	Green BH	Hirons JW	Glover JW	Chaplin A
	2	3	4	5	6	7	8	9	10	11													
	2	3	4	5	6	7	8	9	10	11													
	2	3	6	5		7	11	9	10		4	8											
	2	3	4	5	6	7	11	9	10			1	8										
	2	3	4	5	6	7	11	9	10			1	8										
	2	3	4	5	6	7	8	9	10	11		1											
	2	3	6	5		7	11	9	10		4	1	8										
		3	6	5		7	11	9			1	8	2	4	10								
		2		5	6	7	11	9			1		4	10	3	8							
		2		5	6	7		11	9	1		4	10	3									
		2		6	7	8	5	9	11	1		4	10	3									
	2			5		7	8	6	9	1		4	10	3	11								
	2			5		7	11		9	1		4	10	3	8	6							
		2		5	6	7			10		9	1			3	8	11						
	4			6	7	10			11		9	1			3	8	2	5					
		4			7			10	11	5	9	1			3	8	2	6					
		5	6	7			10	11	9	1			3	8	2	4							
		5	6	7		11			9	1		10	3	8	2	4							
		5	6	7		10	11	9	1		4	3	8	2									
		5	6	7		10	11	9	1		4	3	8	2									
		5	6	7		10	11	9	1		4	3	8	2									
		5	6	7		10	11	9	1		4	3	8	2									
		5	6	7		10	11	9	1		4	3	8	2									
		5	6	7		10	11	9	1		4	3	8	2									
		5	6	7		10	11	9	1		4	3	8	2									
		5	6	7		10	11	9	1		4	3	8	2									
		5	6	7		10	11	9	1		4	3	8	2									
		5	6	7		10		11	9	1		4	3	8	2								
		5	6	7		10		11	9	1		4	3	8	2								
Apps	10	16	9	31	28	33	16	14	28	22	4	21	31	6	1	23	9	26	23	2	14	4	
Goals		2	1	2	3		8	1		8		2				6	2		4				

	...ington J	Galán A	Wassell H	Dougherty J	Wigmore W	Howard H	Adamsmith WC	Leonard AR	McBeaha R	Wilcox FJ	Field CWF	Hartwell AW	Jones WH	Robinson AC	Robertson J	Birmead WH	Beer WU	Windridge JF	Stokes F	Green BH	Hirons JW	Glover JW	Chaplin A
		2		5	6	7	10		11			1	9		4		3	8					
		2		5	6	7	8		11			1		4	10	3	9						
	2	6	5		7			9	11		8	1		4	10	3							
		5	6	7		10	11	2	9	1		4		3	8								
Apps	3	1	4	3	4	2		4	2	1	2	4	1		4	2	4	3					
Goals	1				1	1			1														

League Table

	P	W	D	L	F	A	Pts
Sheffield Wednesday	34	20	7	7	48	28	47
Manchester City	34	19	6	9	71	45	44
Everton	34	19	5	10	59	32	43
Newcastle United	34	18	6	10	58	45	42
Aston Villa	34	17	7	10	70	48	41
Sunderland	34	17	5	12	63	49	39
Sheffield United	34	15	8	11	62	57	38
Wolverhampton W	34	14	8	12	44	66	36
Nottingham Forest	34	11	9	14	57	57	31
Middlesbrough	34	9	12	13	46	47	30
Small Heath	34	11	8	15	39	52	30
Bury	34	7	15	12	40	53	29
Notts County	34	12	5	17	37	61	29
Derby County	34	9	10	15	58	60	28
Blackburn Rovers	34	11	6	17	48	60	28
Stoke	34	10	7	17	54	57	27
Liverpool	34	9	8	17	49	62	26
West Bromwich Albion	34	7	10	17	36	60	24

Division One

Secretary-manager: Alfred Jones

Blues' first three League games of the season ended in 2–1 defeats and all of their three goals came from the penalty spot. The fourth game also had a 2–1 score-line, this time in Blues' favour!

John Bird – a stalwart in Birmingham League football – made his only senior appearance for Blues in the last game of the season at Stoke. With Dougherty, Wigmore and Hartwell all unavailable, the Blackheath-born defender was called up at the last minute and put in a sound performance in a 1–0 defeat.

Blues won two local Cups this season: they beat Wolves 4–0 in the Staffordshire Cup final and West Bromwich Albion 7–2 in the Birmingham Senior Cup final. A crowd of 8,500 saw Tommy Jones score a hat-trick against the Baggies.

In April 1905, Blues signed cricketer-footballer Arthur Mounteney from Leicester Fosse.

Match No.	Date		Venue	Opponents	Result		Scorers	Attendance
1	Sep	3	A	Manchester City	L	1-2	Green (pen)	24,00
2		10	H	Notts County	L	1-2	Beer (pen)	15,0
3		17	A	Sheffield United	L	1-2	Beer (pen)	14,0
4		24	H	Newcastle United	W	2-1	Jones 2	13,00
5	Oct	1	A	Preston North End	D	2-2	Wilcox, McRoberts	10,0
6		8	H	Middlesbrough	W	2-1	Field, Beer (pen)	10,00
7		15	A	Wolverhampton Wan.	W	1-0	Wilcox	8,0
8		22	H	Bury	W	5-0	Wilcox, Field, Green 2, McRoberts	15,0
9		29	A	Aston Villa	L	1-2	Wilcox	40,00
10	Nov	5	H	Blackburn Rovers	W	2-0	Wigmore, Green	15,0
11		12	A	Nottingham Forest	W	2-0	McRoberts, Jones	8,00
12		19	H	Sheffield Wednesday	W	2-1	Jones, Green	15,00
13		26	A	Sunderland	W	4-1	Wilcox, Jones 2, Green	12,00
14	Dec	3	H	Woolwich Arsenal	W	2-1	Dougherty, Jones	12,00
15		10	A	Derby County	L	0-3		6,0
16		17	H	Everton	L	1-2	Jones	18,00
17		26	A	Middlesbrough	W	1-0	McRoberts	10,0
18		31	H	Manchester City	W	3-1	Jones 2, Wilcox	15,00
19	Jan	2	A	Bury	D	1-1	Green	9,00
20		7	A	Notts County	D	0-0		8,00
21		14	H	Sheffield United	W	2-0	Jones, Wilcox	12,00
22		21	A	Newcastle United	W	1-0	Tickle	24,0
23		28	H	Preston North End	W	2-0	Wilcox 2	15,00
24	Feb	11	H	Wolverhampton Wan.	W	4-1	Wilcox 3, Green	15,00
25		25	H	Aston Villa	L	0-3		32,00
26	Mar	4	H	Blackburn Rovers	W	4-1	Jones 2 (1 pen), Field, Beer	5,00
27		11	H	Nottingham Forest	L	1-2	Field	8,00
28		18	A	Sheffield Wednesday	L	1-3	Green	12,00
29		25	H	Sunderland	D	1-1	Jones	12,00
30	Apr	1	A	Woolwich Arsenal	D	1-1	Jones	18,00
31		8	H	Derby County	W	2-0	Green, Jones	12,00
32		15	A	Everton	L	1-2	Hartwell	20,00
33		22	H	Stoke	L	0-1		15,00
34		29	A	Stoke	L	0-1		2,00
							Appearance
							Goa

FA Cup

R1	Feb	4	H	Portsmouth	L	0-2		25,00
							Appearance	

Lineup / appearances grid (player columns left to right): ...lin AC, Glover JW, Stokes F, Beer WJ, Wigmore W, Howard H, Tickle CH, Green BH, Jones WH, Wilcox FJ, Field CWF, Athersmith WC, Dougherty J, McRoberts R, Hartwell AW, Windridge JE, Jones TT, Harvey C, Sellman A, Bird J

...lin AC	Glover JW	Stokes F	Beer WJ	Wigmore W	Howard H	Tickle CH	Green BH	Jones WH	Wilcox FJ	Field CWF	Athersmith WC	Dougherty J	McRoberts R	Hartwell AW	Windridge JE	Jones TT	Harvey C	Sellman A	Bird J
2	3	4	5	6	7	8	9	10	11										
2	3	4	5	6		8	9	10	11	7									
2	3	4	5	6		8	9	10	11	7									
2	3	4	5			8	9	10	11		6	7							
2	3	4	5			8	9	10	11		6	7							
2	3	4				8	9	10	11		6	7	5						
2	3	4				8		9	11		6	7	5	10					
	3	4	5			8	9	10	11		6	7	2						
2	3	4	5			8	9	10	11		6	7							
2	3	4	5		7	8	9		11		6			10					
2	3	4	5			8	9	10	11		6	7							
2	3	4	5			8	9	10	11		6	7							
	3	4	5		8	7	9	10	11		6		2						
	3	4	5			8	9	10	11		6	7	2						
	3	4	5		7	8	9	10			6		2		11				
	3	4	5			8	9	10	11	7	6		2						
	3	4	5	6		8	9	10	11			7	2						
	3	4	5	6		8	9	10	11			7	2						
	3	4	5	6		8	9	10	11	7			2						
	3	4	5			8	9	10	11		6		2						
	3	4	5		7	8	9	10	11		6		2						
2	3		5	6	7	8	9	10			4				11				
2	3	4	5		7	8	9	10			6			11					
2	3	4	5		7	8	9	10	11		6								
2	3	4	5		7	8	10			11	6		9						
2	3	4	5		7	8	9		11		6		10						
2	3	4	5			8	9		11		6	7	10						
2	3	4	5	6		8	9		11				10		7				
2	3	4	5	6		8	9		11				10						
2	3		4	7	8	9	10	11		6		5							
2	3		4	7	8	9	10			6		5	11						
2	3	4		6	7	8		10	11		5	9							
2	3	4		6	7	8		11				9	10			5			
24	34	31	28	13	16	34	30	27	30	5	25	14	15	10	2	1	1		
	4	1		1	10	16	12	4			1	4	1						

...lin AC	Glover JW	Stokes F	Beer WJ	Wigmore W	Howard H	Tickle CH	Green BH	Jones WH	Wilcox FJ	Field CWF	Athersmith WC	Dougherty J	McRoberts R	Hartwell AW	Windridge JE	Jones TT	Harvey C	Sellman A	Bird J
2	3		5		7	8	9	10		6			11		4				
1	1		1		1	1	1	1		1			1		1				

League Table

	P	W	D	L	F	A	Pts
Newcastle United	34	23	2	9	72	33	48
Everton	34	21	5	8	63	36	47
Manchester City	34	20	6	8	66	37	46
Aston Villa	34	19	4	11	63	43	42
Sunderland	34	16	8	10	60	44	40
Sheffield United	34	19	2	13	64	56	40
Small Heath	34	17	5	12	54	38	39
Preston North End	34	13	10	11	42	37	36
Sheffield Wednesday	34	14	5	15	61	57	33
Woolwich Arsenal	34	12	9	13	36	40	33
Derby County	34	12	8	14	37	48	32
Stoke	34	13	4	17	40	58	30
Blackburn Rovers	34	11	5	18	40	51	27
Wolverhampton W	34	11	4	19	47	73	26
Middlesbrough	34	9	8	17	36	56	26
Nottingham Forest	34	9	7	18	40	61	25
Bury	34	10	4	20	47	67	24
Notts County	34	5	8	21	36	69	18

1905-06

Division One

Secretary-manager: Alfred Jones

Match No.	Date		Venue	Opponents	Result		Scorers	Attendance
1	Sep	2	H	Preston North End	D	1-1	W.H.Jones	25,0
2		9	A	Newcastle United	D	2-2	Green, Wilcox	28,0
3		16	H	Aston Villa	W	2-0	W.H.Jones, Mounteney	30,0
4		23	A	Liverpool	L	0-2		24,0
5		30	H	Sheffield United	W	2-0	Wilcox, Mounteney	18,0
6	Oct	7	A	Notts County	D	0-0		15,0
7		14	H	Stoke	W	2-0	W.H.Jones 2	8,0
8		21	A	Bolton Wanderers	W	1-0	W.H.Jones	20,0
9		28	H	Woolwich Arsenal	W	2-1	Beer, WH.Jones	15,0
10	Nov	4	A	Blackburn Rovers	L	1-5	Corman	8,0
11		11	H	Sunderland	W	3-0	Anderson, W.H.Jones, Tickle	15,0
12		18	A	Wolverhampton Wan.	D	0-0		5,0
13		25	A	Everton	W	2-1	W.H.Jones, Anderson	10,0
14	Dec	2	H	Derby County	W	3-1	Tickle, Mounteney, Wigmore	18,0
15		9	A	Sheffield Wednesday	L	2-4	Tickle, W.H.Jones	8,0
16		16	H	Nottingham Forest	W	5-0	Wilcox 3, Harper, WH.Jones	12,0
17		23	A	Manchester City	L	1-4	Green	15,0
18		25	A	Middlesbrough	L	0-1		18,0
19		26	H	Middlesbrough	W	7-0	Green 5, W.H.Jones, Williamson (og)	15,0
20		28	A	Sheffield United	L	0-3		4,0
21		30	A	Preston North End	L	0-3		8,0
22	Jan	1	A	Bury	L	0-1		12,0
23		6	A	Newcastle United	L	0-1		8,0
24		20	A	Aston Villa	W	3-1	Mounteney, W.H.Jones, Dougherty	40,0
25		27	H	Liverpool	W	1-0	Mounteney	20,0
26	Feb	10	H	Notts County	W	4-2	Mounteney, Green, W.H.Jones 2	8,0
27		17	A	Stoke	D	2-2	W.H.Jones 2	5,0
28	Mar	3	A	Woolwich Arsenal	L	0-5		20,0
29		17	A	Sunderland	L	1-3	Anderson	15,0
30		24	H	Wolverhampton Wan.	D	3-3	Mounteney, W.H.Jones 2	5,0
31		26	H	Bolton Wanderers	L	2-5	Mounteney, Tickle	10,0
32	Apr	7	A	Derby County	D	0-0		4,0
33		9	H	Everton	W	1-0	Mounteney	10,0
34		14	H	Sheffield Wednesday	W	5-1	Tickle 3, W.H.Jones 2	8,0
35		16	H	Bury	L	0-3		8,0
36		21	A	Nottingham Forest	L	1-2	W.H.Jones	8,0
37		23	H	Blackburn Rovers	W	3-0	Mounteney, Smith, Green	10,0
38		28	H	Manchester City	W	3-2	Green, W.H.Jones, Edmondson (og)	3,0
							Appearanc	
							Two own-goals	Go

FA Cup

R1	Jan	13	H	Preston North End	W	1-0	Beer	10,0
R2	Feb	3	A	Stoke	W	1-0	W.H.Jones	19,0
R3		24	A	Tottenham Hotspur	D	1-1	Harper	28,0
rep		28	H	Tottenham Hotspur	W	2-0	Green, Mounteney	34,0
R4	Mar	10	H	Newcastle United	D	2-2	Green, W.H.Jones	27,0
rep		14	A	Newcastle United	L	0-3		39,0

R3 replay and R4 replay a.e.t.

Appearanc

Go

256

Birmingham — Appearances & Goals Grid

Wilson AC	Glover JW	Stokes F	Beer WJ	Wigmore W	Dougherty J	Tickle CH	Green BH	Jones WH	Wilcox FJ	Field CWF	Mounteney A	Jones A	Hartwell AW	Anderson GE	Corran F	Howard H	Harper RRB	Bulmead WH	Southall G	Shufflebotham J	Smith J	Keans JH
2	3	4	5	6	7	8	9	10	11													
2	3	4	5	6	7	8	9	10	11													
2	3	4	5	6		7	9	10	11	8												
2	3	4	5	6		7	9	10	11	8												
2	3	4	5	6		7	9	10	11	8												
2	3	4	5	6		7	9		11	8	9											
	3	4	5	6		7	9	10	11	8		2										
2	3	4	5	6		7	9	10		8		11										
2	3	4	5	6		7	9			8		11	10									
2	3	4	5	6		7	9			8		11	10									
2	3	4	5	6	7	8	9					11	10									
2	3		5	6	7	8	9					11	10	4								
2	3	4	5	6	7	8	9					11	10									
2	3	4	5	6	7	8	9	10				11										
2	3	4	5	6	7	8	9	10				11			7							
2	3	4	5	6	7	8	9	10				11										
2	3	4	5	6	7	8	9			10		11										
2		4	5	6	7	8	9			10	9	2	11	6		7						
2		4	5	6		8	9	10				3	11			7						
2		4	5	6		8	9	10				3	11			7						
	3	4	5		8			10	9		2	11	6			7						
2		4	5		7	8	9	10				3	11	6								
	3	4	5		8		10		9		2	11	6			7						
2			5	6		8	9	10				3	11	4		7						
2		4	5	6		8	9	10				3	11			7						
2	3	4			8	9		10				5	11			7						
2	3	4		6		8	9	10				5	11			7						
2			6			9	10			8	5	11	4			7	3					
	3	4	5		8	9		10			2	11	6			7						
	3		5		7	8	9	10			2	11	6	4								
2	3		5		7	8	9	10	11			6	4									
2	3		5	8	4	9		10				6		7		11						
2	3		6	8	4	9		10				5		7		11						
2	3		6	8	4	9		10				5		7		11						
2	3		6	8	4	9		10						7		11	5					
2			6	7	4	9		10				5		3	11			8				
2	3		6	7	8	9		11				5						10	4			
2	3		6	7	8	9		11				5						10	4			
32	**31**	**26**	**28**	**31**	**20**	**36**	**35**	**17**	**7**	**25**	**4**	**19**	**23**	**15**	**3**	**15**	**2**	**5**	**1**	**3**	**2**	
		1	1	1	7	10	22	5		10		3	1		1			1				

Wilson AC	Glover JW	Stokes F	Beer WJ	Wigmore W	Dougherty J	Tickle CH	Green BH	Jones WH	Wilcox FJ	Field CWF	Mounteney A	Jones A	Hartwell AW	Anderson GE	Corran F	Howard H	Harper RRB	Bulmead WH	Southall G	Shufflebotham J	Smith J	Keans JH
2	3	4	5	6		8	9			11	10			7								
2	3	4	5			8	9	10		11	6			7								
2	3	4	5	6		8	9	10		11				7								
2	3	4	5			8	9	11	10			6		7								
2	3	4	5			8	9	10		11	6			7								
2	3	4	5			8	9	10		11	6			7								
6	**6**	**6**	**6**	**2**		**6**	**6**	**1**		**5**	**5**	**5**		**6**								
			1			2	2			1				1								

League Table

	P	W	D	L	F	A	Pts
Liverpool	38	23	5	10	79	46	51
Preston North End	38	17	13	8	54	39	47
Sheffield Wednesday	38	18	8	12	63	52	44
Newcastle United	38	18	7	13	74	48	43
Manchester City	38	19	5	14	73	54	43
Bolton Wanderers	38	17	7	14	81	67	41
Birmingham	38	17	7	14	65	59	41
Aston Villa	38	17	6	15	72	56	40
Blackburn Rovers	38	16	8	14	54	52	40
Stoke	38	16	7	15	54	55	39
Everton	38	15	7	16	70	66	37
Woolwich Arsenal	38	15	7	16	62	64	37
Sheffield United	38	15	6	17	57	62	36
Sunderland	38	15	5	18	61	70	35
Derby County	38	14	7	17	39	58	35
Notts County	38	11	12	15	55	71	34
Bury	38	11	10	17	57	74	32
Middlesbrough	38	10	11	17	56	71	31
Nottingham Forest	38	13	5	20	58	79	31
Wolverhampton W	38	8	7	23	58	99	23

Division One

Secretary-manager: Alfred Jones

Did you know that?

St Andrew's was officially opened on Boxing Day for the League game with Middlesbrough and Benny Green scored the first goal at the new ground, for Blues v Preston, three days later. He was presented with a piano for his effort – and legend has it that the player had already found a buyer for the instrument!

Blues played Preston at Deepdale in temperatures of 90 degrees F (32.2 degrees C) on the opening day of the season.

The first FA Cup tie staged at St Andrew's was the semi-final encounter between Arsenal and Sheffield Wednesday in March. The Owls won 3–1 in front of 35,940 spectators.

Blues beat neighbours Aston Villa 4–0 in the final of the Lord Mayor of Birmingham Charity Cup.

Match No.	Date		Venue	Opponents	Result		Scorers	Attendance
1	Sep	1	A	Preston North End	L	0-2		12,0
2		3	H	Bristol City	D	2-2	Green, Mounteney	12,0
3		8	H	Newcastle United	L	2-4	W.H.Jones, Beer	20,0
4		15	A	Aston Villa	L	1-4	Mounteney	45,0
5		22	H	Liverpool	W	2-1	W.H.Jones, Mounteney	10,0
6		29	A	Bristol City	D	0-0		15,0
7	Oct	6	H	Notts County	W	2-0	Stokes, Kearns	10,0
8		13	A	Sheffield United	L	0-2		10,0
9		20	H	Bolton Wanderers	W	4-2	W.H.Jones 2, Beer (pen), Anderson	15,0
10		27	A	Manchester United	L	1-2	W.H.Jones	12,0
11	Nov	3	H	Stoke	W	2-1	W.H.Jones 2	8,0
12		10	A	Blackburn Rovers	L	0-1		12,0
13		17	H	Sunderland	W	2-0	W.H.Jones, Tickle	10,0
14		24	H	Derby County	W	2-1	Anderson, Wigmore	10,0
15	Dec	1	A	Everton	L	0-3		14,0
16		8	H	Woolwich Arsenal	W	5-1	Green 2, W.H.Jones 2, Beer	19,0
17		15	A	Sheffield Wednesday	W	1-0	Beer	10,0
18		22	H	Bury	W	3-1	Mounteney 2, Wigmore	6,0
19		25	A	Manchester City	L	0-1		14,0
20		26	H	Middlesbrough	D	0-0		32,0
21		29	H	Preston North End	W	3-0	Green 2, W.H.Jones	25,0
22	Jan	1	A	Middlesbrough	L	0-1		20,0
23		5	A	Newcastle United	L	0-2		28,0
24		19	H	Aston Villa	W	3-2	Glover, Mounteney, Green	60,0
25		26	A	Liverpool	L	0-2		14,0
26	Feb	9	A	Notts County	D	2-2	W.H.Jones 2	10,0
27		16	H	Sheffield United	D	0-0		12,0
28	Mar	2	H	Manchester United	D	1-1	Morris	20,0
29		9	A	Stoke	L	0-3		3,0
30		11	A	Bolton Wanderers	W	3-2	Tickle, Green, Mounteney	5,0
31		16	H	Blackburn Rovers	W	2-0	W.H.Jones, Tickle	10,0
32		23	A	Sunderland	L	1-4	Anderson	15,0
33		29	H	Manchester City	W	4-0	Green, Gooch, Anderson, W.H.Jones	16,0
34		30	A	Derby County	D	1-1	Wigmore	5,0
35	Apr	6	H	Everton	W	1-0	Green	12,0
36		13	A	Woolwich Arsenal	L	1-2	Glover	15,0
37		25	H	Sheffield Wednesday	D	1-1	Morris	10,0
38		27	A	Bury	L	0-1		5,0

Appearance
Goa

FA Cup

R1	Jan 12	A	Liverpool	L	1-2	Green (pen)	20,0

Appearance
Goa

Glover JW	Stokes F	Beer WJ	Wigmore W	Dougherty J	Tickle CH	Green BH	Jones WH	Mounteney A	Anderson GE	Kirby C	Harper RBG	Kearns JH	Dorrington J	Smith J	Halworth A	Jones A	Southall G	McCafferty W	Corran F	Hartwell AW	Morris A	Eyre E	Gooch PG	Harvey C
2	3	4	5	6	7	8	9	10	11															
2	3	4	5	6	7	8	9	10	11															
2	3	4	5	6		8	9	10	11	7														
2	3	4	5	6		8	9	10	11		7													
2	3	4	5	6		8	9	10	11		7													
	3	4	5	6		8	9	10	11	7		2												
	3	4	5	6		8	9	10	11	7		2												
	2	6	5	4		8	9	10	11	7		3	1											
2	3	4	5	6	8	7		9	10	11														
2	3	4	5	6	8	7		9		11		10												
2	3	4	5		8	7		9	10	11			6											
2	3	4	5		8	7		9	10	11			6											
2	3	4	5			7		9	10	11			6		8									
2	3	4	5	6		8	9	10	7									11						
2	3	4	5	6		8	9	10	7									11						
2	3	4	5	6		8	9	10	7									11						
2	3	4	5	6		8	9	10	7									11						
2	3	4	5	6		8	9	10										11	7					
2	3	4	5	6		8	9	10	7									11						
2	3	4	5	6		7	9	10	11										8					
2	3	4	5	6		7	9	10	11										8					
2	3	6	5	4		10	9	8	7	11														
2	3	4	5			8	9	10	11	7									6					
2		4	5			7	9	10				3						11	8	6				
2	3	4	5			8	7	9				10						11	6					
3		4				8	7	9	11			2	10						6	5				
2	3	4	5			7	8	9				1							6		10	11		
2	3	4	5			7	8					11							6		10		9	
2	3	4	5	6	7	8	9			11									10					
2	3	4	5	6	7	8	9			11									10					
2	3	4	5	6	7	8	9			11									10					
2	3	4	5	6	7	8	10			11												9		
2	3	4	5	6	10	8	9			11													7	
2	3	4	5	6	7	8	9			11									10					
2	3	4	5			7	8	10											6			11	9	
2	3	4	5			7	8	9		11									6	10				
	2	6	5	4	11	10	9			7				3					8					
43	**37**	**38**	**37**	**26**	**19**	**38**	**38**	**25**	**31**	**1**	**7**	**9**	**2**	**3**	**1**	**1**	**9**	**4**	**13**	**1**	**3**	**2**	**3**	**1**
2	1	4	3		3	9	15	6	5					1							2	1		

Glover JW	Stokes F	Beer WJ	Wigmore W	Dougherty J	Tickle CH	Green BH	Jones WH	Mounteney A	Anderson GE	Kirby C
2	3	4	5	6		8	9	10	11	7
1	1	1	1	1		1	1	1	1	1
										1

League Table

	P	W	D	L	F	A	Pts
Newcastle United	38	22	7	9	74	46	51
Bristol City	38	20	8	10	66	47	48
Everton	38	20	5	13	70	46	45
Sheffield United	38	17	11	10	57	55	45
Aston Villa	38	19	6	13	78	52	44
Bolton Wanderers	38	18	8	12	59	47	44
Woolwich Arsenal	38	20	4	14	66	59	44
Manchester United	38	17	8	13	53	56	42
Birmingham	38	15	8	15	52	52	38
Sunderland	38	14	9	15	65	66	37
Middlesbrough	38	15	6	17	56	63	36
Blackburn Rovers	38	14	7	17	56	59	35
Sheffield Wednesday	38	12	11	15	49	60	35
Preston North End	38	14	7	17	44	57	35
Liverpool	38	13	7	18	64	65	33
Bury	38	13	6	19	58	68	32
Manchester City	38	10	12	16	53	77	32
Notts County	38	8	15	15	46	50	31
Derby County	38	9	9	20	41	59	27
Stoke	38	8	10	20	41	64	26

Division One

Secretary-manager: Alfred Jones

Blues spent £1,000 on a player for the first time when signing utility forward and Yorkshire county cricketer Alonso Drake from Sheffield United in December.

Walter Corbett, who joined Blues in July 1907, won a soccer gold medal for Great Britain at the 1908 Olympic Games.

In the 36th minute of Blues' home game with Nottingham Forest in February a gust of wind blew the roof off one of the stands. The referee abandoned the match with the scores level at 1–1.

Blues retained the Lord Mayor of Birmingham Charity Cup by defeating rivals Aston Villa in the final for the second year running, this time by 5–2.

Match No.	Date		Venue	Opponents	Result		Scorers	Attendance
1	Sep	4	A	Middlesbrough	L	0-1		16,
2		7	H	Preston North End	W	2-0	Mounteney, Wigmore	10,
3		14	A	Bury	L	0-1		14,
4		16	H	Bury	L	0-1		12
5		21	H	Aston Villa	L	2-3	Eyre, Tickle	45
6		28	A	Liverpool	W	4-3	Green, Mounteney 2, Eyre	20
7	Oct	5	H	Middlesbrough	L	1-4	Green	16
8		12	A	Sheffield United	L	0-1		13,
9		19	H	Chelsea	D	1-1	Green	20
10		26	A	Nottingham Forest	D	1-1	Green	12
11	Nov	2	H	Manchester United	L	3-4	Jones, Eyre 2	20
12		9	A	Blackburn Rovers	L	0-1		6
13		16	H	Bolton Wanderers	W	2-1	Green, Eyre	15
14		23	A	Newcastle United	L	0-8		20
15	Dec	7	H	Sunderland	L	0-2		10
16		14	A	Woolwich Arsenal	D	1-1	Green	3
17		21	H	Sheffield Wednesday	W	2-1	Drake, Jones	12
18		25	H	Manchester City	W	2-1	Eyre, Bluff	12
19		26	H	Notts County	D	0-0		20
20		27	A	Notts County	D	0-0		12
21		28	A	Bristol City	D	0-0		10
22	Jan	4	A	Preston North End	D	1-1	Jones	8
23		18	A	Aston Villa	W	3-2	Eyre, Green, Drake	39
24		25	H	Liverpool	D	1-1	Mounteney	18
25	Feb	8	H	Sheffield United	D	0-0		16
26		15	A	Chelsea	D	2-2	Jones, Eyre	17
27		29	A	Manchester United	L	0-1		10
28	Mar	7	H	Blackburn Rovers	D	1-1	Mounteney	5
29		14	A	Bolton Wanderers	L	0-1		13
30		18	A	Everton	L	1-4	Tickle	10
31		21	H	Newcastle United	D	1-1	Tickle	20
32		28	H	Everton	W	2-1	Jones, Beer	15
33		30	H	Nottingham Forest	W	1-0	Jones	2
34	Apr	4	A	Sunderland	L	0-1		16
35		11	H	Woolwich Arsenal	L	1-2	Beer	15
36		17	A	Manchester City	L	1-2	Mounteney	25
37		18	A	Sheffield Wednesday	W	4-1	Jones, Beer, Anderson, Green	8
38		25	H	Bristol City	L	0-4		4

Appearances
G

FA Cup

R1	Jan	11	A	West Bromwich Albion	D	1-1	Jones	36
rep		15	H	West Bromwich Albion	L	1-2	Eyre	24

Appearances
G

	Glover JW	Stokes F	Beer WJ	Wigmore W	Corran F	Tickle CH	Green BH	Jones WH	Mountenay A	Anderson GE	Eyre E	Daughtery J	Popham WW	Corbett WS	Gooch PG	Morris A	Higgins JB	Travers JE	Dorrington J	Holmes E	Kearns JH	Hartwell AW	King HE	Bluff EU	Drake AR	Fairman R	Handley TH	Mouse GS
	2	3	4	5	6	7	8	9	10	11																		
	2	3	4	5	6	7	8	9	10		11																	
	2	3	4	5	6	7	8	9	10		11																	
	2	3	4	5		8	9		10		11	6	7															
	2	3	4	5	10	7	8		9		11	6																
		3	4	5	10	7	8		9		11	6		2														
		3	4	5	10		8		9	11		6		2	7													
	2	3	4	5	6	8	9			11	7						10											
	2	3	4	5	6	8	9			11	7							10										
	2	3		5	6	10	8			11	7		4		9													
	2	3	4	5	6	10	8	9		11	7																	
	2	3	4	5	6	10	8	9		11	7								1									
	2	3	4	5	6	10	8			11	7								1	9								
	2		4		6	10	8			11	7								1	9								
	2	3		5	6	8	4		10	11	7								1	9								
		3	4	5	6		7		9	11									1		2		8	10				
		3	4	5	6		8	9		11	7								1		2			10				
		3	4	5	6		7		9	11									1		2		8	10				
		4			8	9		11		6	7								1		3	10			2	5		
		4	5		8		9		11	6	7	3							1		2			10				
		3	4	5	6	7	8	9		11									1		2			10				
		4	5		7	6		9		11		2							1		3		8	10				
		4	5		7	6		9		11		2							1		3		8	10				
		3	4	5		7	6	9		11									1		2		8	10				
		3	4	5		7	6	9	10	11									1		2		8					
		3		5	6		4	9	8	11		7							1		2			10				
			5	6	7		4	9	8	11			2						1		3			10				
		3	4	5		7	6	9	10	11									1		2		8					
		3	4	5	6		7	8	9	10	11								1		2							
		3	5		6	8	4	10	9		11	7							1		2							
		4	5		8	6	9	10	11			7	2						1		3							
		4	5		8	6	9	10	11			7	2						1		3							
		4	5		7	6	9	8	11	10									1		3				2			
	3	8	5		7	6	9	10		11			4						1		2							
	3	4	5	6	7	8	9	10		11									1		2							
		4	5	6		7	9	10	11											3			8		2			
	3	4	5	6		7	9	10	11										1		2						8	
	13	28	34	35	26	31	36	23	25	8	31	6	17	11	1	1	1	1	24	2	23	1	1	9	11	3	1	1
		3	1		3	8	7	6	1	8														1	2			

	Glover JW	Stokes F	Beer WJ	Wigmore W	Corran F	Tickle CH	Green BH	Jones WH	Mountenay A	Anderson GE	Eyre E	Daughtery J	Popham WW	Corbett WS	Gooch PG	Morris A	Higgins JB	Travers JE	Dorrington J	Holmes E	Kearns JH	Hartwell AW	King HE	Bluff EU	Drake AR	Fairman R	Handley TH	Mouse GS
	3	4	5	6	7	8	9			11									1		2				10			
	4	5	6	7	8	9			11			2							1		3				10			
	1	2	2	2	2	2	2		2			1							2		2				2			
							1		1																			

League Table

	P	W	D	L	F	A	Pts
Manchester United	38	23	6	9	81	48	52
Aston Villa	38	17	9	12	77	59	43
Manchester City	38	16	11	11	62	54	43
Newcastle United	38	15	12	11	65	54	42
Sheffield Wednesday	38	19	4	15	73	64	42
Middlesbrough	38	17	7	14	54	45	41
Bury	38	14	11	13	58	61	39
Liverpool	38	16	6	16	68	61	38
Nottingham Forest	38	13	11	14	59	62	37
Bristol City	38	12	12	14	58	61	36
Everton	38	15	6	17	58	64	36
Preston North End	38	12	12	14	47	53	36
Chelsea	38	14	8	16	53	62	36
Blackburn Rovers	38	12	12	14	51	63	36
Woolwich Arsenal	38	12	12	14	51	63	36
Sunderland	38	16	3	19	78	75	35
Sheffield United	38	12	11	15	52	58	35
Notts County	38	13	8	17	39	51	34
Bolton Wanderers	38	14	5	19	52	58	33
Birmingham	38	9	12	17	40	60	30

Division Two

Manager: Alex Watson

In July 1908, Blues signed Yorkshire-born full-back Frank Womack from Rawmarsh FC. He would remain at St Andrew's until May 1928, making well over 500 appearances for the club.

Billy Beer had a goal disallowed in Blues' 3–2 League defeat at Clapton Orient in February… the referee said the ball had passed outside the upright when, in fact, it went between the posts and then through a hole in the side of the net.

Vivian Woodward scored twice and missed a penalty for Spurs in their 4–0 drubbing of Blues in November.

In the return fixture with Spurs which ended 3–3, the Steel brothers, Bobby and Danny, both netted for the London club.

Match No.	Date		Venue	Opponents	Result		Scorers	Attendance
1	Sep	2	H	Bolton Wanderers	W	2-0	Eyre 2	8,0
2		5	A	Gainsborough Trinity	W	3-1	Eyre 2, W.H.Jones	5,0
3		7	H	Bradford Park Avenue	W	3-1	Smith, Fairman, W.H.Jones	10,0
4		12	H	Grimsby Town	W	3-1	W.H.Jones, Green (pen), Smith	15,0
5		19	A	Fulham	D	1-1	Green	38,0
6		26	H	Burnley	W	2-0	Fairman, W.H.Jones	20,0
7	Oct	6	A	Bradford Park Avenue	W	2-1	Beer, Baddeley (og)	8,0
8		10	H	Wolverhampton Wan.	D	1-1	Smith	20,0
9		17	A	Oldham Athletic	L	0-2		14,0
10		24	H	Clapton Orient	W	1-0	Williams	10,0
11		31	A	Leeds City	L	0-2		15,0
12	Nov	7	H	Barnsley	W	2-1	Green, W.H.Jones	10,0
13		14	A	Tottenham Hotspur	L	0-4		20,0
14		21	H	Hull City	L	1-2	Beer	5,0
15		28	A	Derby County	W	2-1	Moore, Mounteney	10,0
16	Dec	5	H	Blackpool	D	2-2	Chapple, Smith	7,0
17		12	A	Chesterfield	L	2-4	Mounteney, Anderson	5,0
18		19	H	Glossop	L	1-2	Smith	5,0
19		25	A	Stockport County	W	4-2	Chapple 4	10,0
20		26	A	West Bromwich Albion	D	1-1	King	38,0
21		28	H	West Bromwich Albion	D	0-0		30,0
22	Jan	1	A	Bolton Wanderers	L	1-2	Beer	23,0
23		2	H	Gainsborough Trinity	D	2-2	King, Beer	10,0
24		9	A	Grimsby Town	W	3-0	Williams 2, Chapple	5,0
25		23	H	Fulham	L	1-3	Beer	9,0
26		30	A	Burnley	D	1-1	Beer	7,0
27	Feb	13	A	Wolverhampton Wan.	L	0-2		10,0
28		20	H	Oldham Athletic	W	2-0	Beer 2	12,0
29		27	A	Clapton Orient	L	2-3	King, Bumphrey	7,0
30	Mar	13	A	Barnsley	L	1-3	King	4,
31		20	H	Tottenham Hotspur	D	3-3	King, Mounteney, Daykin	8,0
32		27	A	Hull City	L	1-4	Bumphrey	8,0
33	Apr	3	H	Derby County	D	1-1	King	4,0
34		9	A	Stockport County	L	2-3	Chapple, Lowe	7,0
35		10	A	Blackpool	L	0-2		3,0
36		12	H	Leeds City	W	1-0	Bumphrey	3,0
37		17	H	Chesterfield	W	3-0	Mounteney 3	1,5
38		24	A	Glossop	L	1-3	Mounteney	5

Appearanc
One own-goal   Go

FA Cup

R1	Jan	16	H	Portsmouth	L	2-5	Chapple (pen), King	18,8

Appearanc
Go

	Burlington J	Corbett WS	Beer WJ	Wigmore W	Fairman R	Green BH	Smith WA	Jones WH	Mountney A	Eyre E	Womack F	Stokes F	Williams JW	Hanna WH	Travers JE	Wilcox JM	Lowe CB	Moore GS	Anderson BE	Chapple FJ	Dayton T	King HE	Kerns F	Handley TH	Box A	Bumpfrey J	Jones CT	Gartner AE
	2	3	4	5	6	7	8	9	10	11																		
	2	4	5	6	7	8	9	10	11	3																		
	2	3	4	5	6	7	8	9		11		10																
	2	3	4	5	6	7	8	9		11		10																
	2	3	4	5	6	7	8	9	10	11																		
	2	3	4	5	6	7	8	9		11		10																
		3	4	5	6	7	8	9		11		10	2															
	2	3	4		6	5	8	9		11		10		7														
	2	4		6	7	8	9	5	11		10	3																
	2	4		6	7	8	9	5	11		10	3																
	2	5		6	4	8	10		11	3				7	9													
	2	4		5	6	8		9		11	3			7	10													
	2	3	4	5	6	8		9		11				7	10													
	2	5		4	8				9	11	3	9	6	7	10													
	2	3	5		6	4	9			11				10			7		8									
	2	3	5		6	4	9			8				7				11	10									
	2	5		4			9				3			7		8		11	10	6								
	2	3	4	5		8	9							7				11	10	6								
	2	4	5		9					3				7				11	10	6	8							
	2	3	4	5	9					3				7				11	10	6	8							
	2	3	4	5	9					3								11	10	9	7	8						
	2	4	5	6						3				7				11	10	9	7	8						
	2	4	5	6		9				3	7							11	10	6	8							
	2	4		7					9		3							11	10	6	8		5					
	2		4	7					9		3							11	10	6	8		5					
	2	9	4							3				7					10	6			5		1	8	11	
	2		4				11			3				7					10	6			5		1	8		
	2	9	4							3				7				11	6	10			5		1	8		
		9	4						2	3				7				11		6	10		5		1	8		
		4	5					2		3				7	10			11		6	9			8				
	4									2	3			7	10					6	9			8				
		4	5			7	11			2	3							10			9	6		8				
		4	5				6			2	3								10		9			8				
		4		6			11			2	3							8		10		9	5	7				
		4		6			11			2	3							8		10		9	5	7				
		4		6			11			2	3							8		10	6	9	5	7		4		
							11			2	3							8		10	6	8	5			4		
					9	11				2	3							7		10	6	8	5					
Apps	15	27	33	23	19	18	17	18	16	15	14	12	23	3	1	18	11	2	12	19	17	19	1	12	4	12	1	2
Goals		8		2	3	5	5	7	4		3							1	1		7	1	6			3		

	Burlington J	Corbett WS	Beer WJ	Wigmore W	Fairman R	Green BH	Smith WA	Jones WH	Mountney A	Eyre E	Womack F	Stokes F	Williams JW	Hanna WH	Travers JE	Wilcox JM	Lowe CB	Moore GS	Anderson BE	Chapple FJ	Dayton T	King HE	Kerns F	Handley TH	Box A	Bumpfrey J	Jones CT	Gartner AE
	2	3	4	5					9									7			11	10	6	8				
	1	1	1	1					1									1			1	1	1	1				
																						1	1					

Division Two

Manager: Alex Watson

Match No.	Date	Venue	Opponents	Result		Scorers	Attendance
1	Sep 4	H	Oldham Athletic	D	2-2	Millington, Beer	20,00
2	11	A	Barnsley	L	1-5	Chapple	3,00
3	13	H	Glossop	D	2-2	Lowe, Millington	3,00
4	18	H	Fulham	D	1-1	Chapple	12,00
5	25	A	Burnley	L	0-2		5,00
6	Oct 2	A	Leeds City	L	1-2	Freeman	14,00
7	9	A	Wolverhampton Wan.	L	2-4	Buckley, Chapple	10,00
8	16	H	Gainsborough Trinity	W	5-0	Millington 2, Needham 3	10,00
9	23	A	Grimsby Town	W	2-0	Freeman, Wilcox	5,00
10	30	H	Manchester City	D	1-1	Freeman	18,00
11	Nov 6	A	Leicester Fosse	L	1-3	Freeman	10,00
12	13	H	Lincoln City	W	1-0	Needham	5,00
13	20	A	Clapton Orient	L	0-3		9,00
14	27	H	Blackpool	L	1-2	Chapple	1,00
15	Dec 4	A	Hull City	L	0-7		6,00
16	11	H	Derby County	L	1-3	Freeman	5,00
17	18	A	Stockport County	D	1-1	Lappin	4,00
18	25	A	Glossop	L	1-4	Chapple	5,00
19	27	A	West Bromwich Albion	L	1-3	Millington	12,10
20	28	H	Bradford Park Avenue	L	0-1		15,00
21	Jan 1	H	West Bromwich Albion	L	0-1		15,50
22	8	A	Oldham Athletic	D	1-1	Lappin	8,00
23	22	A	Barnsley	W	2-1	Freeman, Chapple	5,00
24	29	A	Fulham	D	0-0		10,00
25	Feb 12	A	Leeds City	L	1-2	Freeman	10,00
26	19	H	Wolverhampton Wan.	W	1-0	Freeman	2,00
27	26	A	Gainsborough Trinity	L	0-1		3,00
28	28	H	Burnley	W	2-1	Chapple, Freeman	1,00
29	Mar 5	H	Grimsby Town	L	2-4	Needham, Chapple	14,00
30	12	A	Manchester City	L	0-3		15,00
31	19	H	Leicester Fosse	W	2-1	Burton, Buckley	10,00
32	26	A	Lincoln City	L	2-3	Burton, Millington	5,00
33	28	A	Bradford Park Avenue	L	0-5		8,00
34	Apr 2	H	Clapton Orient	L	1-2	Burton	8,00
35	9	A	Blackpool	L	0-2		3,00
36	16	H	Hull City	L	0-2		8,00
37	23	A	Derby County	L	1-3	Millington	5,00
38	30	H	Stockport County	W	3-0	Freeman, Millington, Lowe	3,00

Appearance
Goa

FA Cup

R1	Jan 15	H	Leicester Fosse	L	1-4	Lappin	15,1

Appearance
Goa

Player columns (left to right):
...ington J, Womack F, Stokes F, Barr WJ, Buckley FC, Dalton T, Wade JM, Millington CJH, King HE, Chapple FJ, Layton HH, Corbett WS, Miles JR, Humphrey J, Gardner AE, McCourty W, Lowe CB, Freeman WD, Wigmore W, Box A, Needham J, Banks FW, Preston J, Frith RE, Burton JH, Currier W

League Table

	P	W	D	L	F	A	Pts
Manchester City	38	23	8	7	81	40	54
Oldham Athletic	38	23	7	8	79	39	53
Hull City	38	23	7	8	80	46	53
Derby County	38	22	9	7	72	47	53
Leicester Fosse	38	20	4	14	79	58	44
Glossop	38	18	7	13	64	57	43
Fulham	38	14	13	11	51	43	41
Wolverhampton W	38	17	6	15	64	63	40
Barnsley	38	16	7	15	62	59	39
Bradford Park Avenue	38	17	4	17	64	59	38
West Bromwich Albion	38	16	5	17	58	56	37
Blackpool	38	14	8	16	50	52	36
Stockport County	38	13	8	17	50	47	34
Burnley	38	14	6	18	62	61	34
Lincoln City	38	10	11	17	42	69	31
Clapton Orient	38	12	6	20	37	60	30
Leeds City	38	10	7	21	46	80	27
Gainsborough Trinity	38	10	6	22	33	75	26
Grimsby Town	38	9	6	23	50	77	24
Birmingham	38	8	7	23	42	78	23

Division Two

Manager: Bob McRoberts

Match No.	Date		Venue	Opponents	Result		Scorers	Attendance
1	Sep	3	A	Fulham	L	0-3		25,00
2		10	H	Bradford Park Avenue	W	1-0	McKay	18,00
3		17	A	Burnley	D	2-2	Millington, Jones	10,00
4		24	H	Gainsborough Trinity	D	1-1	Jones	12,00
5	Oct	1	A	Leeds City	D	1-1	Bonthron (pen)	8,00
6		8	H	Stockport County	L	1-3	Jones	10,00
7		15	A	Derby County	L	0-1		10,00
8		22	H	Barnsley	W	1-0	Freeman	10,00
9		29	A	Leicester Fosse	L	0-2		10,00
10	Nov	5	H	Wolverhampton Wan.	L	1-3	Foxall	20,00
11		12	A	Chelsea	D	2-2	Jones, Wigmore	25,00
12		19	H	Clapton Orient	L	0-1		14,00
13		26	A	Blackpool	L	1-3	Kidd	4,00
14	Dec	3	H	Glossop	L	1-2	Jones	2,00
15		10	A	Lincoln City	W	1-0	Firth	6,00
16		17	H	Huddersfield Town	W	2-1	Gallimore, Hall	5,00
17		24	A	Bolton Wanderers	L	1-5	Hall	8,00
18		26	A	Hull City	L	1-4	Hall	10,00
19		27	H	West Bromwich Albion	D	1-1	Hall	37,52
20		31	H	Fulham	D	1-1	Hall	14,00
21	Jan	7	A	Bradford Park Avenue	D	2-2	Firth, Hall	10,00
22		21	H	Burnley	D	1-1	Jones	10,00
23		28	A	Gainsborough Trinity	L	0-1		3,00
24	Feb	4	H	Leeds City	W	2-1	Foxall, Powell	15,00
25		13	A	Stockport County	L	1-3	Buckley	3,00
26		18	H	Derby County	W	2-0	Jones, Foxall	15,00
27		25	A	Barnsley	W	3-2	Jones, Hall 2	2,50
28	Mar	4	H	Leicester Fosse	W	1-0	Buckley	10,00
29		11	A	Wolverhampton Wan.	L	1-3	Hall	5,00
30		18	H	Chelsea	W	2-1	Hall, Kidd	27,00
31		25	H	Clapton Orient	L	1-2	Hall	6,00
32	Apr	1	H	Blackpool	W	2-0	McKay, Hall	13,00
33		8	A	Glossop	L	1-2	Jones	1,50
34		14	H	Hull City	W	1-0	Hall	10,00
35		15	H	Lincoln City	L	0-1		10,00
36		17	A	West Bromwich Albion	L	0-1		27,04
37		22	A	Huddersfield Town	L	1-7	Jones	9,00
38		29	H	Bolton Wanderers	W	2-1	Millington, Jones	15,00
							Appearance	
							Goal	

FA Cup

R1	Jan	14	H	Oldham Athletic	D	1-1	Hall (pen)	28,82
rep		17	A	Oldham Athletic	L	0-2		6,40
							Appearance	
							Goal	

Birmingham

Players (columns, left to right): Jerningham J, Bentham RP, Henderson CG, Corbett WS, Buckley FC, Darkin T, Firth RE, Millington CJH, Abbott W, Foxall F, Gallimore G, Jones T, McKay J, Gardner AE, Freeman WD, Bumphrey J, Draper H, Womack F, Lowe CB, Kidd JW, Lindon AE, Males JR, Wigmore W, Hall JH, Robertson G, Greer TG, Batey HP, Powell HH, Wilcox JM

Jer	Ben	Hen	Cor	Buc	Dar	Fir	Mil	Abb	Fox	Gal	Jon	McK	Gar	Fre	Bum	Dra	Wom	Low	Kid	Lin	Mal	Wig	Hal	Rob	Gre	Bat	Pow	Wil
2	3	4	5	6	7	8	9	10	11																			
2	3	4	5	6	7	8			11	9	10																	
2	3		5	6	7	8		10	11	9		4																
2	3	4	5	6	7	8		10		9	11																	
2	3	4	5	6	7	10			9	11		8																
2	3	4	5	6		8		11	9				7	10															
2		4	5	6		7			9			8		10	3	11													
2		4	5	6	7			9				8		11	3	10													
2		4	5	6		8		10	11	9			7		3														
2		5	6					10	11	9		4	7		3		8											
			2	7				10	11	9		4			3		8	1	5	6								
			2	7			7	10	11			4		9		3	8	1	6	5								
			2	7				10	11	9		4			3		8	1	6	5								
		2	5	6	7			10	11	9		4			3		8											
		5	6	7				10		9	11	4			3		8			2								
		5	2	7				11	10			4			3		8		6			9						
		5	2	7				11	10			4			3		8		6			9						
		2	5	6	7			11		10		4			3		8					9						
		5	6	7				11		10		4			3		8		2			9						
			5	7			10	11				4			3		8					9	6					
		5	2	7				11		10		4			3		8					9	6					
		2				7		11		10		4	8		3			1		5			6	9				
				7				11		10		4			3	8		1	5	2	9	6						
		5	4		7			11							3				2	9	6			1	8	10		
		5	4		7			11							3		1		2	9	6				8	10		
2		5			7			11		9		4			3		8					6		1		10		
		5	2		7			11		10		4			3	8			9	6				1				
		5	2		7			11		10		4			3	8			9	6				1				
		5	2		7			11		10			4		3	8			9	6				1				
		5	2		7			11		10			4		3	8	1		9	6								
			2		7			10	11				4		3	8		5	9	6		1						
			2		7			11	9	10			4		3	8		5		6		1						
		5	4		7			10	11						3	8		2	9	6		1						
		5	4		7		10		11						3	8		2		6		1	9					
		5	2		7			10	11				4		3	8			9	6		1						
		5	2		7			11	10				4		3	8			9	6		1						
		5	2		7			10	11				4		3	8			9	6								
3	11	6	11	30	35	17	25	1	21	18	28	15	18	4	12	3	32	2	26	7	6	14	19	19	1	12	4	2
1			2		2	2		3	1	11	2		1					2			1	13				1		

Goals / additional rows:

2			5	7				11		10	4				3		8			9	6							
			2	7			7			11	4				3		8		5	9	6				10			
2	1			2	1	1		1		2	2				2		2		1	2	2				1			
																				1								

League Table

	P	W	D	L	F	A	Pts
West Bromwich Albion	38	22	9	7	67	41	53
Bolton Wanderers	38	21	9	8	69	40	51
Chelsea	38	20	9	9	71	35	49
Clapton Orient	38	19	7	12	44	35	45
Hull City	38	14	16	8	55	39	44
Derby County	38	17	8	13	73	52	42
Blackpool	38	16	10	12	49	38	42
Burnley	38	13	15	10	45	45	41
Wolverhampton W	38	15	8	15	51	52	38
Fulham	38	15	7	16	52	48	37
Leeds City	38	15	7	16	58	56	37
Bradford Park Avenue	38	14	9	15	53	55	37
Huddersfield Town	38	13	8	17	57	58	34
Glossop	38	13	8	17	48	62	34
Leicester Fosse	38	14	5	19	52	62	33
Birmingham	38	12	8	18	42	64	32
Stockport County	38	11	8	19	47	79	30
Gainsborough Trinity	38	9	11	18	37	55	29
Barnsley	38	7	14	17	52	62	28
Lincoln City	38	7	10	21	28	72	24

Division Two

Manager: Bob McRoberts

Match No.	Date		Venue	Opponents	Result		Scorers	Attendance
1	Sep	2	H	Bradford Park Avenue	L	2-3	Kidd 2 (1 pen)	20,000
2		9	A	Fulham	L	1-2	Hall	12,000
3		11	H	Barnsley	L	1-3	Millington	5,000
4		16	H	Derby County	L	0-4		12,000
5		23	A	Stockport County	L	0-2		7,000
6		30	A	Leeds City	W	4-3	Hall 4	10,000
7	Oct	7	A	Wolverhampton Wan.	L	0-1		12,000
8		14	H	Leicester Fosse	W	4-0	Hall 2, Graham 2	12,000
9		21	A	Gainsborough Trinity	D	0-0		3,000
10		28	H	Grimsby Town	D	2-2	Hall (pen), Gildea	15,000
11	Nov	4	A	Nottingham Forest	W	1-0	Graham	14,000
12		11	H	Chelsea	L	1-4	Gibson	20,000
13		18	A	Clapton Orient	L	0-2		4,000
14		25	H	Bristol City	D	0-0		10,000
15	Dec	2	A	Burnley	D	1-1	Jones	14,000
16		9	A	Huddersfield Town	L	2-3	Kidd, Millington	3,500
17		16	H	Blackpool	W	2-1	Hall, Kidd	4,000
18		23	A	Glossop	L	0-2		2,000
19		25	A	Hull City	L	0-4		10,000
20		26	H	Hull City	W	5-1	Kidd 2, Millington, Hall, Graham	10,000
21		30	A	Bradford Park Avenue	L	0-3		15,000
22	Jan	6	H	Fulham	L	1-3	Tinkler	7,000
23		27	H	Stockport County	W	2-0	Conlin, Robertson	12,000
24	Feb	3	H	Gainsborough Trinity	D	2-2	Jones, Hall	10,000
25		10	H	Wolverhampton Wan.	W	3-1	Hall 3 (1 pen)	20,000
26		17	A	Leicester Fosse	L	2-5	Conlin, Jones (pen)	10,000
27		21	A	Derby County	W	1-0	Gardner	5,000
28	Mar	2	A	Grimsby Town	L	0-1		5,000
29		9	H	Nottingham Forest	W	4-2	Jones 2, Hastings, Hall	12,000
30		16	A	Chelsea	W	2-0	Hall, Robertson	30,000
31		23	H	Clapton Orient	W	4-0	Hall 3, Jones (pen)	10,000
32		30	A	Bristol City	L	1-2	Hastings	5,000
33	Apr	5	A	Leeds City	D	0-0		5,000
34		6	H	Burnley	W	4-0	Hall, Reed 2, Hastings	35,000
35		8	A	Barnsley	L	0-1		5,000
36		13	H	Huddersfield Town	W	1-0	Hall	10,000
37		20	A	Blackpool	L	0-1		3,000
38		27	H	Glossop	W	2-0	Robertson 2	6,000
							Appearances	
							Goals	

FA Cup

R1	Jan	13	H	Barnsley	D	0-0		19,500
rep		22	A	Barnsley	L	0-3		12,000
							Appearances	

Appearance and goals grid (players listed across the top):

Dorrington J	Ball W	Womack F	Bumphrey J	Wigmore W	Daykin T	Millington CJH	Kidd JW	Hall JH	Webb S	McKay J	Bailey HP	Gardner AE	Morris DJ	George W	Greer TS	Robertson G	Gibson WF	Gibson RS	Jones T	Conlin J	Graham H	Green A	Crossthwaite H	Hastie IS	Tinkler AA	McClure A	Bates HJ	Jones WH	Hastings W	Reed A
1	2	3	4	5	6	7	8	9	10	11																				
		3	5		2	6	7	8		11			4	10	1	9														
	2	3	5			7	8	9		11	1		4	10		6														
	2	3	8		4	7	10	9		11	1					6	5													
	2	3				7		9			1	4				6	5	8	10	11										
	2	3	4			7		9			1					6	5	8		11	10									
	2	3	4			7		9			1					6	5	8		11	10									
		2	4			7		9			1					6	5	8		11	10	3								
	2	3	4			7		9			1					6	5	8		11	10									
	2	3	4			7	8				1					6	5	9		11	10									
	2	3	4				7	9			1					6	5	8		11	10		1							
		3	4		2			9			1					6	5	8	11	10				7						
		3	4		2	7		9			1					6	5	8	10	11										
1		3	4		2	7		9								6	5	8		11										
1		3	4		2	7	10	9								6	5	8		11										
		3	4		2	7	10	9		1						6	5	8		11										
	2	3	4			7	10	9		1							5			11	8			6						
		3	4		2	7	10	9		1							5			11	8			6						
		3			2	7	10	9		1	4						5			11	8			6						
1		3			2	7	10	9			4						5			11	8			6						
		3			2	7	10			1	4				6	5				11	8			9						
	2	3						9		1	4				10					11					6	5	7	8		
	2	3				7		9		1	4				10					11					6	5		8		
	2	3	4			7		9		1					10											5		8	11	
	2	3	6					9			4				10								1			5	7	8	11	
	2	3	6					9			4				10			11					1		5			8	7	
	2	3	6					9		1	4				10		7								5			8	11	
	2	3	6					9		1	4				10		7								5			8	11	
	2	3	6					9		1	4				10		7								5			8	11	
	2	3	6					9			4				10		7						1		5			8	11	
	2	3	6					9		1	4				10		7								5			8	11	
	2	3	6					8		1	4				10		7								5				11	9
	2	3	6					10		1	4				8		7								9	5			11	
	2	3	6					8		1	4				10		7								5				11	9
	2	3	6					8		1	4						7								5				11	9
	2	3	6					8		1	4						7								5	10			11	9
	2	3	6					8		1	4				10		7								5				11	9
4	26	38	31	3	13	22	14	35	3	4	29	22	3	1	1	30	18	22	3	21	12	1	4	1	19	7	2	11	14	4
			3					6			21					1				4	1	1			1	2	4		1	5	3	2

Additional (cup) fixtures:

Dorrington J	Ball W	Womack F	Bumphrey J	Wigmore W	Daykin T	Millington CJH	Kidd JW	Hall JH	Webb S	McKay J	Bailey HP	Gardner AE	Morris DJ	George W	Greer TS	Robertson G	Gibson WF	Gibson RS	Jones T	Conlin J	Graham H	Green A	Crossthwaite H	Hastie IS	Tinkler AA	McClure A	Bates HJ	Jones WH	Hastings W	Reed A
	2	3			6	7	10	9				1	4				5			11							8			
	2	3			6	7	10	9				1	4				5	8		11										
	2	2				2	2	2				2	2				2	1		2							1			

League Table

	P	W	D	L	F	A	Pts
Derby County	38	23	8	7	74	28	54
Chelsea	38	24	6	8	64	34	54
Burnley	38	22	8	8	77	41	52
Clapton Orient	38	21	3	14	61	44	45
Wolverhampton W	38	16	10	12	57	33	42
Barnsley	38	15	12	11	45	42	42
Hull City	38	17	8	13	54	51	42
Fulham	38	16	7	15	66	58	39
Grimsby Town	38	15	9	14	48	55	39
Leicester Fosse	38	15	7	16	49	66	37
Bradford Park Avenue	38	13	9	16	44	45	35
Birmingham	38	14	6	18	55	59	34
Bristol City	38	14	6	18	41	60	34
Blackpool	38	13	8	17	32	52	34
Nottingham Forest	38	13	7	18	46	48	33
Stockport County	38	11	11	16	47	54	33
Huddersfield Town	38	13	6	19	50	64	32
Glossop	38	8	12	18	42	56	28
Leeds City	38	10	8	20	50	78	28
Gainsborough Trinity	38	5	13	20	30	64	23

Division Two

Manager: Bob McRoberts

The two 4–0 defeats suffered by Blues at Leeds City in the League and Manchester City in the FA Cup, could have been worse! Both teams missed a penalty, both hit the woodwork twice and in the Cup game, former Derby County goalkeeper Horace Bailey, an England international at full and amateur levels and also an Olympic gold medal-winner at soccer, produced at least six brilliant saves.

Again Blues called up five different players to lead the attack this season, including Alf Tinkler, normally a centre-half, who played against Wolves at Molineux in January. He had a hand in one of Billy Jones's two goals in the 2–2 draw.

John Ballantyne, a Scotsman signed from Vale of Leven, made his debut for Blues just 24 hours after arriving at St Andrew's. A diminutive outside-right, standing 5ft 4ins tall, he was a late replacement for Richard Gibson and did well in the 2–1 home win over Grimsby Town on the last day of the League season.

Match No.	Date		Venue	Opponents	Result		Scorers	Attendance
1	Sep	7	A	Bradford Park Avenue	D	0-0		14,000
2		9	H	Fulham	W	2-1	Robertson, Hall	12,000
3		14	H	Wolverhampton Wan.	D	0-0		3,000
4		21	A	Leicester Fosse	W	2-1	Jones, Robertson	12,000
5		28	H	Stockport County	D	1-1	Hall	20,000
6	Oct	5	A	Preston North End	L	0-1		8,000
7		12	H	Burnley	W	3-0	Jones, Hastings, Hall	15,000
8		19	A	Hull City	W	2-1	Jones, Robertson	10,000
9		26	H	Glossop	D	0-0		5,000
10	Nov	2	A	Clapton Orient	W	2-0	Bumphrey, Jones	10,000
11		9	H	Lincoln City	W	4-1	Hall 2, Jones, Bumphrey	35,000
12		16	A	Nottingham Forest	L	1-3	Jones	16,000
13		23	H	Bristol City	W	3-0	Hastings, Robertson, A.R.Smith	20,000
14		30	H	Blackpool	W	3-2	Hall, Gardner, Robertson	10,000
15	Dec	7	A	Huddersfield Town	D	0-0		7,500
16		14	H	Leeds City	D	2-2	A.W.Smith, Tinkler	20,000
17		21	A	Grimsby Town	D	2-2	Robertson, Jones	5,000
18		25	H	Barnsley	W	3-1	Gardner, Robertson 2	35,000
19		26	H	Bury	L	1-2	A.W.Smith	10,000
20		28	H	Bradford Park Avenue	D	1-1	Jones	20,000
21	Jan	1	A	Bury	L	0-3		6,222
22		4	A	Wolverhampton Wan.	D	2-2	Jones 2	7,000
23		18	H	Leicester Fosse	W	5-1	A.R.Smith, Hall 2, Jones, King (og)	15,000
24		25	A	Stockport County	W	1-0	Jones	4,000
25	Feb	8	H	Preston North End	L	0-1		35,000
26		15	A	Burnley	L	0-3		8,000
27		22	H	Hull City	W	3-1	Duncan, Robertson, Jones	10,000
28	Mar	1	A	Glossop	W	2-0	Jones, Robertson	3,000
29		8	H	Clapton Orient	D	1-1	Duncan	14,000
30		15	H	Lincoln City	W	1-0	Duncan	8,000
31		22	H	Nottingham Forest	W	2-0	Reed 2	4,000
32		24	A	Fulham	L	2-3	Robertson, Duncan	8,000
33		25	A	Barnsley	L	0-1		10,000
34		29	A	Bristol City	W	3-0	Reed 2, Robertson	5,000
35	Apr	5	A	Blackpool	L	0-2		3,000
36		12	H	Huddersfield Town	W	3-2	Jones 2, Robertson	10,000
37		19	A	Leeds City	L	0-4		8,000
38		26	H	Grimsby Town	W	2-1	Reed 2	6,000

Appearances

One own-goal

Goals

FA Cup

R1	Jan	11	A	Manchester City	L	0-4		17,442

Appearances

Ray HP	Ball W	Womack F	Gardner AE	Tinkler AA	Bumphrey J	Gibson RS	Jones WH	Hall JH	Robertson G	Smith AR	Dorrington J	Reed A	Hastings W	Crossthwaite H	McClure A	Fairman R	Smith AW	Bates HJ	Spriggs C	Roulson J	Smith JF	Morgan WAL	Duncan CS	Ballantyne J
2	3	4	5	6	7	8	9	10	11															
2	3	4	5	6	7	8	9	10	11	1														
2	3	4	5	6	7	8	9	10	11															
2	3	4	5	6	7	8	9	10	11															
2	3	4	5	6	7	8	9	10	11															
2	3	4	5	6		10	9		7		8	11												
2	3	4	5	6		8	9		7		10	11												
2	3	4	5	6		8	9	10	7		11		1											
2	3	4		6		8	9	10	7		11				5									
2	3	4		6		8	9	10	7		11		1		5									
2	3	4		6		8	9	10	7		11		1		5									
2		4		6		8	9		7		10	11	1		5	3								
2		4	5	6		8	9	10	7		11		1			3								
2		4	5	6	8		9	10	7		11		1			3								
2		4	5	6			9	10	7		8	11	1			3								
2	3	4	5	6		8		10	7			11		9										
2	3	4	5	6		8		10			11		1	9	7									
2	3	4	5	6		8		10	7		11		1	9										
2	3	4	5	6		8		10	7		11		1	9										
2		4	5	6		8		10	7			1		3	9		11							
2		4		6		8		10	7			1	5	3	9		11							
2			9			8			7			5	3	9		11	4		6	10				
2			6			8	9		7			1	5	3		11	4			10				
2	3	4	5			8	9		7			1			11				6	10				
2	3	4	5		7	8	9		11			1							6	10				
2	3					8	9	10	7		11	1	5				4	6						
2	3		6			8	7	10	11			1	5				4				9			
2	3		6			8	7	10	11			1	5				4				9			
2	3		6			8	7	10	11			1	5				4				9			
2	3		6	7				10	11			1	5				4				9			
	3		4	6	7			10	11		8		1	5	2						9			
	3		4	6	7			10	11		8		1	5	2						9			
2	3		5	6	7	9			11		8	1					4			10				
2	3		4	6	7	9		10	11		8		1	5										
2	3		4	6	7	9		10	11		8		1	5										
2	3		4	6	7	9		10	11		8		1	5										
2	3		4	6	7	9		10	11		8		1	5										
2	3		4	6		9		10	11		8		1	5							7			
36	30	23	27	34	15	33	22	30	37	1	13	15	28	19	10	6	1	5	8	4	5	6	1	
		2	1	2				16	8		13	2		6	2		2					4		

Ray HP	Ball W	Womack F	Gardner AE	Tinkler AA	Bumphrey J	Gibson RS	Jones WH	Hall JH	Robertson G	Smith AR	Dorrington J	Reed A	Hastings W	Crossthwaite H	McClure A	Fairman R	Smith AW	Bates HJ	Spriggs C	Roulson J	Smith JF	Morgan WAL	Duncan CS	Ballantyne J
2		4	5	6		8	9	10	7		11				3									
1		1	1	1		1	1	1	1		1				1									

League Table

	P	W	D	L	F	A	Pts
Preston North End	38	19	15	4	56	33	53
Burnley	38	21	8	9	88	53	50
Birmingham	38	18	10	10	59	44	46
Barnsley	38	19	7	12	57	47	45
Huddersfield Town	38	17	9	12	66	40	43
Leeds City	38	15	10	13	70	64	40
Grimsby Town	38	15	10	13	51	50	40
Lincoln City	38	15	10	13	50	52	40
Fulham	38	17	5	16	65	55	39
Wolverhampton W	38	14	10	14	56	54	38
Bury	38	15	8	15	53	57	38
Hull City	38	15	6	17	60	55	36
Bradford Park Avenue	38	14	8	16	60	60	36
Clapton Orient	38	10	14	14	34	47	34
Leicester Fosse	38	13	7	18	49	65	33
Bristol City	38	9	15	14	46	72	33
Nottingham Forest	38	12	8	18	58	59	32
Glossop	38	12	8	18	49	68	32
Stockport County	38	8	10	20	56	78	26
Blackpool	38	9	8	21	39	69	26

Division Two

Manager: Bob McRoberts

Match No.	Date		Venue	Opponents		Result	Scorers	Attendance
1	Sep	3	H	Stockport County	W	3-2	Reed 2, Hastings	13,0
2		6	H	Bradford Park Avenue	L	1-2	Jones	20,0
3		13	A	Notts County	L	1-5	A.W.Smith	12,0
4		20	H	Leicester Fosse	W	1-0	Ballantyne	20,0
5		27	A	Wolverhampton Wan.	L	0-1		20,0
6	Oct	4	H	Hull City	D	1-1	Hastings	9,0
7		11	A	Barnsley	D	1-1	Gibson	9,0
8		18	H	Bury	W	1-0	Neilson	15,0
9		25	A	Huddersfield Town	L	0-7		10,0
10	Nov	1	H	Lincoln City	W	2-0	A.W.Smith, Hodges	18,0
11		8	A	Blackpool	D	2-2	A.W.Smith, Walker	4,0
12		15	H	Nottingham Forest	W	2-0	Bumphrey, Walker	15,0
13		22	A	Woolwich Arsenal	L	0-1		30,0
14		29	H	Grimsby Town	L	1-2	Walker	12,0
15	Dec	6	A	Fulham	L	0-1		10,0
16		13	A	Bristol City	W	2-1	Gibson, Walker	5,0
17		20	H	Leeds City	L	0-2		15,0
18		25	H	Glossop	W	6-0	Walker 2, Foster, Hall 2, Bumphrey	25,0
19		26	A	Glossop	L	1-4	Walker	2,0
20		27	A	Bradford Park Avenue	L	1-5	Morgan	6,0
21	Jan	1	A	Stockport County	L	0-2		8,0
22		3	H	Notts County	W	2-1	Morgan, Pointon	10,0
23		17	A	Leicester Fosse	D	0-0		6,0
24		24	H	Wolverhampton Wan.	W	4-1	Reed, Duncan, Ballantyne, Morgan	30,0
25	Feb	7	A	Hull City	D	0-0		9,0
26		14	H	Barnsley	D	0-0		18,0
27		24	H	Bury	L	1-3	Gibson	4,1
28		28	H	Huddersfield Town	L	1-4	A.R.Smith	15,0
29	Mar	7	A	Lincoln City	D	1-1	Morgan	8,0
30		14	H	Blackpool	D	0-0		7,0
31		21	A	Nottingham Forest	L	1-3	Hall	5,0
32		28	H	Woolwich Arsenal	W	2-0	A.W.Smith 2	17,8
33	Apr	4	A	Grimsby Town	W	2-0	A.W.Smith 2	8,0
34		10	H	Clapton Orient	W	2-0	Hall, A.W.Smith	30,0
35		11	A	Fulham	L	0-1		20,0
36		13	A	Clapton Orient	D	2-2	Walker, Hall	12,0
37		18	H	Bristol City	D	2-2	W.Smith, A.W.Smith	15,0
38		25	A	Leeds City	L	2-3	A.W.Smith, Gardner	10,0

Appearanc
Goa

FA Cup

R1	Jan	10	H	Southend United	W	2-1	Duncan 2	18,0
R2		31	H	Huddersfield Town	W	1-0	Morgan	45,0
R3	Feb	21	H	Queen's Park Rangers	L	1-2	Duncan	35,0

Appearanc
Goa

Ball W	Womack F	Edwards EA	McClure A	Bumphrey J	Ballantyne J	Duncan CS	Hall JH	Reed A	Hastings W	Tinkler AA	Jones WH	Smith AW	Smith AR	Crossthwaite H	Roulson J	Robertson G	Gibson RS	Foster AW	Neilson PM	Hodges FC	Walker WB	Fairman R	Smith JE	Morgan WAL	Hauser S	Porson TS	Stanton A	Baron PH	Robb WB	Gardner AE	Smith W	Eyre E	Wardridge JE
2	3	4	5	6	7	8	9	10	11																								
2	3	4		6	7		9	10	11		5	8																					
2	3	4		6	7	10					5	8	9	11																			
2	3	5			7						6	8	9	11		1	4	10															
2	3	5			7				11		6	8	9			1	4	10															
2	3	6							11		5	8	9			1	4		7	10													
2	3	5		6			8				4	9				1		10	7		11												
2	3	5		6				8			4	9				1		10	7		11												
2	3	5		6				8			4	9				1		10	7		11												
2	3		5								6	9	10	11	1	4		7			8												
2	3		5								6		10	11	1	4		7			8	9											
	3		5	6									10	11	1	4		7			8	9	2										
2	3		5										10	11	1	4		7			8	9		6									
2	3		5										10	11	1	4		7			8	9		6									
	3		5	6									10	11	1	4		7			8	9	2										
	3		5	6			8					4		11	1			7				9	2		10								
	3		5	6			8					4		11	1			7				9	2		10								
2	3		5	6			8					4		11	1			7	10			9											
2	3		5	6			8					4	10	11	1			7				9											
	3	4	5	11														7			8	9	2	6	10	1							
2	3		5			9							4					7			8				6	10	11						
2		5			7	9	8					4													10	1	11	3	6				
2	3		5	4		9	8		11							7									10	1			6				
2	3			4	7	9		8	11	5															10	1			6				
2	3			4	7	9		8	11	5															10	1			6				
2	3			4	7	8			11	5								9							10	1			6				
	3	5	4			9			11							7			8						10		2	6	1				
2	3	5		4	7	9								11					8						10	1			6				
2	3	5		4	7	9	8		11																10	1			6				
	3	5		4	7	9	8	10										2							1		11		6				
2	3	5		4	7		8				9														10	1	11		6				
2	3			7		8	10				9	11		6													5	1	4				
2	3			7		8					9			6											1		5		4	10	11		
2	3		6	7		8		5			9														1				4	10	11		
2	3			7				5			9								10						1		6		4	8	11		
	3			7		8							6							9					1		2	5	4		11	10	
2	3			7		5					9														1			6	4	8	11	10	
2		5						7			9														1		3	6	4	8	11	10	
30	36	15	16	23	19	12	17	8	11	21	9	18	14	17	12	5	18	2	3	10	12	6	4	14	16	4	4	16	2	7	5	6	3
			2	2	1	5	3	2		1	10	1					3			1	8			4		1				1	1		

Ball W	Womack F	Edwards EA	McClure A	Bumphrey J	Ballantyne J	Duncan CS	Hall JH	Reed A	Hastings W	Tinkler AA	Jones WH	Smith AW	Smith AR	Crossthwaite H	Roulson J	Robertson G	Gibson RS	Foster AW	Neilson PM	Hodges FC	Walker WB	Fairman R	Smith JE	Morgan WAL	Hauser S	Porson TS	Stanton A	Baron PH	Robb WB	Gardner AE	Smith W	Eyre E	Wardridge JE
2	3		5	4		9	8		11							7									10	1			6				
2	3		4				8	11	5							7			9						10	1			6				
2	3		5	4	7	8			11										9						10	1			6				
3	3		2	3	1	2	1	1	3							2			2						3	3			3				
						3													1														

Division Two

Manager: Bob McRoberts

Match No.	Date		Venue	Opponents	Result		Scorers	Attendance
1	Sep	2	A	Nottingham Forest	D	1-1	W.Smith	5,0
2		5	A	Leicester Fosse	L	0-1		4,0
3		12	H	Barnsley	W	2-0	Eyre, A.W.Smith	10,0
4		19	A	Glossop	D	3-3	Tinkler, A.W.Smith, Gibson	5
5		26	H	Wolverhampton Wan.	L	1-2	Gibson	20,0
6	Oct	3	A	Fulham	W	3-2	Windridge, A.W.Smith 2	12,0
7		10	H	Stockport County	L	0-1		12,0
8		17	A	Hull City	D	0-0		7,0
9		24	H	Leeds City	W	6-3	A.W.Smith 3, Barton, Windridge, Gibson	8,0
10		31	A	Clapton Orient	D	1-1	Gibson	8,
11	Nov	7	H	Arsenal	W	3-0	A.W.Smith 2, Gibson	15,0
12		14	A	Derby County	L	0-1		7,0
13		21	H	Lincoln City	W	2-0	Gibson, A.W.Smith	5,0
14		28	H	Blackpool	W	3-0	Gibson, W.Smith, A.W.Smith	5,0
15	Dec	5	A	Grimsby Town	L	0-1		4,
16		12	H	Huddersfield Town	W	1-0	Duncan	12,0
17		19	H	Bristol City	W	3-2	Barton, A.W.Smith, Gibson	4,0
18		25	H	Bury	W	1-0	Gibson	20,0
19		26	A	Bury	W	3-1	Toulson 2, Windridge	5,0
20		28	H	Nottingham Forest	W	3-0	A.W.Smith 2 (1 pen), Hodges	25,0
21	Jan	2	H	Leicester Fosse	W	2-0	Gibson, Windridge	16,0
22		23	H	Glossop	W	11-1	A.W.Smith 4, Windridge 5 (1 pen), Eyre, Hodges	8,0
23	Feb	13	A	Stockport County	L	1-3	A.W.Smith	4,0
24		27	A	Leeds City	L	0-2		7,0
25	Mar	1	H	Fulham	W	1-0	Barton	5,0
26		6	A	Clapton Orient	W	1-0	A.W.Smith	15,0
27		8	A	Barnsley	L	1-2	Roulson	3,0
28		13	A	Arsenal	L	0-1		19,0
29		20	H	Derby County	L	0-2		18,0
30		24	H	Hull City	D	2-2	Reed, A.W.Smith	5,
31		27	A	Lincoln City	W	1-0	Morgan	3,0
32	Apr	2	A	Preston North End	L	0-2		10,0
33		5	H	Preston North End	D	1-1	Hodges	10,0
34		10	A	Grimsby Town	W	3-0	Windridge, Barton, Roulson (pen)	10,0
35		14	A	Blackpool	L	1-3	W.Smith	5,
36		17	A	Huddersfield Town	D	0-0		4,0
37		19	A	Wolverhampton Wan.	D	0-0		8,0
38		24	H	Bristol City	D	1-1	Windridge	10,0

Appearanc
Go

FA Cup

R1	Jan	9	H	Crystal Palace	D	2-2	A.W.Smith, Eyre	18,0
rep		16	H	Crystal Palace	W	3-0	Gibson, Tinkler, A.W.Smith	17,0
R2		30	A	Brighton & Hove Albion	D	0-0		9,0
rep	Feb	6	H	Brighton & Hove Albion	W	3-0	Gibson, Morgan, A.W.Smith	28,0
R3		20	H	Oldham Athletic	L	2-3	Gibson, Hodges	39,0

R1 replay and R2 a.e.t.
R1 replay at Birmingham by arrangement.

Appearanc
Go

Appearance grid — Birmingham

	Ball W	Womack F	Bumphrey J	Tratter AA	Barton PH	Gibson RS	Smith W	Walker W	Winthldge JE	Eyre E	Edwards EA	Smith AW	Morgan WAL	Reed A	Gardner AE	Hall JH	McClure A	Duncan CS	Reaton J	Hodges FC	Spriggs C	Stanton A
	2	3	4	5	6	7	8	9	10	11												
	2	3	4	5	6	7	8	9	10	11												
	2	3	4	5		7	8		10	11	6	9										
	2	3	4	5	6	7	8			11			9	10								
	2	3	4	5	6	7	8			11			9	10								
	2	3	4	5	6	7	8		10	11			9									
	2	3	4	5	6	7	8		10	11			9									
	2	3	4	5	6	7			10	11			9		8							
	2	3	4	5	6	7			10	11			9	8								
	2	3		5	6	7	10			11			9		4	8						
	2	3		5	6	7	10			11			9		4	8						
	2	3		5	6	7	10			11			9		4	8						
	2	3			6	7	10			11			9		4	8	5					
	2	3			6	7	8		10	11			9		4		5					
	2	3	4		6	7	8		10	11			9				5					
	2	3	4	5	6	7	8		10	11								9				
	2	3	4	5	6	7	8		10	11			9									
	2	3		5	6	7	8		10	11			9		4							
	2	3		5	6	7			10				9		4	8	11					
	2	3		5	6	7			10				9		4	8	11	2				
		3		5	6	7			10				9		4	8	11	2				
	2	3		5	6	7			10	11			9		4	8						
		3		5	6	7			9	10					4	8	11	2				
	2	3		5	6	7			9	10					4	8	11					
	2	3	6		5	7		8		11					9	4						
	2	3			5	7		8			9	10			4		11					
	2	3	6		5	7		8				10			9	4		11				
	2	3		5	6	7			10	11					9	4	8					
	2	3		5	6	7			10			9				4	8	11				
	2	3		5	7				10		6	9	11			4	8					
	2		6	5	3	7			9	10						4	8	11				
	2	3		5	6	7			10	11		9				4	8					
	2	3		5	6	7			10		9		11			4	8					
	2	3	6	5	9	7	11		10							4	8					
	2	3	6		9	7	11		10					5		4	8					
	2	3		5	6	7			10	11			9			4	8					
	2	3	6		5	7	11		10				9			4	8					
	2	3		5	7	11			10				9			4	8					
	36	37	18	29	37	38	21	5	26	23	2	30	8	3	6	4	4	21	17	9	2	
		1	4	10	3		11	2		21	1	1			1	4	3					

	Ball W	Womack F	Bumphrey J	Tratter AA	Barton PH	Gibson RS	Smith W	Walker W	Winthldge JE	Eyre E	Edwards EA	Smith AW	Morgan WAL	Reed A	Gardner AE	Hall JH	McClure A	Duncan CS	Reaton J	Hodges FC	Spriggs C	Stanton A
	2	3		5	6	7			10	11			9			4	8					
	2	3		5	6	7			10	11			9			4	8					
	2	3		5	6	7			10	11			9			4	8					
	2	3		5	6	7			9	10						4	8	11				
		3		5	6	7			9	10		2				4	8	11				
	4	5		5	5	5			3	2		5	2	1		5	5	2				
		1		3					1	3	1						1					

League Table

	P	W	D	L	F	A	Pts
Derby County	38	23	7	8	71	33	53
Preston North End	38	20	10	8	61	42	50
Barnsley	38	22	3	13	51	51	47
Wolverhampton W	38	19	7	12	77	52	45
Arsenal	38	19	5	14	69	41	43
Birmingham	38	17	9	12	62	39	43
Hull City	38	19	5	14	65	54	43
Huddersfield Town	38	17	8	13	61	42	42
Clapton Orient	38	16	9	13	50	48	41
Blackpool	38	17	5	16	58	57	39
Bury	38	15	8	15	61	56	38
Fulham	38	15	7	16	53	47	37
Bristol City	38	15	7	16	62	56	37
Stockport County	38	15	7	16	54	60	37
Leeds City	38	14	4	20	65	64	32
Lincoln City	38	11	9	18	46	65	31
Grimsby Town	38	11	9	18	48	76	31
Nottingham Forest	38	10	9	19	43	77	29
Leicester Fosse	38	10	4	24	47	88	24
Glossop	38	6	6	26	31	87	18

1915-16

Midland Section: Principal Competition

Opponents	H	A
Barnsley	2–0	1–2
Bradford City	1–1	1–1
Bradford Park Avenue	1–2	3–2
Chesterfield Town	2–2	3–0
Grimsby Town	3–0	0–3
Huddersfield Town	2–1	1–2
Hull City	4–2	1–0
Leeds City	1–1	1–1
Leicester Fosse	2–1	1–1
Lincoln City	0–0	2–3
Nottingham Forest	1–0	4–0
Notts County	4–0	1–1
Rotherham County	1–3	2–8
Sheffield United	5–0	0–0
Sheffield Wednesday	4–1	2–0

Summary:

Venue	P	W	D	L	F	A	Pts	Pos
Home	15	9	4	2	33	14	22	
Away	15	5	5	5	23	24	15	
Totals	30	14	9	7	56	38	37	3rd

Midland Section: Subsidiary Competition

Opponents	H	A
Leicester Fosse	5–1	2–4
Nottingham Forest	4–3	3–3
Notts County	1–1	2–0

Summary:

Venue	P	W	D	L	F	A
Home	3	2	1	0	10	5
Away	3	1	1	1	7	7
Totals	6	3	2	1	17	12

Appearances (all games):

B. Anstey* 3, W. Ball 34, J. Barratt* 1, J. Bell* 1, E. Best 10, S. Bowser* 13, W. Brelsford* 1, A. Brooks* 3, S. Brooks* 9, C. Buckley* 1, W. Charles 1, H. Dobson* 1, W. Clarke 1, F. Crowe 1, C. Duncan 1, H. Edgley* 1, E. Edwards 33, H. Foxall 1, B. Freeman* 1, A. Gardner 19, R. Gibson 1, J. Griffiths 3, H. Hampton* 1, S. Hauser 4 W. Hooton 1, J. Hopkins* 2, J. Hubbard 1, C. Jephcott* 17, A. Lindon* 1, A. McClure 31, W. McCourty 1, A. Mercer 11, H. Middlemiss* 1, H. Montgomery* 13, T. Moore 1, W. Morgan 5, A. Newman 2, A. Osborne* 2, H. Pearson* 13, E. Peers* 12, J. Roulson 12, A. Smith 14, A. Turner 10, W. Walker 2, C. Wallace* 3, T. Weston* R. Westwood 2, G. Whent 1, J. Whitehouse 35, G. Wild 1, F. Womack 34, J. Wootton* 4, H. Yarnall.
* Denotes guest player.

Goalscorers:

Whitehouse 23, Montgomery 6, Bell 5, Bowser 5, Turner 4, Edwards 3, Jephcott 3, Mercer 3, Roulson 3, S. Brooks 2, Morgan 2, Walker 2, Ball 1, Buckley 1, Crowe 1, Freeman 1, Gardner 1, Hopkins 1, McClure 1, Moore 1, Wallace 1, opponents 3.

Wartime Blues

...ues did not play any competitive matches in season 1916–17

...idland Section: Principal Competition

...ponents	H	A
...arnsley	3–1	3–3
...radford City	2–1	3–0
...radford Park Avenue	2–0	0–1
...hesterfield Town	2–2	3–0
...rimsby Town	0–1	2–2
...uddersfield Town	2–1	2–4
...ull City	2–1	2–1
...eeds City	3–1	0–1
...icester Fosse	0–0	0–3
...ncoln City	5–0	3–3
...ottingham Forest	1–1	1–2
...otts County	7–2	3–3
...otherham County	2–1	0–1
...heffield United	4–1	1–3
...heffield Wednesday	4–1	2–0

...ummary:

...nue	P	W	D	L	F	A	Pts	Pos
...ome	15	11	3	1	39	14	25	
...way	15	4	4	7	25	27	12	
...tals	30	15	7	8	64	41	37	3rd

...idland Section: Subsidiary Competition

...ponents	H	A
...icester Fosse	1–0	1–1
...ottingham Forest	0–0	0–1
...otts County	3–2	1–5

...ummary:

...nue	P	W	D	L	F	A
...me	3	2	1	0	4	2
...way	3	0	1	2	2	7
...tals	6	2	2	2	6	9

...pearances (all games):

Ball 20, A. Baines 1, P. Barton 4, J. Beard 1, J. Bell* 11, E. Best 2, S. Bowser* 29, D. Boxley 6, T. Butler 26, ...Cooper* 6, F. Crowe 7, A. Crump 1, G. Davies 1, E. Edwards 15, J. Elkes 3, T. Evans 2, A. Gardner 23, R. Gibson 2, ...Godfrey 1, J. Godfrey 1, J. Harper 2, F. Hawley* 2, H. Howell* 1, G. Hunter* 8, C. Jephcott* 12, H. Johnson* 2, ...Lees* 1, A. Lindon 25, A. McClure 3, A. Mercer* 3, W. Morgan 1, H. Montgomery* 3, A. Newman 2, ...Pennington* 2, S. Richardson* 1, A. Robinson 1, J. Roulson 9, C. Sambrooke 1, J. Scorgie 1, D. Shea* 1, ...Sheldon 2, J. Short 1, A. Smith 20, S. Stevens* 15, R. Tinsley* 1, C. Wallace 1, J. Whitehouse 23, T. White 4, ...Williams 1, A. Wilson* 8, F. Womack 28, J. Wootton 27.
...Denotes guest player.

...alscorers:

...tler 12, Stevens 12, Whitehouse 8, Boxley 4, Wootton 4, Bell 3, Smith 3, Bowser 2, Gibson 2, Morgan 2, ...ontgomery 2, J. Godfrey 1, Jephcott 1, Lees 1, McClure 1, Mercer 1, Richardson 1, Roulson 1, Shea 1, ...nsley 1.

Midland Section: Principal Competition

Opponents	H	A
Barnsley	7–0	1–2
Bradford City	5–1	3–2
Bradford Park Avenue	2–0	1–1
Coventry City	3–1	3–1
Grimsby Town	4–0	4–1
Huddersfield Town	1–0	0–1
Hull City	5–1	3–0
Leeds City	4–2	1–3
Leicester Fosse	0–2	4–0
Lincoln City	3–0	0–1
Nottingham Forest	2–3	0–1
Notts County	0–7	0–2
Rotherham County	2–0	2–0
Sheffield United	4–1	3–1
Sheffield Wednesday	4–2	1–0

Summary:

Venue	P	W	D	L	F	A	Pts	Pos
Home	15	12	0	3	46	20	24	
Away	15	8	1	6	26	16	17	
Totals	30	20	1	9	72	36	41	2nd

Midland Section: Subsidiary Competition

Opponents	H	A
Leicester Fosse	3–0	4–2
Nottingham Forest	1–0	3–1
Notts County	0–3	2–1

Summary:

Venue	P	W	D	L	F	A
Home	3	2	0	1	4	3
Away	3	3	0	0	9	4
Totals	6	5	0	1	13	7

Appearances (all games):

W. Ball 30, P. Barton 5, R. Bennett 1, D. Brown* 5, C. Buchan* 2, T. Butler 1, A. Cooper* 15, F. Crowe 6, G. Davies 27, C. Duncan 1, E. Edwards 2, J. Elkes 3, A .Gardner 26, R. Gibson 11, F. Gillott 1, B. Godfrey 17, J. Godfrey 28, J. Harper* 1, F. Hawley* 21, A. Hill 1, G. Hunter* 13, H. Johnson* 1, G. Jones 5, A. Kay 6, A. McClure 14, A. Mackenzie 1, R. Milsom 1, W. Morgan 21, A. Newman 1, F. Osborne 1, J. Pennington* 1, W. Robb 1, J. Roulson 13, J. Scorgie 3, A. Sheldon 2, J. Short 5, A. Smith 6, A.W. Smith 2, D. Tremelling 2, W. Walker 29, T. White 3, J. Whitehouse 29, A. Wilson* 2, F. Womack 30.
* Denotes guest player.

Goalscorers:

J Godfrey 26, Whitehouse 17, Walker 15, Brown 5, Davies 5, Morgan 3, Short 3, AW Smith 3, Hunter 2, Crowe 1, Elkes 1, Gardner 1, Gibson 1, Hawley 1, McClure 1.

Wartime Review

Blues played a total of 106 competitive matches during World War One, winning 58, drawing 20 and losing 28, with a goal average of 223 for and 140 against.

The biggest home attendance during the hostilities was 26,000 versus Leeds City in November 1917, while the average gate that season was 13,000, compared with 11,000 in 1915–16 and 10,500 in 1918–19.

Frank Womack made 92 appearances in total, Jackie Whitehouse 87, William 'Kosher' Ball 84, Albert Gardner 68 and Ernie Edwards 50. Whitehouse top-scored with 48 goals, Joe Godfrey netted 27 and Billy Walker 17.

Guest players for Blues during the war included five from West Bromwich Albion, two of them England internationals Sid Bowser and Jesse Pennington; four from Aston Villa, among them Harry Hampton who would later join Blues; three from Wolves and also Charlie Buchan from Sunderland.

Division Two

Manager: Frank Richards

Did you know that?

The time Blues produced a full matchday programme (other than a single card) was for their home League game with Hull City in August. Some 5,000 were printed.

The cheapest admission price to stand on the terraces for a home game at St Andrew's this season was one shilling.

In March 1920, Joe Lane, a burly centre-forward, was signed from Blackpool for a club record fee of £3,600. He scored twice on his home debut against Nottingham Forest.

Two months later, Blues signed George Liddell on a professional contract. He was to remain at the club, as a player and manager, until 1939.

Match No.	Date		Venue	Opponents	Result		Scorers	Attendance
1	Aug	30	H	Hull City	W	4-1	Gibson, Walker, Godfrey, Whitehouse	20,0
2	Sep	1	A	South Shields	L	0-1		12,0
3		6	A	Hull City	D	0-0		10,0
4		10	H	South Shields	W	4-0	Millard 2, Morgan 2	15,0
5		13	H	Coventry City	W	4-1	Morgan, Whitehouse, Millard 2	20,0
6		20	A	Coventry City	W	3-1	Millard 2, Whitehouse	16,0
7		27	H	Huddersfield Town	W	4-2	Elkes 2, Whitehouse, Burkinshaw	20,0
8	Oct	4	A	Huddersfield Town	D	0-0		6,0
9		11	H	Blackpool	W	4-2	Walker, Whitehouse, Elkes, Jones (og)	16,0
10		18	A	Blackpool	L	0-3		8,0
11		25	H	West Ham United	L	0-1		30,0
12	Nov	1	A	West Ham United	W	2-1	Short, Millard	20,0
13		8	H	Wolverhampton Wan.	W	2-0	Short 2	20,0
14		15	A	Wolverhampton Wan.	W	2-0	Millard, Short	14,0
15		22	H	Rotherham County	D	2-2	Morgan, Barton	20,0
16		29	A	Rotherham County	W	3-0	Short, Millard 2	12,0
17	Dec	6	A	Stoke	W	1-0	Short	15,0
18		13	H	Stoke	W	2-1	Short 2	30,0
19		20	A	Grimsby Town	W	3-0	Millard 2, Morgan	6,0
20		25	H	Leicester City	L	0-1		20,0
21		26	H	Leicester City	L	0-1		25,0
22		27	H	Grimsby Town	W	4-0	Morgan, Elkes, Burkinshaw, Millard (pen)	20,0
23	Jan	3	A	Bristol City	D	1-1	Millard	12,0
24		17	A	Bristol City	W	1-0	Davies	30,0
25		24	H	Stockport County	D	1-1	Elkes	30,0
26	Feb	7	H	Barnsley	D	0-0		30,0
27		14	A	Barnsley	W	5-0	Barton, Hampton 2, Gibson, Whitehouse	12,0
28		28	A	Nottingham Forest	W	2-1	Hampton 2	9,0
29	Mar	6	A	Lincoln City	D	2-2	Hampton, Lane (pen)	9,0
30		10	H	Nottingham Forest	W	8-0	Hampton 4, Lane 2, Burkinshaw 2	15,0
31		13	H	Lincoln City	W	7-0	Davies, Lane 3, Hampton, Whitehouse, Atkin (og)	30,0
32		15	A	Stockport County	L	1-2	Robson (og)	5,0
33		20	A	Bury	L	0-1		20,0
34		27	H	Bury	L	0-2		30,0
35	Apr	3	A	Port Vale	W	3-1	Hampton, Lane, Elkes	15,0
36		5	A	Fulham	W	2-1	Short, Russell (og)	18,0
37		6	H	Fulham	W	2-0	Jones 2	20,0
38		10	H	Port Vale	W	3-0	Lane, Elkes 2	30,0
39		17	A	Clapton Orient	L	1-2	Lane	18,0
40		24	H	Clapton Orient	W	2-1	Short, Lane	20,0
41		26	A	Tottenham Hotspur	D	0-0		35,0
42	May	1	H	Tottenham Hotspur	L	0-1		40,0

Appearanc

Four own-goals   Go

FA Cup

R1	Jan	10	H	Everton	W	2-0	Burkinshaw, Whitehouse	44,0
R2		31	H	Darlington	W	4-0	Millard, Whitehouse 3	47,0
R3	Feb	21	A	Liverpool	L	0-2	Barton	50,0

Appearanc

Go

Player appearance / line-up chart (columns left-to-right):

Tremelling RD · Ball W · Womack F · Poulson J · McClure A · Baron PH · Gibson RS · Walker WB · Godfrey J · Whitehouse JC · Morgan WAL · Burkinshaw L · Millard AAR · Evans TE · Elkes AJE · Gardner AE · Watson JS · Whitt VTW · Short JJ · Rea A · Davies G · Peart JG · Wilson AR · Hawley RV · Hampton JH · Lane JC · Jones A · Mumford WR

T	Ba	Wo	Po	Mc	Br	Gi	Wa	Go	Wh	Mo	Bu	Mi	Ev	El	Ga	Wt	Wi	Sh	Re	Da	Pe	Ws	Ha	Hm	La	Jo	Mu
	2	3	4	5	6	7	8	9	10	11																	
	2	3	4	5	6	7	8	9	10	11																	
	2	3	4	5	6	7	8	9	10	11																	
	2	3	4	5	6		8		10	11	7		9														
	2	3	4	5	6		8		10	11	7		9														
	2	3	4	5	6		8		10	11	7		9														
	2	3		5	6			9	10	11	7	4	8														
	2	3	6		5			9	10	11	7		8	4													
		3	4	5	6			9	10	11	7		8		2												
		3	4	5	6			9	10	11	7		8		2												
		3	4	5	6			9	10	11	7		8		2												
		3	4	5	6	7			10	11			9	2	8												
		3	4	5	6	7			10	11				2	8	9											
		3	4	5	6					11			9	2	8	10	7										
		3	4	5	6					11			10	2	8		7	9									
1	2	3	4	5	6				11	7	9				10		8										
1	2	3	4	5	6				11	7	9				10		8										
1	2	3	4	5	6				11	7					10		8	9									
1		3		4	5	6			10	11	7	9			8												
1		3		4	5	6			10	11	7	5			8												
1	2	3	4		6				10	11	7	5		9	8												
1	2	3	4		6				10	11	7	9		8													
1	2	3	4		6				10		7	9		8		11			5								
1	2	3	4	5	6				10	11	7	9		8													
1	2	3	4	5	6	8			10	11	7	9															
1	2	3	4	5	6	8			10	11	7											9					
1		3			6	8			10	11	7	4		2							5	9					
		3	4		6	8				11	7	5		2								9	10				
		3	6						10		7	5	4	2			11					8	9				
1		3	4		6				10		7	5		2			11					8	9				
1		3	4		6				10		7	5		2			11					8	9				
1		6		3					10		7	5	4	2			11					8	9				
		3	4	5	6	7			10							2	11					8	9				
1		3	4		6				2					5		10	11					7		8	9		
1		3		6					2				5	4	10	7	11							8	9		
1		3		6					2			7	5	4	10		11								9	8	
1		3	4		6				2			7	5		10		11								9	8	
1		3	4		6				2			7	5		10		11								9	8	
1		3	4	5					10			7		8			11								9		2
1		3	4		6				10			7		8			11								9		2
1		3	4	5	6				10			7	8				11								9		2
Tot	2	20	39	38	24	41	10	11	3	36	28	32	29	6	16	1	2	11	16	3	16	3	2	3	10	14	3	3
			2	2	2		1	7	6	4	14		8					10		2					11	10	2

Cup matches:

T	Ba	Wo	Po	Mc	Br	Gi	Wa	Go	Wh	Mo	Bu	Mi	Ev	El	Ga	Wt	Wi	Sh	Re	Da	Pe	Ws	Ha	Hm	La	Jo	Mu
1	2	3	4		6				10	11	7	5		9					8								
1	2	3	4		6				10	11	7	9															
1	2	3	4	5	6	8			10	11	7							9									
3	3	3	3	2	3	2			3	3	3	2	1		1			1									
				1					4			1	1														

League Table

	P	W	D	L	F	A	Pts
Tottenham Hotspur	42	32	6	4	102	32	70
Huddersfield Town	42	28	8	6	97	38	64
Birmingham	42	24	8	10	85	34	56
Blackpool	42	21	10	11	65	47	52
Bury	42	20	8	14	60	44	48
Fulham	42	19	9	14	61	50	47
West Ham United	42	19	9	14	47	40	47
Bristol City	42	13	17	12	46	43	43
South Shields	42	15	12	15	58	48	42
Stoke	42	18	6	18	60	54	42
Hull City	42	18	6	18	78	72	42
Barnsley	42	15	10	17	61	55	40
Port Vale	42	16	8	18	59	62	40
Leicester City	42	15	10	17	41	61	40
Clapton Orient	42	16	6	20	51	59	38
Stockport County	42	14	9	19	52	61	37
Rotherham County	42	13	8	21	51	83	34
Nottingham Forest	42	11	9	22	43	73	31
Wolverhampton W	42	10	10	22	55	80	30
Coventry City	42	9	11	22	35	73	29
Lincoln City	42	9	9	24	44	101	27
Grimsby Town	42	10	5	27	34	75	25

Division Two

Manager: Frank Richards

Match No.	Date	Venue	Opponents	Result		Scorers	Attendance
1	Aug 28	A	South Shields	L	0-3		20,000
2	30	H	Hull City	W	5-1	Crosbie 2, Barton, Lane 2	25,000
3	Sep 4	H	South Shields	D	1-1	Whitehouse	35,000
4	6	A	Hull City	L	0-1		13,000
5	11	A	Cardiff City	L	1-2	Crosbie	30,000
6	18	H	Cardiff City	D	1-1	Whitehouse	45,000
7	25	A	Leicester City	L	0-3		17,000
8	Oct 2	H	Leicester City	W	5-0	Lane 2, Hampton 3	12,000
9	9	A	Blackpool	L	0-3		10,000
10	16	H	Blackpool	W	3-0	Whitehouse 2, Lane	50,000
11	23	A	Sheffield Wednesday	W	2-1	Whitehouse 2	25,000
12	30	H	Sheffield Wednesday	W	4-0	Crosbie, Whitehouse, Hampton, Lane	30,000
13	Nov 6	A	Wolverhampton Wan.	W	3-0	Burkinshaw, Crosbie, McClure	20,000
14	13	H	Wolverhampton Wan.	W	4-1	Hampton 2, Barton, Lane	35,000
15	20	A	Stoke	W	2-1	Hampton 2	20,000
16	27	H	Stoke	W	3-0	Lane, Burkinshaw, Crosbie	16,000
17	Dec 4	H	Coventry City	W	3-2	Whitehouse 2, Lawrence (og)	25,000
18	11	A	Coventry City	W	4-0	Burkinshaw, Lane, Hampton 2	22,000
19	18	H	Leeds United	W	1-0	McClure	25,000
20	25	A	West Ham United	D	1-1	Bradford	23,000
21	27	H	West Ham United	W	2-1	Hampton 2	60,017
22	Jan 1	A	Leeds United	L	0-1		22,000
23	15	A	Stockport County	W	3-0	Crosbie, Lane, Whitehouse	12,000
24	22	H	Stockport County	W	5-0	Lane 2, Crosbie, Whitehouse, Liney	35,000
25	Feb 5	H	Notts County	W	2-1	Burkinshaw 2	40,000
26	12	A	Clapton Orient	D	1-1	Burkinshaw	18,000
27	16	A	Notts County	D	0-0		14,000
28	19	H	Clapton Orient	D	0-0		20,000
29	26	A	Bury	W	1-0	Hampton	25,000
30	Mar 5	H	Bury	W	4-0	Crosbie 2, Linley, Barton	40,000
31	12	A	Bristol City	W	1-0	Lane	22,000
32	19	H	Bristol City	D	0-0		30,000
33	25	A	Fulham	L	0-5		40,000
34	26	H	Barnsley	L	1-3	Hampton	40,000
35	29	H	Fulham	W	1-0	Booth	30,000
36	Apr 2	A	Barnsley	D	1-1	Davies	19,000
37	9	H	Nottingham Forest	W	3-0	Crosbie, Lane 2	30,000
38	16	A	Nottingham Forest	D	1-1	Crosbie	14,000
39	23	H	Rotherham County	W	3-2	Crosbie 2, Davies	35,127
40	30	A	Rotherham County	D	1-1	Barton	17,000
41	May 2	H	Port Vale	W	4-0	Hampton, Davies 2, Barton	25,000
42	7	A	Port Vale	W	2-0	Hampton, Davies	10,000

One own-goal

Appearances
Goals

FA Cup

R1	Jan 8	A	Luton Town	L	1-2	Barton	12,700

Appearances
Goals

Appearance & goalscorers grid — Birmingham

	Tremelling RD	Ball W	Womack F	Liddell GM	Millard AAR	Barton PH	Birtchenhaw L	Crosbie JA	Lane JC	Whitehouse JC	Morgan WAL	Jones JW	Rodson J	McClure A	Davies G	Booth R	White VTW	Hampton JH	Gibson RS	Elkes AJE	Davis J	Bradford J	Linley E	Haslie S
	2	3	4	5	6	7	8	9	10	11														
		3			6	7	8	9	10	11	2	4	5											
		3			6	7	8	9	10	11	2	4	5											
		3			6	7	8	9	10	11	2	4	5											
		3			6	7	8	9	10		2	4	5	11										
		3			6	7	8	9	10		2		5	11	4									
		3			6		8	9	7	11		4	5				2	10						
		3			6		8	9		11		4	5				2	10	7					
			6	3			8	9		11		4	5				2	10	7					
					6		8	9		11	3	4	5				2	10	7					
		2			6	7	8	9		11	3	4	5				10							
		2			6	7	8	9		11	3	4	5				10							
		2			6	7	8	9		11	3	4	5							10				
		2			6	7	8	9		11	3	4	5				10							
		2			6	7	8	9		11	3	4	5				10							
		2			6		8			11	3	4	5				9	7	10					
		2			6	7	8			11	3	4	5				10		9					
		2			6	7	8			11	3	4	5				10		9					
		2			6	7	8			11	3	4	5				10		9					
		2			6	7	8	9	10		3	4								5		11		
		2			6	7	8	9	10		3		5							4		11		
		2			6	7	8	9	10		3		5							4		11		
		2			6	7	8	9	10		3		5							4		11		
		2			6	7	8	9	10		3		5							4		11	1	
		2			6	7	8	9			3		5				10			4		11	1	
		2			6		8	9			3		5				10	7		4		11	1	
		2			6	7	8	9			3		5				10			4		11	1	
	2				6	7	8	9			3		5							4		11	1	
	2	3			6	7	8	9			4		5				10					11	1	
	2				6	7	8	9			3	4	5				10					11	1	
		2			6	7	8				3		5		4		10	9				11	1	
		2			6	7	8		10		3		5				11	4		9			1	
		2	6			7	8	9	10		3		5				11	4					1	
		2			6	7	8	9			3		5				11	4				10		
		2			6	7	8	9			3	4	5				11					10		
		2			6	7	8	9	10		3		5				11			4				
		2			6	7	8	9	10		3		5				11			4				
		2			6	7	8		10		3		5				11			4		9	1	
Apps	4	38	2	41	35	42	34	33	5	37	22	40	6	4	29	7	2	11	4	12	12			
Goals		5	6	14	15	11			2	5	1		16			1	2							
		2			6	7	8		11		3	4	5				10		9					
		1			1	1	1		1		1	1	1				1		1					
					1																			

1921-22

Division One

Manager: Frank Richards

Match No.	Date	Venue	Opponents	Result		Scorers	Attendance
1	Aug 27	H	Burnley	L	2-3	Elkes 2	40,00
2	29	A	Chelsea	W	2-1	Elkes, Hampton	25,00
3	Sep 3	A	Burnley	L	1-3	Elkes	35,00
4	5	H	Chelsea	W	5-1	Whitehouse 2, Elkes 2, Crosbie	30,00
5	10	A	Everton	L	1-2	Crosbie	30,00
6	17	H	Everton	D	1-1	Whitehouse	30,00
7	24	A	Sunderland	L	1-2	Whitehouse	30,00
8	Oct 1	H	Sunderland	W	1-0	Whitehouse	30,00
9	8	H	Huddersfield Town	L	0-2		40,11
10	15	A	Huddersfield Town	L	0-1		15,00
11	22	H	Bolton Wanderers	D	1-1	Crosbie	20,00
12	29	A	Bolton Wanderers	W	2-1	Bradford 2	21,56
13	Nov 5	H	Arsenal	L	0-1		30,00
14	12	A	Arsenal	L	2-5	Whitehouse, Bradford	30,00
15	19	A	Blackburn Rovers	D	1-1	Bradford	25,00
16	26	H	Blackburn Rovers	W	1-0	Burkinshaw	20,00
17	Dec 3	A	Oldham Athletic	W	1-0	Cameron	14,00
18	10	A	Oldham Athletic	W	3-0	Whitehouse, Liddell, Crosbie	30,00
19	17	H	Sheffield United	W	2-1	Elkes, Whitehouse	30,00
20	24	A	Sheffield United	W	2-1	Whitehouse, Lane	25,00
21	26	A	West Bromwich Albion	L	0-1		49,48
22	27	H	West Bromwich Albion	L	0-2		44,50
23	31	H	Cardiff City	L	0-1		30,00
24	Jan 14	A	Cardiff City	L	1-3	Crosbie	35,00
25	21	H	Newcastle United	L	0-4		15,00
26	Feb 4	H	Liverpool	L	0-2		10,00
27	8	A	Newcastle United	W	1-0	Harvey	22,00
28	11	A	Liverpool	L	0-1		30,00
29	18	H	Manchester United	L	0-1		20,00
30	25	A	Manchester United	D	1-1	Bradford	40,00
31	Mar 11	A	Aston Villa	D	1-1	Liddell	52,34
32	15	H	Aston Villa	W	1-0	Crosbie	34,19
33	18	A	Middlesbrough	D	1-1	Crosbie	20,00
34	25	H	Middlesbrough	W	4-3	Bradford 2, Crosbie, Hampton	15,00
35	Apr 1	H	Tottenham Hotspur	L	0-3		34,23
36	8	A	Tottenham Hotspur	L	1-2	Hampton	19,63
37	14	A	Manchester City	L	0-1		35,00
38	15	A	Bradford City	W	2-1	Bradford 2	25,00
39	18	H	Manchester City	W	3-1	McClure, Bradford, Hampton	30,00
40	22	H	Bradford City	W	1-0	Foxall	25,00
41	May 1	A	Preston North End	D	2-2	Crosbie 2	10,00
42	6	H	Preston North End	L	0-2		20,00

Appearance

Goals

FA Cup

Did not enter

Player appearance / shirt-number grid

Walker S	Womack F	Jones JW	Gregool G	McClure A	Barton PH	Harvey WHT	Hampson JH	Luns JC	Bates AJE	Linley E	Dixon DP	Cameron ES	Tremelling RD	Hunter W	Crosbie JA	Whitehouse JC	Burkinshaw L	Booth R	Neil PWH	Liddell GM	Bradford J	Daws J	Rhodon J	Thompson L	Deacon H	Dawes G	Barratt J	Firwall FH	Ashurst EA	White VH
	2	3	4	5	6	7	8	9	10	11																				
		3	4	5	6	7	8		10	11	2	9																		
	2		4	5	6	7			10	11		9	1	3	8															
	2		4	5	6				10	11			1	3	8	9														
	2	3		5	6				10	11			1	3	8	9	7													
	2	3		5		7	10	11					1		8	9	4			6										
	2	3	5		6	7	10	11					1		8	9	4													
	2	3	5		6	7							1		8	9	4													
	2	3	4	5	6								1		8	9				4										
	2	3		5	6		10						1		8	9	7			6										
	2	3	5		7	10	9						1		11					9										
	2	3	5		7	8	10				9	1		11	7					6		4									
	2	3	5		8	10					9	1		11	7					6		4									
	2	3	5		7		10	9				1		8	11					6		4									
	2	3	5		7		9	10				1		8	11					6		4									
	2		5	6	7		9				10	1	3	8	11							4									
	2				9	10						1	3	8	11		7	6		5	4										
	2		5		9							1	3	8	11		7	6				4		10							
	2		5		7	10	9					1	3	8	11		6					4		10							
	2		5		7			11				1	3	8	9		6					4									
	2		5	6	7		9		11		10	1	3	8								4									
	2	3			6	7				11		1		10						5	9	4				8	11				
	2	3			6	7				1			8	10					5	9		4					11				
	2	3			6	7				1			8	10					5	9		4					11				
	2	3			6	7			11		1		8						5	9		4		10							
	2	3	5	6					11		1		10						4	9	8										
		3	5	6							1		8	10					4	9		2				7	11				
		3	5	6	10						1		8						4	9		2				7	11				
		3	5	6		10					1		8							9		4				7	11	2			
		3	5	6	4	10					1		8							9						7	11	2			
		3	5	6		10					1		8							9		4				7	11	2			
		3	5		8	10					1									9		4				7	11	2	6		
5	3				9						1		8	10						4						7	11	2	6		
	3	5	6		10						1		8	11					9	4						7		2			
	3	5	6		10						1		8						9	4						7	11	2			
	3	5	6		9	10					1		8							4						7	11	2			
	3	5	6		9	10					1		8							4						7	11	2			
	2	3	5	6		10	9					1		8							4						7	11				
8	30	33	10	35	29	21	18	19	16	17	2	6	39	9	34	25	4	2	5	20	17	12	15	2	2	3	12	11	9	2
		1			1	4	1	7		1				1	10	9	10			2	1						1			

League Table

	P	W	D	L	F	A	Pts
Liverpool	42	22	13	7	63	36	57
Tottenham Hotspur	42	21	9	12	65	39	51
Burnley	42	22	5	15	72	54	49
Cardiff City	42	19	10	13	61	53	48
Aston Villa	42	22	3	17	74	55	47
Bolton Wanderers	42	20	7	15	68	59	47
Newcastle United	42	18	10	14	59	45	46
Middlesbrough	42	16	14	12	79	69	46
Chelsea	42	17	12	13	40	43	46
Manchester City	42	18	9	15	65	70	45
Sheffield United	42	15	10	17	59	54	40
Sunderland	42	16	8	18	60	62	40
West Bromwich Albion	42	15	10	17	51	63	40
Huddersfield Town	42	15	9	18	53	54	39
Blackburn Rovers	42	13	12	17	54	57	38
Preston North End	42	13	12	17	42	65	38
Arsenal	42	15	7	20	47	56	37
Birmingham	42	15	7	20	48	60	37
Oldham Athletic	42	13	11	18	38	50	37
Everton	42	12	12	18	57	55	36
Bradford City	42	11	10	21	48	72	32
Manchester United	42	8	12	22	41	73	28

Division One

Manager: Frank Richards

Did you know that?

Blues netted only seven goals in their first 10 League games and all were scored by Joe Bradford.

Albert Rawson, signed from Sheffield United, scored in each of his first five League games for Blues, three of his six goals coming against his former club. His presence and performances certainly went a long way in helping the team stave off relegation.

Billy Walker netted two penalties in Aston Villa's 3–0 victory in March.

When losing at Sheffield United in February, Blues suffered a record eighth successive League defeat. Harry Johnson scored four goals for the Blades.

In May, Blues defender Alec McClure was sent off in a friendly against Real Madrid in Spain... for telling his goalkeeper (Dan Tremelling) where to stand when facing a penalty!

Match No.	Date	Venue	Opponents	Result		Scorers	Attendance
1	Aug 26	A	Chelsea	D	1-1	Bradford	40,00
2	28	H	Newcastle United	L	0-2		35,00
3	Sep 2	H	Chelsea	L	0-1		35,00
4	6	H	Newcastle United	D	0-0		35,00
5	9	A	Manchester City	W	1-0	Bradford	25,00
6	13	H	Stoke	W	2-0	Bradford 2	20,00
7	16	H	Manchester City	L	0-1		30,00
8	23	A	Bolton Wanderers	L	0-3		17,68
9	30	H	Bolton Wanderers	W	2-0	Bradford 2	25,00
10	Oct 7	A	Blackburn Rovers	D	1-1	Bradford	25,00
11	14	H	Blackburn Rovers	D	1-1	Whitehouse	30,00
12	21	A	Middlesbrough	L	1-2	Whitehouse	15,00
13	28	H	Middlesbrough	W	2-0	Bradford, Foxall	25,00
14	Nov 4	H	Cardiff City	D	0-0		30,00
15	11	A	Cardiff City	D	1-1	Watkins	25,00
16	18	H	Nottingham Forest	W	2-0	Bradford, Linley	30,00
17	25	A	Nottingham Forest	D	1-1	Bradford	15,00
18	Dec 2	H	Arsenal	W	3-2	Foxall, Linley 2	29,77
19	9	A	Arsenal	L	0-1		30,00
20	16	H	Everton	D	1-1	Foxall	20,00
21	23	A	Everton	L	1-2	Bradford	20,00
22	25	H	Huddersfield Town	D	0-0		20,00
23	26	A	Huddersfield Town	L	0-4		20,00
24	30	A	Sunderland	L	3-5	Bradford, Whitehouse 2	12,00
25	Jan 6	H	Sunderland	L	1-2	Barratt	30,00
26	20	H	West Bromwich Albion	L	0-2		32,18
27	27	A	West Bromwich Albion	L	0-1		25,12
28	Feb 3	A	Oldham Athletic	L	0-2		9,00
29	10	H	Oldham Athletic	L	2-3	Bradford 2	8,54
30	17	A	Sheffield United	L	1-7	Rawson	12,00
31	Mar 3	A	Preston North End	W	3-2	Rawson, Bradford, Crosbie	12,00
32	10	H	Preston North End	W	1-0	Rawson	30,00
33	12	H	Sheffield United	W	4-2	Rawson 2, Dawes, Bradford	12,00
34	17	H	Aston Villa	W	1-0	Rawson	50,00
35	24	A	Aston Villa	L	0-3		40,00
36	31	H	Liverpool	L	0-1		35,00
37	Apr 2	A	Stoke	D	0-0		22,00
38	7	A	Liverpool	D	0-0		28,00
39	14	H	Tottenham Hotspur	W	2-1	Rawson, McClure	25,00
40	21	A	Tottenham Hotspur	L	0-2		16,35
41	28	H	Burnley	W	1-0	Bradford	19,40
42	May 5	A	Burnley	W	2-0	Bradford, Rawson	10,00
						Appearance	
						Goal	

FA Cup

R1	Jan 13	A	Huddersfield Town	L	1-2	Bradford	27,30
						Appearance	
						Goal	

Birmingham — Appearances and goals grid (player columns left to right):

Tremelling RD · Womack F · Jones JW · Liddall GM · McClure A · Barton PH · Barratt J · Crosbie JA · Bradford J · Whitehouse JC · Foxall FH · Daws J · Dale RA · Sharp F · Linley E · Waddell GB · Watkiss ET · Bettbury CE · Hunter W · Ashurst EA · Thompson L · Rawson AN · Samson AA · Clark W · Harvey WHT · Lane MAE

Tre	Wom	Jon	Lid	McC	Bar PH	Bar J	Cro	Bra	Whi	Fox	Daw	Dal	Sha	Lin	Wad	Wat	Bet	Hun	Ash	Tho	Raw	Sam	Cla	Har	Lan
	2	3	4	5	6	7	8	9	10	11															
	2	3	4	5	6	7	8	9	10	11															
	2	3	6	5		7	8	9	10	11	4														
	2	3		5		7	8	9					4		6	10	11								
	2	3	4	5		7	8	9							6	10	11								
	2	3	4	5		7	8	9							6	10	11								
	2	3	4	5	6	7	8	9								10	11								
	2	3	4	5	6	7	8	9								10	11								
	2	3	4	5	6	7	8	9	10	11															
	2	3	4	5	6	7	8	9	10	11															
	2	3	6	5		7	8	9	10	11			4												
	2	3	6	5		7	8	9	10	11			4												
	2	3	6	5		7	8	9	10	11		4													
	2	3	6	5		7	8	9		4				11		10									
	2	3		5	6		8		9		4			11		10	7								
	2	3		5	6	8	9				4			11		10	7								
	2	3		5	6	8	9				4			11		10	7								
	2	3		5	6		9			11	4					10	8	7							
	2	3		5	6	8	9			11	4					10		7							
	2	3		5	6		9			11	4					10	8	7							
	2	3		5	6		9	8		11	4					10		7							
	2	3		6			9	8		11	5	4				10		7							
	2	3		6		8	9	11		5						10			7	4					
	2	3		6	7		9	8	11	5	4					10									
		3		5	6	7		9	8	11	4					10				2					
		3	6	5		7	8	9	10		4					11				2					
		3	6	5			9	8	11		4					10		7	2						
		3		5	6	8		9	10		4					10		7	2		11				
	2	3	6	5	10		9				4	8				11		7							
	2	3		5	6	8	10				4			11				7			9				
		3		5	6	8	10	11			4							7		2	9	1				
		3		5	6	8	10				4							7		2	9		11			
		3		5	6	8	10			4										2	9		11	7		
		3		5	6	8	10			4										2	9		11	7		
		3		5	6	7	8	10			4									2	9		11			
3			5	6		8				4					10				2	9		11	7		
	3	5		6		8				4					10				2	9		11	7		
		3		5	6	8	10			4										2	9		11	7		
		3	6	5		8	10			4				11						2	9			7		
		3	4	5	6	8	10							11						2	9			7		
		3		5	6		9				4			11						2	8	1		7	10	
		3		5	6		9				4			11						2	8			7	10	
27	41	19	38	31	18	32	39	16	17	15	22	5	26	2	8	15	1	16	1	13	2	7	9	2	
		1			1	1	18	4	3	1						3		1		8						

Tre	Wom	Jon	Lid	McC	Bar PH	Bar J	Cro	Bra	Whi	Fox	Daw	Dal	Sha	Lin	Wad	Wat	Bet	Hun	Ash	Tho	Raw	Sam	Cla	Har	Lan
	3		5	6	11	8	9	7			4			10				2							
	1		1	1	1	1	1	1			1			1				1							
								1																	

League Table

	P	W	D	L	F	A	Pts
Liverpool	42	26	8	8	70	31	60
Sunderland	42	22	10	10	72	54	54
Huddersfield Town	42	21	11	10	60	32	53
Newcastle United	42	18	12	12	45	37	48
Everton	42	20	7	15	63	59	47
Aston Villa	42	18	10	14	64	51	46
West Bromwich Albion	42	17	11	14	58	49	45
Manchester City	42	17	11	14	50	49	45
Cardiff City	42	18	7	17	73	59	43
Sheffield United	42	16	10	16	68	64	42
Arsenal	42	16	10	16	61	62	42
Tottenham Hotspur	42	17	7	18	50	50	41
Bolton Wanderers	42	14	12	16	50	58	40
Blackburn Rovers	42	14	12	16	47	62	40
Burnley	42	16	6	20	58	59	38
Preston North End	42	13	11	18	60	64	37
Birmingham	42	13	11	18	41	57	37
Middlesbrough	42	13	10	19	57	63	36
Chelsea	42	9	18	15	45	53	36
Nottingham Forest	42	13	8	21	41	70	34
Stoke	42	10	10	22	47	67	30
Oldham Athletic	42	10	10	22	35	65	30

Division One

Manager: Billy Beer

Match No.	Date		Venue	Opponents	Result		Scorers	Attendance
1	Aug	25	H	Aston Villa	W	3-0	Bradford 2, Lane	41,30
2		29	A	Liverpool	L	2-6	Bradford 2	15,00
3	Sep	1	A	Aston Villa	D	0-0		59,15
4		5	H	Liverpool	W	2-1	Lane, Bradford	30,00
5		8	H	Sunderland	L	0-2		40,00
6		10	H	Bolton Wanderers	L	0-3		15,00
7		15	A	Sunderland	D	1-1	Rawson	28,00
8		22	H	Arsenal	L	0-2		20,00
9		29	A	Arsenal	D	0-0		35,00
10	Oct	6	H	Blackburn Rovers	D	1-1	Bradford	24,00
11		13	A	Blackburn Rovers	L	1-4	Bradford	20,00
12		20	H	Huddersfield Town	L	0-1		20,00
13		27	A	Huddersfield Town	L	0-1		10,00
14	Nov	3	A	West Ham United	L	1-4	Bradford	20,00
15		10	H	West Ham United	W	2-0	Bradford, Islip	30,00
16		17	H	Notts County	D	0-0		15,00
17		24	A	Notts County	D	1-1	Bradford	14,00
18	Dec	1	A	Everton	L	0-2		18,00
19		8	H	Everton	L	0-1		15,00
20		15	A	West Bromwich Albion	D	0-0		24,78
21		22	H	West Bromwich Albion	D	0-0		14,00
22		26	H	Manchester City	W	3-0	Lane, Bradford, Harvey	35,00
23		29	A	Tottenham Hotspur	D	1-1	Bradford (pen)	25,00
24	Jan	1	A	Bolton Wanderers	D	1-1	Cringan	35,00
25		5	H	Tottenham Hotspur	W	3-2	Bradford, Cringan, Lane	25,00
26		19	H	Nottingham Forest	L	0-2		15,00
27		26	A	Nottingham Forest	D	1-1	Islip	12,00
28	Feb	9	A	Burnley	W	2-1	Cringan, Bradford	10,00
29		16	H	Middlesbrough	W	2-1	Bradford 2	20,00
30		23	A	Middlesbrough	W	1-0	Islip	15,00
31		27	H	Burnley	W	2-1	Bradford 2	14,50
32	Mar	1	H	Preston North End	W	2-0	Bradford 2	20,00
33		8	A	Preston North End	L	0-1		17,00
34		15	A	Chelsea	D	1-1	Ashurst	30,00
35		22	H	Chelsea	W	1-0	Briggs	25,00
36	Apr	5	H	Newcastle United	W	4-1	Bradford 2, Crosbie, Linley	20,00
37		9	A	Newcastle United	L	1-2	Bradford	8,00
38		12	A	Sheffield United	W	2-0	Bradford, Linley	8,00
39		18	A	Manchester City	L	0-1		30,00
40		19	H	Sheffield United	L	0-1		15,00
41		26	A	Cardiff City	L	0-2		15,00
42	May	3	H	Cardiff City	D	0-0		33,14
							Appearance	
							Goa	

FA Cup								
R1	Jan	12	A	Huddersfield Town	L	0-1		30,92
							Appearance	

Appearances and goals grid (1923–24)

Willig RD	Ashurst EA	Jones JW	Dale RA	McClure A	Barton PH	Harvey WHT	Crosbie JA	Bradford J	Lane MAE	Clark W	Womack F	Davis J	Rawson AN	Crispin JA	Phoenix AE	Linley E	Liddell GM	Islip E	Briggs GR	Hoyland W	Hunter W	Russell CJ	Dixon DP	Harris WN
2	3	4	5	6	7	8	9	10	11															
2	3	4	5	6	7	8	9	10	11															
	3	4	5	6	7	8	9	10	11	2														
	3	4	5	6	7	8	9	10	11	2														
	3	4	5	6	7	8	9	10	11	2														
	3	4	5	6	7	8	9	10	11	2														
	3		5		6	7		9		11	2		4		8	10								
	3	4	5	6	7		9			11	2				8	10								
	3		5		6	7	8			11	2		4	9		10								
	3		5		6	7		9		11	2		4	8		10								
2	3		5	6	7		9		11		4	8		10										
2	3		5	6	7	8		11		9		10	4											
2			6	7	8	9	10	11	3			5			4									
2		4		6	7	8	9	10	11	3			5											
2			6	7	8	9		11	3	4	5				10									
2			6	7	8	9		11	3	4	5				10									
2			6	7	8	9		11	3	4	5				10									
2			6	7	8	9		11	3	4	5				10									
2		4	6	7		9	11		3		5	8			10									
2		4	6	7	8	9		11	3		5				10									
2		4	6	7	8	9		11	3		5				10									
2		4	6	7		9	8		3		5	11			10									
2	3	4	6	7		9	8				5	11			10									
2		4	6	7		9	8		3		5	11			10									
2		4	6	7		9			3		5	11			10	8								
2	3	4	6			9					5	11			10	8	7							
2		4	6		8	9		11	3		5				10		7							
2		4	6		8	9		11	3		5				10		7							
2		4	6		8	9		11	3		5				10		7							
2		4	6		8	9		11	3		5				10		7							
	3	4	6	7	8	9		11	2		5				10									
	3	4	6	7	8	9			2		5	11			10									
9	3	4	6	7	8	9			2		5	11			10									
2	3	4	6	7	8						5	11			10	9								
2	3	4	6	7	8	9					5	11			10									
2		4		7	8	9		3			5	11			10			6						
2		4		7	8	9					5	11			10									
2	3	4		7	8	9					5	11	6				10							
	4		7	8			3			5	11	6	9				10	2						
2		6		8	9		3			5	11	4	10		7									
2	3	4	6		8	9		3			5	11			10				7					
31	22	34	9	39	35	31	37	13	25	31	8	6	31	3	18	6	27	3	6	1	2	1	1	
1			1	1	24	4			1	3		2		3	1									

Willig RD	Ashurst EA	Jones JW	Dale RA	McClure A	Barton PH	Harvey WHT	Crosbie JA	Bradford J	Lane MAE	Clark W	Womack F	Davis J	Rawson AN	Crispin JA	Phoenix AE	Linley E	Liddell GM	Islip E	Briggs GR	Hoyland W	Hunter W	Russell CJ	Dixon DP	Harris WN
2		4		6	7		9	8		3		5		11		10								
1		1		1	1		1	1		1		1		1		1								

League Table

	P	W	D	L	F	A	Pts
Huddersfield Town	42	23	11	8	60	33	57
Cardiff City	42	22	13	7	61	34	57
Sunderland	42	22	9	11	71	54	53
Bolton Wanderers	42	18	14	10	68	34	50
Sheffield United	42	19	12	11	69	49	50
Aston Villa	42	18	13	11	52	37	49
Everton	42	18	13	11	62	53	49
Blackburn Rovers	42	17	11	14	54	50	45
Newcastle United	42	17	10	15	60	54	44
Notts County	42	14	14	14	44	49	42
Manchester City	42	15	12	15	54	71	42
Liverpool	42	15	11	16	49	48	41
West Ham United	42	13	15	14	40	43	41
Birmingham	42	13	13	16	41	49	39
Tottenham Hotspur	42	12	14	16	50	56	38
West Bromwich Albion	42	12	14	16	51	62	38
Burnley	42	12	12	18	55	60	36
Preston North End	42	12	10	20	52	67	34
Arsenal	42	12	9	21	40	63	33
Nottingham Forest	42	10	12	20	42	64	32
Chelsea	42	9	14	19	31	53	32
Middlesbrough	42	7	8	27	37	60	22

Division One

Manager: Billy Beer

Match No.	Date		Venue	Opponents		Result	Scorers	Attendance
1	Aug	30	H	Everton	D	2-2	Linley, Crosbie	35,0
2	Sep	3	H	Tottenham Hotspur	L	0-2		18,0
3		6	A	Sunderland	L	0-4		25,0
4		8	H	Bolton Wanderers	W	1-0	Howarth (og)	12,0
5		13	H	Cardiff City	W	2-1	Bradford 2	20,0
6		15	H	Notts County	W	1-0	Bradford	12,0
7		20	A	Preston North End	L	0-1		20,0
8		27	H	Burnley	W	1-0	Cringan	20,0
9	Oct	4	A	Leeds United	W	1-0	Islip	24,0
10		11	H	Aston Villa	W	1-0	Islip	48,0
11		18	A	West Bromwich Albion	D	1-1	Islip	35,6
12		25	A	Huddersfield Town	W	1-0	Bradford	18,0
13	Nov	1	H	Blackburn Rovers	D	1-1	Bradford	10,0
14		8	A	West Ham United	W	1-0	Bradford (pen)	30,0
15		15	H	Sheffield United	D	1-1	Crosbie	27,0
16		22	A	Newcastle United	L	0-4		30,0
17		29	H	Liverpool	W	5-2	Bradford 3 (1 pen), Barton, Islip	30,0
18	Dec	6	A	Nottingham Forest	D	1-1	Bradford (pen)	10,0
19		13	H	Bury	L	0-1		20,0
20		20	A	Manchester City	D	2-2	Bradford, Islip	40,
21		25	H	Arsenal	W	2-1	Crosbie, Islip	36,0
22		26	A	Arsenal	W	1-0	Islip	40,0
23		27	A	Everton	L	1-2	Islip	30,0
24	Jan	1	A	Bolton Wanderers	L	0-3		27,0
25		3	H	Sunderland	W	2-1	Crosbie, Barton	30,0
26		17	A	Cardiff City	L	0-1		8,0
27		24	H	Preston North End	W	3-0	Linley, Briggs 2	20,0
28	Feb	2	A	Burnley	L	2-3	Briggs, Devlin	6,0
29		7	H	Leeds United	D	0-0		26,0
30		14	A	Aston Villa	L	0-1		60,0
31		28	H	Huddersfield Town	L	0-1		12,0
32	Mar	14	H	West Ham United	D	1-1	Crosbie	20,0
33		16	H	West Bromwich Albion	D	0-0		20,0
34		21	A	Sheffield United	L	3-4	Islip, Briggs, Liddell	16,0
35		28	A	Newcastle United	D	1-1	Cringan	36,0
36	Apr	2	A	Blackburn Rovers	L	1-7	Islip	3,
37		4	A	Liverpool	D	1-1	Briggs	18,0
38		10	A	Tottenham Hotspur	W	1-0	Crosbie	30,4
39		11	H	Nottingham Forest	D	1-1	Briggs	20,0
40		18	A	Bury	W	4-1	Briggs 2, Scriven, Crosbie	12,0
41		25	H	Manchester City	W	2-1	Scriven, Crosbie	15,0
42	May	2	A	Notts County	W	1-0	Islip	8,0

							Appearanc
				One own-goal			Go

FA Cup

	Date		Venue	Opponents		Result	Scorers	Attendance
R1	Jan	10	H	Chelsea	W	2-0	Briggs 2	32,0
R2		31	H	Stockport County	W	1-0	Harris	36,0
R3	Feb	21	A	Liverpool	L	1-2	Briggs	44,0

							Appearanc
							Go

	Windling DR	Ashurst E	Jones JW	Dale R	Cringan J	Barton P	Harvey W	Crosbie J	Bradford J	Islip E	Linley E	Womack F	Morgan J	Liddell G	Devlin T	Russell J	Scriven A	Harris WJ	Harvey E	Briggs G	Bruce H	Dixon D	Hunter W	Sykes A
		2	3	4		5	6	7	8	9	10	11												
		2	3	4		5	6	7	8	9	10	11												
			3	4			6	7	8	9	10	11	2	5										
			3			5	6	7		9			2		4	8	10	11						
			3			5	6	7	8	9			2		4		10	11						
		2	3			5	6	7	8	9			2		4		10	11						
	9		3			5	6		8	10			2		4			11	7					
			3			5	6	7	8	9	10		2		4			11						
			3			5	6	7	8	9	10		2		4			11						
			3			5	6	7	8	9	10		2		4			11						
			3			5	6	7	8	9	10		2		4			11						
			3			5	6	7	8	9	10		2		4			11						
			3			5	6		8	9	10		2		4			11	7					
			3			5	6		8	9	10		2		4			11	7					
	7		3			5	6		8	9	10	11	2		4									
			3			5	6		8	9	10	11	2		4		7							
			3			5	6		8	9	10	11	2		4		7							
	2		3	4	5			8	9		11		6		10		7							
			3			5	6		8	9	10	11	2		4		7							
			3			5	6		8	9	10	11	2		4		7							
			3			5	6		8		10	11	2		4		7		9					
			3			5	6		8		10	11	2		4		7		9					
			3	5			6		8	9	10	11	2		4		7							
			3	5			6		8	9	10	11	2		4		7							
			3	6	5				8			11	2		4		10		9					
			3	6	5				8		10		2		4		11	7	9					
			3	6	5				8			11	2	10			7		9	4				
			3	6	5		7	8			10	11	2		4				9					
			3	6	5				8		10	11	2		4		7		9					
	2		3	6	5			8	10		11		4				7		9					
		6	3		5			8			10	11	3		4			7	9		2			
			3	6	5			8			10	11	2		4				7	9				
			3	6	5			8			10	11	2		4				7	9				
			3	4	5	6		8			10	11	2						7	9				
			3	6				8			10		2		4		11		7	9		5		
			3	6				8			10		2		4		11		7	9		5		
			3	6				8			10		2		4		11		7	9		5		
			3	6				8			10		2		4		11		7	9		5		
			3	6				8			10		2		4		11		7	9		5		
			3					8			10		2		4		11		7	9		5	6	
	7	41	22	33	25	13	40	24	34	24	37	1	37	2	5	19	16	12	19	1	1	6	1	
			2	2			8	11	11	2			1	1		2			8					
			3			5	6		8			10	11	2		4				7		9		
			3			5	6		8			10		2		4		11	7			9		
			3	6	5				8	10	11	2		4				7			9			
			3	1	3	2		2	1	2	3	3		3				1	3			3		
																			1			3		

Division One

Manager: Billy Beer

In the League away against Aston Villa in October, Blues trailed 3–0 with 11 minutes to play but fought back to earn a point, equalising with just 30 seconds remaining.

Outside-left Louis Page, playing as an emergency centre-forward, scored six goals for Burnley in their 7–1 win at St Andrew's in April. This was Blues' heaviest home defeat at that time, eventually repeated by West Bromwich Albion in 1960.

Goalkeeper Harry Hibbs made his League for Blues in the 3–0 defeat by Arsenal on the last day of the season.

In September, Blues beat Real Madrid 3–0 in a friendly at St Andrew's.

Blues and Coventry City drew 2–2 in the final of the Lord Mayor of Coventry Charity Cup. Each club held the trophy for six months.

Match No.	Date		Venue	Opponents	Result		Scorers	Attendance
1	Aug	29	A	Sunderland	L	1-3	Bradford	27,2
2		31	H	Manchester City	W	1-0	Bradford	17,56
3	Sep	5	H	Blackburn Rovers	W	2-0	Islip, Bradford	14,20
4		9	A	Everton	D	2-2	Harris, Islip	15,8
5		12	A	Bury	L	1-2	Bradford	16,0
6		16	H	Huddersfield Town	L	1-3	Scriven	16,3
7		19	H	Notts County	L	0-1		3,9
8		21	H	Everton	W	3-1	Bradford 2, Briggs	8,9
9		26	H	West Bromwich Albion	W	3-0	Islip 2, Briggs	26,48
10	Oct	3	A	Sheffield United	L	1-4	Bradford	23,1
11		10	H	Cardiff City	W	3-2	Crosbie, Bradford, Briggs	24,3
12		17	A	Aston Villa	D	3-3	Bradford 2, Spiers (og)	52,25
13		24	H	Leicester City	D	1-1	Islip	28,0
14		31	A	Newcastle United	W	3-1	Islip 2, Crosbie	26,4
15	Nov	7	H	Bolton Wanderers	L	0-1		22,1
16		14	A	Manchester United	L	1-3	Crosbie	23,5
17		21	H	Liverpool	W	2-0	Briggs, Crosbie	17,0
18	Dec	5	H	Leeds United	W	2-1	Scriven, Crosbie	13,4
19		7	A	Burnley	L	1-3	Briggs	5,8
20		12	A	West Ham United	D	2-2	Cringan (pen), Bradford	12,7
21		19	H	Arsenal	W	1-0	Briggs	26,8
22		25	H	Tottenham Hotspur	W	3-1	Bradford 3	29,5
23		26	A	Tottenham Hotspur	L	1-2	Bradford	44,4
24		28	A	Huddersfield Town	L	1-4	Bradford	16,5
25	Jan	1	A	Bolton Wanderers	L	3-5	Bradford 2, Harris	22,2
26		2	H	Sunderland	W	2-1	Briggs, Russell	22,4
27		16	A	Blackburn Rovers	D	4-4	Bradford 3, Harris	14,7
28		23	H	Bury	L	2-3	Briggs, Crosbie	12,7
29	Feb	6	A	West Bromwich Albion	L	1-5	Harris	23,2
30		13	H	Sheffield United	W	2-0	Linley, Briggs	15,7
31		20	A	Cardiff City	L	0-2		18,8
32		27	H	Aston Villa	W	2-1	Briggs 2	38,2
33	Mar	3	A	Notts County	L	0-3		8,1
34		6	A	Leicester City	L	0-1		23,5
35		13	H	Newcastle United	D	1-1	Crosbie	24,3
36	Apr	2	A	Manchester City	W	4-2	Briggs 2, Linley, Crosbie	49,9
37		3	A	Liverpool	D	2-2	Bradford 2 (1 pen)	24,8
38		10	H	Burnley	L	1-7	Bradford	16,6
39		17	A	Leeds United	D	0-0		12,1
40		19	H	Manchester United	W	2-1	Bradford, Jones	8,9
41		24	H	West Ham United	W	1-0	Bradford	12,5
42	May	1	A	Arsenal	L	0-3		22,2
							Appearanc	
							One own-goal	Goa

FA Cup

R3	Jan	9	H	Grimsby Town	W	2-0	Russell, Briggs	36,0
R4		30	A	South Shields	L	1-2	Bradford (pen)	17,0
							Appearanc	
							Goa	

Womack F	Jones JW	Liddell GM	Cringan JA	Barton PH	Briggs GR	Crosbie JA	Bradford J	Islip E	Linley E	Hunter W	Dale RA	Scriven A	Harris WN	Bowden F	Russell CJ	Ashurst EA	Bruce H	Castle FC	Hibbs HE
2	3	4	5	6	7	8	9	10	11										
2	3	4	5	6	7	8	9	10	11										
2	3	4			7	8	9	10		5	6	11							
2	3			6		8	9	10		5	4	11	7						
2	3	4				8	9	10		5	6	11	7						
2	3	4	5	6	9	8		10				11	7						
2	3	4	5	6	9	8	10					11	7						
2	3	4	5	6	10	8	9					11	7						
2	3	4	5	6	10	8	9	11					7						
2	3	4	5	6	10	8	9	11					7						
2	3	4	5	6	10	8	9	11					7						
2	3	4	5	6	10	8	9	11					7						
2	3	4	5	6	10	8	9	11					7						
2	3	4	5		11	8	9	10			6		7						
2	3	4	5		11	8	9	10			6		7						
2	3	4	5		11	8	9	10			6		7						
2	3	4	5		10	8	9				6	11	7						
2	3	4	5		9	8			10		6	11	7						
2	3		5	6	9	8			10		4	11	7						
2	3	4	5		10	8	9				6	11	7						
2	3	4	5		10	8	9				6	11	7						
2	3	4	5		10	8	9				6	11	7						
2	3	4	5			8	9		10		6		7	11					
2	3	4		6	10	8	9			5			7		11				
		4		3	8		9		10	5	6		7		11	2			
	3	4		6	10	8	9			5			7		11	2			
2	3	4	5	6	10	8	9						7		11				
2	3	4	5	6	10	8	9						7		11				
3		4	5		9	8		10			6		7		11	2			
2	3	4			9	8			10	5	6		7		11				
2	3	4		6	9	8			10	5			7		11				
2	3	4			9	8			10	5	6		7		11				
2	3			6	9	8			10	5	4		7		11				
2	3	4			9	8			10	5	6		7		11				
2	3	4	9			8			10	5	6		7		11				
2	3	4			9	8	10		11	5	6		7						
2	3	4	8		9		10		11	5	6		7						
2	3	4			9	8	10		11	5	6		7						
2	3	4		5		8	9				6	11	7		10				
	2	4		3		8	9			5		11	7		10		6		
2	3	4	5			8	10			6		11	7					9	
2	3	4	5			8	10		11	6			7					9	1
39	40	39	27	21	34	40	32	15	16	18	24	15	39	1	14	3	1	2	1
	1		1		13	8	26	7	2			2	4		1				

Womack F	Jones JW	Liddell GM	Cringan JA	Barton PH	Briggs GR	Crosbie JA	Bradford J	Islip E	Linley E	Hunter W	Dale RA	Scriven A	Harris WN	Bowden F	Russell CJ	Ashurst EA	Bruce H	Castle FC	Hibbs HE
	3	4		6	10	8	9			5			7		11	2			
	3	4	5		11	8	9	10			6		7			2			
	2	2	1	1	2	2	2	1		1	1		2		1	2			
					1		1								1				

League Table

	P	W	D	L	F	A	Pts
Huddersfield Town	42	23	11	8	92	60	57
Arsenal	42	22	8	12	87	63	52
Sunderland	42	21	6	15	96	80	48
Bury	42	20	7	15	85	77	47
Sheffield United	42	19	8	15	102	82	46
Aston Villa	42	16	12	14	86	76	44
Liverpool	42	14	16	12	70	63	44
Bolton Wanderers	42	17	10	15	75	76	44
Manchester United	42	19	6	17	66	73	44
Newcastle United	42	16	10	16	84	75	42
Everton	42	12	18	12	72	70	42
Blackburn Rovers	42	15	11	16	91	80	41
West Bromwich Albion	42	16	8	18	79	78	40
Birmingham	42	16	8	18	66	81	40
Tottenham Hotspur	42	15	9	18	66	79	39
Cardiff City	42	16	7	19	61	76	39
Leicester City	42	14	10	18	70	80	38
West Ham United	42	15	7	20	63	76	37
Leeds United	42	14	8	20	64	76	36
Burnley	42	13	10	19	85	108	36
Manchester City	42	12	11	19	89	100	35
Notts County	42	13	7	22	54	74	33

Division One

Manager: Billy Beer (to March), then Bill Harvey

Blues gave a club debut to right-back Joe Smith in September. Signed from neighbours West Bromwich Albion four months earlier, he had made 471 appearances for the Baggies in 16 years, won a League championship medal in 1920 and played three times for England, once in a Victory international.

In 27 of the 44 first-class games played by Blues this season, either Joe Bradford or George Briggs or both featured on the scoresheet.

Briggs was absent only once this season. He suffered concussion in the first game against Blackburn Rovers and was replaced by Fred Castle for the second, a 5–2 defeat at Leicester.

Centre-half Eli Wood made his only appearance for Blues this season. Replacing Jimmy Cringan, he had a nightmare in the 3–0 defeat by Arsenal in April.

Harry Hibbs conceded six goals in his only League appearance this season at Tottenham, having let in three in his previous game for the club at Arsenal.

Match No.	Date		Venue	Opponents	Result		Scorers	Attendance
1	Aug	28	H	Blackburn Rovers	W	3-1	Briggs, Bradford 2	24,09
2		30	A	Leicester City	L	2-5	Bradford, Harris	23,88
3	Sep	4	H	Huddersfield Town	W	2-0	Bradford 2	19,89
4		11	H	Sunderland	W	2-0	Briggs 2	28,03
5		13	H	Sheffield Wednesday	D	0-0		13,67
6		18	A	West Bromwich Albion	W	2-1	Briggs 2	26,69
7		20	H	Everton	W	1-0	Briggs	11,41
8		25	H	Bury	D	2-2	Briggs 2	24,00
9	Oct	2	A	Bolton Wanderers	L	0-1		20,00
10		9	A	Tottenham Hotspur	L	1-6	Bradford	29,39
11		16	H	Derby County	W	1-0	Harris	23,14
12		23	A	Manchester United	W	1-0	Harris	32,01
13		30	H	Aston Villa	L	1-2	Crosbie	48,10
14	Nov	6	A	Cardiff City	L	0-1		10,59
15		13	H	Burnley	W	1-0	Bradford	11,20
16		20	A	Newcastle United	L	1-5	Briggs	30,05
17		27	H	Leeds United	W	2-0	Harris, Bradford	19,70
18	Dec	4	A	Liverpool	L	1-2	Briggs	27,88
19		11	H	Arsenal	D	0-0		22,98
20		18	A	Sheffield United	L	3-4	Briggs, Harris, Bradford	19,09
21		25	A	West Ham United	L	0-1		27,98
22		27	H	West Ham United	L	0-2		39,20
23	Jan	1	A	Leicester City	W	2-1	Bradford 2	31,27
24		15	A	Blackburn Rovers	L	2-3	Islip, Scriven	10,17
25		22	H	Huddersfield Town	L	1-3	Thirlaway	16,77
26	Feb	5	H	West Bromwich Albion	W	1-0	Bradford	29,68
27		12	A	Bury	L	1-3	Islip	11,95
28		16	A	Sunderland	L	1-4	Briggs	10,52
29		26	H	Tottenham Hotspur	W	1-0	Cringan	21,14
30	Mar	5	A	Derby County	L	1-4	Crosbie	15,15
31		12	H	Manchester United	W	4-0	Bradford 2, Crosbie, Scriven	14,39
32		19	A	Aston Villa	L	2-4	Bond, Scriven	49,33
33	Apr	2	A	Burnley	W	2-0	Bradford, Crosbie	12,67
34		4	H	Bolton Wanderers	W	6-1	Crosbie 2, Bradford, Briggs, Scriven, Cringan	6,32
35		9	H	Newcastle United	W	2-0	Bradford, Bond	27,91
36		16	A	Leeds United	L	1-2	Bradford	18,70
37		18	A	Everton	L	1-3	Taylor (og)	32,88
38		19	A	Sheffield Wednesday	D	4-4	Scriven, Bradford, Liddell, Briggs	17,72
39		23	H	Liverpool	W	3-0	Briggs, Bradford, Bond	14,91
40		27	H	Cardiff City	L	1-2	Bradford	23,68
41		30	A	Arsenal	L	0-3		22,61
42	May	7	H	Sheffield United	L	2-3	Bradford, Biggs	10,95

Appearance
One own-goal Goal

FA Cup

R3	Jan	8	H	Manchester City	W	4-1	Bradford, Islip, Crosbie, Briggs	39,50
R4		29	A	Southampton	L	1-4	Briggs	15,80

Appearance
Goal

Player appearance and goalscoring grid (shirt numbers by match). Column headers read vertically:

Walling RD	Womack F	Jones JW	Liddell DM	Cringan JA	Barton PH	Harris WW	Crosbie JA	Briggs GR	Bradford J	Thirlaway WJ	Castle FC	Dale RA	Smith J	Russell CJ	Hibbs HE	Hunter W	Scriven A	Islip E	Bond B	Owen W	Harvey E	Bruce H	Oates AW	Leslie AJ	Wood EE	Isherwood H
2	3	4	5	6		7	8	9	10	11																
2	3	4	5	6		7	8		10	11	9															
2	3	4				7	8	9	10	11		6														
2	3	4	5			7	8	9	10	11		6														
2	3	4	5			7	8	9	10	11		6														
2	3	4	5			7	8	9	10	11		6														
	3	4	5			7	8	9		11		6	2	10												
	3	4	5			7	8	9		11		6	2	10												
	3	4	5			7	8	9		11		6	2	10												
	3	4	5			7	8	9		11		6	2	10	1											
	4	5	3			7	8	9	10	11		6	2													
	4	5	3			7	8	9	10	11		6	2													
	4	5	3			7	8	9	10	11		6	2													
	4	5	3			7	8	9	10	11		6	2													
	4		3			7	8	9	10	11		6	2		5											
	4		3			7	8	9	10	11		6	2		5											
	4		3			7	8	9	10	11		6	2		5											
	4		3			7	8	9	10	11		6	2		5											
	4	5	3			7	8	9	10			6	2			11										
	4	5	3			7	8	9	10			6	2			11										
3		4			6	7	8	9	10			2				11										
3		4			6		8	9		7		2				10	11									
2	3	4	5	6			8	9	10							11	7									
2	3	4	5	6			8	9								11	10	7	1							
2	3	4	5	6			8	9	11							10		7	1							
2		4	5	3			8		10	9		6				11	7	1								
2		4	5	3			8	9				6		11		10	7	1								
2			5	3			8		10	9						11	7	1		4						
2		4	5	3			8	9	11			6					7		10							
2		4	5	3			8		10	9	11		6				7									
2		4	5	3			8		10	9		6				11		7								
2		4	5	3			8	9				6				11	10	7								
2		4	5	3			8		10	9		6				11		7								
2		4	5	3			8		10	9		6				11		7								
2		4	5	3			8		10	9		6				11		7								
	3	4	5				8		10	9		2				11		7				6				
2		4	5	3			8		10	9						11		7				6				
2		4	5	3	8			10	9							11		7				6				
2		4	5	3			8		10	9						11		7				6				
2		4	5				8		10	9		3				11		7				6				
3		4					8		10	9						11		7			2		6	5		
		4	5				8		10	9						11		7			2		6		3	
26	**14**	**41**	**35**	**30**	**22**	**39**	**41**	**34**	**22**	**1**	**29**	**17**	**6**	**1**	**6**	**17**	**7**	**19**	**5**	**1**	**3**	**1**	**7**	**1**	**1**	**1**
	1	2			5	6	16	22	1			5	2	3												

Walling RD	Womack F	Jones JW	Liddell DM	Cringan JA	Barton PH	Harris WW	Crosbie JA	Briggs GR	Bradford J	Thirlaway WJ	Castle FC	Dale RA	Smith J	Russell CJ	Hibbs HE	Hunter W	Scriven A	Islip E	Bond B	Owen W	Harvey E	Bruce H	Oates AW	Leslie AJ	Wood EE	Isherwood H
2	3	4	5	6			8		10	9						11	7									
2	3	4	5				8	7	9	11		6				10	1									
2	2	2	2	1		2	2	2	1		1		2	1	1											
				1		2	1						1													

League Table

	P	W	D	L	F	A	Pts
Newcastle United	42	25	6	11	96	58	56
Huddersfield Town	42	17	17	8	76	60	51
Sunderland	42	21	7	14	98	70	49
Bolton Wanderers	42	19	10	13	84	62	48
Burnley	42	19	9	14	91	80	47
West Ham United	42	19	8	15	86	70	46
Leicester City	42	17	12	13	85	70	46
Sheffield United	42	17	10	15	74	86	44
Liverpool	42	18	7	17	69	61	43
Aston Villa	42	18	7	17	81	83	43
Arsenal	42	17	9	16	77	86	43
Derby County	42	17	7	18	86	73	41
Tottenham Hotspur	42	16	9	17	76	78	41
Cardiff City	42	16	9	17	55	65	41
Manchester United	42	13	14	15	52	64	40
Sheffield Wednesday	42	15	9	18	75	92	39
Birmingham	42	17	4	21	64	73	38
Blackburn Rovers	42	15	8	19	77	96	38
Bury	42	12	12	18	68	77	36
Everton	42	12	10	20	64	90	34
Leeds United	42	11	8	23	69	88	30
West Bromwich Albion	42	11	8	23	65	86	30

Division One

Manager: Bill Harvey

Joe Bradford's four goals in the 4–4 draw at Blackburn in September were all scored with powerful right-foot shots. The Blues striker also hit a post and had two more efforts cleared off the line.

England schoolboy international left-back Ron Stainton was injured on his debut for Blues against Bolton in October. Although he served the club for five years, he never played for the first team again.

Long-serving captain Frank Womack, who had been at the club since 1908, made his 515th and final appearance for Blues in the 2–0 home defeat by Newcastle United in April.

Former Blues player Elias Ashurst died in December after an 18-month illness.

Match No.	Date	Venue	Opponents	Result		Scorers	Attendance
1	Aug 27	A	Tottenham Hotspur	L	0-1		37,40
2	29	H	Huddersfield Town	W	3-1	Bradford 2, Harris	16,4
3	Sep 3	H	Manchester United	D	0-0		25,8
4	7	A	Sunderland	L	2-4	Bond, Bradford	23,0
5	10	A	Everton	L	2-5	Bradford. Briggs	37,3
6	17	H	Cardiff City	L	1-3	Bond	23,7
7	24	A	Blackburn Rovers	D	4-4	Bradford 4	15,3
8	Oct 1	H	Bolton Wanderers	D	1-1	Harris	15,9
9	8	A	Sheffield Wednesday	W	3-2	Briggs 2, Bradford	19,9
10	15	H	Middlesbrough	W	3-2	Bradford, Bloxham, Briggs	17,1
11	22	H	Bury	D	2-2	Harris, Bradford	11,9
12	29	A	Sheffield United	L	1-3	Bond	17,1
13	Nov 5	H	Aston Villa	D	1-1	Crosbie	47,6
14	12	A	Burnley	L	1-2	Bradford	14,6
15	19	H	Arsenal	D	1-1	Crosbie	10,0
16	26	A	Portsmouth	D	2-2	Crosbie 2	18,5
17	Dec 3	H	Leicester City	L	0-2		24,2
18	10	A	Liverpool	W	3-2	Davies, Briggs 2	24,2
19	17	H	West Ham United	L	1-2	Bradford	18,2
20	24	A	Derby County	L	1-4	Bradford	8,5
21	26	H	Sunderland	D	1-1	Davies	20,1
22	31	H	Tottenham Hotspur	W	3-2	Bradford 2, Briggs	11,6
23	Jan 2	A	Newcastle United	D	1-1	Briggs	34,4
24	7	A	Manchester United	D	1-1	Briggs	16,8
25	21	H	Everton	D	2-2	Ellis, Briggs	33,6
26	Feb 4	H	Blackburn Rovers	W	2-1	Bradford 2	21,4
27	11	A	Bolton Wanderers	L	2-3	Bradford, Crosbie	11,7
28	22	A	Cardiff City	L	1-2	Briggs	10,7
29	25	A	Middlesbrough	D	1-1	Firth	18,3
30	Mar 3	A	Bury	W	3-2	Bradford 2, Briggs	13,1
31	7	H	Sheffield Wednesday	W	1-0	Ellis	12,0
32	10	H	Sheffield United	W	4-1	Briggs 3, Bond	22,8
33	17	A	Aston Villa	D	1-1	Bradford	59,3
34	24	H	Burnley	W	4-0	Bradford 3, Crosbie	23,6
35	31	A	Arsenal	D	2-2	Crosbie, Ellis	13,9
36	Apr 7	A	Portsmouth	W	2-0	Bond, Ellis	32,9
37	9	A	Huddersfield Town	L	0-2		28,7
38	10	H	Newcastle United	L	0-2		23,4
39	14	A	Leicester City	L	0-3		17,5
40	21	H	Liverpool	W	2-0	Bradford 2	16,0
41	28	A	West Ham United	D	3-3	Bradford 2, Briggs	17,9
42	May 5	H	Derby County	W	2-1	Curtis, Carr (og)	16,4
						Appearance	
						One own-goal	Goa

FA Cup

R3	Jan 14	H	Peterborough & Fletton	W	4-3	Davies, Bradford 3	38,1
R4	28	A	Wrexham	W	3-1	Randle (pen), Davies 2	12,2
R5	Feb 18	A	Manchester United	L	0-1		52,5
						Appearance	
							Goa

Player columns (left to right):

Tremelling RD · Womack F · Barton PH · Liddell GM · Cringan JA · Leslie AJ · Bond B · Harris WN · Bradford J · Briggs GR · Threlfall W · Smith J · Bruce H · Dale RA · Johnston A · Crosbie JA · Coxford J · Stanton RG · Bloxham A · Firth J · Randle J · Davies SC · Ellis WT · Hibbs HE · Morrall GR · Curtis ER · Pike TE

Trem	Wom	Bart	Lidd	Crin	Lesl	Bond	Harr	Brad	Brig	Thre	Smith	Bruce	Dale	John	Cros	Coxf	Stan	Blox	Firth	Rand	Dav	Ellis	Hibbs	Morr	Curt	Pike
1	2	3	4	5	6	7	8	9	10	11																
1		3	4	5	6	7	8	9	10	11	2															
1		3	4	5	6	7	8	9	10	11	2															
1		3			6	7	8	9	10		2			4	5		11									
1		3	4		6	7	8	9	10		2			5	11											
1		4			6	7	11	9	10		2	3		5		8										
1		4			6	7	8	9	10	11	2	3			5											
1		4			6	7	8	9	10	11	2						5									
1		3	4		6			8	9	10	2			11		5		7								
1		3			6			8	9	10	2		4	11		5		7								
1	3		5	6	7	8	9	10		2		4	11													
1	3	5		6	7		9	10		2		4	11		8											
1	3		5	6	7		9	10		2		4	11	8												
1		5	6	7		9	10		2		4	11	8				3									
1		5	6	7		9	10		2			11	8			3	4									
1		4	6	7			10		2				8	5		3	9	11								
1		5	6			9		2				8	4	7		3	10	11	1							
1		4	5	6		9	7	2				8				3	10	11								
1		4	5	6		9	7	2				8				3	10	11								
2		5	6	7		9						8				3	10	11	4							
2	4	5	6		9	7					8				3	10	11	1								
2	4	5	6	11	9	7					8				3	10		1								
2		5	6	11	9	7					8				3	10		1	4							
2		5	6	8	9	7					8				3	10	11	1	4							
2		5	6		9	7					8				3	10	11		4							
1		5	6		9	7	2				8				3	10	11	1	4							
1		4	5	6		9	7	2				8				3	10	11	1	4						
1		5	6		9	7	2				8				10	3		11	1	4						
1		2	5	6		9	7					8				10	3		11	4						
1	5	2		6		9	7					8				10	3		11	4						
1	5	2		6		9	7					8				10	3		11							
1	5		4	6	7		9		2			8					3		11			10				
1	5	2	4	6			9	7				8					3		11			10				
1	5	2	4	6			9	7				8					3	9	11			10				
1	5	2	4	6	7							8					3		11			10				
1	5	4		6	7			9		2		8					3					10				
1		4		6	11		9	7		2		8	5				3					10				
1	2	5	4		6	11		9	7		2		8				3			8		10				
1		2			6			9	7				8	5				3		11	4	10				
1	5	4		6			9	7	2			8					3					10	11			
1	5	4		6			9	7	2			8					3					10	11			
1	5	4		6	7		10	9	2								3					8	11			
Apps 4	15	16	25	25	42	24	11	37	40	5	27	3	8	9	28	8	1	3	6	29	14	20	8	10	11	3
Goals					5	3	29	16							7						1	1		2	4		1

F.A. Cup

Trem	Wom	Bart	Lidd	Crin	Lesl	Bond	Harr	Brad	Brig	Thre	Smith	Bruce	Dale	John	Cros	Coxf	Stan	Blox	Firth	Rand	Dav	Ellis	Hibbs	Morr	Curt	Pike
1	2			5	6	7		9				8				3	10	11		4						
			5	6			9	7				8				3	10	11	1		4					
	4	5	6			9	7					8				3	10	11	1							
1	1			1	3	3	1		3	2		2				3	3	3	2	2						
								3									1	3								

League Table

	P	W	D	L	F	A	Pts
Everton	42	20	13	9	102	66	53
Huddersfield Town	42	22	7	13	91	68	51
Leicester City	42	18	12	12	96	72	48
Derby County	42	17	10	15	96	83	44
Bury	42	20	4	18	80	80	44
Cardiff City	42	17	10	15	70	80	44
Bolton Wanderers	42	16	11	15	81	66	43
Aston Villa	42	17	9	16	78	73	43
Newcastle United	42	15	13	14	79	81	43
Arsenal	42	13	15	14	82	86	41
Birmingham	42	13	15	14	70	75	41
Blackburn Rovers	42	16	9	17	66	78	41
Sheffield United	42	15	10	17	79	86	40
Sheffield Wednesday	42	13	13	16	81	78	39
Sunderland	42	15	9	18	74	76	39
Liverpool	42	13	13	16	84	87	39
West Ham United	42	14	11	17	81	88	39
Manchester United	42	16	7	19	72	80	39
Burnley	42	16	7	19	82	98	39
Portsmouth	42	16	7	19	66	90	39
Tottenham Hotspur	42	15	8	19	74	86	38
Middlesbrough	42	11	15	16	81	88	37

1928-29

Division One

Manager: Leslie Knighton

Match No.	Date	Venue	Opponents	Result		Scorers	Attendance
1	Aug 25	H	Manchester City	W	4-1	Bond, Bradford, Ellis, Briggs	26,91
2	27	A	Leicester City	L	3-5	Briggs, Crosbie, Ellis	22,589
3	Sep 1	A	Huddersfield Town	D	0-0		19,897
4	8	H	Everton	L	1-3	Briggs	36,069
5	10	H	Leicester City	W	1-0	Briggs	11,449
6	15	A	Arsenal	D	0-0		30,118
7	22	H	Blackburn Rovers	W	4-0	Bradford 2, Briggs 2	23,047
8	29	A	Sunderland	W	4-3	Bradford 3, Bond	26,980
9	Oct 6	H	Derby County	L	1-4	Bond (pen)	27,029
10	13	A	Sheffield Wednesday	L	0-3		21,671
11	20	A	Manchester United	L	0-1		17,522
12	27	H	Aston Villa	L	2-4	Cringan, Bradford	36,26
13	Nov 3	A	Liverpool	W	2-1	Curtis, Bradford	33,647
14	10	H	West Ham United	D	2-2	Bradford, Hicks	17,323
15	17	A	Newcastle United	L	0-1		29,566
16	24	H	Burnley	L	3-6	Briggs, Bradford, Hicks	13,071
17	Dec 1	A	Cardiff City	W	4-1	Hicks 2, Firth, Crosbie	13,691
18	8	H	Sheffield United	D	2-2	Bradford 2	17,760
19	22	H	Leeds United	W	5-1	Bradford 3, Liddell, Hicks	16,05
20	25	H	Bolton Wanderers	L	0-2		31,358
21	26	A	Bolton Wanderers	L	2-6	Pike, Bradford	22,117
22	29	A	Manchester City	W	3-2	Pike 2, Bradford	28,365
23	Jan 5	A	Huddersfield Town	L	1-2	Barkas (pen)	20,042
24	19	A	Everton	W	2-0	Hicks 2	26,273
25	Feb 2	A	Blackburn Rovers	L	1-4	Ellis	13,387
26	9	H	Sunderland	W	1-0	Pike	17,022
27	16	A	Derby County	D	2-2	Bond, Mills	12,522
28	23	H	Sheffield Wednesday	W	4-1	Bond, Mills, Hicks, Bradford	28,599
29	Mar 2	H	Manchester United	D	1-1	Hicks	16,738
30	9	A	Aston Villa	W	2-1	Mills, Crosbie	56,528
31	13	H	Arsenal	D	1-1	Hicks	11,001
32	16	H	Liverpool	D	0-0		20,61
33	20	A	Bury	L	1-3	Bradford	7,296
34	23	A	West Ham United	L	1-2	Firth	15,25
35	29	A	Portsmouth	L	1-3	Ellis	25,136
36	30	H	Newcastle United	D	0-0		21,052
37	Apr 1	H	Portsmouth	W	1-0	Bradford	16,266
38	6	A	Burnley	L	0-4		13,730
39	13	H	Cardiff City	D	0-0		12,997
40	20	A	Sheffield United	L	2-3	Hicks 2	14,382
41	27	H	Bury	W	3-2	Crosbie, Bradford 2	12,905
42	May 4	A	Leeds United	W	1-0	Briggs	8,15

Appearances
Goals

FA Cup

R3	Jan 12	H	Manchester City	W	3-1	Briggs, Bradford 2	25,008
R4	26	A	Chelsea	L	0-1		56,953

Appearances
Goals

Player appearance / shirt-number grid (shirt numbers shown per match; blank = did not play)

Tremelling RD	Liddell GM	Randle J	Cringan JA	Barton PH	Leslie AJ	Bond B	Crosbie JA	Briggs GR	Bradford J	Ellis WT	Frith J	Curtis ER	Dale RA	Hibbs HE	Pike TE	Hicks GW	Cantrell J	Smith J	Birch J	Morrall GR	Barkas E	Mills BR	Horsman W	Riley H
2	3	4	5	6	7	8	9	10	11															
2	3	4	5	6	7	8	9		11	10														
2	3	4	5	6	7	8	9	10	11															
2	3	4	5	6	7	8	9		11	10														
2	3	4	5	6	7	8	9		11		10													
2	3	5		6	7	8	9		11		10	4												
2	3	5		6	7	8	9	10	11			4	1											
2	3	5		6	7	8	9	10	11			4												
2	3	5		6	7	8	9	10	11			4												
2	3	5		6	7	8	9		11		10	4												
2	3	5		6	7	8	9	10				4	1	11										
2	3	5		6	7	8	9	10				4	1		11									
2	3	4		6		8	7	9	10				1		11	5								
2	3	4		6		8	7	9	10				1		11	5								
2	3	4		6	7		9		8	10			1		11	5								
2	3	4		6	7		10	9	8						11	5								
4	3	5		6		8	7	9	10						11		2							
4	3	5		6		8	7	9	10						11		2							
4	3	5		6		8	7	9					10	11			2							
4	3	5		6		8	7	9					10	11			2							
4	3			6	8	7	9						10	11					2	5				
4	3			6		8	7	9					10	11						5	2			
4	3	5		6	11	8	7	9					10								2			
4	3			6	7	8						1	9	11	6					5	2			
4	3			6	7	8			10			1	10	11						5	2	9		
4	3			6	7	8			10			1	10	11						5	2	9		
4	3			6	7	8			10			1		11						5	2	9		
4	3			6	7	8			10			1		11						5	2	9		
4	3			6		8	7	10				1		11						5	2	9		
	3				8	7	10	4	6		1			11						5	2	9		
4	3			6		8		10		7		1		11						5	2	9		
	3			6		8		10		4			11							5	2	9	7	
2	3			6		8	7	9		4			10	11						5				
	3				8		10	4	6		1			11						2	9	7		
4	3			6	7	8	9	10						11	5					2				
2	3			6		8	7	10		4				11						5		9		
2	3			6		8	9	10		4			1	11						5		7		
4	3			6		8	7	9	10			1		11						5	2			
4	3			6		8	7	9			1	10	11							5	2			
4	3			6		8	10	9					11							5	2	7		
4	3			6		8	10	9					11							5	2		7	
40	**41**	**22**	**5**	**38**	**22**	**38**	**35**	**32**	**12**	**12**	**10**	**7**	**18**	**12**	**30**	**7**	**4**	**1**	**19**	**18**	**11**	**3**	**1**	
1	1			5	4	8	22	4	2	1			4	12					1	3				

Cup matches:

Tremelling RD	Liddell GM	Randle J	Cringan JA	Barton PH	Leslie AJ	Bond B	Crosbie JA	Briggs GR	Bradford J	Ellis WT	Frith J	Curtis ER	Dale RA	Hibbs HE	Pike TE	Hicks GW	Cantrell J	Smith J	Birch J	Morrall GR	Barkas E	Mills BR	Horsman W	Riley H
4	3	5		6		8	7	9				1	10	11						2				
4	3	5			7	8		9				1	10	11						6	2			
2	2	2		1	1	2		2				2	2	2						1	2			

League Table

	P	W	D	L	F	A	Pts
Sheffield Wednesday	42	21	10	11	86	62	52
Leicester City	42	21	9	12	96	67	51
Aston Villa	42	23	4	15	98	81	50
Sunderland	42	20	7	15	93	75	47
Liverpool	42	17	12	13	90	64	46
Derby County	42	18	10	14	86	71	46
Blackburn Rovers	42	17	11	14	72	63	45
Manchester City	42	18	9	15	95	86	45
Arsenal	42	16	13	13	77	72	45
Newcastle United	42	19	6	17	70	72	44
Sheffield United	42	15	11	16	86	85	41
Manchester United	42	14	13	15	66	76	41
Leeds United	42	16	9	17	71	84	41
Bolton Wanderers	42	14	12	16	73	80	40
Birmingham	42	15	10	17	68	77	40
Huddersfield Town	42	14	11	17	70	61	39
West Ham United	42	15	9	18	86	96	39
Everton	42	17	4	21	63	75	38
Burnley	42	15	8	19	81	103	38
Portsmouth	42	15	6	21	56	80	36
Bury	42	12	7	23	62	99	31
Cardiff City	42	8	13	21	43	59	29

1929-30

Division One

Manager: Leslie Knighton

Did you know that?

Joe Bradford scored three hat-tricks in eight days in September 1929 – two for Blues in League games against Blackburn Rovers (lost 7–5) and Newcastle United (won 5–1) and one (which was a five-timer) for the Football League against the Irish League.

Syd Puddefoot scored four of Blackburn's seven goals in that thrilling 12-goal encounter at Ewood Park in September.

The first two of Ken Tewksbury's five appearances in goal for Blues came this season. The England amateur international played well in the 1–1 draw at Newcastle on his debut, but was at fault for two of the goals in the 4–2 home defeat by Derby three days later. He married the daughter of a Blues director, W.H. Bull.

Match No.	Date	Venue	Opponents	Result		Scorers	Attendance
1	Aug 31	A	Aston Villa	L	1-2	Bradford	36,83
2	Sep 4	H	West Ham United	W	4-2	Bradford 3, Barkas	13,30
3	7	H	Huddersfield Town	W	4-1	Bradford 2, Curtis, Liddell	24,83
4	14	A	Sheffield United	L	2-4	Curtis, Barkas	16,52
5	16	A	West Ham United	W	1-0	Bradford	13,26
6	21	H	Newcastle United	W	5-1	Bradford 3, Curtis, Crosbie	25,70
7	28	A	Blackburn Rovers	L	5-7	Bradford 3, Crosbie 2	18,94
8	Oct 5	H	Middlesbrough	D	1-1	Bradford	23,14
9	12	A	Liverpool	D	1-1	Curtis	35,85
10	17	A	Leicester City	L	1-2	Curtis	13,35
11	19	H	Leeds United	L	0-1		20,06
12	26	H	Sheffield Wednesday	W	1-0	Hicks	27,22
13	Nov 2	A	Burnley	L	1-3	Curtis	11,06
14	9	H	Arsenal	L	2-3	Bradford, Crosbie	33,90
15	16	A	Bolton Wanderers	D	0-0		15,92
16	23	H	Everton	D	0-0		13,88
17	30	A	Derby County	L	1-3	Curtis	13,5
18	Dec 7	H	Manchester City	W	3-0	Curtis, Haywood 2	15,94
19	14	A	Portsmouth	L	1-2	Barkas	17,97
20	21	H	Sunderland	W	3-1	Hicks, Haywood, Briggs	16,32
21	25	A	Manchester United	D	0-0		18,62
22	26	H	Manchester United	L	0-1		35,68
23	28	A	Aston Villa	D	1-1	Crosbie	33,22
24	Jan 4	A	Huddersfield Town	D	1-1	Hicks	14,59
25	18	H	Sheffield United	W	2-1	Curtis, Bradford	23,47
26	Feb 1	H	Blackburn Rovers	L	1-2	Bradford	18,52
27	8	A	Middlesbrough	L	1-5	Haywood	16,96
28	15	H	Liverpool	W	1-0	Haywood	10,90
29	22	H	Leeds United	W	1-0	Haywood	17,70
30	Mar 8	H	Burnley	W	2-0	Bradford, Cringan	19,48
31	15	A	Arsenal	L	0-1		32,17
32	22	H	Bolton Wanderers	W	3-1	Blyth 2, Bradford	18,26
33	29	A	Everton	W	4-2	Crosbie, Bradford, Blyth, Briggs	28,54
34	Apr 2	A	Newcastle United	D	1-1	Morrall	18,11
35	5	H	Derby County	L	2-4	Briggs, Robinson	13,60
36	12	H	Manchester City	W	4-1	Fillingham 2, Hicks, Briggs	25,72
37	18	A	Grimsby Town	L	1-2	Morrall	19,88
38	19	H	Portsmouth	W	1-0	Fillingham	11,96
39	22	H	Grimsby Town	L	0-2		18,48
40	26	A	Sunderland	L	0-2		15,46
41	28	A	Sheffield Wednesday	D	1-1	Blyth	9,31
42	May 3	H	Leicester City	W	3-0	Bradford 3	12,79

Appearance
Goa

FA Cup

R3	Jan 11	H	Bolton Wanderers	W	1-0	Morrall	36,0
R4	25	A	Arsenal	D	2-2	Briggs 2	43,22
rep	29	H	Arsenal	L	0-1		47,52

Appearance
Goa

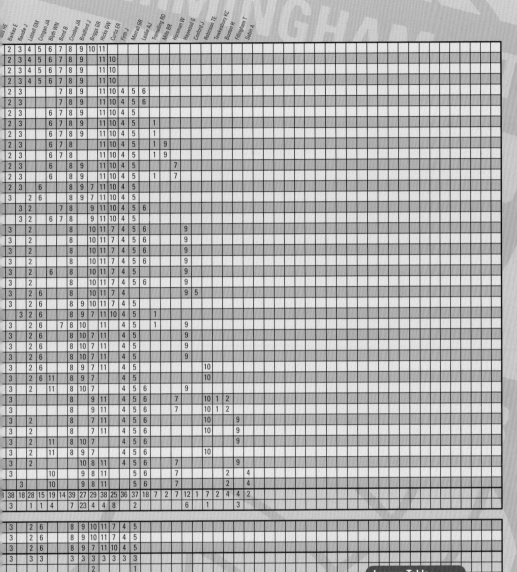

League Table

	P	W	D	L	F	A	Pts
Sheffield Wednesday	42	26	8	8	105	57	60
Derby County	42	21	8	13	90	82	50
Manchester City	42	19	9	14	91	81	47
Aston Villa	42	21	5	16	92	83	47
Leeds United	42	20	6	16	79	63	46
Blackburn Rovers	42	19	7	16	99	93	45
West Ham United	42	19	5	18	86	79	43
Leicester City	42	17	9	16	86	90	43
Sunderland	42	18	7	17	76	80	43
Huddersfield Town	42	17	9	16	63	69	43
Birmingham	42	16	9	17	67	62	41
Liverpool	42	16	9	17	63	79	41
Portsmouth	42	15	10	17	66	62	40
Arsenal	42	14	11	17	78	66	39
Bolton Wanderers	42	15	9	18	74	74	39
Middlesbrough	42	16	6	20	82	84	38
Manchester United	42	15	8	19	67	88	38
Grimsby Town	42	15	7	20	73	89	37
Newcastle United	42	15	7	20	71	92	37
Sheffield United	42	15	6	21	91	96	36
Burnley	42	14	8	20	79	97	36
Everton	42	12	11	19	80	92	35

Division One

Manager: Leslie Knighton

Match No.	Date		Venue	Opponents	Result		Scorers	Attendance
1	Aug	30	H	Sheffield United	W	3-1	Morrall, Briggs, Bradford	20,6
2	Sep	1	A	Leicester City	L	1-2	Briggs	14,3
3		6	A	Derby County	D	0-0		15,6
4		10	H	Newcastle United	D	1-1	Bradford	13,8
5		13	H	Manchester City	W	3-2	Briggs 2, Bradford	11,1
6		17	A	Newcastle United	D	2-2	Briggs, Morrall	19,9
7		20	A	Portsmouth	D	2-2	Hicks, Briggs	16,0
8		27	H	Arsenal	L	2-4	Briggs, Roberts (og)	31,6
9	Oct	4	A	Blackburn Rovers	L	1-2	Horsman	14,7
10		11	H	Blackpool	D	1-1	Curtis	23,4
11		18	A	Aston Villa	D	1-1	Briggs	55,4
12		25	H	Chelsea	W	6-2	Bradford 2, Curtis, Briggs 2, Crosbie	17,2
13	Nov	1	A	Manchester United	L	0-2		11,4
14		8	H	West Ham United	L	0-2		20,1
15		15	A	Middlesbrough	D	1-1	Curtis	11,8
16		22	H	Grimsby Town	W	4-1	Fillingham, Firth 3	13,6
17		29	A	Bolton Wanderers	L	0-2		15,3
18	Dec	6	H	Huddersfield Town	W	2-0	Bradford, Curtis	16,0
19		13	A	Sheffield Wednesday	L	1-9	Briggs	21,2
20		20	H	Liverpool	W	2-0	Briggs 2	16,1
21		25	H	Leeds United	L	0-1		24,9
22		26	A	Leeds United	L	1-3	Curtis	12,3
23		27	A	Sheffield United	L	1-3	Cringan	24,2
24	Jan	3	H	Derby County	L	1-2	Curtis	14,5
25		17	A	Manchester City	L	2-4	Bradford, Gregg	19,9
26		28	H	Portsmouth	W	2-1	Briggs, Bradford	6,5
27		31	A	Arsenal	D	1-1	Bradford	30,9
28	Feb	7	H	Blackburn Rovers	W	4-1	Bradford 4	23,6
29		18	A	Blackpool	W	1-0	Crosbie	10,1
30		21	H	Aston Villa	L	0-4		49,6
31	Mar	7	A	Manchester United	D	0-0		17,6
32		16	A	West Ham United	W	2-1	Firth, Bradford	8,5
33		21	H	Middlesbrough	L	1-2	Jarvis (og)	20,3
34		25	A	Chelsea	L	0-1		12,9
35		28	A	Grimsby Town	L	1-4	Fillingham	10,9
36	Apr	3	A	Sunderland	L	0-1		18,1
37		4	H	Bolton Wanderers	L	0-2		18,0
38		6	H	Sunderland	W	1-0	Gregg	11,2
39		11	A	Huddersfield Town	L	0-1		10,9
40		15	A	Liverpool	D	0-0		6,0
41		18	H	Sheffield Wednesday	W	2-0	Gregg, Curtis	16,4
42	May	2	H	Leicester City	W	2-1	Curtis, Bradford	14,7
								Appearance
				Two own-goals				Goa

FA Cup

	Date		Venue	Opponents	Result		Scorers	Attendance
R3	Jan	10	A	Liverpool	W	2-0	Curtis, Bradford	40,5
R4		24	H	Port Vale	W	2-0	Bradford 2	44,1
R5	Feb	14	H	Watford	W	3-0	Bradford, Curtis 2	49,75
R6		28	H	Chelsea	D	2-2	Bradford, Curtis	55,25
rep	Mar	4	A	Chelsea	W	3-0	Firth, Bradford 2	74,3
SF		14	N	Sunderland	W	2-0	Curtis 2	43,5
F	Apr	25	N	West Bromwich Albion	L	1-2	Bradford	90,3

SF at Elland Road, Leeds. Final at Wembley Stadium.

Appearance
Goal

Appearances Grid

	Gibbins HE	Liddell GM	Barkas E	Firth J	Morrall GR	Cringan J	Briggs GR	Crosbie JA	Bradford J	Byrth WN	Hicks GW	Haywood G	Curtis ER	Fillingham T	Horsman W	Boston H	Tewkesbury KC	Leslie AJ	Tremelling RG	Randle J	Lane H	Stoker L	Thorogood J	Gregg RE	Morfitt JW	Bond B	Robinson TE	Calladine CF
2	3	4	5	6	7	8	9	10	11																			
2	3	4	5	6	7	8			11	9	10																	
2	3	4		6	7	8	9		11		10	5																
2	3	4		6	7	8	9		11		10	5																
2	3	4		6	9	8	10		11			5	7															
	3	4	5	6	9	8			11		10		7	2														
	3	4	5		9	8			11		10	6	7	2														
	3	4	5		9	8		11			10	6	7	2	1													
	3	4	5		9	8					11		7	2		6												
2	3		5	4	9	8	10				11		7		6													
2	3		5	4	9	8	10				11		7		6													
2	3		5	4	9	8	10				11		7		6													
2	3		5	4	9	8	10				11		7		6													
2	3		5	4	9	8	10				11		7		6													
2	3		5	4		8	10		9	11			7		6													
2		10	5	4		8			11	9		7			6	1	3											
2			5	4			10		11	9	7			6		3	8											
2			5	6		8			10	9	7			3		4	11											
2			5	6	10	8		11	9	7	3				4													
2			5	4	9	8		10		7			6		3		11											
2	4	5	6	9	8		10			7			3				11											
2	4	5	6	8		9	10			7			3				11											
	2	5	6	9	8		10	4	7			1	3				11											
2	5		6		8		9					1	3	7	4	11	10											
2	3		5	4	7	8	9		11			6				10												
	3		5	4	7	8	9		11				2		6		10											
2	3	10	5	4	7	8	9		11			6																
2	3		5	4		8	9		11		7	6				10												
	3	6	5	4		8	9		11	5	7		2			10												
2		6		4	8		9	11	5	7			3			10												
	10		4	7		9	11	5		6	3		8															
	3	10	5	4	7		9	11	6		2		8															
2	3	10	5	4	7			11		6			8	9														
	3	10	5	6	9			11	4	7	2		8															
2	3	10	5	6	9			11	9		6	1																
2	3	10		4	9	8		11	5	7		6																
	3	4		9	8		11	5		2		6				7	10											
	3	10		7			9	5		6		2	4	11	8													
	3	10			11	5	7		6		2	4	8			9												
	3		8		9	11	5		6		2	4	10	7														
2	3	8	5		11	9		6		4	10	7																
2	3		5	4	7	8	9		11			6				10												
29	33	25	31	34	32	31	22	2	7	4	40	21	25	10	1	24	5	13	2	7	7	15	1	3	1	1	
	4	2	1		15	2	14		1		8	2	1				3											

	Gibbins HE	Liddell GM	Barkas E	Firth J	Morrall GR	Cringan J	Briggs GR	Crosbie JA	Bradford J	Byrth WN	Hicks GW	Haywood G	Curtis ER	Fillingham T	Horsman W	Boston H	Tewkesbury KC	Leslie AJ
2	3		5	4	10	8	9		11			7				6		
2	3		5	4	7	8	9		11			6				10		
2	3		5	4		8	9		11	7		6				10		
2	3		5	4		8	9		11			6				10		
2	3	10	5	4	7	8	9		11			6						
2	3	10	5	4	7	8	9		11			6						
2	3		5	4	7	8	9		11			6				10		
7	7	2	7	7	6	7	7		7			2				7		4
		1					8					6						

League Table

	P	W	D	L	F	A	Pts
Arsenal	42	28	10	4	127	59	66
Aston Villa	42	25	9	8	128	78	59
Sheffield Wednesday	42	22	8	12	102	75	52
Portsmouth	42	18	13	11	84	67	49
Huddersfield Town	42	18	12	12	81	65	48
Derby County	42	18	10	14	94	79	46
Middlesbrough	42	19	8	15	98	90	46
Manchester City	42	18	10	14	75	70	46
Liverpool	42	15	12	15	86	85	42
Blackburn Rovers	42	17	8	17	83	84	42
Sunderland	42	16	9	17	89	85	41
Chelsea	42	15	10	17	64	67	40
Grimsby Town	42	17	5	20	82	87	39
Bolton Wanderers	42	15	9	18	68	81	39
Sheffield United	42	14	10	18	78	84	38
Leicester City	42	16	6	20	80	95	38
Newcastle United	42	15	6	21	78	87	36
West Ham United	42	14	8	20	79	94	36
Birmingham	42	13	10	19	55	70	36
Blackpool	42	11	10	21	71	125	32
Leeds United	42	12	7	23	68	81	31
Manchester United	42	7	8	27	53	115	22

1931-32

Division One

Manager: Leslie Knighton

Did you know that?

Blues goalkeeper Harry Hibbs lost six teeth after colliding with Huddersfield's centre-forward Harry Davis during the League game at Leeds Road in April.

Blues gained revenge for the previous season's FA Cup final defeat by West Bromwich Albion by doubling up over the Baggies, winning both League games 1–0 over Christmas.

Goalkeeper Jimmy Mittell played in four League games for Blues this season and was on the losing side each time. He conceded 12 goals and had a real 'stinker' at Manchester City, being responsible for two of the five which went past him.

Ernie Curtis literally 'smashed' in two penalties in Blues' 3–0 home League victory over Middlesbrough in March. With his first kick, the ball struck the stanchion holding up the net and came back to him near the spot. His second went in off the underside of the crossbar.

Match No.	Date		Venue	Opponents	Result		Scorers	Attendance
1	Aug	29	A	Everton	L	2-3	Briggs, Curtis	39,14
2	Sep	2	H	Newcastle United	W	4-1	Briggs 2, Curtis, Bradford	12,31
3		5	H	Arsenal	D	2-2	Bradford 2 (1 pen)	26,81
4		12	A	Blackpool	D	1-1	Hicks	19,06
5		16	A	Sunderland	W	3-2	Crosbie, Bradford, Briggs	20,37
6		19	H	Sheffield United	L	1-3	Crosbie	22,72
7		23	H	Sunderland	D	0-0		9,76
8		26	A	Blackburn Rovers	W	2-1	Bradford, Jones (og)	11,00
9	Oct	3	H	Portsmouth	W	2-1	Bradford 2	20,74
10		10	A	Derby County	L	1-2	Morrall	12,12
11		17	H	Grimsby Town	W	2-1	Gregg, Bradford	16,31
12		24	A	Middlesbrough	L	0-2		9,22
13		31	H	Bolton Wanderers	D	2-2	Bradford 2	16,16
14	Nov	7	A	Sheffield Wednesday	L	1-5	Bradford	12,43
15		14	H	Leicester City	W	2-0	Grosvenor, Bradford	14,22
16		21	A	Aston Villa	L	2-3	Smith 2	44,94
17		28	H	Huddersfield Town	W	5-0	Smith 2, Curtis, Bradford, Briggs	18,05
18	Dec	5	A	Liverpool	L	3-4	Briggs, Grosvenor, Smith	19,84
19		12	H	West Ham United	W	4-1	Bradford 2, Curtis 2	19,72
20		19	A	Chelsea	L	1-2	Bradford	17,55
21		25	A	West Bromwich Albion	W	1-0	Curtis	37,90
22		26	H	West Bromwich Albion	W	1-0	Bradford	57,80
23	Jan	2	H	Everton	W	4-0	Haywood 2, Curtis, Bradford	26,25
24		16	A	Arsenal	L	0-3		37,84
25		30	A	Sheffield United	L	0-1		22,45
26	Feb	3	H	Blackpool	W	3-0	Curtis, Grosvenor, Bradford	5,82
27		6	H	Blackburn Rovers	W	2-1	Bradford, Curtis	19,50
28		17	A	Portsmouth	L	1-2	Haywood	7,99
29		20	H	Derby County	D	1-1	Curtis	17,39
30		27	A	Grimsby Town	D	1-1	Horsman	9,45
31	Mar	5	H	Middlesbrough	W	3-0	Curtis 2 (2 pens), Crosbie	18,69
32		12	A	Bolton Wanderers	L	1-5	Keating	11,00
33		19	H	Sheffield Wednesday	L	1-2	Grosvenor	17,27
34		26	A	Leicester City	L	1-3	Smith	15,58
35		28	A	Manchester City	L	1-2	Briggs	19,80
36		29	H	Manchester City	L	1-5	Bradford	12,60
37	Apr	2	H	Aston Villa	D	1-1	Smith	35,67
38		9	A	Huddersfield Town	D	1-1	Briggs	9,56
39		16	H	Liverpool	W	3-1	Bradford 2, Grosvenor	9,42
40		23	A	West Ham United	W	4-2	Briggs 2, Curtis, Smith	10,90
41		30	H	Chelsea	W	4-0	Grosvenor, Smith, Briggs, Bradford	14,86
42	May	7	A	Newcastle United	W	3-0	Bradford 2, Smith	10,75
								Appearance
				One own-goal				Goa

FA Cup

R3	Jan	9	H	Bradford City	W	1-0	Bradford	37,74
R4		23	A	Grimsby Town	L	1-2	Bradford	17,98
								Appearance
								Goa

Birmingham — Season appearances/goals grid

	Liddell GM	Barkas E	Stoker L	Morrall GR	Leslie AJ	Briggs GR	Crosbie JA	Smith GH	Bradford J	Curtis ER	Randle J	Gregg RE	Fillingham T	Hicks GW	Keating RE	Cringan JA	Horsman W	Calladine CF	Tewkesbury KC	Grosvenor AT	Thorogood J	Smith SJ	Firth J	Bioton H	Haywood G	Mittell JA	Wellington SP
2	3	4	5	6	7	8		9	10	11																	
2		4	5	6	7	8		9	11	3	10																
2		4	5	6	7	8		9	11	3	10																
2	3	4	5		7	8		9		10	6	11															
	3	4	5		7	8		9	11	2	10	6															
	3	4	5		7	8		9	11	2	10	6															
2	3	4	5		7	8		9	10		6		11														
2	3	4			8		9	11		10	6				5	7											
2	3	4			8		9	11		10	6				5	7											
2	3	4	5				7		10	6	11				9												
2	3	4	5		7	8	9		10	6	11				1												
2	3	4	5		7			9	11	10					6		8										
2	3	4	5		7			11	10						6		8	9									
2	3	4	5		7	8		9	10						6		8										
2	3	4	5		7			11	10						6		8	9									
2	3	4	5		7			10	11	3					6		8	9									
2		4	5		7			10	11						6		8	9									
2	3	4	5		7			10	11						6		8	9									
2	3		5		7			9	11	10	6				8			4									
2	3		5		7	8		10	11						6			9	4								
2	3	4	5		7			10	11						6		8	9									
2	3		5		7	8		9	11		10	6				8					4						
2	3		5		7	8		9	11		10	6				8				9	4						
2	3	4	5		7			10	11						6				8	9							
3		4			7			10	11			5			6				8			2	9				
3		4	5		7			10	11						6				8	9		2	9				
3		4	5					10	11						6	7			8	9		2					
		4	5					10	11						3	7			8		6	2	9				
3		4	5					10	11							7			8		6	2	9				
		4	5					10	11	3					6	7			8			2	9				
3		4	5					10	11						6	7			8			2	9				
3		4	5						11	10					6	7			8			2	9				
3		4	5			8			11					9	6	7					10	2					
3		4	5			8			11					9	6	7					10	2					
3		4	5				9	11							6	7			8		10	2		1			
3		4	5		7			10	11						6				8	9		2		1			
3		4			7			10	11		5				6				8	9		2		1			
3		4			7			9	11		5				6				8		10	2		1			
2		4	5		7			10	11			6			3				8	9							
2		5			7			10	11			6			3				8	9	4						
2		4	5		7			10	11			6			3				8	9							
2		4	5		7			10	11			6			3				8	9							
2		4	5		7			10				6			3				8	11	9				6		
		4	5		7			10				6			3				8	11	9		2		6		
37	**19**	**39**	**37**	**3**	**30**	**15**	**1**	**37**	**35**	**6**	**16**	**17**	**1**	**5**	**30**	**11**	**2**	**2**	**26**	**5**	**15**	**9**	**15**	**7**	**4**	**2**
1		11	3		26	13		1	1		1				6				10			3					

3		4	5		7			10	11						6				8	9		2					
2	3	4	5		7			10	11						6				8	9							
2	1	2	2		2			2	2						2				2	2		1					
									2																		

1932-33

Division One

Manager: Leslie Knighton

Match No.	Date		Venue	Opponents	Result		Scorers	Attendance
1	Aug	27	H	Arsenal	L	0-1		31,5
2		31	A	Manchester City	L	0-1		20,6
3	Sep	3	A	Everton	L	1-4	Grosvenor	27,5
4		7	H	Manchester City	W	3-0	Briggs, Bradford 2	13,4
5		10	H	Blackpool	W	2-1	Curtis (pen), Bradford	16,0
6		17	A	Derby County	D	2-2	Bradford, Briggs	16,3
7		24	H	Blackburn Rovers	W	3-1	Grosvenor, Curtis, Gregg	19,8
8	Oct	1	A	Leeds United	D	1-1	Thorogood	14,1
9		8	H	Sheffield Wednesday	W	2-1	Thorogood, Grosvenor	14,9
10		15	A	West Bromwich Albion	L	0-1		29,3
11		22	A	Aston Villa	L	0-1		52,1
12		29	H	Middlesbrough	L	1-4	Bradford	9,0
13	Nov	5	A	Chelsea	L	2-4	Grosvenor, Curtis (pen)	25,6
14		12	H	Huddersfield Town	L	0-2		14,2
15		19	A	Sheffield United	L	1-2	Briggs	10,3
16		26	H	Wolverhampton Wan.	D	0-0		22,8
17	Dec	3	A	Bolton Wanderers	D	2-2	Bradford, Briggs	8,9
18		10	H	Liverpool	W	3-0	Gregg 3	11,2
19		17	A	Leicester City	D	2-2	Cringan, Gregg	11,9
20		24	H	Portsmouth	W	4-0	Grosvenor 2, Bradford, Gregg	15,7
21		26	A	Newcastle United	L	1-2	Curtis	41,7
22		27	H	Newcastle United	L	1-2	J. Richardson (og)	29,3
23		31	A	Arsenal	L	0-3		37,8
24	Jan	7	H	Everton	W	4-0	Haywood 3, Grosvenor	17,3
25		21	A	Blackpool	W	1-0	Calladine	10,3
26	Feb	1	H	Derby County	W	3-1	Gregg, Curtis, Haywood	9,6
27		4	A	Blackburn Rovers	L	0-2		7,4
28		11	H	Leeds United	W	2-1	Haywood, Curtis (pen)	22,1
29	Mar	8	H	Aston Villa	W	3-2	Briggs, Bradford, Grosvenor	24,8
30		11	A	Middlesbrough	D	2-2	Bradford, Curtis	14,6
31		18	H	Chelsea	D	0-0		19,6
32		25	A	Huddersfield Town	D	0-0		8,6
33	Apr	1	H	Sheffield United	W	4-1	Curtis 2, Bradford 2	11,0
34		5	A	Sheffield Wednesday	D	1-1	Curtis	6,0
35		8	A	Wolverhampton Wan.	L	0-1		25,2
36		14	A	Sunderland	L	0-1		14,6
37		15	H	Bolton Wanderers	W	2-1	Bradford 2	13,5
38		17	H	Sunderland	W	2-0	Curtis, Bradford	12,5
39		22	A	Liverpool	L	0-1		14,0
40		26	H	West Bromwich Albion	D	1-1	Briggs	16,5
41		29	H	Leicester City	L	0-4		8,8
42	May	6	A	Portsmouth	D	1-1	Grosvenor	11,4

Appearance
One own-goal   Goa

FA Cup

R3	Jan	14	H	Preston North End	W	2-1	Gregg, Grosvenor	29,4
R4		28	H	Blackburn Rovers	W	3-0	Curtis 2, Haywood	25,6
R5	Feb	18	A	Middlesbrough	D	0-0		27,7
rep		22	H	Middlesbrough	W	3-0	Gregg, Haywood, Curtis	29,1
R6	Mar	4	A	West Ham United	L	0-4		44,2

Appearance
Goa

Appearances & Goals Grid

	Ashe	Boston H	Cringan JA	Slater L	Morrall GR	Fillingham T	Briggs GR	Grosvenor AT	Smith SJ	Bradford J	Curtis ER	Harris J	Firth J	Horsman W	Gregg RE	Smith B	Thorogood J	Lea IG	Haywood G	Robinson TE	Barkas E	Calladine CF	Mitrell JA	White FRH
	2	3	4	5	6	7	8	9	10	11														
	2		4	5	6	7	8	9	10	11	3													
	2		4	5			8	9	10	11	3	6	7											
	2		4	5		7	8		9	11	3	6		10										
	2		4	5		7	8		9	11	3	6		10										
	2		4	5	6	7	8		9	11				10	3									
	2		4	5	6	7	8		9	11				10	3									
	2			5	6	7	8			9		4		10	3	11								
	2		4	5		7	8			10					3	11	6	9						
	2		4	5		7	8	9						10	3	11	6							
	2		4	5	6	7	8		9					10	3	11								
	2		4	5	6	7	8		9					10	3	11								
	2		4	5	6		8			7				10	3	11		9						
	2		4	5	6		8									11		9	3					
	2		4	5	6	7	8	9			10					11			3					
	2		4	5	6	7	8	9	10							11			3					
	2	6	4	5		7	8		9	11				10					3					
	2	6	4	5		7	8		9	11				10					3					
	2		4	5		7	8		9	11				10					3	6				
	2		4		5	7	8			11				10	3		9			6				
	2		4	5		7	8		9	11				10					3	6				
	2		4		5	7	8			11				10			9		3	6				
	2		4		5	7	8			11				10			9		3	6				
	2		4	5		7	8			11							9	10	3	6				
	2		4	5		7	8			11				10			9		3	6				
	2		4	5		7	8			11				10			9		3	6				
	2		4	5		7	8			11				10			9		3	6				
	2		4	5		7	8		9	11				10					3	6				
	2		4	5		7	8		9	11				10					3	6				
	2		4	5		7	8		9	11				10					3	6				
	2			5		7	8		9	11				10		4			3	6	1			
	2			5		7	8		9	11				10		4			3	6	1			
	2			5		9	8		11	7				10		4			3	6				
	2		4	5		8			11	7	10					9			3	6				
	2		4	5		8			11	7	10					9			3	6				
	2		4	5		7	8		9	11				10					3	6				
	2		4	5		7	8		9	11				10					3	6				
	2		4	5		7	8		9	11				10					3	6				
	2	6	4		5		8		11	7				10					3					
	2		4	5		8			9	11	7								3	6		10		
	2		4	5		7	8		9	11				10		9			3	6				
	2		4	5		7	8		9	11				10					3	6				
Apps	42	5	38	38	15	35	42	6	26	36	4	5	6	34	9	9	5	11	3	28	22	2	1	
Goals			1			6	9		14	11				7		2		5			1			

	Ashe	Boston H	Cringan JA	Slater L	Morrall GR	Fillingham T	Briggs GR	Grosvenor AT	Smith SJ	Bradford J	Curtis ER	Harris J	Firth J	Horsman W	Gregg RE	Smith B	Thorogood J	Lea IG	Haywood G	Robinson TE	Barkas E	Calladine CF	Mitrell JA	White FRH
	2		4	5		7	8			11				10			9		3	6				
	2		4	5		7	8			11				10			9		3	6				
	2		4	5		7	8			11				10			9		3	6				
	2		4	5		7	8			11				10			9		3	6				
	5		5	5		5	5			5				5			5		5	5	5			
							1			3				2			2							

Division One

Manager: George Liddell

Match No.	Date		Venue	Opponents	Result		Scorers	Attendan
1	Aug	26	A	Arsenal	D	1-1	Bradford	44,6
2		30	H	Manchester City	L	0-1		20,0
3	Sep	2	H	Everton	D	2-2	Haywood, Grosvenor	25,2
4		6	A	Manchester City	L	0-1		19,3
5		9	A	Middlesbrough	W	3-0	Horsman, Bradford 2	11,5
6		16	H	Blackburn Rovers	W	2-0	S.J.Smith, Curtis (pen)	20,7
7		23	A	Newcastle United	D	0-0		21,6
8		30	H	Leeds United	W	4-0	Bradford, Grosvenor, S.J.Smith, Curtis	21,5
9	Oct	7	A	Derby County	L	0-4		17,4
10		14	H	West Bromwich Albion	L	0-1		29,9
11		21	H	Wolverhampton Wan.	D	0-0		31,9
12		28	A	Stoke City	D	1-1	Roberts	17,6
13	Nov	4	H	Liverpool	L	1-2	Roberts	17,9
14		11	A	Portsmouth	W	2-0	White, Fillingham	16,9
15		18	A	Sunderland	D	1-1	Lea	15,2
16		25	A	Chelsea	D	1-1	White	17,8
17	Dec	2	H	Aston Villa	D	0-0		34,7
18		9	A	Tottenham Hotspur	L	2-3	Roberts, White	26,1
19		23	H	Huddersfield Town	D	0-0		9,7
20		25	A	Sheffield United	L	1-2	Roberts	25,6
21		26	H	Sheffield United	W	4-2	White, Robertson, Roberts, Bradford	28,9
22		30	H	Arsenal	D	0-0		34,7
23	Jan	2	A	Sheffield Wednesday	L	1-2	McGurk	12,7
24		6	A	Everton	L	0-2		20,5
25		20	H	Middlesbrough	D	0-0		20,3
26		29	A	Blackburn Rovers	L	1-3	McGurk	5,9
27	Feb	3	H	Newcastle United	L	1-2	McGurk	16,3
28		10	A	Leeds United	L	0-1		14,7
29		21	H	Derby County	W	2-1	S.J.Smith, Mangnall	12,3
30		24	A	West Bromwich Albion	W	2-1	Roberts, White	24,5
31	Mar	3	H	Wolverhampton Wan.	L	0-2		27,3
32		10	H	Stoke City	L	0-1		21,9
33		17	A	Liverpool	L	1-4	Moffatt	30,5
34		24	H	Portsmouth	W	3-1	Barkas (pen), Guest, Mangnall	13,4
35		28	H	Leicester City	W	3-0	Sharman (og), Moffatt, Mangnall	7,8
36		31	A	Sunderland	L	1-4	Booton (pen)	14,1
37	Apr	3	H	Sheffield Wednesday	W	3-0	Catlin (og), Roberts, Guest	24,0
38		7	H	Chelsea	L	0-3		29,1
39		14	A	Aston Villa	D	1-1	Calladine	34,1
40		21	H	Tottenham Hotspur	W	2-0	Whatley (og), Calladine	24,5
41		28	A	Leicester City	W	7-3	Moffatt, Guest 3, Mangnall, Roberts, Jones (og)	16,9
42	May	5	H	Huddersfield Town	L	1-3	Barkas (pen)	14,7
							Appearanc	
				Four own-goals				Goa

FA Cup

R3	Jan	13	H	Sheffield United	W	2-1	Robertson, Haywood	33,1
R4		27	H	Charlton Athletic	W	1-0	Morrall	30,2
R5	Feb	17	H	Leicester City	L	1-2	Haywood	48,5
							Appearanc	
								Goa

Player Appearances Grid

	Booton H	Barkas E	Stoker L	Morrall GR	Calladine CF	McGurk FR	Grosvenor T	Bradford J	Smith SJ	Guest WF	Haywood G	Curtis ER	Horsman W	Gregg RE	Firmingham T	Evans L	Roberts F	White F	Liss G	Robertson J	Thorogood J	Smith B	Shaw F	Crick F	Mangnall D	Moffatt S	Crogan JA	Sykes J
	2	3	4	5	6	7	8	9	10	11																		
	2	3	4	5	6	7	8	9	10	11																		
	2	3	4	5	6	7	8	10		9	11																	
	2	3	4	5	6		8	9				11	7	10														
	2	3	4		6		8	10			9	11	7			5												
	2	3	4		6		8	10	9			11	7			5												
	2	3	4		6	7	8	10	9			11				5												
	2	3	4		6	7	8	10	9			11				5												
	2	3	4		6	7	8	10	9			11				5												
	2	3	4		6	7		10	8		9	11				5	1											
	2	3	4		6	7	8	10								5		9	11									
	2	3	4		6	7	8	10								5		9	11									
	2	3	4		6	7	8	10								5		9	11									
	2	3	4		6		8			7		9					10	11	5									
	2	3	4		6		8			7		9					10	11	5									
	2	3	4		6		8			7		5	1				10	11	9									
	2		4	5	6			8	9			7		3			10	11										
	2		4	5	6			8	9			7		3			10	11										
	2	3	4	5	6			8				7					10	11	9									
	2	3		5	6			8				7					10	11	4	9								
	2	3	4	5	6			8				7					10	11	9									
	2	3	4	5	6			8				7					10	11	9									
	2	3	4	5	6	8				7							10		9	11								
	2	3	4	5	10					7							6		9	11								
	2	3	8	5	10				11	9		7		6					4									
		4	5	6	7		9		11						2		10				3	8						
	3	4	5	6	7		10		11						2		9					8						
	2	3	4	5	6	7		8		11							10						1	9				
	2	3	4	5	6	7		8									10	11					1	9				
	2	3	4	5	6	7		8									10	11					1	9				
	2		4	5	6	7		8								3	10	11						9				
	2	3	4	5	6	7		8									10	11						9				
	2	3	4	5	6		8										10						9	7				
	2	3	4	5	6		8		11								10						9	7				
	2		4	5	6		8		11										10	1	9	7	3					
	2		4	5	6		8		11										10	1	9	7	3					
	2	3	4		6			11		7		5		8					10	1	9							
		3	4		6		9	11		7		5		8					10	1			2					
	2	3		5	6		10	11				9		8		4				1		7						
	2	3	4	5	6		10	11				9		8								7						
	2	3	4	5	6		10	11						8					9	7								
	2	3		5	6		10	11						8						9	7			4				
Apps	39	36	39	28	42	18	18	31	10	16	4	8	17	1	22	2	28	17	6	6	2	2	6	9	12	8	3	1
Goals	1	2		2	3	2	5	3	5	1	2	1		1	8	5	1	1						4	3			

	Booton H	Barkas E	Stoker L	Morrall GR	Calladine CF	McGurk FR	Grosvenor T	Bradford J	Smith SJ	Guest WF	Haywood G	Curtis ER	Horsman W	Gregg RE	Firmingham T	Evans L	Roberts F	White F	Liss G	Robertson J	Thorogood J	Smith B	Shaw F	Crick F	Mangnall D	Moffatt S	Crogan JA	Sykes J
	2	3	4	5	6			11	9			7					10			8								
	2	3	4	5	6		8		11			7					10			9								
	2	3	4	5	6		8		9	7					10			11				1						
Apps	3	3	3	3	3			2		2	2		3				2	1		2	1			1				
Goals				1					2								1											

League Table

	P	W	D	L	F	A	Pts
Arsenal	42	25	9	8	75	47	59
Huddersfield Town	42	23	10	9	90	61	56
Tottenham Hotspur	42	21	7	14	79	56	49
Derby County	42	17	11	14	68	54	45
Manchester City	42	17	11	14	65	72	45
Sunderland	42	16	12	14	81	56	44
West Bromwich Albion	42	17	10	15	78	70	44
Blackburn Rovers	42	18	7	17	74	81	43
Leeds United	42	17	8	17	75	66	42
Portsmouth	42	15	12	15	52	55	42
Sheffield Wednesday	42	16	9	17	62	67	41
Stoke City	42	15	11	16	58	71	41
Aston Villa	42	14	12	16	78	75	40
Everton	42	12	16	14	62	63	40
Wolverhampton W	42	14	12	16	74	86	40
Middlesbrough	42	16	7	19	68	80	39
Leicester City	42	14	11	17	59	74	39
Liverpool	42	14	10	18	79	87	38
Chelsea	42	14	8	20	67	69	36
Birmingham	42	12	12	18	54	56	36
Newcastle United	42	10	14	18	68	77	34
Sheffield United	42	12	7	23	58	101	31

Division One

Manager: George Liddell

Did you know that?

Fred Harris, who was signed in March 1933, scored on his Blues debut against Aston Villa on the opening day of the season. He would remain at St Andrew's until May 1950, captaining the side several times while scoring 68 goals in 312 appearances.

Two-nil down at home to Grimsby, Blues fought back to win 3–2 with Charlie Wilson Jones heading the winning goal in the 63rd minute.

Fred Harris's hat-trick in the FA Cup tie against Coventry City was the first by a Blues player in this competition since January 1928, when Joe Bradford netted three times against non-League side Peterborough & Fletton United.

Dave Mangnall's hat-trick in the nine-goal thriller at Liverpool in October was the first by a Blues player in an away defeat since September 1929 when Joe Bradford's three-goals counted for nothing in a 7–5 reverse at Blackburn.

Match No.	Date		Venue	Opponents	Result		Scorers	Attendance
1	Aug	25	H	Aston Villa	W	2-1	Harris, Guest	53,9
2		29	A	West Bromwich Albion	W	2-1	Sandford (og), Bradford	22,0
3	Sep	1	A	Stoke City	L	0-2		29,6
4		3	H	West Bromwich Albion	L	1-2	White	22,0
5		8	H	Manchester City	L	1-3	Mangnall	24,8
6		15	A	Middlesbrough	W	1-0	Bradford	15,4
7		22	A	Blackburn Rovers	W	1-0	White	11,8
8		29	A	Arsenal	L	1-5	White	47,8
9	Oct	6	H	Portsmouth	W	2-1	Mangall 2	20,9
10		13	A	Liverpool	L	4-5	Booton (pen), Mangall 3	21,4
11		20	H	Chelsea	L	0-1		22,5
12		27	A	Wolverhampton Wan.	L	1-3	Mangnall	22,4
13	Nov	3	H	Leicester City	L	2-3	Jones 2	16,7
14		10	A	Derby County	D	1-1	Guest	20,0
15		17	H	Grimsby Town	W	3-2	Jones 2, Guest	18,6
16		24	A	Preston North End	W	1-0	Roberts	17,6
17	Dec	1	H	Tottenham Hotspur	W	2-1	Jones, Guest	20,5
18		8	A	Sunderland	L	1-5	Barkas (pen)	22,0
19		15	H	Huddersfield Town	L	0-4		16,5
20		22	A	Everton	L	0-2		20,1
21		25	A	Sheffield Wednesday	L	1-2	Mangnall	23,4
22		26	H	Sheffield Wednesday	L	0-4		24,4
23		29	A	Aston Villa	D	2-2	Mangnall 2	40,7
24	Jan	5	H	Stoke City	D	0-0		22,6
25		19	A	Manchester City	D	0-0		31,6
26	Feb	2	A	Blackburn Rovers	L	1-3	Harris	12,2
27		6	H	Middlesbrough	W	4-2	White 2, Jones 2	5,7
28		9	H	Arsenal	W	3-0	Jones, Bradford, Harris	50,1
29		23	H	Liverpool	L	1-3	Harris	22,0
30	Mar	6	A	Chelsea	D	2-2	Guest, Harris	13,0
31		9	H	Wolverhampton Wan.	D	1-1	Jones	19,9
32		16	A	Leicester City	L	1-2	Stoker	18,5
33		23	H	Derby County	W	3-2	Jones 3	11,6
34		30	A	Grimsby Town	L	3-4	White 2 (1 pen), Bradford	9,8
35	Apr	6	H	Preston North End	W	3-0	White 3 (1 pen)	15,7
36		10	H	Portsmouth	L	1-2	White	8,6
37		13	A	Tottenham Hotspur	D	1-1	Jones	27,1
38		19	A	Leeds United	D	1-1	Jones	14,7
39		20	H	Sunderland	D	2-2	White, Jones	21,8
40		22	H	Leeds United	W	3-1	Calladine, Harris 2	18,0
41		27	A	Huddersfield Town	D	2-2	Harris 2	9,1
42	May	4	H	Everton	L	2-3	White, Jones	16,6

							Appearance
				One own-goal			Goal

FA Cup

R3	Jan	12	H	Coventry City	W	5-1	Harris 3, Mangnall, Guest	40,3
R4		26	A	Southampton	W	3-0	White, Fillingham, Guest	28,2
R5	Feb	21	H	Blackburn Rovers	W	2-1	Whiteside (og), White	35,0
R6	Mar	2	A	Burnley	L	2-3	Jones, White	47,6

							Appearance
				One own-goal			Goal

Player appearance / line-up grid (shirt numbers by match). Column headers (left to right):

1. …us HE · 2. Boxton H · 3. Hubbard AA · 4. Staker L · 5. Morrall GR · 6. Calladine CF · 7. Moffatt SH · 8. Harris F · 9. Mangnall D · 10. Bradford J · 11. Guest WF · 12. Clack FE · 13. Jones CW · 14. White FRH · 15. McGurk FR · 16. Finnighann T · 17. Lea JG · 18. Small SJ · 19. Barkas E · 20. Grosvenor AT · 21. Crowther R · 22. Holmes WH · 23. Horsman W · 24. Roberts F · 25. Dearson DJ · 26. Devine JC · 27. Smith B · 28. Steel WG · 29. Morris S

…HE	Box	Hub	Sta	Mor	Cal	Mof	Har	Mng	Bra	Gue	Cla	Jon	Whi	McG	Fin	Lea	Sml	Bar	Gro	Cro	Hol	Hor	Rob	Dea	Dev	Smi	Ste	Mor
2	3	4	5	6	7	8	9	10	11																			
2	3	4	5	6	7	8	9	10	11	1																		
2	3	4	5	6	7	8	9		11		10																	
2	3	4	5	6	7	8	9		11			10																
2	3	4	5	6		8	9	10		11	7																	
2		7	5	6		8	9		11		3	4																
2		7	5	6		8	10		11		3	4	9															
2		7	5	6		8	10		1		11		3	4	9													
2		4	5	6	7	10	9		11									3	8									
2		4	5	6	7	10	9		11									3	8									
2		4		6	7	10	9		11									3	8	5								
2		4	5	6	7	8	10		9	11								3										
2		4	5	6		10	8		1	9	11							3		7								
2		4	5			10		11		9				6				3	8		7							
2		4	5	10			11		9									3	8		7							
2		4	5	6				9	11									3	8		7	10						
2		4	5	6		10		11		9								3	8		7							
2		4	5	6		10		11		9								3	8		7							
2		4	5	6		10		11		9								3			7	8						
2		4		6		10	8		9	11								3	5		7							
2		4		6		9	10		11									3	5		7	8						
2		4		10		11		9										3	5	7	8							
2			6	8		9	10	11		7		5	4		3													
2	4		6		8	9		11	1		7		5		3							10						
2	4		6		8	9		11			7		5		3							10						
2			6		8	9		11			7		5	4	3							10	3					
2	4		6		8		10	11	1	9	7		5		3													
2	4				8		10	11		9	7		5		3							6						
2	4		6		8				9	7		5		3						11		10						
2	4	5	6		8	9		11						3								10						
2	4		6		8			11	1	9	7		5		3							10						
2	4		6		8			11	1	9	7	5		3							10	3						
	4		6	7	8			11		9		5		3							10	2						
	4	5	6		8		10	11	1	9	7		3									2						
	4	5	6		8			1	9	7		3										2	11					
	4	5			8		10	11	9	7		3								6		2						
	4	5			8		10		9	7		3								6		2	11					
	4	5	6				11	9	7		3									10		2						
2		5	6				11	9	7			4						8	10		3							
	5	6		8			11	9	7		4	3						10	2									
		6		8			10	9	7	5	4	3								2	11							
	4		6		8		10	11	9	7		5		3							2							
33	**5**	**37**	**26**	**38**	**10**	**30**	**25**	**15**	**27**	**9**	**26**	**32**	**1**	**17**	**9**	**2**	**30**	**8**	**4**	**1**	**10**	**1**	**4**	**14**	**1**	**11**	**3**	
1		1		1		9	10	4	5		16	13			1			1										

Lower block:

…HE	Box	Hub	Sta	Mor	Cal	Mof	Har	Mng	Bra	Gue	Cla	Jon	Whi	McG	Fin	Lea	Sml	Bar	Gro	Cro	Hol	Hor	Rob	Dea	Dev	Smi	Ste	Mor
2	4		6		8	9		10	11		7	5			3													
2	4		6		8	9		10	11		7	5			3													
2	4		6		8		10	11	9	7		5			3													
2	4		6		8		10	11	9	7		5			3													
4	4		4		4	2	4	4		2	4	4			4													
				3	1		2		1	3		1																

League Table

	P	W	D	L	F	A	Pts
Arsenal	42	23	12	7	115	46	58
Sunderland	42	19	16	7	90	51	54
Sheffield Wednesday	42	18	13	11	70	64	49
Manchester City	42	20	8	14	82	67	48
Grimsby Town	42	17	11	14	78	60	45
Derby County	42	18	9	15	81	66	45
Liverpool	42	19	7	16	85	88	45
Everton	42	16	12	14	89	88	44
West Bromwich Albion	42	17	10	15	83	83	44
Stoke City	42	18	6	18	71	70	42
Preston North End	42	15	12	15	62	67	42
Chelsea	42	16	9	17	73	82	41
Aston Villa	42	14	13	15	74	88	41
Portsmouth	42	15	10	17	71	72	40
Blackburn Rovers	42	14	11	17	66	78	39
Huddersfield Town	42	14	10	18	76	71	38
Wolverhampton W	42	15	8	19	88	94	38
Leeds United	42	13	12	17	75	92	38
Birmingham	42	13	10	19	63	81	36
Middlesbrough	42	10	14	18	70	90	34
Leicester City	42	12	9	21	61	86	33
Tottenham Hotspur	42	10	10	22	54	93	30

Division One

Manager: George Liddell

Match No.	Date		Venue	Opponents	Result		Scorers	Attendance
1	Aug	31	A	Wolverhampton Wan.	L	1-3	Harris	33,45
2	Sep	4	A	Leeds United	D	0-0		13,27
3		7	H	Arsenal	D	1-1	Devine	42,80
4		11	H	Leeds United	W	2-0	Jones, White	14,29
5		14	A	Manchester City	L	1-3	Guest	32,33
6		18	A	West Bromwich Albion	D	0-0		18,04
7		21	H	Stoke City	L	0-5		19,90
8		28	A	Blackburn Rovers	W	2-1	Jones, Harris	13,17
9	Oct	5	H	Chelsea	W	2-1	Harris, Craig (og)	22,62
10		12	A	Liverpool	W	2-1	Harris, Jones	28,99
11		19	A	Sheffield Wednesday	L	1-3	White	13,47
12		26	H	Portsmouth	W	4-0	White, Harris 2, Jones	24,45
13	Nov	2	A	Preston North End	L	1-3	Harris	16,23
14		9	H	Brentford	W	2-1	Jones, Stoker	28,67
15		16	A	Derby County	D	2-2	Calladine, Harris	23,89
16		23	H	Aston Villa	D	2-2	Jones 2	60,25
17		30	A	Bolton Wanderers	L	0-2		21,68
18	Dec	7	H	Huddersfield Town	W	4-1	Jones 2, White, Guest	21,63
19		14	A	Middlesbrough	W	2-0	Jones 2	15,06
20		21	H	Everton	W	4-2	Jones (og), Harris, White, Loughran	16,99
21		25	A	Grimsby Town	L	0-1		11,81
22		26	H	Grimsby Town	D	1-1	Guest	28,97
23		28	H	Wolverhampton Wan.	D	0-0		37,87
24	Jan	4	A	Arsenal	D	1-1	Jones	44,53
25		18	H	Manchester City	L	0-1		23,16
26	Feb	1	H	Blackburn Rovers	W	4-2	Guest, Harris 2, Jennings	23,68
27		3	A	Stoke City	L	1-3	Jones	11,58
28		8	A	Chelsea	D	0-0		30,26
29		15	H	Liverpool	W	2-0	Jones, Harris	21,80
30		29	A	Brentford	W	1-0	Harris	20,52
31	Mar	7	H	Bolton Wanderers	D	0-0		20,17
32		14	A	Portsmouth	W	3-0	Harris, Morris 2	15,84
33		21	H	Derby County	L	2-3	Jones, Barkas (pen)	25,50
34		28	A	Aston Villa	L	1-2	Fillingham	49,53
35	Apr	4	H	Preston North End	D	0-0		15,81
36		10	A	Sunderland	L	1-2	Harris	40,66
37		11	A	Huddersfield Town	L	0-1		9,75
38		13	H	Sunderland	L	2-7	Loughran, Clarke	21,69
39		18	H	Middlesbrough	W	1-0	Harris	17,07
40		22	H	Sheffield Wednesday	W	4-1	Jones 3, Harris	9,08
41		25	A	Everton	L	3-4	Jones, Guest, Dearson	18,32
42	May	2	H	West Bromwich Albion	L	1-3	Barkas (pen)	18,31

Appearance

Two own-goals

Goal

FA Cup

R3	Jan	11	A	Barnsley	D	3-3	White, Jones, Harris	29,33
rep		15	H	Barnsley	L	0-2		34,00

Appearance

Goal

Appearances & goalscorers grid (shirt numbers by player and match)

Wilba HE	Barkas E	Steel WG	Stoker L	Morrall GR	Calladine CF	White FRH	Harris F	Jones CW	Devine JC	Guest WF	Bioxton H	Morris S	Lea IG	Filingham T	Drantzon DJ	Loughran JL	Grosvenor AT	Duck FE	Hughes WM	Syvea JG	Jennings DB	Clarke AW	Trigg C	Richardson EW	Olney JF	Small SJ
2	3	4	5	6	7	8	9	10	11																	
2	3	4	5	6	7	8	9	10	11																	
	3	4	5	6	7	8	9	10	11	2																
	3	4	5	6	7	8	9	10	11	2																
	3	4	5	6	7	8	9	10	11	2																
	3	4	5	6	7	8	9	10	11	2																
	3	4	5	6	7	8	9	10			2	11														
2	3					7	10	9	6	11			4	5	8											
2	3	4				7	10	9		11			5			6	8									
2	3	4				7	10	9		11			5			6	8									
2	3	4				7	10	9		11			5			6	8									
2	3	4				7	10	9		11			5			6	8									
2	3	4				7	10	9		11	8		5			6										
2	3	4		11		7	10	9	8				5			6										
2	3	4		11		7	10	9					5			6	8									
2		4				7	10	9	8	11		3	5			6										
	3	4				7	10	9		11	2		5			6	8									
2	3	4				7	10	9		11			5			6	8	1								
2	3	4				7	10	9	8	11			5			6										
2	3	4				7	10	9		11			5			6	8									
2	3	4					10	9		11			5	7		6	8									
2	3	4					10	9	7	11			5			6	8									
2							10	9	8	11			5			6		3	4	7						
2	3	4					10	9	8	11			5			6				7						
2	3	4					10	9		11			5	8		6	7									
2	3	4	5				10	9	8	11						6	7									
2	3	4	5				10	9	8				11			6	7									
2	3	4	5				10	9	8				11			6	7									
2	3	4	5				10	9					11			6	7	8								
2	3	4					10	9	8				11	5		6										
2	3	4					10	9	8				11	5		6										
		4					10	9	8	11			5			3	6	7	2							
	4	5					10		8	11			3		1	6	7	9	2							
2	3	4	5				10	9	8	11						6	7									
	3	4	5				10	9	8				11			6	7	2								
2	3	4					10		8	11			5		1	6	7	9								
2	3	4	5				10		8	11					1	6	7									
	3		5				10	9					8	4		1	6	7		2	11					
2			5				10	9		11			8	4		1	3	6	7							
2		4					10		11				8		1	3	6	7		5	9					
5	32	36	38	17	9	22	42	39	24	30	7	9	1	24	6	23	14	7	4	15	18	3	4	1	1	1
2			1	5	17	19	1	5			2		1	1	2							1	1			

Wilba HE	Barkas E	Steel WG	Stoker L	Morrall GR	Calladine CF	White FRH	Harris F	Jones CW	Devine JC	Guest WF	Bioxton H	Morris S	Lea IG	Filingham T	Drantzon DJ	Loughran JL	Grosvenor AT	Duck FE	Hughes WM	Syvea JG	Jennings DB	Clarke AW	Trigg C	Richardson EW	Olney JF	Small SJ
2	3	4				7	10	9	8	11			5			6		1								
2		4				7	10	9		11			5			6	8	3								
2	1	2				2	2	2	1	2			2			2	1	1	1							
						1	1	1																		

Division One

Manager: George Liddell

Match No.	Date		Venue	Opponents	Result		Scorers	Attendance
1	Aug	29	H	Portsmouth	W	2-1	Dearson, Morris	24,91
2	Sep	2	A	West Bromwich Albion	L	2-3	Morris, Jones	26,37
3		5	A	Chelsea	W	3-1	Morris, Harris, Dearson	32,80
4		9	H	West Bromwich Albion	D	1-1	Harris	23,81
5		12	H	Stoke City	L	2-4	Jennings, Harris	14,31
6		16	A	Manchester City	D	1-1	Morris	20,28
7		19	A	Charlton Athletic	D	2-2	Jones, Morris	35,42
8		26	H	Grimsby Town	L	2-3	Jones, Harris	21,98
9	Oct	3	A	Liverpool	L	0-2		23,89
10		10	H	Leeds United	W	2-1	Jones, Harris	23,83
11		17	H	Huddersfield Town	W	4-2	Fillingham, Jones, White 2 (1 pen)	25,05
12		24	A	Everton	D	3-3	Brunskill, Harris, Morris	26,94
13		31	H	Bolton Wanderers	D	1-1	Morris	23,28
14	Nov	7	A	Brentford	L	1-2	Dearson	22,90
15		14	H	Arsenal	L	1-3	Devine	39,94
16		21	A	Preston North End	D	2-2	White 2 (1 pen)	16,89
17		28	H	Sheffield Wednesday	D	1-1	Millership (og)	17,99
18	Dec	5	A	Manchester United	W	2-1	White, Jones	16,55
19		12	H	Derby County	L	0-1		8,89
20		19	A	Wolverhampton Wan.	L	1-2	Clarke	19,24
21		25	H	Sunderland	W	2-0	Harris, Jones	37,19
22		26	A	Portsmouth	L	1-2	Jones	32,02
23		28	A	Sunderland	L	0-4		17,30
24	Jan	2	H	Chelsea	D	0-0		17,67
25		9	A	Stoke City	L	0-2		15,31
26		23	H	Charlton Athletic	L	1-2	White	16,97
27	Feb	2	A	Grimsby Town	D	1-1	Harris	6,77
28		6	H	Liverpool	W	5-0	Morris, Beattie, Jennings, Harris, White	21,73
29		13	A	Leeds United	W	2-0	Beattie, Morris	13,67
30		20	A	Huddersfield Town	D	1-1	Beattie	10,33
31		27	H	Everton	W	2-0	Beattie, White	21,15
32	Mar	6	A	Bolton Wanderers	D	0-0		21,57
33		13	H	Brentford	W	4-0	Morris 2, White, Harris	30,51
34		20	A	Arsenal	D	1-1	Beattie	46,08
35		26	A	Middlesbrough	L	1-3	Clarke	24,95
36		27	H	Preston North End	W	1-0	Harris	26,35
37		29	H	Middlesbrough	D	0-0		28,62
38	Apr	3	A	Sheffield Wednesday	W	3-0	Morris 2, Richards	20,80
39		10	H	Manchester United	D	2-2	Clarke, Beattie	19,13
40		17	A	Derby County	L	1-3	Morris	10,80
41		24	H	Wolverhampton Wan.	W	1-0	Jennings (pen)	22,11
42	May	1	H	Manchester City	D	2-2	Morris, Clarke	17,32
								Appearance
							One own-goal	Goal

FA Cup

R3	Jan	16	A	Stoke City	L	1-4	Morris	31,48
								Appearance
								Goal

Appearance and goalscoring grid (Birmingham):

Mills HE	Trigg C	Steel WG	Stoker L	Fillingham T	Sykes JG	Jennings DB	Dearson DJ	Jones CW	Harris F	Morris S	Snall SJ	Devine JC	Butler H	Barkas E	Clack F	Lea IG	Richardson SW	White FRH	Laughran JL	Brunskill NH	Clarke AW	Guest WF	Olney JF	Beattie JM	Kendrick K	Richards DT	Hughes WM	Sykes EA
2	3	4	5	6	7	8	9	10	11																			
2	3	4	5	6	7	8	9	10	11																			
2	3	4	5	6	7	8		10	11	9																		
2	3		5	6	7	8		10	11	9	4																	
2	3			6	7	8	9	10	11		4	5																
2				6	7	8	9	10	11		4	5	3															
2				6	7	8	9	10	11		4	5	3															
2				6	7	8	9	10	11		4		3	1	5													
2		4	5			8	9	10	11				6		3	7												
2		4	5			8	9	10	11				6		3	7												
2		4	5	11		9	10						3			7	6	8										
2	3	4			9	10	11								5	7	6	8										
2	3	4	5		9	10	11									7	6	8										
2	3		5	8	9	10	11				4					7	6											
2	3		5	8	9		11		10							7	6											
2	3	4	5	6		8	9	10	11							7												
2	3	4	5	6		8	9	10	11							7												
2		4	5	6		8	9		11				3			7				10								
2		4	5	6		8	9		11				3			7				10								
2		4		6	8		9		11				3		5	7				10								
2		4		6		8	9	10					3		5	7					11							
2		4	5	6		8	9	10	11				3			7												
2	3		5			10	9					8				7	6	4		11								
	2		5	6			8						3	1	4	7	10	9		11								
2		4					10	11					3			7	6					5	8	9				
2			5		8		10	11		6			3			7	4						9					
2			5		8		10	11		6			3			7	4						9					
2			5		8		10	11		6			3			7	4						9					
2			5		8		10	11		6			3			7	4						9					
2	3		5		8		10	11		6						7	4						9					
2	3		5		8		10	11		6						7	4						9					
2			5		8		10	11					3			7	4						9	6				
2			5				10			8			3			7	4	11					9	6				
2			5		8		10						3		7		4	11					9	6				
2			5		7	8	10										4	11					9	6	3			
2			5		7	8	10	11									4						9	6	3			
2			5		8		10	11									4	7					9	6	3			
				8			10	11						1			4	7		5	9			6	3	2		
2			5		8		10	11									4	7					9	6	3			
	2		5	8			11			6		3				7	4	10					9					
	2	6	5	8			11									7	4	10					9		3			
38	17	19	32	17	25	22	22	35	35	3	17	3	22	3	6	2	27	8	21	11	3	2	17	1	8	6	1	
		1			3	3	8	11	15		1							9	1	4			6		1			

Cup appearances and goals:

Mills HE	Trigg C	Steel WG	Stoker L	Fillingham T	Sykes JG	Jennings DB	Dearson DJ	Jones CW	Harris F	Morris S	Snall SJ	Devine JC	Butler H	Barkas E	Clack F	Lea IG	Richardson SW	White FRH	Laughran JL	Brunskill NH	Clarke AW	Guest WF	Olney JF
2				6	7			10	11			3		5		9	4	8					
1			1	1				1	1			1		1		1	1	1					
									1														

League Table

	P	W	D	L	F	A	Pts
Manchester City	42	22	13	7	107	61	57
Charlton Athletic	42	21	12	9	58	49	54
Arsenal	42	18	16	8	80	49	52
Derby County	42	21	7	14	96	90	49
Wolverhampton W	42	21	5	16	84	67	47
Brentford	42	18	10	14	82	78	46
Middlesbrough	42	19	8	15	74	71	46
Sunderland	42	19	6	17	89	87	44
Portsmouth	42	17	10	15	62	66	44
Stoke City	42	15	12	15	72	57	42
Birmingham	42	13	15	14	64	60	41
Grimsby Town	42	17	7	18	86	81	41
Chelsea	42	14	13	15	52	55	41
Preston North End	42	14	13	15	56	67	41
Huddersfield Town	42	12	15	15	62	64	39
West Bromwich Albion	42	16	6	20	77	98	38
Everton	42	14	9	19	81	78	37
Liverpool	42	12	11	19	62	84	35
Leeds United	42	15	4	23	60	80	34
Bolton Wanderers	42	10	14	18	43	66	34
Manchester United	42	10	12	20	55	78	32
Sheffield Wednesday	42	9	12	21	53	69	30

Division One

Manager: George Liddell

Did you know that?

Blues drew a record 18 League games this season. This was equalled in 1971–72.

As the weeks ticked by, it was a toss-up between Blues and West Bromwich Albion as to who would be relegated with Manchester City. Blues beat the Baggies 2–1 at home, but lost 4–3 away, and by winning their last two games, at Brentford and Leicester, George Liddell's side stayed up while Albion went down, finishing up two points worse off than Blues.

The two regular full-backs for Blues this season were two 17-year-olds, Cyril Trigg and Billy Hughes. They had played together for the first time in the local derby against Aston Villa on 28 March 1936, but now they were first-choice selections in front of goalkeeper Harry Hibbs.

Seven different players were used in the centre-forward position this season, including giant centre-half Tom Fillingham against Arsenal in April.

Match No.	Date		Venue	Opponents	Result		Scorers	Attendance
1	Aug	28	A	Stoke City	D	2-2	Richards, Morris	27,656
2	Sep	1	H	Middlesbrough	W	3-1	Beattie 3	19,297
3		4	H	Portsmouth	D	2-2	Morris, White	28,462
4		8	A	Middlesbrough	D	1-1	Jones	18,831
5		11	A	Chelsea	L	0-2		34,072
6		15	H	Leicester City	W	4-1	Jones 3, White	14,441
7		18	H	Charlton Athletic	D	1-1	Jones	31,631
8		25	A	Preston North End	L	1-2	White	25,066
9	Oct	2	H	Grimsby Town	D	2-2	Jones, Morris	25,644
10		9	A	Leeds United	L	0-1		20,698
11		16	A	Sunderland	L	0-1		24,615
12		23	H	Derby County	W	1-0	Brunskill	23,992
13		30	A	Manchester City	L	0-2		16,829
14	Nov	6	H	Huddersfield Town	D	2-2	Dearson 2	21,541
15		13	A	Blackpool	W	3-0	Clarke 2, Morris	13,975
16		20	H	Wolverhampton Wan.	W	2-0	Dearson, Kendrick	35,272
17		27	A	Bolton Wanderers	D	1-1	Clarke	21,999
18	Dec	4	H	Arsenal	L	1-2	Morris	18,440
19		11	A	Everton	D	1-1	Morris	17,018
20		18	H	Brentford	D	0-0		22,533
21		27	H	Liverpool	D	2-2	Morris, Kendrick	39,563
22	Jan	1	H	Stoke City	D	1-1	Jones	25,130
23		15	A	Portsmouth	D	1-1	Beattie	19,482
24		22	H	Chelsea	D	1-1	Jones	18,480
25		29	A	Charlton Athletic	L	0-2		21,246
26	Feb	5	H	Preston North End	L	0-2		24,908
27		12	A	Grimsby Town	L	0-4		9,256
28		19	H	Leeds United	W	3-2	Dearson 2, White (pen)	20,403
29		26	H	Sunderland	D	2-2	Madden, Harris	25,960
30	Mar	5	D	Derby County	D	0-0		14,533
31		12	H	Manchester City	D	2-2	Harris 2	23,078
32		19	A	Huddersfield Town	L	1-2	Dearson	15,365
33		26	H	Blackpool	D	1-1	Harris	19,902
34	Apr	2	A	Wolverhampton Wan.	L	2-3	Jones, Phillips	27,420
35		6	A	Liverpool	L	2-3	Harris, Jennings	14,656
36		9	H	Bolton Wanderers	W	2-0	Harris, Phillips	19,889
37		15	H	West Bromwich Albion	W	2-1	Dearson 2	34,631
38		16	A	Arsenal	D	0-0		35,161
39		18	A	West Bromwich Albion	L	3-4	Jennings, Phillips 2	34,406
40		23	H	Everton	L	0-3		22,224
41		30	A	Brentford	W	2-1	Harris, Jennings (pen)	14,609
42	May	7	A	Leicester City	W	4-1	Dearson, Clarke, White 2	13,255

Appearances
Goals

FA Cup

R3	Jan	8	H	Blackpool	L	0-1		40,321

Appearances

Hibbs HE	Trigg C	Hughes WM	Brunskill NH	Fillingham T	Richards DT	White FRH	Jennings DB	Beattie JM	Deanson DJ	Morris S	Calrke AW	Cdlck FE	Jones DW	Steel WG	Shaw L	Stoker L	Kendrick K	Bellamy SC	Harris F	Butler H	Kelly J	Madden O	Philips C	Perr HC
1	2	3	4	5	6	7	8	9	10	11														
1	2	3	4	5	6	7	8	9	10	11														
1	2	3	4	5	6	7	8	9			11	10												
	2	3	4	5	6	7	8	10		11		1	9											
	2	3	4	5	6	7	8	9		11		1	10											
1	2		4	5	6	7		8	10	11		9	3											
1	2		4	5	6	7		8	10	11		9	3											
1	2		4	5	6	7		8	10	11		3	9											
	3	4	5	6	7		8		11	10		9	2											
	3	4	5	6	7		8		11	10		9												
	2	3	4	5	6	10	7	8		11		9												
1	2	3	4	5	6	10	8	9		11	7													
1	2		4	5		7	11	9	8		10			3		6								
1	2	3	4	5	6	7		10	8	11					9									
1		3	4	5	6		8	10	11	7				9	2									
	2	3	4	5	6		8	10	11	7	1			9										
	2	3	4		6		8	10	11	7	1			5	9									
	2	3	4	5	6		8	10	11	7				9										
	2	3	4	5	6		9	8	11	7						10								
	2	3	4	5	6		8	11	7					9		10								
	2	3	4	5	6		8	11	7					9		10								
	2	3	4		6	7	11	8			9					10	5							
	2	3	4		6	11		10		7	9			8			5							
	2	3	4		6	11		10		7	9					5	8							
	2	3	4	5	6	11		10		7	1	9				8								
	2	3	4		6	7		10			9					5	8	11						
	2	3		6	7			10		9			4			8	5	11						
	2	3		5	6	7		8			4					10		9	11					
	2	3		5	6	7		8			4					10		9	11					
	2	3		5	6	7		8			4					10		9	11					
	2	3		5	6	7		8	11			4				10		9						
	3		5	6	7	8		10			2	4				9		11						
	3	4	5	6	7		8	11	1		2					10		9						
	3	4	5	6	11		8		1	9	2					10		7						
	3	5			11	6		8		1	9	2	4			10		7						
	3	5			11	6		8		9	2	4				10		7						
	2	5	11		7	6		8			3	4				10		9						
	2	5	9	11	6		8		7		3	4				10								
	2	5	6	7	4		8			3						10		11	9					
	2	5		7	6		8			3						10		11	9	4				
	2	5	6	11	4		8		9	3						10		7						
	2	5		11	4		8		7	9	3	6				10								
4	35	32	35	31	35	35	18	19	35	22	17	8	18	16	2	13	7	1	19	5	8	7	9	1
		1		6	3	4	9	7	4	9				2	7				1	4				

Hibbs HE	Trigg C	Hughes WM	Brunskill NH	Fillingham T	Richards DT	White FRH	Jennings DB	Beattie JM	Deanson DJ	Morris S	Calrke AW	Cdlck FE	Jones DW	Steel WG	Shaw L	Stoker L	Kendrick K	Bellamy SC	Harris F	Butler H	Kelly J	Madden O	Philips C	Perr HC
	2	3	4		6	7	11		8				9				10	5						
	1	1	1		1	1	1		1				1				1	1						

League Table

	P	W	D	L	F	A	Pts
Arsenal	42	21	10	11	77	44	52
Wolverhampton W	42	20	11	11	72	49	51
Preston North End	42	16	17	9	64	44	49
Charlton Athletic	42	16	14	12	65	51	46
Middlesbrough	42	19	8	15	72	65	46
Brentford	42	18	9	15	69	59	45
Bolton Wanderers	42	15	15	12	64	60	45
Sunderland	42	14	16	12	55	57	44
Leeds United	42	14	15	13	64	69	43
Chelsea	42	14	13	15	65	65	41
Liverpool	42	15	11	16	65	71	41
Blackpool	42	16	8	18	61	66	40
Derby County	42	15	10	17	66	87	40
Everton	42	16	7	19	79	75	39
Huddersfield Town	42	17	5	20	55	68	39
Leicester City	42	14	11	17	54	75	39
Stoke City	42	13	12	17	58	59	38
Birmingham	42	10	18	14	58	62	38
Portsmouth	42	13	12	17	62	68	38
Grimsby Town	42	13	12	17	51	68	38
Manchester City	42	14	8	20	80	77	36
West Bromwich Albion	42	14	8	20	74	91	36

Division One

Manager: George Liddell

Match No.	Date		Venue	Opponents	Result		Scorers	Attendance
1	Aug	27	H	Sunderland	L	1-2	Jennings (pen)	32,11
2		31	A	Leeds United	L	0-2		13,57
3	Sep	3	A	Manchester United	L	1-4	Harris	22,22
4		7	H	Leicester City	W	2-1	Kelly, Jones	14,09
5		10	H	Stoke City	L	1-2	Harris	26,51
6		12	A	Leicester City	L	1-2	Farrage	10,77
7		17	A	Chelsea	D	2-2	Brown (pen), Jones	39,50
8		24	H	Preston North End	L	1-3	Farrage	26,22
9	Oct	1	A	Charlton Athletic	D	4-4	Harris 2, Duckhouse, White	20,03
10		8	H	Bolton Wanderers	L	0-2		21,85
11		15	H	Derby County	W	3-0	White 2, Brown	27,85
12		22	A	Grimsby Town	L	0-1		11,02
13		29	H	Aston Villa	W	3-0	Harris 2, Brown	55,30
14	Nov	5	A	Wolverhampton Wan.	L	1-2	Phillips	30,71
15		12	H	Everton	W	1-0	Phillips	27,54
16		19	A	Huddersfield Town	L	1-3	Morris	14,63
17		26	H	Portsmouth	W	2-0	Jennings (pen), Dearson	20,31
18	Dec	3	A	Arsenal	L	1-3	Jennings (pen)	33,71
19		10	H	Brentford	W	5-1	White 4, Phillips	23,33
20		17	A	Blackpool	L	1-2	White	11,85
21		24	A	Sunderland	L	0-1		14,55
22		26	H	Middlesbrough	W	2-1	Morris, Trigg	17,95
23		27	H	Middlesbrough	D	2-2	Harris, Phillips	33,53
24		31	H	Manchester United	D	3-3	Jennings, Phillips, Dearson	20,78
25	Jan	14	A	Stoke City	L	3-6	Jennings (pen), Harris, Duckhouse	14,41
26		28	A	Preston North End	L	0-5		18,47
27	Feb	4	H	Charlton Athletic	L	3-4	Harris 3	29,72
28		18	A	Derby County	W	1-0	Brown	15,41
29		22	A	Bolton Wanderers	L	0-3		11,69
30		25	H	Grimsby Town	D	1-1	Craven	23,23
31	Mar	4	A	Aston Villa	L	1-5	Dearson	40,87
32		11	H	Wolverhampton Wan.	W	3-2	Harris, Morris, Jones	48,97
33		18	A	Everton	L	2-4	Harris, Jones	29,68
34		29	H	Huddersfield Town	D	1-1	Jones	8,97
35	Apr	1	A	Portsmouth	L	0-2		21,91
36		7	A	Liverpool	L	0-4		31,74
37		8	H	Arsenal	L	1-2	Kendrick	33,25
38		10	H	Liverpool	D	0-0		15,06
39		15	A	Brentford	W	1-0	Jones	15,29
40		22	H	Blackpool	W	2-1	Craven, Harris	21,81
41		26	H	Chelsea	D	1-1	Brown	28,63
42		29	H	Leeds United	W	4-0	Brown, Scaife (og), Morris 2	12,52

| | | | | | | | | Appearance |
| | | | | | | One own-goal | | Goal |

FA Cup

R3	Jan	7	H	Halifax Town	W	2-0	Jennings, Phillips	23,52
R4		21	H	Chelmsford City	W	6-0	Harris 2, Brown, Jennings, Madden 2	44,49
R5	Feb	11	H	Everton	D	2-2	Madden 2	67,34
rep		15	A	Everton	L	1-2	Harris	64,79

| | | | | | | | | Appearance |
| | | | | | | | | Goal |

Player Appearances Grid

Hillas HE	Tingi C	Steel WG	Jennings DB	Merrick RW	Hallsall WG	Phillips C	Deacon DJ	Morsland AG	Harris F	Morris S	Hughes WM	Bannwski NH	White RH	Jones CW	Kelly J	Farrage TD	Brown J	Rochards DT	Duchhouse E	Madden G	Wheeler WJ	Shaw R	Clack FE	Butler H	Craven C	Sykes EA	Bye JH	Turner AD	Bodle H	Shaw J	Kendrick K
2	3	4	5	6	7	8	9	10	11																						
2	3	4	5	6	7	8	9	10	11																						
2	3	4	5	6	7	8	9	10	11																						
	2		5	6		8					3	4		7	9	10	11														
	2		5		6		8				3	4		9	10	11	7														
	2		5		6		8				3	4	10	9		11	7														
	2		5	6		8					3	4		9	10	11	7														
	2		5	6		8					3	4		9	10	11	7														
2				4		8					3	5	7				11	6	9	10											
2			5	4		8					3		7	9			11	6		1	10										
2		8		5	9	4		10			3		7				11	6			1										
2	3	8		5	9	6		10				4	7				11				1										
2		8		5	9	4		10			3		7				11	6			1										
2		8	5		9	4		10			3		7				11	6			1										
2		7		5	9	4		10			3		8				11	6			1										
2		8			9	4		10	11	3		7				6				1	5										
2		8			4	9	10				3		7				11	6			1	5									
2		8		5		4		10			3		7	9			11	6			1										
2			5	9	4		10				3		7				11	6			1	8									
2	3		5	9	4		10					7				11	6			1	8										
2		7	5	9	4		10				3					11	6			1	8										
2			5	9	4			7	3							11	6	9	10	1	8										
	5		8	4		10		3								7	6	9		1	11	2									
3	7	5		9	4		10				3					11	6			1	8	2									
	7	5		4		10		3								11	9			6	1	8	2								
	7	5			3								9				11		10	6	1	8	2	4							
2		7	4	9	8	10		3								11				6	1			5							
2		7	5		4	9	3									11	6	10			1	8									
2		4	5		9	11	3									7	6	10			1	8					10				
2		4	5		9	11	3									7	6				1	8							6		
2		7	5		4	10	3					9				11					1	8			5	6					
2		8		4	10	11	3					9				7					1			5	6						
2		8		4	10	11	3					9	11	7							1			5	6						
	7		8	10	11	3						9					6		1				2	5	4						
	8		4	10	3							9				11			1				2	5	6	7					
		4	10	3								9				11			1			8	2	5	6	7					
2	8		4	10	11	3						9				7			1					5	6						
2	7		4	10	3							9				11					8			5	6						
2	7		4	10	11	3						9				8					8			5	6						
2		4	10	11	3							9				7					8			5	6						
2	3		4	10	11	3						9				7				6	8			5							
30	**11**	**29**	**13**	**21**	**15**	**39**	**4**	**37**	**14**	**35**	**7**	**13**	**21**	**4**	**7**	**34**	**19**	**4**	**5**	**5**	**5**	**24**	**2**	**17**	**7**	**1**	**12**	**1**	**11**	**2**	
1		**5**			**5**	**3**			**14**	**5**				**8**	**6**	**1**	**2**	**6**		**2**				**2**					**1**		

7	5		9		10	3						11	6					1			8	2	4								
7	5		4		9	3						11			10			6	1		8	2									
2	7		5	4		9	3					11	6		10			1			8										
2	7		5	4		9	3					11	6		10			1			8										
2	4	2	2	1	3		4	4				4	3		3		1	4		4	2	1									
	2		1			3						1			1		4														

League Table

	P	W	D	L	F	A	Pts
Everton	42	27	5	10	88	52	59
Wolverhampton W	42	22	11	9	88	39	55
Charlton Athletic	42	22	6	14	75	59	50
Middlesbrough	42	20	9	13	93	74	49
Arsenal	42	19	9	14	55	41	47
Derby County	42	19	8	15	66	55	46
Stoke City	42	17	12	13	71	68	46
Bolton Wanderers	42	15	15	12	67	58	45
Preston North End	42	16	12	14	63	59	44
Grimsby Town	42	16	11	15	61	69	43
Liverpool	42	14	14	14	62	63	42
Aston Villa	42	16	9	17	71	60	41
Leeds United	42	16	9	17	59	67	41
Manchester United	42	11	16	15	57	65	38
Blackpool	42	12	14	16	56	68	38
Sunderland	42	13	12	17	54	67	38
Portsmouth	42	12	13	17	47	70	37
Brentford	42	14	8	20	53	74	36
Huddersfield Town	42	12	11	19	58	64	35
Chelsea	42	12	9	21	64	80	33
Birmingham	42	12	8	22	62	84	32
Leicester City	42	9	11	22	48	82	29

Division Two

Manager: George Liddell

Match No.	Date	Venue	Opponents	Result		Scorers	Attendance
1	Aug 26	A	Tottenham Hotspur	D	1-1	Brown	28,36
2	30	H	Leicester City	W	2-0	Farrage, Sharman (og)	13,84
3	Sep 2	H	Burnley	W	2-0	Dearson, Duckhouse	15,90

Appearance
One own-goal Goa

Competition abandoned due to outbreak of World War Two.

Midland Regional League

Opponents	H	A
Coventry City	2–4	1–3
Coventry City	2–0	-
Coventry City	0–0	-
Leicester City	0–0	1–2
Leicester City	3–3	3–1
Luton Town	5–4	2–1
Luton Town	4–1	2–4
Northampton Town	3–1	1–1
Northampton Town	-	3–1
Northampton Town	-	0–3
Walsall	2–1	2–1
Walsall	8–1	2–1
West Brom. Albion	-	1–4
West Brom. Albion	-	1–6
West Brom. Albion	-	0–3
West Brom. Albion	-	2–2
Wolverhampton W.	-	3–2
Wolverhampton W.	0–1	1–3
Wolverhampton W.	-	2–6

Blues played every team four times.

League Cup

Opponents	H	A
Arsenal	-	2–1*
Newport County	5–2	2–2
Reading	2–0	2–0
West Ham United	-	2–4*

* Games played at White Hart Lane.

Appearances (all games):

J. Allen* 1, J. Bate* 1, S. Bellamy 4, H. Bodle 23, F. Broome* 17, E. Brown 1, J. Brown 23, J. Bye 26, C. Craven 9
G. Cummings* 4, F. Deakin* 4, D. Dearson 27, R. Devey* 3, E. Duckhouse 9, G. Edwards* 10, T. Farrage 3, R. Foulkes
F. Gardner 2, A. Godden 11, F. Guest* 6, F. Harris 28, H. Hibbs 12, W. Hughes 26, R. Iverson* 7, D. Jennings 8,
C. Wilson Jones 20, D. Kernick* 1, J. Martin* 2, A. Massie* 4, G. Merrick 1, S. Morris 1, F. Moss* 1, F.W. Moss
W. Quinton 24, S. Rowley 1, R. Shaw 13, C. Trigg 25, A. Turner 26, J. Wheeler 24.
* Denotes guest player

Goalscorers:

Bodle 12, Wilson Jones 11, Trigg 11, Brown 6, Duckhouse 6, Broome 5, Godden 5, Dearson 4, Edwards 4, Guest 2,
Turner 2, Bye 1, Farrage 1, Gardner 1, Harris 1, Jennings 1, opponents 3.

Seasonal summary of games played:

Venue	P	W	D	L	F	A
Home	15	10	3	2	40	18
Away	22	8	4	10	36	52
Totals	37	18	7	12	76	70

2	3	4	5	6	7	8	9	10	11	
2	3	4	5	6	7	8	9	10	11	
2	3	4	5	6	7	8	9	10	11	
3	3	3	3	3	3	3	3	3	3	
					1	1	1		1	

1940-41

League (South) First and Second Championships

Opponents	H	A
Cardiff City	3–2	2–5
Leicester City	1–2	1–2
Luton Town	-	5–2
Mansfield Town	4–1	1–4
Northampton Town	-	1–2
Nottingham Forest	2–1	3–2
Notts County	-	3–3
Stoke City	6–2	0–5
Walsall	-	3–6
West Brom. Albion	1–3	2–1

League (South) Cup

Opponents	H	A
Leicester City	-	3–3
Leicester City replay	-	2–3

Both games played at Filbert Street.

Appearances (all games):

.Batty* 1, H. Bodle 1, J. Brown 7, J. Bye 6, C. Craven 4, F. Deakin14, R. Devey 4, G. Eastham* 6, R. Foulkes 14, . Galley 1, F. Gardner 12, J. Gill* 5, A. Godden 6, F. Harris 13, W. Hughes 12, D. Jennings 12, C. Wilson Jones 12, . Kernick* 4, G. Merrick 13, S. Morris 1, F.W. Moss 1, H. Pearce 2, W. Quinton 16, R. Shaw 3, W. Thayne* 1, . Trigg 12, A. Turner 3, J. Wheeler 5.
Denotes guest player.

Goalscorers:

Trigg 20, Dearson 6, Gardner 3, Wilson Jones 3, Harris 2, Bye 1, Bodle 1, Craven 1, Eastham 1, Godden 1, Gill 1, Jennings 1, Shaw 1, opponent 1.

Seasonal summary of games played:

Venue	P	W	D	L	F	A
Home	6	4	0	2	17	11
Away	12	3	2	7	26	38
Totals	18	7	2	9	43	49

1942-43

League (North) First and Second Championships

Opponents	H	A
Aston Villa	2–1	1–2
Aston Villa	-	0–1
Chesterfield	-	1–1
Coventry City	1–0	2–2
Coventry City	3–1	0–1
Derby County	0–5	1–3
Leicester City	2–1	1–0
Leicester City	5–0	1–2
Northampton Town	0–2	1–4
Northampton Town	1–0	0–1
Stoke City	1–0	3–1
Walsall	4–3	0–1
Walsall	2–1	2–1
Walsall	1–0	1–1
West Brom. Albion	3–0	3–4
West Brom. Albion	5–3	4–0
Wolverhampton W.	1–0	1–1

League (North) Cup

Opponents	H	A
Coventry City	3–1	0–1
Northampton Town	2–4	1–5
West Brom. Albion	0–1	1–2

Appearances (all games):

J. Acquaroff* 31, G. Ainsley* 1, S. Bartram* 1, J. Bate* 1, S. Batty* 2, S. Bellamy 1, H. Bodle 1, J. Bray* 1, J. Brown 3, D. Buttens 1, J. Bye 3, S. Chapman* 1, G. Collins* 2, J. Collins 2, C. Craven 24, H. Davy 4, F. Deakin * D. Dearson 23, R. Devey 2, L. Dolphin 2, E. Eden 7, R. Finan* 1, R. Ford 1, J. Gill 7, W. Goffin* 1, W. Guest* 2, E. Hapgood* 1, G. Hardwick* 1, F. Harris 4, W Hughes 1, P. Jenkins 1, D. Jennings 37, C. Wilson Jones 6, S. King 1, C. Lewis 6, J. McCormick* 28, W. McEwan* 3, G. Merrick 35, N. Middleton 2, E. Millichap 2, F. Mitchell* 16, F.W. Moss 1, S. Ottewell* 13, W. Pears 2, T. Pearson* 2, J. Pope 1, W. Quinton 30, E. Richards 3, G. Robinson* 2 L. Romp 1, J. Shaw 1, R. Shaw 31, J. Shelton* 1, E. Sibley* 1, T. Smith 1, F. Sweeney 1, G. Tranter 2, J. Trickett 1 C. Trigg 5, A. Turner 32, P. Vause* 1, G. Watton 14, F. Watts 1, W. Webster* 1.
* Denotes guest player.

Goalscorers:

Acquaroff 8, Dearson 7, Ottewell 7, Wilson Jones 6, Craven 5, McCormick 5, Watton 5, McEwan 2, Bate 1, Brown 1, Eden 1, Gill 1, Harris 1, Lewis 1, Richards 1, Romp 1, R. Shaw 1, Trickett 1, Turner 1, opponents 3.

Seasonal summary of games played:

Venue	P	W	D	L	F	A
Home	18	13	0	5	34	24
Away	20	4	4	12	25	35
Total	38	17	4	17	59	59

Wartime Blues

League (North) First and Second Championships

Opponents	H	A
Aston Villa	2–1	0–3
Coventry City	0–0	1–2
Derby County	3–3	3–5
Leicester City	3–0	2–2
Northampton Town	1–3	1–2
Northampton Town	3–1	5–0
Stoke City	2–0	1–1
Walsall	5–1	4–2
West Brom. Albion	3–0	3–1
Wolverhampton W.	4–2	0–3

League (North) and Midland Cup Competitions

Opponents	H	A
Aston Villa	1–1	2–1
Coventry City	-	3–0
Leicester City	3–1	1–2*
Manchester City	0–0	0–1
Manchester United	3–1	1–1+
Northampton Town	5–1	-
Stoke City	4–1	1–4
Walsall	5–0	2–2
West Brom. Albion	4–0	1–1
Wolverhampton W.	2–1	2–0

* After extra-time.
+ Played at Maine Road.

Appearances (all games):

Acquaroff* 13, R. Barnett 4, H. Bodle 4, R. Bright* 27, J. Bye 4, C. Craven 6, E. Day 1, D. Dearson 30, P. Doherty* 4, Dolphin 1, R. Faulkner* 1, H. Gee 2, A. Godden 2, K. Green 7, J. Hackett 1, F. Harris 4, L. Hayward* 2, G. Hinsley* 5, W. Hughes 5, D. Jennings 26, W.V. Jones 1, T. McKillop* 1, G. Merrick 38, N. Middleton 2, F. Mitchell 11, . Montgomery 1, L. Morgan* 1, S. Morris 2, A. Mulraney* 33, S. Ottwell* 1, T. Peacock* 1, W. Quinton 24, . Redwood* 1, C. Revell* 1, N. Roberts 2, T. Roberts 16, R. Shaw 32, T. Sibley 2, M. Sinclair* 1, S. Stanton 7, Stanton 1, J. Trickett 1, C. Trigg 30, A. Turner 32, H. Turner* 27.
Denotes guest player.

Goalscorers:

Trigg 35, Mulraney 14, Bright 10, Dearson 5, T. Roberts 4, Hinsley 3, Shaw 3, Acquaroff 2, Bodle 1, Bye 1, Doherty 1, Faulkner 1, Gee 1, Godden 1, Jennings 1, Mitchell 1, Morris 1, Revell 1.

Seasonal summary of games played:

Venue	P	W	D	L	F	A
Home	19	14	4	1	53	17
Away	19	6	5	8	33	33
Totals	38	20	9	9	86	50

League (North) First and Second Championships

Opponents	H	A
Aston Villa	3–2	1–1
Aston Villa	0–3	0–5
Coventry City	1–2	1–0
Coventry City	5–1	2–1
Leicester City	3–3	1–0
Northampton Town	0–0	1–2
Northampton Town	2–2	2–0
Nottingham Forest	4–1	0–0
Port Vale	4–0	0–3
Stoke City	1–1	0–0
Walsall	2–2	1–4
West Brom. Albion	2–0	4–1
West Brom. Albion	4–1	3–2
Wolverhampton W	1–0	4–0
Wolverhampton W.	0–0	1–2

League (North) Cup

Opponents	H	A
Aston Villa	0–1	1–3
Northampton Town	4–0	1–2
West Brom. Albion	1–1	0–4
Walsall	3–1	2–0
Wolverhampton W.	0–0	0–1*

* Game lasted 153 minutes.

Midland League Cup

Opponents	H	A
Coventry City	1–2	2–2

Lost 4–3 on aggregate.

Appearances (all games);

H. Adams 1, R. Bell 1, R. Barnett 1, J. Berry 2, H. Bodle 4, W. Booth* 6, R. Bright* 19, A. Clements 1, C. Craven 12, D. Dearson 38, J. Elliott 1, K. Faulkner 14, J. Fenton 1, A. Garrett* 1, J. Greatrix 1, F. Harrow 6, W. Harris 1, W. Hicklin 11, D. Hipkins 10, W. Hughes 7, N. Jenks 2, D. Jennings 40, C. Jordan* 1, D. Kernick* 3, S. King 3, S.G. King 3, R. Lewes 3, A. Marriott 4, G. Martin 1, D. Massart 9, J. Matthews 2, G. Merrick 38, W. Metcalf * 5, F. Mitchell 7, F. Micheson 1, S. Morris 3, A. Mulraney 37, R. Murrell 2. H. O'Donnell* 3, A. Pope* 1, W. Quinton 12, T. Roberts 2, R. Shaw 30, T. Sibley 2, S. Small* 24, S. Smith 1, S. Stanton 14, D. Trentham* 1, C. Trigg 22, A. Turner 39, H. Turner* 1, F. White* 10, I. Williams 1.
* Denotes guest player.

Goalscorers:

Trigg 22, Massart 9, Mulraney 7, Bright 4, White 4, Small 3, Bodle 2, Dearson 2, Faulkner 2, Lewis 2, Kernick 2, Craven 1, Harris 1, Hipkins 1, Matthews 1, Shaw 1, A. Turner 1, opponents 3

Seasonal summary of games played:

Venue	P	W	D	L	F	A
Home	21	9	8	4	41	23
Away	21	8	4	9	27	33
Totals	42	17	12	13	68	56

Wartime Blues

Football League (South)

Opponents	H	A
Arsenal	0–1	3–0
Aston Villa	3–1	2–2
Brentford	1–0	1–2
Charlton Athletic	1–0	0–0
Chelsea	5–2	3–2
Coventry City	2–0	3–2
Derby County	1–0	2–0
Fulham	2–0	2–3
Leicester City	6–2	1–0
Luton Town	3–2	3–0
Millwall	4–0	1–5
Newport County	3–2	1–0
Nottingham Forest	3–1	0–1
Plymouth Argyle	0–1	3–2
Portsmouth	1–0	4–3
Southampton	4–0	1–1
Swansea Town	5–0	4–2
Tottenham Hotspur	8–0	1–0
West Brom. Albion	4–0	0–0
West Ham United	0–1	2–3
Wolverhampton W.	0–1	3–3

FA Cup

Opponents	H	A
Bradford Park Ave.	6–0	2–2
Derby County	-	1–1*
Derby County	-	0–4+
Portsmouth	1–0	0–0
Sunderland	3–1	0–1
Watford	5–0	1–1

* Semi-final played at Hillsborough.
+ replay played at Maine Road.
(See also Blues in other competitions)

Appearances (League only):

R. Bodle 40, D. Dearson 34, E. Ditchburn* 1, N. Dougall 38, E. Duckhouse 26, G. Edwards 38, F. Harris 39, W. Hughes 4, N. Jenks 2, D. Jennings 41, C. Wilson Jones 27, S. King 2, R. Laing 2, D. Massart 11, I. McPherson 1, G. Merrick 39, F. Mitchell 26, A. Mulraney 38, S. Owen 5, R. Shaw 2, S. Stanton 1, C. Trigg 1, A. Turner 40, F. White 4.
*Guest player.

Goalscorers (League only):

Wilson Jones 20, Bodle 16, Edwards 13, Mulraney 13, Dougall 10, Massart 9, Duckhouse 6, Harris 2, Turner 2, White 2, Dearson 1, Laing 1, Mitchell 1.

Seasonal summary of games played (including FA Cup)

Venue	P	W	D	L	F	A
Home	25	21	0	4	71	15
Away	27	11	9	7	44	40
Totals	52	32	9	11	115	55

Wartime Review

Blues were lying in second place in Division Two when the League programme was abandoned three games int[o] the 1939–40 season. Entering the Midland Regional League, the team did well and finished a creditable third despite having to play all their home games on a neutral ground between October and March when St Andrew'[s] was closed by the authorities because of the threat of air raids on the city. These were difficult times for the clu[b] and when travelling south to play Luton Town at Kenilworth Road in February 1940, the team coach crashe[d] through a traffic island during the black out, but thankfully no one on board was injured.

St Andrew's re-opened on 23 March 1940, and the visitors Walsall beat Blues 2–1 in front of 12,000 spectator[s] At the end of this season the legendary Blues goalkeeper Harry Hibbs announced his retirement. A benefit matc[h] was staged at St Andrew's in April and 15,000 fans saw Blues and Aston Villa draw 1–1.

In 1940–41, Blues entered the Football League (South) but were only able to complete 16 matches and tw[o] Cup games because of bomb damage to St Andrew's. The summer of 1941 saw further enemy bombs dropped o[n] the ground, and Blues were asked to stage games there only at the start and end of the season when the weathe[r] would be at its best. This, however, did not happen, and Blues played only friendly matches until resuming th[e] League (North) in August 1942.

During the 1942–43 campaign Blues played all their 'home' games at Villa Park, and it was not until Augus[t] 1943 that they returned to St Andrew's, which had suffered another devastating blow in January 1942. The mai[n] stand was burned down following an incident in which a fireman threw a bucket of petrol over a burning brazie[r] thinking it was full of water! Repair work was carried out in stages, and the stand was not finally completed unt[il] 1946.The players, meanwhile, soldiered on, and in 1943–44 had one of the best seasons of wartime footbal[l] winning 20 and drawing nine of the 38 games played and scoring 86 goals.

The following season was a mixed one for the team, but there were signs that events in Europe were takin[g] a turn for the better and that serious competitive football might return sooner rather than later. In June 194[5] Harry Storer was appointed Blues' manager. Two month later, a crowd of 30,000 saw West Ham United visit S[t] Andrew's for the start of the new Football League (South) programme, a competition that was interpreted a[s] being a 'transitional season', enabling all the clubs in the country to get their playing squads ready and signe[d] up for the resumption of normal League football the following season.

Blues certainly got back into a routine quickly – almost completing the double! They reached the semi-finals of the FA Cup, which was reintroduced after a six-year break, and won the League (South) Championship, edging out second city neighbours Aston Villa on goal-average after a titanic battle that went t[o] the very last day.

The crowds increased rapidly and, in fact, Blues' 10 FA Cup games were attended by a aggregate total of 388,451, with their two semi-final clashes with Derby County being watched by 145,420 fans.

Facts & Figures

- On 14 October 1939, Blues played two friendly matches – losing 1–0 at Wolves and 3–2 at Stoke.

- Cyril Trigg (five goals) scored Blues' first Wartime League hat-trick in the 6–2 League (South) win over Stoke City in November 1940.

- England beat Wales 2–1 at bomb-damaged St Andrew's in October 1941. Don Dearson (Blues) missed a penalty for the Welsh.

- Syd Ottewell (Chesterfield) was the first guest player to score a hat-trick for Blues in the war, obliging in the 5–3 win over West Bromwich Albion in April 1943.

- In the summer of 1943 Blues added City to the club's name, to become Birmingham City.

- Trigg (35 goals) top-scored for Blues in 1943–44. He found the net in 22 of the team's 38 matches and netted four times in the 5–0 win over Walsall in April.

- Wolves beat Blues 1–0 at Molineux in a second-round, second-leg League (North) Cup tie on 14 April 1945. The winning goal was scored by England international Bill Morris in the 63rd minute of extra-time. Both teams and the referee agreed to play to a finish when the scoresheet was blank at the end of normal time.

In October 1945 Blues defender Ted Duckhouse scored from fully 50 yards in the 8–0 League (South) victory over Tottenham Hotspur – Blues' biggest win in World War Two.

Blues recorded 18 consecutive home victories between 3 September 1945 and 9 March 1946.

On the last day of the 1945–46 season Blues had to beat Luton away to pip rivals Aston Villa to the League (South) Championship. They did it in style, winning 3–0 with goals by Harold Bodle, Frank Mitchell (penalty) and Jock Mulraney. Blues and Villa finished level on 61 points, but Blues edged the title on goal-average by 0.206 of a goal – 96–45 against Villa's 106–58.

Arthur Turner (186), Dennis Jennings (174), Gil Merrick (172) and Don Dearson (166) made most appearances for Blues during World War Two.

Cyril Trigg (88), Charlie Wilson Jones (40) and Jock Mulraney (34) were the three top goalscorers. Trigg was leading marksman in 1940–41 (20 goals), 1943–44 (35) and 1944–45 (22).

The biggest attendance at St Andrew's during the war was 56,615 versus Charlton Athletic in February 1946. There were 63,820 fans present for the local derby encounter away to Aston Villa in January 1946.

Among the many guest players who appeared for Blues during the hostilities were internationals Jimmy Allen, Frank Broome, George Cummings and Alex Massie (all of Aston Villa), Eddie Hapgood (Arsenal), George Hardwick (Middlesbrough), Bert Turner (Charlton), Jackie Bray and Peter Doherty (Manchester City) and George Eastham (Blackpool), plus goalkeepers Ted Ditchburn (Spurs) and Sam Bartram (Charlton) and forward Jack Acquaroff (Norwich City).

Tom Farrage, who played for Blues in 1939–40, was killed in action in 1944. He was a pilot with the Army Air Corps.

Not including the 10 FA Cup games from the previous season, Blues played 215 'other' competitive wartime games between 1939 and 1946. They won 107, drew 39 and lost 69, scored 428 goals and conceded 335.

1946-47

Division Two

Manager: Harry Storer

328

Did you know that?

Inside-forward Alex McIntosh, who had played for Wolves in the 1939 FA Cup Final, was one of a handful of Blues debutants this season.

Albert Stubbins scored a hat-trick for League champions-elect Liverpool in their 4–1 FA Cup quarter-final win over Blues at Anfield.

Harold Bodle scored his only hat-trick for Blues in the 6–1 home win over Plymouth Argyle. He might well have scored five that afternoon as he also struck a post and had two more goal-bound efforts kicked off the line.

Due to the Arctic weather conditions, Blues did not play a single League or Cup game between 23 December and 4 March.

Match No.	Date		Venue	Opponents	Result		Scorers	Attendance
1	Aug	31	A	Tottenham Hotspur	W	2-1	Jones 2	51,25
2	Sep	4	H	Leicester City	W	4-0	Jones 2, Mulraney, Dougall	29,32
3		7	H	Burnley	L	0-2		42,30
4		12	A	Leicester City	L	1-2	Mulraney	20,95
5		14	A	Barnsley	L	1-3	Mulraney	28,21
6		18	A	West Bromwich Albion	L	0-3		30,18
7		21	H	Newport County	D	1-1	Bodle	28,83
8		25	H	West Bromwich Albion	W	1-0	Dearson	50,53
9		28	A	Southampton	L	0-1		24,92
10	Oct	5	H	Nottingham Forest	W	4-0	Bodle, Trigg, Edwards 2	35,09
11		12	H	Coventry City	D	0-0		29,37
12		19	A	Chesterfield	W	1-0	Jones	18,74
13		26	H	Millwall	W	4-0	Bodle, Trigg 2, Dougall	23,24
14	Nov	2	A	Bradford Park Avenue	L	0-2		21,63
15		9	H	Manchester City	W	3-1	Dougall, Mulraney, Trigg	37,74
16		16	A	West Ham United	W	4-0	Bodle, Edwrds 2, Trigg	24,71
17		23	H	Sheffield Wednesday	W	3-1	Trigg 2, Dougall	32,42
18		30	A	Fulham	W	1-0	Trigg	20,79
19	Dec	7	H	Bury	W	3-0	Duckhouse, Dougall, Edwards	30,34
20		14	A	Luton Town	W	3-1	Trigg 3	21,76
21		21	H	Plymouth Argyle	W	6-1	Bodle 3, Mulraney 2, Edwards	26,73
22		25	H	Swansea Town	W	3-1	Dougall, Bodle, Feeney (og)	31,30
23		26	A	Swansea Town	L	0-1		20,00
24		28	H	Tottenham Hotspur	W	1-0	Mulraney	44,17
25	Jan	4	A	Burnley	L	0-1		36,28
26		18	H	Barnsley	L	1-2	Duckhouse	41,40
27	Feb	1	H	Southampton	W	3-1	Trigg 2, Mulraney	32,87
28		15	H	Coventry City	W	2-0	Trigg 2	43,55
29		22	H	Chesterfield	D	0-0		26,13
30	Mar	15	A	Manchester City	L	0-1		55,65
31		22	H	West Ham United	W	3-0	McIntosh, Mitchell (pen), Trigg	29,93
32		29	A	Sheffield Wednesday	L	0-1		27,43
33	Apr	4	A	Newcastle United	D	2-2	McIntosh, Bodle	57,25
34		5	H	Fulham	W	2-1	Hall, Goodwin	28,19
35		7	H	Newcastle United	W	2-0	Bodle, Trigg	42,40
36		12	A	Bury	L	0-2		18,88
37		19	H	Luton Town	W	1-0	Goodwin	27,31
38		26	A	Plymouth Argyle	W	2-0	Edwards, Bodle	23,33
39	May	3	H	Bradford Park Avenue	W	4-0	Dougall, Bodle 2, Mitchell (pen)	23,08
40		10	A	Nottingham Forest	D	1-1	Harris	16,04
41		17	A	Millwall	W	2-0	McIntosh, Dougall	24,08
42		26	A	Newport County	W	3-0	Bodle 2, Dougall	12,02

Appearance
One own-goal Goa

FA Cup

	Date		Venue	Opponents	Result		Scorers	Attendance
R3	Jan	11	A	Fulham	W	2-1	Jones, Dorman	22,39
R4		25	H	Portsmouth	W	1-0	Harris	50,15
R5	Feb	8	H	Manchester City	W	5-0	Bodle, Trigg 2, Mitchell (pen), Mulraney	56,05
R6	Mar	1	A	Liverpool	L	1-4	Mitchell (pen)	51,91

Appearance
Goa

Player appearance/line-up grid (columns left to right):

	Birnick G	Dearson D	Hughes W	Harris F	Duckhouse E	Mitchell F	Mulraney A	Dougall N	Jones CW	Badis H	Edwards G	Owen S	Massart D	Jennings D	Turner A	Trigg C	Goodwin JW	Davey R	Shaw R	Dorman D	McIntosh A	Hall F	Pantley D	Wheeler WJ	Faulkner AG
		2	3	4		5	6	7	8	9	10	11													
		2	3			5	6	7	8		10	11	4												
		2	3			5	6	7	8		10	11	4	9											
				2		6	7	8	9	10	11	4			3	5									
	4	3		9		6	7	8	10		11			5	2										
		2	3			6	7		9	10	11	4			5		8								
		2	3			6	7		9	10	11	4					8	5							
	4	3		2		6		8	9	10	11				5		7								
	4	3				6		8	9	10	11				5	2	7								
		2	3			6	7	8		10	11				5	9		4							
		2	3			6		8		10	11				5	9	7		4						
	3					6		8		10	11	9		5	2	7		4							
		2	3			6	7	8		10	11				5	9		4							
		2	3			6	11	8		10	11				5	9	7		4						
		2	3	4		6	7	8		10	11				5	9									
		2	3	4		6	7	8		10	11				5	9									
		2	3	4		6	7	8		10	11				5	9									
		2	3	4		6	7	8		10	11				5	9									
		2	3	4	9	6	7	8		10	11				5										
		2	3	4		6	7	8		10	11				5	9									
	3			4	2	6	7	8		10	11				5	9									
	3			4	2	6	7	8		10	11				5	9									
	3			4		6	7	8		10	11			2	5	9									
	2			4		6	7	8		10	11			3	5	9									
	2			4		6	7	8			11			3	5	9			10						
	6		4	9			7	10			11			3	5	2		8							
			4	2	6		7			10	11			3	5	9				8					
			4	2	6	7	8			10	11			3	5	9				8					
			4	2	6		8			10	11			3	5	9	7								
		3	4	9	6	7	8			11				2	5				10						
		3	4	5	6	7	8			11				2		9			10						
		3	4	5	6	7	8			11				2		9			10						
		3	4	5	6		7			10	11	9		2				8							
		3	4	5	6					10	11			2		7		8	9						
		3	4	5	6					10				2	7			8	9	11					
		3	4	5	6					10				2	7			8	9	11					
		3	4		6		9			10	11		2	5	7			8							
		3	4	5	6		9			10	11		2		7			8							
		3	4	5	6		9			10	11		2		7			8							
			4	5	6		9			10	11		3	2	7			8							
			4	5	6		9			10	11		3	2				8		1	7				
			4	5	6		9			10	11		3					8			7				

Totals:

| | 1 | 25 | 28 | 29 | 25 | 41 | 27 | 35 | 9 | 36 | 39 | 5 | 3 | 18 | 27 | 29 | 15 | 1 | 5 | 2 | 14 | 3 | 2 | 1 | 2 |
| (goals) | 1 | | 1 | 2 | 2 | 8 | 9 | 5 | 15 | 7 | | | | | | | 17 | 2 | | | | 3 | 1 | | |

Cup section:

	6		4	9			7			10		11			3	5	2					8			
	6		4	2			7	8			10	11			3	5	9								
			4	2	6	7	8			10	11			3	5	9									
			4	2	6	7	8			10	11			3	5	9									
	2		4	4	2	4	3	1		3	4		4	4	4						1				
			1		2	1		1	1					2							1				

League Table

	P	W	D	L	F	A	Pts
Manchester City	42	26	10	6	78	35	62
Burnley	42	22	14	6	65	29	58
Birmingham City	42	25	5	12	74	33	55
Chesterfield	42	18	14	10	58	44	50
Newcastle United	42	19	10	13	95	62	48
Tottenham Hotspur	42	17	14	11	65	53	48
West Bromwich Albion	42	20	8	14	88	75	48
Coventry City	42	16	13	13	66	59	45
Leicester City	42	18	7	17	69	64	43
Barnsley	42	17	8	17	84	86	42
Nottingham Forest	42	15	10	17	69	74	40
West Ham United	42	16	8	18	70	76	40
Luton Town	42	16	7	19	71	73	39
Southampton	42	15	9	18	69	76	39
Fulham	42	15	9	18	63	74	39
Bradford Park Avenue	42	14	11	17	65	77	39
Bury	42	12	12	18	80	78	36
Millwall	42	14	8	20	56	79	36
Plymouth Argyle	42	14	5	23	79	96	33
Sheffield Wednesday	42	12	8	22	67	88	32
Swansea Town	42	11	7	24	55	83	29
Newport County	42	10	3	29	61	133	23

1947-48

Division Two

Manager: Harry Storer

Match No.	Date	Venue	Opponents	Result		Scorers	Attendance
1	Aug 23	H	Barnsley	L	2-3	Bodle, Mitchell (pen)	37,917
2	25	A	Coventry City	W	1-0	Aveyard	30,556
3	30	A	Plymouth Argyle	W	3-0	Dougall, Bodle, Aveyard	24,178
4	Sep 3	H	Coventry City	D	1-1	Bodle	36,544
5	6	H	Luton Town	W	2-1	Bodle, Aveyard	40,032
6	10	A	Newcastle United	D	0-0		35,358
7	13	A	Brentford	W	2-1	Trigg, Edwards	25,523
8	17	A	Newcastle United	L	0-1		51,704
9	20	H	Leicester City	W	1-0	Dougall	36,491
10	27	A	Leeds United	W	1-0	Trigg	37,139
11	Oct 4	H	Fulham	W	3-1	Bodle, Trigg 2	39,758
12	11	H	Chesterfield	D	0-0		37,918
13	18	A	West Ham United	D	0-0		32,228
14	25	A	Bury	W	2-0	Bodle, Dougall	34,806
15	Nov 1	A	Southampton	L	0-2		27,243
16	8	H	Doncaster Rovers	W	3-0	Goodwin 2, Bodie	31,052
17	15	A	Nottingham Forest	W	2-0	McIntosh, Goodwin	33,364
18	22	H	Bradford Park Avenue	W	4-3	Ottewell 2, Goodwin, Mitchell (pen)	29,020
19	29	A	Cardiff City	L	0-2		39,648
20	Dec 6	H	Sheffield Wednesday	W	1-0	Westlake (og)	31,217
21	13	A	Tottenham Hotspur	W	2-1	Garrett, Dougall	52,730
22	20	A	Barnsley	W	1-0	Bodle	18,880
23	25	A	Millwall	D	0-0		25,794
24	27	H	Millwall	W	1-0	Goodwin	45,985
25	Jan 3	H	Plymouth Argyle	D	1-1	Goodwin	35,480
26	17	A	Luton Town	W	1-0	Bodle	19,697
27	31	H	Brentford	D	0-0		37,542
28	Feb 14	H	Leeds United	W	5-1	Laing 2, Stewart 2, Dorman	39,955
29	21	A	Fulham	D	1-1	Bodle	13,164
30	28	A	Chesterfield	W	3-0	Stewart, Dougall, Bodle	15,844
31	Mar 6	H	West Ham United	L	0-1		43,709
32	13	A	Bury	D	1-1	Edwards	23,420
33	20	H	Southampton	D	0-0		39,730
34	27	A	Doncaster Rovers	D	0-0		25,370
35	29	H	West Bromwich Albion	W	4-0	Stewart, Bodle 2, Trigg	47,074
36	30	A	West Bromwich Albion	D	1-1	Bodle	51,945
37	Apr 3	H	Nottingham Forest	W	2-1	Stewart, Mitchell (pen)	38,227
38	10	A	Bradford Park Avenue	W	2-1	Mitchell (pen), Stewart	16,782
39	17	H	Cardiff City	W	2-0	Trigg, Bodle	52,278
40	19	A	Leicester City	D	0-0		31,937
41	24	A	Sheffield Wednesday	D	0-0		25,789
42	May 1	H	Tottenham Hotspur	D	0-0		35,569

Appearances

One own-goal

Goals

FA Cup

R3	Jan 10	H	Notts County	L	0-2		53,322

Appearances

Player appearance / line-up grid (shirt numbers 1–11 per match). Column headings (left to right):

Merrick GH · Trigg C · Southam JH · Harris F · Duckhouse E · Michael FR · Gooden JW · McIntosh A · Dougall C · Badie H · Edwards G · Quinton W · Aveyard W · McDonnell M · Hughes JN · Green K · Berry LJ · Jennings DB · Ottwell S · Garrett ACE · Wheeler WJ · Stewart JG · Durnan DJ · Laing RS · Badham J

Me	Tr	So	Ha	Du	Mi	Go	McI	Do	Ba	Ed	Qu	Av	McD	Hu	Gr	Be	Je	Ot	Ga	Wh	St	Dr	La	Bd
2	3	4		5	6	7		8		9	10	11												
2		4	5	6	7		8		10	11		3	9											
2		4	5	6	7		8		10	11		3	9											
2		4	5	6	7		8		10	11		3	9											
2		4		6			8		10	11		3	9	5	7									
2		4		6			8		10	11		3	9	5	7									
9		4		6			8		10	11	3			5	7	2								
9		4		6			8		10	11	3			5		2	7							
	4	9	6				8		10	11	3			5		2	7							
9		4	2	6		7	8		10	11				5		3								
9		4	2	6		8	7		10	11				5		3								
	4	5	6		8	7		10	11	9				2		3								
	4	2	6		8		10			9	5		3	7		11								
9		4	2	6	7		8		10				5		3									
	4	9	6		8	7		10	11				5		2		3							
	4	9		7			8	10	11				5		2		3	6						
	4		6	7	10	9			11			5		2		3	8							
	4			6	7	10	9			11			5		2		3	8						
2		4	5	6	7		8			11				3	10	9								
	4	5	6	7	8		10	11				2		3		9	1							
	4	5	6	7		8	10	11				2		3		9	1							
	4	5	6	7		8	10	11				2		3		9	1							
	4	5	6	7		8	10	11				2		3		9	1							
	4	5	6	7		8	10	11				2		3		9	1							
	4	5	6	7	8	9	10	11				2		3			1							
9		4	5	6		8	10	11				2		3			7							
9		4	5	6			10	11				2		3			7	8						
9		4	5	6			10					2		3			7	8	11					
9		4	5	6			10					2		3			7	8	11					
	4	5	6			9	10					2		3			7	8	11	4				
	4	5	6			9	10					2		3			7	8	11	4				
	4	5	6		8	10	11					2		3		9	7							
	4	5	6		8	10	11					2		3		9	7							
9		4	5	6			10	11				2		3			7	8						
9		4	5	6			10	11				2		3			7	8						
9		4	5	6			10	11				2		3			7	8						
9		4	5	6		8	10	11				2		3			7							
9		4	5	6		8	10	11				2		3			7							
9		4	5	6		8	10	11				2		3			7							
9		4	5	6		8	10	11				2		3			7							
9		4	5	6		8	10	11				2		3			7							
9		4	5	6		8	10	11				2		3			7							
25	**1**	**40**	**36**	**41**	**16**	**9**	**34**	**39**	**37**	**8**	**7**	**13**	**3**	**35**	**3**	**29**	**5**	**8**	**6**	**17**	**8**	**4**	**2**	
6		**4**	**6**	**1**	**5**	**14**	**2**		**3**					**2**		**3**				**2**	**1**		**7**	**1**

Additional rows (lower block):

Me	Tr	So	Ha	Du	Mi	Go	McI	Do	Ba	Ed	Qu	Av	McD	Hu	Gr	Be	Je	Ot	Ga	Wh	St	Dr	La	Bd
9		6	5	10	7		8		11					2		3			1				4	
1		1	1	1	1		1		1					1		1			1				1	

League Table

	P	W	D	L	F	A	Pts
Birmingham City	42	22	15	5	55	24	59
Newcastle United	42	24	8	10	72	41	56
Southampton	42	21	10	11	71	53	52
Sheffield Wednesday	42	20	11	11	66	53	51
Cardiff City	42	18	11	13	61	58	47
West Ham United	42	16	14	12	55	53	46
West Bromwich Albion	42	18	9	15	63	58	45
Tottenham Hotspur	42	15	14	13	56	43	44
Leicester City	42	16	11	15	60	57	43
Coventry City	42	14	13	15	59	52	41
Fulham	42	15	10	17	47	46	40
Barnsley	42	15	10	17	62	64	40
Luton Town	42	14	12	16	56	59	40
Bradford Park Avenue	42	16	8	18	68	72	40
Brentford	42	13	14	15	44	61	40
Chesterfield	42	16	7	19	54	55	39
Plymouth Argyle	42	9	20	13	40	58	38
Leeds United	42	14	8	20	62	72	36
Nottingham Forest	42	12	11	19	54	60	35
Bury	42	9	16	17	58	68	34
Doncaster Rovers	42	9	11	22	40	66	29
Millwall	42	9	11	22	44	74	29

Division One

Manager: Harry Storer (to November); Bob Brocklebank (from January)

Did you know that?

Centre-forward Fred Slater unfortunately broke his leg in the 10th minute of his Blues debut against Huddersfield Town in November.

Blues failed to score in half of their 42 League games this season, having two separate sequences of five games without a single goal.

Jackie Stewart's four goals against Manchester City in mid-September was the most scored by a Blues winger at senior level for 60 years – since Ted Devey fired in a four-timer against Burton Wanderers in an FA Cup game in December 1888.

Former Blues forward Jack Peart died in September while manager of Fulham.

Match No.	Date		Venue	Opponents	Result		Scorers	Attendance
1	Aug	21	A	Wolverhampton Wan.	D	2-2	Bodie, Trigg	54,36
2		25	H	Middlesbrough	D	0-0		37,86
3		28	H	Chelsea	W	1-0	Stewart	48,26
4	Sep	1	A	Middlesbrough	D	1-1	Garrett	34,01
5		4	A	Everton	W	5-0	Trigg 2, Stewart 2, Garrett	49,19
6		8	A	Manchester City	L	0-1		29,95
7		11	H	Preston North End	W	1-0	Garrett	43,49
8		15	H	Manchester City	W	4-1	Stewart 4	35,59
9		18	A	Burnley	D	2-2	Trigg, Bodie	34,08
10		25	H	Stoke City	W	2-1	Harris, Dougall	48,89
11	Oct	2	A	Charlton Athletic	D	1-1	Garrett	56,29
12		9	A	Bolton Wanderers	D	0-0		45,49
13		16	H	Liverpool	L	0-1		42,33
14		23	A	Blackpool	L	0-1		25,12
15		30	H	Derby County	L	0-1		52,12
16	Nov	6	A	Arsenal	L	0-2		61,57
17		13	H	Huddersfield Town	W	1-0	Hepplewhite (og)	35,20
18		20	A	Manchester United	L	0-3		48,32
19		27	H	Sheffield United	L	1-2	Hall	32,85
20	Dec	4	A	Aston Villa	W	3-0	Stewart 2, Bodie	62,42
21		11	H	Sunderland	D	0-0		28,24
22		18	H	Wolverhampton Wan.	L	0-1		39,65
23		25	H	Newcastle United	W	2-0	Trigg, Roberts	42,11
24		27	A	Newcastle United	L	0-1		49,45
25	Jan	1	A	Chelsea	L	0-2		28,85
26		22	H	Preston North End	D	0-0		31,89
27	Feb	5	H	Burnley	D	0-0		34,00
28		12	H	Everton	D	0-0		35,09
29		19	A	Stoke City	L	1-2	Harris	25,97
30		26	H	Charlton Athletic	W	1-0	Stewart	35,50
31	Mar	5	H	Bolton Wanderers	D	0-0		20,73
32		12	A	Liverpool	L	0-1		43,75
33		19	H	Manchester United	W	1-0	Boyd	46,81
34		26	A	Sheffield United	L	0-4		25,76
35	Apr	2	H	Arsenal	D	1-1	Jordan	38,86
36		9	A	Huddersfield Town	D	0-0		18,85
37		15	A	Portsmouth	L	1-3	Dorman	38,45
38		16	H	Blackpool	D	1-1	Jordan	34,720
39		18	H	Portsmouth	W	3-0	Badham, Stewart, Hindmarsh (og)	29,98
40		23	A	Derby County	L	0-1		25,54
41		30	H	Aston Villa	L	0-1		45,12
42	May	7	A	Sunderland	D	1-1	Roberts	28,00
								Appearances
						Two own-goals		Goals

FA Cup

R3	Jan	8	H	Leicester City	D	1-1	Roberts	41,29
rep		15	A	Leicester City	D	1-1	Bodle	35,36
rep2		17	H	Leicester City	L	1-2	Dorman	31,60

R3 and R3 replay a.e.t.

Appearances
Goals

Appearance Grid

Merrick GH	Green K	Jennings DB	Harris F	Duckhouse E	Badham J	Stewart JG	Dougal C	Trigg C	Bodle H	Edwards G	Garrett ACE	McKee F	Hughes JN	Laing RS	Mitchell FR	Dorman DJ	McDowell M	Slater F	Hall F	Roberts H	Berry JJ	Goodwin JW	Boyd LA	Evans H	Daley J	Ferris RG	Jordan JW	Robertson WH	Quinton W	Southam JH
2	3	4	5	6	7	8	9	10	11																					
2	3	4	5	6	7	8	9	10	11																					
2	3	4	5	6	7	8	9	10	11																					
2	3	4	5	6	7	8	9		11	10																				
2	3	4	5		7	8	9		10	6	11																			
2	3	4	5		7	8	9		10	6	11																			
2	3	4	5		7	8	9		10	6	11																			
2	3	4	5		7	8	9		10	6		11																		
2	3	4	5		7	8	9		10	6		11																		
2	3	4	5		7	8	9		11	10	6																			
2	3	4	5		7	8	9		11	10	6																			
2	3	4	5		7	8	9		11	10	6																			
2	3	4	5		7	8	9		11	10	6																			
2	3	4	5		7		9		10					11	6	8														
2	3	4	5		7	8			10					11	6		9													
2	3	4	5		7		9	10						11	6	8														
2	3	4	5	6	7			10		8		11				5														
2	3	4			7			10		9	8	11	6				5													
2	3		5		7			10		6	8	4		9	11															
2	3	4	5			8	9	10		6				11	7															
2	3	4	5			8		10		6			9	11	7															
2	3	4	5			8	9	10		6				11	7															
2	3	4	5				8	9	10	6				11	7															
2	3	4	5				8	9	10	6				11	7															
2	3	4	5				10	9		6				11	7	8														
3		6	5				9	2	8					11	7		4	10												
3		6	5				9	2	8					11	7		4	10												
3		6	5		7	8	2	10						11		4			9											
	3	6	5		7	8	2	10						11		4			9											
3		10	5	4	8		2							11	7	6		9												
3		10	5	4	8		2							11	7	6		9												
3		10	5	2	8			9						11	7	4			6											
3		10			2	8			5	9				11	7	4			6											
3		4			2	8			5	9				11	7				6	10										
2	3	10	5	4	7					11						10					9	6	8	1						
2	3	10	5	4	7					11											9	6	8	1						
2	3		5	4	7					11	10								7		9	6	8							
2	3		5	9	8					11	4								7			6	10							
3			5	9	10					11	4	2							7			6	8							
3			5	9						11	4	2							7			6	8							
3		10	5	9	7						4	2				11				6			10	8						
41	30	36	39	18	37	24	23	18	8	11	11	3	14	11	10	9	3	2	17	16	1	9	2	7	11	9	1	0	0	
	2			1	11	1	5	3		4					1				1	2		1				2				

Cup

Merrick GH	Green K	Jennings DB	Harris F	Duckhouse E	Badham J	Stewart JG	Dougal C	Trigg C	Bodle H	Edwards G	Garrett ACE	McKee F	Hughes JN	Laing RS	Mitchell FR	Dorman DJ	McDowell M	Slater F	Hall F	Roberts H	Berry JJ	Goodwin JW	Boyd LA	Evans H	Daley J	Ferris RG	Jordan JW	Robertson WH	Quinton W	Southam JH
2		4	5	6		8	9	10								11	7										3			
3		4	5				9		6				8			11	7		10										2	
3		4	5			9			6				8			11	7		10								1		2	
3		3	3	1		1	2	2		2			2			3	3		2							1	1	2		
									1							1			1											

League Table

	P	W	D	L	F	A	Pts
Portsmouth	42	25	8	9	84	42	58
Manchester United	42	21	11	10	77	44	53
Derby County	42	22	9	11	74	55	53
Newcastle United	42	20	12	10	70	56	52
Arsenal	42	18	13	11	74	44	49
Wolverhampton W	42	17	12	13	79	66	46
Manchester City	42	15	15	12	47	51	45
Sunderland	42	13	17	12	49	58	43
Charlton Athletic	42	15	12	15	63	67	42
Aston Villa	42	16	10	16	60	76	42
Stoke City	42	16	9	17	66	68	41
Liverpool	42	13	14	15	53	43	40
Chelsea	42	12	14	16	69	68	38
Bolton Wanderers	42	14	10	18	59	68	38
Burnley	42	12	14	16	43	50	38
Blackpool	42	11	16	15	54	67	38
Birmingham City	42	11	15	16	36	38	37
Everton	42	13	11	18	41	63	37
Middlesbrough	42	11	12	19	46	57	34
Huddersfield Town	42	12	10	20	40	69	34
Preston North End	42	11	11	20	62	75	33
Sheffield United	42	11	11	20	57	78	33

Division One

Manager: Bob Brocklebank

Veteran Dennis Jennings, aged 39 years, 9 months and 17 days, became the oldest player ever to appear in a senior game for Blues when he lined-up against Wolves at Molineux on the last day of the season. It wasn't a happy farewell for Dennis, however, as Blues, trailing 5–0 at half-time, eventually lost 6–1, their worst defeat of the season and their heaviest in the League since 1936.

Blues failed to score a single goal in six League games between 1 October and 5 November. They 'fired' 21 blanks during the season.

Not once did Blues score more than two goals in any one of their 43 competitive matches this season. They managed only eight twos.

For the first time in his career, goalkeeper Gil Merrick was an ever-present between the posts. He would play in all 42 League games in 1950-51 and 41 in 1951–52.

Match No.	Date	Venue	Opponents	Result		Scorers	Attendance
1	Aug 20	H	Chelsea	L	0-3		45,06
2	24	H	West Bromwich Albion	W	2-0	Dailey 2	46,94
3	27	A	Stoke City	L	1-3	Capel	28,11
4	31	A	West Bromwich Albion	L	0-3		50,36
5	Sep 3	H	Burnley	L	0-1		36,34
6	10	A	Sunderland	D	1-1	Dailey	48,55
7	14	H	Wolverhampton Wan.	D	1-1	Dailey	46,43
8	17	H	Liverpool	L	2-3	Brennan, Dailey	37,85
9	24	A	Arsenal	L	2-4	Berry 2	50,85
10	Oct 1	H	Bolton Wanderers	D	0-0		33,14
11	8	H	Portsmouth	L	0-3		37,94
12	15	A	Huddersfield Town	L	0-1		22,87
13	22	H	Everton	D	0-0		32,20
14	29	A	Middlesbrough	L	0-1		33,2
15	Nov 5	H	Blackpool	L	0-2		34,04
16	12	A	Newcastle United	L	1-3	Slater	30,1
17	19	H	Fulham	D	1-1	Brennan	20,16
18	26	A	Manchester City	L	0-4		30,6
19	Dec 3	H	Charlton Athletic	W	2-0	Stewart, Berry	28,48
20	10	A	Aston Villa	D	1-1	Brennan	45,00
21	17	A	Chelsea	L	0-3		28,67
22	24	H	Stoke City	W	1-0	Higgins	28,72
23	26	H	Derby County	D	2-2	Capel, Stewart	45,47
24	27	A	Derby County	L	1-4	Brennan	36,45
25	31	A	Burnley	D	1-1	Dailey	25,47
26	Jan 14	H	Sunderland	L	1-2	Dailey	32,09
27	21	A	Liverpool	L	0-2		37,66
28	Feb 4	H	Arsenal	W	2-1	Dailey, Brennan	34,03
29	18	A	Bolton Wanderers	L	0-1		30,38
30	25	A	Portsmouth	L	0-2		28,09
31	Mar 4	H	Huddersfield Town	W	2-1	Dailey, Brennan	26,23
32	11	A	Fulham	D	0-0		24,97
33	18	H	Manchester City	W	1-0	Brennan	29,96
34	25	A	Blackpool	D	1-1	Stewart	20,73
35	Apr 1	H	Newcastle United	L	0-2		37,24
36	7	A	Manchester United	W	2-0	Stewart, Berry	48,99
37	8	A	Everton	D	0-0		46,82
38	10	H	Manchester United	D	0-0		35,86
39	15	H	Middlesbrough	D	0-0		31,57
40	22	A	Charlton Athletic	L	0-2		42,42
41	29	H	Aston Villa	D	2-2	Trigg 2	24,86
42	May 6	A	Wolverhampton Wan.	L	1-6	Trigg	42,93
						Appearance	
						Goa	

FA Cup

R3	Jan 7	A	Swansea Town	L	0-3		18,99
						Appearance	

Player appearance / line-up grid (shirt-number positions by match)

	Warrick GH	Trigg C	Green K	Dornan DJ	Duckhouse E	Harris F	Stewart JG	Brennan RA	Daley J	Capel TA	McKee F	McDonald M	Boyd LA	Ferris RO	Barry AJ	Badham J	Atkins AW	Jordan JW	Laing RS	Evans H	Jennings DB	Carr DH	Havenga WS	Slater F	Roberts H	Higgins JT	O'Hara EP	Blake AJ	Warhurst R
	2	3	4	5	6	7	8	9	10	11																			
		3		5		7	8	9	10		2	4	6	11															
		3		5		7	8	9	10		2	4	6	11															
		3		5		7	8	9	10		2	4	6	11															
		3				7		9	10	4			6			2	5	8	11										
		3				7	8	9	10	5	4	6	11	2															
		3	4			7	8	9		10	5		6	11	2														
		3	4			7	8	9		10	5		6	11	2														
		3	4			7	8	9	10		5		6	11	2														
	2	3		4		8		9	10		5		7	6			11												
	2	3		4			8	9	10		5		11	7	6														
	2						10	9		6	5		11	7	4		8		3										
						11	10	9			4		8	6	5			3	2	7									
	2		6		7	10			11		4		8	9	5		3												
	2			6		10			4			7	5	8		3		9	11										
	2		5	6		10					7	4	8		11	3		9											
	2		5	6		10			7			4	8			3			9	11									
	2		5	6		10			7			4	8			3			9	11									
				6	7	10			11	2	5	8			3	4			9										
		6			7	10			4		11	2	5	8		3			9										
	3				7	10			4	6	11	2	5	8			9												
	3	6			7	10			4		11	2	5	8			9												
	3				7	10			4	6	11	2	5	8			9												
	2				7	10				6	11	4	5	8		3		9											
	5	6					9		8		7	2			10	3	4		11										
	2				7	8	9		4		11	5			10	3													
	2	6			7	8	9		4		11	5			10	3													
	2	6			7	10	9		4		11	5	8			3													
		6	2		7	10	9		4		11	5		8						3									
	3	4	2	10	8		9		6		7	5							11										
	2	8			10	9			4	6	7	5							11	3									
		8			7	10	9		4	6		2	5						11										
		4			7	10	9			6	8	2	5			3									11				
		8			7	10	9		4	6	11	2	5			3													
					7	10	9		4	6	8	2	5			3		11											
	9				7	8			4	6	11	2	5			10	3												
	9		2		8				4	6	7		5			10	3	11											
	9		2		8				4	6	7		5			10	3									11			
	9	2	5		8				4	6	7					10	3									11			
	9	2	5		7	10			4	6	11			8			3												
	9	2	5	10	7	8			4	6	11						3												
	9	2	5	10	7	8			4	6	11						3												
Apps	12	29	16	15	12	31	39	8	8	10	27	25	39	28	20	15	1	9	25	3	1	2	7	8	2	2	3		
Goals		3				4	7	9	2				4										1	1					

Cup appearances / goals

	Dornan DJ	Duckhouse E	Brennan RA	Daley J	Boyd LA	Ferris RO	Atkins AW	Laing RS	Carr DH
Apps	5	6	8	9	7	2	10	3 4	11
Goals	1	1	1	1	1	1	1 1 1		1

Division Two

Manager: Bob Brocklebank

Young, promising full-back Jeff Hall, who would go on and play for England, made his League debut against Bury in January – the first of 264 appearances for the club.

Blues played four in Festival of Britain Matches in 1951. They lost two at home to Airdrieonians 5–3 and Dinamo Yugoslavia 2–0 and won two in Ireland against Home Farm 2–1 and Cork Athletic 5–2.

Cyril Trigg, who played 140 senior games for Blues at right-back between March 1936 and January 1950, finished up as the team's leading scorer this season, with 19 goals in League and Cup.

Match No.	Date		Venue	Opponents	Result		Scorers	Attendance
1	Aug	19	A	Swansea Town	W	1-0	Boyd	25,0
2		23	H	Leicester City	W	2-0	Trigg, Smith	28,34
3		26	H	Grimsby Town	D	1-1	Powell	33,0
4		28	A	Leicester City	W	3-1	Trigg, Smith, Stewart	31,29
5	Sep	2	A	Notts County	W	1-0	Smith	34,64
6		6	H	Coventry City	D	1-1	Higgins	24,7
7		9	H	Preston North End	W	1-0	Smith	32,63
8		11	A	Coventry City	L	1-3	Berry	30,44
9		16	A	Bury	L	1-4	Dorman	16,80
10		23	H	Queen's Park Rangers	D	1-1	Heath (og)	26,58
11		30	A	Chesterfield	D	1-1	Trigg	12,33
12	Oct	7	A	Southampton	W	2-0	Smith, Green	25,49
13		14	H	Barnsley	W	2-0	Smith, Boyd	26,61
14		21	A	Brentford	L	1-2	Trigg	19,27
15		28	H	Blackburn Rovers	W	3-2	Trigg, Smith, Stewart	24,55
16	Nov	4	A	Hull City	L	2-3	Trigg 2	32,03
17		11	H	Doncaster Rovers	L	0-2		26,72
18		18	A	Sheffield United	L	2-3	Smith, Stewart	23,87
19		25	H	Luton Town	W	3-0	Higgins 2, Smith	18,60
20	Dec	2	A	Leeds United	L	0-3		23,35
21		9	H	West Ham United	W	3-1	Higgins, Stewart, Smith	18,18
22		16	H	Swansea Town	W	5-0	Trigg 3, Stewart, Berry	15,64
23		23	A	Grimsby Town	D	1-1	Smith	13,14
24		25	A	Manchester City	L	1-3	Trigg	40,17
25		26	H	Manchester City	W	1-0	Trigg	32,09
26		30	H	Notts County	L	1-4	Stewart	33,77
27	Jan	13	A	Preston North End	L	0-1		30,66
28		20	H	Bury	D	3-3	Trigg 2, Stewart	25,65
29	Feb	3	A	Queen's Park Rangers	L	0-2		12,25
30		17	H	Chesterfield	W	2-1	Trigg, Higgins	33,76
31		28	H	Southampton	W	2-1	Trigg, Stewart	12,55
32	Mar	3	A	Barnsley	W	2-0	Dailey, Stewart	15,45
33		17	A	Blackburn Rovers	W	3-2	Dailey 2, Higgins	28,11
34		23	H	Cardiff City	D	0-0		15,05
35		24	H	Hull City	W	2-1	Dailey, Boyd	27,5
36		26	H	Cardiff City	L	1-2	Rowley	36,99
37		31	A	Doncaster Rovers	W	1-0	Trigg	16,09
38	Apr	7	H	Sheffield United	W	3-0	Higgins, Rowley, Warhurst	21,97
39		14	A	Luton Town	D	1-1	Warhurst	16,32
40		21	H	Leeds United	L	0-1		23,80
41		25	H	Brentford	D	1-1	Smith	13,64
42		28	A	West Ham United	W	2-1	Rowley, Ferris	12,39
								Appearance
				One own-goal				Goa

FA Cup

R3	Jan	6	H	Manchester City	W	2-0	Stewart, Higgins	30,09
R4		27	A	Derby County	W	3-1	Stewart, Trigg, Smith	37,38
R5	Feb	10	H	Bristol City	W	2-0	Stewart, Trigg	47,83
R6		24	H	Manchester United	W	1-0	Higgins	50,76
SF	Mar	10	N	Blackpool	D	0-0		71,89
rep		14	N	Blackpool	L	1-2	Smith	70,11

SF at Maine Road, Manchester. SF replay at Goodison Park, Liverpool.

	Appearance
	Goa

Player appearances and goals grid — Birmingham City

Mirick GH	Badham J	Green K	Boyd LAM	Atkins AW	Dorman DJ	Berry RJ	Powell A	Trigg C	Smith WH	Roberts H	Stewart JS	Higgins JT	McKee F	Warhurst R	Kinsey HR	Maton R	Farris RO	Hall JJ	Rowley KF	Dailey J	O'Hara EP
2	3	4	5	6	7	8	9	10	11												
2	3	4	5	6	7	8	9	10	11												
2	3	4	5	6	11	8	9	10		7											
2	3	4	5	6	11	8		10		7	9										
2	3	4	5	6	11	8		10		7	9										
2	3	4	5		7	8		10	11		9	6									
2	3	4	5		7	8		10	11		9	6									
2	3	4	5	8	11	7		10			9	6									
2	3	4	5		7	8		10	11		9										
2	3	4	5	6	7	8	9	10	11												
2	3	4	5	6	7	8	9	10	11												
2	3	4	5	6	7		9	10	11	8											
2	3	4	5	6	11	8	9	10		7											
2	3	4	5	6	11	8	9	10		7											
2	3	4	5	6	11	8	9	10		7											
2	3	4	5		11	9	8		7												
2	3	4	5		11	9	10		7	8			10								
2	3		5		11	9	10		7	8					6	4					
	2	4	5		11	9	10		7	8					3	6					
	2	4	5		11	9	10		7	8					3	6					
	2	4	5		11	9	10		7	8					3	6					
	2	4	5		11	9	10		7	8					3	6					
3	2	4	5		11	9	10		7	8						6					
3	2	4	5		11	9	10		7	8						6					
2		4	5	8	11	9		7	10						3	6					
		4	5		11	9	10		7						3	6	2	8			
2			5	4	11	9	10		7	8					3	6					
	2	4	5		11	9	10		7	8					3	6					
2	3	4	5		11	9	10		7	8						6					
2	3	4	5		11		10		7	8						6			9		
2	3	4	5		7		10		8							6			9		11
2	3	4	5		7		10		8							6			9		11
2	3	4	5		7				8	6								10	9		11
2	3	4	5		7				8	6								10	9		11
3	2	4	5		7	9			8	11						6		10			
3	2		5	4	7	9			8	11						6		10			
3	2		5	4	7	9			8	11						6		10			
	2		5	4	7	9			8	11				3	6			10			
4	2		5		11	9	10	7	8						3	6					
3	2	4	5		11		10		7							6		8	9		
35	**39**	**36**	**42**	**21**	**42**	**15**	**30**	**35**	**10**	**25**	**28**	**3**	**9**	**1**	**10**	**20**	**1**	**8**	**6**	**4**	
1	3		1	2	1	17	12		9	7		2			1				3	4	

Mirick GH	Badham J	Green K	Boyd LAM	Atkins AW	Dorman DJ	Berry RJ	Powell A	Trigg C	Smith WH	Roberts H	Stewart JS	Higgins JT	McKee F	Warhurst R	Kinsey HR	Maton R	Farris RO	Hall JJ	Rowley KF	Dailey J	O'Hara EP
	2	4	5	8	11	9		7	10						3	6					
2		4	5		11	9	10		7	8					3	6					
2		4	5		11	9	10		7	8					3	6					
2	3	4	5		11	9	10		7	8						6					
3	2	4	5		11	9	10		7	8						6					
5	4	6	6	1	6	6	5		6	6					3	6					
					2	2			3	2											

Division Two

Manager: Bob Brocklebank

Match No.	Date	Venue	Opponents	Result		Scorers	Attendance
1	Aug 18	H	Bury	W	2-1	Trigg, Higgins	23,86
2	22	H	Leeds United	D	1-1	Ferris	17,80
3	25	A	Leicester City	L	0-4		24,46
4	29	A	Leeds United	D	1-1	Purdon	15,09
5	Sep 1	H	Nottingham Forest	L	0-2		23,19
6	3	A	Sheffield Wednesday	D	1-1	Higgins	32,50
7	8	A	Brentford	L	0-1		25,02
8	12	H	Sheffield Wednesday	D	0-0		13,89
9	15	H	Doncaster Rovers	D	2-2	Badham, Dorman	16,22
10	22	A	Everton	W	3-1	Briggs, Purdon, Wardle	37,12
11	29	H	Southampton	D	1-1	Briggs	25,78
12	Oct 6	H	Swansea Town	D	1-1	Higgins	28,00
13	13	A	Coventry City	D	1-1	Rowley	23,58
14	20	H	West Ham United	W	2-1	Stewart, Briggs	20,29
15	27	A	Sheffield United	L	2-4	Rowley, Stewart	31,19
16	Nov 3	H	Barnsley	W	2-1	Briggs, Stewart	19,18
17	10	A	Hull City	W	1-0	Briggs	27,48
18	17	H	Blackburn Rovers	L	0-1		22,33
19	24	A	Queen's Park Rangers	W	2-0	Briggs, Smith	14,94
20	Dec 1	H	Notts County	W	2-0	Smith 2	26,55
21	8	A	Luton Town	W	4-2	Purdon, Smith, Stewart, Warhurst	15,93
22	15	A	Bury	L	0-3		12,34
23	22	H	Leicester City	W	2-0	Briggs, Wardle	22,22
24	25	H	Rotherham United	W	4-0	Smith 3, Purdon	27,55
25	26	A	Rotherham United	W	2-1	Briggs, Badham	22,33
26	29	A	Nottingham Forest	W	1-0	Briggs	34,31
27	Jan 5	H	Brentford	L	1-2	Wardle	28,36
28	19	A	Doncaster Rovers	W	5-0	Murphy 3, Briggs, Stewart	20,24
29	26	H	Everton	L	1-2	Stewart	32,96
30	Feb 9	A	Southampton	L	0-2		18,64
31	16	A	Swansea Town	L	0-4		24,22
32	Mar 1	H	Coventry City	W	3-1	Briggs, Stewart, Murphy	33,00
33	8	A	West Ham United	W	1-0	Briggs	24,0
34	15	H	Sheffield United	W	3-0	Triggs, Murphy 2	28,00
35	22	A	Barnsley	W	2-1	Murphy, Stewart	14,31
36	29	H	Hull City	D	2-2	Smith, Briggs	14,64
37	Apr 5	A	Blackburn Rovers	W	4-1	Smith, Briggs 2, Dailey	19,11
38	11	H	Cardiff City	W	3-2	Briggs, Green, Sherwood (og)	32,94
39	12	H	Queen's Park Rangers	W	1-0	Trigg	28,22
40	14	A	Cardiff City	L	1-3	Briggs	25,4
41	19	A	Notts County	L	0-5		24,3
42	26	H	Luton Town	W	3-1	Briggs, Purdon, Stewart	28,8

Appearance

One own-goal   Goal

FA Cup

R3	Jan 12	A	Fulham	W	1-0	Briggs	49,5
R4	Feb 2	H	Leyton Orient	L	0-1		25,8

Appearance

Goal

Player appearance grid (shirt numbers by match). Column headings (left to right):

Merrick GH · Hall LJ · Green K · Boyd IAM · Badham J · Ferris RD · Stewart JG · Higgins JT · Trigg C · Rowley KF · Berry RJ · Atkins AV · Purton EJ · Dailey J · Smith WH · Warhurst R · Wardle W · Martin R · Dorman DJ · Briggs TH · Murphy P · Watts JV · Newman JHG · Robertson WH

Mer	Hal	Gre	Boy	Bad	Fer	Ste	Hig	Tri	Row	Ber	Atk	Pur	Dai	Smi	War	Wdl	Mar	Dor	Bri	Mur	Wat	New	Rob
2	3	4	5	6	7	8	9	10	11														
2	3	4	5	6	7	8	9	10	11														
	3	4	2	6	7	8	9	10	11	5													
	3	4	2	6	7			11	5	8	9	10											
	3	4	2	6	7		10		5	8	9			11									
	3	4	2	6	7	10	9	11		5	8												
	3	4	2		7	8	9		5					10	6	11							
	2	4	9		7				5					10	6	11	3	8					
	2	4	9	10	7				5						6	11	3	8					
		4	2	10	7				5	8					6	11	3		9				
2		4	5	10	7				8						6	11	3		9				
2		4		7	8			10						5	6	11	3		9				
	4	2		7	8			10		5					6	11	3		9				
	4	2		7	8			10		5					6	11	3		9				
	4	2		7	8			10		5					6	11	3		9				
	4	2		7	8			10		5					6	11	3		9				
2		4	5		7			10					8		6	11	3		9				
2		4	5		7			10					8		6	11	3		9				
	2	4		7						5	8			10	6	11	3		9				
	2	4	3		7					5	8			10	6	11			9				
	2	4	3		7					5	8			10	6	11			9				
	2	4	3		7					5	8			10	6	11			9				
	2	4	3		7					5	8			10	6	11			9				
	2	4	3		7					5	8			10	6	11			9				
	2	4	7							5	8			10	6	11	3		9				
	2	4	3		7					5	8			10	6	11			9				
	2		4		7					5	8			10	6	11	3		9				
	2		4		7					5					8	6	11	3	9	10			
	2		4		7					5					8	6	11	3	9	10			
	2		4	6	7					5	8					11	3		9	10			
	2		5		7								8		6	11	3		9	10	4		
	2	4	3		7		9							6	11			8	10		5		
	2	4	3	5	7		9							6	11			8	10				
	2	4	3	5	7		9							6	11			8	10				
	2	4	3	5	7									9	6	11		8	10				
	2	4	3							5		7		9	6	11		8	10				
	2	4	3							5		7		9	6	11		8	10			1	
	2	4	3		7		9			5					6	11		8	10				
	2	4	3		7		9			5					6	11		8	10				
	2	4	3				9					5		7	6	11		8	10				
	2	4	3				9			5					7	6	11		8	10			
	2	4		5	7					10				8	6		3		9	11			
6	33	37	39	14	37	10	12	12	4	31	19	5	19	36	35	19	2	33	15	1	1	1	1
	1		2	1	9	3	3	2		5	1	9	1	3		1		18	7				

Mer	Hal	Gre	Boy	Bad	Fer	Ste	Hig	Tri	Row	Ber	Atk	Pur	Dai	Smi	War	Wdl	Mar	Dor	Bri	Mur	Wat	New	Rob
	2		4		7		9			5				10	6	11	3		8				
	2		4		7					5				8	6	11	3		9	10			
	2		2		2		1			2				2	2	2	2		2	1			
																			1				

League Table

	P	W	D	L	F	A	Pts
Sheffield Wednesday	42	21	11	10	100	66	53
Cardiff City	42	20	11	11	72	54	51
Birmingham City	42	21	9	12	67	56	51
Nottingham Forest	42	18	13	11	77	62	49
Leicester City	42	19	9	14	78	64	47
Leeds United	42	18	11	13	59	57	47
Everton	42	17	10	15	64	58	44
Luton Town	42	16	12	14	77	78	44
Rotherham United	42	17	8	17	73	71	42
Brentford	42	15	12	15	54	55	42
Sheffield United	42	18	5	19	90	76	41
West Ham United	42	15	11	16	67	77	41
Southampton	42	15	11	16	61	73	41
Blackburn Rovers	42	17	6	19	54	63	40
Notts County	42	16	7	19	71	68	39
Doncaster Rovers	42	13	12	17	55	60	38
Bury	42	15	7	20	67	69	37
Hull City	42	13	11	18	60	70	37
Swansea Town	42	12	12	18	72	76	36
Barnsley	42	11	14	17	59	72	36
Coventry City	42	14	6	22	59	82	34
Queen's Park Rangers	42	11	12	19	52	81	34

Division Two

Manager: Bob Brocklebank

Match No.	Date		Venue	Opponents	Result		Scorers	Attendance
1	Aug	23	A	Rotherham United	D	1-1	Purdon	15,2
2		27	A	Luton Town	W	1-0	Briggs	20,2
3		30	H	Fulham	L	1-4	Briggs	29,5
4	Sep	3	H	Luton Town	D	2-2	Briggs, Murphy	17,4
5		6	A	West Ham United	W	2-1	Higgins, Murphy	23,9
6		10	A	Leeds United	W	1-0	Rowley	14,1
7		13	H	Leicester City	W	3-1	Briggs, Murphy, Rowley	29,4
8		17	H	Leeds United	D	2-2	Rowley 2	18,3
9		20	A	Notts County	L	0-2		24,5
10		27	H	Southampton	W	2-0	Rowley 2	21,8
11	Oct	4	A	Bury	L	0-3		16,0
12		11	A	Swansea Town	D	1-1	Purdon	21,0
13		18	H	Huddersfield Town	L	0-2		26,4
14		25	A	Sheffield United	D	2-2	Murphy, Wardle	28,3
15	Nov	1	H	Barnsley	W	3-1	Murphy, Rowley (pen), Stewart	19,9
16		8	A	Lincoln City	D	1-1	Trigg	16,2
17		15	H	Hull City	W	4-3	Trigg (pen), Murphy, Stewart, Cox	17,5
18		22	A	Blackburn Rovers	W	2-1	Murphy 2	18,5
19		29	H	Nottingham Forest	L	0-5		17,7
20	Dec	6	A	Everton	D	1-1	Murphy	23,8
21		13	H	Brentford	W	3-1	Trigg, Murphy 2	9,9
22		20	H	Rotherham United	W	4-0	Trigg (pen), Purdon, Murphy, Wardle	11,9
23		25	H	Plymouth Argyle	W	4-0	Purdon, Murphy 2, Stewart	31,6
24		27	A	Plymouth Argyle	L	1-2	Trigg (pen)	25,2
25	Jan	3	A	Fulham	L	1-3	Purdon	21,5
26		17	H	West Ham United	W	2-0	Trigg, Purdon	21,7
27		24	A	Leicester City	W	4-3	Murphy 3, Trigg	27,4
28	Feb	7	A	Notts County	W	3-2	Trigg 2 (2 pens), Murphy	24,5
29		21	H	Bury	L	0-2		26,0
30	Mar	7	A	Huddersfield Town	D	1-1	Ferris	28,6
31		11	H	Swansea Town	L	1-4	Purdon	7,1
32		14	H	Sheffield United	L	1-2	Cox	22,3
33		21	A	Barnsley	W	3-1	Badham, James 2	7,4
34		28	H	Lincoln City	D	2-2	Trigg (pen), Stewart	13,4
35	Apr	3	A	Doncaster Rovers	L	0-1		18,0
36		4	A	Hull City	L	0-2		23,4
37		6	H	Doncaster Rovers	W	2-1	Lane, Boyd	12,0
38		11	H	Blackburn Rovers	L	1-2	Cox	18,3
39		15	A	Southampton	D	1-1	Warhurst	18,3
40		18	A	Nottingham Forest	W	2-0	Lane, Boyd	16,3
41		25	H	Everton	W	4-2	Boyd 2, Murphy, Stewart	17,0
42	May	1	A	Brentford	W	2-1	Lane, Murphy	8,5
							Appearanc	
							Go	

FA Cup

R3	Jan	14	A	Oldham Athletic	W	3-1	Murphy 3	26,5
R4		31	A	Sheffield United	D	1-1	Purdon	43,7
rep	Feb	4	H	Sheffield United	W	3-1	Murphy 2, Wardle	29,5
R5		14	A	Chelsea	W	4-0	Purdon 2, Trigg, Murphy	45,8
R6		28	H	Tottenham Hotspur	D	1-1	Wardle	52,3
rep	Mar	4	A	Tottenham Hotspur	D	2-2	Ferris, Boyd	59,5
rep2		9	H	Tottenham Hotspur	L	0-1		50,8

R6 replay a.e.t.

R6 replay 2 at Molineux.

Appearanc

Go

Appearances Chart

Winnick GH	Green K	Martin R	Boyd LAM	Badham J	Warhurst R	Stewart JG	Purdon EJ	Briggs TH	Murphy P	Wardle W	Cox G	Watts JW	Newman JHG	Higgins JT	Ferris RD	Rowley KF	Smith WH	Schofield JR	Trigg C	Atkins AW	Bannister K	Metcalfe J	Hall JJ	Costigane J	James JE	Lane JG
2	3	4	5	6	7	8	9	10	11																	
2	3	4	5	6	7	8	9	10				11														
2	3	4	5		7	8	9	10				11	6													
2	3	4			7		9	10				11	6	5	8											
2	3	4		6			9	11		7					8	5	10									
2	3	4		6			9	8		7					11	5	10									
2	3	4		6		11	9	8		7						5	10									
2	3	4		6		11	9	8		7						5	10									
2	3	4		6	7	10	9					11		5				8								
2	3	4	5	6			9	8	11	7							10									
2	3	4	5	6			9	8	11	7							10		1							
2	3	4	5	6		10	9	8	11	7							10		1							
2	3	4	5	6	7	10	9	8				11														
2	3	4	5	6	7		9	8	11								10									
2	3	4	5	6	7			8	11								10									
2	3	4	5	6	7		8	10	11								9									
2	3	4	5	6	7		8	10				11					9									
2	3	4		6	7		8	10				11				1	9									
2	3	4		6	7		8	10				11					9	5								
2	3		6	7			10			11			8				9	5	4							
2	3	4		6	7	8		10	11					5			9									
3		6		7	8		10	11					5				9		4		2					
3		6		7	8		10	11					5				9		4		2					
3		6		7	8		10	11					5				9		4		2					
3		6		7	8		10	11					5				9		4		2					
3		6		7	8		10				5						9		4		2		8			
3	6			7	9				5									2	4	11		8	10			
3	4	5		7			11	8				6					9				2		10			
3	6	9					11	7		5		10							4		2		8			
3	6		5		7		10	11					8				9		4		2					
3	6	9		7			10		11		5		8		1				4		2					
3	4		6	7	10			11	8		5					1	9				2					
3	4		6	7	10			11	8		5					1					2		9			
3	4		6	7	10			11	8		5					1					2		9			
3	8	7	6				10	11				5				1			4		2		9			
3	8		6	7			10		11			5				1			4		2		9			
3	8		6	7			10	11				5							4		2		9			
3	8		6	7			10	11				5							4		2		9			
42	24	40	18	31	33	22	17	34	25	23	3	7	4	23	8	1	7	19	3	14	2	16	2	3	6	
	4	1	1	5	7	4	20	2	3					1	1	7		10				2	3			

Winnick GH	Green K	Martin R	Boyd LAM	Badham J	Warhurst R	Stewart JG	Purdon EJ	Briggs TH	Murphy P	Wardle W	Cox G	Watts JW	Newman JHG	Higgins JT	Ferris RD	Rowley KF	Smith WH	Schofield JR	Trigg C	Atkins AW	Bannister K	Metcalfe J	Hall JJ	Costigane J	James JE	Lane JG
3	4		6	7	8		10	11				5					9				2					
3	6		8	7	9		10	11				5							4		2					
3	6		8	7	9		10	11				5							4		2					
3	6		11	7	8		10					5					9		4		2					
3	6		8	7	8			11				5					9		4		2					
3	6	4	10	7				11				5					9				2		8			
3	6	5		7	8			11				10					9		4		2					
7	7	2	6	7	6		4	6				7					5		5		7		1			
	1			3			6	2				1					1									

League Table

	P	W	D	L	F	A	Pts
Sheffield United	42	25	10	7	97	55	60
Huddersfield Town	42	24	10	8	84	33	58
Luton Town	42	22	8	12	84	49	52
Plymouth Argyle	42	20	9	13	65	60	49
Leicester City	42	18	12	12	89	74	48
Birmingham City	42	19	10	13	71	66	48
Nottingham Forest	42	18	8	16	77	67	44
Fulham	42	17	10	15	81	71	44
Blackburn Rovers	42	18	8	16	68	65	44
Leeds United	42	14	15	13	71	63	43
Swansea Town	42	15	12	15	78	81	42
Rotherham United	42	16	9	17	75	74	41
Doncaster Rovers	42	12	16	14	58	64	40
West Ham United	42	13	13	16	58	60	39
Lincoln City	42	11	17	14	64	71	39
Everton	42	12	14	16	71	75	38
Brentford	42	13	11	18	59	76	37
Hull City	42	14	8	20	57	69	36
Notts County	42	14	8	20	60	88	36
Bury	42	13	9	20	53	81	35
Southampton	42	10	13	19	68	85	33
Barnsley	42	5	8	29	47	108	18

Division Two

Manager: Bob Brocklebank

Did you know that?

Ted Purdon scored after 15 seconds in Blues' 4–0 win over Plymouth in September.

All six goals in the Blues-Everton game in December were scored in the second-half, four of them in the space of 10 minutes.

Peter Murphy's hat-trick came in nine minutes against Luton in September.

Fulham led after just 14 seconds in the League game at St Andrew's.

Blues centre-half Trevor Smith conceded a 59th-minute own-goal on his debut at Derby in October.

Blues scored five goals in 26 first-half minutes of their home game v Brentford.

Match No.	Date		Venue	Opponents	Result		Scorers	Attendance
1	Aug	19	H	Hull City	W	2-0	Murphy, Govan	23,84
2		22	H	Swansea Town	W	6-0	Purdon 2, Murphy 3, Kinsey	26,81
3		24	A	Plymouth Argyle	D	2-2	Kinsey, Govan	21,01
4		29	A	Rotherham United	L	0-1		12,67
5	Sep	2	H	Plymouth Argyle	W	3-0	Purdon, Kinsey, Stewart	21,44
6		5	H	Leicester City	L	1-2	Stewart	30,97
7		9	H	Luton Town	W	5-1	Murphy 3, Purdon 2	18,88
8		12	A	Stoke City	L	2-3	Purdon, Hall	22,95
9		16	A	Luton Town	L	0-2		12,23
10		19	H	Fulham	D	2-2	Purdon 2	21,13
11		26	A	West Ham United	W	2-1	Purdon, Kinsey	36,09
12	Oct	3	H	Leeds United	D	3-3	Kinsey, Murphy, Govan	26,43
13		10	H	Lincoln City	W	1-0	Stewart	21,94
14		17	A	Bristol Rovers	D	1-1	Purdon	33,63
15		24	H	Brentford	W	5-1	Purdon, Kinsey, Murphy, Govan, Bragg (og)	23,58
16		31	A	Derby County	W	4-2	Purdon, Stewart, Murphy, Astall	18,27
17	Nov	7	H	Blackburn Rovers	D	0-0		24,60
18		14	A	Doncaster Rovers	L	1-3	Kinsey	16,58
19		21	H	Bury	D	0-0		20,72
20		28	A	Oldham Athletic	W	3-2	Kinsey, Astall, Govan	18,26
21	Dec	5	H	Everton	W	5-1	Trigg, Murphy, Astall 2, Clinton (og)	23,55
22		12	A	Hull City	L	0-3		19,75
23		19	A	Swansea Town	W	3-1	Rowley 2, Purdon	12,49
24		25	H	Notts County	W	3-0	Rowley 2, Govan	30,48
25		26	A	Notts County	L	1-2	Astall	20,98
26	Jan	2	H	Rotherham United	L	2-3	Purdon 2	16,78
27		16	A	Leicester City	W	4-3	Murphy, Rowley, Govan 2	34,70
28		23	H	Stoke City	W	1-0	Kinsey	26,20
29	Feb	6	A	Fulham	L	2-5	Trigg 2 (1 pen)	20,54
30		13	H	West Ham United	W	2-0	Cochrane, Astall	22,71
31		20	A	Leeds United	D	1-1	Rowley	22,80
32		27	A	Lincoln City	W	1-0	Lane	13,92
33	Mar	6	H	Bristol Rovers	D	1-1	Boyd	25,33
34		13	A	Brentford	L	0-2		12,58
35		20	H	Derby County	W	3-0	Trigg 2 (2 pens), Stewart	18,21
36		27	A	Bury	D	1-1	Stewart	11,29
37	Apr	3	H	Oldham Athletic	W	2-1	Murphy, Boyd	15,84
38		10	A	Blackburn Rovers	L	0-3		31,99
39		16	A	Nottingham Forest	D	1-1	Kinsey	25,28
40		17	H	Doncaster Rovers	L	0-1		15,26
41		19	H	Nottingham Forest	D	2-2	Lane, Stewart	14,62
42		24	A	Everton	L	0-1		62,86

Appearance

Two own-goals Goal

FA Cup

R3	Jan	9	A	Wolverhampton Wan.	W	2-1	Murphy, Rowley	36,78
R4		30	A	Ipswich Town	L	0-1		25,08

Appearance

Goal

342

Player appearance / line-up grid

	Merrick GH	Hall JJ	Green K	Boyd LAM	Badham J	Warhurst R	Stewart JG	Kinsey N	Purdon EJ	Murphy P	Green A	Martin R	Bannister K	Newman JHG	Schofield JR	Astall G	Smith T	Wells JW	Trigg C	Rowley JW	Lane JG	Cox G	Cochrane J	James JE	Hall D	Squires B	Atkins AW	Allen GH
	1	2	3	4	5	6	7	8	9	10	11																	
		2			5	6	7	8	9	10	11	3	4															
		2			5	6	7	8	9	10	11	3	4															
	1	2		4	5	6	7	8	9	10	11	3																
		2	5			6	7	8	9	10	11	3	4															
		2	5			6	7	8	9	10	11	3	4															
		2	5			6	7	8	9	10	11	3	4															
	7	2	5			6		8	9	10	11	3	4															
		2	5			6	7	8	9	10	11	3	4															
		2	6				7	8	9	10	11	3	4	5														
	1	2	3	4	5	6		8	9	10	11				7													
	1	2	3	4	5	6		8	9	10	11				7													
		2	3	4		6		8	9	10	11				7	5												
		2	3	4		6	8		9	10	11				7	5												
		2	3	4		6	8		9	10	11				7	5												
	1	2	3	4		6		8	9	10	11			5	7													
		2	4		6		8	9	10	11	3				7	5												
		2	3			6		8		10	11				7	5	4	9										
		2	3			6		8		10	11				7	5	4	9										
		2	3			6		8		10	11				7	5	4	9										
		2	3	4		6		8	9		11				7	5				10								
		2	3	4		6		8	9		11				7	5				10								
		2	3	4		6		8	9		11				7	5	1			10								
		2	3	4		6		8	9		11				7	5				10								
		2	3	4		6		8		9	11		5		7					10								
		2	3	4		6		8			11				7	5			9	10								
		2	3	4		6	7	10		8	11					5		9										
		2	3	4		6			10						7	5			8	9	11							
		2	3			6		8			11				7	5	4		10	9								
		2	3	8		6			10	11					7	5	4		9									
		2	3	8		6			10	11					7	5	4		9									
		2	3	6	4			8		10					7	5				9	11							
		2	3	6		7	4		8					11	5		9	10										
		2	3	6		7	4		8				1	11	5		9	10										
		2	3	6		7	4		10	11			1	8	5		9											
		2	3	4		6		8		10	11				7	5			9									
		2	4		6	7	8			11	3				5		9		10									
		2	4		6	7	8			11	3				5		9		10									
		2	4		6	7	8			11					5		9		10				3					
		2		6	7	8			11	3				5	4	9		10										
	8	32	39	35	7	37	22	37	23	32	38	13	8	7	4	24	24	7	11	8	8	1	1	2	1	1	1	1
	1		2			7	10	15	13	8						6					5	6	2		1			

	Merrick GH	Hall JJ	Green K	Boyd LAM	Badham J	Warhurst R	Stewart JG	Kinsey N	Purdon EJ	Murphy P	Green A	Martin R	Bannister K	Newman JHG	Schofield JR	Astall G	Smith T	Wells JW	Trigg C	Rowley JW	Lane JG	Cox G	Cochrane J	James JE	Hall D	Squires B	Atkins AW	Allen GH
	1	2	3	6			4		8	11		5		7						10	9							
	2	3	4		6		8		9	11		5		7	5					10								
	2	2	2	2		1		2		2	2			1		2	1			2	1							
											1						1											

League Table

	P	W	D	L	F	A	Pts
Leicester City	42	23	10	9	97	60	56
Everton	42	20	16	6	92	58	56
Blackburn Rovers	42	23	9	10	86	50	55
Nottingham Forest	42	20	12	10	86	59	52
Rotherham United	42	21	7	14	80	67	49
Luton Town	42	18	12	12	64	59	48
Birmingham City	42	18	11	13	78	58	47
Fulham	42	17	10	15	98	85	44
Bristol Rovers	42	14	16	12	64	58	44
Leeds United	42	15	13	14	89	81	43
Stoke City	42	12	17	13	71	60	41
Doncaster Rovers	42	16	9	17	59	63	41
West Ham United	42	15	9	18	67	69	39
Notts County	42	13	13	16	54	74	39
Hull City	42	16	6	20	64	66	38
Lincoln City	42	14	9	19	65	83	37
Bury	42	11	14	17	54	72	36
Derby County	42	12	11	19	64	82	35
Plymouth Argyle	42	9	16	17	65	82	34
Swansea Town	42	13	8	21	58	82	34
Brentford	42	10	11	21	40	78	31
Oldham Athletic	42	8	9	25	40	89	25

Division Two

Manager: Bob Brocklebank (to October); Arthur Turner (from November)

Three teams, Blues, Luton Town and Rotherham United, all finished level on 54 points at the top of the Second Division this season. Blues, the champions, and Luton were subsequently promoted with better goal-averages than Rotherham.

Liverpool's 9–1 drubbing by Blues in December remains their heaviest League defeat to date.

Jackie Lane, dribbling past six opponents, scored a brilliant individual goal against Plymouth at St Andrew's in April.

Blues' famous forward-line of Astall, Kinsey, Brown, Murphy and Govan played together for the first time in the 2–0 home win over Swansea in October.

Trevor Smith became Blues' first England Under-23 international this season when capped against Italy.

Match No.	Date		Venue	Opponents	Result		Scorers	Attendance
1	Aug	21	A	Stoke City	L	1-2	Warhurst	27,82
2		25	H	Bristol Rovers	W	2-1	Kinsey, Rowley	25,890
3		28	H	Rotherham United	W	3-1	Govan 2, Warhurst	27,26
4		30	A	Bristol Rovers	D	1-1	Warhurst	26,21
5	Sep	4	A	Luton Town	L	0-1		16,34
6		8	H	Ipswich Town	W	4-0	Kinsey 2, Warmington, Astall	21,23
7		11	H	Hull City	D	0-0		23,84
8		15	A	Ipswich Town	W	2-1	Warmington, Murphy	16,74
9		18	A	Lincoln City	D	1-1	Kinsey	14,58
10		25	H	Bury	L	1-3	Lane	21,24
11	Oct	2	A	Leeds United	L	0-1		21,20
12		9	A	Fulham	L	1-2	Astall	30,29
13		16	H	Swansea Town	W	2-0	Murphy 2	19,99
14		30	H	Derby County	D	1-1	Brown	20,56
15	Nov	6	A	West Ham United	D	2-2	Murphy 2	25,36
16		13	H	Blackburn Rovers	W	3-1	Brown, Astall, Govan	23,82
17		20	A	Plymouth Argyle	L	0-1		19,20
18		27	H	Port Vale	W	7-2	Brown, Murphy 3,,Kinsey 2, Govan	16,35
19	Dec	4	A	Notts County	L	2-3	Murphy, Govan	13,47
20		11	H	Liverpool	W	9-1	Brown 3, Lane, Murphy 2, Astall 2, Govan	17,06
21		18	H	Stoke City	W	2-0	Brown, Govan	22,42
22		25	H	Nottingham Forest	L	0-1		33,00
23		27	A	Nottingham Forest	W	2-0	Murphy, Burkitt (og)	25,87
24	Jan	1	A	Rotherham United	W	2-0	Kinsey, Govan	17,16
25	Feb	5	H	Lincoln City	D	3-3	Murphy 2, Kinsey	20,31
26		12	A	Bury	W	1-0	Brown	12,54
27	Mar	2	H	Leeds United	W	2-0	Lane, Govan	10,77
28		5	A	Swansea Town	W	3-0	Lane, Kinsey, Boyd	22,56
29		16	H	Doncaster Rovers	W	4-1	Kinsey, Murphy, Astall, Warhurst	6,44
30		19	A	Derby County	D	0-0		19,48
31		26	H	West Ham United	L	1-2	Brown	9,13
32		30	H	Fulham	W	3-2	Lane, Astall 2	9,68
33	Apr	2	A	Blackburn Rovers	D	3-3	Lane, Murphy, Kinsey	27,67
34		8	A	Middlesbrough	W	5-2	Lane, Brown 2, Govan 2	32,51
35		9	H	Plymouth Argyle	W	3-1	Kinsey, Lane, Govan	25,07
36		11	H	Middlesbrough	W	3-0	Kinsey, Murphy, Govan	23,65
37		16	A	Port Vale	L	0-2		24,03
38		20	H	Luton Town	W	2-1	Murphy 2	34,61
39		23	H	Notts County	D	1-1	Brown	28,01
40		25	A	Hull City	W	3-0	Bradbury 2, Govan	12,84
41		30	A	Liverpool	D	2-2	Brown, Astall	38,06
42	May	4	A	Doncaster Rovers	W	5-1	Brown, Murphy, Astall 2, Govan	21,30

One own-goal

Appearances
Goals

FA Cup

R3	Jan	8	A	Hull City	W	2-0	Kinsey, Brown	25,920
R4		29	H	Bolton Wanderers	W	2-1	Govan, Wheeler (og)	56,85
R5	Feb	19	H	Doncaster Rovers	W	2-1	Brown 2	57,80
R6	Mar	12	H	Manchester City	L	0-1		57,96

One own-goal

Appearances
Goals

344

Player columns (left to right): Merrick GH, Green K, Allen GH, Boyd LAM, Newman JHG, Warhurst R, Astall G, Kinsey N, Lane JG, Rowley KF, Govan A, Murphy P, Smith T, Warmington PJ, Cox G, Hill D, Badham J, Watts JW, Martin R, Hall JJ, Stewart JG, Schofield JR, Brown E, Bradbury W, James J

League Table

	P	W	D	L	F	A	Pts
Birmingham City	42	22	10	10	92	47	54
Luton Town	42	23	8	11	88	53	54
Rotherham United	42	25	4	13	94	64	54
Leeds United	42	23	7	12	70	53	53
Stoke City	42	21	10	11	69	46	52
Blackburn Rovers	42	22	6	14	114	79	50
Notts County	42	21	6	15	74	71	48
West Ham United	42	18	10	14	74	70	46
Bristol Rovers	42	19	7	16	75	70	45
Swansea Town	42	17	9	16	86	83	43
Liverpool	42	16	10	16	92	96	42
Middlesbrough	42	18	6	18	73	82	42
Bury	42	15	11	16	77	72	41
Fulham	42	14	11	17	76	79	39
Nottingham Forest	42	16	7	19	58	62	39
Lincoln City	42	13	10	19	68	79	36
Port Vale	42	12	11	19	48	71	35
Doncaster Rovers	42	14	7	21	58	95	35
Hull City	42	12	10	20	44	69	34
Plymouth Argyle	42	12	7	23	57	82	31
Ipswich Town	42	11	6	25	57	92	28
Derby County	42	7	9	26	53	82	23

Division One

Manager: Arthur Turner

Match No.	Date	Venue	Opponents		Result	Scorers	Attendance
1	Aug 20	H	Manchester United	D	2-2	Kinsey, Astall	37,61
2	24	A	Newcastle United	D	2-2	Murphy, Astall	34,47
3	27	A	Sheffield United	W	3-0	Brown, Kinsey, Murphy	23,29
4	31	H	Newcastle United	W	3-1	Brown, Murphy, Warhurst	38,36
5	Sep 3	H	Preston North End	L	0-3		47,01
6	5	A	Aston Villa	D	0-0		56,93
7	10	A	Burnley	L	2-3	Kinsey, Astall	22,80
8	17	H	Luton Town	D	0-0		31,01
9	21	A	Aston Villa	D	2-2	Brown, Astall	32,64
10	24	A	Charlton Athletic	L	0-2		21,91
11	Oct 1	H	Tottenham Hotspur	W	3-0	Brown, Murphy, Clarke (og)	31,32
12	8	H	Sunderland	L	1-2	Hudgell (og)	37,94
13	15	A	Portsmouth	W	5-0	Brown 3, Kinsey, Govan	28,95
14	22	H	Manchester City	W	4-3	Lane, Murphy, Govan, Boyd	28,39
15	29	A	Wolverhampton Wan.	L	0-1		47,00
16	Nov 5	H	Chelsea	W	3-0	Astall 2, Boyd	30,49
17	12	A	Blackpool	L	0-2		21,96
18	19	H	Huddersfield Town	W	5-0	Brown 2, Murphy, Astall, Warhurst	24,84
19	26	A	Cardiff City	L	1-2	Brown	23,63
20	Dec 3	H	Arsenal	W	4-0	Kinsey 2, Brown, Astall,	35,76
21	10	A	Bolton Wanderers	L	0-6		15,79
22	17	A	Manchester United	L	1-2	Brown	27,93
23	24	H	Sheffield United	L	0-2		23,82
24	26	H	Everton	W	6-2	Brown 2, Kinsey 3, Govan	25,54
25	27	A	Everton	L	1-5	Astall	42,23
26	31	A	Preston North End	D	1-1	Astall	25,83
27	Jan 14	H	Burnley	L	1-2	Kinsey	27,38
28	21	A	Luton Town	W	1-0	Brown	18,97
29	Feb 4	H	Charlton Athletic	W	4-0	Brown 3, Kinsey	24,44
30	11	A	Tottenham Hotspur	W	1-0	Astall	26,14
31	25	H	Portsmouth	W	3-2	Kinsey 2, Boyd	31,95
32	Mar 7	A	Huddersfield Town	D	1-1	Brown	9,22
33	10	H	Wolverhampton Wan.	D	0-0		45,16
34	21	A	Chelsea	W	2-1	Kinsey, Govan	12,63
35	24	H	Blackpool	L	1-2	Murphy	47,93
36	31	A	Manchester City	D	1-1	Murphy	44,77
37	Apr 2	H	West Bromwich Albion	W	2-0	Brown, Murphy	38,89
38	3	A	West Bromwich Albion	W	2-0	Murphy 2	35,85
39	7	H	Cardiff City	W	2-1	Brown, Baker (og)	37,15
40	14	A	Arsenal	L	0-1		31,77
41	18	A	Sunderland	L	0-1		14,82
42	21	H	Bolton Wanderers	W	5-2	Kinsey, Warmington, Astall, Wheeler 2 (2 og)	29,64

Five own-goals

Appearance
Goal

FA Cup

R3	Jan 7	A	Torquay United	W	7-1	Astall, Brown 3, Kinsey, Murphy 2	18,73
R4	28	A	Leyton Orient	W	4-0	Brown 2, Murphy, Finney	24,72
R5	Feb 18	A	West Bromwich Albion	W	1-0	Murphy	57,21
R6	Mar 3	A	Arsenal	W	3-1	Astall, Murphy, Brown	67,87
SF	17	N	Sunderland	W	3-0	Kinsey, Astall, Brown	65,10
F	May 5	N	Manchester City	L	1-3	Kinsey	98,98

SF at Hillsborough, Final at Wembley Stadium.

Appearance
Goal

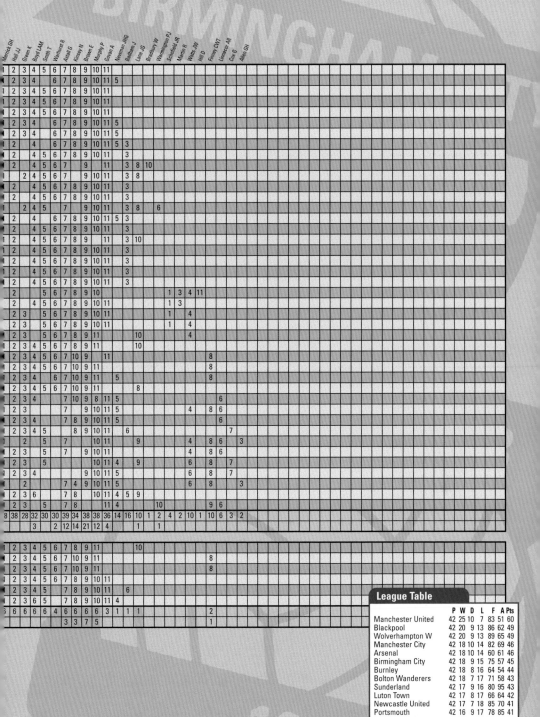

Division One

Manager: Arthur Turner

Match No.	Date		Venue	Opponents	Result		Scorers	Attendance
1	Aug	18	A	Manchester United	D	2-2	Govan, Jones (og)	32,958
2		22	A	Portsmouth	W	3-1	Astall, Govan 2	33,307
3		25	H	Arsenal	W	4-2	Brown, Murphy 2, Govan	37,197
4		29	A	Portsmouth	W	4-3	Govan 3, Astall	25,686
5	Sep	1	A	Burnley	L	0-2		25,531
6		5	H	Newcastle United	W	6-1	Kinsey, Murphy 2, Govan 3	32,506
7		8	H	Preston North End	W	3-0	Govan 3	44,458
8		15	A	Chelsea	L	0-1		40,530
9		22	H	Cardiff City	W	2-1	Kinsey, Govan	39,931
10		29	A	Wolverhampton Wan.	L	0-3		44,191
11	Oct	6	H	Bolton Wanderers	D	0-0		29,614
12		13	A	Leeds United	D	1-1	Larkin	34,460
13		20	H	Luton Town	W	3-0	Brown 2, Orritt	31,783
14		27	A	Aston Villa	L	1-3	Astall	54,922
15	Nov	3	H	Blackpool	D	2-2	Astall, Govan	35,597
16		10	A	Manchester City	L	1-3	Kinsey	21,005
17		17	H	Charlton Athletic	W	4-2	Brown, Kinsey, Astall, Murphy	27,564
18		24	A	Sunderland	W	1-0	Orritt	33,807
19	Dec	1	H	Tottenham Hotspur	D	0-0		38,035
20		8	A	Everton	L	0-2		29,579
21		15	H	Manchester United	W	3-1	Brown 2, Orritt	36,146
22		22	A	Arsenal	L	0-4		28,644
23		25	H	Sheffield Wednesday	W	4-0	Brown, Murphy, Astall, Govan	24,380
24		29	H	Burnley	W	2-0	Brown, Govan	31,733
25	Jan	1	A	Newcastle United	L	2-3	Brown, Govan	29,383
26		12	A	Preston North End	L	0-1		19,430
27		19	H	Chelsea	L	0-1		30,157
28	Feb	2	A	Cardiff City	W	2-1	Brown, Astall	16,854
29		9	H	Wolverhampton Wan.	D	2-2	Astall, Govan	45,915
30		20	A	Bolton Wanderers	L	1-3	Astall	11,284
31	Mar	9	H	Everton	L	1-3	Brown	23,881
32		16	A	Blackpool	L	1-3	Brown	17,610
33		30	A	Charlton Athletic	L	0-1		17,839
34	Apr	3	A	Luton Town	D	0-0		12,881
35		6	H	Sunderland	L	1-2	Brown	24,548
36		10	H	Aston Villa	L	1-2	Murphy	29,852
37		13	A	Tottenham Hotspur	L	1-5	Astall	33,512
38		20	H	Leeds United	W	6-2	Brown 2, Govan 3, Astall	30,642
39		22	A	West Bromwich Albion	D	0-0		18,755
40		23	H	West Bromwich Albion	W	2-0	Kinsey, Govan	30,332
41		27	H	Manchester City	D	3-3	Brown, Govan, Phoenix (og)	23,742
42		29	A	Sheffield Wednesday	L	0-3		13,845

Appearances
Two own-goals Goals

FA Cup

R3	Jan	5	A	Carlisle United		3-3	Murphy 2, Astall	27,445
R3		9	H	Carlisle United		4-0	Brown, 2, Kinsey, Astall	56,458
R4		26	A	Southend United		6-1	Murphy, Govan 3, Cox, Lawler (og)	28,964
R5	Feb	16	A	Millwall		4-1	Kinsey 2, Govan, Brown	41,988
R6	Mar	2	H	Nottingham Forest		0-0		57,827
rep		7	A	Nottingham Forest		1-0	Murphy	36,488
SF		23	N	Manchester United		0-2		65,107

SF played at Hillsborough.

Appearances
One own-goal Goals

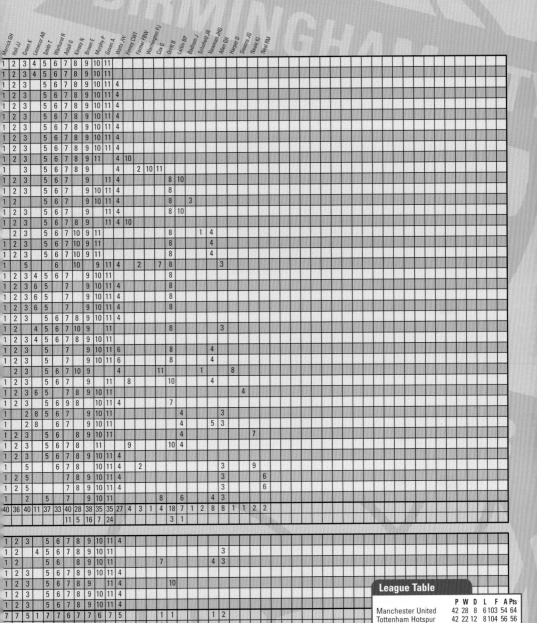

League Table

	P	W	D	L	F	A	Pts
Manchester United	42	28	8	6	103	54	64
Tottenham Hotspur	42	22	12	8	104	56	56
Preston North End	42	23	10	9	84	56	56
Blackpool	42	22	9	11	93	65	53
Arsenal	42	21	8	13	85	69	50
Wolverhampton W	42	20	8	14	94	70	48
Burnley	42	18	10	14	56	50	46
Leeds United	42	15	14	13	72	63	44
Bolton Wanderers	42	16	12	14	65	65	44
Aston Villa	42	14	15	13	65	55	43
West Bromwich Albion	42	14	14	14	59	61	42
Chelsea	42	13	13	16	73	73	39
Birmingham City	42	15	9	18	69	69	39
Sheffield Wednesday	42	16	6	20	82	88	38
Everton	42	14	10	18	61	79	38
Luton Town	42	14	9	19	58	76	37
Newcastle United	42	14	8	20	67	87	36
Manchester City	42	13	9	20	78	88	35
Portsmouth	42	10	13	19	62	92	33
Sunderland	42	12	8	22	67	88	32
Cardiff City	42	10	9	23	53	88	29
Charlton Athletic	42	9	4	29	62	120	22

1957-58

Division One

Manager: Arthur Turner (to February); then joint manager with Pat Beasley

Match No.	Date		Venue	Opponents	Result		Scorers	Attendance
1	Aug	24	H	Aston Villa	W	3-1	Brown, Kinsey, Murphy	50,780
2		28	A	Nottingham Forest	D	1-1	Brown	29,705
3		31	A	Chelsea	L	1-5	Brown	43,806
4	Sep	4	H	Nottingham Forest	L	0-2		26,852
5		7	H	Newcastle United	L	1-4	Hellawell	29,784
6		11	H	Tottenham Hotspur	D	0-0		26,488
7		14	A	Burnley	L	1-3	Neal	20,522
8		18	A	Tottenham Hotspur	L	1-7	Brown	35,292
9		21	H	Preston North End	W	3-1	Neale, Murphy, Govan (pen)	24,894
10		28	A	Sheffield Wednesday	L	3-5	Orritt 2, Murphy	20,129
11	Oct	1	A	West Bromwich Albion	D	0-0		39,738
12		5	H	Manchester City	W	4-0	Murphy 3, Brown	28,059
13		12	H	Wolverhampton Wan.	L	1-5	Astall	43,005
14		19	A	Arsenal	W	3-1	Orritt, Neal 2	39,031
15		26	H	Bolton Wanderers	W	5-1	Brown 2, Orritt, Murphy, Watts	26,225
16	Nov	2	A	Luton Town	L	0-3		17,316
17		9	H	Sunderland	L	2-3	Murphy, Govan	25,315
18		16	A	Everton	W	2-0	Murphy 2	34,875
19		23	H	Blackpool	D	0-0		32,178
20		30	A	Leeds United	D	1-1	Orritt	21,358
21	Dec	7	H	Manchester United	D	3-3	Kinsey, Murphy, Astall	35,191
22		14	A	Leicester City	D	2-2	Kinsey, Astall	28,680
23		21	A	Aston Villa	W	2-0	Brown, Kinsey	41,118
24		26	H	West Bromwich Albion	L	3-5	Brown, Hooper (pen), Neal	48,396
25		28	H	Chelsea	D	3-3	Brown, Murphy 2	37,436
26	Jan	11	A	Newcastle United	W	2-1	Brown, Kinsey	34,825
27		18	H	Burnley	L	2-3	Murphy, Hooper	22,281
28	Feb	1	A	Preston North End	L	0-8		21,511
29		22	A	Wolverhampton Wan.	L	1-5	Murphy	36,941
30	Mar	1	H	Arsenal	W	4-1	Brown 2, Murphy, Hooper	26,834
31		5	A	Manchester City	D	1-1	Murphy	30,655
32		8	A	Bolton Wanderers	L	0-1		18,309
33		12	H	Sheffield Wednesday	W	1-0	Orritt	15,937
34		15	H	Luton Town	D	1-1	Orritt	25,225
35		22	A	Blackpool	L	2-4	Astall, Hooper (pen)	11,549
36		29	H	Everton	W	2-1	Hooper 2	21,628
37	Apr	4	A	Portsmouth	L	2-3	Murphy, Hooper	33,075
38		5	A	Sunderland	W	6-1	Murphy, Astall, Brown, Hooper, Orritt 2	34,184
39		7	H	Portsmouth	W	4-1	Brown, Orritt, Murphy, Hooper	23,380
40		12	H	Leeds United	D	1-1	Orritt	23,112
41		19	A	Manchester United	W	2-0	Hooper, Green	39,215
42		26	H	Leicester City	L	0-1		27,607
							Appearances	
							Goals	

FA Cup

R3	Jan	8	A	York City	L	0-3		19,750
							Appearances	

Player Appearance Grid

	Whitehead JR	Hall LJ	Green K	Watts JW	Smith T	Neal RM	Astall G	Kinsey N	Brown E	Murphy P	Govan A	Merrick GH	Hallawell MS	Mullard CJ	Neale KJ	Larkin BP	Allen GH	Newman JHG	Orrit B	Farmer FBW	Houghton HB	Hooper H	Jennie DWL	Sessions JG
	2	3	4	5	6	7	8	9	10	11														
	2	3	4	5	6	7	8	9	10	11	1													
	2	3	4	5	6	7	8	9	10	11	1													
	2	3	4	5	6	7	8	9	10	11														
	2	3	4	5	6		8	9	10	11			7											
	2	3	4	5	10	7		9		11	1			6	8									
	2	3	4	5	10	7		9		11	1			6	8									
	2	3		5	10	7	8	9		11	1			6		4								
	2	7		6			8		3	10	11	1			9		4	5						
		2		5	6	7	8			10	11	1					3	4	9					
	2	3	4		6	7			9	10	11	1						5	8					
	2	3	4		6	7			9	10	11	1						5	8					
	2	3	4		6	7			9	10	11	1						5	8					
		3	6	5	10	7			9	11		1						4	8	2				
		3	6	5	10	7			9	11				4					8	2				
		3	6	5	10	7			9	11		1		4					8	2				
		3	6	5	4	7			9	10	11	1							8	2				
	2		4	5	6	7			9	10	11	1							8	3				
	2		4	5	6	7			9	10	11	1							8	3				
	2		4	5	6				9	10	11	1							8	3	7			
	2			5	6	11	8	9	10			1			4				3		7			
	2			5	6	11	8	9	10			1			4				3		7			
	2			5	6	11	8	9	10			1			4				3		7			
	2			5	6	11	8	9	10			1			4				3		7			
	2	3		5	6				10	11	1				4						7			
	2			5	6	11	8		10						4	3				9	7			
	2		6	5	4		8	9			11	1				3					7	10		
	2		6	5				9	10	11	1				4			8	3		7			
	2	3		5	6	7			9	10		1			4			8			11			
	2	3		5	6	7			9	10		1			4			8			11			
	2	3			6	7			9	10		1			4			8			11	5		
	2	3		5	6	7			9			1			4			8			11	10		
	2	3		5	6	7				8					4			9			11	10		
	2	3	4	5	6	7			9	10								8			11			
	2	3	4	5	6	7			9						8						10	11		
	2	3	4	5	6	7			9	10								8			11			
	2	3		5	6	8		10	9						4					11	7			
	2	3		5	6	11		9	10						4					8	7			
	2	3		5	6	11		9	10						4					8	7			
	2	3			6	11			10						4					9	7	8	5	
	2	3			6	11			10						4					9	7	8		
4	37	31	22	37	40	37	15	37	36	20	28	1	3	3	22	4	6	25	13	2	2	22	5	2
	1	1		4	5	5	15	20	2		1		1					11				10		

	Whitehead JR	Hall LJ	Green K	Watts JW	Smith T	Neal RM	Astall G	Kinsey N	Brown E	Murphy P	Govan A	Merrick GH	Hallawell MS	Mullard CJ	Neale KJ	Larkin BP	Allen GH	Newman JHG	Orrit B	Farmer FBW	Houghton HB	Hooper H	Jennie DWL	Sessions JG
	2		4	5	6	11	8	9	10			1							3		7			
	1		1	1	1	1	1	1	1			1							1		1			

League Table

	P	W	D	L	F	A	Pts
Wolverhampton W	42	28	8	6	103	47	64
Preston North End	42	26	7	9	100	51	59
Tottenham Hotspur	42	21	9	12	93	77	51
West Bromwich Albion	42	18	14	10	92	70	50
Manchester City	42	22	5	15	104	100	49
Burnley	42	21	5	16	80	74	47
Blackpool	42	19	6	17	80	67	44
Luton Town	42	19	6	17	69	63	44
Manchester United	42	16	11	15	85	75	43
Nottingham Forest	42	16	10	16	69	63	42
Chelsea	42	15	12	15	83	79	42
Arsenal	42	16	7	19	73	85	39
Birmingham City	42	14	11	17	76	89	39
Aston Villa	42	16	7	19	73	86	39
Bolton Wanderers	42	14	10	18	65	87	38
Everton	42	13	11	18	65	75	37
Leeds United	42	14	9	19	51	63	37
Leicester City	42	14	5	23	91	112	33
Newcastle United	42	12	8	22	73	81	32
Portsmouth	42	12	8	22	73	88	32
Sunderland	42	10	12	20	54	97	32
Sheffield Wednesday	42	12	7	23	69	92	31

1958-59

Division One

Joint managers: Arthur Turner and Pat Beasley (to September); then Beasley only.

Did you know that?

Blues scored five times in 19 minutes either side of half-time in their 7–1 win at Nottingham Forest in March...having been 1–0 down!

On 4 April, England right-back Jeff Hall, aged 29, died from polio, having played his last game for Blues against Portsmouth two weeks earlier.

The Middlesbrough-Blues third round FA Cup tie at Ayresome Park in January was abandoned after an hour's play with the scores level at 1–1. Blues won the replay 1–0.

Gil Merrick captained Blues in the 3–0 home defeat by Nottingham Forest.

The former Blues centre-half Sid Owen (Luton Town) was voted Footballer of the Year in 1960 – after leading the Hatters to the FA Cup Final.

Former Blues player and manager Bob McRoberts died on 27 February.

Match No.	Date		Venue	Opponents	Result		Scorers	Attendance
1	Aug	23	A	Aston Villa	D	1-1	Murphy	55,19
2		27	A	West Bromwich Albion	D	2-2	Brown, Houghton	46,46
3		30	H	Luton Town	L	0-1		31,94
4	Sep	3	H	West Bromwich Albion	L	0-6		35,98
5		6	A	Bolton Wanderers	L	0-2		24,70
6		10	A	Leeds United	D	0-0		25,22
7		13	H	Burnley	W	2-1	Brown, Murphy	23,92
8		17	H	Leeds United	W	4-1	Brown 4	24,06
9		20	A	Preston North End	L	0-3		24,25
10		27	H	Leicester City	W	4-2	Gordon, Murphy, Hooper, Astall (pen)	33,32
11	Oct	4	A	Everton	L	1-3	Murphy	39,40
12		11	A	West Ham United	W	2-1	Hooper, Neal	29,13
13		18	H	Nottingham Forest	L	0-3		31,61
14		25	A	Wolverhampton Wan.	L	1-3	Astall	36,15
15	Nov	1	H	Portsmouth	D	2-2	Brown, Taylor	23,72
16		8	A	Blackburn Rovers	L	2-3	Brown, Larkin	28,80
17		15	H	Newcastle United	W	1-0	Larkin	28,75
18		22	H	Tottenham Hotspur	W	4-0	Larkin 2, Hooper, Taylor	28,70
19		29	H	Manchester United	L	0-4		28,65
20	Dec	6	A	Chelsea	L	0-1		27,77
21		13	H	Blackpool	W	4-2	Jackson, Gordon, Larkin, Astall	17,24
22		20	H	Aston Villa	W	4-1	Jackson 2, Astall (pen), Neal	31,85
23		26	H	Manchester City	W	6-1	Jackson 2, Gordon, Larkin 2, Taylor	34,29
24		27	A	Manchester City	L	1-4	Jackson	29,27
25	Jan	3	A	Luton Town	W	1-0	Neal	15,53
26		31	A	Burnley	W	1-0	Gordon	22,10
27	Feb	7	H	Preston North End	W	5-1	Orritt, Gordon, Larkin 2, Astall	21,23
28		21	H	Everton	W	2-1	Larkin, Hooper	22,66
29		28	H	West Ham United	W	3-0	Larkin 2, Neal	19,91
30	Mar	7	A	Nottingham Forest	W	7-1	Stubbs 2, Gordon, Astall 2, Hooper, Watts	18,97
31		14	H	Wolverhampton Wan.	L	0-3		37,72
32		18	A	Leicester City	W	4-2	Stubbs 3, Gordon	15,41
33		21	A	Portsmouth	D	1-1	Larkin	18,17
34	Apr	8	H	Bolton Wanderers	L	1-3	Stubbs	24,60
35		11	H	Tottenham Hotspur	W	5-1	Stubbs, Gordon, Larkin, Hooper (pen), Baker (og)	20,55
36		14	H	Arsenal	W	4-1	Stubbs, Larkin 2, Astall	25,79
37		18	A	Manchester United	L	0-1		43,00
38		20	H	Blackpool	L	0-2		12,26
39		22	H	Blackburn Rovers	W	3-0	Larkin 2, Taylor	22,95
40		25	H	Chelsea	W	4-1	Gordon 2, Hooper, Taylor	19,58
41		29	A	Newcastle United	D	1-1	Hooper	19,77
42	May	4	A	Arsenal	L	1-2	Stubbs	25,95

							Appearance
						One own-goal	Goal

FA Cup

R3	Jan	24	A	Middlesbrough		1-0	Harris (og)	36,58
R4		28	H	Fulham		1-1	Jackson	42,67
rep	Feb	4	A	Fulham		3-2	Hooper 2, Larkin	27,52
R5		14	H	Nottingham Forest		1-1	Astall	55,30
rep		18	A	Nottingham Forest		1-1	Gordon	39,43
rep2		23	H	Nottingham Forest		0-5		34,45

R5 replay a.e.t. R5 replay 2 at Filbert Street, Leicester.

							Appearance
						One own-goal	Goal

352

Appearances & Goals Chart

Merrick GH	Hall JJ	Green K	Larkin BP	Smith T	Neal RM	Hooper H	Orritt B	Brown E	Murphy P	Taylor BJ	Sissons JG	Houghton HB	Watts JW	Jones DWC	Schofield JR	Gordon JDS	Astall G	Halsowell MS	Farmer FBW	Allen GH	Jackson AJ	Stubbs RG	Hume WS
2	3	4	5	6	7	8	9	10	11														
2	3	4		6	7	10	9		11	5	8												
2	3	4		6	7	10	9		11	5	8												
2	3	4		6	7	8	9	10	11	5													
2	3	4	9	10	7	8		11	5		6												
2	3		6	7		9	10	11	5		4	8											
2	3		6	7		9	10	11	5		4	8											
2	3		6	7		9	10	11	5		4	8											
2	3		6	7		9	10	11	5		4	8	1										
2	3		6	7		9	10		5		4				8	11							
2	3		6			9	10		5		4				8	11	7						
2	3		6	7	10	9	11		5		4				8								
2	3		6	7	10	9			5		4				8								
	3	6		10			9		11	5	4				8	7	2						
2	3	6			7		9	10	11	5	4				8								
2		10	5	6	7		9		11		4				8	7			3				
2		10	5	6					11		4				8				3		9		
		10	5	6	7		9		11		4		1		8				2	3			
		10	5	6	7		9		11		4		1		8				2	3			
2		10	5	6			9		11		4				8	7			3				
2		10	5	6					11		4				8	7			3		9		
2		10	5	6					11		4				8	7			3		9		
2		10	5	6					11		4				8	7			3		9		
2		10	5	6					11		4				8	7			3		9		
		10	5	6			11				4				8	7		2	3		9		
2		10	5	6	11	9					4				8	7			3				
2		10	5	6	11	9					4				8	7			3				
2		10	5	6	11	9					4		1		8	7			3				
2		10		6	11				5		4				8	7			3		9		
2		10	5	6	11						4				8	7			3		9		
2		10	5	6	11						4				8	7			3		9		
2		10	5		11						4				8	7		2	3		9		
2		10	5		11						4				8	7		2	3		9		
		10	5	6	11						4				8	7		2	3		9		
		10	5	6	11						4				8	7		2	3		9		
		10	5	6	11						4				8	7		2	3		9		
		10	5	6	11						4				8	7		2	3		9		
		9	5	6	10				11		4				8	7		2	3				
		9	5	6	10				11		4		1		8	7		2	3				
			5	6	10				11		4		1		8	7		2	3		9		
			5	6	10				11		4		1		8	7		2	3		9		
			6		10				11	5	4		1		8	7		2	3		9		
29	**15**	**31**	**27**	**39**	**34**	**12**	**17**	**10**	**26**	**16**	**2**	**38**	**4**	**8**	**33**	**26**	**1**	**13**	**27**	**6**	**12**	**2**	
	18			**4**	**8**	**1**	**8**	**4**	**5**			**1**	**1**		**10**	**8**				**6**	**9**		

Merrick GH	Hall JJ	Green K	Larkin BP	Smith T	Neal RM	Hooper H	Orritt B	Brown E	Murphy P	Taylor BJ	Sissons JG	Houghton HB	Watts JW	Jones DWC	Schofield JR	Gordon JDS	Astall G	Halsowell MS	Farmer FBW	Allen GH	Jackson AJ	Stubbs RG	Hume WS
2		10	5	6					11		4				8	7			3		9		
2		10	5	6					11		4				8	7			3				
2		10	5	6	11						4				8	7			3		9		
2		10	5	6	11	9					4				8	7			3				
2		10	5	6	11	7					4				8				3		9		
2		10	5	6	11	9					4				8	7			3				
6		**6**	**6**	**6**	**4**	**3**			**2**		**6**				**6**	**5**			**6**	**4**			
		1			**2**										**1**	**1**				**1**			

League Table

	P	W	D	L	F	A	Pts
Wolverhampton W	42	28	5	9	110	49	61
Manchester United	42	24	7	11	103	66	55
Arsenal	42	21	8	13	88	68	50
Bolton Wanderers	42	20	10	12	79	66	50
West Bromwich Albion	42	18	13	11	88	68	49
West Ham United	42	21	6	15	85	70	48
Burnley	42	19	10	13	81	70	48
Blackpool	42	18	11	13	66	49	47
Birmingham City	42	20	6	16	84	68	46
Blackburn Rovers	42	17	10	15	76	70	44
Newcastle United	42	17	7	18	80	80	41
Preston North End	42	17	7	18	70	77	41
Nottingham Forest	42	17	6	19	71	74	40
Chelsea	42	18	4	20	77	98	40
Leeds United	42	15	9	18	57	74	39
Everton	42	17	4	21	71	87	38
Luton Town	42	12	13	17	68	71	37
Tottenham Hotspur	42	13	10	19	85	95	36
Leicester City	42	11	10	21	67	98	32
Manchester City	42	11	9	22	64	95	31
Aston Villa	42	11	8	23	58	87	30
Portsmouth	42	6	9	27	64	112	21

Division One

Manager: Pat Beasley

Match No.	Date	Venue	Opponents		Result	Scorers	Attendance
1	Aug 22	H	Wolverhampton Wan.	L	0-1		41,2
2	26	H	Newcastle United	W	4-3	Stubbs, Gordon, Orritt, Hooper (pen)	26,9
3	29	A	Tottenham Hotspur	D	0-0		45,2
4	Sep 2	A	Newcastle United	L	0-1		35,3
5	5	H	Manchester United	D	1-1	Watts	38,2
6	9	H	Chelsea	D	1-1	Larkin	28,1
7	12	A	Preston North End	L	2-3	Stubbs, Neal	18,9
8	16	A	Chelsea	L	2-4	Hooper (pen), Scott (og)	31,6
9	19	H	Leicester City	L	3-4	Hooper 2 (1 pen), Smith	24,9
10	26	A	Burnley	L	1-3	Orritt	23,8
11	Oct 3	H	Leeds United	W	2-0	Barrett, Taylor	25,3
12	10	H	Sheffield Wednesday	D	0-0		21,7
13	17	A	Nottingham Forest	W	2-0	Stubbs, Gordon	24,9
14	24	H	Fulham	L	2-4	Gordon 2	26,6
15	31	A	Arsenal	L	0-3		34,4
16	Nov 7	H	Luton Town	D	1-1	Barrett	19,0
17	14	A	Everton	L	0-4		19,1
18	21	H	Blackpool	W	2-1	Larkin, Hooper	24,7
19	28	A	Blackburn Rovers	L	1-2	Barrett	20,5
20	Dec 5	H	Manchester City	W	4-2	Gordon 2, Barrett, Hooper	18,6
21	12	A	Bolton Wanderers	L	1-4	Hooper	16,0
22	19	A	Wolverhampton Wan.	L	0-2		22,3
23	26	H	West Ham United	W	2-0	Astall, Hooper	29,7
24	28	A	West Ham United	L	1-3	Astall	26,1
25	Jan 2	H	Tottenham Hotspur	L	0-1		27,5
26	16	A	Manchester United	L	1-2	Larkin	47,6
27	23	H	Preston North End	W	2-1	Larkin, Neal	24,1
28	Feb 6	A	Leicester City	W	3-1	Weston, Hume, Hooper	25,8
29	27	A	Manchester City	L	0-3		23,4
30	Mar 5	H	Nottingham Forest	W	4-1	Gordon 2, Neal, Hooper	24,8
31	9	A	Leeds United	D	3-3	Hume, Hooper, McConnell (og)	8,5
32	12	A	Fulham	D	2-2	Gordon, Hooper	25,2
33	19	H	Bolton Wanderers	L	2-5	Weston, Gordon	24,1
34	26	A	Luton Town	D	1-1	Weston	13,6
35	Apr 2	H	Everton	D	2-2	Gordon, Astall	24,8
36	9	A	Blackpool	W	1-0	Gordon	13,5
37	16	H	Arsenal	W	3-0	Murphy 2, Gordon	27,2
38	18	H	West Bromwich Albion	L	1-7	Gordon	28,6
39	19	A	West Bromwich Albion	D	1-1	Gordon	37,8
40	23	A	Sheffield Wednesday	W	4-2	Murphy 2, Astall, Hooper	25,3
41	27	H	Burnley	L	0-1		37,0
42	30	H	Blackburn Rovers	W	1-0	Gordon	24,4
							Appearanc
			Two own-goals				Goa

FA Cup

R3	Jan 9	A	Watford	L	1-2	Hooper	31,5
							Appearanc
							Goa

Schofield JR	Farmer FBW	Allen GH	Watts JW	Smith T	Neal RM	Astall G	Gordon JDS	Stubbs RG	Orritt B	Hooper H	Taylor BJ	Larkin BP	Hellawell MS	Sissons JG	Merrick GH	Barrett JG	Wright PDJ	Weston DP	Hume WS	Rudd WT	Murphy P
	2	3	4	5	6	7	8	9	10	11											
	2	3	4	5	6	7	8	9	10	11											
	2	3	4	5	6		8	9	10	7	11										
	2	3	4	5	6		8	9	10	7	11										
	2	3	4	5	6		8	9	11	7		10									
	2	3	4	5	6		8	9	11	7		10									
	2	3	4	5	6		8	9	11	7		10									
	2	3	4	5	6		8	9	10	11			7								
	2		4	5	6		8	9	10	11			7	3							
	2		4	5	6		8		10	11		9	7	3	1						
	2		4	5	6		8	9		7	11			3	1	10					
	2		4	5	6		8		9	7	11	10		3							
	2	3	4				8	9		7	11	6		5		10					
		3	4	5	6		8	9			11		7	2		10					
	2	3	4	5	6		8		9	7	11					10					
	2	3	4	5	6		8		9	7	11					10					
	2	3	4	5			8	9	10	11		6	7								
	2	3	4	5	6		8	9		11		10	7								
		3	4	5	6		9			11		10	7			8	2				
	2	3	4	5	6		9			11		10	7			8					
	2	3		5	6		9		4	11		10	7			8					
	2	3	4	5	6		9			11		10	7			8					
	2	3	4	5		7	10	9		11		6				8					
	2	3	4	5	6	7	8	9		11		10									
	2	3	4	5	6	7	8	9		11		10									
	2	3	4	5	6	7						8						9	10	11	
	2	3	4	5	6	7						8						9	10	11	
	2	3	4	5	6					7		8						9	10	11	
	2	3	4	5	6		8			7		10						9		11	
	2	3	4	5	6	7	8	9		11									10		
	2	3	4	5	6	7	8			11								9	10		
	2	3	4	5	6	7	8			11								9	10		
	2	3	4	5	6		8			11			7					9	10		
	2	3	4	5	6	7	8			11								9	10		
	2	3	4	5	6	7	8		10	11								9			
	2	3	4	5	6	7	8			11								9			10
	2	3	4	5	6	7	8			11								9			10
	2	3	4	5	6	7	8			11								9			10
	2	3	4	5	6	7	8			11								9			10
	2	3	4	5	6	7	8			11								9			10
	3		4	5	6	7	8			11				2				9			10
	3		4	5	6	7	8			11				2				9			10
	40	36	41	41	39	19	39	18	16	39	8	19	11	8	2	10	1	16	8	4	7
			1	1	3	4	16	3	2	13	1	4				4		3	2		4
	2	3	4	5	10	7		9		11		6				8					
	1	1	1	1	1	1		1		1		1				1					
										1											

League Table

	P	W	D	L	F	A	Pts
Burnley	42	24	7	11	85	61	55
Wolverhampton W	42	24	6	12	106	67	54
Tottenham Hotspur	42	21	11	10	86	50	53
West Bromwich Albion	42	19	11	12	83	57	49
Sheffield Wednesday	42	19	11	12	80	59	49
Bolton Wanderers	42	20	8	14	59	51	48
Manchester United	42	19	7	16	102	80	45
Newcastle United	42	18	8	16	82	78	44
Preston North End	42	16	12	14	79	76	44
Fulham	42	17	10	15	73	80	44
Blackpool	42	15	10	17	59	71	40
Leicester City	42	13	13	16	66	75	39
Arsenal	42	15	9	18	68	80	39
West Ham United	42	16	6	20	75	91	38
Everton	42	13	11	18	73	78	37
Manchester City	42	17	3	22	78	84	37
Blackburn Rovers	42	16	5	21	60	70	37
Chelsea	42	14	9	19	76	91	37
Birmingham City	42	13	10	19	63	80	36
Nottingham Forest	42	13	9	20	50	74	35
Leeds United	42	12	10	20	65	92	34
Luton Town	42	9	12	21	50	73	30

Division One

Manager: Gil Merrick

On their way to reaching the Inter Cities Fairs Cup Final, Blues beat Inter Milan 2–1 in the first leg of the semi-final in the San Siro Stadium in May. This was the last time Inter would lose at home against an English club for 47 years, until Arsenal recorded a 2–0 victory there in the Champions League in March 2008.

Goalkeeper Johnny Schofield fractured his skull during the League game with Manchester United in November.

Colin Withers conceded six goals on his Blues debut at Spurs, who were 3–0 up after 14 minutes.

Burnley fielded five reserves when they beat Blues 1–0 in April…and Johnny Schofield was carried off with a fractured skull during the home game with Manchester United in November. Bryan Orritt took over in goal and performed miracles as Blues recorded a famous 3–1 victory.

It was now five shillings to stand on the terraces at St Andrew's.

Former Barcelona and Spanish international Emilio Aldecoa Gomez (capped v Republic of Ireland in 1948) was named coach at St Andrew's in 1961.

Match No.	Date		Venue	Opponents	Result		Scorers	Attendance
1	Aug	20	A	Bolton Wanderers	D	2-2	Gordon, Hooper	20,54
2		24	A	West Bromwich Albion	W	2-1	Rudd, Hooper	32,10
3		27	H	Sheffield Wednesday	D	1-1	Hooper	27,19
4		31	H	West Bromwich Albion	W	3-1	Gordon, Astall, G.Williams (og)	37,87
5	Sep	3	A	Fulham	L	1-2	Rudd	19,29
6		6	A	Arsenal	L	0-2		20,06
7		10	H	Preston North End	L	1-3	Gordon	24,43
8		14	H	Arsenal	W	2-0	Stubbs 2	22,90
9		17	A	Burnley	L	1-2	Cummings (og)	20,74
10		24	H	Nottingham Forest	W	3-1	Gordon, Singer, Astall	26,65
11	Oct	1	A	Manchester City	L	1-2	Singer	27,66
12		8	A	West Ham United	L	3-4	Rudd, Hellawell 2	15,95
13		15	H	Chelsea	W	1-0	Hellawell	23,33
14		22	A	Aston Villa	L	2-6	Hellawell, Thomson (og)	44,72
15		29	H	Wolverhampton Wan.	L	1-2	Showell (og)	32,28
16	Nov	5	A	Blackburn Rovers	L	0-2		13,46
17		12	H	Manchester United	W	3-1	Gordon, Taylor, Neal	31,56
18		19	A	Tottenham Hotspur	L	0-6		46,01
19		26	H	Leicester City	L	0-2		25,82
20	Dec	3	A	Blackpool	W	2-1	Hellawell 2	11,72
21		10	H	Everton	L	2-4	Neal, Stubbs	27,71
22		17	H	Bolton Wanderers	D	2-2	Harris 2	19,05
23		24	A	Newcastle United	D	2-2	Hellawell, Neal	20,35
24		26	H	Newcastle United	W	2-1	Bloomfield, Hellawell	29,43
25		31	A	Sheffield Wednesday	L	0-2		22,99
26	Jan	14	H	Fulham	W	1-0	Singer	23,26
27		21	A	Preston North End	W	3-2	Bloomfield, Hellawell, Singer	7,66
28	Feb	11	A	Nottingham Forest	L	0-1		23,54
29		25	H	West Ham United	W	4-2	Harris 2 (1 pen), Bloomfield, Neal	16,85
30	Mar	4	A	Chelsea	L	2-3	Gordon, Astall	27,77
31		11	H	Aston Villa	D	1-1	Singer	41,66
32		18	A	Wolverhampton Wan.	L	1-5	Singer	23,8
33		22	H	Manchester City	W	3-2	Harris (pen), Bloomfield 2	18,09
34		25	H	Blackburn Rovers	D	1-1	Hellawell	19,30
35		31	A	Cardiff City	W	2-0	Harris (pen), Orritt	16,33
36	Apr	1	A	Everton	L	0-1		31,8
37		3	H	Cardiff City	W	2-1	Harris, Orritt	20,00
38		8	H	Tottenham Hotspur	L	2-3	Harris 2 (1 pen)	40,90
39		15	A	Manchester United	L	1-4	Foulkes (og)	28,3
40		22	H	Blackpool	L	0-2		17,8
41		27	H	Burnley	L	0-1		15,0
42		29	A	Leicester City	L	2-3	Harris, Singer	19,92
								Appearance
							Five own-goals	Goa

FA Cup

R3	Jan	7	A	Nottingham Forest	W	2-0	Singer 2	19,9
R4		28	H	Rotherham United	W	4-0	Singer 2, Neal, Harris	31,9
R5	Feb	18	H	Leicester City	D	1-1	Harris (pen)	53,5
rep		22	A	Leicester City	L	1-2	Harris	41,9
								Appearance
								Goa

League Cup

R2	Oct	31	A	Bradford Park Avenue	W	1-0	Hellawell	4,7
R3	Nov	14	H	Plymouth Argyle	D	0-0		15,3
rep		16	A	Plymouth Argyle	L	1-3	Wyatt (og)	14,1
								Appearanc
							One own-goal	Goa

Player columns (left to right): Schofield JR, Farmer FBW, Allen BH, Watts JW, Smith T, Neal RM, Astall G, Gordon JDS, Weston DP, Rudd WT, Hooper H, Stubbs RG, Beard M, Singer DJ, Sissons JG, Hellawell MS, Barrow RJ, Orritt B, Taylor BJ, Withers CC, Bloomfield JH, Harris J, Hennessey WT, Foster WA

League Table

	P	W	D	L	F	A	Pts
Tottenham Hotspur	42	31	4	7	115	55	66
Sheffield Wednesday	42	23	12	7	78	47	58
Wolverhampton W	42	25	7	10	103	75	57
Burnley	42	22	7	13	102	77	51
Everton	42	22	6	14	87	69	50
Leicester City	42	18	9	15	87	70	45
Manchester United	42	18	9	15	88	76	45
Blackburn Rovers	42	15	13	14	77	76	43
Aston Villa	42	17	9	16	78	77	43
West Bromwich Albion	42	18	5	19	67	71	41
Arsenal	42	15	11	16	77	85	41
Chelsea	42	15	7	20	98	100	37
Manchester City	42	13	11	18	79	90	37
Nottingham Forest	42	14	9	19	62	78	37
Cardiff City	42	13	11	18	60	85	37
West Ham United	42	13	10	19	77	88	36
Fulham	42	14	8	20	72	95	36
Bolton Wanderers	42	12	11	19	58	73	35
Birmingham City	42	14	6	22	62	84	34
Blackpool	42	12	9	21	68	73	33
Newcastle United	42	11	10	21	86	109	32
Preston North End	42	10	10	22	43	71	30

Division One

Manager: Gil Merrick

Match No.	Date	Venue	Opponents	Result		Scorers	Attendance
1	Aug 19	H	Fulham	W	2-1	Harris, Bloomfield	25,387
2	22	A	Nottingham Forest	L	1-2	Harris	19,486
3	26	A	Sheffield Wednesday	L	1-5	Bloomfield	29,931
4	30	H	Nottingham Forest	D	1-1	Harris	21,095
5	Sep 2	H	Leicester City	L	1-5	Bloomfield	21,977
6	6	A	West Bromwich Albion	D	0-0		20,541
7	9	A	Ipswich Town	L	1-4	Singer	20,017
8	16	H	Burnley	L	2-6	Hellawell, Bloomfield	18,764
9	20	H	West Bromwich Albion	L	1-2	Hellawell	23,931
10	23	A	Arsenal	D	1-1	Harris (pen)	31,749
11	30	H	Bolton Wanderers	W	2-1	Auld, Bloomfield	17,214
12	Oct 7	H	Wolverhampton Wan.	L	3-6	Harris, 2 (1 pen), Bloomfield	29,159
13	14	A	Manchester United	W	2-0	Orritt, Hellawell	30,674
14	21	A	Chelsea	W	3-2	Bloomfield 2, Harris	20,095
15	28	A	Aston Villa	W	3-1	Harris 2, Orritt	49,532
16	Nov 4	H	Blackpool	D	1-1	Orritt	21,450
17	11	A	Blackburn Rovers	L	0-2		12,083
18	18	H	West Ham United	W	4-0	Bloomfield, Orritt, Harris (pen), Auld	20,682
19	25	A	Sheffield United	L	1-3	Harris	16,838
20	Dec 2	H	Cardiff City	W	3-0	Leek 2, Hellawell	20,959
21	9	A	Tottenham Hotspur	L	1-3	Leek	32,509
22	16	H	Fulham	W	1-0	Leek	12,730
23	23	H	Sheffield Wednesday	D	1-1	Leek	19,109
24	26	H	Manchester City	D	1-1	Leek	21,926
25	Jan 13	A	Leicester City	W	2-1	Harris, Auld	22,691
26	20	H	Ipswich Town	W	3-1	Leek 2, Baxter (og)	26,968
27	Feb 3	A	Burnley	L	1-7	Auld	24,047
28	10	H	Arsenal	W	1-0	Harris	27,787
29	17	A	Bolton Wanderers	L	2-3	Auld, Leek	13,308
30	24	A	Wolverhampton Wan.	L	1-2	Leek	29,665
31	Mar 3	H	Manchester United	D	1-1	Leek	25,817
32	9	A	Chelsea	D	1-1	Leek	23,959
33	17	H	Aston Villa	L	0-2		43,489
34	24	A	Blackpool	L	0-1		11,854
35	30	H	Blackburn Rovers	W	2-1	Hellawell, Leek	17,431
36	Apr 6	A	West Ham United	D	2-2	Bloomfield, Lynn	22,668
37	11	A	Manchester City	W	4-1	Harris, Bloomfield, Leek, Hellawell	21,941
38	14	H	Sheffield United	W	3-0	Harris 2 (1 pen), Hellawell	19,514
39	20	A	Everton	L	1-4	Leek	47,506
40	21	A	Cardiff City	L	2-3	Leek 2	8,608
41	24	H	Everton	D	0-0		21,910
42	28	H	Tottenham Hotspur	L	2-3	Beard, Leek	29,614
							Appearances
			One own-goal				Goals

FA Cup

	Date	Venue	Opponents	Result		Scorers	Attendance
R3	Jan 6	H	Tottenham Hotspur	D	3-3	Harris 2, Leek	46,096
rep	10	A	Tottenham Hotspur	L	2-4	Harris, Leek	62,917
							Appearances
							Goals

League Cup

	Date	Venue	Opponents	Result		Scorers	Attendance
R1	Sep 13	H	Swindon Town	D	1-1	Neal	11,596
rep	25	A	Swindon Town	L	0-2		13,063
							Appearances
							Goals

Withers CC	Farmer FBW	Beard M	Watts JW	Smith T	Neal RM	Hellawell MS	Bloomfield JH	Harris J	Rudd WT	Auld R	Foster WA	Hennessey WT	Orritt B	Allen GH	Stubbs RG	Singer DJ	Taylor BJ	Schofield JR	Sissons JG	Lynn S	Leek K	Wright PDJ	Bullock PL	Thwaites D
	2	3	4	5	6	7	8	9	10	11														
		3	4	5	6	7	8	9	10	11	2													
		3		5	6	7	8	9		11	2	4	10											
		6		5	4	7	8	9		11	2			3	10									
		6		5	4	7	8	9		11	2			3	10									
		6	4	5		7	8	9		11	2			3		10								
		6	4	5		7	8	9			2			3		10	11							
	2	6		5	4	7	10	9						3	8		11	1						
	2	6		5		7	10	9		11		4			8			1	3					
	2	6		5		7	10	9		11		4	8					1	3					
	2	6		5		7	8	9		11		4	10					1	3					
	2	6		5		7	10	9				4	8				11	1	3					
	2	6				7	8	9		11	5	4	10					1	3					
		6				7	8	9		11	5	4	10					1	3	2				
		6		5		7	8	9		11		4	10					1	3	2				
		6		5		7	8	9		11		4	10					1	3	2				
		6		5		7		9		11		4	10		8			1	3	2				
		6		5		7	8	9		11		4	10					1	3	2				
		6		5		7		9		11		4	8					1	3	2	10			
		6		5		7		9		11		4	8					1	3	2	10			
		6		5		7		9		11		4	8					1	3	2	10			
		6		5		7		9		11		4	8					1	3	2	10			
		6		5		7		9		11		4	8					1	3	2	10			
		6		5		7		9		11		4	8					1	3	2	10			
		6		5		7	8	9		11		4						1	3	2	10			
		6		5		7	8	9		11		4						1	3	2	10			
		6		5		7	8	9		11		4						1	3	2	10			
		6		5		7	8	9		11	2	4						1	3		10			
		6		5		7	8	9		11	2	4						1	3		10			
		6		5		7	8					4	11		9			1	3	2	10			
		6		5		7	8			11		4			9			1	3	2	10			
		6		5		7	8	9		11		4						1	3	2	10			
		6		5		7	8	9		11		4						1	3	2	10			
		6		5		7	8	9		11		4						1	3	2	10			
		6		5		7	8	9		11		4						1	3	2	10			
		6		5		7	8	9		11		4						1	3	2	10			
		6	4	5		7	8	9		11	2							1	3		10			
		6		5		7	8	9		11	2	4						1	3		10			
	2	6		5		7	8	9		11		4						1	3		10			
		6		5		7	8	9		11	2	4						1			10	3		
		6				7	8			11	5	4						1	3		10	2	9	
		6		5		7	8	9		11	2	4						1	3		10			
	8	42	5	39	6	42	35	39	2	38	15	34	17	5	7	2	3	35	33	21	24	2	1	0
		1				7	11	16		5			4			1				1	18			

Withers CC	Farmer FBW	Beard M	Watts JW	Smith T	Neal RM	Hellawell MS	Bloomfield JH	Harris J	Rudd WT	Auld R	Foster WA	Hennessey WT	Orritt B	Allen GH	Stubbs RG	Singer DJ	Taylor BJ	Schofield JR	Sissons JG	Lynn S	Leek K	Wright PDJ	Bullock PL	Thwaites D
		6		5		7		9		11		4	8					1	3	2	10			
		6		5		7		9		11		4	8					1	3	2	10			
		2		2		2		2		2		2	2					2	2	2	2			
								3													2			

Withers CC	Farmer FBW	Beard M	Watts JW	Smith T	Neal RM	Hellawell MS	Bloomfield JH	Harris J	Rudd WT	Auld R	Foster WA	Hennessey WT	Orritt B	Allen GH	Stubbs RG	Singer DJ	Taylor BJ	Schofield JR	Sissons JG	Lynn S	Leek K	Wright PDJ	Bullock PL	Thwaites D
	2	6		5	4	7	8							3	9	10	11	1						
	2	6		5		7	10	9				4	8					1	3					11
	2	2		2	1	2	2	1				1	1	1	1	1	1	2	1					1
					1																			

League Table

	P	W	D	L	F	A	Pts
Ipswich Town	42	24	8	10	93	67	56
Burnley	42	21	11	10	101	67	53
Tottenham Hotspur	42	21	10	11	88	69	52
Everton	42	20	11	11	88	54	51
Sheffield United	42	19	9	14	61	69	47
Sheffield Wednesday	42	20	6	16	72	58	46
Aston Villa	42	18	8	16	65	56	44
West Ham United	42	17	10	15	76	82	44
West Bromwich Albion	42	15	13	14	83	67	43
Arsenal	42	16	11	15	71	72	43
Bolton Wanderers	42	16	10	16	62	66	42
Manchester City	42	17	7	18	78	81	41
Blackpool	42	15	11	16	70	75	41
Leicester City	42	17	6	19	72	71	40
Manchester United	42	15	9	18	72	75	39
Blackburn Rovers	42	14	11	17	50	58	39
Birmingham City	42	14	10	18	65	81	38
Wolverhampton W	42	13	10	19	73	86	36
Nottingham Forest	42	13	10	19	63	79	36
Fulham	42	13	7	22	66	74	33
Cardiff City	42	9	14	19	50	81	32
Chelsea	42	9	10	23	63	94	28

Division One

Manager: Gil Merrick

Match No.	Date		Venue	Opponents	Result		Scorers	Attendance
1	Aug	18	A	Tottenham Hotspur	L	0-3		51,146
2		21	A	Arsenal	L	0-2		34,004
3		25	H	Leyton Orient	D	2-2	Bullock, Hellawell	23,411
4		29	H	Arsenal	D	2-2	Leek, Lynn (pen)	27,038
5	Sep	1	A	Manchester United	L	0-2		40,618
6		8	H	Burnley	W	5-1	Leek, Hellawell 2, Bloomfield, Bullock	24,463
7		12	A	West Bromwich Albion	L	0-1		25,560
8		15	A	Sheffield Wednesday	L	0-5		22,259
9		19	H	West Bromwich Albion	D	0-0		28,660
10		22	H	Fulham	W	4-1	Leek, Harris, Lynn (pen), Auld	20,439
11		29	A	Leicester City	L	0-3		22,216
12	Oct	6	A	West Ham United	L	0-5		21,150
13		13	H	Manchester City	D	2-2	Stubbs, Regan	21,114
14		24	A	Wolverhampton Wan.	W	2-0	Leek 2	26,226
15		27	H	Aston Villa	W	3-2	Lynn (pen), Leek 2	42,228
16	Nov	3	A	Sheffield United	W	2-0	Hellawell, Stubbs	19,188
17		10	H	Nottingham Forest	D	2-2	Harris, Leek	22,024
18		17	A	Ipswich Town	W	5-1	Harris 2, Auld, Leek 2	16,778
19		24	H	Liverpool	L	0-2		27,050
20	Dec	1	A	Blackpool	D	1-1	Leek	12,955
21		8	H	Blackburn Rovers	D	3-3	Bloommfield, Leek 2	16,108
22		15	H	Tottenham Hotspur	L	0-2		36,623
23		22	A	Leyton Orient	D	2-2	Bloomfield 2	11,646
24	Mar	2	A	Manchester City	L	1-2	Harris	28,798
25		9	H	Wolverhampton Wan.	L	3-4	Lynn 2 (2 pens), Auld	18,219
26		16	A	Aston Villa	L	0-4		40,400
27		23	H	Sheffield United	L	0-1		18,050
28		30	H	Sheffield Wednesday	D	1-1	Auld (pen)	12,279
29	Apr	3	H	Bolton Wanderers	D	2-2	Leek 2	13,200
30		6	A	Ipswich Town	L	0-1		16,756
31		13	A	Nottingham Forest	W	2-0	Leek 2	15,556
32		15	A	Everton	D	2-2	Bloomfield, Leek	50,122
33		16	H	Everton	L	0-1		29,719
34		20	H	Blackpool	L	3-6	Bloomfield, Leek, Auld	15,396
35		24	A	Bolton Wanderers	D	0-0		12,949
36		27	A	Blackburn Rovers	L	1-6	Auld	9,482
37	May	1	H	West Ham United	W	3-2	Auld, Hennessey, Harris	14,410
38		4	A	Fulham	D	3-3	Hellawell, Harris, Auld	20,179
39		8	A	Liverpool	L	1-5	Leek	23,684
40		10	H	Manchester United	W	2-1	Bloomfield 2	21,855
41		14	A	Burnley	L	1-3	Bloomfield	14,350
42		18	H	Leicester City	W	3-2	Harris, Auld, Lynn (pen)	23,971
							Appearances	
							Goals	

FA Cup

	Date		Venue	Opponents	Result		Scorers	Attendance
R3	Mar	5	H	Bury	D	3-3	Leek, Harris, Lynn (pen)	37,913
rep		7	A	Bury	L	0-2		16,525
							Appearances	
							Goals	

League Cup

	Date		Venue	Opponents	Result		Scorers	Attendance
R2	Sep	26	H	Doncaster Rovers	W	5-0	Leek 2, Bloomfield, Harris, Auld	11,384
R3	Oct	15	A	Barrow	D	1-1	Wolstenholme	6,289
rep		29	H	Barrow	W	5-1	Harris 2, Stubbs, Leek, Arrowsmith (og)	11,765
R4	Nov	14	H	Notts County	W	3-2	Lynn (pen), Harris, Auld	13,187
R5	Dec	11	H	Manchester City	W	6-0	Lynn 2 (1 pen), Leek, Auld, Leivers (og), Sear (og)	18,012
SF1	Mar	27	H	Bury	W	3-2	Bullock, Leek, Auld	11,293
SF2	Apr	8	A	Bury	D	1-1	Leek	9,177
F1	May	23	H	Aston Villa	W	3-1	Leek 2, Bloomfield	31,902
F2		27	A	Aston Villa	D	0-0		37,949

Final won 3-1 on aggregate.

Three own-goals

Appearances		
Goals		

Column headers (player names, vertical):
Schofield JR, Lynn S, Sissons JG, Hennessey WT, Smith T, Beard M, Hallwell MS, Bullock PL, Harris J, Leek K, Auld R, Thwaites D, Stubbs RG, Bloomfield JH, Watts JV, Winters CC, Sharples B, Foster WA, Regan MJ, Farrell EJP, Green CR, Rushton BVE, Wolstenholme T

Schofield JR	Lynn S	Sissons JG	Hennessey WT	Smith T	Beard M	Hallwell MS	Bullock PL	Harris J	Leek K	Auld R	Thwaites D	Stubbs RG	Bloomfield JH	Watts JV	Winters CC	Sharples B	Foster WA	Regan MJ	Farrell EJP	Green CR	Rushton BVE	Wolstenholme T
1	2	3	4	5	6	7	8	9	10	11												
1	2	3	4	5	6	7	8	9	10		11											
1	2	3	4	5	6	7	8		10		11	9										
1	2	3	4	5	6	7			10		11	9	8									
1	2	3	4	5	6	7		9	10	11			8									
1	2	3	4	5	6	7	10		9		11		8									
1	2	3	4	5	6	7	10		9		11		8									
1	2	3	4	5		7	10		9		11		8	6								
	2		4		6	7		9	10	11			8		1	3	5					
	2		4		6	7		9	10	11			8		1	3	5					
	2		4		6	7		9	10	11			8		1	3	5					
	3		4	5	6	7	8	9	10	11					1		2					
	2	3	4	5	6	7	10			11		8			1			9				
	2	3	4	5	6	7		9	10	11		8			1							
	2	3	6	5		7		9	10	11		8	4	1								
	2	3	6	5		7		9	10	11		8	4	1								
	2	3	6	5		7		9	10	11		8	4	1								
	2	3	5	6		7		9	10	11		8	4	1								
	2	3	6	5		7		9	10	11		8	4	1								
	2	3	6	5			8	9	10	11			4	1					7			
	2	3	6	5				9	10	11		8	4	1					7			
	2		4	5	6	7		9	10	11		8		1						3		
	2		4		6	7		9	10	11		8		1		5				3		
	2		4	5	6	7		9	10	11		8		1						3		
	2		4	5	6	7		9	10	11		8		1						3		
	2		4	5	6	7	9		10	11		8		1						3		
			6	5	3	7	9		10	11		8	4							2		
			6	5	3	7	9		10	11		8	4							2		
			6	5	3	7	9		10	11		8	4							2		
			6	5	3	7			10	11		8	4				9			2		
			4	5		6	7		9	10	11		8							3	2	
			4		6	7		9	10	11		8	5							3	2	
			4	5	6	7			10	11		8								3	2	
			4	5	6	7	9		10	11		8		1						3	2	
	2		4	5	6	7		9	10	11		8		1						3		
	2		4	5	6	7		9	10	11		8		1						3		
	2		4	5	6	7		9	10	11		8		1						3		
	2		4	5	6	7		9	10	11		8		1						3		
	2		4	5	6	7		9	10	11		8		1						3		
	2		4	5	6	7		9	10	11		8		1						3		
8	33	17	42	37	34	40	14	29	41	36	6	12	28	13	24	3	5	2	2	17	9	0
6		1			5	2	8	20	9		2	9			1							

	2		4	5	6	7		9	10	11		8		1						3		
	2		4	5	6	7		9	10	11		8		1						3		
	2		2	2	2	2		2	2	2		2		2						2		
	1							1	1													

	2		4		6	7		9	10	11		8			1	3	5					
	2	3	4	5	6	7			11	8			1				9				10	
	2	3		5		7		9	10	11		8	4	1							6	
	2	3	6	5		7		9	10	11		8	4	1								
	2		6	5	3	7		9	10	11		8	4	1								
			6	5	3	7	9		10	11		8	4						2			
			4		6	7			10	11		8	5				9		3	2		
	2		4	5	6	7		9	10	11		8								3		
	2		4	5	6	7		9	10	11		8								3		
	7	3	8	7	7	9	1	6	8	9		3	6	5	5	1	1	2		3	2	
	3					1	4	8	4			1	2								1	

League Table

	P	W	D	L	F	A	Pts
Everton	42	25	11	6	84	42	61
Tottenham Hotspur	42	23	9	10	111	62	55
Burnley	42	22	10	10	78	57	54
Leicester City	42	20	12	10	79	53	52
Wolverhampton W	42	20	10	12	93	65	50
Sheffield Wednesday	42	19	10	13	77	63	48
Arsenal	42	18	10	14	86	77	46
Liverpool	42	17	10	15	71	59	44
Nottingham Forest	42	17	10	15	67	69	44
Sheffield United	42	16	12	14	58	60	44
Blackburn Rovers	42	15	12	15	79	71	42
West Ham United	42	14	12	16	73	69	40
Blackpool	42	13	14	15	58	64	40
West Bromwich Albion	42	16	7	19	71	79	39
Aston Villa	42	15	8	19	62	68	38
Fulham	42	14	10	18	50	71	38
Ipswich Town	42	12	11	19	59	78	35
Bolton Wanderers	42	15	5	22	55	75	35
Manchester United	42	12	10	20	67	81	34
Birmingham City	42	10	13	19	63	90	33
Manchester City	42	10	11	21	58	102	31
Leyton Orient	42	6	9	27	37	81	21

Division One

Manager: Gil Merrick

Match No.	Date	Venue	Opponents	Result		Scorers	Attendance
1	Aug 24	H	Bolton Wanderers	W	2-1	Lynn (pen), Hellawell	24,817
2	28	A	Leicester City	L	0-3		27,694
3	31	A	Fulham	L	1-2	Lynn (pen)	21,260
4	Sep 4	H	Leicester City	W	2-0	Leek, Hellawell	23,851
5	7	H	Manchester United	D	1-1	Harley	36,874
6	11	H	West Bromwich Albion	L	0-1		34,666
7	14	A	Burnley	L	1-2	Harris	20,350
8	18	A	West Bromwich Albion	L	1-3	Harris	29,662
9	21	H	Ipswich Town	W	1-0	Beard	19,095
10	28	A	Sheffield Wednesday	L	1-2	Thomson	18,233
11	Oct 2	A	Tottenham Hotspur	L	1-6	Auld	37,649
12	5	H	Everton	L	0-2		23,593
13	19	A	Sheffield United	L	0-3		18,974
14	26	H	Wolverhampton Wan.	D	2-2	Woodfield (og), Harley	24,843
15	Nov 2	A	Chelsea	W	3-2	Harley, P.Bullock, Auld	22,974
16	5	A	Arsenal	L	1-4	Bloomfield	23,499
17	9	H	Blackpool	W	3-2	Bloomfield, Auld, Lynn	17,536
18	16	A	Blackburn Rovers	L	0-3		14,813
19	23	H	Nottingham Forest	D	3-3	Auld 2, Smith	18,161
20	30	A	Stoke City	L	1-4	Auld	27,260
21	Dec 7	H	West Ham United	W	2-1	Auld, Lynn (pen)	15,483
22	14	A	Bolton Wanderers	W	2-0	Leek, Hellawell	9,663
23	21	H	Fulham	D	0-0		13,915
24	28	H	Arsenal	L	1-4	Harley	23,377
25	Jan 11	A	Manchester United	W	2-1	Harley, M.Bullock	44,919
26	18	H	Burnley	D	0-0		15,917
27	Feb 1	A	Ipswich Town	L	2-3	Regan, Farmer	13,349
28	8	H	Sheffield Wednesday	L	1-2	Harley	15,479
29	18	A	Everton	L	0-3		36,252
30	22	A	Liverpool	L	1-2	Leek	41,823
31	29	H	Tottenham Hotspur	L	1-2	Thomson	28,433
32	Mar 7	A	Wolverhampton Wan.	L	1-5	Harley	16,421
33	13	H	Blackburn Rovers	D	2-2	Leek, Auld	15,809
34	20	A	Blackpool	L	0-3		10,203
35	28	A	Chelsea	L	3-4	Thwaites 2, Auld	14,485
36	30	A	Aston Villa	W	3-0	Hellawell, Harris, Lynn (pen)	25,797
37	31	H	Aston Villa	D	3-3	Lynn (pen), Leek, Bloomfield	28,069
38	Apr 4	A	Nottingham Forest	L	0-4		13,897
39	11	H	Stoke City	L	0-1		19,914
40	17	A	West Ham United	L	0-5		22,108
41	22	H	Liverpool	W	3-1	Lynn (pen), Leek, Hellawell	22,630
42	25	H	Sheffield United	W	3-0	Smith, Auld, Lynn (pen)	26,202
							Appearances
						One own-goal	Goals

FA Cup

R3	Jan 4	H	Port Vale	L	1-2	Beard	21,618
							Appearances
							Goals

League Cup

R2	Sep 25	A	Norwich City	L	0-2		16,781
							Appearances

Player appearances grid — Birmingham City

Wilburn CC	Lynn S	Green CR	Foster WA	Smith T	Hennessey WT	Hellawell MS	Bloomfield JH	Harley A	Leek K	Auld R	Beard M	Bullock PL	Harris J	Rushton BWE	Farrell GJP	Thomson RGMcK	Scofield JR	Thwaites D	Martin RB	Anderson GT	Bullock ME	Farmer MC	Regan MJ	Vincent JV
2	3	4	5	6	7	8	9	10	11															
2	3	4	5	6	7	8	9	10	11															
2	3		5	4	7	8	9		11	6	10													
2	3		5	4	7	8	9	10	11	6														
2	3		5	4	7	8	9	10	11	6														
2	3		5	4	7	8	9	10	11	6														
2	3	4	5		7	10			11	6	8	9												
	3		5	4	7	8	9	10		6			11	2										
	3	5		4	7	8	9	10		6			2	11										
	3	5		4	7	8	9			6			2		10									
2	3		5	4	7		9		11	6	10				8	1								
2	3		5	4	7		9		11	6	8				10	1								
2	3	5		4	7		9		10	8					6		11							
2	3		5	4	7	8	9			6	10				11									
2	3		5	4	7	8	9		11	6	10													
2	3		5	4	7	8	9		11	6	10													
2	3		5	4	7	8	9		11	6	10													
2	3	5		4	7	8		10	11	6	9													
2	3		5	4	7	8		10	11	6	9													
2	3		5		7	8	9	10	11	6					4									
2	3		5	4	7	8		10	11	6					9									
2	3		5	4	7	8		10	11	6					9									
2	3		5	4	7	8		10	11	6					9									
2	3		5		7	8	9	10	11	6					4									
2		5	4		8			11	6				10						3	7	9			
2		5	4	7		8		11	6				10						3		9			
2		5	4	7	8								10		11	3				6	9			
2	5		4	7	8	10			6						11	3					9			
2		5	4	7	8	9	10		6						11	3								
	3		5	4	7	8		10		6					9	11	2							
	3		5	4	7	8		10	7	6					9	11	2							
	3		5	4	7		8	10	11	6					9		2							
	3		5	4	7		8	10	11	6					9		2					8		
	3		5	4	7			10	11	6					9		2					8		
	3		5	4	7			10	11	6					9		2					8		
	3		5	4	7	8			11	6					10		2			9				
2	3	5		4	7	8		10	11	6		9												
2	3	5		4	7	8		10	11	6		9												
2	3	5		4	7	8		10	11	6		9												
2	9		5	4	7	8			11	3					6		10							
2		5	4	7	8		9	11							6	1	10	3						
2	6	5	4	7	8			10	11						9			3						
2	6	5	4	7	8			9	11						10	1		3						
33	33	14	34	39	40	34	32	26	34	36	11	5	3	1	21	4	10	14	1	2	1	3	2	
8			2		5	3	7	6	10	1	1	3		2		2			1	1	1			

Wilburn CC	Lynn S	Green CR	Foster WA	Smith T	Hennessey WT	Hellawell MS	Bloomfield JH	Harley A	Leek K	Auld R	Beard M	Bullock PL	Harris J	Rushton BWE	Farrell GJP	Thomson	Scofield	Thwaites	Martin	Anderson	Bullock ME	Farmer	Regan	Vincent
2	3		5	4	7	8		10	11	6					9									
1	1		1	1	1	1		1	1	1					1									
						1																		
	3		5	4	7	8	9	10		6			2	11										
	1		1	1	1	1	1	1		1			1	1										

League Table

	P	W	D	L	F	A	Pts
Liverpool	42	26	5	11	92	45	57
Manchester United	42	23	7	12	90	62	53
Everton	42	21	10	11	84	64	52
Tottenham Hotspur	42	22	7	13	97	81	51
Chelsea	42	20	10	12	72	56	50
Sheffield Wednesday	42	19	11	12	84	67	49
Blackburn Rovers	42	18	10	14	89	65	46
Arsenal	42	17	11	14	90	82	45
Burnley	42	17	10	15	71	64	44
West Bromwich Albion	42	16	11	15	70	61	43
Leicester City	42	16	11	15	61	58	43
Sheffield United	42	16	11	15	61	64	43
Nottingham Forest	42	16	9	17	64	68	41
West Ham United	42	14	12	16	69	74	40
Fulham	42	13	13	16	58	65	39
Wolverhampton W	42	12	15	15	70	80	39
Stoke City	42	14	10	18	77	78	38
Blackpool	42	13	9	20	52	73	35
Aston Villa	42	11	12	19	62	71	34
Birmingham City	42	11	7	24	54	92	29
Bolton Wanderers	42	10	8	24	48	80	28
Ipswich Town	42	9	7	26	56	121	25

Division One

Manager: Joe Mallett

Match No.	Date		Venue	Opponents	Result		Scorers	Attendance
1	Aug	22	A	Nottingham Forest	L	3-4	Harley, Hellawell, Lynn (pen)	26,264
2		26	H	Fulham	D	2-2	Leek, Lynn (pen)	20,719
3		29	H	Stoke City	L	1-2	Lynn (pen)	20,667
4	Sep	2	A	Fulham	L	1-3	Beard	13,100
5		5	A	Tottenham Hotspur	L	1-4	Thomson	34,809
6		9	H	West Bromwich Albion	D	1-1	Thomson	26,568
7		12	W	Burnley	W	2-1	Thomson, Lynn (pen)	16,890
8		16	A	West Bromwich Albion	W	2-0	Auld, Williams (og)	24,535
9		19	A	Sheffield United	L	1-3	Thomson	16,390
10		26	H	Everton	L	3-5	Leek, Hellawell, Hennessey	21,240
11		30	A	Wolverhampton Wan.	W	2-0	Lynn, Leek	21,439
12	Oct	10	H	Liverpool	D	0-0		19,922
13		17	A	Sheffield Wednesday	L	2-5	Hennessey, Auld	15,345
14		24	H	Blackpool	W	3-0	Vowden, Leek, Lynn (pen)	15,916
15		31	A	Blackburn Rovers	L	1-3	Harley	13,722
16	Nov	7	H	Arsenal	L	2-3	Leek, Vowden	20,607
17		14	A	Leeds United	L	1-4	Thomson	32,274
18		21	H	Chelsea	L	1-6	Jackson	19,802
19		28	A	Leicester City	D	4-4	Thwaites, Vowden, Thomson 2 (1 pen)	15,848
20	Dec	5	H	Sunderland	W	4-3	Thomson, Thwaites, Sharples, Jackson	13,564
21		12	H	Nottingham Forest	D	1-1	Thomson	14,011
22		16	A	Manchester United	D	1-1	Thwaites	25,939
23		26	H	West Ham United	W	2-1	Lynn, Thwaites	23,324
24		28	A	West Ham United	L	1-2	Sharples	23,850
25	Jan	2	H	Tottenham Hotspur	W	1-0	Beard	33,830
26		16	A	Burnley	L	0-2		9,970
27		23	H	Sheffield United	D	1-1	Foster	16,670
28	Feb	6	A	Everton	D	1-1	Fenton	34,030
29		13	H	Aston Villa	L	0-1		32,490
30		24	A	Liverpool	L	3-4	Vowden, Fenton, Thwaites	39,250
31		27	H	Sheffield Wednesday	D	0-0		12,130
32	Mar	6	A	Blackpool	L	1-3	Vowden	11,460
33		13	H	Wolverhampton Wan.	L	0-1		18,746
34		17	A	Stoke City	L	1-2	Vowden	12,920
35	Apr	3	A	Chelsea	L	1-3	Lynn (pen)	28,970
36		6	A	Arsenal	L	0-3		16,040
37		10	H	Leicester City	W	2-0	Vowden, Jackson	12,460
38		12	A	Aston Villa	L	0-3		36,870
39		17	A	Sunderland	L	1-2	Lynn (pen)	31,950
40		19	H	Manchester United	L	2-4	Vowden, Thwaites	28,910
41		24	H	Blackburn Rovers	D	5-5	Vowden, Beard 3, Lynn (pen)	8,870
42		26	H	Leeds United	D	3-3	Vowden, Beard, Thwaites	16,630
								Appearance
							One own-goal	Goal

FA Cup

R3	Jan	9	A	West Ham United	L	2-4	Jackson, Thwaites	31,050
								Appearance
								Goal

League Cup

R2	Sep	23	H	Chelsea	L	0-3		15,250
								Appearance

Appearance & Goals Grid

Withers CC	Lynn S	Green CR	Foster WA	Smith T	Beard M	Hellawell MS	Jackson A	Harley A	Leek K	Thwaites D	Hennessey WT	Auld R	Martin RB	Schofield JR	Vincent JV	Vowden GA	Sharples B	Bullock PL	Fenton R	Page ME	Fraser JC	Beel WJL
1	2	3	4	5	6	7	8	9	10	11												
1	2	3	4	5	6	7	8	9	10	11												
1	2	3	4	5	6		7	9		11	8	10										
1	2	3	4	5	6	7		9			8	10	11									
1	2			5		6	7	8		10		4	9	11	3							
	2			5		6	7	8		10		4	9	11	3	1						
	2			5		6	7	8		10		4	9	11	3	1						
	2			5		6	7	8		10		4	9	11	3	1						
	2			5		6	7	8		10		4	9	11	3	1						
	2			5		6	7	8		10		4	9	11	3	1						
	2			5		6	7	8		10		4	9	11	3	1						
	2			5		6	7	8		10		4	9	11	3	1						
	2			5		6	7	8				4	9	11	3	1	10					
	2			5		6	7			10		4	9	11	3	1		8				
	2			5		6	7	10				4	9	11	3	1		8				
	2			5		6				10	7	4	9	11	3	1		8				
		2	5			6	7			10		4	9	11	3	1		8				
		2	5			6	7	10				4	9	11	3	1		8				
	2		5			6		7				11	4	9		3	1		10	8		
	2	3	5			6		7				11	4	9			1		10	8		
	2	3	5			6		7				11	4	9			1		10	8		
	2		5			6		7				11	4		10	3	1		9	8		
	2	3	5			6		7				11	4		10		1		9	8		
	2	3	5			6		7				11	4			1		10	8	9		
	2	3	5			6		7				11		4		10	4			9	8	
	2	3	5			6		7				11	4	9			1		10		7	8
	2	3	5			6		11				4	9			1		10			7	8
	2	3	5			6		11				4	9			1		10		8		7
	2	3	5			6						11	4	9		1		10				8
	2		5			6		7				11	4			1	8	10	3		9	
	2		5			6		7				11	4			1	8	10	3		9	
	2		5			6		7				11	4			1	8	10	3		9	
	2	3	5					7				11	4			1	8	10	6		9	
	2	3	5					7				11	4			1		9		8		10
	2		5					7				11	4			1		10	3	9	6	8
	2		5		10			7				11	4			1		9	3		6	8
	2		5		10			7				11	4		8			9	3		6	
	2	3	5		10			7				11	4		8		1	9			6	

Totals

5	38	22	42	4	39	16	36	5	14	26	38	25	17	20	36	5	27	19	1	7	6	8	5	1
10		1			6	2	3	2	5		7	2	9	2				10	2			2		

League Table

	P	W	D	L	F	A	Pts
Manchester United	42	26	9	7	89	39	61
Leeds United	42	26	9	7	83	52	61
Chelsea	42	24	8	10	89	54	56
Everton	42	17	15	10	69	60	49
Nottingham Forest	42	17	13	12	71	67	47
Tottenham Hotspur	42	19	7	16	87	71	45
Liverpool	42	17	10	15	67	73	44
Sheffield Wednesday	42	16	11	15	57	55	43
West Ham United	42	19	4	19	82	71	42
Blackburn Rovers	42	16	10	16	83	79	42
Stoke City	42	16	10	16	67	66	42
Burnley	42	16	10	16	70	70	42
Arsenal	42	17	7	18	69	75	41
West Bromwich Albion	42	13	13	16	70	65	39
Sunderland	42	14	9	19	64	74	37
Aston Villa	42	16	5	21	57	82	37
Blackpool	42	12	11	19	67	78	35
Leicester City	42	11	13	18	69	85	35
Sheffield United	42	12	11	19	50	64	35
Fulham	42	11	12	19	60	78	34
Wolverhampton W	42	13	4	25	59	89	30
Birmingham City	42	8	11	23	64	96	27

Division Two

Manager: Joie Mallett (to December); then Stan Cullis

Match No.	Date	Venue	Opponents	Result		Scorers	Attendance
1	Aug 21	H	Crystal Palace	W	2-1	Thwaites 2	19,20
2	25	H	Middlesbrough	D	1-1	Beard	16,77
3	28	A	Preston North End	D	3-3	Vowden, Beard 2	16,39
4	31	A	Middlesbrough	D	1-1	Vowden	17,30
5	Sep 4	H	Charlton Athletic	D	2-2	Jackson (pen), Beard	15,32
6	8	H	Leyton Orient	D	2-2	Vowden, Thomson	7,59
7	11	A	Plymouth Argyle	L	1-6	Vowden	10,77
8	13	A	Leyton Orient	L	1-2	Thomson	7,11
9	18	H	Portsmouth	L	1-3	Beard	11,79
10	25	A	Bolton Wanderers	W	2-1	Thomson, Vowden	12,11
11	Oct 9	H	Norwich City	W	1-0	Jackson	11,62
12	16	A	Bury	L	1-5	Darrell	8,18
13	23	H	Southampton	L	0-1		11,69
14	30	A	Derby County	L	3-5	Bullock, Vincent, Page	12,46
15	Nov 6	H	Cardiff City	W	4-2	Lynn (pen), Bullock, Jackson, Thomson	10,74
16	13	A	Carlisle United	L	0-1		10,24
17	20	H	Coventry City	L	0-1		25,95
18	27	A	Bristol City	L	0-2		13,72
19	Dec 4	H	Manchester City	W	3-1	Thwaites, Jackson, Vowden	10,44
20	11	A	Rotherham United	W	4-3	Vowden 3, Jackson	10,68
21	18	H	Bury	W	4-0	Thwaites 2, Thomson, Fenton	10,99
22	28	H	Huddersfield Town	W	2-1	Thwaites, Vowden	19,76
23	Jan 1	A	Norwich City	D	2-2	Vowden, Fenton	15,29
24	8	H	Carlisle United	W	2-1	Beard, Vowden	14,99
25	29	A	Crystal Palace	L	0-1		14,09
26	Feb 5	H	Preston North End	D	1-1	Jackson	14,05
27	19	A	Charlton Athletic	L	1-2	Thwaites	13,74
28	26	H	Plymouth Argyle	W	1-0	Thomson	13,11
29	Mar 5	A	Southampton	W	1-0	Thwaites	18,29
30	12	A	Portsmouth	W	1-0	Vowden	12,36
31	15	A	Huddersfield Town	L	0-2		19,15
32	19	H	Bolton Wanderers	L	0-1		13,77
33	26	A	Ipswich Town	W	1-0	Beard	9,35
34	Apr 2	A	Cardiff City	W	3-1	Vowden 2, Carver (og)	8,15
35	9	H	Derby County	D	5-5	Hockey, Beard 2 (1 pen), Saxton (og), Vowden	13,07
36	11	H	Wolverhampton Wan.	D	2-2	Vowden, Vincent	28,90
37	12	A	Wolverhampton Wan.	L	0-2		32,51
38	16	H	Coventry City	L	3-4	Jackson, Vowden, Fenton	27,11
39	22	H	Bristol City	L	1-3	Beard (pen)	11,73
40	30	A	Manchester City	L	1-3	Vowden	28,40
41	May 3	H	Ipswich Town	W	4-1	Fenton 2, Jackson, Vowden	9,33
42	7	H	Rotherham United	W	3-0	Hockey, Vowden, Barber	11,46

Appearances
Sub appearances
Two own-goals
Goal

FA Cup

R3	Jan 22	H	Bristol City	W	3-2	Vowden 2, Thomson	24,34
R4	Feb 12	H	Leicester City	L	1-2	Thwaites	46,68

Appearances
Goal

League Cup

R2	Sep 22	A	Mansfield Town	L	1-2	Beard	9,34

Appearances
Goals

Player columns (left to right): Harriot J · Martin RB · Green CR · Wylie RM · Foster WA · Hennessey WT · Jackson A · Vowden GA · Beard M · Thomson RG McK · Thwaites D · Sharples B · Fraser JC · Page ME · Schofield JR · Vincent JV · Fenton R · Lynn S · Darrell MA · Bullock ME · Hockey TJ · Balter E

Har	Mar	Gre	Wyl	Fos	Hen	Jac	Vow	Bea	Tho	Thw	Sha	Fra	Pag	Sch	Vin	Fen	Lyn	Dar	Bul	Hoc	Bal
1	2	3	4	5	6	7	8	9	10	11											
1	2	3	4	5	6	7	9	8	10	11											
1	2	3	4	5	6	7	9	8	10	11	12										
1		3		5	4	7	9	8	10	11	6	2									
1		3		5	4	7	9	8	10	11	6	2									
1		3		5	6	7	8	10	9	11		2	4								
1		3	4	5	6	7	8	10	9	11		2									
	3		10	5	6	7	9		8			2	4	1	11						
	3		10	5	6		9	8		11		2	4	1		7					
	3	2	4		6	11	8	10	9			1		7	5						
	3	2	4		6	11	8	10	9			1		7	5						
	3	2	4		6	11	9	10				1		7	5	8					
		3	4		5	7			11		2	6	1	8				10	9		
		3	4		5	7			11		2	6	1	8				10	9		
1			4	5		7		8	11		2	6			3	10	9				
1			4	5	6	7		8	11		2				3	10	9				
1	3	2	4	5		8		9	11		6					10		7			
1	3	2	4	5		8	10	6		11	12			9				7			
1	3		4	5		8	10	6	9	11		2						7			
1	3		4	5		8	10	6	9	11		2						7			
1	3		4	5		8	10	6	9	11		2		12				7			
1	3		4	5		8	10	6		11		2						7			
1	3		4	5		8	10	6	9	11		2		12				7			
1	3		4	5		8	10	6		11		2		9				7			
1	3		4	5		8	10	6	9	11		2						7			
1	3			5		8	10	6	9	11		2	4					7			
1	3		4	5		8	10	6	9	11		2						7			
1	3		4	5		8	10	6	9	11		2						7			
1	3		4	5		8	10	6	9	11		2						7			
1	3		4	5		8	10	6	9	11		2						7			
1	3		4	5		8	10	6	9	11		2						7			
1	3		4	5		7	10	6		11		2		8	9						
1	3		4	5		7	10	6		11		2		8	9			12			
1	3		4	5		7	10	6	12			2		8	9			11			
1	3		4	5		7	10	6				2		8	9			11			
1	3		4	5		7	10	6	9			2		8				11			
1	3		4	5		7	10	6				2		8	9			11			
1	3		4	5		7	10	6				2		8	9			11			
1	3	2	4	5		7	10	6						8	9			11			
1	3		4	5		11	10	6				2			9			7	8		
1	3		4	5		11	10	6				2			9			7	8		
35	34	15	38	37	15	40	38	36		30	2	33	8	7	11	15	5	6	4	24	2
										1		1	1				2			1	
						8	21	10	6	8			1		2	5	1	1	2	2	1

Har	Mar	Gre	Wyl	Fos	Hen	Jac	Vow	Bea	Tho	Thw	Sha	Fra	Pag	Sch	Vin	Fen	Lyn	Dar	Bul	Hoc	Bal
1	3		4	5		8	10	6	9	11		2						7			
1	3		4	5		8	10	6	9	11		2						7			
2	2		2	2		2	2	2	2	2		2						2			
						2		1	1												

Har	Mar	Gre	Wyl	Fos	Hen	Jac	Vow	Bea	Tho	Thw	Sha	Fra	Pag	Sch	Vin	Fen	Lyn	Dar	Bul	Hoc	Bal
	3	4	10		6	11		9				2		1	8	7	5				
	1	1	1		1	1		1				1		1	1	1	1				
								1													

League Table

	P	W	D	L	F	A	Pts
Manchester City	42	22	15	5	76	44	59
Southampton	42	22	10	10	85	56	54
Coventry City	42	20	13	9	73	53	53
Huddersfield Town	42	19	13	10	62	36	51
Bristol City	42	17	17	8	63	48	51
Wolverhampton W	42	20	10	12	87	61	50
Rotherham United	42	16	14	12	75	74	46
Derby County	42	16	11	15	71	68	43
Bolton Wanderers	42	16	9	17	62	59	41
Birmingham City	42	16	9	17	70	75	41
Crystal Palace	42	14	13	15	47	52	41
Portsmouth	42	16	8	18	74	78	40
Norwich City	42	12	15	15	52	52	39
Carlisle United	42	17	5	20	60	63	39
Ipswich Town	42	15	9	18	58	66	39
Charlton Athletic	42	12	14	16	61	70	38
Preston North End	42	11	15	16	62	70	37
Plymouth Argyle	42	12	13	17	54	63	37
Bury	42	14	7	21	62	76	35
Cardiff City	42	12	10	20	71	91	34
Middlesbrough	42	10	13	19	58	86	33
Leyton Orient	42	5	13	24	38	80	23

Did you know that?

Blues were 2–0 down after 35 minutes of their League game against Wolves in December but came back to win 3–2, top-scorer Geoff Vowden netting the 88th-minute winner. This was the first double over Wolves for 46 years.

Blues were always in front in their nine-goal thriller at Portsmouth in August. They lead 3–0 after 40 minutes.

Blues conceded six goals against Spurs for the second time in four years.

Jim Herriot became only the fifth Blues goalkeeper to be an ever-present in a League season.

In August 1966, the 'Beau Brummie' Club for ardent supporters was officially opened.

Match No.	Date		Venue	Opponents	Result		Scorers	Attendance
1	Aug	20	A	Wolverhampton Wan.	W	2-1	Murray 2	26,80
2		24	A	Portsmouth	W	5-4	Murray, Bridges, Beard (pen), Vowden 2	16,934
3		27	H	Norwich City	W	2-1	Vowden, Murray	25,51
4		30	H	Portsmouth	W	3-0	Pack (og), Thomson, Vowden	23,49
5	Sep	3	A	Coventry City	D	1-1	Vowden	36,40
6		7	H	Plymouth Argyle	D	1-1	Murray	19,00
7		10	H	Bury	L	1-3	Thomson	22,44
8		17	A	Preston North End	L	0-3		13,57
9		24	H	Rotherham United	L	2-3	Bridges, Thomson	19,51
10		27	H	Plymouth Argyle	D	0-0		18,31
11	Oct	1	A	Millwall	L	1-3	Vowden	15,77
12		8	A	Ipswich Town	L	2-3	Vowden, Thomson	15,12
13		15	H	Bristol City	W	4-0	Vowden, Murray, Ford (og), Thwaites	15,35
14		22	A	Carlisle United	L	0-2		10,90
15		29	H	Blackburn Rovers	D	1-1	Beard	17,62
16	Nov	5	A	Bolton Wanderers	L	1-3	Hockey	10,03
17		12	H	Charlton Athletic	W	4-0	Vowden 2, Bullock, Vincent	14,02
18		19	A	Derby County	W	2-1	Thomson, Beard	17,38
19		26	H	Crystal Palace	W	3-1	Vowden, Vincent, Bullock	16,82
20	Dec	3	A	Huddersfield Town	L	1-3	Bullock	14,93
21		10	H	Cardiff City	L	1-2	Bullock	17,04
22		17	H	Wolverhampton Wan.	W	3-2	Bridges, Bullock, Vowden	27,54
23		26	H	Northampton Town	W	3-0	Vincent 2, Vowden	24,30
24		27	A	Northampton Town	L	1-2	Bridges	15,43
25		31	A	Norwich City	D	3-3	Bridges, Bullock, Vowden	15,26
26	Jan	7	A	Coventry City	D	1-1	Curtis (og)	36,31
27		14	A	Bury	W	2-0	Bridges 2	6,95
28		21	H	Preston North End	W	3-1	Vowden, Bridges 2	18,48
29	Feb	4	A	Rotherham United	L	2-3	Hockey, Leggat	10,93
30		11	H	Millwall	W	2-0	Bullock, Bridges	18,00
31		25	H	Ipswich Town	D	2-2	Vincent, Thomson	18,49
32	Mar	4	A	Blackburn Rovers	L	0-1		14,90
33		18	H	Carlisle United	L	1-2	Vincent	17,61
34		25	A	Bristol City	L	1-3	Vincent	20,59
35		27	H	Hull City	W	2-1	Isherwood, Beard	17,06
36		28	A	Hull City	W	2-0	Murray 2	23,12
37	Apr	1	H	Bolton Wanderers	D	2-2	Vowden, Murray	18,18
38		15	H	Derby County	W	2-0	Bridges 2	15,20
39		22	A	Crystal Palace	L	1-2	Bridges	13,06
40		28	H	Huddersfield Town	L	0-1		14,38
41	May	6	A	Cardiff City	L	0-3		12,67
42		12	A	Charlton Athletic	L	0-1		10,14

		Appearances	
		Sub appearances	
	Three own-goals	Goal	

FA Cup

	Date		Venue	Opponents	Result		Scorers	Attendance
R3	Jan	28	H	Blackpool	W	2-1	Vowden, Thomson	27,60
R4	Feb	18	A	Rotherham United	D	0-0		15,72
rep		21	H	Rotherham United	W	2-1	Hockey, Bridges	35,48
R5	Mar	11	A	Arsenal	W	1-0	Vowden	40,66
R6	Apr	8	H	Tottenham Hotspur	D	0-0		51,46
rep		12	A	Tottenham Hotspur	L	0-6		52,30

Appearance	
Sub appearances	
Goal	

League Cup

	Date		Venue	Opponents	Result		Scorers	Attendance
R2	Sep	13	A	Nottingham Forest	D	1-1	Vowden	19,27
rep		20	H	Nottingham Forest	W	2-1	Bridges, Vowden	21,51
R3	Oct	4	H	Ipswich Town	W	2-1	Beard (pen), Hockey	15,11
R4		26	A	Grimsby Town	W	4-2	Bridges 2, Fenton, Vowden	11,29
R5	Dec	7	A	Sheffield United	W	3-2	Vincent, Bullock, Hockey	15,02
SF1	Jan	17	H	Queen's Park Rangers	L	1-4	Bridges	34,29
SF2	Feb	7	A	Queen's Park Rangers	L	1-3	Barber	24,60

Appearance	
Sub appearance	
Goal	

	P	W	D	L	F	A	Pts
Coventry City	42	23	13	6	74	43	59
Wolverhampton W	42	25	9	8	88	48	58
Carlisle United	42	23	6	13	71	54	52
Blackburn Rovers	42	19	13	10	56	46	51
Ipswich Town	42	17	16	9	70	54	50
Huddersfield Town	42	20	9	13	58	46	49
Crystal Palace	42	19	10	13	61	55	48
Millwall	42	18	9	15	49	58	45
Bolton Wanderers	42	14	14	14	64	58	42
Birmingham City	42	16	8	18	70	66	40
Norwich City	42	13	14	15	49	55	40
Hull City	42	16	/	19	77	72	39
Preston North End	42	16	7	19	65	67	39
Portsmouth	42	13	13	16	59	70	39
Bristol City	42	12	14	16	56	62	38
Plymouth Argyle	42	14	9	19	59	58	37
Derby County	42	12	12	18	68	72	36
Rotherham United	42	13	10	19	61	70	36
Charlton Athletic	42	13	9	20	49	53	35
Cardiff City	42	12	9	21	61	87	33
Northampton Town	42	12	6	24	47	84	30
Bury	42	11	6	25	49	83	28

Division Two

Manager: Stan Cullis

Did you know that?

Blues used four centre-halves this term: Brian Sharples (seven games), Malcolm Page (9), Winston Foster (22) and ex-Villa defender John Sleeuwenhoek (12).

Seven goals were scored in 30 second-half minutes when Hull were beaten 6–2 in September.

Two-nil down, Millwall scored three times in the last 20 minutes to win at St Andrew's in September.

Blues struck five times in 29 minutes either side of half-time in their 6–1 home win over Huddersfield Town in December.

In the return fixture at Leeds Road, Blues hit back from 2–0 down to win 3–2, Geoff Vowden striking a last-minute decider.

David Exall became the first commercial manager of Birmingham City FC.

Match No.	Date		Venue	Opponents	Result		Scorers	Attendance
1	Aug	19	H	Bolton Wanderers	W	4-0	Bridges 2, Vincent, Hockey	23,53
2		26	A	Huddersfield Town	W	3-2	Vincent, Vowden 2	14,22
3		29	A	Middlesbrough	D	1-1	Vincent	25,81
4	Sep	2	H	Ipswich Town	D	0-0		25,46
5		4	H	Hull City	W	6-2	Bridges, Beard (pen), Murray, Pickering, Vowden, Vincent	25,93
6		9	A	Carlisle United	D	1-1	Vowden	11,20
7		16	H	Blackburn Rovers	D	1-1	Bridges	28,97
8		23	A	Blackpool	L	0-1		25,57
9		26	H	Middlesbrough	W	6-1	Pickering 2, Vincent, Bridges, Beard (pen), Vowden	28,88
10		30	H	Millwall	L	2-3	Pickering, Vincent	30,56
11	Oct	7	A	Aston Villa	W	4-2	Bridges 2, Beard (pen), Vowden	50,06
12		14	H	Portsmouth	D	2-2	Pickering, Vowden	26,24
13		21	A	Norwich City	L	2-4	Bridges, Vowden	16,49
14		28	H	Rotherham United	W	4-1	Vowden, Bridges 3	21,47
15	Nov	4	A	Derby County	D	2-2	Vincent, Bridges	25,48
16		11	H	Preston North End	W	3-0	Vincent 2, Bridges	27,66
17		18	A	Cardiff City	W	3-1	Vincent, Bridges, Murray	13,67
18		25	H	Crystal Palace	W	1-0	Vincent	27,53
19	Dec	2	A	Charlton Athletic	L	1-3	Bridges	13,89
20		9	H	Queen's Park Rangers	W	2-0	Hazell (og), Pickering	25,28
21		16	A	Bolton Wanderers	D	1-1	Farrimond (og)	10,46
22		23	H	Huddersfield Town	W	6-1	Pickering 2, Vincent, Leggat, Vowden, Bridges	26,16
23		26	H	Bristol City	W	4-1	Briggs (og), Leggat, Bridges, Vowden	40,42
24		30	A	Bristol City	L	1-3	Vincent	23,49
25	Jan	6	A	Ipswich Town	L	1-2	Vowden	16,70
26		13	H	Carlisle United	L	1-3	Vowden	21,68
27		20	A	Blackburn Rovers	W	2-1	Vowden, Pickering	17,93
28	Feb	3	H	Blackpool	L	1-2	Wylie	29,64
29		10	A	Millwall	D	1-1	Vowden	13,96
30		24	H	Aston Villa	W	2-1	Bridges 2	45,28
31	Mar	2	A	Portsmouth	W	2-1	Pickering, Foster	27,83
32		16	H	Norwich City	D	0-0		28,95
33		23	A	Rotherham United	D	1-1	Pickering	16,02
34	Apr	2	H	Derby County	W	3-1	Vowden, Bridges, Richardson (og)	29,32
35		6	A	Preston North End	D	0-0		16,82
36		13	H	Cardiff City	D	0-0		29,04
37		15	A	Plymouth Argyle	W	2-1	Vowden, Pickering	13,88
38		16	H	Plymouth Argyle	D	2-2	Wylie, Page	29,3
39		20	A	Crystal Palace	D	0-0		14,94
40	May	4	A	Queen's Park Rangers	L	0-2		25,88
41		7	H	Charlton Athletic	W	4-0	Bridges 2, Vincent, Pickering	19,91
42		11	A	Hull City	W	1-0	Wilson (og)	10,34

Appearance
Sub appearance
Five own-goals   Goa

FA Cup

R3	Jan	27	A	Halifax Town	W	4-2	Pickering, Vowden, Bridges, Beard (pen)	18,1
R4	Feb	17	H	Orient	W	3-0	Vowden 2, Bridges	29,32
R5	Mar	9	A	Arsenal	D	1-1	Vowden	455
rep		12	H	Arsenal	W	2-1	Bridges 2	515
R6		30	H	Chelsea	W	1-0	Pickering	51,57
SF	Apr	27	N	West Bromwich Albion	L	0-2		60,83

SF at Villa Park.   Appearance
Sub appearance
Goa

League Cup

R2	Sep	13	A	Plymouth Argyle	W	2-0	Vowden, Hockey	10,03
R3	Oct	11	A	Derby County	L	1-3	Bridges	24,8

Appearance
Goa

Player columns (left-to-right):

Herriot, J · Murray AG · Martin RB · Wylie RM · Sharples B · Beard M · Bridges BJ · Vincent JV · Pickering F · Vowden GA · Hockey TJ · Green CR · Thomson RDMcK · Page ME · Tivell TK · Fenton R · Lugg G · Slauswnhoek JC · Foster WA · Summerill PE · Darrell MA · Thwaites D

Her	Mur	Mar	Wyl	Sha	Bea	Bri	Vin	Pic	Vow	Hoc	Gre	Tho	Pag	Tiv	Fen	Lug	Sla	Fos	Sum	Dar	Thw
2	3	4	5	6	7	8	9	10	11												
2	3	4	5	6	7	8	9	10	11												
2	3	4	5	6	7	8	9	10	11												
2	3	4	5	6	7	8	9	10	11												
2	12	4	5	6	7	8	9	10	11	3											
2		4	5	6	7	8	9	10	11	3	12										
2	12	4		6	7	8	9	10	11	3		5									
2	12	4		6	7	8	9	10	11	3		5									
2	3	4		6	7	8	9	10	11			5									
2	3	4		6	7	8	9	10	11			5									
2		4		6	7	8	9	10	11	3		5									
2		4		6	7	8	9	10	11	3		5	1								
2	3			6	7	8	9	10	11			5	1	4							
	2	4	5	6	7	8	9	10	11	3					12						
2		4		6	7	8	9	10	11	3	4					5					
2		4		6	7	8	9	10	11	3						5					
2		4		6	7	8	9	10	11	3						5					
2		4		6	7	8	9	10	11	3						5					
2		4		6	7	8	9	10	11	3						5					
2		4		6	7	8	9	10	11	3						5					
2		4		6	7	8	9	10	11	3		12	5								
2		4		6	7	8	9	10		3		11	5								
2	3	4		6	7	8	9	10				11	5								
2	3	4		6	7	8	9	10	11			5									
2		4		6	7	8	9	10	11	3		5									
2		4		6	11	8	9	10	7	3						5					
2		4		6	11	8	9	10	7	3						5					
2		4		6	11	8	9	10	7	3	12					5					
2		4		6	7	8	9	10		3	11					5					
2	3	4		6	7		9	8	11		10					5					
2	3				7	8	9	10		6		4				5	11				
2	3	4		6	7		9	8	11		10					5		12			
2	12	4		6	11		9	7	8	3	10					5					
8	3	4		6	11	7	9		2	10					12	5					
8	3	4		6	11	12	9	7		2	10					5					
2	3	4		6	11		9	8		10				7		5					
2	3	4		6	11		9	8		10				7		5					
2	3	4		6	11	8	9			10						5		7			
2	12	4		6	11	8	9	7		3	10					5					
2	3	4		6	7	11	9	8			10					5					
2	3	4		6	7	11	9	8			10					5					
40	21	39	7	41	42	36	42	40	30	26	1	20	2	1	4	12	16	1	0	1	
	5				1					1	1			3			1				
2		2		3	22	14	13	17	1		1			2		1					

Her	Mur	Mar	Wyl	Sha	Bea	Bri	Vin	Pic	Vow	Hoc	Gre	Tho	Pag	Tiv	Fen	Lug	Sla	Fos	Sum	Dar	Thw
2		4		6	11	8	9	10	7	3						5					
2	2	4		6	7	8	9	10		3		11				5					
2	3	4		6	7	8	9	10	11							5					
2	3	4		6	7		9	10	11			8				5					
2	12	4		6	11		9	7	8	3						5					
2	3	4		6	11		9	7		8		10				5					
5	4	6		6	6	3	6	6	3	5		4				6					
	1																				
				1	4			2	4												

Her	Mur	Mar	Wyl	Sha	Bea	Bri	Vin	Pic	Vow	Hoc	Gre	Tho	Pag	Tiv	Fen	Lug	Sla	Fos	Sum	Dar	Thw
2		4		6	7	8	9	10	11	3		5									
2	3	4		6	7	8	9	10	11			5									
2	1	2		2	2	2	2	2	2	1		2									
		1			1	1															

League Table

	P	W	D	L	F	A	Pts
Ipswich Town	42	22	15	5	79	44	59
Queen's Park Rangers	42	25	8	9	67	36	58
Blackpool	42	24	10	8	71	43	58
Birmingham City	42	19	14	9	83	51	52
Portsmouth	42	18	13	11	68	55	49
Middlesbrough	42	17	12	13	60	54	46
Millwall	42	14	17	11	62	50	45
Blackburn Rovers	42	16	11	15	56	49	43
Norwich City	42	16	11	15	60	65	43
Carlisle United	42	14	13	15	58	52	41
Crystal Palace	42	14	11	17	56	56	39
Bolton Wanderers	42	13	13	16	60	63	39
Cardiff City	42	13	12	17	60	66	38
Huddersfield Town	42	13	12	17	46	61	38
Charlton Athletic	42	12	13	17	63	63	37
Aston Villa	42	15	7	20	54	64	37
Hull City	42	12	13	17	58	73	37
Derby County	42	13	10	19	71	78	36
Bristol City	42	13	10	19	48	62	36
Preston North End	42	12	11	19	43	65	35
Rotherham United	42	10	11	21	42	76	31
Plymouth Argyle	42	9	9	24	38	72	27

Division Two

Manager: Stan Cullis

Geoff Vowden became the first substitute to score a League hat-trick – for Blues against Huddersfield Town in September.

Phil Summerill scored a hat-trick in seven minutes (72–79) in Blues' 5–2 win over Hull in November.

Fred Pickering struck the second-fastest goal ever by a Blues player when he netted after just 13 seconds against Portsmouth at St Andrew's in August.

Blues led Fulham 3–0 at home after 25 minutes but were pegged back to 3–3 before eventually winning 5–4, thanks mainly to Jimmy Greenhoff's four-timer.

Denis Law celebrated his 29th birthday by scoring a hat-trick in Manchester United's 6–2 FA Cup replay victory over Blues.

Match No.	Date		Venue	Opponents		Result	Scorers	Attendance
1	Aug	10	H	Norwich City	L	1-2	Pickering	27,71
2		17	A	Crystal Palace	L	2-3	Vincent, Vowden	17,67
3		20	A	Charlton Athletic	L	1-3	Vincent	14,22
4		24	H	Portsmouth	W	5-2	Pickering 2, Vowden, Summerill, Tindall (og)	23,91
5		28	A	Cardiff City	L	0-4		14,96
6		31	A	Preston North End	L	1-4	Greenhoff	13,11
7	Sep	7	H	Huddersfield Town	W	5-1	Greenhoff, Pickering, Vowden 3	25,00
8		14	A	Middlesbrough	L	1-3	Vincent	17,39
9		17	H	Bury	L	1-3	Greenhoff	24,17
10		21	H	Aston Villa	W	4-0	Summerill, Vincent, Greenhoff, Vowden	40,52
11		28	A	Carlisle United	W	3-2	Greenhoff, Summerill, Green	7,62
12	Oct	5	H	Fulham	W	5-4	Vincent, Greenhoff 4	28,44
13		8	H	Cardiff City	W	2-0	Vincent, Greenhoff	28,23
14		12	A	Bristol City	D	0-0		19,57
15		19	H	Millwall	L	1-2	Greenhoff (pen)	29,77
16		26	A	Derby County	L	0-1		34,21
17	Nov	2	H	Oxford United	L	0-1		23,46
18		9	A	Blackburn Rovers	L	2-3	Pickering 2	11,72
19		16	H	Blackpool	W	1-0	Summerill	22,20
20		23	A	Bolton Wanderers	D	0-0		7,17
21		30	H	Hull City	W	5-2	Greenhoff, Pickering, Summerill 3	21,35
22	Dec	7	A	Sheffield United	L	0-2		14,33
23		14	H	Bristol City	W	2-0	Pickering 2	18,95
24		21	A	Millwall	W	3-1	Darrell, Vincent, Pickering	12,65
25		26	A	Fulham	L	0-2		13,19
26	Jan	11	A	Oxford United	W	2-1	Pickering, Summerill	11,58
27		14	H	Derby County	D	1-1	Pickering,	39,97
28		18	H	Blackburn Rovers	W	3-1	Coddington (og), Robinson (pen), Pickering	27,18
29	Feb	1	A	Blackpool	L	1-2	James (og)	11,29
30	Mar	1	A	Norwich City	D	1-1	Vowden	15,89
31		4	H	Sheffield United	D	2-2	Beard, Pickering	25,12
32		8	H	Crystal Palace	L	0-1		25,29
33		15	A	Portsmouth	D	0-0		15,55
34		21	H	Preston North End	W	3-1	R.Latchford 2, Summerill	22,02
35		25	H	Bolton Wanderers	W	5-0	Vincent, Summerill 3, Beard	20,45
36		29	A	Huddersfield Town	D	0-0		8,10
37	Apr	5	H	Carlisle United	W	3-0	Hockey, Greenhoff 2	22,39
38		7	H	Charlton Athletic	D	0-0		25,88
39		8	A	Bury	W	2-1	Summerill 2	5,81
40		12	A	Aston Villa	L	0-1		53,64
41		15	A	Hull City	W	2-1	Hockey, Vincent	8,70
42		19	H	Middlesbrough	W	3-1	Summerill 2, G.Smith (og)	25,89

	Appearance
	Sub appearance
Four own-goals	Goal

FA Cup

R3	Jan	4	H	Lincoln City	W	2-1	Pickering, Robinson (pen)	31,42
R4		25	A	Sheffield Wednesday	D	2-2	Pickering, Thwaites	52,00
rep		28	H	Sheffield Wednesday	W	2-1	Pickering, Beard	51,46
R5	Feb	11	H	Manchester United	D	2-2	Beard, Robinson (pen)	51,68
rep		24	A	Manchester United	L	2-6	Greenhoff, Summerhill	61,93

	Appearance
	Sub appearance
	Goal

League Cup

R2	Sep	3	H	Chelsea	L	0-1		31,53

	Appearance
	Sub appearance

Player columns (left to right):
Hartnett J, Murray AG, Green CR, Wylie RM, Sharples B, Beard M, Hockey TJ, Vincent JV, Pickering F, Page ME, Bridges BJ, Sleeuwenhoek JC, Vowden GA, Martin RB, Darrell MA, Summerill PE, Foster WA, Greenhoff J, Robinson D, Thwaites D, Pendrey GJS, Thomson RA, Latchford RD, Latchford DB

Ha	Mu	Gr	Wy	Sh	Be	Ho	Vi	Pi	Pa	Br	Sl	Vo	Ma	Da	Su	Fo	Gf	Ro	Tw	Pe	Th	LR	LD
	2	3	4	5		6	7	8	9	10	11												
	2	3	4			6	7	12	9	8	11	5	10										
	2	3	4			6	7	11	9	10		5	8										
		3			6		8	9	4		5	7	2	10	11								
		3			6		8	9	4		5	7	2	10	11								
	2	3			6	7	11	9	4				10	12		5	8						
	2	3	4		6		8	10	7			12			11	5	9						
	2	3	4		6		7	9	10			12			11	5	8						
	2	3	4		7	9	6			10				11	5	8							
		4			6	7	10	3			9	2		11		8	5						
	3				6	7	10	4			9	2		11		8	5						
		4			6	7	8	3			10	2		11		9	5						
	3	4			6	7	11		10		9	2		12		8	5						
	3	4			6	7	11		10		9	2				8	5						
	3	4			6	7	11	9	12		10	2				8	5						
12					6	7	10	4			9	2		11	3	8	5						
7	3				6	11	10	9	4		8	2		12			5						
	3	4			6	11	10	9			7	2		8	5								
	3				6	7	10	4			9	2		11		8	5						
	3	4				7	10	9	6		2				8	5							
	3	4				7	10	9	6		2	11			8	5							
	3	4				7	10	9	6		2			11		8	5						
12	3	4				7	10	9	6		2			11		8	5						
	3	4				7	10	9	6		2	11			8	5							
	3	4				7	10	9	6		2			11		8	5						
	3	4			6	7	10	9		12		2	11		8	5							
	3	4				7	10	9		5		2	11		8	6							
		4			3	7	10	9		5		2			8	6	11						
	3				6	7	10	9	4		2			8	5	11							
	3	8			6	7	11	9		10	2			5									
	3	8			6	7	11	9		5	10	2			4								
		3			6	4	10	9		7	2		11		8	5	12						
					6	10	7	9	4		12	2		11		8	5		3				
		4			6	10	8	5			2		11		7			3	9				
		4			10	8	9			2		11		7	5	6	3						
		6			10		9	5		2	12	11		7		4	3	8					
		3			10	8	9	4			11		7	5	6	2							
		3			10	8	9			12		11	7	5	6	2							
		4				8	9	2		7		10	11		5	6	3		1				
		4				10	8	9	2		7		11		5	6	3		1				
			4	10	8			5			2		11	7		6	3	9		1			
			6	10	8			5			7	2	11			4	3	9		1			
8	28	26	1	32	37	40	32	33	2	7	22	31	4	28	5	31	29	2	8	10	4	4	
2					1		1	4	1	1	2		1										
	1			2	2	9	14			7		1	16		14	1		2					

Ha	Mu	Gr	Wy	Sh	Be	Ho	Vi	Pi	Pa	Br	Sl	Vo	Ma	Da	Su	Fo	Gf	Ro	Tw	Pe	Th	LR	LD
		3	4			7		9	6		2	10	11		8	5							
		3			6	7	10	9	4	12		2			8	5	11						
		3			6	10	7	9	4			2			8	5	11						
		3	6			12	10	7	9	4		2			8	5	11						
		3	6			11	10	7	9	4		2		12	8	5							
		5	3		4	5	4	5	5		0	5	1	1		5	5	3					
		1						1				1											
		2			3						1				1	2	1						

Ha	Mu	Gr	Wy	Sh	Be	Ho	Vi	Pi	Pa	Br	Sl	Vo	Ma	Da	Su	Fo	Gf	Ro	Tw	Pe	Th	LR	LD
	2	3	4			6		8	9	10		7	12		11	5							
	1	1	1			1		1	1	1		1	0		1	1							
										1													

League Table

	P	W	D	L	F	A	Pts
Derby County	42	26	11	5	65	32	63
Crystal Palace	42	22	12	8	70	47	56
Charlton Athletic	42	18	14	10	61	52	50
Middlesbrough	42	19	11	12	58	49	49
Cardiff City	42	20	7	15	67	54	47
Huddersfield Town	42	17	12	13	53	46	46
Birmingham City	42	18	8	16	73	59	44
Blackpool	42	14	15	13	51	41	43
Sheffield United	42	16	11	15	61	50	43
Millwall	42	17	9	16	57	49	43
Hull City	42	13	16	13	59	52	42
Carlisle United	42	16	10	16	46	49	42
Norwich City	42	15	10	17	53	56	40
Preston North End	42	12	15	15	38	44	39
Portsmouth	42	12	14	16	58	58	38
Bristol City	42	11	16	15	46	53	38
Bolton Wanderers	42	12	14	16	55	67	38
Aston Villa	42	12	14	16	37	48	38
Blackburn Rovers	42	13	11	18	52	63	37
Oxford United	42	12	9	21	34	55	33
Bury	42	11	8	23	51	80	30
Fulham	42	7	11	24	40	81	25

Division Two

Manager: Stan Cullis (to March)

Match No.	Date	Venue	Opponents	Result		Scorers	Attendance
1	Aug 9	A	Leicester City	L	1-3	Summerill	35,168
2	16	H	Oxford United	L	1-3	Summerill	27,067
3	19	H	Portsmouth	D	1-1	Summerill	24,976
4	23	A	Blackpool	L	0-2		17,495
5	27	A	Hull City	D	0-0		12,242
6	30	H	Queen's Park Rangers	W	3-0	Murray 3	32,660
7	Sep 6	A	Bolton Wanderers	L	0-2		11,303
8	13	H	Sheffield United	W	2-1	Vincent, Murray	27,201
9	16	H	Norwich City	W	3-1	Murray, Summerill 2	26,408
10	20	A	Charlton Athletic	W	1-0	Hateley	13,999
11	27	H	Carlisle United	D	1-1	Summerill	28,781
12	Oct 4	A	Bristol City	L	0-2		18,694
13	8	A	Oxford United	L	0-2		12,621
14	11	H	Blackburn Rovers	W	3-0	Vowden 2, Summerill	25,602
15	18	A	Aston Villa	D	0-0		54,405
16	25	H	Cardiff City	D	1-1	Hateley	28,287
17	Nov 1	A	Watford	W	3-2	Vincent, Vowden, Murray	17,436
18	8	H	Swindon Town	W	2-0	Vowden, Murray	28,391
19	12	A	Portsmouth	D	1-1	Murray	16,508
20	15	A	Preston North End	L	1-4	Hateley	9,692
21	22	H	Millwall	W	2-0	Hateley, Vincent	22,564
22	Dec 6	H	Huddersfield Town	D	2-2	Vowden, Murray	24,956
23	13	A	Sheffield United	L	0-6		17,332
24	16	A	Middlesbrough	L	2-4	Hateley, Murray	17,020
25	26	H	Blackpool	L	2-3	James (og), Hateley	29,548
26	27	A	Queen's Park Rangers	L	1-2	Page	15,688
27	Jan 10	A	Charlton Athletic	W	3-0	Vincent, Beard, Johnston	18,031
28	17	A	Carlisle United	L	3-4	Summerill 3	7,912
29	31	H	Bristol City	D	2-2	Vincent, Summerill	20,421
30	Feb 14	H	Leicester City	L	0-1		28,232
31	21	A	Cardiff City	L	1-3	Bell (og)	21,887
32	24	H	Bolton Wanderers	W	2-0	Vincent, Summerill	19,489
33	28	H	Watford	D	0-0		22,790
34	Mar 4	H	Blackburn Rovers	D	1-1	Mulraney (og)	8,639
35	11	A	Millwall	L	2-6	Hockey, Murray (pen)	7,825
36	14	H	Middlesbrough	D	0-0		17,974
37	21	A	Huddersfield Town	L	0-2		18,502
38	28	H	Preston North End	W	1-0	Vowden	16,465
39	30	A	Aston Villa	L	0-2		41,694
40	31	A	Swindon Town	L	1-4	Summerill	21,098
41	Apr 4	H	Hull City	L	2-4	R.Latchford, Martin	13,530
42	15	A	Norwich City	L	0-6		12,134

Appearances
Sub appearances
Three own-goals   Goals

FA Cup

R3	Jan 3	A	Chelsea	L	0-3		45,088

Appearances

League Cup

R2	Sep 3	A	Brighton & Hove Albion	L	0-2		24,232

Appearances

374

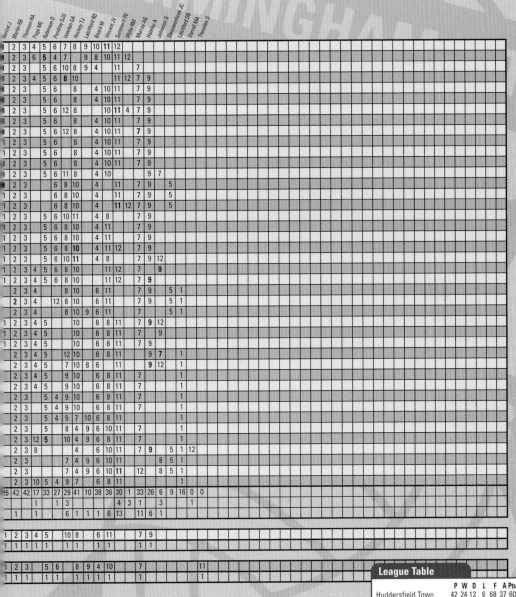

Herriot J · Martin RB · Thomson RA · Page ME · Robinson D · Pendrey GJS · Vowden GA · Hockey TJ · Latchford RD · Beard M · Vincent JV · Summerill PE · Wylie RM · Murray AG · Hateley A · Johnston G · Sleeuwenhoek JC · Latchford DB · Darrell MA · Thwaites D

League Table

	P	W	D	L	F	A	Pts
Huddersfield Town	42	24	12	6	68	37	60
Blackpool	42	20	13	9	56	45	53
Leicester City	42	19	13	10	64	50	51
Middlesbrough	42	20	10	12	55	45	50
Swindon Town	42	17	16	9	57	47	50
Sheffield United	42	22	5	15	73	38	49
Cardiff City	42	18	13	11	61	41	49
Blackburn Rovers	42	20	7	15	54	50	47
Queen's Park Rangers	42	17	11	14	66	57	45
Millwall	42	15	14	13	56	56	44
Norwich City	42	16	11	15	49	46	43
Carlisle United	42	14	13	15	58	56	41
Hull City	42	15	11	16	72	70	41
Bristol City	42	13	13	16	54	50	39
Oxford United	42	12	15	15	35	42	39
Bolton Wanderers	42	12	12	18	54	61	36
Portsmouth	42	13	9	20	66	80	35
Birmingham City	42	11	11	20	51	78	33
Watford	42	9	13	20	44	57	31
Charlton Athletic	42	7	17	18	35	76	31
Aston Villa	42	8	13	21	36	62	29
Preston North End	42	8	12	22	43	63	28

Division Two

Manager: Freddie Goodwin

Did you know that?

Trevor Francis was 16 years, four months and 16 days old when he scored four goals for Blues in the League win over Bolton Wanderers in February 1971.

Malcolm Beard was sent-off in his last game for Blues at Millwall in December.

Phil Summerill scored the fastest-ever goal by a Blues player – netting after 12 seconds of the home game with Watford in March.

Four goals came in the first 17 minutes of QPR's 5–2 win over Blues in October.

Francis's goal at Leyton Orient in March was the first conceded by the London club in 563 minutes of League action.

Blues came back from 2–0 down to win 3–2 at Wrexham two in the League Cup.

Match No.	Date	Venue	Opponents	Result		Scorers	Attendance
1	Aug 15	H	Queen's Park Rangers	W	2-1	Summerill, Vowden	30,785
2	22	A	Carlisle United	W	3-0	Vincent, R.Latchford 2	9,244
3	29	H	Luton Town	D	1-1	Vowden	30,141
4	Sep 1	H	Middlesbrough	L	0-1		27,769
5	5	A	Cardiff City	L	0-2		21,690
6	12	H	Oxford United	D	1-1	Francis	22,346
7	19	A	Portsmouth	L	0-1		18,037
8	26	H	Charlton Athletic	D	1-1	Summerill	20,767
9	29	A	Bristol City	L	1-2	Summerill	15,979
10	Oct 3	A	Hull City	W	1-0	R.Latchford	17,582
11	10	H	Sheffield United	L	0-1		22,374
12	17	A	Queen's Park Rangers	L	2-5	R.Latchford 2	13,074
13	20	A	Leicester City	D	0-0		25,381
14	24	A	Watford	L	1-2	Vowden	14,707
15	31	H	Swindon Town	W	2-1	Vincent, Robinson	18,502
16	Nov 7	A	Sunderland	L	1-2	Summerill	16,095
17	14	H	Orient	W	1-0	Page	14,937
18	21	A	Bolton Wanderers	L	0-3		7,432
19	28	H	Norwich City	D	2-2	Vincent, Summerill	13,630
20	Dec 5	A	Millwall	L	1-2	Summerill	8,560
21	12	H	Sheffield Wednesday	W	1-0	R.Latchford	14,239
22	19	H	Carlisle United	W	1-0	Francis	15,670
23	26	A	Blackburn Rovers	D	2-2	Bowker, Francis	8,787
24	Jan 9	H	Bristol City	W	2-0	Taylor, R.Latchford	15,292
25	16	A	Leicester City	W	4-1	R.Latchford 2, Bowker, Summerill	25,657
26	30	A	Norwich City	D	2-2	Summerill 2	11,411
27	Feb 6	H	Millwall	W	3-1	Page, Summerill (pen), Francis	21,893
28	13	A	Sheffield Wednesday	D	3-3	Francis 2, R.Latchford	12,791
29	20	H	Bolton Wanderers	W	4-0	Francis 4	25,600
30	27	A	Swindon Town	W	2-1	Francis 2	20,094
31	Mar 6	H	Watford	W	2-0	Summerill, Francis	27,605
32	13	A	Orient	W	2-0	Francis, Summerill	11,167
33	20	H	Sunderland	W	3-1	Summerill 2 (1 pen), Page	34,194
34	27	H	Cardiff City	W	2-0	Francis, Summerill	49,025
35	Apr 3	A	Luton Town	L	2-3	R.Latchford, Summerill	25,172
36	9	A	Oxford United	L	0-1		16,027
37	10	H	Blackburn Rovers	W	1-0	Campbell	25,572
38	13	H	Hull City	D	0-0		33,109
39	17	A	Sheffield United	L	0-3		29,364
40	24	H	Portsmouth	D	1-1	R.Latchford	19,440
41	27	A	Middlesbrough	D	0-0		12,802
42	May 1	A	Charlton Athletic	D	1-1	R.Latchford	10,742

Appearances
Sub appearances
Goals

FA Cup

	Date	Venue	Opponents	Result		Scorers	Attendance
R3	Jan 2	A	Huddersfield Town	D	1-1	Summerill (pen)	26,486
rep	5	H	Huddersfield Town	L	0-2		26,558

Appearances
Sub appearances
Goals

League Cup

	Date	Venue	Opponents	Result		Scorers	Attendance
R1	Aug 18	H	Wrexham	D	3-3	Murray, Vowden, Vincent	21,623
rep	26	A	Wrexham	W	3-2	Vowden, Vincent, Hockey	17,019
R2	Sep 9	A	Colchester United	D	1-1	Summerill	8,085
rep	15	H	Colchester United	W	2-1	Vowden, Summerill	17,606
R3	Oct 6	H	Nottingham Forest	W	2-1	Summerill 2	23,015
R4	27	A	Bristol Rovers	L	0-3		21,426

Appearances
Sub appearances
Goals

Appearances / Line-up Grid

Kelly MJ	Thomson RA	Pendrey GJS	Hockey TJ	Hynd JRS	Robinson D	Murray AG	Vowden GA	Latchford RD	Vincent JV	Summerill PE	Hartley A	Francis TJ	Martin RB	Page ME	Green CR	Sheerswheek JC	Bowker K	Bratez M	Campbell AJ	Latchford DB	Thwaites D	Taylor G	Harrison M	Smith G	Johnston G	Darrell MA
1	2	3	4	5	6	7	8	9	10	11																
1	2	3	4	5	6	7	8	9	10		11															
1	2	3	4	5	6	7	8	9	10	11																
1	2	3	4	5	6	7	8	9	10	11																
1	2	3	4	5	6	7	8	**9**	10	11		12															
	3	7	5	6			8	9		11		10	2	4													
	10	4	9	6		8			11			7	2		3	5											
	12	4	5	6		8			10	11	9	7	2		**3**												
	3	4	5	6			8	9	10	11		7	2														
	3	4	5	6			8	9	10	11		2			7												
2	3	4	5	6	7	8	9	10	11			12															
2		8	5	4		12	9	10	11		3				6	7											
3		8	5			4	9	10	11		2				6	7	1										
	3		5			4	**9**	10	11		2	12			6	8	1	7									
	3	4	5	6	7	9		10	11		2				8												
	3	4	5	6	7		**10**	11			2	9			12	8											
	3	8	5	6			9				2	4			10	7											
3		8	5	6			**9**	12	11		2	4			10	7											
3		8		5		9		10	11		2	4			6	7											
3		8	5		**9**	12	10	11			2	4			6	7											
		3	5	6		9		12		8	2	4			10	**7**		11									
		3	5	6		9				8	2	4			10			11	7								
		3	5	6		9				8	2	4			10			11	7								
		3	5	6		9		10			2	4			8	**7**	1	12	11								
	12	3	5			9		10		**2**	4			8		7	1		11	6							
	3			5		9		10		2	4			8		7	1		11	6							
		3	5	6		9		10		8	2	4				7	1		11								
		3	5	6		9		10		8	2	4				7	1		11								
		3	5	6		9		10		**8**	2	4			12	7	1		11								
		3	5	6		9		10		8	2	4				7			11								
		3	5	6		9		10		8	2	4				7			11								
		3	5	6		9		10		8	2					7			11	4							
			5	6		9		10		8	2	3				7			11	4							
			5	6		9		10		8	2	3				7			11	4							
	12		5	6		9		10		**8**	2	3				7			11	4							
	12		5	6		9		10		**8**	2	3				7			11	4							
			5	6		9		10		8	2	3				7			11	4							
			5	6		9		10		8	2	3				7			11	4							
			5	6		9		10		8	2	3				7			11	4							
	4		5	6		9		10		8	2	3				7			11								
	10		5	6			9			2	3			8		7			11	4							
		5	6		9		10			8	2	3				7			8	11							

Totals:

11	24	24	40	38	8	16	35	16	38	2	21	36	27	2	1	8	7	29	8	5	21	2	9			
	4					1	1	1		1		1				2	1		1							
			1		3	13	13	3	16		16			2		2		1		1						

League Table

	P	W	D	L	F	A	Pts
Leicester City	42	23	13	6	57	30	59
Sheffield United	42	21	14	7	73	39	56
Cardiff City	42	20	13	9	64	41	53
Carlisle United	42	20	13	9	65	43	53
Hull City	42	19	13	10	54	41	51
Luton Town	42	18	13	11	62	43	49
Middlesbrough	42	17	14	11	60	43	48
Millwall	42	19	9	14	59	42	47
Birmingham City	42	17	12	13	58	48	46
Norwich City	42	15	14	13	54	52	44
Queen's Park Rangers	42	16	11	15	58	53	43
Swindon Town	42	15	12	15	61	51	42
Sunderland	42	15	12	15	52	54	42
Oxford United	42	14	14	14	41	48	42
Sheffield Wednesday	42	12	12	18	51	69	36
Portsmouth	42	10	14	18	46	61	34
Orient	42	9	16	17	29	51	34
Watford	42	10	13	19	38	60	33
Bristol City	42	10	11	21	46	64	31
Charlton Athletic	42	8	14	20	41	65	30
Blackburn Rovers	42	6	15	21	37	69	27
Bolton Wanderers	42	7	10	25	35	74	24

1971-72

Division Two

Manager; Freddie Goodwin

Match No.	Date	Venue	Opponents	Result		Scorers	Attendance
1	Aug 14	A	Sunderland	D	1-1	Bowker	9,749
2	21	H	Carlisle United	W	3-2	Summerill, Barker, Campbell	26,254
3	28	A	Portsmouth	L	0-1		14,729
4	Sep 1	A	Hull City	L	0-1		16,746
5	4	H	Charlton Athletic	W	4-1	Francis, R.Latchford 3	25,231
6	11	A	Luton Town	D	0-0		14,678
7	18	H	Bristol City	W	1-0	R.Latchford	28,745
8	25	A	Blackpool	D	1-1	Francis	22,610
9	28	H	Watford	W	4-1	R.Latchford 3, Francis	28,095
10	Oct 2	H	Oxford United	D	0-0		31,759
11	9	A	Queen's Park Rangers	L	0-1		16,039
12	16	H	Sunderland	D	1-1	R.Latchford	27,341
13	19	A	Swindon Town	D	1-1	R.Latchford	14,265
14	23	H	Preston North End	D	2-2	R.Latchford, Francis	28,956
15	30	A	Burnley	D	1-1	R.Latchford	17,170
16	Nov 6	H	Orient	W	2-0	Hatton, R.Latchford	27,349
17	13	A	Norwich City	D	2-2	Campbell (pen), R.Latchford	24,094
18	20	A	Millwall	L	0-3		15,724
19	27	H	Fulham	W	3-1	R.Latchford 2, Hatton	25,545
20	Dec 4	A	Middlesbrough	D	0-0		15,671
21	11	H	Sheffield Wednesday	D	0-0		29,272
22	18	A	Charlton Athletic	D	1-1	Hatton	8,313
23	27	H	Cardiff City	W	3-0	Pendrey, Hatton, Francis	40,793
24	Jan 1	A	Bristol City	L	0-1		17,452
25	8	H	Portsmouth	W	6-3	Hatton 2, R.Latchford 2, Campbell (pen), Francis	22,410
26	22	A	Watford	W	1-0	Francis	10,884
27	29	H	Swindon Town	W	4-1	Francis, R.Latchford 2, Hatton	27,824
28	Feb 12	A	Preston North End	D	0-0		17,794
29	19	H	Burnley	W	2-0	Taylor, Hatton	32,035
30	Mar 4	H	Norwich City	W	4-0	Hatton 2, R.Latchford, Hynd	40,895
31	11	H	Queen's Park Rangers	D	0-0		35,557
32	21	A	Carlisle United	D	2-2	Hatton, R.Latchford	12,279
33	25	H	Luton Town	W	1-0	Hatton	34,395
34	31	A	Oxford United	W	1-0	Hatton	18,990
35	Apr 1	A	Cardiff City	D	0-0		23,667
36	4	H	Blackpool	W	2-1	R.Latchford, Francis	45,181
37	8	H	Millwall	W	1-0	R.Latchford	43,483
38	18	A	Fulham	D	0-0		16,555
39	22	H	Middlesbrough	D	1-1	Francis	37,202
40	25	H	Hull City	W	2-0	Campbell (pen), Francis	40,749
41	29	A	Sheffield Wednesday	W	2-1	Hatton, Francis	27,990
42	May 2	A	Orient	W	1-0	R.Latchford	33,383

Appearances
Sub appearances
Goals

FA Cup

R3	Jan 15	H	Port Vale	W	3-0	Hynd, Francis 2	32,937
R4	Feb 5	H	Ipswich Town	W	1-0	R.Latchford	40,707
R5	26	H	Portsmouth	W	3-1	Hatton, R.Latchford 2	43,888
R6	Mar 18	H	Huddersfield Town	W	3-1	Page, R.Latchford, Hatton	52,470
SF	Apr 15	N	Leeds United	L	0-3		54,724

SF at Hillsborough, Sheffield.

Appearances
Sub appearances
Goal

League Cup

R2	Sep 7	A	Queen's Park Rangers	L	0-2		15,037

Appearances

Birmingham City — Appearances & Goals Grid

Kelly MJ	Martin RB	Page ME	Swan G	Hynd JRS	Pendrey GJS	Campbell AJ	Bowker K	Latchford RD	Summed PE	Taylor G	Robinson D	Phillips SE	Latchford DB	Francis TJ	Burns K	Carroll TR	Hatton RJ	Hatland SC	Cooper PD	Harrison M	O'Grady M	Whitehead AJ
2	3	4	5	6	7	8	9	10	**11**	12												
2	3	4	5	6	7	**8**	9	10	11													
2	3	4	5	6	7	**8**	9	10	11	12			1									
2	3	4	5	11	7		9	10		6				**8**	12							
2	3	4	5	6	7		9	10	11					8								
2	3	4	5	10	7		9		6	11				8								
2	4	12	5	3	7		9	11	6	10				8								
2	4	12	5	3	7		9	**11**	6	10				8								
2	4		5	3	7		9	11	6	10				8								
2	4		5	3	7		9	10	6	11				8								
2	4	11	5	3	7		9	12	6	10				8								
2	4		5	3	7		9	10	11	6				8								
2	4	10	5	3	7		9	12	11	6				8								
2	4	10	5	3	7		9	11	6					8								
	4	11	5	3	7		9							8	6	2	10					
	4		5	3	7		9	11						8	6	2	10					
	6		5	3	7		9	11						8	4	2	10					
	4	11	5	3	7		9							8	6	2	10					
	4		5	3	7	11	9							8	6	2	10					
	4		5	3	7	11	9							8	10	2		6				
	4		5	3	7	11	9							8	10	2		6				
	4		5	3	7		9		11					8		2	10	6				
	4		5	3	7		9		11			1		8		2	10	6				
	4		5	3	7		9	11				1		8		2	10	6				
	4	12	5	3	7		9		11			1		8		2	10		1	6		
	4		5	3	7		9		11			1		8		2	10	6	1			
12	4		5	3	7		9		11					8		2	10	6	1			
	4		5	3	7		9		11					8		2	10	6	1			
	4		5	3	7		9		11					8		2	10	6	1			
		4	5	**3**	7		9		11			1		8		2	10	6			12	
	4		5	3	7		9		11			1		8		2	10	6				
	4		5	3	7		9		11			1		8		2	10	6				
	2	4	5	3	7		9		11			1		8			10	6				
	4	11	5	3	7		**9**	12				1		8		2	10	6				
	4	11	5	3	7		9					1		8		2	10	6				
	4	11	5	3	7		9							8		2	10	6	1			
	4	11	5	**3**	7		9		12					8		2	10	6	1			
	2	4	5		7		9							8		3	10	6	1		11	
	2	4	5		7		9		12					8		3	10		1	**11**	6	
12	4	5		3	7		9		11					8		2	10	**6**	1			
		4	5	3	7		9		11					8		2	10		1		6	
		4	5	3	7		9		11					8		2	10		1		6	
9	14	38	22	42	40	42	6	42	7	27	10	6	11	39	7	27	26	19	12	1	2	3
1	1	3							2	3	2	1		1				1				
		1	1	4	2	23	1	1				12		15								

Kelly MJ	Martin RB	Page ME	Swan G	Hynd JRS	Pendrey GJS	Campbell AJ	Bowker K	Latchford RD	Summed PE	Taylor G	Robinson D	Phillips SE	Latchford DB	Francis TJ	Burns K	Carroll TR	Hatton RJ	Hatland SC	Cooper PD	Harrison M	O'Grady M	Whitehead AJ
	4		5	3	7		9		11					8		2	10	6	1			
	4		5	3	7		9		11					8		2	10	6	1			
	4	12	5	3	7		9		11			1		8		2	10	6				
	4		5	3	7		9		11			1		8		2	10	6				
	4	11	5	3	7		**9**	12						8		2	10	6	1			
5	1	5	5	5	5		5		4			2	5			5	5	5	3			
	1								1													
1		1					4						2			2						

Kelly MJ	Martin RB	Page ME	Swan G	Hynd JRS	Pendrey GJS	Campbell AJ	Bowker K	Latchford RD	Summed PE	Taylor G	Robinson D	Phillips SE	Latchford DB	Francis TJ	Burns K	Carroll TR	Hatton RJ	Hatland SC	Cooper PD	Harrison M	O'Grady M	Whitehead AJ
2	3	4	5	6	7		9	10	11					1	8							
1	1	1	1	1	1		1	1	1					1	1							

League Table

	P	W	D	L	F	A	Pts
Norwich City	42	21	15	6	60	36	57
Birmingham City	42	19	18	5	60	31	56
Millwall	42	19	17	6	64	46	55
Queen's Park Rangers	42	20	14	8	57	28	54
Sunderland	42	17	16	9	67	57	50
Blackpool	42	20	7	15	70	50	47
Burnley	42	20	6	16	70	55	46
Bristol City	42	18	10	14	61	49	46
Middlesbrough	42	19	8	15	50	48	46
Carlisle United	42	17	9	16	61	57	43
Swindon Town	42	15	12	15	47	47	42
Hull City	42	14	10	18	49	53	38
Luton Town	42	10	18	14	43	48	38
Sheffield Wednesday	42	13	12	17	51	58	38
Oxford United	42	12	14	16	43	55	38
Portsmouth	42	12	13	17	59	68	37
Orient	42	14	9	19	50	61	37
Preston North End	42	12	12	18	52	58	36
Cardiff City	42	10	14	18	56	69	34
Fulham	42	12	10	20	45	68	34
Charlton Athletic	42	12	9	21	55	77	33
Watford	42	5	9	28	24	75	19

Division One

Manager: Freddie Goodwin

Match No.	Date		Venue	Opponents	Result		Scorers	Attendance
1	Aug	12	H	Sheffield United	L	1-2	R.Latchford	37,390
2		15	H	Newcastle United	W	3-2	McFaul (og), Hope, R.Latchford	35,831
3		19	A	Ipswich Town	L	0-2		17,775
4		23	A	Tottenham Hotspur	L	0-2		30,798
5		26	H	Crystal Palace	D	1-1	Francis	31,066
6		30	A	West Bromwich Albion	D	2-2	Hatton, R.Latchford	37,108
7	Sep	2	A	Wolverhampton Wan.	L	2-3	Hope, Burns	32,539
8		9	H	Manchester City	W	4-1	R.Latchford 3, Campbell	32,983
9		16	A	Derby County	L	0-1		33,753
10		23	H	Everton	W	2-1	R.Latchford, Francis	37,133
11		26	A	Arsenal	L	0-2		30,003
12		30	A	West Ham United	L	0-2		26,482
13	Oct	7	H	Chelsea	D	2-2	Hope, R.Latchford	38,756
14		14	A	Manchester United	L	0-1		52,104
15		21	H	Southampton	D	1-1	Roberts	30,757
16		28	A	Coventry City	D	0-0		35,304
17	Nov	4	H	Tottenham Hotspur	D	0-0		38,504
18		11	A	Newcastle United	L	0-3		26,042
19		18	A	Stoke City	W	2-1	R.Latchford 2	23,040
20		25	H	Norwich City	W	4-1	Pendrey, Hope, Want, Hatton	32,890
21	Dec	2	A	Liverpool	L	3-4	Taylor, Hope, R.Latchford	45,407
22		9	A	Leicester City	D	1-1	Calderwood	32,481
23		16	A	Leeds United	L	0-4		25,275
24		23	H	Arsenal	D	1-1	Bowker	32,721
25		26	A	Everton	D	1-1	R.Latchford	39,363
26		30	H	Ipswich Town	L	1-2	Hatton	32,705
27	Jan	27	A	Manchester City	L	0-1		31,877
28	Feb	10	H	Derby County	W	2-0	R.Latchford, Francis	38,096
29		17	A	Sheffield United	W	1-0	Francis	22,220
30		17	H	Wolverhampton Wan.	L	0-1		43,759
31	Mar	3	A	Chelsea	D	0-0		26,259
32		6	A	Crystal Palace	D	0-0		26,014
33		10	H	Manchester United	W	3-1	R.Latchford, Hatton, Campbell (pen)	51,278
34		17	A	Southampton	L	0-2		14,612
35		24	H	Coventry City	W	3-0	Hatton, R.Latchford, Taylor	34,775
36		31	A	Norwich City	W	2-1	R.Latchford 2	23,899
37	Apr	7	H	Liverpool	W	2-1	R.Latchford, Hatton	48,114
38		14	A	Leicester City	W	1-0	Campbell	27,652
39		21	H	Stoke City	W	3-1	Page, Francis, Hatton	32,513
40		23	H	West Ham United	D	0-0		36,942
41		28	H	West Bromwich Albion	W	3-2	R.Latchford	36,784
42		30	H	Leeds United	W	2-1	Francis, Burns	34,449

Appearances
Sub appearances
One own-goal   Goals

FA Cup

R3	Jan	13	A	Swindon Town	L	0-2		17,373

Appearances
Sub appearances

League Cup

R2	Sep	5	H	Luton Town	D	1-1	R.Latchford	20,962
rep		13	A	Luton Town	D	1-1	Campbell	13,806
rep2		19	N	Luton Town	W	1-0	Francis	11,451
R3	Oct	3	H	Coventry City	W	2-1	Francis, og (Barry)	27,803
R4		31	A	Blackpool	L	0-2		13,332

R2 replay a.e.t.
R2 replay at the County Ground, Northampton.

Appearances
Sub appearances
One own-goal   Goals

Birmingham City

Appearances and goals grid (player columns, left to right):

	Cooper PD	Carrol TR	Want AG	Campbell AJ	Hynd JRS	Harland SC	Hope R	Francis TJ	Latchford RD	Hatton RJ	Taylor G	Pendrey GJS	Page ME	Kelly MJ	Whitehead AJ	Summerill PE	Howett DJ	Burns K	Latchford DB	Martin RB	Roberts JG	Calderwood J	Bowker K	Smith G	Phillips SE	Hendrie PE	Robinson D
	1	2	3	4	5	6	7	8	9	10	11																
	1	2	3	4	5	6	7	8	9	10	11	12															
	1	2	3	4	5	6		8	9	10	11	7	12														
		2	3	4	5	6		8	9		11	7	10	1													
			3	4	5	6	10	8	9		11	7		1	2	12											
			3	4	5	6	10		9	8	11	7		1					2								
			3	4	5	6	10		9	8	11	7		1			2	12									
		2	3	4	5	6	10	8	9		11		7						12	1							
	2		4	5		10	8	9	11		3	6							7	1							
	2		4	5		10	8	9	11	12	3	6							7	1							
			4	5		10	8	9	11	12	3	6							7	1	2						
			4	5	12	10	8	9		11	3	6							7	1	2						
	2	3	12	5			7	8	9			10	6			11			4	1							
	2	3	12	5			10	8	9			11	4						7	1		6					
	2			5		7	8	9	10	11		3	4						1			6					
	2			5	6	7	8	9	10	11		3	4						1								
				6	7	8	9	10	11		3	4						1	2	5							
		3	8		6	7		9	10	11	4					12	1	2	5								
		3			5	6	7		9	10	11	4						1	2	8							
		3			5	6	7		9	10	11	4						1	2	8							
		3			5	6	7		9	10	11	4		1					1	2	8						
		3	7	5		6		9	10	11	4		1					6	8	2							
		3		5				9	10	11	4		1					6	8	2	7						
		3		5	6	11	8	9			4							1			2	7	10				
		3		5	6	8		9		11	4							1			2	7	10				
		3		5	6	8		9	12	11	4							1			2	7	10				
		3	12	5		10		9	8	11		4						1	2	6		7					
			7	5			8	9	10	11	3	4				12		1	2	6							
			7	5			8	9	10	11	3	4						1	2	6							
			7	5			8	9	10	11	3	4				12		1	2	6							
			7	5			8	9	10	11	3	4						1	2	6							
			7	5			8	9	10	11	3	4						1	2	6							
			7	5			8	9	10	11	3	4						1	2	6							
			7	5			8	9	10	11	3	4						1	2	6							
			7	5			8	9	10	11	3	4						1	2	6							
			7	5			8	9	10	11	3	4						1	2	6							
			7	5			8	9	10	11	3	4						1	2	6							
			7	5			8	9	10	11	3	4						1	2	6							
			7	5			8	9		11	3	4						10	1	2	6						
			7	5		12	8	9		11	3	4						10	1	2	6						
			7	5		11	8	9			3	4						10	1	2	6			12			
Totals	3	11	20	29	40	18	24	31	42	31	34	39	26	7	1	1	2	9	32	23	21	5	5	5	3	0	
		3			1	1				1	2	1		1					1						1		
	1	3	1			5	6	19	7	2	1	1		3						1	1	1					

Substitutes / cup appearances:

	3		5	6	10	8		9	12	11	4	2							1				7				
	1		1	1	1	1		0	1	1									1				1				
								1																			

	1		3	4	5	6	10	8		9		11	7						2	12							
	2			4	5	6	10	8	9	11	12	3							7	1							
	2			4	5		10	8	9	11		3	6						7	1							
		3	4	5			8	9			10	6			11				7	1	2						
	2				6	7	8	9	10	11	3	4							12	1			5				
	3	2	4	4	3	4	5	5	3	2	5	3			1		1	3	4	1			1				
										1									2								
		1					2	1																			

Division One

Manager: Freddie Goodwin

Manchester United's goalkeeper Alex Stepney scored the winning goal from the penalty spot on 66 minutes v Blues at Old Trafford in October.

This season saw Bob Hatton net Blues' first hat-trick in the League Cup – in an 11 minute spell (77–88) in the 4–2 replay victory over Blackpool in October.

In the Texaco Cup tie against Stoke City in October, substitute goalkeeper Ritchie Blackmore saved two penalties as Blues won the shoot-out 3–1 after a 0–0 draw.

In the next round, Jimmy Smith of Newcastle was sent off in the first minute of the 3–1 replay defeat at St James' Park.

Trevor Francis's winning penalty in the League Cup replay against Newcastle came in the eighth minute of extra-time.

Following an injury to Gary Sprake, Bob Latchford kept goal for Blues from the 42nd minute in their 2–1 home win over Wolves in October.

Match No.	Date		Venue	Opponents	Result		Scorers	Attendance
1	Aug	25	A	Manchester City	L	1-3	Hatton	35,88
2		28	H	Tottenham Hotspur	L	1-2	Hatton	37,75
3	Sep	1	H	Derby County	D	0-0		34,89
4		5	A	Chelsea	L	1-3	Page	25,66
5		8	A	Leeds United	L	0-3		39,74
6		11	H	Chelsea	L	2-4	Hatton, Taylor	30,252
7		15	H	Liverpool	D	1-1	R.Latchford	35,71
8		22	A	Queen's Park Rangers	D	2-2	R.Latchford, Burns	18,70
9		29	H	Ipswich Town	L	0-3		26,91
10	Oct	6	A	Arsenal	L	0-1		23,91
11		13	H	Wolverhampton Wan.	W	2-1	Francis (pen), Burns	34,97
12		20	A	Manchester United	L	0-1		48,93
13		27	H	Everton	L	0-2		31,18
14	Nov	3	A	Sheffield United	D	1-1	Hynd	19,33
15		10	H	Southampton	D	1-1	Hatton	25,29
16		17	A	Stoke City	L	2-5	Hynd, R.Latchford	19,17
17		24	H	Leicester City	W	3-0	R.Latchford 3	27,71
18	Dec	8	H	Newcastle United	W	1-0	Burns	25,42
19		15	H	West Ham United	W	3-1	Burns 2, Hatton	23,76
20		22	A	Ipswich Town	L	0-3		15,45
21		26	H	Coventry City	W	1-0	R.Latchford	33,42
22		29	H	Leeds United	D	1-1	R.Latchford	50,45
23	Jan	1	A	Derby County	D	1-1	Hatton	31,18
24		12	A	Liverpool	L	2-3	R.Latchford 2	39,09
25		19	H	Manchester City	D	1-1	R.Latchford	31,40
26	Feb	2	H	West Ham United	D	0-0		27,94
27		6	A	Tottenham Hotspur	L	2-4	England (og), Phillips	14,34
28		16	A	Wolverhampton Wan.	L	0-1		33,82
29		23	H	Arsenal	W	3-1	Gallagher, Hatton, Francis	29,82
30	Mar	2	A	Coventry City	W	1-0	Hatton	27,86
31		9	A	Everton	L	1-4	Hatton	33,94
32		16	H	Manchester United	W	1-0	Gallagher	37,76
33		20	A	Norwich City	L	1-2	Styles	18,30
34		23	A	Southampton	W	2-0	Burns, Francis	23,34
35		30	H	Sheffield United	W	1-0	Hatton	27,87
36	Apr	6	A	Leicester City	D	3-3	Burns 3	28,48
37		12	A	Burnley	L	1-2	Campbell	17,03
38		13	H	Stoke City	D	0-0		29,46
39		16	H	Burnley	D	2-2	Hatton 2	36,54
40		20	A	Newcastle United	D	1-1	Francis	34,06
41		23	H	Queen's Park Rangers	W	4-0	Taylor, Francis 2, Kendall	39,16
42		27	H	Norwich City	W	2-1	Hatton, Burns	44,18

Appearance
Sub appearances
One own-goal   Goals

FA Cup

R3	Jan	5	H	Cardiff City	W	5-2	Francis, R.Latchford 2, Hatton 2	22,43
R4		26	A	Queen's Park Rangers	L	0-2		23,36

Appearances
Goals

League Cup

R2	Oct	9	A	Blackpool	D	1-1	Burns	7,94
rep		16	H	Blackpool	W	4-2	Burns, Hatton 3	16,88
R3		30	H	Newcastle United	D	2-2	R.Latchford 2	13,02
rep	Nov	7	A	Newcastle United	W	1-0	Francis (pen)	19,27
R4		21	A	Ipswich Town	W	3-1	R.Latchford 3	12,24
R5	Dec	19	H	Plymouth Argyle	L	1-2	Hatton	15,27

R3 replay a.e.t.

Appearance
Sub appearances
Goals

Player columns (left to right):

Latchford DB, Martin RB, Pendrey GJS, Page ME, Hynd JRS, Burns K, Campbell AJ, Francis TJ, Latchford RD, Hatton RJ, Taylor G, Roberts JS, Cooper PD, Calderwood J, Phillips SE, Hope R, Want AG, Clarke D, Gallagher JA, Sprake G, Kelly MJ, Hendrie PF, Jenkins JL, Kendall H, Styles A

League Table

	P	W	D	L	F	A	Pts
Leeds United	42	24	14	4	66	31	62
Liverpool	42	22	13	7	52	31	57
Derby County	42	17	14	11	52	42	48
Ipswich Town	42	18	11	13	67	58	47
Stoke City	42	15	16	11	54	42	46
Burnley	42	16	14	12	56	53	46
Everton	42	16	12	14	50	48	44
Queen's Park Rangers	42	13	17	12	56	52	43
Leicester City	42	13	16	13	51	41	42
Arsenal	42	14	14	14	49	51	42
Tottenham Hotspur	42	14	14	14	45	50	42
Wolverhampton W	42	13	15	14	49	49	41
Sheffield United	42	14	12	16	44	49	40
Manchester City	42	14	12	16	39	46	40
Newcastle United	42	13	12	17	49	48	38
Coventry City	42	14	10	18	43	54	38
Chelsea	42	12	13	17	56	60	37
West Ham United	42	11	15	16	55	60	37
Birmingham City	42	12	13	17	52	64	37
Southampton	42	11	14	17	47	68	36
Manchester United	42	10	12	20	38	48	32
Norwich City	42	7	15	20	37	62	29

1974-75

Division One

Manager: Freddie Goodwin

Match No.	Date		Venue	Opponents	Result		Scorers	Attendance
1	Aug	17	H	Middlesbrough	L	0-3		32,10
2		20	H	Leicester City	L	3-4	Burns, Francis 2 (1 pen)	27,66
3		24	A	Leeds United	L	0-1		30,82
4		28	A	Leicester City	D	1-1	Francis	24,01
5		31	H	Wolverhampton Wan.	D	1-1	Burns	33,78
6	Sep	7	A	Queen's Park Rangers	W	1-0	Gallagher	16,05
7		14	H	Derby County	W	3-2	Hatton, Francis 2 (2 pens)	27,34
8		21	A	Carlisle United	L	0-1		12,69
9		25	A	West Ham United	L	0-3		25,49
10		28	H	Arsenal	W	3-1	Burns, Hatton 2	25,58
11	Oct	5	H	Coventry City	L	1-2	Francis (pen)	30,28
12		12	A	Luton Town	W	3-1	Francis 3	15,09
13		15	H	Leeds United	W	1-0	Francis	36,51
14		19	H	Newcastle United	W	3-0	Burns, Styles, Hatton	33,33
15		26	A	Sheffield United	L	2-3	Hatton, Styles	21,63
16	Nov	2	H	Chelsea	W	2-0	Hatton, Kendall	30,76
17		9	A	Burnley	D	2-2	Rodway (og), Taylor	16,07
18		16	H	Manchester City	W	4-0	Kendall, Hatton 2, Burns	35,14
19		23	A	Tottenham Hotspur	D	0-0		27,76
20		30	A	Everton	L	1-4	Calderwood	38,36
21	Dec	7	H	Stoke City	L	0-3		33,99
22		14	A	Middlesbrough	L	0-3		23,73
23		21	H	Liverpool	W	3-1	Taylor, Kendall (pen), Hatton	26,60
24		26	A	Derby County	L	1-2	Hatton	26,12
25		28	H	Ipswich Town	L	0-1		30,26
26	Jan	11	A	Stoke City	D	0-0		26,15
27		18	H	Everton	L	0-3		32,28
28	Feb	1	H	Burnley	D	1-1	Emmanuel	24,99
29		8	A	Chelsea	L	1-2	Hatton	18,14
30		18	H	Tottenham Hotspur	W	1-0	Hatton	24,24
31		22	A	Manchester City	L	1-3	Taylor	33,24
32	Mar	1	A	Wolverhampton Wan.	W	1-0	Hendrie	28,25
33		15	A	Arsenal	D	1-1	Burns	17,84
34		18	H	West Ham United	D	1-1	Bryant	34,00
35		22	H	Queen's Park Rangers	W	4-1	Francis, Campbell, Hatton, Calderwood	32,83
36		25	H	Carlisle United	W	2-0	Francis, Burns	33,76
37		29	A	Liverpool	L	0-1		49,45
38	Apr	1	A	Ipswich Town	L	2-3	Burns, Hatton	27,41
39		12	A	Coventry City	L	0-1		24,16
40		19	H	Luton Town	L	1-4	Francis	28,75
41		26	A	Newcastle United	W	2-1	Kendall, Pendry	24,78
42		29	H	Sheffield United	D	0-0		33,67

								Appearance
								Sub appearance
							One own-goal	Goal

FA Cup

	Date		Venue	Opponents	Result		Scorers	Attendance
R3	Jan	4	A	Luton Town	W	1-0	Kendall	17,54
R4		25	A	Chelsea	W	1-0	Burns	36,65
R5	Feb	15	H	Walsall	W	2-1	Hatton, Burns	45,88
R6	Mar	8	H	Middlesbrough	W	1-0	Hatton	47,26
SF	Apr	5	N	Fulham	D	1-1	Gallagher	54,16
rep		9	N	Fulham	L	0-1		35,20

SF replay a.e.t.

SF at Hillsborough, SF replay at Maine Road, Manchester.

		Appearance
		Sub appearance
		Goal

League Cup

	Date		Venue	Opponents	Result		Scorers	Attendance
R2	Sep	11	A	Crewe Alexandra	L	1-2	Gallagher	7,19

		Appearance
		Sub appearance
		Goal

League Table

	P	W	D	L	F	A	Pts
Derby County	42	21	11	10	67	49	53
Liverpool	42	20	11	11	60	39	51
Ipswich Town	42	23	5	14	66	44	51
Everton	42	16	18	8	56	42	50
Stoke City	42	17	15	10	64	48	49
Sheffield United	42	18	13	11	58	51	49
Middlesbrough	42	18	12	12	54	40	48
Manchester City	42	18	10	14	54	54	46
Leeds United	42	16	13	13	57	49	45
Burnley	42	17	11	14	68	67	45
Queen's Park Rangers	42	16	10	16	54	54	42
Wolverhampton W	42	14	11	17	57	54	39
West Ham United	42	13	13	16	58	59	39
Coventry City	42	12	15	15	51	62	39
Newcastle United	42	15	9	18	59	72	39
Arsenal	42	13	11	18	47	49	37
Birmingham City	42	14	9	19	53	61	37
Leicester City	42	12	12	18	46	60	36
Tottenham Hotspur	42	13	8	21	52	63	34
Luton Town	42	11	11	20	47	65	33
Chelsea	42	9	15	18	42	72	33
Carlisle United	42	12	5	25	43	59	29

Appearance grid column headers

Latchford DB · Martin RB · Pendrey GJS · Kendall H · Hynd JRS · Roberts JG · Campbell AJ · Francis TJ · Burns K · Hatton RJ · Page ME · Taylor G · Styles A · Gallagher JA · Sbraga R · Bryant SP · Calderwood J · Phillis SE · Hendon PF · Emmanuel JG · Clarke D · Merton RS · Sprake G · Want AG · Kelly MJ · Smith ILT

1975-76

Division One

Manager: Freddie Goodwin (to September); then Willie Bell

Match No.	Date		Venue	Opponents	Result		Scorers	Attendance
1	Aug	16	A	Leicester City	D	3-3	Hatton, Kendall 2 (1 pen)	25,54
2		19	H	Manchester United	L	0-2		33,17
3		23	H	Everton	L	0-1		26,81
4		26	A	Middlesbrough	L	0-2		22,42
5		30	A	Ipswich Town	L	2-4	Hatton 2	22,65
6	Sep	6	H	Queen's Park Rangers	D	1-1	Kendall	27,30
7		13	A	Wolverhampton Wan.	L	0-2		25,14
8		20	H	Burnley	W	4-0	Campbell, With, Kendall, Francis	25,83
9		23	H	Newcastle United	W	3-2	Withe 2, Francis (pen)	31,16
10		27	A	Aston Villa	L	1-2	Francis	53,78
11	Oct	4	H	Sheffield United	W	2-0	Hatton, Francis	26,12
12		11	A	Liverpool	L	1-3	Hatton	36,53
13		18	H	Leeds United	D	2-2	Francis, Gallagher	33,77
14		25	A	Norwich City	L	0-1		19,60
15	Nov	1	H	West Ham United	L	1-5	Francis	28,47
16		8	A	Manchester City	L	0-2		28,32
17		15	H	Arsenal	W	3-1	Francis (pen), Withe, Hatton	21,65
18		22	A	Leeds United	L	0-3		26,64
19		29	A	Coventry City	L	2-3	Burns, Kendall (pen)	21,80
20	Dec	6	H	Derby County	W	2-1	Burns, Page	30,62
21		13	A	Everton	L	2-5	Kendall, Withe	20,18
22		20	H	Leicester City	W	2-1	Francis (pen), Withe	21,89
23		26	A	Tottenham Hotspur	W	3-1	Francis 2, Withe	21,65
24		27	H	Stoke City	D	1-1	Hatton	37,16
25	Jan	10	H	Wolverhampton Wan.	L	0-1		28,55
26		17	A	Queen's Park Rangers	L	1-2	Francis	16,75
27		31	A	Manchester United	L	1-3	Withe	50,72
28	Feb	7	H	Middlesbrough	W	2-1	Kendall, Hatton	18,59
29		14	H	Manchester City	W	2-1	Gallagher, Kendall	22,44
30		21	A	Arsenal	L	0-1		20,90
31		28	H	Norwich City	D	1-1	Francis (pen)	22,35
32	Mar	6	A	West Ham United	W	2-1	Withe, Emmanuel	19,86
33		13	H	Liverpool	L	0-1		31,79
34		20	H	Coventry City	D	1-1	Francis (pen)	22,95
35		27	A	Derby County	L	2-4	Francis, Needham	28,16
36	Apr	3	H	Aston Villa	W	3-2	Hibbitt, Burns, Francis	46,25
37		7	A	Newcastle United	L	0-4		18,90
38		10	A	Burnley	L	0-1		13,67
39		13	H	Ipswich Town	W	3-0	Francis (pen), Hibbitt, Burns	20,49
40		17	H	Tottenham Hotspur	W	3-1	Gallagher, Francis, Burns	30,6
41		19	A	Stoke City	L	0-1		19,92
42	May	4	A	Sheffield United	D	1-1	Hibbitt	30,78

Appearance
Sub appearance
Goa

FA Cup

R3	Jan	3	A	Portsmouth	D	1-1	Francis	19,41
rep		6	H	Portsmouth	L	0-1		26,10

Appearance
Sub appearance
Goa

League Cup

R2	Sep	9	H	Leyton Orient	W	4-0	Gallagher, Morton, Hatton, Want	18,23
R3	Oct	7	H	Wolverhampton Wan.	L	0-2		29,82

Appearance
Sub appearance
Goa

Player appearance grid (Birmingham City)

	Latchford DB	Osborne IL	Bryant SP	Kendall H	Gallagher JA	Roberts JG	Calderwood J	Phillips SE	Hendrie PF	Hatton RJ	Taylor G	Want AG	Hynd JRS	Burns K	Francis TJ	Pendry GJS	Martin RB	Hope R	Withe P	Hibbitt TA	Campbell AJ	Page ME	Styles A	Emmanuel JG	Smith SJ	Needham JP	Morton R
		2	3	4	5	6	7	8	9	10	11																
		2	3	4	5			**8**	9	7	10	11	6	12													
			3	4	5	12		**9**	7	10	8	2		6	8	11											
			3	4	5					10				6	8	11	2	7	9								
			3	4	5					10				6	8		2	7	9	11							
			3	4	5	6				10					8		2	7	9	11							
			3	4	5					10				6	8		2		9	11	7						
			3	4	5					10				6	8	12	**2**		9	11	7						
		2		4	5					10		3		6	8	12			**9**	11	7						
			3	4	5					10				6	8		2		9	11	7						
			3		5					10	11	12		6	**8**	4	2		9		7						
				4	5					10	12			6	8	3	2		**9**	11	7						
				4	5	6				10	11			8		3	2			9	7						
				4	**5**	6				10	12			9	8	3	2			11	7						
				4	5					10				6	8	3	2		9	11	7						
		2	3	4	5					10	11			6	8	7			9								
		2	3	4	5		8		11	10				6		7			9								
			8	4	5			7		10		3		6					9	11							
		2		4	5					10		3		6	8				9	11	7						
		2	12	4	5					10		3		6	8				9	**11**	7						
		2		4	5					10		3		6	8	7			9	11							
		2	7	4	5					10		3		6	8				9	11							
		2	7	4	5					10		3		6	8				9	11							
					5		4			10		3		6	8		2		9			7	11				
				4	5		12			10		3		**6**	8		2		9			7	11				
				4	5		10			12				6	8		2		9	**11**		7	3				
			3	4	5					10	11			6	8		2				9		7				
				4	5		11			10				6	8		2		9			7	3				
				4	5		11			9				6	8		2		10			7	3	12			
				4	5		11			10				6	8		2		9			2	3	7			
				4	5		12							6	8		2		9	**11**		10	3	7			
			4	5			7			12		3			8	6	2		9	11		10				1	
				4	5					10					8	6	2			11		7	3		1	9	
				4	5					9		3			8	6	2			11		**7**	10			12	
				4	**5**		2			12		6		9	8					11			3	7		10	
				4		6				9		5		10		12		8	11		2	3	7				
		10		5		2				6	8						9	11		4	3	7				
				5		2					6		9	8			10	11		4	3	7				
				5		2			12		6		9	8			10	**11**		4	3	7				
		11		5		2					6		9	8			10			4	3	7				
			4	5		12					6		9	8			10	**11**		2	3	7				
Apps	10	19	36	41	5	15	4	5	33	7	20	0	36	35	14	22	3	32	27	9	19	16	10	2	2		
Sub		1				2	3			4	2	1	1		3								1		1		
Gls			8	3					8					5	17				9	3	1	1			1	1	

FA Cup

				4	5					10	12			6	8	**3**	2		9	11				7			
			3	4	5					10				**6**	8	12	2		9	11	7						
		1	2	2						2	0			2	2	1	2		2	2	1				1		
												1				1											
				1							1			1							1						

League Table

	P	W	D	L	F	A	Pts
Liverpool	42	23	14	5	66	31	60
Queen's Park Rangers	42	24	11	7	67	33	59
Manchester United	42	23	10	9	68	42	56
Derby County	42	21	11	10	75	58	53
Leeds United	42	21	9	12	65	46	51
Ipswich Town	42	16	14	12	54	48	46
Leicester City	42	13	19	10	48	51	45
Manchester City	42	16	11	15	64	46	43
Tottenham Hotspur	42	14	15	13	63	63	43
Norwich City	42	16	10	16	58	58	42
Everton	42	15	12	15	60	66	42
Stoke City	42	15	11	16	48	50	41
Middlesbrough	42	15	10	17	46	45	40
Coventry City	42	13	14	15	47	57	40
Newcastle United	42	15	9	18	71	62	39
Aston Villa	42	11	17	14	51	59	39
Arsenal	42	13	10	19	47	53	36
West Ham United	42	13	10	19	48	71	36
Birmingham City	42	13	7	22	57	75	33
Wolverhampton W	42	10	10	22	51	68	30
Burnley	42	9	10	23	43	66	28
Sheffield United	42	6	10	26	33	82	22

Division One

Manager: Willie Bell

Did you know that?

Forward Roy McDonough, who made two appearances for Blues in 1976–77, was sent off 21 times during his playing career.

A player from each side scored a hat-trick in the 3–3 draw between Blues and Arsenal at St Andrew's – Trevor Francis and Malcolm Macdonald.

Jim Montgomery saved Charlie George's 87th-minute penalty on his Blues debut in the 0–0 draw at Derby in March.

Two players were sent off in the 2–1 win over Aston Villa in May – Leighton Phillips for the visitors and Joe Gallagher for Blues.

Frank Worthington scored for Leicester as Kenny Burns bagged a hat-trick in Blues' 6–2 win at Filbert Street in December.

Playing in only his second international, Francis scored for England in a 5–0 win over Luxembourg.

Match No.	Date		Venue	Opponents	Result		Scorers	Attendance
1	Aug	21	A	Manchester United	D	2-2	Burns, Styles	58,89
2		24	H	Leeds United	D	0-0		35,51
3		28	H	Liverpool	W	2-1	Francis, Gallgher	33,22
4	Sep	4	A	Norwich City	L	0-1		18,50
5		11	H	West Bromwich Albion	L	0-1		39,45
6		18	A	Aston Villa	W	2-1	Burns, Connolly	50,08
7		25	A	Coventry City	L	1-2	Burns	26,37
8	Oct	2	H	Derby County	W	5-1	Burns 4, Connolly	29,19
9		16	H	Middlesbrough	W	3-1	Gallagher, Burns, Francis (pen)	27,74
10		20	A	Tottenham Hotspur	L	0-1		20,19
11		23	A	Newcastle United	L	2-3	Gallagher, Francis (pen)	31,71
12		26	A	Bristol City	W	1-0	Burns	21,47
13		30	H	Queen's Park Rangers	W	2-1	Burns, Francis	31,47
14	Nov	6	A	Arsenal	L	0-4		23,06
15		20	A	Stoke City	L	0-1		21,48
16		27	H	Manchester City	D	0-0		29,72
17	Dec	4	A	Leicester City	W	6-2	Emmanuel, Francis, Burns 3, Rofe (og)	20,38
18		7	H	Ipswich Town	L	2-4	Connolly, Burns	31,16
19		11	H	Sunderland	W	2-0	Jones, Francis	24,59
20		18	A	Everton	D	2-2	Francis, Hibbitt	32,53
21		27	H	West Ham United	D	0-0		39,97
22	Jan	18	H	Arsenal	D	3-3	Francis 3	23,24
23		22	H	Manchester United	L	2-3	Francis, Emmanuel	35,31
24	Feb	2	A	Leeds United	L	0-1		22,80
25		5	A	Liverpool	L	1-4	Burns	41,07
26		12	H	Norwich City	W	3-2	Burns 2, Broadhurst	21,80
27		28	A	West Bromwich Albion	L	1-2	Francis	28,63
28	Mar	5	H	Coventry City	W	3-1	Francis, Connolly, Emmanuel	22,60
29		12	A	Derby County	D	0-0		25,25
30		19	H	Tottenham Hotspur	L	1-2	Connolly	23,39
31		22	A	Middlesbrough	D	2-2	Francis 2	16,43
32	Apr	2	H	Newcastle United	L	1-2	Fox	20,28
33		8	A	West Ham United	D	2-2	Gallagher, Francis	28,16
34		9	H	Bristol City	W	3-0	Francis 3 (2 pens)	19,62
35		11	A	Ipswich Town	L	0-1		29,02
36		16	H	Stoke City	W	2-0	Francis, Burns	19,55
37		19	A	Manchester City	L	1-2	Burns	36,20
38		30	H	Leicester City	D	1-1	Kendall	20,83
39	May	7	A	Sunderland	L	0-1		34,18
40		10	H	Aston Villa	W	2-1	Hibbitt, Francis (pen)	43,72
41		14	H	Everton	D	1-1	Kendall	22,66
42		23	A	Queen's Park Rangers	D	2-2	Kendall, McDonough	14,97

Appearance
Sub appearance
One own-goal
Goa

FA Cup

R3	Jan	8	H	Portsmouth	W	1-0	Kendall	31,5.
R4		29	H	Leeds United	L	1-2	Burns	38,6

Appearance
Sub appearance
Goa

League Cup

R2	Aug	31	A	Blackpool	L	1-2	Pendrey	12,2

Appearance
Goa

Player columns (left to right):
Latchford DB · Page ME · Styles A · Kendall H · Gallagher JA · Want AG · Peredon GJS · Francis TJ · Burns K · Hibbitt TA · Jones GK · Calderwood J · Emmanuel JG · Withe P · Connolly J · Rathbone MJ · Bergia R · Broadhurst K · Fox SD · Montgomery J · McDonough R

Latch.	Page	Styles	Kend.	Gall.	Want	Pere.	Fran.	Burns	Hibb.	Jones	Cald.	Emm.	Withe	Conn.	Rath.	Berg.	Broad.	Fox	Mont.	McD.
2	3	**4**	5	6	7	8	9	10	11	12										
2	3		5	6	4	8	9	10	**11**	7	12									
2	3	4	5	6	7	8	10	11				9								
2	3	4	5	6	7	8	10	11				9								
2	3	4	5	6		8	10	7				9	11							
2	3	**4**	5	6		8	9	10	7	12			11							
2	3		5	6		8	9	4	10	7			11							
2	3		5	6	12	8	9	4	10	7			11							
2	3		5	6	12	8	9	4	10	7			11							
2	**3**		5		6	8		10	7	4	9		11	12						
	3		5		6	8	9	10	7	**4**	12		11	2						
3		5		6	8	9	10	7		4			11	2						
2	3		5		6	8	9	10	7	4			11							
2	3		5	6		8	9	10	7	4			11							
2	3		5	6	4	8	9	10	**7**	12			11							
2	3		5	6	7	8	9	10				4	11							
2	3		5	6	4	8	9	10				7	11							
2	3		5	6	**4**	8	9	10				7	11	12						
4	3		5		6	8	9	10	7				11	2						
2	3	4	5	6		8	9	10	7				11							
6	3	4	5		8	9	10	7					11	2						
2		4	5	6		8		10	7		9		11	3						
	3	4	5	6		8		10	7		9		11	2						
2		4	5		8	9	10	7				11	3	6						
6	3	4	5		8	9	10	7				11	2							
2	3	4	5	6		8	9	10				11			7					
2		5	6		8	9	10		4	11			3	**7**	12					
2		**5**	6		8	9	10	7	4	12		11	3							
	3	**4**		6	12	8	5	10		9		11	2			7	1			
	4	5		3	8	6	10	9	7			11	2			1				
	4	5	6	3	**8**		10		2	7	9		12	11	1					
2	3	4	5	**6**		8		10	11	12		9			7	1				
	4	5	6	3	8	9	10		2	7		11				1				
	4	5	6	3	8	9	10	7	2			11				1				
	4		6	3	**8**	9	10	7			12	11	2	5		1				
	4	5	6	3	8	9	10	7	2			11				1				
	4		6	3	8	9	10	7	2	12		11		**5**		1				
	4	**5**		3	8	9	10	7	2			11	12	6		1				
	4			3	8	9	10	7	2			11		5		1	6			
4		5		3	8	9	10	7	2			11		6						
5	4			3	8	9	10	7	2			11		6						
2		4	**5**		3	8		10		7	12	11		6			1	9		
31	**24**	**25**	**37**	**29**	**24**	**42**	**36**	**42**	**30**	**22**	**10**	**3**	**37**	**13**	**8**	**2**	**3**	**12**	**2**	
	1	3	4						3					4	6		3	1	1		

Goals:

Latch.	Page	Styles	Kend.	Gall.	Want	Pere.	Fran.	Burns	Hibb.	Jones	Cald.	Emm.	Withe	Conn.	Rath.	Berg.	Broad.	Fox	Mont.	McD.
6	**3**	4	5	12		8	9	10	7				11	2						
6	**3**	4	5			8	9	10	7				11	2						
2	2	2	2	0		2	2	2	2				2	2						
				1																
	1				1															

2		4	5	6	7	8		10	11				9		3					
1		1	1	1	1	1		1	1				1		1					
			1																	

League Table

	P	W	D	L	F	A	Pts
Liverpool	42	23	11	8	62	33	57
Manchester City	42	21	14	7	60	34	56
Ipswich Town	42	22	8	12	66	39	52
Aston Villa	42	22	7	13	76	50	51
Newcastle United	42	18	13	11	64	49	49
Manchester United	42	18	11	13	71	62	47
West Bromwich Albion	42	16	13	13	62	56	45
Arsenal	42	16	11	15	64	59	43
Everton	42	14	14	14	62	64	42
Leeds United	42	15	12	15	48	51	42
Leicester City	42	12	18	12	47	60	42
Middlesbrough	42	14	13	15	40	45	41
Birmingham City	42	13	12	17	63	61	38
Queen's Park Rangers	42	13	12	17	47	52	38
Derby County	42	9	19	14	50	55	37
Norwich City	42	14	9	19	47	64	37
West Ham United	42	11	14	17	46	65	36
Bristol City	42	11	13	18	38	48	35
Coventry City	42	10	15	17	48	59	35
Sunderland	42	11	12	19	46	54	34
Stoke City	42	10	14	18	28	51	34
Tottenham Hotspur	42	12	9	21	48	72	33

1977-78

Division One

Manager: Willie Bell (to September); Sir Alf Ramsey (to March); then Jim Smith

Match No.	Date	Venue	Opponents	Result		Scorers	Attendance
1	Aug 20	H	Manchester United	L	1-4	Hibbitt	28,005
2	24	A	Chelsea	L	0-2		18,108
3	27	A	Leeds United	L	0-1		24,551
4	Sep 3	H	Liverpool	L	0-1		28,239
5	10	A	Middlesbrough	W	2-1	Francis 2	19,240
6	17	H	Newcastle United	W	3-0	Connolly, Bertschin 2	19,259
7	24	A	West Bromwich Albion	L	1-3	Connolly	29,115
8	Oct 1	A	Aston Villa	W	1-0	Bertschin	45,436
9	4	H	Queen's Park Rangers	W	2-1	Francis 2	21,304
10	8	H	Coventry City	D	1-1	Francis (pen)	27,412
11	15	A	Ipswich Town	L	2-5	Francis 2	21,313
12	22	H	Derby County	W	3-1	Hibbitt 2, Towers	23,108
13	29	A	Arsenal	D	1-1	Bertschin	31,355
14	Nov 5	H	Wolverhampton Wan.	W	2-1	Francis, Hibbitt	28,103
15	12	A	Everton	L	1-2	Bertschin	37,743
16	19	H	Leicester City	D	1-1	Francis	21,206
17	26	A	Norwich City	L	0-1		16,803
18	Dec 3	H	Nottingham Forest	L	0-2		29,925
19	10	A	Manchester City	L	0-3		36,671
20	17	H	Everton	D	0-0		22,177
21	26	A	West Ham United	L	0-1		25,573
22	27	H	Bristol City	W	3-0	Gallagher, Towers, Francis	24,111
23	31	H	Chelsea	L	4-5	Bertschin, Francis 2, Hibbitt	19,871
24	Jan 2	A	Manchester United	W	2-1	Dillon, Francis	53,500
25	14	H	Leeds United	L	2-3	Bertschin, Connolly	23,701
26	21	A	Liverpool	W	3-2	Emmanuel, Bertschin, Francis (pen)	48,400
27	Feb 4	H	Middlesbrough	L	1-2	Gallagher	14,302
28	25	A	Aston Villa	W	1-0	Francis	33,679
29	28	H	West Bromwich Albion	L	1-2	Francis	26,636
30	Mar 4	A	Coventry City	L	0-4		22,922
31	15	A	Newcastle United	D	1-1	Francis	19,491
32	18	H	Derby County	W	3-1	Connolly, Francis, Bertschin	19,840
33	21	H	Arsenal	D	1-1	Francis	22,081
34	25	A	Bristol City	W	1-0	Francis	21,432
35	28	H	West Ham United	W	3-0	Francis 2 (1 pen), Bertschin	23,553
36	Apr 1	A	Wolverhampton Wan.	W	1-0	Francis	19,924
37	8	H	Norwich City	W	2-1	Gallagher, Francis	20,854
38	11	H	Ipswich Town	D	0-0		19,281
39	15	A	Leicester City	W	4-1	Hibbitt, Pendrey, Bertschin, Francis	15,431
40	22	H	Manchester City	L	1-4	Sbragia	25,296
41	25	A	Queen's Park Rangers	D	0-0		16,041
42	29	A	Nottingham Forest	D	0-0		37,621
						Appearance	
						Sub appearance	
						Goal	

FA Cup

R3	Jan 7	H	Wigan Athletic	W	4-0	Francis 2, Bertschin 2	29,200
R4	Feb 1	A	Derby County	L	1-2	Bertschin	31,950
						Appearance	
						Goal	

League Cup

R2	Aug 30	H	Notts County	L	0-2		14,99
						Appearance	

Player appearance and goalscoring grid (Birmingham City).

Column headers (left to right):

Montgomery J · Calderwood J · Pardry GJS · Towers MA · Howard P · Page ME · Jones BK · Francis TJ · Bertaschin KE · Hibbit TA · Connolly J · Went AG · Styles A · Rathbone MJ · Brathurst K · Emmanuel JG · Fox SD · Shogia R · Dillon KP · Gallagher JA · Latchford DB · Smith S

Mont	Cald	Pard	Tow	How	Page	Jones	Fran	Bert	Hibb	Conn	Went	Styles	Rath	Brath	Emm	Fox	Shog	Dillon	Gall	Latch	Smith
1	2	3	4	5	6	7	8	9	10	11											
1	2	3	4	5		7	8	9	10	11	6										
1	2	3	4	5		7	8	9	10	11	6	12									
1		3	4	5	11		8	9	10		2	6	12	7							
1		3	4				8	9	10	6	2	7	11	5							
1		3	4	5	2		8	9	10	12	6		7	11							
1			4	5	2		8	9	10	7	3		6	11							
1	2	3	4	5			8	9	10	6		7	11								
1	2	3		5	4		8	9	10	7	6	11									
1	2	3		5	4	12	8	9	10	7	6	11									
1	2	3	7	5	4		8	9	10		6	11									
1	2	3	4	5	7		8	9	10		6	11									
1	2	3	4	5	7		8	9	10	12	6	11									
1	2	3	4		7		8	9	10	6		11	5								
1	2	3	4		7		8	9	10	12	6	11	5								
1	2	3	4		7	12	8	9	10	6		5	11								
1	2	3		5	7		8	9	10	6		4	11								
1	2	3	12	5	7		8	9	10	6		4	11								
1	2	3	4	5	7		8	9	10	6		12	11								
1	2	3	4	5	7		8	9	10	6		11									
1	2	3	4	5	7		8	9	10	6		11									
1	2	3	4	5	7		8	9	10	12		11	6								
1	2	3	4	5	7		8	9	10	12		11	6								
1	2		4	5			8	9	10	7	3			11	6						
		3	4	6	2		8	9	10	7				11	5						
	2	3	4	6			8	9	10				7		11	5					
	2	3	4	6			8	9	10				7		11	5					
	2		4	6	12		8	9	10		3			7		11	5				
		2		4	6		8	9	10		3	7				11	5	1			
	1		2		4	6	8	9	10		3	7		12	11	5					
	2	3	4	6	7		8	9	10	11						5					
	2	3	4	6	7		8	9	10	11						5					
	2	3	4	6	7		8	9	10	11						5					
	2	3	4	6	7		8	9	10	11				12		5					
	2	3	4	6	7		8	9	10					11		5					
	2	3	4	6	7		8	9	10			12	11			5					
	2	3	4	6	7		8	9	10	12				11		5					
	2	3	4	6	7		8	9	10	12				11		5					
	2	3	4	6			8	9	10				11		7	5					
	2	3	4				8	9	10				11	6	7	5					
		3	4		2		8	9				6	10	11		7	5				
	2	3					8	9	10			6	4	11		7	5				
Apps																					
1	36	37	37	35	29	3	42	42	41	12	18	5	2	9	20	10	5	16	21	1	
Sub	1		1	2				8		1		1	2	1		1					
Goals	1	2		25	11	6	4			1		1	1	3							

Cup rows:

	2		4	5			8	9	10				7		3			11	6		
	2	3	4	6			8	9	10					7		11	5	1			
	2	1	2	2			2	2	2	1		1		1		2	2	1			
					2	3															

| | 2 | 3 | 4 | 5 | 11 | 7 | 8 | 9 | 10 | | 6 | | | | | | | | | | |
| | 1 | 1 | 1 | 1 | 1 | 1 | 1 | 1 | 1 | | 1 | | | | | | | | | | |

League Table

	P	W	D	L	F	A	Pts
Nottingham Forest	42	25	14	3	69	24	64
Liverpool	42	24	9	9	65	34	57
Everton	42	22	11	9	76	45	55
Manchester City	42	20	12	10	74	51	52
Arsenal	42	21	10	11	60	37	52
West Bromwich Albion	42	18	14	10	62	53	50
Coventry City	42	18	12	12	75	62	48
Aston Villa	42	18	10	14	57	42	46
Leeds United	42	18	10	14	63	53	46
Manchester United	42	16	10	16	67	63	42
Birmingham City	42	16	9	17	55	60	41
Derby County	42	14	13	15	54	59	41
Norwich City	42	11	18	13	52	66	40
Middlesbrough	42	12	15	15	42	54	39
Wolverhampton W	42	12	12	18	51	64	36
Chelsea	42	11	14	17	46	69	36
Bristol City	42	11	13	18	49	53	35
Ipswich Town	42	11	13	18	47	61	35
Queen's Park Rangers	42	9	15	18	47	64	33
West Ham United	42	12	8	22	52	69	32
Newcastle United	42	6	10	26	42	78	22
Leicester City	42	5	12	25	26	70	22

Division One

Manager: Jim Smith

Blues won only six League games this season – a club record.

Malcolm Briggs had the shortest League career as a Blues player, replacing Alan Buckley for the last three minutes against Manchester City in May.

Three World Cup-winners played in the Spurs-Blues game in October: Ricardo Villa and Ossie Ardiles for the home side and Alberto Tarantini for Blues.

Goalkeeper Jim Montgomery made the 600th appearance of his career in the defeat at Leeds in September.

The first £1 million transfer in Britain took place at 2.40pm on 9 February when Blues sold Trevor Francis to Nottingham Forest.

Mark Dennis became the first Blues player to be sent off against the same team twice in one season – Wolves.

Keith Bertschin broke his leg twice this season (v Derby and QPR)

In June 1979, Carlos Francis became the first Black player to join Blues.

Match No.	Date		Venue	Opponents	Result		Scorers	Attendance
1	Aug	19	A	Manchester United	L	0-1		56,139
2		22	H	Middlesbrough	L	1-3	Bertschin	24,409
3		26	H	Derby County	D	1-1	Givens	21,973
4	Sep	2	A	Bolton Wanderers	D	2-2	Francis 2	20,284
5		9	H	Liverpool	L	0-3		31,740
6		16	A	Norwich City	L	0-4		15,701
7		23	H	Chelsea	D	1-1	Givens	18,458
8		30	A	Leeds United	L	0-3		23,331
9	Oct	7	H	Manchester City	L	1-2	Ainscow	18,378
10		14	A	Tottenham Hotspur	L	0-1		41,230
11		21	H	Aston Villa	L	0-1		36,145
12		28	A	Coventry City	L	1-2	Givens	25,429
13	Nov	4	A	West Bromwich Albion	L	0-1		32,130
14		11	H	Manchester United	W	5-1	Dillon, Buckley 2, Givens, Calderwood	23,550
15		18	A	Derby County	L	1-2	Givens	24,720
16		21	H	Bolton Wanderers	W	3-0	Dillon, Buckley, P.Jones (og)	21,643
17		25	H	Bristol City	D	1-1	Tarantini	21,152
18	Dec	2	A	Southampton	L	0-1		18,957
19		9	H	Everton	L	1-3	Buckley	23,391
20		16	A	Nottingham Forest	L	0-1		25,224
21		26	A	Wolverhampton Wan.	L	1-2	Buckley	26,872
22		30	A	Arsenal	L	1-3	Francis (pen)	27,877
23	Feb	3	A	Chelsea	L	1-2	Bertschin	22,511
24		10	H	Leeds United	L	0-1		17,388
25		13	A	Liverpool	L	0-1		35,207
26		24	H	Tottenham Hotspur	W	1-0	Towers	20,980
27	Mar	3	A	Aston Villa	L	0-1		42,419
28		6	H	Queen's Park Rangers	W	3-1	Buckley, Towers (pen), Broadhurst	12,605
29		10	H	Coventry City	D	0-0		17,528
30		24	A	Middlesbrough	L	1-2	Givens	15,013
31		27	H	Norwich City	W	1-0	Givens	12,166
32		31	A	Bristol City	L	1-2	Gallagher	16,453
33	Apr	3	H	Ipswich Town	D	1-1	Gallagher	12,449
34		7	H	Southampton	D	2-2	Barrowclough 2 (1 pen)	12,825
35		14	A	Wolverhampton Wan.	D	1-1	Ainscow	20,550
36		17	A	Ipswich Town	L	0-3		17,677
37		21	H	Nottingham Forest	L	0-2		22,189
38		24	H	West Bromwich Albion	D	1-1	Gallagher	19,897
39		28	A	Everton	L	0-1		23,048
40	May	1	A	Manchester City	L	1-3	Lynex	27,366
41		5	H	Arsenal	D	0-0		14,015
42		7	A	Queen's Park Rangers	W	3-1	Buckley 2, Dark	9,600

Appearances
Sub appearances
One own-goal   Goals

FA Cup

R3	Jan	6	H	Burnley	L	0-2		19,034

Appearances
Sub appearances

League Cup

R2	Aug	29	H	Southampton	L	2-5	Gallagher, Francis	18,464

Appearances
Sub appearances
Goals

	Montgomery J	Calderwood J	Emmanuel JG	Towers MA	Gallagher JA	Bradbury K	Barrowclough SJ	Ainscow A	Bertaschin KE	Givens DJ	Fox SD	Francis TJ	Page ME	Pandey GJS	Freeman N	Rathbone MJ	Howard P	Dillon KP	Dennis ME	Van Den Hauwe PWR	Tarantini A	Buckley AP	Roch BD	Dent TC	Ivey PHW	Lynex SC	Briggs M
	2	3	4	5	6	7	**8**	9	10	11	12																
	2	3	4	5	6	7	12	9	11	**10**	**8**																
		7		5	6	4	11	9	10		8	2	3														
	2	12	4	5		7	10		9		8			1	3	6	11										
	2	10	8	5		7	12		9	11			3	1		6	4										
		10	8	5	6	12	7		9	11			1	3		**2**	4										
		10	6	5	2	11	7		9	8		3				4											
		10	6	5		2		8	9	11	7					4	3										
		10	6	5		11	8		9	12	7					4	3	**2**									
		10	5	12	11	8			9		7	6				**4**	3	2									
	8	10		5	2				9	11	7	6				3		4									
	2	10	4	5		11			9		7	6	1			3		8									
	2	10	4	**5**		11			9		7	1		12	3		6	8									
	10		4	5					9	11	6		1		7	3		2	8								
	10		4	5		12			9	11	6		1		7	3		2	8								
	10		4	5					9	11	6		1		7	3		2	8								
	8		**4**	5		12			9	11	6		1		7	3		2	10								
	7		4	5					9	11	6		1		8	3	**2**		10								
	2		4	5		12			9	11	8	6	1		7	3			10								
1	2			5		11	12		9		8	6			7	3			**10**	4							
		4	5		11			**9**		8	6			10	3		2	12	7							
1		7		5					9		8	6			11	3		2	10	4							
1		12	5	4			7	9		8	6	3			11			2	**10**								
		4	5		**7**	8	9			2		1		11	3		6	10	12							
		4	5			8	9	12		2		1		11	3		6	10	**7**							
		4	5		7	8	9			2		1		10	3		6	12	**11**							
		4	5	11		7	8	9		2		1		10	3		6									
		4	5	12		**7**	**8**	9		2	3	1		10			6	11								
3		4	5		11	7		9		2	1			10			6	8									
		4	5		11	7		9		2	1		6	10	3			8								
		4	5	12	10	7		9		2	6	1		11	3		**8**									
12		4	5	8	11	7		**9**		2		1		10	3		6									
9		4	5		11	7				2		1		10	3		6	8									
8			5	4	11	7		9		2			1	**10**	3			6		12							
		4	5	2	7	8		9			1		11	3	12	6	**10**									
2		4	5		11	7		9		10		1			6	3	**8**		12								
1	2		4	5		10	8		9		7			11	**3**		6	12									
2			5		11	7		9			4			10	3	6		8									
2		**5**		11	8		9			4				7	3	6		10		12							
2			5		10	7				1		3	6		4		**8**			9	11	12				
2			5		**10**	7		9			1		6	11	3	4		12		8						
2			5		12		7				1			10	3	6		8			12	11	4			
3	24	12	31	41	13	26	27	9	38	13	8	32	9	29	2	35	31	7	23	24	3	2	3	2	0		
	1	1			3	3	4		1	1	1		1		1		4		3	2	1					
	1		2	3	1	2	2	2	7		3			2			1	8		1	1					

1			4	5	2			12	11		**8**	6					7	3		10	9						
1			1	1	1			0	1		1	1					1	1		1	1						
									1																		

1		4	12	5	6	7	10	9	11		8	**2**	3														
1		1	0	1	1	1	1	1	1		1	1	1														
		1																									
			1						1																		

League Table

	P	W	D	L	F	A	Pts
Liverpool	42	30	8	4	85	16	68
Nottingham Forest	42	21	18	3	61	26	60
West Bromwich Albion	42	24	11	7	72	35	59
Everton	42	17	17	8	52	40	51
Leeds United	42	18	14	10	70	52	50
Ipswich Town	42	20	9	13	63	49	49
Arsenal	42	17	14	11	61	48	48
Aston Villa	42	15	16	11	59	49	46
Manchester United	42	15	15	12	60	63	45
Coventry City	42	14	16	12	58	68	44
Tottenham Hotspur	42	13	15	14	48	61	41
Middlesbrough	42	15	10	17	57	50	40
Bristol City	42	15	10	17	47	51	40
Southampton	42	12	16	14	47	53	40
Manchester City	42	13	13	16	58	56	39
Norwich City	42	7	23	12	51	57	37
Bolton Wanderers	42	12	11	19	54	75	35
Wolverhampton W	42	13	8	21	44	68	34
Derby County	42	10	11	21	44	71	31
Queen's Park Rangers	42	6	13	23	45	73	25
Birmingham City	42	6	10	26	37	64	22
Chelsea	42	5	10	27	44	92	20

Division Two

Manager: Jim Smith

On the opening day of the season, Blues led Fulham 3–0 at half-time only to lose 4–3, Gordon Davies scoring the winner in the 83rd minute.

Winger Willie Johnston, who played for Blues this season, was sent-off 22 times during his career – possibly a world record!

Colin Todd and Archie Gemmill both made the 500th League appearance of their respective careers, the latter celebrating by scoring a penalty against his former club Preston.

In October, Dutch international Johan Cruyff played for Los Angeles Aztecs in a 1–0 friendly defeat at St Andrew's, Terry Lees scoring the winning penalty.

On his retirement in May 1980, former Blues winger Gordon Taylor was appointed secretary of the PFA.

Match No.	Date		Venue	Opponents	Result		Scorers	Attendance
1	Aug	18	H	Fulham	L	3-4	Evans, Dillon, Bertschin	19,330
2		22	A	Sunderland	L	0-2		25,877
3		25	A	Cardiff City	W	2-1	Evans 2	11,465
4	Sep	1	H	Bristol Rovers	D	1-1	Dillon	15,320
5		8	A	Chelsea	W	2-1	Lynex, Curbishley	17,711
6		15	H	Charlton Athletic	W	1-0	Lynex	16,155
7		22	A	Orient	D	2-2	Lynex, Curbishley	5,550
8		29	H	Newcastle United	D	0-0		19,967
9	Oct	6	A	Preston North End	D	0-0		10,772
10		9	H	Sunderland	W	1-0	Lynex	18,960
11		13	A	Wrexham	L	0-1		13,693
12		20	H	Swansea City	W	2-0	Lynex, Gemmill	18,624
13		27	H	Shrewsbury Town	W	1-0	Ainscow	17,869
14	Nov	3	A	Fulham	W	4-2	Gemmill (pen), Givens 2, Lock (og)	8,336
15		10	H	Cambridge United	W	1-0	Lynex	17,120
16		17	A	Watford	L	0-1		14,378
17		24	A	Luton Town	W	3-2	Bertschin 3	13,720
18	Dec	1	H	Leicester City	L	1-2	Gallagher	25,748
19		8	A	Notts County	D	1-1	Lynex	11,383
20		15	H	Burnley	W	2-0	Worthington 2	13,997
21		21	A	Oldham Athletic	L	0-1		6,728
22		29	H	Cardiff City	W	2-1	Worthington, Bertschin	16,682
23	Jan	1	H	Queen's Park Rangers	W	2-1	Ainscow, Gemmill	25,963
24		12	A	Bristol Rovers	L	0-1		9,351
25	Feb	2	A	Charlton Athletic	W	1-0	Gemmill	6,821
26		9	H	Orient	W	3-1	Bertschin 3	17,474
27		20	A	Newcastle United	D	0-0		27,069
28		23	H	Wrexham	W	2-0	Dillon, Evans	19,302
29		29	A	Swansea City	W	1-0	Lynex	16,363
30	Mar	8	H	Shrewsbury Town	L	0-1		14,801
31		11	H	Chelsea	W	5-1	Broadhurst, Borota (og), Dillon, Ainscow 2	27,297
32		15	H	Preston North End	D	2-2	Gemmill (pen), Worthington	19,548
33		22	A	Cambridge United	L	1-2	Smith (og)	6,805
34		29	H	Watford	W	2-0	Bertschin, Gemmill (pen)	16,582
35	Apr	1	H	Oldham Athletic	W	2-0	Gemmill, Ainscow	17,118
36		5	A	Queen's Park Rangers	D	1-1	Dillon	16,609
37		7	H	West Ham United	D	0-0		28,377
38		12	A	Leicester City	L	1-2	Gemmill (pen)	26,075
39		19	H	Luton Town	W	1-0	Bertschin	23,662
40		22	A	West Ham United	W	2-1	Ainscow, Bertschin	36,167
41		26	A	Burnley	D	0-0		10,388
42	May	3	H	Notts County	D	3-3	Bertschin, Curbishley, Dillon	33,863

	Appearances
	Sub appearances
Three own-goals	Goals

FA Cup

R3	Jan	5	H	Southampton	W	2-1	Bertschin, Gallagher	24,548
R4		26	H	Middlesbrough	W	2-1	Gemmill (pen), Bertschin	29,152
R5	Feb	16	A	Tottenham Hotspur	L	1-3	Bertschin	49,936

	Appearances
	Sub appearances
	Goals

League Cup

R2	Aug	28	H	Preston North End	W	2-1	Ainscow, Dillon	13,660
R2s	Sep	4	A	Preston North End	W	1-0	Lynex	11,043
R3		26	H	Exeter City	L	1-2	Ainscow	13,669

	Appearances
	Sub appearances
	Goals

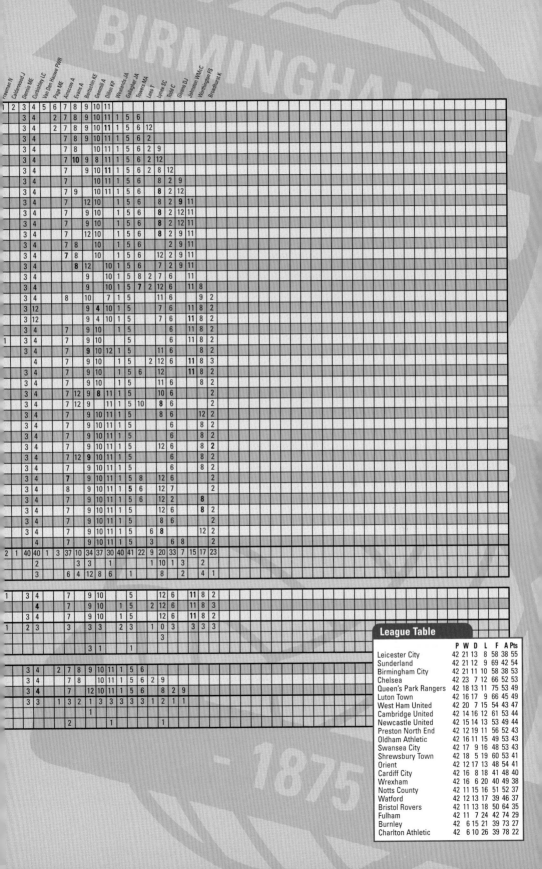

League Table

	P	W	D	L	F	A	Pts
Leicester City	42	21	13	8	58	38	55
Sunderland	42	21	12	9	69	42	54
Birmingham City	42	21	11	10	58	38	53
Chelsea	42	23	7	12	66	52	53
Queen's Park Rangers	42	18	13	11	75	53	49
Luton Town	42	16	17	9	66	45	49
West Ham United	42	20	7	15	54	43	47
Cambridge United	42	14	16	12	61	53	44
Newcastle United	42	15	14	13	53	49	44
Preston North End	42	12	19	11	56	52	43
Oldham Athletic	42	16	11	15	49	53	43
Swansea City	42	17	9	16	48	53	43
Shrewsbury Town	42	18	5	19	60	53	41
Orient	42	12	17	13	48	54	41
Cardiff City	42	16	8	18	41	48	40
Wrexham	42	16	6	20	40	49	38
Notts County	42	11	15	16	51	52	37
Watford	42	12	13	17	39	46	37
Bristol Rovers	42	11	13	18	50	64	35
Fulham	42	11	7	24	42	74	29
Burnley	42	6	15	21	39	73	27
Charlton Athletic	42	6	10	26	39	78	22

1980-81

Division One

Manager: Jim Smith

Did you know that?

August 1980 saw Blues' first ever family day out when 6,000 supporters turned up to look behind the scenes at St Andrew's.

Blues goalkeeper Tony Coton saved John Hawley's penalty after just 50 seconds of his League debut against Sunderland at St Andrew's in December.

During the course of this season Blues played a total of 73 first-team matches (including friendlies)... a club record.

In November, England beat Australia 1–0 in a B international at St Andrew's in front of just 3,292 fans. Blues defender Joe Gallagher set up Alan Sunderland's goal for England.

The legendary Joe Bradford died on 6 September, aged 79.

Match No.	Date		Venue	Opponents	Result		Scorers	Attendance
1	Aug	16	H	Coventry City	W	3-1	Curbishley 2, Dillon	21,877
2		20	A	Nottingham Forest	L	1-2	Worthington	26,561
3		23	H	Manchester United	D	0-0		28,661
4		30	A	Southampton	L	1-3	Worthington	21,683
5	Sep	6	A	Liverpool	D	1-1	Worthington	27,042
6		13	A	Brighton & Hove Alb.	D	2-2	Curbishley, Bertschin	15,767
7		20	H	West Bromwich Albion	D	1-1	Givens	22,016
8		27	A	Norwich City	D	2-2	Ainscow, Worthington	13,561
9	Oct	4	A	Wolverhampton Wan.	L	0-1		22,777
10		7	H	Arsenal	W	3-1	Worthington, Dillon, Lynex	15,511
11		11	H	Aston Villa	L	1-2	Worthington (pen)	33,879
12		18	A	Manchester City	W	1-0	Gemmill (pen)	30,041
13		25	H	Stoke City	D	1-1	Bertschin	16,535
14	Nov	1	A	Middlesbrough	W	2-1	Worthington 2	13,292
15		8	H	Crystal Palace	W	1-0	Bertschin	16,910
16		11	H	Nottingham Forest	W	2-0	Worthington 2	22,433
17		15	A	Coventry City	L	1-2	Curbishley	18,429
18		22	H	Tottenham Hotspur	W	2-1	Curbishley, Ainscow	24,817
19		29	A	Everton	D	1-1	Ainscow	22,274
20	Dec	6	H	Leicester City	L	1-2	Scott (og)	18,479
21		13	A	Aston Villa	L	0-3		41,101
22		20	H	Ipswich Town	L	1-3	Ainscow	16,161
23		26	A	Leeds United	D	0-0		19,214
24		27	H	Sunderland	W	3-2	Worthington, Bertschin, Gemmill	19,005
25	Jan	10	A	Tottenham Hotspur	L	0-1		24,909
26		13	H	Ipswich Town	L	1-5	Worthington	21,149
27		17	H	Southampton	L	0-3		16,491
28		31	A	Manchester United	L	0-2		39,081
29	Feb	7	H	Brighton & Hove Alb.	W	2-1	Curbishley, Evans	13,691
30		14	A	Liverpool	D	2-2	Ainscow, Evans	32,199
31		20	H	Norwich City	W	4-0	Ainscow, Gemmill, Evans 2	14,686
32		28	A	West Bromwich Albion	D	2-2	Ainscow, Worthington	24,848
33	Mar	17	H	Wolverhampton Wan.	W	1-0	Worthington	20,005
34		21	H	Manchester City	W	2-0	Worthington, Evans	16,160
35		28	A	Stoke City	D	0-0		14,624
36		31	A	Arsenal	L	1-2	Worthington	17,431
37	Apr	4	H	Middlesbrough	W	2-1	Evans, Broadhurst	12,472
38		11	A	Crystal Palace	L	1-3	Ainscow	11,122
39		18	A	Sunderland	L	0-3		20,158
40		21	H	Leeds United	L	0-2		14,505
41		25	A	Leicester City	L	0-1		13,666
42	May	2	H	Everton	D	1-1	Evans	12,863

Appearances	
Sub appearances	
One own-goal	Goals

FA Cup

	Date		Venue	Opponents	Result		Scorers	Attendance
R3	Jan	3	H	Sunderland	D	1-1	Bertschin	23,098
rep		7	A	Sunderland	W	2-1	Bertschin, Evans	27,793
R4		24	A	Coventry City	L	2-3	Ainscow, Worthington (pen)	29,492

R3 replay a.e.t.

Appearances	
Sub appearances	
	Goals

League Cup

	Date		Venue	Opponents	Result		Scorers	Attendance
R2	Aug	26	H	Bristol City	W	2-1	Ainscow, Gemmill (pen)	12,163
R2s	Sep	2	A	Bristol City	D	0-0		6,958
R3		23	H	Blackburn Rovers	W	1-0	Gallagher	14,580
R4	Oct	28	H	Ipswich Town	W	2-1	Ainscow, Worthington (pen)	18,968
R5	Dec	2	A	Liverpool	L	1-3	Bertschin	30,236

Appearances	
Sub appearances	
	Goals

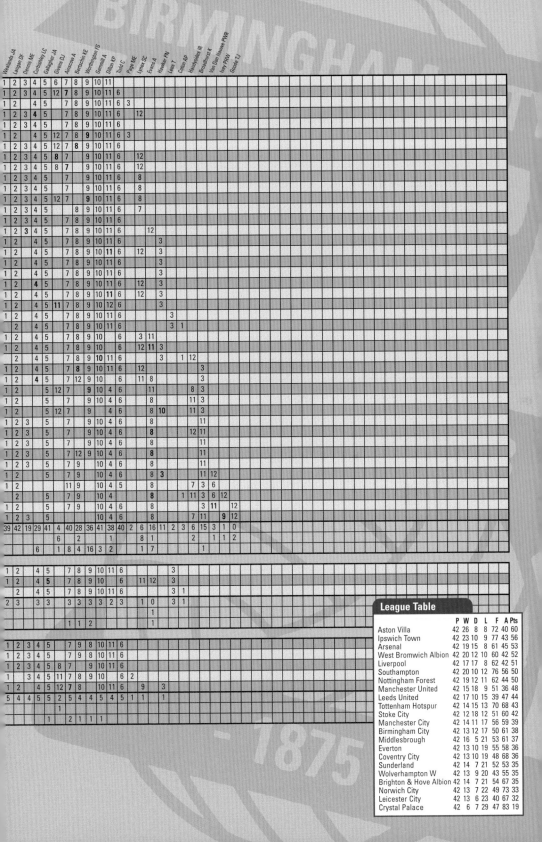

League Table

	P	W	D	L	F	A	Pts
Aston Villa	42	26	8	8	72	40	60
Ipswich Town	42	23	10	9	77	43	56
Arsenal	42	19	15	8	61	45	53
West Bromwich Albion	42	20	12	10	60	42	52
Liverpool	42	17	17	8	62	42	51
Southampton	42	20	10	12	76	56	50
Nottingham Forest	42	19	12	11	62	44	50
Manchester United	42	15	18	9	51	36	48
Leeds United	42	17	10	15	39	47	44
Tottenham Hotspur	42	14	15	13	70	68	43
Stoke City	42	12	18	12	51	60	42
Manchester City	42	14	11	17	56	59	39
Birmingham City	42	13	12	17	50	61	38
Middlesbrough	42	16	5	21	53	61	37
Everton	42	13	10	19	55	58	36
Coventry City	42	13	10	19	48	68	36
Sunderland	42	14	7	21	52	53	35
Wolverhampton W	42	13	9	20	43	55	35
Brighton & Hove Albion	42	14	7	21	54	67	35
Norwich City	42	13	7	22	49	73	33
Leicester City	42	13	6	23	40	67	32
Crystal Palace	42	6	7	29	47	83	19

Division One

Manager: Jim Smith (to February); then Ron Saunders

Did you know that?

Blues' Cyrille Regis scored a hat-trick for West Bromwich Albion in the 3–3 draw at St Andrew's. Frank Worthington netted a late equaliser for Blues.

By holding Tottenham 1–1 at White Hart Lane in April, Blues set a club record of 32 away League games without a win.

Alan Ball (Southampton) and Mark Dennis (Blues) were both sent off in the League game at St Andrew's in October.

In January, Blues beat the Baggies 2–0 to win the *Sports Argus* Arctic Cup Final which was staged on the island of Guernsey in front of 2,658 spectators.

Future Blues striker Paul Moulden scored 289 goals in 40 matches this season while playing for Bolton Lads' Club.

Match No.	Date		Venue	Opponents	Result		Scorers	Attendance
1	Aug	29	A	Everton	L	1-3	Van Mierlo	33,550
2	Sep	1	H	Ipswich Town	D	1-1	Evans	17,321
3		5	H	Nottingham Forest	W	4-3	Broadhurst, Evans, Whatmore 2	19,035
4		12	A	Middlesbrough	L	1-2	Whatmore	13,167
5		19	H	Manchester City	W	3-0	Evans 3	20,109
6		22	A	Arsenal	L	0-1		19,588
7		26	A	Aston Villa	D	0-0		41,098
8	Oct	3	H	West Ham United	D	2-2	Langan, Dillon	22,294
9		10	H	Southampton	W	4-0	Whatmore 2, Worthington 2	16,938
10		17	A	Manchester United	D	1-1	Worthington (pen)	48,800
11		24	A	Stoke City	L	0-1		15,399
12		31	H	West Bromwich Albion	D	3-3	Evans, Gemmill, Worthington (pen)	21,601
13	Nov	7	A	Brighton & Hove Alb.	D	1-1	Evans	18,409
14		21	H	Wolverhampton Wan.	L	0-3		18,673
15		28	A	Swansea City	L	0-1		15,096
16	Dec	5	H	Notts County	W	2-1	Evans 2 (1 pen)	11,914
17	Jan	5	A	Ipswich Town	L	2-3	Broadhurst, Van Mierlo	19,336
18		9	A	Nottingham Forest	L	1-2	Worthington	15,906
19		26	H	Coventry City	D	3-3	Broadhurst, Evans 2	13,023
20		30	A	Manchester City	L	2-4	Worthington 2	28,438
21	Feb	6	H	Middlesbrough	D	0-0		10,715
22		13	A	West Ham United	D	2-2	Van Mierlo, Whatmore	22,512
23		16	H	Sunderland	W	2-0	Van Mierlo, Worthington	10,863
24		20	H	Aston Villa	L	0-1		32,817
25		27	A	Southampton	L	1-3	Worthington (pen)	20,620
26	Mar	6	H	Manchester United	L	0-1		19,637
27		13	H	Stoke City	W	2-1	Hawker, Curbishley	12,018
28		20	A	West Bromwich Albion	D	1-1	Evans	20,936
29		23	H	Tottenham Hotspur	D	0-0		17,708
30		27	H	Brighton & Hove Alb.	W	1-0	Harford	13,234
31		30	A	Liverpool	L	1-3	Harford	24,224
32	Apr	6	H	Everton	L	0-2		12,273
33		10	H	Leeds United	L	0-1		14,497
34		12	A	Sunderland	L	0-2		14,821
35		17	A	Wolverhampton Wan.	D	1-1	Harford	18,964
36		24	H	Swansea City	W	2-1	Broadhurst, Harford	14,973
37		28	A	Tottenham Hotspur	D	1-1	Harford	25,470
38	May	1	A	Notts County	W	4-1	Evans 2, Phillips, Harford	10,704
39		4	H	Arsenal	L	0-1		13,428
40		8	H	Liverpool	L	0-1		26,381
41		12	A	Leeds United	D	3-3	Harford 2, Evans	18,583
42		15	A	Coventry City	W	1-0	Harford	15,925

Appearances
Sub appearances
Goals

FA Cup

R3	Jan	2	H	Ipswich Town	L	2-3	Worthington (pen), Curbishley	17,236

Appearances
Sub appearances
Goals

League Cup

R2	Oct	6	H	Nottingham Forest	L	2-3	Whatmore, Worthington	14,330
R2s		28	A	Nottingham Forest	L	1-2	Evans	16,316

Appearances
Sub appearances
Goals

Player columns (left to right): Weelands JA · Langan DF · Dennis ME · Broadhurst K · Hawker PN · Todd C · Bracken BJPM · Dillon KP · Evans A · Gemmill A · Van Mierlo AWM · Handysides IR · Whatmore N · Worthington FS · Van Den Hauwe PWR · Curbishley LC · Coton AP · Scott BS · Jones R · Phillips LM · Stevenson WB · Limley DIV · MacDowall DJ · Harford MG

	Wee	Lan	Den	Bro	Haw	Tod	Bra	Dil	Eva	Gem	VMi	Han	Wha	Wor	VDH	Cur	Cot	Sco	Jon	Phi	Ste	Lim	Mac	Har
1	2	3	4	5		**7**	8	9	10	11	12													
1	2	3		5		6	**7**	4	9	10	11		8											
1	2	3	5			6	**7**	4	9	10	11	12	8											
1	2	3	5			6	**7**	4	9	10	11	12	8											
1	2	3		5		6	4	**9**			**11**	10	8	12										
	2	3	5			6	4	**9**	10	11	12		8	12										
1	2	3	5			6	**7**	4		10	11	12	8	9										
1	2	3	5			6	**7**	4		10	11	12	8	9										
1	2	3	5			6	**7**	4		10	11		8	9										
	3	5	3		6	**7**	4	8	10	11		8	9	2										
		5	3	6	7		4	8	10	**11**	12		9	2	4									
		5	6	7				8	10	11	3		9	2	4	1								
2	3			6	**7**			8	10	11	12		9	5	4	1								
2	3			6			7		10	**11**	12	8	9	5	4	1								
2	3	6					7	9	10		8			5	4	1								
2	3	5		6			7		10	11		8	9	4		1								
2		5		6	3	7			10	11		8	9	4		1								
2		11		6		4	8	3	7				9	5	10	1								
2	3	10		6		4	8		11				9	5	7									
1	2	3	6				4	8	10		11		9		7		5							
2	**3**	6				7	11	8	9	12	4			5	1	10								
2		6					11	7	8	9	3	4		5	1	10								
2		6					11	7	8	9	3	4		5	1	10								
2		6			10		11	**7**	8	9	3	4		5	1	12								
2		3		**7**	12	9		11				10	6	5			4							
1	2		3	4			7	9	11		8			10	6	5		12						
1	2	10	12	**8**	7	9		11				3	6	5			4							
1	2	10	3		7	9		11				4	6	5		8								
1	2	10	3		7	8		11				4	6	5		4	9							
1	2	10	3		7	**8**		11	12			4	6	5			9							
	2	3			8	10	**7**		11			4	6	5	12		9							
1		2	3		8	10		12	11			4	6	5	7		9							
1		10	3	**11**	8		7					4	6	5	12	2	9							
2		3			8		7	11				5	**6**	1	12		4	9						
2		10	3		8		11				7	12	5	6	1		4	9						
2		3			8		11	7			12	4	6	1		**10**	5	9						
2		3			8		11	7				5	6	1		**10**	4	9						
2		**3**			8		11	7				5	6	1		12	4	9						
2		10	3		8		11	7				5	6	1			4	9						
2		10	3		8		11	7				5	6	1			4	9						
2		3			8	**11**		7	12			5	6	1			**10**	9						
3	36	17	35	19	17	35	29	19	40	8	22	18	30	29	15	14	4	7	12	0	2	12	
	1			1					12	2	1		1	4	1				9				

Substitute appearances:
| | 1 | | | | 1 | | | | | 1 | 15 | 1 | 4 | | | 6 | 9 | | 1 | | | | 9 |

Goals:
	2	3	5		6		7	9	10	11	12		8			**4**	1						
	1	1	1			1	1	1	1				1			1	1						
									1														
								1					1										

	2	3	5		6	7	4		10	11			8	9									
1		5	3	6	**7**	4	8	10	11	12			9	2									
2	1	1	2	1	2	2	1	2	2	0	1	2	1										
									1														
					1				1	1													

Division One

Manager: Ron Saunders

Did you know that?

Kevin Bremner played for five different clubs in four different divisions of the Football League this season. He appeared, in turn, for Colchester United, Blues, Wrexham, Plymouth Argyle and Millwall.

A stray dog on the pitch caused the Manchester City-Blues League game to be held up for 10 minutes.

Paul Mariner (Ipswich Town) was sent-off in the League game at St Andrew's.

During the course of the season Blues scored a winning goal in the 88th minute on three separate occasions…v Arsenal (h) and Coventry City and Sunderland (a).

Blues won the 100th League meeting with Everton by a goal to nil.

Blues reached the final of 'Soccer 6' at the NEC by beating Ipswich and Nottingham Forest.

Former Blues player Jimmy Bloomfield died on 3 April, aged 49.

Match No.	Date		Venue	Opponents	Result		Scorers	Attendance
1	Aug	28	A	Manchester United	L	0-3		48,67
2		31	H	Liverpool	D	0-0		20,97
3	Sep	4	H	Stoke City	L	1-4	Curbishley	14,39
4		8	A	Norwich City	L	1-5	Broadhurst	13,00
5		11	A	West Ham United	L	0-5		18,75
6		18	H	Coventry City	W	1-0	Evans	11,68
7		25	A	Brighton & Hove Alb.	L	0-1		9,84
8	Oct	2	H	Watford	D	1-1	Summerfield	13,87
9		9	H	Luton Town	L	2-3	Langan (pen), Brazier	13,77
10		16	A	Nottingham Forest	D	1-1	Bremner	14,52
11		23	H	Ipswich Town	D	0-0		12,05
12		30	A	Arsenal	D	0-0		20,69
13	Nov	6	H	West Bromwich Albion	W	2-1	Dillon (pen), Blake	18,52
14		13	A	Notts County	D	0-0		9,11
15		20	A	Manchester City	D	0-0		23,17
16		27	H	Sunderland	W	2-1	Evans, Ferguson	12,37
17	Dec	4	A	Everton	D	0-0		13,70
18		11	H	Southampton	L	0-2		11,19
19		18	A	Tottenham Hotspur	L	1-2	Langan	20,94
20		27	H	Aston Villa	W	3-0	Blake, Handysides, Ferguson	43,86
21		29	A	Swansea City	D	0-0		11,84
22	Jan	1	H	Manchester City	D	2-2	Ferguson 2	16,36
23		3	A	Stoke City	D	1-1	Phillips	15,41
24		15	H	Manchester United	L	1-2	Dillon (pen)	19,33
25		22	A	Liverpool	L	0-1		30,98
26	Feb	5	H	West Ham United	W	3-0	Harford, Ferguson, Gayle	12,53
27		26	H	Nottingham Forest	D	1-1	Harford	12,98
28	Mar	5	A	Ipswich Town	L	1-3	Dennis	16,45
29		15	H	Arsenal	W	2-1	Van Den Hauwe, Dillon	11,27
30		19	A	West Bromwich Albion	L	0-2		20,68
31		22	A	Watford	L	1-2	Ferguson	14,22
32		26	H	Notts County	W	3-0	Ferguson 2 (1 pen), Harford	11,74
33	Apr	2	H	Swansea City	D	1-1	Stevenson (pen)	13,59
34		4	A	Aston Villa	L	0-1		40,89
35		9	H	Norwich City	L	0-4		11,73
36		12	H	Luton Town	L	1-3	Hopkins	12,86
37		16	A	Coventry City	W	1-0	Phillips	10,22
38		23	H	Everton	W	1-0	Hopkins	11,04
39		30	A	Sunderland	W	2-1	Harford, Blake (pen)	14,81
40	May	2	A	Brighton & Hove Alb.	D	1-1	Handysides	16,13
41		7	H	Tottenham Hotspur	W	2-0	Harford, Halsall	18,94
42		14	A	Southampton	W	1-0	Harford	20,32
							Appearance	
							Sub appearance	
							Goal	

FA Cup

R3	Jan	8	A	Walsall	D	0-0		12,69
rep		11	H	Walsall	W	1-0	Summerfield	14,77
R4		29	A	Crystal Palace	L	0-1		12,32

R3 replay a.e.t.

							Appearance	
							Sub appearance	
							Goal	

League Cup

R2	Oct	5	A	Shrewsbury Town	D	1-1	Handysides	5,00
R2s		26	H	Shrewsbury Town	W	4-1	Curbishley 2, Evans, Dillon	7,86
R3	Nov	9	H	Derby County	W	3-1	Curbishley, Dillon (pen), Handysides	12,47
R4		30	A	Burnley	L	2-3	Evans, Handysides	10,40

							Appearance	
							Sub appearance	
							Goal	

lyth JA	Langan DF	Hawker PN	Scott GS	Van Den Hauwe PWR	Broadhurst K	Van Mierlo AWM	Carrodus F	Harford MG	Curbishley LC	Francis CE	Evans A	Hagan J	Dillon KP	Dennis ME	Summerfield K	Phillips LM	Stevenson WB	Blake NLG	Whatmore N	Handysides IR	Brazier CJ	Bremner KJ	Mumford WE	Coton AP	Ferguson MJ	Gayle HA	Kuhl M	Halsall M	Hopkins RA
	2	3	4	5	6	7	8	9	10	11																			
	2	3	4	5	6	7	11	9	10		8	12																	
	2	3	4	5	6	7	11	9	10				8																
	2		**4**	5	6		11	9	10			12	8	3	7														
		4		**5**		7	11	9	10			2	8	3	12	6													
	2								10	12	8	7		**3**		6	4	5	9	11									
	2						7		10	12	**8**	3				6	4	5	9	11									
	2			3	6		7		10				8		12		4	5		**11**	9								
	2			3	6				10				8				4	5		11	9	7							
					6		12		**10**			3	7				4	5		11	9	8	2						
				3	6				10				7				4	5		11	9	8	2						
				3	**6**				10		8	2	7				4	5		11	9	12		1					
				3	6				10			2	7				4	5		11	8			1	9				
				3	6				10	8		2	7					5		11	4			1	9				
				3	6				10	12		2	7				4	5		11	8			1	9				
					6				10		8	2	7	3			4	5		11					9				
				3	6				10		8		7				4	5		11	2			1	9				
				3	**6**				10		8	2	7				4	5		11	12			1	9				
	10			3	6			8				2	7	11			4	5		12				1	**9**				
	2			3	6			9	10				7				4	5		11				1	8				
	2			3	6			8	10				7				4	5		11				1	9				
	2				6			8	10			4	7	3				5		11				1	9				
	2				6			9	10				7	3		8	4	5		11				1					
					6			9	10			2	7	3	8		4	5		11				1					
					6			9	10			2	7	3	12			5		**11**	4			1		8			
	2				6			9	10				11	3			4	5						1	8	7			
					6			9	10			2	11	3			4	5						1	8	7			
				12	6			9	**10**			2	11	3			4	5						1	8	7			
				6				9	10			2	11	3			4	5		8				1		7			
				6				9	10			2	11				4	5						1		7	3	8	
								9	10			2	11	3			4	5						1	8	7		6	
				6				9				2		3			4	5						1	8	7		10	11
				6				9				2		3		8	4	5		12				1		**7**		10	11
				6				9				2		3			4	5						1	8	7		10	11
				6	2			9				3				12	4	5		**7**				1	8			10	11
				2	**6**			9				3				12	4	5						1	8	7		10	11
				2				9				4		3		6		5		12				1	**8**	7		10	11
				2	12			9				4		3		6		5		8						**7**		10	11
				2	7			9				4		3		6		5		8				1				10	11
				2				9				4		3		6	12	5		7					**8**			10	11
				7				9				2		3		6	4	5		8				1				10	11
				7				9				2		3		6	4	5		8				1			10		11
4	14	4	4	30	28	4	7	29	30	2	7	30	27	23	2	11	30	37	2	26	10	3	2	28	20	13	2	12	11
				1	1		1			3		2			3	2	1			3	1	1							
	2			1	1			6	1		2		3	1	1	2	1	3		2	1	1			8	1		1	2

lyth JA	Langan DF	Hawker PN	Scott GS	Van Den Hauwe PWR	Broadhurst K	Van Mierlo AWM	Carrodus F	Harford MG	Curbishley LC	Francis CE	Evans A	Hagan J	Dillon KP	Dennis ME	Summerfield K	Phillips LM	Stevenson WB	Blake NLG	Whatmore N	Handysides IR	Brazier CJ	Bremner KJ	Mumford WE	Coton AP	Ferguson MJ	Gayle HA	Kuhl M	Halsall M	Hopkins RA
					6			**9**	10			2	7	3		8	4	5		11	12			1					
					6				10			2	7	3	12		4	5		11	**8**			1	9				
					6			9	10			2	7	3	**11**			5		12	4			1		8			
					3			2	3			3	3	3	1	1	2	3		2	2			3	1	1			
															1					1	1								
															1														

lyth JA	Langan DF	Hawker PN	Scott GS	Van Den Hauwe PWR	Broadhurst K	Van Mierlo AWM	Carrodus F	Harford MG	Curbishley LC	Francis CE	Evans A	Hagan J	Dillon KP	Dennis ME	Summerfield K	Phillips LM	Stevenson WB	Blake NLG	Whatmore N	Handysides IR	Brazier CJ	Bremner KJ	Mumford WE	Coton AP	Ferguson MJ	Gayle HA	Kuhl M	Halsall M	Hopkins RA
	2			3	6		12		10				8		**7**		4	5		11	9								
				3	6				10		8		7				4	5		11	9		2						
				3	6				10			2	7				4	5		11	8			1	9				
					6				10		8	**2**	7			12	4	5		11	3			1	9				
	1			3	4		0		4		2	2	4		1	0	4	4		4	4		1	2	2				
							1									1													
									3		2		2							3									

League Table

	P	W	D	L	F	A	Pts
Liverpool	42	24	10	8	87	37	82
Watford	42	22	5	15	74	57	71
Manchester United	42	19	13	10	56	38	70
Tottenham Hotspur	42	20	9	13	65	50	69
Nottingham Forest	42	20	9	13	62	50	69
Aston Villa	42	21	5	16	62	50	68
Everton	42	18	10	14	66	48	64
West Ham United	42	20	4	18	68	62	64
Ipswich Town	42	15	13	14	64	50	58
Arsenal	42	16	10	16	58	56	58
West Bromwich Albion	42	15	12	15	51	49	57
Southampton	42	15	12	15	54	58	57
Stoke City	42	16	9	17	53	64	57
Norwich City	42	14	12	16	52	58	54
Notts County	42	15	7	20	55	71	52
Sunderland	42	12	14	16	48	61	50
Birmingham City	42	12	14	16	40	55	50
Luton Town	42	12	13	17	65	84	49
Coventry City	42	13	9	20	48	59	48
Manchester City	42	13	8	21	47	70	47
Swansea City	42	10	11	21	51	69	41
Brighton & Hove Albion	42	9	13	20	38	68	40

1983-84

Division One

Manager: Ron Saunders

Match No.	Date		Venue	Opponents	Result		Scorers	Attendance
1	Aug	27	A	West Ham United	L	0-4		19,72
2		30	A	Notts County	L	1-2	Harford	11,03
3	Sep	3	H	Watford	W	2-0	Hopkins, Halsall	11,93
4		6	H	Stoke City	W	1-0	Blake (pen)	13,72
5		10	A	Wolverhampton Wan.	D	1-1	Wright (pen)	15,93
6		17	H	Ipswich Town	W	1-0	Gayle	13,15
7		24	A	Everton	D	1-1	Gayle	15,25
8	Oct	1	H	Leicester City	W	2-1	Harford, Rees	15,21
9		15	A	Aston Villa	L	0-1		39,31
10		22	H	Tottenham Hotspur	L	0-1		18,93
11		29	A	West Bromwich Albion	W	2-1	Harford, Gayle	20,10
12	Nov	5	H	Coventry City	L	1-2	Blake	16,16
13		12	A	Luton Town	D	1-1	Hopkins	11,11
14		19	A	Queen's Park Rangers	L	1-2	Harford	10,82
15		26	H	Sunderland	L	0-1		11,94
16	Dec	3	A	Liverpool	L	0-1		24,79
17		10	H	Norwich City	L	0-1		9,97
18		17	A	Southampton	L	1-2	Stevenson	15,24
19		26	H	Nottingham Forest	L	1-2	Rogers	14,48
20		27	A	Arsenal	D	1-1	Hopkins	25,64
21		31	A	Watford	L	0-1		14,40
22	Jan	2	H	Everton	L	0-2		10,00
23		14	A	West Ham United	W	3-0	Harford, Hopkins, Halsall	10,33
24		21	A	Ipswich Town	W	2-1	Harford, Butcher (og)	12,88
25	Feb	4	A	Leicester City	W	3-2	Peake (og), Wright (pen), Gayle	13,77
26		7	H	Manchester United	D	2-2	Wright (pen), Hopkins	19,99
27		11	H	Wolverhampton Wan.	D	0-0		14,31
28		25	A	Tottenham Hotspur	W	1-0	Harford	23,56
29		28	H	West Bromwich Albion	W	2-1	Broadhurst, Rees	16,78
30	Mar	3	A	Coventry City	W	1-0	Gayle	13,69
31		17	A	Stoke City	L	1-2	Gayle	13,50
32		20	H	Luton Town	D	1-1	Wright (pen)	9,59
33		24	H	Notts County	D	0-0		9,04
34		31	H	Aston Villa	W	2-1	Stevenson, Gayle	23,99
35	Apr	7	A	Manchester United	L	0-1		39,89
36		14	H	Queen's Park Rangers	L	0-2		10,25
37		21	A	Nottingham Forest	L	1-5	Harford	15,32
38		23	H	Arsenal	D	1-1	Kuhl	11,18
39		28	A	Sunderland	L	1-2	Wright (pen)	13,06
40	May	5	H	Liverpool	D	0-0		18,81
41		7	A	Norwich City	D	1-1	Gayle	12,11
42		12	H	Southampton	D	0-0		16,44

Appearance
Sub appearance
Two own-goals   Goa

FA Cup

R3	Jan	7	A	Sheffield United	D	1-1	Wright (pen)	17,20
R3		10	H	Sheffield United	W	2-0	Wright (pen), Harford	10,88
R4		28	A	Sunderland	W	2-1	Harford, Kuhl	21,22
R5	Feb	18	H	West Ham United	W	3-0	Wright (pen), Hopkins, Rees	29,57
R6	Mar	10	H	Watford	L	1-3	Terry (og)	40,22

Appearance
One own-goal   Goa

League Cup

R2	Oct	5	A	Derby County	W	3-0	og (Watson), Rees, Gayle	13,1
R2s		25	H	Derby County	W	4-0	Harford 3, Gayle	7,78
R3	Nov	8	H	Notts County	D	2-2	Handysides, Phillips	10,48
rep		22	A	Notts County	D	0-0		8,2
rep2		29	H	Notts County	D	0-0		9,6
rep3	Dec	5	A	Notts County	W	3-1	Harford, Hopkins 2	7,3
R4		20	H	Liverpool	D	1-1	Harford	17,4
rep		22	A	Liverpool	L	0-3		11,6

R3 replay and replay 2 a.e.t.

Appearance
Sub appearance
One own-goal   Goa

Lobon AP	Hagan J	Stevenson WB	Blake NLG	Wright W	Broadhurst K	Hampden IR	Phillips LM	Harford MG	Van Den Hauwe PWR	Rees AA	Halsall M	McCarrick MB	Gayle HA	Mumford WE	Rogers KP	Kuhl M	Muir LJ	Linton I	Roberts BJF	Kendall MI
1	2	3	4	5		7		9	10	11	12									
1	2		4	5	6	12	8	9	3	11	7	10								
1	2		4	5	6		8	9	3	11	7	10								
1	2		4	5	6		8	9	3	11	7	10	12							
1	2		4	5	6		8	9	3	11	7	10		12						
	12	4	5	6		8	9	3		11	10	7	2							
	12	4	5	6	6	8	9	3		11	10	7	2							
1	2		4	5		8	9	3	11	6	10	7								
1	2	12	4	5	6		9	3	11	8	10	7								
1	2	6	4	5		12	9	3	11	8	10	7								
1	2	6	4	5		8	9	3	11	10	7									
1	2	6	4	5		8	9	3	11	10	7									
1	2	6	4	5		8	9	3	11	7	12									
1	2	6	4	5	10	8	3	11		7	9									
1	2	6	4	5	10	8	9	3	11	7										
1	2	6	4	5	10	8	9	3	11	7										
1	2		5		8	9	3	11	6	7	4	10								
1	2	11	4	5		8	9	3	6	7	10									
1	2	6	4	5		8	9	3	7	11	12									
1	2		4	5		9	3	11	7	12	10	8	6							
1	2	8	4	5		9	3	11	7	12	10	6								
	6	4	5	3		9	8	11	7	10	2									
	8	4	5	6	12	9	3	11	7	2	10									
	2	4	5	6		9	3	11	10	7	8									
	4	5	6		9	3	11	12	10	2	7	8								
	4	5	6		9	3	11	10	2	7	8									
	12	4	5	6		9	3	11	10	2	7	8								
	8	4	5	6	10	9	3	11	7	2										
6	10	4	5		11	9	3		7	2	8									
12	10	4	5	6		9	3	11	2	7	8									
12	10	4	5	6		9	3	11	2	7	8									
3		4	5	6		9	10	11	12	7	8	2								
3		4	5	6		9	8	11	10	7	2									
3		5	6		9	8	11	10	12	7	4	2								
3	6	4			8	11	10	9	7	5	2									
3	6	4	5		9	8	10	11	7	12	2									
12	8	4	5	6		9	3	11	10	7	2									
11	8	4	5	12		9	3		10	7	6	2								
4		5	6		9	3	11	2	7	10	12	8	1							
4		5		9	3	11	2	7	10	8	6									
2		4	5		9	3	11	7	10	8	6									
2		4	5		9	3	11	12	7	10	8	6								
2		4	5		3	11	9	6	7	10	8									
30	21	39	40	22	4	18	39	42	32	22	21	32	3	8	20	1	3	11	1	
3	4		1	1	2			3		3	1	2	1	2		1				
	2	2	5	1		8		5	2	2		8		1	1					

Lobon AP	Hagan J	Stevenson WB	Blake NLG	Wright W	Broadhurst K	Hampden IR	Phillips LM	Harford MG	Van Den Hauwe PWR	Rees AA	Halsall M	McCarrick MB	Gayle HA	Mumford WE	Rogers KP	Kuhl M	Muir LJ	Linton I	Roberts BJF	Kendall MI
	2	4	5	6		9	3	11	10	7	8									
	2	4	5	6		9	3	11	10	7	8									
	4	5	6		9	3	11	10	2	7	8									
10	4	5	6		9	3	11	7	2	8										
10	4	5	6		9	3	11	2	7	8										
4	5	5	5		5	5	5	1	3	3	4	5								
3			2			1	1		1											

2	12	4	5		8	9	3	11	6	10		7								
2	6	4	5		8	9	3	11		10		7								
2	6	4	5	9	8		3	11		10		7								
2	6	4	5		8	9	3	11		12		7			10					
2	6	4	5		8	9	3	11				7				10				
2	6	4	5		8	9	3	11	6			7			10					
2	6	4	5		8	9	3		11	12	7			10						
2	6	4	5		8	9	3	11	10		7									
8	6	8	8		1	8	7	8	7	3	4	0	8		3	1				
	1							1	1											

League Table

	P	W	D	L	F	A	Pts
Liverpool	42	22	14	6	73	32	80
Southampton	42	22	11	9	66	38	77
Nottingham Forest	42	22	8	12	76	45	74
Manchester United	42	20	14	8	71	41	74
Queen's Park Rangers	42	22	7	13	67	37	73
Arsenal	42	18	9	15	74	60	63
Everton	42	16	14	12	44	42	62
Tottenham Hotspur	42	17	10	15	64	65	61
West Ham United	42	17	9	16	60	55	60
Aston Villa	42	17	9	16	59	61	60
Watford	42	16	9	17	68	77	57
Ipswich Town	42	15	8	19	55	57	53
Sunderland	42	13	13	16	42	53	52
Norwich City	42	12	15	15	48	49	51
Leicester City	42	13	12	17	65	68	51
Luton Town	42	14	9	19	53	66	51
West Bromwich Albion	42	14	9	19	48	62	51
Stoke City	42	13	11	18	44	63	50
Coventry City	42	13	11	18	57	77	50
Birmingham City	42	12	12	18	39	50	48
Notts County	42	10	11	21	50	72	41
Wolverhampton W	42	6	11	25	27	80	29

Division Two

Manager: Ron Saunders

Defender Pat Van den Hauwe was booked after just 22 seconds (for a foul on future Blues player Mark Ward) in the away game at Oldham in August.

Billy Wright's 23rd-minute penalty against Middlesbrough in December was the first scored at St Andrew's for 510 minutes!

Blues clinched promotion with two games still remaining.

Unfortunately the last home game of the season against Leeds United was marred by rioting which resulted in the death of a boy when a brick wall collapsed on him. A total of 96 police officers were also injured in the incident and the second half began 30 minutes late.

Blues' teenagers were defeated over two legs in the FA Youth Cup semi-final by Newcastle United.

Match No.	Date		Venue	Opponents	Result		Scorers	Attendance
1	Aug	25	A	Oldham Athletic	W	1-0	Clements (og)	5,30?
2	Sep	1	H	Wimbledon	W	4-2	Clarke 2, Ferguson, Hopkins	10,44
3		4	H	Fulham	W	1-0	Clarke	6,03
4		8	A	Crystal Palace	W	2-0	Clarke, Hopkins	6,52
5		15	H	Carlisle United	W	2-0	Clarke, Harford	11,74
6		18	H	Portsmouth	L	0-1		18,04
7		22	A	Wolverhampton Wan.	W	2-0	Hopkins, Kuhl	16,69
8		29	H	Huddersfield Town	W	1-0	Hopkins	11,48
9	Oct	6	A	Brighton & Hove Alb.	L	0-2		13,69
10		13	H	Blackburn Rovers	L	0-2		12,75
11		20	A	Notts County	W	3-1	Clarke 2, Harford	5,78
12		27	H	Oxford United	D	0-0		20,42
13	Nov	3	H	Shrewsbury Town	D	0-0		9,80
14		10	A	Manchester City	L	0-1		25,36
15		17	A	Charlton Athletic	L	1-2	Morley	4,85
16		24	H	Barnsley	D	0-0		9,50
17	Dec	1	A	Cardiff City	W	2-1	Morley 2	5,05
18		8	H	Middlesbrough	W	3-2	Wright (pen), Saxby (og), Rees	8,00
19		15	A	Leeds United	W	1-0	Clarke	15,85
20		22	A	Wimbledon	W	2-1	Geddis 2	3,67
21		26	H	Grimsby Town	W	2-1	Platnauer, Geddis	14,18
22		29	H	Fulham	D	2-2	Clarke, Hopkins	11,83
23	Jan	1	A	Sheffield United	W	4-3	Clarke, Hopkins, Geddis, West (og)	16,57
24	Feb	2	A	Huddersfield Town	W	1-0	Geddis	7,46
25		23	A	Shrewsbury Town	L	0-1		7,17
26	Mar	2	A	Oxford United	W	3-0	Clarke 2, Geddis	11,58
27		5	H	Oldham Athletic	L	0-1		10,48
28		9	H	Notts County	W	2-1	Clarke, Hopkins	9,07
29		12	A	Carlisle United	L	1-2	Clarke	4,09
30		16	A	Blackburn Rovers	L	1-2	Rees	10,55
31		19	H	Manchester City	D	0-0		18,00
32		23	H	Brighton & Hove Alb.	D	1-1	Hopkins	8,98
33		30	H	Wolverhampton Wan.	W	1-0	Geddis	10,23
34	Apr	5	A	Grimsby Town	L	0-1		6,93
35		8	H	Sheffield United	W	4-1	Daly, Clarke 2, Kennedy	10,23
36		13	A	Portsmouth	W	3-1	Geddis 3	23,99
37		16	H	Crystal Palace	W	3-0	Clarke, Geddis, Kennedy	10,72
38		20	H	Charlton Athletic	W	2-1	Wright (pen), Kennedy	10,69
39		27	A	Barnsley	W	1-0	Geddis	6,75
40	May	4	A	Cardiff City	W	2-0	Hopkins, Kennedy	15,86
41		6	A	Middlesbrough	D	0-0		7,84
42		11	H	Leeds United	W	1-0	Kuhl	24,87

Appearance
Sub appearance
Three own-goals   Goa

FA Cup

R3	Jan	5	H	Norwich City	D	0-0		12,94
rep		23	A	Norwich City	D	1-1	Wright	11,88
rep2		26	H	Norwich City	D	1-1	Geddis	11,75
rep3		28	A	Norwich City	L	0-1		12,39

Replay and replay 2 a.e.t.   Appearance
Sub appearance
Goa

League Cup

R2	Sep	25	H	Plymouth Argyle	W	4-1	Clarke, Hopkins, Harford, Rees	7,96
R2s	Oct	9	A	Plymouth Argyle	W	1-0	Clarke	4,65
R3		30	H	West Bromwich Albion	D	0-0		17,6?
rep	Nov	7	A	West Bromwich Albion	L	1-3	Shearer	16,71

Appearance
Sub appearance
Goa

Player columns (left to right):
Cotton AP, Roberts BLF, Van Den Hauwe PWR, Wright W, Hagan J, Daly GA, Stevenson WB, Clarke W, Ferguson MJ, Gorman PA, Hopkins RA, Kuhl M, Armstrong KC, Harford MG, Halsall M, McDonough JM, Bremner DG, Seaman DA, Jones MAW, Rees AA, Shearer PA, Ranson R, Linford JR, Morley WA, Platnauer NR, Gleeds D, Russell GF, Prudhoe M, Kennedy AJ, Storer S, Brown I

Cot	Rob	VDH	Wri	Hag	Dal	Ste	Cla	Fer	Gor	Hop	Kuh	Arm	Har	Hal	McD	Bre	Sea	Jon	Ree	She	Ran	Lin	Mor	Pla	Gle	Rus	Pru	Ken	Sto	Bro
1	2	3	4	5	6	7	8	9	10	11																				
1	2	3	4	5	6	7	10	9	8	11	12																			
1	2	3	4	12	6		8		10	11	7	5	9																	
1	2	3	4		6		8		10	11	7	5	9																	
	2	3	4		6				11	7	5	9	10																	
	2	3	4	12	6		8		11	7	5	9	10																	
1		3	4	2	6		8	10	11	7	5	9	12																	
	2		4	3	6		8		11	7	5	9		1	10															
	3		4	7	6				12	5	9			10	1	2	11													
	2		4	3	6		8		11	7	5	9		10	1															
	2		4	3	6		8		11		5	9		10	1	7														
	2		4	3	6		8		11		5	9		10	1	7														
	2		4	3	6		8		11	5	9			10	1	7		12												
		4	3				8		2	11	7	5	9		10	1		12	6											
6		4	3				8			7	5			10	1		12			2	9	11								
	2		4	3			8		9	6	5			10	1					7	12	11								
	3		4	6			8		11		5			10	1		9			2	7									
	3		4	6			8		7		5			10	1		9			2		11								
	3		4		6		8		11		5			10	1		9			2			7							
	3		4		6		8		11		5			9	1					2			7	10						
	3		4	12	7		8		11		5			9	1					2			6	10						
	3		4		7		8		11		5			9	1					2			6	10						
	3		4	12	6		8		11		5			9	1					2			7	10						
	3		4	12	6		8		11		5			9	1					2			7	10						
	3		4	5			8		11	6				9	1					2			7	10						
	3		4	5			8		11	6				9	1	7				2				10						
	3		4	12			8		11	6	5			9	1	7				2			10							
	3		4	12			8		11		5			9	1	6		10	2		7									
	3		4	6			8		11		5			9	1			12	2		7	10								
	3		4					11		6	5			9	1	12	8		2		7	10								
	3		4		8			11		6	5				1	7			2			10	9							
	3		4		12	8	9	11		6	5				1	7			2			10								
	3		4		7	6	8	11						9	1				2			10								
	3		4	5	7	6	8	11						9	1		12		2			10								
	3		4	5	7		8	11		6				9					2					1	10					
	3		4		7		8	11		6	5			9	1				2			10					12			
	3		4	9	7		8	11		6	5			1					2			10					12			
	3		4	8	7		9	11		6	5			1		12			2			10								
	3		4		7		8	11		6	5			9	1				2			10					12			
	3		4		7		8	11		6	5			9	1				2			10								
	3		4	12	7		8	11		6	5			1					2		9	10								
	3		4	7			8	11		6	5			9	1				2			10								
41	6	42	21	29	6	40	2	6	39	25	36	12	2	1	30	33	9	5	2	28	1	4	11	18	1	1	4			
			8	1					2		1			1	4	2	1			3										
	2		1	17	1		9	2		2				2				3	1	12			4							

	3		4	5	6		8		11					9	1				2			7	10							
	3		4	12	6		8		11		5			9	1				2			7	10							
	3		4	12	6		8		11		5			9	1				2			7	10							
	3		4		6		8		11		5			9	1				2			7	10							
	4		4	1	4		4			4	3			4	4				4			4	4							
			2																											
		1																					1							

	3		4	3	6		8		11	7	5	9	10							12					1					
	2		4	3			8			7	5	9	6		10	12								1		11				
	2		4	3	6		8			11	5	9		10	7							1								
2		4	3				6	11	7	5			10		8	9								1		12				
4		4	4	2		3		1	2	4	4	3	2		3		1	1	1					4	1	0				
														1	1											1				
				2				1				1			1	1														

League Table

	P	W	D	L	F	A	Pts
Oxford United	42	25	9	8	84	36	84
Birmingham City	42	25	7	10	59	33	82
Manchester City	42	21	11	10	66	40	74
Portsmouth	42	20	14	8	69	50	74
Blackburn Rovers	42	21	10	11	66	41	73
Brighton & Hove Albion	42	20	12	10	54	34	72
Leeds United	42	19	12	11	66	43	69
Shrewsbury Town	42	18	11	13	66	53	65
Fulham	42	19	8	15	68	64	65
Grimsby Town	42	18	8	16	72	64	62
Barnsley	42	14	16	12	42	42	58
Wimbledon	42	16	10	16	71	75	58
Huddersfield Town	42	15	10	17	52	64	55
Oldham Athletic	42	15	8	19	49	67	53
Crystal Palace	42	12	12	18	46	65	48
Carlisle United	42	13	8	21	50	67	47
Charlton Athletic	42	11	12	19	51	63	45
Sheffield United	42	10	14	18	54	66	44
Middlesbrough	42	10	10	22	41	57	40
Notts County	42	10	7	25	45	73	37
Cardiff City	42	9	8	25	47	79	35
Wolverhampton W	42	8	9	25	37	79	33

BIRMINGHAM - 1875

1985-86

Division One

Manager: Ron Saunders (to January); then John Bond

Match No.	Date	Venue	Opponents	Result		Scorers	Attendance
1	Aug 17	H	West Ham United	W	1-0	Hopkins	11,164
2	20	A	Watford	L	0-3		14,029
3	24	A	Chelsea	L	0-2		16,534
4	26	H	Oxford United	W	3-1	Kennedy, Briggs (og), Hopkins	10,575
5	31	A	Everton	L	1-4	Kennedy	28,066
6	Sep 3	H	Manchester City	W	1-0	Geddis	11,714
7	7	H	Aston Villa	D	0-0		24,971
8	14	A	Ipswich Town	W	1-0	Geddis	11,528
9	21	H	Leicester City	W	2-1	Geddis 2	9,834
10	28	A	Queen's Park Rangers	L	1-3	Armstrong	8,411
11	Oct 5	H	Sheffield Wednesday	L	0-2		11,717
12	19	A	West Bromwich Albion	L	1-2	Kennedy	13,553
13	26	H	Coventry City	L	0-1		9,267
14	Nov 2	A	Luton Town	L	0-2		8,550
15	9	H	Newcastle United	L	0-1		8,162
16	16	A	Southampton	L	0-1		12,167
17	23	H	Liverpool	L	0-2		15,062
18	30	A	Arsenal	D	0-0		16,673
19	Dec 7	H	Watford	L	1-2	Wright (pen)	7,048
20	14	A	West Ham United	L	0-2		17,481
21	21	H	Chelsea	L	1-2	Platnauer	10,594
22	26	H	Nottingham Forest	L	0-1		10,376
23	28	A	Manchester City	D	1-1	Geddis	24,955
24	Jan 1	A	Manchester United	L	0-1		43,099
25	11	H	Ipswich Town	L	0-1		6,856
26	18	H	Everton	L	0-2		10,502
27	Feb 1	A	Oxford United	W	1-0	Clarke	9,066
28	8	H	West Bromwich Albion	L	0-1		11,514
29	16	A	Coventry City	D	4-4	Kuhl, Kennedy 2, Whitton	14,356
30	Mar 1	H	Queen's Park Rangers	W	2-0	Clarke (pen), Hopkins	7,093
31	8	A	Sheffield Wednesday	L	1-5	Geddis	17,491
32	12	A	Leicester City	L	2-4	Clarke, Whitton	8,451
33	15	H	Tottenham Hotspur	L	1-2	Kennedy	9,394
34	22	A	Aston Villa	W	3-0	Clarke 2, Whitton	26,694
35	29	H	Manchester United	D	1-1	Handysides	22,551
36	31	A	Nottingham Forest	L	0-3		12,130
37	Apr 6	H	Luton Town	L	0-2		8,836
38	12	A	Newcastle United	L	1-4	Hopkins	20,334
39	16	H	Tottenham Hotspur	L	0-2		9,351
40	19	H	Southampton	L	0-2		5,835
41	26	A	Liverpool	L	0-5		42,025
42	May 3	H	Arsenal	L	0-1		6,239

Appearance
Sub appearance
One own-goal   Goal

FA Cup

R3	Jan 14	H	Altrincham	L	1-2	Hopkins	6,633

Appearance
Sub appearance
Goal

League Cup

R2	Sep 24	A	Bristol Rovers	W	3-2	Wright 2 (2 pens), Geddis	4,331
R2s	Oct 8	H	Bristol Rovers	W	2-1	og (Tanner), Kennedy	3,686
R3	29	H	Southampton	D	1-1	Kennedy	4,836
rep	Nov 6	A	Southampton	L	0-3		9,086

Appearance
Sub appearance
One own-goal   Goal

Appearance and goalscoring grid (player columns):

Seaman DA · Ranson R · Roberts BLF · Wright W · Armstrong KC · Daly GA · Bremner DG · Clarke W · Jones MAW · Geddis D · Hopkins RA · Kuhl M · Hagan J · Kennedy AJ · Dickie JA · Premsier NR · Jenkins LR · Ranson W · Rees AA · Russell GR · Gorton WF · Whitton SP · Smalley MA · Handysides IR · Frain JW · Storer SJ

Sea	Ran R	Rob	Wri	Arm	Daly	Bre	Cla	Jon	Ged	Hop	Kuhl	Hag	Ken	Dic	Pre	Jen	Ran W	Rees	Rus	Gor	Whi	Sma	Han	Fra	Sto
1	2	3	**5**	6	7	8	9	10	11	12															
1	2	3	4	6	7	8	**9**	10	11	12	5														
1	2		4	5		7	8	3	**10**	11	6		9	12											
1	2		4	5		7	8	3	10	11	6		9												
1	2		4	5		7	8	3	10	11	6		9												
1	**2**	12	4	5		7	8	3	10	11	6		9												
1		2	4	5			8	3	10	11	6		9	7											
1	2	8	4				3	10	11	**6**	5	9	9	7	12										
1	2	8	4	5		7		3	10	11			9	6											
1		2	4	5		7	8	3	10	11			9	**6**	12										
1		2	4	5		7		**3**	10	11	8	6	9		12										
1	2		4	5		7		3		11	6		9	12	10	**8**									
1	2	7	4	**5**				3	10	11	6	8	9		12										
1	2	8		5		7		3	10	11	6	4	9												
1	2	3		5		7	8		10			4	9	6		11									
1	2	3	7	5			8		10		6	4	9	12		11									
1	2	3	8	5		7			10	11	6	4	9				12								
1	2	3	6	5		7	8	**9**		11	12	4	9	8											
1	2	3	6	5		7		**10**		11	12	4	9	8											
1	2	3	6			7		**10**		5	4														
1	2	3				7	**8**	11	12		4	9													
1	2	3				7	**8**			11	6	4	9	12					10	5					
1	2					7	8			11	6	4							10	5					
1		2	3	9		7	8			11	6	4							10	5					
1	2	**3**	9			7	8			11	6	4		12					4	5	10				
1	2		5			7	8			11	6		9	3					4	10					
1	2		5				8			11	6	7		3						4	10	9			
1		2					8	**9**	11	6	4	12	3	7						5	10				
1		2					8	**9**	11	6	4		3	7						5	10	12			
1	6	**2**	10				8		11	12	4		3	9						5			7		
1		2					8		11	6	4	**10**	3	9						5		12	7		
2	37	31	29	22	2	32	28	19	25	38	33	31	27	18	12	1	2	4	0	8	5	7	6	1	2
	2							1		4		5	5	5		4	1				1		2		
		1	1				5		6	4	1		6		1				3			1			

League Table

	P	W	D	L	F	A	Pts
Liverpool	42	26	10	6	89	37	88
Everton	42	26	8	8	87	41	86
West Ham United	42	26	6	10	74	40	84
Manchester United	42	22	10	10	70	36	76
Sheffield Wednesday	42	21	10	11	63	54	73
Chelsea	42	20	11	11	57	56	71
Arsenal	42	20	9	13	49	47	69
Nottingham Forest	42	19	11	12	69	53	68
Luton Town	42	18	12	12	61	44	66
Tottenham Hotspur	42	19	8	15	74	52	65
Newcastle United	42	17	12	13	67	72	63
Watford	42	16	11	15	69	62	59
Queen's Park Rangers	42	15	7	20	53	64	52
Southampton	42	12	10	20	51	62	46
Manchester City	42	11	12	19	43	57	45
Aston Villa	42	10	14	18	51	67	44
Coventry City	42	11	10	21	48	71	43
Oxford United	42	10	12	20	62	80	42
Leicester City	42	10	12	20	54	76	42
Ipswich Town	42	11	8	23	32	55	41
Birmingham City	42	8	5	29	30	73	29
West Bromwich Albion	42	4	12	26	35	89	24

1986-87

Division Two

Manager: John Bond (to May)

Match No.	Date		Venue	Opponents	Result		Scorers	Attendance
1	Aug	23	A	Stoke City	W	2-0	Hemming (og), Whitton	11,548
2		25	H	Bradford City	W	2-1	Mortimer 2	7,003
3		30	H	Derby County	D	1-1	Clarke	12,209
4	Sep	3	A	Brighton & Hove Alb.	L	0-2		9,955
5		6	A	Sheffield United	D	1-1	Bremner	10,297
6		13	H	Huddersfield Town	D	1-1	Clarke	6,934
7		20	A	Hull City	L	2-3	Clarke 2	6,851
8		27	H	Ipswich Town	D	2-2	Clarke 2	7,227
9	Oct	4	H	Barnsley	D	1-1	Kennedy	6,427
10		11	A	Portsmouth	L	0-2		11,252
11		18	H	Crystal Palace	W	4-1	Overson, Bremner, Whitton, Clarke	5,987
12		25	A	Sunderland	L	0-2		15,533
13	Nov	1	A	West Bromwich Albion	L	2-3	Clarke, Lynex	15,029
14		8	H	Oldham Athletic	L	1-3	Clarke (pen)	6,082
15		15	A	Millwall	W	2-0	Rees, Clarke	4,795
16		21	H	Leeds United	W	2-1	Bremner, Clarke	7,863
17		29	A	Grimsby Town	W	1-0	Whitton	4,734
18	Dec	6	H	Blackburn Rovers	D	1-1	Clarke	6,428
19		13	A	Shrewsbury Town	L	0-1		4,797
20		19	H	Sheffield United	W	2-1	Clarke 2 (1 pen)	5,007
21		26	A	Reading	D	2-2	Clarke, Lynex	7,662
22		29	H	Millwall	D	1-1	Mortimer	8,006
23	Jan	1	H	Plymouth Argyle	W	3-2	Kuhl, Mortimer, Clarke	8,696
24		3	A	Bradford City	D	0-0		8,679
25		24	H	Stoke City	D	0-0		10,643
26	Feb	7	A	Derby County	D	2-2	Bremner, Whitton	16,836
27		14	H	Brighton & Hove Alb.	W	2-0	Rees 2	6,439
28		21	A	Ipswich Town	L	0-3		10,169
29		28	H	Hull City	D	0-0		6,858
30	Mar	3	A	Huddersfield Town	D	2-2	Rees, Whitton	5,177
31		14	H	Crystal Palace	L	0-6		6,171
32		21	H	Portsmouth	L	0-1		9,823
33		28	A	Barnsley	D	2-2	Whitton, Wigley	4,688
34		31	H	Sunderland	W	2-0	Whitton, North	5,563
35	Apr	4	A	Oldham Athletic	D	2-2	Whitton, Linighan (og)	6,555
36		12	H	West Bromwich Albion	L	0-1		11,158
37		18	A	Plymouth Argyle	D	0-0		13,372
38		20	H	Reading	D	1-1	Frain	5,427
39		25	A	Leeds United	L	0-4		19,133
40	May	2	H	Grimsby Town	W	1-0	Whitton	4,457
41		5	A	Blackburn Rovers	L	0-1		5,622
42		9	H	Shrewsbury Town	L	0-2		7,724

Appearances

Sub appearances

Two own-goals   Goals

FA Cup

R3	Jan	10	A	Ipswich Town	W	1-0	Mortimer	11,616
R4		31	A	Walsall	L	0-1		14,811

Appearances

Goals

League Cup

R2	Sep	23	A	Middlesbrough	D	2-2	Whitton, Mortimer	9,412
R2s	Oct	7	H	Middlesbrough	W	3-2	Whitton, Clarke 2	4,978
R3		29	A	Tottenham Hotspur	L	0-5		15,542

R2s a.e.t.

Appearances

Sub appearances

Goals

Appearances & goals grid (player columns, left to right):

1	Hansbury R
2	Jones MAW
3	Dicks JA
4	Hagen J
5	Dawson VD
6	Kuhl M
7	Bremner DG
8	Rees AA
9	Whitton SP
10	Mortimer DG
11	Hopkins RA
12	Clarke LW
13	Handyside IR
14	Roberts BLF
15	Stace SJ
16	Peer D
17	Goda RE
18	Ranson R
19	Kennedy AJ
20	Williams TE
21	Geddis D
22	Russell MC
23	Lynex SC
24	Bird AL
25	Hart PA
26	Timlinson P
27	North MW
28	Wigley S
29	Ashley KM
30	Frain JW

League appearances (totals row), in the same column order:

31, 5, 33, 12, 34, 23, 40, 27, 39, 33, 3, 24, 19, 23, 3, 1, 5, 16, 5, 29, 2, 3, 10, 6, 1, 11, 4, 11, 7, 2

Substitute appearances row: 1 · · · · · · · · · · · 3 · 1 1 3 1 · 1 · 4 · · · · 2 · 1 1 ·

Goals row: · · 1 1 4 4 9 4 · 16 · · · · · · · 1 · · · · 2 · · · 1 1 · ·

League Table

	P	W	D	L	F	A	Pts
Derby County	42	25	9	8	64	38	84
Portsmouth	42	23	9	10	53	28	78
Oldham Athletic	42	22	9	11	65	44	75
Leeds United	42	19	11	12	58	44	68
Ipswich Town	42	17	13	12	59	43	64
Crystal Palace	42	19	5	18	51	53	62
Plymouth Argyle	42	16	13	13	62	57	61
Stoke City	42	16	10	16	63	53	58
Sheffield United	42	15	13	14	50	49	58
Bradford City	42	15	10	17	62	62	55
Barnsley	42	14	13	15	49	52	55
Blackburn Rovers	42	15	10	17	45	55	55
Reading	42	14	11	17	52	59	53
Hull City	42	13	14	15	41	55	53
West Bromwich Albion	42	13	12	17	51	49	51
Millwall	42	14	9	19	39	45	51
Huddersfield Town	42	13	12	17	54	61	51
Shrewsbury Town	42	15	6	21	41	53	51
Birmingham City	42	11	17	14	47	59	50
Sunderland	42	12	12	18	49	49	48
Grimsby Town	42	10	14	18	39	59	44
Brighton & Hove Albion	42	9	12	21	37	54	39

Division Two

Manager: Garry Pendrey

Did you know that?

Blues recorded their first win on a plastic pitch at Oldham in October.

All four goals in the Simod Cup tie with Derby were scored in the space of 18 extra-time minutes.

Crystal Palace hit five goals in 33 minutes when they crushed Blues 6–0 at Selhurst Park.

Goalkeeper Martin Thomas fractured his cheekbone in the drawn game at Middlesbrough in March; Andy Kennedy took over between the posts.

Neil Sproston, aged 16, made his Blues debut v Middlesbrough (home).

Ian Handysides' last goal for Blues (before he was forced to give up the game through illness) earned a point at Reading in March.

Substitutions

Bold player replaced by No. 12.
Underlined player replaced by No. 14.

Match No.	Date		Venue	Opponents	Result		Scorers	Attendance
1	Aug	15	H	Stoke City	W	2-0	Rees 2	13,137
2		22	A	Aston Villa	W	2-0	Handysides, Rees	30,870
3		29	H	Bournemouth	D	1-1	Kennedy	8,284
4	Sep	1	A	Millwall	L	1-3	Rees	6,758
5		5	H	Crystal Palace	L	0-6		7,011
6		12	A	Swindon Town	W	2-0	Handysides, Whitton	9,128
7		15	H	Blackburn Rovers	W	1-0	Whitton	6,032
8		19	H	Shrewsbury Town	D	0-0		7,183
9		26	A	Plymouth Argyle	D	1-1	McElhinney (og)	8,912
10		30	A	West Bromwich Albion	L	1-3	Kennedy	15,399
11	Oct	3	H	Huddersfield Town	W	2-0	Whitton 2	6,282
12		10	H	Reading	D	2-2	Kennedy, Whitton	6,147
13		17	A	Bradford City	L	0-4		12,256
14		20	A	Sheffield United	W	2-0	Withe 2	9,287
15		24	H	Middlesbrough	D	0-0		7,404
16		31	A	Oldham Athletic	W	2-1	Whitton (pen), Frain	5,488
17	Nov	3	A	Barnsley	W	2-0	Whitton 2	6,622
18		7	A	Hull City	L	0-2		7,901
19		14	H	Leicester City	D	2-2	Whitton 2	8,666
20		21	A	Manchester City	L	0-3		22,690
21		28	A	Ipswich Town	W	1-0	Frain	6,718
22	Dec	5	A	Leeds United	L	1-4	Kennedy	15,987
23		12	H	Aston Villa	L	1-2	Kennedy	27,789
24		19	A	Blackburn Rovers	L	0-2		8,542
25		26	H	Plymouth Argyle	L	0-1		9,166
26		28	A	Shrewsbury Town	D	0-0		6,367
27	Jan	1	A	Bournemouth	L	2-4	Dicks, Wigley	7,963
28		2	H	Swindon Town	D	1-1	Childs	7,829
29		16	A	Stoke City	L	1-3	Kennedy	10,076
30	Feb	6	A	Crystal Palace	L	0-3		8,809
31		9	H	Millwall	W	1-0	Whitton	5,878
32		27	A	Huddersfield Town	D	2-2	Whitton, Robinson	5,441
33	Mar	5	H	Bradford City	D	1-1	Whitton	8,101
34		8	H	West Bromwich Albion	L	0-1		12,331
35		12	A	Reading	D	1-1	Handysides	6,598
36		19	H	Oldham Athletic	L	1-3	Wigley	6,012
37		26	A	Middlesbrough	D	1-1	Atkins	15,465
38	Apr	2	H	Hull City	D	1-1	Williams	7,059
39		5	A	Leicester City	L	0-2		13,541
40		9	H	Sheffield United	W	1-0	Kennedy	7,046
41		23	A	Barnsley	D	2-2	Whitton (pen), Jeffels (og)	4,949
42		30	H	Manchester City	L	0-3		8,014
43	May	2	A	Ipswich Town	L	0-1		11,127
44		6	H	Leeds United	D	0-0		6,024

Appearances
Sub appearances
Two own-goals   Goals

FA Cup

	Date		Venue	Opponents	Result		Scorers	Attendance
R3	Jan	9	A	Gillingham	W	3-0	Greenall (og), Williams, Handysides	9,267
R4		30	A	Barnsley	W	2-0	Rees, Wigley	13,219
R5	Feb	20	H	Nottingham Forest	L	0-1		34,494

Appearances
Sub appearances
One own-goal   Goals

League Cup

	Date		Venue	Opponents	Result		Scorers	Attendance
R1	Aug	18	A	Mansfield Town	D	2-2	Handysides, Whitton	4,425
R1s		25	H	Mansfield Town	L	0-1		6,054

Appearances
Sub appearances
Goals

Player columns (left to right):

Gosden AL · Ranson R · Dicks JA · Williams TE · Overson VD · Handysides IR · Bremner DG · Kennedy AJ · Whiton SP · Rees AA · Wigley S · Roberts BLF · Bird AL · Childs GPC · Trewick J · Hansbury R · Frain JW · Wilna P · Sproson NR · Rusell GR · Robinson CR · Yates MJ · Sturridge PM · Atkins IL · Langley KJ · Ashley KM · Morris R · Tait FR

Gos	Ran	Dic	Wil	Ove	Han	Bre	Ken	Whi	Ree	Wig	Rob	Bir	Chi	Tre	Han	Fra	Wil	Spr	Rus	Rob	Yat	Stu	Atk	Lan	Ash	Mor	Tai
1	2	3	4	5	6	7	8	9	10	11																	
1		3	4		6	7	8	9	10	11	2																
1		3	4		6	7	8		10	11	2	5	12														
1		3	4	5	6	7	8	9	10	11	2	12															
1		3		5		7	8	9	10	11	2	4	12	6													
1	2	3	4	5	8	7		9	10	11			12	6														
	2	3	4	5	8	7	14	9	10			12	6	1													
	2	3	4	5	8	7	12	9		11			1	6	10												
	2	3	4	5	8	7	12	9	10	11			6	1													
	2	3	4	5	8	7	14	9	10	11	5	12	6	1													
1		3	4	5	8	7	12	9	10	11	2		6														
1	2	3	4	5	8	7	12	9	10	11			6														
1	2	3	4	5	8	7			10	11			9														
1	2	3	4	5	8			10	11			7	6		12	9											
1	2	3	4	5	8	7			11			10	6		12	9	14										
1	2	3	4	5		7		9		11	12		8			6	10										
1	2	3		5		7		9	12	11	4		8			6	10										
1	2	3		5		7		9	14	11	4		8			6	10										
1	2	3		5		7		9	12	11	4		8	6			10										
1	2	3	5		7	12	9	10	11	4			8	6													
1	2		5		12	7	10	9	14	11	4		8	3		6											
1	2		5	10	7	9		4	11	12	8	3		6		14											
1	2		5	10	7	9		11	4	8	3		6	12													
1	2	3		5	4	7	9		11	8		6		10													
1	2	3		5		7	9	12	10	11	4		8	6													
	2	3		5		10	9		11	4		8	6	1	7												
	2	3	5		7	12	9		11	4		8	6	1			10										
1	2	3	5		7	10	9		11	4		8			6												
	2	3	6	5	11	7	9		12		4		8	10	1												
	2	3	4	5	14	7		9	10	11			8	6	1			12									
	2	3	4	5	6	7		9		11			8		1			10									
	2	3	4	5	6	7		9	12	11			8		1			10									
	2	3	4	5		7		9		11			8		1	6		10	12								
	2	3	4	5		7		9		11			8		1			12	10								
	2	3	4	5	10	7			11	8			6	1				9									
	2		4	5	10	7	12		11	3			8	6	1			9									
	2		4	5	10	7	12		11	3				1				9			6	8					
	2		4	5	10	7		9		11	3			12	1			14			6	8					
	2		4	5		14		9		11	3	12	7	1			10				6	8					
	2		4	5		10	9		11	3			7	1							6	8					
	2	4	5	10	7	12	9		11	3		14		1						6	8						
	2		5	10		7	9		11	3	4	14		1						6	8	12					
	2		5	10			12		11	3	4	14	7	1			9		8		6	8					
		4		7			9		11	3	5		1	2				10			6	8		12	14		
22	**38**	**32**	**33**	**37**	**28**	**37**	**15**	**32**	**17**	**43**	**26**	**6**	**23**	**25**	**22**	**12**	**8**	**0**	**6**	**3**	**1**	**3**	**8**	**7**	**0**	**0**	**0**
			2		13	1	6		1	3	9	1		2		1	3	1	2				1	1	1		
	1	1		3		7	14	4	2		1			2	2		1				1						

League Table

	P	W	D	L	F	A	Pts
Millwall	44	25	7	12	72	52	82
Aston Villa	44	22	12	10	68	41	78
Middlesbrough	44	22	12	10	63	36	78
Bradford City	44	22	11	11	74	54	77
Blackburn Rovers	44	21	14	9	68	52	77
Crystal Palace	44	22	9	13	86	59	75
Leeds United	44	19	12	13	61	51	69
Ipswich Town	44	19	9	16	61	52	66
Manchester City	44	19	8	17	80	60	65
Oldham Athletic	44	18	11	15	72	64	65
Stoke City	44	17	11	16	50	57	62
Swindon Town	44	16	11	17	73	60	59
Leicester City	44	16	11	17	62	61	59
Barnsley	44	15	12	17	61	62	57
Hull City	44	14	15	15	54	60	57
Plymouth Argyle	44	16	8	20	65	67	56
Bournemouth	44	13	10	21	56	68	49
Shrewsbury Town	44	11	16	17	42	54	49
Birmingham City	44	11	15	18	41	66	48
West Bromwich Albion	44	12	11	21	50	69	47
Sheffield United	44	13	7	24	45	74	46
Reading	44	10	12	22	44	70	42
Huddersfield Town	44	6	10	28	41	100	28

Division Two

Manager: Garry Pendrey (to April); then Dave Mackay

Did you know that?

Aston Villa fired 13 goals past Blues in the space of six weeks between late September and early November 1988. Villa won 2–0 and 5–0 in home and away League Cup games and 6–0 in a Simod Cup tie.

The 5–3 home defeat by Barnsley in October included scoring sequences of two goals in three minutes (24–26), three in three (56–59) and two in one (89).

In the first League meeting between the two clubs since 1902, Walsall scored five goals in 27 minutes to batter bewildered Blues into submission.

Only 4,026 fans attended the Blues v Swindon Town League game in mid-April – the lowest crowd for a home game since April 1913.

Blues' average home League attendance of 6,289 was the lowest-ever at St Andrew's.

Match No.	Date		Venue	Opponents	Result		Scorers	Attendance
1	Aug	27	A	Watford	L	0-1		12,656
2	Sep	3	H	Leicester City	L	2-3	Walsh (og), Robinson	7,932
3		10	A	Oldham Athletic	L	0-4		5,810
4		17	H	Sunderland	W	3-2	Atkins, Robinson, Childs	6,871
5		20	A	Walsall	L	0-5		8,780
6		24	A	Blackburn Rovers	L	0-3		7,562
7	Oct	1	H	Barnsley	L	3-5	Atkins, Langley, Robinson	4,892
8		4	H	Plymouth Argyle	L	0-1		4,435
9		8	A	Bournemouth	W	1-0	Frain	6,186
10		15	H	West Bromwich Albion	L	1-4	Bremner	10,453
11		22	A	Manchester City	D	0-0		20,205
12		25	H	Stoke City	L	0-1		6,262
13		29	A	Swindon Town	L	1-2	Atkins (pen)	6,937
14	Nov	5	H	Portsmouth	D	0-0		5,866
15		12	A	Oxford United	L	0-3		5,600
16		19	A	Hull City	D	1-1	Langley	5,134
17		22	H	Leeds United	D	0-0		6,168
18		26	H	Ipswich Town	W	1-0	Whitton	5,932
19	Dec	3	A	Bradford City	D	2-2	Whitton, Richards	9,503
20		10	H	Crystal Palace	L	0-1		6,523
21		16	A	Chelsea	L	1-4	Whitton	7,897
22		26	A	Shrewsbury Town	D	0-0		7,347
23		31	A	Brighton & Hove Alb.	L	0-4		9,324
24	Jan	2	H	Oldham Athletic	D	0-0		5,998
25		14	A	Leeds United	L	0-1		21,843
26		21	H	Watford	L	2-3	Whitton 2 (1 pen)	6,396
27	Feb	4	A	Plymouth Argyle	W	1-0	Robinson	7,721
28		11	H	Bournemouth	L	0-1		6,444
29		18	H	Manchester City	L	0-2		11,707
30		25	A	West Bromwich Albion	D	0-0		16,148
31		28	A	Stoke City	L	0-1		7,904
32	Mar	4	H	Oxford United	D	0-0		4,954
33		11	A	Portsmouth	L	0-1		8,110
34		18	H	Walsall	W	1-0	Wigley	6,558
35		25	A	Leicester City	L	0-2		9,464
36		27	H	Shrewsbury Town	L	1-2	Sturridge	4,964
37	Apr	1	A	Sunderland	D	2-2	Frain, Yates	10,927
38		4	A	Chelsea	L	1-3	Richards	14,796
39		8	H	Brighton & Hove Alb.	L	1-2	Sturridge	4,579
40		15	A	Barnsley	D	0-0		6,464
41		18	H	Swindon Town	L	1-2	Peer	4,026
42		22	H	Blackburn Rovers	W	2-0	Robinson, Yates	5,813
43		29	A	Ipswich Town	L	0-4		9,998
44	May	1	H	Bradford City	W	1-0	Frain	4,735
45		6	H	Hull City	W	1-0	Yates	4,686
46		13	A	Crystal Palace	L	1-4	Sturridge	17,581

	Appearances
	Sub appearances
One own-goal	Goals

FA Cup

R3	Jan	7	H	Wimbledon	L	0-1		10,431

	Appearances
	Sub appearances

League Cup

R1	Aug	30	A	Wolverhampton Wan.	L	2-3	Thompson (og), Bird	11,007
R1s	Sep	6	H	Wolverhampton Wan.	W	1-0	Whitton	8,981
R2		27	H	Aston Villa	L	0-2		21,177
R2s	Oct	12	A	Aston Villa	L	0-5		19,753

R1s a.e.t.

	Appearances
	Sub appearances
One own-goal	Goals

League Table

	P	W	D	L	F	A	Pts
Chelsea	46	29	12	5	96	50	99
Manchester City	46	23	13	10	77	53	82
Crystal Palace	46	23	12	11	71	49	81
Watford	46	22	12	12	74	48	78
Blackburn Rovers	46	22	11	13	74	59	77
Swindon Town	46	20	16	10	68	53	76
Barnsley	46	20	14	12	66	58	74
Ipswich Town	46	22	7	17	71	61	73
West Bromwich Albion	46	18	18	10	65	41	72
Leeds United	46	17	16	13	59	50	67
Sunderland	46	16	15	15	60	60	63
Bournemouth	46	18	8	20	53	62	62
Stoke City	46	15	14	17	57	72	59
Bradford City	46	13	17	16	52	59	56
Leicester City	46	13	16	17	56	63	55
Oldham Athletic	46	11	21	14	75	72	54
Oxford United	46	14	12	20	62	70	54
Plymouth Argyle	46	14	12	20	55	66	54
Brighton & Hove Albion	46	14	9	23	57	66	51
Portsmouth	46	13	12	21	53	62	51
Hull City	46	11	14	21	52	68	47
Shrewsbury Town	46	8	18	20	40	67	42
Birmingham City	46	8	11	27	31	76	35
Walsall	46	5	16	25	41	80	31

Player columns (left to right): Godden AL, Ranson R, Roberts BLF, Atkins IL, Bird AL, Tarwick J, Bremner DG, Langley KJ, Whitton SP, Robinson CR, Wigley S, Frain JW, Overson VD, Childs BPC, Mona R, Vans MJ, Clarkson IS, Tait PR, Thomas MR, Peer D, Richards CL, Sturridge SA, Ashley KM, Hansbury R, Frain MC, Hopkins RA, Burton MJ, Russell GR, Elliott AR

Division Three

Manager: Dave Mackay

Match No.	Date		Venue	Opponents	Result		Scorers	Attendance
1	Aug	19	H	Crewe Alexandra	W	3-0	Yates, Sturridge, Bailey	10,447
2		26	A	Bristol City	L	0-1		8,938
3	Sep	2	H	Swansea City	W	2-0	Bailey, Hopkins	8,071
4		9	A	Shrewsbury Town	L	0-2		4,714
5		16	H	Tranmere Rovers	W	2-1	Bailey, Gordon	8,604
6		23	A	Brentford	W	1-0	Sturridge	5,386
7		26	H	Walsall	W	2-0	Bailey (pen), Tait	10,834
8		30	A	Blackpool	L	2-3	Sturridge, Gleghorn	5,681
9	Oct	7	A	Rotherham United	L	1-5	Sturridge	4,676
10		14	H	Northampton Town	W	4-0	Bailey 2 (1 pen), Gleghorn 2	8,731
11		17	A	Chester City	L	0-4		1,890
12		21	H	Huddersfield Town	L	0-1		7,951
13		28	A	Bury	D	0-0		3,383
14		31	A	Cardiff City	D	1-1	Sturridge	7,468
15	Nov	4	A	Reading	W	2-0	Sturridge, Hicks (og)	3,527
16		11	H	Leyton Orient	D	0-0		7,491
17		25	H	Bolton Wanderers	W	1-0	Bailey (pen)	8,081
18	Dec	1	A	Wigan Athletic	L	0-1		2,506
19		16	H	Preston North End	W	3-1	Frain, Bailey, Yates	6,391
20		26	A	Bristol Rovers	D	0-0		6,573
21		30	A	Notts County	L	2-3	Atkins (pen), Bailey	7,786
22	Jan	1	H	Fulham	D	1-1	Gleghorn	8,932
23		13	H	Bristol City	L	0-4		11,277
24		20	A	Crewe Alexandra	W	2-0	Bailey, Sturridge	4,681
25		27	H	Shrewsbury Town	L	0-1		7,461
26	Feb	9	A	Tranmere Rovers	L	1-5	Bailey (pen)	6,033
27		13	A	Swansea City	D	1-1	Madden	3,603
28		17	H	Wigan Athletic	D	0-0		5,473
29		24	A	Bolton Wanderers	L	1-3	Gordon	7,618
30	Mar	3	H	Mansfield Town	W	4-1	Bailey 2, Sturridge, Ashley	5,746
31		6	H	Blackpool	W	3-1	Peer, Bailey (pen), Sturridge	7,085
32		10	A	Walsall	W	1-0	Gleghorn	6,036
33		13	H	Brentford	L	0-1		8,169
34		17	H	Rotherham United	W	4-1	Atkins, Sturridge, Gordon, Tait	6,985
35		20	A	Northampton Town	D	2-2	Peer, Gleghorn	4,346
36		24	H	Chester City	D	0-0		7,584
37		31	A	Huddersfield Town	W	2-1	Bailey, Gleghorn	5,837
38	Apr	3	A	Mansfield Town	L	2-5	Bailey, Gleghorn	4,164
39		7	H	Bury	D	0-0		6,808
40		10	A	Cardiff City	W	1-0	Hopkins	3,322
41		14	A	Fulham	W	2-1	Hopkins, Gleghorn	4,568
42		16	H	Bristol Rovers	D	2-2	Matthewson, Hopkins	12,438
43		21	A	Preston North End	D	2-2	Bailey 2	7,680
44		24	H	Notts County	L	1-2	Hopkins	10,533
45		28	A	Leyton Orient	W	2-1	Peer, Hopkins	5,691
46	May	5	H	Reading	L	0-1		14,278

				Appearances
				Sub appearances
			One own-goal	Goals

FA Cup

	Date		Venue	Opponents	Result		Scorers	Attendance
R1	Nov	18	A	Leyton Orient	W	1-0	Sturridge	4,063
R2	Dec	9	A	Colchester United	W	2-0	Gleghorn 2	3,858
R3	Jan	6	H	Oldham Athletic	D	1-1	Gleghorn	13,131
rep		10	A	Oldham Athletic	L	0-1		9,982

				Appearances
				Sub appearances
				Goals

League Cup

	Date		Venue	Opponents	Result		Scorers	Attendance
R1	Aug	22	H	Chesterfield	W	2-1	Atkins, Bailey	6,722
R1s		29	A	Chesterfield	D	1-1	Bailey	3,313
R2	Sep	19	H	West Ham United	L	1-2	Sproson	10,987
R2s	Oct	4	A	West Ham United	D	1-1	Atkins	12,187

				Appearances
				Sub appearances
				Goals

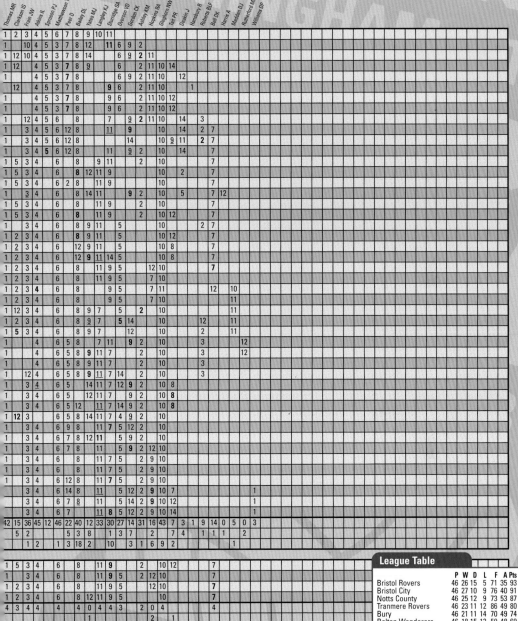

League Table

	P	W	D	L	F	A	Pts
Bristol Rovers	46	26	15	5	71	35	93
Bristol City	46	27	10	9	76	40	91
Notts County	46	25	12	9	73	53	87
Tranmere Rovers	46	23	11	12	86	49	80
Bury	46	21	11	14	70	49	74
Bolton Wanderers	46	18	15	13	59	48	69
Birmingham City	46	18	12	16	60	59	66
Huddersfield Town	46	17	14	15	61	62	65
Rotherham United	46	17	13	16	71	62	64
Reading	46	15	19	12	57	53	64
Shrewsbury Town	46	16	15	15	59	54	63
Crewe Alexandra	46	15	17	14	56	53	62
Brentford	46	18	7	21	66	66	61
Leyton Orient	46	16	10	20	52	56	58
Mansfield Town	46	16	7	23	50	65	55
Chester City	46	13	15	18	43	55	54
Swansea City	46	14	12	20	45	63	54
Wigan Athletic	46	13	14	19	48	64	53
Preston North End	46	14	10	22	65	79	52
Fulham	46	12	15	19	55	66	51
Cardiff City	46	12	14	20	51	70	50
Northampton Town	46	11	14	21	51	68	47
Blackpool	46	10	16	20	49	73	46
Walsall	46	9	14	23	40	72	41

Division Three

Manager: Dave Mackay (to January); then Lou Macari (to June)

Following elimination by Brentford, this was the first season in modern times that Blues had failed to reach the third round of the FA Cup.

Ex-Blues striker Wayne Clarke hit a 29-minute hat-trick in Shrewsbury's 4–1 League win at Gay Meadow. This defeat ended an unbeaten run of 13 matches.

Nigel Gleghorn took over in goal when Martin Thomas was injured in the 57th minute of Blues' 1–0 win at Chester in November.

It was £4.50 to stand up and at least £10 to sit down at St Andrew's this season.

Former Blues goalkeeper Paul Cooper retired in May, having saved 25 penalties over a period of 20 years from 1971.

Another ex-player, Frank Worthington, retired after 25 years as a professional.

Former player Ian Handysides died on 17 August, aged 27.

Match No.	Date	Venue	Opponents	Result		Scorers	Attendance
1	Aug 25	A	Cambridge United	W	1-0	Gleghorn	6,338
2	Sep 1	H	Leyton Orient	W	3-1	Bailey, Hopkins, Moran	5,847
3	8	A	Stoke City	W	1-0	Gleghorn	16,135
4	15	H	Bury	W	1-0	Peer	7,344
5	18	H	Exeter City	D	1-1	Bailey	7,703
6	22	A	Wigan Athletic	D	1-1	Tait	3,904
7	29	H	Preston North End	D	1-1	Bailey	7,154
8	Oct 2	A	Fulham	D	2-2	Overson, Matthewson	4,011
9	6	A	Reading	D	2-2	Matthewson, Sturridge	5,695
10	13	H	Southend United	D	1-1	Sturridge	9,333
11	20	H	Grimsby Town	D	0-0		10,123
12	23	A	Crewe Alexandra	D	1-1	Gleghorn	4,449
13	27	A	Shrewsbury Town	L	1-4	Bailey	6,150
14	Nov 3	H	Huddersfield Town	L	1-2	Tait	7,412
15	10	A	Chester City	W	1-0	Hopkins	2,273
16	24	H	Bournemouth	D	0-0		7,416
17	Dec 1	A	Swansea City	L	0-2		4,896
18	15	H	Rotherham United	W	2-1	Overson, Tait	4,734
19	21	A	Tranmere Rovers	L	0-1		5,054
20	26	H	Brentford	L	0-2		6,612
21	29	H	Bolton Wanderers	L	1-3	Bailey	7,318
22	Jan 1	A	Mansfield Town	W	2-1	Gayle 2	3,654
23	5	A	Bradford City	D	1-1	Frain (pen)	6,315
24	12	A	Leyton Orient	D	1-1	Sturridge	4,701
25	19	H	Cambridge United	L	0-3		5,859
26	26	H	Bury	W	1-0	Sturridge	3,009
27	Feb 2	A	Exeter City	W	2-0	Gayle 2	5,154
28	5	H	Wigan Athletic	D	0-0		5,319
29	13	A	Bradford City	L	0-2		4,776
30	16	A	Bournemouth	W	2-1	Sturridge, Mundee (og)	6,330
31	23	H	Chester City	W	1-0	Dolan	6,702
32	Mar 2	H	Swansea City	W	2-0	Sturridge, Rodgerson	6,903
33	9	A	Rotherham United	D	1-1	Frain (pen)	5,028
34	12	H	Fulham	W	2-0	Peer, Gleghorn	8,083
35	16	A	Preston North End	L	0-2		5,334
36	18	A	Southend United	L	1-2	Gleghorn	6,328
37	23	H	Reading	D	1-1	Rodgerson	6,795
38	30	A	Brentford	D	2-2	Frain, Gleghorn	6,757
39	Apr 2	H	Tranmere Rovers	W	1-0	Yates	7,675
40	7	A	Bolton Wanderers	L	1-3	Gayle	11,280
41	13	H	Mansfield Town	D	0-0		7,635
42	16	H	Stoke City	W	2-1	Matthewson, Hopkins	6,729
43	20	A	Grimsby Town	D	0-0		8,842
44	27	H	Crewe Alexandra	L	0-2		6,429
45	May 4	H	Shrewsbury Town	L	0-1		6,256
46	11	A	Huddersfield Town	W	1-0	Gayle	5,195

Appearances	
Sub appearances	
One own-goal	Goals

FA Cup

	Date	Venue	Opponents	Result		Scorers	Attendance
R1	Nov 17	H	Cheltenham Town	W	1-0	Sturridge	7,942
R2	Dec 12	H	Brentford	L	1-3	Aylott	5,072

Appearances	
Sub appearances	
	Goals

League Cup

	Date	Venue	Opponents	Result		Scorers	Attendance
R1	Aug 28	H	Bournemouth	L	0-1		5,110
R1s	Sep 4	A	Bournemouth	D	1-1	Downs (pen)	4,490

Appearances	
Sub appearances	
	Goals

Player columns (left to right):

Thomas MR · Ashley KM · Downs G · Frain JW · Overson VD · Matthewson T · Peer D · Bailey DL · Hopkins RA · Gleghorn NW · Tait PR · Sturridge SA · Fox MC · Moran R · Clarkson IS · Rutherford MR · Aylott TKC · Gordon CK · Gayle J · Rodgerson I · Dolan EJ · Frances SR · Bell DK · Yates MJ · O'Reilly GM · Robinson PJ · Williams GP

	Tho	Ash	Dow	Fra	Ove	Mat	Pee	Bai	Hop	Gle	Tai	Stu	Fox	Mor	Cla	Rut	Ayl	Gor	Gay	Rod	Dol	Fra	Bel	Yat	O'R	Rob	Wil
	2	3	4	5		6	7	8	9	10	11	12															
	2	3	4			6	7	8	9		10	11	14	5	12												
	2	3	4			6	7	8			10	11	12	5		9											
		3	4	5		6	7	8	14	10	11		9			2	2										
	3		4	5		6	7	8		10	11	9				2	2										
		4	5	3			8	7	10	11	9				2	12											
	12	4	5	3	7	8	9			11			6		2	10											
	10	4	5	3	7	8			11	9	6	12	2														
	3	4	5	6	7	8	11	10		9			2														
	3	4	5	6	7	8	11	10		9			2														
	3	4	5	6	7	8	2	10	11	9	12																
	3	4	5	6	7	12	2	10	11	8						9											
		4	5	3		12	7	10	11	8	6		2	14	9												
	3	4	5	6	7	12	2	10	11	8						9											
	3	4	5	6	7	8	2	10	11				12				9										
	3	4	5	6	7	8	2	10		11			12			9											
	3	4	5	6	12	14		10	11				2		9		8	7									
		3	5	6		7	8		10	11			2		9		12	4									
		3	5	6		7	8		10	11		12	2		9		14	4									
		4	5	3	7	12		10		11	6				9		8	2									
		4	5	3	7	8		10					6				9	2	11								
		4	5	3	7	8		10		12			6				9	2	11								
		4	5	3				10	7	8	6		12				9	2	11								
		4	5	3		10				8	6		2		9			7	11	14							
		3	5	6	7	4		10		11			9				8	2									
			6	7	4	3	10		11				5				9	8	2								
			6	7	4	3	10		11				5		9		8	2	14	12							
		5	6	7	8	4	10		11				3		9		2		12								
		3	5	6	7	8		10		11			2		9		4	12									
		3	5	6	7			10		11			2		9		4	8									
		3	5	6		7	12	10		11			2		9		8	4	14								
		3	5	6	7		12	10		11			2		9		8	4	14								
		3	5	6	7	4		10		11			2		9		8										
		3	5	6	7	9		10		11		12	2				8			4							
		3	5	6	7		11	10				12	2		9		8			4							
		3	5	6	7			10		11		12	2				8	9		4							
		3	5	6				10		11			2	14	9		7	12			4	8					
		3	5	6	7				11				10				8	9		4	2						
		3	5	6	7			11					10	12			8	9		4	2						
		3	5	6	7		12	10		11			2		8		4		14	9							
		3	5	6		11		10					2	8	12		4			7	9						
		3		6	7		12	10		11			2	8			4			5	9	1					
		3		6	7			11		10			2	8	12		4			5	9	1					
		3	5	6	12	14		11		10			2				7	4			9						
		3	5	6	4			11		10			2				7			8	9						

Appearance totals (bold = full appearances):

	5	3	16	42	40	46	37	25	18	42	17	33	9	2	34	1	23	3	20	25	5	0	1	8	1	9	1
		1			3	7	5			5	2	6	3	2	2	2		5	3		1						
		3	2	3	2	5	3	6	3	6			1				6	2	1		1						

(Further supplementary rows below main grid)

		3	4	5		6	7	8	2	10	11	9					12							1			
		3	4	5		6	7	8		10		11		2	12	9											
		2	2	2	2	2	2	2	1	2	1	2		1			0	0	1					1			
																	1	1									
												1						1									

	1	2	3	4	5	6	7	8	9	10	11	12															
	1	2	3	4		6	7	8	9	10	11	14	5	12													
	2	2	2	1	2	2	2	2	2	2	0	1	0														
												2		1													
	1																										

League Table

	P	W	D	L	F	A	Pts
Cambridge United	46	25	11	10	75	45	86
Southend United	46	26	7	13	67	51	85
Grimsby Town	46	24	11	11	66	34	83
Bolton Wanderers	46	24	11	11	64	50	83
Tranmere Rovers	46	23	9	14	64	46	78
Brentford	46	21	13	12	59	47	76
Bury	46	20	13	13	67	56	73
Bradford City	46	20	10	16	62	54	70
Bournemouth	46	19	13	14	58	58	70
Wigan Athletic	46	20	9	17	71	54	69
Huddersfield Town	46	18	13	15	57	51	67
Birmingham City	46	16	17	13	45	49	65
Leyton Orient	46	18	10	18	55	58	64
Stoke City	46	16	12	18	55	59	60
Reading	46	17	8	21	53	66	59
Exeter City	46	16	9	21	58	52	57
Preston North End	46	15	11	20	54	67	56
Shrewsbury Town	46	14	10	22	61	68	52
Chester City	46	14	9	23	46	58	51
Swansea City	46	13	9	24	49	72	48
Fulham	46	10	16	20	41	56	46
Crewe Alexandra	46	11	11	24	62	80	44
Rotherham United	46	10	12	24	50	87	42
Mansfield Town	46	8	14	24	42	63	38

Division Three

Caretaker manager: Bill Coldwell (to August); then Terry Cooper

Did you know that?

In the home League game against West Bromwich Albion (lost 3–0), Trevor Matthewson saw red in the 12th minute – possibly the earliest dismissal of a Blues player ever.

Two-nil down after 15 minutes at home to Chester, Blues stormed back to win 3–2 with Nigel Gleghorn netting a 77th-minute decider.

The Blues-Stoke City League game in February was halted by a pitch invasion with barely a minute remaining. The scores were level at 1–1, but after referee Roger Wiseman had asked for the stadium to be emptied, he brought both teams back onto the pitch to play out the remaining 60 seconds.

In August, Blues signed Robert Taylor from Norwich City. In October he was sold to Leyton Orient and after spells with Brentford and Gillingham, was transferred to Manchester City for £1.5 million in 1999–2000. He scored over 120 goals after being 'given away' by Blues!

Match No.	Date	Venue	Opponents	Result		Scorers	Attendance
1	Aug 17	H	Bury	W	3-2	Gayle, Gleghorn, Okenla	9,0
2	24	A	Fulham	W	1-0	Rodgerson	4,7
3	31	H	Darlington	W	1-0	Sturridge	8,7
4	Sep 3	A	Hull City	W	2-1	Rodgerson, Sturridge	4,8
5	7	A	Reading	D	1-1	Sturridge	6,6
6	14	H	Peterborough Utd.	D	1-1	Cooper	9,4
7	17	H	Chester City	W	3-2	Frain (pen), Gleghorn, Sturridge	8,1
8	21	A	Hartlepool United	L	0-1		4,6
9	28	H	Preston North End	W	3-1	Matthewson, Rodgerson, Gleghorn	8,2
10	Oct 5	A	Shrewsbury Town	D	1-1	Gleghorn	7,0
11	12	H	Stockport County	W	3-0	Donowa, Cooper, Drinkell	12,3
12	19	H	Wigan Athletic	D	3-3	Rodgerson, Gleghorn, Sturridge	9,6
13	26	A	West Bromwich Albion	W	1-0	Drinkell	26,1
14	Nov 2	H	Torquay United	W	3-0	Gleghorn (pen), Sturridge, Donowa	9,4
15	6	A	Brentford	D	2-2	Sturridge, Cooper	8,7
16	9	A	Huddersfield Town	L	2-3	Matthewson, Gleghorn	11,6
17	23	H	Exeter City	W	1-0	Gleghorn	11,3
18	30	H	Bradford City	W	2-0	Peer, Gleghorn	10,4
19	Dec 14	A	Bournemouth	L	1-2	Paskin	6,0
20	21	H	Fulham	W	3-1	Rodgerson 2, Gleghorn	8,8
21	26	A	Darlington	D	1-1	Rodgerson	4,4
22	28	A	Bury	L	0-1		4,2
23	Jan 1	H	Hull City	D	2-2	Gleghorn, Paskin	12,9
24	4	A	Stoke City	L	1-2	Beckford	19,0
25	11	H	Leyton Orient	D	2-2	Cooper, Paskin	10,4
26	18	A	Swansea City	W	2-0	Rodgerson, Rowbotham	4,1
27	Feb 8	H	West Bromwich Albion	L	0-3		27,5
28	11	A	Bradford City	W	2-1	Gleghorn, Sturridge	7,0
29	15	H	Bournemouth	L	0-1		10,8
30	22	A	Leyton Orient	D	0-0		6,0
31	29	H	Stoke City	D	1-1	Frain (pen)	22,1
32	Mar 3	H	Swansea City	D	1-1	Rowbotham	9,4
33	10	A	Brentford	W	1-0	Matthewson	13,2
34	17	A	Bolton Wanderers	D	1-1	Rodgerson	7,3
35	21	H	Huddersfield Town	W	2-0	Gleghorn, Sturridge	12,4
36	24	A	Torquay United	W	2-1	Matthewson, Rowbotham	2,4
37	28	A	Exeter City	L	1-2	Hicks	5,2
38	31	A	Peterborough Utd.	W	3-2	Matthewson, Frain (pen), Sturridge	12,0
39	Apr 4	H	Reading	W	2-0	Frain (pen), Rowbotham	12,2
40	11	A	Chester City	W	1-0	Gleghorn	4,8
41	14	H	Bolton Wanderers	W	2-1	Frain (pen), Rennie	14,4
42	18	H	Hartlepool United	W	2-1	Matthewson, Gleghorn	13,6
43	21	A	Preston North End	L	2-3	Gleghorn, Rennie	7,7
44	25	H	Shrewsbury Town	W	1-0	Gleghorn	19,8
45	28	A	Wigan Athletic	L	0-3		5,9
46	May 2	A	Stockport County	L	0-2		7,8

Appearance
Sub appearance
Goa

FA Cup

R1	Nov 16	A	Torquay United	L	0-3		4,12

Appearance
Sub appearance

League Cup

R1	Aug 21	A	Exeter City	W	1-0	Rodgerson	4,07
R1s	27	H	Exeter City	W	4-0	Hicks, Peer, Gleghorn, Yates	6,17
R2	Sep 25	A	Luton Town	D	2-2	Rodgerson, Gleghorn	6,31
R2s	Oct 8	H	Luton Town	W	3-2	Peer, Gleghorn 2	13,25
R3	29	H	Crystal Palace	D	1-1	Sturridge	17,27
rep	Nov 19	A	Crystal Palace	D	1-1	Gleghorn	10,69
rep2	Dec 3	A	Crystal Palace	L	1-2	Peer	11,38

R3 replay a.e.t.

Appearance
Sub appearance
Goa

Squad appearance grid — player list (left to right):

Thomas MR, Clarkson IS, Matthewson T, Frain JW, Hicks M, Marsden PJ, Rodgerson I, Gayle J, Peer D, Gingham NW, Sturridge SA, Vance MJ, Otania F, Dolan EJ, Donowa BL, Arlott TKC, Cooper MN, Atkins IL, Jones PT, Tait PR, Dinmall KS, Carter TD, Plaskin WU, Cheeseworth JA, Hogan TE, Miller AJ, Rowbotham D, Breckford JN, Francis SR, Rennie D, O'Neill A, Dearston KC, Sale MD, Foy DL

```
 1  2  3  4  5  6  7        8  9     10 11 12 14
 1  2     3  5  6  7        9 10 11     4 12  8
 1  2     3  5  6  7  8  9 10 11    12  4
 1  2     3  5  6  7        9 10 11     4  8
 1  2     3  5  6  7        9 10 11     4  8 12
 1  2     3  5  6        9 10 11  7     4  8 12 14
 1  2     3  5  6  7        9 10 11     4  8
 1  2     3  5  6  7        9 10 11     4  8
 1  2  3  8  5  6  7        9 10 11     4  9
 1  2  3  8  5  6  7      14 10 11     4  9      12
 1  2  3  8  5  6  7        10 11   12  4        9
 1  2  3  8  5  6  7     12 10 11   14  4        9
 1  2  3  8  5  6        10 11     7  4          9
 1  2  3  8  5  6      4 10 11     7             9
 1  2  3  8  5  6 14  12 10 11     7  4          9
 1  2  3  8  5  6  7   4 10 11        9 12
    2  5  3     6  7   4 10 11        9  8    1 12
    2  5  3     6  7   4 10 11  11    9       8  1 12
    2  5  3 12  6  7   4 10            9      8   11 1 14
    2  5  3     6  7   4 10 11        8       9   1
    2 12  3  5  6  7   4 10 11        8       9   1
       3  2  5  6  7   10 11  12    8    4 14     9   1
       3  2  5  6  7   10     12      4           9   1  8 11
    2  6  3  5     7  8 10     12      4          9   1 11
    2  6  3  5     7  8 10          4             9   1 11 12
    2  6  3  5     7 14 10 12        9  4         9   1 11 12
    2  6     5     7   10 11        9  4  3       1  8
    2  6     5     7   10 11        9  4  3 12    1  8 14
    2       11     5   10  4        9     3  8    1             6
    2     3  5  6  7   10 11  12      8       1  9      4 14
    2     3  5  6  7   10     12      8       1  9   14 4 11
    2  6  3  5     7   10 11  12  14  8       1  9      4
       6  3  5  2  7   10            12 11  8 1  9      4
    2  3  8  5  6  7   10 11          12        9      4    1
       3  8  5  6  7   10 11            2       9      4    1
    2  3  8  5  6  7   10 11            12      9      4    1 14
    2  6  3  5     7   10 11          8         9      4    1 12
    2  6  3  5        10 11          8          9   12 4  7 1
    2  6  3  5        10 11          8          9      4 12 1  7
    2  6  3  5 14  7  10 11          8          9      4    1
    2  6  3  5        10 11  7       8          9      4    1 12
    2  6  3  5 12     10 11  14      8  9       7      4    1
    2  6  3  5 12  7  10 11          8          9      4    1
    2  6  3  5  9  7  10 11          8          12     4    1 14
    2  6  3  5 14  7  10 12          8          9      4    1 11
```

Appearance totals:
```
6 42 35 44 41 31 38 2 18 46 38 1 2 1 20 2 27 5 0 10 5 2 8 1 0 15 21 2 0 17 2 12 2
   1    4  1  1  3    2 1 5 1 6    3 1 2         2   1     1 2 3   2   4
   6  5  1        9  1 1 17 10 1   2 4       2   3       4 1       2
```

Cup/play-off appearances (lower blocks):
```
1 2   3 5 6 7     12 10 11       9  4
1 1 1 1 1 1 1      0  1  1       1  1
          1
```
```
1 2   3 5 6 7      9 10 11  4 12 8
1 2   3 5 6 7      9 10 11  4 14 8    12
1 2 3 8 5 6 7      9 10 11  4
1 2 3 8 5 6        9 10 11  4
1 2 3 8 5 6      4 10 11  7         9        12
1 2 5 3   6 7    4 10 11  14        8        12
  2 5 3 12 6 7   4 10 11            9    8 1 14
6 7 5 7 5 7 6    7 7 7 2 1 2 5 0    0  2   2 0  0
              1            3 1 1 1    1       1        1
              1 2     3 5 1 1
```

Division One

Manager: Terry Cooper

Did you know that?

In a real ding-dong game at St Andrew's in mid-April, Blues led Swindon Town 4–1 before conceding five goals in the last half-hour to lose 6–4.

Goalkeeper Martin Thomas was sent off after conceding a penalty in the FA Cup defeat at Reading. Trevor Matthewson took over and saved Jimmy Quinn's spot-kick.

Darren Roberts scored a first-half hat-trick in front of the live TV cameras when Wolves beat Blues 4–0 at St Andrew's in September.

Four players were sent off in the last five minutes of the Anglo-Italian Cup game against Bari at St Andrew's. David Speedie (on loan from Southampton) and Louie Donowa both saw red for Blues, and Montanari and Brambati for Bari.

Former Blues favourite Cyril Trigg died on 9 April, aged 76.

On 5 March, multi-millionaire publisher David Sullivan announced he was the new owner of Birmingham City and that Karren Brady would be managing-director.

Match No.	Date		Venue	Opponents	Result		Scorers	Attendance
1	Aug	16	H	Notts County	W	1-0	Donowa	10,614
2		22	A	Cambridge United	W	3-0	Rennie 2, Donowa	4,837
3		30	H	Grimsby Town	W	2-1	Gleghorn, Rowbotham	6,807
4	Sep	1	H	Southend United	W	2-0	Tait, Beckford	8,324
5		5	A	Portsmouth	L	0-4		12,152
6		12	A	Millwall	D	0-0		8,587
7		19	A	Luton Town	D	1-1	Rowbotham	8,48
8		27	H	Wolverhampton Wan.	L	0-4		14,39
9	Oct	3	A	Oxford United	D	0-0		7,09
10		10	H	Leicester City	L	0-2		14,44
11		17	A	Tranmere Rovers	L	0-4		7,90
12		24	H	Bristol Rovers	W	2-1	Frain (pen), Matthewson	9,87
13	Nov	1	A	Charlton Athletic	D	0-0		4,42
14		4	H	Newcastle United	L	2-3	Speedie, Potter	14,37
15		7	A	Bristol City	L	0-3		10,01
16		21	A	Barnsley	L	0-1		5,60
17		28	A	West Ham United	L	1-3	Rodgerson	15,00
18	Dec	5	A	Brentford	L	1-3	Frain	8,58
19		12	A	Derby County	L	1-3	Speedie	16,66
20		19	H	Watford	D	2-2	Frain, Peschisolido	7,18
21	Jan	9	H	Luton Town	W	2-1	Frain (pen), Gayle	9,60
22		12	A	Swindon Town	D	0-0		13,45
23		17	A	Wolverhampton Wan.	L	1-2	Tait	13,56
24		22	H	Peterborough Utd.	W	2-0	Frain (pen), Gayle	10,27
25		27	A	Southend United	L	0-4		4,06
26		30	H	Cambridge United	L	0-2		9,42
27	Feb	6	A	Notts County	L	1-3	Potter	8,55
28		9	H	Millwall	D	0-0		8,50
29		13	H	Portsmouth	L	2-3	Sturridge, Peschisolido	10,93
30		20	A	Grimsby Town	D	1-1	Gayle	5,23
31		28	A	Leicester City	L	1-2	Matthewson	10,28
32	Mar	6	H	Oxford United	W	1-0	Peschisolido	11,10
33		9	A	Peterborough Utd.	L	1-2	Peschisolido	7,60
34		13	H	Bristol City	L	0-1		15,61
35		16	H	Sunderland	W	1-0	Peschisolido	10,93
36		20	A	Brentford	W	2-0	Peschisolido 2	7,53
37		23	H	Barnsley	W	3-0	Moulden, Saville 2	12,66
38		28	A	Newcastle United	D	2-2	Rodgerson, Saville	27,13
39	Apr	3	H	West Ham United	L	1-2	Saville	19,05
40		6	H	Derby County	D	1-1	Moulden	15,42
41		10	A	Sunderland	W	2-1	Moulden, Saville	16,38
42		12	H	Swindon Town	L	4-6	Frain, Peer, Moulden, Saville	17,90
43		17	A	Watford	L	0-1		9,18
44		24	H	Tranmere Rovers	D	0-0		15,28
45	May	1	A	Bristol Rovers	D	3-3	Mardon, Smith, Saville	5,14
46		8	H	Charlton Athletic	W	1-0	Moulden	22,23

Appearance
Sub appearance
Goal

FA Cup

R1	Nov	15	A	Reading	L	0-1		766

Appearance
Sub appearance

League Cup

R1	Aug	18	A	Exeter City	D	0-0		3,03
R1s		25	H	Exeter City	L	1-4	Sale	5,71

Appearance
Sub appearance
Goal

Player columns: Looney AR, Clarkson IS, Frain JW, Rennie D, Rogers DJ, Marsden PJ, Donowa BL, Tait PR, Sale MD, Gleghorn NW, Sturridge SA, Rodgerson I, Hicks M, Cooper MN, Beckford JN, Rowbotham D, Matthewson T, Peer D, Seatey LJ, Holmes P, Gayle J, Speedie DR, Potter GS, Peschisolido PP, Fenwick P, Fitzpatrick PJ, Quinn SJ, Foy DL, Thomas MR, Catlin R, Hiley SP, Parris GMR, Mousden PAJ, Smith D, Dryden RA, Saville AV, Scott RP

League Table

	P	W	D	L	F	A	Pts
Newcastle United	46	29	9	8	92	38	96
West Ham United	46	26	10	10	81	41	88
Portsmouth	46	26	10	10	80	46	88
Tranmere Rovers	46	23	10	13	72	56	79
Swindon Town	46	21	13	12	74	59	76
Leicester City	46	22	10	14	71	64	76
Millwall	46	18	16	12	65	53	70
Derby County	46	19	9	18	68	57	66
Grimsby Town	46	19	7	20	58	57	64
Peterborough United	46	16	14	16	55	63	62
Wolverhampton W	46	16	13	17	57	56	61
Charlton Athletic	46	16	13	17	49	46	61
Barnsley	46	17	9	20	56	60	60
Oxford United	46	14	14	18	53	56	56
Bristol City	46	14	14	18	49	67	56
Watford	46	14	13	19	57	71	55
Notts County	46	12	16	18	55	70	52
Southend United	46	13	13	20	54	64	52
Birmingham City	46	13	12	21	50	72	51
Luton Town	46	10	21	15	48	62	51
Sunderland	46	13	11	22	50	64	50
Brentford	46	13	10	23	52	71	49
Cambridge United	46	11	16	19	48	69	49
Bristol Rovers	46	10	11	25	55	87	41

Division One

Manager: Terry Cooper (to December); then Barry Fry

Match No.	Date		Venue	Opponents	Result		Scorers	Attendance
1	Aug	14	A	Charlton Athletic	L	0-1		7,788
2		22	H	Wolverhampton Wan.	D	2-2	Saville, Peschisolido	15,117
3		28	A	Barnsley	W	3-2	Smith 2, Shutt	7,241
4		31	H	Crystal Palace	L	2-4	Peschisolido 2	13,856
5	Sep	4	H	Derby County	W	3-0	Frain, Saville 2	15,992
6		12	A	Leicester City	D	1-1	Peschisolido	10,366
7		18	H	Grimsby Town	D	1-1	Donowa	12,108
8		25	H	Luton Town	D	1-1	Shutt	11,801
9	Oct	2	A	Middlesbrough	D	2-2	Peschisolido 2	13,801
10		9	A	Sunderland	L	0-1		19,265
11		16	H	Watford	W	1-0	Wallace	12,823
12		19	H	Bolton Wanderers	W	2-1	Shutt, Phillips (og)	12,071
13		23	A	Peterborough Utd.	L	0-1		7,575
14		31	H	Millwall	W	1-0	Shutt	9,377
15	Nov	2	H	Bristol City	L	0-3		9,192
16		6	H	Nottingham Forest	L	0-3		16,996
17		20	H	Portsmouth	L	0-1		11,896
18		27	A	Tranmere Rovers	L	0-3		9,915
19	Dec	4	A	Nottingham Forest	L	0-1		22,061
20		11	A	Crystal Palace	L	1-2	Saville	11,935
21		18	H	Charlton Athletic	W	1-0	Lowe	13,714
22		26	A	Stoke City	L	1-2	Peschisolido	16,563
23		28	H	West Bromwich Albion	W	2-0	Saville (pen), Peschisolido	28,228
24	Jan	1	A	Southend United	L	1-3	Peschisolido	10,731
25		3	H	Oxford United	D	1-1	Donowa	15,142
26		11	A	Notts County	L	1-2	Cooper	7,212
27		15	A	Watford	L	2-5	Willis, McGavin	7,636
28		22	H	Sunderland	D	0-0		15,884
29	Feb	5	H	Peterborough Utd.	D	0-0		15,140
30		12	A	Millwall	L	1-2	Saville	9,538
31		19	H	Notts County	L	2-3	Frain (pen), Saville	12,913
32		22	A	Wolverhampton Wan.	L	0-3		24,931
33		26	A	Derby County	D	1-1	Claridge	16,624
34	Mar	5	H	Barnsley	L	0-2		15,382
35		12	H	Grimsby Town	L	0-1		5,405
36		15	H	Leicester City	L	0-3		14,681
37		19	A	Luton Town	D	1-1	Claridge	7,690
38		26	H	Middlesbrough	W	1-0	Saville	12,409
39		29	A	Oxford United	L	0-2		8,393
40	Apr	2	H	Stoke City	W	3-1	Willis, Claridge, Ward	13,568
41		9	H	Southend United	W	3-1	Saville, Willis, Doherty	14,307
42		16	H	Bristol City	D	2-2	Donowa, Claridge (pen)	20,316
43		23	A	Portsmouth	W	2-0	Willis, Claridge (pen)	11,101
44		27	A	West Bromwich Albion	W	4-2	Saville, Donowa, Claridge 2	20,316
45		30	A	Bolton Wanderers	D	1-1	Willis	13,602
46	May	8	A	Tranmere Rovers	W	2-1	Donowa, Garnett (og)	15,210

Appearances
Sub appearances
Two own-goals   Goals

FA Cup

R3	Jan 8	H	Kidderminster Harr.	L	1-2	Harding	19,668

Appearances
Sub appearances
Goals

League Cup

R1	Aug 17	H	Plymouth Argyle	W	3-0	Frain, Parris, Peschisolido	9,304
R1s	24	A	Plymouth Argyle	L	0-2		3,659
R2	Sep 21	H	Aston Villa	L	0-1		27,815
R2s	Oct 6	A	Aston Villa	L	0-1		35,856

Appearances
Sub appearances
Goals

League Table

	P	W	D	L	F	A	Pts
Crystal Palace	46	27	9	10	73	46	90
Nottingham Forest	46	23	14	9	74	49	83
Millwall	46	19	17	10	58	49	74
Leicester City	46	19	16	11	72	59	73
Tranmere Rovers	46	21	9	16	69	53	72
Derby County	46	20	11	15	73	68	71
Notts County	46	20	8	18	65	69	68
Wolverhampton W	46	17	17	12	60	47	68
Middlesbrough	46	18	13	15	66	54	67
Stoke City	46	18	13	15	57	59	67
Charlton Athletic	46	19	8	19	61	58	65
Sunderland	46	19	8	19	54	57	65
Bristol City	46	16	16	14	47	50	64
Bolton Wanderers	46	15	14	17	63	64	59
Southend United	46	17	8	21	63	67	59
Grimsby Town	46	13	20	13	52	47	59
Portsmouth	46	15	13	18	52	58	58
Barnsley	46	16	7	23	55	67	55
Watford	46	15	9	22	66	80	54
Luton Town	46	14	11	21	56	60	53
West Bromwich Albion	46	13	12	21	60	69	51
Birmingham City	46	13	12	21	52	69	51
Oxford United	46	13	10	23	54	75	49
Peterborough United	46	8	13	25	48	76	37

Division Two

Manager: Barry Fry

A total of 21 players were used by Blues manager Barry Fry during the 2–1 friendly win against Walsall at the Bescot Stadium in July.

The first 'golden goal' to decide a Wembley Cup Final was scored in the 13th minute of extra-time by Paul Tait for Blues against Carlisle in the Auto-Windscreen Shield in April. Tait was also the scorer of Blues' first-ever 'golden goal' – the 97th minute winner in the semi-final v Swansea three weeks earlier.

Blues beat Huddersfield Town in the first-ever game at the Alfred McAlpine Stadium in May, and victory also clinched the Second Division Championship.

A throw-in this season by Tait was measured at 41 metres, one of the longest-ever in League football.

Slough Town were drawn at home in the first round of the FA Cup but elected to stage the game at St Andrew's.

Blues goalie Ian Bennett kept a club record 19 clean sheets in the League this season (27 overall). He bettered his League record in 1997–98 with 21.

Blues amassed a club record 89 League points this season.

Match No.	Date		Venue	Opponents	Result			Scorers	Attendance
1	Aug	13	A	Leyton Orient	L	1-2		Claridge	7,578
2		20	H	Chester City	W	1-0		Donowa	12,188
3		27	A	Swansea City	W	2-0		Claridge 2	5,807
4		30	H	Wycombe Wanderers	L	0-1			14,305
5	Sep	3	H	Plymouth Argyle	W	4-2		Regis 2, Tait, Wallace	13,202
6		10	A	Oxford United	D	1-1		Claridge	8,072
7		13	A	Rotherham United	D	1-1		Bull	3,574
8		18	H	Peterborough Utd.	W	4-0		Dominguez, Tait, Bull 2	10,600
9		24	H	Hull City	D	2-2		Claridge (pen), Dominguez	12,192
10	Oct	1	A	Wrexham	D	1-1		Claridge	6,012
11		8	H	Huddersfield Town	D	1-1		Bull	15,265
12		15	A	Brighton & Hove Alb.	W	1-0		Donowa	11,004
13		22	A	Brentford	W	2-1		Ward, Shearer	7,779
14		29	H	Bristol Rovers	W	2-0		Claridge, Bull	15,886
15	Nov	1	H	Crewe Alexandra	W	5-0		Claridge, Donowa, Hunt 3	14,212
16		5	A	Shrewsbury Town	W	2-0		Bull, Hunt	5,949
17		19	H	Bournemouth	D	0-0			15,477
18		26	A	Stockport County	W	1-0		Hunt	5,577
19	Dec	10	A	Chester City	W	4-0		Lowe, Claridge, Daish, McGavin	3,946
20		17	H	Leyton Orient	W	2-0		Donowa 2	20,022
21		26	H	Cambridge United	D	1-1		Otto	20,743
22		28	A	Cardiff City	W	1-0		Otto	7,420
23		31	H	Blackpool	W	7-1		Claridge 2, Donowa 2, Lowe, Parris, Bradshaw (og)	18,025
24	Jan	2	A	Bradford City	D	1-1		Cooper	10,539
25		14	A	York City	L	0-2			6,828
26	Feb	4	H	Stockport County	W	1-0		Dinning (og)	17,160
27		11	A	Crewe Alexandra	L	1-2		Donowa	6,359
28		18	H	York City	W	4-2		Francis 2, Shearer, Otto	14,846
29		21	A	Bournemouth	L	1-2		Francis	6,024
30		25	H	Wrexham	W	5-2		Francis 2, Shearer, Donowa, Otto	18,884
31	Mar	4	A	Hull City	D	0-0			9,854
32		11	H	Swansea City	L	0-1			16,191
33		18	A	Wycombe Wanderers	W	3-0		Shearer, Claridge, Evans (og)	7,289
34		21	H	Oxford United	W	3-0		Francis, Claridge, Daish	19,781
35		25	A	Peterborough Utd.	D	1-1		Shearer	8,796
36		29	A	Bristol Rovers	D	1-1		Claridge	7,851
37	Apr	1	H	Rotherham United	W	2-1		Francis, Shearer	16,077
38		4	A	Blackpool	D	1-1		Claridge	4,944
39		11	H	Shrewsbury Town	W	2-0		Claridge 2	18,366
40		15	H	Cardiff City	W	2-1		Ward (pen), Tait	17,455
41		17	A	Cambridge United	L	0-1			5,317
42		19	A	Plymouth Argyle	W	3-1		Whyte, Claridge 2	8,550
43		26	H	Brentford	W	2-0		Francis, Daish	25,581
44		29	H	Brighton & Hove Alb.	D	3-3		Ward, Shearer, Dominguez	19,006
45	May	2	H	Bradford City	D	0-0			25,139
46		6	A	Huddersfield Town	W	2-1		Claridge, Tait	18,775
								Appearances	
								Sub appearances	
							Three own-goals	Goals	

FA Cup

	Date		Venue	Opponents	Result			Scorers	Attendance
R1	Nov	12	H	Slough Town	W	4-0		Shearer 2, McGavin 2	13,394
R2	Dec	2	H	Scunthorpe United	D	0-0			13,832
rep		14	A	Scunthorpe United	W	2-1		Cooper, McGavin	6,280
R3	Jan	7	H	Liverpool	D	0-0			25,326
rep		18	A	Liverpool	D	1-1		Otto	36,275

R3 replay lost 0-2 on penalties a.e.t.

								Appearances	
								Sub appearances	
								Goals	

League Cup

	Date		Venue	Opponents	Result			Scorers	Attendance
R1	Aug	16	A	Shrewsbury Town	L	1-2		Daish	5,049
R1s		23	H	Shrewsbury Town	W	2-0		Claridge (pen), Saville	9,847
R2	Sep	20	A	Blackburn Rovers	L	0-2			14,517
R2s	Oct	4	H	Blackburn Rovers	D	1-1		McGavin	16,275

								Appearances	
								Sub appearances	
								Goals	

Bennett M · Hiley SP · Dryden RA · Ward MW · Shearer PA · Whyte CA · Lowe K · Claridge SE · Saville AV · Willis RC · Dorowa BL · Regis DR · Domingeuz JMM · Scott RP · Daish LS · Harding PJ · Doherty N · Frain JW · De Souza MJL · Tait PR · Wallace DL · Small B · Bull GW · Poole GJ · Hunt JR · McGavin SJ · Barnett DK · Cooper GJ · Howell DC · Otto RJ · Parris GMR · Bailey MJ · Francis KMD · Robinson SE · Webb ML · Williams PA · Hendon M · Bass JDM · Moulden PAJ

League Table

	P	W	D	L	F	A	Pts
Birmingham City	46	25	14	7	84	37	89
Brentford	46	25	10	11	81	39	85
Crewe Alexandra	46	25	8	13	80	68	83
Bristol Rovers	46	22	16	8	70	40	82
Huddersfield Town	46	22	15	9	79	49	81
Wycombe Wanderers	46	21	15	10	60	46	78
Oxford United	46	21	12	13	66	52	75
Hull City	46	21	11	14	70	57	74
York City	46	21	9	16	67	51	72
Swansea City	46	19	14	13	57	45	71
Stockport County	46	19	8	19	63	60	65
Blackpool	46	18	10	18	64	70	64
Wrexham	46	16	15	15	65	64	63
Bradford City	46	16	12	18	57	64	60
Peterborough United	46	14	18	14	54	69	60
Brighton & Hove Albion	46	14	17	15	54	53	59
Rotherham United	46	14	14	18	54	61	56
Shrewsbury Town	46	13	14	19	54	62	53
Bournemouth	46	13	11	22	49	69	50
Cambridge United	46	11	15	20	52	69	48
Plymouth Argyle	46	12	10	24	45	83	46
Cardiff City	46	9	11	26	46	74	38
Chester City	46	6	11	29	37	84	29
Leyton Orient	46	6	8	32	30	75	26

Division One

Manager: Barry Fry

The new all-seater, £7.4 million Tilton Road stand at St Andrew's was officially opened on 15 November. Blues drew 1–1 with Aston Villa before 19,766 fans.

Derby's 4–1 win at St Andrew's was their first on Blues soil for 47 years.

All of Blues' goals in their 5–0 win at Barnsley were scored in a 30-minute spell after half-time. The Tykes finished with nine men and Steve Claridge missed a penalty for Blues.

Blues were 2–0 up, then 4–2 down before drawing 4–4 at Sheffield United in August.

Three former West Bromwich Albion players – Steve Bull, Don Goodman and Andy Thompson – scored for Wolves against Blues in March.

Ex-Blues winger Dave Smith netted the winning penalty for West Bromwich Albion in the shoot-out at the end of the Anglo-Italian Area final at St Andrew's.

In a pre-season home friendly v Liverpool (for the TNT Inter Trophy) the 13,178 fans saw 38 players used during the 94 minutes of action – 23 by Blues!

Match No.	Date	Venue	Opponents	Result		Scorers	Attendance
1	Aug 12	H	Ipswich Town	W	3-1	Tait, Otto, Bowen	18,910
2	19	A	Charlton Athletic	L	1-3	Bowen	9,710
3	26	H	Norwich City	W	3-1	Hunt 3 (1 pen)	19,267
4	30	A	Huddersfield Town	L	2-4	Ward 2	12,305
5	Sep 2	A	Barnsley	W	5-0	Hunt (pen), Claridge, Forsyth, Doherty, Charlery	11,121
6	9	H	Crystal Palace	D	0-0		19,403
7	12	H	Stoke City	D	1-1	Hunt	19,005
8	17	A	West Bromwich Albion	L	0-1		17,854
9	23	A	Watford	D	1-1	Finnan	9,422
10	30	H	Oldham Athletic	D	0-0		17,269
11	Oct 8	A	Southend United	W	2-0	Claridge 2	17,491
12	14	A	Portsmouth	W	1-0	Claridge	10,009
13	21	H	Grimsby Town	W	3-1	Claridge 2, Charlery	16,445
14	29	A	Port Vale	W	2-1	Claridge, Tait	8,875
15	Nov 4	H	Millwall	D	2-2	Castle, Charlery	23,016
16	11	A	Reading	W	1-0	Charlery	10,203
17	18	A	Luton Town	D	0-0		7,920
18	21	H	Derby County	L	1-4	Ward (pen)	19,417
19	26	H	Leicester City	D	2-2	Hunt 2 (1 pen)	17,350
20	Dec 2	A	Southend United	L	1-3	Claridge	7,770
21	9	H	Watford	W	1-0	Francis	16,790
22	16	A	Oldham Athletic	L	0-4		6,602
23	23	H	Tranmere Rovers	W	1-0	Hunt	18,439
24	26	A	Sheffield United	D	1-1	Francis	17,668
25	Jan 14	H	Charlton Athletic	L	3-4	Edwards, Hunt (pen), Forsyth	18,539
26	20	A	Ipswich Town	L	0-2		12,388
27	Feb 4	A	Norwich City	D	1-1	Otto	12,612
28	17	A	Stoke City	L	0-1		15,709
29	20	H	Barnsley	D	0-0		14,168
30	27	A	Crystal Palace	L	2-3	Bowen 2	13,415
31	Mar 2	H	Sheffield United	L	0-1		16,799
32	5	H	Wolverhampton Wan.	W	2-0	Devlin 2 (1 pen)	22,051
33	9	A	Tranmere Rovers	D	2-2	Hunt, Legg	8,696
34	12	H	Huddersfield Town	W	2-0	Devlin, P.Barnes	15,296
35	17	H	Sunderland	L	0-2		23,251
36	20	H	West Bromwich Albion	D	1-1	Hunt	19,147
37	23	A	Wolverhampton Wan.	L	2-3	Devlin 2 (1 pen)	26,256
38	30	A	Grimsby Town	L	1-2	P.Barnes	5,773
39	Apr 2	H	Portsmouth	W	2-0	Devlin (pen), P.Barnes	14,886
40	6	H	Port Vale	W	3-1	Tait, P.Barnes, Peschisolido	17,469
41	10	A	Millwall	L	0-2		9,271
42	13	H	Luton Town	W	4-0	Francis, Devlin, P.Barnes 2	15,426
43	16	A	Sunderland	L	0-3		19,831
44	20	A	Derby County	D	1-1	Breen	16,757
45	27	A	Leicester City	L	0-3		19,702
46	May 5	H	Reading	L	1-2	P.Barnes	16,233
						Appearances	
						Sub appearances	
						Goals	

Substitutions
Bold player replaced by No. 12.
Underlined player replaced by No. 13.
Italic player replaced by No. 14.

FA Cup

R3	Jan 6	H	Wolverhampton Wan.	D	1-1	Poole	21,349
R3	17	A	Wolverhampton Wan.	L	1-2	Hunt	28,088
						Appearances	
						Sub appearances	
						Goals	

League Cup

R1	Aug 15	H	Plymouth Argyle	W	1-0	Cooper	7,964
R1s	22	A	Plymouth Argyle	W	2-1	Edwards, Hunt	6,529
R2	Sep 20	H	Grimsby Town	W	3-1	Daish, Hunt, Claridge	7,446
R2s	Oct 3	A	Grimsby Town	D	1-1	Bowen	3,280
R3	24	H	Tranmere Rovers	D	1-1	McGreal (og)	13,752
rep	Nov 8	A	Tranmere Rovers	W	3-1	Charlery 2, Rushfeldt	9,151
R4	29	A	Middlesbrough	D	0-0		28,031
rep	Dec 20	H	Middlesbrough	W	2-0	Francis 2	19,878
R5	Jan 10	A	Norwich City	D	1-1	Francis	13,028
rep	24	H	Norwich City	W	2-1	Daish, Bowen	21,097
SF1	Feb 11	H	Leeds United	L	1-2	Francis	24,781
SF2	25	A	Leeds United	L	0-3		35,435
R3 replay a.e.t.						Appearances	
						Sub appearances	
			One own-goal			Goals	

League Table

	P	W	D	L	F	A	Pts
Sunderland	46	22	17	7	59	33	83
Derby County	46	21	16	9	71	51	79
Crystal Palace	46	20	15	11	67	48	75
Stoke City	46	20	13	13	60	49	73
Leicester City	46	19	14	13	66	60	71
Charlton Athletic	46	17	20	9	57	45	71
Ipswich Town	46	19	12	15	79	69	69
Huddersfield Town	46	17	12	17	61	58	63
Sheffield United	46	16	14	16	57	54	62
Barnsley	46	14	18	14	60	66	60
West Bromwich Albion	46	16	12	18	60	68	60
Port Vale	46	15	15	16	59	66	60
Tranmere Rovers	46	14	17	15	64	60	59
Southend United	46	15	14	17	52	61	59
Birmingham City	46	15	13	18	61	64	58
Norwich City	46	14	15	17	59	55	57
Grimsby Town	46	14	14	18	55	69	56
Oldham Athletic	46	14	14	18	54	50	56
Reading	46	13	17	16	54	63	56
Wolverhampton W	46	13	16	17	56	62	55
Portsmouth	46	13	13	20	61	69	52
Millwall	46	13	13	20	43	63	52
Watford	46	10	18	18	62	70	48
Luton Town	46	11	12	23	40	64	45

Division One

Manager: Trevor Francis

Match No.	Date	Venue	Opponents		Result	Scorers	Attendance
1	Aug 18	H	Crystal Palace	W	1-0	Devlin	18,765
2	24	A	Sheffield United	D	4-4	Devlin (pen), Newell, Furlong, Hunt	16,332
3	Sep 7	A	Tranmere Rovers	L	0-1		8,548
4	10	H	Oldham Athletic	D	0-0		17,228
5	14	H	Stoke City	W	3-1	Furlong 2, Legg	18,612
6	21	A	Manchester City	L	0-1		26,757
7	28	H	Queen's Park Rangers	D	0-0		17,430
8	Oct 8	A	Huddersfield Town	L	0-3		10,904
9	12	H	Bradford City	W	3-0	Devlin 2, Hunt	25,157
10	15	A	Ipswich Town	W	1-0	Bowen	15,664
11	18	A	Oxford United	D	0-0		7,586
12	26	H	Norwich City	L	2-3	Devlin 2	18,869
13	29	A	Portsmouth	D	1-1	Furlong	6,334
14	Nov 2	A	Port Vale	L	0-3		8,388
15	13	H	Bolton Wanderers	W	3-1	Furlong, Bowen, Todd (og)	17,033
16	17	A	Wolverhampton Wan.	W	2-1	Breen, Legg	22,627
17	20	A	Charlton Athletic	L	1-2	Legg	8,650
18	23	H	Swindon Town	W	1-0	Furlong	16,559
19	26	A	Reading	D	0-0		8,407
20	30	A	Norwich City	W	1-0	O'Connor	12,764
21	Dec 3	H	Barnsley	D	0-0		24,004
22	7	H	Grimsby Town	D	0-0		17,513
23	20	A	Southend United	D	1-1	Devlin	4,889
24	Jan 10	A	Stoke City	L	0-1		9,965
25	18	H	Reading	W	4-1	Devlin 2 (1 pen), Furlong, Gilkes (og)	15,363
26	29	A	Queen's Park Rangers	D	1-1	Devlin	12,138
27	Feb 1	A	Bolton Wanderers	L	1-2	Devlin	16,737
28	4	H	West Bromwich Albion	L	2-3	Devlin (pen), O'Connor	21,600
29	8	H	Portsmouth	L	0-3		15,897
30	23	H	Port Vale	L	1-2	Devlin (pen)	13,192
31	26	A	Swindon Town	L	1-3	Ablett	8,082
32	Mar 1	A	Grimsby Town	W	2-1	O'Connor, Forster	5,439
33	4	H	Wolverhampton Wan.	L	1-2	Forster	19,838
34	8	H	Southend United	W	2-1	O'Connor (pen), Forster	13,189
35	11	H	Manchester City	W	2-0	Furlong (pen), Francis	20,084
36	16	A	West Bromwich Albion	L	0-2		15,972
37	22	H	Sheffield United	D	1-1	Legg	14,969
38	29	A	Crystal Palace	W	1-0	Grainger	17,114
39	31	H	Charlton Athletic	D	0-0		14,525
40	Apr 5	A	Barnsley	W	1-0	Grainger	13,048
41	8	A	Oldham Athletic	D	2-2	Furlong, Grainger	5,942
42	12	H	Huddersfield Town	W	1-0	Jenkins (og)	14,394
43	15	H	Tranmere Rovers	D	0-0		22,364
44	19	A	Bradford City	W	2-0	Devlin, Furlong	15,123
45	26	H	Oxford United	W	2-0	Devlin, Bowen	16,019
46	May 4	A	Ipswich Town	D	1-1	Devlin	20,490

					Appearances
					Sub appearances
			Three own-goals		Goals

FA Cup

	Date	Venue	Opponents		Result	Scorers	Attendance
R3	Jan 4	H	Stevenage Borough	W	2-0	Devlin (pen), Francis	15,365
R4	25	H	Stockport County	W	3-1	Devlin, Furlong, Francis	18,487
R5	Feb 15	H	Wrexham	L	1-3	Bruce	21,511

					Appearances
					Sub appearances
					Goals

League Cup

	Date	Venue	Opponents		Result	Scorers	Attendance
R1	Aug 21	A	Brighton & Hove Albion	W	1-0	Devlin (pen)	5,132
R1s	Sep 4	H	Brighton & Hove Albion	W	2-0	Newell 2	20,05
R2	18	A	Coventry City	D	1-1	Furlong	11,82
R2s	24	H	Coventry City	L	0-1		15,281

					Appearances
					Sub appearance
					Goal

Appearance / Scorer Grid

	Bennett IM	Poole GJ	Ablett GI	Bruce SR	Breen GP	Tait PR	Devlin PJ	Newell MC	Furlong PA	Horne B	Legg A	Hunt JR	Otto RJ	Castle SC	Johnson MO	Holland CJ	Dinnowa BL	Breen JP	Edwards AD	Finnan SJ	Gabbiadini M	Frain JV	Jackson MA	Sutton SJ	O'Connor MJ	Cooke TJ	Francis KMD	Bass JDM	Grainger MR	Brown KJ	Limpar AE	Foster NM	Barnett IM	Robinson SE	Hughes B	Wassall DPJ
	1	2	3	4	5	**6**	7	8	9	10	11	12	13																							
	1	2	3	4	5		7	**8**	9	10	11	12			6	13																				
	1	2	3	4	5			8	9	10	11	13			6		12																			
	1	2	3	4	5		7	8	9	10	13	11			6	12																				
	1	2	3	4	5	13	8	9	10	11		12		6	14	7																				
	1			4	5		7		9	10	11	13		3	6	12	8		2																	
	1		3	4			7	8	9	10	11	6		14	5		12	13	2																	
	1		3	4	5		7		9	10	11	8			6		12		2																	
	1	13	3	4	5		7		9	10	11	8			6		12	2	14																	
	1	2	3	4	5	**8**	7		9	10	11				6		13		12																	
	1	2	**3**	4	5	14	7	13	9	10	12		8		6		11																			
	1	2	3	4	5	12	7		9					8		6		11		10																
	1		3	4	5			9	10	11				13	12	6	8					2														
	1			4		5	11	7	14	**9**	10	12			3	6		8	13			2														
	1	14	4	5	8	12	13	**9**	10	**7**				3	6		11					2														
		4		5	8	12	13	9	10	**7**				3	6		11					2	1													
		12	**4**	5	8		**7**		9	10	7			3	6		11					2	1													
		4		5	8	12		9	10	7	14			3	6		11	13				2	1													
		4		5	12			9	10	7	13			3	6		11					2	1	8	14											
		4	14	5	13				10	7	9			3	6		11					2	1	8	12											
		5	4	14	13			9	10					3	6		11					2	1	8	7	12										
	1	5	4	12	8	14		9	10					**3**	6		11					2		7	13											
	1		4		8	7		12	10	9					5		11							6			13	3	2							
	1		5	4		7		9	10		11				12	6								8		13		3	2							
	1		5	4		7		9	10	11					13	6								8		12		3	2	13						
	1		5		7		9	10	13					4	6								8		12		3	2	11	14						
	1		5	4		7	9	13	10						14	6							8				3	2	11	12						
	1		5	4		7	9	13	10	11	12				3								8				14	2		6						
	1		5	4		9	12	10		14					6	8							11				13	3	2		7					
	1		5	4	8		9	14	10						6	12							11				13	2	3		7					
	1		5	4	**8**			14	10						3	13							6				9	2	12		11	7				
	1		5	4	8				10									7					11				13	3	2		6	12				
	1		**5**	**4**	8	13		10							12			11					7		9	3	2		6		14					
	1		5		8	7		9		4								11					12	2	3				6		10					
	1		5		12	7		9							4	14		11					13	2	3				8		10	6				
	1		5		8	7		9		14					4			11					13	2	3				6	12	10					
	1		5		13	7		9							4			11					12	2	3				6	8	10	5				
	1	12		13	7		9								4			11					14	2	3				6	8	10	5				
	1		5		8	7			14						4	11							12	2	3						13	10	6			
	1		5		8	7		9			13				4								12	2	3							10	6			
	1		5		12	7		9		14					4	11							13	2	3						8	10	6			
	1		5	13		7			14						4			12					9	**2**	3						8	10	6			
	1		5	4		7			13						6			11					9	12							8	10	2			
Apps	40	9	39	30	20	17	32	11	37	33	22	6	1	28	28	0	19	1	3	0	1	10	6	24	1	4	11	21	11	3	4	6	6	10	8	
Sub		1		3	2	9	6	4	6		11	6	3	4	7	4	6	2		2			3	15	2	2		1	3	1						
Gls		1		1		16	1	10		4	2		3					4	1	1		3		4	1		1	3		3						

Cup matches (lower blocks)

	Bennett IM	Poole GJ	Ablett GI	Bruce SR	Breen GP	Tait PR	Devlin PJ	Newell MC	Furlong PA	Horne B	Legg A	Hunt JR	Otto RJ	Castle SC	Johnson MO	Holland CJ	Dinnowa BL	Breen JP	Edwards AD	Finnan SJ	Gabbiadini M	Frain JV	Jackson MA	Sutton SJ	O'Connor MJ	Cooke TJ	Francis KMD	Bass JDM	Grainger MR	Brown KJ	Limpar AE	Foster NM	Barnett IM	Robinson SE	Hughes B	Wassall DPJ
	1		5	4		8	7			10	12				13	**6**		11						9	2	**3**										
	1		5	4	2		**7**		9	10	8	**11**			14	6		13					12		3											
	1		**5**	4			7	13	9	10	8				3	6		12										2	11							
	3		3	3	1	1	3	0	2	3	2	1			1	3		1					1	1	2	1		1	1							
								1						2		2											1									
				1			2		1																											

	Bennett IM	Poole GJ	Ablett GI	Bruce SR	Breen GP	Tait PR	Devlin PJ	Newell MC	Furlong PA	Horne B	Legg A	Hunt JR	Otto RJ	Castle SC	Johnson MO	Holland CJ	Dinnowa BL	Breen JP	Edwards AD	Finnan SJ	Gabbiadini M	Frain JV	Jackson MA	Sutton SJ	O'Connor MJ	Cooke TJ	Francis KMD	Bass JDM	Grainger MR	Brown KJ	Limpar AE	Foster NM	Barnett IM	Robinson SE	Hughes B	Wassall DPJ
	1	2	3	4	5		7	**8**	9	10	**11**	12			6	13																				
	1	2	3	4	5		7	8	9	10	11	13			6	12																				
	1	2	3	4	5	13	12	8	9	10	11				6			**7**																		
	1		3	4	5		7	8	9	10	13				6				**11**	12	**2**															
	4	3	4	4	4	0	3	4	4	4	3	0			4	0		1	1	1	1															
				1				1		1	2				2			1																		
					1	2	1																													

League Table

	P	W	D	L	F	A	Pts
Bolton Wanderers	46	28	14	4	100	53	98
Barnsley	46	22	14	10	76	55	80
Wolverhampton W	46	22	10	14	68	51	76
Ipswich Town	46	20	14	12	68	50	74
Sheffield United	46	20	13	13	75	52	73
Crystal Palace	46	19	14	13	78	48	71
Portsmouth	46	20	8	18	59	53	68
Port Vale	46	17	16	13	58	55	67
Queen's Park Rangers	46	18	12	16	64	60	66
Birmingham City	46	17	15	14	52	48	66
Tranmere Rovers	46	17	14	15	63	56	65
Stoke City	46	18	10	18	51	57	64
Norwich City	46	17	12	17	63	68	63
Manchester City	46	17	10	19	59	60	61
Charlton Athletic	46	16	11	19	52	66	59
West Bromwich Albion	46	14	15	17	68	72	57
Oxford United	46	16	9	21	64	68	57
Reading	46	15	12	19	58	67	57
Swindon Town	46	15	9	22	52	71	54
Huddersfield Town	46	13	15	18	48	61	54
Bradford City	46	12	12	22	47	72	48
Grimsby Town	46	11	13	22	60	81	46
Oldham Athletic	46	10	13	23	51	66	43
Southend United	46	8	15	23	42	86	39

Division One

Manager: Trevor Francis

Match No.	Date	Venue	Opponents	Result		Scorers	Attendance
1	Aug 9	H	Stoke City	W	2-0	Devlin, Ndlovu	20,608
2	23	H	Reading	W	3-0	Bruce, Devlin, Ndlovu	16,495
3	29	A	Stockport County	D	2-2	Devlin, Francis	6,260
4	Sep 2	A	Tranmere Rovers	W	3-0	Hughes, Ndlovu, Furlong	6,620
5	9	A	Huddersfield Town	W	1-0	Furlong	9,477
6	14	H	Sunderland	L	0-1		17,478
7	20	A	Middlesbrough	L	1-3	Furlong	30,125
8	27	A	Sheffield United	D	0-0		20,553
9	Oct 4	H	Crewe Alexandra	L	0-1		16,548
10	12	H	Wolverhampton Wan.	W	1-0	Marsden	17,822
11	18	A	Bury	L	1-2	Grainger	5,700
12	22	A	Charlton Athletic	D	1-1	Devlin	10,070
13	25	H	Oxford United	D	0-0		16,352
14	28	H	Ipswich Town	D	1-1	Bruce	16,778
15	Nov 1	A	Queen's Park Rangers	D	1-1	Furlong	12,715
16	4	H	Bradford City	D	0-0		14,554
17	8	H	Norwich City	L	1-2	Devlin (pen)	15,464
18	15	A	Nottingham Forest	L	0-1		19,610
19	23	A	West Bromwich Albion	L	0-1		18,444
20	29	H	Portsmouth	W	2-1	Furlong 2	17,738
21	Dec 6	A	Port Vale	W	1-0	Cottee	7,509
22	13	H	Manchester City	W	2-1	Forster, O'Connor	21,014
23	20	A	Swindon Town	D	1-1	Forster	10,900
24	26	A	Ipswich Town	W	1-0	McCarthy	17,510
25	28	H	Tranmere Rovers	D	0-0		19,533
26	Jan 10	A	Stoke City	W	7-0	Hughes 2, Furlong 3, McCarthy, Forster	14,940
27	17	H	Huddersfield Town	D	0-0		17,850
28	27	H	Stockport County	W	4-1	Furlong 3, McCarthy	17,118
29	31	A	Reading	L	0-2		10,315
30	Feb 7	H	Middlesbrough	D	1-1	McCarthy	20,634
31	17	A	Crewe Alexandra	W	2-0	Hughes, Adebola	5,559
32	22	H	Sheffield United	W	2-0	Grainger, Johnson	17,965
33	25	H	Bury	L	1-3	Johnson	20,021
34	28	A	Wolverhampton Wan.	W	3-1	Ndlovu 2 (1 pen), Adebola	25,591
35	Mar 4	A	Norwich City	D	3-3	Ndlovu 2, Adebola	9,815
36	7	H	Queen's Park Rangers	W	1-0	Adebola	18,298
37	10	A	Sunderland	D	1-1	Adebola	36,869
38	14	A	Bradford City	D	0-0		16,392
39	21	H	Nottingham Forest	L	1-2	Ndlovu (pen)	24,663
40	28	H	West Bromwich Albion	W	1-0	Johnson	23,260
41	Apr 4	A	Portsmouth	D	1-1	Adebola	14,591
42	11	H	Port Vale	D	1-1	Ndlovu	17,193
43	13	A	Manchester City	W	1-0	Adebola	29,569
44	18	H	Swindon Town	W	3-0	Hughes, Furlong 2	17,016
45	25	A	Oxford United	W	2-0	Furlong (pen), Ford (og)	8,811
46	May 3	H	Charlton Athletic	D	0-0		25,877
						Appearances	
						Sub appearances	
					One own-goal	Goals	

FA Cup

R3	Jan 3	A	Crewe Alexandra	W	2-1	Furlong 2 (1 pen)	4,607
R4	24	H	Stockport County	W	2-1	Hughes 2	15,882
R5	Feb 14	A	Leeds United	L	2-3	Ablett, Ndlovu	35,463
						Appearances	
						Sub appearances	
						Goals	

League Cup

R1	Aug 12	A	Gillingham	W	1-0	Francis	5,241
R1s	26	H	Gillingham	W	3-0	Devlin, Ndlovu, Furlong	7,92
R2	Sep 17	H	Stockport County	W	4-1	Devlin 2 (1 pen), Hughes, Robinson	4,900
R2s	23	A	Stockport County	L	1-2	Furlong (pen)	2,074
R3	Oct 14	A	Arsenal	L	1-4	Hey	27,09
R3 a.e.t.						Appearances	
						Sub appearances	
						Goals	

Birmingham City — Appearances & Goals Grid

	Bennett IM	Wassall DPJ	Grainger MR	Bruce SR	Ablett GI	O'Connor MJ	Devlin PJ	Hey A	Hughes B	Robinson SE	Ndlovu P	Holland CJ	Francis KMD	Johnson MO	Bass JDM	Furlong PA	McCarthy JD	Marsden C	Forster NM	Cottee AR	Charlton ST	Adebola B	Purse DJ	Furnton HL	Gill JM	Poole K
	1	2	3	4	5	6	7	8	9	10	11	13	14	12												
	1	2	3	4	5	6	7	8	10		11	14	12	13		9										
	1	2	6	4	5	7	12		10	8	11		13	3		9										
	1	2	3	4	5	6	7	8	10		11	13	12	14		9										
	1	2	3	4	5	6	7	8	10		11	12	13			9										
	1	2	3	4	5	6	7		10		11	14	13	12		9	8									
	1	4	3		5	14	7		10		11	6	12	13	2	9	8									
	1	2	3	4	5	6	14	7	10		11		12	13		9	8									
	1	2	3	4	5	6	12	7	10		11		9			8										
	1		3	4	5	11	7	13	10		12				2	9	8	6								
	1	2	3	4	5	10	7	9		14	11		13	12		8	6									
	1	4	10		5		12		8	11	13	14	3	2		7	6	9								
	1	2	3	4	5		12		10	8	11	9				7	6	12								
	1		3	4	5		7		8	11	9					10	6	12								
	1	4	11		5		12		8				3	2	9	7	6	10								
	1		3	4	5		7		12	8	11				2	9	10	6	13							
	1		3	4	5		7		10	12			13	11	2	9	7	6		14						
	1	4	3		5	11	7		12	8			13	2	9	10	6			14						
	1		3	4	5		13		8	12			11	2	9	7	6		10							
	1			4	5		12		10	8	13		3	2	9	7	6		11							
	1			4	5		12		10	8	14		3	2	9	7	6		11	13						
	1		4	5	6	9			10	8	11	13	12	2		7		14		3						
	1	12	4	5	6				10	8		13	2			7		9	11	3						
	1	12	4	5	6				10	8	11	13		2		7		9		3						
	1			4	5	8			10	8	12		13	14	2	9	7	6	11	3						
	1			4	5	8			10		13			12	9	7	6	11	3							
	1			4	5	8			10		12	14	13	2	9	7	6	11	3							
	1		3	4	5				10	8		13	12	9	7	6	11									
	1		3	4	5				10	8	13	14		2	9	7	6	11								
	1			4	5	8			10			13	2	9	7	6	11	3	12							
	1	6	4		8				10		11	13		5	2	7		14	3	9	12					
	1	6	4		8				10	12	11			5	2	7		13	3	9	14					
	1	6		5	8				10		11			12	2	7	13	14	3	9	4					
	1	13	4	5	8				10	12	11			2		7	6	14	3	9						
	1		4	5					10	8	11			2		7	6	12	3	9						
	1	13	4		8				10		11			5	2	7	6	12	3	9						
	1	10	4		8				12		11			5	2	7	6		3	9						
	1	10	4		8				13		11			5	2	7	6	12	3	9						
	1	10	4	12	8				13		11			5	2	7	6		3	9						
	1	12	4	14	8				10					5	2	7	6	11	3	9	13					
	1	13		5	8				10	12	11			2		7	6	14	3	9	4					
	1		4		8				10		11			5	2	7	6	14	3	9						
	1		4		8				10	13	11			5	2	7	6	14	3	9	12					
	1		4		8				10	12				5		11	7	6	13	3	9	14	2			
	1		4		8				10	12	14			5		11	7	6		3	9	13	2			
	1		4		8				13		10			5		11	7	6	14	3	9	12	2	1		
Apps	45	14	27	40	34	32	13	8	34	17	29	2	2	22	30	24	41	31	12	4	23	16	2	0	3	1
Sub		6		2	1	9	1	6	8	10	8	18	16		1		1	16	1	1	1	6	1			
Goals		2	2		1	5		5		9		1	3		15	4	1	3	1		7					

	Bennett IM	Wassall DPJ	Grainger MR	Bruce SR	Ablett GI	O'Connor MJ	Devlin PJ	Hey A	Hughes B	Robinson SE	Ndlovu P	Holland CJ	Francis KMD	Johnson MO	Bass JDM	Furlong PA	McCarthy JD	Marsden C	Forster NM	Cottee AR	Charlton ST	Adebola B	Purse DJ	Furnton HL	Gill JM	Poole K
	1		3	4	5	8			10				13	12	2	9	7	6	11							
	1		3	4	5	8			10	14	12		13		2	9	7	6	11							
	1		6	4	5	8	12		10		11		13	2		7		9		3						
3		3	3	3	3	0		3	1	1		0	0	3	2	3	2	3		1						
			1						1		1		2				2	2								
			1					2		1						2										

	Bennett IM	Wassall DPJ	Grainger MR	Bruce SR	Ablett GI	O'Connor MJ	Devlin PJ	Hey A	Hughes B	Robinson SE	Ndlovu P	Holland CJ	Francis KMD	Johnson MO	Bass JDM	Furlong PA	McCarthy JD	Marsden C	Forster NM	Cottee AR	Charlton ST	Adebola B	Purse DJ	Furnton HL	Gill JM	Poole K
	1	4	13		5	6	7		10	8	11			12	3	2	9									
	1	2	3	4	5		7	8	10		11	6	13	12		9										
	1	4	3		5		7		10	8	11	6	12	13	2	9										
	1	4	3		5	6	7		10	8	11		12	13	2	9										
	1	2	3	4	5	6	7	8		10	11	9	14	13	12											
5	5	4	2	5	3	5	2	4	4	5	3	0	1	3	4											
		1								5	4	1														
				3	1			1	1	1	1		2													

League Table

	P	W	D	L	F	A	Pts
Nottingham Forest	46	28	10	8	82	42	94
Middlesbrough	46	27	10	9	77	41	91
Sunderland	46	26	12	8	86	50	90
Charlton Athletic	46	26	10	10	80	49	88
Ipswich Town	46	23	14	9	77	43	83
Sheffield United	46	19	17	10	69	54	74
Birmingham City	46	19	17	10	60	35	74
Stockport County	46	19	8	19	71	69	65
Wolverhampton W	46	18	11	17	57	53	65
West Bromwich Albion	46	16	13	17	50	56	61
Crewe Alexandra	46	18	5	23	58	65	59
Oxford United	46	16	10	20	60	64	58
Bradford City	46	14	15	17	46	59	57
Tranmere Rovers	46	14	14	18	54	57	56
Norwich City	46	14	13	19	52	69	55
Huddersfield Town	46	14	11	21	50	72	53
Bury	46	11	19	16	42	58	52
Swindon Town	46	14	10	22	42	73	52
Port Vale	46	13	10	23	56	66	49
Portsmouth	46	13	10	23	51	63	49
Queen's Park Rangers	46	10	19	17	51	63	49
Manchester City	46	12	12	22	56	57	48
Stoke City	46	11	13	22	44	74	46
Reading	46	11	9	26	39	78	42

1998-99

Division One

Manager: Trevor Francis

Match No.	Date		Venue	Opponents	Result		Scorers	Attendance
1	Aug	8	A	Port Vale	W	2-0	Furlong, Adebola	10,465
2		16	H	Crystal Palace	W	3-1	O'Connor (pen), Adebola, Forster	16,699
3		22	A	Sheffield United	W	2-0	Adebola, Forster	17,528
4		29	H	Barnsley	D	0-0		19,825
5		31	A	Bradford City	L	1-2	Ndlovu	13,910
6	Sep	5	H	Bury	W	1-0	Adebola	15,935
7		8	H	Stockport County	W	2-0	Marsden, Hughes	16,429
8		12	A	Bolton Wanderers	L	1-3	Rowett	19,637
9		19	H	Grimsby Town	L	0-1		17,563
10		26	A	Norwich City	L	0-2		16,584
11		29	A	Portsmouth	W	1-0	O'Connor (pen)	11,843
12	Oct	3	H	Tranmere Rovers	D	2-2	M.Johnson 2	17,189
13		10	A	Watford	D	1-1		10,096
14		17	H	Crewe Alexandra	W	3-1	O'Connor (pen), Furlong, Ndlovu	20,087
15		20	H	Swindon Town	D	1-1	Marsden	19,485
16		25	A	Queen's Park Rangers	W	1-0	Adebola	10,272
17		31	H	Huddersfield Town	D	1-1	Ndlovu	19,170
18	Nov	7	A	West Bromwich Albion	W	3-1	Adebola, Ndlovu 2	19,472
19		14	H	Oxford United	L	0-1		18,216
20		22	A	Wolverhampton Wan.	L	1-3	Furlong	23,037
21		28	H	Bristol City	W	4-2	M.Johnson, Ndlovu, Forster 2	17,577
22	Dec	5	A	Ipswich Town	L	0-1		15,901
23		12	A	Oxford United	W	7-1	Furlong 2, Ndlovu, Grainger, Hughes, Rowett 2	7,189
24		19	H	Sunderland	D	0-0		22,095
25		26	H	Sheffield United	W	1-0	Furlong (pen)	22,005
26		28	A	Bury	W	4-2	O'Connor, Furlong 2, Adebola	7,024
27	Jan	9	A	Port Vale	W	1-0	Furlong	18,632
28		16	A	Barnsley	D	0-0		17,114
29		31	H	Bradford City	W	2-1	Furlong 2 (1 pen)	19,291
30	Feb	6	A	Crystal Palace	D	1-1	Furlong (pen)	15,996
31		13	A	Stockport County	L	0-1		9,056
32		21	H	Bolton Wanderers	D	0-0		26,051
33		27	A	Grimsby Town	W	3-0	Adebola, Ndlovu, Rowett	7,807
34	Mar	2	H	Norwich City	D	0-0		20,749
35		6	H	Portsmouth	W	4-1	Adebola 2, Forster, Hughes	20,613
36		9	A	Tranmere Rovers	W	1-0	M.Johnson	7,184
37		13	H	West Bromwich Albion	W	4-0	Adebola 2, Ndlovu, Grainger	29,060
38		20	A	Huddersfield Town	D	1-1	M.Johnson	14,667
39	Apr	2	A	Crewe Alexandra	D	0-0		5,582
40		5	H	Watford	L	1-2	Holdsworth	24,877
41		10	A	Swindon Town	W	1-0	Rowett	8,896
42		17	H	Wolverhampton Wan.	L	0-1		28,143
43		20	H	Queen's Park Rangers	W	1-0	Forinton	20,886
44		24	A	Bristol City	W	2-1	Ndlovu, Grainger (pen)	15,845
45	May	2	H	Ipswich Town	W	1-0	Furlong	27,685
46		9	A	Sunderland	L	1-2	Grainger	41,393

							Appearances	
							Sub appearances	
							Goals	

Play-offs

SF1	May	16	A	Watford	L	0-1		18,535
SF2		20	H	Watford	W	1-0	Adebola	29,100

Lost 6-7 on penalties after extra time in second leg.

							Appearances	
							Sub appearances	
							Goals	

FA Cup

R3	Jan	2	A	Leicester City	L	2-4	Adebola, Robinson	19,846

							Appearances	
							Sub appearances	
							Goals	

League Cup

R1	Aug	11	H	Millwall	W	2-0	M.Johnson, Adebola	14,13.
R1s		19	A	Millwall	D	1-1	Adebola	4,47.
R2	Sep	15	A	Macclesfield Town	W	3-0	Marsden, Forster, Rowett	2,27.
R2s		22	H	Macclesfield Town	W	6-0	Askey (og), Marsden, M.Johnson, Ndlovu 2, Rowett	3,44.
R3	Oct	28	H	Wimbledon	L	1-2	Marsden	11,84.

							Appearances	
							Sub appearance	
One own-goal							Goal	

432

Player columns (left to right): Bennett IM, Gill JM, Charlton ST, Marsden C, Ablett GI, Johnson MO, McCarthy JD, O'Connor MJ, Furlong PA, Adebola B, Ndlovu P, Granger MR, Forster NM, Holland CJ, Hughes B, Purse DJ, Rowett G, Robinson SE, Johnson A, Poole K, Bass JDM, Marsh STP, Wassall DPJ, Hyde G, Holdsworth DG, Bradbury LM, Forinton HL

Bennett IM	Gill JM	Charlton ST	Marsden C	Ablett GI	Johnson MO	McCarthy JD	O'Connor MJ	Furlong PA	Adebola B	Ndlovu P	Granger MR	Forster NM	Holland CJ	Hughes B	Purse DJ	Rowett G	Robinson SE	Johnson A	Poole K	Bass JDM	Marsh STP	Wassall DPJ	Hyde G	Holdsworth DG	Bradbury LM	Forinton HL
1	2	3	4	5	6	7	8	9	10	11	12	13														
1	2	3	4	5	6	7	8		9	11	12	13		10	14											
1		3	4	5	6	7	8		9	11	10	12	13		14	2										
1		3	4	5	6	7	8		9	12	11	10				2										
1			4	5	6	7	8		9	11	3	10			12	2	14	13									
1			4	5	6		8		9		3	11	13	10	14	2	7	12									
1			4	5	6	12	8		9		3	11		10	13	2	7	14									
1			4	5	6	11	8			9	3	12	13	10	14	2	7										
1		3	4	5		6	7	8		9	11	10	12			14	2	13									
1		3	4	5	6	7	8		9	11	10	12				2	11										
			3	4	5	6	7	8		9	11	10	12			2			1								
			3	4	5	6	7	8		9	11	10	12			14	2	13		1							
		11	5			6		8	9	10	12	3	13			4	2	7		1	14						
		3	6	5	13	12	8	9	10	11						4	2	7		1							
		3	5	13		6	7	10	9	8	11			12		4	2			1							
		3	5	14	6	7	10	9	8	11				12	13	4	2			1							
		3	6	5	13	7		9	14	11	11	10			8	4	2	12		1							
			5	13	6	7		9	8	11	3	12	10			4	2	14		1							
	13	5		6	7		9	8	11	13	14	10	12	4	2			1									
	3	5		6	7		9		11	12	13	8	10	8	4	2			1								
		3		6	7				11	5	9	8	12	4	2	10	13		1								
		5	6	7	8	12		11	3		9	10	13		2	4		1	14								
		5	6	7	10	9	8	11	3	14		12		2	4		1		13								
		5	6	7	10	9	8	11					2	4	1		3	12									
		5	6	7	10	9	8	11	12	13			2	4	1		3										
		5	6	7	10	9	8	11	12			13	2	4	1		3										
		5	6	7	10	9	8	11	13	12			2	4	1		3										
	2		5	6	7		10	9	8	11	12		13	2	4	1		3									
		3		5	6	7	10	9	8	11	12	14		13	2	4	1										
		3		6	7	10	9	8	11			13		12	5	2	4		1								
		3			8	9	14	11	6	13		10	4	5	12		1	2			7						
		3		6	13	8	9	12	11	7	14		10		5		1	2			4						
		3		6	7	8	9	12	11			10		5	13		1	2			4						
		3		6	14	8	9	7	11	13	12	14		10		5		1	2			4					
		3		6	14	8	13	9	12	7	11			10		5		1	2			4					
		3		6	12	8	13	9	11	7	14			10		5		1	2			4					
		3		6	7	8	12	9	11	4	13			10		5	14	1	2			4					
		3		6	7	8			11	4	13			10		2	12		1				5	9	14		
		3		6	12	8			11	7	13			10		1	2			4	5	9	14				
			6	7	12			9	13	3	8			10		2	11		1			4	5				
			6	7	8		9	11	3					10		2	13	1			14	4	5	12			
			6	7				11	3		13	10		10		2	8	1		14	4	5	9	12			
			6	12		13		11	3			10				2	8	1	7			4	5	9			
			6	7		9	12	13	3			10		14	2	8		1				4	5	11			
		3		6	7	12	9	13	14	8				10		2			1				4	5	11		
0	3	27	20	23	43	35	35	24	33	37	30	8	7	20	11	42	20	0	36	9	6	0	13	8	6	0
	1		3	2	8	2	5	6	6	10	25	7	8	9		11	4		2	1	3			1	3	
		2		5		4	13	13	10	4	5		3		5												

(Substitutes used / goals blocks)

Bennett IM	Gill JM	Charlton ST	Marsden C	Ablett GI	Johnson MO	McCarthy JD	O'Connor MJ	Furlong PA	Adebola B	Ndlovu P	Granger MR	Forster NM	Holland CJ	Hughes B	Purse DJ	Rowett G	Robinson SE	Johnson A	Poole K	Bass JDM	Marsh STP	Wassall DPJ	Hyde G	Holdsworth DG	Bradbury LM	Forinton HL
			6	7	8	9	12	13	4			3		11			2	4		1				5	10	
			6	7	8	9	4	11	3		13	10	12	2		1							5	14		
			2	2	2	2	1		2		1	1	0	2	1		2			2	1					
								1	1			1		1						1						
									1																	

(Lower block)

			5	6	7	10	9	8	11	12	14			13		2	4		1		3					
			1	1	1	1	1	1	1	0	0			0		1	1		1		1					
									1	1																
									1																	

(Bottom block)

Bennett IM	Gill JM	Charlton ST	Marsden C	Ablett GI	Johnson MO	McCarthy JD	O'Connor MJ	Furlong PA	Adebola B	Ndlovu P	Granger MR	Forster NM	Holland CJ	Hughes B	Purse DJ	Rowett G	Robinson SE	Johnson A	Poole K	Bass JDM	Marsh STP	Wassall DPJ	Hyde G	Holdsworth DG	Bradbury LM	Forinton HL
1	2	3	4	5	6	7	8		10	11		9	13	12												
1			4	5	6	7	8		9	11	3	13	12	10	14	2										
1		4	5	6	7	8		9	3	10	12					2	11	14					13			
1		3	4		6	7	8		11	14		13		5	2	10	12						9			
		3	6	5		7		9	8	11		12	10		4	2			1							
4	1	3	5	4	4	5	4	1	4	4	2	2	1	1	2	4	2	0	1			1				
									1	2	4	1	1		2								1			
		3		2			2	2		1			2													

League Table

	P	W	D	L	F	A	Pts
Sunderland	46	31	12	3	91	28	105
Bradford City	46	26	9	11	82	47	87
Ipswich Town	46	26	8	12	69	32	86
Birmingham City	46	23	12	11	66	37	81
Watford	46	21	14	11	65	56	77
Bolton Wanderers	46	20	16	10	78	59	76
Wolverhampton W	46	19	16	11	64	43	73
Sheffield United	46	18	13	15	71	66	67
Norwich City	46	15	17	14	62	61	62
Huddersfield Town	46	15	16	15	62	71	61
Grimsby Town	46	17	10	19	40	52	61
West Bromwich Albion	46	16	11	19	69	76	59
Barnsley	46	14	17	15	59	56	59
Crystal Palace	46	14	16	16	58	71	58
Tranmere Rovers	46	12	20	14	63	61	56
Stockport County	46	12	17	17	49	60	53
Swindon Town	46	13	11	22	59	81	50
Crewe Alexandra	46	12	12	22	54	78	48
Portsmouth	46	11	14	21	57	73	47
Queen's Park Rangers	46	12	11	23	52	61	47
Port Vale	46	13	8	25	45	75	47
Bury	46	10	17	19	35	60	47
Oxford United	46	10	14	22	48	71	44
Bristol City	46	9	15	22	57	80	42

1999-2000

Division One

Manager: Trevor Francis

Match No.	Date		Venue	Opponents	Result		Scorers	Attendance
1	Aug	7	H	Fulham	D	2-2	Hughes, Lazaridis	24,042
2		14	A	Norwich City	W	1-0	McCarthy	15,261
3		21	H	Port Vale	W	4-2	Hughes 2, Furlong 2	18,089
4		27	A	Stockport County	L	0-2		6,115
5		30	H	Crewe Alexandra	W	5-1	M.Johnson, McCarthy, Furlong, Holdsworth, Ndlovu	24,085
6	Sep	5	A	Bolton Wanderers	D	3-3	Furlong 2, Holdsworth	11,668
7		11	H	West Bromwich Albion	D	1-1	A.Johnson	25,495
8		18	A	Ipswich Town	W	1-0	Furlong (pen)	19,758
9		25	H	Queen's Park Rangers	W	2-0	Furlong 2 (2 pens)	18,748
10	Oct	2	A	Charlton Athletic	L	0-1		19,753
11		8	A	Walsall	L	0-1		7,164
12		16	H	Crystal Palace	W	2-0	Purse, McCarthy	21,582
13		19	H	Manchester City	L	0-1		22,128
14		23	A	Grimsby Town	D	1-1	Wreh	6,266
15		27	A	Queen's Park Rangers	D	2-2	Marcelo 2	11,196
16		30	H	Charlton Athletic	W	1-0	Hughes	19,172
17	Nov	6	A	Portsmouth	D	2-2	M.Johnson, Lazaridis	12,756
18		20	A	Barnsley	L	1-2	McCarthy	14,886
19		23	H	Tranmere Rovers	W	3-1	Grainger (pen), Hyde, Marcelo	21,132
20		27	H	Swindon Town	D	1-1	Grainger	22,620
21	Dec	4	A	Fulham	D	0-0		12,290
22		17	A	Wolverhampton Wan.	L	1-2	Hughes	19,724
23		26	H	Sheffield United	L	0-2		22,874
24		28	A	Nottingham Forest	L	0-1		20,821
25	Jan	3	H	Huddersfield Town	W	1-0	Hughes	19,958
26		15	H	Norwich City	W	2-0	Grainger 2	21,007
27		22	A	Port Vale	L	1-3	Hughes	7,702
28		29	H	Stockport County	W	2-1	Hughes, Holdsworth	17,150
29	Feb	5	A	Crewe Alexandra	W	3-2	Hughes, Adebola, O'Connor (pen)	6,269
30		12	H	Bolton Wanderers	W	2-1	Adebola, Rankin	18,426
31		15	H	Blackburn Rovers	W	1-0	O'Connor	20,719
32		19	A	Swindon Town	W	4-1	Grainger, Purse, Adebola, Rankin	7,591
33		27	H	Ipswich Town	D	1-1	Mowbray (og)	20,493
34	Mar	4	A	West Bromwich Albion	W	3-0	Adebola 2, Marcelo	17,029
35		7	H	Portsmouth	W	1-0	Marcelo	19,593
36		11	A	Tranmere Rovers	L	1-2	Rowett	9,232
37		18	H	Barnsley	W	3-1	Holdsworth, Rankin 2	25,108
38		22	A	Blackburn Rovers	L	0-1		18,096
39		25	A	Sheffield United	W	2-1	Kozluk (og), Hughes	15,486
40	Apr	1	H	Wolverhampton Wan.	W	1-0	Holdsworth	29,050
41		8	A	Huddersfield Town	D	0-0		16,961
42		15	H	Nottingham Forest	L	0-1		23,000
43		22	A	Crystal Palace	W	2-0	Austin (og), Furlong	17,144
44		24	H	Walsall	W	2-0	Furlong 2 (1 pen)	24,628
45		28	A	Manchester City	L	0-1		32,062
46	May	7	H	Grimsby Town	D	0-0		25,263
							Appearances	
							Sub appearances	
				Three own-goals			Goals	

Play-offs

SF1	May	13	H	Barnsley	L	0-4		26,492
SF2		18	A	Barnsley	W	2-1	Rowett, Marcelo	19,050
							Appearances	
							Sub appearances	
							Goals	

FA Cup

R3	Dec	11	A	Watford	W	1-0	Rowett	8,144
R4	Jan	8	A	Everton	L	0-2		25,405
							Appearances	
							Sub appearances	
							Goals	

League Cup

R1	Aug	10	H	Exeter City	W	3-0	Richardson (og), Adebola, A.Johnson	18,976
R1s		24	A	Exeter City	W	2-1	Richardson (og), O'Connor	2,338
R2	Sep	14	H	Bristol Rovers	W	2-0	O'Connor (pen), Holdsworth	17,457
R2s		21	A	Bristol Rovers	W	1-0	Rowett	5,456
R3	Oct	12	H	Newcastle United	W	2-0	Purse, O'Connor (pen)	19,795
R4	Nov	30	H	West Ham United	L	2-3	Grainger, Hyde	17,728
							Appearances	
							Sub appearances	
				Two own-goals			Goals	

Player columns (left to right):
Poole K, Rowett G, Grainger MR, Hughes B, Purse DJ, Johnson MO, McCarthy JD, Adebola B, Furlong PA, O'Connor MJ, Lazaridis S, Furinton HT, Holland CJ, Johnson A, Holdsworth DG, Hyde G, Ndlovu P, Newton EJ, Breacher J, Bennett J, Bennett MM, Johnston A, Haarhoff JP, Bass JDM, Gill JJM, West C, Marcelo, Charlton ST, Dyson JG, Robinson SE, Ramlin I, Carrick M, Myhre T, Campbell SP, Vassall DPJ, Knight R

League Table

	P	W	D	L	F	A	Pts
Charlton Athletic	46	27	10	9	79	45	91
Manchester City	46	26	11	9	78	40	89
Ipswich Town	46	25	12	9	71	42	87
Barnsley	46	24	10	12	88	67	82
Birmingham City	46	22	11	13	65	44	77
Bolton Wanderers	46	21	13	12	69	50	76
Wolverhampton W	46	21	11	14	64	48	74
Huddersfield Town	46	21	11	14	62	49	74
Fulham	46	17	16	13	49	41	67
Queen's Park Rangers	46	16	18	12	62	53	66
Blackburn Rovers	46	15	17	14	55	51	62
Norwich City	46	14	15	17	45	50	57
Tranmere Rovers	46	15	12	19	57	68	57
Nottingham Forest	46	14	14	18	53	55	56
Crystal Palace	46	13	15	18	57	67	54
Sheffield United	46	13	15	18	59	71	54
Stockport County	46	13	15	18	55	67	54
Portsmouth	46	13	12	21	55	66	51
Crewe Alexandra	46	14	9	23	46	67	51
Grimsby Town	46	13	12	21	41	67	51
West Bromwich Albion	46	10	19	17	43	60	49
Walsall	46	11	13	22	52	77	46
Port Vale	46	7	15	24	48	69	36
Swindon Town	46	8	12	26	38	77	36

Division One

Manager: Trevor Francis

Match No.	Date	Venue	Opponents	Result		Scorers	Attendance
1	Aug 12	A	Queen's Park Rangers	D	0-0		13,926
2	18	H	Fulham	L	1-3	Sonner	21,659
3	26	A	Nottingham Forest	W	2-1	Eaden, Marcelo	18,820
4	28	H	Barnsley	W	4-1	Hughes, Holdsworth, Grainger (pen), Ndlovu	17,160
5	Sep 9	H	Sheffield United	W	1-0	O'Connor (pen)	21,493
6	12	H	Preston North End	W	3-1	Ndlovu, A.Johnson, O'Connor (pen)	16,464
7	17	A	West Bromwich Albion	D	1-1	Horsfield	19,858
8	23	H	Tranmere Rovers	W	2-0	Grainger, Horsfield	17,640
9	Oct 1	A	Watford	L	0-2		12,355
10	8	A	Crewe Alexandra	W	2-0	Hughes, Marcelo	6,829
11	14	H	Crystal Palace	W	2-1	Adebola, Burchill	17,191
12	17	H	Stockport County	W	4-0	Grainger (pen), Horsfield, Burchill 2	15,579
13	22	A	Sheffield Wednesday	L	0-1		14,695
14	25	H	Gillingham	W	1-0	Marcelo	26,044
15	28	A	Portsmouth	D	1-1	Adebola	15,218
16	Nov 4	H	Bolton Wanderers	D	1-1	Grainger (pen)	20,043
17	7	A	Norwich City	L	0-1		13,900
18	18	H	Burnley	W	3-2	O'Connor, Adebola, Burchill	19,641
19	25	H	Huddersfield Town	W	2-1	Lazaridis, Horsfield	22,120
20	Dec 2	A	Gillingham	W	2-1	M.Johnson, Horsfield	9,247
21	9	H	Wimbledon	L	0-3		16,778
22	17	A	Wolverhampton Wan.	W	1-0	Adebola	19,938
23	23	H	Queen's Park Rangers	D	0-0		24,311
24	26	A	Blackburn Rovers	L	1-2	Purse	24,899
25	Jan 1	H	Nottingham Forest	L	0-2		20,034
26	13	A	Barnsley	W	3-2	M.Johnson, Lazaridis, Marcelo	13,631
27	27	A	Fulham	W	1-0	Grainger	15,482
28	Feb 3	H	Norwich City	W	2-1	Hughes, Purse (pen)	18,551
29	10	A	Sheffield United	L	1-3	Horsfield	19,313
30	17	H	West Bromwich Albion	W	2-1	O'Connor, Adebola	25,025
31	20	A	Preston North End	W	2-0	Grainger, A.Johnson	14,864
32	Mar 2	H	Watford	W	2-0	Eaden, Hughes	20,724
33	6	A	Crystal Palace	W	2-1	Upson (og), Adebola	13,987
34	10	H	Crewe Alexandra	W	2-0	Purse (pen), A.Johnson	28,042
35	14	H	Blackburn Rovers	L	0-2		29,150
36	17	A	Stockport County	L	0-2		7,176
37	20	A	Grimsby Town	D	1-1	A.Johnson	4,843
38	24	H	Sheffield Wednesday	L	1-2	Horsfield	19,733
39	Apr 1	H	Wolverhampton Wan.	L	0-1		24,003
40	7	A	Wimbledon	L	1-3	Marcelo	6,619
41	10	A	Tranmere Rovers	L	0-1		8,084
42	13	A	Bolton Wanderers	D	2-2	Marcelo, O'Connor	15,025
43	16	A	Portsmouth	D	0-0		23,304
44	21	A	Burnley	D	0-0		17,057
45	28	H	Grimsby Town	W	1-0	Marcelo	24,822
46	May 6	A	Huddersfield Town	W	2-1	Woodhouse 2	19,290

Appearances
Sub appearances
One own-goal   Goals

Play-offs

SF1	May 13	H	Preston North End	W	1-0	Eaden	29,072
SF2	17	A	Preston North End	L	1-2	Horsfield	16,928

Lost 2-4 on penalties a.e.t. in the second leg

Appearances
Sub appearances
Goals

FA Cup

R3	Jan 6	A	Manchester City	L	2-3	Grainger, Adebola	19,380

Appearances
Sub appearances
Goals

League Cup

R1	Aug 22	A	Southend United	W	5-0	Eaden, M.Johnson, Hughes, Marcelo, Adebola	3,69_
R1s	Sep 5	H	Southend United	D	0-0		9,507
R2	19	A	Wycombe Wanderers	W	4-3	Horsfield 2, A.Johnson 2	2,537
R2s	26	H	Wycombe Wanderers	W	1-0	Ndlovu	8,960
R3	Oct 31	A	Tottenham Hotspur	W	3-1	Adebola 2, Burchill	27,096
R4	Nov 29	H	Newcastle United	W	2-1	M.Johnson, Adebola	18,520
R5	Dec 12	H	Sheffield Wednesday	W	2-0	Sonner, Adebola	22,911
SF1	Jan 9	A	Ipswich Town	L	0-1		21,684
SF2	31	H	Ipswich Town	W	4-1	Grainger, Horsfield 2, A.Johnson	28,624
F	Feb 25	N	Liverpool	N	1-1	Purse (pen)	73,500

SF2 a.e.t., 2-1 at 90 minutes.
Final at Millennium Stadium Cardiff.
Final lost 4-5 on penalties a.e.t.

Appearances
Sub appearances
Goals

Player columns (left to right): Bennett MM, Eaden NJ, Johnson MO, Hughes B, Holdsworth DG, Purse DJ, Lazaridis S, Grainger MR, Horsfield GM, Somner DJ, Ndlovu P, Marcelo, Williams J, Johnson A, Gill JM, O'Connor MJ, Adebola B, Birmnos D, Robinson SE, Charles GA, Hyde G, Burchill MJ, Edghill RA, Jenkins SR, Poole K, Woodhouse C, McCarthy JD, Tiler C, Atkinson P, Furlong PA, Pollock J, Bass JDM

League Table

	P	W	D	L	F	A	Pts
Fulham	46	30	11	5	90	32	101
Blackburn Rovers	46	26	13	7	76	39	91
Bolton Wanderers	46	24	15	7	76	45	87
Preston North End	46	23	9	14	64	52	78
Birmingham City	46	23	9	14	59	48	78
West Bromwich Albion	46	21	11	14	60	52	74
Burnley	46	21	9	16	50	54	72
Wimbledon	46	17	18	11	71	50	69
Watford	46	20	9	17	76	67	69
Sheffield United	46	19	11	16	52	49	68
Nottingham Forest	46	20	8	18	55	53	68
Wolverhampton W	46	14	13	19	45	48	55
Gillingham	46	13	16	17	61	66	55
Crewe Alexandra	46	15	10	21	47	62	55
Norwich City	46	14	12	20	46	58	54
Barnsley	46	15	9	22	49	62	54
Sheffield Wednesday	46	15	8	23	52	71	53
Grimsby Town	46	14	10	22	43	62	52
Stockport County	46	11	18	17	58	65	51
Portsmouth	46	10	19	17	47	59	49
Crystal Palace	46	12	13	21	57	70	49
Huddersfield Town	46	11	15	20	48	57	48
Queen's Park Rangers	46	7	19	20	45	75	40
Tranmere Rovers	46	9	11	26	46	77	38

Division One

Manager: Trevor Francis (to October); then Steve Bruce

Into the Play-offs for the fourth successive season, at long last Blues celebrated with a final victory, thus clinching a place in the Premiership for the first time.

On 23 September, Blues played their 4,000th game in the Football League but sadly they lost against Preston North End.

Marcelo's hat-trick in the 4–0 win over Bradford City came in just 12 minutes.

Darren Huckerby bagged four of Manchester City's six goals against Blues in the League Cup tie at Maine Road.

Blues finished with only nine men when beating Walsall 2–1 at the Bescot Stadium in August.

Former player Stan Harland died on 2 September, ex-Blues manager Stan Cullis on 28 February and Stan Lynn on 28 April.

Match No.	Date		Venue	Opponents	Result		Scorers	Attendance
1	Aug	11	A	Wimbledon	L	1-3	B.Hughes	9,142
2		19	H	Millwall	W	4-0	Eaden, Horsfield, B.Hughes 2	19,091
3		25	A	Walsall	W	2-1	Mooney, Horsfield	7,245
4		27	H	Stockport County	W	2-1	Grainger, Mooney (pen)	18,478
5	Sep	8	H	Sheffield Wednesday	W	2-0	B.Hughes, A.Johnson	19,421
6		15	A	Manchester City	L	0-3		31,714
7		18	H	Burnley	L	2-3	A.Johnson 2	18,426
8		23	H	Preston North End	L	0-1		23,004
9		26	A	Watford	D	3-3	Grainger, Horsfield, B.Hughes	13,091
10		29	A	Crewe Alexandra	D	0-0		7,314
11	Oct	13	A	Barnsley	W	3-1	Horsfield, Furlong, Marcelo	11,910
12		17	A	Nottingham Forest	D	0-0		18,210
13		20	H	Bradford City	W	4-0	Sonner, Marcelo 3	25,011
14		23	H	Gillingham	W	2-1	Horsfield 2	27,101
15		26	A	Grimsby Town	L	1-3	Marcelo	5,419
16		30	A	Portsmouth	D	1-1	Marcelo	15,612
17	Nov	4	H	Rotherham United	D	2-2	Branston (og), Horsfield	28,436
18		7	H	West Bromwich Albion	L	0-1		23,554
19		17	A	Sheffield United	L	0-4		15,686
20		25	H	Coventry City	W	2-0	Marcelo 2	18,279
21		30	A	Gillingham	D	1-1	Marcelo	8,575
22	Dec	8	H	Norwich City	W	4-0	Mooney 3 (1 pen), Marcelo	17,310
23		11	H	Crystal Palace	W	1-0	Mooney (pen)	20,119
24		16	A	Wolverhampton Wan.	L	1-2	Marcelo	21,482
25		22	H	Walsall	W	1-0	Purse (pen)	20,127
26		26	H	Sheffield Wednesday	W	1-0	Horsfield	24,335
27		29	A	Stockport County	W	3-0	Mooney, Marcelo, Vickers	5,827
28	Jan	1	H	Nottingham Forest	D	1-1	Mooney	19,770
29		10	A	Millwall	D	1-1	Mooney	11,856
30		19	H	Wimbledon	L	0-2		17,766
31		29	A	West Bromwich Albion	L	0-1		25,266
32	Feb	16	H	Barnsley	W	1-0	John	19,208
33		23	H	Watford	W	3-2	Purse, Mooney 2 (1 pen)	18,059
34		26	A	Burnley	W	1-0	Mooney	13,504
35	Mar	2	A	Preston North End	L	0-1		15,543
36		5	H	Manchester City	L	1-2	M.Johnson	24,160
37		9	H	Wolverhampton Wan.	D	2-2	Devlin, John	22,104
38		12	A	Bradford City	W	3-1	Purse, Horsfield, John	13,105
39		15	A	Norwich City	W	1-0	John	18,258
40		24	A	Coventry City	D	1-1	Horsfield	17,945
41		30	H	Grimsby Town	W	4-0	B.Hughes 2, John	23,249
42	Apr	1	A	Crystal Palace	D	0-0		19,598
43		7	H	Portsmouth	D	1-1	John	25,030
44		10	H	Crewe Alexandra	W	3-1	Mooney, Carter, John	28,615
45		13	A	Rotherham United	D	2-2	Grainger, Beech (og)	10,536
46		21	H	Sheffield United	W	2-0	Grainger, Horsfield	29,178

Appearances
Sub appearances
Two own-goals
Goals

Play-offs

SF1	Apr	28	H	Millwall	D	1-1	B.Hughes	28,282
SF2	May	2	A	Millwall	W	1-0	John	16,391
F		12	N	Norwich City	D	1-1	Horsfield	71,597

Final at the Millennium Stadium, Cardiff.
Final won 4-2 on penalties a.e.t.

Appearances
Sub appearances
Goals

FA Cup

R3	Jan	5	A	Liverpool	L	0-3		40,875

Appearances
Sub appearances

League Cup

R1	Aug	22	H	Southend United	W	3-0	Whelan (og), Mooney 2 (1 pen)	12,015
R2	Sep	11	A	Bristol Rovers	W	3-0	M.Johnson, B.Hughes, A.Johnson	5,582
R3	Oct	10	A	Manchester City	L	0-6		13,912

Appearances
Sub appearances
Goals

Player columns (left to right):
Vaesen NJ-T, Gill JM, Grainger MR, Sonner DJ, Purse DJ, Johnson MO, Eaton NJ, Mooney TJ, Horsfield GM, O'Connor MJ, Lazaridis S, Hughes B, Holdsworth DG, Furlong PA, Woodhouse C, Marcelo, Kelly AT, Johnson A, Burrows D, Bragstad BO, Luntala T, Hutchinson J, Ferrari CE, Fleming C, Vickers SH, Bennett IM, Hyde G, Kenna JJ, McCarthy JD, Bak A, Carter DA, Devlin PJ, John S, Johnson DM, Williams TA, Tebily O, Hughes ME, Poole K

League Table

	P	W	D	L	F	A	Pts
Manchester City	46	31	6	9	108	52	99
West Bromwich Albion	46	27	8	11	61	29	89
Wolverhampton W	46	25	11	10	76	43	86
Millwall	46	22	11	13	69	48	77
Birmingham City	46	21	13	12	70	49	76
Norwich City	46	22	9	15	60	51	75
Burnley	46	21	12	13	70	62	75
Preston North End	46	20	12	14	71	59	72
Wimbledon	46	18	13	15	63	57	67
Crystal Palace	46	20	6	20	70	62	66
Coventry City	46	20	6	20	59	53	66
Gillingham	46	18	10	18	64	67	64
Sheffield United	46	15	15	16	53	54	60
Watford	46	16	11	19	62	56	59
Bradford City	46	15	10	21	69	76	55
Nottingham Forest	46	12	18	16	50	51	54
Portsmouth	46	13	14	19	60	72	53
Walsall	46	13	12	21	51	71	51
Grimsby Town	46	12	14	20	50	72	50
Sheffield Wednesday	46	12	14	20	49	71	50
Rotherham United	46	10	19	17	52	66	49
Crewe Alexandra	46	12	13	21	47	76	49
Barnsley	46	11	15	20	59	86	48
Stockport County	46	6	8	32	42	102	26

Premier League

Manager: Steve Bruce

The highest position Blues achieved this season was 11th in late November following a 1–1 home draw with Tottenham. Their lowest was 19th.

Stern John had the pleasure of scoring Blues' first 'PL' goal – a penalty in the 1–1 draw at Everton.

Geoff Horsfield was the hero in the local derby against his future club, West Bromwich Albion, when he netted a dramatic last-minute winner at St Andrew's in March.

Clinton Morrison scored 90th-minute goals for Blues to earn a 2–2 draw at Liverpool and a 1–0 victory at Sunderland.

Former Blues goalkeeper David Seaman retired in May, having made 1,020 appearances in a career which began with Leeds United in 1979.

Match No.	Date		Venue	Opponents	Result		Scorers	Attendance
1	Aug	18	A	Arsenal	L	0-2		38,018
2		24	H	Blackburn Rovers	L	0-1		28,563
3		28	A	Everton	D	1-1	John (pen)	37,197
4		31	H	Leeds United	W	2-1	D.Johnson, Devlin	27,164
5	Sep	11	A	Liverpool	D	2-2	Morrison 2	43,113
6		16	H	Aston Villa	W	3-0	Morrison, Enckelman (og), Horsfield	29,505
7		21	A	Middlesbrough	L	0-1		29,869
8		28	H	Newcastle United	L	0-2		29,072
9	Oct	5	A	West Ham United	W	2-1	John 2	35,010
10		19	A	West Bromwich Albion	D	1-1	Moore (og)	27,021
11		26	H	Manchester City	L	0-2		29,316
12	Nov	2	H	Bolton Wanderers	W	3-1	Purse, Horsfield, Savage	27,224
13		9	A	Chelsea	L	0-3		35,237
14		17	H	Fulham	D	0-0		26,164
15		23	A	Sunderland	W	1-0	Morrison	38,803
16		30	H	Tottenham Hotspur	D	1-1	Kenna	29,505
17	Dec	7	A	Southampton	L	0-2		31,132
18		15	A	Fulham	W	1-0	Kirovski	14,962
19		21	H	Charlton Athletic	D	1-1	Devlin (pen)	28,837
20		26	H	Everton	D	1-1	Kirovski	29,505
21		28	A	Manchester United	L	0-2		67,640
22	Jan	1	A	Leeds United	L	0-2		40,034
23		12	H	Arsenal	L	0-4		29,505
24		18	A	Blackburn Rovers	D	1-1	John	23,331
25	Feb	1	A	Bolton Wanderers	L	2-4	Savage, Morrison	24,288
26		4	H	Manchester United	L	0-1		29,475
27		8	H	Chelsea	L	1-3	Savage (pen)	29,475
28		23	H	Liverpool	W	2-1	Morrison, Clemence	29,449
29	Mar	3	A	Aston Villa	W	2-0	Horsfield, Lazaridis	42,602
30		16	A	Manchester City	L	0-1		34,596
31		22	H	West Bromwich Albion	W	1-0	Horsfield	29,449
32	Apr	5	A	Tottenham Hotspur	L	1-2	Devlin (pen)	36,058
33		12	H	Sunderland	W	2-0	Hughes, Dugarry	29,132
34		19	A	Charlton Athletic	W	2-0	Savage (pen), Dugarry	25,732
35		21	H	Southampton	W	3-2	Hughes, Dugarry 2	29,115
36		26	H	Middlesbrough	W	3-0	Lazaridis, Dugarry, Clemence	28,821
37	May	3	A	Newcastle United	L	0-1		52,146
38		11	H	West Ham United	D	2-2	John, Horsfield	29,505

Appearances
Sub appearances
Two own-goals Goals

FA Cup

R3	Jan	5	A	Fulham	L	1-3	John	9,203

Appearances
Sub appearances
Goals

League Cup

R2	Oct	2	A	Leyton Orient	W	3-2	John 3	3,615
R3	Nov	5	H	Preston North End	L	0-2		12,241

Appearances
Sub appearances
Goals

Vaesen NJ-T	Kenna JJ	Grainger MR	Cunningham KE	Purse DJ	Tebily O	Johnson DM	John S	Horsfield GM	Cisse A	Hughes B	Carter DA	Lazaridis S	Mooney TJ	Savage RW	Morrison CH	Devlin PJ	Powell DA	Kirovski J	Vickers SH	Woodhouse C	Sadler M	Fagan CA	Johnson MO	Hutchinson J	Coly F	Dugarry C	Clemence SN	Clapham JR	Bennett IM	Upson MJ	Swierczewski P	Marriott A
1	2	3	4	5	6	7	8	9	10	11	12	13																				
1		3	6	5	2	7	8	9	10	11	4	12	13																			
1	12	3	6	5	2	7	8	9	10	11	13			4	14																	
1	2	3	6	5		11	8	12	10	13		14		4	9	7																
1	2	3	6	5		11	8	12		10	13	14		4	9	7																
1	2	3	6	5		11	8	12	10	14				4	9	7	13															
1	2	3	6	5		11	8	13	10			12		4	9	7		14														
1	2		6	5		11	8	14	10		3			4	9	7	13	12														
1	2		6	5		11	8	12	10			3		4	9	7	13															
1	2				6		8	12		14	3	11		4	9	7	10		5	13												
1	2			5	6		8	12	10	13		3		4	9	7	11	14														
1	2		6	5			8	12	10	14		11		4	9	7	13				3											
1	3		6	5	2		8	13	10	14		12		4	9	7	11															
1	3		6	5	2		8	9	10	12		11		4	13	7		14														
1	3		6	5	2	14	8		10	13		11		4	9	7	12															
1	3		6	5	2	12	8		10	13		11		4	9	7		14														
1	3		6	5	2	7	8		10	4	12	11			9			13				14										
1	3		6	5	2	7		9	10	14				4	8		12	11		13												
1	3		6		2	7		9	10			12		4	8	13		11	5													
1	2		6			11		9	10	14		12		4	13	7		8	5				3									
1	2		6					12	10			11		4	9	7	13	8		14	3		5									
1	2	3				11		12	10					4	9	7	13	8					6	5								
1	3	12				7	8							4		13		14	5				6		2	9	10	11				
	2					7	14		10			11		4	9	12		13	5				6			8		3	1			
	2		6				12					11		4	9	7		13								8	10	3	1	5		
1	2		6			7	8					12		4	9	14		13								11	10	3		5		
1	2		6			7		9				11		4	13	14										8	10	3		5	12	
1	2		6			7		13			12	11		4	9	14										8	10	3		5		
1	2		6			7		12			14	11		4	9	13										8	10	3		5		
	2		6			7	14	12				11		4	9	13										8	10	3	1	5		
	2		6			11	13	12			14			4	9	7										8	10	3	1	5		
	2		6			11	8	9			14	12				7		13								4	10	3		5		1
	2		6				12	9		4	13	11				7		14								8	10	3	1	5		
	2		6	14		7	12	9		11				4		13										8	10	3	1	5		
	2		6			7	14	9		11		12		4		13										8	10	3	1	5		
	2		6			7	14	9		11		12		4		13										8	10	3	1	5		
	2			5		7	14	9		11		13		4									12			8	10	3	1	6		
	2			5		7	12	9		14		11		4		13										8	10	3	1	6		
27	36	8	31	19	12	28	20	15	21	10	3	17	0	33	24	20	3	5	5	0	2	0	5	1	1	16	15	16	10	14	0	1
	1	1		1		2	10	16		12	9	13	1		4	12	8	12		3		1	1								1	
	1			1		1	5	5		2		2		4	6	3		2								5	2					

1	6	3				11	12			14				4	9	7	10	8				13		5	2							
1	1	1				1	0			0				1	1	1	1	1				0		1	1							
							1			1												1										
							1																									

	2			5		12	8	9				3					7	11	6	4	10	13							1			
			6		2			9		7	10	11			8		4	13			3	12		5					1			
	1		1	1	1	0	1	2		1	1	2			1		2	1	1	1	2	0		1					2			
						1												1				2										
							3																									

League Table

	P	W	D	L	F	A	Pts
Manchester United	38	25	8	5	74	34	83
Arsenal	38	23	9	6	85	42	78
Newcastle United	38	21	6	11	63	48	69
Chelsea	38	19	10	9	68	38	67
Liverpool	38	18	10	10	61	41	64
Blackburn Rovers	38	16	12	10	52	43	60
Everton	38	17	8	13	48	49	59
Southampton	38	13	13	12	43	46	52
Manchester City	38	15	6	17	47	54	51
Tottenham Hotspur	38	14	8	16	51	62	50
Middlesbrough	38	13	10	15	48	44	49
Charlton Athletic	38	14	7	17	45	56	49
Birmingham City	38	13	9	16	41	49	48
Fulham	38	13	9	16	41	50	48
Leeds United	38	14	5	19	58	57	47
Aston Villa	38	12	9	17	42	47	45
Bolton Wanderers	38	10	14	14	41	51	44
West Ham United	38	10	12	16	42	59	42
West Bromwich Albion	38	6	8	24	29	65	26
Sunderland	38	4	7	27	21	65	19

Premier League

Manager: Steve Bruce

Did you know that?

After winning 2–0 at Portsmouth in late September, Blues rose to fourth place in the Premiership – their highest position in the top flight of English football since 1955.

Stern John scored a dramatic 90th-minute equaliser for Blues in League games against Newcastle United (home) in late January and Aston Villa (away) in February.

Blues completed their first double in the Premiership in March with a 2–0 home win over Bolton Wanderers, having won 1–0 at the Reebok Stadium in October.

A record crowd for the re-designed St Andrew's of 29,588 witnessed Blues' 3–0 defeat by the reigning champions Arsenal in November.

Match No.	Date		Venue	Opponents	Result		Scorers	Attendance
1	Aug	16	H	Tottenham Hotspur	W	1-0	Dunn (pen)	29,358
2		23	A	Southampton	D	0-0		31,656
3		30	A	Newcastle United	W	1-0	Dunn	52,006
4	Sep	14	H	Fulham	D	2-2	Forssell 2	27,250
5		20	A	Leeds United	W	2-0	Savage (pen), Forssell	34,305
6		27	A	Portsmouth	W	2-0	Clemence, Lazaridis	29,057
7	Oct	4	A	Manchester United	L	0-3		67,633
8		14	H	Chelsea	D	0-0		29,460
9		19	H	Aston Villa	D	0-0		29,546
10		25	A	Bolton Wanderers	W	1-0	Forssell	25,023
11	Nov	3	H	Charlton Athletic	L	1-2	Dugarry	27,225
12		8	A	Wolverhampton Wan.	D	1-1	Forssell	28,831
13		22	H	Arsenal	L	0-3		29,588
14		30	A	Liverpool	L	1-3	Forssell	42,683
15	Dec	6	H	Blackburn Rovers	L	0-4		29,354
16		13	A	Leicester City	W	2-0	Morrison, Forssell	30,639
17		26	H	Manchester City	W	2-1	Kenna, Forssell	29,520
18		28	A	Everton	L	0-1		39,631
19	Jan	7	A	Tottenham Hotspur	L	1-4	Savage (pen)	30,016
20		10	H	Southampton	W	2-1	Kenna, Clemence	29,071
21		18	A	Chelsea	D	0-0		41,073
22		31	H	Newcastle United	D	1-1	John	29,513
23	Feb	8	A	Manchester City	D	0-0		46,967
24		11	H	Everton	W	3-0	Johnson, Lazaridis, Forssell	29,004
25		22	A	Aston Villa	D	2-2	John, Forssell	40,061
26	Mar	3	H	Middlesbrough	W	3-1	Savage, Forssell, M.Taylor	29,369
27		6	H	Bolton Wanderers	W	2-0	Forssell, Hughes	28,003
28		13	H	Leicester City	L	0-1		29,491
29		20	A	Middlesbrough	L	3-5	Morrison, Forssell 2	30,244
30		27	H	Leeds United	W	4-1	Forssell 2 (1 pen), Hughes 2	29,069
31	Apr	3	A	Fulham	D	0-0		14,667
32		10	H	Manchester United	L	1-2	Grainger	29,548
33		12	A	Portsmouth	L	1-3	John	20,104
34		17	A	Charlton Athletic	D	1-1	Morrison	25,206
35		25	H	Wolverhampton Wan.	D	2-2	Morrison, Forssell	29,494
36	May	1	A	Arsenal	D	0-0		38,061
37		8	H	Liverpool	L	0-3		29,533
38		15	A	Blackburn Rovers	D	1-1	John	26,070
							Appearances	
							Sub appearances	
							Goals	

FA Cup

R3	Jan	3	H	Blackburn Rovers	W	4-0	Clemence, Morrison, Forssell, Hughes	18,688
R4		24	H	Wimbledon	W	1-0	Hughes	22,159
R5	Feb	14	A	Sunderland	D	1-1	Forssell	24,966
rep		25	H	Sunderland	L	0-2		25,645
R5 replay a.e.t.							Appearances	
							Sub appearances	
							Goals	

League Cup

R2	Sep	23	A	Blackpool	L	0-1		7,370
							Appearances	
							Sub appearances	

Player appearance and goals grid (player columns, left to right):
Taylor MS (Maik), Kenna JJ, Clapham JR, Savage RW, Purse DJ, Cunningham KE, Johnson DM, Dugarry C, Horsfield GM, Clemence SN, Dunn DJI, Tebily O, Devlin PJ, John S, Upson MJ, Morrison CH, Lazaridis S, Cisse A, Forssell MK, Figueroa LG, Carter DA, Hughes B, Kirovski J, Taylor M (Martin), Barrowman A, Granger MR

	Tay MS	Kenna	Clap	Sav	Purse	Cunn	John DM	Dug	Hors	Clem	Dunn	Teb	Dev	John S	Upson	Morr	Laz	Cisse	Fors	Fig	Cart	Hugh	Kir	Tay M	Barr	Gra
1	1	2	3	4	5	6	7	8	9	10	11	14	13	12												
2	1	2	3	4		6	7		9	10	11		14		8	5	13	12								
3	1	2	3	4		6	7		12	10	8	14		9	5		11	13								
4	1	2	3	4	5		7			10	11	12		8	6	14	13		9							
5		3	4		6	2	8		10	7	13			5	14	11	12	9								
6		3	4		6	2	8		10	7	13			5	11	12	9	14								
7		3		6	2	8		10	7	14			5		11	4	9		12	13						
8		3		6	7	8		10	9	2		13	5		11	4				12						
9		3	4		6	2	8		10	7	14		5	13	11	12	9		1							
10	12	3		6		8		10	7	2		5	14	11	4	9		13								
11		3		6		8		10	7	2	14	5	13	11	4	9		12								
12		3	4		6	2	8		10	7		13	5		12	9		11								
13		3	7		6	2		10	8		12	5	13	11	4	9		14								
14		3	4		6	2	8		10	7	12		5	14	11	4	9		1		13					
15		2	3	4		6	7	8		14	10	5			12	11	13	9								
16		2	3	4		6	7		10	11			14	5	8	12	13	9								
17	2		4		6	7		10	11			12	5	8	3	14	9			13						
18	2		4			6	7		8	5	12	3	13	9			11	14								
19	3		4	5	6	2		10	7	12		8		9		11	13	14								
20	3			5	6	7		10	4	2		8		9		13	11	12								
21	3		4	5	6	7		10		2	8	9	12		14	11	13									
22	3		4	5	6	7			2		12	8	11		9	10										
23	3	13	4	5	6	7	12			2		8	14	11		9		10								
24		4	5	6	7	12			2		13	3	8	11	9		10	14								
25	3		4	5	6	7	8		10	12	2		14	13	9		11									
26	12		4		6	7		10		2		13	3	8		9		14	11	5						
27	12		4	6	7			10		2		13	3	8	14	9		11	5							
28		4		6		10		2		12	3	8	11	9		7	5	13								
29		6	7		10			12	5	8	11	9		4	2	3										
30		6	7		10		13		12	5	8	11	9		4	2	3									
31		14	4	6	7		12		13	5	8	11	9		10	2	3									
32		13	4	6	7		10		14	5	8	3	9		11	2	12									
33		11	4	6	7		13	2	8	3	14	9		12	10	5										
34		3	4	6	7		10		12	5	8		9		11	2										
35		3	4	6	7		10		12	5	8	11	9		12	2										
36		3	4	6	7		10	8	2	12	5	9	11		1	13										
37		3	4	6	7		10		2	12	5	8	11	14	9		1	13								
38		3	4	6	7		10		2	12	5	8	11		9		12	6								
App	14	22	31	9	36	35	12	2	32	20	17	0	7	30	19	25	5	32	0	4	1	17	0	11	0	3
Sub	3	3				2	1	3	1	10	2	22		13	5	10		1	2	4	9	6	1	1	1	
Gls	2		3			1	1		2	2			4	2		17		3	1	1						

League / cup section:

	2		4		6	7		10	11		5	8	3		9		13	12	14							
	3	13	4	5	6	7		10	2		8		9		12		11									
	2		4	5	6	7	12			3	8	11	13	9		14	10									
	3		4	5	6	7		12	10	2		13	8		9		14	11								
App	4	0	4	3	4	4	0	1	3	2	1	2	4	2	0	3	0	3	0							
Sub		1			1			1			1		1	1		3	1	1								
Gls	2		3				1	1		2		2														

	3		6	2		10	7		8	5	9	11	4	12	13			14								
	1		1	1		1	1		1	1	1	1	1	0	0			0								
											1	1														

Premier League

Manager: Steve Bruce

This season, Blues boss Steve Bruce signed his son Alex Bruce from Blackburn Rovers.

Runners-up Arsenal were leading Blues 1–0 with 10 minutes remaining of the final Premiership game of the season at St Andrew's. The Uruguayan international Walter Pandiani, signed from the Spanish club Deportivo La Coruna, duly equalised before Emile Heskey struck home a last-gasp winner.

Early goals by Clinton Morrison (nine minutes) and David Dunn (12) paved the way for a 2–1 away win over rivals Aston Villa in December. And then, for the first time since 1977–78, Blues completed the League double over the foe from Aston with a 2–0 home win in March, future Villa player Emile Heskey being one of Blues' scorers on a day of celebration!

Robbie Savage scored one of the earliest penalties ever awarded to Blues – in the fourth minute of the derby against West Bromwich Albion in December.

Match No.	Date		Venue	Opponents	Result		Scorers	Attendance
1	Aug	14	A	Portsmouth	D	1-1	Savage	20,021
2		21	H	Chelsea	L	0-1		28,559
3		24	H	Manchester City	W	1-0	Heskey	28,551
4		28	A	Tottenham Hotspur	L	0-1		35,290
5	Sep	11	A	Middlesbrough	L	1-2	Heskey	30,252
6		18	H	Charlton Athletic	D	1-1	Yorke	27,400
7		25	A	Bolton Wanderers	D	1-1	Izzet	23,692
8	Oct	3	H	Newcastle United	D	2-2	Upson, Yorke	29,021
9		16	H	Manchester United	D	0-0		29,221
10		24	A	Southampton	D	0-0		27,568
11		30	A	Crystal Palace	L	0-1		28,916
12	Nov	6	A	Liverpool	W	1-0	Anderton	42,669
13		13	H	Everton	L	0-1		28,388
14		21	A	Blackburn Rovers	D	3-3	Savage, Dunn, Anderton	20,290
15		27	H	Norwich City	D	1-1	Morrison	29,120
16	Dec	4	A	Arsenal	L	0-3		38,064
17		12	A	Aston Villa	W	2-1	Morrison, Dunn	41,329
18		18	H	West Bromwich Albion	W	4-0	Savage (pen), Heskey, Morrison, Anderton	28,880
19		26	H	Middlesbrough	W	2-0	Heskey, Morrison	29,082
20		28	A	Fulham	W	3-2	Savage, Heskey, Carter	18,706
21	Jan	1	A	Newcastle United	L	1-2	Heskey	52,222
22		4	H	Bolton Wanderers	L	1-2	Upson	27,171
23		15	A	Charlton Athletic	L	1-3	Melchiot	26,111
24		22	H	Fulham	L	1-2	Volz (og)	28,512
25	Feb	2	H	Southampton	W	2-1	Blake (pen), Pandiani	28,797
26		5	A	Manchester United	L	0-2		67,831
27		12	H	Liverpool	W	2-0	Gray, Pandiani (pen)	29,318
28		26	A	Crystal Palace	L	0-2		23,371
29	Mar	6	A	West Bromwich Albion	L	0-2		25,744
30		20	H	Aston Villa	W	2-0	Heskey, Gray	29,382
31	Apr	2	H	Tottenham Hotspur	D	1-1	Carter	29,304
32		9	A	Chelsea	D	1-1	Pandiani	42,031
33		16	H	Portsmouth	D	0-0		28,880
34		20	A	Manchester City	L	0-3		42,450
35		23	A	Everton	D	1-1	Heskey	36,820
36		30	H	Blackburn Rovers	W	2-1	Heskey, Blake	28,620
37	May	7	A	Norwich City	L	0-1		25,471
38		15	H	Arsenal	W	2-1	Heskey, Pandiani	29,300
							Appearance	
							Sub appearance	
					One own-goal		Goal	

FA Cup

R3	Jan	8	H	Leeds United	W	3-0	Heskey, Carter 2	25,15
R4		30	A	Chelsea	L	0-2		40,37
							Appearance	
							Sub appearance	
							Goal	

League Cup

R2	Sep	21	H	Lincoln City	W	3-1	Gronkjaer, Morrison, Savage (pen)	14,52
R3	Oct	27	H	Fulham	L	0-1		26,37
							Appearance	
							Sub appearance	
							Goal	

League Table

	P	W	D	L	F	A	Pts
Chelsea	38	29	8	1	72	15	95
Arsenal	38	25	8	5	87	36	83
Manchester United	38	22	11	5	58	26	77
Everton	38	18	7	13	45	46	61
Liverpool	38	17	7	14	52	41	58
Bolton Wanderers	38	16	10	12	49	44	58
Middlesbrough	38	14	13	11	53	46	55
Manchester City	38	13	13	12	47	39	52
Tottenham Hotspur	38	14	10	14	47	41	52
Aston Villa	38	12	11	15	45	52	47
Charlton Athletic	38	12	10	16	42	58	46
Birmingham City	38	11	12	15	40	46	45
Fulham	38	12	8	18	52	60	44
Newcastle United	38	10	14	14	47	57	44
Blackburn Rovers	38	9	15	14	32	43	42
Portsmouth	38	10	9	19	43	59	39
West Bromwich Albion	38	6	16	16	36	61	34
Crystal Palace	38	7	12	19	41	62	33
Norwich City	38	7	12	19	42	77	33
Southampton	38	6	14	18	45	66	32

Premier League

Manager: Steve Bruce

Match No.	Date	Venue	Opponents		Result	Scorers	Attendance
1	Aug 13	A	Fulham	D	0-0		16,550
2	20	H	Manchester City	L	1-2	Butt	26,366
3	23	H	Middlesbrough	L	0-3		27,998
4	27	A	West Bromwich Albion	W	3-2	Heskey 2, Jarosik	23,993
5	Sep 10	H	Charlton Athletic	L	0-1		26,846
6	17	A	Portsmouth	D	1-1	Jarosik	19,319
7	24	H	Liverpool	D	2-2	Warnock (og), Pandiani	27,733
8	Oct 2	A	Arsenal	L	0-1		37,891
9	16	H	Aston Villa	L	0-1		29,312
10	22	A	Blackburn Rovers	L	0-2		18,341
11	29	H	Everton	L	0-1		26,554
12	Nov 5	A	Newcastle United	L	0-1		52,191
13	26	A	Sunderland	W	1-0	Gray	32,442
14	Dec 5	H	West Ham United	L	1-2	Heskey	24,010
15	10	H	Fulham	W	1-0	Butt	27,597
16	17	A	Manchester City	L	1-4	Jarosik	41,343
17	26	A	Tottenham Hotspur	L	0-2		36,045
18	28	H	Manchester United	D	2-2	Clapham, Pandiani	28,459
19	31	A	Chelsea	L	0-2		40,652
20	Jan 2	H	Wigan Athletic	W	2-0	Melchiot, Pennant	29,189
21	14	A	Charlton Athletic	L	0-2		26,312
22	21	H	Portsmouth	W	5-0	Jarosik, Pennant, Upson, Forssell (pen), Dunn	29,138
23	Feb 1	A	Liverpool	D	1-1	Alonso (og)	43,851
24	4	H	Arsenal	L	0-2		27,075
25	13	A	West Ham United	L	0-3		31,294
26	25	H	Sunderland	W	1-0	Heskey	29,251
27	Mar 4	A	Middlesbrough	L	0-1		28,141
28	11	H	West Bromwich Albion	D	1-1	Forssell (pen)	28,041
29	18	H	Tottenham Hotspur	L	0-2		26,398
30	26	A	Manchester United	L	0-3		69,070
31	Apr 1	H	Chelsea	D	0-0		26,364
32	4	H	Bolton Wanderers	W	1-0	Jarosik	26,493
33	8	A	Wigan Athletic	D	1-1	Dunn	18,669
34	16	A	Aston Villa	L	1-3	Sutton	40,158
35	19	H	Blackburn Rovers	W	2-1	Butt, Forssell	25,282
36	22	A	Everton	D	0-0		35,420
37	29	H	Newcastle United	D	0-0		28,337
38	May 7	A	Bolton Wanderers	L	0-1		26,275

Appearances
Sub appearances
Two own-goals   Goals

FA Cup

R3	Jan 7	A	Torquay United	D	0-0		5,974
R3	17	H	Torquay United	W	2-0	Forssell, Jarosik	24,655
R4	28	A	Reading	D	1-1	Dunn	23,762
rep	Feb 7	H	Reading	W	2-1	Gray, Forssell	16,644
R5	19	A	Stoke City	W	1-0	Forssell	18,765
R6	Mar 21	H	Liverpool	L	0-7		27,371

Appearances
Sub appearances
Goals

League Cup

R2	Sep 20	A	Scunthorpe United	W	2-0	Forssell 2 (1 pen)	6,101
R3	Oct 26	H	Norwich City	W	2-1	Pennant, Jarosik	28,822
R4	Nov 29	A	Millwall	D	2-2	Gray, Heskey	7,731
R5	Dec 20	H	Manchester United	L	1-3	Jarosik	20,454

R4 won 4-3 on penalties a.e.t.

Appearances
Sub appearances
Goals

446

League player appearance grid for Birmingham City.

Column headers (players):
Taylor MS (Maik), Melchiot M, Clapham JR, Butt N, Upson MJ, Cunningham KE, Pennant JJ, Pandiani WG, Heskey EWI, Clemence SN, Gray JR, Forssell MK, Morrison CH, Lazaridis S, Izzet MK, Tebily O, Jarosik J, Johnson DM, Kilkenny NM, Taylor M (Martin), Dunn DJI, Vaesen NJ-T, Painter M, Briley MM, Sutton CR, Bruce AS, Latka M, Campbell DJ, Sadler M, Nafti M, Till P, Ojr SU

League Table

	P	W	D	L	F	A	Pts
Chelsea	38	29	4	5	72	22	91
Manchester United	38	25	8	5	72	34	83
Liverpool	38	25	7	6	57	25	82
Arsenal	38	20	7	11	68	31	67
Tottenham Hotspur	38	18	11	9	53	38	65
Blackburn Rovers	38	19	6	13	51	42	63
Newcastle United	38	17	7	14	47	42	58
Bolton Wanderers	38	15	11	12	49	41	56
West Ham United	38	16	7	15	52	55	55
Wigan Athletic	38	15	6	17	45	52	51
Everton	38	14	8	16	34	49	50
Fulham	38	14	6	18	48	58	48
Charlton Athletic	38	13	8	17	41	55	47
Middlesbrough	38	12	9	17	48	58	45
Manchester City	38	13	4	21	43	48	43
Aston Villa	38	10	12	16	42	55	42
Portsmouth	38	10	8	20	37	62	38
Birmingham City	38	8	10	20	28	50	34
West Bromwich Albion	38	7	9	22	31	58	30
Sunderland	38	3	6	29	26	69	15

The Championship

Manager: Steve Bruce

Did you know that?

Blues scored inside the last 10 minutes of 16 League matches this season, including eight winners or point-savers.

Blues won 26 League games this season – a club record. Their previous best was 25 in 1946–47, 1984–85 and 1994–95.

Blues recorded their biggest-ever win at Newcastle by thumping the Geordies 5–1 in a third round FA Cup replay. James Milner (United) and Matthew Upson (Blues) played against each other at St James' Park and were members of the England squad at the 2010 World Cup in South Africa. Obafemi Martins (United) also appeared in the World Cup (for Nigeria).

Blues paid a club record £6.8 million for Jermaine Pennant from Liverpool in July.

Match No.	Date		Venue	Opponents	Result		Scorers	Attendance
1	Aug	5	H	Colchester United	W	2-1	Campbell, Bendtner	24,238
2		9	A	Sunderland	W	1-0	Forssell (pen)	26,668
3		12	A	Stoke City	D	0-0		12,347
4		19	H	Crystal Palace	W	2-1	Larsson, Bendtner	20,223
5		26	A	Cardiff City	L	0-2		20,109
6	Sep	9	H	Hull City	W	2-1	Campbell, Bendtner	19,228
7		12	A	Queen's Park Rangers	W	2-0	N'Gotty, Jerome	10,936
8		16	H	Ipswich Town	D	2-2	Dunn, Campbell	20,841
9		23	A	Leeds United	L	2-3	Warner (og), Bendtner	18,898
10		30	A	Leicester City	D	1-1	McSheffrey	18,002
11	Oct	14	A	Luton Town	L	2-3	Danns, Campbell	9,275
12		17	H	Norwich City	L	0-1		20,537
13		21	A	Derby County	W	1-0	Clemence	25,673
14		28	H	West Bromwich Albion	W	2-0	McSheffrey 2	21,009
15		31	A	Coventry City	W	1-0	Bendtner	27,212
16	Nov	4	A	Plymouth Argyle	W	1-0	Jaidi	17,008
17		11	H	Barnsley	W	2-0	Danns, McSheffrey	19,344
18		18	A	Wolverhampton Wan.	D	1-1	McSheffrey	22,256
19		25	A	Burnley	W	2-1	Campbell, Bendtner	12,889
20		29	A	Southampton	L	3-4	Jerome, Bendtner, Jaidi	21,889
21	Dec	2	H	Plymouth Argyle	W	3-0	Bendtner, McSheffrey, Upson	22,592
22		9	H	Preston North End	W	3-1	McSheffrey 3 (1 pen)	23,159
23		16	A	Sheffield Wednesday	W	3-0	Clemence, Jerome, McSheffrey	26,083
24		23	A	Southend United	W	4-0	Campbell, Clemence, Jaidi, McSheffrey	9,781
25		26	H	Queen's Park Rangers	W	2-1	Jerome, Upson	29,431
26		29	H	Luton Town	D	2-2	Danns, McSheffrey	24,642
27	Jan	1	A	Ipswich Town	L	0-1		22,436
28		30	H	Southend United	L	1-3	P.Clarke (og)	19,177
29	Feb	3	A	Colchester United	D	1-1	Clemence	5,918
30		11	H	Stoke City	W	1-0	McSheffrey	15,854
31		17	A	Crystal Palace	W	1-0	Jerome	17,233
32		20	H	Sunderland	D	1-1	Campbell	20,941
33		24	A	Hull City	L	0-2		18,811
34		27	H	Leeds United	W	1-0	Bendtner	18,363
35	Mar	4	H	Cardiff City	W	1-0	Larsson	28,223
36		9	H	Derby County	W	1-0	Vine	20,962
37		13	A	Norwich City	L	0-1		23,504
38		18	A	West Bromwich Albion	D	1-1	Johnson	21,434
39	Apr	1	A	Coventry City	W	3-0	Campbell 2, Jaidi	25,424
40		7	H	Burnley	L	0-1		28,777
41		9	A	Barnsley	L	0-1		15,857
42		14	A	Southampton	W	2-1	Bendtner, Jaidi	19,754
43		17	A	Leicester City	W	2-1	Larsson, Jaidi	24,290
44		22	A	Wolverhampton Wan.	W	3-2	Jerome, Bendtner, Cole	22,754
45		28	H	Sheffield Wednesday	W	2-0	Jerome, Larsson	29,317
46	May	6	A	Preston North End	L	0-1		16,832

Appearances
Sub appearances
Two own-goals   Goals

FA Cup

	Date		Venue	Opponents	Result		Scorers	Attendance
R3	Jan	6	H	Newcastle United	D	2-2	Campbell, Larsson	16,444
rep		17	A	Newcastle United	W	5-1	McSheffrey, Solano (og), N'Gotty, Larsson, Campbell	26,099
R4		27	H	Reading	L	2-3	Larsson, Martin.Taylor	20,014

Appearances
Sub appearances
One own-goal   Goals

League Cup

	Date		Venue	Opponents	Result		Scorers	Attendance
R1	Aug	22	H	Shrewsbury Town		1-0	Larsson	12,426
R2	Sep	19	H	Wrexham		4-1	Jerome, McSheffrey 2, Bendtner	10,491
R3	Oct	24	A	Sheffield United		4-2	Campbell, Bendtner, Jerome, Larsson	10,584
R4	Nov	8	H	Liverpool		0-1		23,06

R2 a.e.t.

Appearances
Sub appearances
Goal

Taylor MS (Maik)	Kelly SMD	Sadler M	Danns NA	N'Gotty B	Tebily O	Johnson DM	Dunn DJI	Forssell MK	Campbell DJ	Clemence SN	Jerome CZ	Larsson SB	Bendtner N	Muamba FN	Nafti M	Jaidi RBA	McSheffrey G	Doyle CA	Gray JR	Kilkenny NM	Taylor M (Martin)	Painter M	Upson MJ	Vine RL	Cole AA
1	2	3	4	5	6	7	8	9	10	11	14	13	12												
1	2	3	14	5	6	7	12	9		13		11	10	4	8										
1	2	3	13	5	6	7	12	9		14		11	10	4	8										
1	2	3	13	5		7	4	14	9			12	10		8	6	11								
	2	3		5		7	8		9		13	12	10		4	6	11	1							
1			12	5		2	8		9			7	10		4	6	11		3	13					
1			7	5		2	8		9		12	3	10	4		6	11			13	14				
1			7	5		2	8	13	9		10	3			4	6	11			14	12				
1			7		12	2	8		9		14	13	10		4	6	11				5	3			
1	2	3	14		5			13	9		12	7	10	8	4	6	11								
1	2	3	7	5				13	9		10	14		8	4	6	11			12					
1		3	7	5	2		8		9		10	14		4		6	11		13	12					
1	2	3	14			7	8			11	12	13	9		4	6	10				5				
1	2	3	14			7				8	10	12	9	4	13	6	11				5				
1	2	3	7						13	8	10	12	9	4		6	11				5				
1	2	3	7							8	10	12	9	4	14	6	11		13		5				
1	2	3	12						14	8	10	7	9	4	13	6	11				5				
1	2	3	13							8	10	7	9	4	12	6	11				5				
1	2	3	8						13	11		7	9	4	12	6	10				5		14		
1	2	3	8						14	11	12	7	9	4	13	6	10				5				
1	2	3	13						12	8	10	7	9		4	6	11						5		
1	2	3							13	8	10	7	9	4	12	6	11						5		
1	2	3	13						14	8	10	7	9		4	6	11			12			5		
1	2	3	12			7			9	8			10	14	4	6	11			13			5		
1	2	3				7			9	8	12	14	10	13	4	6	11						5		
1	2	3	12						13		10	7	9	8	4	6	11			14			5		
1	2	3	13			7			9	8		12	10	4			11				6		5		
1		3		2		7			14	13	9	8		12	4		11				6		5	10	
		3		2		7			14	8	9	13	12	4		6	11	1			5			10	
		3		2		7				8	10	12	9	4		6	11	1			5			13	
		3	14	2		7				8	10	12	9	4		6	11	1			5			13	
		3	13	2					14	8	10	7	9	4		6	11	1			5			12	
	12	3	4	2					9	8	10	7	13			6	11	1			5			14	
	2	3		6						8	12	7	9	4	13		11	1	14		5			10	
	2	3		6						8	13	7	9	4	12		11	1			5			10	
	2	3		6		12				8	13	7	9	4			11	1			5			10	
	2	3				7		13		8	12	11	9	4		6		1	14		5			10	
	2	3				7			12	8	13	14	9	4		6		1	11		5			10	
	2	3				7			12	8	10	4	9	14	13	6		1			5			11	
	2	3	14			7			12		13	8	9		4	6	11	1			5			10	
	3		13	2		7			8		9		12	4		6	11	1	14		5			10	
	3			2		7			14	8			10	4	13	6	11	1			5			12	9
	3			2					13	8	12	7	10	4	14	6	11	1			5				9
	3			2						8	12	7	10	4	13	6	11	1			5			14	9
	3			2						8	13	7	10	4	12	6	11	1			5			14	9
	3			2		12			14	8	13	7	10		4	6	11	1			5				9
27	35	36	11	25	5	24	9	3	15	31	20	27	38	30	18	38	40	19	2	0	29	1	8	10	5
	1		18		1	2	2	5	17	3	18	16	4	4	14				5	8	2		1	7	
			3	1		1	1	1	9	4	7	4	11			6	13						2	1	1
1	2	3	13			7			9			8	10	4		6	11			14	12		5		
1		3	13	2		7			9		10	8		4	12		11			14	6		5		
1		3	14	2		7			9		10	8	12	4			11			13	6		5		
3	1	3	0	2		3			3		2	3	1	3	0	1	3			0	2		3		
			3										1		1					3	1				
				1					2			3					1				1				
	14		4					9	13	11	10	2	12	8		6		1	3	7	5				
	2				6		14	9	13		10	7	12	4			11	1		8	5	3			
	2	3	4						9		10	7	12	8		6		1	11	13	5				
1	2	3	8						9		10	7	12	14	4	6	13		11		5				
1	3	2	3		1		0	2	2	1	4	4	0	3	1	3	1	3	3	2	4	1			
	1						1		2				4	1			1			1					
									1		2	2	2				2								

League Table

	P	W	D	L	F	A	Pts
Sunderland	46	27	7	12	76	47	88
Birmingham City	46	26	8	12	67	42	86
Derby County	46	25	9	12	62	46	84
West Bromwich Albion	46	22	10	14	81	55	76
Wolverhampton	46	22	10	14	59	56	76
Southampton	46	21	12	13	77	53	75
Preston North End	46	22	8	16	64	53	74
Stoke City	46	19	16	11	62	41	73
Sheffield Wednesday	46	20	11	15	70	66	71
Colchester United	46	20	9	17	70	56	69
Plymouth Argyle	46	17	16	13	63	62	67
Crystal Palace	46	18	11	17	59	51	65
Cardiff City	46	17	13	16	57	53	64
Ipswich Town	46	18	8	20	64	59	62
Burnley	46	15	12	19	52	49	57
Norwich City	46	16	9	21	56	71	57
Coventry City	46	16	8	22	47	62	56
Queens Park Rangers	46	14	11	21	54	68	53
Leicester City	46	13	14	19	49	64	53
Barnsley	46	15	5	26	53	85	50
Hull City	46	13	10	23	51	67	49
Southend United	46	10	12	24	47	80	42
Luton Town	46	10	10	26	53	81	40
Leeds United	46	13	7	26	46	72	36

Premier League

Caretaker manager: Eric Black (to November); then Alex McLeish (Manager)

Match No.	Date	Venue	Opponents	Result		Scorers	Attendance
1	Aug 12	A	Chelsea	L	2-3	Forssell, Kapo	41,590
2	15	H	Sunderland	D	2-2	McShane (og), O'Connor	24,898
3	18	H	West Ham United	L	0-1		24,961
4	25	A	Derby County	W	2-1	Jerome 2	31,117
5	Sep 1	A	Middlesbrough	L	0-2		22,920
6	15	H	Bolton Wanderers	W	1-0	Kapo	28,124
7	22	A	Liverpool	D	0-0		44,215
8	29	H	Manchester United	L	0-1		26,526
9	Oct 7	A	Blackburn Rovers	L	1-2	Jerome	19,316
10	20	A	Manchester City	L	0-1		45,688
11	27	H	Wigan Athletic	W	3-2	Ridgewell, Kapo 2 (1 pen)	27,661
12	Nov 3	A	Everton	L	1-3	Kapo	35,155
13	11	H	Aston Villa	L	1-2	Forssell	26,539
14	24	H	Portsmouth	L	0-2		22,089
15	Dec 2	A	Tottenham Hotspur	W	3-2	Larsson, McSheffrey (pen), Jerome	35,635
16	8	A	Newcastle United	L	1-2	Jerome	49,948
17	15	H	Reading	D	1-1	Forssell	27,300
18	22	A	Bolton Wanderers	L	0-3		19,111
19	26	H	Middlesbrough	W	3-0	Downing (og), Forssell, McSheffrey (pen)	24,094
20	29	H	Fulham	D	1-1	Larsson	28,923
21	Jan 1	A	Manchester United	L	0-1		75,459
22	12	A	Arsenal	D	1-1	O'Connor	60,037
23	19	A	Chelsea	L	0-1		26,567
24	29	A	Sunderland	L	0-2		37,670
25	Feb 2	H	Derby County	D	1-1	Larsson	25,924
26	9	A	West Ham United	D	1-1	McFadden (pen)	34,884
27	23	H	Arsenal	D	2-2	McFadden 2 (1 pen)	27,195
28	Mar 1	H	Tottenham Hotspur	W	4-1	Larsson, Forssell 3	26,055
29	12	A	Portsmouth	L	2-4	Larsson, Muamba	20,138
30	17	H	Newcastle United	D	1-1	McFadden	25,777
31	22	A	Reading	L	1-2	Zarate	24,085
32	29	H	Manchester City	W	3-1	McSheffrey (pen), Zarate 2	22,962
33	Apr 5	A	Wigan Athletic	L	0-2		17,926
34	12	H	Everton	D	1-1	Zarate	25,923
35	20	A	Aston Villa	L	1-5	Forssell	42,584
36	26	H	Liverpool	D	2-2	Larsson, Forssell	29,252
37	May 3	A	Fulham	L	0-2		25,308
38	11	H	Blackburn Rovers	W	4-1	Muamba, Jerome 2, Murphy	26,668

Appearances
Sub appearances
Two own-goals   Goals

FA Cup

R3	Jan 5	A	Huddersfield Town	L	1-2	O'Connor	13,410

Appearances
Sub appearances
Goals

League Cup

R2	Aug 28	H	Hereford United	W	2-1	McSheffrey, O'Connor	10,185
R3	Sep 26	A	Blackburn Rovers	L	0-3		9,205

Appearances
Sub appearances
Goals

Player columns (left to right):
Doyle CA · Kelly SMD · Queudrue F · Nafti M · Ridgewell LM · Djourou-Gbadjere JD · Larsson SB · Muamba FN · Forssell MK · Kapo OM-Q · McSheffrey G · Parnaby S · de Ridder DBF · Jerome CZ · O'Connor GL · Jaidi RBA · Sadler M · Taylor M (Marrin) · Mehmeta BO · Schmitz R · Patricio IVR · Dans NA · Kingson RPF · Johnson DM · McFadden JH · Zarate MM · Murphy DP · Taylor MS (Mark) · Vine RL · Aluko S

1	2	3	4	5	6	7	8	9	10	11	12	14	13																
1	3		4	5	6	7	8	9	10	11	2			13	12														
1	3			4	5		7	8	9	11	12	2		13	10	6	14												
	3		13	5	4	12	8	9	7	11	2			10		6	14	1											
	3		14	5	4	7	8	9	11	12	2			10	13	6		1											
	2	3	4	5	6	7	8		10	11			9	14		1	12	13											
	2	3	4	5	6	7			10	12			9	13		1	11	14	8										
	2	3	4	5	6	7	8		10	11			9	14		1		13	12										
	2	3	4	5	6	7	8		10	11			9	12		1		13	14										
	2	3	4	5		8			10	11	12	9	13			1	6	7	14										
	2	3	4	5		13	8		10	14		7	9	12		1	6	11											
	2		4	5	6	11	8	14	10	13		7	9	12		1	3												
	2		4	5	6	13	8	12	10			7	9	14		1	3	11											
	2		4	5	6		8	9	10	11		7		12		1	3			1									
	2		4	5	6	10	8	13	14	11	12	7	9			1	3												
	2		4	5		10	8	13	12	11		7	9		3	1	6												
	2		5		8	4	9		11			10	12		3	1	6			7									
	2			4	10	8		12	11			9	13	6	3	1	5			7									
	2	3	13	5		8	4	9		11			10	12		1				7									
	2	3	12	5		8	4	9		11		13	10	14	6	1				7									
	2	3	4	5		7	8	13		11		12	9	10	6	1		14											
	2	3		5		7	4	14	11	13	12		9	10		1	6			8									
	2	3		5		7	4	13	11				9	10		1	6			8	12								
	2	3		5		7	4	12	11				9			1	6			8	10	13							
	2			5		7	4		11					9		1				8	10	12	3	6					
	2			5		7	4	9		11	13		12			1				8	10		3	6					
	2		14	5		7	4	9	11		12					1				8	10	13	3	6					
	2			5		7	4	9		11		14		6		1				8	10	13	3						
	2			5		7	4	9		11			14		6	1				8	12	10	3						
	2			5		7	4	9		11	12		13		6	1				8	10	14	3						
	2	4	5		7	8	9		11			13	12	6		1						10	3						
	2	5			7	4	9		11	12			13	6		1				8		10	3						
	2	12			7	4	9		11	14		13		6		1				8		10	3	5					
	2	4	5		7	8	9		11			12	13	6		1					10	14	3						
	2	4	5			8	13	12	11			7		6		1					10	9	3						
	2	12	4	5		7	8	9	11	13				6		1					10	14	3						
	2	12		5		7	4	9	11			14		6		1				8	10	13	3						
	2	13	5		7	4	9	11	14			12		6		1				8		10	3						
3	38	14	19	35	13	32	37	21	22	24	4	6	21	5	18	3	34	1	12	4	0	1	17	10	6	14	4		
		2	7			3		9	4	8	9	4	12	18		2		1	3	3	2			2	8				
				1		6	2	9	5	3			7	2										4	4	1			

	2	3		5		8	4	9		11		7	12	10	6		1												
	1	1		1		1	1	1		1		1	0	1	1		1												
													1																
														1															

	6		4	5		7			11	2			9		3				8	1					10	12			
2					9				2	7			10	6	3		13	14	4	1	8			5	11				
0	1		1	1		1		1	2	1		2	1	2		0	0	2	2	1			1	2	0			
1													1	1										1					
												1		1															

League Table

	P	W	D	L	F	A	Pts
Manchester United	38	27	6	5	80	22	87
Chelsea	38	25	10	3	65	26	85
Arsenal	38	24	11	3	74	31	83
Liverpool	38	21	13	4	67	28	76
Everton	38	19	8	11	55	33	65
Aston Villa	38	16	12	10	71	51	60
Blackburn Rovers	38	15	13	10	50	48	58
Portsmouth	38	16	9	13	48	40	57
Manchester City	38	15	10	13	45	53	55
West Ham United	38	13	10	15	42	50	49
Tottenham Hotspur	38	11	13	14	66	61	46
Newcastle United	38	11	10	17	45	65	43
Middlesbrough	38	10	12	16	43	53	42
Wigan Athletic	38	10	10	18	34	51	40
Sunderland	38	11	6	21	36	59	39
Bolton	38	9	10	19	36	54	37
Fulham	38	8	12	18	38	60	36
Reading	38	10	6	22	41	66	36
Birmingham City	38	8	11	19	46	62	35
Derby County	38	1	8	29	20	89	11

2008-09

The Championship

Manager: Alex McLeish

Match No.	Date	Venue	Opponents	Result		Scorers	Attendance
1	Aug 9	H	Sheffield United	W	1-0	Phillips	24,019
2	16	A	Southampton	W	2-1	O'Connor, Phillips	18,925
3	23	H	Barnsley	W	2-0	Phillips, O'Connor	17,413
4	30	A	Norwich City	D	1-1	Larsson	24,229
5	Sep 13	H	Doncaster Rovers	W	1-0	Jerome	18,165
6	16	A	Bristol City	W	2-1	Carey (og), Jerome	18,456
7	20	H	Blackpool	L	0-1		20,983
8	27	A	Cardiff City	W	2-1	McFadden, Owusu-Abeyie	18,304
9	30	A	Derby County	D	1-1	Owusu-Abeyie	29,743
10	Oct 4	H	Queen's Park Rangers	W	1-0	Phillips	18,498
11	18	A	Burnley	D	1-1	Jerome	13,809
12	21	H	Crystal Palace	W	1-0	O'Connor	17,706
13	25	H	Sheffield Wednesday	W	3-1	O'Connor 2, Phillips	17,300
14	28	A	Queen's Park Rangers	L	0-1		13,594
15	Nov 3	H	Coventry City	L	0-1		17,215
16	8	A	Nottingham Forest	D	1-1	McFadden	21,415
17	15	H	Charlton Athletic	W	3-2	McFadden, Phillips, Queudrue	20,071
18	21	A	Swansea City	W	3-2	Bent, Phillips 2	16,956
19	25	H	Ipswich Town	W	2-1	Ridgewell, Phillips	15,689
20	29	A	Wolverhampton Wan.	D	1-1	Jerome	26,329
21	Dec 6	H	Watford	W	3-2	Bent, Jerome, Phillips	18,174
22	9	A	Plymouth Argyle	W	1-0	Carsley	10,446
23	13	A	Preston North End	L	0-1		10,943
24	20	H	Reading	L	1-3	Phillips	19,695
25	26	A	Ipswich Town	W	1-0	McFadden	23,536
26	28	H	Swansea City	D	0-0		21,836
27	Jan 17	H	Cardiff City	D	1-1	Bowyer	19,853
28	24	A	Blackpool	L	0-2		8,105
29	27	H	Derby County	W	1-0	Carsley	15,330
30	31	A	Sheffield Wednesday	D	1-1	Phillips	18,409
31	Feb 7	H	Burnley	D	1-1	Phillips	16,763
32	14	H	Nottingham Forest	W	2-0	Bent, Fahey	17,631
33	21	A	Coventry City	L	0-1		22,637
34	24	A	Crystal Palace	D	0-0		12,847
35	Mar 1	A	Sheffield United	L	1-2	Morgan (og)	24,232
36	4	H	Bristol City	W	1-0	Queudrue	17,551
37	7	H	Southampton	W	1-0	Fahey	16,735
38	10	A	Barnsley	D	1-1	M.Taylor	11,295
39	14	A	Doncaster Rovers	W	2-0	Jerome, Bouazza	11,482
40	21	H	Norwich City	D	1-1	Jerome	18,159
41	Apr 6	H	Wolverhampton Wan.	W	2-0	Jerome, O'Connor	25,935
42	11	A	Charlton Athletic	D	0-0		20,022
43	13	H	Plymouth Argyle	D	1-1	Queudrue	19,323
44	18	A	Watford	W	1-0	Jerome	16,180
45	25	H	Preston North End	L	1-2	Fahey	24,825
46	May 3	A	Reading	W	2-1	Phillips, Fahey	23,879
						Appearances	
						Sub appearances	
					Two own-goals	Goals	

FA Cup

R3	Jan 13	H	Wolverhampton Wan.	L	0-2		22,232
						Appearances	
						Sub appearances	

League Cup

R1	Aug 13	A	Wycombe Wanderers	W	4-0	Nafti, Jerome, Larsson, Owusu-Abeyie	2,735
R2	26	A	Southampton	L	0-2		11,331
						Appearances	
						Sub appearances	
						Goals	

452

This is an appearance/lineup grid for Birmingham City. Player column headers (left to right):

1. Taylor MS (Maik)
2. Parnaby S
3. Murphy DP
4. Nafti M
5. Ridgewell LM
6. Taylor M (Martin)
7. Larsson SB
8. Carsley L
9. Bent M
10. McFadden JH
11. McSheffrey G
12. Phillips KM
13. O'Connor GL
14. Jerome CZ
15. Owusu-Abeyie Q
16. Kelly SMO
17. Agustien K
18. Jaidi RBA
19. Queudrue F
20. Wilson JA
21. Hunt N
22. Johnson DM
23. Sinclair SA
24. Bowyer L
25. Bouazza H
26. Fahey K
27. Costly C
28. Carr S
29. De La Cruz U
30. Doyle CA
31. Traore D
32. Mutch JJE
33. Sinnott RA

1	2	3	4	5	6	7	8	9	10	11	12	13	14																			
1	2	3	4	5	6	7	8	9	10	**11**	12	13	14																			
1	2	3	**4**	5	6	7	8	13	11			14	9	12	*10*																	
1	**2**	3		5	6	7	4	13	11	14	*10*	9			8	12																
1	2	3		5	6	7	4	12	11	13	10			**9**		8																
1	2	3	4	5	6	7	8	13	12			*10*		9	**11**	14																
1	2	3		5	6	7	**4**	12	10	11				9	14	13	*8*															
1	*3*		5	6	7	4	12	10	*11*	13			9	14	2	**8**																
1	2	3		5		7	4	**11**			14	13	*9*	*10*		8	6															
1	2	3	4	5			8	13	**11**		14	12	*9*	*10*		7	6															
1	2	3	12	5		7	**4**		13			*10*	9	14	**11**		8	6															
1	2	**3**		5	6	7	4		13			10	*9*	14	11		*8*		12													
1	2			5	6	7	4	12				10	9	*11*			*8*		3	13												
1	2		12	5	6	*7*	4	14	13			*10*	9	**11**			8		3													
1	**2**		4	5	6		8	14	11			10	*9*	13			7		3	12												
1			5		7	4	13	11				10		*9*	14		**8**	6	3	12		2										
1			3	5	7	4	9	10				13		12			**8**	6		11		2										
1		12	5	14	7	4	*9*	11				**10**		13				6	*3*	8		2										
1		4	5		7	8	9	*10*				12	14	**11**			13	6	*3*	8		2										
1	14	12	5		7	**4**	9	11				10					13	6	*3*	8		2										
1	11	12	5			4	*9*	7				10		13	14			6	*3*	8		**2**										
1	13			5	7	4	**9**					10		12	11		14	6	*3*	8		2										
1	7			5		4	9					10		12	11		14	6	**3**	8		2										
1	13	11		5		4	**9**					10		12	7		14	6	*3*	8		2										
1	2	3			7	4	13	**11**				10		9	12			5	6	8												
1	2	11		5		4	13	*10*				9				7	6	**3**				12	8									
1	2	11		5		4	9	7				**10**		13	12			6	*3*			14	8									
1		3		5		12	4	14				10		9		2	6			**7**	8	11	13									
1	2		5		7	4		12				13		9			6	*3*		**11**	8	10	14									
1	3		5	6	2	4		**9**				10		12				13	8	11	7											
1	2	3		5	6	12	4	14				10		*9*					7	8	11	13										
1	3		5	6	2	4			10			*9*						7	8	**11**	13	12										
1	3		5	6	2	4	9					**10**		12				11	8	14	7	13										
1	3		5	6	2	4	10					9						11	8	12	7	13										
1	3		5		4		9					12				6			14	**11**	8	13	7	**10**	2							
1	3					4	9	13				12				6	5			*7*		11	8	**10**	2							
1			5	7	4	**10**						9				6	3			13	8		11	12	2							
1			5	7	4	**10**						9				6	3			13	8	14	11	12	2							
1			5	7	4							9				6	3		8	12		13	11	**10**	2							
1		5		7	4				12	**9**						6	*3*			14	8	*10*	11		2	13						
1	14		5		7	4		13	**10**	9						6	*3*			12	8	**11**			2							
1	3		5		7	4		12		**10**	13	9				6				8	14	11			2							
1	3		5		**7**	4		13	14	12				10	9	6				4	8	*10*	11		2							
1	3	**5**		7			14			10	*9*					6	13			4	8		**11**		2		12					
1	3			**7**				10		12	9	13				6	*5*			4	8		11		2		1	14				
1				**7**				10		13	9	12				6	5			4	8		11		2			3				
1	3		5	12	4			**7**			*10*	14	*9*			6					8		11		2			3				

Totals rows:

45	19	28	6	36	23	35	41	16	22	5	24	10	25	12	2	13	30	23	8	0	9	8	8	17	9	15	3	13	0	1	2
	2	2	5		1	3		17	8	13	12	6	18	7	3	5		2	2	1	2	1	6		7	4	5		1	1	1
		1	1		1	2	3	4		14	6	9	2			3				1	1	4									

Lower block (goals / cards):

1	2			5			4	**10**				9				13	7	6	3	8		12									11	
1	1			1			1	1				1				0	1	1	1	1		0									1	
												1				1			1												

Second lower block:

	2	**3**	4	5	6	7	8		*11*	*10*	9	13	14			12										1						
	2	3		5			4	9		*11*	12	**10**		8	6	7										1		13				
	2	2	1	2	1	1	2	1		2	1	2	0	1	1	1		0							2	0		0				
										1		1	1		1	1		1								1						
		1		1							1		1	1																		

Premier League

Manager: Alex McLeish

Match No.	Date	Venue	Opponents	Result		Scorers	Attendance
1	Aug 16	A	Manchester United	L	0-1		75,062
2	19	H	Portsmouth	W	1-0	McFadden (pen)	19,922
3	22	H	Stoke City	D	0-0		21,694
4	29	A	Tottenham Hotspur	L	1-2	Bowyer	35,318
5	Sep 13	H	Aston Villa	L	0-1		25,196
6	19	H	Hull City	W	1-0	O'Connor	23,759
7	26	H	Bolton Wanderers	L	1-2	Phillips	28,671
8	Oct 3	A	Burnley	L	1-2	Larsson	20,102
9	17	A	Arsenal	L	1-3	Bowyer	60,082
10	24	H	Sunderland	W	2-1	Ridgewell, McFadden	21,723
11	Nov 1	H	Manchester City	D	0-0		21,462
12	9	A	Liverpool	D	2-2	Benitez, Jerome	42,560
13	21	H	Fulham	W	1-0	Bowyer	23,659
14	29	A	Wolverhampton Wan.	W	1-0	Bowyer	26,668
15	Dec 5	A	Wigan Athletic	W	3-2	Larsson 2, Benitez	18,797
16	12	H	West Ham United	W	1-0	Bowyer	28,203
17	15	H	Blackburn Rovers	W	2-1	Jerome 2	23,187
18	20	A	Everton	D	1-1	Larsson	33,660
19	26	H	Chelsea	D	0-0		28,958
20	28	A	Stoke City	W	1-0	Jerome	27,211
21	Jan 9	H	Manchester United	D	1-1	Jerome	28,907
22	27	A	Chelsea	L	0-3		41,293
23	30	H	Tottenham Hotspur	D	1-1	Ridgewell	27,238
24	Feb 7	H	Wolverhampton Wan.	W	2-1	Phillips 2	24,165
25	10	A	West Ham United	L	0-2		34,458
26	21	A	Fulham	L	1-2	Baird (og)	21,758
27	27	H	Wigan Athletic	W	1-0	McFadden (pen)	25,921
28	Mar 9	A	Portsmouth	W	2-1	Jerome 2	18,465
29	13	H	Everton	D	2-2	Jerome, Gardner	24,579
30	20	A	Sunderland	L	1-3	Jerome	37,962
31	24	A	Blackburn Rovers	L	1-2	McFadden	23,856
32	27	H	Arsenal	D	1-1	Phillips	27,039
33	Apr 4	H	Liverpool	D	1-1	Ridgewell	27,909
34	11	A	Manchester City	L	1-5	Jerome	45,209
35	17	H	Hull City	D	0-0		26,669
36	25	A	Aston Villa	L	0-1		42,788
37	May 1	H	Burnley	W	2-1	Jerome, Benitez	24,578
38	9	A	Bolton Wanderers	L	1-2	McFadden	22,863

Appearances
Sub appearances
One own-goal   Goals

FA Cup

R3	Jan 2	A	Nottingham Forest	D	0-0		20,975
rep	12	H	Nottingham Forest	W	1-0	Ferguson	9,399
R4	23	A	Everton	W	2-1	Ferguson, Benitez	30,875
R5	Feb 13	A	Derby County	W	2-1	Dann, Ridgewell	21,043
R6	Mar 6	A	Portsmouth	L	0-2		20,456

Appearances
Sub appearances
Goals

League Cup

R2	Aug 25	A	Southampton	W	2-1	Carsley, Bowyer	11,753
R3	Sep 22	A	Sunderland	L	0-2		20,576

Appearances
Sub appearances
Goals

Hart J	Carr S	Vignal G	Carsley L	Johnson R	Queudrue F	Larsson SB	Ferguson B	Jerome CZ	McFadden JH	Fahey K	O'Connor GL	Benitez C	O'Shea J	Parnaby S	Phillips KM	Bowyer L	Taylor MS (Maik)	McSheffrey G	Tainio T	Dann S	Ridgewell LM	Johnson DM	Michel	Gardner C	Espinoza G	Sammons A	Preston D	Jervis J
1	2	3	4	5	6	7	8	**9**	10	11	12	13	14															
1	2	**3**		5	6	7	4	9	11	8	*10*	14		12	13													
1	2			5	6	13	4		11	7	9	12		3	**10**	8												
1	2		**4**	5	6	7	8		10		9	12		3		11		13										
1			*12*	5	6	2	4		**10**	11	9	13		3	14	8			7									
1	2			5			4			11	12	9		3		8		**10**	7	6								
1	2	3		5		7	4			11	12	9			13	8			**10**	6								
1	2			5	**3**	13	4		10	11	9				14	8			7	6	12							
1	2		*4*	5		7	8	**9**	10		12				14	11		13		6	3							
1	2		14	5		7	4	9	**11**		12	10				8		13		6	3							
	2			5		7	4	9	**11**	12		10			13	8	1			6	3							
1	2	13	12	5		7		9	11			*10*				8		14	**4**	6	3							
1	2			5		7	4	9	11	12		**10**				8				6	3							
1	2			5		7	4	9	11	12		**10**				8				6	3							
1	2			5		7	4	**9**	11	12		10				8				6	3							
1	2			5		7	4	9	11	12		**10**			13	8				6	3							
1	2			5		7	4	9	**11**	12		10				8				6	3							
1	2	13		5		7	4	9	**11**	12		10				8				6	3							
1	2			5		7	4	9	**11**	12		10				8				6	3	13						
1	2			5		**7**	4	9	11	12		10				8				6	3							
1	2			5		**7**	4	9	11	12		10				8				6	3							
1	2			5		7	4	**9**	11	12		10				8				6	3		13					
1	2			5		**7**	4	9	11	12		10				8				6	3		13					
1	2			5		7	4	9	*11*	14		**10**			12	8				6	3			13				
1	2			5			4	9	12	**11**					10	8				6	3		13	7				
1	2			5		**7**	*4*	9	10	11					13	8				6	3		14	12				
1	2			5		7	4	*9*	**10**	11					12	8				6	3		14	13				
1				5		13	4	9	14	11		*10*		**2**					12	6	3		8	7				
1	2			5		12	4	9	13	11		10				8				6	3			**7**				
1	2			5			4	9	12	11		**10**			13	14				6	3		*8*	7				
1	2			5		12	4	9	10	*11*		13			14	8				6	3			**7**				
1	2			5			4	9	**10**	11		12			13	8				6	3			7				
1	2			5			4	9	**10**	11					12	8				6	3			7				
	2			5		12	4	*9*	10	11		14			13	8	1			6	3			7				
1	2			5		13	4	9	**10**	11					12	8				6	3			7				
1	2	3		5		**11**	4	9	10	13				12	14	8					6			*7*				
1		3	14	5		7	4	*9*	**11**	13		10		2		8					6		12					
1	2	3		5		**7**	4	9	11	13		12				8					6		10					
36	35	6	3	38	6	26	37	32	32	18	5	21	0	6	2	34	2	1	5	30	30	0	3	10				
		2	4			7			4	16	5	9	1	2	17	1		4	1		1	1	6	3				
						4		11	5		1	3			4	5					3			1				

Hart J	Carr S	Vignal G	Carsley L	Johnson R	Queudrue F	Larsson SB	Ferguson B	Jerome CZ	McFadden JH	Fahey K	O'Connor GL	Benitez C	O'Shea J	Parnaby S	Phillips KM	Bowyer L	Taylor MS (Maik)	McSheffrey G	Tainio T	Dann S	Ridgewell LM	Johnson DM	Michel	Gardner C	Espinoza G	Sammons A	Preston D	Jervis J
1		3	4	5			8	9		11		14		**2**	*10*	13		12			6	7						
1	2			5		7	4	9	*11*	12		10			13	**8**				6	3	14						
1	2			5		7	4		10	11		**9**				8		13		6	3							12
1	2			5		**7**	4	9	*11*	12		10			13	8				6	3			14				
1	2			5		7	4	9	10	**11**		13			12	8				6	3			14				
5	4	1	1	5		4	5	4	4	3		3		1	1	4		0		4	5	1		0				0
										2		2			3	1		2				1		2				1
							2					1								1	1							

Hart J	Carr S	Vignal G	Carsley L	Johnson R	Queudrue F	Larsson SB	Ferguson B	Jerome CZ	McFadden JH	Fahey K	O'Connor GL	Benitez C	O'Shea J	Parnaby S	Phillips KM	Bowyer L	Taylor MS (Maik)	McSheffrey G	Tainio T	Dann S	Ridgewell LM	Johnson DM	Michel	Gardner C	Espinoza G	Sammons A	Preston D	Jervis J
	2		4		6	7			12		13	9	**11**	3		8	1	10							5			
							4			13	9		7	*2*	10	12	1	11		6	3				5	8	14	
	1		1		1	1	1		0	0	1	1	2	2	1	1	2	2		1	1				2	1	0	
									1	1	1					1											1	
			1													1												

League Table

	P	W	D	L	F	A	Pts
Chelsea	38	27	5	6	103	32	86
Manchester United	38	27	4	7	86	28	85
Arsenal	38	23	6	9	83	41	75
Tottenham Hotspur	38	21	7	10	67	41	70
Manchester City	38	18	13	7	73	45	67
Aston Villa	38	17	13	8	52	39	64
Liverpool	38	18	9	11	61	35	63
Everton	38	16	13	9	60	49	61
Birmingham City	38	13	11	14	38	47	50
Blackburn Rovers	38	13	11	14	41	55	50
Stoke City	38	11	14	13	34	48	47
Fulham	38	12	10	16	39	46	46
Sunderland	38	11	11	16	48	56	44
Bolton	38	10	9	19	42	67	39
Wolverhampton	38	9	11	18	32	56	38
Wigan Athletic	38	9	9	20	37	79	36
West Ham United	38	8	11	19	47	66	35
Burnley	38	8	6	24	42	82	30
Hull City	38	6	12	20	34	75	30
Portsmouth	38	7	7	24	34	66	18

Blues' Record in League Football 1889–2010

Season	P	W	D	L	F	A	Pts	Pos
Football Alliance								
1889–90	22	9	3	10	62	49	21	7th
1890–91	22	7	2	13	38	66	16	10th
1891–92	22	12	5	5	53	36	29	3rd
3 seasons	66	28	10	28	153	151	66	n/a
Football League								
Division Two								
1892–93	22	17	2	3	90	35	36	1st
1893–94	28	21	0	7	103	44	42	2nd
Division One								
1894–95	39	9	7	14	50	74	25	12th
1895–96	30	8	4	18	39	79	20	15th
Division Two								
1896–97	30	16	5	9	69	47	37	4th
1897–98	30	16	4	10	58	50	36	6th
1898–99	34	17	7	10	85	50	41	8th
1899–1900	34	20	6	8	78	38	46	3rd
1900–01	34	19	10	5	57	24	48	2nd
Division One								
1901–02	34	11	8	15	47	45	30	17th
Division Two								
1902–03	34	24	3	7	74	36	51	2nd
Division One								
1903–04	34	11	8	15	39	52	30	11th
1904–05	34	17	5	12	54	38	39	7th
1905–06	34	17	7	14	65	59	41	7th
1906–07	38	15	8	15	52	52	38	9th
1907–08	38	9	12	17	40	60	20	20th
Division Two								
1908–09	38	14	9	15	58	61	37	11th
1909–10	38	8	7	23	42	78	23	20th
1910–11	38	12	8	18	42	64	32	16th
1911–12	38	14	6	18	55	59	34	12th
1912–13	38	18	10	10	59	44	46	3rd
1913–14	38	12	10	16	48	60	34	14th
1914–15	38	17	9	12	62	39	43	5th
1915–19 *Competition suspended due to World War One*								

Season	P	W	D	L	F	A	Pts	Pos
1919–20	42	24	8	10	85	34	56	3rd
1920–21	42	24	10	8	79	38	58	1st
Division One								
1921–22	42	15	7	20	48	60	37	18th
1922–23	42	13	11	18	41	57	37	17th
1923–24	42	13	13	16	41	49	39	14th
1924–25	42	17	12	13	49	53	46	8th
1925–26	42	16	8	18	66	81	40	14th
1926–27	42	17	4	21	64	73	38	17th
1927–28	42	13	15	14	70	75	41	11th
1928–29	42	15	10	17	68	77	40	15th
1929–30	42	16	9	17	67	62	41	11th
1930–31	42	13	10	19	55	70	36	19th
1931–32	42	18	8	16	78	67	44	9th
1932–33	42	14	11	17	57	57	39	13th
1933–34	42	12	12	18	54	56	36	20th
1934–35	42	13	10	19	63	81	36	19th
1935–36	42	15	11	16	61	63	41	12th
1936–37	42	13	15	14	64	60	41	12th
1937–38	42	10	18	14	58	62	38	18th
1938–39	42	12	8	22	62	84	32	21st
1939–46 *Competition suspended due to World War Two*								
Division Two								
1946–47	42	25	5	12	74	33	55	3rd
1947–48	42	22	15	5	55	24	59	1st
Division One								
1948–49	42	11	15	16	36	38	37	17th
1949–50	42	7	14	21	31	67	28	22nd
Division Two								
1950–51	42	20	9	13	64	53	49	4th
1951–52	42	21	9	12	67	56	51	3rd
1952–53	42	19	10	13	71	66	48	6th
1953–54	42	18	11	13	78	58	47	7th
1954–55	42	22	10	10	92	47	54	1st
Division One								
1955–56	42	18	9	15	75	57	45	6th
1956–57	42	15	9	18	69	69	39	12th
1957–58	42	14	11	17	76	89	39	13th
1958–59	42	20	6	16	84	68	46	9th
1959–60	42	13	10	19	63	80	36	19th
1960–61	42	14	6	22	62	84	34	19th
1961–62	42	14	10	18	65	81	38	17th
1962–63	42	10	13	19	63	90	33	20th
1963–64	42	11	7	24	54	92	29	20th
1964–65	42	8	11	23	64	96	27	22nd
Division Two								
1965–66	42	16	9	17	70	75	41	10th

Season	P	W	D	L	F	A	Pts	Pos
1966–67	42	16	8	18	70	66	40	10th
1967–68	42	19	14	9	83	51	52	4th
1968–69	42	18	8	16	73	59	44	7th
1969–70	42	11	11	20	51	78	33	18th
1970–71	42	17	12	13	58	48	46	9th
1971–72	42	19	18	5	60	31	56	2nd
Division One								
1972–73	42	15	12	15	53	54	42	10th
1973–74	42	12	13	17	52	64	37	19th
1974–75	42	14	9	19	53	61	37	17th
1975–76	42	13	7	22	57	75	33	19th
1976–77	42	13	12	17	63	61	38	13th
1977–78	42	16	9	17	55	60	41	11th
1978–79	42	6	10	26	37	64	22	21st
Division Two								
1979–80	42	21	11	10	58	38	53	3rd
Division One								
1980–81	42	13	12	17	50	61	38	13th
1981–82*	42	10	14	18	53	61	44	16th
1982–83	42	12	14	16	40	55	50	17th
1983–84	42	12	12	18	39	50	48	20th
Division Two								
1984–85	42	25	7	10	59	33	82	2nd
Division One								
1985–86	42	8	5	29	30	73	29	21st
Division Two								
1986–87	42	11	17	14	47	59	50	19th
1987–88	44	11	15	18	41	66	48	19yh
1988–89	46	8	11	27	31	76	35	23rd
Division Three								
1989–90	46	18	12	16	60	59	66	7th
1990–91	46	16	17	13	45	49	65	12th
1991–92	46	23	12	11	69	52	81	2nd
Division One *(new construction of League format)*								
1992–93	46	13	12	21	42	52	40	19th
1993–94	46	13	12	21	52	69	51	22nd
Division Two								
1994–95	46	25	14	7	84	37	89	1st
Division One								
1995–96	46	15	13	18	61	64	58	15th
1996–97	46	17	15	14	52	48	66	10th
1997–98	46	19	17	10	60	35	74	7th
1998–99	46	23	12	11	66	37	81	4th
1999–2000	46	22	11	13	65	44	77	5th
2000–01	46	23	9	14	59	48	78	5th
2001–02	46	21	13	12	70	49	76	5th

Season	P	W	D	L	F	A	Pts	Pos
Premier League								
2002–03	38	13	9	16	41	49	48	13th
2003–04	38	12	14	12	43	48	50	10th
2004–05	38	11	12	15	40	46	45	12th
2005–06	38	8	10	20	28	50	34	18th
League Championship								
2006–07	46	26	8	12	67	42	86	2nd
Premier League								
2007–08	38	8	11	19	46	62	35	19th
League Championship								
2008–09	46	23	14	9	54	37	83	2nd
Premier League								
2009–10	38	13	11	14	38	47	50	9th

* Three points for a win rule was introduced for the 1981–82 season.

Blues' Complete Record of League Results
1892–2010 inclusive:

Division	Seasons	P	W	D	L	F	A
Premier League	6	228	65	67	96	236	302
First Division	50	2,030	651	501	888	2,785	3,249
2/1/Championship	47	1,906	847	460	599	3,002	2,363
3/2 Football League	4	184	82	55	47	258	197
Totals:	107	4,358	1,645	1,083	1,630	6,272	6,158

BLUES' RECORD AGAINST OTHER CLUBS

Details include all Premier League games but not Football Alliance fixtures, Test Matches or Play-offs.

ARSENAL

Venue	P	W	D	L	F	A
Home	61	30	15	16	113	79
Away	61	4	18	39	38	119
Total	122	34	33	55	151	198

ASTON VILLA

Venue	P	W	D	L	F	A
Home	54	22	13	19	80	72
Away	54	14	14	26	68	94
Totals	108	36	27	45	148	166

BARNSLEY

Venue	P	W	D	L	F	A
Home	32	19	7	6	56	29
Away	32	13	8	11	49	47
Totals	64	32	15	17	105	76

BLACKBURN ROVERS

Venue	P	W	D	L	F	A
Home	52	32	8	12	99	61
Away	52	7	11	34	69	131
Totals	104	39	19	46	168	191

BLACKPOOL

Venue	P	W	D	L	F	A
Home	38	20	8	10	88	51
Away	38	7	8	23	31	64
Totals	76	27	16	33	119	115

BOLTON WANDERERS

Venue	P	W	D	L	F	A
Home	57	30	14	13	100	63
Away	57	7	17	33	54	121
Totals	114	37	31	46	154	184

BOOTLE

Venue	P	W	D	L	F	A
Home	1	1	0	0	6	2
Away	1	1	0	0	4	1
Totals	2	2	0	0	10	3

BOURNEMOUTH (AFC)

Venue	P	W	D	L	F	A
Home	5	0	3	2	1	3
Away	5	2	0	3	7	9
Totals	10	2	3	5	8	12

BRADFORD CITY

Venue	P	W	D	L	F	A
Home	11	7	4	0	17	4
Away	11	4	4	3	13	14
Totals	22	11	8	3	30	18

BRADFORD PARK AVENUE

Venue	P	W	D	L	F	A
Home	8	4	1	3	16	11
Away	8	2	2	4	7	19
Totals	16	6	3	7	23	30

BRENTFORD

Venue	P	W	D	L	F	A
Home	14	7	3	4	25	13
Away	14	8	2	4	19	15
Totals	28	15	5	8	44	28

BRIGHTON & HOVE ALBION

Venue	P	W	D	L	F	A
Home	7	3	3	1	11	8
Away	7	1	2	4	4	12
Totals	14	4	5	5	15	20

BRISTOL CITY

Venue	P	W	D	L	F	A
Home	24	12	8	4	41	25
Away	24	8	5	11	22	31
Totals	48	20	13	15	63	56

BRISTOL ROVERS

Venue	P	W	D	L	F	A
Home	6	3	3	0	10	6
Away	6	0	5	1	6	7
Totals	12	3	8	1	16	13

BURNLEY

Venue	P	W	D	L	F	A
Home	42	22	7	13	71	52
Away	42	6	11	21	40	80
Totals	84	28	18	38	112	132

BURTON SWIFTS

Venue	P	W	D	L	F	A
Home	7	6	0	1	20	7
Away	7	6	1	0	20	6
Totals	14	12	1	1	40	13

BURTON UNITED

Venue	P	W	D	L	F	A
Home	1	1	0	0	2	0
Away	1	1	0	0	1	0
Totals	2	2	0	0	3	0

BURTON WANDERERS

Venue	P	W	D	L	F	A
Home	1	1	0	0	3	2
Away	1	1	0	0	6	2
Totals	2	2	0	0	9	4

BURY

Venue	P	W	D	L	F	A
Home	32	16	5	11	50	39
Away	32	10	4	18	36	54
Totals	64	26	9	29	86	93

CAMBRIDGE UNITED

Venue	P	W	D	L	F	A
Home	4	1	1	2	2	6
Away	4	2	0	2	5	3
Totals	8	3	1	4	7	9

CARDIFF CITY

Venue	P	W	D	L	F	A
Home	29	16	9	4	44	24
Away	29	10	2	17	32	46
Totals	58	26	11	21	76	70

CARLISLE UNITED

Venue	P	W	D	L	F	A
Home	9	6	1	2	16	9
Away	9	2	2	5	13	15
Totals	18	8	3	7	29	24

CHARLTON ATHLETIC

Venue	P	W	D	L	F	A
Home	27	14	8	5	39	25
Away	27	3	9	15	22	41
Totals	54	17	17	20	61	66

CHELSEA

Venue	P	W	D	L	F	A
Home	40	13	12	15	63	62
Away	40	6	12	22	42	75
Totals	80	19	24	37	105	137

CHESTER CITY

Venue	P	W	D	L	F	A
Home	4	3	1	0	5	2
Away	4	3	0	1	6	4
Totals	8	6	1	1	11	6

CHESTERFIELD

Venue	P	W	D	L	F	A
Home	7	4	3	0	12	5
Away	7	2	4	1	9	7
Totals	14	6	7	1	21	12

COLCHESTER UNITED

Venue	P	W	D	L	F	A
Home	1	1	0	0	2	1
Away	1	0	1	0	1	1
Totals	2	1	1	0	3	2

COVENTRY CITY

Venue	P	W	D	L	F	A
Home	23	11	7	5	38	21
Away	23	8	6	9	29	30
Totals	46	19	13	14	67	51

CREWE ALEXANDRA

Venue	P	W	D	L	F	A
Home	10	7	2	1	33	7
Away	10	5	4	1	19	7
Totals	20	12	6	2	52	14

CRYSTAL PALACE

Venue	P	W	D	L	F	A
Home	20	13	2	5	29	20
Away	20	5	5	10	18	31
Totals	40	18	7	15	47	51

DARLINGTON

Venue	P	W	D	L	F	A
Home	1	1	0	0	1	0
Away	1	0	1	0	1	1
Totals	2	1	1	0	2	1

DARWEN

Venue	P	W	D	L	F	A
Home	4	4	0	0	21	4
Away	4	0	2	2	5	8
Totals	8	4	2	2	26	12

DERBY COUNTY

Venue	P	W	D	L	F	A
Home	47	24	11	12	85	65
Away	47	8	17	22	49	89
Totals	94	32	28	34	134	154

DONCASTER ROVERS

Venue	P	W	D	L	F	A
Home	8	5	2	1	24	7
Away	8	4	1	3	14	6
Totals	16	9	3	4	38	13

EVERTON

Venue	P	W	D	L	F	A
Home	58	18	18	22	81	83
Away	58	6	16	36	64	130
Totals	116	24	34	58	145	213

EXETER CITY

Venue	P	W	D	L	F	A
Home	2	1	1	0	2	1
Away	2	1	0	1	3	2
Totals	4	2	1	1	5	3

FULHAM

Venue	P	W	D	L	F	A
Home	36	16	12	8	63	51
Away	36	11	11	14	40	54
Totals	72	27	23	22	103	105

GAINSBOROUGH TRINITY

Venue	P	W	D	L	F	A
Home	10	6	4	0	37	12
Away	10	4	3	3	13	8
Totals	20	10	7	3	50	20

GILLINGHAM

Venue	P	W	D	L	F	A
Home	2	2	0	0	3	1
Away	2	1	1	0	3	2
Totals	4	3	1	0	6	3

GLOSSOP (NORTH END)

Venue	P	W	D	L	F	A
Home	10	5	3	2	28	9
Away	10	3	1	6	12	21
Totals	20	8	4	8	40	30

GRIMSBY TOWN

Venue	P	W	D	L	F	A
Home	35	18	9	8	70	40
Away	35	7	9	19	37	50
Totals	70	25	18	27	107	90

HARTLEPOOL UNITED

Venue	P	W	D	L	F	A
Home	1	1	0	0	2	1
Away	1	0	0	1	0	1
Totals	2	1	0	1	2	2

HUDDERSFIELD TOWN

Venue	P	W	D	L	F	A
Home	46	24	8	14	79	52
Away	46	9	18	19	38	71
Totals	92	33	26	33	117	123

HULL CITY

Venue	P	W	D	L	F	A
Home	27	14	10	3	57	32
Away	27	9	6	12	22	40
Totals	54	23	17	15	79	72

IPSWICH TOWN

Venue	P	W	D	L	F	A
Home	29	12	10	7	39	29
Away	29	8	1	20	31	60
Totals	58	20	11	27	70	89

LEEDS CITY

Venue	P	W	D	L	F	A
Home	7	4	1	2	16	13
Away	7	0	2	5	4	14
Totals	14	4	3	7	20	27

LEEDS UNITED

Venue	P	W	D	L	F	A
Home	41	24	11	6	78	37
Away	41	7	12	22	27	61
Totals	42	31	23	28	105	98

LEICESTER CITY (FOSSE)

Venue	P	W	D	L	F	A
Home	59	31	10	18	108	75
Away	59	18	11	30	97	117
Totals	118	49	21	48	205	192

LEYTON ORIENT (CLAPTON, ORIENT)

Venue	P	W	D	L	F	A
Home	18	10	6	2	29	13
Away	18	4	7	7	22	26
Totals	36	14	13	9	51	39

LINCOLN CITY

Venue	P	W	D	L	F	A
Home	17	13	2	2	51	12
Away	17	9	6	2	29	20
Totals	34	22	8	4	80	32

LIVERPOOL

Venue	P	W	D	L	F	A
Home	49	21	13	15	77	52
Away	49	7	11	31	60	110
Totals	98	28	24	46	137	162

LOUGHBOROUGH TOWN

Venue	P	W	D	L	F	A
Home	4	4	0	0	16	0
Away	4	2	1	1	5	4
Totals	8	6	1	1	21	4

LUTON TOWN

Venue	P	W	D	L	F	A
Home	26	14	8	4	55	26
Away	26	11	8	7	34	32
Totals	52	25	16	11	89	58

MANCHESTER CITY (ARDWICK)

Venue	P	W	D	L	F	A
Home	65	39	12	14	138	78
Away	65	9	11	43	55	128
Totals	130	48	23	57	193	206

MANCHESTER UNITED (NEWTON HEATH)

Venue	P	W	D	L	F	A
Home	46	15	18	13	66	70
Away	46	9	8	29	34	72
Totals	92	24	26	42	100	142

MANSFIELD TOWN

Venue	P	W	D	L	F	A
Home	2	1	1	0	4	1
Away	2	1	0	1	4	6
Totals	4	2	1	1	8	7

MIDDLESBROUGH

Venue	P	W	D	L	F	A
Home	46	25	13	8	85	49
Away	46	10	15	21	51	70
Totals	92	35	28	29	136	119

MIDDLESBROUGH IRONOPOLIS

Venue	P	W	D	L	F	A
Home	1	1	0	0	2	1
Away	1	0	0	1	0	3
Totals	2	1	0	1	2	4

MILLWALL

Venue	P	W	D	L	F	A
Home	14	9	3	2	25	9
Away	14	3	4	7	15	24
Totals	28	12	7	9	40	33

NEW BRIGHTON TOWER

Venue	P	W	D	L	F	A
Home	3	3	0	0	9	2
Away	3	0	2	1	2	6
Totals	6	3	2	1	11	8

NEWCASTLE UNITED

Venue	P	W	D	L	F	A
Home	46	21	11	14	77	59
Away	46	8	14	24	47	86
Totals	92	29	25	38	124	145

NEWPORT COUNTY

Venue	P	W	D	L	F	A
Home	1	0	1	0	1	1
Away	1	1	0	0	3	0
Totals	2	1	1	0	4	1

NORTHAMPTON TOWN

Venue	P	W	D	L	F	A
Home	2	2	0	0	7	0
Away	2	0	1	1	3	4
Totals	4	2	1	1	10	4

NORTHWICH VICTORIA

Venue	P	W	D	L	F	A
Home	2	2	0	0	14	2
Away	2	2	0	0	13	0
Totals	4	4	0	0	27	2

NORWICH CITY

Venue	P	W	D	L	F	A
Home	26	14	6	6	46	27
Away	26	4	10	12	27	48
Totals	52	18	16	18	63	75

NOTTINGHAM FOREST

Venue	P	W	D	L	F	A
Home	43	17	10	16	72	58
Away	43	12	14	17	48	54
Totals	46	29	24	33	120	112

NOTTS COUNTY

Venue	P	W	D	L	F	A
Home	26	15	6	5	44	25
Away	26	5	8	13	26	48
Totals	52	20	14	18	70	73

OLDHAM ATHLETIC

Venue	P	W	D	L	F	A
Home	12	4	4	4	15	13
Away	12	4	3	5	12	21
Totals	24	8	7	9	27	34

OXFORD UNITED

Venue	P	W	D	L	F	A
Home	13	4	6	3	13	8
Away	13	6	3	4	17	11
Totals	26	10	9	7	30	19

PETERBOROUGH UNITED

Venue	P	W	D	L	F	A
Home	4	2	2	0	7	1
Away	4	1	1	2	5	6
Totals	8	3	3	2	12	7

PLYMOUTH ARGYLE

Venue	P	W	D	L	F	A
Home	14	8	4	2	31	12
Away	14	7	4	3	19	15
Totals	28	15	8	5	50	27

PORT VALE (BURSLEM)

Venue	P	W	D	L	F	A
Home	14	11	1	2	45	14
Away	14	6	2	6	18	23
Totals	28	17	3	8	63	37

PORTSMOUTH

Venue	P	W	D	L	F	A
Home	42	25	10	7	81	42
Away	42	12	14	16	58	63
Totals	84	37	24	23	139	105

PRESTON NORTH END

Venue	P	W	D	L	F	A
Home	40	24	8	8	77	41
Away	40	5	11	24	34	77
Totals	80	29	19	32	111	118

QUEEN'S PARK RANGERS

Venue	P	W	D	L	F	A
Home	22	16	5	1	36	11
Away	22	5	8	9	24	30
Totals	44	21	13	10	60	41

READING

Venue	P	W	D	L	F	A
Home	10	3	5	2	16	12
Away	10	3	5	2	12	11
Totals	20	6	10	4	28	23

ROTHERHAM UNITED (TOWN, COUNTY)

Venue	P	W	D	L	F	A
Home	14	10	2	2	41	20
Away	14	5	6	3	24	22
Totals	28	15	8	5	65	42

SHEFFIELD UNITED

Venue	P	W	D	L	F	A
Home	49	28	9	12	86	45
Away	49	11	8	30	64	109
Totals	98	39	17	42	150	154

SHEFFIELD WEDNESDAY

Venue	P	W	D	L	F	A
Home	39	20	14	5	61	28
Away	39	10	7	22	54	96
Totals	78	30	21	27	115	124

SHREWSBURY TOWN

Venue	P	W	D	L	F	A
Home	9	3	2	4	5	6
Away	9	1	3	5	4	10
Totals	18	4	5	9	9	16

SOUTH SHIELDS (GATESHEAD)

Venue	P	W	D	L	F	A
Home	2	1	1	0	5	1
Away	2	0	0	2	0	4
Totals	4	1	1	2	5	5

SOUTHAMPTON

Venue	P	W	D	L	F	A
Home	19	9	6	4	26	20
Away	19	5	3	11	15	25
Totals	38	14	9	15	41	45

SOUTHEND UNITED

Venue	P	W	D	L	F	A
Home	6	4	1	1	11	6
Away	6	1	1	4	8	13
Totals	12	5	2	5	19	19

STOCKPORT COUNTY

Venue	P	W	D	L	F	A
Home	18	14	2	2	42	13
Away	18	5	3	10	18	26
Totals	36	19	5	12	60	39

STOKE CITY

Venue	P	W	D	L	F	A
Home	42	21	10	11	55	42
Away	42	7	9	26	42	71
Totals	84	28	19	37	97	113

SUNDERLAND

Venue	P	W	D	L	F	A
Home	52	25	13	14	74	58
Away	52	10	7	35	53	107
Totals	104	35	20	49	127	165

SWANSEA CITY (TOWN)

Venue	P	W	D	L	F	A
Home	14	8	4	2	28	10
Away	14	7	3	4	17	13
Totals	28	15	7	6	45	23

SWINDON TOWN

Venue	P	W	D	L	F	A
Home	10	5	3	2	20	13
Away	10	4	3	3	14	13
Totals	20	9	6	5	34	26

TORQUAY UNITED

Venue	P	W	D	L	F	A
Home	1	1	0	0	3	0
Away	1	1	0	0	2	1
Totals	2	2	0	0	5	1

TOTTENHAM HOTSPUR

Venue	P	W	D	L	F	A
Home	40	18	9	13	54	43
Away	40	8	6	26	36	86
Totals	80	26	15	39	90	129

TRANMERE ROVERS

Venue	P	W	D	L	F	A
Home	10	5	4	1	11	7
Away	10	3	1	6	10	17
Totals	20	8	5	7	21	24

WALSALL (TOWN SWIFTS)

Venue	P	W	D	L	F	A
Home	11	10	1	0	38	7
Away	11	6	1	4	19	15
Totals	22	16	2	4	57	22

WATFORD

Venue	P	W	D	L	F	A
Home	14	8	3	3	26	15
Away	14	3	2	9	13	24
Total	28	11	5	12	39	39

WEST BROMWICH ALBION

Venue	P	W	D	L	F	A
Home	57	20	15	22	70	73
Away	57	14	18	25	59	78
Totals	114	34	33	47	129	151

WEST HAM UNITED

Venue	P	W	D	L	F	A
Home	41	23	8	10	72	41
Away	41	14	10	17	53	77
Totals	82	37	18	27	125	118

WIGAN ATHLETIC

Venue	P	W	D	L	F	A
Home	6	3	3	0	9	5
Away	6	1	2	3	5	10
Totals	12	4	5	3	14	15

WIMBLEDON

Venue	P	W	D	L	F	A
Home	3	1	0	2	4	7
Away	3	1	0	2	4	7
Totals	6	2	0	4	8	14

WOLVERHAMPTON WANDERERS

Venue	P	W	D	L	F	A
Home	59	22	19	18	84	80
Away	59	14	8	37	62	110
Totals	118	36	27	55	146	190

WREXHAM

Venue	P	W	D	L	F	A
Home	2	2	0	0	7	2
Away	2	0	1	1	1	2
Totals	4	2	1	1	8	4

WYCOMBE WANDERERS

Venue	P	W	D	L	F	A
Home	1	0	0	1	0	1
Away	1	1	0	0	3	0
Totals	2	1	0	1	3	1

YORK CITY

Venue	P	W	D	L	F	A
Home	1	1	0	0	4	2
Away	1	0	0	1	0	2
Totals	2	1	0	1	4	4

All details correct up to May 2010

Blues in the FA Cup (1881-82 to 1888-89)

Here are details of Blues' FA Cup results prior to 1892 when they joined the Football League.

1881–82
Round 1
17 Oct v Derby Town (h) 4–1
Slater (2), Hards, A. James
1,000
Bodenham; Gessey, Summers; T. James,
Teychenne, F. James; Hards, Rotherham,
A. James, Whitehead, Slater

Round 2
3 Dec v Wednesbury Old Athletic (a) 0–6
3,000
Bodenham; Gessey, Summers; T. James,
Tatton, F. James; Hards, Rotherham,
Teychenne, Whitehead, Slater

1882–83
PL Bye

Round 1
11 Nov v Stafford Road Works (h) 3–3
Slater (2), T. James
2,000
Vale; Elliman, T. James; Morgan, F. James,
Jones; Hards, Stanley, Green, Kingston,
Slater

Round 2 replay
18 Nov v Stafford Road Works (a) 2–6
Stanley, Hards
1,000
Vale; Bailey, Taylor; T. James, Morgan,
Rotherham; Hards, A. Stanley, Jones, Green,
Slater

1883–84
Round 1
20 Oct v Birmingham Excelsior (h) 1–1
A. James
1,500
Hedges; Elliman, Taylor; F. James, Gessey,
T. James; A. James, A. Stanley, Jones, Clayon,
Slater

Round 1 replay
11 Nov v Birmingham Excelsior (n*) 2–3
A. James, Stanley
2,000
Hedges; Elliman, Taylor; F. James, Gessey,
T. James; A. James, A. Stanley, Jones,
Clayton, Hards
* Played at the Aston Lower Grounds

1884–85
Round 1
8 Nov v Birmingham Excelsior (a) 0–2
2,000
Clarke; Elliman, Hare; T. James, Felton,
F. James; A. James, Morris, Simms, A. Stanley,
Willetts

1885–86
Round 1
31 Oct v Burton Wanderers (h) 9–2
*Stanley (4), Davenport (2), Evetts, A. James,
Morris*
1,000
Hedges; Jones, Evetts; F. James, Simms,
Felton; A. James, Davenport, A. Stanley,
Figures, Morris

Round 2
4 Nov v Darwen (h) 3–1
Felton, Morris, Stanley
2,000
Hedges; Hare, Evetts; F. James, Simms,
Felton; Morris, Davenport, A. Stanley, Hill,
Figures

Round 3
12 Dec v Derby County (h) 4–2
3,000
Hedges; Hare, Evetts; F. James, Simms,
Felton; Morris, Davenport, A. Stanley, Hill,
Figures

Round 4 Bye

Round 5
16 Jan v Davenham (h) 2–1
Figures, Davenport
6,000
Hedges; Hare, Evetts; F. James, Simms,
Felton; Morris, Davenport, A. Stanley, Hill,
Figures

Round 6
13 Feb v Redcar (h) 2–0
Davenport (2)
6,000
Hedges; Hare, Evetts; F. James, Simms,
Felton; Morris, Davenport, A. Stanley, Hill,
Figures

Semi-final
6 Mar v West Bromwich Albion (n*) 0–4
4,100
Hedges; Hare, Evetts; F. James, Simms, Felton;
Morris, Davenport, A. Stanley, Hill, Figures
* Played at the Aston Lower Grounds

1886–87
Round 1
30 Oct v Mitchell's St George (a) 1–3
Price
5,000
Charsley; Hare, Lovesey; Price, Simms,
Barlow; Morris, W. Stanley, A. Stanley, Hill,
Figures

1887–88
Round 1
15 Oct v Aston Unity (h) 6–1
Smith (2), *Figures, W. Dixon (2), Stanley*
2,000
Charsley; Evetts, Barlow; G. Dixon, Hare,
Morris; W. Dixon, Adams, Smith, A. Stanley,
Figures

Round 2
5 Nov v Aston Villa (a) 0–4
12,000
Charsley; Evetts, Barlow; Farley, Simms,
Morris; W. Dixon, Adams, Smith, A. Stanley,
Figures

1888–89
Pr 1 Bye

Pr 2
27 Oct v Burslem Port Vale (h) 3–2
Watson (2), Hill
2,000
Charsley; A. Morris, Speller; H. Morris,
Jenkyns, Simms; G. Short, A. Stanley,
W. Devey, Hill, Watson

Pr 3
17 Nov v Leek (h) 4–0
Hill, Jenkyns, Devey, Stanley
3,000
Charsley; A. Morris, Speller; H. Morris,
Jenkyns, Simms; G. Short, A. Stanley,
W. Devey, Hill, Watson

Pr 4
8 Dec v Burton Wanderers (h) 9–0
E. Devey (4), W. Devey (4), Short
2,000
Charsley; A. Morris, Speller; H. Morris,
Jenkyns, Simms; G. Short, A. Stanley,
W. Devey, Hill, E. Devey

Round 1
2 Feb v West Bromwich Albion (h) 2–3
Hill (2)
3,034
Charsley; A. Morris, Speller; H. Morris,
Jenkyns, E. Devey; G. Short, A. Stanley,
W. Devey, Watson, Hill

FACT FILE
● For reaching the 1886 semi-final each
Blues player received 2s 6d…1s for a taxi
to the ground and 1s 6d for a meal!

● Blues qualified for the semi-final before
their arch-rivals Aston Villa, who had to
wait until March before they took on
and beat Glasgow Rangers.

● The unregistered player who appeared
against Wednesbury Old Athletic in
the second round of the 1890–91
competition was Charlie Short (ex-
Aston Gas) who actually scored one of
Blues' goals!

BLUES' £1 MILLION PLAYERS

Here are details of certain players bought and sold by Blues for £1 million or more:

Players Signed

Fee	Player	From	When
£6 million	Nikola Zigic	Valencia	May 2010
£5.9 million	Ben Foster	Manchester United	July 2010
£5.75 million	James McFadden	Everton	January 2008
£5.5 million	David Dunn	Blackburn Rovers	July 2003
£5 million	Roger Johnson	Cardiff City	June 2009
£4.25 million	Clinton Morrison	Crystal Palace	August 2002
£4 million	Fabrice Muamba	Arsenal	May 2007
£3.5 million	Emile Heskey	Liverpool	July 2004
£3.5 million	Craig Gardner	Aston Villa	January 2010
£3 million	Mikael Forssell	Chelsea	July 2005
£3 million	Cameron Jerome	Cardiff City	June 2006
£3 million	Gary McSheffrey	Coventry City	August 2006
£3 million	Olivier Kapo	Juventus	June 2007
£3 million	Michel	Sporting Gijon	January 2010
£2.7 million	Garry O'Connor	Lokomotiv Moscow	July 2007
£2.5 million	Robbie Savage	Leicester City	May 2002
£2.5 million	Luciano Figueroa	Rosario Central	August 2003
£2.5 million	Rowan Vine	Luton Town	January 2007
£2.25 million	Geoff Horsfield	Fulham	July 2000
£2.2 million	Jesper Gronkjaer	Chelsea	July 2004
£2 million	Radhi Jaidi	Bolton Wanderers	August 2006
£2 million	Liam Ridgewell	Aston Villa	August 2007
£2 million	Franck Queudrue	Fulham	August 2007
£1.85 million	Jon McCarthy	Port Vale	September 1997
£1.6 million	Stan Lazaridis	West Ham United	July 1999
£1.6 million	Peter Ndlovu	Coventry City	July 1997
£1.5 million	Paul Furlong	Chelsea	July 1996
£1.5 million	Aliou Cissé	Montpellier	July 2002
£1.5 million	Maik Taylor	Fulham	March 2004
£1.5 million	David Murphy	Hibernian	January 2008
£1.25 million	Martin Taylor	Blackburn Rovers	February 2004
£1.25 million	Robbie Blake	Burnley	January 2005

Fee	Player	From	When
£1.2 million	David Holdsworth	Sheffield United	March 1999
£1.1 million	Marcus Bent	Charlton Athletic	July 2008
£1 million	Gary Rowett	Derby County	August 1998
£1 million	Dele Adebola	Crewe Alexandra	February 1998
£1 million	Curtis Woodhouse	Sheffield United	January 2001
£1 million	Tom Williams	Peterborough United	March 2002
£1 million	Matthew Upson	Arsenal	January 2003
£1 million	Jamie Clapham	Ipswich Town	January 2003
£1 million	Medhi Nafti	Racing Santander	January 2005
£1 million	Sebastian Larsson	Arsenal	January 2007

* Initial fee was £5.5 million, which would rise to £7.75 millon after a set number of appearances.
NB: Christian Benitez left Birmingham City in May 2010 after his season loan spell had expired.
It was anticipated that the Ecuadorian international would be Blues' record signing, but the deal
never materialised and he returned to his parent club, Santos Laguna, agreeing a new three-year
contract.

Players Sold

Fee	Player	To	When
£6.7 million	Jermaine Pennant	Liverpool	July 2006
£6 million	Matthew Upson	West Ham United	January 2007
£5.5 million	Emile Heskey	Wigan Athletic	July 2006
£5.5 million	Fabrice Muamba	Bolton Wanderers	June 2008
£3.1 million	Robbie Savage	Blackburn Rovers	January 2005
£3 million	Gary Rowett	Leicester City	June 2000
£2.5 million	Gary Breen	Coventry City	January 1997
£2.5 million	Olivier Kapo	Wigan Athletic	July 2008
£2.2 million	David Dunn	Blackburn Rovers	January 2007
£2.1 million	'DJ' Campbell	Leicester City	July 2007
£2 million	Clinton Morrison	Crystal Palace	August 2005
£1.8 million	Jose Dominguez	Sporting Lisbon	August 1995
£1.5 million	Liam Daish	Coventry City	February 1996
£1.5 million	Darren Carter	West Bromwich Albion	July 2005
£1.2 million	Steve Claridge	Leicester City	March 1996
£1.18 million	Trevor Francis	Nottingham Forest	February 1997
£1 million	Geoff Horsfield	Wigan Athletic	September 2003
£1 million	Rowan Vine	Queen's Park Rangers	January 2008

ABANDONED AND POSTPONED MATCHES

Over the years most clubs face the prospect of having a game abandoned and quite often have matches postponed well before the scheduled kick-off time.

Here are details of Blues' fixtures which were called off by the referee while already in progress:

Football League

10 January 1903 v Manchester City (a) abandoned after 83 mins, fog, Blues 1–0 up, lost replay 4–0.
22 February 1908 v Nottingham Forest (h) abandoned 36 mins, high winds, 1–1, Blues won replay 1–0.
16 December 1933 v Sheffield Wednesday (h) abandoned 70 mins, fog, Blues 2–1 up, won replay 3–0.
22 February 1936 v Sheffield Wednesday (h) abandoned 36 mins, snow, Blues 1–0 up, won replay 4–1.
15 February 1958 v Manchester City (a) abandoned 40 mins, fog, 1–1, replay 1–1.
2 January 2002 v Crewe Alexandra (h) abandoned 58 mins, waterlogged pitch, 0–0, Blues won replay 3–1.

FA Cup

10 January 1959 v Middlesbrough (a) abandoned 60 mins, snow, 1–1, Blues won replay 1–0.
25 February 1963 v Bury (h), abandoned at half-time, dangerous pitch with Blues 1–0 up, replay 3–3.

Texaco Cup

28 November 1973 v Newcastle United (a) abandoned 100 mins, bad light, 1–1, lost replay 3–1.

Lord Mayor of Birmingham Charity Cup Final

3 May 1905 v Aston Villa (a) abandoned 50 mins, bad weather, Villa 1–0 up, no replay.

Friendlies

10 Sepember 1881 v Darlaston All Saints (h) abandond 60 mins, 'no contest', Blues 16–0 up.
26 August 1882 v Walsall Town (h) abandoned, 70 mins, heat exhaustion, Blues 4–3 up.
26 January 1884 v Wolves (h) abandoned 75 mins, bad light, Wolves 1–0 up.
23 January 1898 v Aston Villa (a) abandoned, 70 mins, bad weather, Villa 4–0 up.
9 March 1899 v Leek (a) abandoned 76 mins, poor weather, Blues 2–1 up.
6 March 1909 v Aston Villa (a) abandoned 67 mins, heavy rain, Villa 2–1 up.
8 August 1981 v Crystal Palace (a) abandoned 70 mins, floodlight failure, Palace 1–0 up
29 December 1981 v Weymouth (a) abandoned after 83 mins, waterlogged pitch, Blues 3–1 up.
18 August 1984 v NAC Breda (a) abandoned 80 mins, poor light, 1–1 at time.

Postponed Matches

The Birmingham City v Bury third-round FA Cup tie, scheduled to take place on Saturday 5 January 1963, was postponed no fewer than 14 times before it finally got underway seven weeks later on 25 February. Then the tie was abandoned at half-time because of a frozen pitch, and in the end it was completed on 7 March 1963 when Bury won a replay 2–0 at Gigg Lane.

Appearance Records

Here are the details of the top appearance-makers for Blues in the named competitions. Where applicable (since 1965) all substitute appearances have been included in the totals:

Football League

(qualification 250)

491	Frank Womack
485	Gil Merrick
414	Joe Bradford
409	Johnny Crosbie
401	Ken Green
382	Dan Tremelling
365	Trevor Smith
358	Harry Hibbs
351	Malcolm Beard
339	Malcolm Page
332	Ray Martin
331	Percy Barton
329	Frank Wigmore
323	George Liddell
306	Garry Pendrey
298	George Briggs
286	Joe Gallagher
283	Nat Robinson
282	Fred Harris
280	Trevor Francis
268	Cyril Trigg
261	Jimmy Cringan
260	Ned Barkas
256	Len Boyd

FA Cup

(qualification 20)

56	Gil Merrick
35	Ken Green
35	Trevor Smith
33	Jeff Hall
31	Joe Bradford
30	Fred Harris
30	Harry Hibbs
29	Malcolm Page
28	Ned Barkas
28	Percy Barton
27	Gordon Astall
27	Harry Morris
27	Billy Walton
26	George Briggs

26	Walter Wigmore
25	Malcolm Beard
25	Len Boyd
24	Jimmy Cringan
24	Peter Murphy
24	Frank Womack
23	Johnny Crosbie
23	George Morrall
23	Nat Robinson
23	Cyril Trigg
23	Roy Warhurst
22	Chris Charsley
22	Dennis Jennings
22	George Liddell
22	Eddie Stanley
21	Joe Gallagher
21	Caesar Jenkyns
20	Trevor Francis
20	Jim Herriot
20	Noel Kinsey

Football League Cup

(qualification 10)

24	Malcolm Beard
23	Garry Pendrey
19	Trevor Francis
19	Ray Martin
17	Joe Gallagher
17	Roger Hynd
17	Bob Latchford
15	Colin Green
14	Kevin Dillon
14	Malcolm Page
12	Trevor Smith
11	Bertie Auld

Inter-Cities Fairs Cup

(qualification 10)

18	Trevor Smith
17	Brian Farmer
17	Johnny Watts
15	George Allen
14	Dick Neal

12	Johnny Schofield
11	Johnny Gordon
11	Mike Hellawell
11	Bryan Orritt
10	Gil Merrick

Football Alliance

(qualification 20)

64	Fred Speller
61	Ted Devey
56	Caesar Jenkyns
51	Jack Hallam
46	Fred Wheldon
42	Jack Bayley
40	Will Devey
40	Harry Morris
37	Chris Charsley
32	Billy Walton
31	Tommy Hands
25	Fred Heath
22	Billy Ollis
21	Walter Gittins
21	Billy Pratt

Other Competitions

(qualification 10)

19	Jim Hagan
14	Bob Hatton
14	Garry Pendrey
12	Malcolm Page
11	Alan Campbell
11	Tony Want
10	Gordon Taylor

World War One

(qualification 50)

92	Frank Womack
87	Jack Whitehouse
84	Billy Ball
68	Albert Gardner
50	Ernie Edwards

World War Two
(qualification 90)

176	Arthur Turner
166	Don Dearson
164	Dennis Jennings
164	Gil Merrick
111	Ray Shaw
108	Jock Mulraney
95	Cyril Trigg
92	Fred Harris

All Major Competitions
(top 15)

551	Gil Merrick
515	Frank Womack
445	Joe Bradford
443	Ken Green
432	Johnny Crosbie
430	Trevor Smith
405	Malcolm Beard
395	Dan Tremelling
394	Malcolm Page
388	Harry Hibbs
374	Ray Martin
360	Garry Pendrey
355	Frank Wigmore
349	Percy Barton
345	George Liddell

All Senior Games (including wartime)
(top 15)

715	Gil Merrick
607	Frank Womack
445	Joe Bradford
443	Ken Green
432	Johnny Crosbie
430	Trevor Smith
405	Malcolm Beard
404	Fred Harris
395	Dan Tremelling
394	Malcolm Page
388	Harry Hibbs
386	Cyril Trigg
376	Dennis Jennings
374	Ray Martin
360	Garry Pendrey

Fact File

- Colin Todd made 649 League appearances during his career, Frank Worthington made 757, Howard Kendall 613 and Jim Montgomery 608.
- Goalkeeper 'Nat' Robinson holds the record for most ever-presents – four seasons: 1899–1900, 1901–02, 1904–05 and 1905–06.
- Gil Merrick made 145 consecutive appearances for Blues between April 1949 and March 1952 (136 in the Football League).

Blues in Europe

Inter-Cities Fairs Cup 1956–61

Blues were one of the first British clubs to enter a major European Competition when they participated in the Inter-Cities Fairs Cup in 1956.

This is Blues' full record in this now defunct competition:

1956–58 tournament

Played in groups, the top club in each one qualified for the semi-finals

Group B
16 May 1956 v Inter Milan (a) 0–0
Merrick, Badham, Green, Watts, Newman, Warmington, Cox, Kinsey, Brown, Murphy, Govan.
Attendance: 8,000

21 May 1956 v Zagreb Select (a) 1–0
Brown
Merrick, Badham, Allen, Boyd, Newman, Warhurst, Lane (Cox), Finney, Brown, Kinsey, Murphy.
Attendance: 12,000

3 Dec 1956 v Zagreb Select (h) 3–0
Orritt, Brown, Murphy
Merrick, Farmer, Allen, Watts, Green, Warhurst, Cox, Orritt, Brown, Murphy, Govan.
Attendance: 40,144

17 Apr 1957 v Inter Milan (h) 2–1
Govan 2
Merrick, Hall, Green, Watts, Smith, Warhurst, Astall, Kinsey, Brown, Murphy, Govan.
Attendance: 34,461

Final Group B table

	P	W	D	L	F	A	Pts
Birmingham	4	3	1	0	6	1	7
Inter Milan	4	2	1	1	6	2	5
Zagreb Select	4	0	0	4	0	9	0

Semi-final first leg
23 Oct 1957 v Barcelona (h) 4–3
Murphy 2, Brown, Orritt
Merrick, Farmer, Allen, Larkin, Smith, Watts, Astall, Orritt, Brown, Neal, Murphy.
Attendance: 30,791

Semi-final second leg
13 Nov 1957 v Barcelona (a) 0–1 (agg. 4–4)
Merrick, Hall, Allen, Larkin, Smith, Neal, Astall, Kinsey, Brown, Murphy, Govan.
Attendance: 60,000

Semi-final replay
26 Nov 1957 v Barcelona (on Basle, Switzerland) 1–2
Murphy
Merrick, Hall, Farmer, Watts, Smith, Neal, Astall, Orritt, Brown, Murphy, Govan.
Attendance: 20,000

1958–60 tournament

First round, first leg
14 Oct 1958 v Cologne Select (a) 2–2
Neal, Hooper
Merrick, Hall, Green, Watts, Sissons, Neal, Hooper, Gordon, Brown, Orritt, Murphy.
Attendance: 12,000

First round, second leg
11 Nov 1958 v Cologne Select (h) 2–0 (agg 4–2)
Larkin, Taylor
Merrick, Hall, Allen, Watts, Smith, Neal, Hooper, Gordon, Brown, Larkin, Taylor.
Attendance: 20,266

Second round, first leg
6 May 1959 v Dinamo Zagreb (h) 1–0
Larkin
Schofield, Farmer, Allen, Watts, Sissons, Neal, Hooper, Gordon, Stubbs, Larkin, Taylor.
Attendance: 21,411

Second round, second leg
24 May 1959 v Dinamo Zagreb (a) 3–3 (agg 4–3)
Larkin 2, Hooper
Schofield, Farmer, Allen, Watts, Smith, Neal, Astall, Gordon, Stubbs, Larkin, Hooper.
Attendance: 50,000

Semi-final first leg
7 Oct 1959 v Union St Gilloise (a) 4–2
Hooper, Gordon, Barrett, Orritt
Merrick, Sissons, Farmer, Watts, Smith, Neal, Hooper, Gordon, Orritt, Barrett, Taylor.
Attendance: 20,000

Semi-final second leg
11 Nov 1959 v Union St Gilloise (h) 4–2 (agg 8–4)
Gordon 2, Larkin, Hooper (pen)
Schofield, Farmer, Allen, Watts, Smith, Larkin, Hellawell, Barrett, Gordon, Hooper, Taylor.
Attendance: 14,152

Final first leg
29 Mar 1960 v Barcelona (h) 0–0
Schofield, Farmer, Allen, Watts, Smith, Neal, Astall, Gordon, Weston, Orritt, Hooper.
Attendance: 40,524

Final second leg
4 May 1960 v Barcelona (a) 1–4 (agg 1–4)
Hooper
Schofield, Farmer, Allen, Watts, Smith, Neal, Astall, Gordon, Weston, Murphy, Hooper.
Attendance: 75,000

1960–61 tournament
First round, first leg
19 Oct 1960 v Ujpesti Dozsa (h) 3–2
Gordon 2, Astall
Schofield, Farmer, Allen, Watts, Sissons, Neal, Hellawell, Rudd, Gordon, Singer, Astall.
Attendance: 23,381

First round, second leg
26 Oct 1960 v Ujpesti Dozsa (a) 2–1 (agg 5–3)
Rudd, Singer
Schofield, Farmer, Allen, Watts, Smith, Neal, Hellawell, Barlow, Gordon, Singer, Rudd.
Attendance: 25,000

Second round, first leg
23 Nov 1960 v Boldklub Copenhagen (a) 4–4
Gordon 2, Singer 2
Schofield, Farmer, Allen, Watts, Smith, Neal, Hellawell, Gordon, Singer, Bloomfield, Taylor.
Attendance: 2,500

Second round, second leg
7 Dec 1960 v Boldklub Copenhagen (h) 5–0 (agg 9–4)
Stubbs 2, Harris, Bloomfield, Hellawell
Withers, Farmer, Allen, Watts, Sissons, Neal, Hellwell, Stubbs, Harris, Bloomfield, Taylor.
Attendance: 22,486

Semi-final first leg
19 April 1961 v Inter Milan (a) 2–1
Harris, Balleri (og)
Withers, Farmer, Allen, Hennessey, Smith, Neal, Hellawell, Stubbs, Harris, Bloomfield, Orritt.
Attendance: 20,000

Semi-final second leg
3 May 1961 v Inter Milan (h) 2–1 (agg 4–2)
Harris 2
Schofield, Farmer, Allen, Hennessey, Smith, Neal, Hellawell, Orritt, Harris, Bloomfield, Auld.
Attendance: 29,530

Final first leg
27 Sep 1961 v AS Roma (h) 2–2
Hellawell, Orritt
Schofield, Farmer, Sissons, Hennessey, Foster, Beard, Hellawell, Bloomfield, Harris, Orritt, Auld.
Attendance: 21,005

Final second leg
11 Oct 1961 v AS Roma (a) 0–2 (agg 2–4)
Schofield, Farmer, Sissons, Hennessey, Smith,
Beard, Hellawell, Bloomfield, Harris, Singer,
Orritt.
Attendance: 50,000

1961–62 tournament
First round
Birmingham City received a bye.

Second round, first leg
15 Nov 1961 v RCD Espanyol (a) 2–5
Bloomfield, Harris (pen)
Schofield, Lynn, Sissons, Hennessey, Smith,
Beard, Hellawell, Bloomfield, Harris, Orritt,
Auld.
Attendance: 60,000

Second round, second leg
**7 Dec 1961 v RCD Espanyol (h) 1–0 (agg
3–5)**
Auld
Schofield, Lynn, Sissons, Hennessey, Smith,
Beard, Hellawell, Orritt, Harris, Leek, Auld.
Attendance: 16,874

**Blues' complete record in the Inter Cities
Fairs Cup: 1956–62**

Venue	P	W	D	L	F	A
Home	12	10	2	0	29	11
Away	12	4	4	4	21	25
Neutral	1	0	0	1	1	2
Totals	25	14	6	5	51	38

Top scorers: Johnny Gordon 7, Jimmy Harris
5, Harry Hooper 5, Bunny Larkin 4, Bryan
Orritt 4.
Most appearances: Trevor Smith 18, Brian
Farmer 17, Johnny Watts 17.
Biggest crowd: 75,000 v Barcelona, Nou
Camp, May 1960.
Lowest crowd: 2,500 v Boldklub Copenhagen,
November 1960.

GOALSCORERS

Top 10 all-time Blues scorers (major competitions)

267	Joe Bradford
133	Trevor Francis
127	Peter Murphy
113	Fred Wheldon
107	George Briggs
102	Billy Jones
92	Geoff Vowden
90	Eddie Brown
86	Bob McRoberts
84	Bob Latchford

Top 10 League scorers

249	Joe Bradford
118	Trevor Francis
107	Peter Murphy
99	Billy Jones
98	George Briggs
74	Eddie Brown
71	Johnny Crosbie
70	Bob McRoberts
68	Bob Latchford
67	Cyril Trigg

Top 10 FA Cup scorers

17	Joe Bradford
16	Will Devey
14	Peter Murphy
13	Eddie Brown
12	Bob McRoberts
12	Eddie Stanley
12	Fred Wheldon
11	Billy Walton
9	Ernie Curtis
8	George Briggs

Top five League Cup scorers

8	Ken Leek
8	Geoff Vowden
6	Mick Harford
6	Bob Latchford
5	Bob Hatton

Top five European scorers

7	Johnny Gordon
5	Jimmy Harris
5	Harry Hooper
4	Bunny Larkin
4	Bryan Orritt

Top five wartime scorers (1915–19)

48	Jack Whitehouse
26	Joe Godfrey
17	Billy Walker
12	Tom Butler
12	Stan Stevens

Top 10 wartime scorers (1939–46*)

88	Cyril Trigg
40	Charlie Wilson Jones
34	Jock Mularaney
32	Harold Bodle
23	Don Dearson
17	George Edwards
14	Dave Massart
11	Bob Bright
9	Neil Dougall
8	Jack Acquaroff

* Not including FA Cup in 1945–46

Top five Football Alliance scorers (1889–92)

33	Will Devey
31	Fred Wheldon
21	Jack Hallam

FACT FILE

- Walter Abbott holds the club record for most goals in a season: 42 in 1898–99 (34 in the League, eight in the FA Cup).
- Joe Bradford scored in every round of the FA Cup in 1930–31.
- Trevor Francis scored in eight consecutive League games (13 goals in total) between 6 February and 27 March 1971.

BLUES IN OTHER COMPETITIONS

Anglo-Italian Cup
1971–72
Group A
1 Jun v Lanerossi Vicenza (a) 0–0
Cooper, Page, Want, Smith, Hynd, Harland, Campbell, Hope, R. Latchford, Hatton, Taylor.
Attendance: 3,000

4 Jun v Sampdoria (a) 1–2
Campbell (pen)
Cooper, Page, Want, Smith, Hynd, Harland, Campbell, Hope (Pendrey), R. Latchford, Hatton, Taylor (Summerill).
Attendance: 15,000

7 Jun v Lanerossi Vicenza (h) 5–3
Latchford 2, Francis, Hatton, Taylor
Cooper (Kelly), Page, Want, Pendrey, Hynd, Harland, Campbell, Francis, R. Latchford, Hatton, Taylor.
Attendance: 23,642

10 Jun v Sampdoria (h) 2–0
Latchford, Hatton
Kelly, Page, Want (Whitehead), Pendrey, Hynd, Harland, Campbell, Francis, R. Latchford, Hatton, Taylor.
Attendance: 19,510
* *Blues finished fourth in the English group and failed to qualify for the Final.*

1992–93
Preliminary Rounds
15 Sep v Sunderland (a) 1–0
Sale
Gosney, Clarkson, Frain, Matthewson, Hicks, Rogers, Donowa, Tait, Sale, Gleghorn, Rowbotham.
Attendance: 5,871

29 Sep v Cambridge United (h) 3–3
Gleghorn, Frain, Sale
Thomas, Clarkson, Frain, Matthewson, Hicks, Rogers, Rodgerson, Tait (Sale), Donowa, Gleghorn, Sturridge (Rowbotham).
Attendance: 3,102

Intermediate Stage, Group A
11 Nov v AS Bari (h) 1–0
Cooper
Sealey, Tait (Donowa), Frain, Matthewson, Rogers, Potter, Rodgerson, Gayle (Peschisolido), Speedie, Cooper, Sturridge.
Attendance: 4,970

2 Dec v AC Cesena (a) 2–1
Frain (pen), Sturridge
Thomas, Clarkson, Frain, Tait, Rogers, Potter, Rodgerson, Gayle (Peschisolido), Speedie, Cooper, Sturridge.
Attendance: 2,090

8 Dec v Ascoli Calcio (h) 1–1
Sturridge
Sealey, Clarkson, Potter, Rennie, Hicks, Matthewson, Rodgerson, Tait, Speedie, Sale (Donowa), Sturridge.
Attendance: 3,963

16 Dec v Lucchese (a) 0–3
Sealey, Clarkson, Potter, Rennie, Hicks, Matthewson, Rodgerson, Gayle, Rowbotham, Tait, Peschisolido.
Attendance: 139

1993–94
Preliminary Rounds
1 Sep v Stoke City (a) 0–2
Miller, Scott, Rogers, Peer, Clarkson, Mardon, Fenwick, Tait, Moulden (Robinson), Morgan (Black), Potter.
Attendance: 8,633

14 Sep v Wolverhampton Wanderers (h) 2–2
Wratten 2
Miller, Hicks, Potter, Fenwick, Whyte, Mardon, McMinn, Tait (Wratten), Black, Smith, Donowa.
Attendance: 2,710

1995–96
Group A
5 Sep v Genoa (h) 2–3
Bowen 2
Bennett; Hiley, Johnson; Castle (Doherty), Edwards, Whyte; Hunt, Bowen, Charlery (Martin), Ward, Cooper (Forsyth).
Attendance: 20,430

11 Oct v Perugia (a) 1–0
Castle
Bennett; Poole, Cooper; Castle, Edwards,
Johnson; Hunt (Martin), Claridge, Rae
(Tait), Otto (Richardson), Finnan.
Attendance: 1,200

15 Nov v Ancona (a) 2–1
Edwards, Tentoni og
Bennett; Forsyth, Johnson (Cooper); Castle
(Richardson), Edwards, Daish; Hunt,
Charlery, Rushfeldt, Otto, Tait (Finnan).
Attendance: 1,500

13 Dec v Cesena (h) 3–1
Hunt, Claridge, Donowa*
Bennett (Griemink); Poole, Frain; Forsyth,
Edwards (Rae), Richardson, Hunt, Claridge,
Francis (Charlery), Preece, Donowa.
Attendance: 7,813
* Some reference books give Tamburini own-goal.

Area Semi-final
30 Jan v West Bromwich Albion (h) 2–2
(Blues lost 4-1 on penalties)
Poole, Bull
Griemink; Poole, Finnan; Forsyth, Edwards,
Johnson; Hunt, Bowen (S. Barnes), Bull, Otto
(Claridge), Tait.
Attendance: 9,113

Anglo-Scottish Tournament
1977–78
Group A
5 Aug v Plymouth Argyle (a) 1–1
Craven (og)
Montgomery, Rathbone, Pendrey, Towers,
Page, Want, Jones, Francis, Bertschin,
Hibbitt, Connelly.
Attendance: 5,176

9 Aug v Bristol Rovers (a) 1–1
Francis
Montgomery, Page, Pendrey, Towers, Sbragia,
Want, Jones (Calderwood), Francis,
Bertschin, Hibbitt, Connelly.
Attendance: 2,317

12 Aug v Bristol City (h) 1–0
Francis
Montgomery, Rathbone, Pendrey, Page,
Sbragia, Want, Jones, Francis, Bertschin,
Hibbitt, Connelly.
Attendance: 9,512

1979–80
Group A
4 Aug v Bristol City (h) 0–4
Wealands, Calderwood (Van den Hauwe),
Page, Curbishley, Gallagher, Lees, Lynex,
Evans, Bertschin, Towers, Dillon.
Attendance: 7,631

6 Aug v Plymouth Argyle (a) 1–1
Bertschin
Freeman, Van den Hauwe, Page, Curbishley,
Gallagher, Lees, Lynex, Evans, Bertschin,
Calderwood (Dillon), Aincow.
Attendance: 3,137

8 Aug v Fulham (a) 5–0
Bertschin 2, Evans, Ainscow, Dillon
Freeman (Wealands), Calderwood, Page,
Curbishley, Gallagher, Van den Hauwe,
Aincow, Evans, Bertschin, Gemmill, Dillon.
Attendance: 3,137

Texaco Cup
1973–74
First round, first leg
19 Sep v Stoke City (a) 0–0
Cooper (Kelly), Gallagher, Want, Campbell,
Hynd, Whitehead, Hope (Emmanuel),
Pendrey, Hatton, Phillips, Bryant.
Attendance: 9,530

First round, second leg
**2 Oct v Stoke City, (h) 0–0 (agg 0–0,
Birmingham won 3–1 on penalties)**
D. Latchford (Blackmore), Osborne, Want,
Burns, Gallagher, Roberts, Calderwood,
Campbell, Francis, Hatton (Emmanuel),
Phillips.
Attendance: 13,433

Second round, first leg
22 Oct v Newcastle United (h) 1–1
Latchford
Kelly, Clarke, Want, Pendrey, Gallagher,
Roberts, Burns, Francis, R. Latchford (Hope),
Hatton, Taylor.
Attendance: 12,422

Second round, second leg
28 Nov v Newcastle United (a) 1–1 (match abandoned after 100 minutes because of bad light)
Bowker
D. Latchford, Martin, Gallagher, Want, Whitehead, Roberts, Calderwood, Jenkins, Bowker, Phillips, Taylor.
Attendance: 5,529

Replay
5 Dec v Newcastle United (a) 1–3 (agg 2–4)
Francis
D. Latchford, Gallagher, Want (Clarke), Jenkins, Hynd, Burns, Campbell, Francis, R. Latchford, Hatton, Hendrie.
Attendance: 9,762

1974–75
Group 1
3 Aug v West Bromwich Albion (a) 0–0
D. Latchford, Martin, Pendrey, Kendall, Gallagher, Roberts, Campbell, Morton, Burns, Hatton, Hendrie.
Attendance: 18,643

7 Aug v Peterborough United (a) 1–1
Taylor
D. Latchford (Sprake), Page, Pendrey, Kendall, Gallagher, Roberts, Hendrie, Morton (Sbragia), Burns, Hatton, Taylor.
Attendance: 8,915

10 Aug v Norwich City (h) 3–1
Campbell, Francis, Hatton
D. Latchford (Sprake), Martin, Pendrey, Kendall, Sbragia, Roberts, Campbell, Francis (Hendrie), Burns, Hatton, Page.
Attendance: 14,847

Second round, first leg
17 Sep v Ayr United (h) 3–0
Burns 2, Calderwood
D. Latchford, Martin (Hope), Styles, Calderwood, Gallagher, Pendrey, Campbell, Francis, Burns, Hatton, Taylor.
Attendance: 12,327

Second round, second leg
2 Oct v Ayr United (a) 0–0 (agg 3–0)
D. Latchford, Calderwood, Bryant, Kendall, Hynd, Pendrey, Hendrie, Phillips (Hope), Allen, Hatton, Taylor.
Attendance: 4,992

Semi-final first leg
23 Oct v Newcastle United (a) 1–1
Hatton
D. Latchford, Hynd, Styles, Kendall, Gallagher, Pendrey, Campbell (Emmanuel), Calderwood, Burns, Hatton, Taylor.
Attendance: 20,556

Semi-final second leg
6 Nov v Newcastle United (h) 1–4 (agg 2–5)
Burns
D. Latchford, Martin, Pendrey, Kendall, Gallagher, Page, Campbell, Phillips (Taylor), Burns, Hatton, Calderwood.
Attendance: 17,754

Full Members' Cup
1986–87
Round 1
1 Oct v Brighton & Hove Albion (a) 3–0
Clarke, Kuhl, O'Regan (og)
Hansbury, Ranson, Dicks (Williams), Hagan, Overson, Rees, Bremner, Clarke, Whitton, Mortimer (Kuhl), Cooke.
Attendance: 3,794

Round 2
4 Nov v Charlton Athletic (a) 2–3
Geddis, Shirtliff (og)
Hansbury, Jones (Rees), Dicks, Russell, Overson, Kuhl, Bremner, Clarke, Whitton, Geddis, Lynex (Hagan).
Attendance: 821

Simod Cup

1987–88

First round

25 Nov v Derby County (a) 1–3

Whitton

Godden, Ranson, Trewick, Williams, Frain, Bird, Bremner, Childs (Rees), Whitton, Kennedy (Ashley), Wigley.

Attendance: 8,277

1988–89

First round

9 Nov v Aston Villa (a) 0–6

Thomas, Frain, Roberts, Atkins, Bird, Langley, Bremner, Childs, Yates, Sturridge (Morris), Wigley.

Attendance: 8,324

Leyland DAF Trophy

1989–90

Preliminary rounds

28 Nov v Aldershot (a) 0–3

Thomas, Ashley, Frain, Atkins, Clarkson (Tait), Matthewson, Bell, Bailey, Sturridge, Gleghorn, Langley.

Attendance: 1,148

12 Dec v Hereford United (h) 1–0

Atkins

Thomas, Clarkson (Roberts), Frain, Atkins, Overson, Matthewson, Bell, Bailey, Yates (Deakin), Gleghorn, Langley.

Attendance: 3,168

1990–91

Preliminary rounds

6 Nov v Walsall (a) 1–0

Skipper (og)

Thomas, Hopkins, Downs, Frain, Overson, Matthewson, Peer, Sturridge (Bailey), Aylott (Clarkson), Gleghorn, Tait.

Attendance: 5,053

27 Nov v Lincoln City (h) 2–0

Clarke (og), Sturridge

Thomas, Clarkson, Downs, Frain, Overson, Matthewson, Peer, Bailey, Gayle, Gleghorn, Sturridge.

Attendance: 2,922

First round

18 Feb v Swansea City (h) 0–0 (Blues won 4–2 on penalties)

Thomas, Clarkson, Frain, Rodgerson, Overson, Matthewson, Peer, Dolan, Aylott (Harris), Gleghorn, Sturridge.

Attendance: 3,555

Southern Area quarter-final

26 Feb v Mansfield Town (h) 2–0

Matthewson, Gayle

Thomas, Clarkson, Frain, Rodgerson, Overson, Matthewson, Peer, Dolan (Gayle), Aylott, Gleghorn (Bailey), Sturridge.

Attendance: 5,358

Southern Area semi-final

5 Mar v Cambridge United (h) 3–1

Peer, Gleghorn, Overson

Thomas, Clarkson, Frain, Rodgerson, Overson, Matthewson, Peer, Gayle, Aylott, Gleghorn, Sturridge.

Attendance: 9,429

Southern Area Final first leg

26 Mar v Brentford (h) 2–1

Rodgerson, Gayle

Thomas, Clarkson, Frain, Yates, Overson, Matthewson, Peer, Gayle, Rodgerson (Robinson), Gleghorn, Sturridge.

Attendance: 16,219

Southern Area Final second leg

9 Apr v Brentford (a) 1–0

Sturridge

Thomas, Clarkson, Frain, Peer, Overson, Matthewson, Robinson, Yates, Gayle (Aylott), Gleghorn, Sturridge.

Attendance: 8,745

Final

26 May v Tranmere Rovers (Wembley) 3–2

Gayle 2, Sturridge

Thomas, Clarkson, Frain, Yates, Overson, Matthewson, Peer, Gayle, Robinson, Gleghorn, Sturridge (Bailey).

Attendance: 58,756

Autoglass Trophy
1991–92
Preliminary rounds
18 Dec v Stoke City (a) 1–3
Tait
Cheesewright, Clarkson, Frain, Peer, Hicks, Mardon, Rodgerson, Tait, Atkins (Okenla), Gleghorn, Cooper.
Attendance: 5,932

7 Jan v Walsall (h) 0–1
Miller, Clarkson, Frain, Cooper, Hicks, Matthewson, Rodgerson, Peer, Beckford, Gleghorn, Okenla (Hogan).
Attendance: 5,239

Auto Windscreens Shield
1994–95
First round
27 Sep v Peterborough United (a) 5–3
Bull, Dominguez, Hunt 3
Price, Scott, Frain, Ward, Barnett, Daish, Hunt, Claridge, Bull (McGavin), Poole, Dominguez (Wallace).
Attendance: 2,044

Second round
18 Oct v Walsall (h) 3–0
Shearer 2, Donowa
Bennett, Poole, Donowa, Ward, Barnett, Daish, Hunt, Claridge (McGavin), Bull, De Souza (Doherty), Shearer.
Attendance: 10,089

Third round
29 Nov v Gillingham (h) 3–0
McGavin, Poole, Tait
Bennett, Poole, Whyte, Ward (Lowe), Barnett, Daish, Donowa (Cooper), Claridge, McGavin, Dominguez, Tait.
Attendance: 17,028

Fourth round
10 Jan v Hereford United (h) 3–1
Claridge, Ward (pen), Otto
Bennett, Poole, Cooper, Ward, Barnett, Daish, Donowa, Claridge, Lowe (Dominguez), Otto, Shearer.
Attendance: 22,351

Southern Area semi-final
31 Jan v Swansea City (h) 3–2 (aet/sudden death)
Claridge, Francis, Tait
Bennett, Scott, Cooper, Ward, Barnett, Whyte, Donowa (Dominguez), Claridge, Francis, Otto, Lowe (Tait).
Attendance: 20,326

Southern Area Final first leg
28 Feb v Leyton Orient (h) 1–0
Shearer
Bennett, Poole, Cooper, Tait (Whyte), Barnett, Daish, Donowa, Saville (McGavin), Francis, Otto, Shearer.
Attendance: 24,002

Southern Area Final second leg
14 Mar v Leyton Orient (a) 3–2 (agg 4–2)
Claridge 2, Williams
Bennett, Poole, Whyte, Ward, Barnett, Daish, Esteves (Tait), Claridge, Robinson, Otto (Doherty), Williams.
Attendance: 10,830

Final
23 Apr v Carlisle United (Wembley) 1–0 (aet/sudden death)
Tait
Bennett, Poole, Cooper, Ward, Barnett, Daish, Hunt, Claridge, Francis (Donowa), Otto, Shearer (Tait).
Attendance: 76,663

Test Matches
1892–93
22 Apr v Newton Heath (Stoke) 1–1
Wheldon
Charsley, Bayley, Pumfrey, Ollis, Jenkyns, G. Short, Hallam, Walton, Mobley, Wheldon, Hands.
Attendance: 4,000

Replay
27 Apr v Newton Heath (Sheffield) 2–5
Walton, Mobley
Charsley, Bayley, Pumfrey, Ollis, Jenkyns, G. Short, Hallam, Walton, Mobley, Wheldon, Morris.
Attendance: 6,000

1893–94
26 Apr v Darwen (Stoke) 3–1
Hallam, Walton, Wheldon
Charlsey, Purves, G. Short, Ollis, Jenkyns, E. Devey, Hallam, Walton, Mobley, Wheldon, Hands.
Attendance: 3,000

1895–96
18 Apr v Liverpool (a) 0–4
Meates, Lester, Oliver, Farnall, Leake, Fraser, Mobley, Robertson, Jones, Wheldon, Hands.
Attendance: 20,000

20 Apr v Liverpool (h) 0–0
Meates, Lester, Oliver, Walton, Leake, Fraser, Hallam, Robertson, Jones, Wheldon, Hands.
Attendance: 5,000

25 Apr v Manchester City (a) 0–3
Meates, Lester, Oliver, Farnall, Leake, Fraser, Hallam, Robertson, Jones, Wheldon, Hands.
Attendance: 9,500

27 Apr v Manchester City (h) 8–0
Jones 3, Wheldon 3, Abbott, Hallam
Roach, Lester, Dunlop, Farnall, Leake, Fraser, Hallam, Robertson, Jones, Abbott, Wheldon.
Attendance: 2,000

FA Cup
1945–46
Third round, first leg
5 Jan v Portsmouth (h) 1–0
Flewin (og)
Merrick, Duckhouse, Jennings, Harris, Turner, Mitchell, Mulraney, Dougall, Jones, Bodle, Edwards.
Attendance: 33,845

Third round, second leg
9 Jan v Portsmouth (a) 0–0 (agg 1–0)
Merrick, Duckhouse, Jennings, Harris, Turner, Mitchell, Mulraney, Dougall, Jones, Bodle, Edwards.
Attendance: 23,716

Fourth round, first leg
26 Jan v Watford (h) 5–0
Mulraney 3, Jones, Bodle
Merrick, Duckhouse, Jennings, Harris, Turner, Mitchell, Mulraney, Dougall, Jones, Bodle, Edwards.
Attendance: 25,054

Fourth round, second leg
30 Jan v Watford (a) 1–1 (agg 6–1)
Jones
King, Duckhouse, Jennings, Harris, Turner, Mitchell, Mulraney, Dougall, Jones, Bodle, Edwards.
Attendance: 6,126

Fifth round, first leg
9 Feb v Sunderland (a) 0–1
Merrick, Duckhouse, Jennings, Harris, Turner, Mitchell, Mulraney, Dougall, Jones, Bodle, Edwards.
Attendance: 44,820

Fifth round second leg
13 Feb v Sunderland (h) 3–1 (agg 3–2)
Jones 2, Mulraney
King, Duckhouse, Jennings, Harris, Turner, Mitchell, Mulraney, Dougall, Jones, Bodle, Edwards.
Attendance: 39,880

Sixth round, first leg
2 Mar v Bradford Park Avenue (a) 2–2
Dougall, Jones
Merrick, Duckhouse, Jennings, Harris, Turner, Mitchell, Mulraney, Dougall, Jones, Bodle, Edwards.
Attendance: 19,732

Sixth round, second leg
9 Mar v Bradford Park Avenue (h) 6–0 (agg 8–2)
Dougall 2, Bodle 2, Mulraney 2
Merrick, Duckhouse, Jennings, Harris, Turner, Mitchell, Mulraney, Dougall, Jones, Bodle, Edwards.
Attendance: 49,858

Semi-final
23 Mar v Derby County (Hillsborough) 1–1
Mulraney
Merrick, Duckhouse, Jennings, Harris, Turner, Mitchell, Mulraney, Dougall, Jones, Bodle, Edwards.
Attendance: 65,013

Semi-final replay
27 Mar v Derby County (Maine Road) 0–4 (aet)
Merrick, Duckhouse, Jennings, Harris, Turner, Mitchell, Mulraney, Dougall, Jones, Bodle, Edwards.
Attendance: 80,407

1972–73
Third/fourth-place Play-off
5 Aug v Stoke City (h) 0–0 (Blues won 4–3 on penalties)
Cooper, Carroll, Want, Campbell, Hynd, Harland, Hope, Francis, R. Latchford, Hatton, Taylor.
Attendance: 25,841

Football League Play-offs
1999–2000
Semi-final first leg
13 May v Barnsley (h) 0–4
Myhre, Rowett, M. Johnson, Hughes, Purse (Ndlovu), Holdsworth, Grainger, O'Connor, Furlong (Adebola), A. Johnson (Marcelo), Lazaridis.
Attendance: 26,492

Semi-final second leg
18 May v Barnsley (a) 2–1 (agg 2–5)
Rowett, Marcelo
Myhre, Rowett, M. Johnson (Lazaridis), Gill Holdsworth, Purse, Hughes, Marcelo, Furlong (A. Johnson), O'Connor, Ndlovu.
Attendance: 19,050

2000–01
Semi-final first leg
13 May v Preston North End (h) 1–0
Eaden
Bennett, Atherton, Woodhouse (Hughes), Sonner, Purse, M. Johnson, Eaden (McCarthy), O'Connor (Holdsworth), Horsfield, Marcelo, Lazaridis.
Attendance: 29,072

Semi-final second leg
17 May v Preston North End (a) 1–2 (agg 2–2, PNE won 4–2 on penalties)
Horsfield
Bennett, Atherton (Lazaridis), Grainger, Sonner, Purse, M. Johnson, McCarthy (Eaden), O'Connor (Hughes), Horsfield, Marcelo, Woodhouse.
Attendance: 16,928

2001–02
Semi-final 1st leg
28 Apr v Millwall (h) 1–1
Hughes
Vaesen, Kenna, Grainger, B. Hughes, Purse, Tebily, D Johnson, Carter, Horsfield, John, Mooney (Lazaridis).
Attendance: 28,282

Semi-final 2nd leg
2 May v Millwall (a) 1–0 (agg 2–1)
John
Vaesen, Kenna, Grainger, B. Hughes, Purse, Vickers, Devlin, Tebily, Horsfield (A. Johnson), John, Mooney (Lazaridis).
Attendance: 16,391

Final
12 May v Norwich City (Wembley) 1–1 (aet), Blues won 4–2 on penalties)
Horsfield
Vaesen, Kenna, Grainger, B. Hughes, Vickers (Carter), M. Johnson, Devlin, Tebily, Horsfield (A. Johnson), John, Mooney (Lazaridis).
Attendance: 71,597

BLUES' NON-COMPETITIVE MATCHES

Over the course of time Blues have played literally hundreds of non-competitive matches (friendlies, tour games, testimonials, benefits) both in the UK and abroad. Many were contested before the introduction of League football, and here is an unofficial list of results of many of these games. For general information, a 'Football League and Cup' season ends on 30 June and therefore all games in any one season were played between 1 July and 30 June.

NB: The results of some of the early games (certainly those played between 1875 and 1880) are subject to confirmation, as newspaper reports give conflicting details. Also, Walsall Town and Walsall Swifts were different clubs prior to 1888 when they amalgamated to become Walsall Town Swifts. Since 1895 the club has been known as Walsall.
Ivan Barnsley and Dave Drage have been most helpful with this section.

1875–76
Blues 1 Holte Wanderers 1
(12-a-side game, Blues' first-ever 'match')
Blues 2 Hockley Belmont 1
(Blues' first-ever win)
Blues 1 Stafford Road 1
Blues 1 St George's 0
Bordesley Green Methodists 0 Blues 1

1876–77
Blues 2 Nechells 0
Blues 5 Aston Manor 0
Blues 1 Saltley College 1
Aston Unity 1 Blues 0
(Blues' first-ever defeat)
Calthorpe 2 Blues 1

1877–78
Blues 5 Saltley College
(First game at Muntz Street)
Blues 10 St Luke's 0
Blues 10 Walsall Swifts 2
Blues 9 Lion Works (Aston) 0
Coventry 0 Blues 8

1878–79
Blues 0 Walsall Town 0
Blues 1 Excelsior 3
Blues 2 Stafford Road 1

Excelsior 1 Blues 0
St Phillips 0 Blues 2

1879–80
Blues 1 Aston Villa 0
(Blues' first game against Villa)
Aston Villa 4 Blues 1
Calthorpe 0 Blues 4
Wednesbury Town 2 Blues 0

1880–81
Blues 4 Excelsior 3
Wednesbury Old Athletic 4 Blues 0
Blues 4 Wednesbury Strollers 1
Blues 12 Bloxwich 0
Aston Unity 4 Blues 2

1881–82
Blues 0 Walsall Town 3
Blues 5 Excelsior 1
Nottingham Forest 3 Blues 2
Wednesbury Strollers 4 Blues 1
Excelsior 5 Blues 1
Blues 4 Derby Town 1
Wednesbury Old Athletic 6 Blues 0
Blues 4 Elwells 0
Blues 8 Birmingham St George's 3
Blues 3 Wednesbury Strollers 2
Blues 16 Darlaston All Saints 0

The referee abandoned this game after 60
minutes, declaring it 'no contest' after Blues
had scored eight goals in 14 minutes
immediately after half-time.

1882–83

Blues 0 Nottingham Forest 4
Blues 6 Derby St Luke's 0
Blues 0 Walsall Town 1
Blues 0 Walsall Swifts 3
Druids 1 Blues 2
Blues 1 Staveley 1
Blues 0 Accrington 3
Blues 3 Chesterfield Spiral 0
Stafford Road 1 Blues 1
Leek Town 2 Blues 5
Blues 4 Wednesbury Old Athletic 1
Walsall Swifts 1 Blues 5
Blues 3 Saltley College 0
Staveley 1 Blues 3
Blues 0 Nottingham Forest 2
Accrington 4 Blues 1
Blues 1 West Bromwich Albion 5
(First game v WBA)
Walsall Town 2 Blues 4
(Game abandoned after 70 minutes; players
suffering with heat exhaustion in
temperatures of 100 degrees)
Blues 18 Elwells 1
(Eddie Stanley scored seven goals for Blues)

1883–84

Aston Villa 4 Blues 0
Stoke 9 Blues 1
Walsall Swifts 3 Blues 3
Blues 1 Walsall Town 1
Nottingham Forest 3 Blues 2
Blues 1 Druids 1
Walsall Town 1 Blues 1
Blues 9 Notts Wanderers 1
Accrington 2 Blues 1
Blues 2 Great Harlow 0
Blues 2 Long Eaton Rangers 2
Church 2 Blues 1
Blues 1 Stoke 1
Blues 0 Wolves 1
Blues 3 Nottingham Forest 2
Blues 1 Church 2

Blues 2 Wednesbury Strollers 2
Blues 5 Stafford Rangers 2
Great Lever 4 Blues 0
Blues 1 Aston Unity 2
Blues 3 Stafford Road 0
Blues 1 Wednesbury Town 1

1884–85

Notts Rangers 5 Blues 5
Blues 0 West Bromwich Albion 2
Blues 2 Aston Unity 2
Blues 5 Wednesbury Town 1
Walsall Town 3 Blues 0
Blues 0 Excelsior 3
Wolves 2 Blues 0
Blues 5 Leek Town 4
Blues 8 Wednesbury Strollers 2
Blues 2 Burslem Port Vale 0
Blues 1 Stafford Road 1
Blues 3 Birmingham Junior Ass. 2
Wellington 1 Blues 0
Nottingham Forest 3 Blues 0
Burton Wanderers 2 Blues 1
Leek Town 4 Blues 3
Blues 0 Wolves 1
Blues 3 Aston Villa 4
Blues 2 Walsall Swifts 2
Blues 0 Wolves 0
Burslem Port Vale 5 Blues 1
Blues 3 Birmingham St George's 1
Blues 3 Burton Wanderers 4
Blues 1 Walsall Town 1
Blues 2 Aston Unity 3
Wednesbury Town 6 Blues 1
Blues 0 Nottingham Forest 0

1885–86

Blues 0 Nottingham Forest 2
Blues 6 Burton Wanderers 3
Birmingham St George's 6 Blues 1
Derby County 6 Blues 0
Stafford Road 2 Blues 1
Blues 0 Excelsior 1
Blues 4 Junction Street School 2
Blues 5 Birmingham Junior Ass. 0
Burton Wanderers 2 Blues 1
Blues 3 Stafford Road 0
Blues 6 Aston Unity 3

Blues 1 Stoke 3
Blues 3 Stafford Rangers 1
Blues 2 Derby Midland 2
Nottingham Forest 1 Blues 2
Blues 3 Birmingham St George's 0
Excelsior 1 Blues 1
Blues 2 Derby Junction Street 1
Blues 5 Excelsior 0
Blues 0 West Bromwich Albion 7
Blues 1 Aston Villa 8
(Albert Brown scored six goals for Villa)
Aston Villa 7 Blues 0
Stoke 2 Blues 1

1886–87
Blues 3 Halliwell (Sheffield) 0
Blues 0 Nottingham Forest 2
Blues 2 Long Eaton Rangers 4
Blues 4 Derby St. Luke's 1
Walsall Town 1 Blues 0
Blues 1 Aston Villa 1
Aston Unity 1 Blues 0
Blues 5 Wellington St George's 2
Wolves 4 Blues 1
Stafford Road 1 Blues 6
Blues 0 Excelsior 2
Blues 0 Mitchell St George's 3
Blues 2 Birmingham Junior Ass. 2
Jardines FC (Notts) 3 Blues 0
Aston Villa 3 Blues 2
Blues 2 Burton Wanderers 0
Blues 1 Aston Unity 1
Derby Midland 2 Blues 1
Blues 1 Walsall Town 0
Blues 1 Derby Midland 0
Blues 4 Aston Unity 3
Aston Villa 7 Blues 0
Stoke 2 Blues 0

1887–88
Walsall Town 3 Blues 0
Blues 3 Stafford Rangers 2
Blues 4 Jardines FC (Notts) 0
Blues 4 Davenham 1
Oldbury Town 2 Blues 4
Blues 0 London Casuals 2
Blues 4 Excelsior 0
Oldbury Town 2 Blues 0

Blues 1 Walsall Town 0
Derby Midland 0 Blues 1
Blues 2 Wolves 3
Blues 6 Rotherham Town 2
Grimsby Town 3 Blues 0
Blues 0 Oldbury Town 1
Blues 7 Burton Wanderers 1
Long Eaton Rangers 7 Blues 3
Blues 3 Macclesfield 2
Blues 15 Long Eaton Rangers 0
(Austin Smith and Alf Stanley scored five
goals each)
Aston Villa 4 Blues 1
Gainsborough Trinity 2 Blues 0
Blues 0 Oldbury Town 1
Blues 3 Great Bridge Unity 1
Notts Rangers 2 Blues 1
Blues 5 Aston Unity 0
Blues 4 Notts Rangers 3
Blues 4 Stafford Rangers 0
Blues 2 Walsall Town 3
Blues 4 Witton (Lancs) 3
Blues 4 Aston Shakespeare 0
Blues 4 Aston Unity 2
Blues 5 Derby Junction 2
Blues 9 Burton Swifts 0
Blues 1 Walsall Swifts 0

1888–89
Leek Town 1 Blues 2
Blues 2 Witton (Lancs) 1
Blues 5 Jardines FC (Notts) 1
Blues 5 Great Marlow 1
Derby Junction 3 Blues 1
Blues 10 Oldbury Town 1
Derby Midland 1 Blues 1
Blues 7 Chirk 1
Blues 6 Loughborough Town 0
Blues 0 Birmingham St George's 2
Blues 4 Davenham 1
Blues 6 Long Eaton Rangers 2
West Bromwich Albion 4 Blues 1
Blues 1 West Bromwich Albion 2
Blues 2 Leek Town 1
Blues 3 Nottingham Forest 0
Newton Heath 1 Blues 0
Darwen 3 Blues 1
Blues 3 Derby Junction 2

1889–90

Blues 4 Kidderminster Harriers 1
Blues 4 Aston Villa 0
Stoke 2 Blues 0
Blues 2 Stoke 1
Blues 4 Past XI 1
Blues 3 Burslem Port Vale 1
Blues Burton Swifts 0
Blues 4 Jardines FC (Notts) 1
Long Eaton Rangers 0 Blues 2
Burslem Port Vale 3 Blues 4
Blues 2 Derby Junction 0
Kidderminster Harriers 0 Blues 3
Blues 2 Aston Villa 2
Blues 6 Great Marlow 1
Aston Villa 1 Blues 0

1890–91

Aston Villa 0 Blues 4
Blues 3 Warwick County 0
Blues 5 Burslem Port Vale 1
Blues 2 Aston Villa 2
Blues 4 Kidderminster Harriers 1
Aston Villa 3 Blues 0
Middlesbrough Ironopolis 6 Blues 1
Blues 3 Wolves 2
Walsall Town Swifts 6 Blues 1
Blues 2 Birmingham St George's 0
West Bromwich Albion 3 Blues 1
Blues 3 West Bromwich Albion 3
Blues 2 West Bromwich Albion 1
Blues 4 Aston Villa 5

1891–92

Wolves 2 Blues 0
Blues 3 Wolves 3
Aston Villa 3 Blues 0
Newton Heath 7 Blues 2
Blues 7 Bolton Wanderers 0
Royal Arsenal 1 Blues 2
Blues 1 Preston North End 3
Blues 4 West Bromwich Albion 0
Aston Villa 5 Blues 1

1892–93

Blues 4 Birmingham & District XI 3
Blues 1 Derby County 0
Blues 4 Gainsborough Trinity 1

Aston Villa 3 Blues 2
Blues 4 Bolton Wanderers 3
Royal Arsenal 3 Blues 1
Blues 2 Nottingham Forest 3
Blues 0 Middlesbrough 2
Middlesbrough Ironopolis 2 Blues 1
Blues 3 Darwen 2
Blues 4 West Bromwich Albion 1
West Bromwich Albion 4 Blues 1
Blues 5 West Bromwich Albion 0 (Caesar
Jenkyns benefit)
Blues 4 Stoke 2

1893–94

Everton Reserves 5 Blues 1
Marlow 2 Blues 2
Blues 2 Nottingham Forest 2
Blues 3 Aston Villa 3
Sherwood Foresters 0 Blues 3

1894–95

Home Farm 0 Blues 3
Ardwick 2 Blues 1
Notts County 3 Blues 3
Woolwich Arsenal 3 Blues 4
Blues 1 West Bromwich Albion 3 (Fred
Wheldon benefit)

1895–96

Blues 1 Aston Villa 3 (Ted Devey benefit)
Leyton FC 3 Blues 8
Aston Villa 1 Blues 2
Walsall 3 Blues 2 (Sam Holmes benefit)
Leicester Fosse 3 Blues 2
Blues 3 Notts County 4
Blues 2 Walsall 3

1896–97

Aston Villa 3 Blues 1
Blues 2 Wolves 0 (at Crystal Palace)
Millwall Athletic 9 Blues 1
Blues 2 Hibernian 5
Aston Villa 1 Blues 1 (Jack Elliott benefit)
New Brompton 4 Blues 1
Blues 2 Aston Villa 1 (Billy Walton benefit)
Blues 5 Liverpool 1
Grimsby Town 2 Blues 1
Blues 5 West Bromwich Albion 1
Blues 7 Bolton Wanderers 0

1897–98
Blues 3 Burton Wanderers 0
Blues 4 Lincoln City 0
Blues 2 Notts County 3
Blues 6 Wellingborough 0
Aston Villa 4 Blues 0 (abandoned after 70 mins)
West Herts 2 Blues 2
Walsall 0 Blues 2
Blues 0 Aston Villa 3
Blues 3 Walsall 2
Blues 3 Small Heath reserves 1
Blues 8 West Bromwich Albion 3 (Alex
Leake benefit)

1898–99
Blues 1 West Bromwich Albion 0
Blues 2 Leek Town 1
Gainsborough Trinity 0 Blues 1

1899–1900
Blues 6 Everton XI 2
Bristol Rovers 2 Blues 0
Aston Villa 5 Blues 2
Reading 1 Blues 0
Blues 1 West Bromwich Albion 1

1900–01
Bristol City 2 Blues 0
Blues 3 Nottingham Forest 1

1901–02
Selected XI 7 Blues 3 (William Pratt benefit)
Chesterfield 4 Blues 2
Blues 6 Brierley Hill Alliance 2
Blues 1 Leicester Fosse 0
West Bromwich Albion 2 Blues 0 (Jack
Paddock benefit)
Aston Villa 1 Blues 1 (Ibrox Park Disaster
Fund)

1902–03
Aston Villa 4 Blues 2
West Bromwich Albion 3 Blues 2
(Warwickshire CCC fund)
Aston Villa 4 Blues 1

1903–04
Bristol Rovers 3 Blues 2
New Brompton 2 Blues 2
Blues 1 Coventry City 2

1905–06
Blues 5 Old Heathens 2 (local Charity
match)

1906–07
Corinthians 2 Blues 1
Bristol City 3 Blues 2
Reading 3 Blues 3

1907–08
Norwich City 5 Blues 2

1908–09
Treharris 2 Blues 4
Blues 3 Wolves 0 (Marsh Cup)

1911–12
Blues 0 Sheffield United 4
Aston Villa XI 4 Blues XI 4 (local Charity
match)

1912–13
First overseas tour to Denmark
Copenhagen Select XI 1 Blues 0
Copenhagen Select XI 5 Blues 4

1913–14
Blues 2 Cambridge/Oxford University XI 3
Blues 4 Airdrieonians 1

1915–16
Blues 2 Footballers' Battalion 3
Blues 0 Chris Buckley's XI 2
Blues 0 Jesse Pennington's XI 3
Blues 6 Royal Fusiliers 1
Blues 3 Footballers' Battalion 1
Blues 4 Coventry City 1
Blues 5 West Yorkshire Regiment 2
Coventry City 1 Blues 1
Blues 8 3rd Light Infantry Brigade 0
Blues 2 Wolves 5
Blues 1 RAMC XI 1
Wolves 2 Blues 2
Blues 2 RAMC 2

1916–17
Coventry City 3 Blues 3 (Lord Mayor's
Prisoner of War Fund)
Blues 3 West Bromwich Albion 1
(Sportsman's Motor Ambulance Fund)

West Bromwich Albion 0 Blues 1
(Sportsman's Motor Ambulance Fund)
Harborne Lynwood 2 Blues 2 (James
Whittall benefit)

1917–18
Blues 10 Army XI 1 (at Rugeley)
Blues 1 Coventry City 3
Blues 1 Jimmy Windridge's XI 2

1918–19
Aston Villa 1 Blues 2 (County FA Find)
Coventry City 2 Blues 3 (County FA Fund)
Blues 2 Coventry City 1

1920–21
Blues 3 Coventry City 1
Blues 1 Aston Villa 1 (Lord Mayor's
Unemployment Fund)

1921–22
Blues 5 Corinthians 0
Bristol City 3 Blues 3

1922–23
Spain tour
Real Madrid 0 Blues 3
CD Europa 3 Blues 5 (in Barcelona)
CD Europa 3 Blues 4 (in Madrid)
CD Europa 2 Blues 8 (in Valencia)
Spanish Army Select XI 1 Blues 5
Atletico Madrid 1 Blues 3
Real Sociedad 0 Blues 1
Real Sociedad 3 Blues 2
CD Europa 1 Blues 6 (in Barcelona)

Blues 1 Manchester United 1

1923–24
Spain tour
CD Europa 2 Blues 2 (in Barcelona)
CD Europa 1 Blues 1 (in Madrid)
CD Europa 2 Blues 1 (in Valencia)
Athletic Bilbao 1 Blues 2
Athletic Bilbao 1 Blues 2
Valencia 3 Blues 1
Valencia 2 Blues 1

British Army 1 Blues 2
Blues 1 Coventry City 1

1924–25
Spain tour
CF Barcelona 1 Blues 0
CF Barcelona 2 Blues 0
Real Madrid 2 Blues 3
Spanish Select 0 Blues 1

Corinthians 0 Blues 2
Blues 4 Coventry City 1
Blues 3 Corinthians 0

1925–26
Blues 8 Glentoran 2
(Joe Bradford scored 4 goals)
Blues 3 Real Madrid 0
Corinthians 1 Blues 0
Coventry City 2 Blues 2
Blues 1 Corinthians 0
Aston Villa 6 Blues 3

1927–28
Blues 2 Coventry City 2

1929–30
European tour
Sparta Rotterdam 1 Blues 2
Copenhagen Select XI 2 Blues 0
Copenhagen Select XI 1 Blues 2
Copenhagen Select XI 4 Blues 5
Berlin Select XI 0 Blues 5

1930–31
German tour
Proutien Munster 1 Blues 2
Essen Select XI 0 Blues 1
Armenia Sports Club 1 Blues 8
Munich Select XI 1 Blues 3

Blues 2 Corinthians 1

1931–32
European tour
Mannheim Select XI 2 Blues 1
Bohemians (Czech) 1 Blues 2
IK Staplar 2 Blues 8

AIK Stockholm 0 Blues 3
Copenhagen Select XI 3 Blues 4
Gothenburg 0 Blues 2

1935–36
Oxford University 2 Blues 5

1938–39
Blues 6 Celtic 1
Chelmsford City 0 Blues 6
Coventry City 2 Blues 0 (Football League
Jubilee)

1939–40
Coventry City 3 Blues 2 (Football League
Jubilee)
Leicester City 6 Blues 4
Newport County 2 Blues 2
Shrewsbury Town 1 Blues 1
Chesterfield 3 Blues 2
QPR 2 Blues 3
Stoke City 3 Blues 2
Worcester City 0 Blues 2
Notts County 1 Blues 0
Shrewsbury Town 1 Blues 3
Chester 1 Blues 1
Cardiff City 4 Blues 5
Manchester United 6 Blues 2
Blues 2 West Bromwich Albion 2
Blues 2 Aston Villa 1
Wolves 1 Blues 0
Blues 2 Aston Villa 1 (Harry Hibbs
testimonial)

1940–41
Blues 1 RAF XI 1
Blues 3 Services XI 3
Worcester City 2 Blues 4
Chester 3 Blues 3
Blues 0 Aston Villa 3

1941–42
Aston Villa 4 Blues 0
Blues 2 Derby County 2
Wolves 0 Blues 3
RAF XI 1 Blues 1 (at Villa Park)
Blues 2 Aston Villa 1
Chester 3 Blues 3
Walsall 0 Blues 0
Blues 0 Leicester City 3 (at Villa Park)

Blues 2 Leicester City 4
Coventry City 4 Blues 2
West Bromwich Albion 4 Blues 1
Blues 3 Czech Army XI 2
Blues 4 Wolves 0
Blues 2 Aldershot Army XI 4
Blues 4 Northampton Town 1
Blues 7 Birmingham Works AFA 0
Blues 2 All Welsh XI 3
Aston Villa 7 Blues 0
Blues 4 Czech Army XI 0
Blues 3 British Army 6
West Bromwich Albion 4 Blues 1
Blues 0 Aston Villa 1
Aston Villa 4 Blues 1
Wolves 2 Blues 4
Blues 5 Wolves 0
Blues 3 RAF XI 1
Blues 2 RAF XI 0
Derby County 2 Blues 2

1942–43
Blues 1 RAF XI 1

1945–46
Sweden tour
FF Malmo 3 Blues 2
AIK Stockholm 1 Blues 2
AFK Gothenburg 0 Blues 1
Elfsburg 1 Blues 2

Services XI 2 Blues 0 (in Germany)

1946–47
Blues 3 AC Sparta 1
(Sparta, Czech League and Cup-winners)

1947–48
Switzerland tour
La Chaux De Fonds 2 Blues 3
Berne Select 0 Blues 2
FC Basel 0 Blues 5
Young Boys Zurich 1 Blues 1
FC Lucerne 0 Blues 1

Aston Villa 2 Blues 1
Portsmouth 1 Blues 0
Dundee United 1 Blues 5

1948–49
Leyton Orient 0 Blues 2

1949–50
Blues 2 AIK Stockholm 2
Aston Villa 3 Blues 1
Blues 1 Bury 2

1950–51
Festival of Britain
Blues 3 Airdrieonians 5
Blues 0 Dinamo Yugoslavia 2
Home Farm (Dublin) 1 Blues 2
Cork Athletic 2 Blues 5

Worcester City 2 Blues XI 2
Crewe Alexandra XI 3 Blues 3
(Tony Waddington testimonial)

1951–52
Holland/Denmark/Germany tour
FC Eintracht 2 Blues 4
Staernet 1 Blues 3
Danish Select 1 Blues 2
Arminia 0 Blues 5
Breda 1 Blues 3
Flensburg 2 Blues 5

Aston Villa 3 Blues 2

1952–53
Aston Villa 1 Blues 1 (Coronation Cup)
Hereford United 3 Blues 2

1954–55
Torquay United 2 Blues 3
Crewe Alexandra 4 Blues 1

1955–56
Coventry City 2 Blues 2
Torquay United 2 Blues 3

1956–57
Edinburgh Select 2 Blues 1 (at Tynecastle)
Blues 3 Borussia Dortmund 3
(opening of St Andrew's floodlights)

1957–58
Blues 4 Sampdoria 2
Valencia 3 Blues 0

1958–59
Switzerland tour
Grenchen/Biel XI 0 Blues 3
Schaffhausen 0 Blues 7
FC Lucerne 2 Blues 5

Blues 5 Bela Vista 0

1959–60
Spain tour
CD Athletica 2 Blues 0
FC Sevilla 1 Blues 1

Blues 2 Valencia 3
Dunfermline Athletic 5 Blues 2
Blues 1 All Star XI 5 (Jeff Hall Memorial match)
Blues 1 Dundee 2

1960–61
North America tour
Hamilton Steelers 2 Blues 4 (in Ontario)
Calgary All Stars 2 Blues 11 (in Calgary)
Third Lanark 2 Blues 3 (in Toronto)
Montreal Cantalia 1 Blues 0 (in Montreal)
Third Lanark 4 Blues 1 (in New York)
Third Lanark 1 Blues 1 (in Vancouver)
Victoria All Stars 2 Blues 5 (in Victoria, Canada)
British Columbia 1 Blues 5 (in Vancouver)
FC Rheims 1 Blues 2 (in Toronto)

1961–62
Blues 2 Torquay United 0
Cambridge City 0 Blues 2
Stirling Albion 1 Blues 3 (opening of floodlights)
Blues 3 Bratislava 2

1962–63
Shrewsbury Town 3 Blues 2
Blues 1 Coventry City 2 (Public Charity match)

Swindon Town 4 Blues 2 (first game for seven weeks)
Drumcondra 2 Blues 0

1963–64
Germany tour
Fortuna Dusseldorf 2 Blues 2
Rheinddahlen 3 Blues 6
Wuppertal 1 Blues 5

Blues 2 Drumcondra 0
Blues 5 Ferencvaros 1
Southend United 4 Blues 2
Blues 4 Distillery 0 (Trevor Smith benefit)

1964–65
Ireland tour
Distillery 1 Blues 6
Portadown 1 Blues 4

Kidderminster Harriers 1 Blues 2
Peterborough United 2 Blues 1

1965–66
Spain tour
Lerida 3 Blues 1
CD Europa 0 Blues 2 (in Barcelona)
Huelva 2 Blues 1

1966–67
Stratford Town 0 Blues XI 3
Notts County 2 Blues 2
Walsall 1 Blues 2
Oxford United 1 Blues 1

1967–68
Switzerland/France tour
FC Lucerne 2 Blues 6
Racing Club Strasburg 1 Blues 2
Biel Bien 4 Blues 3

Blues 4 ex-Blues XI 3 (Johnny Schofield testimonial)

1968–69
Blues 12 International XI 8 (Malcolm Beard testimonial)

Peterborough United 3 Blues 3
Swansea Town 1 Blues 0
Blues 0 Hibernian 2 (18,000 crowd)
Corby Town 1 Blues 1 (testimonial)
Brierley Hill Alliance 1 Blues 4 (Bob Beech testimonial)

1969–70
Bournemouth 3 Blues 0
Aldershot 2 Blues 2
Reading 0 Blues 2 (opening of floodlights)
Blues 3 Asanta Kotoko 0
Blues 12 International XI 8 (Malcolm Beard testimonial)
Blues 2 West Bromwich Albion 2
Blues 2 Slovan Bratislava 0
Blues 2 Manchester City 3 (Ron Wyle testimonial)

1970–71
Holland tour
Holland Sports XI 0 Blues 2
DFC Dordrecht 0 Blues 1
RC Haarlem 0 Blues 0

Bristol Rovers 0 Blues 1
Tranmere Rovers 0 Blues 0
Plymouth Argyle 2 Blues 1 (Winston Foster testimonial)

1971–72
Ireland tour
Shamrock Rovers 0 Blues 2
Cork Hibernians 0 Blues 1

Swansea Town 0 Blues 3
Merthyr Tydfil 0 Blues 1
Aston Villa 2 Blues 1
Blues 3 Wolves 4 (Ray Martin testimonial)
Stoke City 2 Blues 2 (Arthur Turner testimonial)
Brighton & Hove Albion 2 Blues 2 (Geoff Sidebottom testimonial)

1972–73
North America tour
Baltimore Bays 2 Blues 7
New York Cosmos 0 Blues 3
Toronto Metros 2 Blues 3

Australasia tour
Tahiti 1 Blues 3
Tahiti Combined XI 2 Blues 4
Queensland XI 0 Blues 5
New South Wales XI 1 Blues 2

Portsmouth 0 Blues 2
Preston North End 0 Blues 1

1973–74
Cardiff City 1 Blues 3 (opening of new
grandstand)
Malines FC (Belgium) 2 Blues 1
Fulham 0 Blues 0
WBA/Aston Villa XI 2 Blues/Wolves XI 1
(Tony Brown testimonial)

1974–75
FC Lens 0 Blues 1
Martinique XI 0 Blues 0
Martinique XI 1 Blues 1
Blues/Midlands XI 4 England XI 3
(Birmingham Bombings Fund)

1975–76
Denmark tour
FC Viking 0 Blues 1
FC Hamarkameraten 0 Blues 6
Valerengens 2 Blues 2

Cardiff City 1 Blues 4
Plymouth Argyle 0 Blues 0
Blues 1 Celtic 0
(Club's centenary game at St Andrew's,
14,670 crowd)

1976–77
Belgium/Holland tour
FC Beveren 0 Blues 3
Liege 0 Blues 2
De Graafschap 1 Blues 0

Blues 4 Australia 1
Alvechurch 3 Blues 2 (opening of floodlights)

1977–78
Blues 3 ex-Blues XI 3 (Malcolm Page
testimonial)

Oxford United 0 Blues 1
Weymouth 0 Blues 2 (Stuart Morgan
testimonial)

1978–79
La Linea Tournament, Gibralter
Real Zaragoza 0 Blues 1 (s/f)
Sporting Gijon 1 Blues 2 (final)

Blues 1 Ajax Amsterdam 0
Blues 1 West Bromwich Albion 1 (in
Guernsey)
Blues 4 West Bromwich Albion 0 (Garry
Pendrey testimonial)
Walsall 0 Blues 1
Brierley Hill 0 Blues 4
Portsmouth 0 Blues 1
Dundalk 2 Blues 1
Wigan Athletic 0 Blues 0
Port Vale 0 Blues 1 (Tommy McLaren
testimonial)
Newport County 2 Blues 2 (Keith Saunders
testimonial)

1979–80
Boston United 0 Blues 1
Blues 1 Los Angeles Aztecs 1 (Johan Cruyff
played for Aztecs)
Blues 8 Blues Past XI 3 (Dave Latchford
testimonial)
Blues 5 Omonia FC 0
Aston Villa 2 Blues 3 (Ron Saunders
testimonial)
FC Lucerne 2 Blues 3

1980–81
Sweden tour
JFK Hallaby 3 Blues 2
Vanesborgs 0 Blues 1
Forstat Vara SK 3 Blues 5
Skarblaka 0 Blues 11

South America tour
Columbia XI 4 Blues 1
Honduras XI 2 Blues 2
Guatemala XI 2 Blues 2
Peru 1 Blues 2
Peru XI 1 Blues 2

Blues 1 Tilburg Willem 3

Barnet 2 Blues 1

Hednesford Town 1 Blues 4

Poole Town 0 Blues 5 (Poole's centenary match)

Norwich City 0 Blues 2 (at Boston Utd. FC)

Kuwait National XI 3 Blues 0

Blues 0 Kuwait National XI 2

Blues 3 Aston Villa 6 (Joe Gallagher testimonial)

Blues 10 Lucerne 1 (Tony Evans & Archie Gemmill scored hat-tricks)

Blues 0 Tampa Bay Rowdies 0

Aldershot 1 Blues 4 (Andy Needham testimonial)

Weymouth 0 Blues 8 (Jimmy McCafferty testimonial)

Worcester City 0 Blues XI 1 (B Williams testimonial)

Scunthorpe United 2 Blues 4

Newport County 2 Blues 1

1981–82
Holland tour
Waganingen 2 Blues 2

Willem II 1 Blues 1

FC Groningen 1 Blues 1

Cardiff City 0 Blues 0

Hereford United 2 Blues 1 (Herefordshire Cup)

Charlton Athletic 0 Blues 2

Crystal Palace 1 Blues 0 (abandoned, 70 mins; floodlight failure)

Torquay United 1 Blues 2

QPR 2 Blues 1 (Hollman testimonial at Wellingborough)

Bolton Wanderers 1 Blues 1

Arnold Town 1 Blues XI 4

Blues 1 FC Groningen 1

Weymouth 1 Blues 3 (abandoned, 83 minutes, waterlogged pitch)

Blues 2 West Bromwich Albion 1 (Sports Argus Arctic Cup in Guernsey)

Sheffield United 2 Blues 1

Reaading 2 Blues 2 (at Bournemouth)

1982–83
Forest Green Rovers 1 Blues 2

Walsall 0 Blues 3

Shrewsbury Town 1 Blues 1

AP Leamington 1 Blues 4 (Mick Harford hat-trick)

1983–84
Sweden tour
Gallivare 2 Blues 1

Ranea 0 Blues 5

Alvsbyn IF 0 Blues 1

Haparanda 0 Blues 5

Cardiff City 1 Blues 2

1984–85
Holland tour
De Graafschap 0 Blues 0

Kon Sint Niklas FC 1 Blues 0

Veendam 0 Blues 4

NAC Breda 1 Blues 1 (abandoned 80 mins.)

1985–86
Port Vale 1 Blues 1

Bristol Rovers 1 Blues 1

Blues 2 Derby County 1

Blues 3 Aston Villa 3 (Kevan Broadhurst testimonial; Blues won on penalties)

1986–87
Weymouth 3 Blues 3

Bournemouth 0 Blues 1

Yeovil Town 0 Blues 0

Bideford Town 0 Blues 3

Blues 0 Coventry City 0

Bristol City 0 Blues 1

1987–88
Aston Villa 5 Blues 2 (Football League Centenary match)

Bristol City 3 Blues 1

Blues 1 Oxford United 2

Hednesford Town 1 Blues XI 1

1988–89
Boston United 2 Blues XI 0

Blues 2 Manchester United 5 (Ian Handysides testimonial)

Blues 0 Arsenal 4
Stockport County 1 Blues 2

1989–90
VS Rugby 2 Blues XI 1
Nuneaton Borough 1 Blues XI 5
Alvechurch 0 Blues XI 2
Blues 1 Middlesbrough 2
Highgate United 0 Blues XI 3

1990–91
Blues 0 Middlesbrough 2
Kidderminster Harriers 1 Blues XI 1
Blues 0 Luton Town 1
Highgate United 1 Blues XI 2

1991–92
Ireland tour
Athlone Town 0 Blues 1
Ballinsloe 0 Blues 4
Galway 0 Blues 3
Kilkenny 0 Blues 1
Waterford 0 Blues 3
Cobh Ramblers 1 Blues 1

Highgate United 1 Blues XI 1
Cinderford Town 1 Blues XI 3 (opening of floodlights)
Blues XI 2 Ron Atkinson's XI 3 (Frank Worthington testimonial)

1992–93
Ireland tour
Cobh Ramblers 0 Blues 3
Athlone Town 0 Blues 1
Sligo Rovers 0 Blues 3
Kilkenny 1 Blues 2
Galway 4 Blues 3

Highgate United 2 Blues XI 4
Rocester 0 Blues XI 3
Blues 3 Real Sociedad 4
Blues 1 Real Mallorca 1 (IF tournament s/f)
Blues 1 Coventry City 0 (IF tournament final)
Walsall 0 Blues 3
Aston Villa 2 Blues 0 (Jimmy Dugdale testimonial)

Aston Villa 2 Blues 2
West Bromwich Albion 0 Blues 1
(Martyn Bennett testimonial – 70-minute match only)

1993–94
Italy tour
Pisa 0 Blues 1
Chiamcano 1 Blues 4
AS Siena 1 Blues 0
Carrese & Massese 4 Blues 1
(Carresse played in first half, Massese in second)

Hereford United 1 Blues 1
Barnet 3 Blues 6 (Evans testimonial)
Telford United 1 Blues 1
Coventry City 2 Blues 1 (Lloyd McGrath testimonial)
Tiverton Town 3 Blues XI 3 (testimonial)
Blues 2 Norwich City 3
Blues 1 Liverpool 1 (ICC Cup)

1994–95
Blues 1 Aston Villa 1 (opening of 'new' St Andrew's)
Kettering Town 0 Blues 4
Stevenage Borough 1 Blues 6
Aylesbury United 1 Blues XI 2
Telford United 0 Blues 2
Bedford Town 1 Blues XI 0
Grimsby Town 3 Blues 3
Notts County 2 Blues 0 (at Walsall)
Colchester United 5 Blues 2
Walton & Hersham 1 Blues XI 1
Walsall 1 Blues 2 (21 players used by Blues)
Blues 1 Nottingham Forest 4 (double celebration match)
Aston Villa 2 Blues 0 (Paul McGrath testimonial)

1995–96
Whyteleafe FC 1 Blues 5
Blues 0 Liverpool 1
Enfield 0 Blues 4
Blues 1 Celtic 0
Blues 1 Sheffield Wednesday 3

Blues 0 Aston Villa 6 (John Frain
testimonial)
Blues 1 Aston Villa 1 (opening of £7.4m
Tilton Rd. stand)
Blues 1 Manchester United 0
Blues 0 Chelsea 3
Blues 0 West Bromwich Albion 0
Barrow 2 Blues 2 (testimonial at Holker
Street)
Kidderminster Harriers 1 Blues 4 (Richard
Forsyth testimonial)
Coventry City 1 Blues 1 (Brian Borrows
testimonial)

1996–97
Walsall 1 Blues 1
Blues 1 Everton 2
Blues 1 Arsenal 0
Wycombe Wanderers 1 Blues 2
Stockport County 4 Blues 0

1997–98
Blues 0 Aston Villa 0
Notts County 1 Blues 0
Blues 2 Newcastle United 3
Blues 1 Derby County 0
Yeovil Town 1 Blues 1
Walsall 3 Blues 3
Hednesford Town 0 Blues 1

1998–99
Exeter City 0 Blues 4
Plymouth Argyle 1 Blues 1
Blues 4 Tottenham Hotspur 2
Blues 4 Manchester United 3
(Peter Ndlovu hat-trick for Blues)
Peterborough United 1 Blues 1
Blues 4 Sheffield Wednesday 0
Hednesford Town 1 Blues XI 3

1999–2000
Blackpool 0 Blues 1
Blues 0 Leeds United 0
Cheltenham Town 1 Blues 3
Blues 1 Chelsea 1
Rushden & Diamonds 2 Blues XI 1
Blues 3 Coventry City 1
Hednesford Town 1 Blues 5

2000–01
Cheltenham Town 0 Blues 4
Oxford United 0 Blues 3
Blues 0 Tottenham Hotspur 1
Stoke City 2 Blues 1
Hednesford Town 1 Blues 3

2001–02
Bristol Rovers 2 Blues 1
Chesterfield 0 Blues 3
Cheltenham Town 3 Blues 1
Kidderminster Harriers 1 Blues 2
QPR 0 Blues 1

2002–03
Scotland tour
Livingston 2 Blues 1
Motherwell 2 Blues 1
Partick Thistle 1 Blues 2

Exeter City 0 Blues 1
Forest Green Rovers 0 Blues 6
Tranmere Rovers 0 Blues 7
Stoke City 0 Blues 2
Blues 1 Deportivo Alaves 1
Blues 2 Jamaica XI 1 (Ian Bennett
testimonial)

2003–04
Malaysia Cup
Newcastle United 2 Blues 1 (s/f)
Malaysia XI 0 Blues 4 (3rd/4th Play-off)

Burton Albion 0 Blues 4
Port Vale 2 Blues 0
Burnley 2 Blues 2
Walsall 1 Blues 3
Blues 0 Real Mallorca 0
Cardiff City 1 Blues 0 (Len Ashurst
testimonial)

2004–05
Germany tour
VfB Possneck 0 Blues 5
FC Erzgebirge AUE 1 Blues 0
SPVGVB Weiden 1 Blues 4
SSV Ulm 1 Blues 0

Cheltenham Town 1 Blues 1
Sheffield Wednesday 0 Blues 1
Blues 9 Celebrity XI 2 (MG Rover fund)
Hull City 1 Blues 4
Exeter City 0 Blues 2
Blues 1 CA Osasuna 1

2005–06
Norway tour
Egersunds IK 0 Blues 2
FK Viking 0 Blues 1
Brann Bergen 4 Blues 0

Derby County 0 Blues 4
Northampton Town 1 Blues 0
QPR 2 Blues 1
Peterborough United 2 Blues 1
Deportivo La Coruna 'B' 0 Blues 1
Deportivo La Coruna 2 Blues 0
Blues 6 Martin Grainger's XI 2 (M Grainger
testimonial)

2006–07
Spain/Gibraltar tour
San Pedro 0 Blues 6
Newcastle Gibralter 0 Blues 6
Malaga 3 Blues 4

Burton Albion 1 Blues 5
Blues 0 Tottenham Hotspur 2
Blues 1 FC Nancy 1

2007–08
Germany Tour
Hohenlohe Auswahl 0 Blues 2
FC Heidenheim 1846 0 Blues 1
FC Schweinfurt '05 2 Blues 5

Walsall 0 Blues 2
Peterborough United 0 Blues 3
Sheffield Wednesday 0 Blues 2

2008–09
Germany/Austria tour
Kirchbeg 0 Blues 7
Victoria Plazen 1 Blues 3
Nuremberg 1 Blues 2

Gillingham 0 Blues 2
Forest Green Rovers 0 Blues 1
Leicester City 2 Blues 3
Blues 1 Fulham 1

2009–10
Austria Tour
Vfb Stuttgart 2 Blues 0
GC Augsburg 2 Blues 0
Al Hilal 3 Blues 0

Burton Albion 3 Blues XI 2
Crewe Alexandra 4 Blues 1
Hednesford Town 0 Blues XI 0
Dagenham & Redbridge 0 Blues 1
Nottingham Forest 2 Blues 1
Cheltenham Town 0 Blues 4
Blues 0 Sporting Gijon 0

2010–11
Far East Tour
Hong Kong XI 2 Blues 3
Liaoning 0 Blues 2
Beijing Gouan 0 Blues 1
Derby County 1 Blues 2
MK Dons 2 Blues 3
Northampton Town 2 Blues XI 2
Blues 0 Real Mallorca 1
Harrow Borough 3 Blues XI 4

INTERNATIONAL BLUES

Unless stated otherwise, the figure shown in brackets alongside each player's name, refers to the number of caps (including substitute appearances) he gained for his country during his career as a Birmingham City (Small Heath) player only. And please note that before 1924 there was only one Ireland national team. After that, the Republic of Ireland became a separate entity although, until after World War Two, players born in the Republic could also play for Northern Ireland in the Home International Tournament. An asterisk (*) alongside the number of caps won by that player means he was still adding to his total at 2010.

FULL INTERNATIONALS

Australia
Stan Lazaridis (33)

Canada
Lyndon Hooper (5), Paul Peschisolido (7)

Cayman Islands
Martyn O'Connor (2)

England
Gordon Astall (2), Percy Barton (7), Joe Bradford (12), Chris Charsley (1), Wally Corbett (3), Trevor Francis (12), Tom Grosvenor (3), Jeff Hall (17), Mike Hellawell (2), Emile Heskey (3), Harry Hibbs (25), Gil Merrick (23), Trevor Smith (2), Lew Stoker (3), Dan Tremelling (1), Matthew Upson (7)

Finland
Mikael Forrsell (2)

Ivory Coast
Olivier Tebily (4)

Jamaica
Michael Johnson (7)

Northern Ireland
Bobby Brennan (3), Jackie Brown (3), Ray Ferris (3), Damien Johnson (42), Jon McCarthy (5), Danny Sonner (1), Maik Taylor (54*)

Poland
Poitr Swierczewski (2)

Republic of Ireland
Eric Barber (1), Gary Breen (6), Tommy Carroll (9), Kenny Cunningham (32), Gerry Daly (5), Colin Doyle (2), Keith Fahey (2*), Don Givens (14), Jimmy Higgins (1), Stephen Kelly (5), David Langan (10), Clinton Morrison (2)

Scotland
Kenny Burns (8), Johnny Crosbie (1), Paul Devlin (10), Archie Gemmill (10), Jim Herriot (8), James McFadden (7*), Frank McGurk (1), Gary O'Connor (1)

Serbia
Nikola Zigic (3*)

Sweden
Sebastian Larsson (23*)

Trinidad & Tobago
Stern John (1)

Tunisia
Radhi Jaidi (4), Medhi Nafti (11)

Turkey
Muzzy Izzet (1)

Wales
Ernie Curtis (2), Don Dearson (3), George Edwards (6), Sidney Evans (1), Colin Green (15), Terry Hennessey (16), Billy Hughes (10), Caesar Jenkyns (4), Charlie Wilson Jones (1), Fred Jones (1), Noel Kinsey (3), Ken Leek (5), Andy Legg (2), Seymour Morris (5), Malcolm Page (28), Aubrey Powell (1), Tony Rees (1), Dai Richards (6), John Roberts (15), Robbie Savage (14), Gray Sprake (5), Byron Stevenson (4)

Zimbabwe
Peter Ndlovu (5)

Under-20

Argentina
Mauro Zarate (1)

England
Darren Carter (2), Asa Hall (5), Andrew Johnson (2), Neil Kilkenny (1)

Under-21 Internationals (from 1976)

England
Keith Bertschin (3), Alan Curbishley (1), Mark Dennis (3), Kevin Dillon (1), Howard Gayle (3), David Seaman (10)

Northern Ireland
David Howland (1)

Republic of Ireland
Colin Doyle (1), James O'Shea (6*), Marcus Painter (1)

Wales
Tony Rees (1)

Under-23 Internationals (1954–76)

England
Trevor Francis (5), Jimmy Greenhoff (4), Bob Latchford (2), Dick Neal (1), Trevor Smith (15)

Scotland
Kenny Burns (2), Jimmy Calderwood (1)

Wales
Gary Emmanuel (1), Colin Green (4), Terry Hennessey (6), Bryan Orritt (3), Malcolm Page (6)

B Internationals

England
Len Boyd (1), Joe Gallagher (1), Ken Green (2), Jeff Hall (1), Trevor Smith (2)

Great Britain (v Rest of Europe)
Billy Hughes (1)

United Kingdom (Olympic Games)
Wally Corbett (3)

Young England (v England)
Jeff Hall (1), Dick Neal (1), Trevor Smith (1)

FA XI
Gil Merrick (1)

FA Tours
Jeff Hall (1955 to West Indies), Wally Harris (1926 to Canada), Billy Harvey (1920 to South Africa), Harry Hibbs (1926 to Canada), Billy Smith (1951 to Australia), Ken Tewksbury (1931 to Canada), Frank Womack (1925 to Australia)

FA of Ireland
Ray Ferris (1953 tour to Canada)

Football League
Gordon Astall (1), Joe Bradford (5), Jack Glover (2), Ken Green (2), Tom Grosvenor (1), Fred Harris (1), Jeff Hall (1), Harry Hibbs (3), Harry Hooper (1), Billy Jones (1), Jack Jones (1), Alec McClure (1), Gil Merrick (11), Billy Morgan (1), Nat Robinson (2), Trevor Smith (2), Lew Stoker (1), Charlie Tickle (1), Dan Tremelling (2), Sid Wharton (1), Fred Wheldon (2), Walter Wigmore (1), Frank Womack (1)

Football League XI
Trevor Francis (1), Fred Wheldon (1), Frank Womack (1)

VICTORY AND WARTIME INTERNATIONALS

England
Billy Ball (1)

Scotland
Neil Dougall (1)

Wales
Don Dearson (15), George Edwards (2), Billy Hughes (14)

OTHER INTERNATIONALS (UNOFFICIAL)

England
Harry Hibbs (1) Alex Leake (1), Frank Mitchell (1), Billy Morgan (1), Billy Smith (1), Sid Wharton (1)

Scotland
Neil Dougall (1)

All-Ireland
Tommy Carroll (1)

APTC XI
Gil Merrick (1)

Birmingham Association
Will Edden (7), Billy Edmunds (4), Arthur James (2)

Players' Union XI
Walter Wigmore (1)

AMATEUR INTERNATIONALS

England
Horace Bailey (4), Wally Corbett (18), Billy Harvey (3), Sid Hauser (1), J. Slater (2), Ken Tewksbury (4)

INTERNATIONAL TRIALS

The Rest (v England)
Percy Barton (2), Joe Bradford (1), Wally Harris (1), Harry Hibbs (1), Lew Stoker (2)

England (v The Rest)
Percy Barton (1), Joe Bradford (1), Tom Grosvenor (1), Harry Hibbs (2)

North (v South)
Percy Barton (1), Joe Bradford (1), Billy Jones (1), Jack Jones (1), Alex Leake (1), Nat Robinson (1), Frank Stokes (1), Fred Wilcox (1)

South (v England)
Percy Barton (2), Frank Womack (1)

South (v North)
Frank Womack (1)

Anglo-Scots (v Home Scots)
Johnny Crosbie (3)

Professionals (v Amateurs)
Joe Bradford (1), Billy Harris (1), Nat Robinson (1), Frank Stokes (1), Frank Womack (1)

Possibles (v Probables)
Lew Stoker (1)

England Amateur (for North v South)
Tom Pointon (1)

Youth Internationals (Under-16, Under-17, Under-18)
England
Sone Aluko, Malcolm Beard, Ronnie Bird, Jack Butland, Darren Carter, Mark Dennis, Kevin Dillon, Neil Duce, Tony Elliott, Trevor Francis, Anthony Gibson, Asa Hall, Ian Handysides, Phil Hawker, Andrew Johnson, Davey Jones, Neil Kilkenny, Bob Latchford, Jordan Mutch, Sonny Parker, Stuart Parker, Paul Passey, Krystian Pearce, Steve Phillips, Graham Potter, Mick Rathbone, Nathan Redmond, Jonathan Roach, Matthew Sadler, Ashley Sammons, Steve Smith, Phil Summerill, Dennis Thwaites, Johnny Vincent, James Williams, Nigel Winterburn

New Zealand
James Haarhoff (1)

Northern Ireland
Frank McKeown (2)

Republic of Ireland
Colin Doyle, David Joyce, James O'Brien, Marcus Painter

Scotland
Andrew Barrowman

FA Youth XI
Ray Martin (1)

Staffordshire County & County FA
George Briggs, Dicky Dale, Billy Edmunds, Will Edden, Arthur James, David Keys, Jack Lee, James H. Sparrow

Schoolboy Internationals
* Several players represented their country when on schoolboy forms with Birmingham City.

The following players all won full international honours with other clubs either before joining or after leaving Blues:

Algeria	Hameur Bouazza
Argentina	Luciano Figueroa, Alberto Tarantini
Australia	Neil Kilkenny, Stan Lazaridis
Canada	Paul Fenwick, Lyndon Hooper, Paul Peschisolido
Cayman Islands	Isaiah Rankine
Czech Republic	Jiri Jarosik
Denmark	Nicklas Bendtner, Jesper Gronkjaer

Ecuador	Christian Benitez, Ulises De La Cruz, Giovanni Espinoza
England	Walter Abbott, Darren Anderton, Charlie Athersmith, Horace Bailey, Ray Barlow, Johnny Berry, Lee Bowyer, Barry Bridges, Frank Buckley, Nicky Butt, Michael Carrick, Gary Charles, Chris Charsley, Andy Cole, Jimmy Conlin, Tony Cottee, David Dunn, Ben Foster, Trevor Francis, Billy George, Harry Hampton, Mick Harford, Joe Hart, Emile Heskey, Dennis Hodgetts, Andrew Johnson, Bob Latchford, Alex Leake, Lewis Lodge, Tony Morley, Syd Owen, Mike O'Grady, Fred Pentland, Kevin Phillips, Fred Pickering, William C. Rose, David Seaman, Joe Smith, Chris Sutton, Bobby A. Thomson, Colin Todd, Tony Towers, Matthew Upson, Danny Wallace, Fred Wheldon, Jimmy Windridge, Nigel Winterburn, Peter Withe and Frank Worthington.
Finland	Mikael Forssell, Teemu Tianio
France	Christophe Dugarry, Olivier Kapo, Bruno N'Gotty, Franck Queudrue
Ghana	Richard Kingson, Quincy Owusu-Abeyei
Holland	Bud Brocken, Mario Melchiot, Toine Van Mierlo
Honduras	Carlos Costly, Wilson Palacios
Ivory Coast	Olivier Tebily
Jamaica	Michael Johnson, Darryl Powell
Liberia	Christopher Wreh
Mali	Djimi Traore
Nigeria	Sone Aluko, Folorunso Okenla
Northern Ireland	Gary Breen, Bobby Brennan, Jackie Brown, Tony Capaldi, Michael Hughes, Damien Johnson, Owen Madden, Jon McCarthy, Jimmy McLaughlin, Danny Sonner, Maik Taylor
Norway	Bjorn Otto Bragstad, Thomas Myhre
Poland	Arek Bak, Piotr Swierczewski
Portugal	Jose Dominguez
Republic of Ireland	Eric Barber, Gary Breen, Jackie Brown, Alex Bruce, Stephen Carr, Tommy Carroll, Lee Carsley, Kenny Cunningham, Garry Daly, Steve Finnan, Curtis Fleming, Don Givens, Alan Kelly, Stephen Kelly, Jeff Kenna, David Langan, Jim McDonagh, Owen Madden, Clinton Morrison, John Sheridan
St Lucia	Ken Charlery
Scotland	Bertie Auld, Jim Blyth, Des Bremner, Danny Bruce, Mark Burchill, Kenny Burns, John Connolly, Johnny Crosbie, Barry Ferguson, Archie Gemmill, Bobby Hope, Allan Johnston, Willie Johnston, Graham Leggatt, Nigel Quashie, Bruce Rioch, Billy Robb, James Robertson, David Speedie
Serbia	Nikola Zigic
Senegal	Aliou Cissé, Ferdinand Coly, Salif Diao
Spain	Borja Oubina
Sweden	Anders Limpar
Switzerland	Johan Djourou-Gradjere
Trinidad & Tobago	Stern John, Dwight Yorke
Tunisia	Radhi Jaidi, Medhi Nafti
Turkey	Muzzy Izzet
USA	Jovan Kirovski
Uruguay	Walter Pandiani
Wales	Jason Bowen, John Cornforth, Erbnie Curtis, Stan Davies, George Edwards, Len Evans, Robert Evans, David Giles, Jack Hallam, Terry Hennessey, Trevor Hockey, Brian Horne, Steve Jenkins, Caesar Jenkyns, Andy Legg, Noel Kinsey, Ken Leek, Andy Marriott, Charlie Phillips, Aubrey Powell, Dai Richards, John Roberts, Gray Sprake, Byron Stevenson, Martin Thomas, Pat Van den Hauwe
Zimbabwe	Peter Ndlovu

INTERNATIONAL TALK BACK

- Among other international footballers who have been associated with Birmingham City (not as players) are ex-managers Pat Beasley, Terry Cooper, Stan Cullis, Harry Storer and Sir Alf Ramsey (all England) and Willie Bell, Dave Mackay, Lou Macari and Alex McLeish (Scotland); assistant manager/coach Roy Aitken (Scotland) and coaches George Blackburn, Peter Bonetti, Tony Brown, Dave Fairhurst, Mick Mills, Nigel Spink and Chris Woods (all England), Bobby Ferguson (Scotland), Emilio Aldecoa Gomez (Spain) and Mark Bowen (Wales).
- The former Blues goalkeeper Mike Kelly was on the England coaching staff.
- Welshman Caesar Jenkyns was the first Blues player to represent his country in a full international (v Ireland at Bangor in February 1892).
- Goalkeeper Chris Charsley was the first Blues player to appear for England (v Ireland on 25 February 1893 at Perry Barr, Aston).
- Johnny Crosbie was the first Blues player to win a Scotland cap (v England in April 1922 at Villa Park).
- Jackie Brown was the first Irish international from Blues (capped against Scotland in 1938), and Jimmy Higgins was the first from the Republic of Ireland to gain international recognition (playing against Argentina in 1951).
- Trevor Smith was Birmingham's first England Under-23 player, capped v Italy in 1954, while the club's first Under-21 debutant was Keith Bertschin for England v Scotland in 1977.
- Len Boyd was the first B international capped as Blues player. He started for England against Holland in 1951–52.
- Blues' most-capped players (while at the club) have been goalkeeper Maik Taylor (55 for Northern Ireland at 2010), midfielder Damien Johnson (42 for Northern Ireland), winger Stan Lazaridis (33 for Australia), right-back Kenny Cunningham (32 for the Republic of Ireland), the versatile Malcolm Page (28 for Wales) and goalkeepers Harry Hibbs (25) and Gil Merrick (23) for England.
- Goalkeeper Harry Hibbs, with 25 appearances for his country, is Blues' most capped England player.
- Blues' forward Billy Smith scored 13 goals in five matches while on tour with the FA party in Australia in the summer of 1951.
- Blues' defender Don Dearson occupied eight different positions for Wales and Stan Davies six during their respective international careers. Davies actually took over in goal during one game.
- Dearson unfortunately missed a penalty for Wales against England in a wartime international at St Andrew's in 1941. England won 2–1.
- During 1897 and 1898, England inside-forward Fred Wheldon was on the winning side in each of his four internationals. He scored in three of them – netting a hat-trick in a 6–0 win over Ireland, hitting a brace in a 3–0 victory over Wales and notching one goal in the 3–1 triumph over Scotland.
- During their careers both Owen Madden and Jackie Brown won caps for Northern Ireland and the Republic of Ireland.
- Blues' winger Wallace Norman Harris made 12 appearances for the FA XI on their tour to Canada in 1926, scoring six goals.
- Harry Hibbs made 10 appearances for the FA side on the 1931 tour to Canada. He was accompanied to North America by Blues' reserve 'keeper Ken Tewkesbury, a student at Birmingham University who registered as an amateur at St Andrew's. He played in seven games.
- Radhi Jaidi has won over 100 caps for Tunisia and Stern John likewise for Trinidad & Tobago.
- Blues goalkeeper and Young Player of the Year for 2010, Jack Butland helped England Under-17s win the European Championship in 2010.

Blues in Local Competitions

Birmingham Senior Cup

Blues first entered this competition in 1878–79, losing 1–0 to Calthorpe in the opening round. Their first victory followed in October 1879 when they beat Wednesbury Old Athletic (away) 2–1.

In November 1886 Blues beat Coseley 13–0 – their biggest win in the competition. Three years earlier they had beaten Dudley 11–0 and in 1885 whipped Sandwell 10–3.

One of their heaviest defeats came at Wolves in 1896, when they lost 8–2 at Molineux.

Up to the mid-1920s, Blues usually fielded their strongest team, but thereafter their line-up comprised a mixture of first and second-team players. And since the late 1940s, to date, the reserves have mainly been in action, although for the 1983 and 1996 Finals against Aston Villa both teams put out strong sides. Ian Handysides scored the vital goal in 1983, and Jason Bowen and Ricky Otto were on target in 1996. Four players were sent-off in this latter Final – the Blues trio of John Cornforth, Ian Jones and Paul Peschisolido and Ben Petty of Villa.

The Birmingham Senior Cup is now called the Aston Villa Cup.

Blues have so far appeared in 15 Finals, the details of which are as follows:

Season	Opposition	Result		Att:
1904–05	West Bromwich Albion	won	7–2	8,500
1905–06	Aston Villa	lost	3–1	11,000
1906–07	Wolverhampton W	won	5–3	8,000
1914–15	Stoke	won	2–0	5,000
1919–20	Stoke reserves	won	3–0	3,000
1920–21	Stoke reserves	won	5–1	2,500
1921–22	Wellington Town	won	2–1	3,000
1982–83	Aston Villa	won	1–0	11,763
1991–92	VS Rugby	lost	3–0	1,000
1995–96	Aston Villa	won	2–0	1,773
1998–99	Wolverhampton W	won	4–1	1,324
1999–2000	Walsall	won	1–0	1,769
2002–03	Moor Green	won	2–0 (aet)	1,065
2004–05	Redditch United	lost	3–2	1,308
2007–08	Burton Albion	won	5–0	2,012

* Both clubs fielded their Youth teams in these two Finals.

Lord Mayor of Birmingham Charity Cup

This trophy was first played for in 1881–82, and since then Blues have appeared in 22 Finals, winning (or sharing the prize) on 12 occasions. Here are the results of all 22 Finals:

1891–92	Wolverhampton W	lost	2–1	4,000
1892–93	Aston Villa	lost	3–2	4,000
1894–95	Aston Villa	lost	5–3	7,000
1903–04	Aston Villa	lost	4–2	5,000
1904–05	Aston Villa	lost	1–0*	4,500
1905–06	Aston Villa	drew	1–1+	8,000
1906–07	Aston Villa	won	4–0	12,000
1907–08	Aston Villa	won	5–2	10,000

1909–10	Aston Villa	lost	2–1	12,500
1918–19	Aston Villa	won	4–1	6,116
1920–21	West Bromwich Albion	drew	2–2+	8,067
1921–22	West Bromwich Albion	lost	2–0	7,545
1923–24	Aston Villa	drew	3–3+	15,360
1924–25	West Bromwich Albion	lost	3–1	9,934
1926–27	Aston Villa	lost	4–2	9,798
1927–28	Aston Villa	lost	3–2	8,540
1928–29	Aston Villa	lost	2–1	11,220
1933–34	Aston Villa	won	2–0	10,876
1934–35	Aston Villa	won	2–1	6,334
1935–36	Aston Villa	won	4–2	5,509
1936–37	Aston Villa	drew	2–2+	10,144
1937–38	Coventry City	drew	1–1+	6,340

* This game was abandoned after 50 minutes, no result, trophy shared.
+ Trophy shared

Staffordshire Senior Cup

This is one of the oldest competitions in Midlands football. Prior to World War Two most clubs fielded their first team but since 1946, with the odd exception, all of the major League clubs have chosen their reserve side.

Blues have played in nine Staffordshire Cup Finals, the details of which are as follows:

1904–05	Wolverhampton W	won	4–0	3,000
1905–06	West Bromwich Albion	won	6–2	4,000
1908–09	Aston Villa	lost	5–0	6,000
1911–12	Burslem Port Vale	lost	2–0	6,000
1912–13	Aston Villa	lost	2–0†	4,500
1914–15	Aston Villa	won	1–0	3,000
1919–20	Port Vale	lost	1–0	4,000
1926–27	Walsall reserves	lost	2–1	2,000
1936–37	Wolverhampton W reserves	lost	4–1	2,000

† After 1–1 draw

Walsall Senior Cup

This was the first trophy won by Blues.
They have appeared in three Finals, as follows:

1882–83	Walsall Swifts	won	4–1	1,000
1900–01	West Bromwich A reserves	drew	1–1*	1,500
1903–04	West Bromwich A	won	5–0†	1,000

* Trophy shared
† After 0–0 draw

Lord Mayor of Coventry Cup

Blues entered this competition four times between the wars and reached the Final once.

1925–26	Coventry City (a)	drew	2–2*	4,000

* Each club held the Cup for six months.

MATCH SUMMARY

Summaries of all competitive games played by Blues: 1881 to 2010

Premier League (seasons 2002–06; 2007–08; 2009–10)

Venue	P	W	D	L	F	A
Home	114	44	38	32	143	118
Away	114	21	29	64	93	184
Totals	228	65	67	96	236	302

Football League (seasons 1892–1915; 1919–39; 1946–2002; 2006–07; 2008–09)

Venue	P	W	D	L	F	A
Home	2,065	1,078	503	484	3,720	2,271
Away	2,065	502	513	1,050	2,316	3,585
Totals	4,130	1,580	1,016	1,534	6,036	5,856

Football Alliance (seasons 1889–92)

Venue	P	W	D	L	F	A
Home	33	19	5	9	99	52
Away	33	6	7	20	56	117
Totals	66	25	12	29	155	169

FA Cup (seasons 1881–2010)

Venue	P	W	D	L	F	A
Home	167	98	*29	40	372	179
Away	139	44	31	64	187	218
Neutral	19	2	4	13	14	38
Totals	315	144	*64	117	573	435

* Won one game on penalties v Stoke City, 1973

Football League Cup (under various titles: seasons 1960–2010)

Venue	P	W	D	L	F	A
Home	88	51	14	23	169	98
Away	86	28	24	34	108	134
Neutral	2	1	*1	0	2	1
Totals	176	80	*39	57	279	233

* Lost one game on penalties, Final v Liverpool, 2001

Inter-Cities Fairs Cup (seasons 1955–62)

Venue	P	W	D	L	F	A
Home	12	10	2	0	29	11
Away	12	4	4	4	21	25
Neutral	1	0	0	1	0	1
Totals	25	14	6	5	51	38

Test Matches (seasons 1891–92, 1892–93, 1895–96)

Venue	P	W	D	L	F	A
Home	2	1	1	0	8	0
Away	2	0	0	2	0	7
Neutral	3	1	1	1	6	7
Totals	7	2	2	3	14	14

Play-offs (seasons 1998–2002)

Venue	P	W	D	L	F	A
Home	4	2	1	1	3	5
Away	4	2	0	2	4	4
Neutral	1	0	*1	0	1	1
Totals	9	4	*2	3	8	10

* Won one game on penalties, Final v Norwich City, 2002

Anglo-Italian Tournament (seasons 1971–72, 1992–94, 1995–96)

Venue	P	W	D	L	F	A
Home	9	4	*4	1	21	15
Away	8	4	1	3	7	9
Totals	17	8	*5	4	28	24

* Lost one game on penalties after draw v West Bromwich Albion, 1996

Anglo-Scottish Cup (seasons 1977–78, 1979–80)

Venue	P	W	D	L	F	A
Home	3	2	0	1	6	4
Away	3	0	3	0	3	3
Totals	6	2	3	1	9	7

Texaco Cup (seasons 1973–75)

Venue	P	W	D	L	F	A
Home	5	2	2	1	10	6
Away	7	0	6	1	4	6
Totals	12	2	8	2	14	12

Autoglass Trophy (season 1991–92)

Venue	P	W	D	L	F	A
Home	1	0	0	1	0	1
Away	1	0	0	1	1	3
Totals	2	0	0	2	1	4

Auto Windscreens Shield (season 1994–95)

Venue	P	W	D	L	F	A
Home	6	6	0	0	16	5
Away	1	1	0	0	5	3
Neutral	1	1	0	0	1	0
Totals	8	8	0	0	22	8

Full Members' Cup (season 1986–87)

Venue	P	W	D	L	F	A
Home	1	1	0	0	3	0
Away	1	0	0	1	2	3
Totals	2	1	0	1	5	3

Simod Cup (season 1987–88)

Venue	P	W	D	L	F	A
Away	2	0	0	2	1	9

Leyland DAF Trophy (seasons 1989–91)

Venue	P	W	D	L	F	A
Home	6	5	*1	0	10	2
Away	3	2	0	1	2	3
Neutral	1	1	0	0	3	2
Totals	10	8	*1	1	15	7

* Won one game on penalties after draw v Swansea City

Wartime (competition matches only)
1915–19

Venue	P	W	D	L	F	A
Home	53	38	8	7	134	55
Away	53	20	12	21	89	85
Totals	106	58	20	28	223	140

* Blues did not play any competitive matches in 1916–17

1939–46*

Venue	P	W	D	L	F	A
Home	99	67	14	18	238	104
Away	113	39	24	50	183	223
Neutral	3	1	1	1	7	8
Totals	215	107	39	69	428	335

*Blues did not play any competitive matches in 1941–42.
*FA Cup games played in 1945–46 not included.

OVERALL SUMMARY OF GAMES PLAYED:

Venue	P	W	D	L	F	A
Home	2,687	1,436	*631	620	5,000	2,956
Away	2,666	678	656	1,332	3,101	4,661
Neutral	31	7	*8	16	34	58
Totals	5,384	2,321	*1,295	1,968	8,135	7,675

BLUES' SENDINGS-OFF

Here is an unofficial list of Blues' players who have been sent-off in senior first team matches.

Premier League

Aliou Cissé	v Arsenal (a)	18 August 2002
Olivier Tebily	v West Brom Albion (a)	19 October 2002
Geoff Horsfield	v Charlton Athletic (a)	21 December 2002
Matthew Upson	v Newcastle United (a)	3 May 2003
Darren Purse	v Fulham (h)	14 September 2003
Maik Taylor	v Manchester United (a)	4 October 2003
Christophe Dugarry	v Blackburn Rovers (h)	6 December 2003
Maik Taylor	v Portsmouth (a)	12 April 2004
Kenny Cunningham	v Liverpool (h)	8 May 2004
Damien Johnson	v Charlton Athletic (h)	18 September 2004
Muzzy Izzet	v Everton (h)	13 November 2004
Damien Johnson	v Norwich City (a)	7 May 2005
Nicky Butt	v Portsmouth (a)	17 September 2005
Neil Kilkenny	v Liverpool (h)	24 September 2005
Kenny Cunningham	v Arsenal (a)	2 October 2005
Nico Vaesen	v Manchester City (a)	17 December 2005
Muzzy Izzet	v Tottenham Hotspur (a)	26 December 2005
Damien Johnson	v Liverpool (a)	1 February 2006
Emile Heskey	v Arsenal (h)	4 February 2006
Martin Taylor	v Arsenal (h)	23 February 2008
Franck Queudrue	v Manchester City (h)	29 March 2008
Damien Johnson	v Wigan Athletic (a)	5 April 2008
Barry Ferguson	v Manchester City (h)	1 September 2009

Football League/Championship

Caesar Jenkyns	v Liverpool (h)	14 October 1893
Caesar Jenkyns	v. Liverpool (h)	29 December 1894
Caesar Jenkyns	v Derby County (a)	30 March 1895
Sid Wharton	v Gainsborough Trinity (h)	19 January 1901
Walter Wigmore	v. Sunderland (a)	17 March 1906
Fred Chapple	v Wolverhampton W. (a)	13 February 1911
Wally Hastings	v Leeds City (a)	5 April 1912
James Bumphrey	v Barnsley (a)	11 October 1913
Jack Jones	v Rotherham County (a)	30 April 1921
Percy Barton	v Arsenal (a)	12 November 1921
Percy Barton	v Newcastle United (h)	26 August 1922
James Daws	v Newcastle United (a)	6 September 1922
Percy Barton	v Bolton Wanderers (a)	23 September 1922
Percy Barton	v Sunderland (h)	3 January 1925
Bertie Mills	v Burnley (a)	6 April 1929
Ned Barkas	v Burnley (a)	2 November 1929
Johnny Watts	v Everton (a)	14 November 1959
Jimmy Harris	v Newcastle United (h)	26 December 1960
Alex Harley	v Sheffield Wednesday (a)	28 September 1963
Bertie Auld	v Fulham (h)	21 December 1963
Terry Hennessey	v Stoke City (h)	11 April 1964
Bertie Auld	v Liverpool (h)	22 April 1964
Winston Foster	v Wolverhampton W. (a)	30 September 1964
Trevor Hockey	v Blackburn Rovers (a)	20 January 1968
Fred Pickering	v Crystal Palace (a)	17 August 1968
Ron Wylie	v Charlton Athletic (a)	20 August 1968
Johnny Vincent	v Blackburn Rovers (h)	18 January 1969

Malcolm Beard	v Millwall (a)	5 December 1970
Bob Latchford	v Middlesbrough (a)	4 December 1971
Bob Hatton	v Sheffield United (a)	17 February 1973
Archie Styles	v Carlisle United (a)	21 September 1974
Archie Styles	v Manchester United (a)	31 January 1976
Gary Jones	v Arsenal (a)	6 November 1976
Joe Gallagher	v Aston Villa (h)	10 May 1977
Garry Pendrey	v Liverpool (h)	9 September 1978
Garry Pendrey	v Coventry City (a)	28 October 1978
Mark Dennis	v Wolves (a)	26 December 1978
Mark Dennis	v Wolves (h)	14 April 1979
Colin Todd	v Charlton Athletic (a)	2 February 1980
Colin Todd	v West Ham United (a)	22 April 1980
Mark Dennis	v Nottingham Forest (a)	28 August 1980
Frank Worthington	v Everton (a)	29 November 1980
Mark Dennis	v Southampton (h)	10 October 1981
Kevan Broadhurst	v West Brom Albion (a)	20 March 1982
Kevin Dillon	v Stoke City (h)	4 September 1982
Jim Blyth	v Nottingham Forest (a)	16 October 1982
David Langan	v Stoke City (a)	3 January 1983
Mark Dennis	v Notts County (h)	26 March 1983
Robert Hopkins	v Notts County (a)	30 August 1983
Mick Harford	v Stoke City (a)	17 March 1984
Mick Harford	v Sunderland (a)	28 April 1984
Robert Hopkins	v Portsmouth (h)	18 September 1984
Ken Armstrong	v Everton (a)	31 August 1985
Wayne Clarke	v Newcastle United (h)	9 November 1985
Steve Whitton	v Sheffield United (a)	6 September 1986
Tommy Williams	v Crystal Palace (a)	14 March 1987
Vince Overson	v Blackburn Rovers (h)	15 September 1987
Vince Overson	v West Brom Albion (h)	15 October 1988
Kevin Langley	v Leyton Orient (a)	28 April 1990
Trevor Matthewson	v West Brom Albion (h)	8 February 1992
Mark Cooper	v Stockport County (a)	2 March 1992
Ian Clarkson	v Bristol City (a)	7 November 1992
Darren Rowbotham	v Bristol City (a)	7 November 1992
John Gayle	v Swindon Town (a)	12 January 1993
Darren Rogers	v Derby County (h)	6 April 1993
Paul Mardon	v Sunderland (a)	9 October 1993
Chris Whyte	v Bolton Wanderers (h)	19 October 1993
Dave Barnett	v West Brom Albion (h)	28 December 1993
Andy Saville	v Southend United (a)	1 January 1994
Steve Claridge	v Watford (a)	15 January 1994
Gary Cooper	v Watford (a)	15 January 1994
Dave Barnett	v Derby County (a)	26 February 1994
Gary Cooper	v Brighton & Hove A (h)	29 April 1995
Gary Poole	v Manchester City (a)	21 September 1996
Paul Devlin	v Bolton Wanderers (h)	13 November 1996
Martin Grainger	v Bolton Wanderers (a)	1 February 1997
Martin O'Connor	v Crystal Palace (a)	29 March 1997
Paul Furlong	v Huddersfield Town (h)	12 April 1997
Darren Wassall	v Sheffield United (a)	27 September 1997
Paul Furlong	v Reading (a)	31 January 1998
Chris Marsden	v Reading (a)	31 January 1998
Michael Johnson	v Nottingham Forest (a)	21 March 1998
Simon Charlton	v Swindon Town (h)	20 October 1998
Peter Ndlovu	v Huddersfield Town (h)	31 October 1998
Graham Hyde	v Norwich City (h)	2 March 1999
Gary Rowett	v Huddersfield Town (a)	20 March 1999
Graham Hyde	v Bolton Wanderers (a)	5 September 1999
Darren Purse	v Portsmouth (a)	6 November 1999
Martyn O'Connor	v Wolves (h)	1 April 2000

Bryan Hughes	v Wolves (h)	1 April 2000
Martin Grainger	v Gillingham (a)	2 December 2000
Martin Grainger	v Walsall (a)	25 August 2001
Danny Sonner	v Walsall (a)	25 August 2001
Danny Sonner	v West Brom Albion (h)	7 November 2001
Curtis Woodhouse	v Millwall (a)	10 January 2002
Darren Purse	v Sheffield United (h)	21 April 2002
Cameron Jerome	v Colchester United (h)	5 August 2006
Nicklas Bendtner	v Queens Park Rangers (a)	12 September 2006
Bruno N'Gotty	v Ipswich Town (h)	16 September 2006
Damien Johnson	v Leeds United (a)	23 September 2006
Radhi Jaidi	v Hull City (a)	24 February 2007
Gary McSheffrey	v Derby County (h)	9 March 2007
Julian Gray	v West Brom Albion (a)	18 March 2007
Neil Danns	v Barnsley (a)	9 April 2007
Fabrice Muamba	v Sheffield Wednesday (h)	28 April 2007
Medhi Nafti	v Doncaster Rovers (h)	13 September 2008
Nigel Quashie	v Charlton Athletic (h)	15 November 2008
David Murphy	v Swansea City (h)	28 December 2008
Lee Carsley	v Wolverhampton W. (h)	6 April 2009
Maik Taylor	v Plymouth Argyle (h)	13 April 2009
Lee Bowyer	v Preston North End (h)	25 April 2009

FA Cup

Walter Wigmore	v Manchester United (h)	16 December 1903
Billy Morgan	v Liverpool (h)	21 February 1920
Mark Cooper	v Torquay United (a)	16 November 1991
Martin Thomas	v Reading (a)	15 November 1992
Paul Devlin	v Wrexham (h)	15 February 1997
Aliou Cissé	v Sunderland (a)	3 February 2004
Radhi Jaidi	v Newcastle United (h)	6 January 2007

League Cup

Kevan Broadhurst	v Nottingham Forest (h)	28 October 1981
Mickey Halsall	v Plymouth Argyle (a)	9 October 1984
Tony Rees	v West Brom Albion (a)	7 November 1984
Eamonn Dolan	v Exeter City (a)	21 August 1991
Paul Tait	v Aston Villa (a)	6 October 1993
Gary Cooper	v Tranmere Rovers (h)	24 October 1995
Gary Poole	v Norwich City (h)	24 January 1996
Darren Wassall	v Arsenal (a)	14 October 1997
Geoff Horsfield	v Preston North End (h)	5 November 2002

Inter-Cities Fairs Cup

Bryan Orritt	v Zagreb XI (h)	3 December 1956
Trevor Smith	v Dinamo Zagreb (a)	24 May 1959
Johnny Gordon	v Ujpesti Dosza (a)	26 October 1960
Jimmy Harris	v RCD Espanyol (h)	7 December 1961
Bertie Auld	v RCD Espanyol (h)	7 December 1961

Anglo-Italian Cup

David Speedie	v AS Bari (h)	11 November 1992
Louie Donowa	v AS Bari (h)	11 November 1992
John Gayle	v Luchesse (a)	6 December 1992

Auto Windscreens Shield

Chris Whyte	v Swansea City (h)	31 January 1995

Football League Play-offs

David Holdsworth	v Watford (h)	20 May 1999

Others

Alex McClure	v Real Madrid (a) Fr	1 July 1923
Garry Pendrey	v Holland Sports (a) Fr	5 August 1970
Trevor Hockey	v RFC Haarlem (a) Fr	9 August 1970
Don Givens	v Real Zaragoza (a) LLT	5 August 1978
Keith Bertschin	v FC Groningen (a) Fr	8 August 1981
John Cornforth	v Aston Villa (h) BSC	8 May 1996
Ian Jones	v Aston Villa (h) BSC	8 May 1996
Paul Peschisolido	v Aston Villa (h) BSC	8 May 1996

Fact File

- Damien Johnson has been sent off a record five times during his Blues career.
- Blues had a record seven sendings-off in season 2005–06, all in the Premier League.
- Five different Blues players were sent off in Inter-Cities Fairs Cup games over a period of five years: 1956–61. Two were dismissed in the same match.
- Trevor Matthewson was ordered-off as early as the 12th minute of the home League game with West Bromwich Albion in February 1992 – possibly the earliest ever dismissal of a Blues player at competitive level.
- Malcolm Beard's dismissal at Millwall in 1970 came in his last match for Blues.
- Mark Dennis was sent-off in both home and away League games against Wolves in season 1978–79 – the only Blues player to meet this fate! Dennis was sent off 14 times during his professional career.
- Scottish international left-winger Willie Johnston was dismissed on 22 occasions during his playing days. He assisted Blues in 1979–80.
- Utility forward Roy McDonough, a Blues player in the mid-1970s, was sent off 21 times during his 23-year playing career from 1974–97.
- Winger Peter Ndlovu was sent off for 'diving' versus Huddersfield Town in October 1998. His red card was later rescinded.
- Aliou Cisse was sent off in Blues' first-ever Premier League game against Arsenal at The Emirates Stadium in August 2002. His red card was also rescinded on appeal.
- Four players were sent off in the Birmingham Senior Cup final of 1996 between Blues and Aston Villa at St Andrew's – three from the home side, plus Ben Petty of Aston Villa.
- Defender Alex McClure was sent off in Blues' friendly against Real Madrid in Spain in 1923 for telling his goalkeeper Dan Tremelling where to stand when facing a penalty!
- The first player to be sent off while representing Wales in a full international was future Blues midfielder Trevor Hockey, then of Norwich City, who was dismissed against Poland in September 1973.
- Before joining Blues, Byron Stevenson was sent off playing for Wales against Turkey in 1979.
- Jason Crowe, making his Arsenal debut as a last-minute substitute against Blues in a League Cup tie in October 1997, was sent off 33 seconds into extra-time, having touched the ball just once.
- Jim Smith (Newcastle United) was dismissed in the very first minute of the Texaco Cup encounter with Blues at St James' Park in December 1973 – probably the quickest sending off ever in a game involving Blues.

BLUES' ODDITIES

- Blues were disqualified from the FA Cup in 1890–91 after it was revealed they had fielded an ineligible player (Charlie Short) in their 2–0 win over Wednesbury Old Athletic. Short was not registered at the time.
- Hibbs was the only footballer to receive a testimonial during World War Two – Blues against Aston Villa in April 1940.
- Brothers Ted and Will Devey each scored four goals in Blues' 9–0 FA Cup win over Burton Wanderers on 8 December 1888 – a competition record.
- Don Dearson and Stan Davies, who both played for Birmingham and Wales, appeared in every position between them in full internationals. Davies acted as a stand-in goalkeeper.
- Ron Saunders managed three League clubs, all in the Midlands, that were within a five-mile radius of each other – Aston Villa, Blues and West Bromwich Albion.
- In the late 1940s/early 1950s manager Harry Storer signed Martin O'Donnell three times for three different clubs. He secured his services for Coventry City, Blues and Derby County.
- Manager Arthur Turner did a similar thing when he signed forward Bill Finney for Blues, Stoke City and Crewe Alexandra in the 1950s.
- Blues pipped Aston Villa by 0.206 of a goal to win the Football League (South) Championship in 1945–46.
- Chris Charsley kept goal for Blues in 1886–87, played for England at both amateur and senior levels and was a police officer who later became Chief Constable of Coventry.
- Winger Jock Mulraney scored twice in the space of 70 first-half seconds of Blues' fourth-round first-leg FA Cup clash against Watford at St Andrew's on 26 January 1946. Just 20 seconds after that he struck a post…if he had scored it would have been the quickest hat-trick ever recorded in first-class football. Blues won the game 5–0, and Jock eventually knocked in his third goal late on.
- A friendly between Walsall Town and Blues in August 1882 was abandoned after 70 minutes when players complained of heat exhaustion. Blues were leading 4–3 at the time.
- After the end of his playing career, Gary Charles, who was on loan to Blues in 2000, struggled with alcoholism. He was twice imprisoned – first for drink driving and soon afterwards for cutting off his electronic tag to go on holiday to the Costa del Sol. Then, in September 2005, he was arrested and charged with assault on a woman in a taxi office in Clay Cross, Derbyshire. However, after the jury failed to reach a verdict, a retrial was ordered. Between the trials Charles was jailed again, this time for turning up at court in a drunken state. At a later hearing, he admitted he had an on-going drink problem, and after being found guilty he was subsequently fined and handed a suspended sentence and a community service order. In December 2006, Charles was in trouble again. This time he was jailed for 12 months after committing a public order offence.

- Blues have achieved something which very few other clubs have failed to do – beat the top two clubs in Spain! They twice defeated Real Madrid in home and away friendlies in the mid-1920s and then, in an Inter-Cities Fairs Cup game in 1957, they were 4–3 victors over Barcelona at St Andrew's.

- Outside-left Alex Govan scored five hat-tricks in competitive matches for Blues in season 1956–57 – no other winger has achieved such a feat. Some 50 years or so earlier, in 1898–99, Blues forward Walter Abbott netted a club record six hat-tricks (five in the League, one in the FA Cup) and in September 1929 Joe Bradford hit three hat-tricks for Blues and one (five goals) for the Football League against the Irish League. He ended that campaign with four trebles for Blues.

- Three other players have scored four hat-tricks in a season for Blues – Frank Mobley in 1893–94, Joe Godfrey in 1918–19 (wartime) and Cyril Trigg in 1944–45 (also in wartime). Joe Bradford holds the record for most hat-tricks for the club in all competitions – total 13 (12 League, one FA Cup). Trigg claimed a total of 12 (two League, 10 wartime).

- In 1941–42 Blues opted out of playing in the Regional League and Cup competitions. They chose to play friendly matches instead – when a team could be assembled!

- In 1930, Blues manager Leslie Knighton had a bid of £10,000 turned down by Arsenal for inside-forward Alex James.

- In the early 1930s Blues had four England 'international' goalkeepers on their books – Harry Hibbs and Dan Tremelling (full), Ken Tewksbury (amateur) and Arthur Slater (junior).

- Blues signed Argentinian striker Luciano Figueroa in 2002 from Rosario Central – after UEFA cancelled his transfer to the Spanish club Osasuna.

- The only Blues player to score in the penalty shoot-out in both the Worthington Cup Final of 2001 and League Play-off Final in 2002 was Stan Lazaridis.

- David Wiseman and his son, Jack, were associated with Birmingham City Football Club for a total of 103 years. David, an OBE, was a director from 1928 to 1976 and club president until his death in 1978, at the age of 93. Jack became a director in 1956 and was later chairman and vice-chairman. He was 92 when he died in 2009 while still in office. Jack's son, Michael, a director at St Andrew's since 1997, is now the club's vice-president.

- Goalkeeper Gil Merrick served Blues as a player for a record 22 years (1938–60). Full-back Frank Womack spent almost 20 years at St Andrew's (1908–28) and the versatile Cyril Trigg was a Blues player for 19 years (1935–54).

- The last-ever game played at the club's old ground, Muntz Street, was a Birmingham League fixture against West Bromwich Albion on 25 December 1906. A crowd of 1,200 saw Blues win 5–2.

BIRMINGHAM CITY FIRSTS

- The first goal scored for Blues (Small Heath) was in the 12-a-side friendly 2–2 draw with Holte Wanderers on 30 November 1875.
- Eddie Stanley scored Blues' first FA Cup hat-trick – in a 9–2 home win over Burton Wanderers on 31 October 1885.
- Blues won their first-ever League game on 3 September 1892 against Burslem Port Vale by 5–1 before a crowd of 2,500.
- Will Devey became the first Blues player to score as many as six goals in a competitive game when he struck a double hat-trick in the 12–0 Alliance League win over Nottingham Forest on 8 March 1890.
- Arsenal's first-ever competitive game was an FA Cup tie against Blues on 16 January 1892. The match kicked off 25 minutes late due to the referee losing his way to the ground, and after Chris Charsley had saved Bernard Shaw's weak penalty (the first given away by Blues in a senior game, incidentally) the Gunners were eventually blitzed away to the tune of 5–1.

RESERVES, ACADEMY & YOUTH TEAMS

Blues' second XI was first established in 1879 and for several years played only friendly matches. Today the reserves play in the Premier Reserve League (South).

The club's Academy, which was established in its current form in 1999, trains boys in age groups from Under-9s through to Under-18s, running a team covering the latter age-group in the Premier Academy League.

Blues' reserves were initially based in the Birmingham & District League (from 1893), and finished runners-up in their third season, repeating the feat in 1907 and 1921. In 1915 they were runaway winners of the League, scoring 160 goals in 34 games with Charlie Duncan netting a record 52.

In 1921–22, following the reorganisation associated with the formation of the Third Division North, Blues' second string joined the Central League, which consisted at the time of reserve teams of the majority of the Northern-based Football League clubs.

However, in 1947–48 Blues lost their place to Barnsley and as a result joined the Football Combination, the equivalent reserve League for teams in the southern half of the country. They eventually rejoined an expanded Central League in 1982.

Since 1999–2000, the competition in which the second team plays depends on the standing of the club's first team. Relegation from the Premier League for the first team in 2006 meant that Blues' reserves dropped out of the Premier Reserve League into the Central League, which they won at the first attempt and were subsequently promoted back to the Premier League. And it has been up and down again since then.

Nowadays, the club enters its reserve XI in the Birmingham Senior (Aston Villa) Cup, which it has won on 12 occasions, most recently in 2008 when Burton Albion were thrashed 5–0 (see Blues in Other Competitions).

The reserve team's playing staff consists of younger players and those on the fringe of the first-team squad, augmented by first-team players recovering from injury and academy players gaining experience. The team plays most of its matches at Damson Park, the home ground of Solihull Motors, yet occasionally they do play at St Andrew's…and when they do, there is usually a high attendance present. The Academy team uses the club's training ground at Wast Hills, Kings Norton, for their home games.

At the start of the 2010–11 season, Richard Beale was acting manager of Blues' second team, while Terry Westley was in charge of the club's Academy. First-team coaches Andy Watson and Peter Grant are also involved with the players. The players' fitness coach is Andy Kalinins, and the goalkeeping coach is Dave Watson (ex-Barnsley).

FA YOUTH CUP

The FA Youth Challenge Cup is a competition run by the Football Association for Under-18 sides. Only those players between the age of 15 and 18 on 31 August of the current season are eligible to take part. It is dominated by the youth sides of professional teams, mostly from the Premier League, but attracts over 400 entrants from throughout the country.

Blues' youngsters have reached the final of the competition just once, in season 1966–67. Their opponents, Sunderland, ran out clear winners over two legs, winning 1–0 at St Andrew's and by the same score at Roker Park. The Blues team for both games was: Dave Latchford; Reynolds, Beckett; Lee, Saunders, Garry Pendrey; Rushworth, Dorsett, Bob Latchford, Keith Bowker and Jones. Colin Suggett, Billy Hughes and Derek Forster were in Sunderland's line-up.

In 1984–85 Blues reached the semi-final stage but once again fell victims to a team from the North-East, this time losing over two legs to Newcastle United. It was more semi-final disappointment for Blues as recently as 2008–09, when once again they succumbed at the semi-final stage, going down 6–1 on aggregate to a strong Liverpool team who won 3–0 at St Andrew's and 3–1 at Anfield. Manchester United knocked Blues out of the competition three times in six seasons, winning 3–2 in 2001–02, 2–0 in 2005–06 and 2–0 again in the quarter-finals in 2006–07.

Several players have progressed through Birmingham City's youth team to become full internationals, among them four England stars: Trevor Francis, Andrew Johnson, Bob Latchford and Nigel Winterburn.

No Mean Rivals
Birmingham City v Aston Villa

The two 'second city' clubs first met in a friendly on 27 September 1879, Blues (Small Heath) winning by 'one goal and a disputed goal to nil'. Aston Villa won the first competitive game – a second-round FA Cup tie played at their Wellington Road ground on 5 November 1887 – by 4–0, and the Villans also triumphed in the first-ever League encounter, winning a Division One match 2–1 on 1 September 1894. The return fixture, later in the month, ended 2–2 when both teams converted a penalty.

On 7 September 1895 10 goals (the most in any Blues-Villa game) were scored in the First Division fixture at Wellington Road. Villa won 7–3 in front of 14,000 fans. The return fixture at Muntz Street, seven weeks later, resulted in a 4–1 win for Villa.

Blues' first League win over Villa came on 16 September 1905 – 2–0 at Muntz Street. The first 'Birmingham' derby at St Andrew's took place on 19 January 1907 when a crowd of 45,000 saw Villa win 3–2. In a League game at Villa Park on 17 October 1925 Blues were trailing 3–0 with 11 minutes remaining, yet rallied and scored three times in a dramatic final spell to draw the match.

In 1928 Villa made headlines by signing centre-forward Tom 'Pongo' Waring from Tranmere Rovers. He made his first appearance in a claret-and-blue shirt in a reserve game at St Andrew's against Birmingham which attracted a crowd of 23,000. Waring scored a hat-trick in a 6–3 win.

The last League game before World War Two took place at Villa Park on 4 March 1939. Blues were outplayed as Jackie Martin scored a hat-trick in Villa's 5–1 win before a crowd of 40,874.

Blues beat Villa 2–1 in a 'farewell' match for goalkeeper Harry Hibbs in April 1940. This was the only wartime benefit game. Blues and Villa battled it out for the Football League (South) title in 1945–46. In the end it was Blues who took the prize, edging out their arch-rivals by just 0.206 of a goal. The most significant clash, however, certainly in recent times, was the 1963 League Cup Final, which took place not long after Villa had whipped Blues 4–0 in a League game. Blues won the two-legged encounter 3–1 on aggregate to claim their only major domestic honour to date.

The first-ever Second Division meeting between the clubs took place on 7 October 1967 when Blues won 4–2 at Villa Park in front of 50,067 fans. During the late 1970s and early 1980s Blues and Villa met regularly in the First Division, and there were some tremendous battles. Blues won 3–2 at St Andrew's in April 1976, completed the double over their arch-rivals in 1976–77 and 1977–78, lost twice to Villa in 1978–79 and again in 1980–81 (the season when Villa won the League title).

Reigning European Cup champions Villa were then beaten 3–0 in December 1982, 2–1 in March 1984 and 3–0 again in a vital relegation encounter at Villa Park in March 1986. In-form Villa whipped Blues 7–0 on aggregate in a 1988–89 League Cup tie, and in the same season Blues crashed 6–0 at Villa Park in a Simod Cup game.

Although the Premier League was introduced in 1992, it was 10 years before Blues and Villa met at this level. Then, in 2002–03, it was Blues who came out on top, winning 3–0 at home (when Villa 'keeper Peter Enckleman conceded a bizarre own-goal from a throw-in) and 2–0 away when Villa had two players sent off – Dion Dublin for head-butting Robbie Savage and Joey Guðjónsson for a reckless two-footed tackle on Matthew Upson.

Blues doubled up again in 2004–05, winning 2–1 at Villa Park and 2–0 at St Andrew's. The very next season Villa responded with a double over Villa! The local derby on 20 April 2008 ended in a 5–1 home victory for Villa, the biggest winning margin for either side in a League match for 40 years. Unfortunately, and certainly disappointingly for Blues fans, the last two meetings, in 2009–10, ended in two 1–0 wins for Villa who, in fact, have won the last six League meetings between the two clubs.

Players who have appeared for both clubs at competitive level

Malcolm Beard, Noel Blake, Frank Buckley, Frank Carrodus, Fred Chapple, Gary Charles, Wally Corbett, Frank Cornan, Will Devey, Edmund Eyre, Fred Foxall, Billy George, Cammie Fraser, Craig Gardner, David Geddis, Harry Hampton, Charles Hare, Roly Harper, Tony Hateley, Trevor Hockey, Dennis Hodgetts, Robert Hopkins, Lee Jenkins, Mark Jones, Jack Kearns, Alec Leake, Albert Lindon, Ivor Linton, Stan Lynn, Alex McClure, Ray Martin, Charlie Millington, Tony Morley, Dennis Mortimer, Jock Mulraney, Jim Murray, Charlie Phillips, Kevin Phillips, Arthur Phoenix, Kevin Poole, Tony Rees, Liam Ridgewell, Bruce Rioch, Phil Robinson, John Slueewenhoek, Bryan Small, Chris Sutton, Ken Tewksbury, Bobby Thomson, George Travers, Geoff Vowden, Fred Wheldon, Jack Wilcox, Peter Withe, Colin Withers and Ron Wylie.

* Several players from both clubs guested for their opposite number during both wars. Ron Saunders managed both clubs; Bob Brocklebank played for Villa and managed Blues; Harry Parkes played for Villa and was a director of both clubs; ex-Blues star Don Dorman scouted for both clubs; Doug Ellis was a director of Blues and director and chairman of Villa; Graham Leggatt played for Blues and coached at Villa; Keith Bradley and Keith Leonard both played for Villa and later coached with Blues; and Ray Shaw was a Blues player and trainer and Villa trainer and physiotherapist.

Blues' Playing Record against Aston Villa
League/Premier League

Venue	P	W	D	L	F	A
Home	54	22	13	19	80	72
Away	54	14	14	26	68	94
Totals	108	36	27	45	148	166
FA Cup						
Home	2	0	1	1	0	4
Away	1	0	0	1	0	1
Totals	3	0	1	2	0	5
League Cup						
Home	3	1	0	2	3	4
Away	3	0	1	2	0	6
Totals	6	1	1	4	3	10
Simod Cup						
Away	1	0	0	1	0	6
Wartime						
Home	7	4	1	2	11	10
Away	8	1	2	5	7	18
Totals	15	5	3	7	18	28

Overall Record

H/A	133	42	32	59	169	215

Blues Extra
Message From The Club President

In an interview with Blues' press officer Chris Kershaw and *Birmingham Mail* journalist Colin Tattum during the club's pre-season trip to the Far East in 2010, President Carson Yeung talked about the ongoing pride he has in being the owner of Birmingham City.

'I am proud to be the first Chinese owner of a Premier League club' said Mr Yeung from inside his exquisite home in Hong Kong.

'I am very happy about this. I am very happy for our race, our country and what I bought is exactly what I wanted to do.

'Birmingham is very popular already in Hong Kong and China. And my dream is that I will promote Birmingham City to be a strong team in a few years. But I am not in a rush at the moment. I have said before that I would buy good players for not just this season, but for many seasons.

'It is important my team is strong in the future. We have to do it by steps. I don't want us to be number one tomorrow; it has to be done by steps.

'The team is going better each day; that is the right way for us to improve.'

Mr Yeung added: 'Maybe a quarter, or maybe even a half, of my life is to do with Birmingham City. It's because I love the club.

'Yes, sure I am here for the long-term. Some people might not think this, but it's true.

'The fact is, you can see it. By what has been done so far and what we are trying to do.

'All the fans love me now, they know me. I'm a "work-hard" guy. I think they know what I am like.

'My business holds 96 per cent of the football club. We try to put in a lot of effort, to help the management and the team.

'Last season, you have to respect what we did. But this season, we want to be doing even better.

'Now we have bought in a few players, we would also like to increase our options by signing a midfielder, a left-back and even a right-back for my target team.'

The amiable but extremely focused club President finished with this message to all Blues' fans: 'I'll take care of you and will make you very happy. I'll make Birmingham City a successful club, now and in the future.'

Pass Master

Barry Ferguson attempted more passes – over 2,000 – than any other player in the Premier League in 2009–10. A total of 1,372 were completed.

New Recruit

Alex McLeish secured striker Matt Derbyshire on a season's loan from Olympiakos in mid-August 2010. Born in Blackburn on 14 April 1986, he played for Great Harwood Town, Blackburn Rovers, Plymouth Argyle (loan) and Wrexham (loan) before joining Olympiakos CFP, also on loan, in January 2009. Five months later, having helped his team win the Greek League and Cup double, he signed for the Piraeus club on a permanent basis. When Derbyshire arrived at St Andrew's he had already netted 55 goals in 143 club appearances.

On Loan

Midfielder Jordon Mutch joined Championship side Watford on loan in August 2010. He assisted both Doncaster Rovers and Hereford United in 2009–10.

Also in August, Jake Jervis agreed a six-month loan spell with Notts County.

Good Start

With Ben Foster and substitute Nikola Zigic making their debuts, Blues started the 2010–11 Premier League campaign with a spirited 2–2 draw at Sunderland, managed by former St Andrew's favourite Steve Bruce. 2–0 down, and playing against 10 men following Lee Cattermole's sending-off, Alex McLeish's side fought back to earn a point with late goals from Scott Dann (77 minutes) and Liam Ridgewell (88).

A week later Foster brilliantly saved Morten Gamst Pedersen's penalty, Matt Derbyshire made his debut against his old club and Craig Gardner scored twice as Blues beat Blackburn Rovers 2–1.

Next up in the League it was Bolton Wanderers, followed by West Bromwich Albion, Wigan and then Everton and Arsenal. The first 'second-city' derby of the season, at Villa Park, was set for 30 October.

Experience In Depth

At the start of 2010–11, Blues' first-team players had accumulated over 5,000 League appearances between them. Leading the way was Maik Taylor with a total of 569, followed by Kevin Phillips, 480, Marcus Bent 465, Lee Bowyer 432, Barry Ferguson 363, Stephen Carr 353, Roger Johnson 314, James McFadden 251, Gary O'Connor 225, Cameron Jerome 214, Liam Ridgewell 186, David Murphy 174, Sebastian Larsson 152, Michel 147, Stuart Parnaby 139, Scott Dann 136, Nikola Zigic 109, Ben Foster 107, Keith Fahey 76, Craig Gardner 72, Colin Doyle 41, Jordon Mutch 21, James O'Shea 11 and Enric Valles 4.

* Matt Derbyshire arrived at the club with 112 League appearances under his belt.

MANAGER OF THE MONTH

Alex McLeish was named Premier League Manager of the Month for December 2009.

PLAYER OF THE YEAR

Barry Ferguson was voted Blues' players' Player of the Year for 2009–10.

INTERNATIONAL ROUND-UP

Goalkeeper Jack Buckland, aged 17 years and 6ft 3in tall, was upgraded to Under-21 level by England's Academy manager and ex-Blues defender Noel Blake for the game against Slovakia on 2 September. He faced his St Andrew's colleague Jakub Hronec during the match.

Ben Foster was set to keep goal for England in the friendly with Hungary at Wembley in early August but withdrew through injury. Former Blues loanee Joe Hart took over and played well in a 2–1 win.

CLUB BADGES

Birmingham City has had three different official club crests. From 1905 (the year City was added to the club's name) until 1972, the Birmingham coat of arms was the badge on the players' shirts, although it was not always displayed in competitive matches. The second crest – designed by Burntwood-based Blues fan Michael Wood – was formed by intertwining the letters 'BCFC' and was featured in the centre of the player's penguin-design shirts. This remained as the club's official badge/logo for only five years. The club's third and current badge has been in evidence for 33 years and is universally known as the 'Globe Crest', recognised throughout the footballing world.

MILESTONE

During the 2010–11 season Blues will play Liverpool for the 100th time at League level. They were scheduled to meet Roy Hodgson's team at St Andrew's for the 99th meeting on 11 September and at Anfield on 23 April 2011.

Season 2010–11 will see Aston Villa, Birmingham City, West Bromwich Albion and Wolverhampton Wanderers play against each other in top-flight football for the first time in 27 years. They last met in 1983–84 when Liverpool won the Championship and Blues and Wolves were relegated!

First Meeting

Blues met Rochdale for the first time in the club's history in the second round of the Carling sponsored League Cup in August 2010. A crowd of 6,431 at St Andrew's saw Blues win 3–2, with McFadden (pen), Murphy and Derbyshire the goalscorers.

Blues Ladies FC

For information regarding women's football, please contact:
Birmingham City Ladies
c/o Stratford Town FC
Knights Lane, Tiddington
Stratford-upon-Avon, Warwickshire
CV37 7B
Tel: 01789 269336

Deadline Day Deals

Blues manager Alex McLeish expressed his delight at signing no fewer than three international players on the final day of the August 2010 transfer window. The triple swoop saw the club land the services of the Belarus midfielder and former Arsenal star Alexander Hleb on a season-long loan from Barcelona.

Czech Republic international Martin Jiranek arrived for an undisclosed fee on a one-year deal from Spartak Moscow and Chilean winger Jean Beausejour was secured from Club America of Mexico on a three-year contract.

A delighted McLeish said: 'We've been working hard for a long time to enhance the squad and bring in extra quality and in the players we have signed today we believe we have done exactly that as all of them are international players.

'Competition for places is becoming intense and that can only be good. It keeps everyone on their toes. Building a squad is an ongoing process and is something we'll continue to work hard to do.

'I'd like to take this opportunity to thank the club's Board for their support in helping me bring players to the club during the transfer window.'

Hleb and Beausejour are the first to play for Blues from Belarus and Chile. Jiri Jarosik was the first from the Czech Republic.

ALSO: on 31 August 2010, Blues' striker Marcus Bent joined Wolverhampton Wanderers on a four-month loan.

LATE NEWS: On the international front, Gary O'Connor received a late call up to Scotland's squad for the 2012 European Championship qualifiers, accompanying his St Andrew's colleague James McFadden, while Ben Foster was part of England's set-up.

ROLL OF HONOUR

Ivan Barnsley

Robin Barnsley

Russell Barnsley

Sarah Manton

Neil Manton

Max Manton

Paul Willis

Danilo 'Dan' Ronzani

Harold McDonough

Mick Sherry

Malcolm McHenry

John Westwood

Pete Flamingo

Russell Faulkner

Adam 'Lurkio' Phillips

James Cross

Alan Prosser (Hednesford)

Stanley Bushell

Anthony Bushell

Laurence McGann

Keith McGann

Ashley & George Ward

Leslie Steenton

Joe Morgan

Ray Whitehouse

Rob Lecrass

Peter Mcnally

Steve Jennings

Christopher Gaze

Ben Little

Jake Dolan

Des Ponsonby

Barry & Adam Ross

Steve Amos

David Spionkop McCaffrey

Bradley Priddey

Peter Drew

Alan R. Ayres

Helen Dunphy

Steve Caron

James Caron

Matthew Caron

Daniel Caron

Steve Neale

Stuart Ellis

Matthew Freeman

Paul Hughes

Tony Cotter

Peter George Young

Judy Puddy

Steve & Di Sorrell

Phil Smith

David Galvin

A.N. Davis

David Cottrill

Andrew Reilly

John Edward Hatton

Jejz Lynch

Patricia Aves

Tom Prendergast

Stephen Barritt

Lee 'Wiggy' Bennett

Alfred Butler

Paul Joseph Thompson

Steve Carter

Geoff Perry

Crathorn Family

Codnor Blue Noses S&M&L&H

James Mountford

Alan Mountford

John Reeves

Darrel James Kennedy

Russell Newns

Phil Stokes

Ian Stokes

Oscar Stokes

Neil Cottrell

Dave Hukins

William Frankum

Liam O'Doherty

Peter Don Gough

Michael Brownhill

Cayden Tyler Mellerick

Ray Guest

Martin Smallwood

Gerard Samuels

www.joysandsorrows.co.uk

Paul Cuffe

Carl Anthony William Buxton

George Dyson

Wilf Styles